Drummer Boy

Isaiah Van Horn Revolutionary
War Veteran and Pioneer of
Indiana County
Pennsylvania

by

J. Derald Morgan, Ph D, PE

authorHOUSE®

AuthorHouse™
1663 Liberty Drive
Bloomington, IN 47403
www.authorhouse.com
Phone: 833-262-8899

Published by AuthorHouse 01/27/2021

ISBN: 978-1-4567-4277-5 (sc)
ISBN: 978-1-4567-4279-9 (hc)
ISBN: 978-1-4567-4278-2 (e)

Library of Congress Control Number: 2011902365

Preface

"Forget the past; do not dwell on it. See, I am doing a new thing!
Now it springs up; do you not see it?I am making a way in the
desert and streams in the wasteland."

Isaiah 43:18-19

This scripture may indeed be a strange way to begin a book of
family history. The book you are holding in your hand is more than
a book of family history. It is a remarkable story of a people
stepping out on faith to follow their God figuratively, on their way
through the desert and up the streams in the wasteland.

Isaiah was chosen by his father to be the drummer for his company
of militia drawn from the good men of Bucks County who saw a
new thing springing up, **The United States of America.** A land
free from the tyranny of oppressive taxation and unbridled and
arbitrary rules of the King of England. Isaiah's father gave his life
for the cause leaving a young family to make way for themselves.
From this I have drawn the title of the book Drummer Boy.

I wish that I had writings to validate the struggles of the family as
this new country was emerging. However, we do not have anything
but snipits of information from which we can imagine and
formulate in our own minds the progression of the family. Clearly
they did not dwell on the past. Isaiah married, started a family and
moved to Western Pennsylvania. Not exactly a desert but at the
time of his migration, a dangerous and unknown wilderness ripe for
home steading and expansion of this new nation.

What we do know is that Isaiah followed in the pathway of the
Lord. He is listed as the 6th Elder of Gilgal Church, a congregation
of the United Presbyterian Church, established in a remote and
untamed area of the United States of America in the early 1800s. In
fact if you go there today it is still in a very remote part of the
country. I was fortunate enough to be in the area on Sunday and
attended this church with a group of Christians that were

representative of the salt of the earth.

In the 1790 Census, there is an Isaiah Van Horn in Hopewell, Newton, Tyborn, and West Pennsboro, Cumberland, Pennsylvania with 1-2-1 listing. Most likely Isaiah was in Cumberland, PA in 1790 as Cumberland was one of 8 counties in PA and included what is now Indiana County, PA. West Pennsboro Township of the existing Cumberland County is nearly half way from Bucks County to Indiana County.

In 1796 or 97 Isaiah and family moved to what is now Wheatfield Township, Indiana Cnty, PA. In 1804, he owned a farm in East Mahoning Township, about one mile east of Georgeville. It is said that he planted the orchard that is so productive on this farm.

Since I am dedicating this book to my maternal grandmother I have added the ancestors of her mother to this book.

I hope that you enjoy the many snipits of history of the ancestors and descendents of Isaiah. This is the story of a Revolutionary War Drummer Boy, a true Patriot, and his ancestors and descendents.

J. Derald Morgan, PhD, PE, FIEE, FNAFE, CESB Forensic Eng.

Table of Contents

Introduction

This is a book about the descendants of a young lad, Isaiah Van Horn, that served as "Drummer" in his father's, Captain Henry Van Horn, militia company that was raised in 1776 from Bucks County, PA. Following the war and after marrying and starting a family he moved to Indiana County, PA in the late 1700s or early 1800s where he lived the rest of his life. It should be noted that after the completion of the Revolutionary War that 73 patriots made Indiana County their home along with Isaiah Van Horn, Although he was not an educated man he was a solid hard working citizen that is the life blood of a strong America. He had the pioneer spirit that was so essential to the expansion of the county after the Revolutionary War.

The following description of the History of Indiana County is taken directly from the description of the history on the web site of the Historical and Genealogical Society of Indiana County with additions and editing by the author.

The recorded history of Indiana County begins around 1727, when James Le Tort, a French Huguenot trader, set up a trading post for the Indians near what is now the town of Shelocta, in the western part of the county. Various other traders and Indian fighters traveled through the county in the 1700's, including the famous frontiersmen, Conrad Weiser, Peter Shaver, William Franklin, son of Benjamin Franklin, and John Harris, Sr., who established Harris's Ferry on the present site of Harrisburg.

In 1756, during the French and Indian War, Lt. Col. John Armstrong led a force of 307 men from Fort Shirley, in present Huntingdon County, to attack Kittanning Path, an Indian trail which roughly parallels U.S. Route 422 through Indiana County. This route which was renamed the Armstrong Trail, is now preserved by The Armstrong Trail Society and a portion of it in Indiana County has been marked with signs and used for hiking and nature study.

The southern portion of the county was purchased from the Iroquois Six Nations in 1768, in the first Treaty of Fort Stanwix by Thomas and Richard Penn, sons of William Penn. The line of this purchase, extending across the center of Indian County, is known as the Purchase Line and is commemorated today by a monument in the town of Cherry Tree, marking the corner of the Purchase. There were only eight counties in the 86 year old Commonwealth at that time and this lower part of Indiana County was included in Cumberland County. In 1771, Bedford was formed out of Cumberland County and two years later, Westmoreland County was carved out of Bedford County. Both of these counties included what is now Indiana County.

In 1784, the Penns signed the second Treaty of Fort Stanwix with the Indians and purchased the northern section of the county which became part of Northumberland County. In 1795, Lycoming County was created out of part of Northumberland County, so the northern portion of Indiana County was for a time part of Lycoming County. Indiana County traces its parentage from five other counties! The two parts of Indiana County, north and south of the Purchase Line, were joined when the county was created by the Pennsylvania Legislature in 1803. With the formation of the county, competition developed among various areas for the honor of having the county seat. This was settled in 1805 when George Clymer of Philadelphia, a signer of both the Declaration of Independence and the Constitution, donated out of his considerable holdings 250 acres of land in the center of the county to be used as a county seat. This cinched the title for the town of Indiana which by 1810 had a population of 125.

In 1806, the official business of the county was transferred from Greensburg when the first session of the Indiana County Court was held on the second floor of Peter Sutton's Tavern in the town of Indiana. Three years later the first Court House was built. According to the census of 1810, the new county had a population of 1,214. The first newspaper was started in 1814 and hewed to the Federalist line in politics. The town of Indiana became a borough in 1816, the same year Pittsburgh was incorporated as a city.

Transportation was developing in the county in the early 1800's. In 1807, the Frankstown Road was improved and tolls were charged when it became a turnpike. In 1825, the fabulous financial success of the Erie Canal in New York State and of the Schuylkill Canal which connected Pottsville and Philadelphia, ushered in the Canal Age. The construction of the Pennsylvania Canal to link Philadelphia and Pittsburgh with a system of waterways and railways began in 1826. The Conemaugh River was an important link in the section from Johnstown to Pittsburgh. By 1829, the first canal boats were passing the Indiana County towns of Blairsville and Saltsburg and by 1834, the canal was opened it full length. Within 30 years the canal had been replaced by railroads and the State government was almost bankrupt as a result of the canal building fever. A spur line of the Pennsylvania Railroad was completed in Indiana in 1856.

In the 1830's and 1840's Indiana County became a hotbed of abolitionism. The Center Township Anti-Slavery Society was organized in 1838, and an abolition newspaper, The Clarion Freedom, was established in 1843. The county was on one of the mail lines of the Underground Railroad and many prominent citizens risked their lives by harboring runaway slaves. A fervent Indiana abolitionist, Dr. Robert Mitchell, was convicted by a Federal Court in 1847, and fined for helping slaves. During the Civil War, Indiana County sent several regiments of troops to fight for the Union.

Houses of worship in the county represent many religious denominations. Bethel Presbyterian Church is believed to be the oldest Protestant Church and dates back to 1788. **Another early church was Gilgal United Presbyterian Church established in 1806 with Isaiah Van Horn being one of the first elders, listed as the 6th elder. Many of the Van Horns and their related families are buried**

7

in the Gilgal Cemetery.

As has been told about 1800 settlers began to locate north of the purchase line in the region technically named Mahoning. **The earliest included Isaiah Van Horn, William work, John Leasure, Robert Brady, James Thompson, James Irving, James Park, William P. Brady, Matthew Wyncoop, William Hopkins and Joshua Lewis.** These Pioneers realized they needed a church where they could worship together. Not all were church members but all favored a Presbyterian Church. They found a central spot on a hill above the Little Mahoning , a knoll sloping gradually to a spring of of clear sparkling water. When the church was completed the honor of naming it was given to the pioneer woman Martha Thompson. She chose the name Gilgal because she believed the Jordan of their trials was providentially crossed and this spot a bit of Cannan.

The oldest Catholic Church is St. Patrick's in Pine Township, built in 1827, but the deed for the land was given in 1806.

In 1855, a Normal School for training teachers was begun in the old Indiana Academy and in the basement of a church. By 1870, a movement had started for the founding of a state Normal School which bore fruit in 1875, when Indiana State Normal School was established. It became a four-year State Teacher's College in 1927, and began granting degrees.

The county's first major industry was the manufacture of salt, made from evaporating salt water pumped from wells. The salt boom in the southwestern part of the county accounted for the name of the town of Saltsburg.

Bituminous coal was being dug from exposed outcropping as early as 1795, but there is no record of the date or location of the first mine. However, coal mining soon rivaled farming as the backbone of the county's economy. Several iron furnaces were built in the 1830's and 1840's, but ceased operations when timber from which charcoal was made gave out. By 1905, coke production became a major industry with the construction of beehive ovens at Ernest.

Another industry started in 1914, with the building of the McCreary tire plant in Indiana.

After the disastrous St. Patrick's Day flood in 1936, a movement was begun to assure that protection of Pittsburgh from further ravages. In 1946, construction was started by the Army Corps of Engineers on the mammoth Conemaugh Dam on the Conemaugh River near Blairsville. Several towns were demolished and moved out of the way and two railroad tunnels and old Pennsylvania Canal tunnel were sealed. The work took seven years to complete and the finished project is the largest flood control dam in the Allegheny River system.

Yellow Creek Park was created in 1963, located along on one of the first 'highways' in the state, the Kittanning Path, used by the Delaware and Shawnee Nations and by early settlers. The park includes 3,140 acres and provides numerous recreational activities.

More recently, Indiana became know as the birthplace of film star, Jimmy Stewart and as the Christmas Tree Capitol of the world. Visitors and locals alike can relive Indiana County's past by visiting the area's many historical sites including: Four scenic covered bridges, including the newly rededicated Thomas Bridge, the longest in the county and the only one still in use today; Tunnelview Historic Site, featuring the remains of past railroads, canals and the third tunnel ever built in America, the Pennsylvania Canal tunnel and aqueduct; historic Saltsburg, where you can relive life in a booming canal town of the 1800's.

Historic structures from the late 1800's like Ebenezer Church, Bethel Church, the Silas M. Clark House, and historic downtown Indiana.

And, of course, Smicksburg Amish Settlement."

These features, along with the county's rich history, make Indiana County one of the top scenic spots to visit in Pennsylvania!

According to an article about Smicksburg and Mahonings by

Cortlandt W. W. Elkin, MD the lands of Indiana County were obtained by the pioneer families in one of three ways: Purchase of land from the Pennsylvania state land office that opened in 1769, receipt of a land grant or patent for military service or the purchase of land grants from large land holding companies like the Holland Company. The well known Holland Land Company was made up of eleven wealthy merchants from Amsterdam who had, in 1792, purchased thousands of acres of land in what is now Indiana and Armstrong counties.

Several of the farms and land holdings of the pioneer families that were obtained by one or more of the three methods given above near the end of the 18th and the beginning of the 19th Century are: the Jacob Wilhelm and J. B. Work farms that were obtained from military patents given to General William Ford in 1787 and 1785 respectively; the Allen farm patented in 1785 in West Mahoning at the fork of the Mahonings; the Work farms in East Mahoning in 1804; the Leisure farm in East Mahoning in 1802; the James Chambers farm in North Mahoning; the William Travis farm in West Mahoning at the site of the Old Good Mill on Little Mahoning in 1806; Michael Lantz farm on Ross Run in South Mahoning obtained in 1799; **the Van Horn farms in East Mahoning near Georgeville in 1804**; the Spencer farm in West Mahoning; the Marshall farms at Glade Run in Armstrong County and in South Mahoning, Indiana County in 1820; the Christopher Wells farm in South Mahoning; the Weamer farm in South Mahoning in 1802; Jerimiah Criag farm in East Mahoning 1813; the Archibald Smitten farm in North Mahoning of 1812; the Asa Crossman farm near Georgeville 1806; the North farm in North Mahoning patented to Henry Geddis in 1798; the Robert Jordan farm on the Smicksburg-Punxsutawney road in 1807; the Dilts tracts in North Mahoning of 1800 at the "Dilts Mill" and Davidsville; Jonathan Ayers land at Mahoning P.O. in East Mahoning patented in 1800 to William P. Brady and the site of a famous tavern in the early days and later of Ayers P.O.; the Hopkins farm in East Mahoning 1860; the William Niel (Neal) in West Mahoning near North Point in 1807 as well as the sites at Smicksburg purchased by Charles Coleman of Marchand purchased by Archibald Smitten of Davidsville purchased by Soloman Sprankle all having been purchased from the Holland Land Company.

Looking over the list of the families found above and those found in the list of taxables in the area in 1807 we find the names of these families who are even today active in the affairs of the area or have left to make their contributions to the growth of the United States throughout the entire country. Names of prominence in Indiana County and in this genealogical work are the **Ayers, Brady, Black, Crossman, Davis, Dilts, Ewings, Hoovers, Hopkins, Jamison, Justis, Kilpatrick, Leasure, Lewis, McHenry, Niels (Neals), Pearce, Parks, Smith, Thompson, Van Horn (Van Horne), Warden, Wells, Work and Wyncoop** as well as many others that came later to join these pioneers. One finds these family names on numerous ballots for elected office, lists of jurors and grand jurors, buyer and sellers of land, materials and supplies.

And then there was Armagh, Indiana Cnty, PA a place where the authors grandmother, great grand father and gggrandfather Van Horn resided. The information about Armagh herein is from the Armagh Area Bicentennial 1792-1992:

"Armagh, Ireland 1792 - Mrs. Parker was married to William Parker, son of Lord Parker of Belfast, Ireland. William died leaving his wife with four children. Some time after the death of William, his widow fell in love with James Graham who was the caretaker of her estate. It was said that Graham was a fine man but not of noble blood. Feeling the pressure of the social status, Mrs. Parker sold her estate and married James Graham and made plans to set sail to the New World.

The eight families set sail from New Castle, Ireland on two ships the "Minerva" mastered by Charles Forrest (burthern 400 tons) and "Renown" mastered by William Loth (burthern 450 tons). It was said to be a long and frightful trip to their new homeland.

They landed in Philadelphia on July 21, 1792 by way of the North Atlantic Delaware Bay and onto the Market Street Wharf, Irish immigrants were not well accepted on the Eastern seaboard and were often told to move west.

After obtaining the necessary provisions for the trip West, they were off to find a new area to call home. The exact date is not known when they left Philadelphia area, but we can be sure it took some time to procure the necessary implements to start a new life in the new country.

It was noted as the group of Irish families were traveling West, the roads were terrible and crossing some streams was next to impossible. Wheel blocks had to be used coming down Chickoree Mountain. These were chain and wooden block devices used to keep the back wheels of wagons from turning.

On September 1, 1792, the Irish group had made their way to a place known as Plainfield. The group liked the lay of the land. It reminded them of Armagh, Ireland. It was decided by the group to travel west no further. Mr. Graham said he would try to find the owner of the land and get approval to stay as Fall was fast approaching and shelters had to be built. It is recorded that Robert Douglas had obtained Patten from said Commonwealth of Pennsylvania, being the area known as Plainfield. James Gibson bought this area of Plainfield in 1790 and sold the area to James and wife Margaret in 1798 for a total sum of $16.00. The area of Plainfield was now officially Armagh. The town was surveyed by Joseph McCarthy with lots layed out to the size of 66 feet front and 165 feet deep. First lots sold were to William Parker. The first child born in the new town was Jeannette Fee on August 22, 1793.

In the summer and fall of 1799, a subscription school was taught in the village by Robert Davis, an old Revolutionary soldier. The scholars who attended this first school were: Katie Tomb, Hugh Tomb, John Tomb, Elizabeth Fee, Jeannette Fee, Josias Fee and Elizabeth Carr. The only books were those of the teacher. Letters were pasted on a board with a handle on it in the shape of a paddle. A log building was used for the school house and was located south from the center of town near where the Old

Presbyterian Church now sits.

The first tavern was opened by James Graham in a rude log cabin. In 1800 the first blacksmith shop was opened by Peter Dyke, which reportedly did a good business."

Indiana Countians have served their country proudly and well in all of its military conflicts. It is interesting to note that 3,680 or 11% of the population of the county volunteered for service during the Civil War in combat units and the number is larger by 1,000 to 1,500 if militia units are added to the number. A surprising 21 to 24% of the county population participated in World War II amounting to 13 to 15,000 men and women in combat units. This has been reported to be the highest percentage of population of any county in the United States. Many of the descendants of Isaiah have stood up and been counted among those who answer the call of service to their country.

Some additional facts about Indiana County, Pennsylvania and the Van Horn family are as follows:

Indiana County Census Totals

1820 - 8,882
1830 - 14.252
1840 - 20,782
1850 - 27,170
1860 - 33,687
1870 - 36,138
1880 - 40,527
1890 - 42,175
1900 - 42,556
1910 - 66,210
1920 - 80,910
1930 - 75,395
1940 - 79,854
1950 - 77,106
1960 - 75,366

1970 - 79,451
1980 - 92,281
1990 - 89,994

Indiana County Community Facts

The 1990 Census report indicates that Indiana, PA is a close knit community of quiet neighborhoods and friendly individuals who care about the future of the area. Convenient shopping, vast recreational areas, and sophisticated cultural offerings combine to help the community grow and prosper, while still maintaining its small-town charm. The 2000 census gives the population as 89,605 and the 2009 estimate is 87,629.

The Indiana Community size is 43.3 square miles (White Township/Indiana Boroughs: 15 square miles) the County is comprised of 24 Townships and 15 Boroughs with a total County size of 829 square miles.

From the 2009 Census Estimate for Indiana County, PA:

Percentage of Population by Age: Under 5 years = 4.9%, 65 and over = 15.6% with 96.4% White.

Over 85% are high school graduates.

Median Household Income is $49, 532

Median Value of individual home $92,700 with 70.9% home ownership and 2.37 persons per household.

In 1840 there were 411 Van Horn families in the census with the most living in Pennsylvania. There were 127 in PA, 69 in OH, 63 in NJ and 62 in NY. There were 38 of these Van Horn families in Bucks County and and 7 in Indiana County, PA. Today most Van Horns live in Pennsylvania and California.

14

In the Civil War there were 528 Union and 71 Confederate Van Horn Soldiers. These Soldiers served in the Pennsylvania Units of the 104th Infantry, 3rd Artillery, 1st Light Artillery.

In 1880 we again find the most of the Van Horn households in Pennsylvania. There were 235 PA Van Horn households distributed with 49 in Philadelphia, 30 in Bucks and 12 in Indiana and 9 in Allegheny Counties, PA. The majority of the Indiana and Allegheny County families were descendants of Isaiah Van Horn. In this census the primary Van Horn employment was farmer, farm laborer or worker, laborer and then carpenter, blacksmith, teamsters and machinists. In 1880 the average workday was 10 hours and a worker made $1 to $3 per day.

In 1917-1918 there were 1,608 Van Horns men that registered for the Draft. The most were registered in Philadelphia County(49) with Allegheny County(17) registering the 3rd most Van Horns.

In 1920 there were 2,331 US Van Horn households, 48 % owned their homes and 82% were literate. There were 5 states in which Van Horns were 100% literate. The literacy rate in 1920 of the Van Horn family members far exceeded the literacy rate of the general population. In every age group except for one (76-85) the Van Horn households that owned their home was significantly higher than the general population. Of these households there were in the counties of Philadelphia(87), Allegheny(21) and in Indiana(14). These Van Horn households were distributed with 365 in PA, 227 in OH, 185 in NY, 175 in NJ and 159 in MI.

It is interesting to note that in 1880 82.5% of the heads of Van Horn households were married and in 1920 the percentage was the same. In 1880 the ratio of females to males was 2,575 to 2,766 or 48.2% female. In 1920 it was 3,193 to 3,335 or 48.9% females.

15

During the Second World War 216 Van Horn Draft Registrants are listed in the 1942 old man draft registration. The youngest was 45 and the oldest was 64. 529 Van Horn enlisted for service in the WW II. Of these 402 enlisted for the duration of the war. The majority enlisted in 1942. Over 70% of the enlistees were single with most of the age between 18 and 25.

In the 2000 Census we find that Van Horn families were distributed as follows: 487 PA, 458 CA, 448 OH, 338 FL and 307 in MI. The cities in PA with the largest number of Van Horn households were Philadelphia(22) and Pittsburgh(15).

According to data the life expectancy of Van Horns is about the same as the general population. This ranged from about 40 in 1939 to over 75 in the year 2000.

In 2000 there were 5,742 Van Horn households in the Census. This makes this the 2,141th largest named household in the US.

The above material is taken from the Historical and Genealogical Society of Indiana County, PA web site, Cortlandt W. W. Elkins Article, the US Census web site and The Van Horn Name in History published by the Generations Network, Inc and edited and amended by Dr. J. Derald Morgan.

This book is dedicated to:

My Maternal Grandmother

Leafy Fern Van Horn

Leafy Fern Van Horn
Abt 1910

Author's Notes

In order to read this book the author suggests that you look over the items in these notes so that you understand some of the terms used in the material and some of the difference used for abbreviations or indexing with which the reader may not be familiar.

1. In order to provide privacy for all of the living people listed in the book you will find for their birth dates, marriage dates and other personally identifiable information the statement "Private" is substitued. For example data for birth date and place is given as follows: b. Private. This may also be true if the author does not know the death date of the person and they have been born within 100 years of this publication.

2. The bold number by each name is the reference number for each person in this portion of the family history work. It can be used to find that person in earlier or later parts of the history.

3. The superscript number by each name after the reference number gives the number of generations from the reference ancestor or descendant. For example of you are looking at the descendants of Isaiah Van Horn and you see the number 12 beside the name this person is then in the 12th generation from Isaiah Van Horn. Isaiah Van Horn then would be that persons 11th great grandfather.

4. The superscript number given by a fact is the reference number for the endnotes. The author has diligently sought to find a reference for every name and every fact in this work. There are over 5,000 references included in this work. Where there is no reference for a person or the facts for that person, the author has been unable to obtain any verification for the person and their relationships. There may be errors of fact as a result of not being able to validate the persons facts. A great many people have been included that are

in this category as the relationships have been aquired by various sources but not verified. Any corrections along with verification are of interest to the author and changes will be made in future editions or ammendments to this work. Note that for many of the persons included where the facts are marked the author has a reference that validates the relationship but it is not indicated as the fact is not given for those who are living to protect their personally indentifiable information.

5. Abbreviations:

1. Aft.   - After a given date
2. b.   - Born
3. Bef.   - Before a given date
4. Brig. - Brigade
5. Cnty   - County
6. Cpl.   - Military Rank of Corporal
7. d.   - Died
8. d/o   - Daughter of
9. DAC   - Daughter of the American Colonists
10. DAR   - Daughters of the American Revolution
11. Dau   - daughter
12. Dec'd - deceased
13. Div. - division
14. Exr. - executor of an estate
15. Exrs. - executors of an estate
16. Extx. - executrix of an estate
17. Fams - families
18. g.gf - great grandfather
19. g.gm - great grandmother
20. gd.   - granddaughter
21. gf.   - grandfather
22. gm.   - grandmother
23. gs.   - grandson
24. Inf   - Infantry
25. m.   - Married

26. Mil.   - Military
27. p.   - page
28. pp.   - pages
29. PV   - Pennsylvania Volunteer
30. PVI   - Pennsylvania Volunteer Infantry
31. Pvt.   - Military Rank of Private
32. Ref.   - reference
33. Reg.   - Regiment
34. Rt.   - Rural Mail Route
35. s/o   - Son of
36. SAR   - Sons of the American Revolution
37. Ser.   - serial
38. Twp.   - Township
39. Vol.   - Volume
40. w/o   - with out
41. wf   - wife
42. wid/o   - widow of
43. Wit.   - witness
44. Co.   -Military or Business Company occasionally
              a county when copied from other works

CAPTAIN HENRY VAN HORNE'S COMPANY.

Muster Roll of Captain Henry VanHorn's Company of Militia, commanded by Col. Joseph Kirkbride, Newtown, in Bucks county, January 22, 1777.

Captain.

Henry Van Horn, December 6, 1776.

First Lieutenant.

Robert Ramsey, December 6, 1776.

Second Lieutenant.

Thomas Huston, December 6, 1776.

Ensign.

Abram Johnson, December 6, 1776.

Sergeant.

Andrew McMinn, December 6, 1776.

Corporal.

John Vance, December 27, 1776.

Drummer.

Isaiah Van Horn, December 6, 1776.

Privates.

John Price, December 26, 1776.
Joshua Van Horn, December 6, 1776.
David McMorris, December 14, 1776.
James McMorris, January 5, 1777.
James Sharkey, December 26, 1776.
Archibald McCorkell, December 26, 1776.
David Riddle, December 6, 1776.
Peter Lafferton, December 6, 1776.
Patrick Hunter, December 26, 1776.
William Bateman, January 3, 1777.
Thomas Harper, January 3, 1777.
Eman Scott, December 26, 1776.
Abram Slack, December 26, 1776.
Jeremiah Van Horn, January 3, 1777.
John Johnson, December 6, 1776.
Robert Watson, January 17, 1777.
Robert McDowell, December 26, 1776.

Mustered them of Captain Van Horn's Company: 1 Captain. 2 Lieutenants, 1 Ensign, 1 Sergeant, 1 Corporal, 1 Drummer, and 17 Privates.

LOD[k]. SPROGELL, *M. M. G. of P.*

Drummer.

Isaiah Van Horn, December 6, 1776.

Privates.

John Price, December 26, 1776.
Joshua Van Horn, December 6, 1776.
David McMorris, December 14, 1776.
James McMorris, January 5, 1777.
James Sharkey, December 26, 1776.
Archibald McCorkell, December 26, 1776.
David Riddle, December 6, 1776.
Peter Lafferton, December 6, 1776.
Patrick Hunter, December 26, 1776.
William Bateman, January 3, 1777.
Thomas Harper, January 3, 1777.
Eman Scott, December 26, 1776.
Abram Slack, December 26, 1776.
Jeremiah Van Horn, January 3, 1777.
John Johnson, December 6, 1776.
Robert Watson, January 17, 1777.
Robert McDowell, December 26, 1776.

Mustered them of Captain Van Horn's Company: 1 Captain, 2 Lieutenants, 1 Ensign, 1 Sergeant, 1 Corporal, 1 Drummer, and 17 Privates.

LOD'K SPROGELL, M. M. G. of P.

(c.) We and each of us the undernamed Substitutes in the second Class of Bucks County Militia doth hereby Acknowledge that we have rec'd of and from Samuel Smith Sub. Lieutenant of the County aforesaid the sum annexed to each of our Names, which is the full consideration stipulated for our Bounty for the Term of Two Months. Witness our hands this 7th Day of August, 1777, at Billings Port—— We say Rec'd severally by us.

	Dollars.	c.
James & Wallace, his mark.	40	15	0
John + Hamblton, his mark.	60	22	10
patrick his Koncs, mark.	40	15	

Captain Henry Van Horn's Muster Roll showing his son
Isaiah Van Horn as Drummer Boy

Historic Newtown Part III 1775-1783 250th Anniversary of Newtown by Edward Roberts Barnsley

Historic Newtown, Part III, 1775-1783

On April 19, 1775, there was shed at Lexington, Massachusetts, the first blood in the War of the Revolution, a war which terminated in the separation of the American colonies from Great Britain, and in their change from this humble character and condition, to that of free and independent States.

Shortly after this battle, the citizens of Bucks County responded to the call of the Continental Congress, and 51 residents of Newtown formed themselves into a Company under the captaincy of Francis Murray. The following is the Roll of Newtown Company on August 21, 1775:

FRANCIS MURRAY, *Captain.*

ROBERT RAMSEY, *First Lieutenant.*

JOSEPH GRIFFITHS, *Second Lieutenant.*

JAMES ALLEN.
JOHN ATKINSON, JR.

JOHN BAILEY.
WILLIAM BATEMAN.
GEORGE HOPKINS BURDEN.

JOHN DALTON.
SMITH DAVIDS.
JOSEPH DYER.

JOHN EASTWICK.

JOHN GREGG.

FRANCIS HARRISON.
THOMAS HARVEY.
JAMES HUSTON.
PATRICK HUSTON.
THOMAS HUSTON.

ABRAHAM JOHNSTON.
GEORGE JOHNSTON.
JOHN JOHNSTON.

PETER LEFFERTSON.
ABRAHAM LOWELL.
HENRY LOWELL.
THOMAS LOWRIE.

ARCHIBALD MCCORKEL.
JAMES MCCOY.

ROBERT MCDOWELL.
CHARLES MCLAUGHLIN.
ANDREW MCMINN.
DAVID MCMORRIS.
JOHN MOODY.
JOHN MURFITS.
WILLIAM MURFITS.

SOLOMON PARK.
JOHN PRICE.

JOHN RANDALL.
JOHN REEDER.
JOHN RONEY.

EMAN SCOTT.
JAMES SHIRKEY.
ABRAM STARK.

SAMUEL TALBERT.
ANTHONY TEATE.
NATHANIEL TWINING.

HENRY VANHORN.
JOHN VANHORN.
JOSHUA VANHORN.
CHRISTIAN VANHORNE.

ROBERT WATSON.

THOMAS YARDLEY.

24

64   HISTORIC NEWTOWN

Not all of the Newtown citizens, however, were military
minded. The following list of 73 Non-Associators shows the
names of those who refused to bear arms.

NON-ASSOCIATORS, NEWTOWN, PA., AUGUST 21, 1775

JOHN ASHBURN.

DAVID BARTON.
JAMES BOYD.
JOHN BOYD, at JOSEPH WORSTALL'S.
JAMES BRIGGS.
JAMES BRIGGS, JR.
MOSES BRIGGS.
WILLIAM BRIGGS.
ABNER BUCKMAN.
BENJAMIN BUCKMAN.
JACOB BUCKMAN.
JAMES BUCKMAN.
JOHN BUCKMAN, JR.
JOSEPH BUCKMAN, JR.
THOMAS BUCKMAN, JR.
WILLIAM BUCKMAN, JR.

GEORGE CAMPBELL.
SAMUEL CAREY.
ASA CAREY.
SAMPSON CARY.

SAMUEL DOAN.
JOSEPH DUNN.
RALPH DUNN.

HENRY ELBY.

SAMUEL HARVEY.
JESSE HICKS.
JOSEPH HICKS.
ROBERT HILLBORN.
SAMUEL HILLBORN.
RICHARD HOVENDEN.
ANDREW HUNTER.

WILLIAM KING, doctor.

DAVID LEE.
WILLIAM LEVINS.
HENRY LEWIS.

MILES MARTINDALE.
JOHN MARTINDELL.

JOSEPH MARTINDELL.
STRICKLAND MARTINDELL.
PATRICK MCCALLA.
JAMES MCMORRIS.
AMOS MITCHELL.
JOHN MITCHELL.
WILLIAM MORGAN.
HENRY MULLIN, living with DAVID
  TWINING.

JOSEPH NEEDER, with DAVID TWIN-
  ING.

JOHN PASTE.
WILLIAM PATTON, at SAMUEL HILL-
  BORN'S.
ABRAM PENQUITE.

GEORGE SPIRE, at THOS. YARDLEY'S.
DAVID STORY.
JOHN STORY.
THOMAS STORY.
DANIEL STRADLING.
JOSEPH STRADLING.

JOHN TAYLOR.
PETER TAYLOR.
STACEY TAYLOR.
TIMOTHY TAYLOR.
WILLIAM TAYLOR.
ROBERT THOMAS.
ROBERT THOMAS, JR.
JAMES TOMLINSON.
JOHN TOMLINSON.
RICHARD TOMLINSON.
WILLIAM TOMLINSON.
JOHN TOOL.
DAVID TWINING.
JACOB TWINING.

JOHN VANCE.
JOSEPH VERNON.

JOSEPH WORSTALL.

SAMUEL YARDLEY.

Newtown and vicinity seems to have been a hot bed of
Toryism all through the Revolution. In the Fall of 1776 the

25

British Loyalists held an election at Newtown which very much excited the Council of Safety, and brought from them more or less of a reprimand upon Judge Wynkoop for permitting such an affair to be conducted. The inspectors of this election were: Will Minkham, John Story, James Shaw, and Thomas Smith. The clerks were: William Linton, Thomas Ross, and William Atkinson. William Biles dispersed the tickets, and John Windar, clerk of the court, issued the proclamation. The following letters* pertain to this election:

Bucks County, Neshamoney, October 2th, 1776.
To the Councel of Saftey, in Philadelphia.

Gentelmen,
Noe Doubt you have heard of an Election ben held yesterday by the torey partey at Nuetowr, in this County, the Bearer, Captⁿ Sempell, I have sent to inform you of what he knows concerning the affear, as he was at the Election.

From yr most Obedt Hu'ble
Servt,
WILLIAM BAXTER, Lt. Colⁿ.

In Council of Safety, Philadᵃ, 3d Oct. 1776.
To Henry Wynkoop, Esq.

Sir,
We are Informed that some evil minded persons, disaffected to the present Government, have attempted to prevent its Establishment, by supporting the late Government under the Authority of the King of Great Britain, for wᶜʰ purpose they have proceeded to an Election of Representatives under the said authority, in Contempt and defiance of the authority of the good people of this State. As such a Measure, if carried into Execution, cannot fail to defeat this virtuous Opposition to the Tyranny of the King of Great Britain, it behoves us to take Effectual Measures to punish such contumacious Offenders against this State. You are therefore desired to make enquiry concerning the Said Election, & of the persons who are principally concern'd therein, & communicate the same to this Board as soon as you conveniently can.

By order of the Council.

In the treasurer's reports for that year we find the sequel to this matter, in entries such as these, under dates of October 23rd, 24th, and 25th:

The Council of Pennsylvania directs Mr. Nesbit, the treasurer, to pay Major McMaster £6, and charge the same to the State for expenses concerning the Bucks County election; Capt. John Jameson, 8£, 15s 10 d., and Capt. Thos. Wier 6£ 0s. 4d., the expenses of their respective companies in going to Newtown to suppress the election there on October 1st and 2d, and to disperse the people.

The payments were made on the avouchment of Lieut. Col. William Baxter, who commanded the Second Battalion.

*Pennsylvania Archives, First Series, Vol. V, p. 31 and 32.

Because Newtown was the County Seat and conveniently situated between the opposing forces, it was frequently the rendezvous for exchange of prisoners of war. On December 8, 1776, Lewis Nicola, Town Major of Philadelphia, issued orders* for:

> A corporal & 6 men to parade tomorrow morning, at 7 o'clock, under the court-house, to escort a party of English soldiers to Newtown in Bucks County.

The guard returned by the 16th, and Major Nicola issued an order requiring them to turn in their arms to him on the following morning.

When General Wilkinson came to Newtown from Philadelphia on the afternoon of December 25, 1776, he said that he was surprised to learn that Washington had transferred his quarters to Newtown. By transferring his quarters (not headquarters) to that place, Washington meant simply that he had sent his secretary to Newtown with his papers and other articles of value for a place of safety, or at least greater security than the farm house near Jericho mountain. It was not until after the battle and victory at Trenton the following day, December 26th, that Washington came to Newtown. The *Pennsylvania Journal* of 1781 says that after the battle, Washington with his army and prisoners recrossed the Delaware at the same ferry he had crossed on his march to Trenton on the morning of that day. The private soldiers were marched off immediately to Newtown. The 23 officers, however, remained in a chamber in the Ferry House where, according to their own account, they passed a miserable night. Next morning they were escorted to Newtown by Col. Weedon. At Newtown, the officers were quartered at inns and private houses; the soldiers in the Presbyterian Church and the jail. On December 27, 1776, an officer on Washington's staff wrote the following in his diary:

> Here we are back in our camp with the prisoners and trophies. Washington is keeping his promise; the soldiers (Hessians) are in the Newtown meeting-house and other buildings. He has just given directions for tomorrow's dinner. All the captured Hessian officers are to dine with him. He bears the Hessians no malice, but says they have been sold by their Grand Duke to King George and sent to America, when if they could have their own way they would be peaceably living in their own country.

Apparently, however, only four of the Hessian officers actually had the pleasure of dining with Washington. The remainder being entertained by Lord Stirling at the House of

*Pennsylvania Archives, First Series, Vol. V, p. 96.

Amos Strickland, Sr., [Brick Hotel]. Concerning this event Lieut. Piel, one of the Hessians, wrote:

> We had scarce seated ourselves, when a long dark meager looking man, whom we took for the parson of the place, stepped forth and held a discourse in German, setting forth the justice of the American side of the war. He told us he was born in Hanover, and said the King of England was nothing but the elector of Hanover. Lord Stirling seeing we were not much edified by the preacher, took us with him to visit General Washington. The latter received us very courteously, but as he could only speak English, we could not understand much of what he said. He invited four of our officers to dine with him, the rest dined with Lord Stirling.

When The Hessians were brought to Newtown they were greatly alarmed by a report, that was in some way raised among them, that the Americans killed and ate their prisoners. The panic would have become serious if it had not fortunately happened that a German was found in Northampton township who could talk to them and obtain their confidence. It is seen from the following letter written to the Council of Safety, by Clement Biddle, Deputy Quarter Master General, that the 1,000 Hessian privates were only in Newtown on the nights of the 26th and the 27th. They were sent to Philadelphia on the 28th where they arrived two days later.

> Headquarters, Newtown.
> December 28, 1776.

> His Excellency, Gen. Washington has commanded me to send forward the prisoners taken at Trenton to pass through Philadelphia, to Lancaster, and I have sent them with a guard, under the conduct of Captain Murray (an officer of this state lately released from New York) with directions to furnish them provisions and quarters on the road. I have the pleasure to inform you the number of prisoners is near 1,000, that their arms, six brass field pieces, eight standards of colors, a number of swords, cartouch boxes, taken by the happy expedition are safely arrived at and near this place.

The Hessian officers were kept in Newtown until the 30th, when Washington left. On this date they were paroled, concerning which Biddle wrote to the Council:

> Newtown,
> December 30, 1776.

> Enclosed is a copy of the parole signed by the Hessian officers who are forwarded by command of His Excellency, Gen. Washington to Philadelphia to be sent to Lancaster or such places as you direct.

The original of this Parole of Honor signed by 20 of the captive Hessian officers at Washington's Headquarters, Newtown, on December 30, 1776, is preserved among the Horatio Gates papers in the archives of the New York Historical Society, 170 Central Park West, New York City. By their permission the following verbatim copy of the same is hereby reproduced:

We the Subscribers Hessian Officers made prisoners of War by the American Army under Command of His Excellency General Washington at Trenton on the 26 Inst. being allowed our Liberty under such Restrictions as to place As may be from time to time appointed do give Our parole of Honour that we will remain at the place and within the limits appointed for us by his Excellency the General the Honorable Congress, Council of safety or Commissary of prisoners of War, peacably behaving ourselves and by no way Send or give Intelligence to the British or Hessian Army or speak or do any thing disrespectfull or Ingurous to the American States while we remain Prisoners of war.

We will also restrain our Servants and Attendants Who are allowed to remain with us as far as in Our power to the same Conditions.

F. SCHEFFER, *lieutenant colonel.*	DE LOEWENSTEIN, *captain.*
J. A. VON HANSTEIN, *major.*	FOBBE, *lieutenant.*
A. C. STEDING, *captain.*	F. FISCHER, *lieutenant of artillery.*
KELLER, *lieutenant.*	DE DRACK, *ensign.*
PIEL, *lieutenant.*	J. J. MALTHAUS, *major.*
MOLLER, *lieutenant.*	BRUBACH, *captain.*
GRAEBE, *ensign.*	KINEN, *lieutenant.*
VON ZENGEN HENDRICH.	FLECK, *ensign.*
VON HOBE, *ensign.*	KLEINSCHMIT, *ensign.*
DE BIESENROUT, *captain.*	SCHROEDER, *ensign.*

Washington's Headquarters in Newtown were in a brownstone house at the southwest corner of Sycamore Street and Washington Avenue then belonging to the widow Harris. It was in this house that Washington wrote his two letters* to Congress giving them the official report of the Battle of Trenton. This Headquarters House, the second on the site, was torn down in 1862, according to General W. W. H. Davis, and the present building constructed sometime during the Civil War by Alexander German. This present structure, the third on the site, is believed to have been built out of the stone of the Headquarters House, and to have been constructed along similar lines and on the same foundations as the older building.

John Harris, Esq., the husband of Hannah Harris, Washington's hostess, was born in 1717 and settled in Newtown as early as 1750. Seven years later, on May 5, 1757, Harris bought 53 acres of land from Benjamin Twining, tailor. This farm was part of the town lot patented to Thomas Rowland on Fourth Month 1, 1685, and by various conveyances passed to Stephen Twining, the first settler, who improved it and built the tan yard before alluded to. Benjamin Twining was the son of Nathaniel Twining, and grandson of the said Stephen Twining.

John Harris, storekeeper, had evidently rented the Twining farm before he bought it in 1757, as he was living on it at the time of purchase. He carried on farming, tanning, and storekeeping. The store was not in a part of the farm house, but some

*These were printed in the *Newtown Enterprise* on August 4 and 11, 1932.

distance back, along what is now known as the Swamp Road. In 1760, Harris was elected secretary of the Library Company, which he had helped to organize, and with which he later became prominently associated. In 1764, Harris was appointed Justice of the Peace, an office he held until his death nine years later. On September 21, 1767, he purchased from Nelson Jolly, grandson of Henry Nelson, deceased, a 61-acre farm that he called the Upper Farm, located on the west side of the Common, north of his first purchase. The Presbyterian Church stands on the southeast corner of his Upper Farm. Gradually Harris became a considerable land owner, owning over 500 acres in the county. About 257 acres lay in Newtown, and as much in Upper Makefield, part of which was bought from the trustees of the London Company and the remainder from the Manor of Highlands.

John Harris took an active part in the building of the Presbyterian Church in 1769, and was one of the principal managers and the ticket seller of the lottery by which the money was raised for construction of the same. He married Hannah Stewart, daughter of Charles Stewart, of Upper Makefield township, and· they had seven children: John, Ann, Sarah, Elizabeth, Mary, Rachel, and Hannah. Harris died August 13, 1773,· aged 56; and was buried in the Newtown Presbyterian Graveyard. His widow continued to live at the homestead many years after his death. The slave census of 1780 shows that Hannah owned 11 slaves, three times as many as anyone else in the township. In 1787 she went to Kentucky to get her share of her brother William Stewart's estate. When and where she died is not known to the writer.

General Washington left Newtown on December· 30th in advance of his troops, crossed the Delaware at McKonkey's Ferry, and marched with them to Trenton, where battle was given Lord Cornwallis on January 2, 1777; following up the advantage gained there, he routed the British at Princeton the next day, and sent them retreating across New Jersey. In the meanwhile Lord Stirling, who had accompanied Washington in his successful expedition against the Hessians, had taken a cold thereby, and was now laid up at Newtown with rheumatism. He was, however, placed in command of the post, and watched the fords of Bucks County. He was there for about two weeks, and from his correspondence it is learned that many prisoners captured at Princeton passed through Newtown enroute for Lancaster. Tradition has it that Lord Stirling made his headquarters in Justice's House, the brown-stone building at No. 107 south State

*Records of Presbyterian Church.

Street. The following letters* of his are supposed to have been written in this building:

Newtown, Jan^u 4th, 1777.

Sir,

I have not yet been able to learn the particulars of General Washington's last Expedition into New Jersey. But he Certainly has gained some Considerable advantage, the 17th & 55th Regiments were completely routed near Prince Town, the 40th which was left in the Colledge 'tis probable were either taken prisoners or fled to Brunswick. Gen¹ Washington's army passed thro' Prince Town about nine o'clock A. M., and the Enemy's army arrived there about 2 o'clo' P. M., from Trenton. Our people took about 20 Waggon loads of Baggage belonging to the latter, which must greatly distress them. I was Ill with the Rheumatism before our first expedition to Trentown, but the fatigue & hardships I endured for forty hours in the worst weather I ever saw—rendered me unfit for further duty in the field, Gen¹ Washington therefore placed me here to do the best I could to secure the ferries & upper part of the Country against any Surprise or to pass above. I will do the best I can, with the few I have to Command.

Thomas Watson a man of very good Character, has made my heart bleed for him; he has refused the Continental Money for Hay Necessary for the Subsistence of our troops, I confined him, he is a good man by all account: I have relaced him, I have suffered him on his parol to go & abide with his family; 'till your further order I do not like to meddle with these Civil matters & for God Sake take them of my Shoulders.

I have a Number of prisoners from the Enemys Army pouring in upon me, (thank God) but tell me what I am to do with them, there is no Room for them here, I wish we may have as many more as will puzzle you what to do with, this is the first line I have been able to scrawl since I passed the Delaware last.

Most respectfully, yours,

STIRLING.

New Town,
Jan. 6, 1777.

Chairman of the Council of Safety,
Philadelphia.
Sir,

The three persons whose Names are on foot hereof were brought to me as Deserters from our Army; by their own Confession they left it while in pursuit of the Enemy; they belong to the 3d Battalion of the Philadelphia Militia, and I send them to you in order that they may be made a proper example of to their fellow Citizens. I am your most Humble Servant.

STIRLING.

Deserters Names are
James Reynols,
Patrick Marony,
Henry Bell.

P. S. Lieutenant Wilmot, of the British Light horse, is Just brot in wounded. I shall send him on to four lane End to morrow. There are a Number of prisoners of war here, & more Coming in. I should be glad to have your opinion where it will be best to send them.

*Pennsylvania Archives, First Series, Vol. V, pp. 157, 166 and 175.

Isaiah Van Horn Pioneer of Indiana County, Pennsylvania

New Town, Jany. 8th, 1777.

Robert Morris, Esq.

My dear Sir:

I have been very Ill at this place for some days past owing to what I suffered in our Expedition to Trenton on the 26 Decr. In a Letter I have Just received from General Stephen, dated at Trenton this morning, in which are the following words. "There is a report that General How intends to push towards Delaware, and for Philadelphia, with 7000 men, which he has made up from his different Posts to reinforce his army in the Jersey's, and in his turn will take no notice of General Washington being in his rear. This is said, my Lord, to be authentic Intelligence." If it should prove, our best chance is by vigilance to prevent their crossing the River, for I have no Troops with me except some trifling Guards of Militia. I have taken every precaution to keep the boats on this side, but if this severe weather continues the river will be Passable on the Ice in many places; it will, therefore, be necessary to Collect all the Troops we can, and have them ready to oppose the Passage of the River, or Join General Washington as occasion may require. I now write to Col. Weedon, who is at Philada to Collect all the recovered sick of the whole army from wherever they are. I am told there are some Maryland Troops on their way to Philada, and two Regiments of Virginia Troops at the Head of the Bay. I know not what orders any of them are under. But I think they had all be better ordered up as soon as Possible, wherefore, unless you know that Congress have destined them otherwise, I must request the favour of you to forward the Inclosed Letters to the Commanding Officers of all those Troops to come forward as soon as Possible, and to the Commissary of Provisions to provide properly for them. Be pleased also to Communicate this to the Council of Safety & Board of War.

I have the Honor to be, &.,

STIRLING.

In order to save I must request the favr of you to desire the board of war to direct the Commissarie to make the necessary Preparation of Provisions & ammunition. If any of them are in want of arms, I have some Hundreds—please to direct and forward the others.

On January 12, 1777, Capt. Henry Vanhorne made a return of his company of militia commanded by Col. Joseph Kirkbride, of Newtown, with the dates of their enlistment. This roll is as follows:

Henry Vanhorne, captain	Dec. 6, 1776
Robert Ramsey, 1st lieut.	Dec. 6, 1776
Thomas Huston, 2d lieut.	Dec. 6, 1776
Abram Johnson, ensign	Dec. 6, 1776
Andrew McMinn, sergeant	Dec. 6, 1776
John Vance, corporal	Dec. 6, 1776
Isaiah Vanhorn, drummer	Dec. 6, 1776
Joshua Vanhorn, private	Dec. 6, 1776
David Riddle, private	Dec. 6, 1776
Peter Leffertson, private	Dec. 6, 1776
John Johnson, private	Dec. 6, 1776
David McMorris, private	Dec. 14, 1776
John Price, private	Dec. 26, 1776

James Sharkey, private...............................Dec. 26, 1776
Archibald McCorkle, private..........................Dec. 26, 1776
Patrick Hunter, private..............................Dec. 26, 1776
Eman Scott, private..................................Dec. 26, 1776
Abram Slack, private.................................Dec. 26, 1776
Robert McDowell, private.............................Dec. 26, 1776
William Bateman, private............................Jan. 3, 1777
Thomas Harper, private..............................Jan. 3, 1777
James Vanhorn, private..............................Jan. 3, 1777
James McMorris, private........................ .....Jan. 5, 1777
Robert Watson, private..............................Jan. 17, 1777

Newtown, after these incidents, so far as is known, lapsed into a quiescent state, but the correspondence shows that during the following summer of 1777, the militia was making considerable preparations for marching and for collecting blankets and other equipment. In this connection, Col. Joseph Kirkbride wrote* on May 18, 1777:

> Our Quota of Blankits (which I expect is nearly rais'd and Lodg'd at Newtown) will amount to between 5 & £600.

Another letter† reads:

New Town, Bucks Co., 31th July, 1777.

Timothy Matlack, Esq.,
Secretary to Honorable the Executive Council.
Philadelphia.
Sir,

> According to my directions from Colonel Kirkbride I have sent by Samuel Rees, Waggoner, One Hundred of the best & cleanest Blankets of those collected in our County, the remainder, about 200 shall send (this Morning) to Thomas Jink's Fulling, who says if the Weather continues Dry he will compleat them in a Week. At which time shall expect Orders for the delivery of them.

I am with real regard,

Sir, your Most Humble Serv't,

JOHN BENEZET.

On Saturday morning, September 20, 1777, the wounded Marquis de Lafayette passed through Newtown enroute to Bethlehem. He was conveyed in the carriage of Henry Laurens, and had probably spent the previous night at Four Lanes' End, [Langhorne].

Notwithstanding the vigilance of the militia which encircled Philadelphia during the British occupation of the City, raiding parties of British and American Tories occasionally penetrated their lines. In one of these instances a troop of British Light

*Pennsylvania Archives, First Series, Vol. V. p. 342.
†Idem, p. 469.

33

Horse raided Jenks' Fulling Mill in Middletown township, and captured at Newtown Francis Murray, who had, according to Edward McMasters, secreted himself in an empty sugar hogshead in the cellar of his store at the southeast corner of State Street and Centre Avenue. The following letter‡ written by the colonel of Murray's regiment describes this raid:

Camp, Feb'ʸ 21st, 1778.

His Excellency Thomas Wharton, Junr., Esqr.,
Lancaster.

Sir,

    I am much concern'd to Inform your Excellency that an Express arrived in Camp yesterday afternoon, with the disagreeable news of a party of Light Horse belonging to the Enemy, consisting of about Forty, pushed up to Newtown, Bucks County, and took my Major, with a small party of men, Prisoners, and all the cloathing I had laid up there for my Regiment. My hopes of getting my Regiment genteelly and well cloathed this campaigne are vanish'd, unless your Excellency & the Council will assist me in it, which I must Intreat in the strongest manner. I really hop'd sir, my own activity would have saved you this trouble, but 'tis my misfortune to find all my good intentions frustrated by this most unlucky blow. My poor fellows are in a most deplorable situation at present, scarcely a shirt to one of their Backs, & equally distress'd for the other necessarys; but they bear it patiently, and however they may suffer for the want, I must say, I would rather wait a few weeks untill I could get all their cloathing together.

    I now send Mr. Howel 22 ℔ Thread; 57 Groce Coat, & 42 Groce Vest Buttons; 326⅝ yards Tow linin; 7 p'es Shalloon, & 4 p'es blue Broad cloth, Cont'g, 63½ yards (trimmings I was sending to New town for the Cloths); these things I must request he will make the best use of in his power for my men; they are sufficient for the trimming of 300 suits cloathes, which I could wish to be blue and red if possible, as I know White cannot now be obtained.

    As I write Mr. Howel on the subject, I shall not trouble your Excellency farther, well knowing every exertion is now making use of by the Council to have their Troops well cloathed.

    I am with great respect
        and Esteem, your
            Excellencys most
                obed't hu'ble serv't,
                    WALTER STEWART,
                    Col. 13th P. Reg't.

    New town is 24 miles from Philad'a, and the Militia are posted at Bustle Town, which makes this a most daring attempt on their side, and an unfortunate one on mine.

                        W. S.

    General Washington himself was very much alarmed over this affair and wrote the following* from Valley Forge on February 23, 1778:

    The insolence of the disaffected in Philadelph'a and Bucks Counties has arisen to a very alarming Height. They have seized and carried off a number of respectable inhabitants in those Counties, and such officers of

‡Idem, Vol. VI, p. 295.
*Pennsylvania Archives, First Series, Vol. VI, p. 291.

the Army as fell in their way,† among others, Major Murray, of the 13th Pennsylvania Regiment, who was at Newtown with his family. What adds to the misfortune is, that they carried off near 2000 y^ds of Cloth which had been collected in the County, and was making up for the Regiment. In the last Paragraph of your letter you say that the Cloathing coming to Camp is for the 3^d, 6th, 9th, and 12th Regiments, as you expected that the 13th would be otherwise supplied. You probably had the Cloth in Newtown in View when you wrote, but that being lost, you will undoubtedly make proper provision for that Regiment.

The following item is taken from page 5 of the Account* of Joseph Kirkbride, lieutenant of Bucks County:

> Paid for the pay and rations of a guard under the command of Capt. Thomas Huston, conducting British prisoners from Newtown to Philadelphia in 1778, and for a hire of a baggage waggon, April 8, 1779 . . . . . 50£-14-0.

In 1778 when the Continental Army lay encamped at Valley Forge and the British occupied Philadelphia, a conference was held at Newtown to arrange a cartel for the exchange of prisoners of war. General Washington and Sir William Howe each appointed a commission for the purpose. The American Commissioners were: Col. William Grayson, Lieut. Col. Alexander Hamilton, Lieut. Col. Robert H. Harrison of Washington's staff, and Elias Boudinot, Esq. The British Commissioners were: Col. Charles O'Hara of the Cold Stream Guards, Col. Humphrey Stevens of the First Regiment of Foot, and Capt. Richard Fitzpatrick of the Third Regiment of Foot. Each Commission was attended by an escort of 12 Light Dragoons, the American troop being under command of Capt. Robert Smith of Baylor's Regiment.

The Commissioners met first at Germantown on March 31, 1778, but adjourned to Newtown on April 6th, and assembled at Strickland's Hotel [Brick Hotel]. They remained at Newtown until the 12th, but failed to come to an agreement. In a letter written by Col. Boudinot after the conference was over, he says of the British Commissioners:

> We were very sociable, but had previously obtained the character of our opponents, and were convinced they depended much on out-drinking us. We knew that Col. Grayson was a match for them and therefore left all that part of the business to him. They sat down often while we were preparing to go, till they could scarcely sit upright. Just before sundown they were put on their horses and went for the city.

The robbery of the county treasurer at Newtown by the

† Lieut. Henry Marsits and Ensign Joseph Cox were two of the others captured. [E. R. B.]
* Published at Philadelphia in 1786.

Doans and their confederates on the night of October 22, 1781, was one of the most exciting events of the day. John Hart, then treasurer, rented the house that is now in the possession of George W. Brown. Early that evening Moses Doan rode through the town to see if the situation was favorable, and about ten o'clock the house of the treasurer was surrounded, and Mr. Hart made prisoner. While sentinels kept watch outside and over the treasurer, others of the gang ransacked his house. Then, obtaining the keys of the treasurer's office, and one of them putting on Mr. Hart's hat and carrying his lighted lantern, as was his wont, the robbers went to the office, where they stole all the public money to be found. They got, in all 735£, 17s and 19½ d. in specie, and £1,307 in paper. That night they divided the spoils at the Wrightstown school house, which stood at the top of the hill and across the Durham Road from the Meeting House.

In the Fall of 1781, apprehension was felt that the movements of the enemy at Staten Island threatened another invasion of Pennsylvania. An alarm was sent out September 11th and 12th to all County Lieutenants to prepare at once to assemble their militia at Newtown. On the 28th the orders came to rendezvous at that point "with the utmost expedition." The Light Horse of Lancaster County; three companies, armed and unarmed, from Berks County; a troop of horse from Cumberland county; two companies from Philadelphia County; and some militia, together with the men of Chester and Bucks counties, turned out and were all encamped at Newtown on October 1, under the command of General Lacey.

When Newtown folk saw the hungry legions gathering, they must have felt some serious misgivings, probably lessons from past experience, to have caused William McCalla, the commissioner of purchases for Bucks county, to write the Council at Philadelphia in this strain:

> General Lacey and the Commissary of Issues at the Post of Newtown are Calling for Meat and other Supplies for the use of that Post and it is not in my Power to Supply them Without I be furnished with money as the People are Determined Not to Sell at Trust.

Fortunately the enemy failed to materialize, so the big scare was soon over. General Lacey on October 16th paid off the troops, and dismissed them after thanking them for mobilizing so quickly. An amusing incident in connection with the disbandment of the post at Newtown, was the meeting of the company of Col. MacVeagh's Philadelphia County Battalion. The day following their discharge, Capt. Bushkirk with Ensign Strine at the head of his company, marching to the tune of "The Rogues' March," proceeded to the quarters of Commissary General Crispin and demanded that each officer's canteen be filled with whiskey for use on the way home. On being refused, they threatened to blow up the powder magazine*. While the Commissary was defending it, Col. MacVeagh appeared upon the scene, paid the price of the rum out of his own pocket, and sent the men away rejoicing. Crispin demanded of General Lacey a courtmartial of these men, and referred him for witnesses to Capt. Craige, foragemaster; Lieut. Taylor, of the Light Horse of Bucks County; and Samuel Davis, quartermaster.

On July 24, 1782, the Council of Safety ordered that Col. Joseph Hart, Lieutenant of Bucks County, be directed to order out 50 men from the county militia to guard the jail at Newtown. In 1790, the Federal Government conducted the first census of the United States. At that time the population of the Bucks County jail was very small, there being only five inmates; namely, four men and one woman.

---

*This was the aforementioned county record office built prior to 1772.

The Hunt for the Van Horn Fortune

A Family Folly

Ok...what's this about the legend of the Van Horn family millions that had so many family members excited in the decades of the 1920s, 30s, & 40s? First, before we explore the farce of the "Van Horn millions" we need some background on the family.

Our last Van Horn ancestor was Mary Van Horn (d.1909). Mary was the mother of Jane (Starner?) who married John Boorem. We can trace Mary's ancestry back to the Dutch immigrant Christian B. Van Horn who settled in the new-world Dutch colony of New Amsterdam (New York) in the mid 1650s. Because the Dutch were meticulous record keepers, we know quite a bit about our early Van Horn ancestors. They left wills, business records, and most importantly for our essay here, land records.

The records tell us, among other things, that the family at one time owned a good chunk of what is modern-day New York City. The records show that the Van Horn family at one time owned pieces of Central Park, Harlem (a Dutch word) and the area around the Wall Street financial district. Of course, in those days these areas were mainly fields and cow pastures. It was the lawful ownership of some of this land that we are concerned with.

As Holland's fortunes faded, England became the dominate power in the New World; New Amsterdam became New York, however the Van Horn family still retained much of its ownership of their former pieces of Dutch New Amsterdam. It seems that family eventually arrived at an arrangement with the (state? city?) whereby it leased out some of its property to settlers for a period of 99 years. At the end of the lease ownership of the land was to revert to the Van Horn family.

To make a long story short, by the time the 99 year lease was up it seems that everybody had forgotten about the arrangement, and ownership of the land was deeded by New York to the people who had occupied the land for (by this time) several generations.

Then, in the early 20th century, the old lease (supposedly) resurfaced (was said to be in the possession of a certain Van Horn family member), and further evidence as to the existence of the lease was (supposedly, again) found in certain court records (which mysteriously disappeared before the hearings on the matter). This was enough to convince some family members that the city of New York had illegally deeded the land to the settlers following the expiration of the 99 year lease. Attorney's were hired to look into the matter, with a number of results which will be discussed later.

At about the same time there began a rumor that there was a vast Van Horn estate in Holland being held in escrow by the government, just waiting to be claimed by the legitimate descendants. Naturally, this caused further excitement. First, there was the prospect that the family was owed significant compensation for the violation of the 99 year lease by the City of New York, and second, there was the promise of a fortune waiting in Holland as well.

As word spread among the family, descendants were urged to gather in order to discuss what action, if any, was to be taken in regards to these matters. This meeting was the basis for what would become in the mid-1920s the annual Van Horn family reunion.

At this first meeting the main order of business was to form a committee to ascertain if the two claims mentioned above had any validity. It was also decided that in case there was a basis for these claims, it would be wise to begin the process of identifying all Van Horn family members. To do this you had to be able to trace your ancestry back to one of two Van Horn family members, the aforementioned Christian B. Van Horn, or his (bother? cousin?) Abraham Van Horn. The result was an impressive book published in 1928, "The Van Horn Family History," by Francis Marvin, that is loaded with valuable information and lineage for the two main

39

branches of the family. This work has always been by far the most impressive accomplishment of the whole affair, and, despite many inaccuracies, remains a valuable tool for the modern genealogist.

The book includes a synopsis of the family claims and the results of the committee's investigations into those claims; the genealogy section of the book provides a lot more information than a standard listing of descendants with dates of birth, marriage and death. In some instances the information reads like a county history, because it includes short stories and brief sketches of some of the family's more prominent pioneering members.

After about a year's worth of investigation the committee concluded that there was no hope of either of the two claims ever amounting to anything. The alleged lease was never produced, and records that had supposedly been in the possession of the city that may have supported the family's position suddenly disappeared.

Although family members claimed that this-and-that relative had the lease in their possession, or this-and-that relative had actually seen and read the lease, no one was able ever to produce the actual document. Another variation on the story says that the family was preparing to bring the lease in for examination, but it was destroyed in a fire. Several branches of the family (including my own) made this claim. My grandmother told me that her father, Hooker Boorem, always told her that his mother's brother Joe Starner was actually in possession of the lease but it had been burned in a fire.

The result was that when hearings were held in New York to determine the validity of the Van Horn claims, all the family could do was provide testimony from people who said they had seen the document and read the contents. No lease was ever produced. For it's part, the city maintained that although the records showed that the family had at one time owned the land in question, the city had in fact deeded the land to the present owners in a perfectly legal manner. The committee formed by the family to investigate the matter also felt that even if the alleged lease could have been produced and authenticated, the family would still have had great difficulty collecting any damages or compensation from the city.

As for the Van Horn estate in Holland, it appears that there had in fact been a valuable family fortune in Holland during the colonial period. Again, as in the case of the disputed lease, many, many years had passed. If the Dutch government had in fact confiscated the estate for a lack of heirs, they either no longer had a record of it or they weren't prepared to admit to it. Either way, this too became a dead issue.

The committee's conclusion and advice to family members was to give up their attempts to claim money that probably wasn't there in the first place. One can't help but feel that in their recommendation the committee did the family a great service. When one looks at the evidence (or lack thereof) its easy to see that the committee was on solid ground in recommending that family members give up the chase for the alleged Van Horn millions. They were able to cut through the hype and money-induced hysteria and render an objective and honest opinion on the matter, and for that the family should had been grateful. Unfortunately, some family members found it difficult to let go of their dreams.

The problem was that, despite the committee's recommendations, many family members were willing to spend their hard-earned money to continue the pursuit of the Van Horn millions. There were some unsuccessful legitimate attempts to revive the issue, but there were more instances of unscrupulous individuals taking advantage of people still hoping for some kind of windfall. For years afterwards, family members or their "attorney's" went around to descendants asking for a yearly donation to help fund the legal fight to recover the family's fortune. It was simple, if you contributed, you moved to the head of the list if and when the funds were recovered. Unfortunately it appears that my own ancestors fell prey to this ruse as well.

The hunt for the Van Horn millions is, at the same time, one of our most silly and fascinating family stories. The events and characters seem to be the stuff that Hollywood is made of. There were millions of dollars at stake. There were allegations of misconduct on the part of the City of New York and the Dutch government. There was the brave fight by descendants to recover what had been wrongfully taken from the family. There was the tragic fire that had destroyed the lease. There was money collected and spent in pursuit of the millions, and there was a parade of greedy and unscrupulous family members who took advantage of people (or is it that they simply took advantage of people's greedy nature?) No Hollywood script needed here!

Jeffrey L. Thomas

-1-

The Meeting of the Janeson Van Jorn Association held in Guernsey Hall Maron 24th, 1908.

Meeting was called to order by D. T. Scott, Chairman, Mr. Scott read a paper concerning the different lines which have been traced back to Patentees. These lines are as the New York Branch White House B----, Bergen County and Bucks County Branch. The N. Y. Branch has been traced back to Cornelius Jansen and Maria Jansen, the doughter of one of the patentess, under this line there are several families to be traced.

Mrs. Bigert comes under this line and is traced back to Cornelius Jansen. The White House Branch has been successfully traced back to 1759. The Bergen Branch and the White House B----, is where the missing link is. The Bergen County B---- comes down through Lawrence Jansen, one of the patentess and has been successfully traced, his descendants have been found scattered through Pennsylvania. He then stated that the meeting of today was called for purpose of raising funds to find those missing links. Mr. Bender said he thought he had those missing links and had the will of the father of Abraham Van Horn of the White House who was John, a son of Cornelius Jansen, and that he had spent a great deal of time and money in finding this record. He then read an abstract. of the will to John Van Horn which was taken from Page 235, New York abstract of wills. Motion was then made that the meeting adjourn until 1:30 P. M.

Minutes of the Van Horn Estate Meeting in Indiana County

-2-

Afternoon Session. Meeting opened at 1:30 o'clock by
Mr. D. T. Scott. Mr. Gross moves that the committee adjourn
and the meeting be re-opened as a general meeting, in order that
all members of the association may take part and feel at liberty
to do so. Motion carried. Mr. Scott suggests the reading of the
report of the auditing of the committee. Motion made by A. D.
Gardner that the report be receive d and placed on file. Mopion
carried. Motinn made by Mrs. Rambo that the Association be connected with the N. Y. Association; motion seconded and carried.
Mr. Gross with drew his second and asked that an amendment be xxx
made to this motion which is that Mr. Bender be asked to investigate
andreport to the secretary his findings of this accociation in N. Y.
and the committee be governed accordingly by the report of this investigation to be given at the next meeting. Motion seconded by
Mrs. Rambo. Mr. Gardner said that he sould be very reluctant to
join this Association until a thorough inbertigaticn has been made
and suggest leaving a motion of that kind rest. The amendment
made by Mr. Gross concerning the investigation of Mr. Bender's
N. Y. Association carried. Mr. Gross then brought up the subject of the member being allowed to examine the Secretary's books
but not being allowed to make copies, claiming that it was not
right for any of the committee to have vontrol of all this data,
and then made a motion that the motion which was carried in committee
meeting be cancelled and that any one have the privilege of copying
anything that interest their family of anyone whom they represent.
Mr. Van Horn said in Part, "Let any Person in this whole committee
send in their genealogy papers and family papers to this Association
and they can be traded; this Association will not trace their
genealogy for them unless they have paid in money to this Association.

Minutes of the Van Horn Estate Meeting in Indiana County

-3-

Isaac and George Logan born in Indiana County.

Copy of C. H. Van Horn's letter (Sec. of the Janson
Van Horn Association fo Scranton) to Mrs. Gourly of Harrisburg.

Taylor, Pa., Oct. 17th, 1907

Dear Madam:

I really am obliged to ask you pardon for not answering
your letter sooner. I have been awaiting results all fo this
time, and waiting to get the wills in New York City and other
sources. to clinch the genealogy back to the patentees.

We have new wills, marriage records, New York Marriages
records, New Jersey records and all of the New Jersey Histo-
tical Society Proceedings of Patterson N. J. and New York City,
and I have only three more wills to get from the old colonial
wills on file in the Clerk of the Court of Appeals at Albany,
N. Y. From The evidence of records, wehave now in our hands
enough data to connect any branch or family and now the committee is about ready to take up this work. It has been a
hard year's work and most of the people think there has been
nothins done. Rather a thankless position. Your family can
be traced but I have not had the time, having put in the time
on the other end and find we can connect back to the patent
all right with bur only one missing link, bur I think I will
get it when I get what I have sent for.

I think that in the neat future there will be a general
meeting called so that all can see what has been done, it is
a long chapter. I will be pleased to hear from you at any
time and I will answer at once on receipt of yours, etc.
I am very truly yours,

C. H. Van Horn, Sec.

Minutes of the Van Horn Estate Meeting in Indiana County

45

Genealogy and Biographical sketch at the Van Horns in Holland.

The original name Barensten was a noted family of Hooren, a town in the northern part of the Province of Holland. This fact is borne out by the Coat of Arms, a picture of which was obtained. Richard H. Van Horn, Tradition has it, that of the five original brothers who should have inherited equally the vast estate in Holland by the laws of the Netherlands Netherlands The oldest son became the legatee in order to keep up the nobility of the family. The other four brothers left the estate, with it one of the brothers seems to have left his original name. (The only member of which we have any account) Christian Barenaten who married in 1652, came to America, locating at Bergen, and was commissioned at Ft. Delaware, Died of Dysentery in 1658, and was buried at Bergen.

Children of Christian Baranaten and Janetz Hang, his wife.

Bernard Christian Van Horn, (who remained at Bergen).

Captain Cornelius)
Abraham   (from Bergen to Hunderton Co.
Lena   )

These three built the White House, still in possession of thier offspring and a noted landmark today.

The eldest son, Bernard Christian Van Horn, said to have been born in Holland in 1658 in the town of Hooran from which he derived his name, Van meaning from, hence Van Hooren or Van Horn. Barnet or Bernard Van Horn had nine sons and one daughter.

Minutes of the Van Horn Estate Meeting in Indiana County

-2-

CHILDREN

Richard, Born -------	) Abraham, born -------
Christian, " 1681	(Isaac, " -------
Peter, " 1686	) Janitz, " 1696, who married
Barnet or Bernard,Born 1691	(and remained in Bergen.
John, born 1692	)

Seven of these children moved to Bucks County. Among the first marriages were the Van Sants, Cornells, Hagermans, Longshires, Corsans, Woodmans, Burleys, Gillmans, Wyncoops, Van Pelts and Reeder.

Christian B. Van Horn from whom our immediate Branch descends, (born, 1681) married Williemetse Van Dyke.

CHILDREN

Bernard, born 1702	(Catherine, born, 1719
Henry, " 1707	) Jane, " 1721
John, " 1713	(Charity, " 1723
Ann, " 1716	) Christian, " 1728

Henry born in 1707, the second son of Christian, married Susana Van Fleck. Second Henry born 1728, married in 1758 to Elizabeth Van Sant, born -----, died 1775.

Their Children Were

Joshua, born 1759	) Susane, born 1768
Isaiah, " 1760	(Elizabeth, " 1770
Mary, " 1764	) Sarah, " 1775
Christian, " 1766	(Henry, " 1777
	(copy from Mrs. Hall.)

Isaiah Van Horn born in Bucks County, Oct. 24th, 1760, died Aug. 27th, 1844.

CHILDREN

Henry Van Horn	) Isaiah Van Horn
Alexander Van Horn	(William " "
Jane " " (married)	Nancy " "--(married
Joshua " " McElhoes(	Isaac " " Hamilton)
John " 2	) George Logen Van Horn

Henry, Alexander, and Jane were born in Bucks County, Joshua and John " " " Cumberland "/ Isaiah, William and Nancy " " " Westmoreland Co. Prior to formation fo Indiana Co.

Minutes of the Van Horn Estate Meeting in Indiana County

Motion was then made that Mr. Gross be dropped from the committee; motion carried; question called and rising vote tak-
en, 23 in favor of discharging him and 15 for his retainment;
the majority being in favor of discharging him, the motion
was carried and so ordered by Chairman that Mr. Gross be
Dropped.

The question as to how funds were to be raised was then .
taken up. Mr. Johnson Muthersbaugh of Lewiston asked the
amount needed; it was thought about $500,00. It was then sug-
gested that each member pay at that time wat he thought he c
could and then an assessment be made to raise $500.00. Each
member to pay $1.00 or $1.50 per month and in that way enough
money would be raised to meet the running espenses. Motion
was made and carried that assessment be made and a donation
be taken up. There was taken up at this time $63.50.

Mr. Scott suggested that something be done withthe
vacancy caused by the removal of Mr. Gross. Motion made that
Mr. Rev. Azar be made a member of the committee, motion carried.
Mr. Ven Horn suggested that committee be increased and that
Mr. Bender of Philadelphia become a member; motion carried and
accepted by Mr. Bender.

Motion was made by the Rev. Azar that the committee be
given a vote of thanks for their service to the association
by rising vote; motion carried unanimously.

(seal) C. H. Van Horn, Secy.

Minutes of the Van Horn Estate Meeting in Indiana County

Generations from Barnet or Bernard Van Horn direct to
Alexander's grand children.

Barnet or Bernard Van Horn, or Hooren

Christian B. Van Horn, born 1681, (Married Williametze
                                    Van Dyke, died Nov.
                                    25th, 1751.)
Henry Van Horn, born Sept, 15th, 1707,(married Elizaboth
                                    Van Sant) died---

Isaiah VaN Hornm born Oct. 24th, 1760, died Aug. 27, 1844
                 (married Dorcas Logan)

Alexander Van Horn, Born,-----   Died -----
                 (married Mary Wherry)

Minutes of the Van Horn Estate Meeting in Indiana County

INDIANA PEOPLE AND VANHORN ESTATE

James W. VanHorn Has Best Claim for a Share in Rich Lands.

FILED THEIR DOCUMENTS

Papers Setting Forth Relationships Forwarded to Philadelphia Representative.

ONE HEIR MUST BE SHOWN

Should the Van Horn heirs receive all the millions spoken of in the article sent out by Canby Van Horn, of Ambler, near Philadelphia, there are members of the family who would probably be enriched by more than the $30,000 share the claimant referred to says will be his share. One of these is Col. Robert T. Van Horn, a member of the fifth generation of descendants where as Canby belongs to the seventh.

J. W. Van Horn, of No 735 Locust street, is a nephew of Col. Van Horn and the only member of the sixth generation residing here In addition to the seventh generation claimants previously named other Indiana persons who are heirs of equal standing are: Mrs. William McAdoo, of Oak street; Mrs. Madison McLaughlin, of Grant street, and John Houk, of the West End Hotel. All these are direct descendants of Isaiah Van Horn.

The Indiana county branch are descended from Henry Van Horn, grandfather of J. W. Van Horn, who settled near Georgeville almost a century ago. Henry Van Horn married a Thompson and his children are inter-married with the McElhoes, Houk, McLaughlin and other well-known Indiana county families.

In connection with the fight for the $11,000,000 estate in the heart of New York City it is interesting to note that a Philadelphia member of the flamily who in his capacity as a lawyer instituted preliminary work died suddenly when he had gotten but rightly started in the work. It was found afterward that he had died from poisoning, but the manner in wh'ch he received the deadly drug is not known. Following his death many valuable papers relating to the estate were lost and have not as yet re-appeared.

Canby Van Horn and a Mrs. Hall, of Philadelpaia, made a new start and it is through their efforts that the suit has finally been won in court after a twenty years battle. Mrs. Hall solicited funds from the Indiana county Van Horns and has many papers relating to their claims. It is stated that Col. Robert T. Van Horn, the nearest heir, is not interested in the claims of his relatives and does not believe a fortune will be theirs. He formerly edited the Kansas City "Journal" and represented the Corn State in Congress for years.

REGAINS HER SIGHT.

7 Dec 1907 Indiana Evening Gazette

Ancestors of Henry B. VAN HORN

Generation No. 1

1. CAPTAIN Henry B. VAN HORN[1,2], born 02 Oct 1734 in Newtown Twp., Bucks Cnty, PA[2]; died Dec 1777 in Wrightstown, Bucks Cnty, PA[2,3]. He was the son of **2. Henry VAN HORN** and **3. Susanna VAN VLECK**. He married **(1) Elizabeth VAN ZANT**[4] 10 Aug 1758 in Bucks Cnty, PA[4,5]. She was born 1736 in Lower Makefield Twp., Bucks Cnty, PA[6], and died 25 Nov 1807 in Bensalem, Bucks Cnty, PA[6]. She was the daughter of Isaiah VAN ZANT and Gertje Charity VAN HOORN.

Notes for CAPTAIN Henry B. VAN HORN:
The Volume 1 p. 207 Daughters of the American Colonists lists the middle initial as B.

According to the muster roll extracted from the Pennsylvania Archives, 2nd Series, Vol. 14
Captain Henry Van Horne's Company January 22, 1777
Captain: Henry Van Horn
1st Lieutenant: Robert Ramsey
2nd Lieutenant: Thomas Huston
Ensign: Abram Johnson
Sergeant: Andrew McMinn
Corporal: John Vance
Drummer: Isaiah Van Horn (his son)
Privates: Jeremiah Van Horn (relationship unknown) Joshua Van Horn (son) and 15 additional men

---

Henry Van Horn, son of Henry and Susanna (Van Vlecq) Van Horn, was reared on the old homestead purchased by his grandfather, Christian Van Horn, in 1726, and at the death of his father, in 1761, inherited a one-half interest therein with his brother Christian. They made a division of the 252 acres, each conveying to the other 126 acres in 1773. After the reverses on Long Island in November, 1776, and at Fort Washington when the Continental forces were so badly routed and so many of the Bucks county contingent were taken prisoners, Henry Van Horn raised an independent company of militia and was commissioned their captain, December 6 1776, (See Penna. Arch. Vol. XIV p. 175)and took them into the service, He died of camp fever late in 1777.. He married Elizabeth Vansant, daughter of Isaiah and Charity (Van Horn) Van Zant, and they were the parents of eight children: Joshua, born February 21, 1759; Isaiah, born October 24, 1760, was drummer in his father's company, 1776-7; Mary, born May 5, 1764, married Isaac Gillam, died April 18, 1823; Christian, born July 13, 1766; Susanna, born October 9, 1768, married Jesse Willett, who had previously married her sister Sarah; Elizabeth, married an Anderson, and died January 26, 1813; Sarah, born February 7, 1773, married Jesse Willett, died prior to 1809; Henry, born April 5, 1777. Elizabeth the mother, died November 25, 1807, aged about eighty years.

Henry Van Horn, youngest child of Captain Henry and Elizabeth (Vansant) Van Horn, born in Newtown township, April 5, 1777, learned the trade of a carpenter and cabinet maker and located at Yardley, Bucks county, where he followed the trade of a cabinet maker for several years. His Sign uniquely painted is now in possession of his grandson, Richard H. Van Horn, of Lambertville, New Jersey. He also purchased a farm of 93 acres in Lower Makefield in 1805, which, in 1811,he conveyed to his brother-in-law, Isaac Gillam. He purchased a farm of 200 acres in Upper Makefield, near Eagle Tavern, where he resided the balance. of his life. He died in February,. 1849. He married, in 1798,

Isaiah Van Horn Pioneer of Indiana County, Pennsylvania

Hannah Reeder, of Canaan, Upper Makefield, and their six children who grew to maturity were as follows:

1. Abraham, born 1802, married, in 1829, Eliza Hampton, by whom he had one child, Margery. He married (second) Christiana Neald, and a son Henry K. was born in 1834. He married (third) Elizabeth Sampsel. He sold his farm in Upper Makefield and removed to Sandy Spring, Maryland, where he reared a family of thirteen children.

2. Elizabeth, born 1804, married William Ryan, of Upper Makefield, born 1810. They settled near Rocksville, Northampton township, Bucks county, and engaged in the milling business. Three of their children survive: Edward H., born 1832; Mary, born 1835; and Hannah, born 1839.

3. Eleanor H., born 1810, married Cornelius Slack, and settled in Lower Makefield. He was lately a merchant at Dolington. Their children are: Watson, born 1832 ; John H., born 1833; Henry V., born 1836; Jane E., born 1839; Sarah E., born 1841; William H., born 1843; Anna M., born 1847; and Hannah, born 1850.

4. Moses H., born January 15, 1812, at Yardleyville, removed with his parents to Upper Makefield, where he spent his entire life, inheriting at his father's death, in 1849 100 acres of the old homestead. He was a successful farmer and a prominent man in the community, holding many positions of trust and honor. He and his wife and family were lifelong members of the Society of Friends. He married, April 13, 1843, Rebecca Scattergood, born February 7, 1820, daughter of John* and Catherine (Hepburn) Scattergood, of Makefield, who died September 15, 1895. Moses died February 13, 1885. They were the parents of nine children : Richard H., born 1844; Mary Anna, born 1846; Samuel S., born 1848 . ; William T., born 1851 ; George F., and Catharine S., twins, born 1854; Hannah E., born 1857; Benjamin F., born 1860; and Emma L., born 1863.

5. Mary A., born 1816, married Christian Van Horn, born 1814, and settled on a farm near Dolington. Their surviving issue are: Cyrus B, Jane E., Cornelius S., Hannah E., and Callender C.

6. John R., born 1820, married Rebecca Feaster, and settled on a portion of the old homestead in Upper Makefield. Their surviving children are: James P., David F., Emeline, Watson, Martha F., and Joseph F.

RICHARD H. VAN HORN, eldest son of Moses and Rebecca (Scattergood) Van Horn. born at the old homestead of his grandfather, in 1844, was reared on the Upper Makefield farm, acquired a limited education at the public school and later took a course at Union Business College in Philadelphia. After a few years experience in the mercantile business in Philadelphia, he started into that business for himself at Lambertville, New Jersey, in 1868. By strict application to business and a close study of the wants and needs of the community, he soon built up a large trade and his remodeled store in 1884 named "Grand Depot" enjoyed much more than a local reputation and soon outgrew its early modest quarters. In 1877 an adjoining building was added and the volume of business doubled. Seven years later the entire property was remodeled and both stores thrown into one, making a large and commodious department store, and his brother, Samuel S., who had been for some years a clerk in the establishment was given all interest in the business, and the firm name became R. H. Van Horn & Brother. The partnership of the growing establishment extended far beyond the limits of Jersey into their native county, and the country districts and towns of New Jersey. In 1889 the brothers dissolved partnership and Richard H. continued the business alone until 1892, when his son Henry came of age and was admitted as a partner. Ten years later the younger son, Edmori E., becoming of age, also became a partner, and the firm of R. H. Van Horn & Sons, continued to conduct the popular and successful establishment that has grown from its modest beginning of 1868. With the addition of a new building. the floor space of which combined with the original "Grand Depot" covers now (1904) about three quarters of an acre. Richard H. Van Horn married, in 1869, Lydia Beatty Warner, born in 1845, daughter of Edwards Edmunds Warner, of

Philadelphia, and of New England ancestry, and they are the proud parents of two sons. both of whom, as before stated. are members of the firm. Henry E., the eldest, born April 21, 1870, Marrie Era Runkle, of Hunterdon county, New Jersey; and Edmori E., born in October, 1879, married Jessie I Hoffman of the same place. Mr. R. H. Van Horn is all active member of the Society of Friends, having many years since transferred his certificate of membership from Wrightstown Monthly Meeting to Solebury where he and his wife have Lydianna were subsequently appointed elders. Mr. R.H. Van Horn has always shown an active spirit in his town affairs but little interest in "Political Pulls"; he his, however, served in the school board, acted as a member of the board of trade, and at present is next to the oldest director in the Amwell National Bank of Lambertville.

SAMUEL. SCATERGOOD VAN HORN, second son of Moses and Rebecca (Scattergood) VanHorn. whose ancestry his been given in the preceding, was born in Makefield township, Bucks county, Pennsylvania, October 28, 1848, and was reared on the Upper Wakefield farm; acquiring his education at the public schools of that township. In 1870 he went to Lambertville. New Jersey. In 1889 Samuel S. Van Horn embarked in the general merchandise business in Lambertville. where he carried on a successful business for three years. He then purchased his present location, where he has since conducted a successful business. Mr. Van Horn married, in 1888, Ella M.. Dilley, daughter of Louis and Caroline (Larison) Dilley, of Kingwood, Hunterdont county, New Jersey. To this marriage .has been born two sons, Lloyd and Earl. Mr. Van Horn is all extensive real estate owner in Lambertville, owning fifteen resident properties. He is a member of the Society of Friends.

Captain Henry Van Horn was Captain of The Independent Company at Fort Washington, Pa., died 1777.

More About CAPTAIN Henry B. VAN HORN:
Burial: Unknown, Wrightstown, PA
Military service: 1777, Captain of Van Horn's Company of Bucks County, PA militia[7,8]

More About Elizabeth VAN ZANT:
Burial: Unknown, Newtown, Bucks Cnty, PA

More About Henry VAN HORN and Elizabeth VAN ZANT:
Marriage: 10 Aug 1758, Bucks Cnty, PA[9,10]

Generation No. 2

2. Henry VAN HORN[11,12], born Bet. 15 Sep 1704 - 1707 in Newtown Twp., Bucks Cnty, PA; died Jun 1761 in Newtown Twp., Bucks Cnty, PA[13]. He was the son of **4. Christian Barentsen VAN HOORN** and **5. Williamtje VAN DYKE**. He married **3. Susanna VAN VLECK** 19 Oct 1728.
    3. Susanna VAN VLECK[14,15,16], born Bet. 1711 - 1715; died Jun 1776 in Bucks Cnty, PA[17]. She was the daughter of **6. Paulus VAN VLECK** and **7. Jannetje VAN DYKE**.

Notes for Henry VAN HORN:
    According to C. S. Willima's book "Christian Barentsen Van Horn and His Descendants" NY 1911 we find the following:
    Henry b. 1707, m, Susanna Van Vleck dau. of Paulus Van Vleck. Lived in Newtown, Bucks Co., PA. He died in 1761 and is buried in the Feaster Grave Yard. She inherited from her grandfather Hendrick Janse Van Dyck, one half of his real estate, the other half was bequeathed to her Aunt Willemtje, wife of Christian Van Horn.

Isaiah Van Horn Pioneer of Indiana County, Pennsylvania

His will dated Newtown, Bucks Co., PA May 9, 1761. Proved Dec. 10, 1761, makes provision for his wife Susanna--gives to eldest daughter Jane Johnson, youngest daughter Susanna Longshore and to sons Christian and Henry.

Susanna (Van Vleck) Van Horn made her will Apr. 18, 1776, proved June 22, 1776. Names sons and daughters and g.d. Susanna Johnson.

DAC shows birth date as 1707

Pennsylvania Wills, 1682-1834 BUCKS COUNTY Page 74. Henry Vanhorn, of Newtown Twp., Yeoman. May 9, 1761. Proved December 10, 1761. Wife Susanna. Sons Christian and Henry, exrs. Plantation in Newtown. Daus. Jane, eldest, wife of John Johnson, youngest daughter. Susanna Longshore. Wit: George Dunn, Jno. Atkinson, Junr., Wm. Ashburn.

Henry Van Horn born September 15. 1707. died in Newtown township, Bucks county, in 1761. He married his first cousin, Susanna Van Vleck, daughter of Rev. Paulus and Janetje (Van Horn) Van Vleck. She inherited from her grandfather, Hendrick Van Dyck, one half of his real estate, and 173 acres thereof was conveyed to Henry by the same proceedings as in the case of his father. an the latter at his death devised to Henry 200 acres,. in Newtown, and it was devised by the will of Henry in 1761 to his sons , Christian and Henry. Susanna, the widow of Henry, died in 1776. They were the of four children, Christian, who married June 14, 1764, Sarah Vansant; Henry Van Horn, died 1777, married Elizabeth Vansant; Jane. who married John Johnson; and Susannah, who married Euclides Longshore.

More About Henry VAN HORN:
Burial: Unknown, Feaster Graveyard, Bucks Cnty, PA

Notes for Susanna VAN VLECK:
DAC Vol. 3, p.112 the spelling of the name is given as VanVlecq
Will was proved 22 June 1776.

Marriage Notes for Henry VAN HORN and Susanna VAN VLECK:
The Daughters of the American Colonists(DAC) Vol.1, p. 207 lists a marriage date of 1727.

More About Henry VAN HORN and Susanna VAN VLECK:
Marriage: 19 Oct 1728

Children of Henry VAN HORN and Susanna VAN VLECK are:
        i.   Jane VAN HORN[18], died Unknown; married John JOHNSON 25 Dec 1762; died Unknown.

           More About John JOHNSON and Jane VAN HORN:
           Marriage: 25 Dec 1762

      ii.   Susanna VAN HORN[18], died Unknown; married Euclides LONGSHORE 14 Oct 1768; died Unknown.

           More About Euclides LONGSHORE and Susanna VAN HORN:
           Marriage: 14 Oct 1768

iii.   Christian VAN HORN[18,19,20], born 29 Aug 1728 in Newtown Twp., Bucks
       Cnty, PA[21]; died 1777; married Sarah VAN ZANT 14 Jun 1764; born 1740;
       died Bef. 05 Oct 1785.

Notes for Christian VAN HORN:
Christian Van Horn, eldest son of Henry and Susanna (Van Vlecq) Van horn,
born in Newtown Township, Bucks County, married June 14, 1764, Sarah
Vansant, daughter of Isaiah and Charity (Van Horn) Vansant, of Lower
Makefield. Her mother, Charity (Van Horn) Vansant, being a daughter of Peter
and Elizabeth (Gabriels) Van Horn. Christian Van Horn inherited from his
father 126 acres of land in Newtown township, on the Neshaminy Creek, part
of the land purchased by his grandfather, Christian Van Horn in 1726, whereon
he lived until his death in 1777, when it was divided between his sons Henry
and Isaiah.

Sarah (Vansant) Van Horn died in 1785. They were the parents of but two
children, viz.: Henry and Isaiah.

Henry, married, April 26, 1787, Elizabeth McCorkle, and had three children;

  Amos, born March 4, 1792, died at Newtown, September 5, 1823, married,
January 8, 1817, Mercy Starkey;
  Susan, born October 25. 1794, died in Michigan, September 5, 1872, married
Joseph Roberts; and
  Elizabeth, born January 27, 1797, married Joseph Winship, and died at
Newtown, May 12, 1868.

Isaiah Van Horn, second son of Christian and Sarah (Vansant) Van Horn, was
born in Newtown Township, Bucks County, married, December 31, 1794,
Catharine Suber, daughter of John and Catharine (Van Horn) Suber, and his
first cousin. He was adjudged fifty acres of the homestead farm by the orphans'
court in 1787, but on March 15, 1791, sold it to his brother Henry, and on his
marriage in 1794 took up his residence on a farm belonging to the estate of his
father-in-law, Isaiah Vansant, in Upper Makefield, where he died in 1802. His
widow, Catharine, married John Wynkoop, January 31, 1805. The only child of
Isaiah and Catharine(Vansant) Van Horn, was Sarah, born February 29, 1796;
died January 27, 1838. She married (first) on January 16. 1812, Aaron Winder,
and (second) August 24, 1825, Abner Morris. Catharine Wynkoop, the mother,
died in December, 1820. R. Winder Johnson, of Philadelphia, to whom we are
indebted for the above account of the Van Horn family, is a grandson of Aaron
and Sarah (Van Horn) Winder, great-grandson of Isaiah and Catharine (Suber)
Van Horn, great-great-grandson of both Christian and Sarah (Vansant) Van
Horn, and John and Catharine (Van Horn) Suber, and great-great-great-
grandson of Henry and Susanna (Van Vlecq) Van Horn, John and Lena (Van
Pelt) Van Horn, and Isaiah and Charity (Van Horn) Vansant, and great-great-
great-great-Grandson of Christian and Williamiantje (Vandyck) Van Horn, and
Peter and Elizabeth (Gabriells) Vanhorn, the last mentioned Christian and
Peter Van Horn, being sons of Barendt Christianzen Van Hoorn and his wife
Geertje Dircks Classen, and grandsons of Christian Baretzen Van Hoorn and
Jannetje Jans, the pioneer ancestors of the family in America.

Isaac Van Horn, of Solebury township, Bucks county,Pennsylvania, was
commissioned January 1, 1776, ensign of Captain John
Beatty's company, Bucks county's contingent of the Flying Camp Fifth

Pennsylvania Battalion. Colonel Robert Magaw, and was taken prisoner at Fort Washington, November 16, 1776. Exchanged in 1778, and promoted to lieutenant, July 1, 1779; captain, Second Pennsylvania June 19 1781. Retired from service January 1, 1783. Settled in Westmoreland County, Pennsylvania, 1781. Member of seventh and eighth congress, 1801-1803 from Pennsylvania. Receiver of public monies at Zanesville Ohio in 1815. Died in Muskingum county, Ohio, February 2, 1831. Pennsylvania Archives, Second Series.

More About Christian VAN HORN and Sarah VAN ZANT:
Marriage: 14 Jun 1764

  iv. Daniel VAN HORN, born 1729; died Unknown; married Anna BARLLMAN; died Unknown.

1   v. CAPTAIN Henry B. VAN HORN, born 02 Oct 1734 in Newtown Twp., Bucks Cnty, PA; died Dec 1777 in Wrightstown, Bucks Cnty, PA; married Elizabeth VAN ZANT 10 Aug 1758 in Bucks Cnty, PA.

Generation No. 3

4. Christian Barentsen VAN HOORN[22,23], born Bet. 24 Oct 1680 - 21 Oct 1681 in Bergen Cnty, NJ[24]; died Bet. 23 Nov 1751 - 25 Nov 1753 in Nothhampton Twp., Bucks Cnty, PA[24]. He was the son of **8. Barent Christiansen VAN HOORN** and **9. Geertje Dircks CLAUSSEN**. He married **5. Williamtje VAN DYKE** 20 May 1700.
  5. Williamtje VAN DYKE[24,25], born 04 Jul 1681 in Staten Island, NY[26]; died 06 May 1760 in Richboro, Bucks Cnty, PA[26]. She was the daughter of **10. Hendrick Jans VAN DYKE** and **11. Jennetje HEERMANS**.

Notes for Christian Barentsen VAN HOORN:
  The footnote in the Volume 1 of the Daughters of American Colonists on page 207 indicates that Christian Van Horn(1681-1751) was representative to the Provincial Congress from Bucks County, Pa., 1725, 30, 34.

  DAC Vol. 3, p.112 footnotes indicate that Christian (Barendtse) VanHorn (1681-1751) of New Amsterdam, New York, was a fire warden,burgher and landed proprietor. He was born in Holland. Note that this statement is in error as it was his grandfather that was the fire warden and born in Holland.

  DAC Vol. 3, p.112 lists Christian Van Horn (1681-1751), of Bucks County, PA as a member of the Pennsylvania Assembly.

  Member of the Pa. Provencal assembly from 1723-1737 and lived in Bucks Cnty, Pa. He was one of Bucks Counties most outstanding citizens in his time.

  Christian Van Horn. second son of Barendt and Geertje (Dirckse) Van Horn, born at Bergen, New Jersey, October 24. 1681. He married Williamtje Van Dyck, daughter of Hendrick Janse and Jennetje (Heermans) Van Dyck, and granddaughter of Jan Tomasse Van Dyck, who emigrated from Amsterdam in 1652 and settled in New Utrecht, Long Island.
.

Isaiah Van Horn Pioneer of Indiana County, Pennsylvania

Christian Van Horn located in Northampton township, Bucks county, on 294 acres conveyed to him by his father in 1707. In 1737 two hundred acres of the land belonging to the estate of his father-in-law, Hendrick Van Dyck, in Middleton township was conveyed to him by Jeremiah Langhorne, as "straw man" in effecting the transfer from the devices of Van Dyck to Christian Van Horn. He represented Bucks County in the Pennsylvania assembly for the years 1723-1732 and 1734-1737, thirteen years in all. He died November 23, 1751. and his wife May 6, 1760. She was born or. Staten Island, July 4, 1681. The will of Christian Van Horn devised to his eldest son Bernard the home plantation of 205 acres in Northampton, to his son Henry 200 acres on which Henry was living in Newtown, purchased of George and Joseph Randal in 1726; to his son John thirty-two acres in Northampton, to his daughter Charity Van Dure another tract adjoining containing forty-one acres, and to his son Christian 187 acres in Northampton, when he should come of age; the other children receiving their shares of his estate in money. To his son-Barnard he bequeathed his large Bible. This Bible is now in the possession of Dr. Wilmer Krusen, of 127 North Twenty-ninth street, Philadelphia, having descended to him from his ancestors. the Hegemans, John Hegeman having married Jane Van Horn, daughter of Christian, who inherited it from her brother, Barnard Van Horn, who died in 1760, without issue. It was printed at Dordrecht in 1690, and was purchased by Hendrick Van Dyck in December, 1701, and presented to his daughter Williamtje, who married Christian Van Horn. On the fly leaf it contains the record of the birth of the children of Hendrick Van Dyck, those of Christian and Williamtje Van Horn, and those of John and Jannetje (Van Horn) Hegeman.

Notes for Williamtje VAN DYKE:
Williamtje Van Dyck, daughter of Hendrick Janse and Jennetje (Heermans) Van Dyck, and granddaughter of Jan Tomasse Van Dyck, who emigrated from Amsterdam in 1652 and settled in New Utrecht, Long Island. His sixth child. Hendrick Janze, baptized July 2, 1653, married, February 7, 1680 Jannetje Hermans, daughter of Herinan Janse Van Barkeloo, and settled on Staten Island, where he was a constable in 1689 and assessor in 1703. In 1704 he purchased land in Bucks county and removed there. At the organization of Bensalem church, in 1710. he produced a certificate from the Staten Island church. He purchased four tracts of land in Middletown, two of which he retained until his death in 1721, and devised to his daughter Williamtje, wife ,of Christian Van Horn. and his granddaughter Elizabeth Van Vleck. who later married her cousin, Henry Van Horn. He had but two children, Williamtje, and Jannetje, who became the wife of the Reverend Paulus Van Vleck, , the first pastor at Neshaminy.

Death date and place provided by Marge Gardner 7/28/1997 e-mail mgardner@shadowlink.net.

Pennsylvania Wills, 1682-1834 BUCKS COUNTY WILL BOOK 3 Page 13. Williamkee Vanhorn, Northampton. April 25, 1760. Proved May 26, 1760. Daus. Charity Vanduren, Katharine Hagerman, and Jane Hagerman. Granddau. M. Vanhorn and her Bro. and Sis. Dau-in-law Susanna Vanhorn. Granddau. Mimy Corson. Granddau. Williamky Vanduren. Daus. Charity and Jane and Garret Wyncoop, exrs. Wit: Wm. Hibbs, Patience Vanhorn, Jos. Wildman.

More About Christian VAN HOORN and Williamtje VAN DYKE:
Marriage: 20 May 1700

Children of Christian VAN HOORN and Williamtje VAN DYKE are:
      i.   Bernard VAN HOORN, born 19 Feb 1701; died 12 Apr 1760; married Jannetje VAN BOSKERK 31 Dec 1741; died Unknown.

        Notes for Bernard VAN HOORN:
        Barnard Van Horn, born February 19.1701-2, died April 22, 1760. married

Isaiah Van Horn Pioneer of Indiana County, Pennsylvania

December 31, 1741, Jannentje Van Boskerk, had no children.

More About Bernard VAN HOORN and Jannetje VAN BOSKERK:
Marriage: 31 Dec 1741

2   ii.   Henry VAN HORN, born Bet. 15 Sep 1704 - 1707 in Newtown Twp., Bucks Cnty, PA; died Jun 1761 in Newtown Twp., Bucks Cnty, PA; married Susanna VAN VLECK 19 Oct 1728.

      iii.   Charity VAN HOORN[27], born 1710; died Unknown; married Godfrey VAN DUHREN; died Unknown.

Notes for Charity VAN HOORN:
Geertje or Charity, baptized May 21, 1710 married Godfrey Van Duren. who was the first innkeeper at Ruckman's, in Solebury township, Bucks county.

More About Charity VAN HOORN:
Baptised: 21 May 1710

      iv.   Gertie VAN HOORN, born 1710; died Unknown; married Andries BOSKIRK 29 Jul 1741; died Unknown.

More About Gertie VAN HOORN:
Baptised: 06 Jun 1724, Baptised

More About Andries BOSKIRK and Gertie VAN HOORN:
Marriage: 29 Jul 1741

      v.   Antje VAN HOORN, born Abt. 1712; died Unknown.

Notes for Antje VAN HOORN:
Antje of Ann,baptized March 22, 1712. died in infancy.

      vi.   John VAN HOORN, born 08 Dec 1713; died Nov 1760; married Lena VAN PELT 30 May 1739; died Unknown.

Notes for John VAN HOORN:
John Van Horn , born December 8, .1713, married, May 30, 1739. Lena Van Pelt (See Van Pelt Family) and died in 1760.

John and Lena (Van Pelt) Van Horn were the parents of five children, all of whom were baptized at Southampton church, viz.: Catherine, baptized August 11, 1741, married January 12, 1764 John Subers; Christian, baptized October 4. 1743. died young, Willimentje, baptized May 11, 1746, died in infancy; Willimentje, born March 1, 1748; and Joseph, born May 30, 1750, married, January 7, 1773, Ann Searle.

More About John VAN HOORN and Lena VAN PELT:
Marriage: 30 May 1739

      vii. Annetje VAN HOORN, born 19 Jul 1716 in Bucks Cnty, PA; died 08 Aug

1753; married Cornelius CORSON, SR 06 Aug 1735 in Abington, Montgomery Cnty, PA; died Unknown.

Notes for Annetje VAN HOORN:
Ann Van Horn, born July 10, 1716, died 1753. married Cornelius Corson, and had seven children, viz.: Blasndia, baptized March 26, 1738, Willemeynje baptized February 24, 1740; Marytje, baptized May 23, 1742; Jannetje, baptized July 19. 1744; Antje, baptized December 26, 1746; Benjamin, baptized April 13, 1749; and Cornelius, baptized November 16, 1751.

More About Cornelius CORSON and Annetje VAN HOORN:
Marriage: 06 Aug 1735, Abington, Montgomery Cnty, PA

   viii. Cathrine VAN HOORN[27], born 13 Apr 1719; died Unknown; married Henry HAGERMAN 20 Oct 1741; died Unknown.

Notes for Cathrine VAN HOORN:
Catharine Van Horn, born April 13, 1719. married Hendrick Hegeman, and had four children, viz.: Adrien, baptized March 26. 1738; Maria. baptized April 7, 1740; Jannetje, baptized June 6; 1742; Catrintje, baptized March 24, 1745.

More About Henry HAGERMAN and Cathrine VAN HOORN:
Marriage: 20 Oct 1741

   ix. Jane VAN HOORN[27], born 20 May 1721; died 07 Sep 1783; married John HAGERMAN 20 Oct 1741; born 10 Jan 1718; died Unknown.

Notes for Jane VAN HOORN:
Jane Van Horn. born May 10, 1721, died September 7, 1783, married, October 20, 1741, John Hegemony, born January 10, 171i8, and had nine children; Mary, born March 8. 1743; Christian, born August 8. 1745; Henry born January 5, 1748; John , born July 26. 1750; Henry. born January 11, 1753; Benjamin, born November 19, 1755; Adrian, born September 16, 1758; Barnet. born February 23, 1761; and Jane, born May 15, 1765.

More About John HAGERMAN and Jane VAN HOORN:
Marriage: 20 Oct 1741

   x. Geertje VAN HOORN, born 09 Nov 1723; died Unknown.
   xi. Adrian VAN HOORN, born 1726; died Unknown; married Jannetjie; died Unknown.
   xii. Christian VAN HOORN, born 20 Aug 1728; died 17 Dec 1755; married June VAN DUHREN; died Unknown.

More About Christian VAN HOORN:
Baptised: 03 May 1730, Baptised

6. Paulus VAN VLECK[28], died Unknown. He married **7. Jannetje VAN DYKE** 11 Jul 1711 in Philadelphia, PA.
7. Jannetje VAN DYKE, died Unknown. She was the daughter of **10. Hendrick Jans VAN DYKE** and **11. Jennetje HEERMANS**.

Marriage Notes for Paulus VAN VLECK and Jannetje VAN DYKE:

Pennsylvania Archives Series: Series 2; Volume IX; Chapter: Marriage Record of the First
Presbyterian Church of Philadelphia. 1702-1745. - 1760-1803, p. 71

More About Paulus VAN VLECK and Jannetje VAN DYKE:
Marriage: 11 Jul 1711, Philadelphia, PA

Child of Paulus VAN VLECK and Jannetje VAN DYKE is:
  3   i.   Susanna VAN VLECK, born Bet. 1711 - 1715; died Jun 1776 in Bucks Cnty,
               PA; married Henry VAN HORN 19 Oct 1728.

Generation No. 4

   8. Barent Christiansen VAN HOORN[29,30], born Bet. 30 Aug 1651 - 03 May 1655 in
Hoorn, Netherlands[31]; died 1726 in Pennerpoeck, Bergen Cnty, NJ[31]. He was the son of **16.
Christian Barentsen VAN HOORN** and **17. Jannetje JANS**. He married **9. Geertje Dircks
CLAUSSEN** 14 Feb 1679 in Bergen Dutch Reformed Church[31].
   9. Geertje Dircks CLAUSSEN[31,32], born 05 Feb 1662 in Nieuw Amstel(New York), NY;
died 1772. She was the daughter of **18. Dirk CLAUSSEN** and **19. Myrtie ROELOFS**.

Notes for Barent Christiansen VAN HOORN:
His birthday as recorded in Amsterdam is May 14, 1651. The record is from the Lutheran Church
Register in Amsterdam, Netherlands.

Lived in Pemmerpoeck NJ, Bergen Cnty, NJ and later in Bucks Cnty, PA. He lived at Bergen, NJ in
which town he was a farmer and owner of large tracts of land. It was here they raised their family.
On January 14, 1717 he signed a petition to Governor Hunter. All of their children except Jacob and
Dirck moved to Bucks Cnty, PA. Dirck moved to Hackensack, NJ and Jacob remained on the
homestead at Pemmerpoeck.

In 1674 he was taxed on a valuation of 700 Florins.

On March 26, 1677, Barent Christian Van Hoorn of Monkaque, planter, was granted by Gov. Philip
Carteret fifty acres of land and meadow at Pemmerpoeck, NJ, in one deed and eighty-five acres of
meadow or marsh land on the Bay called Kill von Kull (Newark Bay) in Bergen County, NJ.

On September 29, 1697, the proprietors of East Jersey granted him one hundred and sixty acres on
the "Hackingsack" river subject to a yearly quit rent of one half penny for each acre. (This land
joined that of Thomas Lawrensen Van Boskerk).

Barent Christian and his half brother Peter Van Boskerk purchased May 15, 1703, of Robert Heator
for 825 Pounds, one thousand acres on Neshaminy Creek, Bucks County, PA, the division of which
was made in their deed of partition dated September 18, 1707. Two days later Barent conveyed all of
his share to his sons, Peter who was deeded 257 acres and Christian 294 acres.

On the 29th of September, 1707, Barent Christian Van Hoorn of Bergen County, NJ bought for 290
Pounds five hundred and fifty acres in Bucks County, PA, from Thomas Groom, two hundred and
seventy four acres were conveyed to his son Barent Barentsen Van Hoorn on June 17, 1714. He
deeds to his son Abraham Van Hoorn, May 6, 1722, two hundred and ninety acres and on June 7,
1722, to his son Isaac Van Hoorn two hundred and seventy acres; altogether these conveyances
amount to 1381 acres.

Although owning much land in Bucks county, PA, Barent Christian Van Hoorn continued to live in

Isaiah Van Horn Pioneer of Indiana County, Pennsylvania

Bergen county, NJ.

****

A GENEALOGICAL AND PERSONAL HISTORY OF BUCKS COUNTY, PENNSYLVANIA
By William W. H. Davis
Edited by WARREN S. ELY and John W. Jordan
CLEARFIELD COMPANY

Originally prepared under the editorial supervision of Warren S. Ely and John W. Jordan and Published as Volume III of History of Bucks County Pennsylvania, second edition, New York and Chicago, 1906 Reprinted Genealogical Publishing Co., Inc. Baltimore, 1975

PART I

Reprinted in Two Parts for Clearfield Company, Inc. by Genealogical Publishing Co., Inc. Baltimore, Maryland 1994
The publisher gratefully acknowledges the loan of the original volume from the Maryland Historical Society Baltimore, Maryland

Barent Christian Van Horn, eldest son of Christian Barents and Jannetje Jans, as before stated was probably born in Holland, a theory which is borne out by the early date at which he acquired title to land. On March 26, 1667, Governor Philip Carteret granted to Barent Christian, of Menkaque, planter, fifty acres of land at Pembrepach and eighty-five acres on the bay called Kill Van Kull, both in Bergen county. On September 29, 1697, he obtained a grant from the proprietors of East Jersey, 160 acres on "Hackingsack River," joining that of his half brother 'Thomas Lawreinson (Van Boskerk). On May 15, 1703, Barnard Christian and his half brother, Peter Lawrence, purchased 1,000 acres of Robert Heaton, on Neshaminy creek, in Bucks county, which on September 1, 1707, they partitioned between them. Two days later, September 20, 1707, Barnard Christian conveyed his portion to his two sons. Peter and Christian Barnson, Peter receiving 257 acres and Christian 294 acres. On September 29, 1707, Barnard Christian purchased 550 acres in Bucks county, of Thomas Groom, 274 acres of which he conveyed to his son Barnard Barnson, June 17, 1714. He also acquired other land in Bucks county, and on June 2, 1722, conveyed to his son, Isaac Van Horn, 276 acres, and on May 6, 1722, 290 acres to his son, Abraham Van Horn. He thus owned in all 1381 acres of land in Bucks county, though lie continued to live in Bergen county, New Jersey, and died there in 1726. He married. in 1679, at the Bergen Dutch Reformed church, Geertje Dircks, daughter of Dirck Classen, who was baptized in New York, March 5, 1662. The children of Barent Christian Van Horn and Geertje Dirckse were:

Richard Barentsen Van Horn, born at Bergen, New Jersey, died at Hackensack, New Jersey, in 1763; married, April 11, 1704, Elizabeth Garretsen.

Christian Van Horn, born October 24,1685, died in Northampton township, Bucks county, November 23, 1751;

Nicholas Van Horn, born in Bergen county, New Jersey, died in Delaware; he was for a time a resident of Bucks county, and the baptism of two of his children Barnet on July 24, 1715, and Rachel on April 29, 1720, are recorded at Abington Presbyterian church.

Peter Barentsen Van Horn, born at Bergen, 1686, died in Middletown township, Bucks county, February 20, 1750. He married (first) Tryntje (Catharine) Van Dyck, and (second) Elizabeth Gabriels, on May 9, 1706. She was Baptized at Albany, New York, May 12, 1689, and died November 3, 1759. She was a daughter of Gabriel Tomase Struddles. Peter settled on land conveyed to   him by his father in Northampton in 1707 and 1715, and later purchased 425 acres in

Middletown. According to the Rev. Samuel Streng, Peter Van Horn joined the Episcopal church, and was a vestryman of St. James Protestant Episcopal church at Bristol, 1734-7. His children, all with the possible exception of Barnard, his eldest son, being by the second wife Elizibeth, were as follows:

Catherine, baptized June 4, 1710, died 1755, married Thomas Craven, of Warminnister, Bucks county;

Barnard, who married Patience Hellings;

Charity, who married. June 6, 1732, Isaiah Vansant

Jane baptized October 16,1715, married, August 10, 1732, Edmund Roberts ;

Gabriel, baptized March 3, 1716, died 1789, married Martha Breisford;

Elizabeth, who married April 21, 1737, Peter Praul;

Peter, baptized August 25, 1719, married in 1746, Margaret Marshall;

Mary, who married William Gosline , of Bristol, Bucks county;

Benjamin, who married, June 5, 1749, Hannah Davis;

Richard, born 1726, died unmarried, February 1, 1756;

John, twice married. second wife being Mary Collett, a widow; and

Garret, who married Mary Neal, and died in 1801.

Barent Barentsen Van Horn, born in Bergen, New Jersey. April 3, 1691, died in Bucks county, in 1776. He married (first) February 23, 1712, Jannetje Pieters, and (second) January 25, 1726. at Bergen, Elizabeth Klinkenberg. He received by Deed in 1714 276 acres in Northampton township, Bucks county, from his father. He had fourteen children, most of whom married and reared families.

John Van Horn, born in Bergen, New Jersey, 1692, died in Lower Dublin, Philadelphia county, 1758, and is buried in the Vandegrift burying ground. He married Rebecca Vandegrift, daughter of Johannes and Nealke (Volkers) Vandegrift, of Bucks county, and had one son John and six daughters.

Abraham Van Horn, born in Bergen, New Jersey, died in Northampton, Bucks county. in 1773, on farm of 290 acres received by deed from his father in 1722. he married first Mary Dungan, and second Mary Vansciver, and had six sons, Barnard, Isaac, Abraham. David, Jacob, and Jeremiah, and three daughters, Mary, wife of Derrick Krewson, Charity, and Martha, who married a Van Sciver.

Jane Van Horn, born at Bergen. New Jersey, April 18, 1697, married Adrien La Ruc, and resided at Six Mile Run, New Jersey.

Isaac Van Horn, born at Bergen, New Jersey, died in Solebury township, Bucks county, Pennsylvania, in 1760. He married Alice Sleght (or Slack) and had eight children:

Bernard. who married first Sarah Van Pelt and second Jane Slack;

John, who married Catharine Neafie;

Catharine, who married a Van Pelt;

Charity,

Geertje,

Elsie,

Isaac, baptized 1749,* married Alice Neafies;

Jane.

Jacob Van Horn, born at Bergen, New Jersey, died there April 14, 1775. 15. Benjamin Van Horn, born at Bergen, January 10, 1705.

More About Barent VAN HOORN and Geertje CLAUSSEN:

Isaiah Van Horn Pioneer of Indiana County, Pennsylvania

Marriage: 14 Feb 1679, Bergen Dutch Reformed Church[33]

Children of Barent VAN HOORN and Geertje CLAUSSEN are:

  i.   Dirck Barentsen VAN HOORN, born 23 Jan 1680 in Bergen Cnty, NJ; died Dec 1763 in Hackensack, NJ; married Elizabeth Garretsen VAN WAGENEN 11 Apr 1704; died Unknown.

> Notes for Dirck Barentsen VAN HOORN:
> He was an Ensign in the Provincial Army from Bucks Cnty during 1747-48.
> He is also known by the name Richard.
> His will:
> Derrick Van Horn, Saddle River, Hackensack, NJ "very sick"
> Dated May 26, 1733 Probated August 27, 1768
> Children:
> Barent (eldest son) land on NE side of the Great Pond
> Gerret (2ndt son) 20 pounds 13 shillings and 4 pence paid by Barent
> John (3rd son) 20 pounds 13 shillings and 4 pence paid by Barent
> Gertje (eldest daughter) 20 pounds 13 shillings and 4 pence paid by Barent
> Leah (2nd daughter) 20 pounds 13 shillings and 4 pence paid by Barent
> Nelsie (3rd daughter) 20 pounds 13 shillings and 4 pence paid by Barent
>
> To these my 6 children all my land at Wagrave, Bergen County
>
> Wife Elizabeth, mentions nothing for her but the legacies are not to be paid until 5 years after wife's decease
>
> Executors: Brothers Gerret Gerretze and John Gerretze
>
> More About Dirck Barentsen VAN HOORN:
> Lived: Pemmerpoeck and Bergen, NJ
> Religion: Dutch Church in Hackensack, NJ
>
> More About Dirck VAN HOORN and Elizabeth VAN WAGENEN:
> Marriage: 11 Apr 1704

4 ii.   Christian Barentsen VAN HOORN, born Bet. 24 Oct 1680 - 21 Oct 1681 in Bergen Cnty, NJ; died Bet. 23 Nov 1751 - 25 Nov 1753 in Nothhampton Twp., Bucks Cnty, PA; married Williamtje VAN DYKE 20 May 1700.

 iii.   Pieter Barentsen VAN HOORN[34,35], born 19 Apr 1686 in Bergen Cnty, NJ; died Bet. 20 Feb 1749 - 1760 in Middletown Twp., Bucks Cnty, PA; married (1) Tryntje VAN DYKE 09 Mar 1704; died Bef. 1708; married (2) Elizabeth Strudles GABRIELS 09 May 1708; born 1689 in Albany, NY; died 03 Nov 1759.

> Notes for Pieter Barentsen VAN HOORN:
> Peter Barentsen Van Horn, born at Bergen, 1686, died in Middletown township, Bucks county, February 20, 1750. He married (first) Tryntje (Catharine) Van Dyck, and (second) Elizabeth Gabriels, on May 9, 1706. She was Baptized at Albany, New York, May 12, 1689, and died November 3, 1759. She was a daughter of Gabriel Tomase Struddles. Peter settled on land conveyed to him by his father in Northampton in 1707 and 1715, and later purchased 425 acres in Middletown. According to the Rev. Samuel Streng, Peter Van Horn joined the Episcopal church, and was a vestryman of St. James

Protestant Episcopal church at Bristol, 1734-7. His children, all with the possible exception of Barnard, his eldest son, being by the second wife Elizibeth, were as follows:

Catherine, baptized June 4, 1710, died 1755, married Thomas Craven, of Warminnister, Bucks county;

Barnard, who married Patience Hellings;

Charity, who married. June 6, 1732, Isaiah Vansant (see Vansant family)

Jane baptized October 16,1715, married, August 10, 1732, Edmund Roberts ; Gabriel, baptized March 3, 1716, died 1789, married Martha Breisford; Elizabeth, who married April 21, 1737, Peter Praul;

Peter, baptized August 25, 1719, married in 1746, Margaret Marshall;

Mary, who married William Gosline , of Bristol, Bucks county;

Benjamin, who married, June 5, 1749, Hannah Davis;

Richard, born 1726, died unmarried, February 1, 1756;

John, twice married. second wife being Mary Collett, a widow; and

Garret, who married Mary Neal, and died in 1801.

Pennsylvania Wills, 1682-1834 BUCKS COUNTY WILL BOOK 2 Page 181. Pieter Van Hooren, of Middletown, Yeoman. February 12, 1749/50. Proved ---. Wife Elizabeth. 2d. son Gabriel, exr. Eldest son, Bernard, 3d. Peter, 4th Benjamin, 5th Richard, 6th John, 7th Garrett. Eldest daughter. Catharine, wife of Thomas Craven. 2d. Charity, wife of Isaiah Vansant. 3d. Jane, wife of Edmond Roberts. 4th Elizabeth, wife of Peter Praul. 5th Mary, wife of William Gosline. Wit: John Vansandt, Francis Titus, Garret Vansant.

More About Pieter VAN HOORN and Tryntje VAN DYKE:
Marriage: 09 Mar 1704

iv.   Nickolas Barentsen VAN HOORN, born 03 Feb 1688 in Bergen Cnty, NJ; died Unknown in DE; married Elizabeth LAWRENCE; died Unknown.

Notes for Nickolas Barentsen VAN HOORN:
Settled and spent his adult life in the State of Delaware.

v.   Barent Barentsen VAN HOORN, born 03 Apr 1691 in Pemmerpoeck, Bergen Cnty, NJ; died Bet. 1776 - 22 Oct 1779 in Bucks Cnty, PA; married (1) Jannetje PIETERS 23 Feb 1712 in Bergen, Bergen Cnty, NJ; born 03 Oct 1687; died 1750; married (2) Elizabeth KLINKENBERG 11 Nov 1726 in Bergen Cnty, NJ; died Unknown.

Isaiah Van Horn Pioneer of Indiana County, Pennsylvania

Notes for Barent Barentsen VAN HOORN:
Barent Barentsen Van Horn, born in Bergen, New Jersey. April 3, 1691, died in Bucks county, in 1776. He married (first) February 23, 1712, Jannetje Pieters, and (second) January 25, 1726. at Bergen, Elizabeth Klinkenberg. He received by Deed in 1714 276 acres in Northampton township, Bucks county, from his father. He had fourteen children, most of whom married and reared families.

More About Barent VAN HOORN and Jannetje PIETERS:
Marriage: 23 Feb 1712, Bergen, Bergen Cnty, NJ

vi. Johannes Barentsen VAN HOORN, born 05 Feb 1692 in Bergen Cnty, NJ; died 15 Feb 1758 in Lower Dublin, Philadelphia Cnty, PA; married Rebecca VANDEGRIFT 20 Apr 1718 in Philadelphia, PA; died Unknown.

Notes for Johannes Barentsen VAN HOORN:
Settled in Philadelphia early in his life and there reared his family. Had one son John and 6 daughters. He lived in Hackensack, NJ for a while before moving to Bensalem, Bucks County, PA where he bought 107 acres 52 perches of land April 20, 1722 of John Baker. He died in Dublin Philadelphia County, PA and was buried in the Vandegrift ground.

His will is dated December 10, 1757 and proved February 27, 1758. The will mention children as listed and grandchild John Crispin, child of daughter Helena and Susanna and Jane Johnson.

More About Johannes Barentsen VAN HOORN:
Burial: Unknown, VANDEGRIFT burying ground

Marriage Notes for Johannes VAN HOORN and Rebecca VANDEGRIFT:
Publication Title: Pennsylvania Archives Series: Series 2; Volume IX; Chapter Marriage Record of the First Presbyterian Church of Philadelphia. 1702-1745. - 1760-1803.p. 71

More About Johannes VAN HOORN and Rebecca VANDEGRIFT:
Marriage: 20 Apr 1718, Philadelphia, PA

vii. Abraham Barentsen VAN HOORN, born 12 Sep 1695 in Minkaque, Bergen Cnty, NJ; died Bet. 10 Mar 1773 - 1777 in Easton, Bucks, PA; married (1) Mary DUNGAN 06 Jul 1718 in Northampton Cnty, PA; born 1700; died 1750; married (2) Mary VAN SCRIVER Abt. 1751 in Northampton Cnty, PA; born 1732; died 1792.

Notes for Abraham Barentsen VAN HOORN:
Lived in Northampton Cnty,PA and died near what is now Easton, PA.

Abraham Van Horn, born in Bergen, New Jersey, died in Northampton, Bucks county. in 1773, on farm of 290 acres received by deed from his father in 1722. he married first Mary Dungan, and second Mary Vansciver, and had six sons, Barnard, Isaac, Abraham. David, Jacob, and Jeremiah, and three daughters, Mary, wife of Derrick Krewson, Charity, and Martha, who married a Van Sciver

His will was dated February 7, 1770 and was proved April 2, 1773.

More About Abraham VAN HOORN and Mary VAN SCRIVER:
Marriage: Abt. 1751, Northampton Cnty, PA

viii. Jannetje Barents VAN HOORN, born 18 Apr 1697 in Bergen Cnty, NJ; died
Unknown; married Adrian LA RUE 12 Dec 1719; died Unknown.

Notes for Jannetje Barents VAN HOORN:
Member 6 mile run church in Bucks Cnty,PA (Six Mile Run NJ?) April 16,
1711.

More About Adrian LA RUE and Jannetje VAN HOORN:
Marriage: 12 Dec 1719

ix. Isaac Barentsen VAN HOORN, born 02 Jan 1699 in Bergen Cnty, NJ; died
Feb 1760 in Solebury Twp., Bucks Cnty, PA; married Alice SLEIGHT Bef. Jul
1727; died Unknown.

Notes for Isaac Barentsen VAN HOORN:
Resided in Bucks Cnty, PA.

Isaac Van Horn, born at Bergen, New Jersey, died in Solebury township, Bucks
county, Pennsylvania, in 1760. He married Alice Sleght (or Slack) and had eight
children:
 Bernard. who married first Sarah Van Pelt and second Jane Slack;
 John, who married Catharine Neafie;
 Catharine, who married a Van Pelt;
 Charity,
 Geertje,
 Elsie,
 Isaac, baptized 1749,* married Alice Neafies;
 Jane.

Pennsylvania Wills, 1682-1834 BUCKS COUNTY, PA, WILL BOOK 3 Page
27. Isaac Vanhorne, of Solebury, Yeoman. June 5, 1760. Proved August 29,
1760. Wife Alice. Daus. Catharine Van Pelt, Charity and Jane Vanhorne. Sons
Barnard and John (exrs.), 200 acres "I live on.." Isaac, £110 when of age. Wit:
Gysbert Bogart, Crispin Blackfan, David Brown. Signed "Iseeck Van
Hooren.."

Notes for Alice SLEIGHT:
Name has several spellings Sleight, Slegt and Slack

More About Isaac VAN HOORN and Alice SLEIGHT:
Marriage: Bef. Jul 1727

x. Jacob Barentsen VAN HOORN, born 18 Nov 1702 in Bergen, NJ; died 14 Apr
1775 in Bergen, NJ; married Jannetje VAN BOSKIRK 01 Apr 1727; died
Unknown.

Notes for Jacob Barentsen VAN HOORN:
Some sources list this son as Johannis.

More About Jacob VAN HOORN and Jannetje VAN BOSKIRK:
Marriage: 01 Apr 1727

xi. Benjamin Barentsen VAN HOORN, born 10 Jan 1705 in Bergen Cnty, NJ;
died Unknown.

More About Benjamin Barentsen VAN HOORN:
Baptised: 25 Mar 1705, Baptised

10. Hendrick Jans VAN DYKE, died Unknown. He was the son of **20. Jan Tomasse VAN DYKE**. He married **11. Jennetje HEERMANS**.
11. Jennetje HEERMANS, died Unknown.

Children of Hendrick VAN DYKE and Jennetje HEERMANS are:
| 5 | i. | Williamtje VAN DYKE, born 04 Jul 1681 in Staten Island, NY; died 06 May 1760 in Richboro, Bucks Cnty, PA; married Christian Barentsen VAN HOORN 20 May 1700. |
| 7 | ii. | Jannetje VAN DYKE, died Unknown; married Paulus VAN VLECK 11 Jul 1711 in Philadelphia, PA. |

Generation No. 5

16. Christian Barentsen VAN HOORN[36,37]**,** born 1625 in Hoorn, East Friesland, Germany; died 26 Jul 1658 in South River, DE[38]. He was the son of **32. Barent Barents VAN HOORN** and **33. Mary BAERTS**. He married **17. Jannetje JANS** Bet. 20 Apr 1647 - 1652 in Amsterdam, Netherlands[38].
17. Jannetje JANS[38,39]**,** born 1629 in Ultrecht, Netherlands; died 13 Jul 1694 in Bergen Cnty, NJ[40]. She was the daughter of **34. Tuman Jansen JANS** and **35. Neeltje ?**.

Notes for Christian Barentsen VAN HOORN:
The following material is taken directly from THE VAN HORN FAMILY HISTORY by Francis M. Marvin Press Publishing Co, 1929

Christian Barentsen Van Hoorn, who, as was the family custom in Holland, signed his name Van Hoorn, was undoubtedly a brother of Jan Cornellessen Van Hoorn, both of whom came to New Amsterdam. now New York City, in America about 1640, A.D. He married Jannetje Jans.

He came from Hoorn, a city in the North of Holland. He seems to have been a man of undoubted good judgement, as he was frequently appointed referee.

He was appointed on March 10, 1653, by the Burgomasters and Schepens of New Amsterdam to view a house, in regard to the building of which there was some litigation. (This raises the question about the date of immigration which was given as about 1640)

On June 28, 1655, he appears as attorney for Albert Andressen.

Isaiah Van Horn Pioneer of Indiana County, Pennsylvania

On September 5, 1658, he sailed with the expedition from New Netherlands, the object of which was to dispossess the Swedes, who had settled on the South river (Delaware), the settlement was known as Fort Christina, now Wilmington, Delaware.

On October 15, 1655, he was a subscriber to the fund for repairing and strengthening the City Hall, 15 Guilders. He was appointed Fire Warden at Fort Amsterdam, January 18, 1656.

On April 17,1657 he is made a small Burgher.

On August 1, 1657, he is given a patent for a lot of land "By the Land Gate" New Amsterdam (at Broadway and Wall Street).

On November 17, 1657, he is paid 1616 Guilders, 13 Stivers, and mortgage of 1233 Guilders, 17 Stivers for house and lot at New Amsterdam, by Cornelise Janse Plavier, previously bought by Christian Barentsen February 17, 1654, and July 30, 1657.

On May 30, 1658, Hendrick Hendricks, a tailor, acknowledges to owe him 500 Guilders, balance of purchase money for house and lot in New Amsterdam, near the Land Gate, and mortgages said house to satisfy the debt.

At about this time he returned to Wilmington, Delaware, where he and others who had obtained a grant of land on the south side of None Such Creek, a tributary of the Christina, not far from the present Wilmington, Delaware; at the junction of the two streams is Sweet Nut Island, opposite Newport. It was on this grant of land he and his fellow grantees began the erection of a mill.

In the documents relating to the Colonial History of New York, this mill if referred to as a horse mill. Horse power was probably, used when water power from low tides was not available.

It was while building this mill he died. It is not doubted but that he was buried in the old graveyard about a mile from the City of Wilmington, Delaware.

At the time of his death he still held the office of Fire Warden, as on the 23rd of December, 1658, his successor was appointed it being noted in the City records that he had died at South River, (Delaware).

Jannetje Jans, widow and executrix of Christian Barentsen presented to the Court in New Amsterdam an inventory of "all the liabilities and assets as they were at the time of her husbands demise" requesting that Mr. Jacob Alrichs, Director of the City's Colony on the South River, where her husband died, be written to "in order that the chattels which are there may be sent from the south river to this place." The inventory was put into the hands of the Orphanmasters of the City, who were requested to examine and prove the same, and, as far as possible, to effect a settlement.

_____

Minutes of the Orphanmasters of New Amsterdam

Demise of Christian Barentsen VanHorn

August 28, 1658, Orphan master Pieter Wolfersen Van Cowvenhoven produces a letter received through Court Messenger, Pieter Schabanck, which having been opened, was found to have been written and sent by the Hon. Alrichs from the South River and to report the death of Christian Barentsen Van Hoorn on the 26th of July 1658, with a statement by inventory of his estate and the request to assist his widow.

Alrichs writes to Peter Stuyvesant September 5, 1658, "In regard to the widow of Christian Barents, as she desired beyond measure to go there and requested it within three days after her husband's burial, by word of mouth and by writing also that the property which he left behind, might be sold immediately, all of which has been agreed to and permitted at her repeated instances or demands and arranged for the best of the heirs, so that they have been benefited more than usual, by some presents, or words of consolation, as your Honor will have seen from the transmitted letters and account and sale of the property; therefore, there is no cause given the aforesaid widow to complain, but I only advised or proposed to her, that it would be for her best to remain in possession; she should be assisted in finishing the mill, with the income of which through the grist, she would be able to diminish the expenses and live decently and abundantly with her children, on the surplus, besides that she had yet three or four good cows, with sheep and hogs, which also could help her to maintain her family. She and her children should have remained on and inherited the father's estate, which was in good condition, here, wherein the widow and the children could have continued reputably and in (good) position to much advantage, but she would not listen to advice, that she was to be restricted in her inclinations and well-being, which I shall never think of, much less do. This God may grant and give, and I will also ask him to take your Honor and us with our families in his Almighty care and protection, remaining

Your Honor's ever obedient and faithful servant J. Alrichs."

New Amstel, the 5th September, A.D. 1658. To the Noble, Honorable, Worshipful. Wise, very Prudent Mr. Petier Stuyvesant General of New Netherlands, Curacao, etc., Residing in Fort Amsterdam. By Capt. Jacobsen

---

FROM THE RECORDS OF NEW NETHERLAND

"December 18, 1658. Before the Board appeared Burgomaster Olaf Stevensen Cortlandt who is informed by the Orphan master, of the inventory of his property here, made by this widow, wherein the differences appearing with which they do not know what to do, the widow of said Christian Barentsen Van Hoorn, called Jannetje Jans, is called and asked whether the payment for the house near the Land Gate had been received; she answers, yes, by Hendrick Van Dyck who had Power of Attorney from her husband; asked about the payment for the house where Hendrick Hendricksen, the tailor lives, she says not to have received it, but it is still due and charged.

Immigrated to New Amstel (New Amsterdam or New York)

The first record of him being in New Amsterdam is March 10, 1653.

On his marriage intention record filed in Amsterdam, Netherlands he is shown as from Hoorn in Oostland House and that he is a journeyman carpenter.

page 173-175 The American Genealogist

EUROPEAN ORIGIN OF CHRISTIAEN BARENTS VAN HOORN

The present article serves as an addendum to Mr. George Olin Zabriskie's fine series, "Christiaen Barentsen Van Horn and Some of His Earlier Descendants" which began in TAG 43:193 and continued for six Whole Numbers. Mr. Zabriskie has now kindly contributed the results of some successful searching on his behalf of the Dutch expert of the Genealogical Society in Salt Lake City, Mr. Hendrick O. Slok, whose address is 233 East Capitol, Salt Lake City, Utah 84103. Mr. Slok began with examination of the Reformed Dutch registers of Amsterdam and in particular the marriage intention registers 1645-1650. Almost at once he discovered the following under date of 20 April 1647:

Isaiah Van Horn Pioneer of Indiana County, Pennsylvania

Compareerden als voren, Christaen baerentsz. van Hoorn in [Uo]stland Huijs tilqmeegesel out 22 Jaer geen ouders hebbende woon-op de Lindegracht geasst met zijn swaeger Jan Janse & Jannetie Jana van Uijtrecht out 18 Jaer, woon- bijde cathuijsters, geasst met mer moeder Neeltje Jana [signed by marks M and X]. [Translation: "Appeared as before, Chriatiaen baerentsz from Hoorn in [Oolstland House carpenter journeyman age 22 years having no parents residing on the Lindegracht assisted with his brother-in-law Jan Janse & Jannetje Jana, from Uitrecht age 18 years, residing at the cathuijsters, assisted With her mother Neeltje Jana (Film Call No. 113.204."I

This most important record agrees entirely with our knowledge of Christiaen Baerentsen van Horn in America:

174   THE AMERICAN GENEALOGIST

He was a house carpenter and his wife was named Jannetje Jans. The word "cathuijsters" is an allusion to a former Carthusian monastery that once stood in the northwestern part of Amsterdam where the Lindegracht is. Mr. Slok then searched the baptismal registers of the same church for baptisms of their children but found none. Knowing that descendants of this couple were Lutherans, he searched the corresponding registers of the Lutheran Church (Film 113.416), and again struck gold:

9 Mey 1649, Jannetie, Va. [father] Christiaen Barents; Test. Stijnte Jans.
14 Mey 1651, Barent, Va. Christiaen Barents; Test. Machtelt Engels.

This gives us a new child, the only daughter, hitherto unsuspected because she doubtless died soon, but the baptism of Barent is precisely what we should expect since such a child was the eldest son of this couple in America and the date of baptism fits the age very nicely. Moreover, we may suggest that Stijntje Jans may have been a sister of Jannetje Jans. No other children were found, though Mr. Slok searched until 1660, but this is encouraging, since a baptism dated when the family was in America would have dashed our hopes. Neither the Reformed nor the Lutheran registers contain an entry of the actual marriage, and the names of Christiaen and his wife are likewise missing from the Lutheran membership records (Film 16149, pt. 9). A Stintje Jans, wife of Barent Barents, was listed on 23 March 1667; at an earlier date she was simply mentioned by name. The Utrecht Reformed registers were searched for a Neeltje Jans married to a Jan, with perhaps two children, Jan and Jannetje, but the search of the baptismal register was negative. There was an index but it is useless since it was based on the father's family name or patronymic (Film 121,754-5). The marriage registers for the period L616-1630 contained the following (Film 121,783):

Jan Gosensz van Schaij & Neeltje Jans, 18 June 1617.
Johan Bastiaense & Neeltje Jans, 18 June 1623.
Jan van Monsiou & Neeltjen Jana, 30 May 1626
Jan dela Moulje & Neeltgen Jans, 18 Nov. 1627.

One of these four couples may be the right one but so far as we can see, there is no evidence to point to the true father of our Jannetje. The results are very heartening. For the first time we now know that Jannetje Jans' mother was Neeltje Jans, and that she was born in Utrecht.

CHRISTIAEN BARENTS VAN HOORN   175

The area that Christaen came was not the Hoorn in Holland but the one in East Friesland. (This is disputed in the book "The Rev. William Van Horne as a misinterpretation of the record and the use of the term Oosland.) We also get the important baptismal date for Barent Christiaensen Van Hoorn--the fact that his mother was not identified in the record should give us no pause. Moreover, all this information is germane not only to the members of the Christaen Barents Van Hoorn family but also to all the Van Buskirks, since the second husband of Jannetje Jans was Lourens Andriesen, at times called Van Boschkerck, from which his four sons derived their surname. In conclusion I may be pardoned for calling attention to my own article in TAG, supra, 38: 65-69, in which I showed that Evien's statement that Jannetje Jans was "daughter of the Norman" is in error thus clearing the stage for Mr Slok's happy discoveries.

--G. E. McC.
****

A GENEALOGICAL AND PERSONAL HISTORY OF BUCKS COUNTY, PENNSYLVANIA
By William W. H. Davis
Edited by WARREN S. ELY and John W. Jordan
CLEARFIELD COMPANY

Originally prepared under the editorial supervision of Warren S. Ely and John W. Jordan and Published as Volume III of History of Bucks County Pennsylvania, second edition, New York and Chicago, 1906 Reprinted Genealogical Publishing Co., Inc. Baltimore, 1975

PART I

Reprinted in Two Parts for Clearfield Company, Inc. by Genealogical Publishing Co., Inc. Baltimore, Maryland 1994
The publisher gratefully acknowledges the loan of the original volume from the Maryland Historical Society Baltimore, Maryland

pages 92 -98

THE VAN HORN FAMILY. The family of Van Horn has been a prominent one in Bucks county for two centuries, filling important positions in the official, professional and business life of the county in every generation and constantly sending out its representatives to fill! like important positions in other localities and states, its representatives now being found in nearly every state in the Union. The pioneer ancestor of the family was Christian Barendtse. that is Christian, son of Barendt, who it is said came from Hooren, a city of the Zuyder Zee. about twenty-five miles from Amsterdam. The exact date of his arrival in America is not known. He was a carpenter by trade, and the records of New Amsterdam show that he and a fellow craftsman, Auke Jansen, were appointed, March 10, 1653, by the burgomasters and schepens of New Amsterdam to view a house, about the building of which there was some litigation. These records further show that he was frequently appointed a referee during the next four or five years. And he is shown to have contributed towards the strengthening of the city wall on October 15, 1655. He is also said to have been with the force sent out from New Amsterdam, September 5, 1655, against the Swedes and Finns on the south (now Delaware) river, at Fort Christina. On his return to New Amsterdam he was appointed January 18, 1656. a fire warden, in place of Johan Paul Jacquet, who had resigned and "removed to the South River in New Netherlands." On April 17, 1657, he was admitted a "Small Burgher" of New Amsterdam, an honor which carried with it the freedom of trade and a right to membership in the respective guilds of the town, and conferred upon natives of the city, residents there One year and six weeks before the date of the charter, burgher's sons-in-law. city storekeepers, salaried servants of the company and all paying the sum of twenty-five guilders. On August 1, 1657, Christian Barentze, carpenter, was granted by Peter Stuyvesant, director general of New Netherland, a lot in New Amsterdam, by the Land Gate, (now at Broadway and Wall streets) for a house and garden. He also owned several other properties in the neighborhood, some of which are said to have covered a part of the present Trinity churchyard. Probably as a result of his trip to the South river, Christian Barentse and Joost Rugger and possibly others obtained a grant of land on the south side of None Such creek, a tributary of the Chrisiana, near the present site of Wilmington, Delaware; and began the erection thereon of a tide water mill. According to Amos C. Brinton, who has given much

71

attention to the ancient mill sites of Delaware Barentse and Rugger, he began the erection of this mill in 1656.

From the dates previously given, however, as well as from other records, it would appear, that the date of Christian Barentse's, removal to the Delaware was sometime in the year 1657. Contemporary records also refer to the mill as a "horse mill," the truth of the matter being most probably that the horse mill was set up to serve until the tide water mill was completed. The low marshy nature of the land and the turning up of the mud to the sun caused an epidemic from which Barentse died July 26, 1658. A letter written by Vice-Director Jacob Alricks, from New Anistel, (New Castle) to Stuyvesant, tender date of September 5, 1658, and published in documents relating to the Colonial History of New York, vol. xii, p. 224, relates entirely to the affairs of the widow and children of Christian Barentse. It states that the widow had requested within three days of his burial that she desired to return to New Amsterdam, and that the property which he left be sold and that though he consents thereto he "advised and proposed to her that it would be for her best to remain in possession. she should be assisted in completing the mill, with income whereof, which through the grists she would be able to diminish the expenses and live decently and abundantly with her children on the surplus, besides that she had yet three or four cows with sheep and hogs, which also could help, her to maintain her family, she and her children should have remained on and in her and the father's estate, which was in good condition here, wherein the widow with the children could have continued reputably and in position to much advantage; but she would not listen to advice, * * * that she was to be restricted in her inclinations and well being, which I shall never think of, much less do." The wife of Christian Barentse was Jannetje Jans, and it is probable that they were married before coming to America, as the baptism of their eldest child is not recorded in the New York church. On December 12. 1658, Jannetje Jans, widow and executrix of Christian Barents, presented an inventory of his goods and chattels to the court at New Amsterdam, and requested that Vice-Director Alricks, "Director of the City's Colony on the South River, where her husband died, be written to in order that the chattels which are there may be sent from the South river to this place."

The widow married on September 12, 1658, Laurens Andriessen Van Boskerk, who was born in Holstein Denmark. He was a member of Bergen court in 1667, its president in 1682, a member of the governor's council for many years. He died in 1693 and Jannetje on July 13, 1694 They were the parents of four children, Andries, Lourens, Peter, and Thomas, the two latter, according to the Dutch custom, being known as Lourensons, appear later to have become known by the name of Lawrence. Peter joined his half-brother, Barant Christian Van Horn, in his purchase of land in Bucks county in 1703. His Youngest son John married Alce Van Horn, granddaughter of Christian Barents, and his daughter Jannetje, married Cornelius Corson, of Staten Island, and became the ancestress of the Bucks county Corsons. The children of Christian Barents and Jannetje Jans were as follows;

1. Jannetje

2. Barend Christian Van Horn, born in Holland, married Geertje Dircks; died in Bergen county, New Jersey, in 1726.

Barent Christian Van Horn, eldest son of Christian Barents and Jannetje Jans, as before stated was probably born in Holland, a theory which is borne out by the early date at which he acquired title to land. On March 26, 1667, Governor Philip Carteret granted to Barent Christian, of Menkaque, planter, fifty acres of land at Pembrepach and eighty-five acres on the bay called Kill Van Kull,both in Bergen county. On September 29, 1697, he obtained a grant from the proprietors of East Jersey, 160 acres on "Hackingsack River," joining that of his half brother 'Thomas Lawreinson (Van Boskerk). On May 15, 1703, Barnard Christian and his half brother, Peter Lawrence, purchased 1,000 acres of Robert Heaton, on Neshaminy creek, in Bucks county, which on September 1, 1707, they partitioned between them. Two days later, September 20, 1707, Barnard Christian conveyed his portion to his two sons. Peter and Christian Barnson, Peter receiving 257 acres and Christian 294 acres. On September 29, 1707, Barnard Christian purchased 550 acres in Bucks county, of Thomas

Groom, 274 acres of which he conveyed to his son Barnard Barnson, June 17, 1714. He also acquired other land in Bucks county, and on June 2, 1722, conveyed to his son, Isaac Van Horn, 276 acres, and on May 6, 1722, 290 acres to his son, Abraham Van Horn. He thus owned in all 1381 acres of land in Bucks county, though lie continued to live in Bergen county, New Jersey, and died there in 1726. He married. in 1679, at the Bergen Dutch Reformed church, Geertje Dircks, daughter of Dirck Classen, who was baptized in New York, March 5, 1662.

3. Cornelius Van Horn, baptized August 3, 1653, married Margaret Van de Berg, died in Bergen county in 1729.

4. Jan Van Horn, baptized March 18, 1657, married Lena Boone, died in Bergen county.

Notes for Jannetje JANS:
The following is taken directly from the book THE VAN HORN FAMILY HISTORY by Francis M. Martin of Bartonsville, PA.

Jannetje Jans widow of Christian Barentsen Van Hoorn, Married December 12, 1658, as her (2) husband, Laurens Andriessen Van Boskerk, who was born in Holstein, Denmark. He was a member of the Bergen, NJ Court in 1667; President of the same in 1682; and a member of the governor's Council for a number of years. Jannetje took as her fortune to her (2) husband "1400 florins heavy money, 10 Wampum beads for one stiver."

Van Boskerk and his wife made a joint Will dated August 29, 1679; proved March 19 1692-93 by the provisions of which the survivor was to enjoy the whole estate for life. After his and her decease one half of the property was to be devised to the children of Jannetje by her first husband, Christian Barentsen Van Hoorn, and the family by the second marriage, received the remainder.

Jannetje Jans d. July 13, 1694, having survived her (2) husband, Laurens Andriessen Van Boskerk, several months.

More About Christian VAN HOORN and Jannetje JANS:
Marriage: Bet. 20 Apr 1647 - 1652, Amsterdam, Netherlands[40]

Children of Christian VAN HOORN and Jannetje JANS are:
8	i.	Barent Christiansen VAN HOORN, born Bet. 30 Aug 1651 - 03 May 1655 in Hoorn, Netherlands; died 1726 in Pennerpoeck, Bergen Cnty, NJ; married Geertje Dircks CLAUSSEN 14 Feb 1679 in Bergen Dutch Reformed Church.
	ii.	Cornelis Christiansen VAN HOORN, born 03 Aug 1653 in New Amsterdam, NY; died 24 Mar 1729; married Margaret VANDERBURGH 04 Mar 1665 in Hackensack, Bergen Cnty, NJ; died Unknown.

More About Cornelis VAN HOORN and Margaret VANDERBURGH:
Marriage: 04 Mar 1665, Hackensack, Bergen Cnty, NJ

	iii.	Johannes Christiansen VAN HOORN, born 18 Mar 1656; died Unknown; married Lenah BOONE; died Unknown.

18. Dirk CLAUSSEN, born 1616 in Leeuwarden,,Friesland,Netherlands; died 1686 in New Amsterdam, NY. He was the son of **36. Clauses JACOBSEN** and **37. Pietterlie HEERTGENS**. He married **19. Myrtie ROELOFS**.
19. Myrtie ROELOFS, born 1626 in Leeuwarden,,Friesland,Netherlands; died 1676 in New Amsterdam, NY.

Child of Dirk CLAUSSEN and Myrtie ROELOFS is:

9   i.   Geertje Dircks CLAUSSEN, born 05 Feb 1662 in Nieuw Amstel(New York), NY; died 1772; married Barent Christiansen VAN HOORN 14 Feb 1679 in Bergen Dutch Reformed Church.

20. Jan Tomasse VAN DYKE, died Unknown.

Notes for Jan Tomasse VAN DYKE:
Jan Tomasse Van Dyck, who emigrated from Amsterdam in 1652 and settled in New Utrecht, Long Island.
His sixth child. Hendrick Janze, baptized July 2, 1653, married, February 7, 1680 Jannetje Hermans, daughter of Herinan Janse Van Barkeloo, and settled on Staten Island, where he was a constable in 1689 and assessor in 1703. In 1704 he purchased land in Bucks county and removed there. At the organization of Bensalem church, in 1710. he produced a certificate from the Staten Island church. He purchased four tracts of land in Middletown, two of which he retained until his death in 1721, and devised to his daughter Williamtje, wife of Christian Van Horn. and his granddaughter Elizabeth Van Vleck. who later married her cousin, Henry Van Horn. He had but two children, Williamtje, and Jannetje, who became the wife of the Reverend Paulus Van Vleck, , the first pastor at Neshaminy.

Child of Jan Tomasse VAN DYKE is:

10   i.   Hendrick Jans VAN DYKE, died Unknown; married Jennetje HEERMANS.

Generation No. 6

32. Barent Barents VAN HOORN, died Unknown. He married **33. Mary BAERTS** 02 Feb 1625.
    33. Mary BAERTS, died Unknown.

Notes for Barent Barents VAN HOORN:
    In the book a New Jersey Lineage to Christian Barentsen Van Horne by Jean Baber she gives a probable parentage to Christian fro the Registers if the Reformed Church in Harlem, Netherland. The Banns-Hoorn were published 19 January 1625 Barent Barents, young man and Mary Baerts, young daughter, both from Hoorn, married 2 February 1625. Jena Baber notes that there is a gap in church records from 1 January 1624 and 31 December 1626 for baptisms. This is the time period of birth of Christian taken from the Marriage Intention Register in Amsterdam, Netherlands.

More About Barent VAN HOORN and Mary BAERTS:
Marriage: 02 Feb 1625

Child of Barent VAN HOORN and Mary BAERTS is:

16   i.   Christian Barentsen VAN HOORN, born 1625 in Hoorn, East Friesland, Germany; died 26 Jul 1658 in South River, DE; married Jannetje JANS Bet. 20 Apr 1647 - 1652 in Amsterdam, Netherlands.

34. Tuman Jansen JANS, died Unknown. He married **35. Neeltje ?.**
    35. Neeltje ?, died Unknown.

Child of Tuman JANS and Neeltje ? is:

17   i.   Jannetje JANS, born 1629 in Ultrecht, Netherlands; died 13 Jul 1694 in Bergen Cnty, NJ; married (1) Christian Barentsen VAN HOORN Bet. 20 Apr 1647 - 1652 in Amsterdam, Netherlands; married (2) Laurens Andriessen VAN

BOSKERK 12 Dec 1658.

36. Clauses JACOBSEN, born in Leeuwarden, Friesland; died Unknown. He married **37. Pietterlie HEERTGENS**.

37. Pietterlie HEERTGENS, died Unknown.

Notes for Clauses JACOBSEN:
Emigrated to New Amsterdam with his wife and widowed mother in 1653. He was a potter by trade. He became a small burgher in 1657 when he bought a house and lot in New Amsterdam and set up a shop known afterwards as "Pot Baker Corner" a place located near the outlet of the fresh water into the East river.

Child of Clauses JACOBSEN and Pietterlie HEERTGENS is:

  18   i.   Dirk CLAUSSEN, born 1616 in Leeuwarden,,Friesland,Netherlands; died 1686 in New Amsterdam, NY; married Myrtie ROELOFS.

Endnotes

1. Will of Henry Van Horn Bucks County Wills Book 3,p 74.
2. *Sons and Daughters of the Pilgrims, Volume I, p. 448 & 449* , "Electronic."
3. Peterson, Clarence S., *Known Military Dead During the American Revolutionary War,* (Reprint, Baltimore: Genealogical Publishing Co., Inc., 1967.), "Electronic."
4. *Sons and Daughters of the Pilgrims, Volume I, p. 448 & 449* , "Electronic."
5. *New Jersey Marriage Records, 1665-1800, Marriage Licenses, U-V, Page 423* , "Electronic."
6. *Sons and Daughters of the Pilgrims, Volume I, p. 448 & 449* , "Electronic."
7. Pennsylvania Archives, 2nd Series, Volume 14 p. 175.
8. *Pennsylvania Archives Series: Series 5 Volume: V Chapter: Muster Rolls and Papers Relating to the Associators and Militia of the County of Bucks.* .
9. *Sons and Daughters of the Pilgrims, Volume I, p. 448 & 449* , "Electronic."
10. *New Jersey Marriage Records, 1665-1800, Marriage Licenses, U-V, Page 423* , "Electronic."
11. *Sons and Daughters of the Pilgrims, Volume I, p. 448 & 449* , "Electronic."
12. *The Colonial Society of Pennsylvania 1950 , Page 66,* "Electronic."
13. *Sons and Daughters of the Pilgrims, Volume I, p. 448 & 449* , "Electronic."
14. Will of Henry Van Horn Bucks County Wills Book 3,p 74.
15. *Sons and Daughters of the Pilgrims, Volume I, p. 448 & 449* , "Electronic."
16. *The Colonial Society of Pennsylvania 1950 , Page 66,* "Electronic."
17. *The Abridged Compendium of American Genealogy Vol. III, Lineage records,, P. 340,* "Electronic."
18. Will of Henry Van Horn Bucks County Wills Book 3,p 74.
19. *The Colonial Society of Pennsylvania 1950 , Page 66,* "Electronic."
20. *History of Bucks County, PA Volume I, Bucks County Genealogies, Page 95* , "Electronic."
21. *History of Bucks County, PA Volume I, Bucks County Genealogies, Page 95,96 & 97,* "Electronic."
22. *Sons and Daughters of the Pilgrims, Volume I, p. 448 & 449* , "Electronic."
23. *The Colonial Society of Pennsylvania 1950 , Page 66,* "Electronic."
24. *Sons and Daughters of the Pilgrims, Volume I, p. 448 & 449* , "Electronic."
25. *The Colonial Society of Pennsylvania 1950 , Page 66,* "Electronic."
26. *Sons and Daughters of the Pilgrims, Volume I, p. 448 & 449* , "Electronic."
27. Will of Willamentje Van Horn Bucks County Will Book 3, p 13.
28. *The Abridged Compendium of American Genealogy Vol. III, Lineage records,, P. 340,* "Electronic."
29. *Sons and Daughters of the Pilgrims, Volume I, p. 448 & 449* , "Electronic."
30. *The Colonial Society of Pennsylvania 1950 , Page 66,* "Electronic."
31. *Sons and Daughters of the Pilgrims, Volume I, p. 448 & 449* , "Electronic."

32. *The Colonial Society of Pennsylvania 1950 , Page 66*, "Electronic."
33. *Sons and Daughters of the Pilgrims, Volume I, p. 448 & 449* , "Electronic."
34. New Jersey Biographical Sketches, 1665-1800.
35. Sons & Daughters of Pilgrims, Vol III, Lineage of Members, Page 105.
36. *Sons and Daughters of the Pilgrims, Volume I, p. 448 & 449* , "Electronic."
37. *The Colonial Society of Pennsylvania 1950 , Page 66*, "Electronic."
38. *Sons and Daughters of the Pilgrims, Volume I, p. 448 & 449* , "Electronic."
39. *The Colonial Society of Pennsylvania 1950 , Page 66*, "Electronic."
40. *Sons and Daughters of the Pilgrims, Volume I, p. 448 & 449* , "Electronic."

Descendants of Henry B. VAN HORN

Generation No. 1

1. CAPTAIN Henry B.[6] VAN HORN (Henry[5], Christian Barentsen[4] VAN HOORN, Barent Christiansen[3], Christian Barentsen[2], Barent Barents[1])[1,2] was born 02 Oct 1734 in Newtown Twp., Bucks Cnty, PA[2], and died Dec 1777 in Wrightstown, Bucks Cnty, PA[2,3]. He married **Elizabeth VAN ZANT[4]** 10 Aug 1758 in Bucks Cnty, PA[4,5], daughter of Isaiah VAN ZANT and Gertje VAN HOORN. She was born 1736 in Lower Makefield Twp., Bucks Cnty, PA[6], and died 25 Nov 1807 in Bensalem, Bucks Cnty, PA[6].

Notes for CAPTAIN Henry B. VAN HORN:
The Volume 1 p. 207 Daughters of the American Colonists lists the middle initial as B.

According to the muster roll extracted from the Pennsylvania Archives, 2nd Series, Vol. 14 Captain Henry Van Horne's Company January 22, 1777
Captain: Henry Van Horn
1st Lieutenant: Robert Ramsey
2nd Lieutenant: Thomas Huston
Ensign: Abram Johnson
Sergeant: Andrew McMinn
Corporal: John Vance
Drummer: Isaiah Van Horn (his son)
Privates: Jeremiah Van Horn (relationship unknown) Joshua Van Horn (son) and 15 additional men

Henry Van Horn, son of Henry and Susanna (Van Vlecq) Van Horn, was reared on the old homestead purchased by his grandfather, Christian Van Horn, in 1726, and at the death of his father, in 1761, inherited a one-half interest therein with his brother Christian. They made a division of the 252 acres, each conveying to the other 126 acres in 1773. After the reverses on Long Island in November, 1776, and at Fort Washington when the Continental forces were so badly routed and so many of the Bucks county contingent were taken prisoners, Henry Van Horn raised an independent company of militia and was commissioned their captain, December 6 1776, (See Penna. Arch. Vol. XIV p. 175)and took them into the service, He died of camp fever late in 1777.. He married Elizabeth Vansant, daughter of Isaiah and Charity (Van Horn) Van Zant, and they were the parents of eight children: Joshua, born February 21, 1759; Isaiah, born October 24, 1760, was drummer in his father's company, 1776-7; Mary, born May 5, 1764, married Isaac Gillam, died April 18, 1823; Christian, born July 13, 1766; Susanna, born October 9, 1768, married Jesse Willett, who had previously married her sister Sarah; Elizabeth, married an Anderson, and died January 26, 1813; Sarah, born February 7, 1773, married Jesse Willett, died prior to 1809; Henry, born April 5, 1777. Elizabeth the mother, died November 25, 1807, aged about eighty years.

Henry Van Horn, youngest child of Captain Henry and Elizabeth (Vansant) Van Horn, born in Newtown township, April 5, 1777, learned the trade of a carpenter and cabinet maker and located at Yardley, Bucks county, where he followed the trade of a cabinet maker for several years. His Sign uniquely painted is now in possession of his grandson, Richard H. Van Horn, of Lambertville, New Jersey. He also purchased a farm of 93 acres in Lower Makefield in 1805, which, in 1811,he conveyed to his brother-in-law, Isaac Gillam. He purchased a farm of 200 acres in Upper Makefield, near Eagle Tavern, where he resided the balance. of his life. He died in February,. 1849. He married, in 1798,

Isaiah Van Horn Pioneer of Indiana County, Pennsylvania

Hannah Reeder, of Canaan, Upper Makefield, and their six children who grew to maturity were as follows:

1. Abraham, born 1802, married, in 1829, Eliza Hampton, by whom he had one child, Margery. He married (second) Christiana Neald, and a son Henry K. was born in 1834. He married (third) Elizabeth Sampsel. He sold his farm in Upper Makefield and removed to Sandy Spring, Maryland, where he reared a family of thirteen children.

2. Elizabeth, born 1804, married William Ryan, of Upper Makefield, born 1810. They settled near Rocksville, Northampton township, Bucks county, and engaged in the milling business. Three of their children survive: Edward H., born 1832; Mary, born 1835; and Hannah, born 1839.

3. Eleanor H., born 1810, married Cornelius Slack, and settled in Lower Makefield. He was lately a merchant at Dolington. Their children are: Watson, born 1832 ; John H., born 1833; Henry V., born 1836; Jane E., born 1839; Sarah E., born 1841; William H., born 1843; Anna M., born 1847; and Hannah, born 1850.

4. Moses H., born January 15, 1812, at Yardleyville, removed with his parents to Upper Makefield, where he spent his entire life, inheriting at his father's death, in 1849 100 acres of the old homestead. He was a successful farmer and a prominent man in the community, holding many positions of trust and honor. He and his wife and family were lifelong members of the Society of Friends. He married, April 13, 1843, Rebecca Scattergood, born February 7, 1820, daughter of John* and Catherine (Hepburn) Scattergood, of Makefield, who died September 15, 1895. Moses died February 13, 1885. They were the parents of nine children : Richard H., born 1844; Mary Anna, born 1846; Samuel S., born 1848 . ; William T., born 1851 ; George F., and Catharine S., twins, born 1854; Hannah E., born 1857; Benjamin F., born 1860; and Emma L., born 1863.

5. Mary A., born 1816, married Christian Van Horn, born 1814, and settled on a farm near Dolington. Their surviving issue are: Cyrus B, Jane E., Cornelius S., Hannah E., and Callender C.

6. John R., born 1820, married Rebecca Feaster, and settled on a portion of the old homestead in Upper Makefield. Their surviving children are: James P., David F., Emeline, Watson, Martha F., and Joseph F.

RICHARD H. VAN HORN, eldest son of Moses and Rebecca (Scattergood) Van Horn. born at the old homestead of his grandfather, in 1844, was reared on the Upper Makefield farm, acquired a limited education at the public school and later took a course at Union Business College in Philadelphia. After a few years experience in the mercantile business in Philadelphia, he started into that business for himself at Lambertville, New Jersey, in 1868. By strict application to business and a close study of the wants and needs of the community, he soon built up a large trade and his remodeled store in 1884 named "Grand Depot" enjoyed much more than a local reputation and soon outgrew its early modest quarters. In 1877 an adjoining building was added and the volume of business doubled. Seven years later the entire property was remodeled and both stores thrown into one, making a large and commodious department store, and his brother, Samuel S., who had been for some years a clerk in the establishment was given all interest in the business, and the firm name became R. H. Van Horn & Brother. The partnership of the growing establishment extended far beyond the limits of Jersey into their native county, and the country districts and towns of New Jersey. In 1889 the brothers dissolved partnership and Richard H. continued the business alone until 1892, when his son Henry came of age and was admitted as a partner. Ten years later the younger son, Edmori E., becoming of age, also became a partner, and the firm of R. H. Van Horn & Sons, continued to conduct the popular and successful establishment that has grown from its modest beginning of 1868. With the addition of a new building. the floor space of which combined with the original "Grand Depot" covers now (1904) about three quarters of an acre. Richard H. Van Horn married, in 1869, Lydia Beatty Warner, born in 1845, daughter of Edwards Edmunds Warner, of

Philadelphia, and of New England ancestry, and they are the proud parents of two sons. both of whom, as before stated. are members of the firm. Henry E., the eldest, born April 21, 1870, Marrie Era Runkle, of Hunterdon county, New Jersey; and Edmori E., born in October, 1879, married Jessie I Hoffman of the same place. Mr. R. H. Van Horn is all active member of the Society of Friends, having many years since transferred his certificate of membership from Wrightstown Monthly Meeting to Solebury where he and his wife have Lydianna were subsequently appointed elders. Mr. R.H. Van Horn has always shown an active spirit in his town affairs but little interest in "Political Pulls"; he his, however, served in the school board, acted as a member of the board of trade, and at present is next to the oldest director in the Amwell National Bank of Lambertville.

SAMUEL. SCATERGOOD VAN HORN, second son of Moses and Rebecca (Scattergood) VanHorn. whose ancestry his been given in the preceding, was born in Makefield township, Bucks county, Pennsylvania, October 28, 1848, and was reared on the Upper Wakefield farm; acquiring his education at the public schools of that township. In 1870 he went to Lambertville. New Jersey. In 1889 Samuel S. Van Horn embarked in the general merchandise business in Lambertville. where he carried on a successful business for three years. He then purchased his present location, where he has since conducted a successful business. Mr. Van Horn married, in 1888, Ella M.. Dilley, daughter of Louis and Caroline (Larison) Dilley, of Kingwood, Hunterdont county, New Jersey. To this marriage .has been born two sons, Lloyd and Earl. Mr. Van Horn is all extensive real estate owner in Lambertville, owning fifteen resident properties. He is a member of the Society of Friends.

Captain Henry Van Horn was Captain of The Independent Company at Fort Washington, Pa., died 1777.

More About CAPTAIN Henry B. VAN HORN:
Burial: Unknown, Wrightstown, PA
Military service: 1777, Captain of Van Horn's Company of Bucks County, PA militia[7,8]

More About Elizabeth VAN ZANT:
Burial: Unknown, Newtown, Bucks Cnty, PA

Children of Henry VAN HORN and Elizabeth VAN ZANT are:

2   i. Joshua[7] VAN HORN, born 21 Feb 1759 in Bucks Cnty, PA; died Unknown. He married Martha HOWELL; born 05 Jul 1763 in Bucks Cnty, PA; died 1858.

Notes for Joshua VAN HORN:
1790 Census lists one male over 16 one male under 16 and 2 females in the family. Joshua is living next to his brother Henry Van Horn and 2 doors from his mother Elizabeth Van Horn who is a head of family.

More About Joshua VAN HORN:
Military service: 1777, Served in Captain Van Horn's Company of the PA Militia Bucks County, PA. His father's company.

3   ii. Isaiah VAN HORN[9,10,11,12,13], born Bet. 02 - 24 Oct 1760 in Bucks Cnty, PA[14,15]; died Bet. 06 - 27 Aug 1844 in East Mahoning Twp., Indiana Cnty, PA[15,16]. He married Dorcas LOGAN[17,18] 01 Jan 1787 in Bucks Cnty, PA[19]; born Bet. 1765 - 02 Apr 1771 in Feasterville, Bucks Cnty, PA[20]; died 22 Sep 1854 in Mahoning Twp., Indiana Cnty, PA.

Notes for Isaiah VAN HORN:

Was a drummer boy in his father's company in the Army of the Revolution. He married Doris Logan at the close of the revolutionary war and settled in western PA where he raised his family.

In 1790 Census there is an Isaiah Van Horn in Hopewell, Newton, Tyborn, and Westpensboro, Cumberland, Pennsylvania with 1-2-1 listing. Most likely Isaiah was in Cumberland, PA in 1790 as Cumberland was one of 8 counties in PA and included what is now Indiana County, PA.

In 1796 or 97 Isaiah and family moved to what is now Wheatfield Twp., Indiana Cnty, PA. In 1804 he owned a farm in East Mahoning Twp., about one mile east of Georgeville. It is said that he planted the orchard that is so productive on this farm. Reference History of Indiana County, PA p. 479 1880.

Died at the age of 84 according to the records of Gilgal Church.

In the History of Gilgal written May 16, 1861 on page 4 there is a discussion of the eldership of the church. John Work and Joshua Lewis were the ruling elders chosen. some time after William Hopkins and James Thompson were added to the session. The next addition consisted of Isaiah Van Horn and William Work. In the list of Elders he is listed 6th on the roll.

In the summary of his will he lists children as Henry, Alexander, Jane McElhose, Isaiah, George l, and Isaac with executor as Henry Van Horn and Hugh Hamilton, written on 27 April 1839 and Witnessed by James Y. Brady and George L. Van Horn and Probated on 23 September, 1844. Probate 763 Indiana County, PA. Will Book Vol. 1 p. 493.

More About Isaiah VAN HORN:
Burial: Unknown, Gilgal Cemetery, Indiana Cnty, PA Grave marked by DAR in 1893[21]
Military service: 1776, Revolutionary War as Drummer in Father's Milita Unit 2nd Regiment Bucks Cnty, PA[22,23]
Will: 27 Apr 1839, W. Mahoning Twp., Indiana Cnty, PA Vol. 1 p. 493

4   iii.   Mary VAN HORN, born 05 May 1764 in Bucks Cnty, PA; died 12 Apr 1831. She married Isaac GILLAM[24] in Bucks Cnty, PA; born 1760 in Bucks Cnty, PA; died 18 Apr 1823.

Notes for Isaac GILLAM:
In1790 next door to Joseph Gilam in Bucks, Cnty, PA.

5   iv.   Christian VAN HORN, born 13 Jul 1766 in Bucks Cnty, PA; died Bet. 18 Apr 1823 - 14 Aug 1833 in Upper Makefield, Bucks Cnty, PA. He married Elizabeth BURLEY 29 Mar 1787 in Newtown, Bucks Cnty, PA; born Bet. 16 Mar 1770 - 1777 in Newtown, Bucks Cnty, PA; died Bet. 23 Jul 1851 - 1854 in Newtown, Bucks Cnty, PA.

Notes for Elizabeth BURLEY:
In Memory of Elizabeth Van Horn wife of Christian Van Horn who departed this life July 23rd 1854 in the 88th year of her age Birth ??/??/1763 Death 7/23/1851Newtown, PA Spouse: Christian VanHorn Buried Old Presbyterian Church Cemetery Newtown, PA USA

6   v.   Susanna VAN HORN, born 09 Oct 1768 in Newtown, Bucks Cnty, PA; died 06 Jun 1839 in Mercer Cnty, IL. She married Jesse WILLETS Abt. 1802 in Bucks Cnty, PA; born Nov 1770 in Brunswick, Berks Cnty, PA; died 07 Jul 1842 in Mercer Cnty, IL.

7   vi.   Elizabeth VAN HORN, born Bet. 06 May 1770 - 1774 in Bucks Cnty, PA; died 26 Jan 1813. She married ANDERSON; died Unknown.

8   vii.   Sarah VAN HORN, born 07 Feb 1773 in Newtown, Bucks Cnty, PA; died 1799 in Newtown, Bucks Cnty, PA. She married Jesse WILLETS Abt. 1790; born Nov 1770 in Brunswick, Berks Cnty, PA; died 07 Jul 1842 in Mercer Cnty, IL.

9   viii.   Henry VAN HORN, JR[25,26], born 05 Apr 1777 in Newtown Twp., Bucks Cnty, PA[27]; died Feb 1849 in Upper Makefield Twp., Bucks Cnty, PA[27]. He married Hannah REEDER[28,29,30,31] Bet. Feb 1798 - 01 May 1800 in Bucks Cnty, PA[32]; born Bet. 11 Mar 1781 - 1786 in Upper Makefield Twp., Bucks Cnty, PA[33]; died 17 Sep 1867 in Upper Makefield Twp., Bucks Cnty, PA.

More About Henry VAN HORN, JR:
Occupation: Carpenter and Cabinet Maker

Notes for Hannah REEDER:
Living with Rachel Warner in 1850 in Upper Makefield, Bucks Cnty, PA

Endnotes

1. Will of Henry Van Horn Bucks County Wills Book 3,p 74.
2. *Sons and Daughters of the Pilgrims, Volume I, p. 448 & 449* , "Electronic."
3. Peterson, Clarence S., *Known Military Dead During the American Revolutionary War*, (Reprint, Baltimore: Genealogical Publishing Co., Inc., 1967.), "Electronic."
4. *Sons and Daughters of the Pilgrims, Volume I, p. 448 & 449* , "Electronic."
5. *New Jersey Marriage Records, 1665-1800, Marriage Licenses, U-V, Page 423* , "Electronic."
6. *Sons and Daughters of the Pilgrims, Volume I, p. 448 & 449* , "Electronic."
7. Pennsylvania Archives, 2nd Series, Volume 14 p. 175.
8. *Pennsylvania Archives Series: Series 5 Volume: V Chapter: Muster Rolls and Papers Relating to the Associators and Militia of the County of Bucks. .*
9. *Isaiah Van Horn Will 27 April, 1839 Indiana Cnty, PA.*
10. *Interments of the Gilgal Cemetery, Gilgal Church, Indiana Cnty, PA.*
11. *Mahoning, Indiana Cnty, PA 1840 Census p. 122.*
12. *DAR Lineage Book 149 (56430).*
13. DAR National Record Copy of Member Application# 448771.
14. Hamilton, Von Gail, *Work Family History: Twelve Generations of Work in America 1690-1969, Park City, Utah*, (Park City, Utah: Publishers Press, 1969, 614 pgs.).
15. *Interments of the Gilgal Cemetery, Gilgal Church, Indiana Cnty, PA.*
16. *Abstract of Graves of Revolutionary Patriots, Vol.4, Serial: 11831.*
17. *DAR Lineage Book 149 (56430).*
18. *East Mahoning Twp., Indiana Cnty, PA 1850 Census p. 247.*
19. DAR National Record Copy of Member Application # 800118.
20. *East Mahoning Twp., Indiana Cnty, PA 1850 Census p. 247.*
21. DAR National Certificate Record Copy of Member Application , #451294.
22. Pennsylvania Archives, 2nd Series, Volume 14.
23. *Pennsylvania Archives Series: Series 5 Volume: V Chapter: Muster Rolls and Papers Relating to the*

Associators and Militia of the County of Bucks. .

24. *Bucks Cnty, PA 1790 Census p. 186.*

25. The National Society of the Daughters of the American Revolution Volume 94, p. 19.

26. Sons and Daughters of the Pilgrims, Volume I, p. 449.

27. *Sons and Daughters of the Pilgrims, Volume I, p. 448 & 449* , "Electronic."

28. The National Society of the Daughters of the American Revolution Volume 94.

29. *Sons and Daughters of the Pilgrims, Volume I, p. 448 & 449* , "Electronic."

30. *The Pennsylvania Genealogical Magazine Vol III, Marriages Copied from the Docket of Isaac Hicks p. 206*, "Electronic."

31. *History of Bucks County, PA Volume I, Bucks County Genealogies, Page 95,96 & 97*, "Electronic."

32. *The Pennsylvania Genealogical Magazine Vol III, Marriages Copied from the Docket of Isaac Hicks p. 206*, "Electronic."

33. DAR National Record Copy of Member Application # 490300.

Annie and Frank
McElhoes 18 Nov 1934

Eugene R. Van Horn

Pearl Ruth Van
Horn

Marion Catherine Learn

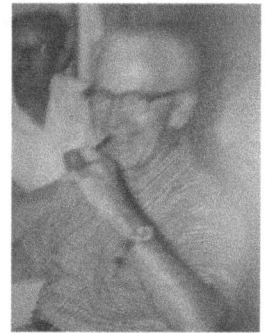

John Simpson Van
Horn

Harold Van Horn

Thelma Van Horn

Harry Bennett and
Irene Simpson Van
Horn

Nellie Van Horn at
19

Bennett Work Van Horn Family

Henry Foster and Matida Van Horn Family

Leafy Fern VanHorn

Leafy & Jennie Van Horn & Elizabeth Wolf

Grandmother Leafy Fern Van Horn Wolf

Rusty and Davene Schimmel with Leafy and Davis Wolf

Ruth Fern Morgan   Johnie Derald Morgan

John Baber Morgan Family

Samuel Cornelius Van Horn

RAN AWAY

From the residence of the subscriber, in East Wheatfield township, Indiana county, on Saturday, July 4th,

SAMUEL VAN HORN,

Aged 16 years; about 5 feet 6 or 7 inches high, fair hair, light complexion and grayish blue eyes, had on when he left steel mixed pants (casimere) nearly black, dark vest, cross buttoned cassimere coat and blue cap.

All persons are hereby warned not to harbor hire or trust said boy. A reasonable reward will be paid any person giving information that will lead to his arrest and return home, or for returning him to his home. All reasonable expenses will be paid in addition.

27:3t.   H. C. VAN HORN

Indiana Progress(Indiana, PA) 23 July 1874

S. C. Van Horn Farm House

S. C. Van Horn Farm in Dallam Cnty, TX

88

Eli Tannehill

Robert Thompson Van Horn

William Wesley Lydick

Mary Van Horn

Ernest Hutzler Family

John Milton Hutzler

Nanie May Hutzler

Roseannah Van Horn and John Hutzler

George W. McBee   Stella Van Horn Sterene

Stella with son Owen and Husband Clifford Serene

Roy, Pearl and Hansine Van
Horn

Nellie and Ovie 1956

Davis, Leafy and Family Wolf

Gilgal Presbyterian Church Indiana County, PA

Isaiah Van Horn Grave Gigal Cemetery

Armaugh UP Church and Cemetery

Liberty Cemetery Bettsville, OH

Isaiah Van Horn Pioneer of Indiana County, Pennsylvania

Emma Ellen Hummel Van Horn Liberty Cemetery Bettsville, OH

Samuel Cornelius and Jennie Hummel Van Horn Dalhart , TX

Harry and Irene Van Horn Grave
Gilgal Cemetery

Harry V. and Agnes M. Van Horn

Sarah Van Horn Gilgal Cemetery

Glen Van Horn Gilgal

James I. Van Horn Gilgal

Henry Foster and Matilda Van
Horn Scottdale

Stella M. Van Horn Headstone

John Work Grave Gilgal Cemetery

Bernadine Braymore Van Horn
Headstone

George P. Van Horn Grave Gilgal
Cemetery

Col. Robert Thompson Van Horn

Merle and Glennetta Van Horn
Tombstone in Gilgal Cemetery

Adela Honeywood Cooley

Donald M and Hazel Henry Van
Horn

97

George Logan and Catherine D.
Van Horn

Bennett Work and Mary Bell
Warden Van Horn

Tirzah Van Horn Headstone

Clair L and Ralph E. Van Horn
Gilgal

Norman and Effie Van Horn Grave
Gilgal Cemetery

Virginia Van Horn and Norman
Brad Talley Gigal Cemetery

Rachel Pounds Van Horn

Bennett Van Horn Tombstone
Gilgal Cemetry

Robert E. Van Horn

Blaine Van Horn Family
Tombstone Gilgal Cemetery

Ralph H. and Anna Van Horn

William G. Van Horn Gilgal

William Work Gilgal

John and Belle Van Horn Gilgal

John Dick Van Horn Scottdale
Cemetery

Robert and Mary Cannon
Thompson Gilgal

A. M. Hopkins and W. L. Work, trustees of the Mahoning United Presbyterian church, petition the court for a preliminary injunction to restrain George Learn, Jeremiah Stowe, Samuel L. Rowe and Casper Aul, from trespassing on plaintiff's property, in East Mahoning township and to stop said parties from working at the erection of buildings on said land. Plaintiffs claims they have been occupying about three acres of land and have a church building thereon erected since 1830, and and that recently the defendants, representing the "Pentecostal Band" or "Holy Rollers," as commonly termed, have taken possession of a portion of the three acres and are now engaged in erecting a frame building to be used as a rival church. Preliminary injunction directed to issue.

W. W. Brilhart, guardian of Bertha, John and George Lydick, was granted an order to pay to the mother $90 and an allowance of $1.25 per week from the funds of John and George each.

12 Nov 1894 Indiana Evening
Gazette (Indiana, PA)

A MONSTER PUMPKIN.

The Grower Promises to Have It At Our Fair.

Vegetable stories are ripe now and a good one on pumpkins comes from East Wheatfild township. Mr. David Wakefield, who resides on the opposite side of the river from Nineveh, has a pumpkin—a monster pumpkin—which is still growing. The last time his neighbors helped him to move it around in order to get its actual size, the cow melon measured 50 inches around the middle and 32 inches in length. It is a perfect specimen and makes one's mouth water for pies when they look at it.

Mr. Wakefield prizes it highly not only on account of its size, but the history of the seed from which it was grown. Of course the pumpkin couldn't help growing big because the vine on which the seed was grown last year, yielded eight wagon loads of pumpkins. We haven't space to go into details about the capacity of the wagon. Mr. Wakefield will have the pumpkin at our fair next month and every farmer should see it.

21 August 1895 Indiana Messenger

MRS. MARY A. VAN HORN.

Mrs. Mary A. Van Horn died at DuBois, on February 22, aged about 84 years. The deceased was the widow of the late Isaiah Van Horn, a resident of East Mahoning township, this county. Mr. Van Horn died 17 years ago, but four daughters and one son survive her. They are as follows: Mrs. Stuchell Lydic, of Deckers Point; Mrs. Andrew McGaughey, of Ambrose; Mrs. Wm. Lydick, of Mitchells Mills; John A., of DuBois, and Mrs. Rose A. Hutsler, of West Virginia. The remains were brought to this county on Thursday and interred in Mahoning church cemetery, in East Mahoning township.

Indiana Progress(Indiana, PA)
March 2, 1898

RECENT DEATHS.

James Wherry VanHorn.

James Wherry VanHorn, for years a resident of West Wheatfield township, died on Saturday. May 19, aged 72 years and six months. In 1847 he was married to Miss Rachel Stewart, who died 24 years ago. Four daughters survive him. They are Mrs. Mary Heisley, of Williamsport; Miss Flora Van Horn, who was his housekeeper and devoted attendant; Mrs. Annie Ashbaugh, of Buffalo, N. Y.; and Mrs. Callie Ballentine, of Derry. Miss Van Horn and Mrs. Ballentine attended their father during the last days of his sickness, Mrs. Heisley not reaching his bedside until two hours before his death and Mrs. Ashbaugh not until three hours after. His grand-daughter, Mrs. Maggie Ashcom, of Conemaugh, was also with him as were three great grand children. Mr. VanHorn was a life-long member of the Presbyterian church, and a member in good standing of the Indiana Lodge of Masons. He was a Republican and has assisted in many a bitter political fight in his community. For 25 years he was engaged in railroad work, and probably enjoyed one of the largest acquaintances among railroad employes of any man in Western Pennsylvania. Mr. VanHorn owned a farm near Centerville for 40 years and by his death that community lost an influential resident and a staunch friend.

Indiana County Gazette (Indiana,
PA) June 6, 1894

101

George Logan Van Horn.

George Logan Van Horn, died at his home in North Po nt on Tuesday, Sept. 14, as the result of a paralytic stroke sustained several years ago. Mr. Van Horn was 68 years of age and was a veteran of the Civil War, having served from August, 1862, until the close of the war. At the battle of Winchester, Virginia, he was wounded in the right leg, taken prisoner," and placed in the Libby prison, and later in the Bell Island prison. The deceased was a member of the United Brethren church: He was born on the old Van Horn homestead, about two miles from where he died. He is survived by his wife and the following children: Miss Tirzale Van Horn, of Ridgway; Mrs. J. C. Serene, Saltsburg; Mrs. W. H. Weiss, Brackenridge; E. M. and A. V. Van Horn, Rural Valley; W. A. Van Horn, Yatesboro. Two sisters, Mrs. Nancy O'Connor, McKees Rocks, and Mrs. Lucy Neale, of Punxsutawney, also survive him. The funeral was held on Saturday.

Indiana County Gazette (Indiana, PA)
22 September 1909

Williamsport, Pa.

Report of Georgeville school for month ending January 7, 1898: Number of pupils enrolled, 47; average attendance, 41; average attendance during term till date, 40; per cent. during month, 90; per cent. of attendance during term till date, 91. Names of those missing no days are: Alice, Bertha, Vesta and Urbie Butler, Nannie Lockard, Annie Hazlette, Essie, Harry and Berton Frederick, Lottie and Wallace Hopkins, Scott and John Roush, James and Harry Van Horn and Waldo Simpson. The following missed only one day during month, Willie Hazlette, Effie Frederick, Charlie Grove, Thomas Sloniger, Paul Hopkins, Wilson Sutter, Lee Van Horn, Homer and Park McManis.

OLIVE NICHOL,
Teacher.

Indiana Progress(Indiana, PA) Jan 26
1898

Recent Deaths.

David S. Wakefield.

David S. Wakefield, a prominent resident of East Wheatfield township, died Satudray, aged 75 years. Death was_due to general debility, he having been seriously ill for a week. With the exception of two years spent in the South with Company D, Fourth Pennsylvania cavalry, he resided in East Wheatfield his entire life. Mr. Wakefield was twice married. His first wife was Miss Tabitha Van Horn, and his second wife was Miss Eliza Robinson, who died about nine years ago. The surviving children are: Mrs. Joseph Davis, of Pittsburg; Mrs. Emanuel Funk, Mrs. Jerome McNeilly, Mrs. William McGinley, George B., and William Wakefield and Mrs. William Wakefield and Mrs. William Rodgers, all of whom reside in the neighborhood of Seward, and Mrs. J. D. Tomb, of East Wheatfield township. He was a brother of A. E. Wakefield, of Johnstown, and of Mrs. Mary Taylor, of Seward. The funeral will be held Tuesday afternoon from the Rodgers home. Services will_be conducted by the Rev. Mr. Noble, pastor of the New Florence M. E. church, and interment will take place in the Wakefield burying ground.

3 May 1909 Indiana Evening Gazette
(Indiana, PA)

With the death of John F. Heisley there passes one who linked the history of early street railway service in Williamsport with the present. One is reminded of the little old cars drawn by a single horse and heralded by a bell attached to the collar of the horse's harness. The driver did duty also as conductor and the passengers dropped their fares in a slot in the front of the car. Mr. Heisley graduated from driver to motorman when the system—if the old horse car line could be called a system—was electrified, and witnessed the extension of the lines and the accompanying development of the outlying sections. He was well and favorably known, had a large circle of friends and will be greatly missed, especially by those who knew him best.

27 Jan 1915 Gazette and Bulletin of
Williamsport

INDIANA PEOPLE AND VANHORN ESTATE

James W. VanHorn Has Best Claim for a Share in Rich Lands.

FILED THEIR DOCUMENTS

Papers Setting Forth Relationships Forwarded to Philadelphia Representative.

ONE HEIR MUST BE SHOWN

Should the Van Horn heirs receive all the millions spoken of in the article sent out by Canby Van Horn, of Ambler, near Philadelphia, there are members of the family who would probably be enriched by more than the $30,000 share the claimant referred to says will be his share. One of these is Col. Robert T. Van Horn, a member of the fifth generation of descendants where as Canby belongs to the seventh.

J. W. Van Horn, of No 735 Locust street, is a nephew of Col. Van Horn and the only member of the sixth generation residing here In addition to the seventh generation other Indiana claimants previously named other Indiana persons who are heirs of equal standing are: Mrs. William McAdoo, of Oak street; Mrs. Madison McLaughlin, of Grant street, and John Houk, of the West End Hotel. All these are direct descendants of Isaiah Van Horn.

The Indiana county branch are descended from Henry Van Horn, grandfather of J. W. Van Horn, who settled near Georgeville almost a century ago. Henry Van Horn married a Thompson and his children are inter-married with the McElhoes, Houk, McLaughlin and other well-known Indiana county families.

In connection with the fight for the $11,000,000 estate in the heart of New York City it is interesting to note that a Philadelphia member of the family who in his capacity as a lawyer instituted preliminary work died suddenly when he had gotten but rightly started in the work. It was found afterward that he had died from poisoning. but the manner in which he received the deadly drug is not known. Following his death many valuable papers relating to the estate were lost and have not as yet re-appeared.

Canby Van Horn and a Mrs. Hall, of Philadelpoia. made a new start and it is through their efforts that the suit has finally been won in court after a twenty years battle. Mrs. Hall solicited funds from the Indiana county Van Horns and has many papers relating to their claims. It is stated that Col. Robert T. Van Horn. the nearest heir. is not interested in the claims of his relatives and does not believe a fortune will be theirs. He formerly edited the Kansas City "Journal" and represented the Corn State in Congress for years.

REGAINS HER SIGHT.

7 Dec 1907 Indiana Evening Gazette (Indiana, PA)

Terrible Death of Young Georgeville Man.

With six other woodsmen George VanHorn, formerly of Georgeville, this county, was burned to death Tuesday morning of last week, in a West Virginia lumber camp. The logging camp was situated near Davis, West Virginia, and was a long two-story frame building, occupied by 35 men who slept up stairs.

The fire broke out in the latter part of the night when all the occupants were in their soundest sleep. One, smelling the smoke, gave the alarm to his comrades and in a moment a wild rush was made for the only means of egress—one narrow doorway. George VanHorn and six others succeeded, after terrible efforts, in fighting their way through the terror-stricken crowd. Once on the stairs they made a wild rush for the fresh air, but the stairs gave away and they were thrown into the midst of the fire. They might have escaped even then but the heat from the resinous pine boards overcame them and they sank back perishing and in a few moments were burned almost to a crisp Many of the remaining members escaped with more or less serious injuries, and some escaped unhurt.

Much trouble was experienced in identifying the burned men, Van Horn being finally recognized by a ring which he wore.

The deceased was a son of Benjamin VanHorn, of Georgeville, and the charred remains were brought to his home Saturday evening. He was aged about 25 years. Funeral services were held Monday afternoon at 2 o'clock. Interment at Gilgal.

The others who perished were Minhale Cronan, aged 60, and John Morris, both of New York; Arthur Hydrick, aged 22, W. Va.; Thomas Hackey, aged 40, of this state and Jack Riley and Forest Maynard, residence unknown.

Indiana Weekly Messenger (Indiana, PA) 29 January 1902

- - - - -

The military record of the Mahonings has been a very commendable one; in fact so many ablebodied men enlisted for service in the Civil War that farming was carried on very largely by children and women. And in the World War the proportion of accepted enlisted and drafted men was reputed to be the highest in Western Pennsylvania. But we may go back to 1840 and find that Mahonings had the following pensioners of the Revolution: John Leasure, John Brady (one of a famous family of fighters and scouts), Isaiah Van Horn, Thomas Neal, James Ewing, James Shields. In the Civil War we find, among others, the following wearers of the Blue: Adam Black, Daniel and Abraham Crissman, Alex Colkitt, Even Lewis, Robt. Jordan, David Neal, Davis A. Lukehart, Aaron Lukehart, Jno. C. Armour, James G. Walker, Enoch Lewis, Wm. Kerr, John Q. Adams Barrett, John Kerr, John Lewis, Samuel Lewis, Thomas Kerr, Chas. Kerr, John Root, Dr. D. R. Crawford, Gilbert Stear, Stewart Byer, Wm. Elkin, Abraham Glenn, Campbell Cassidy, John Weston,—of Smicksburg and West Mahoning; Peter Frech, Conrad Zener, Peter Spencer, James A. Streams, Peter Diltz, Milton Work, Peter Keel, Wm. Work, Robt. Jordan, Jno. L. Neal, James Gourley, James Laughry, Wm. Hazlett, Jas. Hazlett, Hugh Lewis, Silas Work, Samuel Crawford, Asa Croasman, Henry Peffer, Samuel Hazlett, David B. Work, Wm. Meanor—and many others chiefly from East and North Mahoning; Wm. S. Rowland, Noah Seanor, Thos. Lukehart, David Lukehart, Lewis A. Weigh, David R. Lewis, John Lewis, Robt. Suter—mostly from South Mahoning; Samuel Jordan, Joseph Lydick, Jacob Frantz, Arch McBrier, Peter Small, Albert Shafer, Peter Justice, J. S. Neal, David Pringle, Henry Stear, John Stear and many others. Very few of these remain, and practically none participate in the Memorial Day services, but their graves are remembered by their children and those faithful friends who have marked their graves and placed flowers on the sod. Some of the grave stones have sharp epitaphs that remind the reader of the war. For example, the headstone of John L. A. Barrett in the Presbyterian cemetery at Smicksburg bears an inscription that this soldier died as a result of "Jeff Davis's Rebellion."

As for soldiers from the Mahonings in the World War, names are not available at this time; let us hope that they served their country as well as their elders in the Civil War.

- - - - -

Indiana Progress (Indiana, PA) Feb. 26, 1936

Mail Service on the New B., R. & P. Will Supersede the Star Routes.

FIRST RUN NEXT MONDAY

Clerk Will Leave Indiana in the Morning and Return From Punxsutawney That Evening.

COUNTRY HACKS DISCONTINUED

Men Who Have Been Driving to Marion Center and Plumville Are Laid Off.

IS AN EVIL TO THREE TOWNS.

Mail service will be established on the Indiana Branch of the Buffalo, Rochester & Pittsburg next Monday morning. A government clerk will arrive here today and prepare for his new duties.

The new service will result in some radical changes in the postal affairs of Indiana county and result in the abolishment of many rural routes and the passing of such historic stages as those to Marion Center and Plumville.

The mail car will be attached to the B., R. & P. train on the northern trip to Punxsutawney leaving here at 9:30 a. m. and the southern trip from that town arriving here at 5:15. The mail clerk will spend the night here and have a five hour lay-over in Punxsutawney. He will distribute and receive mail ponches from Ernest, Creekside, Homer, Marion Center, Savan, Locust Lane and the towns supplied from those places. His salary will be $800 a year.

Indiana county residents will therefore have but one mail each way every day.

Closed mail ponches will be brought to Indiana from Punxsutawney and points north of that town on the 9 a. m. train and returned to those main line stations on the 5:35 p. m. train.

By the new arrangement Smicksburg, Denton and Plumville will not have direct communication with Indiana, the star route stage to those towns having been discontinued and J. F. Runyan laid off with a month's extra pay as a bonus. The mail to these towns will be sent over the Indiana and West Penn branches of the Pennsylvania and the Allegheny Valley to Mosgrove and then over the Buffalo, Rochester & Pittsburg to Goodville, this county, where a star route mail carrier will receive a pouch containing mail for Smicksburg, Denton and Plumville.

Ernest, Creekside and Chambersville are served by the Plumville carrier at present but they will now be served by the railroad.

The stage coaches that now leave Indiana at 9:15 a. m. and 1 p. m. respectively, for Marion Center will make their last trip tomorrow. These coaches have hauled mail and passengers for over 50 years and their passing away before the railroad mail car has a bit of fond memory for residents of the towns they served.

W. C. Stadtmiller and J. H. Van Horn are the present drivers of the Marion Center stage and they will tomorrow be discharged and given a months extra pay.

Indiana County Gazete December 2, 1904

The Grim Reaper's Harvest.

CORNELIUS HUTCHISON.

On June 18, 1891, East Wheatfield lost one of its most valued citizens in the death of Cornelius Hutchison. The deceased was one who did much for the community in which he lived. He was an industrious, thrifty farmer, and by his careful management had accumulated a considerable amount of real estate and other valuables. Early in life, when the mode of transportation was chiefly by stage, he was one of the careful and responsible drivers on the pike. Often has the remark been made by those riding in his stage, "Hutchison has the ribbons, we can go asleep in safety." This was the good trait of his character, and whatever he did was done well.

His friends and neighbors paid their last tribute of respect to him on Saturday, and showed their esteem for him by the unusually large number who attended his funeral. His body was interred in the burial grounds of the Bethel United Presbyterian church, of which he was a member. Mr. Hutchison was in his seventy-fifth year.

We, with many others, extend our sympathy to the bereaved family.

24 June 1891 Indiana Progress
(Indiana , PA)

He Was Hit Hard.

Wm. Marks, of Marion Center, preferred charges before 'Squire Marlin, of West Indina, Saturday, charging James Van Horn, of that place, with aggravated assault and battery. Marks alleges that they quarreled and that Van Horn struck him on the head with a stone. Marks was in town Saturday and one of his ears was badly cut. High Constable Rupert arrested Van Horn on Monday, and gave bail for his appearance at court. The same day Van Horn preferred charges against Marks for assault and battery.

Indiana Progress(Indiana, PA) May 8
1895

The Shock Killed Him.

Cornelius Hutchison, of Centerville, this county, died one day last week, aged 76 years. A week before his death he was crossing the Pennsylvania railroad, at New Florence, where a freight train had been parted at the crossing. Before his wagon was entirely over the train came together, crushing the rear part of Mr. Hutchison's wagon, and he made a most narrow escape from death. He drove home and took his bed, but never recovered from the shock received at the crossing and died in a week. He was an old canal boatman and well known along the river from Johnstown to Pittsburg.

Room 5. Indiana Public Schools.

24 April 1895 Indiana Messenger
(Indiana, PA)

HIESTAND

Samuel Hiestand, born 1781, in the Page area, went to Ohio, 1804; was justice of Fairfield county, Ohio; a founder of the United Brethren church in Ohio; and made bishop, 1833. He was son of Jacob Hiestand, Mennonite from Pennsylvania, accidentally drowned in the Shenandoah river, and Elizabeth Brumback, descendant of Kempers. Jacob Hiestand's children moved to Ohio. Bishop Hiestand's brother, Rev. Abraham Hiestand, was pioneer minister of Washington county, Indiana. Their brothers, Joseph and John Hiestand, were also ministers. Abraham Hiestand, of the Page area, signs himself, 1794, "minister of the Church of the Mennonite Society." The Hiestands intermarried with Stouter, Bixler, Pilser, Strickler, and others.

Chapter XXX A Pagent of the Golden West

1, 1874, Mary E. Hutchison was united in marriage with James Estep Tomb and for a number of years resided on the farm of Samuel Tomb, father of James E. Tomb Thirty-two years ago Mr. Tomb retired and located in Armagh, where his death occurred in 1912. To this union five sons and a daughter were born, three of whom survive: Ranson Tomb of Johnstown, Robert Bruce Tomb of Armagh and Harry Tomb of Philadelphia Mrs. Tomb is also survived by a half-brother, James J Hutchison of Armagh, three grandchildren and a great-grandson. In her younger days Mrs. Tomb became a member of the Bethel U. P. Church and after her marriage became affiliated with the Armagh Methodist Episcopal Church, where she was a regular attendant until last year. For many years she was a teacherin the Sunday school of the church

7 June 1936 Indiana Democrat
Indiana, PA

Taken Home.

The Johnstown *Tribune* of the 10th says: In the village of Armagh, Indiana county, died, on Tuesday of this week, Mr. Robert Hutchison, grandfather of John H. Cunningham, of the firm of Nutter, Cunningham & Co., of this place, aged nearly eighty-nine years. The deceased was a farmer, and during forty years of his existence resided on the same farm where he departed this life. His father Cornelius Hutchison, died near Lockport, on the Indiana side, about 28 years ago, and by a singular coincidence, was also aged nearly eighty-nine years. The latter was a soldier during the Revolutionary War, and his record for bravery has never been impeached. Near where his son Robert died resides three sons and two daughters, and one son and two daughters have preceded him to the tomb. To-day the remains of Mr. Hutchison were consigned to their last resting-place, near Centerville, in the same burying ground where the ashes of his father and mother repose in peace. The exact date of the birth of deceased was the 10th day of January, 1789.

18 Oct 1877 Indiana Democrat
Indiana , PA

SAMUEL CUNNINGHAM. Attorney.
EXECUTOR'S NOTICE.

Letters testamentary on the estate of James W. VanHorn, late of West Wheatfield township, deceased, having been granted the undersigned, those having claims against said estate are requested to present them duly authenticated for settlement, and those knowing themselves to be indebted are requested to make prompt payment.
FLORA M. VANHORN,
MRS. CAROLINE E. BALLANTYNE,
P. O. Address, Huff.   Executors.
Indiana Co., Pa.

Indiana County Gazette (Indiana, PA
June 27, 1894

DIED.

VANHORN—Near Marion, January 14, 1888, William, son of James T. and Ellen H. Vanhorn, aged 21 years, 1 month and 14 days.

Some two years ago buoyant with life and hope he left home for the far famed West. The picture of health and bodily vigor, promise of long life and prosperity was before him. The early autumn brought him home ailing, but it was thought tender care and loving attention would, restore him to wonted health. Four months of gradual decline and his name has passed from the roll of the living to that of the dead. In early manhood while he was looking into the red of the morning, the evening had grown around him and the night gathered him into its folds. A few hours before he died he called the writer to his side and said, "I long to be at rest." Soon that rest came, "the rest that remaineth for the people of God."

"There is no death. The angel form
Walks o'er the earth with silent tread;
He bears our best loved things away,
And then we call them 'dead.'

"He leaves our hearts all desolate;
He plucks our fairest, sweetest flowers;
Transplanted into bliss they now
Adorn immortal bowers.
        E. G. T.

William Van Horn Obituary

June 21 Bride

MRS. CARLETON BARR

Mrs. Carleton Barr, bride of last Saturday, is the former Romayne McLaughlin, daughter of Mr. and Mrs. Charles T. McLaughlin. She and Carleton V. Barr were married Saturday morning, June 21 in the home of her parents by Harry Burton Boyd, D. D. pastor of the First Presbyterian Church of Indiana.

Romayne McLaughlin BARR

HEART ATTACK IS FATAL FOR BANK OFFICIAL

Cashier, Vice President of Saltsburg Institution Death Victim

WORLD WAR I VET

Owen M. Serene, aged 52, cashier and vice president of the Saltsburg First National bank and a veteran of World War I, died yesterday afternoon at 4:20 in the Latrobe hospital, Latrobe, as the result of a heart attack suffered earlier in the day.

Mr. Serene, who had been a member of the staff of the Saltsburg financial institution for the last 25 years, was well-known throughout the Kiski Valley district. He had been reelected to his offices in the bank only last week.

Stricken in Morning

He suffered the attack, which later claimed his life, yesterday morning.

He was born in North Point on July 15, 1889, a son of James Clifford and Stella Van Horn Serene.

During the first world war he served overseas with Company L, 28th Infantry Division, the Pennsylvania National Guard.

He was a member of St. John's Lutheran church, Saltsburg, the American Legion post of that town, the Indiana post of the Veterans of Foreign Wars, the Apollo Elks and the Saltsburg chapter of the Odd Fellows.

Wife Survives

Survivors include his wife, Ruth Johnston Serene; a daughter, Mary Lou, at home, and his father, James C. Serene.

Friends will be received at the Robinson Funeral home, Saltsburg, after 7 o'clock tonight. Funeral services will be held there Thursday afternoon at 2 o'clok with the Rev. C. E. Stahlman, pastor of St. John's Lutheran church, in charge. Burial will be in the Edgewood cemetery, Saltsburg.

Owen M. Serene Obituary

107

Van Horns Met at North Point.

Sixty-two members of the Van Horn family attended the third annual reunion of the clan on Thursday at the old homestead of the late William Van Horn at North Point. The day was an ideal one for the annual gathering and the members of the family began to arrive at daylight. Those who came by train were taken to the big farm house in carriages and wagons, and by noon they had all arrived and prepared for dinner, which was served under the big trees in the grove. After dinner the real work of the reunion was taken up. J. L. Condron, of Verona, delivered a speech in praise of the committee which had so successfully arranged for the reunion Officers were elected for the next year and a place for next year's reunion will be decided upon later. Those present were: Mrs. Jennie Gallagher, E. M. Van Horn, Isabelle Van Horn, A. V. Van Horn and family, Mrs. Jennie Steward and Harold Van Horn and family, of Rural Valley; M. A. Van Horn, of Marshville; Ont.; Mrs. Clifford Serene and Gwen M. Serene, of Saltsburg; Mrs. Nancy and Zoe Conners, of McKees Rocks; Misses Eleanor and Florence Walter, Mrs. Lucinda Neal, Mrs. R. P. Neal and family, Mr. and Mrs. James M. Condron and son, James, Mrs. R. W. Collins, and George L. Condron, of Punxsutawney; Misses Hazel and Olive Condron, Jacob L. Condron, Russell Ritchey, Roy Beebe, of Verona, Pa.; J. E. Condron and family, of Smicksburg; Mrs. Martha McKillers, Mrs. Annie Black, Mr. and Mrs. Logan Van Horn, Mrs. J. C. Stear, Clyde Neal, Mrs. Frank Reitz and Miss Violet Stear, of North Point; George Travis and family, of Porter, and John Gordon, of Trade City.

...

Indiana Progress(Indiana, PA) 25
August 1909

The Republicans of East Wheatfield township nominated the following ticket on Saturday: Judge, R. G. Cramer; inspector, Charles Nipps; auditor, Fred W. Mack; road supervisors, William Campbell, Levi Foust, Jeff. McBride and David Wakefield; justice of the peace, Thomas Dodd and John E. Brown; school director, James J. Hutchison and Darwin Cassitt; poor overseer, S C. VanHorn.

Indiana Progress(Indiana, PA) Jan.
24, 1900

JOHN A. STEWART.

John A. Stewart died at his home at Washington, D. C., on Monday evening, January 9, 1899, aged 60 years. Mr. Stewart had suffered from grippe which developed into pneumonia, resulting in his death as above stated. Deceased was born in 1839 and was son of the late William G. and Mary G. Stewart, nee Van Horn. When the war of the rebellion opened Mr. Stewart enlisted July 2, 1862, in Captain Creps' company of the 61st regiment, and was discharged March 16, 1865. He was wounded and taken prisoner May 4, 1863, and was again wounded with loss of an arm at Spottsylvania Court House May 12, 1864, and discharged at the date named above. A brother, Henry, was also a member of the 61st regiment and was killed at the battle of the Wilderness. Another brother, Archibald S., served in the signal corps and died with Sherman's army on the march from Atlanta to the sea. The subject of this sketch was a carpenter by trade, but the injuries received in the service of his country prevented him from following that vocation after the close of the war, and in 1865 he was elected county treasurer, which position he filled with credit to himself and the people. After his term as treasurer expired he was collector and treasurer of the borough of Indiana and later in the employ of the First National Bank of this place. Some 12 years ago he was appointed to the position of doorkeeper in the National House of Representatives, which place he held until the time of his death, and was one of the most trusted and respected officers in the House. Deceased was a nephew of A. M., and J. M. Stewart, of Indiana. He was married to Mary, a daughter of Robert Barber, who is a sister of Mrs. L. A. Hollister, of this place, who, with three children, survive him.

The remains will be brought to this place to-morrow and taken to the Presbyterian church, where services will be held at 2 o'clock p. m. Interment at Greenwood.

Indiana Weekly Messenger (Indiana,
PA) 11 January 1899

FIVE GENERATIONS

Of the VanHorn Family Found Under One Roof.

REMARKABLE LONGEVITY

The Trials of a Married Man, Who Wanted to Hear the Returns.

OTHER TALES OF DOMESTIC LIFE

A correspondent at New Florence writes:

There came into my possession a few days ago a group of photo-pictures that I venture to say cannot be duplicated in the State. The group consists of five persons, constituting one family, living under one roof, and representing five generations. Their home is in Indiana county, just across the Conemaugh river opposite the town of New Florence. The home is that of Mr. James W. VanHorn.

Let me give a short description of this unique and interesting family. Mrs. Mary VanHorn, the mother of James, was born in Antrim county, in the north-east of Ireland, in the province of Ulster, November, 1801. Her maiden name was Wherry. She came with her family to this county in 1810 and settled on the farm now owned by Mr. George Leuffer, but a short distance from where she now resides. In 1819 she was married to Alexander VanHorn, with whom she lived happily until his decease in 1871. Mrs. VanHorn is a staunch Presbyterian—she could scarcely be anything else, coming from North Ireland—and has been a member of the church for more than 70 years. Although her mind is somewhat impaired by age, she is a remarkably intelligent lady, and is possessed of a very sweet and lovely disposition.

The next member of this group is Mr. James W. VanHorn, second son of Mrs. Mary VanHorn, who was born on Hallow e'en, 1831, and is now in the 70th year of his age. He was brought up on the farm and received his education in the common schools of the neighborhood.

In 1854 he went South to Atlanta, and was engaged in railroading. When the war of the rebellion broke out he was in Memphis, Tennessee, and although anxious to return North, he was not permitted to do so; he was virtually a prisoner. Here he was compelled to remain and assist in operating the road till June 6, 1862, when Memphis surrendered to our forces. Being now released from exile he came North. In 1866 he went to Williamsport, Pa., where he spent several years, also in railroading. Here Mrs. VanHorn died, after which Mr. VanHorn came back and settled on a farm near New Florence, where he still resides. Twenty-six years of his life were spent on the railroad. He is at the present time a confirmed invalid, being unable to walk without crutches, and even then with great difficulty.

Miss Florence VanHorn, who represents the third generation in this group, is the daughter of Mr. James W. VanHorn, and his housekeeper at the present time. Her position is no sinecure. Beside having the care of an invalid father and a grandmother who is 99 years old, she has the management of a large farm on her hands. All honor to those who devote their lives to caring for the feeble and the aged.

Mrs. Maggie Ashcorn is a granddaughter of James VanHorn, and was brought up almost from her infancy in his family. About three years ago she was married to Mr. Frank Ashcorn and resides in Conemaugh borough. She is, however, spending the summer at her grandfather's. Mrs. Ashcorn has a rollicking, handsome boy, 15 months old, who brings up the rear, and represents the fifth generation of this house.

H.

TRIALS OF A FAMILY MAN.

5 Generations of Van Horns

In loving memory of
Mrs. Stella M. Serene
"There is no Death. What seems so is transition;
This life of mortal breath
Is but a suburb of the life elysian
Whose portal we call Death."

This transition came quietly peacefully, as befitted her life, to Stella M. (Van Horne) Serene, wife of Mr. J. Clifford Serene, President of the First National Bank, Saltsburg, Pa., at the family home, Thursday May 2, 1946, at 7:45 p. m., after an illness of several years. She was daughter of Logan and Catherine (Travis) Van Horne, and was born North Point, Indiana County, Pennsylvania, February 28, 1871.

She had been a resident of Saltsburg, for over forty-five years. Early in life she connected herself with the United Brethren Church at North Point, Pa., and after coming to Saltsburg became an active worker in the Methodist Episcopal Church, participating in all its activities until prevented by ill-health.

She was a member of the Cecelia Rebekah Degree Lodge and took active part in the Ladies' Auxiliary of the American Legion.

Surviving are her husband, J. Clifford Serene, a son, Owen M. Serene, Director and Cashier of the First National Bank, Saltsburg, Pa., a granddaughter, Mary Lou Serene, born January 30, 1894, and Thelma Van Horne, a niece. Of a retiring disposition, only her neighbors or those who met her in her home found out the sterling quality bound up in her life. The neighborhood has lost a friend who will long be remembered.

Mrs. Serene was greatly interested in Red Cross and other activities during the World War and with wonder, for her father, George Logan Van Horne served during the Civil war in the 67th Pennsylvania Volunteers, while on Mr. Serene's side, his father was a member of the 6 Pennsylvania Volunteers. In 1917, her son, their grandson, Owen M. Serene enlisted in Company A 110th Regiment, 28th Division. And on July 30th, 1918, he was badly wounded and gassed while in action and on partial recovery was transferred to General Hospital office at Bordeaux, France, returning to the United States and being discharged in April 1919.

This would explain the great interest Mrs. Serene had in the work of the Ladies' Auxiliary of the American Legion.

Funeral services were conducted at the Robinson Funeral Home, Saltsburg, at 2:30 p. m., Sunday, May 1946, by Rev. Fred M. Bennett, pastor of the Methodist Episcopal Church, Saltsburg.

Her body was laid to rest in Edgewood Cemetery amid the sunshine of a perfect spring day, surrounded by nature's beautiful early flowers, singing birds to await the Resurrection of the just.

"Now the laborer's task is o'er
Now the battle day is past;
Now upon the farther shore,
Lands the voyager at last.
Father, in Thy gracious keeping
Leave we now Thy servant sleeping."

H. F. C.

Stella M. Van Horn Serene Obituary

Couple Held In Incident With Police

REYNOLDSVILLE — incident which started in Punxsutawney and carried over to a Reynoldsville Magistrate's Office in the early hours of Sunday morning resulted in the arrest of a scrappy husband-wife duo from Smicksburg, RD 1.

The incident started when Punxsutawney police stopped Richard Vanhorn, 20, of Smicksburg RD 1 on a traffic violation at 2:50 a.m. Sunday.

While attempting to cite Vanhorn for the traffic violation, Patrolmen John Lowmaster and William Beatty were allegedly assaulted by the Smicksburg area man.

Vanhorn and his wife were then taken before District Magistrate Bill Wescoat in Reynoldsville for his arraignment.

While in the Reynoldsville office of Magistrate Wescoat for the arraignment, Mrs. Joyce Vanhorn, 18, alledgedly assaulted the police officers. The Punxsutawney policemen were then assisted by Reynoldsville Patrolman Gary Basinger in arresting Mrs. Vanhorn on charges of aggravated assault and disorderly conduct.

As a result of the entire incident the Vanhorns were both committed to jail. Richard was sent to the Jefferson County Jail in Brookville in lieu of $5,000 bail while Mrs. Vanhorn was sent to the Punxsutawney Borough Jail in lieu of $2,500 in bail.

Indiana Evening Gazette (Indiana, PA) March 28, 1977

Will Farm in Texas.

Mr. S. C. Van Horn, of East Wheatfield township, has sold his farm near Armagh, to Oliver J. Riggs, of Johnstown. Mr. Van Horn has purchased a ranch of 160 acres in Dallam county, Tex., and will move there next month. He returned just recently from Texas and is well impressed with the climate and country in general and believes that this great agricultural belt offers fine opportunities to those seeking a home sight, and especially to the thrifty farmer with a small capital.

Indiana Progress(Indiana, PA) 7 October 1908

S. C. Van Horn,

PRACTICAL AUCTIONEER, Armagh, Pa.

Sales cried in any part of the county. Contracts made by mail.

Indiana Progress(Indiana, PA) October 7, 1903

S. C. VanHorn

S. C. VanHorn, aged 79 years, a native of East Wheatfield township, died at his home in Dalhart, Tex., on January 6. He was born near Armagh on December 31, 1858, and resided there until about 30 years ago, when he moved to Dalhart. Surviving are his widow, Mrs. Tressa VanHorn, to whom he was united in marriage five years ago; three children by a previous marriage—H. C. Van Horn, of Dalhart, Tex.; Mrs. Leafy Wolf, of Dayton, O.; and Mrs. Nellie Smith, of Guymon, Okla., two grandsons and five granddaughters. A sister, Mrs. Harry Bateman, resides in St. Petersburg, Fla. Mr. VanHorn was laid to rest beside the wife of his youth, in Dalhart cemetery.

Indiana Progress(Indiana, PA) January 20, 1937

ESDAY, OCTOBER 23, 1895.

FIRED THE TABERNACLE.

South Mahoning Youths Held for Court for Disturbing Religious Meetings.

A MOST SENSATIONAL HEARING.

Evangelist Stowe Says a Lighted Cigar Was Applied to His Gospel Tent.

ELEVEN DEFENDANTS GO FREE.

If anybody has any idea that religion is at a discount in South Mahoning township he makes a great mistake. Citizens out there go to church regularly every Sunday, contribute liberally to the collection basket, and have never been known to remain in the back ground when a donation party is suggested for the minister. South Mahoning has been blessed with her share of worshipping places for many years, and, until a few weeks ago, the respect accorded all things religious had never been questioned. Recently, however, troubles arose personally involving almost a score of South Mahoning's young men, and very materially ruffling the usual placidity of the neighborhood.

A short time ago a minister of the Church of God, Rev. Stowe by name, set up a tent near Plumville, and began holding nightly meetings. He was assisted in the work by Rev. Isaiah McCoy, and the two had no other idea than that they had erected their tabernacle in a district ripe for the saving of souls. The meetings were fairly well attended, and the "hallelujahs" of the "Saints" as the ministers style themselves, rang exultingly over South Mahoning's hills. By and by the younger people of the nightly audiences grew weary of too constant attendance at service, and according to Rev. Stowe, took to congregating on the outside. This fact alone would have been overlooked had it not developed into matters more pronounced. Loud talking from the outside disturbed the inside devotions. An occasional stone on the top of the tent cut little rents in the tabernacle and the determined swinging on the ropes by one or two small boys so shook the big oil lamp suspended from the center of the tabernacle as to almost shake the faith of some of the worshipers in the ability of the "Saints" to save. The "Saints" tried to remonstrate. It was no use. The boys would talk and the lamp continued to shake. They tried prayer. A dismal failure resulted, for the next night two of the boys wanted to whip the preacher. Then Rev. Stowe concluded to try earthly remedies, and an information was the result.

Rev. Stowe went before 'Squire George Kellar, of the Fourth ward, and warrants were issued for J. A. Davis, John Little, Findley Blose, Thomas Ashbaugh, Joseph Craft, Sprague VanHorn, John Gallentine, Harry Lukehart, John Warden, Carole Buchanan, William Spencer, John Brewer, Leroy VanHorn, Thomas Mabon, Thomas Frantz and Morris Johnston, 17 of the flower of South Mahoning's youths, and all born of good parents.

Constable Pringle took the warrants and it wasn't very long until he had served them upon all of the boys save two—Findley Blose and Joseph Craft, who eluded the officer and hid in the woods.

The hearing was set for last Saturday morning at 9, and promptly at that time 'Squire Kellar's little office was packed with the accused and the witnesses. Rev. Stowe didn't show up until almost 10. Lawyer Keener was with him, and the battle shortly began. Rev. Stowe was the first witness. He told his story in accordance with the above facts. He said it was the intention to establish a permanent organization in the neighborhood and that considerable money had been subscribed for that purpose. According to his version the first trouble arose when John Gallentine and William Spencer drove into the grounds in which the tabernacle is located on the evening of October 2. "They were loud in their talk," said the preacher, "and continued it in the inside. This was kept up almost every night, to the inconvenience of those at worship, and the general distribution of the "Word." In his efforts to establish the fact that the meetings were of a religious nature. Lawyer Keener displayed a surprising knowledge of ecclesiastical affairs, speaking fluently of "Oxford editions," "Echoes from Glory," etc. Rev. Stowe was finally turned over to attorney Taylor for cross examination. One of the first questions asked him was "Did you ever write a letter to a Mr. Cleaver, admitting the theft of a chicken?" The preacher acknowledged the crime, but said it was 10 years ago, before the doctrines which he now advocated had become instilled into him. Since being "saved" he had offered every reparation of the offense. Generally, he stuck to his original story, and was finally released from further interrogation.

The testimony of Rev. McCoy, Aaron [illegible], G. W. Haslett, William Hawk, R[illegible] Pearce, Taylor Mogle, Harry Elkin and Abram Silver was also taken. Nearly all had something to say about the conduct around the tent, and one man testified that Thomas Ashbaugh set the tent on fire with a cigar.

The case was concluded about five in the evening, and resulted in the release of 11 of the defendants. Jim Little, Harry [...]baugh were the unfortunates who will have to come before the court. John and Jim are the ones who wanted to knock the salvation out of the preacher; Harry stands accused of indulging in an occasional sip of firewater near the tabernacle entrance, and Tom put the business end of his cigar against the tabernacle and burned his way through to glory. The case will come up for trial in December, and South Mahoning will be in full force to testify. The boys gave bail in the sum of $300 for their appearance.

ROBBED THE WIDOW'S HOME,

But the Thieves Couldn't Find Where the Money was Hidden.

During the absence of Mrs. D. Cameron, of Homer City, in Indiana, last Wednesday night, thieves gained an entrance to her dwelling and ransacked the premises. An entrance was gained by breaking out a pane of glass in the kitchen window and undoing the fastening in the inside.

The robbery was discovered on Thursday morning by Mrs. Daniel Cameron, a sister-in-law, who had the keys to the house during the owner's absence. An investigation in the afternoon disclosed the fact that a couple of gold watches and watch cases, two gold rings and a revolver were among the missing articles. The watch cases were found on the street on Friday afternoon and returned to Mrs. Cameron. Every bureau drawer and cupboard had been pillaged, and many minor articles carried away.

It is believed the thieves were in search of money. On Wednesday morning Mrs. Cameron after making some purchases at Flickinger's store, displayed a large roll of bills. The thieves probably believed the money was concealed about the house, and in this surmise they were correct, but their search for it proved fruitless. In a cup in the cupboard was about $16 and the remainder was stowed deep in the pocket of a dress which hung in the wardrobe.

IT WAS FOR BLOOD.

Rival Town Organizations Battle for Football Supremacy.

On Normal grounds last Saturday evening the football teams of the Indiana Athletic Club and the West End Athletic Association battled for supremacy. All the bad blood which is supposed to have existed between the rival parts of town for years seemed to come to the surface in this game on Saturday, and it was biff! bang! from the call of time. The West End lads were the heavier, but their rivals were away ahead in activity. They also showed a greater familiarity with their signals and as a result won in two 25 minute halves. The score was eight to nothing, Earhart missing in his trials for goals after two touch downs.

There is material in the two teams to make one very creditable town aggregation. The boys lined up as follows:

INDIANA A. C.	POSITION.	WEST END A. A.
Thompson	right end	Wiggins
Gibson	right tackle	Walker
Galbie	right guard	Rice, Bid
Ortz	center	Marshall
Wilson	left guard	Balentine, Thomas
Hood	right tackle	Gessler
Myers	left end	Hammers
Miller	quarterback	McClosky (Capt.)
Earhart (Capt)	right half back	Gearhart
Keck	left half back	Lockard
Wood	full back	Balentine, H.

Referee—Campbell; Umpire—Robertson.

MANY PRETTY SIDE WALKS.

Flag Stone and Cement are Pushing the Red Bricks to the Rear.

Shortly before the dissolution of the West Indiana council an order had been issued requiring the building of pavements by property holders on the north side of Philadelphia street, from a short distance east of MacCartney's foundry to about 1,500 feet west. This work has been going on for some time and is now nearly completed.

Of the 1500 feet which will soon be finished about 340 feet will be cement, including the properties of A. S. Cunningham, William Brinkman, Mr. Wachob, W. D. Anthony, Mrs. Collebaugh and C. M. Wood. In addition to this it is said Sutton Bros. will place 300 feet of flag stone pavement along their paper mill property.

All this, of course, will be very pretty, and Third street, in the same neighborhood shows improvement of equal proportions. From the Saltsburg road to Philadelphia street is one continuous flag stone pavement, with the exception of one little strip of cement. Citizens of that end of town have reason to be proud of the improvements which they have made.

Railroad Work is Quiet.

A large number of railroad men who were living in hopes of more railroad being built, left here this week for St. Marys, where 15 miles of road is now under construction. This looks very much as though the railroad building in this section will be at a standstill this winter.—*Glen Campbell Comet.*

Was Taken Sick in Johnstown.

Martin V. Patterson, Saltsburg's well-known citizen, while in Johnstown last week was taken suddenly ill with cramp. He was confined to his room in the Capital Hotel for three days, but on Tuesday evening was improved sufficiently to admit of his going to his home.

Opening of Library Hall.

The theatrical season was opened at Library Hall on last Friday evening by Mr. Joe Sullivan in "Maloney's Mishaps." The audience was away below what it should have been at the season's initial performance. The company was but [...]

23 October 1895 Indiana County Gazette

Report of Hutchison school, East Wheatfield township, for the month ending December 21, 1894; Dillie Cunningham, teacher: Number in attendance, males a5, females 7: average attendance, males 5, females 5; average attendance during term, males 5. females 6; per cent of attendance, males 89. females 72: percent of attendance during term, males 93, females 83; those who missed no days, Coulter Van Horn, Robert Cunningham and Leaffe Van Horn. Visitors, two.

Indiana Progress(Indiana, PA)
January 2, 1895

John N. Van Horn.

John N. Van Horn, a well-known resident of East Mahoning township, died on Wednesday morning with Bright's disease, at the age of 62 years. The deceased was born in South Mahoning township, August 13, 1842, and spent the early part of his life in that section of the county. He was a valiant and efficient soldier of the Civil War, enlisting as corporal in Co. F, 105th P. V., in the fall of 1861, and was wounded and discharged from the command in February, 1863. In June of that year he enlisted as second sergeant in Co. A, Second Batallion, P. V., and was discharged January 21, 1864. On August 26, of the same year, he enlisted as second lieutenant in Co. A, 206th P. V., and was discharged June 26, 1865, at the close of the war. He was united in marriage to Miss Jane Campbell, of near Georgeville, and in 1881 went to South Dakota, where his wife died. Returning to this county in June, 1904, he married Miss Belle Nichol, of near Georgeville, in the fall of that year. His wife and several children survive him.

Indiana Progress(Indiana, PA)
October 30, 1907

AT HUTCHISON SCHOOLHOUSE.

East Wheatfield Teachers Hold Their Second Institute.

The East Wheatfield township teachers held a lively session of institute at the Hutchison schoolhouse on Saturday afternoon. Mr Scott Cribbs presided and Miss Pearl Mack was secretary.

After the address of welcome by Miss Pearl Mack, the first topic, "How to Teach Primary Physiology," was opened by R. C. Walbeck and discussed by a number of other teachers present. "What Preparation Should the Teacher Make Before Entering the Profession?" was the subject opened by R. J. Felton and warmly discussed by others. "Object of Our Township Institutes" was the next topic discussed. Good talks were made by Messrs. T. V. Conrad, J. J. Hutchison and Prof. C. A. Campbell. "Correlation of the Branches" and "Co-operation of the Teacher and Parent" were subjects that were liberally discussed by teachers and others. The program was spiced with recitations by Viola Cunningham, James Gross, Leafy Van Horn, Joe McKelvey, Madge Cunningham and Nellie Van Horn and music by Madge Cunningham and by the school.

The next institute will be held at the Elder schoolhouse December 10. The program will be published in next week's issue of the PROGRESS.

Indiana Progress(Indiana, PA) Nov 23, 1898

Wolf-VanHorn.

Davis M. Wolf and Miss Leary Fern Van Horn, of Dalhart, Texas, were married on Wednesday at the home of the bride's parents, Mr. and Mrs. S. C. Van Horn, who are former residents of East Wheatfield township, this county.

Indiana Progress(Indiana, PA) 28 December 1910

111

John Van Horn.

John Van Horn, aged 44, general foreman of the boiler department of the Edgar Thompson Steel Works at Braddock, died at the family home, 218 Eighth street, Braddock, Sabbath morning at 11:30 o'clock, from pneumonia, which developed last Wednesday night. He was born in Braddock, at the old homestead of the Van Horns 10 yards from his present place of residence, having lived in the immediate neighborhood all his life. He was the eldest son of George Van Horn. Mr. Van Horn had been connected with the boiler department of the Edgar Thompson plant for almost 20 years, 14 of which were spent as general foreman under Superintendent John Noey, and previously as foreman of injectors under the old boiler system. He was married on October 30, 1890 to Miss Alpharetta Weamer, of Indiana, the daughter of Mrs. Eliabeth Weamer, of North Fifth street and of the late David Weamer. Mrs. Anna Thompson and David and Charles Weamer of Indiana, are sister and brothers to the deceased's widow, who is left with one daughter, Miss Jean Van Horn. He also leaves his mother, Mrs. George Van Horn, of Edgewood Park, a brother, Clarence E. Van Horn, of Swissvale, and a sister, Mrs. Joseph A. Hayes, of Swissvale. The funeral services will be held at the Van Horn home this evening at 8 o'clock and the interment will be made in the cemetery near Braddock, Wednesday afternoon at 3 o'clock.

15 Jan 1915 Indiana
Gaazette(Indiana,PA)

AN INTERESTING LETTER

We publish some excerpts from a letter written by Mrs. John Lytle, of Fort Morgan, Colorado. Mrs. Lytle is a daughter of the late Tabitha Van Horn and Moses T. Work and a sister of Mrs. Aaron Steel, of this place. She has a great many friends in this county who will be glad to hear from her through the columns of the Messenger.

She writes: "I take this opportunity to thank you for kind thoughts of me in sending the article on 'Old Gilgal.' We enjoyed it exceedingly. We lived over again the scenes and experiences of the days when, with our mother, we children rode behind on 'old black Sallie' to church on Sabbath morning, through the woods, the dogwoods abloom, the doves a-cooing and the Bob White a-calling. Oh! that seems such a long time ago, but the memory is all so dear to me.

"I also remember I had the great pleasure of many times riding in the buggy with Aunt Mollie and Uncle Robert Thompson to where our road led off through the woods from the main road. They drove a big white horse, much like the one Mr. Caruthers drove. As we count time that is a long time ago, but it seems as but yesterday, as I look back. I love to think of the early days when we were all under the same roof tree, with father and mother. * * *

"I certainly expect to see old Pennsylvania again, but when I cannot say. I have a lot of dear ones there. Our son, Victor and wife are in Pennsylvania and our son, Herbert, in Sacramento, Calif., while our daughter, Helen, is in college at Colorado Springs, Colo., about as far apart as they can get and we about half way between.

"Emma McCreery lives near us and is well. Mrs. Emigh, nee Lizzie Ryckman, of Marion Center, also lives near us. She is far from well. The influenza has been in our community for six weeks, causing many deaths. Schools and churches are closed. Hoping the coming year may be a happy one to you all, I will close by again thanking you for the paper with the article on 'old Gilgal.' I shall preserve it among my treasures.

"Most cordially,
"SARAH WORK LYTLE."

Indiana Weekly Messenger
(Indiana, PA) 12 December
1918

FOUR ESTATES DIVIDED

Bequests Made in Wills Filed During The Last Week.

The will of the late John N. Van Horn, of East Mahoning township, has been filed. He bequeaths to his widow all the household goods, his horse, buggy, sleigh and harness and the interest while she remains his widow on $3000 which he directs be deposited in equal shares in three banks in Indiana. He gives to his daughter, Mrs. Nora Anderson and his son, Claude Van Horn, a judgment note on R. V. Van Horn for $500. The former is to receive $300 and the latter $200. His daughter-in-law, Mrs. Elmira Van Horn, is given a note for $102 which testator held against her. His son, R. C. Van Horn, is given a note for $131.30 which testator held against him. His son, W. B. Van Horn, is given $200 and a note of $400 held against him by testator. His daughter, Mrs. M. H. Gould, is bequeathed $400 and a note for $200 held against her husband by testator. He directs that after the death or remarriage of his widow that the $3,000 deposited in the Indiana banks be paid in equal shares to the following children: Claud, W. B., R. C., Myrrell Gould and Nora Anderson. His executor is directed to pay to W. B. Van Horn $125 to be used in repairing the graves and a like sum is to be expended for the purchase of a monument to mark the grave of the testator. All the balance of his estate is bequeathed to his widow. James M. Nichol is appointed executor. The will is dated April 26, 1907. In a codicil dated October 22, 1907 the testator appoints his son, W. B. Van Horn as one of the executors.

Indiana Progress(Indiana, PA) Dec. 18, 1907

EAST WHEATFIELD.

Hubert Van Horn, of Wilkinsburg, is the guest of his brother, S C. Van Horn.

E. W. Brendlinger, of Morrellville, is visiting his daughter, Mrs. E. A. Johnston.

S. C. Van Horn and wife attended the Free Methodist campmeeting at Blairsville he latter part of last week

Indiana Progress(Indiana, PA) Augus 9, 1899

GRAND JURY RETURNS:

Commonwealth vs. Charles T. Stuchell, carrying concealed weapons, a true bill; Edward L. Kobaugh, f. and b., a true bill; Rosa Bell Johns, concealing the death of a bastard child, a true bill; David A. Lydick, assault and battery, a true bill; Charles Abel, assault and battery, not a true bill and the county pay the costs; James Van-horn, Jr., assault and battery, not a true bill and the prosecutor, William Work, to pay the costs; William Work assault and battery, not a true bill and James Vanhorn, prosecutor, to pay the costs; Alexander W. Fleming, f. and b., a true bill; Matilda Sylvanus, entering a barn, etc.. a true bill; John Marshall, entering a shop with intent to commit a felony, a true bill; Holsey Walker, same, true bill as to one count; Frank Roof, same; true bill.

William North, of Glen Campbell, formerly a citizen of Great Britian, took out his naturalization papers.

Indiana Progress(Indiana, PA) June 5 1895

Miss Tirzah Van Horn, the only sister of Mrs. J. C. Serene, of Saltsbu.g, was accidentalyy killed at Ridgway Sunday on returning from church services. The interment was made in Edgewood cemetery Wednesday of last week. Miss VanHorn has visited in Saltsbu g frequently.

22 March 1923 Indiana Weekly Messanger (Indiana, PA)

The Republicans of East Wheatfield township nominated the following ticket on Saturday: Judge, R. G. Cramer; inspector, Charles Nipps; auditor, Fred W. Mack; road supervisors, William Campbell, Levi Foust, Jeff. McBride and David Wakefield; justice of the peace, Thomas Dodd and John E. Brown; school director, James J. Hutchison and Darwin Cassitt; poor overseer, S C. VanHorn.

Indiana Progress(Indiana, PA) Jan. 24, 1900

DIED.

VANHORN—Near Marion, January 14, 1895, William, son of James T. and Ellen H. Vanhorn, aged 21 years, 1 month and 14 days.

Some two years ago buoyant with life and hope he left home for the far famed West. The picture of health and bodily vigor, promise of long life and prosperity was before him. The early autumn brought him home ailing, but it was thought tender care and loving attention would, restore him to wonted health. Four months of gradual decline and his name has passed from the roll of the living to that of the dead. In early manhood while he was looking into the red of the morning, the evening had grown around him and the night gathered him into its folds. A few hours before he died he called the writer to his side and said, "I long to be at rest." Soon that rest came, "the rest that remaineth for the people of God."

"There is no death. The angel form
Walks o'er the earth with silent tread;
He bears our best loved things away,
And then we call them 'dead.'

"He leaves our hearts all desolate;
He plucks our fairest, sweetest flowers;
Transplanted into bliss they now
Adorn immortal bowers.
E. G. T.

William Van Horn Obituary

GRAND JURY RETURNS:
Commonwealth vs. Charles T. Stuchell, carrying concealed weapons, a true bill; Edward L. Kobaugh, f. and b., a true bill; Rosa Bell Johns, concealing the death of a bastard child, a true bill; David A. Lydick, assault and battery, a true bill; Charles Abel, assault and battery, not a true bill and the county pay the costs; James Vanhorn, Jr., assault and battery, not a true bill and the prosecutor, William Work, to pay the costs; William Work assault and battery, not a true bill and James Vanhorn, prosecutor, to pay the costs; Alexander W. Fleming, f. and b., a true bill; Matilda Sylvanus, entering a barn, etc., a true bill; John Marshall, entering a shop with intent to commit a felony, a true bill; Holsey Walker, same, true bill as to one count; Frank Roof, same; true bill.
William North, of Glen Campbell, formerly a citizen of Great Britian, took out his naturalization papers.

Indiana Progress(Indiana, PA) June 5, 1895

Our old friend, Col. Robt. T. Van-Horn, editor of the Kansas City Journal, has been tendered the Republican nomination in the Fifth Missouri District. In a letter declining the honor, the Colonel writes as follows:

The reasons are personal, not political, and are insuperable. I have done earnest work in the Republican party for more than a quarter of a century, and I am not fitted now for the active duties of such a campaign as must be made to do justice to the Republican cause in this district and the State of Missouri. The result is too important to omit any condition of success.

I look upon Republican success as of the last importance to the people and to the future prosperity of the masses that depend on their personal labor and employment for a living. In some respects I am in advance of the Republican party on these questions, but it is of all political organizations the only one that makes the question of wages an issue paramount. The cry of cheap clothes is a delusion. Give the man or woman who works the money—the highest wages possible and let them settle the question of clothes for themselves.

The American worker gets higher wages than any other on the planet to-day. Why? Because he has the home market of 60,000,000 of people to buy the product of his labor. Open that to all the world and foreign wages come in with foreign wares.

This fact is clear to the common sense of every man, and answers all fine spun theories of doctrinaires and professors who talk and write, but don't work.

Select some man for congress who is thoroughly identified with the principle—one that the workingmen know is right on this question, and you will then have done the best you can do—deserved political confidence and success. I would like to make a canvass on such an issue, but that pleasure is denied me by reasons that I cannot disregard. So my declination must be taken as conclusive and final under any circumstances. Very truly yours, R. T. VAN HORN.

Indiana Weekly Messenger (Indiana, PA) September 26, 1888

George Logan Van Horn CW
Discharge

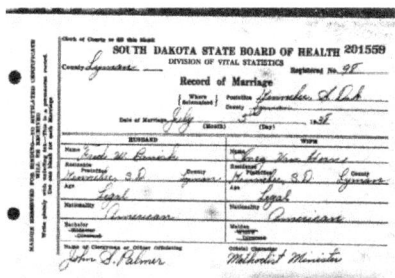

Inez Vernal Van Horn Marriage
Certificate

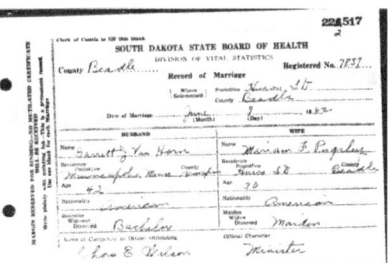

Jesse Garrett Van Horn Marriage
Certificate

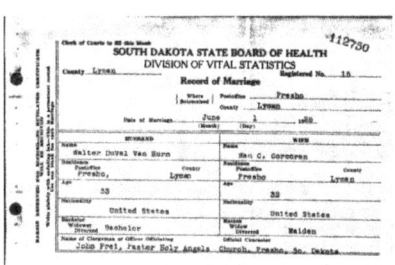

Walter Duval Van Horn Marriage
Certificate

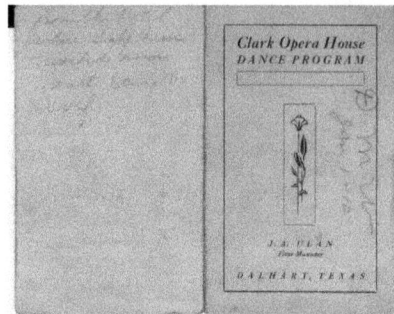

Leafy Van Horn' Dance Card from
Dance where she met Davis Wolf

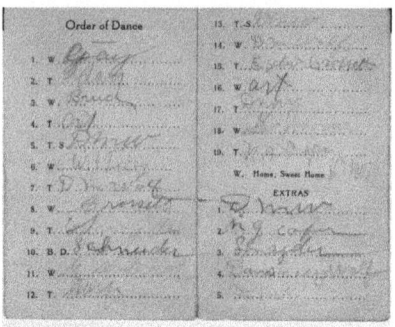

Leafy Van Horn Dance Card Note #
of Davis Wolf's Dances

The Lord is my shepherd; I shall not want.
He maketh me to lie down in green pastures:
He leadeth me beside the still waters.
He restoreth my soul: He leadeth me in the
paths of righteousness for His name's sake.
Yea, though I walk through the valley of
the shadow of death, I will fear no evil:
for thou art with me; Thy rod and
thy staff they comfort me.
Thou preparest a table before me in the presence
of mine enemies: thou anointest my head
with oil; my cup runneth over.
Surely goodness and mercy shall follow me
all the days of my life; and I will
dwell in the house of the Lord forever.
Twenty-third Psalm

IN MEMORY OF
LEAFY FERN WOLF

DATE OF BIRTH
December 17, 1886

DATE OF DEATH
November 18, 1969

FUNERAL SERVICE
Friday, November 21st, 1:30 PM
Meyer & Boehmer Funeral Home

CLERGYMAN
Dr. Emerson D. Bragg

FINAL RESTING PLACE
Miami Valley Memory Gardens

Leafy Van Horn Memorial Program

Descendants of Isaiah VAN HORN

Generation No. 1

1. Isaiah[7] VAN HORN *(Henry B.[6], Henry[5], Christian Barentsen[4] VAN HOORN, Barent Christiansen[3], Christian Barentsen[2], Barent Barents[1])*[1,2,3,4,5] was born Bet. 02 - 24 Oct 1760 in Bucks Cnty, PA[6,7], and died Bet. 06 - 27 Aug 1844 in East Mahoning Twp., Indiana Cnty, PA[7,8]. He married Dorcas LOGAN[9,10] 01 Jan 1787 in Bucks Cnty, PA[11]. She was born Bet. 1765 - 02 Apr 1771 in Feasterville, Bucks Cnty, PA[12], and died 22 Sep 1854 in Mahoning Twp., Indiana Cnty, PA.

Notes for Isaiah VAN HORN:
Was a drummer boy in his father's company in the Army of the Revolution. He married Doris Logan at the close of the revolutionary war and settled in western PA where he raised his family.

In 1790 Census there is an Isaiah Van Horn in Hopewell, Newton, Tyborn, and Westpensboro, Cumberland, Pennsylvania with 1-2-1 listing. Most likely Isaiah was in Cumberland, PA in 1790 as Cumberland was one of 8 counties in PA and included what is now Indiana County, PA.

In 1796 or 97 Isaiah and family moved to what is now Wheatfield Twp., Indiana Cnty, PA. In 1804 he owned a farm in East Mahoning Twp., about one mile east of Georgeville. It is said that he planted the orchard that is so productive on this farm. Reference History of Indiana County, PA p. 479 1880.

Died at the age of 84 according to the records of Gilgal Church.

In the History of Gilgal written May 16, 1861 on page 4 there is a discussion of the eldership of the church. John Work and Joshua Lewis were the ruling elders chosen. some time after William Hopkins and James Thompson were added to the session. The next addition consisted of Isaiah Van Horn and William Work. In the list of Elders he is listed 6th on the roll.

In the summary of his will he lists children as Henry, Alexander, Jane McElhose, Isaiah, George l, and Isaac with executor as Henry Van Horn and Hugh Hamilton, written on 27 April 1839 and Witnessed by James Y. Brady and George L. Van Horn and Probated on 23 September, 1844. Probate 763 Indiana County, PA. Will Book Vol. 1 p. 493.

More About Isaiah VAN HORN:
Burial: Unknown, Gilgal Cemetery, Indiana Cnty, PA Grave marked by DAR in 1893[13]
Military service: 1776, Revolutionary War as Drummer in Father's Milita Unit 2nd Regiment Bucks Cnty, PA[14,15]
Will: 27 Apr 1839, W. Mahoning Twp., Indiana Cnty, PA Vol. 1 p. 493

More About Isaiah VAN HORN and Dorcas LOGAN:
Marriage: 01 Jan 1787, Bucks Cnty, PA[16]

Children of Isaiah VAN HORN and Dorcas LOGAN are:
2.   i.   Henry[8] VAN HORN, b. Bet. 11 Nov 1787 - 25 Jan 1788, Bucks Cnty, PA; d. 18 Sep 1877, Residence of Moses Work, Indiana Cnty, PA.
3.   ii. Alexander VAN HORN, b. Bet. 17 Dec 1789 - 1790, Bucks Cnty, PA; d. 27 Jul 1871, West Wheatfield, Indiana Cnty, PA.

4.   iii.   Jane VAN HORN, b. Bet. 25 Feb - 05 Mar 1792, Cumberland Cnty, PA; d. 13 Sep
                1865, Green Twp., Indiana Cnty, PA.
5.   iv.   Joshua VAN HORN, b. Bet. 17 Aug 1794 - 19 Aug 1795, Cumberland Cnty, PA; d.
                02 Nov 1887, Indiana Cnty, PA.
6.   v.   John VAN HORN, b. Bet. 28 Nov 1796 - 07 May 1797, Cumberland Cnty, PA; d.
                Aft. 1881.
7.   vi.   Isaiah VAN HORN, b. Bet. 20 May 1799 - 02 Mar 1807, Westmoreland, PA or
                Indiana Cnty, PA; d. 15 Nov 1880, East Mahoning, Indiana Cnty, PA.
8.   vii.   William G. VAN HORN, b. Bet. 01 Mar 1800 - 1802, Leggett Farm, West Mahoning
                Twp. Indiana Cnty, PA; d. Bet. 10 - 17 Aug 1882, Indiana Cnty, PA.
9.   viii.   Nancy VAN HORN, b. 02 Oct 1804, East Wheatfield, Indiana Cnty, PA; d. Abt.
                1880.
10.   ix.   Isaac VAN HORN, b. Bet. 20 May 1806 - 11 Apr 1810, Indiana Cnty, PA; d.
                Unknown.
11.   x.   George Logan VAN HORN, b. Bet. 06 - 16 Jan 1813, East Mahoning Twp., Indiana
                Cnty, PA; d. 27 Feb 1901, Georgeville, Indiana Cnty, PA Home of son Bennett W.
                Van Horn.

Generation No. 2

2. Henry[8] VAN HORN *(Isaiah[7], Henry B.[6], Henry[5], Christian Barentsen[4] VAN HOORN, Barent Christiansen[3], Christian Barentsen[2], Barent Barents[1])[17,18,19,20,21,22,23]* was born Bet. 11 Nov 1787 - 25 Jan 1788 in Bucks Cnty, PA[24], and died 18 Sep 1877 in Residence of Moses Work, Indiana Cnty, PA[24]. He married Elizabeth THOMPSON[25,26,27,28,29] 18 Jun 1814, daughter of Robert THOMPSON and Mary CANNON. She was born Abt. 1788 in Londonderry, Ireland[30], and died Bet. 13 Feb - 16 Apr 1858 in Indiana Cnty, PA[30,31].

Notes for Henry VAN HORN:
        In 1850 has his son Henry living with him and his sister in law Mary Thompson born Ireland. Also a Balinda Henderson is in the home. He is a farmer with an estate of $1600.
        In 1860 Census Balinda Henderson age 26 born in PA is housekeeper, Henry is a farmer and his real estate is worth $2000 and personal effects are worth $500. His son Henry and his family is living with him.
        In 1870 he is living with his daughter Tabitha and her husband Moses T. Work.
        4 Oct 1877 the Indiana Progress(Indiana, PA) reports the death of Henry Van Horn on September 18, 1877 in his 90th year. He died at the home of Moses Work. The Indiana Weekly Messenger (Indiana, PA) of the same date states that Henry came to the county in 1803 and located in Mahoning Twp. while the area was a wilderness with wild beasts and occasional Indians. He was one of the original members of Gilgal Presbyterian Church

More About Henry VAN HORN:
Burial: Unknown, Gilgal Cemetry, Gilgal Church, Indiana Cnty, PA
Military service: War of 1812

More About Elizabeth THOMPSON:
Burial: Unknown, Gilgal Cemetery, Indiana Cnty, PA

More About Henry VAN HORN and Elizabeth THOMPSON:
Marriage: 18 Jun 1814

Children of Henry VAN HORN and Elizabeth THOMPSON are:

12.   i.   Mary C.[9] VAN HORN, b. Abt. 1817, Indiana Cnty, PA; d. Bet. 1850 - 1860, Indiana Cnty, PA.
13.   ii.   James Thompson VAN HORN, b. 15 Aug 1819, Indiana Cnty, PA; d. 17 Oct 1900, East Mahoning Twp., Indiana Cnty, PA.
14.   iii.   Tabitha Logan VAN HORN, b. Bet. 27 Sep 1821 - 1822, Indiana Cnty, PA; d. 10 Dec 1890, Ft. Morgan, Morgan Cnty, CO.
15.   iv.   Col. Robert Thompson VAN HORN, b. Bet. 10 - 19 May 1824, Indiana Cnty, PA; d. Bet. 02 - 03 Jan 1916, Evanston Station, Clay Cnty, MO.
      v.   Isaiah VanZant VAN HORN, b. 1826, PA; d. Unknown, Infancy.
      vi.   Dorcas L. VAN HORN, b. Abt. 1828; d. Abt. 1876.
16.   vii.   Henry A. VAN HORN, b. Bet. 1828 - 1829, PA; d. Bet. 27 - 28 Apr 1887, Georgeville, Indiana Cnty, PA.

3. Alexander[8] VAN HORN *(Isaiah[7], Henry B.[6], Henry[5], Christian Barentsen[4] VAN HOORN, Barent Christiansen[3], Christian Barentsen[2], Barent Barents[1])[32,33,34,35,36]* was born Bet. 17 Dec 1789 - 1790 in Bucks Cnty, PA[37], and died 27 Jul 1871 in West Wheatfield, Indiana Cnty, PA[38]. He married Mary WHERRY[39,40,41,42,43,44] 13 May 1819 in Indiana Cnty, PA, daughter of James WHERRY and Mary DICK. She was born Nov 1801 in Antrim, Ulster, Ireland[45], and died 30 Jun 1893 in Indiana Cnty, PA[46].

Notes for Alexander VAN HORN:
     War of 1812 154th Reg 2nd Brig 15th Div PA Mil Pvt 1812-1814
     Found in the Index of Landowners and Joiners of Westmoreland County, PA in the early land survey book, 1769-1905, Westmoreland County, Pennsylvania Survey Books 2-155
     In 1850 a Thomas Campbell is living in the family. George is not in the listing and Alice is shown in the family likely both George and Alice are grandchildren based on the 10 year gap in children.. Alexander is a farmer. He is worth $2000 and his son Alexander is farming with him. Reference Grave Register Indiana Cnty Historical Society
     In 1860 Alexander is a farmer and has a real estate value of $2000 and personal effects of $500. He is living next door to his daughter Tabitha and her family. There is a George Van horn age 14 and born PA living in the family. This could be a son or a grandson.
     In 1870 Alexander is a retired farmer with real estate worth $500 and personal effects valued a $1,000. There is a Phoebe Van Horn age 22 born PA living with the family as well as a Susan Wakefield age 8 born PA, the daughter of Tabitha, also a laborer is living with the family that is unrelated.
     The Indiana Progress(Indiana, PA) of 24 August 1871 gives Alexander's death as 2 July 1871 and he is 81 years and 7 months residing in West Wheatfield Twp., Indiana Cnty, PA. He is buried at the Armagh UP Church Cemetery but the church is no longer on the site of the cemetery.
     Alexander's Will is found in the Indiana Cnty Will Book Vol. 3, p. 576 1871

More About Alexander VAN HORN:
Burial: 27 Jul 1871, Armagh-Bethel UP Cemetery[47,48]
Military service: Bet. 1812 - 1814, War of 1812 Pvt,154th Reg 2nd Brig 15th Div PA Mil[48]

Notes for Mary WHERRY:
     In 1880 living with her son James.
     Mary's Will is in the Indiana Cnty, PA Will Book Vol. 8, p 157 dated1893

More About Mary WHERRY:
Burial: Unknown, Armagh-Bethel UP Cemetery[49]

Religion: Presbyterian

More About Alexander VAN HORN and Mary WHERRY:
Marriage: 13 May 1819, Indiana Cnty, PA

Children of Alexander VAN HORN and Mary WHERRY are:
17.   i.   John Dick[9] VAN HORN, b. Dec 1829, PA; d. 17 Oct 1901, PA.
    ii.   Isaiah VAN HORN[50,51,52], b. 22 May 1820, Indiana Cnty, PA[52]; d. 01 Mar 1895, Stewart Station, Westmoreland Cnty, PA[53,54].

Notes for Isaiah VAN HORN:
In 1880 Isaiah is living with James Van Horn his widowed brother and they are farming together.
Civil War Co I 93rd Reg PVI Pvt 9/19/64-6/20/65. His index card indicated he mustered in 9/15/1864 at Pittsburgh, PA as a Private of age 44.He was 5'11" with light hair, fair complexion and grey eyes. He works at a Roller Manufacturer. He was born in Indiana Cnty, PA. He was wounded 10/19/1864 at Cedar Creek, VA. He was discharged 6/20/1865.
14 September 1892 Indiana Evening Gazette (Indiana, PA) reports that Isaiah Van Horn visited his sister Mrs. Crum last week in Huff Twp., Indiana Cnty, PA
6 March 1895 Indiana Progress (Indiana, PA) Mr. Isaiah Van Horn was buried in the Armagh Cemetery on Monday March 4. He had been living at Stewart Station in Westmoreland county, for the past year but was formerly from this county.

More About Isaiah VAN HORN:
Burial: 04 Mar 1895, Armagh Presbyterian Cemetery Armagh, PA[55]
Military service: Bet. 16 Sep 1864 - 20 Jun 1865, Private Co. I, 93rd PVI know as the Lebanon Infantry
Occupation: Farmer
Veteran: 19 Oct 1864, Wounded in action of the 93rd at Cedar Creek, VA

18.   iii.   James Wherry VAN HORN, b. 31 Oct 1821, PA; d. 19 May 1894, Indiana Cnty, PA or Westmoreland Cnty, PA.
19.   iv.   Henry Coulter VAN HORN, b. 18 Sep 1823, Centerville, PA; d. 19 Jul 1898, East Wheatfield Twp., Indiana Cnty, PA.
    v.   Mary D. VAN HORN, b. 20 Jul 1825, PA; d. 27 Jun 1826, PA.
    vi.   Thomas M. VAN HORN, b. 24 Mar 1827; d. 29 Oct 1868.
20.   vii.   Alexander VAN HORN, JR, b. 18 Jan 1832, PA; d. 27 Jun 1866, Civil War Petersburgh, Va..
21.   viii.   William VAN HORN, b. Bet. 1827 - 31 Dec 1833, PA; d. 09 Nov 1886, Allamakee Cnty, IA.
22.   ix.   Tabitha L. VAN HORN, b. 26 Jul 1836; d. 02 Dec 1862.
    x.   George VAN HORN[56], b. Abt. 1846, PA[56]; d. Unknown.
    xi.   Alice VAN HORN[57], b. Abt. 1847, PA[57]; d. Unknown; m. CRUM; d. Unknown.

4. Jane[8] VAN HORN *(Isaiah[7], Henry B.[6], Henry[5], Christian Barentsen[4] VAN HOORN, Barent Christiansen[3], Christian Barentsen[2], Barent Barents[1])*[58,59,60,61,62] was born Bet. 25 Feb - 05 Mar 1792 in Cumberland Cnty, PA[62], and died 13 Sep 1865 in Green Twp., Indiana Cnty, PA[62]. She married John MCELHOES[63,64] Abt. 1813, son of Isaiah MCELHOES and Nancy SCOTT. He was born 1785 in Cumberland Cnty, PA[65], and died 17 Jan 1857 in Green Twp., Indiana Cnty, PA[66].

Notes for Jane VAN HORN:
Living with daughter Nancy Dilts and family in 1860 age 60 born PA.

Notes for John MCELHOES:
Samuel John's brother is living near his son Isaiah in 1850.

I am not sure if I can be of help, but I have information about the McElhoes family that may fill in some of the gaps. My information was prepared by my great-uncle,Joseph Isaiah McElhoes and given to my father, Waldo Steele McElhoes, when my parents visited Uncle Joe in Home, PA. in the 1960's. According to this info,the first of the McElhoes to come to America from Scotland was John McElhoes He immigrated to Philadelphia and died there circa 1791. According to my calculations,and based on Uncle Joe's info, this John McElhoes was my great, great, great, great,great,grand-father. His son, Isaiah (or Thomas Isaiah) McElhoes, moved from Philadelphia and settled in or around Home, PA. in what is now Indiana Co. but at that time was Westmoreland Co. Two of Isaiah's sons, John and Samuel, moved to Rayne Township. in the late 1700's. That John McElhoes is my great, great, great grand-father and he married Jane Van Horn. They had four children: Isaiah (married Isabelle Kinter);Nancy (married William Dilts); Dorcas (married first Henry Kinter,then William Houck); Susan (married Johnson Lightcap).
The list goes on tracking the lineage to my grand father, Frank Thompson McElhoes who married a widow, Patience Anne Baker, nee Anderson. They migrated to western Canada, producing seven sons on the way, one of whom was my father, Waldo Steele McElhoes.
I have an extra copy of the material Uncle Joe prepared; it's five pages of a form of family tree and three pages of a family history. I don't have a fax but I'm prepared to send it via snailmail to any one interested. Hopefully, this will start an exchange of info and add to my knowledge of the McElhoes family.
Regards; Richard (Dick) McElhoes (the Canadian branch)

More About John MCELHOES:
Burial: Unknown, Washington Church Cemetery, Rayne Twp., Indiana Cnty, PA
Occupation: Farmer and operated a grist mill

More About John MCELHOES and Jane VAN HORN:
Marriage: Abt. 1813

Children of Jane VAN HORN and John MCELHOES are:
23. i. Isaiah[9] MCELHOES, b. 25 Jun 1815, Green Twp., Indiana Cnty, PA; d. 02 Oct 1896, Green Twp., Indiana Cnty, PA.
24. ii. Nancy MCELHOES, b. 06 Mar 1817, Green Twp., Indiana Cnty, PA/Washington Cnty, PA; d. 14 Jul 1893, Kellysburg, Indiana Cnty, PA.
25. iii. Dorcas MCELHOES, b. 08 Sep 1816, PA; d. 10 Apr 1896, Cherry Hill Twp., Indiana Cnty, PA.
26. iv. Susan MCELHOES, b. Bet. 22 Feb 1820 - 1821, Rayne, Indiana Cnty, PA; d. 1901, Rayne, Indiana Cnty, PA.

5. Joshua[8] VAN HORN *(Isaiah[7], Henry B.[6], Henry[5], Christian Barentsen[4] VAN HOORN, Barent Christiansen[3], Christian Barentsen[2], Barent Barents[1])[67,68,69,70,71,72]* was born Bet. 17 Aug 1794 - 19 Aug 1795 in Cumberland Cnty, PA[73], and died 02 Nov 1887 in Indiana Cnty, PA. He married Fanny BRIGGS[74,75,76,77] Abt. 1819[77], daughter of Benjamin BRIGGS and Mary DAVIS. She was born 17 Nov 1795 in Tell Twp., Huntington Cnty, PA[78], and died Bef. 1870 in Indiana Cnty, PA.

Notes for Joshua VAN HORN:
 In 1840 Mahoning Twp., Indiana Cnty, PA 1111101000000/0020110000000 Living next to Peter Christopher and James Wells.
 In 1860 Living next door to Christopher Wells who could be the brother of Martha who married Henry his son. He is worth $1200 in real estate and $650 in personal effects and he is a

farmer. Also living next to Abraham and Sarah Sink.
In 1870 living with son Benjamin B. Van Horn with no occupation.

Notes for Fanny BRIGGS:
Many sources gives her name as Phonia Briggs.

More About Joshua VAN HORN and Fanny BRIGGS:
Marriage: Abt. 1819[79]

Children of Joshua VAN HORN and Fanny BRIGGS are:
27.   i.   Benjamin Briggs[9] VAN HORN, b. Bet. 1819 - 1822, East Mahoning, Indiana Cnty,
              PA; d. 29 Aug 1887, Indiana Cnty, PA.
28.   ii. Christian VAN HORN, b. 05 Aug 1821, Indiana Cnty, PA; d. 24 Jan 1904,
              Armstrong Cnty, PA.
29.   iii. Mary Ann VAN HORN, b. Abt. 1822, Indiana Cnty, PA; d. Aft. 1910.
30.   iv. Henry VAN HORN, b. Bet. 23 Jan 1823 - 1826, Indiana Cnty, PA/KY; d. Bet. 26
              Aug 1883 - 19 Jul 1896, Northern Twp., Franklin Cnty, IL/Indiana Cnty, PA.
31.   v.   Tabitha Dorcas VAN HORN, b. 02 Dec 1827, Plumville, Indiana Cnty, PA; d. 13
              Jan 1920, Punxsutawney, Jefferson Cnty, PA.
32.   vi. Sarah VAN HORN, b. 30 Apr 1830, Indiana Cnty, PA; d. 01 Apr 1886, Franklin
              Cnty, IL.
33.   vii. Samuel H. VAN HORN, b. 1831, Centre Twp., Indiana Cnty, PA; d. 1888, Indiana
              Cnty, PA.
         viii. Miriam VAN HORN[80,81], b. Bet. 1834 - 1840, Indiana Cnty, PA[82]; d. Unknown.

6. John[8] VAN HORN *(Isaiah[7], Henry B.[6], Henry[5], Christian Barentsen[4] VAN HOORN, Barent
Christiansen[3], Christian Barentsen[2], Barent Barents[1])*[83,84,85,86] was born Bet. 28 Nov 1796 - 07 May 1797 in
Cumberland Cnty, PA[87], and died Aft. 1881. He married Thressa HASTINGS[88,89,90] 1824[91],
daughter of James HASTINGS and Margaret DIXSON. She was born 14 Sep 1806 in PA[92,93], and
died 1861[94].

Notes for John VAN HORN:
     In 1850 John is a laborer and has 4 children living in the home. There are 3 others in the home
a Roseanna Wisel, Eliza J. Joslan and Mathew Ritchie.
     In 1880 John is living with his son William and his family on Taggart Street in Allegheny, PA
     1879-1881 Directory of Pittsburgh and Allegheny Cities lists John as a Sexton living at 108
Taggart St the same address of William A. Van Horn his son.

More About John VAN HORN and Thressa HASTINGS:
Marriage: 1824[94]

Children of John VAN HORN and Thressa HASTINGS are:
34.   i.   John Hastings[9] VAN HORN, b. Bet. 1824 - 1827, PA; d. Aft. 1880.
35.   ii. William A. VAN HORN, b. Bet. 1826 - 1832, PA; d. Unknown.
         iii. Christine VAN HORN[95], b. Abt. 1830, PA[95]; d. Unknown.
36.   iv. James Devin VAN HORN, b. 1834, PA; d. 1864, Malvern Hill, VA.

7. Isaiah[8] VAN HORN *(Isaiah[7], Henry B.[6], Henry[5], Christian Barentsen[4] VAN HOORN, Barent*

Isaiah Van Horn Pioneer of Indiana County, Pennsylvania

Christiansen[3], Christian Barentsen[2], Barent Barents[1])[96,97,98,99,100,101] was born Bet. 20 May 1799 - 02 Mar 1807 in Westmoreland, PA or Indiana Cnty, PA[102,103], and died 15 Nov 1880 in East Mahoning, Indiana Cnty, PA[104]. He married Mary Ann HOPKINS[105,106,107,108,109] Abt. 1833, daughter of Robert HOPKINS and Roseanna PATTERSON. She was born Bet. 1800 - 1816 in Indiana Cnty, PA[110,111], and died 22 Feb 1898 in DuBois, Clearfield Cnty, PA[112].

Notes for Isaiah VAN HORN:
Some sources gives his birth as in Westmoreland Cnty, PA
In 1850 he gives his real estate worth as $1150.
In 1860 he gives his real estate a value of $1,500 and his personal effects as $350. He is living near George and Benjamin Van Horn.
In 1880 Isaiah and Mary have returned to Indiana Cnty, PA from WV and are living with the oldest daughter Jane Elizabeth and her family.
9 Dec 1880 Isaiah Van Horn died 15th ult in East Mahoning late of WV have removed from South Mahoning some 10 years ago. Aged 73.
.

More About Isaiah VAN HORN:
Burial: Unknown, East Mahoning Twp., Indiana Cnty, PA

Notes for Mary Ann HOPKINS:
Died age 84

More About Mary Ann HOPKINS:
Burial: Unknown, Mahoning Church Cemetery, East Mahoning Twp., Indiana Cnty, PA
Will: 1893, Indiana Cnty, PA Vol. 8, p. 157

More About Isaiah VAN HORN and Mary HOPKINS:
Marriage: Abt. 1833

Children of Isaiah VAN HORN and Mary HOPKINS are:
37.   i.   Jane Elizabeth[9] VAN HORN, b. 22 Oct 1835, Indiana Cnty, PA; d. 11 Feb 1908, Deckers Point, Indiana Cnty, PA.
38.   ii.   Martha VAN HORN, b. Bet. May 1835 - 1837, Penn Hills, Alegheny Cnty, PA; d. 10 Nov 1920.
39.   iii. Mary P. VAN HORN, b. 27 Apr 1839, Diamondville, Indiana Cnty, PA; d. 17 Oct 1914, Lovejoy, East Mahoning, Indiana Cnty, PA.
40.   iv.   John A. VAN HORN, b. Bet. 1845 - 1855, PA; d. 12 Apr 1922, Dayton, Montgomery Cnty, OH.
41.   v.   Roseannah VAN HORN, b. 24 May 1850, Altoona, Blair Cnty, PA; d. 02 May 1926, Shanghai, Berkeley Cnty, WV.

8. William G.[8] VAN HORN *(Isaiah[7], Henry B.[6], Henry[5], Christian Barentsen[4] VAN HOORN, Barent Christiansen[3], Christian Barentsen[2], Barent Barents[1])[113,114,115,116,117,118,119,120]* was born Bet. 01 Mar 1800 - 1802 in Leggett Farm, West Mahoning Twp. Indiana Cnty, PA[121], and died Bet. 10 - 17 Aug 1882 in Indiana Cnty, PA[121]. He married Rachel POUNDS[121,122,123,124,125] 03 Mar 1827, daughter of George POUNDS and Margaret REDDING. She was born Bet. 03 May 1802 - 1805 in Penn Hills, Alegheny Cnty, PA[126], and died Bet. 02 - 12 Apr 1889 in Indiana Cnty, PA[126].

Notes for William G. VAN HORN:
In 1850 he is a farmer and his farm is worth about $600.
In 1860 he is a farmer with land worth $500 and personal effects of $350. His mother in law

Margaret Pounds age 81 is living in the family.

In 1870 Census William is a farmer with real estate valued at $3,000 and personal effects of $500. His son George his wife and child are living with the family.

In 1880 William and Rachel are living with a servant and a couple of doors from son George and his family.

8 April 1886 there is a notice in the Indiana Progress(Indiana, PA) that 65 acres in West Mahoning Twp. owned by William Van Horn is in jeopardy of being sold for taxes of $7.33 owed on 1883 taxes.

15 Aug 1908 Indiana evening Gazette (Indiana, PA) William Van Horn family reunion on the William Van Horn farm at North Point, Indiana Cnty, PA.

More About William G. VAN HORN:
Burial: Unknown, Gilgal Cemetry, Gilgal Church, Indiana Cnty, PA
Occupation: Farmer

More About Rachel POUNDS:
Burial: Unknown, Gilgal Cemetery Gilgal UP Church Indiana Cnty, PA

More About William VAN HORN and Rachel POUNDS:
Marriage: 03 Mar 1827

Children of William VAN HORN and Rachel POUNDS are:

	i.	John[9] VAN HORN, d. Unknown.
42.	ii.	Martha VAN HORN, b. 20 Feb 1828, PA; d. 04 Jul 1856.
43.	iii.	William G. VAN HORN, JR, b. 11 Sep 1829, PA; d. 09 Nov 1866.
44.	iv.	Margaret J. VAN HORN, b. 19 Jul 1831, PA; d. 04 Mar 1905, Smicksburg, Indiana Cnty, PA.
45.	v.	Catherine VAN HORN, b. Bet. 11 Sep 1832 - 1838, PA; d. 16 May 1905.
46.	vi.	Dorcas VAN HORN, b. 06 Aug 1833, Smicksburg, Indiana Cnty, PA; d. Bet. 15 Mar 1876 - 1889, Smicksburg, Indiana Cnty, PA.
47.	vii.	Nancy VAN HORN, b. Bet. 18 Aug 1835 - 1836, PA; d. 1916, McKees Rock, Allegheny Cnty, PA.
	viii.	Isaiah VAN HORN, b. 24 Oct 1837, PA; d. 07 Nov 1837.
48.	ix.	George Logan VAN HORN, b. 29 Dec 1840, West Mahoning Twp., Indiana Cnty, PA; d. 14 Sep 1909, North Point, Jefferson Cnty, PA.
	x.	Sarah VAN HORN[126,127,128], b. Bet. 25 Dec 1842 - 1846, PA[129]; d. 12 Nov 1877, Indiana Cnty, PA.

More About Sarah VAN HORN:
Burial: Unknown, Gilgal Cemetry, Gilgal Church, Indiana Cnty, PA

49.	xi.	Mary Lucinda VAN HORN, b. Bet. 23 Feb 1844 - 1846, PA; d. Aft. 1909.
	xii.	Charles Milton VAN HORN[129], b. 19 Sep 1848, PA[129]; d. Bet. 31 Aug 1849 - 1850.
50.	xiii.	Samuel Redding VAN HORN, b. Bet. 15 Feb 1850 - 1851, North Point, Indiana Cnty, PA; d. Bet. 13 - 23 May 1906, Brockway, Jefferson Cnty, PA.

9. Nancy[8] VAN HORN *(Isaiah[7], Henry B.[6], Henry[5], Christian Barentsen[4] VAN HOORN, Barent Christiansen[3], Christian Barentsen[2], Barent Barents[1])[130,131,132,133]* was born 02 Oct 1804 in East Wheatfield, Indiana Cnty, PA[134], and died Abt. 1880. She married Hugh HAMILTON[134,135,136] Apr 1819 in Mahoning Twp., Indiana Cnty, PA, son of Robert HAMILTON and Ann THOMPSON. He was born Abt. 1795 in Laught, Tyrone, Ireland[137], and died Abt. 1875 in MD.

Notes for Nancy VAN HORN:
In 1850 Nacy and family are living near to her brothers Henry and George and his husbands family. Hugh is a farmer and their estate is worth $1600.

Notes for Hugh HAMILTON:
In 1860 has Mary Thompson age 81 born Ireland living with him. He is a farmer and has a land value of $1800 and personal effects of $750. A Robert Hamilton is living next door.

More About Hugh HAMILTON:
Occupation: Farmer

More About Hugh HAMILTON and Nancy VAN HORN:
Marriage: Apr 1819, Mahoning Twp., Indiana Cnty, PA

Children of Nancy VAN HORN and Hugh HAMILTON are:

	i.	Robert C.[9] HAMILTON[138], b. Abt. 1828, PA[138]; d. Unknown.
51.	ii.	Dorcas HAMILTON, b. Abt. 1831, PA; d. 08 Apr 1890.
52.	iii.	Margaret HAMILTON, b. 15 Mar 1833, East Mahoning Twp., Indiana Cnty, PA; d. 07 Sep 1874, Indiana Cnty, PA.
	iv.	Jane HAMILTON[138], b. Abt. 1839, PA[138]; d. Unknown.
	v.	Martha A. HAMILTON[139,140], b. Bet. 1841 - 1844, PA[141]; d. Unknown.

10. Isaac[8] VAN HORN *(Isaiah[7], Henry B.[6], Henry[5], Christian Barentsen[4] VAN HOORN, Barent Christiansen[3], Christian Barentsen[2], Barent Barents[1])*[142,143] was born Bet. 20 May 1806 - 11 Apr 1810 in Indiana Cnty, PA[143], and died Unknown. He married Fanny CONINE, daughter of Peter CONINE. She was born Abt. 1801 in Peapack, Somerset Cnty, NJ, and died Unknown.

Notes for Isaac VAN HORN:
In 1860 living with brother George and family.

Child of Isaac VAN HORN and Fanny CONINE is:

	i.	Sarah[9] VAN HORN, d. Unknown.

11. George Logan[8] VAN HORN *(Isaiah[7], Henry B.[6], Henry[5], Christian Barentsen[4] VAN HOORN, Barent Christiansen[3], Christian Barentsen[2], Barent Barents[1])*[144,145,146,147,148,149,150,151] was born Bet. 06 - 16 Jan 1813 in East Mahoning Twp., Indiana Cnty, PA[152], and died 27 Feb 1901 in Georgeville, Indiana Cnty, PA Home of son Bennett W. Van Horn[152,153,154]. He married Mary Brady WYNCOOP[155,156,157,158,159,160] 07 Apr 1842 in East Mahoning Twp., Indiana Cnty, PA, daughter of Matthew WYNCOOP and Elizabeth WORK. She was born Bet. 08 - 11 Dec 1814 in Indiana Cnty, PA[161,162,163], and died 07 Feb 1881 in Indiana Cnty, PA[164].

Notes for George Logan VAN HORN:
In 1850 George has living with him his mother Dorcas who is widowed and his sister in law Jane Wyncoop and his brother Isaiah Van Horn. He is a farmer and his worth is $700. He is living next to his brother Henry and between other relatives.

Mr. Laney AUL is a grandson as well as Mrs. William MCADOO and Mr. and Mrs Robert JOHNSON.

Logan died in his 89th year at the home of his son B. W. Van Horn of old age. The newspaper reports that B. W. is the only living relative at the time of Logan's death.

In 1860 George's brother Isaac is living with the family. also a Jane Wyncoop a domestic age 36 born PA is living in the family. This may be Mary's sister or a Neice. In 1860 George has a real estate value of $2200 and a personal effects worth $800.

During the Civil War George was in the Libby Prison where he spent 6 weeks. He as a member of the 67th Pa Volunteer Infantry.

In 1870 George is a farmer with a real estate value of $16,000 and personal effects of value of $900. A Jane Wyncoop age 1 born PA is living with George, Mary and Bennett.

In 1880 George and Mary are living alone next door to Bennett and his family.

25 July 1888 in a roll given in the Indiana Weekly Messenger (Indiana, PA) Logan Van Horn joins others in agreeing to return to vote with the Republican Party in the coming election.

More About George Logan VAN HORN:
Burial: Unknown, Gilgal Cemetry, Gilgal Church, Indiana Cnty, PA
Military service: 67th Reg PA VI

Notes for Mary Brady WYNCOOP:
Not sure of the 1814 birth date since Matthew and Elizabeth married in 1819.

More About Mary Brady WYNCOOP:
Burial: Unknown, Gilgal Cemetry, Gilgal Church, Indiana Cnty, PA

More About George VAN HORN and Mary WYNCOOP:
Marriage: 07 Apr 1842, East Mahoning Twp., Indiana Cnty, PA
Marriage Place: Gilgal United Presbyterian Church, Maion Center, PA

Children of George VAN HORN and Mary WYNCOOP are:

    i.   Elizabeth[9] VAN HORN[165], b. 26 Jun 1843, Indiana Cnty, PA[166]; d. Bet. 17 Aug 1844 - 1848, Indiana Cnty, PA[166].

        More About Elizabeth VAN HORN:
        Burial: Unknown, Gilgal Cemetry, Gilgal Church, Indiana Cnty, PA

    ii.   Melissa Jane VAN HORN[167,168], b. 27 Jul 1845, Indiana Cnty, PA[169]; d. Bet. 13 - 15 Mar 1860, Indiana Cnty, PA[170].

        More About Melissa Jane VAN HORN:
        Burial: Unknown, Gilgal Cemetery Gilgal UP Church Indiana Cnty, PA
        Cause of Death: Sore throat

53.   iii.   Bennett Work VAN HORN, b. Bet. 13 May 1847 - 1851, Indiana Cnty, PA; d. 01 Feb 1925, Georgeville, Indiana Cnty, PA.

    iv.   Mary Agnes VAN HORN[171], b. Bet. 04 - 13 May 1851, Indiana Cnty, PA[171]; d. 03 Dec 1859, Indiana Cnty, PA[171,172].

        More About Mary Agnes VAN HORN:
        Burial: Unknown, Gilgal Cemetery Gilgal UP Church Indiana Cnty, PA
        Cause of Death: Sore throat

    v.   Margaret Emily VAN HORN[173,174], b. 01 Nov 1852, Indiana Cnty, PA[174]; d. 28 Dec 1859, Indiana Cnty, PA[174,175].

        More About Margaret Emily VAN HORN:
        Burial: Unknown, Gilgal Cemetery Gilgal UP Church Indiana Cnty, PA
        Cause of Death: Sore throat

Generation No. 3

12. Mary C.[9] VAN HORN *(Henry[8], Isaiah[7], Henry B.[6], Henry[5], Christian Barentsen[4] VAN HOORN, Barent Christiansen[3], Christian Barentsen[2], Barent Barents[1])[176,177]* was born Abt. 1817 in Indiana Cnty, PA[177], and died Bet. 1850 - 1860 in Indiana Cnty, PA. She married William G. STEWART[178,179,180,181,182] Abt. 1836, son of John STEWART and Elizabeth ARMSTRONG. He was born 12 Mar 1816 in Armstrong, Indiana Cnty, PA[183], and died Bet. 12 Jan - 02 Nov 1890 in Washington District of Columbia.

Notes for William G. STEWART:
In 1850 Mary's name is given as Martha. A Samuel Stewart age 28 a Physician and Amelia Strock age 12 are living in the home. The two children are James and Henry.

More About William G. STEWART:
Occupation: Physician

More About William STEWART and Mary VAN HORN:
Marriage: Abt. 1836

Children of Mary VAN HORN and William STEWART are:
54. i. John Alexander[10] STEWART, b. 04 May 1839, Indiana Cnty, PA; d. 09 Jan 1899, Washington District of Columbia.
55. ii. Elizabeth Canon STEWART, b. Bet. 1840 - 1843, Indiana Cnty, PA; d. Abt. 1898.
  iii. Henry Van Zandt STEWART[184,185,186], b. Bet. 1841 - 1848, Indiana Cnty, PA[187,188]; d. 05 May 1864, Wilderness, VA.

   Notes for Henry Van Zandt STEWART:
   Henry served with Co "A", 61st PVI; wounded in the battle at Fair Oaks, Va and killed in the battle of Wilderness, VA., May 5th, 1864

   More About Henry Van Zandt STEWART:
   Military service: Company A, 61st Regiment Civil War

  iv. Archibald J. STEWART[189,190], b. Abt. 1845, Indiana Cnty, PA[190]; d. 18 Mar 1865, Sampson Cnty, NC.

   Notes for Archibald J. STEWART:
   Served for 6 months in the Volunteers (which one) and then in the Signal Corps, Died of fever during Sherman's march to the Sea.
   12 Apr 1865 Indiana Progress (Indiana, Pa)

   A.S. STEWART. It is with the deepest feelings of regret that we record the death of this estimable young man--a son of MR. W.G. STEWART, one of our County Commissioners. He died on the evening of the 18th of March, of Typhoid fever, while on the march with our army through North Carolina, having taken sick about the 1st of the month. The circumstances of his death are about these: On the 29th of February, fifty men were detached from the Headquarters of the Army of the Tennessee--among them MR. STEWART--to cut the railroad leading from Camden, South Carolina, to Wilmington, North Carolina. They met the enemy, and were forced to fall back. They were out two days, and on their return to camp, young

127

STEWART complained of severe headache. He constantly grew worse till the 18th ult., when he died. He maintained a cheerful spirit until the last. During his sickness his comrades attended him with great care; and after his death, he was conveyed a day's march along with the army, to a place of burial. His body was interred beneath a spreading grape vine, in a private burial ground owned by a MRS. LANE, in Sampson County, North Carolina, north of Clinton and west of Faisson's Station. His comrades speak of him, as a soldier and a companion, in the warmest terms of praise. He was a worthy and promising young man, and is the second son of MR. STEWART who has been given a sacrifice upon the country's altar in the suppression of the rebellion. Requiescat in pace.

More About Archibald J. STEWART:
Burial: Unknown, Sampson Cnty, NC

56.   v.   Margaretta T. STEWART, b. 25 Jun 1848, Indiana Cnty, PA; d. 06 Feb 1937, Indiana Cnty, PA.

      vi. Kate STEWART[191], b. Abt. 1850, Indiana Cnty, PA; d. Bef. 1937.

13. James Thompson[9] VAN HORN *(Henry[8], Isaiah[7], Henry B.[6], Henry[5], Christian Barentsen[4] VAN HOORN, Barent Christiansen[3], Christian Barentsen[2], Barent Barents[1])*[192,193,194,195] was born 15 Aug 1819 in Indiana Cnty, PA[196,197], and died 17 Oct 1900 in East Mahoning Twp., Indiana Cnty, PA[198]. He married Ellen H. MEANOR[199,200,201,202,203] 03 Jul 1855[204], daughter of William MEANOR. She was born Jun 1837 in Indiana Cnty, PA[205], and died 06 Feb 1918 in East Mahoning Twp., Indiana Cnty, PA[206].

Notes for James Thompson VAN HORN:

    In 1860 Margaret Thompson aged 76 born in Indiana Cnty, PA is living with this family and Susan Meanor age 18 and born Indiana Cnty, PA is also living with the family and is teaching school. His real estate is valued at $3,000 and personal effects at $650.

    5 March 1862 Indiana Messenger Traverse Juror from Rayne Twp.

    In 1870 he is a farmer and his land is worth $16,000 and his personal effects $1300.

One of the founding Elders of the Marion Presbyterian Church. Organizer of the Marion Institute. Received much credit for the construction of a Court House. Was one of the managers of the IC Agricultural Society and assigned to help form the Indiana Agricultural Society.

    He was an Indiana County commissioner for several sessions of the commission.

    In the Indiana Progress(Indiana, PA) of 24 Feb. 1870 he is listed as a commissioner along with John Flemming and James Work the County Clerk. Also listed in the same paper on 3 March 1870, 14 April, 1870, 27 July 1871 for a bridge construction project, 20 Feb. 1873 for amounts paid to James T. Van Horn as a commissioner.

    On 15 Oct.1874 James it is reported that James was elected chair of the county Republican Party.

    8 Feb 1877 James T. Van Horn as the executor advertises in the Indiana Progress(Indiana, PA) the settlement of the estate of John Meanor. 2 Feb 1892 and again in 10 Feb 1892 the Progress reports that James T. Van Horn files the first and final settlement of John Meanor's estate.

    5 & 26 August 1891 J. T. Van Horn is listed in the Indiana Progress(Indiana, PA) as a Grand Juror from East Mahoning Twp.

    9 Sept 1891 the Indiana Progress(Indiana, PA) reports that James T. Van Horn is elected foreman of the Grand Jury.

    Indiana County 175th Anniversary History by Clarence D. Stephenson Vol. 4 p. 65 the follow is found:

    "Van Horn, James T.. b. c. 1819. died 10-1-1900. IC Commissioner, 1869-71. When the Indiana County (IC) Agricultural Society was organized 1-3-1855, he was one of the first managers. One of the first ruling elders when the Presbyterian Church of Marion was organized, 1860. Names

Isaiah Van Horn Pioneer of Indiana County, Pennsylvania

on 8-29-1855 to prepare a Know Nothing platform (Vol 1, 395). One of the organizers of the Marion Institute, 1857. He has been given much credit for completion of the 1870 Courthouse (Vol. III, 225).

From a Brief History of The Political Parties of Indiana county by Charles B. Poydence we find:

"In 1840 James Moorehead, the old Anti-Masonic Leader, began to publish another newspaper called the Clarion of Freedom, which agitated against slavery and started the Indiana County movement of the Abolitionist party.

The Abolitionist movement began in Boston in 1831 with the founding of the Liberator, a newspaper edited by Willima Lloyd Garrison. Two years later, Garrison founded the American Anti-Slavery Society in Philadelphia which became the most radical faction of the Abolitionist movement and included such notables as John Brown, Lucretia Mott, and Wendell Phillips.

Indiana County was a late-comer to the Abolitionist movement but played an active part in it. The leadership here tended to lean toward the radical side, and the movement remained quite strong in the count for a number of years, but began to diminish with the decline of the national movement following the Christiana riots of 1851. A slave owner and United States marshal has arrived in Christiana, Lancaster County, and demanded the return of three fugitive slaves who were hidden on a nearby farm. Instead of turning over the slaves, a mob of whites and Negro freemen attacked the authorities, killed the slave owner, and chased off the marshal. By 1854 most of the Abolitionists had became Whigs. Although they had exercised a strong voice in the county's politics, the Abolitionists were never in control, and Indiana County had remained a Whigs stronghold, voting consistently for Whig Presidential candidates from 1840 to the founding of the Republican party in 1856

Actually , the real power of the Whigs ended in 1854 with the ascendancy of the Know-Nothings. the Know-Nothings were an anti-foreign, anti-Catholic, secret political group which began in New York and Pennsylvania and spread throughout the nation. Their tenure was brief, but their influence was awesome. The party appealed to the popular fear of the increasing number of immigrants into the county (in the thirty years prior to 1855 over five million foreigners, mostly Roman Catholic Iris and Germans came to the United States).

Although the Know-Nothing party had only been in existence since 1852, it had, by 1854, swallowed up the Whigs of Indiana County as well as the rest of the state. The election of the Whig and American candidate Pollack, to the governorship in 1854 was only technically a Whig victory. Actually, it was a victory for the Know Nothings who formed the larger part of the Whig and American alliance.

It as indeed, a strange coalition that formed the Indiana County Whig party in 1856; comprising a union of the Anti Masons, who violently opposed secret societies, and of the Know-Nothings who were themselves members of a secret society. It was a union of the Abolitionists who demanded the immediate emancipation of the slaves and the Whigs who declined and eventually died out in large part because they were reluctant to take a stand against slavery. In 1856 that union was destined to melt into the newly-formed Republican party.

The part of the Republican party that took control in Indiana county was the same radical faction that had sized control of the national movement and nominated John C. Freeman for President of the United States. Its platform had committed the party to the abolition of slavery, and it found support among the Whigs, Free Soilers, and some Northern businessmen and industrial interests who sought to establish economic advantages over the South. In the presidential elections of 1856, Pennsylvania again went Democratic, but Indiana Countians voted for the Republican Freemont by more than a 2 to 1 margin over fellow-Pennsylvanian, James Buchanan. It was to be fifty-four years before the newly-formed Republican party would taste defeat in Indiana county."

Mr V. married Ellen H. Meanor, d/o William Meanor Sr. She d 1918 in her 81st year. their children were James W. ; Gerge H.; Mary m. Samuel Barr; Rachel m Lem S. Brock; Margaret m Douglass; and Elizabeth b. 6-14-1860 not m"

More About James Thompson VAN HORN:
Burial: Unknown, Marion Center

Occupation: Farmer
Will: 1894, Indiana Cnty, PA Vol. 8, p. 284

Notes for Ellen H. MEANOR:
In 1910 she is widowed and has her single daughter Elizabeth living with her. She is the mother of 12 children and in 1910 only 5 are living.

More About Ellen H. MEANOR:
Cause of Death: Pleurisy
Religion: United Presbyterian of Marion Center, Indiana Cnty, PA

More About James VAN HORN and Ellen MEANOR:
Marriage: 03 Jul 1855[207]

Children of James VAN HORN and Ellen MEANOR are:
      i.   Leah[10] VAN HORN[208,209], d. Bet. Oct - Nov 1945.

          Notes for Leah VAN HORN:
          6 March 1907 Leah of Marion Center visited her brother James Van Horn in Indiana according to the Indiana Weekly Messenger (Indiana, PA).

57.   ii.   Mary C VAN HORN, b. 02 Aug 1856, Green Twp., Indiana Cnty, PA; d. 29 Apr 1947, Indiana Cnty, PA.
      iii.   William VAN HORN[210], b. Bet. 1858 - 1859, Indiana Cnty, PA[211]; d. 14 Jan 1883, Marion Center, Indiana Cnty, PA[212].
      iv.   Elizabeth VAN HORN[213,214,215,216,217,218,219], b. Bet. 14 Jun 1859 - 1860, Indiana Cnty, PA[220,221]; d. 22 Oct 1945, Marion Center, Indiana Cnty, PA[221].

          Notes for Elizabeth VAN HORN:
          In 1930 Elizabeth is 69 and is a servant in a private home of Martha Gibson.
          30 May 1918 Indiana Weekly Messenger (Indiana, PA) reports that Elizabeth is the sole heir of Ellen H. Van Horn's estate and is the executrix of the estate.

          More About Elizabeth VAN HORN:
          Burial: Unknown, Marion Center Cemetery, Indiana Cnty, PA
          Organizations: Member of Womens's Christian Temperence Union (WCTU)
          Religion: First Presbyterian Church at Marion Center, PA

58.   v.   James W. VAN HORN, b. 1861, Indiana Cnty, PA; d. 21 Sep 1947, Miami, Dade Cnty, FL.
59.   vi.   Margaret VAN HORN, b. Apr 1864, Indiana Cnty, PA; d. 21 Oct 1909, Twin Falls, ID.
60.   vii.   Rachel VAN HORN, b. Abt. 1868, Indiana Cnty, PA; d. Bet. 1901 - 1909.
61.   viii.   George H. VAN HORN, b. Abt. 1870, Indiana Cnty, PA; d. Aft. 1930.
      ix.   Lizzie A. VAN HORN[222], b. 26 Aug 1872, Indiana Cnty, PA[223]; d. 26 Aug 1881, Marion Center, Indiana Cnty, PA[224].

          More About Lizzie A. VAN HORN:
          Cause of Death: Diphtheria

      x.   HarryVAN HORN, d. Bef. 1909.
      xi.   Homer VAN HORN, d. Bef. 1909.

14. Tabitha Logan[9] VAN HORN *(Henry[8], Isaiah[7], Henry B.[6], Henry[5], Christian Barentsen[4] VAN HOORN, Barent Christiansen[3], Christian Barentsen[2], Barent Barents[1])[225,226,227,228,229]* was born Bet. 27 Sep 1821 - 1822 in Indiana Cnty, PA[230], and died 10 Dec 1890 in Ft. Morgan, Morgan Cnty, CO. She married Moses Thompson WORK[231,232,233,234] 13 May 1847 in Indiana Cnty, PA, son of William WORK and Miriam SCROGGS. He was born 05 Dec 1812 in Mahoning Twp., Indiana Cnty, PA[235,236], and died 02 Mar 1886.

Notes for Tabitha Logan VAN HORN:
Died at the home of Sarah and John Lytle. Dr. Hubert Work returned Tabitha's body to PA for burial

More About Tabitha Logan VAN HORN:
Burial: Unknown, Gilgal Cemetry, Gilgal Church, Indiana Cnty, PA

Notes for Moses Thompson WORK:
Moses Thompson's father died when he was 16, the care of the farm fell to him since the older brothers had married and started homes of their own. The equipment of that day were the wooden plow, the scythe, the sickle and the flail. At the age of 21 he married and three years later build a log cabin and log barn on the farm where he remained for the rest of his life. He was a man of good taste and was a good farmer; he had good address and of fine appearance. He was county Commissioner form 1854 to 1857 and was often the arbitrator to settle disputes between his neighbors. At his home the poor and the simple met with the same warm reception as those more favored with wealth and talent. Moses lost his wife and two younger children within 6 days leaving him with 3 children under the age of 10. It was fortunate that he lived close to other family members. Five of the children of William and Miriam Scroggs Work lived on adjoining farms with most of the others close by. Moses was especially gifted in music and his name is mentioned many times in the records regarding teaching, singing and other musical talents. He and other family members were blessed with musical talents. He was well off financially having real property worth $10,000 and cash of $3,000. His brother's net worth statements compared favorably to those of Moses. His son, Milton a member of the U. P. Church at Mahoning for 60 years was a farmer and stock raiser who specialized in horses, fruit and poultry. He enlisted in the 23rd Regt. of the state Militia in 1862. Milton and Elizabeth had no children.

In 1870 his father in law is living with the family. He has a property value of $10,000 and a personal effects value of $3,000. He is a farmer.

More About Moses Thompson WORK:
Will: 1886, Indiana Cnty, PA Vol. 5, p. 598

More About Moses WORK and Tabitha VAN HORN:
Marriage: 13 May 1847, Indiana Cnty, PA

Children of Tabitha VAN HORN and Moses WORK are:
62.   i.   Elizabeth Francis[10] WORK, b. 01 Sep 1848, East Mahoning Twp.,Indiana Cnty, PA; d. 02 Apr 1926, Des Moines, Polk Cnty, IA.
          ii.   Frances A. WORK[237], b. Bet. 30 Aug 1850 - 1852, Indiana Cnty, PA; d. 25 Aug 1876.
          iii.   Mary S. WORK[237,238,239,240], b. Bet. 05 Oct 1852 - 1854, East Mahoning Twp., Indiana Cnty, PA[241]; d. 18 May 1954, Indiana Cnty, PA; m. Aaron Work STEELE[242,243,244,245], Abt. 1901[246]; b. 14 Jul 1844, East Mahoning Twp., Indiana Cnty, PA[247]; d. 03 Aug 1922, Indiana Cnty, PA[248].

          Notes for Mary S. WORK:
          In 1910 she states in the census that they have been married for 8 years it is a first

131

marriage for both and she is the mother of no children.

More About Mary S. WORK:
Burial: Unknown, Oakland Cemetery, Indiana Cnty, PA

Notes for Aaron Work STEELE:
The last 17 years of his life he was a court crier. He was manager of the Indiana County Agricultural commission for a term. Farmer and Stock raiser.

More About Aaron Work STEELE:
Burial: Unknown, Oakland Cemetery, Indiana Cnty, PA
Employment: Court Crier[249]
Military service: Civil War 2 enlistments
Politics: 1884, Elected County Commission
Religion: Presbyterian

More About Aaron STEELE and Mary WORK:
Marriage: Abt. 1901[249]

	iv.	Ruth WORK, b. 07 Nov 1855, Indiana Cnty, PA; d. 03 Jan 1858.
63.	v.	Sarah Steele WORK, b. 09 Feb 1858, Indiana Cnty, PA; d. 27 Sep 1938, Denver, Denver Cnty, CO.
64.	vi.	Dr. Hubert Robert WORK, b. 03 Jul 1860, Marion Center, Indiana Cnty, PA; d. 14 Dec 1942, Denver, Denver Cnty, CO.
	vii.	Jennie Myrtle WORK[250], b. Bet. 02 Dec 1862 - 1864, Indiana Cnty, PA[250]; d. 24 Dec 1882.

15. Col. Robert Thompson[9] VAN HORN *(Henry[8], Isaiah[7], Henry B.[6], Henry[5], Christian Barentsen[4] VAN HOORN, Barent Christiansen[3], Christian Barentsen[2], Barent Barents[1])*[251,252,253,254,255,256,257,258] was born Bet. 10 - 19 May 1824 in Indiana Cnty, PA[259], and died Bet. 02 - 03 Jan 1916 in Evanston Station, Clay Cnty, MO. He married Adela Honeywood COOLEY[260,261,262,263,264,265,266,267] 22 Dec 1848 in Pomeroy, Meigs Cnty, OH. She was born 18 Jan 1826 in Coolville, Athens Cnty, OH[268], and died 24 Jul 1910 in MO[269].

Notes for Col. Robert Thompson VAN HORN:
Kansas City, MO Alderman, elected Mayor of Kansas City in 1861 and 1864. He was postmaster in Kansas City from 1857 to 1861 resigning when he was elected Mayor. He was elected to Congress in 1864 on the coattails of President Lincoln and was reelected 1866, 1868, 1880 and 1882. He was appointed Collector of Internal Revenue by President Grant a position he held from 1875 to 1881. He was twice a delegate to the Republican National Convention from Missouri. In 1861 with the capture of Fort Jackson by the confederate Army, Col Van Horn raised a battalion of men which he commanded which soon became a regiment. He was wounded at the battle of Lexington and at Corinth while leading his regiment. At Corinth his horse was shot out from under him. He served form 1861 to the end of the war.

Robert Thompson Van Horn (1824-1916) Family Papers (KC297) Native Sons Archives (NSA)

R.T. Van Horn was born in Indiana County, Pennsylvania, to Henry and Elizabeth (Thompson) Van Horn. He apprenticed as a printer and became a journeyman printer from 1843-1855. He also taught school briefly, worked on the Erie Canal, studied law, and operated a steamboat. On December 2, 1848, he married Adela Honeywood Cooley (born January 18, 1826) in Pomeroy, Ohio. They had four sons, only one of whom survived them.

Isaiah Van Horn Pioneer of Indiana County, Pennsylvania

Van Horn came to Kansas City in 1855 and purchased a weekly newspaper called The Enterprise. It was later called the Western Journal of Commerce, and then became the daily Kansas City Journal. Van Horn served as Postmaster of Kansas City from 1857-1861 and was then elected mayor as a Union candidate. During the Civil War, he commanded his own battalion until it merged with another to form the 25th Regiment of the Missouri volunteer infantry. He fought in several battles, including Shiloh, and he was wounded in the Battle of Lexington. Van Horn was elected to the Missouri Senate in 1862 and then once again as mayor of Kansas City in 1864. After holding office locally, he was elected to the U.S. Congress, where he served two terms. While in Congress, he obtained legislation that brought the Hannibal Bridge and crucial railroad service through Kansas City. Upon his return to this area, President U.S. Grant appointed Van Horn a regional tax collector, a post he held until 1881, when the voters returned him to Washington, D.C. for two more terms in Congress. R.T. Van Horn was a city builder who promoted the expansion and improvement of Kansas City. He was a member of many business and civic organizations. His wife, Adela, died July 24, 1910, and he died January 3, 1916.

R.T. and Adela Van Horn's son, Dick, and his wife, Frances McClure Van Horn, had two children--a daughter, Adela Cooley, and a son, Henry Kirkwood. Adela was born October 3, 1876. She attended the University of Chicago and was named a Phi Beta Kappa scholar. In 1919, she served as a Red Cross worker in Europe, and was later a member of the Women's Overseas Service League. Adela was also a member of the Daughters of the American Revolution. She traveled extensively throughout the world. In the late 1950s, she moved to Tucson, Arizona, where she lived in the Coronado Hotel.

The R.T. Van Horn materials were placed in scrapbook form by the Native Sons. WHMC-KC has removed the materials from that format. R.T. Van Horn's papers include correspondence, Civil War service records, business and property records, and some artifacts and ephemera. Much of the correspondence has been transcribed. Adela Cooley Van Horn, his granddaughter, traveled extensively, and the bulk of her materials consists of correspondence, passports, narratives, and photographs. She retained many genealogical records, as well. 1832-1965

VAN HORN, Robert Thompson, a Representative from Missouri; born in East Mahoning, Indiana County, Pa., May 19, 1824; attended the common schools; apprenticed to a printer; moved to Ohio in 1844 and settled in Pomeroy; studied law; was admitted to the bar about 1850 and commenced practice in Pomeroy, Ohio; moved to Kansas City, Mo., in 1855; member of the board of aldermen in 1857; postmaster of Kansas City 1857-1861; established and edited the Kansas City Journal; elected mayor of Kansas City in 1861 and again in 1864; enlisted in the Union Army during the Civil War and served as lieutenant colonel of the Twenty-fifth Regiment, Missouri Volunteer Infantry; member of the State senate 1862-1864; elected as a Republican to the Thirty-ninth, Fortieth, and Forty-first Congresses (March 4, 1865-March 3, 1871); was not a candidate for renomination in 1870; chairman of the Republican State central committee 1874-1876; collector of internal revenue for the sixth district of Missouri 1875-1881; delegate to the Republican National Conventions in 1864, 1868, 1872, 1876, 1880, and 1884; member of the Republican National Committee in 1872 and 1884; elected as a Republican to the Forty-seventh Congress (March 4, 1881-March 3, 1883); successfully contested the election of John C. Tarsney to the Fifty-fourth Congress and served from February 27, 1896, to March 3, 1897; unsuccessful candidate for renomination in 1896; retired from editorship of the Kansas City Journal in 1897; died on his estate, "Honeywood," at Evanston Station, near Kansas City, Mo., January 3, 1916; interment in Mount Washington Cemetery, Kansas City, Mo.

In the Indiana Progress(Indiana, PA) of 11 August 1870 Robert is listed as one of the any editors and publishers that are member of congress.
The Indiana Progress(Indiana, PA) of 15 August 1906 reports that Col. R. T. Van Horn is visiting A. W. Steele noting that Mrs. Steele is his niece.

More About Col. Robert Thompson VAN HORN:
Burial: Unknown, Mt. Washington Cemetery Kansas City, MO
Occupation: Printer, Editor, Publisher and Founder and Owner of the Kansas City Journal and a renowed journalist
Political Office: Mayor of Kansas City, Missouri State Legislator and 4 terms in the House of Representatives US Congress

Notes for Adela Honeywood COOLEY:
In 1860 a C. R. Cooley age 16 born OH is living in the home and is a printer apprentice.
In 1870 a Kate Cooley a Neice age 23 born OH is living with the family.
In 1880 the family is living on Walnut Street in Kansas City and Kate Cooley is still living with the family.
In 1900 she states she is the mother of 4 children of which only one is living. She has been married for 31 years. Kate Cooly is living with the family.

More About Robert VAN HORN and Adela COOLEY:
Marriage: 22 Dec 1848, Pomeroy, Meigs Cnty, OH

Children of Robert VAN HORN and Adela COOLEY are:

      i.   Caleb Henry[10] VAN HORN[270], b. 24 May 1850, Pomeroy, Meigs Cnty, OH[270]; d. 12 Jun 1858, Kansas City, MO.

          Notes for Caleb Henry VAN HORN:
          Indiana Register (Indiana, PA), Extracts April-August, 1858
          29 June 1858 DIED. On the 12th inst., in Kansas City, Missouri, of Scarlatina, CALEB HENRY, oldest son of R.T. AND ADELA VAN HORN, aged 8 years and 19 days.

          More About Caleb Henry VAN HORN:
          Cause of Death: Scarlatina

65.   ii. Richard VAN HORN, b. 15 Nov 1851, Pomeroy, Meigs Cnty, OH; d. Aft. 1930.
      iii. Robert Cannon VAN HORN[271,272,273], b. 26 Jul 1853, Pomeroy, Meigs Cnty, OH[274,275]; d. 12 Nov 1918, Kansas City, Jackson Cnty, MO[276]; m. Kate TIMMEY[277], 13 Aug 1878; b. 29 Jun 1857, Harrisonville, Cass Cnty, MO[277]; d. 20 May 1910[278].

          Notes for Robert Cannon VAN HORN:
          In 1880 he is living in the home of Hamilton Timmey on Charlotte Street in Kansas City, MO listed as a son in law. The only female of age to be his wife is a Kate Timmey age 23 born MO.

          More About Robert Cannon VAN HORN:
          Cause of Death: Consumption
          Occupation: Surveyor, Post Office clerk

          Notes for Kate TIMMEY:
          The 1889-1891 Kansas City City Directory lists a Kate VanHorn as a widow of Robert C. Van Horn living at 406 Charlotte.

More About Robert VAN HORN and Kate TIMMEY:
Marriage: 13 Aug 1878

    iv.   Charles C. VAN HORN[279,280], b. 17 Feb 1861, Kansas City, Jackson Cnty,
          MO[281,282]; d. 25 May 1881[283].

          More About Charles C. VAN HORN:
          Occupation: Type Setter

16. Henry A.[9] VAN HORN *(Henry[8], Isaiah[7], Henry B.[6], Henry[5], Christian Barentsen[4] VAN HOORN,
Barent Christiansen[3], Christian Barentsen[2], Barent Barents[1])*[284,285,286,287,288] was born Bet. 1828 - 1829 in
PA[289,290], and died Bet. 27 - 28 Apr 1887 in Georgeville, Indiana Cnty, PA[291,292]. He married
Amanda JAMES[293,294] Abt. 1851. She was born Bet. 1832 - 1834 in PA[295], and died 06 Jun 1887 in
Indiana Cnty, PA.

Notes for Henry A. VAN HORN:
    In 1850 living with parents. His age is given as 21.
    In 1860 Henry and family are living with his widowed father. He has personal effects worth
$200.
    In 1870 Henry is a farmer and he has real estate worth $4,500 and personal effects of $1,500.
    In 1880 is a widower and his two youngest daughters Elizabeth and Minnie are living with him.
He is 51.
    Known as Harry Van Horn.
    Will date 1899 Indiana Will Book Vol. 9, p. 312

More About Henry A. VAN HORN:
Burial: Unknown, Gilgal Cemertery, Indiana Cnty, PA
Occupation: Laborer, Farmer

Notes for Amanda JAMES:
Indiana Register (Indiana, PA), Extracts May-June, 1867
12 June 1867
VAN HORN. On June 6, MRS. AMANDA VAN HORN, wife of HENRY A. VAN HORN, of
East
Mahoning township, aged above 35 years.

More About Amanda JAMES:
Burial: Unknown, Gilgal Cemetery Gilgal UP Church Indiana Cnty, PA

More About Henry VAN HORN and Amanda JAMES:
Marriage: Abt. 1851

Children of Henry VAN HORN and Amanda JAMES are:
66.   i.   Anna M.[10] VAN HORN, b. Feb 1854, PA; d. Bef. 1941.
67.   ii.   Alice Lucetta VAN HORN, b. 1855, PA; d. Aft. 1899.
        iii.   Thaddeus VAN HORN, b. Feb 1858, Indiana Cnty, PA; d. 17 Mar 1858, Indiana
            Cnty, PA.

            More About Thaddeus VAN HORN:
            Burial: Unknown, Gilgal Cemetery Gilgal UP Church Indiana Cnty, PA

    iv.   Robert Logan VAN HORN[296,297], b. 1859, PA[298]; d. Bef. 1941.

More About Robert Logan VAN HORN:
Lived: Mt. Pleasant, PA

68.   v.   Edith Lee VAN HORN, b. 23 Feb 1862, PA; d. 23 Aug 1941, Georgeville, Indiana Cnty, PA.

69.   vi.   Minnie VAN HORN, b. 27 Jan 1866, Georgeville, Indiana Cnty, PA; d. 08 Aug 1953, Brookville, Jefferson Cnty, PA.

17. John Dick[9] VAN HORN *(Alexander[8], Isaiah[7], Henry B.[6], Henry[5], Christian Barentsen[4] VAN HOORN, Barent Christiansen[3], Christian Barentsen[2], Barent Barents[1])*[299,300,301,302,303] was born Dec 1829 in PA[304], and died 17 Oct 1901 in PA[305]. He married Ann Caroline NEIGHLY[306,307,308,309,310,311] Abt. 1855. She was born Mar 1828 in PA[312], and died Aft. 1910.

Notes for John Dick VAN HORN:
    In 1860 living near Alexander Van Horn. Has land worth $1500 and personal effects of $500. Apparently living in the same household as John Wagner and his large family who is listed as a station master.
    In 1870 John is a merchant and is worth $2000 in real estate and $1500 in personal effects.
    In 1900 living on Quarry Street in Mt. Pleasant, PA. Caroline is the mother of 8 with only 4 living in 1900. They have bee married for 44 years and son James is living with them.

More About John Dick VAN HORN:
Occupation: Farmer, Merchant, Laborer, Day Laborer

Notes for Ann Caroline NEIGHLY:
    In 1910 living with her oldest daughter and her family on Mountain Road in Springfield, Fayette Cnty, PA.

More About John VAN HORN and Ann NEIGHLY:
Marriage: Abt. 1855

Children of John VAN HORN and Ann NEIGHLY are:
70.   i.   Sarah Jane[10] VAN HORN, b. 13 Mar 1859, Normalville, Fayette Cnty, PA; d. 03 Jun 1942, Mill Run, Fayette Cnty, PA.

       ii.   Anna M. VAN HORN[312,313], b. Abt. 1858, PA[314]; d. Unknown.

71.   iii. Henry D. Foster VAN HORN, b. 12 Sep 1860, PA; d. 18 Jan 1935.

      iv. Tabitha VAN HORN[314,315], b. Abt. 1864, PA[316]; d. Unknown.

72.   v.   Albert VAN HORN, b. May 1864, PA; d. Aft. Apr 1942.

      vi. James VAN HORN[317,318], b. Jul 1870, PA[319]; d. Unknown.

          More About James VAN HORN:
          Occupation: Day Laborer

      vii. Edward VAN HORN[319], b. Abt. 1871, PA[319]; d. Unknown.

     viii. ? VAN HORN, d. Unknown.

18. James Wherry[9] VAN HORN *(Alexander[8], Isaiah[7], Henry B.[6], Henry[5], Christian Barentsen[4] VAN HOORN, Barent Christiansen[3], Christian Barentsen[2], Barent Barents[1])*[320,321,322,323,324,325,326] was born 31 Oct 1821 in PA[327], and died 19 May 1894 in Indiana Cnty, PA or Westmoreland Cnty, PA[328,329]. He married Rachel STEWART[330,331] Abt. 1847[332]. She was born 1829 in PA[333], and died Bet. 1870 -

1872 in Indiana Cnty, PA[334].

Notes for James Wherry VAN HORN:
In 1860 James is a laborer and states he has real estate worth $6,600.
In 1880 James is a widower and has two daughters Flora and Margaret living with him as well as his mother and his brother Isaiah Van Horn.
The Indiana Progress(Indiana, PA) reports on 10 Aug. 1876 that James is a grand juror chosen from West Wheatfield Twp.
The Indiana Weekly Messenger (Indiana, PA) of 4 Aug 1880 lists James W. Van Horn of West Wheatfield as a grand juror.
4 Aug. 1880 Indiana Weekly Messenger (Indiana, PA) notes James W. of West Wheatfield is assigned to jury duty.
6 June 1894 Indiana Gazette reports on his death as May 19, 1894 and that he was a railroad man for 25 years and had a farm at Centerville for 40 years.
The Indiana Progress(Indiana, PA) reports Feb 20, 1896 the filing of an account of Flora M. Van Horn and Caroline Balentine the executors of the estate of James W. Van Horn of West Wheatfield Twp., who is deceased.
Will in Indiana Will Book Vol. 8, p. 251 1894

More About James Wherry VAN HORN:
Burial: Unknown, West Fairfield Methodist Cemetery, Fairfield Twp., Westmoreland Co., Pa
Fraternal Organization: Indiana Masonic Lodge
Occupation: Railroad, Policeman, Farmer
Politics: Republican
Religion: Presbyterian

More About James VAN HORN and Rachel STEWART:
Marriage: Abt. 1847[334]

Children of James VAN HORN and Rachel STEWART are:
    i.   Mary V.[10] VAN HORN[335,336,337,338,339,340], b. Jul 1848, PA[341,342]; d. Aft. 1910; m. John F. HEISLEY[343,344,345,346,347], Abt. 1884[348]; b. Apr 1841, PA[349,350,351,352]; d. 25 Jan 1915, Williamsport, Lycoming Cnty, PA[353].

        Notes for Mary V. VAN HORN:
        Lived in Williamsport, PA
        In the 1889 Williamsport Directory Mary is listed as a dressmaker at 443 Hepburn and later at 331 Lycoming street.
        In 1910 Mary and John are living in Williamsport, PA he has been married twice and Mary once and she is the mother of one living child. They have been married for 25 years.
        11 July 1910 Williamsport Gazette and Bulletin Mrs. John Ballantine of Derry visited her sister Mrs. John Heisley of Lycoming Street.

        More About Mary V. VAN HORN:
        Employment: Dressmaking

        Notes for John F. HEISLEY:
        In 1880 living with daughter Maggie and the family of Peter Mutehart. John says he is single not widowed.
        In 1910 lives on Lycoming Street in Williamsport, PA with wife Mary and lodger Emery Carpenter age 62 born PA.

        More About John F. HEISLEY:

Burial: Unknown, Mound Cemetery
Cause of Death: Asphyxiatin
Employment: 1880, Plasterer
Occupation: Motorman Street Railway

More About John HEISLEY and Mary VAN HORN:
Marriage: Abt. 1884[354]

  ii. Florence M. VAN HORN[355,356,357,358,359,360,361,362,363,364,365], b. Nov 1850, PA[366]; d. Aft. 1930.

Notes for Florence M. VAN HORN:
In June 1894 the Indiana County Gazette (Indiana, PA) reports in James' obit that Flora lived with him and was his devoted housekeeper.
In 1900 Florence is living with her niece Margaret Ashcom.
3 Feb 1903 it is reported in the Indiana Progress(Indiana, PA) that Caroline Ballantyne sold 1/4/ of 97 acres to Florence M. Van Horn for $500
30 March 1909 the Indiana Evening Gazette (Indiana, PA) reports that Florence sold a acre in West Wheatfield to PRR Co. for $200.
In 1910 she is single living alone and has her own income.
In 1920 she is single and living with her Neice on 9th Street in New Florence, PA
In 1930 she is single age 79 and living with her nephew by marriage Fran Ashcom in New Florence, PA.

More About Florence M. VAN HORN:
Will: 1893, Named as granddaughter of Mary VAN HORN wife of Alexander VAN HORN

73. iii. Anna I. VAN HORN, b. Jun 1853, PA; d. Aft. 1930.
74. iv. Caroline E. VAN HORN, b. Dec 1856, PA; d. Bet. 1910 - 1920, Westmoreland Cnty, PA.
75. v. Margaret Mary VAN HORN, b. Mar 1868, PA; d. Abt. 1920, PA.

19. Henry Coulter[9] VAN HORN *(Alexander[8], Isaiah[7], Henry B.[6], Henry[5], Christian Barentsen[4] VAN HOORN, Barent Christiansen[3], Christian Barentsen[2], Barent Barents[1])*[367,368,369,370,371,372,373,374,375] was born 18 Sep 1823 in Centerville, PA[376,377], and died 19 Jul 1898 in East Wheatfield Twp., Indiana Cnty, PA[378,379,380]. He married Ellen HUTCHISON[381,382,383,384] 12 Jan 1847, daughter of Robert HUTCHISON and Nancy STEELE. She was born 12 Apr 1825 in East Wheatfield Twp., Indiana Cnty, PA[385,386], and died 26 Dec 1872 in Indiana Cnty, PA[387].

Notes for Henry Coulter VAN HORN:
In 1860 he is a farmer and states his real estate holdings are worth $3500 and his personal effect are $728. He is living 2 farms away from Robert and Agnes Hutchinson who may be the parents of his wife Ellen Hutchinson.
Civil War Co F 2nd Ind Bn Mil 1863 PVI Pvt 7/23/63-1/21/64 was mustered in the 2nd H 83 PVI on 2/15/1865 at Pittsburgh, PA as a Corporal and mustered out on 6/28/1865. He is 6', dark hair, dark complexion, blue eyes and is a farmer born in Indiana Cnty, PA.
In 1870 he is a farmer and his real estate is valued at $5,000 and personal effect as $1,100.
In 1880 he is a farmer and his son Hubert is living with him as well as his niece Ellen(Ellie) Wakefield.
His Obituary says he is 75 and died on July 19, 1892. these dates suggest that Henry was born in 1815.
It is reported in the Indiana Progress(Indiana, PA) that H. C. Van Horn on the date of 16

Isaiah Van Horn Pioneer of Indiana County, Pennsylvania

March 1876 is a member of the county Republican committee. The Progress reports on 20 April 1876 that H. C. Van Horn represents East Wheatfield on the county Republican committee.

1 March 1877 H. C. Van Horn is reported as elected to be one of the 2 supervisors for the East Wheatfield Twp.

28 Feb 1878 H. C. Van Horn is reported in the Indiana Progress(Indiana, PA) as one of the supervisors of East Wheatfield Twp.

16 May 1878 H. C. Van Horn is one of the Grand Jurors listed for the June term of the court. Twp.

13 Feb 1884 H. C. Van Horn is elected an East Wheatfield Director according to the Indiana Weekly Messenger (Indiana, PA).

16 June 1886 the Indiana County Messenger lists the School Board Reports and H.C. Van Horn is the President of the East Wheatfield School Board.

18 & 25 Dec 1889 H. C. Van Horn vs Jacob Heisel is listed in the Indiana Progress(Indiana, PA) as a cause for the December Term of the Court

Indiana Cnty, PA book and Page 28/639 Henry C & Ellen Van Horn, Whtf Twp TO Cornelius HUTCHISON, same11 Feb 1864 Adj: Henry Rodgers & Corn Hutchison $100 E Whtf Twp Orig bo't by Jas Dick, 10 Acres Wit: Jas Wakefield

October 18, 1893 Indiana Weekly Messenger (Indiana, PA) states that H. C, Van Horn of New Florence attended the Barnum Circus at Johnstown and was knocked down and robbed of $6 by Patch O'Connell who is in the Ebensburg Jail awaiting trial.

November 8, 1893 the Indiana County Gazette (Indiana, PA) reports that Patrick O'Connell is sent to he penitentiary for 18 months for robbing H. C. VanHorn of Indiana County under the Stone Bridge in Johnstown

31 Jan 1894 Indiana County Gazette (Indiana, PA) (Indiana, PA) O'Conner is sent to prison for robbing H. C. Van Horn of Indiana county near the Stone Bridge in Johnstown, PA. His term is 18 months.

More About Henry Coulter VAN HORN:
Burial: Unknown, Armagh Presbyterian, Indiana Cnty, PA[388]
Military service: Bet. 25 Jun 1863 - 28 Jun 1865, Private Co. H.2nd PVI and Corporal Co. H. 83rd PVI[388]

Notes for Ellen HUTCHISON:
Robert and Agnes Hutchinson are living 2 locations away from Ellen and Henry in 1860 and both are aged 71 and born in PA.

Died at 47y 8m 14d

More About Ellen HUTCHISON:
Burial: Unknown, Armagh-Bethel UP Cemetery[389]

More About Henry VAN HORN and Ellen HUTCHISON:
Marriage: 12 Jan 1847

Children of Henry VAN HORN and Ellen HUTCHISON are:

76.   i.   Alice Roselia[10] VAN HORN, b. Bet. 21 - 22 Mar 1848, Indiana Cnty, PA; d. 17 Jun 1911.
77.   ii.   William Alexander VAN HORN, b. 21 Mar 1850, Indiana Cnty, PA; d. Aft. 1910.
78.   iii. Mary Agnes VAN HORN, b. 20 Nov 1851, Armagh, Indiana Cnty, PA; d. Bef. 1937.
79.   iv.   Clara Lucinda VAN HORN, b. 27 Apr 1854, Indiana Cnty, PA; d. 26 Jan 1872, East Wheatfield, Indiana Cnty, PA.
80.   v.   Henry Coulter VAN HORN, b. 12 Mar 1855, East Wheatfield, Indiana Cnty, PA; d.

01 Dec 1919, WA.

vi.   Charles Fremont VAN HORN[390,391], b. 15 Mar 1857, Indiana Cnty, PA[391]; d. 1877.

81.   vii.   Samuel Cornelius VAN HORN, b. Bet. 31 Dec 1857 - 1858, Near Armagh, Indiana Cnty, PA; d. 06 Jan 1937, Dalhart, Dallam Cnty, TX.

viii.   Ester Emma VAN HORN[392], b. 19 Sep 1860, Indiana Cnty, PA[392]; d. 20 Jun 1872, East Wheatfield Twp., Indiana Cnty, PA[393].

More About Ester Emma VAN HORN:
Cause of Death: Typhoid Fever

82.   ix.   Tabitha Logan VAN HORN, b. 14 Oct 1862, Indiana Cnty, PA; d. 1950, Pinellas Cnty, FL.

x.   Ellen Caroletta VAN HORN[394], b. 30 Jun 1865, Indiana Cnty, PA[394]; d. 06 Dec 1871.

83.   xi.   Hubert Earl VAN HORN, b. Bet. 21 Aug 1869 - 1870, Indiana Cnty, PA; d. Bef. 1937.

20. Alexander[9] VAN HORN, JR *(Alexander[8], Isaiah[7], Henry B.[6], Henry[5], Christian Barentsen[4] VAN HOORN, Barent Christiansen[3], Christian Barentsen[2], Barent Barents[1])*[395,396,397] was born 18 Jan 1832 in PA[398], and died 27 Jun 1866 in Civil War Petersburgh, Va.. He married Mary E.[398] Abt. 1854. She was born 1834 in PA[398], and died Unknown.

Notes for Alexander VAN HORN, JR:
A farmer living next to his brother James in 1860. He states in the 1860 census he has personal effects valued at $257. A Robert Dunlap age 3 born PA is living with the family. This might be Mary's brother.
Killed in battle in the Civil War at Petersburg, PA.

More About Alexander VAN HORN, JR:
Military service: Civil War Private in Company I 11th Pennsyvania Res. Inf.

More About Alexander VAN HORN and Mary E.:
Marriage: Abt. 1854

Children of Alexander VAN HORN and Mary E. are:
i.   Alexander M.[10] VAN HORN[399,400], b. 1856, PA[400]; d. Unknown.
ii.   Adella VAN HORN[401,402], b. 1858, PA[402]; d. Unknown.

21. William[9] VAN HORN *(Alexander[8], Isaiah[7], Henry B.[6], Henry[5], Christian Barentsen[4] VAN HOORN, Barent Christiansen[3], Christian Barentsen[2], Barent Barents[1])*[403,404] was born Bet. 1827 - 31 Dec 1833 in PA[405], and died 09 Nov 1886 in Allamakee Cnty, IA[406]. He married Mariah[407,408,409] Abt. 1856. She was born 11 Apr 1840 in PA[410,411], and died 06 Mar 1912 in Allamakee Cnty, IA[411].

Notes for William VAN HORN:
    According to Michel Ferris his great grandmother Alice was sent to live with her Uncle William during the Civil War.
    According to the History of Allamakee Cnty, IA William moved to the county from Indiana Cnty, PA in 1857. He is a farmer in section 28 of Jefferson Twp., Allamakee Cnty, IA and his post office is Rossville, IA.

More About William VAN HORN:

Burial: Unknown, Rossville Cemetery, Allamakee Cnty, IA

Notes for Mariah:
    In 1900 she is widowed and living with her single son Samuel R. Van Horn.

More About William VAN HORN and Mariah:
Marriage: Abt. 1856

Children of William VAN HORN and Mariah are:
      i.   Samuel R.[10] VAN HORN[412,413,414], b. 08 Nov 1857, IA[415]; d. 24 Mar 1916, Allamakee Cnty, IA[416].

          More About Samuel R. VAN HORN:
          Burial: Unknown, Rossville Cemetery, Allamakee Cnty, IA

      ii. Albert A. VAN HORN[417], b. 31 Jul 1859, IA[417]; d. 25 Oct 1869, Allamakee Cnty, IA[418].

          More About Albert A. VAN HORN:
          Burial: Unknown, Rossville Cemetery, Allamakee Cnty, IA

      iii. Cora VAN HORN[419], b. Abt. 1868, IA[419]; d. Unknown.
      iv. Wilomina VAN HORN[419,420,421], b. Feb 1871, IA[422]; d. Unknown; m. John F. GAST[423], Aft. 1900; b. Abt. 1872; d. 1949.

          More About John GAST and Wilomina VAN HORN:
          Marriage: Aft. 1900

      v. Edith B. VAN HORN, b. Abt. 1873, IA; d. Unknown.
84.   vi. Frank VAN HORN, b. Abt. 1875, IA; d. Unknown.

22. Tabitha L.[9] VAN HORN (*Alexander*[8], *Isaiah*[7], *Henry B.*[6], *Henry*[5], *Christian Barentsen*[4] *VAN HOORN*, *Barent Christiansen*[3], *Christian Barentsen*[2], *Barent Barents*[1])[424,425,426,427] was born 26 Jul 1836[428], and died 02 Dec 1862. She married David Seba WAKEFIELD[429,430,431,432] Abt. 1854, son of David WAKEFIELD and Susan WILSON. He was born Bet. 1834 - 15 Jan 1835 in PA[433], and died 01 May 1909 in East Wheatfield, Indiana Cnty, PA[434].

Notes for Tabitha L. VAN HORN:
In 1860 she and her husband are living next door to her father mother and brother George. There are 4 children in the family and a Bunevista Wakefiield relationship unknown.

Notes for David Seba WAKEFIELD:
    In 1860 he is living next door to his father in law Alexander Van Horn. He farms and his personal effects are valued at $300.
David's wife Tabitha died in 1862.
    In 1870 he has a new wife with the children of Tabitha in the family and two young children that must be the children of his second marriage. Since Tabitha died in 1862 Susan and John must be her children. The census shows John as a female. The Emily of the 1860 Census must be the Lavina of the 1870 Census. David is a farmer and his land is worth $3000 and personal effects of $700.
    In 1880 a grandson John Brown age 18 is living in the home. David gives his name as D. S. Wakefield.
    27 Jan. 1892 Indiana Cnty Gazette (Indiana, PA) an announcement that on the third Tuesday of February the freemen of East Wheatfield may vote at the Wagon Shop of David Wakefield.

Isaiah Van Horn Pioneer of Indiana County, Pennsylvania

21 August 1895 Indiana Weekly Messenger (Indiana, PA) Mr. Wakefield states he has a pumpkin growing on his East Wheatfield farm that will take the cake and will take a premium at the county fair. This pumpkin measures 50 inches around the middle and 32 inches stem to stem.

More About David Seba WAKEFIELD:
Military service: PA Cav. Co. D 4th Volunteers
Occupation: Farmer

More About David WAKEFIELD and Tabitha VAN HORN:
Marriage: Abt. 1854

Children of Tabitha VAN HORN and David WAKEFIELD are:
  i.   Ellen[10] WAKEFIELD[435,436,437], b. Abt. 1855, PA[438,439]; d. Unknown.
  ii. Margaret WAKEFIELD[440,441], b. Abt. 1856, PA[441]; d. Unknown.
  iii. Mary WAKEFIELD[442,443], b. Abt. 1858, PA[443]; d. Unknown.
  iv. Lavina WAKEFIELD[444,445], b. Abt. Apr 1860, PA[445]; d. Unknown.
  v.   E. Susan WAKEFIELD[446,447,448], b. Bet. 1861 - 1862, PA[448]; d. Unknown.

> Notes for E. Susan WAKEFIELD:
> In1870 Susan is living with her grandparents Alexander and Mary Van Horn. Her mother died shortly after the birth of Susan and her brother or in childbirth.

  vi. John WAKEFIELD, b. Bet. 1861 - 1862, PA; d. Bef. 1880.

23. Isaiah[9] MCELHOES *(Jane[8] VAN HORN, Isaiah[7], Henry B.[6], Henry[5], Christian Barentsen[4] VAN HOORN, Barent Christiansen[3], Christian Barentsen[2], Barent Barents[1])*[449,450,451,452] was born 25 Jun 1815 in Green Twp., Indiana Cnty, PA[453], and died 02 Oct 1896 in Green Twp., Indiana Cnty, PA. He married Isabella KINTER[453,454] Abt. 1839. She was born 31 May 1807 in Green Twp., Indiana Cnty, PA[455], and died 31 Jan 1879 in Indiana Cnty, PA.

Notes for Isaiah MCELHOES:
    In 1870 Isaiah has a value of real estate of $14000 and personal effects of $1000.

More About Isaiah MCELHOES:
Burial: Unknown, Washington Church Cemetery, Rayne Twp., Indiana Cnty, PA
Occupation: Justice of the Peace, Woolen Mill Owner, Farmer

More About Isabella KINTER:
Burial: Unknown, Washington Church Cemetery, Rayne Twp., Indiana Cnty, PA

More About Isaiah MCELHOES and Isabella KINTER:
Marriage: Abt. 1839

Children of Isaiah MCELHOES and Isabella KINTER are:
85.   i.   Jane[10] MCELHOES, b. Mar 1841, Green Twp., Indiana Cnty, PA; d. Aft. 1910.
86.   ii. John Kinter MCELHOES, b. 16 Mar 1845, Green Twp., Indiana Cnty, PA; d. 18 Feb 1908, Indiana Cnty, PA.
87.   iii. James Steele MCELHOES, b. 04 Apr 1847, Green Twp., Indiana Cnty, PA or Elderton, Armonstrong Cnty, PA; d. 08 Aug 1923, Indiana Cnty, PA.
         iv. Elizabth MCELHOES[455], b. Abt. Jan 1850, Indiana Cnty, PA[455]; d. Unknown.
         v.   Sarah Isabella MCELHOES[456,457], b. Bet. 1853 - 1855, Indiana Cnty, PA[458]; d. Unknown; m. James ALLEN, Aft. 1880; d. Unknown.

More About James ALLEN and Sarah MCELHOES:
Marriage: Aft. 1880

    vi.   William R. MCELHOES, b. 28 Jan, Indiana Cnty, PA; d. 28 Aug 1884, Indiana Cnty, PA.

24. Nancy[9] MCELHOES *(Jane[8] VAN HORN, Isaiah[7], Henry B.[6], Henry[5], Christian Barentsen[4] VAN HOORN, Barent Christiansen[3], Christian Barentsen[2], Barent Barents[1])*[459,460,461,462] was born 06 Mar 1817 in Green Twp., Indiana Cnty, PA/Washington Cnty, PA[463], and died 14 Jul 1893 in Kellysburg, Indiana Cnty, PA[464]. She married William DILTS[465,466,467,468] 02 May 1839, son of Peter DILTS and Jane COULTER. He was born 25 Apr 1814 in North Mahoning Twp., Indiana Cnty, PA[469], and died 27 Oct 1861 in Rayne Twp., Indiana Cnty, PA[470].

Notes for Nancy MCELHOES:
    In 1860 her mother is living in the family with an age of 60.

More About William DILTS:
Burial: Unknown, Washington Church Cemetery, Rayne Twp., Indiana Cnty, PA

More About William DILTS and Nancy MCELHOES:
Marriage: 02 May 1839

Children of Nancy MCELHOES and William DILTS are:
    i.   Peter Watson[10] DILTS[471], b. Abt. 1840, Green Twp., Indiana Cnty, PA; d. 1870, Rayne Twp., Indiana Cnty, PA; m. Christeanna KINTER; d. Unknown.

        More About Peter Watson DILTS:
        Burial: Unknown, Washington Church Cemetery, Rayne Twp., Indiana Cnty, PA

    ii.   John Scott DILTS[471], b. Abt. 1842, Green Twp., Indiana Cnty, PA; d. 12 Jan 1864, Green Twp., Indiana Cnty, PA.

        More About John Scott DILTS:
        Burial: Unknown, Washington Church Cemetery, Rayne Twp., Indiana Cnty, PA

    iii.   James Coulter DILTS[471], b. Abt. 1844, Green Twp., Indiana Cnty, PA; d. Unknown; m. Martha MCCALL; d. Unknown.
    iv.   William C. DILTS[471], b. Abt. 1845, Green Twp., Indiana Cnty, PA; d. Unknown; m. Dora COOPER; d. Unknown.
    v.   Jane DILTS[471], b. Abt. 1847, Green Twp., Indiana Cnty, PA; d. 27 Mar 1876, Green Twp., Indiana Cnty, PA.

        More About Jane DILTS:
        Burial: Unknown, Washington Church Cemetery, Rayne Twp., Indiana Cnty, PA

    vi.   Agnes DILTS[471], b. Abt. 1849, PA; d. Unknown; m. Benjamin MCCLUSKEY; d. Unknown.
    vii.   Samuel DILTS[471], b. Abt. 1851, PA; d. Unknown.
    viii.   Tabitha DILTS[471], b. Abt. 1855, PA; d. Unknown.
88.   ix.   Henry Milton DILTS, b. 10 May 1859, Kellysburg, Indiana Cnty, PA; d. 15 Nov 1932, Blairsville, Indiana Cnty, PA.

25. Dorcas[9] MCELHOES *(Jane[8] VAN HORN, Isaiah[7], Henry B.[6], Henry[5], Christian Barentsen[4] VAN HOORN, Barent Christiansen[3], Christian Barentsen[2], Barent Barents[1])*[472,473,474,475] was born 08 Sep 1816 in PA[476], and died 10 Apr 1896 in Cherry Hill Twp., Indiana Cnty, PA. She married (1) Henry D. KINTER[477] Abt. 1840, son of John KINTER and Sarah ROSS. He was born 08 Jun 1812 in Indiana Cnty, PA, and died 10 Jun 1855 in Indiana Cnty, PA. She married (2) William HOUCK[478,479,480] Abt. 1845. He was born 12 Sep 1822 in Bavaria/Prussia[481], and died Aft. 1880.

Notes for Dorcas MCELHOES:
  In 1880 Dorcas is living separately from William with her son John and his wife and Samuel Stewart an apprentice miller. John is an engineer.

More About Dorcas MCELHOES:
Burial: Unknown, Washington Church Cemetery, Rayne Twp., Indiana Cnty, PA

More About Henry KINTER and Dorcas MCELHOES:
Marriage: Abt. 1840

Notes for William HOUCK:
  In 1880 living with 2 children Danial and Fanny. working as a wagon maker and a servant Hannah Bence is in the home.

More About William HOUCK:
Occupation: Farmer, Wagon Maker and Miller

More About William HOUCK and Dorcas MCELHOES:
Marriage: Abt. 1845

Children of Dorcas MCELHOES and William HOUCK are:
89.   i.   William H.[10] HOUCK, b. Abt. 1847, PA; d. Bet. 1880 - 1900.
           ii.   Ann E. HOUCK[481], b. Abt. 1849, PA[481]; d. Unknown.
90.   iii. Daniel HOUCK, b. Apr 1852, PA; d. Unknown.
           iv.   Fanny HOUCK[481,482,483], b. Abt. 1853, PA[484]; d. Unknown.
91.   v.   John HOUCK, b. 25 Jun 1858, PA; d. 21 May 1949, Indiana Cnty, PA.
           vi.   Kate HOUCK[484], b. Abt. 1859, PA[484]; d. Bef. 1870.

26. Susan[9] MCELHOES *(Jane[8] VAN HORN, Isaiah[7], Henry B.[6], Henry[5], Christian Barentsen[4] VAN HOORN, Barent Christiansen[3], Christian Barentsen[2], Barent Barents[1])*[485,486,487] was born Bet. 22 Feb 1820 - 1821 in Rayne, Indiana Cnty, PA[488], and died 1901 in Rayne, Indiana Cnty, PA. She married Johnston LIGHTCAP[489,490,491]. He was born 02 Oct 1811 in Cumberland Cnty, PA[491], and died Dec 1896 in Rayne Twp., Indiana Cnty, PA.

More About Johnston LIGHTCAP:
Burial: Unknown, Marion Center, Indiana Cnty, PA

Children of Susan MCELHOES and Johnston LIGHTCAP are:
92.   i.   Jane T.[10] LIGHTCAP, b. 1847, Rayne Twp., Indiana Cnty, PA; d. 1882.
           ii.   Lucinda LIGHTCAP[492,493,494], b. 1850, East Mahoning, Indiana Cnty, PA[495]; d. 22 Oct 1897, Indiana Cnty, PA[495].

           More About Lucinda LIGHTCAP:
           Religion: Presbyterian

93. iii. John Scott LIGHTCAP, b. 21 Sep 1851, East Mahoning, Indiana Cnty, PA; d. 29 Nov 1929, East Mahoning, Indiana Cnty, PA.

94. iv. Nancy Ann LIGHTCAP, b. 14 Sep 1854, East Mahoning, Indiana Cnty, PA; d. 21 Aug 1943, Indiana Cnty, PA.

v. Silas W. LIGHTCAP[496,497], b. Oct 1856, PA[498]; d. 13 Feb 1911, Philadelphia, PA.

Notes for Silas W. LIGHTCAP:
30 April 1910 Indiana Evening Gazette (Indiana, PA) reports that Silas Lightcap of Dewey, OK is home recovering from a broken arm that occurred when he fell from a swinging bridge.
15 Feb. 1911 Indiana Evening Gazette (Indiana, PA) obituary indicates that he died in a Philadelphia Hospital on 13 Feb. 1911 that he is the son of Johnston and Susan Lightcap and is survived by brothers Harry and Scott and a sister Mrs Robert Mabon with whom he recently lived after returning from several years in the West.

More About Silas W. LIGHTCAP:
Burial: Unknown, Marion Center, PA

vi. Infant LIGHTCAP, b. 02 Oct 1861, Green Twp., Indiana Cnty, PA; d. Unknown.

95. vii. Harry Johnson LIGHTCAP, b. Sep 1864, East Mahoning, Indiana Cnty, PA; d. Unknown.

27. Benjamin Briggs[9] VAN HORN *(Joshua[8], Isaiah[7], Henry B.[6], Henry[5], Christian Barentsen[4] VAN HOORN, Barent Christiansen[3], Christian Barentsen[2], Barent Barents[1])*[499,500,501,502,503,504,505] was born Bet. 1819 - 1822 in East Mahoning, Indiana Cnty, PA[506,507,508]. He married Phoebe NEFF[509,510,511,512,513,514,515] 13 Aug 1842[516], daughter of John NEFF and Sarah PIERCE. She was born Oct 1820 in PA[517,518], and died 05 Feb 1905 in Plumville, South Mahoning Twp., Indiana Cnty, PA[519,520].

Notes for Benjamin Briggs VAN HORN:
In 1860 he is a farmer with personal effects of $350.
Exempted from Civil War service because of a disability
In 1870 he is a farmer with real estate valued at $1,600 and personal effects of $500. His father Joshua is living with the family.
in 1880 he and his wife Phoebe are living next door to his son, Harvey, and his family.
9 Nov. 1876 the Indiana Progress (Indiana, PA) reports that Benjamin Van Horn is to serve for the week on the Travers Jury representing the S. Mahoning Twp.
Will in Indiana Will book Vol 6, p. 169 1887

More About Benjamin Briggs VAN HORN:
Will: 1887, Indiana Cnty, PA Vol. 6, p. 169

Notes for Phoebe NEFF:
Died at the home of her son A. M. Van Horn.

More About Phoebe NEFF:
Burial: 07 Feb 1905, Bertcha Cemetery, Plumville, Indiana Cnty, PA[520]

More About Benjamin VAN HORN and Phoebe NEFF:
Marriage: 13 Aug 1842[521]

Children of Benjamin VAN HORN and Phoebe NEFF are:

96.   i.   Lt. John Neff[10] VAN HORN, b. 13 Aug 1842, Indiana Cnty, PA; d. 22 Oct 1907, Marion Center or Georgeville, Indiana Cnty, PA.
97.   ii. James Harvey VAN HORN, b. Abt. 1851, Indiana Cnty, PA; d. 20 Aug 1921, Kellysburg, Indiana Cnty, PA.
98.   iii. Alexander Milton VAN HORN, b. 20 Jan 1851, South Mahoning Twp., Indiana Cnty, PA; d. 28 May 1944, Homer City, Indiana Cnty, PA.
99.   iv. Sarah S. VAN HORN, b. 27 Dec 1853, Indiana Cnty, PA; d. 29 Jan 1932, Green Twp., Indiana Cnty, PA.
        v.   Rose VAN HORN[522], b. Bef. 1860; d. Aft. 1910.
        vi. Belle VAN HORN[522], b. Bef. 1860; d. Aft. 1910.

        Notes for Belle VAN HORN:
        The Indiana Progress (Indiana, PA) of 14 September 1910 indicates that Rose and Belle Van Horn visited their sister Sarah Lukehart of Barnard during this week. I have added them to the children of Benjamin and Phoebe Va Horn.

28. Christian[9] VAN HORN (*Joshua[8], Isaiah[7], Henry B.[6], Henry[5], Christian Barentsen[4] VAN HOORN, Barent Christiansen[3], Christian Barentsen[2], Barent Barents[1]*)[523,524,525,526,527] was born 05 Aug 1821 in Indiana Cnty, PA[528], and died 24 Jan 1904 in Armstrong Cnty, PA. He married (1) Rachael PEIRCE[528,529] Abt. 1843. She was born Abt. 1824 in PA[530], and died Bet. 1870 - 1880. He married (2) Caroline HOUSER Bet. 1843 - 1880. She died Unknown. He married (3) Sarah[531] Bef. 1880. She was born Abt. 1831 in PA[531], and died Bef. 1900.

Notes for Christian VAN HORN:
    In 1860 living with Enoch Dewey a Farmer. Christion has a value of $200 in real estate and $200 in personal property.
    In 1870 a carpenter with real estate worth $1,200 and personal effects of $750.
    By 1880 Christion has married widow Houser and her 3 daughters are now living with them.
    In 1900 widowed for the second time and living with daughter. This may be Margaret Houser a stepdaughter

More About Christian VAN HORN:
Occupation: Farmer, House Carpenter

More About Christian VAN HORN and Rachael PEIRCE:
Marriage: Abt. 1843

More About Christian VAN HORN and Caroline HOUSER:
Marriage: Bet. 1843 - 1880

More About Christian VAN HORN and Sarah:
Marriage: Bef. 1880

Children of Christian VAN HORN and Rachael PEIRCE are:
100.   i.   John Miles[10] VAN HORN, b. Sep 1845, PA; d. Aft. 1920.
        ii. William H. VAN HORN[532], b. Abt. 1848, PA[532]; d. Unknown.
        iii. Melissa VAN HORN[532,533], b. Abt. 1851, PA[534]; d. Unknown.
        iv. Caroline VAN HORN[534,535], b. Abt. 1852, PA[536]; d. Unknown.
101.   v.   Adessa Levina VAN HORN, b. Oct 1860, PA; d. Unknown.

29. Mary Ann[9] VAN HORN (*Joshua[8], Isaiah[7], Henry B.[6], Henry[5], Christian Barentsen[4] VAN HOORN,*

Barent Christiansen[3], Christian Barentsen[2], Barent Barents[1])[537,538,539,540] was born Abt. 1822 in Indiana Cnty, PA[541], and died Aft. 1910. She married Robert STEWART[541,542,543] 24 Aug 1845 in Gilgal Church, East Mahoning Twp., Indiana Cnty, PA[544]. He was born Abt. 1821 in PA[545], and died Aft. 1880.

Notes for Robert STEWART:
    In 1860 Farmer with land worth $700 and personal effects worth $500.
    In 1870 Lumberman with home worth $2000 and personal effects of $1000.

More About Robert STEWART:
Occupation: Millwright, Lumberman and Farmer

More About Robert STEWART and Mary VAN HORN:
Marriage: 24 Aug 1845, Gilgal Church, East Mahoning Twp., Indiana Cnty, PA[546]

Child of Mary VAN HORN and Robert STEWART is:
    i.   Robert[10] STEWART[547,548], b. Abt. 1854, PA[548]; d. Bef. 1870.

30. Henry[9] VAN HORN *(Joshua[8], Isaiah[7], Henry B.[6], Henry[5], Christian Barentsen[4] VAN HOORN, Barent Christiansen[3], Christian Barentsen[2], Barent Barents[1])[549,550,551,552,553]* was born Bet. 23 Jan 1823 - 1826 in Indiana Cnty, PA/KY[554,555], and died Bet. 26 Aug 1883 - 19 Jul 1896 in Northern Twp., Franklin Cnty, IL/Indiana Cnty, PA[556,557]. He married Martha WELLS[558,559,560] Abt. 1849. She was born Abt. 1832 in PA[561], and died Abt. 1873 in Northern Twp., Franklin Cnty, IL[562].

Notes for Henry VAN HORN:
    In 1860 his personal effects are listed as worth $450 and he is a farmer.
    Some records state he died in IL

More About Henry VAN HORN:
Burial: Unknown, Armagh Presbyterian Church, East Wheatfield Twp., Indiana Cnty, PA
Military service: Bet. 23 Jun 1863 - 21 Jan 1864, Co "F", 1nd Bn ?
Occupation: Farmer

More About Henry VAN HORN and Martha WELLS:
Marriage: Abt. 1849

Children of Henry VAN HORN and Martha WELLS are:
102.	i.	Nathan[10] VAN HORN, b. Abt. 1851, PA; d. Unknown.
	ii.	Samuel Gates VAN HORN, b. 14 Dec 1853, Plumville, Indiana Cnty, PA; d. 1856.
	iii.	Robert W. VAN HORN[563,564], b. 19 Jan 1855, Plumville, Indiana Cnty, PA[565]; d. Abt. 1932.
103.	iv.	Mazella I. VAN HORN, b. 27 Mar 1847, Plumville, Indiana Cnty, PA; d. 30 Jun 1951, West Frankfort, Franklin Cnty, IL.
	v.	Mary E. VAN HORN[565,566], b. Jun 1860, PA[567]; d. 1936, Plumville, Indiana Cnty, PA.
104.	vi.	Abner Briggs VAN HORN, b. Bet. 24 Jul 1865 - 1867, PA; d. 14 Mar 1944.
	vii.	Thomas VAN HORN[568], b. Abt. 1867, PA[568]; d. Unknown.

31. Tabitha Dorcas[9] VAN HORN *(Joshua[8], Isaiah[7], Henry B.[6], Henry[5], Christian Barentsen[4] VAN HOORN, Barent Christiansen[3], Christian Barentsen[2], Barent Barents[1])[569,570,571,572,573,574,575]* was born 02 Dec 1827 in Plumville, Indiana Cnty, PA[576], and died 13 Jan 1920 in Punxsutawney, Jefferson Cnty,

PA. She married Isaac KECK[576,577,578,579] Abt. 1848. He was born Abt. 1817 in PA[580], and died Aft. 1880.

Notes for Tabitha Dorcas VAN HORN:
    In 1900 living with daughter Etta Grube and her family.
    In 1910 she is a housekeeper for James Hunter in Punxsutawney, PA.
    In 1920 widowed and living with youngest son Lynn Keck and his wife Laura.

Notes for Isaac KECK:
    In 1850 and in 1870 his wife's name is Tabitha.
    In 1860 gives wife's name as Dorcas. Is this a second wife or was Tabitha named Tabitha Dorcas. Her grandmother was Dorcas so she may have had two names.
    In 1870 he is a hotel owner and has a real estate value worth $8000 and person effects worth $760.
    In 1880 wife is Tabitha and he is a laborer

More About Isaac KECK:
Occupation: Laborer, Merchant, Farmer and Butcher

More About Isaac KECK and Tabitha VAN HORN:
Marriage: Abt. 1848

Children of Tabitha VAN HORN and Isaac KECK are:
    i.   James Madison[10] KECK[580,581,582,583], b. Feb 1850, Jefferson Cnty, PA[584]; d. 29 Apr 1905, Punxsutawney, Jefferson Cnty, PA.

        More About James Madison KECK:
        Occupation: House Painter

    ii.   W. C. KECK, b. Feb 1850, Jefferson Cnty, PA; d. Unknown.
105.   iii.   George Milton KECK, b. Abt. 1853, Jefferson Cnty, PA; d. 02 Jul 1918, New London, Huron Cnty, OH.
106.   iv.   Martin Luther KECK, b. Feb 1857, Jefferson Cnty, PA; d. Jun 1923, Wilkinsburg, Allegheny Cnty, PA.
    v.   Thomas J. KECK[585], b. Abt. 1858, Jefferson Cnty, PA[585]; d. Bef. 1870.
107.   vi.   Ellen Etta KECK, b. May 1861, Jefferson Cnty, PA; d. 17 May 1902, Punxsutawney, Jefferson Cnty, PA.
    vii.   Charles KECK[586,587], b. Abt. 1863, Jefferson Cnty, PA[588]; d. Unknown.

        More About Charles KECK:
        Occupation: Laborer

108.   viii.   Lynn McKee KECK, b. 28 Mar 1865, Punxsutawney, Jefferson Cnty, PA; d. 02 Aug 1930, Punxsutawney, Jefferson Cnty, PA.

32. Sarah[9] VAN HORN *(Joshua[8], Isaiah[7], Henry B.[6], Henry[5], Christian Barentsen[4] VAN HOORN, Barent Christiansen[3], Christian Barentsen[2], Barent Barents[1])*[589,590,591,592] was born 30 Apr 1830 in Indiana Cnty, PA[593], and died 01 Apr 1886 in Franklin Cnty, IL. She married Jacob SINK[593,594,595] Abt. 09 Aug 1849, son of George SINKS and Margaret ADAMS. He was born 15 May 1827 in Bedford Cnty, PA[596], and died 16 Feb 1902 in Franklin Cnty, IL.

More About Sarah VAN HORN:
Burial: Unknown, Walnut Grove Cemetery, Franklin Cnty, IL

Notes for Jacob SINK:
    In 1870 he is a farmer and has an estate of land worth $1680 and personal effects of $450.
    In 1880 his last name is spelled Sinks. Sarah, Elmer and Margaret are of the home. He is a farmer born in PA as is Sarah.

    Story updated 23 Sep 2009 by Katesson. Changes based on information taken from two obituaries and includes the identification of a second marriage, and confirms Jacob's birth location as being Bedford County, PA, and his birth and death dates.

Jacob Sink is the second child of George Sink and his first (unnamed) wife and was born in St. Clair Township, Bedford County, Pennsylvania. Jacob married first Sarah VanHorn in Indiana County, Pennsylvania, and they had six children. Jacob and Sarah resided in South Mahoning Township, Indiana County, Pennsylvania until they relocated to Township 5, Range 4, Franklin County, Illinois in 1868. Jacob was a Civil War veteran who enlisted 15 Mar 1865 in Company B, 74th Pennsylvania Infantry and served primarily in Washington, DC and West Virginia. Jacob was mustered out on 29 Oct 1865 when the regiment was disbanded. Jacob applied for a Civil War pension in 1898 but we do not know if the pension was granted. After Sarah's death in 1892 Jacob married Melissa E. Wells on 9 August 1893, in Franklin County, Illinois.

Jacob's birth and death dates and locations, and the names of his wives and marriage dates and locations were taken from two published obituaries. The first appears in the March 12, 1902 edition of the Indiana Weekly Messenger newspaper, Indiana, PA. and identifies his birth location as being Bedford County, PA, and the death date of his first wife Sarah Vanhorn, and his marriage date to his second wife, Melissa Wells. The second obituary appears in The Indiana Progress newspaper in Indiana, PA, on March 12, 1902, and identifies his age at the time of his death as being 74 years, 9 months, and 1 day. Using a date calculator and his death age in years, months and days, his birth date was calculated to be 15 May 1827. Both obituaries identify his marriages, his Civil War service, and the relocation from Pennsylvania to Illinois in 1868.

More About Jacob SINK:
Military service: Company B, 74th PA Voluteers Infantry
Occupation: Farmer

More About Jacob SINK and Sarah VAN HORN:
Marriage: Abt. 09 Aug 1849

Children of Sarah VAN HORN and Jacob SINK are:
    i. Mary Ellen[10] SINK[597,598], b. 17 Sep 1851, Indiana Cnty, PA[599]; d. 15 Apr 1917, Franklin, Hamilton Cnty, IL; m. Hiram Benson MCPHERSON[600], 03 Feb 1870, Franklin Cnty, IL[600]; b. 18 Mar 1843, Lower Augusta, Northumberland Cnty, PA[600]; d. 04 Jan 1918, Franklin, Hamilton Cnty, IL.

        Notes for Mary Ellen SINK:
        In 1900 Mary indicates she has not given birth to any children.

        More About Mary Ellen SINK:
        Burial: Unknown, Richardson Hill Cemetery, Hamilton, Franklin, IL

        Notes for Hiram Benson MCPHERSON:
        In the 1870 Census both families are in Franklin Cnty, IL.
        In 1880 they are living in Shelton. Hamilton Cnty, IL and have no children.

In 1900 Mary E. states she is the mother of no children. Hiram is farming.

More About Hiram Benson MCPHERSON:
Occupation: Farmer

More About Hiram MCPHERSON and Mary SINK:
Marriage: 03 Feb 1870, Franklin Cnty, IL[600]

109.	ii.	Sarah Dorcas SINK, b. 15 Sep 1853, Indiana Cnty, PA; d. Bet. 25 Aug 1925 - 1926, Rexford, Thomas Cnty, KS.
110.	iii.	Austin Addison SINK, b. Abt. 1856, Indiana Cnty, PA; d. Bef. 1900.
	iv.	Augustus Gilbert SINK[601,602], b. Abt. 1857, Indiana Cnty, PA[603]; d. Unknown.
111.	v.	Melissa J. SINK, b. Jun 1860, Indiana Cnty, PA; d. Unknown.
112.	vi.	Elmer E. SINK, b. Bet. 29 Jul 1861 - 1863, Indiana Cnty, PA; d. 22 Jan 1898, Franklin Cnty, IL.
113.	vii.	Margaret Emma SINK, b. Bet. 02 Jul 1865 - 1867, Indiana Cnty, PA; d. Aft. 1930.

33. Samuel H.[9] VAN HORN *(Joshua[8], Isaiah[7], Henry B.[6], Henry[5], Christian Barentsen[4] VAN HOORN, Barent Christiansen[3], Christian Barentsen[2], Barent Barents[1])*[604,605,606,607,608,609] was born 1831 in Centre Twp., Indiana Cnty, PA[610,611], and died 1888 in Indiana Cnty, PA. He married (1) Rachel STEELE Bef. 1860. She died Unknown. He married (2) Miriam Work STEELE[612,613,614,615,616,617,618,619] 07 Mar 1860 in Indiana Cnty, PA[620], daughter of Matthew STEELE and Sarah WORK. She was born 02 Mar 1834 in PA[621,622], and died 03 Jul 1908 in East Mahoning, Indiana Cnty, PA[623].

More About Samuel H. VAN HORN:
Burial: Unknown, Mahoning Cemetery Indiana Cnty, PA[624]
Military service: Bet. 23 Jul 1863 - 21 Jan 1864, Civil War Co. A 2nd Ind Bn Mil & 206 P.V.I.[624]

More About Samuel VAN HORN and Rachel STEELE:
Marriage: Bef. 1860

More About Miriam Work STEELE:
Cause of Death: Stroke of Paralysis
Lived: Clayville, PA
Medical Information: Died at home of nephew Elijah Steele

Marriage Notes for Samuel VAN HORN and Miriam STEELE:
Indiana Register (Indiana, PA), Extracts April, 1860
3 April 1860
MARRIED--On the 7th March, by the same, MR. SAMUEL VANHORN, to MISS MIREM STEEL.

More About Samuel VAN HORN and Miriam STEELE:
Marriage: 07 Mar 1860, Indiana Cnty, PA[625]

Children of Samuel VAN HORN and Miriam STEELE are:

114.	i.	Anderson T.[10] VAN HORN, b. 03 Jun 1861, Indiana Cnty, PA; d. Bet. 1908 - 1910, PA.
	ii.	son VAN HORN, b. Mar 1863, Indiana Cnty, PA; d. Mar 1863, Indiana Cnty, PA.
	iii.	daughter VAN HORN, b. Sep 1868, Indiana Cnty, PA; d. Sep 1868, Indiana Cnty, PA.

34. John Hastings[9] VAN HORN *(John[8], Isaiah[7], Henry B.[6], Henry[5], Christian Barentsen[4] VAN HOORN, Barent Christiansen[3], Christian Barentsen[2], Barent Barents[1])*[626,627,628,629] was born Bet. 1824 - 1827 in PA[630], and died Aft. 1880. He married Christina WRIGHT[631,632,633] Abt. 1848. She was born Abt. 1830 in PA[634], and died Aft. 1880.

Notes for John Hastings VAN HORN:
 In 1870 living in Allegheny, PA and has personal effects valued at $1000.
 J. F. Diffenbacher's Directory of Pittsburgh and Allegheny Cities 1884 shown as John H. Van Horn living at 118 Page St. He is a foreman but in what industry is not listed.
 J. F. Diffenbacher's Directory of Pittsburgh and Allegheny Cities 1888 listed as a brakeman living at 159 Sedgwick in Pittsburgh, PA

More About John Hastings VAN HORN:
Occupation: Coal Dealer, Boatman, Mechanic, Steel Mill Worker

More About John VAN HORN and Christina WRIGHT:
Marriage: Abt. 1848

Children of John VAN HORN and Christina WRIGHT are:
      i.   Thirza[10] VAN HORN[634,635], b. Abt. 1850, PA[636]; d. Aft. 1870.
     ii.   Emma VAN HORN[636,637], b. Bet. 1852 - 1853, PA[638]; d. Aft. 1870.
    iii.   Susannah VAN HORN[638,639], b. Abt. 1855, PA[640]; d. Aft. 1870.
    iv.   Maggie VAN HORN[640,641,642], b. Abt. 1857, PA[643]; d. Aft. 1880.

            Notes for Maggie VAN HORN:
            J. F. Diffenbacher's Directory of Pittsburgh and Allegheny Cities 1888 listed as Maggie M. Van Horn at 303 Lyle St. in Pittsburgh. She is a teacher.

     v.   Millie VAN HORN[643,644], b. Abt. 1860, PA[645]; d. Aft. 1880.
    vi.   William VAN HORN[645,646], b. Abt. 1863, PA[647]; d. Aft. 1880.
115.   vii.   Harry V. VAN HORN, b. 02 Feb 1874, PA; d. 11 Nov 1953, PA.

35. William A.[9] VAN HORN *(John[8], Isaiah[7], Henry B.[6], Henry[5], Christian Barentsen[4] VAN HOORN, Barent Christiansen[3], Christian Barentsen[2], Barent Barents[1])*[648,649,650,651] was born Bet. 1826 - 1832 in PA[652], and died Unknown. He married Mary A. SHAFFNIC[653,654] Abt. 1850. She was born Abt. 1833 in PA[655,656], and died Unknown.

Notes for William A. VAN HORN:
 In 1860 he as personal effects valued at $125.
 In 1880 his father is living with him and is listed as a dependant. William is Clerk in the Court House.
 1879-1881 Directory of Pittsburgh and Allegheny Cities lists William A. a clerk and weigh master and living at 108 Taggart St the same address as his father John.
 J. F. Diffenbacher's Directory of Pittsburgh and Allegheny Cities 1884 listed at 108 Taggart St. with occupation as a clerk.

More About William A. VAN HORN:
Occupation: Boatman, Teamster, Clerk in Coal Office

More About William VAN HORN and Mary SHAFFNIC:
Marriage: Abt. 1850

Children of William VAN HORN and Mary SHAFFNIC are:

    i.   Augustus[10] VAN HORN[657,658], b. Abt. 1852, PA[659]; d. Unknown; m. Kate[660]; b. Abt. 1850, PA[660]; d. Unknown.

        Notes for Augustus VAN HORN:
        Boyd's Williamsport City Directory 1871-72 lists an Augustus G. Van Horn rooming at 51 W. Third at that city.

        More About Augustus VAN HORN:
        Occupation: Teamster

    ii.   Sarah R. VAN HORN[661], b. Abt. 1858, PA[661]; d. Unknown.
    iii. Elizabeth VAN HORN[662], b. Abt. 1867, PA[662]; d. Unknown.
    iv. William A. VAN HORN[662], b. Abt. 1874, PA[662]; d. Unknown.

36. James Devin[9] VAN HORN *(John[8], Isaiah[7], Henry B.[6], Henry[5], Christian Barentsen[4] VAN HOORN, Barent Christiansen[3], Christian Barentsen[2], Barent Barents[1])[663,664,665]* was born 1834 in PA[666,667], and died 1864 in Malvern Hill, VA[668]. He married Sarah Jane TAYLOR[668,669] 1859[670]. She was born 1840 in PA[671], and died 1906.

More About James Devin VAN HORN:
Military service: Pvt Co. H PA 1st Regiment CW died 1864
Occupation: Carpenter

More About James VAN HORN and Sarah TAYLOR:
Marriage: 1859[672]

Child of James VAN HORN and Sarah TAYLOR is:
116.   i.   John Hastings[10] VAN HORN, b. Aug 1860, PA; d. Aft. 1930.

37. Jane Elizabeth[9] VAN HORN *(Isaiah[8], Isaiah[7], Henry B.[6], Henry[5], Christian Barentsen[4] VAN HOORN, Barent Christiansen[3], Christian Barentsen[2], Barent Barents[1])[673,674,675,676,677,678,679,680]* was born 22 Oct 1835 in Indiana Cnty, PA[681], and died 11 Feb 1908 in Deckers Point, Indiana Cnty, PA. She married Stuchell LYDICK[682,683,684,685,686,687,688,689] 04 May 1854 in South Mahoning Twp., Indiana Cnty, PA[690], son of John LYDICK and Mary LYDICK. He was born 23 Mar 1834 in East Mahoning Twp., Indiana Cnty, PA[691], and died 05 Feb 1911 in Deckers Point, Indiana Cnty, PA.

Notes for Jane Elizabeth VAN HORN:
    Died at the age of 78 and was the mother of 9 living children and 45 grandchildren at her death.
    In 1900 she states she is the mother of 12 children with 10 living.

More About Jane Elizabeth VAN HORN:
Burial: 14 Feb, Taylorsville Cemetery, Indiana Cnty, PA services by Rev. J. M. Imbrie[692]

Notes for Stuchell LYDICK:
    In 1870 Stuchell is living next door to his brother Joshua and then next is his brother William. He is a carpenter and his land is worth $600 and his personal effects $400.
    In 1910 Stuchell is a widower and is boarding in the home of his son Amos's in laws. He is living with Amos his wife and their daughter in the Barr home.

More About Stuchell LYDICK:
Burial: Unknown, Taylorsville Cemetery, Green Twp., Indiana Cnty, PA[692]
Occupation: Carpenter

More About Stuchell LYDICK and Jane VAN HORN:
Marriage: 04 May 1854, South Mahoning Twp., Indiana Cnty, PA[693]
Marriage date: Ceremony according to Associate Reformed Presbyterian

Children of Jane VAN HORN and Stuchell LYDICK are:

117.	i.	John Albert[10] LYDICK, b. Feb 1855, Indiana Cnty, PA; d. 20 May 1912, Penn Run, Indiana Cnty, PA.
118.	ii.	James Irvin LYDICK, b. 11 Jul 1856, Indiana Cnty, PA; d. Aft. 1930.
119.	iii.	Samuel K. LYDICK, b. 22 Oct 1857, Indiana Cnty, PA; d. Unknown.
	iv.	Wilson T. LYDICK[694], b. 27 Mar 1859, Indiana Cnty, PA[694]; d. 09 Jun 1861, Green Twp., Indiana Cnty, PA.

> More About Wilson T. LYDICK:
> Burial: Unknown, Taylorsville Cemetery, Green Twp., Indiana Cnty, PA[695]

120.	v.	Mary A. LYDICK, b. 01 Apr 1861, Indiana Cnty, PA; d. Aft. 1910.
121.	vi.	Elmer E. LYDICK, b. 25 Feb 1863, Indiana Cnty, PA; d. 30 Jul 1927, Indiana Cnty, PA.
122.	vii.	Martha Jane LYDICK, b. 03 Sep 1865, Indiana Cnty, PA; d. 02 Mar 1943, 1302 Oakland Ave., Indiana, PA.
123.	viii.	Ida Mae LYDICK, b. 11 May 1868, East Mahoning Twp., Indiana Cnty, PA; d. 07 Feb 1945.
124.	ix.	Ira Van LYDICK, b. 16 Jan 1871, Taylorsville, Indiana Cnty, PA; d. 11 Feb 1951, Hyattsville, Prince George Cnty, MD.
	x.	Albert LYDICK, b. Abt. 1872, Indiana Cnty, PA; d. Bef. 1880.
125.	xi.	Ruth E. LYDICK, b. Bet. 12 Oct 1873 - 1876, Indiana Cnty, PA; d. 1904, Green Twp., Indiana Cnty, PA.
	xii.	Edward G. LYDICK, b. 07 Jul 1876, Indiana Cnty, PA; d. 27 Jul 1876, Indiana Cnty, PA.
126.	xiii.	Amos Burton LYDICK, b. 24 May 1878, Indiana Cnty, PA; d. 21 Jun 1954, Johnstown, Cambria Cnty, PA.
127.	xiv.	Jennie B. LYDICK, b. Mar 1879, Indiana Cnty, PA; d. 1906, PA.

38. Martha[9] VAN HORN *(Isaiah[8], Isaiah[7], Henry B.[6], Henry[5], Christian Barentsen[4] VAN HOORN, Barent Christiansen[3], Christian Barentsen[2], Barent Barents[1])*[696,697,698,699,700,701,702] was born Bet. May 1835 - 1837 in Penn Hills, Alegheny Cnty, PA[703], and died 10 Nov 1920[704]. She married (1) William Turner MCCALL[704]. He died 1881[704]. She married (2) Andrew Jackson MCGAUGHEY[705,706,707,708] Abt. 1889, son of William MCGAUGHEY and Mary BLAIR. He was born 23 Feb 1837 in PA[709], and died 1915[710].

Notes for Martha VAN HORN:
    In 1910 Martha indicates that she and Andre have been married 20 years and that she is the mother of 7 children of which only 1 is living in 1910. Since she was 53 at the time of this marriage these must be children by a first marriage.
    In 1900 they are married for 10 years and she has 5 children of which 2 are living.

More About Martha VAN HORN:
Burial: Unknown, Marion Center Cemetery, Indiana Cnty, PA
Lived: 1898, Ambrose, PA

More About Andrew MCGAUGHEY and Martha VAN HORN:
Marriage: Abt. 1889

Child of Martha VAN HORN and William MCCALL is:
128.   i.   Anna[10] MCCALL, b. Abt. 1871, PA; d. Unknown.

39. Mary P.[9] VAN HORN *(Isaiah[8], Isaiah[7], Henry B.[6], Henry[5], Christian Barentsen[4] VAN HOORN, Barent Christiansen[3], Christian Barentsen[2], Barent Barents[1])*[711,712,713,714,715,716,717] was born 27 Apr 1839 in Diamondville, Indiana Cnty, PA[718,719], and died 17 Oct 1914 in Lovejoy, East Mahoning, Indiana Cnty, PA[720]. She married William Wesley LYDICK[721,722,723,724,725] 15 Mar 1864 in South Mahoning, Indiana Cnty, PA, son of John LYDICK and Mary LYDICK. He was born 05 Sep 1839 in Ambrose, Indiana Cnty, PA[726], and died 05 Feb 1911 in Diamondville, East Mahoning, Indiana Cnty, PA.

More About Mary P. VAN HORN:
Burial: Oct 1914, Taylorsville Cemetery, Taylorsville, PA
Cause of Death: Stomach Trouble
Lived: 1898, Mitchell Mills, Indiana Cnty, PA

More About William Wesley LYDICK:
Burial: Unknown, Diamondville & Taylorville Cemetery, Indiana Cnty, PA
Military service: 206th PVI Civil War
Occupation: Laborer

Marriage Notes for Mary VAN HORN and William LYDICK:
Indiana Register (Indiana, PA), Extracts January-April, 1864
23 March 1864.
LYDICK-VANHORN. On March 15th, by J.Y. Brady, esq., [sic] at Glen Oak, LIEUT. W.G. LYDICK, of East Mahoning township, and MISS MOLLIE P. VANHORN, of South Mahoning township.

More About William LYDICK and Mary VAN HORN:
Marriage: 15 Mar 1864, South Mahoning, Indiana Cnty, PA

Children of Mary VAN HORN and William LYDICK are:
            i.   Andrew A.[10] LYDICK, b. 25 Feb 1865; d. 24 Mar 1865.
129.   ii.   Harry Logan LYDICK, b. 20 May 1866, Indiana Cnty, PA; d. 10 Nov 1912.
130.   iii.   Milton Crawford LYDICK, b. 11 Apr 1868, South Mahoning, Indiana Cnty, PA; d. 17 Nov 1934, Green Twp., Indiana Cnty, PA.
131.   iv.   Mary Emma LYDICK, b. 06 Nov 1871, PA; d. 01 Dec 1955.
132.   v.   Joseph Bell LYDICK, b. 30 Aug 1873, Deckers Point, Indiana Cnty, PA; d. 19 Jun 1920.
133.   vi.   Margaret Jane LYDICK, b. 07 Nov 1875, Indiana Cnty, PA; d. 07 Jan 1968.

40. John A.[9] VAN HORN *(Isaiah[8], Isaiah[7], Henry B.[6], Henry[5], Christian Barentsen[4] VAN HOORN, Barent Christiansen[3], Christian Barentsen[2], Barent Barents[1])*[727,728,729,730,731,732] was born Bet. 1845 - 1855 in PA[733,734,735], and died 12 Apr 1922 in Dayton, Montgomery Cnty, OH. He married Jane Narcissa LONG[735,736,737,738,739,740] Aug 1866, daughter of Daniel LONG and Martha WARREN. She was born 05 Aug 1847 in Indiana Cnty, PA[741,742], and died 25 Jan 1932 in Ganotown, Berkeley Cnty, WV.

Notes for John A. VAN HORN:

The History of Indiana County, Pennsylvania p. 292 shows John A. Van Horn as a member of the 43rd PV 1st light artillery 14th reserves and a date of February 24, 1864.

1 June 1909 Indiana Evening Gazette (Indiana, PA) announced that John A. Van Horn was one of the Civil War Veterans to receive a pension of $12/month.

John must have gone with his sister Roseanna to WV as the lived in the same county.

In 1920 John A. Van Horn is an inmate at the Old Soldiers Home in Dayton, OH. He is listed as widowed of age 74 and born in PA.

More About John A. VAN HORN:
Burial: 1922, Dayton, Montgomery Cnty, OH National Cemetery Section 2 Row 22 Site 21
Lived: 1898, DuBois, Indiana Cnty, PA
Military service: PVT ARTILLERY CIVIL WAR

Notes for Jane Narcissa LONG:

In 1880 divorced and living with her mother and step father and 3 of her children although she is listed as a separate residence she is not listed as head of household and rather as a stepchild to Daniel Long.

Narcissa is buried alone in the cemetery. In the 1880 Census she is listed as being divorced with three children. She is also listed as being a servant. I believe after she divorced she was forced to move in with her parents and become a servant in the household. All of her children are listed as being grandchildren to the head of the household. The head of household was Daniel Long although he is listed as her stepfather.

In 1910 she is a widowed lodger living in Gerrardstown, WV with the Bagley(Gageby) family. This is her daughter Florida and her husband.

In 1920 again living with Charles Gageby and Florida and is listed as an aunt. They may be hiding the relationship for some reason.

In 1930 living with her grandson William Gageby in a home she owns worth $500. Her name is given as Alice Van Horn age 82 born in PA with parents born in PA.

More About Jane Narcissa LONG:
Burial: Unknown, Central Chapel Cemetry, Ganotwon, Berkeley Cnty, WV

More About John VAN HORN and Jane LONG:
Divorce: Bef. 1880
Marriage: Aug 1866

Children of John VAN HORN and Jane LONG are:
134.   i.   William[10] VAN HORN, b. Jul 1868, PA; d. Unknown.
          ii.   Francis VAN HORN[743,744,745,746], b. Abt. Sep 1869, PA[747]; d. Aft. 1930; m. Rebecca S.[748,749,750], Abt. 1889; b. Abt. 1867, PA[751]; d. Aft. 1930.

          Notes for Francis VAN HORN:
          If this is Frank Van Horn then he is married to Rebecca and lived in Martinsburg where his mother died.

          In 1910 he is married to R. and both are boarding in Martinsburg. He is a foreman in a Knitting mill. He and Rebecca have been married for 20 years and they have had no children.

          In 1920 he is married to Rebecca S. and both are born in PA as well as are his parents. He is a superintendent in a mill.

          In 1930 he is living with Rebecca in a home on burke Street in Martinsburg, WV that they own worth $7,000 and they have a radio. He is a Superintendent in a Hosiery Mill.

More About Francis VAN HORN:
Employment: 1920, Superintendant Rolling Mill

More About Francis VAN HORN and Rebecca S.:
Marriage: Abt. 1889

        iii.   Delia VAN HORN, b. 1871, Berkeley Cnty, WV; d. Bef. 1880.
        iv.   Sarah VAN HORN[752], b. Abt. 1872, Berkeley Cnty, WV[752]; d. Unknown.
135.   v.   Nora Mary Agnes VAN HORN, b. 29 Dec 1874, PA; d. 24 Oct 1957, Martinsburg, Berkeley Cnty, WV.
136.   vi.   Florida Anna Vrginia VAN HORN, b. 05 Jun 1878, Ganotown, Berkeley Cnty, WV; d. Aft. 1930.

41. Roseannah[9] VAN HORN *(Isaiah[8], Isaiah[7], Henry B.[6], Henry[5], Christian Barentsen[4] VAN HOORN, Barent Christiansen[3], Christian Barentsen[2], Barent Barents[1])*[753,754,755,756,757,758,759,760] was born 24 May 1850 in Altoona, Blair Cnty, PA[761,762,763], and died 02 May 1926 in Shanghai, Berkeley Cnty, WV. She married John William HUTZLER[764,765,766,767,768] 23 Feb 1869 in Martinsburg, Berkeley Cnty, WV, son of Alfred HUTZLER and Hannah WILLIAMS. He was born Bet. 24 Jul 1847 - Jan 1848 in Glengary, Berkeley Cnty, WV/OH[769], and died 19 Jan 1914 in Shanghai, Berkeley Cnty, WV.

More About Roseannah VAN HORN:
Lived: 1898, WV

Notes for John William HUTZLER:
    Living next to his father and brothers and sisters with Rosa in Berkeley Cnty, WV in 1870. They are newly married. He is a farmer
    1900 Rose Anna and John are living with 6 children. they have been married for 30 years and have 10 children all of whom are living.
    Living next to Ernest Hutzler and his wife and children in 1910. Ernest is of the age to be the child of Rose and John.
    According to the Frederick Post (Frederick, MD) 22 Jan 1914 John .W Hutzler died at the home of his son Ernest.

More About John William HUTZLER:
Burial: Unknown, Presbyterian Cemetery, Gerrardstown, Berkeley Cnty, WV

More About John HUTZLER and Roseannah VAN HORN:
Marriage: 23 Feb 1869, Martinsburg, Berkeley Cnty, WV

Children of Roseannah VAN HORN and John HUTZLER are:
137.   i.   Mary Pearl[10] HUTZLER, b. 1870, Shanghai, Berkeley Cnty, WV; d. 28 Aug 1949, Brunswick, MD.
138.   ii.   Charles Strother HUTZLER, b. 21 Aug 1872, Shanghai, Berkeley Cnty, WV; d. 19 Jul 1936, Gerrardstown, Berkeley Cnty, WV.
139.   iii.   William Logan HUTZLER, b. 1874, Shanghai, Berkeley Cnty, WV; d. 09 Dec 1957, Martinsburg, Berkeley Cnty, WV.
140.   iv.   Nannie Mae HUTZLER, b. 14 Mar 1877, Shanghai, Berkeley Cnty, WV; d. 1948, Berkeley Springs, WV.
141.   v.   Ernest Irvin HUTZLER, b. 13 Jul 1879, Shanghai, Berkeley Cnty, WV; d. 1948, Ridgeway, Berkeley Cnty, WV.
142.   vi.   Thettie Jane HUTZLER, b. Bet. 30 Nov 1881 - 1882, Shanghai, Berkeley Cnty, WV; d. 20 Feb 1939, Martinsburg, Berkeley Cnty, WV.

143. vii. John Milton HUTZLER, b. 18 Jul 1884, Shanghai, Berkeley Cnty, WV; d. 24 Jul 1965, Harrisonburg, WV.

   viii. Howard Calvin HUTZLER[770,771], b. Bet. Jan - 26 Jun 1887, Shanghai, Berkeley Cnty, WV[771]; d. Aft. 1949, OH.

144. ix. Harwood Chapman HUTZLER, b. Bet. 26 Jan - Jun 1887, Shanghai, Berkeley Cnty, WV; d. 15 May 1929, Berkeley Cnty, WV.

   x. George Sherman HUTZLER[772,773], b. 11 Jul 1889, Shanghai, Berkeley Cnty, WV[773]; d. 1931, Berkeley Cnty, WV; m. Frances Margaret PALMER[774], 16 Apr 1912, Berkeley Cnty, WV[774]; b. 09 Feb 1892, Berkeley Cnty, WV; d. 01 Feb 1955, Berkeley Cnty, WV.

More About George HUTZLER and Frances PALMER:
Marriage: 16 Apr 1912, Berkeley Cnty, WV[774]

42. Martha[9] VAN HORN *(William G.[8], Isaiah[7], Henry B.[6], Henry[5], Christian Barentsen[4] VAN HOORN, Barent Christiansen[3], Christian Barentsen[2], Barent Barents[1])[775]* was born 20 Feb 1828 in PA[775], and died 04 Jul 1856. She married Aaron HOPKINS[775,776,777,778] Abt. 1846, son of Robert HOPKINS and Roseanna PATTERSON. He was born Abt. 1820 in PA[779], and died Bet. 1880 - 1900.

Notes for Aaron HOPKINS:
 In 1850 living with father, brother and wife and young daughter and son in his father's home. His mother is deceased. Living only a couple of farms from Martha's uncle George Logan Van Horn.
 In 1860 Aaron has a new wife Elizabeth as his first wife is deceased leaving him with 4 young children. He is a farmer and has an estate of $1400 in land and $350 in personal effects.

More About Aaron HOPKINS and Martha VAN HORN:
Marriage: Abt. 1846

Children of Martha VAN HORN and Aaron HOPKINS are:
  i. Martha I.[10] HOPKINS[779,780], b. Abt. 1848, PA[781]; d. Unknown.
  ii. Nancy HOPKINS[782], b. Mar 1850, PA[782]; d. Unknown.
145. iii. James N. HOPKINS, b. Abt. Jun 1850, PA; d. Unknown.
  iv. John Taylor HOPKINS[782,783,784], b. Bet. 1850 - 1852, PA[784]; d. Unknown.
  v. Scott HOPKINS[784,785,786], b. Bet. 1852 - 1854, PA[786]; d. Unknown.

43. William G.[9] VAN HORN, JR *(William G.[8], Isaiah[7], Henry B.[6], Henry[5], Christian Barentsen[4] VAN HOORN, Barent Christiansen[3], Christian Barentsen[2], Barent Barents[1])[787]* was born 11 Sep 1829 in PA[787], and died 09 Nov 1866. He married Maria PATTERSON. She died Unknown.

Notes for William G. VAN HORN, JR:
 According to the 1850 census William and Magaret are twins showing them as the same age and with a parenthesis around both of them. It would indicate that they are both born in about 1831. Other information indicates that they were born about 10 months apart and were not twins.

Children of William VAN HORN and Maria PATTERSON are:
  i. Nathan[10] VAN HORN, b. 1852; d. Unknown.
  ii. Robert W. VAN HORN, b. 1855; d. Unknown.
  iii. Mezella I. VAN HORN, b. 1857; d. Unknown.
  iv. Mary E. VAN HORN, b. 1860; d. Unknown.

44. Margaret J.[9] VAN HORN *(William G.[8], Isaiah[7], Henry B.[6], Henry[5], Christian Barentsen[4] VAN HOORN, Barent Christiansen[3], Christian Barentsen[2], Barent Barents[1])*[787,788,789,790,791] was born 19 Jul 1831 in PA[792], and died 04 Mar 1905 in Smicksburg, Indiana Cnty, PA[793]. She married David STEAR[794,795,796] 1850, son of George STEAR and Catherine FISHER. He was born 03 Aug 1817 in West Mahoning Twp., Indiana Cnty, PA[797], and died 25 Aug 1886 in Smicksburg, Indiana Cnty, PA[798].

Notes for David STEAR:
In 1870 he is a farmer and his land value is $5000 and personal effects $1380.
In 1880 he is a farmer and he has living with him an Enoch C. Stear a dry goods merchant age 47 born PA.

More About David STEAR and Margaret VAN HORN:
Marriage: 1850

Children of Margaret VAN HORN and David STEAR are:
146.   i.   Caroline Widmina[10] STEAR, b. Abt. 1851, PA; d. Aft. 1930.
147.   ii.   David Blanchard STEAR, b. 05 May 1866, Indiana Cnty, PA; d. 04 Sep 1936, Trade City, PA.
148.   iii. Lilly May STEAR, b. 1869, Trade City, Indiana Cnty, PA; d. 14 Sep 1954, Grove City, Mercer Cnty, PA.
149.   iv.   Ambrose Kelly STEAR, b. Mar 1871, PA; d. 24 Nov 1928, Trade City, PA.
150.   v.   Enoch Blair STEAR, b. 31 Oct 1874, Grove City, Mercer Cnty, PA; d. Bef. 04 Sep 1936.
151.   vi.   Van Horn STEAR, b. Bet. 1877 - 1879, PA; d. Aft. 04 Sep 1936.

45. Catherine[9] VAN HORN *(William G.[8], Isaiah[7], Henry B.[6], Henry[5], Christian Barentsen[4] VAN HOORN, Barent Christiansen[3], Christian Barentsen[2], Barent Barents[1])*[799,800,801,802] was born Bet. 11 Sep 1832 - 1838 in PA[803], and died 16 May 1905. She married Jacob L. COON[804,805,806,807] 05 May 1856 in Indiana Cnty, PA, son of Harrison COON and Mary LANTZ. He was born Bet. 19 Dec 1835 - 1836 in Perry Twp., Jefferson Cnty, PA[808], and died 19 Oct 1910 in Punxsutawney, Jefferson Cnty, PA[809].

Notes for Jacob L. COON:
15 Aug 1908 Indiana Evening Gazette (Indiana, PA) Jacob Coon of Plumville is listed as attending the reunion of the William Van Horn family reunion.
In 1910 he indicates he is married for a second time about 3 years earlier but is separated at the time of the census.

More About Jacob L. COON:
Burial: 1910, Perrysville Cemetery
Occupation: 1880, Farmer

Marriage Notes for Catherine VAN HORN and Jacob COON:
Indiana Register, May-June 1856 Extracts 6 May 1856 (Tuesday)
MARRIED. On the 1st inst., by John Chambers, Esq., MR. JACOB L. COON,of North Mahoning township, to MISS CATHERINE VAN HORN, of West Mahoning township.

More About Jacob COON and Catherine VAN HORN:
Marriage: 05 May 1856, Indiana Cnty, PA

Children of Catherine VAN HORN and Jacob COON are:

    i.   Theophilus Albert[10] COON[810,811,812], b. Bet. 1855 - 1856, PA[813]; d. Aft. 1929.

        More About Theophilus Albert COON:
        Employment: 1880, Carpenter

| 152. | ii. | Alice Melissa COON, b. Bet. 1856 - 28 Apr 1858, PA; d. 25 Jun 1918. |

      iii.   Mary COON[814], b. Abt. 1856, PA[814]; d. Bef. 1929.

153.   iv.   Lanieann COON, b. 16 Jun 1859, PA; d. Aft. 1910.

154.   v.   Charles Barclay COON, b. 03 Feb 1862, PA; d. 14 Mar 1904, Pittsburgh, Alleghney Cnty, PA.

155.   vi.   George L. COON, b. 26 Jun 1854, PA; d. 31 Aug 1954.

      vii.   Harry COON[814,815], b. 29 May 1867, PA[816]; d. 25 Nov 1882.

156.   viii.   Augustus Kimmel COON, b. 14 Mar 1869, Perrysville, Jefferson Cnty, PA; d. 19 Sep 1929, Pittsburgh, Alleghney Cnty, PA.

      ix.   Frank COON, b. 16 Dec 1871, PA; d. 02 Nov 1912, Lawton, OK[817].

        More About Frank COON:
        Cause of Death: Cruched by a falling oil drilling derrick in Lawton, OK
        Employment: 1912, Oil Well Driller
        Lived: 1910, Oklahoma

157.   x.   Wade Blair COON, b. Bet. 26 Aug 1873 - 1874, PA; d. 17 Jun 1943, Los Angeles Cnty, CA.

      xi.   Edith R. COON[818], b. 18 Aug 1878, Horatio, Jefferson Cnty, PA[818]; d. 03 Apr 1922, Harrisburg, PA; m. Walker WELLS; b. 1881; d. 26 Dec 1910, Punxsutawney, Jefferson Cnty, PA.

        More About Walker WELLS:
        Burial: Unknown, Greenwood Cemetery, Punxsutawney, Jefferson Cnty, PA

46. Dorcas[9] VAN HORN *(William G.*[8]*, Isaiah*[7]*, Henry B.*[6]*, Henry*[5]*, Christian Barentsen*[4] *VAN HOORN, Barent Christiansen*[3]*, Christian Barentsen*[2]*, Barent Barents*[1]*)*[819,820,821,822] was born 06 Aug 1833 in Smicksburg, Indiana Cnty, PA[823], and died Bet. 15 Mar 1876 - 1889 in Smicksburg, Indiana Cnty, PA. She married George Leroy CONDRON[824,825,826,827] 13 Mar 1855, son of Jacob CONDRON and Elizabeth LOCKHARD. He was born 29 Apr 1824 in PA[828], and died Aft. 1889 in Smicksburg, Indiana Cnty, PA.

Notes for George Leroy CONDRON:
    1860 Census Real Estate $400 and Personal Effects $250. He is a house carpenter and has 4 children one an unnamed infant boy.
    28 February 1878 Indiana Progress (Indiana, PA) George Condron is the Smicksburg, PA assessor.
    8 May 1889 the Indiana Progress(Indiana, PA) reported on a surprise birthday party held the 29th of April in George Condron's home. A pair of willow rockers were given to Mr. and Mrs. Condron by the Rev Streamer and G. H Warren added a speech characteristic of himself, time was spend discussing old times and singing buckwheat notes.

More About George Leroy CONDRON:
Occupation: House Carpenter

Marriage Notes for Dorcas VAN HORN and George CONDRON:
Indiana Register (Indiana, PA) 20 March 1855

MARRIED. On the 13th inst., by C. Lowe, Esq., MR. GEORGE CONDRON, to MISS DAREUS VAN HORN, both of Schmicksburg [sic], Indiana county.

More About George CONDRON and Dorcas VAN HORN:
Marriage: 13 Mar 1855

Children of Dorcas VAN HORN and George CONDRON are:

158.   i.   Laura Jane[10] CONDRON, b. Bet. 24 Oct 1854 - 1855, Smicksburg, Indiana Cnty, PA; d. 08 Oct 1915, Smicksburg, Indiana Cnty, PA.

159.   ii.   James Melantheon CONDRON, b. Mar 1856, Indiana Cnty, PA; d. Unknown.

160.   iii.   William Madison CONDRON, b. 18 Apr 1858, Smicksburg, Indiana Cnty, PA; d. 16 Oct 1918, Punxsutawney, Jefferson Cnty, PA.

        iv.   Jacob Leroy CONDRON[828,829,830,831,832,833], b. Mar 1862, Indiana Cnty, PA[834,835]; d. Aft. 1909; m. Martha Jane[836,837], Abt. 1890; b. May 1867, PA[838,839]; d. Unknown.

Notes for Jacob Leroy CONDRON:
24 Aug 1909 Indiana Evening Gazette (Indiana, PA) 62 descendents of William Van Horn gathered at the home in North Point to hear J. L Condron give the address. In 1930 Jacob L. is living next door to his brother Cornelius and Wife. He is not employed, owns his home worth $15,000 and does not have a radio. He indicates he is married but no wife is listed.

More About Jacob Leroy CONDRON:
Occupation: House Carpenter

More About Jacob CONDRON and Martha Jane:
Marriage: Abt. 1890

161.   v.   Cornelius Elsworth CONDRON, b. 17 Nov 1861, Indiana Cnty, PA; d. 07 Jul 1946, Los Angeles,CA.

        vi.   Marion M. CONDRON[840,841], b. 07 Apr 1865, Indiana Cnty, PA[842]; d. Unknown.

162.   vii.   Charles Gillis CONDRON, b. Abt. 18 Nov 1867, Indiana Cnty, PA; d. 09 Aug 1928, Verona, Allegheny Cnty, PA.

163.   viii.   George A. CONDRON, b. Mar 1870, Indiana Cnty, PA; d. Unknown.

164.   ix.   Olive Florence CONDRON, b. 02 Jul 1872, Indiana Cnty, PA; d. 1945, Jefferson Cnty, PA.

165.   x.   Angus Blanchard CONDRON, b. Jan 1875, Indiana Cnty, PA; d. 25 Nov 1904, PA.

47. Nancy[9] VAN HORN *(William G.[8], Isaiah[7], Henry B.[6], Henry[5], Christian Barentsen[4] VAN HOORN, Barent Christiansen[3], Christian Barentsen[2], Barent Barents[1])*[843,844,845,846,847] was born Bet. 18 Aug 1835 - 1836 in PA[848], and died 1916 in McKees Rock, Allegheny Cnty, PA. She married Jacob B. O'CONNER[849,850,851,852] Abt. 1855. He was born Abt. 1831 in PA[853], and died Bet. 1880 - 1900.

More About Nancy VAN HORN:
Burial: Unknown, Blairsville, Indiana Cnty, PA
Lived: McKees Rock, Allegheny Cnty, PA

More About Jacob B. O'CONNER:
Occupation: Boatman, Baggage Master on Cars, Railroad Clerk

More About Jacob O'CONNER and Nancy VAN HORN:
Marriage: Abt. 1855

Children of Nancy VAN HORN and Jacob O'CONNER are:
  i.   James[10] O'CONNER[853], b. Abt. 1857, Indiana Cnty, PA[853]; d. Bef. 1870.
  ii. Zoe Frances O'CONNER[853,854,855], b. May 1860, Indiana Cnty, PA[856]; d. Unknown.
  iii. Ida Jane O'CONNER[857,858], b. Abt. 1861, Indiana Cnty, PA[859]; d. Unknown.
  iv. Robert Parnold O'CONNER[859,860], b. Abt. 1862, PA[861]; d. Unknown.
  v.   Jacob B. A. O'CONNER[861,862], b. Apr 1863, PA[863]; d. Unknown; m. Kate, Abt. 1894; b. Oct 1856, PA; d. Unknown.

        Notes for Jacob B. A. O'CONNER:
        In 1900 Jacob is given as Park O'Conner. In one census he was listed as Jacob P. A. and in another Jacob B. Because of the birth date and the fact that his sister Zoe and mother Nancy are living with him I have decided that his is the Jacob O'Conner of earlier listings. He is married and has been married for 5 years with no children of this marriage. His mother is a widow and is shown as the mother of only one living child. this is a major error as his mother and sister are living with their mother so at least 2 are living.

        More About Jacob O'CONNER and Kate:
        Marriage: Abt. 1894

  vi. Edward P. O'CONNER[863,864], b. Abt. 1867, PA[865]; d. Unknown.
  vii. Ada Leona O'CONNER[866], b. Abt. 1876, PA[866]; d. Unknown.

48. George Logan[9] VAN HORN *(William G.[8], Isaiah[7], Henry B.[6], Henry[5], Christian Barentsen[4] VAN HOORN, Barent Christiansen[3], Christian Barentsen[2], Barent Barents[1])*[867,868,869,870,871,872] was born 29 Dec 1840 in West Mahoning Twp., Indiana Cnty, PA[873,874], and died 14 Sep 1909 in North Point, Jefferson Cnty, PA[875,876]. He married Catherine Araminta TRAVIS[877,878,879,880] Bef. 1867. She was born Bet. 06 Apr - May 1848 in Ridgeway, Indiana Cnty, PA[881,882,883], and died 24 Dec 1915 in Indiana Cnty, PA[883].

Notes for George Logan VAN HORN:
        In 1870 he is living with his parents and wife and newly born daughter,
        19 May 1870 the Indiana Progress(Indiana, PA) listed the 80 acres of George L. Van Horn of West Mahoning for a tax sale.
        20 April 1876 issue of Indiana Progress(Indiana, PA) includes and item that George L. Van Horn has been mustered out of the military Company G. 67th Regiment of the Pennsylvania volunteers and is farming in North Mahoning Twp. The article was a summary of military service in Indiana Cnty, PA.
        2 May 1906 the Indiana Weekly reports that Logan Van horn is seriously injured due to a premature explosion while working near North Point.
        George Logan VanHorn served with the Union Army, Co. G,67 Reg.PVI in the Civil War. He was a POW at Libby Prison in Richmond,VA from 9 Oct.1862-14 Jul.1865. He was married to Catherine D. Travis They share a tombstone in Northpoint Cemetery, Northpoint, PA.

More About George Logan VAN HORN:
Burial: Unknown, w45 Northpoint Cemetery, Indiana Cnty, PA[884]
Cause of Death: Stroke
Medical Information: Died at home in North Point, PA
Military service: Bet. 19 Sep 1862 - 14 Jul 1865, Civil War Co. G, 67th Regiment P.V.[884]
Religion: United Brethren Church

Notes for Catherine Araminta TRAVIS:
In 1910 is widowed, the mother of 6 children all living and has her own income.
Catherine received a widows veterans pension for the Civil War Service of George Logan Van Horn,

More About Catherine Araminta TRAVIS:
Burial: Unknown, North Point Cemetery, Indiana Cnty, PA

More About George VAN HORN and Catherine TRAVIS:
Marriage: Bef. 1867

Children of George VAN HORN and Catherine TRAVIS are:

i.   Tirzale E.[10] VAN HORN[885,886,887,888,889,890,891], b. Bet. Jan - May 1870, Indiana Cnty, PA[892,893]; d. 11 Mar 1923, Ridgeway, Elk Cnty, PA[894].

Notes for Tirzale E. VAN HORN:
In 1870 her name is Tirsa Van Horn 5 months old in June.
In 1880 she is Tersa E. Van Horn age 10 years.
In 1900 census living with the Brooks family as a lodger. She is single and is a bookkeeper.
15 August 1906 Indiana Progress(Indiana, PA) reported the sale of a lot by J. Dorsey Neal to Tirzah E. Van Horn in West Mahoning for $300.
In 1910 single age 40 bookkeeper for a newspaper and lives with the Barden family on Church Street in Ridgeway, PA.
In 1920 single age 49 as the census was enumerated in January. She owns her home free and clear in Ridgeway, PA on East Main Street. She is not employed on this date. Her name is spelled Tirzah.

More About Tirzale E. VAN HORN:
Burial: 14 Mar 1923, Edgewood Cemetery, Saltsburg, PA
Cause of Death: Struck by a rearing horse while going home from church.
Employment: 1920, Bookkeeper for Newspaper
Lived: Ridgeway, PA

166.   ii.   Stella M. VAN HORN, b. 28 Feb 1871, North Point, Indiana Cnty, PA; d. 02 May 1940, Indiana Cnty, PA.
167.   iii. Anna B. VAN HORN, b. Oct 1872, Indiana Cnty, PA; d. Aft. 22 Sep 1909.
168.   iv.   Elmer Monroe VAN HORN, b. 13 Jan 1877, Indiana Cnty, PA; d. Aft. 1930.
169.   v.   Arnold Wilton VAN HORN, b. Jul 1878, Indiana Cnty, PA; d. 1929, Armstrong Cnty, PA.
170.   vi.   Angus Vanzant VAN HORN, b. 26 Aug 1880, Indiana Cnty, PA; d. Aft. 1920.

49. Mary Lucinda[9] VAN HORN *(William G.[8], Isaiah[7], Henry B.[6], Henry[5], Christian Barentsen[4] VAN HOORN, Barent Christiansen[3], Christian Barentsen[2], Barent Barents[1])*[895,896,897,898,899] was born Bet. 23 Feb 1844 - 1846 in PA[900,901], and died Aft. 1909. She married George NEALE[902,903] 12 Jan 1864, son of John NEIL and Rachel BLOSE. He was born Abt. 1842 in PA[903], and died Bet. 1871 - 1880.

Notes for Mary Lucinda VAN HORN:
In the 1880 census May L is living with 3 daughters and is widowed.

Notes for George NEALE:
In 1870 living in West Mahoning Twp., Indiana Cnty, PA between John and Abraham Neal of the ages that one is likely his father and the other is his uncle. John may be his father as Rachel is

John's wife and George and Lucinda's first daughter is Rachel. George has a valuation of $2500 for land and $550 for personal effects.

More About George NEALE:
Occupation: Farmer

More About George NEALE and Mary VAN HORN:
Marriage: 12 Jan 1864

Children of Mary VAN HORN and George NEALE are:

    i. Mary Rachel[10] NEAL[904,905], b. Abt. 1864, PA[905]; d. Unknown.
    ii. Zoe Wilemina NEAL[906,907,908], b. Abt. 1866, PA[909]; d. Unknown.
    iii. Ruth NEAL[910,911,912], b. Abt. Aug 1869, PA[913]; d. Unknown.
    iv. Nancy Ellen NEAL[914,915], b. 22 Nov 1871, North Point, Indiana Cnty, PA[915]; d. Unknown; m. John Crissman STEAR; d. Unknown.

        Notes for John Crissman STEAR:
        15 Aug 1908 Indiana Evening Gazette (Indiana, PA) John Stear and family are listed as attending the William Van Horn family reunion

50. Samuel Redding[9] VAN HORN *(William G.[8], Isaiah[7], Henry B.[6], Henry[5], Christian Barentsen[4] VAN HOORN, Barent Christiansen[3], Christian Barentsen[2], Barent Barents[1])*[916,917,918] was born Bet. 15 Feb 1850 - 1851 in North Point, Indiana Cnty, PA[919,920], and died Bet. 13 - 23 May 1906 in Brockway, Jefferson Cnty, PA[921]. He married Elizabeth Odessa CRAFT[922,923] Bet. 1870 - 1875 in Brockway, Jefferson Cnty, PA, daughter of William CRAFT and Lydia OHL. She was born 10 Jan 1865 in Brookville, Jefferson Cnty, PA[924], and died 28 Jul 1932 in Falls Creek, Jefferson/Clearfield Cnty, PA or Brockway, Jefferson Cnty, PA.

Notes for Samuel Redding VAN HORN:
    In the Indiana Progress(Indiana, PA) of 8 Oct. 1874 Samuel R. Van Horn is listed as the prosecutor of Benjamin McHenry for assault.

More About Samuel Redding VAN HORN:
Occupation: Well Driller

Notes for Elizabeth Odessa CRAFT:
    In 1910 she is a widow living with her son and his family.

More About Samuel VAN HORN and Elizabeth CRAFT:
Marriage: Bet. 1870 - 1875, Brockway, Jefferson Cnty, PA

Children of Samuel VAN HORN and Elizabeth CRAFT are:

    i. Merril[10] VAN HORN[925], b. Nov 1877, PA[925]; d. Unknown; Adopted child.
171.   ii. Edward Harry VAN HORN, b. 05 Jul 1884, Belleview, Stanton Cnty, PA; d. 28 Jan 1951, Brockway, Jefferson Cnty, PA.

51. Dorcas[9] HAMILTON *(Nancy[8] VAN HORN, Isaiah[7], Henry B.[6], Henry[5], Christian Barentsen[4] VAN HOORN, Barent Christiansen[3], Christian Barentsen[2], Barent Barents[1])*[926,927,928] was born Abt. 1831 in PA[929], and died 08 Apr 1890. She married William Allen STEELE[930,931,932,933] 11 Jun 1851 in Indiana Cnty, PA[934], son of Matthew STEELE and Sarah WORK. He was born 28 Aug 1828 in Centre, Indiana Cnty, PA[935,936], and died 01 Oct 1901.

Notes for William Allen STEELE:
    In 1860 living near his father in law with a land value of $1000 and $250 in personal effects. A James Stewart is living in the home as a farm laborer.
    In 1900 widowed and living with his son Elmer and his family.

More About William Allen STEELE:
Occupation: Farmer

More About William STEELE and Dorcas HAMILTON:
Marriage: 11 Jun 1851, Indiana Cnty, PA[937]

Children of Dorcas HAMILTON and William STEELE are:
172.	i.	Elijah Work[10] STEELE, b. 26 Apr 1852, East Mahoning Twp.,Indiana Cnty, PA; d. 20 Aug 1917.
	ii.	Alice Amelia STEELE[938,939], b. 27 Feb 1854, Indiana Cnty, PA[940]; d. Unknown.
	iii.	Lettice Jane STEELE[940,941], b. 15 Nov 1856, Indiana Cnty, PA[942]; d. Unknown.
	iv.	Hugh Clark STEELE[943], b. 27 Feb 1863, Indiana Cnty, PA; d. Apr 1865, Indiana Cnty, PA.
	v.	Ida Sarah STEELE[943], b. 15 Nov 1868, Indiana Cnty, PA; d. Unknown.
	vi.	Alvord Hamilton STEELE[943], b. 11 Jun 1866, Indiana Cnty, PA; d. Unknown.
173.	vii.	Robert Elmer STEELE, b. 16 Apr 1872, Indiana Cnty, PA; d. Unknown.
	viii.	William Hastings STEELE, b. 13 Oct 1874, Indiana Cnty, PA; d. Unknown.
	ix.	Margaret Ellen STEELE[943], b. 26 Jun 1877, Indiana Cnty, PA; d. 25 Mar 1949; m. Willis Orr SUTTER[943], 01 Jun 1907; d. 06 Dec 1931.

        More About Willis SUTTER and Margaret STEELE:
        Marriage: 01 Jun 1907

52. Margaret[9] HAMILTON *(Nancy[8] VAN HORN, Isaiah[7], Henry B.[6], Henry[5], Christian Barentsen[4] VAN HOORN, Barent Christiansen[3], Christian Barentsen[2], Barent Barents[1])*[944,945] was born 15 Mar 1833 in East Mahoning Twp., Indiana Cnty, PA[946], and died 07 Sep 1874 in Indiana Cnty, PA. She married James Monroe WORK 13 Oct 1853, son of William WORK and Nancy BROWN. He was born 08 Apr 1830 in East Mahoning Twp., Indiana Cnty, PA, and died 23 Nov 1895 in Indiana Cnty, PA.

Notes for James Monroe WORK:
    Indiana county commissioner 182-1874. Teacher, farmer, lumberman, and barn builder. In 1871 he moved to Marion Center and manufactured furniture and blinds for windows. After 17 years in manufacturing he turned to undertaking. He as a Justice of the Peace. In 1863 he enlisted in the PA militia and served briefly on the southern PA border. He was a member of the Mahoning United Presbyterian Church.

More About James WORK and Margaret HAMILTON:
Marriage: 13 Oct 1853

Children of Margaret HAMILTON and James WORK are:
	i.	Rhoda Haseltine[10] WORK, b. 22 Jan 1855, Indiana Cnty, PA; d. 05 Jun 1864.
	ii.	Clara Frances WORK, b. 11 Sep 1856, Indiana Cnty, PA; d. 20 Jun 1864.
	iii.	Jeremiah Walter WORK, b. 12 May 1858, Indiana Cnty, PA; d. 08 Apr 1925; m. Ida Leila WESTON; d. Unknown.
	iv.	Carl Hamilton WORK, b. 15 Sep 1860, Indiana Cnty, PA; d. Unknown.
	v.	Jessie Fremont WORK, b. 01 Aug 1862, Indiana Cnty, PA; d. 18 Dec 1939; m.

James Loughry PARK, JR; d. Unknown.

vi.   Edsell Hale WORK, b. 08 Sep 1865, Indiana Cnty, PA; d. 15 Jul 1869.

vii.   Elizabeth Estella WORK, b. 30 Oct 1868, Indiana Cnty, PA; d. 14 Apr 1910; m.
       Robert Craig MEANOR, Mar 1887; d. 13 Dec 1892.

       More About Robert MEANOR and Elizabeth WORK:
       Marriage: Mar 1887

viii. Lottie Nancy WORK, b. 21 Sep 1869, Indiana Cnty, PA; d. 20 Oct 1956; m. Samuel
       RUGH, 09 Dec 1886; d. Unknown.

       More About Samuel RUGH and Lottie WORK:
       Marriage: 09 Dec 1886

ix.   Mary Carothers WORK, b. 07 Aug 1872, Indiana Cnty, PA; d. 10 Jan 1942; m.
       Austin Lewis GUTHRIE, 09 Apr 1889; d. Unknown.

       More About Austin GUTHRIE and Mary WORK:
       Marriage: 09 Apr 1889

x.   Margaret Hamilton WORK, b. 01 Sep 1874, Indiana Cnty, PA; d. 12 Jul 1942; m.
       Jackson Boggs GUTHRIE, 24 Dec 1895; d. Unknown.

       More About Jackson GUTHRIE and Margaret WORK:
       Marriage: 24 Dec 1895

53. Bennett Work[9] VAN HORN *(George Logan[8], Isaiah[7], Henry B.[6], Henry[5], Christian Barentsen[4] VAN HOORN, Barent Christiansen[3], Christian Barentsen[2], Barent Barents[1])*[947,948,949,950,951,952,953,954,955,956,957,958] was born Bet. 13 May 1847 - 1851 in Indiana Cnty, PA[959,960,961], and died 01 Feb 1925 in Georgeville, Indiana Cnty, PA[962,963]. He married Mary Belle WARDEN[964,965,966,967,968,969,970,971] Bet. 01 Jan 1872 - 1873 in East Mahoning Twp., Indiana Cnty, PA[972], daughter of Robert WARDEN and Caroline MCQUOWN. She was born 27 Feb 1853 in PA[973,974], and died 13 Aug 1932 in Plumville, Indiana Cnty, PA[975,976].

Notes for Bennett Work VAN HORN:
       Civil War Co B 67th Reg PVI Pvt 3/9/65-6/19/65. According to his index card he had dark hair, grey eyes, a fair complexion, was 5'7",was 18 and a farmer.
       In 1880 he is a farmer and is living next door to his parents.
       15 June 1985 B. W. Van Horn elected as President of the Georgeville School Board and H. A. Van Horn as secretary.
       In 1900 he is a farmer, has been married for 27 years and he and his wife have 12 children all living.
       In 1920 Bennett owns his farm free and clear and is living close to his son James and next to Harry B. his grandson Robert age 6 is living with the family.
       In the Feb 6 1895 Indiana Progress(Indiana, PA) B. W. Van Horn is reported to have received no offers for his vote in the contested election.
       14 Feb. 1900 Indiana Progress(Indiana, PA) Bennett Van Horn is called to serve the March Term as a juror.
       12 Nov. 1904 Indiana County Gazette (Indiana, PA) lists B. W. Van Horn as a director of the County Schools.
       14 October 1914 operated on for cancer in Indiana, PA according to the Indiana Progress(Indiana, PA).
       3 March 1921 B. W. Van Horn advertises in the Indiana Progress(Indiana, PA) the sale of his

farm of 107 acres near Georgeville with both surface and coal offered for sale.

29 December 1923 it is reported in the Indiana Evening Gazette (Indiana, PA) that B. W. Van Horn has returned home from New Castle where he underwent 3 weeks of cancer treatments. He is somewhat improved.

More About Bennett Work VAN HORN:
Burial: Unknown, Gilgal Cemetry, Gilgal Church, Indiana Cnty, PA[977]
Military service: Bet. 09 Mar - 19 Jun 1965, 74th Regiment of he Pennsylvania Volunteer Infantry; Co. B, 67 Regiment[977]
Occupation: Farmer

Notes for Mary Belle WARDEN:
In 1910 married 37 years the mother of 13 with 12 living.
16 March 1921 Mrs B. W.. Van Horn advertised a comb fly shuttle loom and organ for sale cheap.
25 April 1929 the Indiana Evening Gazette (Indiana, PA) reports that Belle and grandson Robert have moved from the old Schrecengost property to a smaller place on Main owned by Sylvester Griffith.
In 1930 her grandson Robert is living with her. She rents for $8/month and does not have a radio.
In her obituary her name is given as Mary Belle Nichol Warden Van Horn. Later a correction was printed in the paper removing the Nichol from the name. They are buried together at Gilgal Cemetery.

More About Mary Belle WARDEN:
Burial: Unknown, Gilgal Cemetry, Gilgal Church, Indiana Cnty, PA
Occupation: Weaver
Religion: Gigal Presbyterian Church

More About Bennett VAN HORN and Mary WARDEN:
Marriage: Bet. 01 Jan 1872 - 1873, East Mahoning Twp., Indiana Cnty, PA[978]
Marriage date: At his residence

Children of Bennett VAN HORN and Mary WARDEN are:
174.   i.   Ada Myrtle[10] VAN HORN, b. 29 Aug 1873, Georgeville, Indiana Cnty, PA; d. 21 May 1953, Indiana, Indiana Cnty, PA.

        ii.   George Preston VAN HORN[979,980], b. 16 May 1875, Indiana Cnty, PA[981]; d. 21 Jan 1902, Davis, WV[981].

            More About George Preston VAN HORN:
            Burial: Unknown, Gilgal Cemetery, Indiana Cnty, PA[982,983]
            Cause of Death: Burned to death in a boarding house fire
            Military service: Pvt., Spanish American WarArtillery Btry A 4th Art 1898[983]

175.   iii.   Mary Caroline VAN HORN, b. 11 Apr 1877, Indiana Cnty, PA; d. 13 May 1940, Indiana Cnty, PA.

176.   iv.   Cora Belle VAN HORN, b. 03 Jun 1879, Georgeville, Indiana Cnty, PA; d. 19 Sep 1961, Indiana, Indiana Cnty, PA.

177.   v.   Anna Florence VAN HORN, b. 20 Jun 1881, South Mahoning Twp., Indiana Cnty, PA; d. 04 Jan 1971, Indian Haven, Indiana Cnty, PA.

178.   vi.   Robert Lee Claire VAN HORN, b. 25 Jul 1882, Georgeville, Indiana Cnty, PA; d. 05 Jul 1951, Plumville, Indiana Cnty, PA.

179.   vii.   James Ira VAN HORN, b. 26 Apr 1885, South Mahoning Twp., Indiana Cnty, PA; d. Bet. 10 - 26 Mar 1951, Indiana, Indiana Cnty, PA.

180. viii. Harry Bennett VAN HORN, b. 17 Jun 1887, South Mahoning Twp., Indiana Cnty,
              PA; d. 19 Feb 1976, Indiana Cnty, PA.
181. ix.   Pearl Agnes VAN HORN, b. 24 Jul 1889, Georgeville, Indiana Cnty, PA; d. 03 Oct
              1967, Indiana Cnty, PA.
182. x.   Norman Clarence VAN HORN, b. 22 Oct 1891, Georgeville, Indiana Cnty, PA; d.
              11 Sep 1972, Indiana Cnty, PA.
183. xi.   Dollie Ethel VAN HORN, b. 20 Apr 1894, Indiana Cnty, PA; d. Bet. 30 - 31 Aug
              1976, Indiana Cnty, PA.
184. xii.   Edna Gertude VAN HORN, b. 26 Apr 1898, Indiana Cnty, PA; d. 27 Mar 1987.
185. xiii. Verna Viola VAN HORN, b. 21 Aug 1900, Georgeville, Indiana Cnty, PA; d. 10
              May 1962, Warren, OH.

Generation No. 4

54. John Alexander[10] STEWART *(Mary C.[9] VAN HORN, Henry[8], Isaiah[7], Henry B.[6], Henry[5], Christian Barentsen[4] VAN HOORN, Barent Christiansen[3], Christian Barentsen[2], Barent Barents[1])[984,985,986]* was born 04 May 1839 in Indiana Cnty, PA[987], and died 09 Jan 1899 in Washington District of Columbia[988]. He married Mary BARBER[989,990,991,992] 15 Nov 1884, daughter of Robert BARBER and Amanda PARK. She was born 04 Mar 1852 in Indiana Cnty, PA[993], and died 15 Feb 1940 in Washington District of Columbia[994].

Notes for John Alexander STEWART:
    Individual:Served with Co "A", 61st PVI , wounded near Bank's Ford, VA., May4, 1863, and taken prisoner. Wounded second time at Spottsylvania, May 12, 1864, with loss of left arm and part of right hand.

    27 April 187[1] Indiana Progress, Indiana, Pa

    MR. EDITOR. Please announce that JOHN A. STEWART will be a candidate for County Treasurer at the Republican primary election.
MR. STEWART'S life has been an eventful one. He was a private in Company A, 61st Regt, PV; was wounded in the left arm, causing a compound fracture, and taken a prison at the battle of Chancellorsville, May 4th, 1863, and again at the battle of Spottsylvania Court House was severely wounded, losing his left arm and had part of his right hand shot away, from which he suffered intensely, having to lay all that summer in the hospital at Washington, unable even to lift his hand to his face. In the fall he was brought home on a stretcher, still unable to assist himself in any way. He is totally disabled for labor, and is well qualified for the office. Vote for him.
- -
    John A. Stewart died at his home at Washington, D.C., on Monday evening, January 9, 1899, aged 60 years. Mr. Stewart had suffered from grippe which developed into pneumonia, resulting in his death as above stated. Deceased was born in 1839 and was a son of the late William G. and Mary G. Stewart, nee Van Horn. When the war of the rebellion opened Mr. Stewart enlisted July 2, 1862, in Captain Crep's company of the 61st regiment, and was discharged March 16, 1865, He was wounded and taken prisoner May 4, 1863, and was again wounded with loss of an arm at Spottsylvania Court House May 12, 1864, and discharged at the date named above. A brother, Henry, was also a member of the 61st regiment and was killed at the battle of the Wilderness. Another brother, Archibald S. served in the signal corps and died with Sherman's army on the march from Atlanta to the sea. The subject of this sketch was a carpenter by trade, but the injuries received in the service of his country prevented him from following that vacation after the close of the war, and in 1865, he was elected county treasurer, which position he filled with credit to himself and the people. After his term as treasurer expired he was collector and treasurer of the borough of Indiana and later in the employ of the First National Bank of this place. Some 12 years ago he was appointed

to the position of doorkeeper in the National House of Representatives, which place he held until the time of his death, and was one of the most trusted and respected officers in the House. Deceased was a nephew of A. M. and J.M. Stewart, of Indiana. He was married to Mary, a daughter of Robert Barber, who is a sister of Mrs. L.A. Hollister, of this place, who, with three children, survive him.

The remains will be brought to this place tomorrow and taken to the Presbyterian church, where services will be held at 2 o'clock p.m. Interment at Greenwood.

Indiana Weekly Messenger (Indiana, PA) 1899 January 11

More About John Alexander STEWART:
Burial: Unknown, Greenwood Cemetery
Occupation: Fur Dealer, Collector and Treasurer Indiana, PA, Door Keeper US House of Representatives

Notes for Mary BARBER:
    In 1880 she is single living at home with her parents and siblings. She is occupied as a teacher.
    In 1900 she is found with the 3 children indicated in the obituary of her husband John Stewart. She is widowed and working in securities and real estate. They live on 3rd Street in DC.
    In 1920 she is living on 3rd Street in Washington DC with her daughter Mabel and operating a lodging house. Mable is a government clerk.
    In 1930 living with her single daughter M. Mable who is a teacher, She is a rooming house proprietor and has a home on 3rd Street in Washington, DC she owns worth $7,500.There are 3 roomers at this time in the home.

More About Mary BARBER:
Employment: Securities and Ral Estate
Occupation: 1880, Teacher

More About John STEWART and Mary BARBER:
Marriage: 15 Nov 1884

Children of John STEWART and Mary BARBER are:
186.   i.   Roberta[11] STEWART, b. 23 Mar 1886, Washington District of Columbia; d. Unknown.
187.   ii.   John G. STEWART, b. 30 Dec 1890, Washington District of Columbia; d. Unknown.
          iii.   Mary Mabel STEWART[995,996,997], b. Aug 1892, Washington District of Columbia[998]; d. 01 Jun 1963.

               Notes for Mary Mabel STEWART:
               In 1920 living with her mother Mary B. Stewart On 3rd NE in a home her mother owns free and clear.

               More About Mary Mabel STEWART:
               Employment: 1920, Government Clerk

55. Elizabeth Canon[10] STEWART *(Mary C.[9] VAN HORN, Henry[8], Isaiah[7], Henry B.[6], Henry[5], Christian Barentsen[4] VAN HOORN, Barent Christiansen[3], Christian Barentsen[2], Barent Barents[1])[999,1000]* was born Bet. 1840 - 1843 in Indiana Cnty, PA[1001], and died Abt. 1898. She married Luther Brainard WHITHAM[1002,1003,1004,1005] 23 Dec 1870, son of David WHITTAM and Christina. He was born 28 Mar 1840 in Ohio Cnty, VA/WV[1006], and died 15 Aug 1917.

More About Elizabeth Canon STEWART:
Occupation: Music Teacher

Notes for Luther Brainard WHITHAM:
Lodging with his son in St. Louis, MO in 1900. He is a widower and retired. His son is a teacher.

More About Luther Brainard WHITHAM:
Occupation: Teacher

More About Luther WHITHAM and Elizabeth STEWART:
Marriage: 23 Dec 1870

Children of Elizabeth STEWART and Luther WHITHAM are:
       i.   ?[11] WHITHAM, b. 1872; d. Unknown.
188.   ii. Peregrine Stewart WHITHAM, b. 21 Sep 1875, IL; d. Unknown.
     iii. Mary Stewart WHITHAM, b. 1877; d. Unknown.

56. Margaretta T.[10] STEWART *(Mary C.[9] VAN HORN, Henry[8], Isaiah[7], Henry B.[6], Henry[5], Christian Barentsen[4] VAN HOORN, Barent Christiansen[3], Christian Barentsen[2], Barent Barents[1])*[1007,1008,1009] was born 25 Jun 1848 in Indiana Cnty, PA[1010], and died 06 Feb 1937 in Indiana Cnty, PA[1011]. She married Madison W. MCLAUGHLIN[1012,1013,1014], son of William MCLAUGHLIN and Elizabeth MCCOMB. He was born 01 Jan 1842 in Indiana Cnty, PA[1015], and died Bet. 1900 - 1928.

Notes for Margaretta T. STEWART:
In 1900 a niece Roberta Stewart born March 1886 is living in the family.
6 April 1904 Indiana Progress(Indiana, PA) Margaretta deed is recorded of sale of a lot in Marion center, PA to Horatio Simmons.
17 December 1928 Indiana Evening Gazette (Indiana, PA) states that Margaretta T. McLaughlin will receive a widows pension increase from $30 to $50.

More About Margaretta T. STEWART:
Burial: Unknown, Washington Church Cemetery, Rayne Twp., Indiana Cnty, PA

Notes for Madison W. MCLAUGHLIN:
In 1912 Madison and Margaretta moved from Grant Street Indiana, PA to Pittsburgh and J. A. Titterington moved from Railroad Avenue into the Margaret McLaughlin house on Grant Street as reported by the 10 April 1912 Indiana County Gazette (Indiana, PA).

Children of Margaretta STEWART and Madison MCLAUGHLIN are:
       i.   Howard William[11] MCLAUGHLIN[1015,1016,1017], b. Abt. Dec 1869, Indiana Cnty, PA[1018]; d. Aft. 1937.

           More About Howard William MCLAUGHLIN:
           Lived: 1937, Minneapolis, MN

      ii. Thomas McCord MCLAUGHLIN[1019], b. 25 Feb 1871, Indiana Cnty, PA[1019]; d. Bef. 1908.
     iii. John A. L. MCLAUGHLIN[1019,1020], b. Abt. 1872, Indiana Cnty, PA[1021]; d. Aft. 1937.

           More About John A. L. MCLAUGHLIN:
           Lived: Altoona, Blair Cnty, PA

iv.   Mary Lois MCLAUGHLIN[1022,1023], b. Abt. 1874, Indiana Cnty, PA[1023]; d. Aft. 1908; m. RAY; d. Unknown.

v.   Frank W. MCLAUGHLIN[1023], b. Abt. 1875, Oakmont, Allegheny Cnty, PA[1023]; d. Bef. 1908.

More About Frank W. MCLAUGHLIN:
Military service: 1898, PA Nationa Guard

vi.   Ida A. MCLAUGHLIN[1024,1025], b. Abt. 1877, Indiana Cnty, PA[1025]; d. Aft. 1937; m. LUNGER; d. Unknown.

vii. Roy Harvey MCLAUGHLIN[1026,1027,1028], b. 11 Dec 1880, Indiana Cnty, PA[1029]; d. Aft. 1937.

More About Roy Harvey MCLAUGHLIN:
Lived: 1937, Pittsburgh, PA

viii. Samuel S. MCLAUGHLIN[1030,1031,1032], b. Feb 1883, Indiana Cnty, PA[1033]; d. Aft. 1937.

More About Samuel S. MCLAUGHLIN:
Lived: 1937, Altoona, Blair Cnty, PA

ix.   George G. MCLAUGHLIN[1034,1035], b. Aug 1885, Indiana Cnty, PA[1035]; d. Aft. 1908.

x.   Hansel Clark MCLAUGHLIN[1036,1037], b. Sep 1887, Indiana Cnty, PA[1038,1039]; d. 11 Mar 1908, Indiana Cnty, PA[1040].

Notes for Hansel Clark MCLAUGHLIN:
 According to the 13 November 1907 Indiana County Gazette (Indiana, PA) Clark left with his sister Lois for Bartow, FL he has been suffering with throat problems and it is hoped that the warm climate will be beneficial while he picks the fall orange crop.

xi.   Ernest MCLAUGHLIN, b. 07 Jun 1892, Indiana Cnty, PA; d. Unknown.

57. Mary C[10] VAN HORN (*James Thompson[9], Henry[8], Isaiah[7], Henry B.[6], Henry[5], Christian Barentsen[4] VAN HOORN, Barent Christiansen[3], Christian Barentsen[2], Barent Barents[1]*)[1041,1042,1043,1044,1045,1046,1047,1048,1049] was born 02 Aug 1856 in Green Twp., Indiana Cnty, PA[1050,1051,1052], and died 29 Apr 1947 in Indiana Cnty, PA[1053]. She married Samuel Lydick BARR[1054,1055,1056,1057,1058] 31 Dec 1885 in Green Twp., Indiana Cnty, PA[1059], son of Robert BARR and Catherine LYDICK. He was born 18 Nov 1860 in Green Twp., Indiana Cnty, PA[1060,1061], and died 20 Jan 1939 in Indiana Cnty, PA[1062].

Notes for Mary C VAN HORN:
 5 October 1882 Mary is listed In the Indiana Progress(Indiana, PA) as a teacher from Green Twp. in attendance at the Indiana Institute.
 8 Jan 1885 Mary is listed in the Indiana Progress(Indiana, PA) as the teacher of Indiana School No. 17 Green Twp.

More About Mary C VAN HORN:
Lived: Utah and Clymer, PA

Notes for Samuel Lydick BARR:

In 1910 his mother is living with the family. They have 5 children all living at home and Samuel is a farmer. He and Mary have been married for 24 years.

In 1920 living on an unnamed road in Green Twp., Indiana Cnty, PA. He is a farmer and his daughters Eva and Helen are living with the family along with his widowed daughter in law and his twin grandchildren the children of his deceased son Carlton.

In 1930 living on South 6th Street in Indiana. He is renting for $30/month and has a radio. His daughter in law Nellie and her children are living in the family.

Indiana County 175th Anniversary History by Clarence D. Stephenson Vol. 4 p. 65 the follow is found:

"Mr. B. was know as Professor Barr because he was a teacher for 30 years. He was a member of E. Union Presbyterian Church, Taylorsville, and an elder 41 years; afterward a member of the First Presbyterian Church, Indiana, and Leech Bible class. Served on Indiana Boro Council. Member, Glen Campbell Lodge, I.O.O.F."

He was IC treasurer for 1920 to 1923. In the article quoted above it fails to mention his son Carleton as one of his children.

More About Samuel Lydick BARR:
Migration: Abt. 1920, Indiana, Indiana Cnty, PA
Occupation: Farmer, School Teacher, Salesman Publishing House; Professor
Politics: Indiana Cnty, PA Treasurer[1063]

More About Samuel BARR and Mary VAN HORN:
Marriage: 31 Dec 1885, Green Twp., Indiana Cnty, PA[1064]
Marriage Place: Home of Rev. James Caldwell

Children of Mary VAN HORN and Samuel BARR are:

189.   i.   Stella[11] BARR, b. 31 Mar 1887, Green Twp., Indiana Cnty, PA; d. 06 Jun 1961, Vandergrift, Westmoreland Cnty, PA.

        ii.   Eva BARR[1065,1066,1067,1068], b. 06 Nov 1888, Geen Twp., Indiana Cnty, PA[1069]; d. Aft. 1930.

190.   iii.   Mabel BARR, b. 28 May 1892, Green Twp., Indiana Cnty, PA; d. Aft. 1930.

191.   iv.   Carleton Van Horn BARR, b. 23 Nov 1893, Green Twp., Indiana Cnty, PA; d. Bef. 1920.

192.   v.   Helen C. BARR, b. 22 Oct 1896, Green Twp., Indiana Cnty, PA; d. Dec 1985, Indiana Cnty, PA.

58. James W.[10] VAN HORN *(James Thompson[9], Henry[8], Isaiah[7], Henry B.[6], Henry[5], Christian Barentsen[4] VAN HOORN, Barent Christiansen[3], Christian Barentsen[2], Barent Barents[1])*[1070,1071,1072,1073,1074,1075,1076,1077,1078] was born 1861 in Indiana Cnty, PA[1079,1080,1081], and died 21 Sep 1947 in Miami, Dade Cnty, FL[1082]. He married Melissa B. ALLISON[1083,1084,1085,1086,1087,1088] 1895 in Indiana Cnty, PA, daughter of Robert ALLISON and Mary Caroline. She was born 08 Jun 1865 in Plumville, Indiana Cnty, PA[1089,1090], and died 06 Jun 1930 in Indiana Cnty, PA[1091].

Notes for James W. VAN HORN:

9 Jan 1895 Jas W. Van Horn is listed in the Indiana Progress(Indiana, PA) as having been an ineligible voter even though he is listed as having voted in the election in East Mahoning Twp.

7 Nov. 1900 Indiana Progress(Indiana, PA) listed a purchase of a lot In Marion Center by James Van Horn from J. Horace McGinity for $140.

14 February 1906 the Indiana Weekly Messenger (Indiana, PA) reports that S. M. Jack sold to J. W. Van Horn a lot in Indiana for $500.

Isaiah Van Horn Pioneer of Indiana County, Pennsylvania

22 May 1907 Indiana County Gazette (Indiana, PA) J. W. VanHorn is a delegate for the Prohibition Party.

3 July 1907 the Indiana Gazette reports that J. W. Van Horn erected a dwelling house of 8 rooms on Locust Street in Indiana, PA for a cost of $2000.

In 1910 living in Irwin, PA and visited Plumville with wife and daughter Effie as reported on 16 July 1910 in the Indiana Evening Gazette (Indiana, PA)

In 1920 owns his place with a mortgage and is a farm operator. Living with wife and daughter Effie.

In 8 Aug 1925 J. W. Van Horn announces he will be a candidate for Jury commissioner on the Republican ticket.

In 1930 living with his brother in law S. L. Barr and sister Mary.

1 Nov 1945 Indiana Evening Gazette (Indiana, PA) reports that James formerly of Marion, PA now of Miami, FL came home upon the death of his sister Miss Lee Van Horn of Indiana, PA

More About James W. VAN HORN:
Lived: Locust and also South Seventh Street, Indiana, Indiana Cnty, PA, Irwin, PA and Miami, FL
Occupation: Farmer

Notes for Melissa B. ALLISON:
Indiana Evening Gazette (Indiana, PA) S. M. Jack a lot in Indiana to Melissa B. Van Horn for $475 on 6 February 1907

Indiana Weekly Messenger (Indiana, PA) of March 25, 1908 reports that Melissa Van Horn has sold to John Smail a lot in Indiana for $1500.

More About Melissa B. ALLISON:
Lived: 1909, Irwin, PA

More About James VAN HORN and Melissa ALLISON:
Marriage: 1895, Indiana Cnty, PA

Child of James VAN HORN and Melissa ALLISON is:
    i.   Effie Golda[11] VAN HORN[1092,1093,1094,1095,1096,1097,1098], b. 08 Dec 1896, Marion Center, Indiana Cnty, PA[1099,1100]; d. 22 Sep 1980, Greenvillle, PA[1101].

    Notes for Effie Golda VAN HORN:
    3 January 1914 Indiana Evening Gazette (Indiana, PA) reports that a New Years party was held for the operators of the Huntington and Clearfield Telephone Company and Effie Van Hon is listed among the attendees.

    In 1920 living with mother and father she works as a stenographer in an insurance office.

    In 1930 Effie has living with her her mother and a boarder. She rents for $25/month a house on 12th Street in Indiana, PA and she has a radio.

    5 November 1945 the Indiana Evening Gazette (Indiana, PA) reports on the Plumville East End club Halloween Party and Effie is listed as an attendee.

    More About Effie Golda VAN HORN:
    Burial: Unknown, Oakland Cemetery, Indiana, PA
    Lived: Sharon, PA
    Occupation: Bank Clerk, Insurance company Stenographer, Indiana County Deposit Bank and Employment Security Counselor
    Organizations: DAR; United Ostomy Association; Retired State Employees Association
    Religion: Presbyterian

59. Margaret[10] VAN HORN *(James Thompson[9], Henry[8], Isaiah[7], Henry B.[6], Henry[5], Christian Barentsen[4] VAN HOORN, Barent Christiansen[3], Christian Barentsen[2], Barent Barents[1])*[1102,1103,1104] was born Apr 1864 in Indiana Cnty, PA[1105], and died 21 Oct 1909 in Twin Falls, ID[1106]. She married Thomas J. DOUGLAS[1107,1108,1109,1110,1111] 12 May 1897 in Arapahoe Cnty, CO, son of James DOUGLAS and Margaret. He was born Jun 1867 in Canada[1112], and died Aft. 1920.

Notes for Margaret VAN HORN:
　　23 July 1907 Indiana Evening Gazette (Indiana, PA) Mr and Mrs Douglas of Rockyford, CO stopped to see her brother J. W. Van Horn while on their way to the Jamestown Exposition.
　　27 Oct 1909 Indiana Evening Gazette (Indiana, PA) obituary states that she died of Typhoid and left 3 children the youngest one month old. Her parents James T. and Ellen A. her husband T.J. Douglas and sisters Miss Elizabeth, Mrs S.l. Barr and L. S. Brock and brothers James and George H. Van Horn.

More About Margaret VAN HORN:
Cause of Death: Typhoid Fever
Lived: Rocky Ford, Otero Cnty, CO; Twin Falls, ID

More About Thomas J. DOUGLAS:
Occupation: Farmer; Coal Dealer

More About Thomas DOUGLAS and Margaret VAN HORN:
Marriage: 12 May 1897, Arapahoe Cnty, CO

Children of Margaret VAN HORN and Thomas DOUGLAS are:
　　i.　Mary Ellen[11] DOUGLAS[1112,1113], b. Feb 1898, CO[1114]; d. Unknown.
　　ii.　Robert M. DOUGLAS[1115,1116], b. 09 Dec 1901, Rocky Ford, Otero Cnty, CO[1117]; d. Unknown.

　　　　Notes for Robert M. DOUGLAS:
　　　　In the 1929 passenger list of the ship Malolo he is listed as single.

　　　　More About Robert M. DOUGLAS:
　　　　Lived: 1929, Berkeley, CA

　　iii.　Gail Leigh DOUGLAS[1118], b. Abt. Jun 1903, CO; d. 30 Nov 1906, Rocky Ford, Otero Cnty, CO[1118].

　　　　More About Gail Leigh DOUGLAS:
　　　　Cause of Death: Scarlet Fever

　　iv.　Margaret Van Horn DOUGLAS, b. Bet. 1903 - 1906, CO; d. 16 Nov 1906, Rocky Ford, Otero Cnty, CO[1118].

　　　　More About Margaret Van Horn DOUGLAS:
　　　　Cause of Death: Scarlet Fever

　　v.　Kenneth V. DOUGLAS[1119,1120,1121], b. Abt. Oct 1909, ID; d. Unknown; m. Freida M.[1122], Abt. 1927; b. Abt. 1907, KS[1122]; d. Unknown.

　　　　Notes for Kenneth V. DOUGLAS:
　　　　In 1930 living in Twin Falls, ID in a home he rents for $25 and has a radio.

More About Kenneth V. DOUGLAS:
Employment: 1930, Contractor coffee company

More About Kenneth DOUGLAS and Freida M.:
Marriage: Abt. 1927

60. Rachel[10] VAN HORN *(James Thompson[9], Henry[8], Isaiah[7], Henry B.[6], Henry[5], Christian Barentsen[4] VAN HOORN, Barent Christiansen[3], Christian Barentsen[2], Barent Barents[1])*[1123,1124,1125,1126,1127,1128,1129] was born Abt. 1868 in Indiana Cnty, PA[1130], and died Bet. 1901 - 1909. She married S. Lem BROCK[1131,1132] Aft. 1900. He was born 1862 in PA[1132], and died Unknown.

Notes for Rachel VAN HORN:
    28 August 1889 Rachel Van Horn is listed in the Indiana Progress(Indiana, PA) as a teacher in East Mahoning Schools wages $30 and term opens September 30.
    6 September 1899 Indiana Progress(Indiana, PA) reports that Rachel has vacationed at home is is returning to Pittsburgh.
    27 April 1892 Indiana Gazette reports that the Hazlett M. P. Church has resented Rachel, who is a teacher at the Hazlett School in Montgomery County, a bible. She is the organist at the church.
    In 1930 Rachel is living with the children Waynesburg, PA and rents for $50/month. She indicates she is married although Lem is in CO.

More About Rachel VAN HORN:
Lived: Pittsburgh, PA; Waynesburg, PA; Beaver, PA

Notes for S. Lem BROCK:
    In 1930 Lem is living in Colorado and is the Deputy Assessor for the county government. He is renting for $5/month and is married although Rachel is living back in PA with the family.

More About S. BROCK and Rachel VAN HORN:
Marriage: Aft. 1900

Children of Rachel VAN HORN and S. BROCK are:
    i.   Lester V.[11] BROCK[1132,1133], b. Abt. 1903, PA[1134]; d. Unknown.

          More About Lester V. BROCK:
          Occupation: College Professor

    ii.   Dan S. BROCK[1134,1135], b. Abt. 1906, PA[1136]; d. Unknown.

          More About Dan S. BROCK:
          Occupation: Senior Inspector State Highway Depatment

    iii.   Ruth BROCK[1136,1137], b. Abt. 1908, PA[1138]; d. Unknown.
    iv.   Helen BROCK[1138,1139], b. Bet. 1908 - 1909, PA[1140]; d. Unknown.

61. George H.[10] VAN HORN *(James Thompson[9], Henry[8], Isaiah[7], Henry B.[6], Henry[5], Christian Barentsen[4] VAN HOORN, Barent Christiansen[3], Christian Barentsen[2], Barent Barents[1])*[1141,1142,1143,1144,1145,1146] was born Abt. 1870 in Indiana Cnty, PA[1147], and died Aft. 1930. He married Belle COLEMAN[1147,1148,1149] 22 May 1902 in Denver, Denver Cnty, CO[1150], daughter of J. Nelson COLEMAN. She was born Abt. 1869 in PA[1151], and died Aft. Nov 1930.

Notes for George H. VAN HORN:

30 Sept 1904 Indiana Evening Gazette (Indiana, PA) reports that George H. Van Horn son of James T. Van Horn, ex county commissioner of Indiana Cnty, has been nominated as District Attorney for the Eighth Judicial District of Colorado. He currently lives in Loveland, CO and lived in Marion Center until 8 years ago. He has been practicing law in CO for 3 years.

20 Dec 1928 Indiana Evening Gazette (Indiana, PA) announces that county boy George H. Van Horn gets a judgeship in Weld county, Colorado. He is the brother of J. W. and Miss Elizabeth Van Horn and Mrs S. L. Barr of Indiana.

In the 1930 Census George is age 59 born PA and both parents born PA. He is a lawyer, married and first married at age 32. He is lodging in Greely, Weld Cnty, CO.

More About George H. VAN HORN:
Education: Northern Indiana Normal at Valparaiso, IN and State Normal at Greely, CO
Lived: Vale, CO
Occupation: Attorney, District Attorney 8th Judicial District of Colorado and Judge

Notes for Belle COLEMAN:

16 May 1906 Indiana Progress(Indiana, PA) reports that she visited her father J. N. Coleman of near Clarksburg, PA along with 2 of her children. It is noted she has lived in the west for 10 years

In 1930 she is living in Loveland, CO as a school teacher with her daughter Naomi and son Paul. She owns her home worth $2250 and does not have a radio. She indicates she is married and married at age 30 years. Her husband is lodging in Greely, CO at the time of this census.

More About Belle COLEMAN:
Lived: Nov 1930, Loveland, Larimer Cnty, CO
Occupation: Public School Teacher

More About George VAN HORN and Belle COLEMAN:
Marriage: 22 May 1902, Denver, Denver Cnty, CO[1152]

Children of George VAN HORN and Belle COLEMAN are:

193.   i.   George Henry[11] VAN HORN, b. 02 Jun 1903, Loveland, Larimer Cnty, CO; d. Unknown.

          ii.   Dorthea VAN HORN[1153], b. Abt. 1905, Loveland, Larimer Cnty, CO[1153]; d. Unknown.

          iii.   Naomi VAN HORN[1153,1154], b. Abt. 1907, Loveland, Larimer Cnty, CO[1155]; d. Unknown.

194.   iv.   Paul H. VAN HORN, b. Abt. 1912, Loveland, Larimer Cnty, CO; d. Unknown.

62. Elizabeth Francis[10] WORK *(Tabitha Logan[9] VAN HORN, Henry[8], Isaiah[7], Henry B.[6], Henry[5], Christian Barentsen[4] VAN HOORN, Barent Christiansen[3], Christian Barentsen[2], Barent Barents[1])*[1156,1157,1158,1159,1160,1161] was born 01 Sep 1848 in East Mahoning Twp.,Indiana Cnty, PA[1162,1163], and died 02 Apr 1926 in Des Moines, Polk Cnty, IA. She married Joseph Henderson HOOD[1164,1165] 07 Jan 1869, son of Thomas HOOD and Elizabeth LYTLE. He was born 03 May 1844 in White Twp., Indiana Cnty, PA[1165], and died 07 Jan 1908 in Des Moines, Polk Cnty, IA.

Notes for Elizabeth Francis WORK:
Listed in the 1880 Census as Lizzie.

Notes for Joseph Henderson HOOD:
Joseph was a coal dealer of Home Valley, lived in Indiana county, PA for a time. He was a contractor and builder in Kansas City, MO and then Des Moines, IA.

More About Joseph Henderson HOOD:
Occupation: Coal Dealer

More About Joseph HOOD and Elizabeth WORK:
Marriage: 07 Jan 1869

Child of Elizabeth WORK and Joseph HOOD is:
195. i. Dora Myrtle[11] HOOD, b. 14 Feb 1870, Kellysburg, Indiana Cnty, PA; d. 28 Feb 1933, Evanston, Cook Cnty, IL.

63. Sarah Steele[10] WORK *(Tabitha Logan[9] VAN HORN, Henry[8], Isaiah[7], Henry B.[6], Henry[5], Christian Barentsen[4] VAN HOORN, Barent Christiansen[3], Christian Barentsen[2], Barent Barents[1])[1166,1167,1168,1169,1170]* was born 09 Feb 1858 in Indiana Cnty, PA[1171,1172], and died 27 Sep 1938 in Denver, Denver Cnty, CO. She married (1) ? LYTLE. He died Unknown. She married (2) John Miller LYTLE[1173,1174,1175] 07 May 1878 in Indiana Cnty, PA[1176], son of Thomas LYTLE and Rachel MILLER. He was born 27 May 1851 in Indiana Cnty, PA[1177], and died 15 Jul 1928 in Ft. Morgan, Morgan Cnty, CO.

More About Sarah Steele WORK:
Lived: Ft. Morgan, Morgan Cnty, CO

More About John Miller LYTLE:
Degree: Pittsburgh School of Pharmacy
Employment: Chief of Operarion Telephone Company
Occupation: Druggist

More About John LYTLE and Sarah WORK:
Marriage: 07 May 1878, Indiana Cnty, PA[1178]

Children of Sarah WORK and John LYTLE are:
196. i. Herbert Jolly[11] LYTLE, b. 08 Jun 1880, Marion Center, Indiana Cnty, PA; d. 14 Feb 1962, Alemeda Cnty, CA.
      ii. Victor Von LYTLE[1178,1179,1180,1181,1182], b. 08 Apr 1884, Marion Center, Indiana Cnty, PA[1183]; d. 14 Nov 1969, Los Angeles, Los Angeles Cnty, CA[1184]; m. Josephine O. BONAZZI[1185,1186], Abt. 1913; b. 19 Mar 1889, Rome, Italy; d. Aft. 1949.

           Notes for Victor Von LYTLE:
           Taught at the Oberlin Conservatory of Music.

           More About Victor Von LYTLE:
           Lived: Pennsylvania
           Occupation: Musician and Teacher of Music

           Notes for Josephine O. BONAZZI:
           Taught at Oberlin College 1921-1949.

           More About Victor Von LYTLE and Josephine BONAZZI:
           Marriage: Abt. 1913

      iii. Helen Hortense LYTLE[1187,1188], b. 26 Jan 1897, CO[1188]; d. Aft. 1954; Adopted child.

           Notes for Helen Hortense LYTLE:

Isaiah Van Horn Pioneer of Indiana County, Pennsylvania

In 1918 is attending College in Colorado Springs, CO.

More About Helen Hortense LYTLE:
Lived: Colorado Springs, CO

64. Dr. Hubert Robert[10] WORK *(Tabitha Logan[9] VAN HORN, Henry[8], Isaiah[7], Henry B.[6], Henry[5], Christian Barentsen[4] VAN HOORN, Barent Christiansen[3], Christian Barentsen[2], Barent Barents[1])*[1189,1190,1191,1192,1193] was born 03 Jul 1860 in Marion Center, Indiana Cnty, PA[1194,1195], and died 14 Dec 1942 in Denver, Denver Cnty, CO. He married (1) Laura May ARBUCKLE[1196,1197,1198] 31 Aug 1887. She was born Feb 1850 in Madison, IN[1199], and died May 1924 in Washington, DC[1199]. He married (2) Ethel Reed SPOONER[1200] 05 Dec 1934. She was born 17 Jul 1872 in Central City, CO, and died 04 May 1960.

Notes for Dr. Hubert Robert WORK:
Hubert Work planned to go to California to practice medicine after graduating form the University of PA Medical School in Philadelphia in 1885. He stopped in Greely to visit his cousin, James Work McCreery. While there he contracted typhoid fever, and Mary Melvina Arbuckle McCreery, his cousins wife nursed him until he recovered. During his convalescence, Laura May Arbuckle came to visit her sister and Dr. Work fell in love with her. They were married and moved to Ft. Morgan. Later they located at Pueblo and there founded Woodcroft Hospital, the first mental institution in the Rocky Mountain area. He was a Presbyterian and a Mason.
Dr Work was chairman of Herbert Hoover's Campaign.
In an article on boners by political candidate and their entourages, we find this concerning Hubert Work- On Hoover's campaign train, ex Secretary of the Interior, Hubert Work told a western crowd, "I've spent many delightful hours in your beautiful little city. It is a very genuine pleasure to find myself back in _____," He then whispered to a colleague standing beside him these words which a microphone picked up-"Where the hell are we?"
15 June 1908 Colorado Spring Gazette (Colorado Springs, CO) repots that Hubert Work along with other members of the Colorado Delegation were on their way to the Chicago Republican Convention.
For 1915 Dr. Work paid $699.64 in federal income tax on his 1040 from Pueblo, CO.
Dr. Hubert Work was a lieutenant Colonel in the US Army Medical Corps in WWI was a medical adviser to the Provost Marshall General. He served as President of the AMA; Assistant Postmaster General in 1921; Postmaster General in 1922; Secretary of the interior -1923-1928. One of his first acts in this latter capacity was to clean the department of all traces of the scandal resulting from the leasing of the Teapot Dome in Wyoming naval oil reserve. His reorganization of the department was reputed to have reduced expenditures 129 Million Dollars the first three years of his tenure. He had no tolerance for clock watchers, ordering all the clocks removed from the Interior Department when he became secretary. A close friend of Calvin Coolidge, Dr. Work also fought side by side with the White House Physician to save the life of President Harding. Dr. Work is buried in Arlington Cemetery.
From Wikepedia
Hubert Work (July 3, 1860 – December 14, 1942) was a U.S. administrator and physician. He served as the Postmaster General between 1922 and 1923 in the presidency of Warren G. Harding. He then served as the Secretary of the Interior from 1923-1928 during the administration of Calvin Coolidge.
Work was born in Marion Center, Pennsylvania. Attended medical school at the University of Michigan from 1882-1883, but ultimately received an M.D. from the University of Pennsylvania in 1885. He settled in Colorado and founded Woodcroft Hospital in Pueblo in 1896. In 1920, Work served as president of the advocacy group, the American Medical Association.
Work was active in the Republican Party, having served as the Colorado state chairman in 1912. In 1914, Work ran unsuccessfully in a special election for the United States Senate having been defeated by the Democrat Charles Spalding Thomas, later the governor of Colorado. Work polled

98,728 votes (39 percent) in a multi-candidate to field to Thomas' 102,037 ballots (40.3 percent). This was Colorado's first Senate election by popular vote under the Seventeenth Amendment to the United States Constitution.

He was a Colorado delegate to the Republican National Convention in 1920, and he chaired the Republican National Committee from 1928 to 1929.

During World War I, Work served in the U.S. Army in the Medical Corps and attained the rank of lieutenant colonel.

Work served as the U.S. Assistant Postmaster General from 1921 to 1922 and Postmaster General from 1922 to 1923, under President Harding. He also served as U.S. Secretary of the Interior from 1923 to 1928, under both Harding and Coolidge. During Work's tenure as Secretary of the Interior, American citizenship was formally granted to Native Americans.

He died in Denver and was buried in Arlington National Cemetery in Virginia.

More About Dr. Hubert Robert WORK:
Burial: Unknown, Arlington National Cemetery
Lived: Denver, Denver Cnty, CO

More About Hubert WORK and Laura ARBUCKLE:
Marriage: 31 Aug 1887

More About Hubert WORK and Ethel SPOONER:
Marriage: 05 Dec 1934

Children of Hubert WORK and Laura ARBUCKLE are:
197.   i.   MD Phillip[11] WORK, b. 20 Jun 1888, Ft. Morgan, Morgan Cnty, CO; d. 02 Jul 1952, Las Cruces, Dona Ana Cnty, NM.
         ii.   Frances Mary WORK[1201], b. 10 Aug 1890, Ft. Morgan, Morgan Cnty, CO; d. 08 Aug 1891, Ft. Morgan, Morgan Cnty, CO.
       iii. Hubert Robert WORK, JR[1201], b. 22 May 1894, Pueblo, CO; d. 1895, Ft. Morgan, Morgan Cnty, CO.
198.   iv. Dorcas Logan WORK, b. 30 Sep 1896, Pueblo, CO; d. 02 Feb 1953.
199.   v. Robert Van Horn WORK, b. 23 Apr 1898, Pueblo, CO; d. 23 Aug 1935, Denver, Denver Cnty, CO.

65. Richard[10] VAN HORN *(Robert Thompson[9], Henry[8], Isaiah[7], Henry B.[6], Henry[5], Christian Barentsen[4] VAN HOORN, Barent Christiansen[3], Christian Barentsen[2], Barent Barents[1])*[1202,1203,1204,1205,1206,1207,1208,1209,1210] was born 15 Nov 1851 in Pomeroy, Meigs Cnty, OH[1211,1212], and died Aft. 1930. He married Margaret KIRKWOOD[1213,1214,1215,1216,1217] 15 Nov 1875. She was born Jan 1851 in MO[1218], and died Bef. 1920[1219].

Notes for Richard VAN HORN:
In 1920 Richard is a widower lives on Van Horn Road in a home he owns free and clear with his son, daughter in law and grandson as well as his niece Kate Cooley. There are 2 servants in the home.

In 1930 Richard is a widowed and owns his home worth about $3500. He has a radio. Both is children and his daughter in law and grandson live with him on West VanHorn in Blue Twp., Jackson Cnty, MO.

More About Richard VAN HORN:
Census: Printer, Deputy US Collector, Newspaper Collector, Capitalist Managing

Notes for Margaret KIRKWOOD:
    In 1900 Margaret states she is the mother of 2 and both are living.

More About Richard VAN HORN and Margaret KIRKWOOD:
Marriage: 15 Nov 1875

Children of Richard VAN HORN and Margaret KIRKWOOD are:
      i.   Adela C.[11] VAN HORN[1220,1221,1222,1223,1224,1225,1226], b. 03 Oct 1876, Kansas City, Jackson Cnty, MO[1227,1228]; d. Unknown.
200.   ii. Henry Kirkwood VAN HORN, b. 25 Feb 1878, Kansas City, Jackson Cnty, MO; d. Aft. 1930.

66. Anna M.[10] VAN HORN *(Henry A.[9], Henry[8], Isaiah[7], Henry B.[6], Henry[5], Christian Barentsen[4] VAN HOORN, Barent Christiansen[3], Christian Barentsen[2], Barent Barents[1])[1229,1230,1231,1232]* was born Feb 1854 in PA[1233], and died Bef. 1941. She married (1) Jacob BURKET, JR[1233,1234,1235] Abt. 1870, son of Jacob BURKET and Catherine. He was born 1849 in PA[1236], and died Bef. 1890. She married (2) J. J. HENDERSON[1237] Abt. 1888[1237]. He was born Apr 1831 in PA[1237], and died Unknown.

Notes for Anna M. VAN HORN:
    Living next door to parents in 1870. Married at age 16.
    In 1900 living with her second husband J. J. Henderson, her two sons by her first marriage, William and Jay, and her son by her second marriage, Bob Henderson. There is a Burk Van Horn age 21 born PA and Katy Scott age 32 born PA and married boarding with the family. Living near to Guy Van Horn, her nephew, and his family.

Notes for Jacob BURKET, JR:
    In 1870 living next door to Anna's parents and in 1880 living next door to his elderly parents.

More About Jacob BURKET, JR:
Occupation: Farm Worker, Doctor

More About Jacob BURKET and Anna VAN HORN:
Marriage: Abt. 1870

More About J. J. HENDERSON:
Occupation: Hotel Keeper

More About J. HENDERSON and Anna VAN HORN:
Marriage: Abt. 1888[1237]

Children of Anna VAN HORN and Jacob BURKET are:
      i.   Kitty A.[11] BURKET[1238], b. Abt. 1875, PA[1238]; d. Unknown.
201.   ii. William Alexander BURKET, b. 06 Aug 1878, PA; d. Unknown.
202.   iii. Jay Miller BURKET, b. 21 Feb 1885, Clarington, Forest Cnty, PA; d. Unknown.

Child of Anna VAN HORN and J. HENDERSON is:
    iv. Bob[11] HENDERSON[1239], b. Mar 1891, PA[1239]; d. Unknown.

67. Alice Lucetta[10] VAN HORN *(Henry A.[9], Henry[8], Isaiah[7], Henry B.[6], Henry[5], Christian Barentsen[4] VAN HOORN, Barent Christiansen[3], Christian Barentsen[2], Barent Barents[1])[1240,1241,1242]* was born 1855 in

PA[1243], and died Aft. 1899. She married William Alexander VAN HORN[1244,1245,1246,1247] Abt. 1875, son of Henry VAN HORN and Ellen HUTCHISON. He was born 21 Mar 1850 in Indiana Cnty, PA[1248,1249], and died Aft. 1910.

Notes for Alice Lucetta VAN HORN:
    27 December 1899 the Indiana Weekly Messenger (Indiana, PA) reports that on 15 December 1899 the will of Henry A. Van Horn of Georgeville is filed and his daughter Lucetta receives his house, lot and furniture situated in Georgeville. The will is dated 22 April 1897.
    Name is also given as Lucetta A. Van Horn in 1880 Census

Notes for William Alexander VAN HORN:
    10 April 1895 Indiana Weekly Messenger (Indiana, PA) reports that William G. Ling sells to William P. Van Horn on March 23, 1895 50 acres in East Wheatfield for $3500. I suspect that this sale was to William A not William P. Van Horn.
    12 October 1910 the Indiana Progress(Indiana, PA) states that William has left to visit his sister Mrs. William Bowser in North Dakota.
    William is living next to his father in law Henry Van Horn with his wife Lusetta and their two children.

More About William Alexander VAN HORN:
Occupation: Carpenter, Architect

More About William VAN HORN and Alice VAN HORN:
Marriage: Abt. 1875

Children of Alice VAN HORN and William VAN HORN are:
203.   i.   Guy Wiseman[11] VAN HORN, b. 22 Nov 1877, PA; d. Aft. 1930.
204.   ii.   Harry Burk VAN HORN, b. Oct 1878, PA; d. Unknown.

68. Edith Lee[10] VAN HORN *(Henry A.[9], Henry[8], Isaiah[7], Henry B.[6], Henry[5], Christian Barentsen[4] VAN HOORN, Barent Christiansen[3], Christian Barentsen[2], Barent Barents[1])*[1250,1251,1252,1253,1254,1255,1256] was born 23 Feb 1862 in PA[1257,1258], and died 23 Aug 1941 in Georgeville, Indiana Cnty, PA[1258]. She married William D. SHIELDS[1258,1259,1260,1261] Abt. 1884[1262]. He was born May 1858 in PA[1262], and died 1924[1263].

Notes for Edith Lee VAN HORN:
    In 1910 she is the mother of one child living and her husband is a lumberman and the son is Sylvanius. There is a servant in the home.
    In 1930 she is widowed living on Jefferson Street in Brookfield, PA in a home she owns worth $10,000 and there is a radio in the home. There is a couple rooming with them Peter and Mary Loftus of NY who is an electrical engineer.

More About Edith Lee VAN HORN:
Burial: Unknown, Mt. Taber Cemetery

Notes for William D. SHIELDS:
    In 1920 lives on Jefferson Street in Brookville, PA in a home he owns free and clear. His wife son and daughter in law are of the home. He is a lumberman.

More About William D. SHIELDS:
Occupation: Lumberman, Merchant, Legislator

More About William SHIELDS and Edith VAN HORN:
Marriage: Abt. 1884[1264]

Child of Edith VAN HORN and William SHIELDS is:
     i.   Samuel V.[11] SHIELDS[1265,1266,1267,1268,1269], b. Aug 1885, PA[1270]; d. Aft. Aug
        1941[1271]; m. Helen[1272]; b. Abt. 1896, PA[1272]; d. Unknown.

        Notes for Samuel V. SHIELDS:
        In 1900 he is listed as Samuel O, in 1910 as Sylvanius and in 1920 as Samuel V. in
        1930 as Van S. Shields. His mother Obit lists him as S. Van Horn Shields.
        In 1920 Helen is listed as a daughter in law and in 1930 Van S. is listed as living with
        his mother as single. He has no occupation.

        More About Samuel V. SHIELDS:
        Employment: 1920, Gas Operator
        Lived: Brookville, Jefferson Cnty, PA

69. Minnie[10] VAN HORN *(Henry A.[9], Henry[8], Isaiah[7], Henry B.[6], Henry[5], Christian Barentsen[4] VAN HOORN, Barent Christiansen[3], Christian Barentsen[2], Barent Barents[1])*[1273,1274,1275,1276,1277,1278,1279] was born 27 Jan 1866 in Georgeville, Indiana Cnty, PA[1280,1281,1282], and died 08 Aug 1953 in Brookville, Jefferson Cnty, PA[1282]. She married Dr. Jeremiah Johnson BREWER[1283,1284,1285,1286] 20 Oct 1883 in Marion Center, East Mahoning Twp., Indiana Cnty, PA[1287,1288], son of Christopher BREWER and Mary JOHNSTON. He was born 23 Sep 1856 in Punxsutawney, PA or Delmont, PA[1289,1290], and died 26 Jan 1933 in Brookville Hospital, Brookville, Jefferson Cnty, PA[1290].

More About Minnie VAN HORN:
Burial: 10 Aug 1953, Brookville, Jefferson Cnty, PA

Notes for Dr. Jeremiah Johnson BREWER:
    In 1920 owns his home on Buttonwood Road free and clear. He is a physician with a general practice.

More About Dr. Jeremiah Johnson BREWER:
Cause of Death: Bronchial pneumonia
Occupation: Physician Country Practice

More About Jeremiah BREWER and Minnie VAN HORN:
Marriage: 20 Oct 1883, Marion Center, East Mahoning Twp., Indiana Cnty, PA[1291,1292]
Marriage date: Rev. A. J. Jolly

Children of Minnie VAN HORN and Jeremiah BREWER are:
205.   i.   Anna C.[11] BREWER, b. Mar 1886, PA; d. Aft. 1953.
        ii. Harry Christopher BREWER[1293,1294,1295], b. 10 Aug 1888, PA[1296,1297,1298]; d. Bef.
           1953; m. Fay[1298]; d. Unknown.

           Notes for Harry Christopher BREWER:
           In his WWI Draft Registration he is single, tall, medium build with gray eyes and
           dark hair. He is a farmer lives in Clarington, PA and his father J. J. Brewer is his best
           contact.
           In his WWII Draft Registration he indicates he lives at 246 Euclid Ave in Brookville,
           PA. His contact is Fay Brewer at the same address that is either his wife or a

daughter in 1942. He works for Kone Supply Co in Brookville, PA. His telephone is 755. He is 5'3" tall weighs 147 pounds he is shown as a Negro with black eyes, hair and skin. Since the writing on the physical characteristics page is very different than that on the page with name and address. I think that the records have been mixed as his brother is not shown as Negro.

More About Harry Christopher BREWER:
Lived: Brookville, Jefferson Cnty, PA
Occupation: Pipe Fitter Gas Field

    iii.   Glenn Shields BREWER[1299,1300,1301], b. 06 Jul 1891, PA[1302]; d. Aft. 1953[1303].

Notes for Glenn Shields BREWER:
In his WWII Draft Registration in 1942 he lives in Clarington, PA. He is a farmer and gives the name of the person who would best be able to locate him as his mother Minnie Brewer who also lives in Clarington, PA. He is 5'3" tall and weighs 118 pounds. He has brown eyes and hair and a sallow complexion.
In his WWI registration in 1917 he is single and lists his father as the best contact.

More About Glenn Shields BREWER:
Lived: Clarrington, PA
Occupation: Farmer

    iv.   Augusta BREWER[1304,1305,1306], b. Dec 1893, PA[1307]; d. Aft. 1953; m. Professor Howard E. GAYLEY[1308], Abt. 1926[1308]; b. Abt. 1890, PA[1308]; d. Unknown.

More About Augusta BREWER:
Lived: Brookville, Jefferson Cnty, PA

Notes for Professor Howard E. GAYLEY:
In 1930 living on Tulane Road in Columbus OH in a place that they rent for $55/month. They do not have a radio. He is a college instructor. they have been married about 13 years.

More About Howard GAYLEY and Augusta BREWER:
Marriage: Abt. 1926[1308]

    v.   Florence E. BREWER[1309,1310,1311,1312], b. Jun 1899, PA[1313]; d. Aft. 1953; m. Andrew F. COOK[1314], Abt. 1921[1314]; b. Abt. 1891, PA[1314]; d. Unknown.

More About Florence E. BREWER:
Lived: Coudersport, PA

Notes for Andrew F. COOK:
In 1930 live on Broad Street in New Bethlehem, PA where they are renting for $35/month. They have a radio. He and Florence have been married for about 8 years.

More About Andrew F. COOK:
Employment: 1930, Clerk in Oil Gas Supplier

More About Andrew COOK and Florence BREWER:
Marriage: Abt. 1921[1314]

vi. Alice L. BREWER[1315,1316,1317], b. Abt. 1901, PA[1318]; d. Aft. 1953; m. Leo F. GERBER[1319], 1929[1319]; b. Abt. 1904, PA[1319]; d. Unknown.

More About Alice L. BREWER:
Lived: Columbus, OH

More About Leo F. GERBER:
Occupation: 1930, Grade School Teacher

More About Leo GERBER and Alice BREWER:
Marriage: 1929[1319]

70. Sarah Jane[10] VAN HORN *(John Dick[9], Alexander[8], Isaiah[7], Henry B.[6], Henry[5], Christian Barentsen[4] VAN HOORN, Barent Christiansen[3], Christian Barentsen[2], Barent Barents[1])*[1320,1321,1322,1323,1324,1325,1326] was born 13 Mar 1859 in Normalville, Fayette Cnty, PA[1327], and died 03 Jun 1942 in Mill Run, Fayette Cnty, PA. She married Charles K. BROOKS[1328,1329,1330,1331] 1880[1332], son of George BROOKS and Hannah. He was born 06 Mar 1858 in Normalville, Fayette Cnty, PA[1333], and died Abt. 1949 in Mill Run, Fayette Cnty, PA.

Notes for Sarah Jane VAN HORN:
In 1900 she is the mother of 5 and all 5 are living. Only 4 are enumerated in the 1900 census.

Notes for Charles K. BROOKS:
In 1920 living on Stewart Rd in Springfield, Fayette Cnty, PA in a home he owns free and clear. He is a public school principal.
In 1930 living in Springfield Twp., Fayette Cnty, PA in a home he owns worth $3000 and has a radio.

More About Charles K. BROOKS:
Occupation: 1910, Farmer

More About Charles BROOKS and Sarah VAN HORN:
Marriage: 1880[1334]

Children of Sarah VAN HORN and Charles BROOKS are:
206. i. Clarence Wilbur[11] BROOKS, b. 04 Sep 1882, Mill Run, Fayette Cnty, PA; d. 1958, Mill Run, Fayette Cnty, PA.
  ii. Van E. BROOKS[1335], b. Oct 1885, PA[1336]; d. 1907, Springfield, Fayette Cnty, PA.
  iii. Harold K BROOKS[1337,1338,1339], b. Dec 1887, Springfield, Fayette Cnty, PA[1340]; d. Unknown.
  iv. Leslie Metrezat BROOKS[1340,1341,1342], b. 08 Feb 1890, Springfield, Fayette Cnty, PA[1343]; d. 12 Mar 1976, Clearwater, Pinellas Cnty, FL; m. Jane[1344], Abt. 1923; b. Abt. 1883, KY; d. Aft. 1930.

  More About Leslie BROOKS and Jane:
  Marriage: Abt. 1923

  v. Omer Victor BROOKS, b. Bet. 1880 - 1900, PA; d. Aft. 1900.

71. Henry D. Foster[10] VAN HORN *(John Dick[9], Alexander[8], Isaiah[7], Henry B.[6], Henry[5], Christian Barentsen[4] VAN HOORN, Barent Christiansen[3], Christian Barentsen[2], Barent*

Isaiah Van Horn Pioneer of Indiana County, Pennsylvania

Barents[1])[1345,1346,1347,1348,1349,1350] was born 12 Sep 1860 in PA[1351], and died 18 Jan 1935. He married Matilda TANNEHILL[1351,1352,1353,1354] 17 Sep 1885, daughter of Eli TANNEHILL and Elizabeth GRAHAM. She was born 19 Apr 1863 in PA[1355], and died 21 Jan 1935[1356].

Notes for Henry D. Foster VAN HORN:
   In 1900 lives on Edwin Ave Scottdale, PA.
   In 1910 lives on Spring Street, Scottdale, PA has been married one time for 24 years and he and his wife have 6 children all of whom are living.
   In 1920 living on Spring Street Scottdale, PA and is a roller in a rolling mill. He owns his home free and clear. Somehow Henry is listed as Henry L. Van Horn and born in Massachusetts. This is clearly Henry D. Foster as this person is living in the same place and his wife is Matilda and daughter is Olive but another son is listed that was not on the 1910 census.
   In 1930 he is H. Foster Van Horn. He and Matilda live alone in a home worth $10,000 free and clear and do not have a radio. He married at age 25 and she at age 22. He is listed as being a policeman in a sheet steel mill. I suspect he is a security person. This time the census taker got his birth place correct as Pennsylvania.
   Their daughter Ann Mary had 2 sons Gene and Harold Harkcom. She died while they were babies and Henry and his wife adopted the children.

From John F. Van Horn:
   Henry Foster and Matilda Tannehill Van Horn had six children and later adopted 2 more, the sons of Anna Mary, who died early. The six natural children and their wives were: John Dick Van Horn, born May 19, 1889, married Berdeen Braymer June 15, 1916, died April 12, 1982; Judson Tannehill Van Horn, b. Aug 2, 1887, m. Beatrice Barton June 13, 1919, d. May 16, 1967; Olive Mae Van Horn, b. July 14, 1894, m. Walter Edge, d. July 12, 1981; Hazel Foster Van Horn, b. July 15, 1892, m. William Presley Donaldson Sept. 21, 1917, d. Nov 11, 1980; Anna Mary Van Horn, b. April 11, 1886, m. Harkcom Feb 13, 1913 at age 27; Viola Virginia Van Horn, b. Dec 25, 1890, m. William Price, d. May 13, 1973. The two adopted children, who were given the Van Horn name, were; Eugene Harkcom Van Horn and Harold Harkcom Van Horn. Both were married. Eugene had 1 adopted child and Harold had I believe 2 natural children.

More About Henry D. Foster VAN HORN:
Occupation: Rougher Steel Mill, Roller Sheet Mill

More About Henry VAN HORN and Matilda TANNEHILL:
Marriage: 17 Sep 1885

Children of Henry VAN HORN and Matilda TANNEHILL are:
207.   i.   Annie[11] VAN HORN, b. 11 Apr 1886, Scottdale, Westmoreland Cnty, PA; d. 13 Feb 1913.
208.   ii. Judson Tannehill VAN HORN, b. 02 Aug 1887, Mt. Pleasant, Westmoreland Cnty, PA; d. 27 May 1967, Augusta, Richmond Cnty, GA.
209.   iii. John Dick VAN HORN, b. 19 May 1889, Scottdale, Westmoreland Cnty, PA; d. 14 Apr 1982, Meadville, Crawford Cnty, PA.
210.   iv. Viola Virginia VAN HORN, b. 25 Dec 1890, Scottdale, Westmoreland Cnty, PA; d. 13 May 1973.
211.   v.   Hazel Foster VAN HORN, b. 15 Jul 1892, Scottdale, Westmoreland Cnty, PA; d. 11 Nov 1980.
212.   vi. Olive Mae VAN HORN, b. 14 Jul 1894, Scottdale, Westmoreland Cnty, PA; d. 12 Jul 1981, Greensburg, Westmoreland Cnty, PA.

72. Albert[10] VAN HORN *(John Dick*[9]*, Alexander*[8]*, Isaiah*[7]*, Henry B.*[6]*, Henry*[5]*, Christian Barentsen*[4] *VAN HOORN, Barent Christiansen*[3]*, Christian Barentsen*[2]*, Barent Barents*[1])[1357,1358,1359,1360,1361,1362] was

born May 1864 in PA*1363*, and died Aft. Apr 1942. He married Fannie E.*1364,1365,1366* Abt. 1888*1367*.
She was born Nov 1864 in PA*1367*, and died Bet. 1920 - 1930.

Notes for Albert VAN HORN:
    In 1920 Albert is living with his family on Loughlin Street in Dawson, PA in a home he owns
free and clear. Fanie is the mother of 6 children.
    In 1930 Albert is a widower who lives in his home which he owns worth $6000 and has a radio.
four of his single children are living in the home.

More About Albert VAN HORN:
Occupation: Railroad Agent, Bookkeeper Coal Mine, Auditor Nast Run Railroad, Auditor Steam
Railroad

More About Albert VAN HORN and Fannie E.:
Marriage: Abt. 1888*1367*

Children of Albert VAN HORN and Fannie E. are:
      i.   Laura[11] VAN HORN*1367*, b. Feb 1890, PA*1367*; d. Unknown.
      ii.   Theodore VAN HORN*1367,1368,1369,1370*, b. Aug 1893, Stoystown, PA*1371*; d. Aft. 27
          Apr 1942*1372*.

          Notes for Theodore VAN HORN:
          In his WWI Draft Registration he lives in Dawson and is a Tipple Foreman for a
          Coal company. He is tall slender with grey eyes and brown hair.
          In his WWI I Draft Registration he says he works for F. E. Burdette in Dawson,
          PA. He gives his father as his point of contact so we know he is living. He has hazel
          eyes, brown hair and light complexion.

          More About Theodore VAN HORN:
          Occupation: Clerk General Store, Laborer C&C Company, Laborer Steam Railroad

     iii.   Frank VAN HORN*1373,1374,1375,1376*, b. Mar 1895, PA*1377*; d. Unknown.

          More About Frank VAN HORN:
          Occupation: Clerk PL&E Railroad, Laborer Steam Railroad

     iv.   Katherine VAN HORN*1377,1378,1379,1380*, b. Mar 1897, PA*1381*; d. Unknown.

          More About Katherine VAN HORN:
          Occupation: Clerk PL&E Railroad, Merchant Dry Goods

     v.   Alice VAN HORN*1381,1382,1383*, b. Jan 1899, PA*1384*; d. Unknown.

          More About Alice VAN HORN:
          Occupation: clerk Post Office

     vi.   Caroline VAN HORN*1385,1386,1387*, b. Abt. 1904, PA*1388*; d. Unknown.

73. Anna I.[10] VAN HORN *(James Wherry[9], Alexander[8], Isaiah[7], Henry B.[6], Henry[5], Christian Barentsen[4]*
VAN HOORN, Barent Christiansen[3], Christian Barentsen[2], Barent
Barents[1])[1389,1390,1391,1392,1393,1394,1395,1396] was born Jun 1853 in PA*1397,1398*, and died Aft. 1930. She
married James M. ASHBAUGH*1399,1400,1401,1402* Abt. 1874. He was born Jun 1851 in PA*1403*, and

died Bef. 1930.

Notes for Anna I. VAN HORN:
In 1894 lived in Buffalo, NY.
In 1930 living next door to her son Charles on 10th Street in Niagara Falls, NY in a home she owns worth $12,000.

More About James M. ASHBAUGH:
Occupation: Hardware Merchant, Merchandise Shipper, Civil Engineer Surveying

More About James ASHBAUGH and Anna VAN HORN:
Marriage: Abt. 1874

Children of Anna VAN HORN and James ASHBAUGH are:
    i.   Charles W.[11] ASHBAUGH[1403,1404,1405,1406,1407], b. Sep 1876, PA[1408,1409]; d. Aft. 1930; m. F. Edwina HORNE[1410,1411], Abt. 1913; b. Abt. 1878, NY[1412]; d. Aft. 1930.

        More About Charles W. ASHBAUGH:
        Occupation: Electrician

        More About Charles ASHBAUGH and F. HORNE:
        Marriage: Abt. 1913

    ii.   ? ASHBAUGH[1413], d. Unknown.
    iii. Howard Covode ASHBAUGH[1413,1414,1415], b. 30 Jun 1885, Westmoreland Cnty, PA[1416,1417]; d. Aft. 1942; m. Louise[1418]; b. Abt. 1885, PA[1418]; d. Aft. 1942.

        Notes for Howard Covode ASHBAUGH:
        In his WWI civilian draft registration he is living in Denver, CO.
        In 1920 living in Denver with wife Louise. He is a cereal traveler.
        In 1930 he is living in Omaha, NE and is a salesman for a Food Products Co. He lives with his wife Louise and they rent for $45/month and have a radio.
        In his WWI I civilian draft registration taken in 1942 he is living at 2304 Park Ave., Indianapolis, IN with his wife Louise. He is a self employed wholesale candy dealer. Hie telephone is WAB 4223. He was born in Westmoreland Cnty, PA.

74. Caroline E.[10] VAN HORN *(James Wherry[9], Alexander[8], Isaiah[7], Henry B.[6], Henry[5], Christian Barentsen[4] VAN HOORN, Barent Christiansen[3], Christian Barentsen[2], Barent Barents[1])*[1419,1420,1421,1422,1423,1424,1425] was born Dec 1856 in PA[1426], and died Bet. 1910 - 1920 in Westmoreland Cnty, PA. She married John Wesley BALLANTYNE[1427,1428,1429,1430,1431,1432] Abt. 1877. He was born 07 Jul 1854 in PA[1433], and died Aft. 1930.

Notes for Caroline E. VAN HORN:
In 1894 lived in Derry, PA. Sometimes called Callie.

Notes for John Wesley BALLANTYNE:
In 1920 he lives on North Chestnut Street in Derry, PA. He owns his home free and clear. He is a Hardware Store Merchant. His daughter Gertrude is of the home. He is as of the date of this survey widowed.
In 1930 he is living a 216 North Chestnut Street in Derry, PA. He owns his home worth $18,000 and has a radio. His daughter Mary Gertrude and his sister Margaret M. Ballentyne are living in the home as well as a servant. He is the manger of a hardware store.

More About John Wesley BALLANTYNE:
Occupation: Hardware Merchant, Tinner owns shop and store

More About John BALLANTYNE and Caroline VAN HORN:
Marriage: Abt. 1877

Children of Caroline VAN HORN and John BALLANTYNE are:
       i. Mary Gertude[11] BALLANTYNE[1433,1434,1435,1436], b. Sep 1878, PA[1437]; d. Unknown.
213.   ii. James Van Horn BALLANTYNE, b. 13 Oct 1881, Derry, Westmoreland Cnty, PA; d. 07 Jan 1948, Edgewood, Allegeheny Cnty, PA.
214.   iii. John Wesley BALLANTYNE, b. 21 Jul 1885, Derry, Westmoreland Cnty, PA; d. Unknown.
     iv. Florence BALLANTYNE[1437,1438], b. Jun 1888, PA[1439]; d. Unknown.

          More About Florence BALLANTYNE:
          Employment: Real Estate Stenographer

75. Margaret Mary[10] VAN HORN *(James Wherry[9], Alexander[8], Isaiah[7], Henry B.[6], Henry[5], Christian Barentsen[4] VAN HOORN, Barent Christiansen[3], Christian Barentsen[2], Barent Barents[1])[1440,1441,1442,1443,1444,1445]* was born Mar 1868 in PA[1446], and died Abt. 1920 in PA. She married Benjamin Frank ASHCOM[1447,1448,1449] Abt. 1888, son of John ASHCOM and Mary GOHN. He was born Abt. 1868 in PA[1450], and died Abt. 1930 in New Florence, Westmoreland Cnty, PA.

Notes for Margaret Mary VAN HORN:
    It is not known who are the parents of Margaret. She is known to be a granddaughter of James W. Van Horn through his will and through an article in the Indiana County Gazette (Indiana, PA) September 9, 1891. However the 1880 Census lists her as his daughter. It could be that she is the illegitimate daughter of Flora and the family never discussed this matter.
    In the obit of James, Maggie is given as his granddaughter and that she is Mrs. Ashcom living in Conemaugh, PA.

More About Margaret Mary VAN HORN:
Lived: Conemaugh, PA

Notes for Benjamin Frank ASHCOM:
    In 1920 living on Ninth Street in New Florence in a house he owns with a mortgage. Of the home is his wife, his 2 daughters Florence V. and Grace M. Ashcom as well as his aunt by marriage Florence Van Horn aged 69 and single.
    In 1930 his aunt Florence Van Horn age 72 born PA is living with him and his wife who is apparently his second marriage. He is living on Ninth Street in New Florence, PA in a home he owns worth $3,000.

More About Benjamin Frank ASHCOM:
Occupation: Farmer, Railroad Locomotive Engineer

More About Benjamin ASHCOM and Margaret VAN HORN:
Marriage: Abt. 1888

Children of Margaret VAN HORN and Benjamin ASHCOM are:
215.   i. James Donald[11] ASHCOM, b. 16 Apr 1890, Conemaugh, Cambria Cnty, PA; d. 03 Mar 1968, Johnstown, Cambria Cnty, PA.
      ii. Eugene Wesley ASHCOM[1451,1452,1453], b. 21 Jan 1892, PA[1454]; d. Unknown; m.

Beulah E.*1455*, Abt. 1916, PA; b. 1892, PA*1455*; d. Unknown.

Notes for Eugene Wesley ASHCOM:
WWI draft registration states he lives at 726 Clark St in Johnstown, (Dale) Cambria Cnty, PA. His telephone # is 63-554. He works for the PA Railroad. His wife is Beulah E. Ashcom and she lives at the same address. He is 6'1" weighs 195 # has brown eyes, gray hair and a light complexion and has no disabilities.
In 1930 he lives on Clark Street in a home he owns worth $6000 and has a radio. He and Beulah married when they were both 25. No children are listed. He is a locomotive fireman for a steam railroad.

More About Eugene ASHCOM and Beulah E.:
Marriage: Abt. 1916, PA

216.   iii.   John Raymond ASHCOM, b. 12 Oct 1893, Huff, Indiana Cnty, PA; d. 14 Jul 1965, PA.
        iv.   Florence V. ASHCOM*1456,1457,1458*, b. Jul 1898, PA*1459*; d. Unknown.
        v.   Mary G. ASHCOM*1460,1461*, b. Abt. Dec 1909, PA*1462*; d. Unknown.

76. Alice Roselia[10] VAN HORN *(Henry Coulter[9], Alexander[8], Isaiah[7], Henry B.[6], Henry[5], Christian Barentsen[4] VAN HOORN, Barent Christiansen[3], Christian Barentsen[2], Barent Barents[1])[1463,1464,1465,1466,1467]* was born Bet. 21 - 22 Mar 1848 in Indiana Cnty, PA*1468*, and died 17 Jun 1911. She married Thomas CUMMINGS*1469,1470,1471* Abt. 1865. He was born Bet. 10 Sep 1832 - 1833 in County Meath, Ireland*1472*, and died 01 Nov 1905.

Notes for Alice Roselia VAN HORN:
During the Civil War it is said that Alice was sent to live with her Uncle William in Allamakee County, IA.
In 1900 Alice indicates she is the mother of 7 children of which 5 are living with 4 given in the census.
In 1910 Alice is widowed and is living with her son Thomas who is single and a farmer and her daughter Ellen who is single and a school teacher.

Notes for Thomas CUMMINGS:
In 1870 he is a farmer with a valuation of land as $1700 and personal effects of $600. He states he was born in MD and both parents were foreign born. He later says he was born in Ireland.
He moved to MN between 1880 and 1885 from Iowa. In the 1885 MN census he states both parents were foreign born and he was born in Ireland.

More About Thomas CUMMINGS:
Occupation: farmer

More About Thomas CUMMINGS and Alice VAN HORN:
Marriage: Abt. 1865

Children of Alice VAN HORN and Thomas CUMMINGS are:
217.   i.   Emmett W.[11] CUMMINGS, b. Feb 1868, IA; d. Aft. 1920.
        ii.   Frank CUMMINGS*1472,1473,1474*, b. Sep 1869, IA*1475,1476*; d. Unknown.
218.   iii.   Thomas Patrick CUMMINGS, b. Bet. 14 Aug 1872 - 1874, IA; d. Bet. 1930 - 1940, Koochiching Cnty, MN.
219.   iv.   Charles CUMMINGS, b. 01 May 1879, Forest City, Winnebago Cnty, IA; d. Unknown.
        v.   Ellen M. CUMMINGS*1477,1478*, b. Jul 1887, MN*1479*; d. Unknown; m. HAMMOND;

d. Unknown.

More About Ellen M. CUMMINGS:
Occupation: School Teacher

77. William Alexander[10] VAN HORN *(Henry Coulter[9], Alexander[8], Isaiah[7], Henry B.[6], Henry[5], Christian Barentsen[4] VAN HOORN, Barent Christiansen[3], Christian Barentsen[2], Barent Barents[1])*[1480,1481,1482,1483] was born 21 Mar 1850 in Indiana Cnty, PA[1484,1485], and died Aft. 1910. He married (1) Alice Lucetta VAN HORN[1486,1487,1488] Abt. 1875, daughter of Henry VAN HORN and Amanda JAMES. She was born 1855 in PA[1489], and died Aft. 1899. He married (2) Martha J.[1490,1491] Abt. 1895[1491]. She was born Jun 1860 in PA[1492], and died Aft. 1910.

Notes for William Alexander VAN HORN:
10 April 1895 Indiana Weekly Messenger (Indiana, PA) reports that William G. Ling sells to William P. Van Horn on March 23, 1895 50 acres in East Wheatfield for $3500. I suspect that this sale was to William A not William P. Van Horn.
12 October 1910 the Indiana Progress(Indiana, PA) states that William has left to visit his sister Mrs. William Bowser in North Dakota.
William is living next to his father in law Henry Van Horn with his wife Lusetta and their two children.

More About William Alexander VAN HORN:
Occupation: Carpenter, Architect

Notes for Alice Lucetta VAN HORN:
27 December 1899 the Indiana Weekly Messenger (Indiana, PA) reports that on 15 December 1899 the will of Henry A. Van Horn of Georgeville is filed and his daughter Lucetta receives his house, lot and furniture situated in Georgeville. The will is dated 22 April 1897.
Name is also given as Lucetta A. Van Horn in 1880 Census

More About William VAN HORN and Alice VAN HORN:
Marriage: Abt. 1875

More About William VAN HORN and Martha J.:
Marriage: Abt. 1895[1493]

Children are listed above under (67) Alice Lucetta VAN HORN.

78. Mary Agnes[10] VAN HORN *(Henry Coulter[9], Alexander[8], Isaiah[7], Henry B.[6], Henry[5], Christian Barentsen[4] VAN HOORN, Barent Christiansen[3], Christian Barentsen[2], Barent Barents[1])*[1494,1495,1496,1497,1498,1499] was born 20 Nov 1851 in Armagh, Indiana Cnty, PA[1500], and died Bef. 1937. She married William H. BOWSER[1501,1502,1503,1504] 24 Dec 1874, son of Margaret. He was born 04 Aug 1846 in Ligonier, Westmoreland Cnty, PA[1505], and died 11 Mar 1926 in Milnor, Sargent Cnty, ND.

Notes for Mary Agnes VAN HORN:
In 1900 Mary states she is the mother of 6 with 4 living in 1900. there are 3 living in the family so only one other child is still living. She and William have been married for 25 years.

Notes for William H. BOWSER:
May have served in the Civil War

In 1920 owns his place free and clear. Living with wife and working as a laborer for the railroad.

BLM Land Listing in Sargent Cnty, ND BOWZER WILLIAM 05 131 N 055 W 025 80 251101 PA 7646 10/10/1894

More About William H. BOWSER:
Employment: 1920, Railroad Laborer
Occupation: Farmer

More About William BOWSER and Mary VAN HORN:
Marriage: 24 Dec 1874

Children of Mary VAN HORN and William BOWSER are:

	i.	Ellen[11] BOWSER[1505], b. Abt. 1875, PA[1505]; d. Unknown.
220.	ii.	John A. BOWSER, b. 07 Aug 1877, PA; d. 10 Feb 1951, Dickey Cnty, ND.
	iii.	Margaret BOWSER[1505], b. May 1880, PA[1505]; d. Unknown.
	iv.	Mary M. BOWSER[1506], b. Apr 1882, PA[1506]; d. Unknown.
	v.	Florence Van Horn BOWSER[1507,1508], b. Dec 1891, AR[1509]; d. Unknown.
	vi.	Bertha C. BOWSER[1509,1510], b. Jun 1893, ND[1511]; d. Unknown; m. BOWMAN; d. Unknown.

Notes for Bertha C. BOWSER:
Lived in MN

	vii.	William F. BOWSER, b. Private.

79. Clara Lucinda[10] VAN HORN *(Henry Coulter[9], Alexander[8], Isaiah[7], Henry B.[6], Henry[5], Christian Barentsen[4] VAN HOORN, Barent Christiansen[3], Christian Barentsen[2], Barent Barents[1])[1512,1513]* was born 27 Apr 1854 in Indiana Cnty, PA[1514], and died 26 Jan 1872 in East Wheatfield, Indiana Cnty, PA. She married Joseph KISSINGER[1515] 30 Sep 1869, son of Joseph KISSINGER and Elizabeth. He was born 1847 in PA[1516], and died Unknown.

More About Joseph KISSINGER and Clara VAN HORN:
Marriage: 30 Sep 1869

Child of Clara VAN HORN and Joseph KISSINGER is:

	i.	Minnie A.[11] KISSINGER[1516,1517], b. Jun 1870[1518]; d. Aft. 1900.

Notes for Minnie A. KISSINGER:
In 1880 living with her grandparents. It is uncertain what has become of her parents between 1870 and 1880.

80. Henry Coulter[10] VAN HORN *(Henry Coulter[9], Alexander[8], Isaiah[7], Henry B.[6], Henry[5], Christian Barentsen[4] VAN HOORN, Barent Christiansen[3], Christian Barentsen[2], Barent Barents[1])[1518,1519,1520,1521,1522]* was born 12 Mar 1855 in East Wheatfield, Indiana Cnty, PA[1523], and died 01 Dec 1919 in WA[1524]. He married Hannah M. VAN HORN[1525,1526,1527,1528] Abt. 1887. She was born Jul 1860 in IA[1529], and died Aft. 1922.

Notes for Henry Coulter VAN HORN:
The 1900 census lists Harry Van Horn as the enumerator for Kiona Pct. of Yakima Cnty, WA.

Isaiah Van Horn Pioneer of Indiana County, Pennsylvania

25 March 1914 the Indiana Progress(Indiana, PA) reported that H. C. Van Horn left on Saturday to visit his sister Mrs. Harry Bateman of Wilkinsburg, PA. He has been ill for several months. This item is in the items of East Wheatfield Twp. items of news. Since H. C. Van Horn has a sister married to a Harry Bateman and in Wilkinsburg I have concluded that it is Tabitha L. Van Horn and through this connection in the news found the husband and family of Tabitha.

17 Dec. 1919 Indiana Progress (Indiana, PA) reports that Harry Van Horn of WA died on Dec 1. He was born in East Wheatfield Twp. but went west a number of years ago.

More About Henry Coulter VAN HORN:
Occupation: Farmer
Organizations: Old Boatmen

Notes for Hannah M. VAN HORN:
In 1920 Hannah and Esther are lodgers on 6th Avenue in Seattle, WA and Esther is a School Teacher and Hannah is widowed.
In 1930 Hannah is a widow living on North Sixteenth Street in Seattle, WA in a home she owns worth $4500. Living with her are her two daughters both unmarried.

More About Henry VAN HORN and Hannah VAN HORN:
Marriage: Abt. 1887

Children of Henry VAN HORN and Hannah VAN HORN are:
    i.   Bowen[11] VAN HORN[1529,1530,1531,1532], b. 10 Jul 1889, ND[1533,1534]; d. 17 May 1941, Los Angeles Cnty, CA[1534].

        Notes for Bowen VAN HORN:
        In 1920 lives in Horn Rapids, Benton Cnty, WA and owns his place with a mortgage.
        In 1930 he is a lodger on Highland Place in Monrovia, Los Angles Cnty, CA and is an Agriculture Laborer.

    ii. Elizabeth E. VAN HORN[1535,1536,1537], b. Feb 1891, WA[1538]; d. Unknown.

        Notes for Elizabeth E. VAN HORN:
        In 1920 Elizabeth is a Public School teacher in Elma, WA and is a lodger.

        More About Elizabeth E. VAN HORN:
        Occupation: Public School Teacher

    iii. Esther G. VAN HORN[1538,1539,1540,1541,1542], b. Oct 1893, Benton Cnty, WA[1543]; d. Unknown.

        More About Esther G. VAN HORN:
        Occupation: Assistant Manager Nach Motor Coach Co.

81. Samuel Cornelius[10] VAN HORN *(Henry Coulter[9], Alexander[8], Isaiah[7], Henry B.[6], Henry[5], Christian Barentsen[4] VAN HOORN, Barent Christiansen[3], Christian Barentsen[2], Barent Barents[1])*[1544,1545,1546,1547,1548,1549,1550] was born Bet. 31 Dec 1857 - 1858 in Near Armagh, Indiana Cnty, PA[1551,1552,1553,1554], and died 06 Jan 1937 in Dalhart, Dallam Cnty, TX[1555,1556]. He married (1) Emma Ellen HUMMEL[1557,1558,1559,1560,1561] 24 Apr 1883 in Fremont, OH Reformed Church, Sandusky Cnty, OH, daughter of Christian HUMMEL and Margaret FISHER. She was born 1854 in Sandusky Cnty, OH[1562], and died 04 Jan 1887 in Seneca Cnty, OH[1563]. He married (2) Jennie E. HUMMEL[1564,1565,1566,1567,1568] Abt. 1889 in OH[1569], daughter of Christian HUMMEL and Margaret

FISHER. She was born 11 Aug 1852 in OH[1570,1571,1572,1573], and died 14 Aug 1929 in Dalhart, Dallam Cnty, TX[1574]. He married (3) Teressa[1575] Abt. 1932 in TX[1575]. She died Aft. 06 Jan 1937.

Notes for Samuel Cornelius VAN HORN:
    Emma Hummel Van Horn died shortly after the birth of her second child Leafy Fern Van Horn. Samuel C. Van Horn then married Emma's sister Jennie Hummel.
    In 1920 living in Dalhart,TX on Keeler Street in a home they own free and clear.

    An article in the Indiana Progress(Indiana, PA) of 23 July 1874 H. C. Van Horn writes that Samuel Van Horn has Run Away. He is 16 years of age and is 5 feet 6 or 7 inches tall brown hair, light complexion, grayish blue eyes. He asks that no one harbor Samuel and is willing to pay expenses for his return.
    15 March 1899 the Indiana Weekly Messenger (Indiana, PA) reports that S. C. Van Horn is elected from East Wheatfield Twp. to the county committee.
    7 June 1899 Indiana Progress (Indiana, PA) states that S C. Van Horn is building a coal, wash and wood house.
    9 Aug 1899 Indiana Progress (Indiana, PA) reports that Hubert Van Horn of Wilkinsburg visited his brother S. C. Van Horn. In the same paper it is reported that S. C. and his wife visited the Free Methodists camp meeting at Blairsville the latter part of the previous week.
    24 June 1903 Indiana Progress (Indiana, PA) reported that S. C. Van Horn in a delegation from East Wheatfield participated in the county's centennial activities by exhibiting a pair of millstones from the Findley Mill constructed at Cramer in 1784-85.
    From the Indiana County 175th Anniversary History by Clarence D. Stephenson quotes an article for the Indiana County Gazette (Indiana, PA) of 24 June 1903 states that in the Great Industrial Parade " The Plumville band led North and south Mahoning. North Mahoning was led by Marshall S. C. Van Horn, followed by a number of cavalrymen."
    1 March 1905 S. C. Van Horn election as constable in East Wheatfield Twp., Is reported in the Indiana Progress (Indiana, PA) and the Indiana Weekly Messenger (Indiana, PA) of the same date.
    24 April 1907 the Indiana Progress (Indiana, PA) reports that Constable Samuel C. Van Horn of East Wheatfield Twp. was at the county seat.
    27 November 1907 Indiana Progress (Indiana, PA) reports a sale by S. C. Van Horn to John B. Taylor of 116 acres in East Wheatfield for $29.
    13 May 1908 S. C. Van Horn sells 2 acres in East Wheatfield to C. G. and W. H. Dick for $10 as reported in the Indiana Progress(Indiana, PA).
    11 November 1908 the Indiana Weekly Messenger (Indiana, PA) reports that Mr. and Mrs. S. C. Van Horn have purchased a ranch in the Lone Star State and are leaving soon to raise cattle. Their friends in and about Armagh have gathered to say they good byes and wish them well in their new home.
    11 Nov 1908 the Indiana Evening Gazette (Indiana, PA) reports that the S. C. Van Horn family of Armagh left this day for their new home in Dalhart, TX.
    25 November 1908 the Indiana Weekly Messenger (Indiana, PA) reports that Ex-Patrolman Riggs of Johnstown has purchased the Van Horn farm of 116 acres near Armagh and has taken possession. the Van Horn family has moved to a cattle ranch in Texas.

More About Samuel Cornelius VAN HORN:
Burial: 1937, Elmwood Cemetery, Dalhart. Dallam Cnty, TX
Occupation: Farmer, Labor Foreman Round House

Notes for Emma Ellen HUMMEL:
    In 1880 Emma is a servant in the John King home in Jackson Twp., Sandusky Cnty, OH. She is 24 and born OH. She says her father was born in Germany and mother in PA.
    According to the Fremont Weekly Journal of 7 January 1887 Mrs. Emma Van Horn of Bettsville, died on Tuesday. She formerly lived in the family of James Kridler of this city.

More About Emma Ellen HUMMEL:
Burial: 1887, Liberty Cemetery, Bettsville, OH
Occupation: 1880, Housekeeper

More About Samuel VAN HORN and Emma HUMMEL:
Marriage: 24 Apr 1883, Fremont, OH Reformed Church, Sandusky Cnty, OH

Notes for Jennie E. HUMMEL:
    In 1880 Jennie is a servant in the John Stierwalt home in Fremont, Sandusky Cnty, OH. She is 27 born OH and says her father was born in OH and mother in VA.
    9 May 1900 Indiana Progress (Indiana, PA) reports that Mrs. S. C. Van Horn spent the day in Armagh.
    25 Dec 1901 Indiana Progress (Indiana, PA) newspaper: "Mrs. Trombel of Fremont, is visiting her daughter, Mrs. S. C. Van Horn."
    9 Oct. 1907 the Indiana Progress (Indiana, PA) reports that Mrs. S. C. Van Horn and daughter Nellie were traveling to Ohio and Michigan to visit friends.
    In 1910 and 1920 Jennie states her father was born in Germany and in 1910 her mother was born in MD and in 1920 in VA. In 1900 she states Germany and MD for the birth places.
    In 1910 Jennie, Samuel and Nellie are living two doors from her sister Ida and her family in Dallam Cnty, TX. both families are farming.

More About Jennie E. HUMMEL:
Burial: 15 Aug 1929, Elmwood cemetery, Dalhart. Dallam Cnty, TX

More About Samuel VAN HORN and Jennie HUMMEL:
Marriage: Abt. 1889, OH[1576]

More About Samuel VAN HORN and Teressa:
Marriage: Abt. 1932, TX[1577]

Children of Samuel VAN HORN and Emma HUMMEL are:
221.   i.   Henry Coulter[11] VAN HORN, b. Bet. 07 Sep 1884 - 1885, Warren, Waynesville Cnty, OH; d. 27 Jul 1960, Dalhart, Dallam Cnty, TX.
222.   ii.   Leafy Fern VAN HORN, b. Bet. 17 Dec 1885 - 1886, Bettsville, Liberty Twp., Seneca Cnty, OH; d. 18 Nov 1969, Dayton, Montgomery Cnty, OH.

Child of Samuel VAN HORN and Jennie HUMMEL is:
223.   iii. Nellie Vidella[11] VAN HORN, b. Nov 1893, OH; d. Unknown.

82. Tabitha Logan[10] VAN HORN *(Henry Coulter[9], Alexander[8], Isaiah[7], Henry B.[6], Henry[5], Christian Barentsen[4] VAN HOORN, Barent Christiansen[3], Christian Barentsen[2], Barent Barents[1])*[1578,1579,1580,1581,1582] was born 14 Oct 1862 in Indiana Cnty, PA[1583], and died 1950 in Pinellas Cnty, FL[1584]. She married Harry T. BATEMAN[1585,1586,1587]. He was born Aug 1861 in PA[1588,1589], and died Unknown.

Notes for Tabitha Logan VAN HORN:
    In 1920 listed as Harriett T. Bateman living at 521 5th Ave in St. Petersburg, FL. She is married and owns home with a mortgage and has a grandson Kenneth age 12 born PA living in the home with her. She has no listed employment.
    In 1930 living at 521 Fifth Avenue South in St. Petersburg, FL in a home she owns worth about $5,000 and does not have a radio. She indicates she is married and she was 18 on the date of her first marriage. She and her parents were born in PA and she indicates no employment. Her son

Allen lives on 4th street in St. Petersburg near his mother.

On the passenger list for the SS America sailing from Cherbourg, France May 28,1 931 and arriving in New York June 5, 1931, Tabitha is found listed with the following information: Tabitha L. Bateman, Female, white, age 68, born 1862 Indiana County, PA and living at 521 Fifth Avenue S, St. Petersburg, FL. She sailed with a large group of Gold Star Mothers indicating that she lost a son in WWI. There is a record that shows a Russell L. Bateman of Wilkinsburg, PA a private was killed in the Great War.

More About Tabitha Logan VAN HORN:
Lived: Wilmerding, PA; Roup Station, PA and St. Petersburg, FL

Notes for Harry T. BATEMAN:
In 1910 living on Center Ave. in Wilkinsburg, PA there are 3 lodgers and a servant in the family in addition to the 2 youngest sons.
In 1920 living on Center Ave. in Wilkinsburg, PA Harry, John and Allen are lodgers and Claude, Russell and Tabitha are not listed with them. Harry is a Train Master, John is an accountant with the railroad and Allen is in advertising with a newspaper.

More About Harry T. BATEMAN:
Occupation: Railroad Train Master and Yard Master

Children of Tabitha VAN HORN and Harry BATEMAN are:
  i. John Earle[11] BATEMAN[1589,1590,1591], b. 07 Mar 1883, PA[1592,1593]; d. Unknown; m. Estella F.[1594], Abt. 1908[1594]; b. Abt. 1886, PA[1594]; d. Unknown.

      Notes for John Earle BATEMAN:
      In his WWI Draft Registration he is a riveter at the Baltimore Ft. McHenry Dry Docks and his wife is Estella Bateman.

      More About John Earle BATEMAN:
      Occupation: Order Clerk, Railway brakeman

      More About John BATEMAN and Estella F.:
      Marriage: Abt. 1908[1594]

  ii. Claude BATEMAN[1595], b. Jan 1885, PA[1595]; d. Unknown.

      More About Claude BATEMAN:
      Occupation: Office Boy

  iii. Russell L. BATEMAN[1596,1597], b. May 1891, PA[1598,1599]; d. Bet. 1917 - 1919, WWI[1600].

      More About Russell L. BATEMAN:
      Military service: Killed in WWI
      Occupation: Railroad Clerk

  iv. Allen BATEMAN[1601,1602,1603], b. Aug 1897, PA[1604,1605]; d. Unknown; m. Laura E. FAIR[1605], Abt. 1924; b. Abt. 1882, PA[1605]; d. Unknown.

      Notes for Allen BATEMAN:
      Living one Street over from his mother in 1930. He lives with his wife Laura and his father and law is also living in the home. He is a real estate broker and lives in a home worth $35,000 and has a radio.

Notes for Laura E. FAIR:
Laura's father is living with Laura and Allen in 1930.

More About Allen BATEMAN and Laura FAIR:
Marriage: Abt. 1924

83. Hubert Earl[10] VAN HORN *(Henry Coulter[9], Alexander[8], Isaiah[7], Henry B.[6], Henry[5], Christian Barentsen[4] VAN HOORN, Barent Christiansen[3], Christian Barentsen[2], Barent Barents[1])[1606,1607,1608,1609,1610]* was born Bet. 21 Aug 1869 - 1870 in Indiana Cnty, PA[1611,1612], and died Bef. 1937. He married Ada[1613,1614] Abt. 1896[1615]. She was born Nov 1878 in PA[1615], and died Unknown.

Notes for Hubert Earl VAN HORN:
9 Aug. 1899 Indiana Progress(Indiana, PA) reports that Hubert of Wilkinsburg, Pa visits his brother S. C. Van Horn
In 1910 a lodger with the Killen family. He indicates he is married. He is also listed with his family in Pittsburgh. He is a house carpenter so he may have been working in Indiana Cnty on a construction project. There are 4 boarders living in the home.

More About Hubert Earl VAN HORN:
Occupation: House Carpenter
Politics: 1907, Pittsburgh, PA

Notes for Ada:
2 August 1899 Indiana Progress(Indiana, PA) reported that Mrs. Hubert Van Horn and son Warren were visiting S. C. Van Horn in East Wheatfield.

More About Hubert VAN HORN and Ada:
Marriage: Abt. 1896[1615]

Children of Hubert VAN HORN and Ada are:
    i.   Warren H.[11] VAN HORN[1615,1616], b. Aug 1897, PA[1617]; d. Unknown.

           Notes for Warren H. VAN HORN:
           2 Aug 1899 the Indiana Progress(Indiana, PA) reports that Mrs Hubert Van Horn and son Warren are visiting S. C. Van Horn.
           In 1902 a Warren and William Van Horn are living with William an Catherine Lavis. Warren is 18 and William is 22. They are nephews of William and Catherine Lavis.

    ii.   ? VAN HORN[1617], b. Bet. 1897 - 1900; d. Bef. 1900.
224.   iii. Charles VAN HORN, b. Abt. 1901, PA; d. Unknown.

84. Frank[10] VAN HORN *(William[9], Alexander[8], Isaiah[7], Henry B.[6], Henry[5], Christian Barentsen[4] VAN HOORN, Barent Christiansen[3], Christian Barentsen[2], Barent Barents[1])[1618]* was born Abt. 1875 in IA[1618], and died Unknown. He married Theresa WARD. She died Unknown.

Children of Frank VAN HORN and Theresa WARD are:
    i.   Mabel[11] VAN HORN, b. 1903, SD; d. Unknown.
    ii. Wilhemina VAN HORN, b. 1905, SD; d. Unknown.
    iii. Ward VAN HORN, b. 1906, SD; d. Unknown.
    iv. Francis VAN HORN, b. 1909, SD; d. Unknown.

225.   v.   Mary Gladys VAN HORN, b. 30 Apr 1910, Buffalo, Harding Cnty, SD; d. 15 Aug
              1985, Bozeman, MT.
         vi. LeRoy VAN HORN, d. Unknown.

85. Jane[10] MCELHOES *(Isaiah[9], Jane[8] VAN HORN, Isaiah[7], Henry B.[6], Henry[5], Christian Barentsen[4] VAN HOORN, Barent Christiansen[3], Christian Barentsen[2], Barent Barents[1])*[1619,1620,1621,1622,1623] was born Mar 1841 in Green Twp., Indiana Cnty, PA[1624,1625], and died Aft. 1910. She married George W. COLLINS[1625,1626] Abt. 1881 in Indiana Cnty, PA. He was born Jan 1835 in PA[1627], and died Aft. 1910.

Notes for Jane MCELHOES:
    In 1900 Jane indicates she is the mother of 2 children and both are living.

Notes for George W. COLLINS:
    In 1880 there is a George Collins in the Young Twp. of Indiana County with a wife that died on the 1st of June in 1880. He has 3 children. This George is the same age as the one found in 1900 married to Jane with 2 children. The confusing part is that the census taker indicates that they have been married for 40 years. In 1880 Jane McElhoes is single and living with her father so the marriage mush have been about when she was 40 years of age.
    In 1910 George is farming and his wife Jane and the 2 boys are living in the home. Joseph is widowed and is a butcher and his infant son is in the household. George is a teamster.

More About George COLLINS and Jane MCELHOES:
Marriage: Abt. 1881, Indiana Cnty, PA

Children of Jane MCELHOES and George COLLINS are:
226.   i.   Joseph M.[11] COLLINS, b. Feb 1882, PA; d. Unknown.
         ii. George Edward COLLINS[1627,1628], b. Feb 1885, PA[1629]; d. Unknown.

86. John Kinter[10] MCELHOES *(Isaiah[9], Jane[8] VAN HORN, Isaiah[7], Henry B.[6], Henry[5], Christian Barentsen[4] VAN HOORN, Barent Christiansen[3], Christian Barentsen[2], Barent Barents[1])*[1630,1631,1632] was born 16 Mar 1845 in Green Twp., Indiana Cnty, PA[1633], and died 18 Feb 1908 in Indiana Cnty, PA. He married Margaret Huston THOMPSON[1633,1634] 11 Mar 1868 in Green Twp., Indiana Cnty, PA. She was born 10 Nov 1842 in Indiana Cnty, PA[1635], and died 14 Feb 1902 in Indiana Cnty, PA.

More About John Kinter MCELHOES:
Burial: Unknown, Washington Church Cemetery, Rayne Twp., Indiana Cnty, PA
Military service: Bet. 13 Aug 1864 - 16 Jun 1865, Private company A 206th PA Infantry

More About John MCELHOES and Margaret THOMPSON:
Marriage: 11 Mar 1868, Green Twp., Indiana Cnty, PA

Children of John MCELHOES and Margaret THOMPSON are:
227.   i.   Gertrude[11] MCELHOES, b. 24 Mar 1869, Indiana Cnty, PA; d. 26 Mar 1907, West
              Hickory, PA.
228.   ii. Frank Thomas MCELHOES, b. Bet. 06 - 16 Sep 1872, Rayne Twp., Indiana Cnty,
              PA; d. 22 May 1946, Vancouver, BC, Canada.
229.   iii. Mary Lucetta MCELHOES, b. 01 Dec 1874, PA; d. Unknown.
230.   iv. Robert Roy MCELHOES, b. 13 Jul 1876, Rayne Twp., Indiana Cnty, PA; d. 25 Feb
              1958, Indiana Cnty, PA.
231.   v.   Joseph Isaiah MCELHOES, b. 18 May 1879, Rayne Twp., Indiana Cnty, PA; d. 06
              Sep 1974, Rayne Twp., Indiana Cnty, PA.

232.   vi.   Martha Belle MCELHOES, b. Bet. 31 Oct - 01 Nov 1882, Home, Indiana Cnty, PA;
                   d. 28 Jul 1977, Burnaby, BC Canada.
            vii.   Merle John MCELHOES*1635,1636,1637*, b. 23 Jul 1884, PA*1638*; d. 05 Jul 1942,
                   Burnaby, BC Canada*1639*; m. Ann ENGINEER; d. Unknown.

                   Notes for Merle John MCELHOES:
                   In 1910 he is in Washington working as a Carpenter on a rail road.
                   He registered for the WWI draft in Seattle Washington. He gave his name as John
                   Merle. He is a Structural Iron Worker with Lester Monahan at the Coleman Dock in
                   Seattle, WA. He lists his closest relative as Frank McElhoes in Otter tail, MN.
                   In 1921 he is a bridge carpenter, single, boarding in Holbrook, OR.
                   Also in 1921 the local paper reports that after a long absence and loss of contact
                   with the family he writes to the postmaster asking if any of his relatives still live in
                   Indiana county, PA. He writes from Detroit, MI and shortly thereafter returns to
                   visit with 2 of his brothers who live in Home. PA.
                   According to the Indiana Gazette in April, 1922 he was being assessed for 15A Coal
                   in Plumville Twp.,Indiana Cnty, PA

                   More About Merle John MCELHOES:
                   Burial: 08 Jul 1942, Forest Lawn Memorial Park, Burnaby, BC Canada

87. James Steele[10] MCELHOES *(Isaiah[9], Jane[8] VAN HORN, Isaiah[7], Henry B.[6], Henry[5], Christian
Barentsen[4] VAN HOORN, Barent Christiansen[3], Christian Barentsen[2], Barent Barents[1])1640,1641,1642,1643* was
born 04 Apr 1847 in Green Twp., Indiana Cnty, PA or Elderton, Armonstrong Cnty, PA*1644*, and
died 08 Aug 1923 in Indiana Cnty, PA. He married Orpha RUPPERT*1645* Abt. 1894. She was born
Abt. 1865 in Elderton, Armonstrong Cnty, PA*1645*, and died Unknown.

Notes for James Steele MCELHOES:
        In 1871 James S. is listed as a Grand Juror in the 9 Nov. 1871 Indiana Progress(Indiana, PA).
        In 1910 an Aunt Nancy McCright age 73 is living in the home.

Notes for Orpha RUPPERT:
        In 1910 she is listed as the mother of 3 with 2 living as of that date.

More About James MCELHOES and Orpha RUPPERT:
Marriage: Abt. 1894

Children of James MCELHOES and Orpha RUPPERT are:
233.   i.   George Allen[11] MCELHOES, b. 15 Oct 1895, White Twp., Indiana Cnty, PA; d.
                   Unknown.
            ii.   Marion M. MCELHOES*1645*, b. Abt. 1903, PA*1645*; d. Unknown.
            iii.   ? MCELHOES, d. Unknown.

88. Henry Milton[10] DILTS *(Nancy[9] MCELHOES, Jane[8] VAN HORN, Isaiah[7], Henry B.[6], Henry[5],
Christian Barentsen[4] VAN HOORN, Barent Christiansen[3], Christian Barentsen[2], Barent
Barents[1])1646,1647,1648,1649,1650* was born 10 May 1859 in Kellysburg, Indiana Cnty, PA*1650*, and died 15
Nov 1932 in Blairsville, Indiana Cnty, PA*1651*. He married Charlotte Susan HAMILTON*1652,1653,1654*
03 Jun 1885 in Indiana Cnty, PA. She was born 15 Jan 1863 in Indiana Cnty, PA*1655*, and died 21
Feb 1954 in Blairsville, Indiana Cnty, PA*1655*.

Notes for Henry Milton DILTS:

In 1920 lives on Brady Street in Blairsville, PA in a home he owns free and clear. He is a receiving clerk for the railroad.

More About Henry DILTS and Charlotte HAMILTON:
Marriage: 03 Jun 1885, Indiana Cnty, PA

Children of Henry DILTS and Charlotte HAMILTON are:
234.   i.   Elva Floid[11] DILTS, b. 01 Mar 1886, Kellysburg, Indiana Cnty, PA; d. Aft. 1930.
235.   ii.   Martha Elizabeth DILTS, b. Abt. 1887, PA; d. Unknown.
        iii. Mildred L. DILTS[1656], b. Abt. 1893, PA; d. Unknown.
        iv.   Emerson C. DILTS[1657,1658], b. Abt. 1901, PA; d. Unknown.

        Notes for Emerson C. DILTS:
        In 1920 living with parents and works as a track supervisor for the railroad.

89. William H.[10] HOUCK *(Dorcas[9] MCELHOES, Jane[8] VAN HORN, Isaiah[7], Henry B.[6], Henry[5], Christian Barentsen[4] VAN HOORN, Barent Christiansen[3], Christian Barentsen[2], Barent Barents[1])*[1659,1660,1661] was born Abt. 1847 in PA[1662], and died Bet. 1880 - 1900. He married Regina Anna[1663,1664,1665]. She was born Feb 1846 in PA[1666], and died Unknown.

Notes for Regina Anna:
        In 1900 widowed living alone and farming.

Children of William HOUCK and Regina Anna are:
        i.   Mary A.[11] HOUCK[1666,1667], b. Feb 1870, PA[1668]; d. Unknown.
        ii.   Alice HOUCK[1669], b. Abt. 1871, PA[1669]; d. Unknown.
        iii. Amos F. HOUCK[1669], b. Abt. 1874, PA[1669]; d. Unknown.
        iv.   Joseph A. HOUCK[1669], b. Abt. 1874, PA[1669]; d. Unknown.

90. Daniel[10] HOUCK *(Dorcas[9] MCELHOES, Jane[8] VAN HORN, Isaiah[7], Henry B.[6], Henry[5], Christian Barentsen[4] VAN HOORN, Barent Christiansen[3], Christian Barentsen[2], Barent Barents[1])*[1670,1671,1672,1673] was born Apr 1852 in PA[1674,1675], and died Unknown. He married Ella[1675] Abt. 1895 in PA. She was born Jun 1865 in PA[1675], and died Unknown.

More About Daniel HOUCK and Ella:
Marriage: Abt. 1895, PA

Child of Daniel HOUCK and Ella is:
        i.   William[11] HOUCK[1675], b. Mar 1897, PA[1675]; d. Unknown.

91. John[10] HOUCK *(Dorcas[9] MCELHOES, Jane[8] VAN HORN, Isaiah[7], Henry B.[6], Henry[5], Christian Barentsen[4] VAN HOORN, Barent Christiansen[3], Christian Barentsen[2], Barent Barents[1])*[1676,1677,1678] was born 25 Jun 1858 in PA[1679], and died 21 May 1949 in Indiana Cnty, PA. He married Emma Jane WIDDOWSON[1679]. She was born Abt. 1860 in Cherry Hill Twp., Indiana Cnty, PA[1679], and died Unknown.

More About John HOUCK:
Occupation: 1880, Engineer

Children of John HOUCK and Emma WIDDOWSON are:

    i.   Linda Maude[11] HOUCK, b. 06 Aug 1880, Cherry Hill Twp., Indiana Cnty, PA; d. Unknown.
    ii. Harry Stanley HOUCK, b. 09 Jun 1882, Cherry Hill Twp., Indiana Cnty, PA; d. Unknown.

92. Jane T.[10] LIGHTCAP *(Susan[9] MCELHOES, Jane[8] VAN HORN, Isaiah[7], Henry B.[6], Henry[5], Christian Barentsen[4] VAN HOORN, Barent Christiansen[3], Christian Barentsen[2], Barent Barents[1])[1680,1681,1682,1683]* was born 1847 in Rayne Twp., Indiana Cnty, PA[1684], and died 1882. She married George Stockholm WYNKOOP[1685,1686,1687] 23 Sep 1868 in Green Twp., Indiana Cnty, PA, son of Matthew WYNCOOP and Mary VAN LEAR. He was born 26 Dec 1846 in PA[1688], and died 02 Oct 1897 in Green Twp.,Indiana Cnty, PA[1688].

More About George Stockholm WYNKOOP:
Burial: Unknown, Marion Center, Indiana Cnty, PA
Military service: Bet. 16 Jul - 14 Nov 1864, 1st Bn, Ind Militia 1863

More About George WYNKOOP and Jane LIGHTCAP:
Marriage: 23 Sep 1868, Green Twp., Indiana Cnty, PA

Children of Jane LIGHTCAP and George WYNKOOP are:
    i.   Mary Annie[11] WYNKOOP[1689,1690], b. Abt. 1869, PA[1691]; d. Unknown.
    ii. Susan L. WYNKOOP[1692], b. Abt. 1870, PA[1692]; d. Unknown.
    iii. Robert J. WYNKOOP[1692], b. Abt. 1873, PA[1692]; d. Unknown.
    iv. William C. WYNKOOP[1692], b. Abt. 1878, PA[1692]; d. Unknown.

93. John Scott[10] LIGHTCAP *(Susan[9] MCELHOES, Jane[8] VAN HORN, Isaiah[7], Henry B.[6], Henry[5], Christian Barentsen[4] VAN HOORN, Barent Christiansen[3], Christian Barentsen[2], Barent Barents[1])[1693]* was born 21 Sep 1851 in East Mahoning, Indiana Cnty, PA[1693], and died 29 Nov 1929 in East Mahoning, Indiana Cnty, PA. He married Maria Lucinda BENCE[1694] 16 Nov 1876 in Green Twp., Indiana Cnty, PA. She was born Sep 1858 in PA[1694], and died Unknown.

More About John Scott LIGHTCAP:
Occupation: Blacksmith apprentice

More About John LIGHTCAP and Maria BENCE:
Marriage: 16 Nov 1876, Green Twp., Indiana Cnty, PA

Children of John LIGHTCAP and Maria BENCE are:
236.   i.   William B.[11] LIGHTCAP, b. 18 Jan 1878, PA; d. Sep 1965.
237.   ii. Susana LIGHTCAP, b. 05 Nov 1879, PA; d. Unknown.
        iii. Samuel J. LIGHTCAP, b. 26 Jun 1881, PA; d. 29 Mar 1884, Green Twp., Indiana Cnty, PA.
        iv. Mary J. LIGHTCAP[1694], b. 26 Feb 1883, PA; d. Unknown.
238.   v. Silas Edgar LIGHTCAP, b. Bet. 1884 - 16 Dec 1885, East Mahoning, Indiana Cnty, PA; d. 16 Jul 1918.
        vi. Clara Mabel LIGHTCAP[1694], b. Bet. 29 Mar 1884 - 1887, PA; d. Unknown.
        vii. Florence Maggie LIGHTCAP[1694], b. 04 Nov 1889, PA; d. Unknown.
        viii. Fay R. LIGHTCAP[1694], b. 29 Nov 1891, PA; d. Unknown.
        ix. John Irven LIGHTCAP[1694], b. 11 Jun 1895, PA; d. Unknown.
        x. Harry D. LIGHTCAP[1694], b. Bet. 22 Oct 1896 - 1897, PA; d. Unknown.
        xi. Charles Bence LIGHTCAP, d. Unknown.

94. Nancy Ann[10] LIGHTCAP *(Susan[9] MCELHOES, Jane[8] VAN HORN, Isaiah[7], Henry B.[6], Henry[5], Christian Barentsen[4] VAN HOORN, Barent Christiansen[3], Christian Barentsen[2], Barent Barents[1])[1695,1696,1697]* was born 14 Sep 1854 in East Mahoning, Indiana Cnty, PA[1698], and died 21 Aug 1943 in Indiana Cnty, PA. She married Robert Clair MABON[1699,1700] Abt. 1874. He was born Nov 1849 in PA[1701], and died 24 Jan 1920 in White Twp., Indiana Cnty, PA.

Notes for Nancy Ann LIGHTCAP:
    In 1910 she is the mother of 3 with only 1 living.

More About Robert MABON and Nancy LIGHTCAP:
Marriage: Abt. 1874

Children of Nancy LIGHTCAP and Robert MABON are:
      i.   Silas Merle[11] MABON[1701], b. Mar 1881, PA[1701]; d. 1906.
239.   ii. George Clair MABON, b. Aug 1888, PA; d. 03 Dec 1967, Indiana Cnty, PA.
      iii. ? MABON, d. Bef. 1900.

95. Harry Johnson[10] LIGHTCAP *(Susan[9] MCELHOES, Jane[8] VAN HORN, Isaiah[7], Henry B.[6], Henry[5], Christian Barentsen[4] VAN HOORN, Barent Christiansen[3], Christian Barentsen[2], Barent Barents[1])[1702,1703]* was born Sep 1864 in East Mahoning, Indiana Cnty, PA[1704], and died Unknown. He married Ida M. WYNCOOP[1704,1705]. She was born Apr 1866 in PA[1706], and died Unknown.

Children of Harry LIGHTCAP and Ida WYNCOOP are:
      i.   Bertha[11] LIGHTCAP[1706], b. Dec 1889, PA; d. Unknown.
      ii. Clark S. LIGHTCAP[1706,1707], b. Oct 1891, PA[1707]; d. Unknown.
      iii. Budd E. LIGHTCAP[1708,1709], b. Aug 1893, PA[1709]; d. Unknown.
      iv. Esther L. LIGHTCAP[1710,1711], b. Sep 1897, PA[1711]; d. Unknown.
      v. Sloan B. LIGHTCAP[1711], b. Abt. 1901, PA[1711]; d. Unknown.

96. Lt. John Neff[10] VAN HORN *(Benjamin Briggs[9], Joshua[8], Isaiah[7], Henry B.[6], Henry[5], Christian Barentsen[4] VAN HOORN, Barent Christiansen[3], Christian Barentsen[2], Barent Barents[1])[1712,1713,1714,1715,1716,1717,1718,1719]* was born 13 Aug 1842 in Indiana Cnty, PA[1720,1721], and died 22 Oct 1907 in Marion Center or Georgeville, Indiana Cnty, PA[1722,1723,1724]. He married (1) Mary Jane CAMPBELL[1725,1726,1727] 1868 in Indiana Cnty, PA[1728,1729]. She was born 04 Jan 1848 in PA[1730,1731], and died 28 Feb 1898 in Hatch City, Kennebec Cnty, SD[1732,1733]. He married (2) Martha Belle NICHOL[1734,1735,1736,1737,1738] 23 Nov 1904 in Indiana Cnty, PA[1739], daughter of William NICHOL and Margaret. She was born 17 May 1857 in Green Twp., Indiana Cnty, PA[1740,1741], and died Aug 1942 in Marion Center, Indiana Cnty, PA[1742,1743].

Notes for Lt. John Neff VAN HORN:
    Civil War Co F 105 Reg 2nd Lt Co A 206 Reg PV Cpl 10/26/61-6/26/65 Pensioner for gun shot in the arm at $4/month.
    In 1870 married and one child Claud. His real estate is worth $700 and personal effects $150. He is living in Banks Twp., Indiana Cnty, PA.
    In the Indiana Progress(Indiana, PA) dated 10 September 1874 note is made of the good workmanship of John Van Horn in plastering the house of Augustus Warren in Georgeville, PA.
    31 May 1877 John N. Van Horn is reported by the Indiana Progress(Indiana, PA) to be elected to the county Republican Committee representing Banks Twp.
    21 June 1877 the Progress notes that John N. Van Horn is to report to a meeting of the

Republican committee representing Banks Twp.

28 June 1877 the Progress repeats the meeting call for July 2nd 1877 at 1:00Pm to elect a chairman.

1 August 1878 the Progress reports that Lt. John N. Van Horn called a July 17, 1878 meeting of the Banks Twp. citizens to order for the purpose of electing officers and hearing a speech by Gen. White.

7 November 1878 John N. Van Horn is to serve the 3rd week of December on the Grand Jury for Banks Twp.

23 Feb 1881 the Indiana Progress(Indiana, PA) and the Indiana Weekly Messenger (Indiana, PA) both report that J. N. Van Horn or John N. Van Horn was elected auditor from Banks Twp.

28 September 1881 the Indiana Weekly Messenger (Indiana, PA) reports that there will be a Sunday School picnic on the John Van Horn farm in Banks Twp. on October 8th, 1881 and that there will be good music and eminent speakers.

30 November 1881 the Indiana Weekly Messenger (Indiana, PA) reports that there were 34 tickets sold for the West one of those being to John Van Horn and family of Horton, PA to Kimbal, Dakota.

4 April 1883 Indiana Weekly Messenger (Indiana, PA) it is reported that train tickets were sold to John Van Horn of Horton, PA to Kimbal, Dakota.

7 Jan 1891 the Indiana Progress(Indiana, PA) reports on a letter from John N. Van Horn Sheriff of Bruel Cnty, SD. He states there is no snow and the roads are dry and dusty.

23 November 1904 Indiana Progress(Indiana, PA) marriage licenses listed John N. Van Horn of Hatch City, SD to Belle Nichol of Georgeville, PA.

31 July 1907 the Indiana County Gazette (Indiana, PA) notes that A. W Steele visited J. N. Van Horn who is suffering with diabetes

The History of Indiana County, Pennsylvania p. 302 reports that John N. VanHorn entered as a corporal in the 105th PVI Company F on October 25, 1861 and was discharged on February 6, 1863.

More About Lt. John Neff VAN HORN:
Burial: Unknown, Gilgal Cemetery, Indiana Cnty, PA[1744,1745]
Cause of Death: Diabetes and a compliation of diseases
Lived: Georgeville, Indiana Cnty, PA; South Dakota
Migration: 1881, South Dakota and returned to PA in 1904
Military service: Bet. 26 Oct 1861 - 26 Jun 1865, Co. F 105th Reg; Co. A 206th Rg PVI; Rank Corporal; Co. A, 2nd Bat PVI as Second Sergeant; Co. A, 206th P.V. I. as Second Lieutenant;U.S. Signal Corps, 2ndLt, Co"A" 206th P.V.I[1745]
Occupation: Farmer and House Plasterer; Sheriff Brule Cnty, SD; Rancher

More About John VAN HORN and Mary CAMPBELL:
Marriage: 1868, Indiana Cnty, PA[1746,1747]

Notes for Martha Belle NICHOL:
In1910 and 1920 she is widowed and has her widowed mother and sister Ollive living with her. Her sister has two young children also living in the home.

In 1930 Belle has living with her her widowed sister Olive and her brother James and his wife Myrtle. She owns her home worth $3,000 and does not have a radio.

From news items in the Indiana Progress(Indiana, PA) of Oct. 4, 1905 we learn that one of Belle's sister married Delmar Hamilton. He is the father of the two children living in the home in 1920.

More About Martha Belle NICHOL:
Burial: Unknown, Gilgal Cemetery Gilgal UP Church Indiana Cnty, PA
Lived: 1907, Georgeville, Indiana Cnty, PA

Occupation: Music Teacher, Farmer
Religion: Organist at the Marion Center Presbyterian Church, Indiana Cnty, PA

More About John VAN HORN and Martha NICHOL:
Marriage: 23 Nov 1904, Indiana Cnty, PA[1748]
Marriage Place: Home of Parent Margaret Nichol

Children of John VAN HORN and Mary CAMPBELL are:

	i.	R. Vandall[11] VAN HORN[1749], b. SD; d. Aft. 1907[1749].
240.	ii.	Claude Duval VAN HORN, b. 21 Feb 1869, Indiana Cnty, PA; d. 23 Jun 1937, Lyman Cnty, SD.
241.	iii.	William Burton VAN HORN, b. 20 Nov 1871, Indiana Cnty, PA; d. 12 Oct 1924, Chamberlain, Brule Cnty, SD.
242.	iv.	Robert Campbell VAN HORN, b. 03 Feb 1875, Banks Twp., Indiana Cnty, PA; d. 05 Apr 1943, Kennebec Cnty, SD.
	v.	Emma VAN HORN, b. 21 Jan 1877, Indiana Cnty, PA; d. Unknown.
243.	vi.	Myrreel VAN HORN, b. Jun 1877, Indiana Cnty, PA; d. Aft. 1907, NY, NY.
244.	vii.	Nora VAN HORN, b. 03 Aug 1879, Indiana Cnty, PA; d. Aft. 1930, SD.
	viii.	Etta VAN HORN[1750,1751], b. 21 Jan 1886, Indiana Cnty, PA[1751]; d. Bef. 1907.

97. James Harvey[10] VAN HORN *(Benjamin Briggs[9], Joshua[8], Isaiah[7], Henry B.[6], Henry[5], Christian Barentsen[4] VAN HOORN, Barent Christiansen[3], Christian Barentsen[2], Barent Barents[1])*[1752,1753,1754,1755,1756,1757,1758,1759] was born Abt. 1851 in Indiana Cnty, PA[1760], and died 20 Aug 1921 in Kellysburg, Indiana Cnty, PA[1761]. He married Isabelle FRY[1762,1763,1764] Bet. 1870 - 1874[1764]. She was born Jan 1857 in PA[1765], and died 10 Jan 1919 in Marion Center, Indiana Cnty, PA[1766].

Notes for James Harvey VAN HORN:
    In 1880 Harvey is a farmer and living next door to his parents.
    In 1900 he and Isabella have been married for 26 years. She is the mother of 8 children of which 7 are living.
    15 January 1915 the Weekly Messenger reports that the H. J. Van Horn home was completely destroyed from a fire set by an exploding oil lamp and that a couple of weeks ago their daughter Adda Blystone's home had been completely destroyed also.
    1920 Census widowed and living with his daughter Annie and her husband Ray Kephart in Marion Center.
    25 Aug 1921 the Indiana Weekly Messenger (Indiana, PA) reports his death at the home of his son Denton in Kellysburg.

More About James Harvey VAN HORN:
Burial: 24 Aug 1921, Marion Center, Indiana Cnty, PA
Lived: Marion Center, Indiana Cnty, PA
Occupation: Day Laborer Odd Jobs, Laborer Gas Company

Notes for Isabelle FRY:
    21 September 1891 Indiana Weekly Messenger (Indiana, PA) reports that J. H. Rochester sells to Isabella Van Horn on July 6, 1896 a lot in Marion Center for $75.

More About Isabelle FRY:
Cause of Death: Heart Trouble
Occupation: Laundress at home

More About James VAN HORN and Isabelle FRY:

Isaiah Van Horn Pioneer of Indiana County, Pennsylvania

Marriage: Bet. 1870 - 1874[1767]

Children of James VAN HORN and Isabelle FRY are:

245.   i.   Orin Denton[11] VAN HORN, b. 11 Aug 1874, South Mahoning Twp., Indiana Cnty, PA; d. 11 Mar 1949, Marion Center, Indiana Cnty, PA.

         ii.   Minnie A. VAN HORN[1768,1769,1770], b. Abt. 1876, Indiana Cnty, PA[1771]; d. Bef. 1969; m. BRUSHIER; d. Unknown.

Notes for Minnie A. VAN HORN:
According to Harvey's Obituary Minnie lives in the west.

246.   iii.   Charles Blaine VAN HORN, b. Bet. 01 - 02 Aug 1890, Rayne Twp., Indiana Cnty, PA; d. 01 Nov 1965, Indiana, Indiana Cnty, PA.

        iv.   Homer Park VAN HORN[1772,1773,1774,1775,1776,1777,1778,1779], b. Bet. 26 Mar 1889 - 20 Mar 1890, South Mahoning Twp., Indiana Cnty, PA[1780,1781,1782,1783]; d. 01 Dec 1976, Indiana Haven, Indiana Cnty, PA[1784]; m. Edna Alpha JUART[1785,1786,1787], Abt. 1920; b. 18 May 1901, Plumville, Indiana Cnty, PA[1797]; d. 14 May 1952, Marion Center near Plumville, Indiana Cnty, PA.

Notes for Homer Park VAN HORN:
In 1930 lived on High Street in Marion Center, PA in a home he owns worth $500. A Neice Alberta Van Horn age 7 born PA is living with he and Edna.
In his WWI Draft Registration he is single and states he was born South Mahoning Twp., Indiana Cnty, PA March 20, 1890. He is short, slim and has gray eyes and red hair.
25 April 1923 Park is building a home on a newly purchased lot on High Street in Marion Center according to a report in the Indiana County Progress.
3 Nov. 1937 reported in the Indiana Progress(Indiana, PA) that Park and wife have moved into their new bungalow on North Manor Street in Marion Center.
In his WWI I Draft registration he states he was born in South Mahoning Twp., Indiana County on 26 March 1889. Other sources give his birth as 25 April. He lists Edna as his contact and he is self employed. He is White, 5 feet 8 and 3/4 inches in height and weighs151 pounds, he has blue eyes and gray hair with a ruddy complexion.

More About Homer Park VAN HORN:
Burial: Unknown, Marion Center Cemetery, Indiana Cnty, PA
Lived: Rochester Mills, PA
Occupation: Laborer Saw Mill, Farm Labor, Laborer for Gas Company

More About Edna Alpha JUART:
Burial: Unknown, Marion Center Cemetery, Indiana Cnty, PA
Cause of Death: Self inflicted gun shot wood to the head

More About Homer VAN HORN and Edna JUART:
Marriage: Abt. 1920

        v.   Annie P. VAN HORN[1788,1789,1790,1791,1792], b. Bet. 20 Jul 1891 - 1893, Indiana Cnty, PA[1793]; d. 07 Apr 1969, Rochester Mills, PA[1794]; m. Dean Ray KEPHART[1795,1796], 20 Feb 1918, Indiana, Indiana Cnty, PA[1797,1798]; b. Abt. 1894, PA[1799]; d. 1941[1800].

Notes for Annie P. VAN HORN:
15 January 1913 A. S. McGinty sells 2 lots in Marion Center to Anna P. Van Horn

for $2500 according to the Indiana Progress(Indiana, PA) of this date.

More About Annie P. VAN HORN:
Burial: Unknown, Marion Center Cemetery, Marion Center, Indiana Cnty, PA
Lived: 1937, Marion Center, Indiana Cnty, PA

Notes for Dean Ray KEPHART:
Ray is a coal miner and rents. His father in law Harvey is living with him in 1920.

More About Dean Ray KEPHART:
Lived: Marion Center, Indiana Cnty, PA

More About Dean KEPHART and Annie VAN HORN:
Marriage: 20 Feb 1918, Indiana, Indiana Cnty, PA[1801,1802]
Marriage date: Rev. B W. Hutchinson
Marriage Place: Methodist Parsonage

247.   vi.   Mary Ada VAN HORN, b. Sep 1894, Indiana Cnty, PA; d. Bet. 1969 - 1976.
248.   vii.   Alice Elsie VAN HORN, b. Jun 1896, Indiana Cnty, PA; d. Aft. 1976.
         viii. ? VAN HORN, d. Bef. 1900.

98. Alexander Milton[10] VAN HORN *(Benjamin Briggs[9], Joshua[8], Isaiah[7], Henry B.[6], Henry[5], Christian Barentsen[4] VAN HOORN, Barent Christiansen[3], Christian Barentsen[2], Barent Barents[1])*[1803,1804,1805,1806,1807,1808,1809,1809,1810,1811,1812,1813,1814] was born 20 Jan 1851 in South Mahoning Twp., Indiana Cnty, PA[1815], and died 28 May 1944 in Homer City, Indiana Cnty, PA[1815]. He married Rosalie L. KERNS[1815,1816,1817,1818,1819] 18 Dec 1877 in South Mahoning Twp., Indiana Cnty, PA[1820]. She was born 20 Mar 1859 in Garrets Run, Armstrong Cnty, PA[1820], and died 29 Aug 1917 in Indiana Cnty, PA[1820].

Notes for Alexander Milton VAN HORN:
    21 Feb 1883 the Indiana Weekly Messenger (Indiana, PA) reports the election of Millon Van Horn as Auditor for East Mahoning Twp., Indiana Cnty, PA
    In 1920 he owns his place free and clear. He is widowed and Pluma his daughter is listed as his wife. Neither has an occupation.
    1 Feb 1933 the Indiana Progress(Indiana, PA) reports that A. M. Van Horn has a radio installed in his home.
    22 April 1908 the Indiana Gazette reports that A. M. Van Horn is running for assemblyman on the Socialist Party.(Note he was defeated in several attempts)
    7 April 1909 Indiana Progress(Indiana, PA) reports that George T. Lydick sold to A. M. Van Horn 18 acres in south Mahoning for $500 and Francis E.. Watrus sold to A. M. Van Horn a tract in South Mahoning for $78.30.
    23 October 1912 the Indiana Progress(Indiana, PA) reports that Milton Van Horn is running for the Senate of the State of Pennsylvania as a Socialist.
    13 November 1912 the Indiana Progress(Indiana, PA) reports the vote and Van Horn came in 3rd with 1007 votes.
    29 January 1913 the Indiana Progress(Indiana, PA) reports that A. M. Van Horn is elected Vice President of the Farmers Telephone Company.

More About Alexander Milton VAN HORN:
Burial: Unknown, Berachea Cemetry, Plumville, Indiana Cnty, PA
Lived: 29 Aug 1906, Rossmoyne, PA
Occupation: Plasterer, Farmer

Notes for Rosalie L. KERNS:
In 1900 Rosa state she is the mother of 9 children of which 8 are living.

More About Rosalie L. KERNS:
Cause of Death: Cancer of the stomach

More About Alexander VAN HORN and Rosalie KERNS:
Marriage: 18 Dec 1877, South Mahoning Twp., Indiana Cnty, PA[1820]
Marriage date: Rev. I. W. Shoemaker[1821]
Marriage Place: Brides Home

Children of Alexander VAN HORN and Rosalie KERNS are:
249.   i.   LeRoy Kerns[11] VAN HORN, b. 08 Jul 1878, Indiana Cnty, PA; d. 16 Feb 1954, Youngstown, Mahoning Cnty, OH.
250.   ii.   Sprague L. VAN HORN, b. 23 Sep 1879, Plumville, Indiana Cnty, PA; d. 30 Mar 1951, Ambridge, PA.
251.   iii.   Mary Mae VAN HORN, b. 12 Sep 1882, Indiana Cnty, PA; d. 31 Oct 1967, Meadville, PA.
252.   iv.   George Percy VAN HORN, b. Bet. 06 Sep 1883 - 1884, South Mahoning Twp., Indiana Cnty, PA; d. 12 Jan 1965, Blairsville, Indiana Cnty, PA.
253.   v.   Nellie Gertrude VAN HORN, b. 06 Nov 1885, PA; d. 22 Aug 1964, Indiana, Indiana Cnty, PA.
254.   vi.   Zula L. VAN HORN, b. Mar 1887, Plumville, PA; d. Aft. 1944.
        vii.   Pluma Ruth VAN HORN[1822,1823,1824,1825], b. Dec 1893, PA[1826]; d. Aft. 1953; m. James E. HARE[1827], 04 Feb 1932, Indiana, Indiana Cnty, PA; b. Abt. 1888, VA; d. Unknown.

        Notes for Pluma Ruth VAN HORN:
        15 May 1907 Nellie, Pluma and Russell Van Horn are reported on the sick list according to the Indiana Progress(Indiana, PA).
        24 July 1912 Pluma is appointed Assistant Principal of the Plumville School for the 1912-13 term according to the Indiana County Gazette (Indiana, PA).
        In 1923 a teacher in the Sagamore Schools.
        In 1930 she is shown as a lodger in the home of Dora Boden but her name is struck through. This entry is in the Borough of Salzburg, PA

        More About Pluma Ruth VAN HORN:
        Lived: Indiana, Indiana Cnty, PA
        Occupation: Indiana county Teacher

        Notes for James E. HARE:
        Boarding with Nellie Van Horn Rankin Pluma's sister in 1920.

        More About James E. HARE:
        Military service: WWI Vetern of the US Army 80th Division of the One 315 Artillery
        Occupation: Rochester and Pittsburgh Coal Company of Lucerne, PA
        Organizations: American Legion and Vetran of Foreign Wars

        More About James HARE and Pluma VAN HORN:
        Marriage: 04 Feb 1932, Indiana, Indiana Cnty, PA
        Marriage date: Rev C. C. Fulton
        Marriage Place: Indiana Presbyterian Church, Indiana Cnty, PA

    viii.   Talmage VAN HORN[1828], b. 24 Feb 1897, Indiana Cnty, PA[1829]; d. 02 Jul 1925,

South Mahoning Twp., Indiana Cnty, PA[1829].

More About Talmage VAN HORN:
Burial: Unknown, Baracca Cemetery,Plumville, South Mahoning Twp., Indiana Cnty, PA

255.   ix.   Russell E. VAN HORN, b. Oct 1899, PA; d. Aft. 1944.

99. Sarah S.[10] VAN HORN *(Benjamin Briggs[9], Joshua[8], Isaiah[7], Henry B.[6], Henry[5], Christian Barentsen[4] VAN HOORN, Barent Christiansen[3], Christian Barentsen[2], Barent Barents[1])[1830,1831,1832,1833,1834,1835,1836,1837]* was born 27 Dec 1853 in Indiana Cnty, PA[1838], and died 29 Jan 1932 in Green Twp., Indiana Cnty, PA. She married Turner Thompson LUKEHART[1839,1840,1841] 08 Oct 1874 in Indiana Cnty, PA[1842], son of Jacob LUKEHART and Lena DAVIS. He was born 26 Aug 1853 in Indiana Cnty, PA[1843], and died 03 Mar 1905 in Armstrong Cnty, PA.

Notes for Sarah S. VAN HORN:
    In 1930 widowed and living with her daughter Ethel who is also widowed.

More About Sarah S. VAN HORN:
Lived: 29 Aug 1906, Plumville and Barnards, PA

Notes for Turner Thompson LUKEHART:
    Unknown date and newspaper
    Turner Lukehart died at his home near Barnards, Armstrong county, on Thursday of typhoid pneumonia, aged about 50 years. He is survived by his wife, two sons and two daughters. The deceased was born in South Mahoning township, this county, and has many relatives living in that section. Interment was made in the Mahoning Baptist church cemetery near Plumville, on Sunday.

More About Turner Thompson LUKEHART:
Lived: Plumville and Barnards, PA

Marriage Notes for Sarah VAN HORN and Turner LUKEHART:
Indiana Progress(Indiana, PA) 12 Oct 1874
Marriage- Lukehart-Vanhorn. On the 8th inst. at the M.E. parsonage, by Rev. M.Y. Sleppy. Mr. Turner T. Lukehart, and Miss Sarah S. VanHorn, both of Plumville, Indiana Co., Pa

More About Turner LUKEHART and Sarah VAN HORN:
Marriage: 08 Oct 1874, Indiana Cnty, PA[1844]
Marriage date: Rev. M. J. Sleppy
Marriage Place: ME Parsonage

Children of Sarah VAN HORN and Turner LUKEHART are:
        i.   Nora Ethel[11] LUKEHART[1845,1846], b. 25 Feb 1876, Armstrong Cnty, PA; d. 1959;
              m. (1) Daniel G. BEERS; b. 07 Apr 1864, Dayton, PA; d. 05 Oct 1941, Blairsville,
              Indiana Cnty, PA; m. (2) Robert Dinsmore GRAHAM[1846], 1901; b. 1876; d. 1910.

              Notes for Nora Ethel LUKEHART:
              In 1930 she is widowed and has her mother living with her. She owns her home that

is worth $500. Her occupation is a laundress and takes in laundry in her home.

More About Robert Dinsmore GRAHAM:
Occupation: 1910, House Carpenter

More About Robert GRAHAM and Nora LUKEHART:
Marriage: 1901

256.	ii.	Luther Merle LUKEHART, b. 21 Nov 1877, Armstrong Cnty, PA; d. 18 Oct 1938.
257.	iii.	Bertha Agnes LUKEHART, b. Bet. 02 - 12 Aug 1880, Barnard, Armstrong Cnty, PA; d. 01 Apr 1960, Dayton, Armstrong Cnty, PA.
258.	iv.	Homer Boyd LUKEHART, b. 17 Sep 1888, Armstrong Cnty, PA; d. 19 Feb 1956, Dayton, Armstrong Cnty, PA.

100. John Miles[10] VAN HORN *(Christian[9], Joshua[8], Isaiah[7], Henry B.[6], Henry[5], Christian Barentsen[4] VAN HOORN, Barent Christiansen[3], Christian Barentsen[2], Barent Barents[1])[1817,1848,1849,1850,1851,1852]* was born Sep 1845 in PA[1853,1854], and died Aft. 1920. He married (1) Ann Margaret BARNETT[1854,1855,1856] Abt. 1863, daughter of Seneca BARNETT and Sarah. She was born Abt. 1843 in Porter Twp., Jefferson Cnty, PA[1857], and died Aft. 1920. He married (2) Rachel Margaret PIERCE[1858,1859,1860] Abt. 1880[1861]. She was born May 1864 in PA[1862,1863], and died Aft. 1920.

Notes for John Miles VAN HORN:
In 1860 he is a farmer married with 2 children. He is living with his father and mother and 2 sisters.
In 1900 John is married to Margaret Rachel for 9 years and she is the mother of 8 children 8 living. One is not in the home. Since they have only been married for 9 years only 5 of the children are theirs and the others are Rachel's from her first marriage. John's children by his first wife are older and out of the home.

More About John Miles VAN HORN:
Burial: Unknown, Falls Creek, Jefferson Cnty, PA[1864]
Military service: Bet. 25 Oct 1861 - 06 Feb 1863, Civil War Co. F, 105th PA Inf.[1864]
Occupation: Teamster, Farm Laborer

More About John VAN HORN and Ann BARNETT:
Marriage: Abt. 1863

More About John VAN HORN and Rachel PIERCE:
Marriage: Abt. 1880[1865]

Children of John VAN HORN and Ann BARNETT are:

	i.	Ida[11] VAN HORN[1866,1867], b. Abt. 1865, PA[1868]; d. Unknown.
259.	ii.	Samuel A. VAN HORN, b. Aug 1866, PA; d. Bet. 1920 - 1930.
	iii.	William H. VAN HORN[1869], b. Abt. 1871, PA[1869]; d. Unknown.
	iv.	David M. VAN HORN[1869], b. Abt. 1871, PA[1869]; d. Unknown.
260.	v.	Dessia A. VAN HORN, b. Oct 1875, PA; d. Unknown.
	vi.	Alice V. VAN HORN[1869], b. Abt. 1875, PA[1869]; d. Unknown.
	vii.	Nora Ellie VAN HORN[1869], b. May 1879, PA[1869]; d. Unknown.

Children of John VAN HORN and Rachel PIERCE are:

261.	viii.	Emma H.[11] VAN HORN, b. Nov 1880, PA; d. Unknown.

262.   ix.   Stella Marilla VAN HORN, b. May 1882, PA; d. Aft. 1930.
        x.   Laura A. VAN HORN[1870], b. Nov 1882, PA[1870]; d. Unknown; Stepchild.
263.   xi.   Lilla L. VAN HORN, b. May 1891, PA; d. Unknown.
       xii.   Elvie E. VAN HORN[1870,1871], b. Mar 1893, PA[1872]; d. Unknown.
264.   xiii.   Lester Leona VAN HORN, b. 05 Apr 1895, DuBois, Clearfield Cnty, PA; d. Aft. 1930.
265.   xiv.   Donald Michael VAN HORN, b. 28 Nov 1897, PA; d. 1970, PA.
266.   xv.   Norman Ernest VAN HORN, b. 16 Oct 1899, PA; d. Unknown.

101. Adessa Levina[10] VAN HORN *(Christian[9], Joshua[8], Isaiah[7], Henry B.[6], Henry[5], Christian Barentsen[4] VAN HOORN, Barent Christiansen[3], Christian Barentsen[2], Barent Barents[1])*[1873,1874,1875] was born Oct 1860 in PA[1876], and died Unknown. She married George J. BOSSARD[1876,1877,1878] Abt. 1878. He was born May 1855 in PA[1879], and died Unknown.

Notes for Adessa Levina VAN HORN:
    In 1910 she is the mother of 7 with 6 living at the time of the census. They have been married for 30 years in their first marriage.

More About George BOSSARD and Adessa VAN HORN:
Marriage: Abt. 1878

Children of Adessa VAN HORN and George BOSSARD are:
        i.   Cora[11] BOSSARD[1879,1880], b. 02 Mar 1883, Dayton, Armstrong Cnty, PA[1881,1882]; d. 28 Jan 1962, Kittanning, Armstrong Cnty, PA[1882]; m. Henry RUPP[1882]; d. Unknown.

            More About Cora BOSSARD:
            Cremation: Kittanning Cemetery, Kittanning PA[1882]

       ii.   Elliot BOSSARD[1883], b. Feb 1884, PA[1883]; d. Unknown.
      iii.   Calvin C. BOSSARD[1883], b. Oct 1886, PA[1883]; d. Unknown.
267.   iv.   Harvey S. BOSSARD, b. Mar 1893, PA; d. Unknown.
        v.   Ethel L. BOSSARD[1883,1884,1885], b. Nov 1895, PA[1886]; d. Unknown; m. Gilbert LLOYD[1887]; d. Unknown.
       vi.   Etta BOSSARD[1887], d. Unknown; m. LYLE[1887]; d. Unknown.
      vii.   Arthur Lee BOSSARD[1888,1889], b. Abt. 1903, PA[1890]; d. Unknown.

            Notes for Arthur Lee BOSSARD:
            In 1920 living with his brother Harvey.

            More About Arthur Lee BOSSARD:
            Employment: 1920, Section Hand Steam Railroad

102. Nathan[10] VAN HORN *(Henry[9], Joshua[8], Isaiah[7], Henry B.[6], Henry[5], Christian Barentsen[4] VAN HOORN, Barent Christiansen[3], Christian Barentsen[2], Barent Barents[1])*[1891,1892] was born Abt. 1851 in PA[1893], and died Unknown. He married Theodosia[1894] Abt. 1873. She was born Abt. 1852 in PA[1894], and died Unknown.

More About Nathan VAN HORN:
Occupation: Railroad Brakeman

More About Nathan VAN HORN and Theodosia:

Marriage: Abt. 1873

Children of Nathan VAN HORN and Theodosia are:
  i. Elizabeth[11] VAN HORN[1894], b. Abt. 1875, PA[1894]; d. Unknown.
  ii. Bertha VAN HORN, b. May 1880, PA; d. Unknown.

103. Mazella I.[10] VAN HORN *(Henry[9], Joshua[8], Isaiah[7], Henry B.[6], Henry[5], Christian Barentsen[4] VAN HOORN, Barent Christiansen[3], Christian Barentsen[2], Barent Barents[1])*[1895,1896,1897] was born 27 Mar 1847 in Plumville, Indiana Cnty, PA[1898], and died 30 Jun 1951 in West Frankfort, Franklin Cnty, IL[1899]. She married William Vinson CARLTON[1899] 03 Jun 1875[1899]. He was born 02 Dec 1846 in Equality, Gallatin Cnty, IL[1899], and died 24 May 1914 in Northern Twp., Franklin Cnty, IL[1899].

More About William CARLTON and Mazella VAN HORN:
Marriage: 03 Jun 1875[1899]

Child of Mazella VAN HORN and William CARLTON is:
268. i. Henry Oliver[11] CARLTON, b. 03 Feb 1882, Northern Twp., Franklin Cnty, IL; d. 21 Aug 1966, Benton, Franklin Cnty, IL.

104. Abner Briggs[10] VAN HORN *(Henry[9], Joshua[8], Isaiah[7], Henry B.[6], Henry[5], Christian Barentsen[4] VAN HOORN, Barent Christiansen[3], Christian Barentsen[2], Barent Barents[1])*[1900,1901,1902,1903] was born Bet. 24 Jul 1865 - 1867 in PA[1904], and died 14 Mar 1944. He married (1) Lora Belle KERN. She was born 1881, and died Unknown. He married (2) Lora Bell CLARK[1905,1906] Abt. 1891[1906]. She was born Jun 1873 in IL[1907], and died Unknown.

Notes for Abner Briggs VAN HORN:
  IN 1920 he is divorced. His son Raymond and his wife and son Roy are living in the home.

More About Abner Briggs VAN HORN:
Occupation: 1910, House carpenter

More About Abner VAN HORN and Lora CLARK:
Marriage: Abt. 1891[1908]

Child of Abner VAN HORN and Lora KERN is:
  i. Wynne[11] VAN HORN, b. 1909; d. Unknown.

Children of Abner VAN HORN and Lora CLARK are:
  ii. Goldie[11] VAN HORN[1909,1910], b. Sep 1893, IL[1911]; d. Unknown.
  iii. William Raymond VAN HORN[1912,1913,1914], b. Nov 1896, IL[1915]; d. Unknown; m. Rhoda L.[1915]; b. 1896, IL[1915]; d. Unknown.
  iv. Roy Louis VAN HORN[1915,1916,1917], b. Feb 1900, IL[1918]; d. Unknown.
  v. Everett VAN HORN[1919], b. 1902, IL[1919]; d. Unknown.
  vi. Nola VAN HORN, b. 1904, IL; d. Bef. 1910.
  vii. Lloyd VAN HORN, b. Abt. Oct 1908, IL; d. Unknown.

105. George Milton[10] KECK *(Tabitha Dorcas[9] VAN HORN, Joshua[8], Isaiah[7], Henry B.[6], Henry[5], Christian Barentsen[4] VAN HOORN, Barent Christiansen[3], Christian Barentsen[2], Barent Barents[1])*[1920,1921,1922] was born Abt. 1853 in Jefferson Cnty, PA[1923], and died 02 Jul 1918 in New London, Huron Cnty,

OH. He married Clara[1924] Abt. 1871. She was born Abt. 1851 in PA[1924], and died Unknown.

More About George KECK and Clara:
Marriage: Abt. 1871

Children of George KECK and Clara are:
    i.   Mary E.[11] KECK[1924], b. Abt. 1873, PA; d. Unknown.
    ii. David G. KECK[1924], b. Abt. 1876, PA; d. Unknown.
    iii. Gertrude S. KECK[1924], b. Abt. 1878, PA; d. Unknown.

106. Martin Luther[10] KECK *(Tabitha Dorcas[9] VAN HORN, Joshua[8], Isaiah[7], Henry B.[6], Henry[5], Christian Barentsen[4] VAN HOORN, Barent Christiansen[3], Christian Barentsen[2], Barent Barents[1])*[1925,1926,1927,1928] was born Feb 1857 in Jefferson Cnty, PA[1929], and died Jun 1923 in Wilkinsburg, Allegheny Cnty, PA. He married Marion M.[1930] Abt. 1884. She was born Dec 1860[1930], and died Unknown.

More About Martin Luther KECK:
Occupation: Fruit Tree and Farm Agent, Printer

More About Martin KECK and Marion M.:
Marriage: Abt. 1884

Children of Martin KECK and Marion M. are:
    i.   Leone E.[11] KECK[1930], b. Sep 1887, PA; d. Unknown.
    ii. Norma C. KECK[1930], b. Oct 1889, PA; d. Unknown.
    iii. Ruby M. KECK[1930], b. Aug 1891, PA; d. Unknown.
    iv. Percy A. KECK[1930], b. Dec 1892, PA; d. Unknown.
    v. Marion E. KECK[1930], b. Apr 1894, PA; d. Unknown.
    vi. ? KECK, b. Bef. 1900; d. Unknown.
    vii. ? KECK, b. Bef. 1900; d. Unknown.

107. Ellen Etta[10] KECK *(Tabitha Dorcas[9] VAN HORN, Joshua[8], Isaiah[7], Henry B.[6], Henry[5], Christian Barentsen[4] VAN HOORN, Barent Christiansen[3], Christian Barentsen[2], Barent Barents[1])*[1931,1932,1933] was born May 1861 in Jefferson Cnty, PA[1934], and died 17 May 1902 in Punxsutawney, Jefferson Cnty, PA. She married Means A. GRUBE[1935,1936] Abt. 1890. He was born Sep 1863 in PA[1937], and died Unknown.

Notes for Ellen Etta KECK:
    In 1900 Eta and Means have been married for 9 years and she is the mother of 5 with 5 living. He is a blacksmith and they are renting.

Notes for Means A. GRUBE:
    In 1930 owns home worth $3000 and has a radio. He is living next to his brother in law Lynn Keck.

More About Means A. GRUBE:
Occupation: Blacksmith; Blacksmith for Coal Mine

More About Means GRUBE and Ellen KECK:
Marriage: Abt. 1890

Children of Ellen KECK and Means GRUBE are:

    i.   Lou[11] GRUBE[1937], b. Dec 1891, PA[1937]; d. Unknown.

    ii.   Lee GRUBE[1937], b. Nov 1893, PA[1937]; d. Unknown.

   iii.   Helen R. GRUBE[1937], b. Nov 1895, PA[1937]; d. Unknown.

   iv.   Leonard GRUBE[1937], b. May 1899, PA[1937]; d. Unknown.

    v.   June GRUBE[1937,1938], b. Feb 1900, PA[1939]; d. Unknown.

        Notes for June GRUBE:
        In 1930 June is living with her father and stepmother.

        More About June GRUBE:
        Occupation: Department Store Saleslady

108. Lynn McKee[10] KECK *(Tabitha Dorcas[9] VAN HORN, Joshua[8], Isaiah[7], Henry B.[6], Henry[5], Christian Barentsen[4] VAN HOORN, Barent Christiansen[3], Christian Barentsen[2], Barent Barents[1])*[1940,1941,1942,1943,1944] was born 28 Mar 1865 in Punxsutawney, Jefferson Cnty, PA[1945], and died 02 Aug 1930 in Punxsutawney, Jefferson Cnty, PA. He married Laura Malinda BARNETT[1946,1947,1948] 25 May 1888 in Punxsutawney, Jefferson Cnty, PA, daughter of John BARNETT and Mary DUNMIRE. She was born 10 May 1870 in Punxsutawney, Jefferson Cnty, PA[1949], and died 15 Feb 1943 in Punxsutawney, Jefferson Cnty, PA.

Notes for Lynn McKee KECK:
    In 1920 renting on Belmont Ave in Punxsutawney, PA. He is a brick layer (mason) house builder and in 1920 his mother is living with him and his wife.
    In 1930 living next door to his brother in law Means Grube. He is renting for $15/month.

More About Lynn McKee KECK:
Occupation: Laborer

More About Laura Malinda BARNETT:
Occupation: Dressmaker

More About Lynn KECK and Laura BARNETT:
Marriage: 25 May 1888, Punxsutawney, Jefferson Cnty, PA

Children of Lynn KECK and Laura BARNETT are:

    i.   Hazel May[11] KECK[1950], b. Apr 1890, Punxsutawney, Jefferson Cnty, PA[1951]; d. 08 Oct 1926, Punxsutawney, Jefferson Cnty, PA.

        More About Hazel May KECK:
        Occupation: Music Teacher

269.   ii.   Earl Donovan KECK, b. 08 Apr 1896, Elk Run, Jefferson Cnty, PA; d. 25 Feb 1966, Punxsutawney, Jefferson Cnty, PA.

109. Sarah Dorcas[10] SINK *(Sarah[9] VAN HORN, Joshua[8], Isaiah[7], Henry B.[6], Henry[5], Christian Barentsen[4] VAN HOORN, Barent Christiansen[3], Christian Barentsen[2], Barent Barents[1])*[1952,1953,1954] was born 15 Sep 1853 in Indiana Cnty, PA[1955], and died Bet. 25 Aug 1925 - 1926 in Rexford, Thomas Cnty, KS. She married Hugh Albert MCAFOOS[1956,1957,1958] 27 Feb 1873 in Franklin Cnty, IL[1959], son of John MCAFOOS and Elizabeth SPEACE. He was born 14 Jul 1852 in McEdonia, PA[1960], and died 03 Mar 1942 in Rexford, Thomas Cnty, KS.

Notes for Sarah Dorcas SINK:
In 1900 Sarah states she is the mother of 8 with 7 living. there are 5 children in the home in 1900.

More About Sarah Dorcas SINK:
Burial: Unknown, Hawkeye Cemetery, Decatur Cnty, KS

Notes for Hugh Albert MCAFOOS:
In 1880 living in Franklin Cnty, IL near his father in law. His wife is Dorcus and Albert, Charles and Elsie are of the home. He is a farmer.
In 1930 he is a widower living alone in a home he owns worth $1000 he gives no occupation. He is living in Rexford, Thomas Cnty, KS.
His tombstone in Hawkeye Cemetery in Decatur Cnty, KS gives his name as Hughey A. McAfoos.

More About Hugh Albert MCAFOOS:
Burial: Unknown, Hawkeye Cemetery, Decatur Cnty, KS
Occupation: Carpenter

More About Hugh MCAFOOS and Sarah SINK:
Marriage: 27 Feb 1873, Franklin Cnty, IL[1961]

Children of Sarah SINK and Hugh MCAFOOS are:
270.   i.   Albert Hugh[11] MCAFOOS, b. 17 Nov 1873, Franklin Cnty, IL; d. Unknown.
271.   ii.   Charles Austin MCAFOOS, b. 07 May 1876, Nortern, Franklin Cnty, IL; d. 29 Jan 1962, Holton, Jackson Cnty, KS.
272.   iii.   Elsie Estelle MCAFOOS, b. 03 Sep 1878, Franklin Cnty, IL; d. 08 Apr 1940, Rexford, Thomas Cnty, KS or Goodland, KS.
   iv.   Effie MCAFOOS[1962], b. 07 Aug 1881, Franklin Cnty, IL[1962]; d. Unknown.
   v.   John J. MCAFOOS, b. 12 Feb 1884, Franklin Cnty, IL; d. 1886.

More About John J. MCAFOOS:
Burial: Unknown, Hawkeye Cemetery, Decatur Cnty, KS

273.   vi.   Oscar Alvin MCAFOOS, b. 27 Jun 1887, Thomas Cnty, KS; d. Sep 1974, Santa Fe, Santa Fe Cnty, NM.
   vii.   Clarence Everett MCAFOOS[1962,1963,1964], b. 31 Aug 1890, Thomas Cnty, KS[1965]; d. 21 Feb 1970, Hoxie, Sheridan Cnty, KS; m. Edna PATTERSON[1966], Abt. 1919[1966]; b. Abt. 1879, OH[1966]; d. Unknown.

Notes for Clarence Everett MCAFOOS:
In his WWI draft registration he states he is tall of medium build with blue eyes and light hair. He is a grain buyer and is singe. He is single living and working in Rexford, KS.
In 1930 he owns his place and has a radio. He and Edna have been married about 11 years. He is a general farmer.

More About Clarence MCAFOOS and Edna PATTERSON:
Marriage: Abt. 1919[1966]

274.   viii.   Ella Mary MCAFOOS, b. Bet. 19 Aug 1893 - 1896, Thomas Cnty, KS; d. 14 Dec 1955, Amarillo, Potter Cnty, TX.

110. Austin Addison[10] SINK *(Sarah[9] VAN HORN, Joshua[8], Isaiah[7], Henry B.[6], Henry[5], Christian Barentsen[4] VAN HOORN, Barent Christiansen[3], Christian Barentsen[2], Barent Barents[1])[1967,1968,1969]* was born Abt. 1856 in Indiana Cnty, PA[1970], and died Bef. 1900. He married Malinda FULERTON[1971,1972,1973] Abt. 1877. She was born Jan 1856 in OH[1974], and died Unknown.

Notes for Malinda FULERTON:
In 1900 Malinda is widowed and living with her children. She states she is the mother of 5 of which 4 are living.
In 1910 living with her daughter Althia Johnson. Althia is head of the household and married for 5 years. In the Census Malinda is listed as divorced. She has had 5 children of which 4 are living in 1910.

More About Austin SINK and Malinda FULERTON:
Marriage: Abt. 1877

Children of Austin SINK and Malinda FULERTON are:
275.   i.   Calvin[11] SINK, b. Sep 1879, IL; d. Unknown.
           ii.   Ellen SINK[1974], b. Sep 1881, IL[1974]; d. Unknown.
276.   iii. Althia SINK, b. Nov 1883, IL; d. Unknown.
           iv.   Cora SINK[1974], b. May 1886, IL[1974]; d. Unknown.

111. Melissa J.[10] SINK *(Sarah[9] VAN HORN, Joshua[8], Isaiah[7], Henry B.[6], Henry[5], Christian Barentsen[4] VAN HOORN, Barent Christiansen[3], Christian Barentsen[2], Barent Barents[1])[1975,1976]* was born Jun 1860 in Indiana Cnty, PA[1977], and died Unknown. She married William M. HECK[1978] Abt. 1878. He was born Abt. 1855 in TN[1978], and died Unknown.

More About Melissa J. SINK:
Lived: Jefferson Cnty, IL

More About William HECK and Melissa SINK:
Marriage: Abt. 1878

Child of Melissa SINK and William HECK is:
           i.   Calvin C.[11] HECK[1978], b. Oct 1880, IL[1978]; d. Unknown.

112. Elmer E.[10] SINK *(Sarah[9] VAN HORN, Joshua[8], Isaiah[7], Henry B.[6], Henry[5], Christian Barentsen[4] VAN HOORN, Barent Christiansen[3], Christian Barentsen[2], Barent Barents[1])[1979,1980]* was born Bet. 29 Jul 1861 - 1863 in Indiana Cnty, PA[1981], and died 22 Jan 1898 in Franklin Cnty, IL. He married Rhoda Emaline SMITH[1982] 22 Nov 1883 in Franklin Cnty, IL, daughter of George SMITH and Minerva GIBBS. She was born Bet. Apr 1862 - 30 Mar 1863 in IL[1982], and died 13 Nov 1932 in Franklin Cnty, IL.

More About Elmer SINK and Rhoda SMITH:
Marriage: 22 Nov 1883, Franklin Cnty, IL

Children of Elmer SINK and Rhoda SMITH are:
           i.   Charley O.[11] SINK, b. Abt. 1884; d. 20 Feb 1892.
           ii.   Ella E. SINK[1982], b. Apr 1886, IL[1982]; d. 04 Apr 1965; m. Ross WILLIAMS; b. 07 Aug 1883; d. 09 Jun 1953.
           iii. Norma SINK[1982], b. Mar 1888, IL[1982]; d. Unknown.

Isaiah Van Horn Pioneer of Indiana County, Pennsylvania

277.   iv. Stella SINK, b. Jan 1890, IL; d. Unknown.
278.   v.   Loren Wilson SINK, b. Bet. Nov 1891 - 11 Aug 1893, Franklin Cnty, IL; d. 10 Jan
              1974, Ewing, Franklin Cnty, IL.
279.   vi. William Jacob SINK, b. Jun 1894, IL; d. Unknown.

113. Margaret Emma[10] SINK *(Sarah[9] VAN HORN, Joshua[8], Isaiah[7], Henry B.[6], Henry[5], Christian Barentsen[4] VAN HOORN, Barent Christiansen[3], Christian Barentsen[2], Barent Barents[1])*[1983,1984,1985,1986,1987] was born Bet. 02 Jul 1865 - 1867 in Indiana Cnty, PA[1988], and died Aft. 1930. She married William Sherman COCKRUM[1989,1990,1991] Abt. 1889, son of COCKRUM and Martha. He was born Jan 1866 in IL[1992], and died Aft. 1930.

More About William COCKRUM and Margaret SINK:
Marriage: Abt. 1889

Children of Margaret SINK and William COCKRUM are:
        i.   Oscar[11] COCKRUM[1993,1994], b. Oct 1892, IL[1995]; d. Unknown.
        ii. Eddie COCKRUM[1995,1996], b. Dec 1897, IL[1997]; d. Unknown.
        iii. Owen COCKRUM[1997,1998], b. Dec 1899, IL[1999]; d. Unknown.
        iv. Clyde COCKRUM[2000], b. Abt. 1902, IL[2000]; d. Unknown.

114. Anderson T.[10] VAN HORN *(Samuel H.[9], Joshua[8], Isaiah[7], Henry B.[6], Henry[5], Christian Barentsen[4] VAN HOORN, Barent Christiansen[3], Christian Barentsen[2], Barent Barents[1])*[2001,2002,2003,2004] was born 03 Jun 1861 in Indiana Cnty, PA[2005], and died Bet. 1908 - 1910 in PA. He married Sadie A. KINNAN[2006,2007,2008] 14 Mar 1890 in Indiana, Indiana Cnty, PA[2009], daughter of J. W. KINNAN. She was born Aug 1862 in Deckers Point, Grant Twp., Indiana Cnty, PA[2010], and died Mar 1943 in Punxsutawney, Jefferson Cnty, PA[2011].

Notes for Anderson T. VAN HORN:
      8 February 1895 Indiana Weekly Messenger (Indiana, PA) reports the testimony of Anderson in the vote buying trial of Chales Brown accused of buying votes for a candidate by the name of White. Anderson states he received no money but negotiated with Brown for a payment more than the offer of a days pay and dinner.

More About Anderson T. VAN HORN:
Lived: Clearfield Cnty, PA and Butler Cnty, OH
Occupation: Teamster

Notes for Sadie A. KINNAN:
      In 1900 she is the mother of 6 children and 4 are living. The living children are Harry, Dora, Jospeh and Samuel.
      In 1910 she is a widow and has moved from Clearfield Cnty to Jefferson Cnty, PA she is the mother of 8 of which 5 are living on the date of the census. Living in the home ore Dora, Ord, Clyde and Julie. Ord and Clyde are laborers at Horatio.
      In 1920 she is a widow living on Main Street in Punxsutawney, PA. She owns her home. Living with her are her son Joseph and daughter Julia. She is a truant officer for the school board.

More About Sadie A. KINNAN:
Burial: Unknown, Greenwood Cemetery, Indiana, PA
Employment: Truant Office for the School Board

Marriage Notes for Anderson VAN HORN and Sadie KINNAN:
Indiana Messenger, Indiana PA, March 19, 1890
Mr. Anderson T. VANHORN, of Clearfield county, to Sadie A. KINNAN, of Decker's point, on
March 14, 1890, at the Kinter House, Indiana, by Pastor D. W. Swigart.

More About Anderson VAN HORN and Sadie KINNAN:
Marriage: 14 Mar 1890, Indiana, Indiana Cnty, PA[2012]
Marriage date: D. W. Swigart
Marriage Place: Kinter House

Children of Anderson VAN HORN and Sadie KINNAN are:

    i.   Harry M.[11] VAN HORN[2013], b. Sep 1885, Punxsutawney, Jefferson Cnty, PA; d.
        Bef. 1910.

    ii. Dora B. VAN HORN[2013,2014], b. Dec 1890, Punxsutawney, Jefferson Cnty, PA[2014];
        d. Unknown.

        More About Dora B. VAN HORN:
        Occupation: 1910, Servant

    iii. Joseph W. VAN HORN[2015,2016,2017], b. Bet. 24 Mar 1890 - 1893, Punxsutawney,
        Jefferson Cnty, PA or Mahaffey, Clearfield Cnty, PA[2017,2018]; d. 27 Jun 1976, Oil
        City, PA; m. Margaret LATCHAW[2019], Aft. 1920; d. Aug 1961.

        Notes for Joseph W. VAN HORN:
        In 1920 Joseph is a Lt. in the Marines.

        More About Joseph W. VAN HORN:
        Burial: Unknown, Greenwood Cemetery, Jefferson Cnty, PA[2020]
        Military service: 1920, Marine Corp Officer, Lieutenant

        More About Joseph VAN HORN and Margaret LATCHAW:
        Marriage: Aft. 1920

    iv. Ord VAN HORN[2021], b. Abt. 1892, Punxsutawney, Jefferson Cnty, PA; d. Aft.
        1910.

        Notes for Ord VAN HORN:
        As there is no Ord in the 1900 Census living with the family and yet he is there in
        1910 with Sadie. Joseph was 7 in 1900 and Ord is 17 in 1910 and no Joseph is
        shown. Ord must be the nickname of Joseph.

280.   v.   Samuel Clyde VAN HORN, b. Feb 1896, Punxsutawney, Jefferson Cnty, PA; d. Aft.
        1966.

    vi. Julie VAN HORN[2021,2022], b. Bet. 1901 - 1902, Punxsutawney, Jefferson Cnty,
        PA[2022]; d. Unknown.

        Notes for Julie VAN HORN:
        In 1920 living with her mother and working as a clerk in a dry goods store.

        More About Julie VAN HORN:
        Occupation: Clerk Dry Goods Store

    vii. ? VAN HORN, d. Bef. 1910.

viii.   ? VAN HORN, d. Bef. 1910.

115. Harry V.[10] VAN HORN *(John Hastings[9], John[8], Isaiah[7], Henry B.[6], Henry[5], Christian Barentsen[4] VAN HOORN, Barent Christiansen[3], Christian Barentsen[2], Barent Barents[1])[2023,2024,2025,2026]* was born 02 Feb 1874 in PA[2027], and died 11 Nov 1953 in PA. He married Agnes B. MOYES[2028,2029,2030] Abt. 1892, daughter of George MOYES and Jennie ZERNEY. She was born Abt. 1875 in PA[2031], and died Aft. 1961 in PA.

Notes for Harry V. VAN HORN:
in his WWI Draft Registration he is Harry V. Van Horn, Sr. He is of medium height, medium build and has brown eyes and hair. He states he has 3 fingers missing from his left hand. He works as an Engineer for Carbon Steel company of Pittsburgh, PA. His wife is Aggie Viola.
In 1920 lives on Montrose Hill in O'Hara, PA in a place that he rents. He is a steel mill laborer.
In 1930 owns his home worth $2500 and has a radio. Lives on Oxford Street in O'Hara Twp., PA. Henry Moyes an Uncle is living with the family he is 83 and is the brother of Agnes's father. His son Harry and his family are next door.
We have some variation in the initials of Harry and his son. From Harry V. to Harry C. to Harry Z. The Z is said to stand for Zerney.

More About Harry V. VAN HORN:
Burial: Unknown, Deer Creek Cemetery, Cheswick, Allegheny Cnty, PA Section 2A Row 9 Below Road
Occupation: Stationary Engineer, Laborer Steel Mill, Machine Operator Construction

Notes for Agnes B. MOYES:
Agnes lists her father as being from Scotland. In 1930 her Uncle Henry Moyes born Scotland and parents born Scotland is of the home. I have concluded that this is her father's brother not her mother's brother since her mother was born in Pennsylvania.

More About Agnes B. MOYES:
Burial: Unknown, Deer Creek Cemetery, Cheswick, Allegheny Cnty, PA Section 2A Row 9 Below Road

More About Harry VAN HORN and Agnes MOYES:
Marriage: Abt. 1892

Children of Harry VAN HORN and Agnes MOYES are:
281.   i.   Harry V.[11] VAN HORN, JR, b. 15 Oct 1894, PA; d. 28 Jan 1942.
282.   ii.   Ralph Hastings VAN HORN, b. 14 Aug 1900, PA; d. 06 Apr 1997, Pittsburgh, Alleghney Cnty, PA.
        iii. Viola Agnes VAN HORN[2031,2032], b. 09 Oct 1904, PA[2033]; d. Unknown.

              More About Viola Agnes VAN HORN:
              Occupation: Messinger Steel Mill

        iv.   Lawrence Moyes VAN HORN[2033,2034], b. 01 Jul 1907, PA[2035]; d. 11 Apr 2004, Chicora, Butler Cnty, PA.
        v.   William Wright VAN HORN[2035,2036,2037], b. 24 Oct 1909, PA[2038]; d. Unknown.

              More About William Wright VAN HORN:
              Occupation: Layout Helper Construction

        vi.   Walter Morris VAN HORN[2039,2040], b. Bet. 19 Mar - Dec 1912, PA[2041]; d. 21 Sep

1968, Pittsburgh, Alleghney Cnty, PA[2042]; m. Evelyn Florence HUSTON, 16 Nov 1932, Pittsburgh, Allegheny Cnty, PA; b. 1914; d. 1984.

More About Walter Morris VAN HORN:
Occupation: Machinist Helper Manufacturing

More About Walter VAN HORN and Evelyn HUSTON:
Marriage: 16 Nov 1932, Pittsburgh, Allegheny Cnty, PA

    vii.   Ethel M. VAN HORN, b. Private.

116. John Hastings[10] VAN HORN *(James Devin[9], John[8], Isaiah[7], Henry B.[6], Henry[5], Christian Barentsen[4] VAN HOORN, Barent Christiansen[3], Christian Barentsen[2], Barent Barents[1])*[2043,2044,2045,2046] was born Aug 1860 in PA[2047], and died Aft. 1930. He married Sarah Isabel PALMER[2048,2049,2050,2051] 1886. She was born Mar 1865 in PA[2052], and died Aft. 1930.

Notes for John Hastings VAN HORN:
    In 1920 John and Ella are living alone in Jim Wells Cnty, TX. Their daughter and her husband are living in the same county.
    In 1930 living in Nueces Cnty, TX on a place he owns worth $12,000 and has a radio. His son Arthur is living in the home and daughter Sarah Isabel is living next door with her husband and their daughter.

More About John Hastings VAN HORN:
Occupation: Railroad Brakeman, House Carpenter

More About John VAN HORN and Sarah PALMER:
Marriage: 1886

Children of John VAN HORN and Sarah PALMER are:
    i.   Arthur Palmer[11] VAN HORN[2053,2054,2055,2056], b. 17 Jul 1887, Leetsdale, PA[2057]; d. Aft. 1930.

        Notes for Arthur Palmer VAN HORN:
        In the 1912 Pittsburgh, PA City Directory he lives at 445 Water and is a clerk.
        In his WWI Draft Registration he states he lives at 607 Mesquite, Corpus Christi, TX. He is a Stenographer for the _____City National Bank in corpus Christi, TX. He is single and is Tall, Slender, Slightly built with grey eyes and Brown hair. He indicates he was born in Leetsdale, PA.
        In 1920 he is a bookkeeper for CC Harman. He is single and a boarder on Blucher Street in Corpus Christi, TX.

        More About Arthur Palmer VAN HORN:
        Lived: Corpus Christi, TX
        Military service: Veteran WW I, Lt in Army reserves
        Occupation: Asst. Cashier Bank

283.   ii.   Sarah Isabel VAN HORN, b. Aug 1891, PA; d. Unknown.

117. John Albert[10] LYDICK *(Jane Elizabeth[9] VAN HORN, Isaiah[8], Isaiah[7], Henry B.[6], Henry[5], Christian Barentsen[4] VAN HOORN, Barent Christiansen[3], Christian Barentsen[2], Barent Barents[1])*[2058,2059,2060,2061] was born Feb 1855 in Indiana Cnty, PA[2062], and died 20 May 1912 in Penn

217

Run, Indiana Cnty, PA. He married Rachel A. MCCRACKEN[2063,2064,2065,2065] Abt. 1877[2066]. She was born 03 Dec 1860 in Grant Twp., Indiana Cnty, PA[2067], and died 20 Oct 1945 in Cherry Hill Twp., Indiana Cnty, PA.

More About John Albert LYDICK:
Occupation: Day Laborer Odd Jobs

Notes for Rachel A. MCCRACKEN:
In 1910 Rachel indicates she is the mother of 5 and 3 are living at the time of this census.

More About John LYDICK and Rachel MCCRACKEN:
Marriage: Abt. 1877[2068]

Children of John LYDICK and Rachel MCCRACKEN are:
      i.   Martha[11] LYDICK, b. 1879, PA; d. 1880, PA.
      ii. Annie LYDICK, b. 11 Feb 1881, PA; d. 1899, PA.
284.   iii. William D. LYDICK, b. 06 Mar 1884, Indiana Cnty, PA; d. 1937, PA.
285.   iv. Alice M. LYDICK, b. Mar 1887, PA; d. Unknown.
286.   v.   John Torrence LYDICK, b. Feb 1890, PA; d. Dec 1975, Clymer, Indiana Cnty, PA.

118. James Irvin[10] LYDICK *(Jane Elizabeth[9] VAN HORN, Isaiah[8], Isaiah[7], Henry B.[6], Henry[5], Christian Barentsen[4] VAN HOORN, Barent Christiansen[3], Christian Barentsen[2], Barent Barents[1])*[2069,2070,2071,2072,2073,2074,2075] was born 11 Jul 1856 in Indiana Cnty, PA[2076], and died Aft. 1930. He married Emma STIVER[2076,2077,2078,2079,2080] 1880. She was born Sep 1858 in PA[2081], and died Aft. 1930.

Notes for James Irvin LYDICK:
    In 1880 living next door to his father and mother and his Van Horn grandparents. A Henry H, Honuck age 21 born PA is also living with James and his wife Emma.
    In 1900 he is Irvin J. Lydick and is living with is wife and 3 daughters. They have been married for 22 years and have 3 children all living.

More About James Irvin LYDICK:
Occupation: Carpenter and Farmer

More About James LYDICK and Emma STIVER:
Marriage: 1880

Children of James LYDICK and Emma STIVER are:
      i.   Larsa Jane[11] LYDICK[2082,2083], b. May 1881, PA[2084]; d. Unknown.
      ii. Nora E. LYDICK[2084,2085], b. Dec 1882, PA[2086]; d. Unknown.

          Notes for Nora E. LYDICK:
          In 1910 Nora is living with her parents she is listed as single and indicates she is the mother of 1 but that child is not living in 1910.

      iii. Annie E. LYDICK[2086,2087,2088], b. Nov 1894, PA[2089]; d. Unknown; m. Theodore CYANET[2090], Abt. 1918; b. Abt. 1890, ND[2090]; d. Unknown.

          More About Theodore CYANET and Annie LYDICK:
          Marriage: Abt. 1918

119. Samuel K.[10] LYDICK *(Jane Elizabeth[9] VAN HORN, Isaiah[8], Isaiah[7], Henry B.[6], Henry[5], Christian Barentsen[4] VAN HOORN, Barent Christiansen[3], Christian Barentsen[2], Barent Barents[1])[2091,2092,2093]* was born 22 Oct 1857 in Indiana Cnty, PA[2094,2095], and died Unknown. He married Hannah J. PALMER[2095] Abt. 1879. She was born Oct 1858 in PA[2095], and died Unknown.

More About Samuel K. LYDICK:
Employment: 1900, Tannery Laborer

More About Samuel LYDICK and Hannah PALMER:
Marriage: Abt. 1879

Children of Samuel LYDICK and Hannah PALMER are:
- i. Manda[11] LYDICK[2095], b. Jun 1885, PA[2095]; d. Unknown.
- ii. Miller LYDICK[2095], b. Sep 1888, PA[2095]; d. Unknown.
- iii. Russel LYDICK[2095], b. Sep 1891, PA[2095]; d. Unknown.
- iv. Levi LYDICK[2095], b. Mar 1894, PA[2095]; d. Unknown.
- v. Virginia LYDICK[2095], b. Apr 1900, PA[2095]; d. Unknown.

120. Mary A.[10] LYDICK *(Jane Elizabeth[9] VAN HORN, Isaiah[8], Isaiah[7], Henry B.[6], Henry[5], Christian Barentsen[4] VAN HOORN, Barent Christiansen[3], Christian Barentsen[2], Barent Barents[1])[2096,2097,2098,2099]* was born 01 Apr 1861 in Indiana Cnty, PA[2100], and died Aft. 1910. She married James PALMER[2101,2102] Abt. 1880. He was born Oct 1847 in PA[2103,2104], and died Aft. 1910.

Notes for Mary A. LYDICK:
In 1900 she states she is the mother of 7 with 5 living. There is a married daughter in the home but no son in law.

More About James PALMER and Mary LYDICK:
Marriage: Abt. 1880

Children of Mary LYDICK and James PALMER are:
287. i. Elizabeth Pearl[11] PALMER, b. Jan 1882, PA; d. 23 Jul 1966, Clymer, Indiana Cnty, PA.
- ii. Myrtle J. PALMER[2104], b. Jul 1883, PA[2104]; d. Unknown; m. WISINGER; d. Unknown.
- iii. Burton S. PALMER[2105,2106], b. Aug 1888, PA[2107,2108]; d. Unknown.
- iv. David Edward PALMER[2109,2110], b. Aug 1894, PA[2111,2112]; d. Unknown.
- v. Carl PALMER[2112], b. Nov 1899, PA[2112]; d. Unknown.

121. Elmer E.[10] LYDICK *(Jane Elizabeth[9] VAN HORN, Isaiah[8], Isaiah[7], Henry B.[6], Henry[5], Christian Barentsen[4] VAN HOORN, Barent Christiansen[3], Christian Barentsen[2], Barent Barents[1])[2113,2114,2115,2116,2117]* was born 25 Feb 1863 in Indiana Cnty, PA[2118], and died 30 Jul 1927 in Indiana Cnty, PA. He married Anna FULMER[2119,2120,2121] Abt. 1889 in Green Twp., Indiana Cnty, PA. She was born Dec 1863 in PA[2122], and died Unknown.

Notes for Elmer E. LYDICK:
8 May 1895 Cherryhill-Blair Elmer Lydick is listed as non payment of taxes in the Indiana Weekly Messenger (Indiana, PA). Elmer E. Lydick Green-Blair is also listed for non payment of taxes.
In 1900 living next door to Jos. Lydick unknown relationship and has a nephew Albert Lowman living in the family.

In 1910 living next door to brother Van Lydick.

In 1920 living in a home he owns free and clear. He is a farmer. Two daughters of the home Eva V. and Jessie L. Note that in his obit Jessie is call Maude as well as in the 1910 census.

ELMER E. LYDIC--After a lingering illness from cancer, Elmer E. Lydick, prominent resident of Cherryhill township, died in the Indiana Hospital, Saturday evening about 12 o'clock. He leaves his widow, Mrs. Annie Lydic and three children, Dean, Eva and Maude. Funeral services will be conducted in his late residence Tuesday afternoon at 4 o'clock. The body will be brought to Indiana for interment in Greenwood Cemetery. (News: Aug. 1, 1927)

More About Elmer E. LYDICK:
Burial: 1927, Greenwood Cemetery,Indiana Cnty, PA
Occupation: Blacksmith and Farmer

Notes for Anna FULMER:
In 1900 Anna is the mother of 5 children of which only Charles is living.
In 1910 Annie is the mother of 7 children of which 3 are living.

More About Elmer LYDICK and Anna FULMER:
Marriage: Abt. 1889, Green Twp., Indiana Cnty, PA

Children of Elmer LYDICK and Anna FULMER are:
      i.   Charles Dean[11] LYDICK[2122,2123], b. Aug 1895, PA[2124]; d. Unknown.
     ii.   Eva V. LYDICK[2125,2126], b. Abt. 1900, PA[2126]; d. Unknown.
   iii.   Maude LYDICK[2127,2128], b. Abt. 1903, PA[2128]; d. Unknown.

122. Martha Jane[10] LYDICK *(Jane Elizabeth*[9] *VAN HORN, Isaiah*[8]*, Isaiah*[7]*, Henry B.*[6]*, Henry*[5]*, Christian Barentsen*[4] *VAN HOORN, Barent Christiansen*[3]*, Christian Barentsen*[2]*, Barent Barents*[1]*)*[2129,2130,2131,2132,2133,2134] was born 03 Sep 1865 in Indiana Cnty, PA[2135], and died 02 Mar 1943 in 1302 Oakland Ave., Indiana, PA. She married John A MYERS[2136,2137] Abt. 1885. He was born Aug 1856 in PA, and died Bet. 1910 - 1930.

Notes for Martha Jane LYDICK:
In 1920 she is renting in Richmond Village, Grant Twp., Indiana Cnty, PA. Martha is widowed. She lives with her daughter Lottie B (P) who is single and a public school teacher.

In 1930 she is living on Plum Rd in Hempfield Twp., Westmoreland Cnty, PA with her son Arthur. She rents for $15/month, Arthur is a farm laborer and is single. Living next door is her son Clarence R. Meyers and his family. He is also a farm laborer.

More About Martha Jane LYDICK:
Burial: Unknown, East Union Cemetery, Indiana Cnty, PA

More About John A MYERS:
Occupation: 1900, Stone Mason

More About John MYERS and Martha LYDICK:
Marriage: Abt. 1885

Children of Martha LYDICK and John MYERS are:
      i.   Harvey J.[11] MYERS[2137], b. Abt. 1887, PA; d. Bef. 1970; m. Nellie JEFFERIES; d. Unknown.

           More About Harvey J. MYERS:

Occupation: 1910, Railroad Fireman

    ii.   Arthur Bell MYERS[2138,2139,2140], b. 31 Jan 1889, Purchase Line, PA[2141]; d. Bef. 1970; m. Dorothy HEMMINGER, Aft. 1930; d. Unknown.

Notes for Arthur Bell MYERS:
In his WWI Draft Registration he is single, a farmer, lives on RD#2 Shelocta, PA. He is tall of medium build with grey eyes and black hair.

More About Arthur MYERS and Dorothy HEMMINGER:
Marriage: Aft. 1930

    iii.   Minnie M. MYERS[2142,2143], b. Oct 1890, PA; d. Bef. 1970; m. Gus M. FETTERMAN; d. Unknown.
    iv.   Edgar L. MYERS[2144,2145], b. 19 Apr 1892, PA; d. Bef. 1970; m. Gaye BASH; d. Unknown.

288.   v.   Harry Irvin MYERS, b. 06 Feb 1894, PA; d. 31 Jan 1970, Indiana, Indiana Cnty, PA.
    vi.   Lulu Blanche MYERS[2146,2147], b. 22 May 1895, PA; d. 31 Dec 1958; m. Clair SHANKLE; d. Unknown.
    vii.   Lottie P. MYERS[2148,2149], b. Oct 1896, PA; d. Aft. 1970; m. Richard LEWIS; d. Unknown.
289.   viii.   Joseph Lucas MYERS, b. 14 Mar 1898, PA; d. 19 Apr 1975, Tacoma Park, Montgomery Cnty, MD.
290.   ix.   Clarence R. MYERS, b. Abt. 1902, PA; d. Bef. 1970.
291.   x.   Albert Dennis MYERS, b. Oct 1899, Grant Twp., Indiana Cnty, PA; d. Aft. 1970.

123. Ida Mae[10] LYDICK *(Jane Elizabeth[9] VAN HORN, Isaiah[8], Isaiah[7], Henry B.[6], Henry[5], Christian Barentsen[4] VAN HOORN, Barent Christiansen[3], Christian Barentsen[2], Barent Barents[1])*[2150,2151,2152,2153] was born 11 May 1868 in East Mahoning Twp., Indiana Cnty, PA[2154], and died 07 Feb 1945. She married Wallace Evan SHANKLE[2155,2156] 03 May 1887 in Diamondville, Indiana Cnty, PA[2157,2158], son of Rebecca. He was born Bet. 22 Nov 1853 - 1856 in Arcadia, Indiana Cnty, PA[2159], and died 07 Nov 1932 in Chevy Chase, Indiana Cnty, PA[2160].

More About Wallace Evan SHANKLE:
Burial: Unknown, Taylorsville Cemetery, Inidana Cnty, PA
Cause of Death: Heart Disease
Employment: Coal Mine

More About Wallace SHANKLE and Ida LYDICK:
Marriage: 03 May 1887, Diamondville, Indiana Cnty, PA[2161,2162]

Children of Ida LYDICK and Wallace SHANKLE are:
292.   i.   Thomas Roy[11] SHANKLE, b. 25 Dec 1887, Grant Twp., Indiana Cnty, PA; d. 07 Jan 1974, Indiana, Indiana Cnty, PA.
    ii.   Oliver Gordon SHANKLE[2163,2164,2165], b. 01 Feb 1889, Grant Twp., Indiana Cnty, PA[2166]; d. 02 May 1965, White Twp., Indiana Cnty, PA[2167]; m. Ann Elizabeth BYERS, 09 Jan 1943; b. Abt. 1900; d. 11 Mar 1969.

Notes for Oliver Gordon SHANKLE:
In 1920 and 1930 he is a foundry moulder and is living with his aunt and uncle Van and Myrtle Lydick
In 1942 he is 5ft 6in and weighs 140 pounds has blue eyes and gray hair. Works for

the Indiana Foundry and lives at 411 N. 5th Street in Indiana,.Pa according to his WWI I Draft Registration.

More About Oliver Gordon SHANKLE:
Lived: Apr 1942, 411 N. 5th Street Indiana, PA

More About Oliver SHANKLE and Ann BYERS:
Marriage: 09 Jan 1943

293.   iii.   Elizabeth Mabel SHANKLE, b. Bet. 13 Feb 1889 - 1890, Grant Twp., Indiana Cnty, PA; d. 04 Dec 1969, Indiana Cnty, PA.
         iv.   Emerson Ralph SHANKLE[2168], b. 26 Mar 1891, Grant Twp., Indiana Cnty, PA[2168]; d. 13 Dec 1916, Indiana, Indiana Cnty, PA[2169]; m. Edna LAMBING[2170], 11 Oct 1916, Clymer, Indiana Cnty, PA[2170,2171]; d. Unknown.

               More About Emerson Ralph SHANKLE:
               Burial: Unknown, Taylorsville Cemetery
               Cause of Death: Injured in an explosuion at te Clymer Brick and Fire Clay Company

               More About Emerson SHANKLE and Edna LAMBING:
               Marriage: 11 Oct 1916, Clymer, Indiana Cnty, PA[2172,2173]

294.   v.   Myrtle Mae SHANKLE, b. 10 Aug 1892, Grant Twp., Indiana Cnty, PA; d. 06 Aug 1964, Indiana, Indiana Cnty, PA.
295.   vi.   Eva Jane SHANKLE, b. 06 Sep 1894, Grant Twp., Indiana Cnty, PA; d. 03 Jul 1992, Indiana, Indiana Cnty, PA.
296.   vii. Delsa Joan SHANKLE, b. 31 Jul 1896, Grant Twp., Indiana Cnty, PA; d. 14 Feb 1968, PA.
297.   viii. Ford Russell SHANKLE, b. 09 Apr 1898, Grant Twp., Indiana Cnty, PA; d. 07 Mar 1987, Indiana, Indiana Cnty, PA.
         ix.   Wallace Glenn SHANKLE[2174,2175,2176,2177,2178], b. 21 Oct 1900, Montgomery Twp., Indiana Cnty, PA[2179]; d. 08 Sep 1972, Indiana, Indiana Cnty, PA[2180]; m. MILLER; d. Unknown.

               Notes for Wallace Glenn SHANKLE:
               5 June 1918 Wallace Shankle is listed in the Indiana Evening Gazette (Indiana, PA) as having given $0,50 to the YMCA fund.
               In 1930 lives on Pennsylvania Rd in White Twp., Indiana Cnty, PA owns his home worth $1500 and has a radio. His son Glenn lives in the home.
               22 April 1933 Indiana Evening Gazette (Indiana, PA) Glenn Shankle is one of many men called to the welfare office to pick up their 3 day work card.
               22 Nov 1942 WWI I Enlistment indicates he is single with dependents he is 64 inches tall and weighs 176 pounds he has a grammar school education and is enlisted as a private in the army. In his obituary there is no mention of a wife or dependents. His parents are deceased so they are not his dependents.
               9 September 1972 Indiana Evening Gazette (Indiana, PA) Wallace G. Shankle Obituary does not mention a wife. It gives his parents and brothers Roy T and Ford R and sister Mrs E. Jane McManus as survivors and internment in Taylorsville Cemetery. He died in the Indiana Hospital but was living in Blacklick, Pa.

               More About Wallace Glenn SHANKLE:
               Burial: Unknown, Taylorsville Cemetery

124. Ira[10] Van LYDICK *(Jane Elizabeth*[9] *VAN HORN, Isaiah*[8]*, Isaiah*[7]*, Henry B.*[6]*, Henry*[5]*, Christian Barentsen*[4] *VAN HOORN, Barent Christiansen*[3]*, Christian Barentsen*[2]*, Barent Barents*[1]*)*[2181,2182,2183,2184,2185] was born 16 Jan 1871 in Taylorsville, Indiana Cnty, PA[2186], and died 11 Feb 1951 in Hyattsville, Prince George Cnty, MD. He married Myrtle M. MOORE[2187,2188,2189] Abt. 1891. She was born Abt. 1875 in PA[2190], and died 1934.

Notes for Ira Van LYDICK:
    In 1900 living with parents and son. No wife is given although he states he has been married for 8 years.
    VAN LYDICK died Sunday morning at the home of his son and daughter-in-law, Mr. and Mrs. Frayne Lydick of Hyattsville, Md., after an illness of two weeks. Born June 16, 1871 at Taylorsville, Indiana county, he was the husband of the late Myrtle M. Lydick who preceded him in death 17 years ago. [s/o Stuchell Lydick]. Surviving are three sons: Charles of New York; Frayne of Maryland; Oliver of Indianapolis, Ind.; one daughter, Audrey, wife of Leroy Cunningham of Indiana, Pa.; 26 grandchildren; 19 great grandchildren, and one brother, Bert Lydick of Johnstown. Three sons and two daughters preceded him in death. Friends will be received at the Bell Funeral Home, Wayne avenue, Indiana, after 1·00 p.m. Tuesday, where services will be conducted on Wednesday, Feb. 14, at 1:30 p.m. by Mrs. Joseph Lefebure of Barnsboro. Interment will be in Deckers Point Cemetery. [11 Feb. 1951-News date]

More About Ira Van LYDICK:
Employment: Indiana Foundry Laborer, Coal Miner

Notes for Myrtle M. MOORE:
    In 1910 Myrtle is mother of 6 with 4 living

More About Ira Van LYDICK and Myrtle MOORE:
Marriage: Abt. 1891

Children of Ira Van LYDICK and Myrtle MOORE are:
| | i. | David Myrl[11] LYDICK[2191,2192,2193], b. Abt. 1892, PA[2194]; d. Bef. 1929. |

298.   ii.   Rosaline LYDICK, b. Abt. 09 Jul 1899, PA; d. 26 Mar 1929, Indiana, Indiana Cnty, PA.

        iii.   Charles G. LYDICK[2195,2196,2197], b. Abt. 1904, PA[2198]; d. Aft. 1929.

           Notes for Charles G. LYDICK:
           In 1929 living at Ft Benning, GA.

299.   iv.   Frayne C. LYDICK, b. Abt. 1907, PA; d. Aft. 1929.

        v.   Bernice A. LYDICK[2198,2199], b. Abt. 1912, PA[2200]; d. Aft. 1929.

           Notes for Bernice A. LYDICK:
           In 1929 living in NY.

        vi.   Audrey M. LYDICK[2200,2201,2202], b. Feb 1916, PA[2203]; d. Aft. 1929; m. Leroy CUNNINGHAM; d. Unknown.

        vii.   Oliver G. LYDICK[2203,2204,2205], b. 19 Mar 1917, PA[2206]; d. Aft. 1929.

125. Ruth E.[10] LYDICK *(Jane Elizabeth*[9] *VAN HORN, Isaiah*[8]*, Isaiah*[7]*, Henry B.*[6]*, Henry*[5]*, Christian Barentsen*[4] *VAN HOORN, Barent Christiansen*[3]*, Christian Barentsen*[2]*, Barent Barents*[1]*)*[2207,2208] was born Bet. 12 Oct 1873 - 1876 in Indiana Cnty, PA[2209], and died 1904 in Green Twp., Indiana Cnty, PA.

She married Harry M. WILT[2210] Abt. 1892 in Indiana Cnty, PA[2211], son of David WILT and Mary M.. He was born Nov 1869 in PA[2212], and died Unknown.

Notes for Harry M. WILT:
    In 1910 living with his parents and given as single. His son Paul is also in the home. No mention of other children.
    In 1920 living with his parents in Green Twp., Indiana Cnty, PA widowed. He is a laborer and works out.

More About Harry WILT and Ruth LYDICK:
Marriage: Abt. 1892, Indiana Cnty, PA[2213]

Children of Ruth LYDICK and Harry WILT are:
      i.   Calvin[11] WILT[2214]; b. Jul 1892, PA[2214]; d. Bef. 1982.
300.   ii. Ira Paul WILT, b. Apr 1895, PA; d. 15 May 1982, Indiana Cnty, PA.
     iii. Joseph WILT[2214], b. Aug 1897, PA[2214]; d. Bef. 1982.
     iv. Benjamin O. WILT[2214], b. Apr 1899, PA[2214]; d. Aft. 1982.
     v. Frank WILT, d. Bef. 1982.

126. Amos Burton[10] LYDICK *(Jane Elizabeth[9] VAN HORN, Isaiah[8], Isaiah[7], Henry B.[6], Henry[5], Christian Barentsen[4] VAN HOORN, Barent Christiansen[3], Christian Barentsen[2], Barent Barents[1])*[2215,2216,2217,2218] was born 24 May 1878 in Indiana Cnty, PA[2219,2220], and died 21 Jun 1954 in Johnstown, Cambria Cnty, PA. He married Mary Verne BARR[2221,2222,2223,2224] 1909, daughter of Moses BARR and Jennie C.. She was born Abt. 1890 in PA[2225], and died 28 Feb 1966 in St. Petersburg, FL.

Notes for Amos Burton LYDICK:
    In 1910 Amos is living with his wife and child in the home of her parents.
    In 1930 living with wife and two single children. They rent for $45/month and do not have a radio. Amos was 30 when he married and Mary Verne was 18.
    AMOS BERTON LYDIC, 76, of Johnstown, died in the Conemaugh Valley Memorial Hospital the evening of June 21. He was born May 24, 1878 in Indiana county, the son of Stuchell and Jane Van Horn Lydic. Surviving are his wife, the former Verne Barr; two daughters: Mayne, wife of James Skinner of Barberton, Ohio, and Morna, wife of N. L. Stuver of Johnstown; also six grandchildren. The family will receive friends from 7-9 P.M. Tuesday and 2-4 and 7-9 Wednesday at the H. M. Pickings Sons Mortuary, Johnstown, where services will be conducted at 11 A.M. Thursday. Interment will be in Richland Cemetery.

More About Amos Burton LYDICK:
Burial: Unknown, Richland Cemetery
Occupation: Bet. 1918 - 1930, Blacksmith

Notes for Mary Verne BARR:
    MRS. MARY VERNE LYDIC, 75, of 244 Locust St., Johnstown, died Monday, Feb. 28, 1966, in St. Petersburg, Fla. Born July 13, 1890 in Somerset Co.;, she was a daughter of Moses and Jennie McCoy Barr. She was a member of the American Baptist Church in St. Petersburg. Mrs. Lydic was preceded in death by her husband, Amos, who died in 1954; also two sisters, one brother and one great-.....Survivors include the following daughters: Mrs. James (Mayme) Skinner, Barberton, O.; Mrs. Nathaniel (Mora) Stuver, St. Petersburg, Fla.; six grandchildren; eight great grandchildren. Friends will be received from 2-4 and 7-9 p.m. Friday at the Picking Mortuary, Johnstown, where funeral services will be conducted at 11 a.m. Saturday. Rev. Charles Bray, officiating. Interment will be in Richland Cemetery

More About Mary Verne BARR:
Burial: Unknown, Richland Cemetery
Occupation: 1930, House to House Soap Sales

More About Amos LYDICK and Mary BARR:
Marriage: 1909

Children of Amos LYDICK and Mary BARR are:
    i.   Mary C.[11] LYDICK[2225,2226,2227,2228], b. Jan 1909, PA[2229]; d. Unknown; m. James SKINNER[2230]; d. Unknown.

        More About Mary C. LYDICK:
        Occupation: 1930, House to House Soap Sales

    ii.   Myrna E. LYDICK[2231,2232], b. Abt. 1911, PA[2233]; d. Unknown; m. Nathaniel L. STUVER[2234]; d. Unknown.

        More About Myrna E. LYDICK:
        Occupation: 1930, Grocery Store Saleslady

127. Jennie B.[10] LYDICK *(Jane Elizabeth[9] VAN HORN, Isaiah[8], Isaiah[7], Henry B.[6], Henry[5], Christian Barentsen[4] VAN HOORN, Barent Christiansen[3], Christian Barentsen[2], Barent Barents[1])*[2235,2236] was born Mar 1879 in Indiana Cnty, PA[2237], and died 1906 in PA. She married Thomas A. LAMBING[2238,2239,2240,2241] Abt. 1896 in Indiana Cnty, PA[2242,2243], son of Robert LAMBING and Hannah Maria. He was born Mar 1875 in PA[2244], and died Unknown.

More About Thomas A. LAMBING:
Burial: Unknown, Plum Creek Cemetery, Indiana Cnty, PA
Employment: 1930, Machinist in Coal Mine
Occupation: Fireman Stone Quary

More About Thomas LAMBING and Jennie LYDICK:
Marriage: Abt. 1896, Indiana Cnty, PA[2245,2246]

Children of Jennie LYDICK and Thomas LAMBING are:
        i.   Mary Edna[11] LAMBING[2247,2248], b. Mar 1898, PA[2249,2250]; d. Unknown.
301.   ii.   Mildred Grace LAMBING, b. 03 Jun 1900, Rochester Mills, Indiana Cnty, PA; d. 22 Jan 1987, White Twp., Indiana Cnty, PA.
302.   iii.   Charles A. LAMBING, b. 14 Oct 1904, Green Twp., Indiana Cnty, PA; d. 17 Jan 1979, Natrona Heights, Allegheny Cnty, PA.

128. Anna[10] MCCALL *(Martha[9] VAN HORN, Isaiah[8], Isaiah[7], Henry B.[6], Henry[5], Christian Barentsen[4] VAN HOORN, Barent Christiansen[3], Christian Barentsen[2], Barent Barents[1])*[2251,2252] was born Abt. 1871 in PA, and died Unknown. She married WEAVER[2253]. He died Bef. 1920.

Children of Anna MCCALL and WEAVER are:
    i.   Vada[11] WEAVER[2254], b. Abt. 1901, PA; d. Unknown.
    ii.   Martha WEAVER[2254], b. Abt. 1903, PA; d. Unknown.

129. Harry Logan[10] LYDICK *(Mary P.[9] VAN HORN, Isaiah[8], Isaiah[7], Henry B.[6], Henry[5], Christian Barentsen[4] VAN HOORN, Barent Christiansen[3], Christian Barentsen[2], Barent Barents[1])*[2255,2256,2257] was born 20 May 1866 in Indiana Cnty, PA[2258], and died 10 Nov 1912. He married Mary LONG[2259] 09 Jun 1892 in Indiana Cnty, PA. She was born Dec 1866[2259], and died Unknown.

More About Harry LYDICK and Mary LONG:
Marriage: 09 Jun 1892, Indiana Cnty, PA

Children of Harry LYDICK and Mary LONG are:
- i. Goldie Esther[11] LYDICK[2259], b. 02 Apr 1893, Indiana Cnty, PA; d. Unknown.
- ii. Wesley Long LYDICK[2259], b. 23 Apr 1894, Indiana Cnty, PA; d. Unknown.
- iii. Lulu Leona LYDICK[2259], b. 10 Feb 1897, Indiana Cnty, PA; d. Unknown.
- iv. Mary Elizabeth LYDICK[2259], b. 15 Jan 1900, Indiana Cnty, PA; d. Unknown.
- v. Wilda Jeanette LYDICK[2259], b. 12 Nov 1902, Indiana Cnty, PA; d. Unknown.

130. Milton Crawford[10] LYDICK *(Mary P.[9] VAN HORN, Isaiah[8], Isaiah[7], Henry B.[6], Henry[5], Christian Barentsen[4] VAN HOORN, Barent Christiansen[3], Christian Barentsen[2], Barent Barents[1])*[2260,2261,2262,2263,2264] was born 11 Apr 1868 in South Mahoning, Indiana Cnty, PA[2265], and died 17 Nov 1934 in Green Twp., Indiana Cnty, PA. He married Nettie Alice WALTERMIRE[2266,2267] 12 May 1903 in Indiana Cnty, PA. She was born 23 Nov 1882 in Cherryhill Twp., Indiana Cnty, PA[2268], and died Unknown.

More About Milton Crawford LYDICK:
Burial: Unknown, Diamondville Cemetery, Indiana Cnty, PA
Lived: Lovejoy, Indiana Cnty, PA
Occupation: Farmer

More About Milton LYDICK and Nettie WALTERMIRE:
Marriage: 12 May 1903, Indiana Cnty, PA

Children of Milton LYDICK and Nettie WALTERMIRE are:
- i. Ernest Torrence[11] LYDICK[2268,2269], b. 01 Oct 1903, Green Twp., Indiana Cnty, PA; d. Unknown.
- 303. ii. John Crawford LYDICK, b. 08 Oct 1906, Green Twp., Indiana Cnty, PA; d. Unknown.
- iii. Louise Grace LYDICK[2270,2271], b. 12 Mar 1910, Green Twp., Indiana Cnty, PA; d. Unknown.
- iv. Alta LYDICK, b. Private.

131. Mary Emma[10] LYDICK *(Mary P.[9] VAN HORN, Isaiah[8], Isaiah[7], Henry B.[6], Henry[5], Christian Barentsen[4] VAN HOORN, Barent Christiansen[3], Christian Barentsen[2], Barent Barents[1])*[2272,2273,2274,2275] was born 06 Nov 1871 in PA[2276], and died 01 Dec 1955. She married Harry Melbourn MOCK[2277,2278] 16 Oct 1891 in Indiana Cnty, PA. He was born 22 Jun 1870 in PA[2279], and died Unknown.

More About Mary Emma LYDICK:
Lived: Indiana, Indiana Cnty, PA

Notes for Harry Melbourn MOCK:
Based on age Gertude and Mrytle may be the same person.
1930 living on Benjamine Franklin Highway East White Twp., Indiana Cnty, PA in a house he owns worth $2000 with his wife Emma. He is a coal miner.

More About Harry Melbourn MOCK:
Occupation: farmer, Teamster with Own Team

More About Harry MOCK and Mary LYDICK:
Marriage: 16 Oct 1891, Indiana Cnty, PA

Children of Mary LYDICK and Harry MOCK are:
    i.   Dorothy[11] MOCK, b. 29 May 1892, PA; d. Unknown.
    ii.   Bryston Milton MOCK[2280], b. 14 May 1893, PA[2280]; d. Unknown.
    iii.   Roxie May MOCK[2280], b. Sep 1894, PA[2280]; d. Unknown.
    iv.   Homer Wilford MOCK[2280], b. 19 Jun 1896, PA[2280]; d. Unknown.
    v.   Jay McKinley MOCK[2281,2282], b. 03 May 1900, PA[2283]; d. Unknown.
    vi.   Bruce Guy MOCK[2284], b. 06 Dec 1905, PA[2284]; d. Unknown.
    vii.   Edna MOCK[2285,2286], b. Abt. 1908, PA[2287]; d. Unknown.
    viii.   Gertrude MOCK[2287], b. Abt. 1910, PA[2287]; d. Unknown.
    ix.   Myrtle MOCK[2288], b. Abt. Feb 1910, PA[2288]; d. Unknown.

132. Joseph Bell[10] LYDICK *(Mary P.[9] VAN HORN, Isaiah[8], Isaiah[7], Henry B.[6], Henry[5], Christian Barentsen[4] VAN HOORN, Barent Christiansen[3], Christian Barentsen[2], Barent Barents[1])*[2289,2290,2291] was born 30 Aug 1873 in Deckers Point, Indiana Cnty, PA[2292], and died 19 Jun 1920. He married (1) Margaret Jane FULMER[2293] 07 Dec 1893 in Indiana Cnty, PA. She was born 08 Nov 1875 in Deckers Point, Indiana Cnty, PA[2293], and died Unknown. He married (2) Sidney STOPHEL Aft. 1916. She died Unknown.

More About Joseph Bell LYDICK:
Lived: Clymer, PA
Occupation: Laborer

More About Joseph LYDICK and Margaret FULMER:
Divorce: 25 Apr 1916, Indiana County, Indiana, Pennsylvania
Marriage: 07 Dec 1893, Indiana Cnty, PA

More About Joseph LYDICK and Sidney STOPHEL:
Marriage: Aft. 1916

Children of Joseph LYDICK and Margaret FULMER are:
        i.   Clair J.[11] LYDICK, b. 11 Jul 1894, Indiana Cnty, PA; d. Unknown.
304.   ii.   Blair James LYDICK, b. 15 Nov 1896, Cherryhill Twp., Indiana Cnty, PA; d. 17 Sep 1970, Cherryhill Twp., Indiana Cnty, PA.
305.   iii.   Della Gloria LYDICK, b. 27 Jul 1897, Mitchell Mills, Indiana Cnty, PA; d. Unknown.
306.   iv.   Tero Fulmer LYDICK, b. 03 Mar 1899, Diamondville, Indiana Cnty, PA; d. Unknown.

Child of Joseph LYDICK and Sidney STOPHEL is:
    v.   Leroy Maurice[11] LYDICK, b. Private.

133. Margaret Jane[10] LYDICK *(Mary P.[9] VAN HORN, Isaiah[8], Isaiah[7], Henry B.[6], Henry[5], Christian Barentsen[4] VAN HOORN, Barent Christiansen[3], Christian Barentsen[2], Barent Barents[1])*[2294,2295,2296] was born 07 Nov 1875 in Indiana Cnty, PA[2297], and died 07 Jan 1968. She married Charles

WIDDOWSON[2298] Abt. 1897. He was born Abt. 1875 in PA[2298], and died Bet. 1916 - 1929 in PA.

Notes for Margaret Jane LYDICK:
In 1920 Margaret is widowed and farming. She owns her place free and clear. Her son Donald and 3 youngest children are living with her.

More About Margaret Jane LYDICK:
Lived: Clymer, PA

More About Charles WIDDOWSON:
Occupation: Farmer

More About Charles WIDDOWSON and Margaret LYDICK:
Marriage: Abt. 1897

Children of Margaret LYDICK and Charles WIDDOWSON are:
      i.   Ethel[11] WIDDOWSON[2298], b. Abt. 1897, PA[2298]; d. Unknown.
     ii.   Alva WIDDOWSON[2298], b. Abt. 1899, PA[2298]; d. Unknown.
   iii.   Blanche WIDDOWSON[2298], b. Abt. 1901, PA[2298]; d. Unknown.
   iv.   Donald WIDDOWSON[2298,2299], b. Abt. 1903, PA[2300]; d. Unknown.

            More About Donald WIDDOWSON:
            Occupation: Coal Miner

      v.   Ruth WIDDOWSON[2300], b. Abt. 1904, PA[2300]; d. Unknown.
     vi.   Edith WIDDOWSON[2300], b. Abt. 1907, PA[2300]; d. Unknown.
   vii.   Electa WIDDOWSON, b. Private.
  viii.   Silian S. WIDDOWSON, b. Private.

134. William[10] VAN HORN *(John A.[9], Isaiah[8], Isaiah[7], Henry B.[6], Henry[5], Christian Barentsen[4] VAN HOORN, Barent Christiansen[3], Christian Barentsen[2], Barent Barents[1])*[2301,2302,2303] was born Jul 1868 in PA[2304], and died Unknown. He married Lucy[2305,2306] Abt. 1891. She was born Aug 1872 in WV[2307], and died Unknown.

Notes for William VAN HORN:
    In 1920 the 3 youngest children of William and Lucy are living in the Hedgesville District of Berkeley Cnty, WV with other families as boarders. Something must have happened to William and Lucy before 1920. The two older children are married and the 3 youngest are boarding out with other families. Nothing is found of Sadie.

More About Lucy:
Occupation: Farmer

More About William VAN HORN and Lucy:
Marriage: Abt. 1891

Children of William VAN HORN and Lucy are:
307.   i.   John Wesley[11] VAN HORN, b. 07 Oct 1893, Berkeley Cnty, WV; d. Unknown.
308.   ii.   Daniel H. VAN HORN, b. Sep 1895, WV; d. Unknown.
     iii.   Sadie A. VAN HORN[2307,2308], b. Feb 1899, WV[2309]; d. Unknown.
     iv.   Alonzo Curtis VAN HORN[2310,2311], b. Abt. 1902, WV[2312]; d. Unknown.

            Notes for Alonzo Curtis VAN HORN:

In 1920 Alonzo Curtis is living with the Smiley family in Hedgesville, WV and is a farm laborer.

    v.   Dora F. VAN HORN[2312,2313], b. Abt. 1905, WV[2314]; d. Unknown.

        Notes for Dora F. VAN HORN:
        In the 1920 Census Dora is a boarder with the Buts family in Hedgesville, WV.

    vi.   Berta Blanche VAN HORN[2314,2315], b. Abt. 1907, WV[2316]; d. Unknown.

        Notes for Berta Blanche VAN HORN:
        In 1920 living with the Laing family in Berkeley Cnty, WV. The 3 youngest children of William Van Horn are living in different families in the same neighborhood.

135. Nora Mary Agnes[10] VAN HORN *(John A.[9], Isaiah[8], Isaiah[7], Henry B.[6], Henry[5], Christian Barentsen[4] VAN HOORN, Barent Christiansen[3], Christian Barentsen[2], Barent Barents[1])*[2317,2318,2319,2320,2321] was born 29 Dec 1874 in PA[2322], and died 24 Oct 1957 in Martinsburg, Berkeley Cnty, WV. She married David Brown GAGEBY[2323,2324,2325,2326] Bet. 12 Aug 1892 - 1898, son of James GAGEBY and Virginia GRUBB. He was born 20 Dec 1869 in Bunker Hill, Berkeley Cnty, WV[2327], and died 11 Dec 1944 in Inwood, Berkeley Cnty, WV.

Notes for Nora Mary Agnes VAN HORN:
    In 1930 living with Noran and her family is Jennie Van Horn listed as an aunt age 72 her daughter Margaret Van Horn age 25 and her granddaughter Margarie age 5.

Notes for David Brown GAGEBY:
    In 1930 he is renting for $20/month and has a radio in the house in South Raleigh Street in Martinsburg, WV. He is a salesman in a retail grocery.

More About David Brown GAGEBY:
Cause of Death: Bright's Disease
Occupation: Mail Carrier, Retail Grocery Salesman

More About David GAGEBY and Nora VAN HORN:
Marriage: Bet. 12 Aug 1892 - 1898

Children of Nora VAN HORN and David GAGEBY are:
        i.   Virginia[11] GAGEBY[2327,2328], b. Jun 1888, WV; d. Unknown.
       ii.   Rose Jane GAGEBY[2329,2330,2331], b. Jan 1897, WV[2331]; d. Unknown.
309.   iii.   James Allen GAGEBY, b. Feb 1900, Bunker Hill, Berkeley Cnty, WV; d. 08 Aug 1966, Martinsburg, Berkeley Cnty, WV.
       iv.   Bertha Melissa GAGEBY[2332], b. 20 Jan 1902, WV; d. 15 Aug 1919, Berkeley Cnty, WV.

        More About Bertha Melissa GAGEBY:
        Burial: Unknown, Morgan Chapel Cemetery, Bunker Hill, WV

310.   v.   John Henry GAGEBY, b. 01 Jun 1913, Berkeley Cnty, WV; d. 19 Sep 1981, Biglerville, Adams Cnty, PA.
311.   vi.   Ida May GAGEBY, b. 08 Jul 1904, Berkeley Cnty, WV; d. 14 Nov 1983, Martinsburg, Berkeley Cnty, WV.
       vii.   Edgar Leroy GAGEBY[2332,2333,2334], b. 26 Jan 1907, Berkeley Cnty, WV[2335]; d. 03 Jun 1980, Berkeley Cnty, WV; m. Nellie Mae DEARING; b. 19 Jan 1912, Elkton,

Rockingham Cnty, VA; d. Apr 1967, Berkeley Cnty, WV.

More About Edgar Leroy GAGEBY:
Burial: Unknown, Rosedale Cemetery, Martinsburg, WV
Employment: 1930, Laborer Hosery Mill

More About Nellie Mae DEARING:
Employment: Presser Peter Pan Cleaners

312.   viii.   William Brown GAGEBY, b. 03 Oct 1909, Bunker Hill, Berkeley Cnty, WV; d. 31
                 Dec 1974, Martinsburg, Berkeley Cnty, WV.

136. Florida Anna Vrginia[10] VAN HORN *(John A.[9], Isaiah[8], Isaiah[7], Henry B.[6], Henry[5], Christian Barentsen[4] VAN HOORN, Barent Christiansen[3], Christian Barentsen[2], Barent Barents[1])[2336,2337,2338,2339,2340]* was born 05 Jun 1878 in Ganotown, Berkeley Cnty, WV[2341], and died Aft. 1930. She married (1) Charles Thompson GAGEBY[2342,2343] 12 Feb 1902 in Jones Springs, Berkeley Cnty, WV, son of James GAGEBY and Virginia GRUBB. He was born 22 Sep 1867 in Bunker Hill, Berkeley Cnty, WV[2344], and died Unknown. She married (2) Wesley D. SLONAKER[2345] Aft. 1920. He was born Abt. 1867 in WV, and died Aft. 1930.

Notes for Florida Anna Vrginia VAN HORN:
     In 1900 she is living with her sister Nora and her husband David Gageby and is listed as the sister in law of the head of the house. Her name is given as Dota Van Horn. She married her brother in law's brother Charles Gageby.
     In 1920 Florida is living with her husband Charles and her 3 youngest children. Also in the home is Jennie Van Horn listed as an aunt who is of the age and name of her mother. Her oldest daughter Margaret, who is widowed, and her granddaughter Margie are also living in the home. In 1920 she is living 2 doors from Mr. D. W. Slonaker to whom she is married in 1930.
     In 1930 she is married to Wesley Slonaker and has her two youngest children living with her. Her son William is living with his grandmother two doors away.

Notes for Charles Thompson GAGEBY:
     He may have died between 1920 and 1930 as Florida is remarried in 1930 to Mr. Slonaker who was a near neighbor in 1920.

More About Charles Thompson GAGEBY:
Occupation: Fireman lumber mill and laborer

More About Charles GAGEBY and Florida VAN HORN:
Marriage: 12 Feb 1902, Jones Springs, Berkeley Cnty, WV

More About Wesley SLONAKER and Florida VAN HORN:
Marriage: Aft. 1920

Children of Florida VAN HORN and Charles GAGEBY are:
313.   i.   Margaret Picolla Van Horn[11] GAGEBY, b. Abt. 1894, WV; d. Unknown.
           ii.   John D. GAGEBY[2346,2347], b. Abt. 1904, WV[2348]; d. Unknown.
           iii. George William Francis GAGEBY[2348,2349], b. Abt. 1911, WV[2350]; d. Unknown.

                 Notes for George William Francis GAGEBY:
                 In 1930 living with his grandmother and working as a farm laborer.

           iv.   Mary Catherine GAGEBY, b. Private.

v.   Charles Curtis GAGEBY, b. Private.

137. Mary Pearl[10] HUTZLER *(Roseannah[9] VAN HORN, Isaiah[8], Isaiah[7], Henry B.[6], Henry[5], Christian Barentsen[4] VAN HOORN, Barent Christiansen[3], Christian Barentsen[2], Barent Barents[1])*[2351,2352,2353,2354] was born 1870 in Shanghai, Berkeley Cnty, WV[2355], and died 28 Aug 1949 in Brunswick, MD[2356,2357]. She married George Drury CATLETT[2358,2359,2360,2361] 18 Dec 1888 in Berkeley, Berkeley Cnty, WV, son of Samuel CATLETT and Elsie J.. He was born 1867 in VA[2362], and died Bet. 29 Aug 1949 - Sep 1954[2363,2364].

More About Mary Pearl HUTZLER:
Burial: Unknown, Luthern Cemetery, Middletown, MD

Notes for George Drury CATLETT:
        In 1910 lives on Potomac Ave. He is a locomotive engineer has been married for 21 years and his wife is the mother of 8 children of which 6 are living.
        In 1920 lives on High Street. Says he was born in VA and father US and mother WV.
        In 1930 living on Potomac in Brunswick, MD in a home he owns worth about $3,000 and there is a radio in the home. Living with him are 3 single children John H., Harry S. and Helen.

More About George Drury CATLETT:
Employment: 1920, Railroad Assistant Foreman

More About George CATLETT and Mary HUTZLER:
Marriage: 18 Dec 1888, Berkeley, Berkeley Cnty, WV

Children of Mary HUTZLER and George CATLETT are:
        i.   John H.[11] CATLETT[2365,2366], b. Abt. 1894, MD[2367]; d. Bet. 1930 - 1949.

                Notes for John H. CATLETT:
                John Served in WWI information as follows:
                John H Catlett Race: white Address: Brunswick, Frederick Co. Birth Place: Brunswick, Md.
                Age: 21 yrs 11 mos Comment: Ind 9/26/17 pvt; pvt 1c 2/1/18; wag 7/1/18, 153 Dep Brig; Co L 313 Inf 10/9/17; Co B 307 Am Tn 10/16/17, Hon disch 5/23/19, Overseas 5/19/18 to 5/12/19, Marbache Sector; St Mihiel; Marbache Sector; Meuse-Argonne.

        ii.   Raymond W. CATLETT[2368], b. Abt. 1892, MD[2368]; d. Aft. 1954[2369,2370].
        iii.   Harley S. CATLETT[2371], b. Abt. 1894, MD[2371]; d. Aft. 1949[2372].
        iv.   Harry Samuel CATLETT[2373,2374,2375,2376], b. 01 Oct 1895, MD[2377]; d. May 1976, Middletown, Frederick Cnty, MD[2378].

                Notes for Harry Samuel CATLETT:
                 Harry Served in WWI information as follows:
                Harry S Catlett ,white Address: Brunswick, Frederick Co. Birth Place: Brunswick, Md. Birth Date: 01 Oct 1895 Comment: Ind 7/23/18 pvt, 154 Dep Brig; Co F 71 Inf 8/10/18, Hon disch 1/31/19
                His name is given as well as his birth date and place in his WWI I Draft Registration. His mother is his next of kin and is Mary P. Catlett and she lives at 509 Potomac Street in Brunswick, Frederick Cnty, MD. He lives with his mother and he is a farmer. He is 5 ft 11 inches weighs 187 pounds, has brown eyes and hair and a light complexion. He has scars on his right leg.

314. v. Mary Edith CATLETT, b. Abt. 1898, MD; d. 11 Sep 1954, Brunswick, Frederick
      Cnty, MD.
    vi. Bertha L. CATLETT[2379,2380,2381], b. Abt. 1902, MD[2382]; d. Aft. 1949; m. R. W.
      ATKINSON[2383]; d. Unknown.
    vii. Helen V. CATLETT[2384,2385,2386,2387], b. Abt. 1906, MD[2388]; d. Aft. 1949; m. Ray
      LENHART[2389]; d. Unknown.

      More About Helen V. CATLETT:
      Employment: 1930, School Teacher

138. Charles Strother[10] HUTZLER *(Roseannah[9] VAN HORN, Isaiah[8], Isaiah[7], Henry B.[6], Henry[5],*
Christian Barentsen[4] VAN HOORN, Barent Christiansen[3], Christian Barentsen[2], Barent Barents[1])[2390,2391,2392]
was born 21 Aug 1872 in Shanghai, Berkeley Cnty, WV[2393], and died 19 Jul 1936 in Gerrardstown,
Berkeley Cnty, WV. He married (1) Mary B. LYNN[2394] 10 Jul 1900 in Berkeley Cnty, WV, daughter
of Jacob LYNN. She was born 1879 in VA, and died 1903 in Berkeley Cnty, WV. He married (2)
Laura B. SHROADS[2395,2396] 07 Sep 1907 in Hagerstown, Washington Cnty, MD, daughter of
SHROADS and Martha V.. She was born 20 Sep 1884 in Gerrardstown, Berkeley Cnty, WV[2397], and
died 1979 in Pittsburgh, Allegeheny Cnty, PA.

Notes for Charles Strother HUTZLER:
  In 1920 he is living with his second wife Laura and her mother Martha Srodes as well as his
daughter Katherine. He is a farmer and owns his place free and clear.
  In 1930 living on Gerrardstown Inwood road on a farm he rents and farms. There is no radio
in the home and there are two children Catherine and Fred. He and Laura have been married about
22 years by the ages and age of marriage of Laura. Two houses away an Ethel Van Horn age 40 and
single is living in the home of John Rogers as a boarder.
  from a letter from Mrs. Harry Horner, Sr. written to Mary Crim........"Charley Hutzler worked
on my father's farm and his wife,Nannie, worked for my mother and helped to take care of we three
older children. We all loved her very much and as for Charlie, we thought he was great!" Uncle
Charley's picture reminds you very much of my brother Bud. Charlie's farmed the old Bailey farm on
Rt. 51 across the road from
Dad built our big stone house on the hill.......(Charles Strother was Ernest Hutzler's brother)

More About Charles HUTZLER and Mary LYNN:
Marriage: 10 Jul 1900, Berkeley Cnty, WV

Notes for Laura B. SHROADS:
  PER MARY CRIM Laura had a bad stroke but even in her 90's, she still sewed prolifically.
Paralyzed on her right side, she learned to do many things with her left hand. Lived with her son,
Fred, in Pittsburgh, PA where she died.

More About Charles HUTZLER and Laura SHROADS:
Marriage: 07 Sep 1907, Hagerstown, Washington Cnty, MD

Child of Charles HUTZLER and Mary LYNN is:
    i. Rosalie[11] HUTZLER, b. 1901, WV; d. 1903, Berkeley Cnty, WV.

Children of Charles HUTZLER and Laura SHROADS are:
    ii. Katherine V.[11] HUTZLER[2397,2398], b. Abt. 1912, WV[2399]; d. Unknown.
    iii. Fred Likens HUTZLER[2400], b. 06 Mar 1921, Inwood, WV[2400]; d. 30 Mar 1994,

Pittsburgh, Allegheny Cnty, PA[2401]; m. ?, Private; b. Private.

Notes for Fred Likens HUTZLER:
GENERATION LINE- 1ST. JACOB AND NELLIE DAVIS HUTZLER 1809---
2ND. ALFRED AND HANNAH WILLIAMS HUTZLER 1846---3RD. JOHN
WILLIAM AND ROSEANNA VANHORN HUTZLER 1869---4TH CHARLES
AND LAURA SHROADES HUTZLER 1907---5TH FRED HUTZLER 1921 ---
FRED AND HIS
WIFE LIVED IN PITTSBURG, PA

More About Fred HUTZLER and ?:
Private-Begin: Private

139. William Logan[10] HUTZLER *(Roseannah[9] VAN HORN, Isaiah[8], Isaiah[7], Henry B.[6], Henry[5], Christian Barentsen[4] VAN HOORN, Barent Christiansen[3], Christian Barentsen[2], Barent Barents[1])*[2402,2403] was born 1874 in Shanghai, Berkeley Cnty, WV[2403], and died 09 Dec 1957 in Martinsburg, Berkeley Cnty, WV. He married Odessa MCCARTY[2404,2405] 17 Feb 1901 in Berkeley Cnty, WV. She was born Abt. 1881 in VA[2405], and died Bef. 1930.

Notes for William Logan HUTZLER:
In 1930 a William Logan widowed of the right age and birth location is living in Winchester, VA with the Riley family and a McCarty. He is listed as an Uncle.

More About William Logan HUTZLER:
Employment: Railroad trackman

More About William HUTZLER and Odessa MCCARTY:
Marriage: 17 Feb 1901, Berkeley Cnty, WV

Children of William HUTZLER and Odessa MCCARTY are:
     i.   ?[11] HUTZLER, b. Bet. 1901 - 1910; d. Bef. 1910.
    ii.   ? HUTZLER, b. Bet. 1901 - 1910; d. Bef. 1910.

140. Nannie Mae[10] HUTZLER *(Roseannah[9] VAN HORN, Isaiah[8], Isaiah[7], Henry B.[6], Henry[5], Christian Barentsen[4] VAN HOORN, Barent Christiansen[3], Christian Barentsen[2], Barent Barents[1])*[2406,2407,2408,2409,2410] was born 14 Mar 1877 in Shanghai, Berkeley Cnty, WV[2411], and died 1948 in Berkeley Springs, WV. She married George W. MCBEE[2412,2413,2414,2415,2416] 23 Jun 1897 in Berkeley Cnty, WV, son of William MCBEE and Margaret A.. He was born Jul 1869 in Jefferson Cnty, WV[2417], and died Aft. 1930.

Notes for George W. MCBEE:
In 1920 a granddaughter Ilene is living in the family. She is 1 year 8 months of age and was born in WV. George owns his own place and is a sector foreman on the railroad.
In 1930 owns his home in Bath on John's Run worth $2,000. He is a railroad foreman. He has two sons living at home. His wife is Nannie. Herbert is married and his wife is living with him in his parents home.

More About George W. MCBEE:
Employment: 1910, Railroad Laborer

More About George MCBEE and Nannie HUTZLER:

Marriage: 23 Jun 1897, Berkeley Cnty, WV

Children of Nannie HUTZLER and George MCBEE are:

315.   i.   Forest W.[11] MCBEE, b. Mar 1898, WV; d. Unknown.

        ii.   Anna M. MCBEE[2418,2419], b. Abt. 1900, WV[2420]; d. Unknown.

       iii. Henry G. MCBEE[2420], b. Abt. 1901, WV[2420]; d. Unknown.

       iv. Lebben W. MCBEE[2420,2421], b. Abt. 1903, WV[2422]; d. Unknown.

> Notes for Lebben W. MCBEE:
> IN 1930 a Lilburn McBee is living in Cumberland, Allegheny Cnty, MD working as a railroad clerk and boarding. This is likely our Lebben McBee. He is married but no wife is listed in the census.

       v.   Herbert L. MCBEE[2422,2423,2424], b. Abt. 1905, WV[2425]; d. Unknown; m. Evelyn V.[2426], Abt. 1928; b. Abt. 1911, WV[2426]; d. Unknown.

> More About Herbert L. MCBEE:
> Employment: 1930, Telegraph Operator

> More About Herbert MCBEE and Evelyn V.:
> Marriage: Abt. 1928

       vi. Eual B. MCBEE[2427,2428], b. Abt. Mar 1909, WV[2429]; d. Unknown.

      vii. Ira G. MCBEE[2430,2431], b. Abt. 1912, WV[2432]; d. Unknown.

141. Ernest Irvin[10] HUTZLER *(Roseannah[9] VAN HORN, Isaiah[8], Isaiah[7], Henry B.[6], Henry[5], Christian Barentsen[4] VAN HOORN, Barent Christiansen[3], Christian Barentsen[2], Barent Barents[1])*[2433,2434,2435,2436] was born 13 Jul 1879 in Shanghai, Berkeley Cnty, WV[2437], and died 1948 in Ridgeway, Berkeley Cnty, WV. He married Lillian DUNHAM[2438,2439,2440] 10 Feb 1903 in Hagerstown, Washington Cnty, MD, daughter of Samuel DUNHAM and Heser DANIELS. She was born 06 Jun 1884 in Gerrardstown, Berkeley Cnty, WV[2441], and died 15 Jun 1945 in Inwood, Berkeley Cnty, WV.

Notes for Ernest Irvin HUTZLER:
> In 1920 living with his wife and 6 children He is a farmer and rents his farm.
> In 1930 he owns his place worth $6610 on Ridgeway and Payne Chapel Rd. He is a farmer and has 7 of his 9 children living at home.

More About Ernest HUTZLER and Lillian DUNHAM:
Marriage: 10 Feb 1903, Hagerstown, Washington Cnty, MD

Children of Ernest HUTZLER and Lillian DUNHAM are:

       i.   Dorothy[11] HUTZLER, b. 12 Jul 1904, Gerrardstown, Berkeley Cnty, WV; d. 12 Oct 1904, Gerrardstown, Berkeley Cnty, WV.

316.   ii.   John Harland HUTZLER, b. 03 May 1905, Gerrardstown, Berkeley Cnty, WV; d. 29 Apr 1975, Inwood, Berkeley Cnty, WV.

       iii. Hugh Samuel HUTZLER[2441,2442], b. 22 Apr 1907, Gerrardstown, Berkeley Cnty, WV[2443]; d. 14 Mar 1980, Inwood, Berkeley Cnty, WV; m. Mary Virginia WILSON, 26 Jun 1930, Williamsport, Washington Cnty, MD; b. 03 Sep 1911; d. 27 Apr 1987, Martinsburg, Berkeley Cnty, WV.

> More About Hugh HUTZLER and Mary WILSON:
> Marriage: 26 Jun 1930, Williamsport, Washington Cnty, MD

iv. Ward Irvin HUTZLER[2443,2444], b. 12 Jan 1909, Gerrardstown, Berkeley Cnty, WV[2445]; d. 22 May 1987, Inwood, Berkeley Cnty, WV; m. HOOVER, Private; b. Private.

More About Ward HUTZLER and HOOVER:
Private-Begin: Private

v. Virginia Rose HUTZLER[2445,2446], b. 03 Aug 1910, Gerrardstown, Berkeley Cnty, WV[2447]; d. Jul 1979, Ridgeway, Berkeley Cnty, WV; m. RIDGEWAY; d. Unknown.

vi. Adeline HUTZLER[2447,2448], b. 16 Apr 1912, Gerrardstown, Berkeley Cnty, WV[2449]; d. 29 Nov 1973, Martinsburg, Berkeley Cnty, WV; m. Russell Joe SWARTZ, 01 Sep 1933; b. 15 Mar 1913; d. 29 Oct 1993, Winchester, Frederick Cnty, VA.

More About Russell SWARTZ and Adeline HUTZLER:
Marriage: 01 Sep 1933

vii. Ernestine HUTZLER, b. Private; m. Edgar McLaren RICE, Private; b. 08 Feb 1913; d. 13 Feb 1989, Martinsburg, Berkeley Cnty, WV.

More About Edgar RICE and Ernestine HUTZLER:
Private-Begin: Private

viii. Mary Pearl HUTZLER, b. Private; m. H. B. SCARLETT, Private; b. Private.

More About H. SCARLETT and Mary HUTZLER:
Private-Begin: Private

ix. Paul Martin HUTZLER, b. Private; m. Ann BAILEY, Private; b. Private.

More About Paul HUTZLER and Ann BAILEY:
Private-Begin: Private

142. Thettie Jane[10] HUTZLER *(Roseannah[9] VAN HORN, Isaiah[8], Isaiah[7], Henry B.[6], Henry[5], Christian Barentsen[4] VAN HOORN, Barent Christiansen[3], Christian Barentsen[2], Barent Barents[1])*[2450,2451] was born Bet. 30 Nov 1881 - 1882 in Shanghai, Berkeley Cnty, WV[2451], and died 20 Feb 1939 in Martinsburg, Berkeley Cnty, WV[2452]. She married Jeremiah M. UNGER[2453]. He was born 14 Feb 1881 in Berkeley Cnty, WV, and died 14 Jul 1945 in Shanghai, Berkeley Cnty, WV.

Children of Thettie HUTZLER and Jeremiah UNGER are:
    i. Donald[11] UNGER, b. Private.
    ii. George UNGER, b. Private.
    iii. Paul UNGER, b. Private.

143. John Milton[10] HUTZLER *(Roseannah[9] VAN HORN, Isaiah[8], Isaiah[7], Henry B.[6], Henry[5], Christian Barentsen[4] VAN HOORN, Barent Christiansen[3], Christian Barentsen[2], Barent Barents[1])*[2453,2454,2455,2456,2457] was born 18 Jul 1884 in Shanghai, Berkeley Cnty, WV[2458], and died 24 Jul 1965 in Harrisonburg, WV. He married Olive B. FUSS[2459,2460,2461] 06 Nov 1907 in Berkeley Cnty, WV, daughter of John FUSS and Lydia BEARD. She was born 17 Jul 1885 in Hedgesville, Berkeley Cnty, WV, and died 16 Sep 1959 in New Market, VA.

Notes for John Milton HUTZLER:
   In 1930 owns his home in Ashby, VA worth about $2000 and does not have a radio.

More About John Milton HUTZLER:
Employment: 1930, Railroad Conductor

More About John HUTZLER and Olive FUSS:
Marriage: 06 Nov 1907, Berkeley Cnty, WV

Children of John HUTZLER and Olive FUSS are:
>   i.   Donald Alvin[11] HUTZLER[2462,2463], b. 11 Jun 1909, MD[2464]; d. 23 Apr 1981, CA.
>   ii. Dorthea M. HUTZLER[2465,2466], b. Abt. 1911, MD; d. Unknown.
>   iii. Mary Alice HUTZLER, b. Private.

144. Harwood Chapman[10] HUTZLER *(Roseannah[9] VAN HORN, Isaiah[8], Isaiah[7], Henry B.[6], Henry[5], Christian Barentsen[4] VAN HOORN, Barent Christiansen[3], Christian Barentsen[2], Barent Barents[1])*[2467,2468,2469] was born Bet. 26 Jan - Jun 1887 in Shanghai, Berkeley Cnty, WV[2470], and died 15 May 1929 in Berkeley Cnty, WV. He married Mary Agnes NESMITH[2471,2472] 20 Dec 1906 in Berkeley Cnty, WV. She was born 21 Aug 1882 in Berkeley Cnty, WV, and died Aft. 1930.

Notes for Harwood Chapman HUTZLER:
   In 1920 living on Harwood Ave. in Charlestown renting. He works out as a farm laborer.
   In the 18 May 1929 Frederick Post (Frederick, MD) his death is reported. He died of sugar diabetes. He worked on the McKown Orchard Company. He is survived by his widow the former Miss Nesmith, his children Adrian, Nellie, Trammel and Pittman.

More About Harwood Chapman HUTZLER:
Burial: Unknown, Presbyterian Cemetery, Gerrardstown, Berkeley Cnty, WV

Notes for Mary Agnes NESMITH:
   In 1930 she is a widow with 4 children at home from 21 to 10. She rents for $12/month and works out as a laborer. Her son Adrian is an Orchard worker.

More About Harwood HUTZLER and Mary NESMITH:
Marriage: 20 Dec 1906, Berkeley Cnty, WV

Children of Harwood HUTZLER and Mary NESMITH are:
>   i.   Adrian[11] HUTZLER[2473,2474], b. Abt. 1907, WV[2475]; d. Unknown.
>   ii. Nellie HUTZLER, b. Private.
> 317. iii. Harwood Trammell HUTZLER, b. 17 Nov 1918, Jefferson Cnty, WV; d. 08 Jul 1993, Martinsburg, Berkeley Cnty, WV.
>   iv. Pittman William HUTZLER, b. Private.

145. James N.[10] HOPKINS *(Martha[9] VAN HORN, William G.[8], Isaiah[7], Henry B.[6], Henry[5], Christian Barentsen[4] VAN HOORN, Barent Christiansen[3], Christian Barentsen[2], Barent Barents[1])*[2476,2477,2478] was born Abt. Jun 1850 in PA, and died Unknown. He married Mary C. GRACE[2478]. She was born Abt. 1860 in PA[2478], and died Unknown.

Children of James HOPKINS and Mary GRACE are:
>   i.   Etta Jane[11] HOPKINS[2478], b. Abt. 1877, IA[2478]; d. Unknown.
>   ii. William A. HOPKINS[2478], b. Dec 1879, IA[2478]; d. Unknown.

146. Caroline Widmina[10] STEAR *(Margaret J.[9] VAN HORN, William G.[8], Isaiah[7], Henry B.[6], Henry[5], Christian Barentsen[4] VAN HOORN, Barent Christiansen[3], Christian Barentsen[2], Barent Barents[1])[2479,2480,2481,2482,2483]* was born Abt. 1851 in PA[2484], and died Aft. 1930. She married John M. DILTS[2485,2486,2487] Abt. 1871, son of Peter DILTS and Mary. He was born 27 Mar 1847 in PA[2488], and died Bet. 1920 - 1930.

Notes for Caroline Widmina STEAR:
    In 1900 she is the mother of 13 children of which 9 are living. She and John have been married for 28 years.

More About Caroline Widmina STEAR:
Lived: 1895, Blackwell, OK Territory

Notes for John M. DILTS:
    In 1910 living in Red River, Tillman County, OK. He and Caroline have been married for 38 years. She the mother of 13 with 9 living.
    In 1920 farming in Pueblo Cnty, CO. Living with his wife of 48 years and his 4 youngest children.

More About John M. DILTS:
Employment: 1870, Teaching School
Occupation: 1880, Farmer

More About John DILTS and Caroline STEAR:
Marriage: Abt. 1871

Children of Caroline STEAR and John DILTS are:
	i.	Edwin J.[11] DILTS[2489], b. 08 Mar 1873, PA[2489]; d. Unknown.
318.	ii.	William R. DILTS, b. 12 Jul 1875, PA; d. Unknown.
	iii.	Maggie DILTS, b. Abt. 1877, PA; d. Unknown.
	iv.	Henry K. DILTS[2489,2490], b. 01 May 1879, KS[2491]; d. Aft. 1930.
	v.	John DILTS[2491], b. 14 Aug 1881, KS[2491]; d. Unknown.
	vi.	Arthur DILTS[2491], b. 10 Mar 1888, KS[2491]; d. Unknown; m. Alice, Abt. 1916; b. Abt. 1887, TN; d. Unknown.

        Notes for Arthur DILTS:
        In 1930 he is an oil well driller living in Natrona Cnty, WY with wife Alice.

        More About Arthur DILTS and Alice:
        Marriage: Abt. 1916

| | vii. | Thomas DILTS[2491,2492], b. 12 Sep 1891, KS[2493]; d. Aft. 1930. |

        Notes for Thomas DILTS:
        In 1930 living with his brother Fred and farming.

319.	viii.	Frederick DILTS, b. 17 Aug 1893, OK; d. Aft. 1930.
320.	ix.	Daniel W. DILTS, b. 10 Jul 1896, OK; d. Aft. 1930.
	x.	Lillie M. DILTS[2493,2494], b. 28 Dec 1898, OK[2495]; d. Aft. 1930; m. Hubert WRIGHT[2496], Abt. 1924; b. Abt. 1900, TX[2497]; d. Unknown.

        Notes for Hubert WRIGHT:
        In 1930 living near his brothers in law in Pueblo Cnty, CO. He is farming. His

mother in law Caroline Dilts is living in the home. She is widowed.

More About Hubert WRIGHT and Lillie DILTS:
Marriage: Abt. 1924

147. David Blanchard[10] STEAR *(Margaret J.[9] VAN HORN, William G.[8], Isaiah[7], Henry B.[6], Henry[5], Christian Barentsen[4] VAN HOORN, Barent Christiansen[3], Christian Barentsen[2], Barent Barents[1])*[2498,2499,2500,2501,2502] was born 05 May 1866 in Indiana Cnty, PA[2503,2504], and died 04 Sep 1936 in Trade City, PA[2504]. He married Minerva MCKILLIP[2505,2506] 31 Dec 1885[2507,2508], daughter of William MCKILLIP and Martha NEAL. She was born Abt. 1865 in PA[2509], and died Unknown.

Notes for David Blanchard STEAR:
According to the obit in the Indiana Democrat 9 Sept. 1936 one of his sisters is Mrs. John Lewis of Grove City, PA.
SOCIETY NEWS   GOLDEN WEDDING ANNIVERSARY IN TRADE CITY HOME
Mr. and Mrs. David Blanchard Stear, a prominent couple of the northern part of the county, celebrated their fiftieth wedding anniversary Tuesday evening, December 31, 1935, in their home at Trade City. A bounteous wedding dinner was served to twelve guests in the Stear home. The guests of honor received a number of gifts and congratulation cards from their many friends. During the evening the guests enjoyed musical numbers and a social evening.
Mr. Stear is the son of David and Margaret Van Horn Stear (deceased) of Trade City, one of the pioneer families of that section. Mrs. Stear whose maiden name was Minerva McKillip, is the daughter of William and Martha Neal McKillip (deceased) of West Mahoning township near North Point. The bride and groom of fifty years ago were married in Indiana December 31, 1885, by the Rev. J. Day Brownlee, the attendants were S.G. Coon and Miss May Stear, (now Mrs John Lewis of Grove City) a sister of the groom. Following the wedding a dinner was served in the McKillip home to fifty guests , including relatives and neighbors. There is but one guest of the wedding party of fifty years ago, surviving, and that person is Mrs. John Lewis. Mr. and Mrs. Stear went into housekeeping in Punxsutawney, where the family home was maintained for many years . Two children were born of this union, Caddy (deceased), and Inez, wife of R. Merrill Neville, of 227 South Eleventh street, Indiana. There are two grandchildren, Leasnora and Merrill Neville Jr.

More About David Blanchard STEAR:
Burial: Unknown, North Point Cemetery, Indiana Cnty, PA
Employment: Traveling Salesman

More About David STEAR and Minerva MCKILLIP:
Marriage: 31 Dec 1885[2510,2511]

Children of David STEAR and Minerva MCKILLIP are:
        i.   Caddy[11] STEAR, d. Bef. 1910.
321.   ii.   Inez Ethel STEAR, b. Abt. 1890, PA; d. Mar 1975, Smicksburg, Indiana Cnty, PA.

148. Lilly May[10] STEAR *(Margaret J.[9] VAN HORN, William G.[8], Isaiah[7], Henry B.[6], Henry[5], Christian Barentsen[4] VAN HOORN, Barent Christiansen[3], Christian Barentsen[2], Barent Barents[1])*[2512,2513,2514,2515] was born 1869 in Trade City, Indiana Cnty, PA[2515], and died 14 Sep 1954 in Grove City, Mercer Cnty, PA. She married John Dilts LEWIS[2516,2517] Abt. 1894[2517], son of John LEWIS and Isabella DILTS. He was born 14 Aug 1864 in Frostberg, Jefferson Cnty, PA[2518], and died 08 Feb 1946 in Grove City, Mercer Cnty, PA.

Notes for John Dilts LEWIS:
 In 1910 in Perry, Jefferson Cnty, PA as a farmer with wife and 3 children.
 In 1920 owns his place with a mortgage as a farmer.
 In 1930 renting on Grant Street in Indiana, PA for $36/month and has a radio. He is a laborer doing odd jobs.

More About John LEWIS and Lilly STEAR:
Marriage: Abt. 1894[2519]

Children of Lilly STEAR and John LEWIS are:
     i.   Charles Berton[11] LEWIS[2520], b. 13 Oct 1899, PA[2520,2521]; d. Unknown.

           Notes for Charles Berton LEWIS:
           In his WWI draft registration he is a student living at home at 404 N. Mahoning St. in Punxsutawney, PA. He is of medium height, slender build and has brown hair and blue eyes.

     ii.   Frank Noble LEWIS[2522,2523], b. 27 Sep 1902, PA[2524]; d. 14 Feb 1965.

           Notes for Frank Noble LEWIS:
           In 1930 Frank N. Lewis is a Sailor listed at the Naval Academy and Naval Hospital.

           More About Frank Noble LEWIS:
           Military service: Lt. US Navy WWII

    iii. Eleanor Lucile LEWIS[2524,2525], b. Abt. 1909, PA[2526]; d. Unknown.

149. Ambrose Kelly[10] STEAR *(Margaret J.[9] VAN HORN, William G.[8], Isaiah[7], Henry B.[6], Henry[5], Christian Barentsen[4] VAN HOORN, Barent Christiansen[3], Christian Barentsen[2], Barent Barents[1])*[2527,2528,2529,2530,2531] was born Mar 1871 in PA[2532,2533], and died 24 Nov 1928 in Trade City, PA[2534]. He married Etta MOTTARN[2535,2536,2537,2538] Bet. 1896 - 23 Jun 1898[2539,2540]. She was born Bet. 27 Jul 1876 - Jan 1877 in Worthville, Jefferson Cnty, PA[2541], and died 23 Oct 1965 in Indiana Cnty, PA[2542].

Notes for Ambrose Kelly STEAR:
 In 1900 a Myrtle Mottern age 10 born PA is living with the family. No relationship is given.
 In 1910 living in Greensburg, PA. He and Etta have been married for 13 years. The have 5 children all living as of this date. He is a blacksmith at a harvesting equipment manufacturer. Name is spelled Steer.

More About Ambrose Kelly STEAR:
Employment: 1900, Salesman

Notes for Etta MOTTARN:
 In 1920 Mr. Stear is not listed but Etta is married and living on the family farm with 7 of the children. Monna appears to be married by this time and living with her mother and no husband listed although her name is given as Martin. Her father was born in Germany and mother in Pennsylvania.
 5 Nov 1930 Etta Stear is the administratix of the estate of A. K. Stear and the property to be sold at auction is listed.
 1930 Census Etta is a widow, owns her place, does not have a radio and has her sons farming with her.

More About Ambrose STEAR and Etta MOTTARN:

Marriage: Bet. 1896 - 23 Jun 1898[2543,2544]

Children of Ambrose STEAR and Etta MOTTARN are:

    i.   Alverta[11] STEAR[2545,2546,2547], b. Jun 1898, PA[2548]; d. Unknown.

    ii. Moana STEAR[2548,2549,2550], b. Feb 1900, PA[2551]; d. Unknown; m. MARTIN[2552]; d. Unknown.

    iii. Orcett STEAR[2552,2553], b. Abt. 1901, PA[2554]; d. Unknown.

    iv. Vera STEAR[2555], b. Abt. 1902, PA[2555]; d. Unknown.

    v. Weird A. STEAR[2556,2557,2558], b. Abt. 1903, PA[2559]; d. Unknown.

    vi. Minta STEAR[2560], b. Abt. 1911, PA[2560]; d. Unknown.

    vii. Thelma STEAR, b. Private.

322.   viii. Ermond Lester STEAR, b. Private.

150. Enoch Blair[10] STEAR *(Margaret J.[9] VAN HORN, William G.[8], Isaiah[7], Henry B.[6], Henry[5], Christian Barentsen[4] VAN HOORN, Barent Christiansen[3], Christian Barentsen[2], Barent Barents[1])*[2561,2562,2563,2564,2565,2566] was born 31 Oct 1874 in Grove City, Mercer Cnty, PA[2567,2568], and died Bef. 04 Sep 1936. He married Bertha Katherine[2568,2569,2570,2571] Abt. 1896[2572]. She was born May 1873 in PA[2573], and died Unknown.

Notes for Enoch Blair STEAR:

    In 1910 living on Clarence Street in Lake Charles, LA. He is a lumber salesman.

    In 1920 renting on Clarence in Lake Charles, LA. He is a salesman in an Automobile city. Byron L and McDonald are listed at 631 Clarence in Lake Charles, LA but on a different sheet than with Enock and Bertha K. Stear.

    In 1930 owns his home in Calcasieu Parish, LA and he has a radio. Living in the home are Bertha, Donald E. a son 28 and single as well as Frank N. Stear a grandson age 7 born in LA.

    In his WWI draft registration he is a self employed lumberman living at 631 Pine Street in Lake Charles, LA with wife Bertha Kate. He is of medium height, stout in stature with brown hair and brown eyes.

More About Enoch Blair STEAR:
Employment: House Painter

More About Enoch STEAR and Bertha Katherine:
Marriage: Abt. 1896[2574]

Children of Enoch STEAR and Bertha Katherine are:

323.   i. Byron L.[11] STEAR, b. Mar 1898, PA; d. Unknown.

    ii. Donald E. STEAR[2574,2575,2576], b. Abt. 1912, PA[2577]; d. Unknown.

        More About Donald E. STEAR:
        Employment: 1930, Utilityman Filling station

151. Van Horn[10] STEAR *(Margaret J.[9] VAN HORN, William G.[8], Isaiah[7], Henry B.[6], Henry[5], Christian Barentsen[4] VAN HOORN, Barent Christiansen[3], Christian Barentsen[2], Barent Barents[1])*[2578,2579,2580,2581,2582] was born Bet. 1877 - 1879 in PA[2583,2584], and died Aft. 04 Sep 1936. He married Ernie[2584,2585,2586] Abt. 1901[2587]. She was born Abt. 1876 in PA[2588], and died Unknown.

Notes for Van Horn STEAR:

    In 1920 living on Mahoning Street in Punxsutawney, PA with wife and two children. He is a dry goods merchant.

In 1930 owns his home worth $1500 and does not have a radio.

More About Van Horn STEAR:
Employment: 1910, Laborer Amite Coal Mine
Occupation: 1920, Merchant Dry Goods

More About Van STEAR and Ernie:
Marriage: Abt. 1901[2589]

Children of Van STEAR and Ernie are:
    i.   Faye[11] STEAR[2590,2591,2592], b. Abt. 1903, PA[2593]; d. Unknown.
    ii. Dorothy STEAR[2593,2594], b. Abt. 1905, PA[2595]; d. Unknown.

152. Alice Melissa[10] COON *(Catherine[9] VAN HORN, William G.[8], Isaiah[7], Henry B.[6], Henry[5], Christian Barentsen[4] VAN HOORN, Barent Christiansen[3], Christian Barentsen[2], Barent Barents[1])*[2596,2597,2598,2599] was born Bet. 1856 - 28 Apr 1858 in PA[2600], and died 25 Jun 1918. She married (1) Isaac J. REEVES. He died Unknown. She married (2) John M. LAFFERTY 04 Mar 1875, son of Samuel LAFFERTY and Anna BRETH. He was born 27 May 1857 in East Mahoning Twp., Indiana Cnty, PA, and died 14 Aug 1920.

More About John LAFFERTY and Alice COON:
Marriage: 04 Mar 1875

Child of Alice COON and John LAFFERTY is:
324.   i.   Homer[11] LAFFERTY, b. 18 Sep 1876, PA; d. 1950.

153. Lanieann[10] COON *(Catherine[9] VAN HORN, William G.[8], Isaiah[7], Henry B.[6], Henry[5], Christian Barentsen[4] VAN HOORN, Barent Christiansen[3], Christian Barentsen[2], Barent Barents[1])*[2601,2602,2603,2604] was born 16 Jun 1859 in PA[2605], and died Aft. 1910. She married Reuben H. GOURLEY[2606,2607] 1883[2608]. He was born Jul 1855 in PA[2608], and died Unknown.

Notes for Lanieann COON:
    In 1900 her name is given a Lena A.

Notes for Reuben H. GOURLEY:
    In 1910 living in Harrisburg, PA. He is a Hotel Clerk. He lives on Chestnut with his wife and 4 living children. The children are Nellie a stenographer, M. Blair a grocery merchant, Ellis P. a Hotel Clerk and Maryland who is not employed.

More About Reuben H. GOURLEY:
Employment: 1900, Machine Saleman

More About Reuben GOURLEY and Lanieann COON:
Marriage: 1883[2608]

Children of Lanieann COON and Reuben GOURLEY are:
    i.   Nellie[11] GOURLEY[2608,2609], b. Jun 1885, PA[2610]; d. Unknown.
    ii. M. Blair GOURLEY[2610,2611], b. May 1887, PA[2612]; d. Unknown.
    iii. Ellis P. GOURLEY[2612,2613], b. Jan 1889, PA[2614]; d. Unknown.
    iv. Maryland GOURLEY[2614,2615], b. Jul 1895, MD[2616]; d. Unknown.
    v.   ? GOURLEY, d. Unknown.

154. Charles Barclay[10] COON *(Catherine[9] VAN HORN, William G.[8], Isaiah[7], Henry B.[6], Henry[5], Christian Barentsen[4] VAN HOORN, Barent Christiansen[3], Christian Barentsen[2], Barent Barents[1])[2617,2618]* was born 03 Feb 1862 in PA[2619], and died 14 Mar 1904 in Pittsburgh, Alleghney Cnty, PA. He married Anna BIRDESON. She died Unknown.

Child of Charles COON and Anna BIRDESON is:

325.   i.   Mabel[11] COON, b. Abt. 1901; d. Unknown.

155. George L.[10] COON *(Catherine[9] VAN HORN, William G.[8], Isaiah[7], Henry B.[6], Henry[5], Christian Barentsen[4] VAN HOORN, Barent Christiansen[3], Christian Barentsen[2], Barent Barents[1])[2619,2620]* was born 26 Jun 1854 in PA[2621], and died 31 Aug 1954. He married (1) Jettie C. MCQUOWN 22 Feb 1884 in Punxsutawney, Jefferson Cnty, PA. She died Unknown. He married (2) Minnie Bell BURKETT 03 Jul 1905 in Bull Run, PA. She died Unknown.

More About George L. COON:
Lived: 1910, Washington, PA

More About George COON and Jettie MCQUOWN:
Marriage: 22 Feb 1884, Punxsutawney, Jefferson Cnty, PA

More About George COON and Minnie BURKETT:
Marriage: 03 Jul 1905, Bull Run, PA

Children of George COON and Jettie MCQUOWN are:

    i.   Bertha[11] COON, d. Unknown.
    ii.   Walter Clyde COON, d. Unknown.
    iii.   Cecil COON, d. Unknown.
    iv.   Inez Gay COON, d. Unknown.

Child of George COON and Minnie BURKETT is:

    v.   ?[11] COON, d. Unknown.

156. Augustus Kimmel[10] COON *(Catherine[9] VAN HORN, William G.[8], Isaiah[7], Henry B.[6], Henry[5], Christian Barentsen[4] VAN HOORN, Barent Christiansen[3], Christian Barentsen[2], Barent Barents[1])[2621,2622]* was born 14 Mar 1869 in Perrysville, Jefferson Cnty, PA[2623], and died 19 Sep 1929 in Pittsburgh, Alleghney Cnty, PA[2624]. He married Martha M. SHAFFER. She was born 1867, and died 1949.

More About Augustus Kimmel COON:
Cause of Death: Sudden Heart Attack
Employment: 1929, Allegheny Lumber Company
Lived: 1910, Indiana

Children of Augustus COON and Martha SHAFFER are:

    i.   Catherine[11] COON[2624], b. Abt. 1901; d. Unknown.
    ii.   Edna COON[2624], b. 10 Jun 1889; d. Unknown.
    iii.   M. F. COON[2624], d. Unknown.
    iv.   Jacob Shaffer COON, b. 1904; d. 1905.
    v.   Marion A. COON, b. 04 Oct 1896; d. 22 Mar 1897.

vi.   ? COON, d. Unknown.

157. Wade Blair[10] COON *(Catherine[9] VAN HORN, William G.[8], Isaiah[7], Henry B.[6], Henry[5], Christian Barentsen[4] VAN HOORN, Barent Christiansen[3], Christian Barentsen[2], Barent Barents[1])*[2625,2626,2627,2628] was born Bet. 26 Aug 1873 - 1874 in PA[2629,2630,2631], and died 17 Jun 1943 in Los Angeles Cnty, CA[2632]. He married Bessie Irene MITCHELL[2633,2634,2635] Abt. 1895 in PA[2635], daughter of Eden MITCHELL. She was born 08 Oct 1872 in PA[2636,2637], and died Aug 1965 in Los Angeles Cnty, CA.

Notes for Wade Blair COON:
   In 1900 Albert S. Mitchell a brother in law age 19 born PA is living in the home. This gives us the maiden name of Bess. Wade is a Mechanical Engineer.
   In his WWI draft registration he is a mason working in Stockton, Tooele Cnty, UT. He is of medium height, stout build with brown hair and eyes. He and Bess live in Milford, UT.
   In 1930 lives in Compton, CA on Paulsine Street (sic) in a home he owns worth $4000 and has a radio. He is a construction foreman.

More About Wade Blair COON:
Employment: 1920, Agent Mechanical Engineer
Lived: 1910, Idaho

More About Wade COON and Bessie MITCHELL:
Marriage: Abt. 1895, PA[2637]

Children of Wade COON and Bessie MITCHELL are:
326.   i.   Don Mitchell[11] COON, b. 21 Jan 1896, Punxsutawney, Jefferson Cnty, PA; d. Mar 1962, Compton, Los Angeles Cnty, CA.
327.   ii. Harry L. COON, b. Jun 1898, PA; d. Unknown.
328.   iii. Kimmel B. COON, b. Abt. 1901, PA; d. Aft. 1971.

158. Laura Jane[10] CONDRON *(Dorcas[9] VAN HORN, William G.[8], Isaiah[7], Henry B.[6], Henry[5], Christian Barentsen[4] VAN HOORN, Barent Christiansen[3], Christian Barentsen[2], Barent Barents[1])*[2638,2639,2640,2641,2642] was born Bet. 24 Oct 1854 - 1855 in Smicksburg, Indiana Cnty, PA[2643], and died 08 Oct 1915 in Smicksburg, Indiana Cnty, PA[2644]. She married (1) Samuel Taylor ROBINSON[2645] 21 May 1874 in Smicksburg, Indiana Cnty, PA[2646]. He was born 11 May 1850 in Smicksburg, Indiana Cnty, PA[2647], and died 10 Jul 1893 in Smicksburg, Indiana Cnty, PA. She married (2) Lowery HUGHES[2648] Abt. 1898[2649]. He was born Apr 1856 in PA[2650], and died Unknown.

More About Samuel Taylor ROBINSON:
Occupation: Marble Cutter

More About Samuel ROBINSON and Laura CONDRON:
Marriage: 21 May 1874, Smicksburg, Indiana Cnty, PA[2651]
Marriage date: Rev. G. W. Mechlin

More About Lowery HUGHES:
Occupation: 1900, Grocer

More About Lowery HUGHES and Laura CONDRON:
Marriage: Abt. 1898[2652]

Children of Laura CONDRON and Samuel ROBINSON are:
    i.   Lizzie[11] ROBINSON[2653], b. Abt. 1874, PA[2653]; d. Unknown.
   ii. Oila May ROBINSON[2653,2654,2655], b. Oct 1878, PA[2656]; d. Unknown.
  iii. Joseph Laurie ROBINSON[2657,2658], b. May 1881, PA[2659]; d. Unknown.

        Notes for Joseph Laurie ROBINSON:
        In 1910 Joseph is living with 3 of his sisters, Olie, Lucille and Florence. He is a
        dentist. His sisters Olie and Lucille are salesladies at a department and dry goods
        store.

        More About Joseph Laurie ROBINSON:
        Occupation: 1910, Dentist

   iv. Dolly ROBINSON[2659,2660], b. Jun 1884, PA[2661]; d. Unknown.
    v. Florence ROBINSON[2661,2662], b. Apr 1892, PA[2663]; d. Unknown.

Child of Laura CONDRON and Lowery HUGHES is:
   vi. Lowery[11] HUGHES, JR[2663], b. Sep 1899, PA[2663]; d. Unknown.

159. James Melantheon[10] CONDRON *(Dorcas[9] VAN HORN, William G.[8], Isaiah[7], Henry B.[6], Henry[5], Christian Barentsen[4] VAN HOORN, Barent Christiansen[3], Christian Barentsen[2], Barent Barents[1])*[2664,2665,2666,2667] was born Mar 1856 in Indiana Cnty, PA[2668], and died Unknown. He married Mary Agnes GALBRAITH[2669,2670] 01 Jan 1878 in Smicksburg, Indiana Cnty, PA[2671]. She was born Dec 1854 in PA[2672], and died Unknown.

More About James Melantheon CONDRON:
Occupation: Carpenter

More About James CONDRON and Mary GALBRAITH:
Marriage: 01 Jan 1878, Smicksburg, Indiana Cnty, PA[2673]
Marriage date: Rev. C. T. Steck Officiating

Children of James CONDRON and Mary GALBRAITH are:
    i.   Robert E.[11] CONDRON[2674,2675], b. Abt. 1878, PA[2676]; d. Unknown.
   ii. George L. CONDRON[2676,2677], b. Apr 1880, PA[2678]; d. Unknown.
  iii. Clair CONDRON[2679], b. Jan 1882, PA[2679]; d. Unknown.

160. William Madison[10] CONDRON *(Dorcas[9] VAN HORN, William G.[8], Isaiah[7], Henry B.[6], Henry[5], Christian Barentsen[4] VAN HOORN, Barent Christiansen[3], Christian Barentsen[2], Barent Barents[1])*[2680,2681,2682,2683] was born 18 Apr 1858 in Smicksburg, Indiana Cnty, PA[2684], and died 16 Oct 1918 in Punxsutawney, Jefferson Cnty, PA. He married Margaret Cymisca KUNKLE[2685,2686,2687,2688] Oct 1881 in Smicksburg, Indiana Cnty, PA[2689], daughter of KUNKLE and Jane. She was born Jun 1862 in PA[2690], and died 1942.

Notes for William Madison CONDRON:
According to the 5 October 1887 Indiana Progress(Indiana, PA) W. M. Condron was the contractor for the construction of the house of the Kellysburg Postmaster Mr. McQuilken.

More About William Madison CONDRON:

Occupation: Bet. 1900 - 1910, Marble Agent

Notes for Margaret Cymisca KUNKLE:
    In 1910 married 29 years and his mother of 9 children of which 6 are living in 1910.
    In 1930 living in a home she owns worth $4000 with her oldest and youngest daughters, Myrtle and Jane. both daughters are salesladies in dry goods and womens clothing.

More About William CONDRON and Margaret KUNKLE:
Marriage: Oct 1881, Smicksburg, Indiana Cnty, PA*2691*

Children of William CONDRON and Margaret KUNKLE are:
     i.   Minnie Myrtle[11] CONDRON*2692,2693,2694,2695*, b. May 1882, PA*2696,2697*; d. 1944.
     ii.   Olive Florence CONDRON, b. 1884, PA; d. 1885.
     iii. Laura Elizabeth CONDRON*2698,2699*, b. Jun 1886, PA*2700,2701*; d. 1962; m. Leroy Thompson ANDERSON; d. Unknown.
     iv. Clarence Reed CONDRON, b. 1888, PA; d. 1889.
     v.   Hugh W. CONDRON, b. 1889, PA; d. 1890.

329.   vi. Dollie Irene CONDRON, b. Apr 1890, PA; d. 1958.
330.   vii. Ira Sloan CONDRON, b. 05 Jul 1893, Home, PA; d. 29 Apr 1958.
     viii. Walter Merle CONDRON*2702,2703*, b. Sep 1895, PA*2704,2705*; d. 1918.
     ix. Dorcas Jane CONDRON*2706,2707,2708,2709*, b. Mar 1899, PA*2710,2711*; d. 1934; m. SMEATON, Aft. 1920; b. 1882; d. Unknown.

        More About SMEATON and Dorcas CONDRON:
        Marriage: Aft. 1920

161. Cornelius Elsworth[10] CONDRON *(Dorcas[9] VAN HORN, William G.[8], Isaiah[7], Henry B.[6], Henry[5], Christian Barentsen[4] VAN HOORN, Barent Christiansen[3], Christian Barentsen[2], Barent Barents[1])2712,2713,2714,2715* was born 17 Nov 1861 in Indiana Cnty, PA*2716*, and died 07 Jul 1946 in Los Angeles,CA*2717*. He married Nancy Loretta LNU*2718,2719* Abt. 1889. She was born Abt. 1869 in PA*2720*, and died Abt. 1930.

Notes for Cornelius Elsworth CONDRON:
    15 Aug 1908 Indiana Evening Gazette (Indiana, PA) C.E of Smicksburg and family are listed as attending the family of William Van Horn reunion.
    In 1910 he has taken in two of his brother Angus' children George Leroy and Margaet Loretta.
    In 1930 he is living next to his brother Leroy on Clarion Street in Smicksburg, PA. He owns his own home worth $2,000 and has a radio. He works as a laborer.

More About Cornelius Elsworth CONDRON:
Occupation: Odd Jobs

More About Nancy Loretta LNU:
Occupation: Dressmaker

More About Cornelius CONDRON and Nancy LNU:
Marriage: Abt. 1889

Child of Cornelius CONDRON and Nancy LNU is:
     i.   George L.[11] CONDRON*2720*, b. Abt. 1898, PA*2720*; d. Unknown; Adopted child.

162. Charles Gillis[10] CONDRON *(Dorcas[9] VAN HORN, William G.[8], Isaiah[7], Henry B.[6], Henry[5],*

Christian Barentsen[4] VAN HOORN, Barent Christiansen[3], Christian Barentsen[2], Barent Barents[1])[2721,2722,2723] was born Abt. 18 Nov 1867 in Indiana Cnty, PA[2724], and died 09 Aug 1928 in Verona, Allegheny Cnty, PA. He married Belle Clifford HILL[2725,2726], daughter of Alexander HILL and Emma BARNETT. She was born 26 Apr 1872 in Titiouti, Warren Cnty, PA[2727], and died 03 Jul 1950 in Verona, Allegheny Cnty, PA.

More About Charles Gillis CONDRON:
Occupation: Carpenter

Notes for Belle Clifford HILL:
    In 1930 lives at 446 Parker in Verona a short distance from her married daughter Olive.

Children of Charles CONDRON and Belle HILL are:
	i.	Hazel B.[11] CONDRON[2728], b. Abt. 1890, PA[2728]; d. Unknown.
331.	ii.	Olive Florence CONDRON, b. 25 Aug 1892, Verona, Allegheny Cnty, PA; d. 09 Jul 1977, Oakmont, Allegheny Cnty, PA.
	iii.	George L. CONDRON[2728], b. Abt. 1902, PA[2728]; d. Unknown.
	iv.	Margaret CONDRON[2729,2730], b. Abt. 1906, PA[2731]; d. Unknown.
	v.	Charles Gillis CONDRON, JR[2731,2732], b. Abt. 1909, PA[2733]; d. Unknown; m. Roberta[2733]; b. Abt. 1911, PA[2733]; d. Unknown.
	vi.	Clarence J. CONDRON[2733,2734], b. Abt. 1912, PA[2735]; d. Unknown.

163. George A.[10] CONDRON *(Dorcas[9] VAN HORN, William G.[8], Isaiah[7], Henry B.[6], Henry[5], Christian Barentsen[4] VAN HOORN, Barent Christiansen[3], Christian Barentsen[2], Barent Barents[1])[2736,2737,2738]* was born Mar 1870 in Indiana Cnty, PA[2739], and died Unknown. He married Blanch[2740]. She was born Abt. 1874 in PA[2740], and died Unknown.

Notes for George A. CONDRON:
    In 1920 living in Verona on North Ave in a home he owns free and clear. His nephew Ellsworth is living with him. Also in the house is George's wife and son Edwin.

More About George A. CONDRON:
Occupation: Carpenter Railroad

Child of George CONDRON and Blanch is:
	i.	Edwin[11] CONDRON[2741], b. Abt. 1896, PA[2742]; d. Unknown.

164. Olive Florence[10] CONDRON *(Dorcas[9] VAN HORN, William G.[8], Isaiah[7], Henry B.[6], Henry[5], Christian Barentsen[4] VAN HOORN, Barent Christiansen[3], Christian Barentsen[2], Barent Barents[1])[2743,2744]* was born 02 Jul 1872 in Indiana Cnty, PA[2745], and died 1945 in Jefferson Cnty, PA. She married J. A. WALTER[2746] 12 May 1892 in Smicksburg, Indiana Cnty, PA. He was born Feb 1860 in PA[2746], and died Unknown.

More About J. A. WALTER:
Occupation: Physician

More About J. WALTER and Olive CONDRON:
Marriage: 12 May 1892, Smicksburg, Indiana Cnty, PA

Child of Olive CONDRON and J. WALTER is:
	i.	Eleanor D.[11] WALTER[2746], b. Jul 1896, PA[2746]; d. Unknown.

165. Angus Blanchard[10] CONDRON *(Dorcas[9] VAN HORN, William G.[8], Isaiah[7], Henry B.[6], Henry[5], Christian Barentsen[4] VAN HOORN, Barent Christiansen[3], Christian Barentsen[2], Barent Barents[1])*[2747,2748] was born Jan 1875 in Indiana Cnty, PA[2749], and died 25 Nov 1904 in PA. He married Emma RITCHEY[2750] 1893, daughter of George RITCHEY and Sarah GREY. She was born 22 Jul 1877 in PA[2750], and died 21 Mar 1903 in PA.

More About Angus Blanchard CONDRON:
Burial: Unknown, Ritchey Cemetery, Penn Hill, PA
Occupation: Carpenter

More About Angus CONDRON and Emma RITCHEY:
Marriage: 1893

Children of Angus CONDRON and Emma RITCHEY are:
     i.   Ike[11] CONDRON, d. Unknown.
     ii. Ellsworth E. CONDRON[2750,2751], b. Jan 1895, PA[2752]; d. Unknown.

          Notes for Ellsworth E. CONDRON:
          In 1920 living with Uncle Gorge Condron in Verona, PA. He is a railroad clerk.

     iii. Dorcas Belle CONDRON[2752], b. Nov 1897, PA[2752]; d. Unknown.
     iv. Loretta Margaret CONDRON[2753], b. Abt. 1902, PA[2753]; d. Unknown.

166. Stella M.[10] VAN HORN *(George Logan[9], William G.[8], Isaiah[7], Henry B.[6], Henry[5], Christian Barentsen[4] VAN HOORN, Barent Christiansen[3], Christian Barentsen[2], Barent Barents[1])*[2754,2755,2756,2757,2758,2759,2760] was born 28 Feb 1871 in North Point, Indiana Cnty, PA[2761], and died 02 May 1940 in Indiana Cnty, PA. She married James Clifford SERENE[2762,2763,2764,2765,2766,2767,2768] Abt. 1898, son of William SERENE and Teressa KANEY. He was born Oct 1870 in Saltsburg, Indiana Cnty, PA[2769], and died Aft. 1951 in Saltsburg, Indiana Cnty, PA.

Notes for Stella M. VAN HORN:
     15 Aug 1908 Indiana Evening Gazette (Indiana, PA) Mrs Serene of Saltsburg and son attended William Van Horn family reunion.

More About Stella M. VAN HORN:
Burial: May 1940, Edgewood Cemetery, Saltsburg, PA; Rev Fred M. Bennett Methodis Episcopal
Religion: United Brethren and Methodist Episcopal Churches

Notes for James Clifford SERENE:
     In 1920 living on Indiana Ave. in Saltsburg, PA in a home he owns free and clear. He has a niece living in the home.
     In 1930 owns his home worth $3,000 and has a radio. No employment is listed. J. Clifford and wife Stella M. married when each was 28 years of age.

More About James Clifford SERENE:
Occupation: Bet. 1900 - 1920, Butcher, Merchant Meats

More About James SERENE and Stella VAN HORN:
Marriage: Abt. 1898

Child of Stella VAN HORN and James SERENE is:
332.   i.   Owen Meridith[11] SERENE, b. 15 Jul 1899, North Point or Saltsburg, Indiana Cnty,
               PA; d. 14 Jan 1951, Saltsburg, Indiana Cnty, PA.

167. Anna B.[10] VAN HORN *(George Logan[9], William G.[8], Isaiah[7], Henry B.[6], Henry[5], Christian
Barentsen[4] VAN HOORN, Barent Christiansen[3], Christian Barentsen[2], Barent Barents[1])*[2770,2771,2772] was
born Oct 1872 in Indiana Cnty, PA[2773,2774], and died Aft. 22 Sep 1909. She married W. H.
WEISS[2775,2776] Abt. 1889. He was born Jun 1870 in PA[2776], and died Unknown.

More About Anna B. VAN HORN:
Lived: Brackenridge, PA

More About W. H. WEISS:
Occupation: Engineer

More About W. WEISS and Anna VAN HORN:
Marriage: Abt. 1889

Children of Anna VAN HORN and W. WEISS are:
               i.   Flora[11] WEISS[2776], b. Apr 1891, PA[2776]; d. Unknown.
               ii.   Claude WEISS[2776], b. Mar 1893, PA[2776]; d. Unknown.
               iii. Clara WEISS[2776], b. Mar 1896, PA[2776]; d. Unknown.

168. Elmer Monroe[10] VAN HORN *(George Logan[9], William G.[8], Isaiah[7], Henry B.[6], Henry[5], Christian
Barentsen[4] VAN HOORN, Barent Christiansen[3], Christian Barentsen[2], Barent Barents[1])*[2777,2778,2779,2780,2781]
was born 13 Jan 1877 in Indiana Cnty, PA[2782,2783], and died Aft. 1930. He married Isabel L.
STEWART[2784,2784] Abt. 1903, daughter of Jennie. She died Bef. 1910.

Notes for Elmer Monroe VAN HORN:
        23 May 1894 E. M. Van Horn was elected by the Populist Party to serve as a Congressional
Conferee according to the Indiana Weekly Messenger (Indiana, PA) of this date.
        In his WWI Draft Registration he indicates he is of medium height, medium build with brown
eyes and brown hair. His wife is Isabel L. and he is a farmer.
        In 1910 he is a widower living with his daughter and mother in law.
        In 1930 living with his mother in law and her sister and her granddaughter, her husband and
Roe's great grandson. He is called Roe and has no occupation at the time of the census. His daughter
is living in the household with her husband William Dolby and their son William Dolby.
        14 May 1931 Simpson's Leader-Times (Kittanning, PA) E. M. Van Horn was arrested on a
warrant by William Dolby for pulling a 32 calibre firearm from his pocket and making a threat to kill
him.
        20 May 1931 Simpson's Leader-Times (Kittanning, PA) E. M. Van Horn was given a hearing
for carrying a concealed firearm, pointing firearms and surety of the peace on a charge brought by his
son in law William Dolby.
        23 June 1931 Simpson's Leader-Times (Kittanning, PA) Elmer Van Horn was ordered to find
another home and put up a bond of $30 for his part in pulling a gun on his son in law in his Rural
Valley, PA home. If he does not keep the peace he will have to serve time in the Allegheny Work
House.

More About Elmer Monroe VAN HORN:
Occupation: House Painter

More About Elmer VAN HORN and Isabel STEWART:
Marriage: Abt. 1903

Child of Elmer VAN HORN and Isabel STEWART is:
333.   i.   Mary Isabel[11] VAN HORN, b. Abt. 1905, PA; d. Unknown.

169. Arnold Wilton[10] VAN HORN *(George Logan[9], William G.[8], Isaiah[7], Henry B.[6], Henry[5], Christian Barentsen[4] VAN HOORN, Barent Christiansen[3], Christian Barentsen[2], Barent Barents[1])*[2785,2786,2787,2788,2789,2790] was born Jul 1878 in Indiana Cnty, PA[2791,2792], and died 1929 in Armstrong Cnty, PA. He married Iva C. HILTY[2793,2794,2795] Abt. 1901, daughter of Joseph HILTY and Christena WHITACRE. She was born 22 Mar 1884 in Cowansannock Twp., Armstong Cnty, PA, and died 09 Oct 1973 in Armstrong Cnty, PA.

Notes for Arnold Wilton VAN HORN:
    This family used the name Van Horne instead of the Van Horn by other relatives of the same line. Listed as Wilty A. Van Horne in 1880 Census.
    4 January 1903 The Indiana Messenger states that Arnold Van Horn and wife visited their parents at North Point, Jefferson Cnty, PA.

More About Arnold Wilton VAN HORN:
Burial: Unknown, Rural Valley Cemetery Rural Valley, PA
Occupation: House Painter, Teamster, Farmer

More About Iva C. HILTY:
Burial: Unknown, Rural Valley Cemetery, Armstrong Cnty, PA

More About Arnold VAN HORN and Iva HILTY:
Marriage: Abt. 1901

Children of Arnold VAN HORN and Iva HILTY are:
       i.   Dorothy[11] VAN HORN, b. PA; d. Aft. 1993.
334.   ii.   Homer E. VAN HORN, b. Abt. 1903, PA; d. Aft. 1973.
      iii.   Annie C. VAN HORN[2796], b. Abt. 1904, PA; d. Bef. 1920.
      iv.   Tirza L. VAN HORN[2797,2798], b. Abt. 1906, PA; d. Aft. 1973; m. SCHIMPF; d. Unknown.
      v.   Estella Laura VAN HORN[2799,2800], b. Abt. 1908, PA; d. Bet. 1920 - 1973.
      vi.   Lena Christine VAN HORN[2800], b. 02 Jul 1909, PA; d. 16 May 1993, NuMine, Armstrong Cnty, PA.

          Notes for Lena Christine VAN HORN:
          In his brother Owen's obituary she is called Nina.

          More About Lena Christine VAN HORN:
          Burial: Unknown, Rural Valley Cemetery, Indiana Cnty, PA

      vii.   Audrey VAN HORN, b. Abt. 1910, PA; d. Unknown.
335.   viii.   Nelson Blair VAN HORN, b. 13 Aug 1913, NuMine, Armstrong Cnty, PA; d. 02 Feb 1993, Willoughby, OH.
336.   ix.   Owen DeLone VAN HORNE, b. 06 Mar 1916, Cowansannock Twp., Armstong Cnty, PA; d. 26 Mar 1964, NuMine, Armstrong Cnty, PA.
      x.   Genieve VAN HORN[2801], b. Abt. 1917, PA; d. Aft. 1993; m. MCCOLLUM, Private; b. Private.

More About MCCOLLUM and Genieve VAN HORN:
Private-Begin: Private

337.　　xi.　Ida VAN HORN, b. Abt. 1919, PA; d. Aft. 1993.

170. Angus Vanzant[10] VAN HORN *(George Logan[9], William G.[8], Isaiah[7], Henry B.[6], Henry[5], Christian Barentsen[4] VAN HOORN, Barent Christiansen[3], Christian Barentsen[2], Barent Barents[1])*[2802,2803,2804,2805,2806] was born 26 Aug 1880 in Indiana Cnty, PA[2807,2808], and died Aft. 1920. He married May E. CRAFT[2809,2810] Abt. 1903, daughter of Albert CRAFT and Elizabeth H.. She was born Abt. 1883 in PA[2811], and died Bet. 1910 - 1920.

Notes for Angus Vanzant VAN HORN:
　　In his WWI and WWI I Draft registrations he indicates his name as Ingus and Angus Vanzant Van Horn. In his WWI draft registration he is a coal miner and he lists his sister Stella Serene as his closest relative.
　　In 1920 widowed and boarding with Murray Stewart on 7th Street. He is a carpenter in a coal mine. He is listed as 37 which would be in error.
　　In his WWI I Draft Registration he states that he is self employed as a carpenter and his closest relative is listed as Kelly Hazzlet the son of Thomas Hazzlet a person who must live near him at the time. He lives on a farm in Young Twp., Indiana Cnty, PA and his mailing address is RFD #2 Homer the same as Kelly Hazzlet. He is white 5 foot 11 inches tall and weighs 184 pounds his eyes are blue his hair brown and he is of light complexion.

More About Angus VAN HORN and May CRAFT:
Marriage: Abt. 1903

Children of Angus VAN HORN and May CRAFT are:
　　i.　Harry M.[11] VAN HORN[2811,2812,2813,2814,2815], b. 09 Oct 1904, Indiana Cnty, PA[2816]; d. Unknown.

　　　　Notes for Harry M. VAN HORN:
　　　　In 1910 living with his grandparents.
　　　　In 1920 living with his grandmother near to his father in Armstrong Cnty, PA.
　　　　In 1930 living with his cousin Clarence E. Craft and his wife Ethel. They are both working for an Electrical Manufacturing operation in Erie, PA.

　　　　More About Harry M. VAN HORN:
　　　　Occupation: Machine Hand in Electrical Manufacturing

　　ii.　Thelma I. VAN HORN[2817,2818,2819], b. Bet. 1906 - 1908, PA[2820]; d. Bef. 2000.

　　　　Notes for Thelma I. VAN HORN:
　　　　Living with her aunt and uncle James Clifford Serene in 1920 in Saltsburg, PA.

　　iii.　Dotha C. VAN HORN[2821,2822], b. Abt. 1907, PA[2823]; d. Unknown.

171. Edward Harry[10] VAN HORN *(Samuel Redding[9], William G.[8], Isaiah[7], Henry B.[6], Henry[5], Christian Barentsen[4] VAN HOORN, Barent Christiansen[3], Christian Barentsen[2], Barent Barents[1])*[2824,2825,2826,2827,2828,2829] was born 05 Jul 1884 in Belleview, Stanton Cnty, PA[2830,2831], and died 28 Jan 1951 in Brockway, Jefferson Cnty, PA[2832]. He married Edna Leona MCMINN[2833,2834,2835,2836,2837,2838] 27 Jan 1906 in Westville, PA, daughter of Daniel MCMINN and

Emma LINSENBIGLE. She was born 26 Jun 1885 in Lands Mills, Jefferson Cnty, PA*2839*, and died 20 Dec 1966 in Brockway, Jefferson Cnty, PA or DuBois, Clearfield Cnty, PA*2840,2841*.

Notes for Edward Harry VAN HORN:
    In his WWI Draft Registration he indicates he is tall of medium build with brown eyes and black hair. He lives in Falls Creek is married to Edna Leona and is an Engineer for the BR&P Railroad in Punxsutawney, PA.
    In 1930 Edward and Edna are living alone in Falls Creek, PA in a home they own worth $2,500 and do not have a radio.

More About Edward Harry VAN HORN:
Occupation: Steam Shovel Engineer, Engineer BR&P Railroad,Laborer Glass Factory; Well Driller of Artesian Wells

More About Edna Leona MCMINN:
Cause of Death: Auto Accident
Medical Information: Auto was driven by her son in law the Editor of the Brockway Record
Religion: Presbyterian

More About Edward VAN HORN and Edna MCMINN:
Marriage: 27 Jan 1906, Westville, PA

Children of Edward VAN HORN and Edna MCMINN are:
338.   i.   Mary Emma[11] VAN HORN, b. Abt. 1907, PA; d. Unknown.
339.   ii.   Walter Edward VAN HORN, b. 02 Mar 1909, Punxsutawney, Jefferson Cnty, PA; d. 14 Sep 1994, Jamestown, NY.

172. Elijah Work[10] STEELE *(Dorcas[9] HAMILTON, Nancy[8] VAN HORN, Isaiah[7], Henry B.[6], Henry[5], Christian Barentsen[4] VAN HOORN, Barent Christiansen[3], Christian Barentsen[2], Barent Barents[1])2842,2843,2844,2845,2846* was born 26 Apr 1852 in East Mahoning Twp.,Indiana Cnty, PA*2847*, and died 20 Aug 1917. He married Emma ALDOUS*2848,2849,2850* Abt. 1876, daughter of John ALDOUS. She was born Oct 1852 in PA*2851*, and died 25 Oct 1928.

More About Elijah STEELE and Emma ALDOUS:
Marriage: Abt. 1876

Children of Elijah STEELE and Emma ALDOUS are:
        i.   Edward Telford[11] STEELE*2852*, b. Abt. 1877, East Mahoning Twp.,Indiana Cnty, PA*2852*; d. Unknown.
340.   ii.   Clark Lewis STEELE, b. 08 Oct 1879, East Mahoning Twp.,Indiana Cnty, PA; d. May 1963.
        iii. John Aldous STEELE*2853*, b. 02 May 1884, East Mahoning Twp.,Indiana Cnty, PA*2853*; d. Jul 1972, Rural Valley, Armstrong Cnty, PA.
        iv.   Allen Ester STEELE*2853,2854*, b. 09 Jun 1886, East Mahoning Twp.,Indiana Cnty, PA*2855*; d. Unknown.
341.   v.   Clare Clawson STEELE, b. 18 Oct 1888, East Mahoning Twp.,Indiana Cnty, PA; d. 10 Nov 1964, Punxsutawney, Jefferson Cnty, PA.
        vi.   Lester Donald STEELE*2855,2856*, b. 07 Nov 1893, East Mahoning Twp.,Indiana Cnty, PA*2857*; d. 03 Mar 1974, Marion Center, Indiana Cnty, PA.
        vii. Bessie M. STEELE*2857,2858*, b. Jan 1897, East Mahoning Twp.,Indiana Cnty, PA*2859*; d. Unknown.
        viii. Norman Hamilton STEELE*2860*, b. Abt. 1900, East Mahoning Twp.,Indiana Cnty,

PA[2860]; d. Jul 1970, Pittsburgh, Alleghney Cnty, PA.

173. Robert Elmer[10] STEELE *(Dorcas[9] HAMILTON, Nancy[8] VAN HORN, Isaiah[7], Henry B.[6], Henry[5], Christian Barentsen[4] VAN HOORN, Barent Christiansen[3], Christian Barentsen[2], Barent Barents[1])*[2861,2862] was born 16 Apr 1872 in Indiana Cnty, PA[2863], and died Unknown. He married Sadie[2863] Abt. 1893. She was born Sep 1872 in PA[2863], and died Unknown.

Notes for Robert Elmer STEELE:
    In the 1900 Census Elmer and Sadie have been married for 6 years. they have 2 boys and his father William is widowed and living with the family. His occupation is a farmer.

More About Robert STEELE and Sadie:
Marriage: Abt. 1893

Children of Robert STEELE and Sadie are:
      i.   Glenn F.[11] STEELE[2863], b. Apr 1895, PA[2863]; d. Unknown.
     ii.   Albert B. STEELE[2863], b. Jul 1897, PA[2863]; d. Unknown.

174. Ada Myrtle[10] VAN HORN *(Bennett Work[9], George Logan[8], Isaiah[7], Henry B.[6], Henry[5], Christian Barentsen[4] VAN HOORN, Barent Christiansen[3], Christian Barentsen[2], Barent Barents[1])*[2864,2865,2866,2867,2868,2869,2870,2871] was born 29 Aug 1873 in Georgeville, Indiana Cnty, PA[2872,2873], and died 21 May 1953 in Indiana, Indiana Cnty, PA[2873]. She married William M. MCADOO[2874,2875,2876,2877,2878,2879] 25 Sep 1895 in Indiana Cnty, PA. He was born 01 Feb 1870 in PA[2880], and died Apr 1942 in Indiana Cnty, PA.

Notes for Ada Myrtle VAN HORN:
Sometimes called Addie.

More About Ada Myrtle VAN HORN:
Burial: Unknown, Oakland Cemetery, Indiana, PA
Medical Information: Died at the home of her daughter Esther Ferrier in Indiana, PA
Religion: United Presbyterian Church

Notes for William M. MCADOO:
    14 Oct 1908 Indiana Evening Gazette (Indiana, PA) William a clerk in the John F. Clement's store is reported as having an attack of quinsy and his 12 year old daughter has been suffering from jaundice.
    In 1920 lives on South Sixth Street in Indiana, PA and owns his home free and clear of debt. Charles R. McAdoo a nephew age 18 is living in the home. There are also 2 servants in the household.
    In 1930 William and Ada live on South 6th Street in Indiana, PA in a home he owns worth $8,000. There is a radio in the home. There is also a roomer living with them named Samuel Freeman age 55 born in PA. William is a Grocery Store Merchant.

More About William M. MCADOO:
Occupation: Laborer Planning Mill, Restaurant Proprieter

More About William MCADOO and Ada VAN HORN:
Marriage: 25 Sep 1895, Indiana Cnty, PA

Children of Ada VAN HORN and William MCADOO are:

342.	i.	Hazel B.[11] MCADOO, b. 02 Nov 1895, Indiana Cnty, PA; d. 07 Sep 1985, Monroeville, Allegheny Cty, PA.
343.	ii.	Esther M. MCADOO, b. 20 May 1897, Indiana Cnty, PA; d. 28 Mar 1998, St. Andrew's Village, Indiana, Indiana Cnty, PA.
344.	iii.	Nellie E. MCADOO, b. Abt. 1900, PA; d. Aft. 1998.
345.	iv.	Jane E. MCADOO, b. Abt. 1905, PA; d. Bef. 1998.

175. Mary Caroline[10] VAN HORN *(Bennett Work[9], George Logan[8], Isaiah[7], Henry B.[6], Henry[5], Christian Barentsen[4] VAN HOORN, Barent Christiansen[3], Christian Barentsen[2], Barent Barents[1])*[2881,2882,2883,2884,2885,2886,2887,2888] was born 11 Apr 1877 in Indiana Cnty, PA[2889], and died 13 May 1940 in Indiana Cnty, PA. She married Laney Lawrence AUL[2890,2891,2892,2893,2894,2895,2896,2897,2898,2899,2900,2901,2902] Bet. 15 - 21 May 1895 in East Mahoning Twp., Indiana Cnty, PA[2903], son of Casper AUL and Catherine MCHENRY. He was born Bet. 03 - 13 Sep 1875 in East Mahoning Twp., Indiana Cnty, PA[2904,2905,2906], and died 18 Jun 1955 in Indiana Cnty, PA[2906].

Notes for Mary Caroline VAN HORN:
8 Nov. 1922 Indiana Progress (Indiana, PA) Mr. and Mrs. Laney Aul we guests of her parents Mr. and Mrs. B. W. Van Horn of Rossmoyne.

Notes for Laney Lawrence AUL:
His WWI Draft Registration indicates he lives at 19 Harney Sagamore, PA and his wife is Carrie. He is employed as a stationery engineer with Sagamore Coal and Coke company. He is of medium height, slender build and had brown eyes and hair.

More About Laney Lawrence AUL:
Burial: Unknown, Gilgal Cemetery, Indiana Cnty, PA
Lived: 1933, Marion Center, Indiana Cnty, PA
Occupation: Mine Car Inspector, Power Station Engineer
Religion: Church of God, Indiana, PA

More About Laney AUL and Mary VAN HORN:
Marriage: Bet. 15 - 21 May 1895, East Mahoning Twp., Indiana Cnty, PA[2907]
Marriage date: Married by Squire Samuel Rowe at his residence

Children of Mary VAN HORN and Laney AUL are:

346.	i.	Herbert Riggle[11] AUL, b. 22 Feb 1896, Georgeville, Indiana Cnty, PA; d. 22 Apr 1974, Indiana, Indiana Cnty, PA.
347.	ii.	Curtis Edwin AUL, b. Bet. Nov 1897 - 21 Sep 1898, PA; d. 13 Apr 1972.
348.	iii.	Bertha Della AUL, b. 06 Aug 1899, PA; d. Bet. Jun 1986 - 24 Jun 1988.
349.	iv.	Iva Bell AUL, b. Bet. 11 - 12 Nov 1901, Georgeville, Indiana Cnty, PA; d. 09 Apr 1951, Clearfield, Clearfield Cnty, PA.
350.	v.	Alma Florence AUL, b. 14 Apr 1903, Georgeville, Indiana Cnty, PA; d. 03 Sep 1957, Indiana, Indiana Cnty, PA.
351.	vi.	Mary Jane AUL, b. 04 Sep 1905, Rossmoyne, Indiana Cnty, PA; d. 24 Apr 1978.
	vii.	Mable Mildred AUL[2908,2909], b. 08 Sep 1907, PA[2910]; d. 26 Nov 1917, Punxsutwaney, PA.

More About Mable Mildred AUL:
Cause of Death: Appendicitis
Medical Information: died following the operation

| 352. | viii. | Myrtle Linda AUL, b. Bet. 03 Nov - Dec 1909, PA; d. 13 Feb 1950, Niagra Falls, |

253

Niagra Cnty, NY.

353.   ix.   Lawrence David AUL, b. 27 Jul 1912, Sagamore, Armstrong Cnty, PA; d. 07 Jan 1984, Niagra Falls, Niagra Cnty, NY.

354.   x.   Floyd William AUL, b. Abt. 1914, Sagamore, Armstrong Cnty, PA; d. 02 Dec 1977, Tucson, AZ.

        xi.   Ralph Lee AUL[2911], b. Bet. Nov 1917 - 18 Jan 1918, Sagamore, Armstrong Cnty, PA[2911]; d. 18 Sep 1968; m. Mae SHORT, Private; b. Private.

        More About Ralph AUL and Mae SHORT:
        Private-Begin: Private

        xii.   Twila Ethel AUL, b. Private; m. Albert Miles KERR[2912,2913,2914,2915], Private; d. Unknown.

        More About Albert KERR and Twila AUL:
        Private-Begin: Private

176. Cora Belle[10] VAN HORN *(Bennett Work[9], George Logan[8], Isaiah[7], Henry B.[6], Henry[5], Christian Barentsen[4] VAN HOORN, Barent Christiansen[3], Christian Barentsen[2], Barent Barents[1])*[2916,2917,2918,2919,2920,2921,2922,2923,2924,2925,2925,2926] was born 03 Jun 1879 in Georgeville, Indiana Cnty, PA[2927], and died 19 Sep 1961 in Indiana, Indiana Cnty, PA[2928]. She married Albert Martin SHAFFER[2929,2930,2931,2932,2933,2934] 1900, son of Isaac SHAFFER and Agnes GANETT. He was born 26 Aug 1875 in DuBois, Clearfield Cnty, PA[2935,2936], and died 23 Nov 1941 in Indiana Cnty, PA[2937].

More About Cora Belle VAN HORN:
Burial: Unknown, Beraccha Cemetery, Plumville, PA
Lived: Plumville, PA
Medical Information: Died at her home.
Religion: Plumville, PA United Presbyterian Church

Notes for Albert Martin SHAFFER:
        In 1910 married for 10 years his and Cora's first marriage and they have 4 children all living.
        In 1920 he owns his own home free and clear of debt.
        26 Dec 1936 the Indiana Evening Gazette (Indiana, PA) reports that the family of Mr. and Mrs. Albert Shaffer with sons Clyde and Paul are moving to the Bruce Leisure Farm in Cookport to farm for G. W. Stephens of Barnsboro who is the Assistant Superintendent of the Cambria county Schools. Mr. Shaffer has been employed by the Alta Vista Dairy Farms for the past two years.
        His obituary of 24 Nov 1941 in the Indiana Evening Gazette (Indiana, PA) lists his father as living and his wife surviving as well as children Nelson of Plumville, Claude Shaffer and Mrs Doroty Weaver of Indiana, Mrs Agnes Banks of Homer, Miss Zelda Shaffer of Cleveland, OH, Clyde Shaffer, Camp Shelby and Paul of the home.

More About Albert Martin SHAFFER:
Burial: Unknown, Beraccha Cemetery, Plumville, PA
Occupation: Mine Car Inspector, Laborer General Work, Assistant Engineer Rose Coal Company
Religion: Methodist

More About Albert SHAFFER and Cora VAN HORN:
Marriage: 1900

Children of Cora VAN HORN and Albert SHAFFER are:

355.   i.   Nelson Ernest[11] SHAFFER, b. 26 Feb 1901, Indiana Cnty, PA or Dubois. Clearfield Cnty, PA; d. 12 Jan 1959, Kittanning, Armstrong Cnty, PA.

356.   ii.   Dorothy Bell SHAFFER, b. 13 Nov 1903, DuBois, Indiana Cnty, PA; d. 13 May 1945, Johnstown, Cambria Cnty, PA.

357.   iii.   Agnes Marie SHAFFER, b. 02 Jan 1906, Ernest, Indiana Cnty, PA; d. 26 May 1994, Indiana, Indiana Cnty, PA.

    iv.   Zelda Mae SHAFFER[2938,2939,2940], b. 07 Apr 1908, Indiana Cnty, PA[2941]; d. 06 Jan 1977, Youngstown, Westmoreland Cnty, PA[2942]; m. (1) Peter MARSHALL[2942]; d. Aft. 1977; m. (2) BOWSER, Private; b. Private.

Notes for Zelda Mae SHAFFER:
10 Jan 1977 Indiana Evening Gazette (Indiana, PA) Obituary no children are mentioned and she is survived by her brothers Claude, Clyde and Paul and sister Agnes.

More About Zelda Mae SHAFFER:
Burial: 06 Jan 1977, Green Haven Memorial Gardens, Youngstown, Westmoreland Cnty, PA
Lived: Hubbard and Cleveland, OH

More About BOWSER and Zelda SHAFFER:
Private-Begin: Private

358.   v.   Claude Ellsworth SHAFFER, b. 21 Jun 1910, Indiana Cnty, PA; d. 30 Jun 1981.

359.   vi.   Gladys Rossett SHAFFER, b. Bet. 07 Jan - 26 Feb 1913, Indiana Cnty, PA; d. 17 Mar 1933, Indiana, Indiana Cnty, PA.

    vii.   Clair Wilson SHAFFER, b. 14 Feb 1916, Indiana Cnty, PA; d. 14 Feb 1916, Indiana Cnty, PA.

360.   viii.   Staff Sgt Clyde Sylvester SHAFFER, b. Bet. 07 Dec 1918 - Jan 1919, Plumvile, Indiana Cnty, PA; d. 06 Mar 1998, Dixonville, Indiana Cnty, PA.

    ix.   Paul Benett SHAFFER[2943,2944,2945], b. 30 Dec 1922, Indiana Cnty, PA[2946]; d. Bet. 1994 - 1998.

Notes for Paul Benett SHAFFER:
22 Dec 1945 Indiana Evening Gazette (Indiana, PA) reports that Pvt Paul B. Shaffer of Indiana was discharged of Friday 21 Dec. 1945.

More About Paul Benett SHAFFER:
Military service: Amy stationed in Germany

177. Anna Florence[10] VAN HORN *(Bennett Work[9], George Logan[8], Isaiah[7], Henry B.[6], Henry[5], Christian Barentsen[4] VAN HOORN, Barent Christiansen[3], Christian Barentsen[2], Barent Barents[1])[2947,2948,2949,2950,2951,2952,2953,2954,2955]* was born 20 Jun 1881 in South Mahoning Twp., Indiana Cnty, PA[2956], and died 04 Jan 1971 in Indian Haven, Indiana Cnty, PA[2957]. She married Robert JOHNSTON[2958,2959,2960,2961,2962,2963,2964] 30 Nov 1899[2965]. He was born Bet. 07 Jul 1870 - 1874 in PA[2966], and died 24 Nov 1939 in Indiana Cnty, PA.

More About Anna Florence VAN HORN:
Lived: Plumville, PA

Notes for Robert JOHNSTON:
In 1900 he uses 1870 as birth date and in 1910 and 1920 uses 1874.
In 1920 owns house free and clear.

In 1930 owns his place worth $2500 and does not have a radio. Living 2 doors from daughter Irene and her husband and family.

More About Robert JOHNSTON:
Occupation: Farmer and Coal Miner

More About Robert JOHNSTON and Anna VAN HORN:
Marriage: 30 Nov 1899[2967]

Children of Anna VAN HORN and Robert JOHNSTON are:

361.	i.	William Clair[11] JOHNSTON, b. 28 Apr 1901, Rossmoyne, Indiana Cnty, PA; d. 19 Oct 1986, Rochester Mills, PA.
362.	ii.	Irene Mae JOHNSTON, b. 21 Oct 1904, Georgeville, Indiana Cnty, PA; d. 29 Sep 1969, Punzsutawney, Jefferson Cnty, PA.
363.	iii.	Velma A. JOHNSTON, b. Abt. 1906, Indiana Cnty, PA; d. Aft. 1971.
364.	iv.	Lester Carl JOHNSTON, b. 23 Nov 1911, South Mahoning Twp., Indiana Cnty, PA; d. 17 Sep 1975, Home, PA.
365.	v.	Walter R. JOHNSTON, b. 27 Sep 1918, South Mahoning Twp., Indiana Cnty, PA; d. 05 Jul 1994, Indiana Cnty, PA.

178. Robert Lee Claire[10] VAN HORN *(Bennett Work[9], George Logan[8], Isaiah[7], Henry B.[6], Henry[5], Christian Barentsen[4] VAN HOORN, Barent Christiansen[3], Christian Barentsen[2], Barent Barents[1])*[2968,2969,2970,2971,2972,2973,2974,2975] was born 25 Jul 1882 in Georgeville, Indiana Cnty, PA[2976,2977], and died 05 Jul 1951 in Plumville, Indiana Cnty, PA. He married (1) Mary Ella KROH[2978,2979,2980] 13 Mar 1907 in Indiana Cnty, PA[2981,2982], daughter of Charles KROH and Ella SEANOR. She was born Bet. 03 Aug 1883 - 1885 in PA[2983], and died 22 Oct 1913 in Plumville, Indiana Cnty, PA[2984]. He married (2) Mary Elizabeth BROWN[2985,2986,2987] Nov 1914 in Plumville, PA[2988], daughter of Emery BROWN and Alice DOLBY. She was born Bet. 30 Jan 1894 - 31 Jan 1896 in DuBois, Clearfield Cnty, PA[2989], and died 02 May 1989 in Indian Haven, Indiana Cnty, PA.

Notes for Robert Lee Claire VAN HORN:
In his WWI Draft Registration he indicates he works for the Buffalo and Susquehanna Coal and Coke company. He is of medium height, medium build and has brown eyes and black hair, He lists his contact as his wife Mary Elizabeth Van Horn.
In 1920 owns his home free and clear. He is an electrician in the mines. This is his second wife his first wife having died.
12 Aug 1925 Indiana Evening Gazette (Indiana, PA) states he is of Plumville and visited in Tuesday with Indiana friends.
In 1930 owns his own home worth about $1500 and has a radio.
17 November 1909 the Indiana Progress(Indiana, PA) reports the sale of a lot in Plumville by John St. Clair to Robert L. Van Horn for $500.

More About Robert Lee Claire VAN HORN:
Burial: Unknown, Smicksburg Cemetery, Smicksburg, PA
Occupation: Electrician Coal Mine; B&S Coal Company, Coal Miner
Organizations: UMW of America # 473 of Sagamore, PA
Religion: Methodist

Notes for Mary Ella KROH:
24 April 1907 G. W. Seanor to Minnie Van Horn 8 acres in south Mahoning for $1500 according to the report in the Indiana Weekly Messenger (Indiana, PA).
23 Oct 1913 Indiana Evening Gazette (Indiana, PA) Mrs. Minnie Van Horn wife of Lee Van Horn, died at her home in Plumville, Tuesday evening at 9 o'clock. Death was due to blood

poisoning. She was a member of the Plumville Methodist Episcopal Church, where the funeral services will be held tomorrow (Friday) morning at 10 o'clock. She leaves her husband, four sons and one daughter. Mrs Van Horn was a sister of Mrs. McAdoo of Philadelphia Street
According to William J. Van Horn Minnie was a Seneca Indian.

More About Mary Ella KROH:
Cause of Death: Blood Poisoning
Lived: Plumville, PA

More About Robert VAN HORN and Mary KROH:
Marriage: 13 Mar 1907, Indiana Cnty, PA[2990,2991]
Marriage date: Rev. James Fish
Marriage Place: Home of William McAdoo East Chestnut Street, Georgeville, PA

Notes for Mary Elizabeth BROWN:
According to the census her marriage to Lee Van Horn is her first marriage at age 18.

More About Mary Elizabeth BROWN:
Lived: Plumville, PA

More About Robert VAN HORN and Mary BROWN:
Marriage: Nov 1914, Plumville, PA[2992]

Children of Robert VAN HORN and Mary KROH are:
      i.   Walter Laird[11] VAN HORN[2993,2994,2995,2996,2997,2998], b. 29 Aug 1907, Plumville, Indiana Cnty, PA[2999]; d. Bet. 1961 - 1987; m. Emily WILSON, Private; b. Private.

          Notes for Walter Laird VAN HORN:
          29 April 1936 Real Estate Transfers listed in the Indiana Progress(Indiana, PA) that Laird and Robert L. Van Horn transfer a lot in Plumville to Robert E. Van Horn.

          More About Walter Laird VAN HORN:
          Lived: Niagra Falls, Niagra Cnty, NY
          Occupation: Coal Miner

          More About Walter VAN HORN and Emily WILSON:
          Private-Begin: Private

366.   ii.   Floyd Albert VAN HORN, b. 08 Oct 1908, Plumville, Indiana Cnty, PA; d. 24 Jul 1987, Youngstown, Mahoning Cnty, OH.
367.   iii.   Wilbur Bennett VAN HORN, b. 24 Feb 1910, Plumville, Indiana Cnty, PA; d. 11 Jul 1998, Indiana, Indiana Cnty, PA.
368.   iv.   Olive Marion VAN HORN, b. 24 Dec 1911, Plumville, Indiana Cnty, PA; d. 19 Mar 2000, Portsmouth, VA.
      v.   Harry Brown VAN HORN[3000,3001,3002,3003], b. Abt. 1912, Plumville, Indiana Cnty, PA[3004]; d. Bet. 1989 - 1998.
369.   vi.   Robert VAN HORN, b. 29 Sep 1913, Plumville, Indiana Cnty, PA; d. Aft. 1987.

Children of Robert VAN HORN and Mary BROWN are:
370.   vii.   June Louise[11] VAN HORN, b. 08 Jun 1915, Plumville, Indiana Cnty, PA; d. Aft. 1989.
371.   viii.   Alice Belle VAN HORN, b. 24 Oct 1917, Plumville, Indiana Cnty, PA; d. Bet. 1951 - 1989.

372. ix. Howard Lee VAN HORN, b. 14 Dec 1919, Plumville, Indiana Cnty, PA; d. Jan 1984, Tanawanda, Erie Cnty, NY.

373. x. William Clyde VAN HORN, b. 24 Jan 1922, Plumville, Indiana Cnty, PA; d. Aft. 1998.

374. xi. Hillary Leroy VAN HORN, b. 10 Oct 1924, Plumville, Indiana Cnty, PA; d. 24 Oct 1973, Niagra Falls, Niagra Cnty, NY.

375. xii. Donald Charles VAN HORN, b. 21 Feb 1927, Plumville, Indiana Cnty, PA; d. 2000.

376. xiii. Richard Max VAN HORN, b. 12 Nov 1929, Plumville, Indiana Cnty, PA; d. Bef. 1989.

377. xiv. George Eugene VAN HORN, b. 02 Sep 1931, Plumville, Indiana Cnty, PA; d. Aft. 1998.

xv. Raymond LaVern VAN HORN[3005,3006], b. Bet. 19 Sep 1931 - 1932, Plumville, Indiana Cnty, PA[3007]; d. 21 Oct 1974, Kittanning, Armstrong Cnty, PA[3007].

Notes for Raymond LaVern VAN HORN:
25 May 1950 the Indiana Evening Gazette (Indiana, PA) reports that Raymond who was injured in 1944 in a sledding accident will go to a clinic in New York for rehabilitation. This rehabilitation was provided by the Coal Miners fund and Raymond's father is a coal miner.

More About Raymond LaVern VAN HORN:
Burial: Unknown, Smicksburg, PA
Lived: Plumville, PA

179. James Ira[10] VAN HORN *(Bennett Work[9], George Logan[8], Isaiah[7], Henry B.[6], Henry[5], Christian Barentsen[4] VAN HOORN, Barent Christiansen[3], Christian Barentsen[2], Barent Barents[1])*[3008,3009,3010,3011,3012] was born 26 Apr 1885 in South Mahoning Twp., Indiana Cnty, PA[3013,3014], and died Bet. 10 - 26 Mar 1951 in Indiana, Indiana Cnty, PA. He married Anna L. KLINE[3015,3016] 29 Jul 1913. She was born Abt. 1896 in PA[3017], and died 05 Nov 1946 in Indiana Cnty, PA.

Notes for James Ira VAN HORN:
In his WWI Draft Registration he indicates he is short of medium build with blue eyes and brown hair.

More About James Ira VAN HORN:
Burial: Unknown, Gilgal Cemetery, Indiana County, PA
Lived: Smicksburg, Indiana Cnty, PA
Occupation: Fireman Railroad, Miner Mccombs Coal Company

More About James VAN HORN and Anna KLINE:
Marriage: 29 Jul 1913

Children of James VAN HORN and Anna KLINE are:

378. i. Carrie Etta[11] VAN HORN, b. Abt. 1914, PA; d. 03 Dec 1968, Dixonville, PA.

379. ii. Deloris Belle VAN HORN, b. 04 Sep 1915, East Mahoning Twp., Indiana Cnty, PA; d. 21 Jul 1971, Kittanning, Armstrong Cnty, PA.

380. iii. Arlene May VAN HORN, b. 29 Mar 1918, South Mahoning Twp., Indiana Cnty, PA; d. 19 Dec 1975, Indiana, Indiana Cnty, PA.

180. Harry Bennett[10] VAN HORN *(Bennett Work[9], George Logan[8], Isaiah[7], Henry B.[6], Henry[5], Christian Barentsen[4] VAN HOORN, Barent Christiansen[3], Christian Barentsen[2], Barent Barents[1])*[3018,3019,3020,3021,3022,3023,3024,3025,3026,3027,3028,3029,3030] was born 17 Jun 1887 in South

Mahoning Twp., Indiana Cnty, PA[3031,3032], and died 19 Feb 1976 in Indiana Cnty, PA[3033,3034]. He married Irene Bertha SIMPSON[3035,3036,3037,3038,3039,3040,3041] 25 Dec 1912 in Georgeville, Indiana Cnty, PA[3042,3043], daughter of Wesley SIMPSON and Mary LYTLE. She was born 09 Jul 1889 in East Mahoning Twp., Indiana Cnty, PA[3044,3045], and died 06 Jan 1979 in Indiana, Indiana Cnty, PA[3046].

Notes for Harry Bennett VAN HORN:
In his WWI Draft registration he says he is tall of slender build with blue eyes and brown hair. He works for his father as a farmer and is married with 3 children.
In 1920 owns his farm free and clear an lives next door to his father and mother.
In 1930 owns his own home worth about $1500 and does not have a radio. He can read and write as can his wife. He is a laborer on a Steam Railroad.
January 8, 1962 admitted to the Indiana Hospital.
June 30, 1964 discharged from the Indiana Hospital
20 Dec 1972 Indiana Evening Gazette (Indiana, PA) reports on the 60 Wedding Anniversary listing all 10 children and notes there are 30 grandchildren and 38 great grandchildren as of this date.
According to Annette Kline Grandpap was an avid player of the spoons.

More About Harry Bennett VAN HORN:
Burial: Unknown, Gilgal Cemetry, Gilgal Church, Indiana Cnty, PA
Lived: Smicksburg, PA
Occupation: Steam Railroad Laborer
Religion: Gilgal Presbyterian Church, Indiana County, PA

More About Irene Bertha SIMPSON:
Burial: Unknown, Gilgal Cemetry, Gilgal Church, Indiana Cnty, PA

Marriage Notes for Harry VAN HORN and Irene SIMPSON:
25 December 1912 Indiana Progress(Indiana, PA) reports that a marriage license was taken by Harry B Van Horn and Irene Simpson.

More About Harry VAN HORN and Irene SIMPSON:
Marriage: 25 Dec 1912, Georgeville, Indiana Cnty, PA[3047,3048]
Marriage date: Rev. R. J. Roberts
Marriage Place: Parents Home

Children of Harry VAN HORN and Irene SIMPSON are:
381.   i.   John Simpson[11] VAN HORN, b. 24 Feb 1914, Georgeville, Indiana Cnty, PA; d. 06 Jun 1993, Monroeville or Export, PA.
        ii.   Ralph Emerson VAN HORN[3049,3050,3051], b. 18 Oct 1916, Indiana Cnty, PA[3052,3053]; d. 14 Oct 2000, Hillsdale, Indiana Cnty, PA[3054,3055].

        Notes for Ralph Emerson VAN HORN:
        If this is the Ralph Emerson Van Horn found in the newspapers he was charged with public indecency and indecent assault of a girl going home from school. It is in the papers in 1963 and he is given age of 46.In the 4 Oct 1963 Indiana Gazette it is reported that Ralph Van Horn admitted to charges of a morals charge having molested a 7 year old girl when she was walking home from school on April 1 and later picked up for a public indecency charge by a State trooper.
        In the 27 Nov 1963 Indiana Evening Gazette (Indiana, PA) he is to appear before the Grand Jury on Dec. 4 of that year to stand for charges of indecent exposure and indecent assault.

        More About Ralph Emerson VAN HORN:

259

Burial: Unknown, Gilgal Cemetery Gilgal UP Church Indiana Cnty, PA

382. iii. Walter L. VAN HORN, b. 14 Mar 1917, Smicksburg, Indiana Cnty, PA; d. 21 Feb 2008, Murrysville, Westmoreland Cnty or Smicksburg, Indiana Cnty, PA.
383. iv. Merle Wayne VAN HORN, b. 24 Feb 1919, Indiana Cnty, PA; d. 28 Aug 1948, Tarentum, PA.
384. v. Mary Belle VAN HORN, b. Abt. 1920, Indiana Cnty, PA; d. Aft. 1988.
       vi. Claire L. VAN HORN[3056,3057,3058], b. 22 Jul 1923, South Mahoning Twp., Indiana Cnty, PA[3059,3060]; d. 18 Jun 1988, Indiana, Indiana Cnty, PA[3060].

More About Claire L. VAN HORN:
Burial: Unknown, Gigal Presbyterian Church Cemetery, Indiana Cnty, PA

       vii. Bennett Wesley VAN HORN[3061], b. 1924, Indiana Cnty, PA; d. 1924.

More About Bennett Wesley VAN HORN:
Burial: Unknown, Gilgal Cemetery Gilgal UP Church Indiana Cnty, PA

385. viii. Helen Louise VAN HORN, b. Bet. 13 Jun - Jul 1926, Indiana Cnty, PA; d. 08 Sep 1990, PA.
386. ix. Blaine W. VAN HORN, b. 26 Jan 1928, Indiana Cnty, PA; d. Aft. 2008.
387. x. Twila May VAN HORN, b. Aft. 1930; d. Aft. 2008.

181. Pearl Agnes[10] VAN HORN *(Bennett Work[9], George Logan[8], Isaiah[7], Henry B.[6], Henry[5], Christian Barentsen[4] VAN HOORN, Barent Christiansen[3], Christian Barentsen[2], Barent Barents[1])*[3062,3063,3064,3065,3066,3067,3068,3069] was born 24 Jul 1889 in Georgeville, Indiana Cnty, PA[3070], and died 03 Oct 1967 in Indiana Cnty, PA. She married John Delbert GOOD[3071,3072,3073,3074,3075,3076] 05 Feb 1913 in Marion Center, Indiana Cnty, PA[3077,3078], son of Joshua GOOD and Alice SINK. He was born 21 Oct 1887 in Smicksburg, PA[3079], and died 07 Oct 1980 in Indian Haven, Indiana Cnty, PA.

More About Pearl Agnes VAN HORN:
Lived: Plumville, PA

Notes for John Delbert GOOD:
    In 1930 they own their place worth about $3500.

More About John Delbert GOOD:
Occupation: Farmer

More About John GOOD and Pearl VAN HORN:
Marriage: 05 Feb 1913, Marion Center, Indiana Cnty, PA[3080,3081]
Marriage date: Rev R. J. Roberts
Marriage Place: Home of Minister

Children of Pearl VAN HORN and John GOOD are:
388. i. Lawrence Kenneth[11] GOOD, b. Abt. 29 Jan 1914, South Mahoning Twp., Indiana Cnty, PA; d. 20 Jan 1968, New Castle, PA.
389. ii. Wilbur Dale GOOD, b. 16 Jul 1916, South Mahoning Twp., Indiana Cnty, PA; d. 15 Sep 1991, Indiana, Indiana Cnty, PA.
390. iii. Ernest Glenn GOOD, b. 11 Dec 1920, Sagamore, Armstrong Cnty, PA; d. Aft. 2008.
391. iv. Alice Belle GOOD, b. 14 Apr 1923, Plumville, Indiana Cnty, PA; d. 14 Feb 2008,

Felt Manor, Emporium, Indiana Cnty, PA.
392.   v.   Lola Stella GOOD, b. 17 Oct 1925, Indiana Cnty, PA; d. Aft. 2008.
           vi.   ? GOOD[3081], d. Bef. 1963.

182. Norman Clarence[10] VAN HORN *(Bennett Work[9], George Logan[8], Isaiah[7], Henry B.[6], Henry[5], Christian Barentsen[4] VAN HOORN, Barent Christiansen[3], Christian Barentsen[2], Barent Barents[1])[3082,3083,3084,3085,3086,3087,3088,3089,3090,3091,3092,3093]* was born 22 Oct 1891 in Georgeville, Indiana Cnty, PA[3094,3095], and died 11 Sep 1972 in Indiana Cnty, PA[3096]. He married (1) Edna LANEY[3097,3098] 25 Jul 1917 in Indiana Cnty, PA[3099]. She was born Abt. 1898 in Starford, PA[3100], and died Aft. 1920. He married (2) Effie A. HUMBERSON[3101,3102,3103,3104,3105,3106,3107] 15 Aug 1925 in Friendsville, Garrett Cnty, MD[3108], daughter of HUMBERSON and Alice UMBLE. She was born 19 Sep 1902 in Friendsville, Garrett Cnty, MD[3109], and died 26 Sep 1997 in St. Andrews Village, Indiana, PA[3110,3111].

Notes for Norman Clarence VAN HORN:
    17 September 1917 Indiana Evening Gazette (Indiana, PA) Norman Van Horn of Georgeville is listed as being called for the draft.
    In 1920 living next door to a Laney family that is likely Edna's parents and siblings. Her parents are likely Rush B. and Margaret Laney. He is renting and is a railroad laborer.
    29 Dec 1923 Norman is visiting his parents in Georgeville.
    In 1930 he is renting for $10/month and has been married for 5 years to Effie. He has a sister in law also living in the home Mary Burkett age 14 born PA.
    9 May 1930 Indiana Evening Gazette (Indiana, PA) reports that Norman Van Horn an AEF veteran is now employed by a gas and coal company in Beckley, WV. He is home visiting family on this date.
    10 December 1930 the Indiana Evening Gazette (Indiana, PA) reports that Norman Van Horn of Plumville was one of the hunters who brought in a Buck
    In 1942 he completes the WWI I Draft registration and indicates that he and Effie are living on RFD #2 Smicksburg, PA. He is employed by Hoffman Bros of Punxsutawney, PA. He is 5 foot 7 inches tall weights 155 pounds is of dark complexion with gray eyes and brown hair. His registration was filed in April 1942 at the Carbon Cnty, PA courthouse.

More About Norman Clarence VAN HORN:
Burial: Unknown, Gilgal Cemetery, Indiana Cnty, PA
Military service: WW I
Occupation: Driller Testing Coal, Diamond Driller for Hoffman Drilling Comany of Punxsutawney, PA; Railroad Fireman; Gas and Coal Co. Berkeley Cnty, WV

More About Norman VAN HORN and Edna LANEY:
Marriage: 25 Jul 1917, Indiana Cnty, PA[3112]

Notes for Effie A. HUMBERSON:
    Adopted by Leonard and Ellen Lytle.

More About Effie A. HUMBERSON:
Burial: Unknown, Gilgal Cemetery, Gilgal Church, Indiana Cnty, PA
Hobies: Bingo, Quilting, Chrocheting
Organizations: Loyal Circle Class, Desdemona Rebekah Lodge, Marion Center Senior Citizen Center
Religion: Plumville Presbyterian Church

More About Norman VAN HORN and Effie HUMBERSON:
Marriage: 15 Aug 1925, Friendsville, Garrett Cnty, MD[3113]

Marriage date: Rev. P. W. Arbogast

Children of Norman VAN HORN and Effie HUMBERSON are:
393.   i.   Geraldine[11] VAN HORN, b. Marion Center, Indiana Cnty, PA; d. Aft. 1997.
394.   ii.   Lavona VAN HORN, b. Smicksburg, PA; d. 1992.
395.   iii. Norma Jean VAN HORN, b. Private.
396.   iv.   Virginia E. VAN HORN, b. 10 Aug 1926, PA; d. Bef. 2005.
        v.   ? VAN HORN[3114], b. Abt. 1928, Indiana Cnty, PA; d. 1928, Indiana Cnty, PA[3114].

        More About ? VAN HORN:
        Burial: Unknown, Gilgal Cemetery, Indiana Cnty, PA

397.   vi.   Glenn LeRoy VAN HORN, b. 20 Aug 1933, Smicksburg, PA; d. 31 Jan 1988,
              Kensington, PA.
        vii. Raymond VAN HORN, b. Abt. 1947, Indiana Cnty, PA; d. 20 Oct 1947, Indiana
              Cnty, PA.

        More About Raymond VAN HORN:
        Burial: Unknown, Gilgal Cemetery, Indiana Cnty, PA

183. Dollie Ethel[10] VAN HORN *(Bennett Work[9], George Logan[8], Isaiah[7], Henry B.[6], Henry[5], Christian Barentsen[4] VAN HOORN, Barent Christiansen[3], Christian Barentsen[2], Barent Barents[1])*[3115,3116,3117,3118,3119,3120,3121,3122,3123,3124] was born 20 Apr 1894 in Indiana Cnty, PA[3125], and died Bet. 30 - 31 Aug 1976 in Indiana Cnty, PA. She married Walter Byron FETTERHOFF[3126,3127,3128,3129,3130,3131,3132,3133] 08 Dec 1915 in Smicksburg, Indiana Cnty, PA[3133], son of Elmer BECK and Minnie FETTERHOFF. He was born 21 Jan 1897 in PA[3134,3135], and died 26 Feb 1969 in Trade City, North Mahoning Twp., Indiana Cnty, PA.

More About Dollie Ethel VAN HORN:
Lived: Smicksburg, PA

Notes for Walter Byron FETTERHOFF:
      In his WWI I Draft Registration his birth is given as 21 Jan.1897. He is a self employed farmer Smicksburg, PA. His wife is Dollie Fetterhoff. He is white with grey eyes, brown hair and a ruddy complexion he is about 5 foot 7 inches and weighs about 150 pounds.

More About Walter Byron FETTERHOFF:
Occupation: Coal Miner

More About Walter FETTERHOFF and Dollie VAN HORN:
Marriage: 08 Dec 1915, Smicksburg, Indiana Cnty, PA[3136]
Marriage Place: Luthern Pasonage

Children of Dollie VAN HORN and Walter FETTERHOFF are:
398.   i.   Martin W.[11] FETTERHOFF, b. 26 May 1916, North Mahoning, Indiana Cnty, PA;
              d. 05 Nov 1993, Indiana, Indiana Cnty, PA.
399.   ii.   Ruby L. FETTERHOFF, b. 27 Mar 1918, Trade City, PA; d. 12 Jan 2007, Mulberry
              Square.
        iii. Elmer Byron FETTERHOFF[3137,3138,3139], b. Abt. 1919, PA[3140]; d. Bet. 1993 - 2007;
              m. Loletta Arlene SHIELDS, Private; b. Private.

        Notes for Elmer Byron FETTERHOFF:
        3 July 1941 Indiana Evening Gazette (Indiana, PA) reports that Elmer Byron

Fetterhoff is a county registrant and he lives at RFD #2 Smicksburg, PA.
21 July 1941 Indiana Evening Gazette (Indiana, PA) lists Elmer Byron as a selectee
91-S-19

More About Elmer FETTERHOFF and Loletta SHIELDS:
Private-Begin: Private

	iv.	Bruce C. FETTERHOFF, b. Private.
	v.	Dennis M. FETTERHOFF, b. Private.
400.	vi.	Anna Belle FETTERHOFF, b. Private.
	vii.	Robert FETTERHOFF, b. Private.
401.	viii.	Pearl M. FETTERHOFF, b. Abt. 1924, PA; d. Aft. 2007.

184. Edna Gertude[10] VAN HORN *(Bennett Work[9], George Logan[8], Isaiah[7], Henry B.[6], Henry[5], Christian Barentsen[4] VAN HOORN, Barent Christiansen[3], Christian Barentsen[2], Barent Barents[1])[3141,3142,3143,3144,3145,3146,3147,3148,3149]* was born 26 Apr 1898 in Indiana Cnty, PA[3150], and died 27 Mar 1987. She married Cyrus B. DILTS[3151,3152,3153,3154,3155] 13 Sep 1920 in Indiana Cnty, PA[3156,3157], son of Wilson DILTS and Mary WIDDOWSON. He was born 05 Oct 1896 in Rossmoyne, Indiana Cnty, PA[3158], and died 28 Oct 1985 in Indiana, Indiana Cnty, PA.

Notes for Edna Gertude VAN HORN:
1 September 1915 it is reported in the Indiana Progress(Indiana, PA) that Dollie and Edna visited cousins Max and Roxie Good.
Edna may be listed in two censuses in 1920 one in South Mahoning Twp. and one in Plumville, PA.

More About Edna Gertude VAN HORN:
Lived: Smicksburg and Georgeville, PA
Occupation: Saleslady Clothing Store, Clerk Department Store

Notes for Cyrus B. DILTS:
Name is spelled Diltz in some publications.
In 1930 he is renting for $15 per month and has a radio.
Wilson Dilts of near Plumville died last Saturday in 80th year
Allison Wilson Diltz died at 12:30 last Saturday afternoon, September 5, at his home at Rossmoyne, near Plumville. The cause of his death was heart trouble having been bedfast almost two months. He had been in failing health for several years but had continued his farm operations until his recent illness caused him to take his bed last July.
Mr. Diltz was born in North Mahoning Township, Indiana County, on May 26, 1857, the son of Mr. and Mrs. Henry K. Diltz and was one of ten children five surviving. He was united in marriage to Miss Mary Widdowson, also of Indiana county, in Punxsutawney, in 1882. He had spent his entire life time on his two farms on what is know as White Oak Flat between Georgeville and Plumville being quite successful and was held in high regard by his legion of friends throughout that region. He was a member of the Mahoning Baptist church.
He is survived by widow and their nine children, his death having been the first break in the family circle. The sons and daughters are, namely: Robert H, of Georgeville; Cye and John of near Rossmoyne; Mrs. John Mayo of Carnegie; Mrs. S.B. Irwin of near Punxsutawney; Nannie and June of Fairmont, West Virgina; Mrs. E. J. Pearson, of Conneaut, Ohio; Maye at home. Also surviving are five brothers and sister; Dr. Harry Diltz and Mrs. Belle Miller of Wilkinsburg; Mrs. Ada Work, of California; Mrs J.C. Ribblett of Youngwood; Thomas B. Diltz of Greensburg.
Funeral services were held at the late home at 2:00 o'clock, Tuesday afternoon, in charge of Rev. J. E. McCall of the Dayton United Presbyterian church. The large attendance at the funeral and the many elaborate floral tributes attested for the high esteem in which the deceased was held in his

home community. Burial was made in the family plot in the Gilgal cemetery, near Georgeville. O.J. Nupp, wife and grandson Terry J Carlson of this place, were among the relatives to attend the funeral.

More About Cyrus B. DILTS:
Occupation: Coal Mine Cutter
Social Security Number: 209-01-6152

More About Cyrus DILTS and Edna VAN HORN:
Marriage: 13 Sep 1920, Indiana Cnty, PA[3159,3160]
Marriage date: Rev. Dr. F. W. Hinnitt
Marriage Place: Parsonage of Rev. F. W. Hinnitt on South 6th Street

Children of Edna VAN HORN and Cyrus DILTS are:
      i.   Betty J.[11] DILTS, b. Private; m. Robert J. SMITH, Private; b. Private.

          More About Robert SMITH and Betty DILTS:
          Private-Begin: Private

      ii. Helen L. DILTS, b. Private; m. Harry BYERS, Private; b. Private.

          More About Harry BYERS and Helen DILTS:
          Private-Begin: Private

402.   iii. Marjorie DILTS, b. Private.
      iv. Barbara DILTS, b. Private; m. William BRADY, Private; b. Private.

          More About William BRADY and Barbara DILTS:
          Private-Begin: Private

185. Verna Viola[10] VAN HORN *(Bennett Work[9], George Logan[8], Isaiah[7], Henry B.[6], Henry[5], Christian Barentsen[4] VAN HOORN, Barent Christiansen[3], Christian Barentsen[2], Barent Barents[1])*[3161,3162,3163,3164,3165,3166,3167] was born 21 Aug 1900 in Georgeville, Indiana Cnty, PA[3168], and died 10 May 1962 in Warren, OH[3168]. She married Samuel Andrew OLSON[3169,3170,3171,3172,3173] 06 Nov 1920, son of Thomas OLSON and Theressa WEAVER. He was born 13 Nov 1896 in Valier, Jefferson Cnty, PA[3174], and died 31 May 1951 in Indiana Cnty, PA.

More About Verna Viola VAN HORN:
Lived: Plumville, PA
Medical Information: Died at the home of her son Samuel Olson, Jr. 2153 Brier Street, Warren, OH.
Occupation: Clerk US Post Office

Notes for Samuel Andrew OLSON:
    In 1930 living with his widowed mother his sister and his wife. His mother is the head of the house who owns her home worth $7100 and they have a radio.

More About Samuel Andrew OLSON:
Occupation: Postmaster US Post Office

More About Samuel OLSON and Verna VAN HORN:
Marriage: 06 Nov 1920

Child of Verna VAN HORN and Samuel OLSON is:
403.   i.   Samuel Andrew[11] OLSON, JR, b. 17 Aug; d. Aft. 1962.

Generation No. 5

186. Roberta[11] STEWART *(John Alexander[10], Mary C.[9] VAN HORN, Henry[8], Isaiah[7], Henry B.[6], Henry[5], Christian Barentsen[4] VAN HOORN, Barent Christiansen[3], Christian Barentsen[2], Barent Barents[1])[3175,3176]* was born 23 Mar 1886 in Washington District of Columbia[3177], and died Unknown. She married William C. ADAMS[3178,3179] 11 Nov 1906[3180], son of Chambers ADAMS and Mary A.. He was born Bet. 08 Jan 1874 - 1875 in Utica, Oneida Cnty, NY[3181], and died 06 Jun 1925 in Ft. Smith, AR[3182].

Notes for Roberta STEWART:
    In 1900 listed in Indiana Cnty, PA living with her aunt.

More About William C. ADAMS:
Employment: 1900, Bicycle Repair

More About William ADAMS and Roberta STEWART:
Marriage: 11 Nov 1906[3182]

Child of Roberta STEWART and William ADAMS is:
     i.   Mary[12] ADAMS, b. Private; m. HUGHES[3182], Private; d. Unknown.

          More About HUGHES and Mary ADAMS:
          Private-Begin: Private

187. John G.[11] STEWART *(John Alexander[10], Mary C.[9] VAN HORN, Henry[8], Isaiah[7], Henry B.[6], Henry[5], Christian Barentsen[4] VAN HOORN, Barent Christiansen[3], Christian Barentsen[2], Barent Barents[1])[3183,3184,3185]* was born 30 Dec 1890 in Washington District of Columbia[3186], and died Unknown. He married Margaret K.[3187,3188] Abt. 1919. She was born Abt. 1891 in Ireland[3189], and died Unknown.

Notes for John G. STEWART:
    In 1920 is married and lives on D St. NW in Washington, DC where he rents. He is a chauffeur for a private family.
    In 1930 owns home worth $7950 and has a radio. He is a machinist in a garage. Lives with wife of 10 years and son age 5 at 954 Shepherd Street in Washington,DC.

Notes for Margaret K.:
    In 1920 census indicates she immigrated in 1907 and became a citizen in 1913.

More About John STEWART and Margaret K.:
Marriage: Abt. 1919

Child of John STEWART and Margaret K. is:
     i.   John K.[12] STEWART, b. Private.

188. Peregrine Stewart[11] WHITHAM *(Elizabeth Canon[10] STEWART, Mary C.[9] VAN HORN, Henry[8], Isaiah[7], Henry B.[6], Henry[5], Christian Barentsen[4] VAN HOORN, Barent Christiansen[3], Christian*

Barentsen[2], Barent Barents[1])[3190,3191,3192,3193,3194] was born 21 Sep 1875 in IL[3195,3196], and died Unknown. He married Pauline F. WOODBERRY[3197,3198] Abt. 1912. She was born Abt. 1890 in MA[3199], and died Unknown.

Notes for Peregrine Stewart WHITHAM:
His WWI draft registration has him living at 18 Livingston in New Brunswick, NJ born 21Sept. 1875. He is a draught man for Wright-Martin Aircraft in New Brunswick, NJ on Jersey Ave. His wife is Pauline F. and lives at the same address. He is tall of medium build with grey eyes and light chestnut hair.
In 1920 lists name as Peri Whitman. He is a draught man and lives with wife and 5 year old daughter Pauline E.

More About Peregrine Stewart WHITHAM:
Occupation: Teacher, Actor Stock Company, Salesman Manufacurer of Refrigerators

More About Peregrine WHITHAM and Pauline WOODBERRY:
Marriage: Abt. 1912

Child of Peregrine WHITHAM and Pauline WOODBERRY is:
  i. Pauline E.[12] WHITHAM, b. Private.

189. Stella[11] BARR *(Mary C[10] VAN HORN, James Thompson[9], Henry[8], Isaiah[7], Henry B.[6], Henry[5], Christian Barentsen[4] VAN HOORN, Barent Christiansen[3], Christian Barentsen[2], Barent Barents[1])[3200,3201,3202,3203,3204]* was born 31 Mar 1887 in Green Twp., Indiana Cnty, PA[3205], and died 06 Jun 1961 in Vandergrift, Westmoreland Cnty, PA[3206]. She married David Paul MILLER[3207,3208,3209,3210,3211] 19 Aug 1913 in Penn Run, Indiana Cnty, PA[3212], son of Edward MILLER and Ella A.. He was born 21 May 1885 in West Lebanon, PA[3213], and died 22 Nov 1947 in New Castle, PA[3214].

Notes for Stella BARR:
In 1908 listed as a Junior at Normal. Indiana, PA
In 1909 passed the State Teachers Exam and listed as a graduate of Normal
In 1910 recommended for the 3 day State Teachers Senior Exam and listed as a graduate of Normal from Indiana, PA

More About Stella BARR:
Burial: Unknown, Vandergrift, Westmoreland Cnty, PA Cemetery
Education: 1910, Indiana State College(Normal)
Occupation: School teacher in Indiana, Cambia and Westmoreland Counties, PA
Organizations: Eastern Starr
Religion: Unted Presbyterian Church

Notes for David Paul MILLER:
In 1942 he reports on his draft registration that he lives at 105 W. Adams in Vandegrift, Westmoreland Cnty, PA. His wife is Stella Miller. He works for the Vandergrift Savings and Trust on Grant Street in Vandergrift, PA. He is 5'8" weighs 190# has hazel eyes, brown hair and ruddy complexion. His telephone is Vandergrift 912.
In 1920 he lives at 105 W. Adams in Vandergrift, PA in a home he owns with a mortgage. He is a Paying Teller in a Bank in Vandergrift. His wife is Stella B. and he has two infant daughters.
1930 owns his own home worth $8500 and has a radio.

More About David Paul MILLER:
Occupation: Assistant in Bank

More About David MILLER and Stella BARR:
Marriage: 19 Aug 1913, Penn Run, Indiana Cnty, PA[3215]
Marriage date: Rev. W. J. Sproull

Children of Stella BARR and David MILLER are:
  i.   Helen E.[12] MILLER, b. Private.
  ii. Marian R. MILLER, b. Private; m. KEARNEY, Private; b. Private.

       More About KEARNEY and Marian MILLER:
       Private-Begin: Private

  iii. Marjorie J. MILLER, b. Private.
  iv. Glenna F. MILLER, b. Private.

190. Mabel[11] BARR *(Mary C[10] VAN HORN, James Thompson[9], Henry[8], Isaiah[7], Henry B.[6], Henry[5], Christian Barentsen[4] VAN HOORN, Barent Christiansen[3], Christian Barentsen[2], Barent Barents[1])*[3216,3217,3218] was born 28 May 1892 in Green Twp., Indiana Cnty, PA[3219], and died Aft. 1930. She married Richard L. BOUCHER[3220,3221], son of William W. BOUCHER. He was born Abt. 1890 in PA[3222], and died Unknown.

More About Richard L. BOUCHER:
Occupation: Farmer

Children of Mabel BARR and Richard BOUCHER are:
  i.   Wayne R.[12] BOUCHER, b. Private.
  ii. Meridith E. BOUCHER, b. Private.
  iii. Samuel L. BOUCHER, b. Private.

191. Carleton Van Horn[11] BARR *(Mary C[10] VAN HORN, James Thompson[9], Henry[8], Isaiah[7], Henry B.[6], Henry[5], Christian Barentsen[4] VAN HOORN, Barent Christiansen[3], Christian Barentsen[2], Barent Barents[1])*[3223] was born 23 Nov 1893 in Green Twp., Indiana Cnty, PA[3223], and died Bef. 1920[3224]. He married Nellie M. HANCOCK[3224,3225,3226,3227] Abt. 16 Sep 1914 in Indiana Cnty, PA[3228], daughter of Richard HANCOCK and Mary MARTIN. She was born 16 Jul 1888 in Houtzdale, PA[3229,3230], and died 21 Mar 1954 in Indiana, Indiana Cnty, PA[3230].

More About Nellie M. HANCOCK:
Burial: Unknown, Greenwood Cemetery
Lived: 1949, 598 South 6th Street Indiana, PA

More About Carleton BARR and Nellie HANCOCK:
Marriage: Abt. 16 Sep 1914, Indiana Cnty, PA[3231]

Children of Carleton BARR and Nellie HANCOCK are:
404.   i.   Winifred[12] BARR, b. Private.
405.   ii. Carleton Van Horn BARR, b. Private.

192. Helen C.[11] BARR *(Mary C[10] VAN HORN, James Thompson[9], Henry[8], Isaiah[7], Henry B.[6], Henry[5], Christian Barentsen[4] VAN HOORN, Barent Christiansen[3], Christian Barentsen[2], Barent Barents[1])*[3232,3233,3234] was born 22 Oct 1896 in Green Twp., Indiana Cnty, PA[3235], and died Dec 1985 in Indiana Cnty,

PA[3236]. She married Harry Arlington ALLISON[3237,3238] 20 May 1929 in Penn Run, Cherry Hill Twp., Indiana Cnty, PA. He was born 16 Oct 1893 in Green Twp., Indiana Cnty, PA[3239], and died 03 Feb 1987 in Indiana Cnty, PA.

More About Helen C. BARR:
Occupation: School Teacher

Notes for Harry Arlington ALLISON:
    In 1930 owns his own home worth $5000 and has a radio.

More About Harry Arlington ALLISON:
Occupation: Barber

More About Harry ALLISON and Helen BARR:
Marriage: 20 May 1929, Penn Run, Cherry Hill Twp., Indiana Cnty, PA

Children of Helen BARR and Harry ALLISON are:
406.   i.   Lois Isabell[12] ALLISON, b. Private.
            ii.   Donald Harry ALLISON, b. Private.
            iii. Mary Kathryn ALLISON, b. Private.

193. George Henry[11] VAN HORN *(George H.[10], James Thompson[9], Henry[8], Isaiah[7], Henry B.[6], Henry[5], Christian Barentsen[4] VAN HOORN, Barent Christiansen[3], Christian Barentsen[2], Barent Barents[1])[3240]* was born 02 Jun 1903 in Loveland, Larimer Cnty, CO[3240], and died Unknown. He married Marie WHITFORD 20 Sep 1926 in Denver, Denver Cnty, CO. She died Unknown.

More About George Henry VAN HORN:
Occupation: Farmer, Rancher, County Collector Malheur County, CO

More About George VAN HORN and Marie WHITFORD:
Marriage: 20 Sep 1926, Denver, Denver Cnty, CO

Children of George VAN HORN and Marie WHITFORD are:
            i.   Martha[12] VAN HORN, b. Private.
            ii.   Shirley VAN HORN, b. Private.
            iii. Jeanette VAN HORN, b. Private.

194. Paul H.[11] VAN HORN *(George H.[10], James Thompson[9], Henry[8], Isaiah[7], Henry B.[6], Henry[5], Christian Barentsen[4] VAN HOORN, Barent Christiansen[3], Christian Barentsen[2], Barent Barents[1])[3240,3241,3242]* was born Abt. 1912 in Loveland, Larimer Cnty, CO[3243], and died Unknown. He married V. N. Private. She was born Private.

Notes for Paul H. VAN HORN:
    Lived with son at 2715 Carriage Drive and 225 Big Horn Drive in Estes Park, Larimer Cnty, CO

More About Paul VAN HORN and V. N.:
Private-Begin: Private

Child of Paul VAN HORN and V. N. is:
            i.   H.[12] VAN HORN, b. Private; m. Kimberly J., Private; b. Private.

More About H. VAN HORN and Kimberly J.:
Private-Begin: Private

195. Dora Myrtle[11] HOOD *(Elizabeth Francis[10] WORK, Tabitha Logan[9] VAN HORN, Henry[8], Isaiah[7], Henry B.[6], Henry[5], Christian Barentsen[4] VAN HOORN, Barent Christiansen[3], Christian Barentsen[2], Barent Barents[1])[3244,3245,3246]* was born 14 Feb 1870 in Kellysburg, Indiana Cnty, PA[3247], and died 28 Feb 1933 in Evanston, Cook Cnty, IL[3248]. She married Oliver Ortho SMITH[3249]. He was born 01 Dec 1867 in Des Moines, Polk Cnty, IA, and died 29 Mar 1916.

Notes for Dora Myrtle HOOD:
        In the 1925 Iowa Census Dora is widowed living with her widowed mother and her single daughter. She owns her home free and clear and has $5000 in insurance on the home. The home is on 36 street in Des Moines and is worth $10,000 by her estimate. She has completed 12 years of schooling and is a high school diploma holder.

More About Oliver Ortho SMITH:
Occupation: Architect

Child of Dora HOOD and Oliver SMITH is:
        i.   Edna Elizabeth[12] SMITH[3249,3250], b. 04 Dec 1893, Des Moines, Polk Cnty, IA[3250]; d. Unknown.

                Notes for Edna Elizabeth SMITH:
                Graduate of the University of Chicago; taught for 6 years in Public and 6 years in Private school; was principal of a private school in Des Moines, IA. In 1937, she went to professional decorating school in Chicago and was an interior decorator in Evanston, IL for ten years, Palo Alto, CA for 20 years. She then went with the Allied Arts guild in Menlo Park, CA.
                In 1925 Iowa Census she is 31 single and has 6 years of University or College Education.

196. Herbert Jolly[11] LYTLE *(Sarah Steele[10] WORK, Tabitha Logan[9] VAN HORN, Henry[8], Isaiah[7], Henry B.[6], Henry[5], Christian Barentsen[4] VAN HOORN, Barent Christiansen[3], Christian Barentsen[2], Barent Barents[1])[3251,3252,3253,3254,3255,3256,3257]* was born 08 Jun 1880 in Marion Center, Indiana Cnty, PA[3258], and died 14 Feb 1962 in Alemeda Cnty, CA[3259]. He married Grace J. SNYDER[3260,3261,3262] Abt. 1903, daughter of Samuel SNYDER and Sarah J.. She was born Abt. 1879 in KS[3263], and died Bet. 1920 - 1930.

Notes for Herbert Jolly LYTLE:
        In 1910 his father and mother in law are living in the family. He is a retail druggist and he and Grace have been married for 6 years and have one child Dorcas Grace.
        In 1930 he is renting in Berkley, CA for $45/month and has a radio. He has his single daughter Dorcas living with him.
        In his WWI Draft registration he is living at 514 22nd Street in Sacramento, CA and his wife is Grace J. Lytle. He is of medium build, medium Height and has blue eyes and brown hair. He works as a pharmacist.
        In his WWI I Draft registration he states he is living at 814 E. St in Eureka, Humbolt Cnty, CA and he is working for the Red Cross Pharmacy. His point of contact is his daughter Mrs. Dorcas Oswald living at 2525 Bailey Street in San Jose, CA

More About Herbert Jolly LYTLE:
Employment: Salesman Correpondence School

Lived: Sacramento, CA
Occupation: Chiropodist and Pharmacist or Drugist

More About Herbert LYTLE and Grace SNYDER:
Marriage: Abt. 1903

Child of Herbert LYTLE and Grace SNYDER is:
   i. Dorcas Grace[12] LYTLE[3264,3265,3266,3267], b. 04 Aug 1905, CO[3268]; d. 25 May 1985,
    Lodi, San Joaquin Cnty, CA[3269]; m. Oscar J. OSWALD[3270], Bef. 1936; d. Unknown.

    Notes for Dorcas Grace LYTLE:
    In 1936 living at 2525 Bailey San Jose, CA registered as a republican occupation a
    housewife. Also listed at 819 S. 12th as a housewife. Since her name is Oswald she is
    married before 1936 living with Oscar J. Oswald.
    In 1942 Dorcas and Oscar J. Oswald are living at 2525 Bailey in San Jose, California.
    He is a collector and she a housewife. Both are registered as republicans.
    According to the Work Family History Dorcas's husband was J. D. Oswald.

    More About Dorcas Grace LYTLE:
    Employment: Stenographer California Industrial Accident Commission

    More About Oscar OSWALD and Dorcas LYTLE:
    Marriage: Bef. 1936

197. MD Phillip[11] WORK *(Hubert Robert[10], Tabitha Logan[9] VAN HORN, Henry[8], Isaiah[7], Henry B.[6],*
Henry[5], Christian Barentsen[4] VAN HOORN, Barent Christiansen[3], Christian Barentsen[2], Barent
Barents[1])[3270,3271,3272] was born 20 Jun 1888 in Ft. Morgan, Morgan Cnty, CO[3273], and died 02 Jul 1952
in Las Cruces, Dona Ana Cnty, NM[3274]. He married (1) Ruth HUBBARD. She died Unknown. He
married (2) Helen Taylor TUTTLE[3274,3275] 18 Aug 1916[3276]. She was born 15 Mar 1890 in Denver,
Denver Cnty, CO[3276], and died Unknown.

Notes for MD Phillip WORK:
  He studied in Vienna in 1930 and was Professor and Head of the Department of Neurology at
the University of Colorado from 1936-1943.
  In 1930 he owns his home worth $16,000 and is a physician.

More About MD Phillip WORK:
Burial: Unknown, Arlington National Cemetery[3277]
Degree: Bet. 1909 - 1913, BS University of Pennsylvania and MD

More About Phillip WORK and Helen TUTTLE:
Marriage: 18 Aug 1916[3278]

Children of Phillip WORK and Helen TUTTLE are:
407. i. Sarah[12] WORK, b. Private.
408. ii. Laura May WORK, b. Private.
409. iii. Elizabeth WORK, b. Private.

198. Dorcas Logan[11] WORK *(Hubert Robert[10], Tabitha Logan[9] VAN HORN, Henry[8], Isaiah[7], Henry*
B.[6], Henry[5], Christian Barentsen[4] VAN HOORN, Barent Christiansen[3], Christian Barentsen[2], Barent
Barents[1])[3278,3279,3280] was born 30 Sep 1896 in Pueblo, CO[3281,3282], and died 02 Feb 1953. She

married Albert West BISSELL[3283] 29 Oct 1919, son of West BISSELL and Matilda MAC HOLD. He was born 04 Mar 1891 in Hoboken, NJ[3283], and died 1949.

Notes for Dorcas Logan WORK:
    On March 9 1936 Albert and Dorcas arrived on the Santa Maria at the Port of New Orleans and give their place of residence as 814 Monticello Street in Evanston, IL. It listed their birth dates as March 4, 1891 for Albert and Sept , 1896 for Dorcas as well as place of birth.
    On Feb. 27, 1937 Albert and Dorcas arrive again in New Orleans on the Morazan from Vera Cruz, Mexico. They live at 811 Monticello St, in Evanston, IL. Dorcas's birth date is given as 30 September 1896 in this listing.

More About Dorcas Logan WORK:
Education: Colorado College and Colorado University

Notes for Albert West BISSELL:
    In his WWI Draft Registration he is single living on Block S in Pueblo, CO. He is Assistant Superintendent of a wire mill. He is 5 feet 11 inches of medium build with brown eyes and brown hair,
    In the 1921 Pueblo Colorado City Directory Albert and Dorcas are living at 112 W. Pitkin avenue. He is a steel worker.

More About Albert West BISSELL:
Employment: Assistant Superintendent Blast Furnace at a Steel Works

More About Albert BISSELL and Dorcas WORK:
Marriage: 29 Oct 1919

Child of Dorcas WORK and Albert BISSELL is:
410.   i.   Julia Machold[12] BISSELL, b. Private.

199. Robert Van Horn[11] WORK *(Hubert Robert[10], Tabitha Logan[9] VAN HORN, Henry[8], Isaiah[7], Henry B.[6], Henry[5], Christian Barentsen[4] VAN HOORN, Barent Christiansen[3], Christian Barentsen[2], Barent Barents[1])[3284,3285,3286]* was born 23 Apr 1898 in Pueblo, CO[3287,3288], and died 23 Aug 1935 in Denver, Denver Cnty, CO. He married (1) Louise NORWOOD. She died Unknown. He married (2) Irma Mary WEICKER[3289] Jun 1924, daughter of R. V. WEICKER. She was born Abt. 1903 in CO[3289], and died Unknown.

Notes for Robert Van Horn WORK:
    In his WWI Draft registration he indicates he was born 11 April 1898. He lists his permanent address as Woodcroft Hospital in Pueblo, CO. His occupation is College which one can assume that it means he is a college student. He is tall slender and has blue eyes and brown hair.
    In 1930 living in Denver, CO on E. 25th Street in a home he owns worth $12,500 and has a radio. He and his wife have been married about 5 years and have a son that is 1 year 7 months of age.

More About Robert Van Horn WORK:
Burial: 05 Sep 1935, Arlington National Cemetery Washington, DC Section 4 Site 3026
Employment: Manager Deposits Warehouse
Military service: WWI Private in Coast Artillary

More About Robert WORK and Irma WEICKER:
Marriage: Jun 1924

Child of Robert WORK and Irma WEICKER is:

411.   i.   Hubert Van Horn[12] WORK III, b. 01 Sep 1928, Denver, Denver Cnty, CO; d. 04 Aug 2007, Denver, Denver Cnty, CO or Englewood, Arapahoe Cnty, CO.

200. Henry Kirkwood[11] VAN HORN *(Richard[10], Robert Thompson[9], Henry[8], Isaiah[7], Henry B.[6], Henry[5], Christian Barentsen[4] VAN HOORN, Barent Christiansen[3], Christian Barentsen[2], Barent Barents[1])[3290,3291,3292,3293,3294]* was born 25 Feb 1878 in Kansas City, Jackson Cnty, MO[3295], and died Aft. 1930. He married Mary Frances MCCLURE[3296,3297,3298,3299] 04 Oct 1899. She was born Aug 1878 in MO[3300], and died Aft. 1930.

More About Henry Kirkwood VAN HORN:
Occupation: Bank Clerk, Fire Insurance Agent

More About Henry VAN HORN and Mary MCCLURE:
Marriage: 04 Oct 1899

Children of Henry VAN HORN and Mary MCCLURE are:
      i.   Robert T.[12] VAN HORN[3301,3302,3303], b. 08 Aug 1900, MO[3304,3305]; d. Unknown.

            More About Robert T. VAN HORN:
            Occupation: Insurance Salesman

      ii. ? VAN HORN, b. Private.

201. William Alexander[11] BURKET *(Anna M.[10] VAN HORN, Henry A.[9], Henry[8], Isaiah[7], Henry B.[6], Henry[5], Christian Barentsen[4] VAN HOORN, Barent Christiansen[3], Christian Barentsen[2], Barent Barents[1])[3306,3307,3308,3309,3310]* was born 06 Aug 1878 in PA[3311,3312], and died Unknown. He married Elizabeth R. GROCE[3312,3313] Abt. 1900. She was born Abt. 1879 in PA[3313], and died Bet. 1918 - 1920.

Notes for William Alexander BURKET:
      In his draft registration he is tall of medium build and has hazel blue eyes with brown hair. His wife is Mrs. Elizabeth R. Burkett and he is a driller. They live in Forest Cnty, PA.
      In 1920 he is widowed and has 10 children and his sister in law age 34 single Bertha M. Groce living with the family.

More About William Alexander BURKET:
Occupation: Lumberyard Labor, Driller

More About William BURKET and Elizabeth GROCE:
Marriage: Abt. 1900

Children of William BURKET and Elizabeth GROCE are:
      i.   Wilma M.[12] BURKET[3314,3315], b. Abt. 1900, PA[3316]; d. Unknown.
      ii.   Lillian A. BURKET[3316,3317], b. Abt. 1903, PA[3318]; d. Unknown.
      iii. Harry W. BURKET[3318,3319], b. Abt. 1906, PA[3320]; d. Unknown.
      iv.   Raymond BURKET[3320,3321], b. Abt. 1908, PA[3322]; d. Unknown.
      v.   William Alexander BURKET, JR[3322,3323], b. Abt. 1910, PA[3324]; d. Unknown.
      vi.   Nellie J. BURKET[3324], b. Abt. 1911, PA[3324]; d. Unknown.
      vii. Catherine E. BURKET, b. Private.
      viii. Doyle BURKET, b. Private.
      ix.   Dale BURKET, b. Private.

x.   Bertha J. BURKET, b. Private.

202. Jay Miller[11] BURKET *(Anna M.[10] VAN HORN, Henry A.[9], Henry[8], Isaiah[7], Henry B.[6], Henry[5], Christian Barentsen[4] VAN HOORN, Barent Christiansen[3], Christian Barentsen[2], Barent Barents[1])[3325,3326,3327]* was born 21 Feb 1885 in Clarington, Forest Cnty, PA[3328], and died Unknown. He married Irene HENDERSON[3329,3330] 1909 in PA. She was born Abt. 1880 in PA[3331], and died Unknown.

Notes for Jay Miller BURKET:
His WWI I draft registration indicates he is 5'8" 166 lbs and he has gray eyes and gray hair. His closest relative is Miss Betty Burket which is likely a daughter. He works for Mayburg Chemical in Mayburg, PA.

More About Jay Miller BURKET:
Occupation: Teamster Lumber Woods

More About Jay BURKET and Irene HENDERSON:
Marriage: 1909, PA

Children of Jay BURKET and Irene HENDERSON are:
i.   Darrell C.[12] BURKET[3331,3332], b. Abt. 1902, PA[3333]; d. Unknown; Stepchild.
ii.   Harry Paul BURKET[3333,3334], b. Jan 1910, PA[3335]; d. Unknown.
iii. Elizabeth BURKET, b. Private.
iv.   James B. BURKET[3336], b. Abt. 1902, PA[3336]; d. Unknown.
v.   Fred W. BURKET[3336], b. Abt. Jul 1905, PA[3336]; d. Unknown.

203. Guy Wiseman[11] VAN HORN *(William Alexander[10], Henry Coulter[9], Alexander[8], Isaiah[7], Henry B.[6], Henry[5], Christian Barentsen[4] VAN HOORN, Barent Christiansen[3], Christian Barentsen[2], Barent Barents[1])[3337,3338,3339,3340,3341]* was born 22 Nov 1877 in PA[3342], and died Aft. 1930. He married Cora Estella WILLIAMS[3343,3344,3345,3346] Abt. 1898, daughter of William WILLIAMS and Isabell COON. She was born 26 Oct 1876 in PA[3347], and died 07 Nov 1970.

Notes for Guy Wiseman VAN HORN:
In 1917 in WWI Draft materials he is a lumberman living in Charleston, WV.
In 1920 owns his home in Charleston, WV free and clear. He is living with his wife and 3 daughters. He is employed as a lumberman.
In 1933 was a pall bearer in the funeral of Dr. J. J. Brewer. Lived at this time in Charleston, WV.

More About Guy Wiseman VAN HORN:
Occupation: Laborer, Bookeeeper Lumber Office, Bank President

More About Guy VAN HORN and Cora WILLIAMS:
Marriage: Abt. 1898

Children of Guy VAN HORN and Cora WILLIAMS are:
i.   Mildred L.[12] VAN HORN[3347,3348,3349], b. Jun 1899, PA[3350]; d. Unknown.
ii.   Inez B. VAN HORN[3351,3352], b. Abt. 1902, PA[3353]; d. Unknown.
iii. Edith L. VAN HORN[3353,3354,3355], b. Abt. 1904, PA[3356]; d. Unknown.

204. Harry Burk[11] VAN HORN *(William Alexander[10], Henry Coulter[9], Alexander[8], Isaiah[7], Henry B.[6],*

Henry[5], Christian Barentsen[4] VAN HOORN, Barent Christiansen[3], Christian Barentsen[2], Barent Barents[1])[3357,3358,3359] was born Oct 1878 in PA[3360], and died Unknown. He married Sara G.[3361,3362] Abt. 1902. She was born Abt. 1881 in OH[3363], and died Unknown.

Notes for Harry Burk VAN HORN:
    In 1900 boarding with his aunt Anna and her family.
    In 1910 living on Showers Rd in Clarion, PA married for 7 years. He and Sara have had 4 children of which 2 are living.

More About Harry Burk VAN HORN:
Employment: 1920, Carpenter
Occupation: Coal Miner

Notes for Sara G.:
    In 1910 the mother of 4 with 2 living.

More About Harry VAN HORN and Sara G.:
Marriage: Abt. 1902

Children of Harry VAN HORN and Sara G. are:
412.   i.   Minnie[12] VAN HORN, b. Abt. 1903, PA; d. Unknown.
            ii.   Jennie VAN HORN[3363,3364], b. Abt. 1905, PA[3365]; d. Unknown.
            iii. Evaline VAN HORN[3366], b. Abt. 1912, PA[3366]; d. Unknown.

                  Notes for Evaline VAN HORN:
                  In 1930 there is an Evelyn Van Horn lodging with the Gluck family. Since Hazel is found living with the older sister in 1930 and the parents are not located, it is likely that they died or separated between 1920 and 1930. Evelyn is an Usherette at a theater in Pittsburgh.

            iv.   Hazel VAN HORN, b. Private.

205. Anna C.[11] BREWER *(Minnie[10] VAN HORN, Henry A.[9], Henry[8], Isaiah[7], Henry B.[6], Henry[5], Christian Barentsen[4] VAN HOORN, Barent Christiansen[3], Christian Barentsen[2], Barent Barents[1])[3367,3368,3369]* was born Mar 1886 in PA[3370], and died Aft. 1953. She married Harley G. BENTLEY[3371] Abt. 1911[3371]. He was born Abt. 1888 in NY[3371], and died Unknown.

More About Anna C. BREWER:
Lived: Kane, PA

Notes for Harley G. BENTLEY:
    In 1930 he is the manager of an oil and gas supply company. He lives on Ash Street in Kane, PA in a home he owns worth about $5,000 and has a radio.

More About Harley BENTLEY and Anna BREWER:
Marriage: Abt. 1911[3371]

Children of Anna BREWER and Harley BENTLEY are:
            i.   Deane A.[12] BENTLEY[3371], b. Abt. 1915, PA[3371]; d. Unknown.
            ii.   Max H. BENTLEY, b. Private.

206. Clarence Wilbur[11] BROOKS *(Sarah Jane[10] VAN HORN, John Dick[9], Alexander[8], Isaiah[7], Henry*

B.[6], Henry[5], Christian Barentsen[4] VAN HOORN, Barent Christiansen[3], Christian Barentsen[2], Barent Barents[1])[3372,3373,3374,3375,3376] was born 04 Sep 1882 in Mill Run, Fayette Cnty, PA[3377,3378], and died 1958 in Mill Run, Fayette Cnty, PA. He married Mae STILLWAGON[3378,3379,3380,3381] Abt. 1906. She was born Abt. 1884 in Connelsville, Fayette Cnty, PA[3382], and died 1961 in LaPuenta, CA.

Notes for Clarence Wilbur BROOKS:
WWI Draft Registration lives as 3447 Allendale in Pittsburgh, PA. He works for West Penn Power and wife is Mae who lives at the same address. He is 5 ft 11 inches weighs 145 lbs has brown eyes and gray hair.
In 1920 rents a home on Stueben Street in Crafton, PA. He is a Real Estate Agent. His wife is Emma E. where in the WWI Draft registration and the census of 1910 she is listed as Mae. His brother Harold K. is living in the home with his 5 children.
In 1930 living on Allendale Street in Pittsburgh, PA in a home he owns worth $10000. There is a radio in the home. He is a business agent for a street railway. There are 8 children in the home. May and he have been married for 24 years.

More About Clarence Wilbur BROOKS:
Occupation: 1900, Teacher

Notes for Mae STILLWAGON:
In 1920 name is Emma E. age is about the same as Mae. If Emma is a second wife the only evidence is the gap between children.
Other records give her name as Mary K. Stillwagon, Mary Catherine Stillwagon and Mae S.

More About Clarence BROOKS and Mae STILLWAGON:
Marriage: Abt. 1906

Children of Clarence BROOKS and Mae STILLWAGON are:
	i.	Clarence Wilbur[12] BROOKS, JR[3382,3383,3384], b. Abt. 1907, PA[3385]; d. Unknown.
413.	ii.	Gretchen BROOKS, b. Abt. Jan 1910, PA; d. Unknown.
	iii.	Charles B. BROOKS[3386,3387], b. Abt. 1911, PA[3388]; d. Unknown.
	iv.	Katherine BROOKS, b. Private.
	v.	Vincent K. BROOKS[3389], b. Abt. 1915, PA[3389]; d. Unknown.
	vi.	Robert P. BROOKS, b. Private.
414.	vii.	William Lynn BROOKS, b. 26 Apr 1922, Crafton, Allegheny Cnty, PA; d. 03 Mar 1993, Terra Haute, Vigo Cnty, IN.
	viii.	Raymond BROOKS, b. Private.

207. Annie[11] VAN HORN (Henry D. Foster[10], John Dick[9], Alexander[8], Isaiah[7], Henry B.[6], Henry[5], Christian Barentsen[4] VAN HOORN, Barent Christiansen[3], Christian Barentsen[2], Barent Barents[1])[3390,3391] was born 11 Apr 1886 in Scottdale, Westmoreland Cnty, PA[3392], and died 13 Feb 1913[3393]. She married Carney Vance HARKCOM[3393,3394] Abt. 1903. He was born 01 Feb 1885 in PA[3395], and died Dec 1969 in Revenna, Portage Cnty, OH.

Notes for Carney Vance HARKCOM:
In 1910 living in Scottdale, PA on Edwin Ave. near father in law. He is an engineer in a sheet mill.

More About Carney HARKCOM and Annie VAN HORN:
Marriage: Abt. 1903

Children of Annie VAN HORN and Carney HARKCOM are:
| 415. | i. | Eugene R. HARKCOM[12] VAN HORN, b. 17 Dec 1908, Scottdale, Westmoreland |

Cnty, PA; d. 10 Mar 2007, Altoona, Blair Cnty, PA.

416.   ii.   Harold V. HARKCOM VAN HORN, b. Abt. 1906, Scottdale, Westmoreland Cnty, PA; d. Abt. 1958, PA.

208. Judson Tannehill[11] VAN HORN *(Henry D. Foster[10], John Dick[9], Alexander[8], Isaiah[7], Henry B.[6], Henry[5], Christian Barentsen[4] VAN HOORN, Barent Christiansen[3], Christian Barentsen[2], Barent Barents[1])[3396,3397,3398,3399]* was born 02 Aug 1887 in Mt. Pleasant, Westmoreland Cnty, PA[3400,3401], and died 27 May 1967 in Augusta, Richmond Cnty, GA[3402,3403]. He married Beatrice Elizabeth BARTON[3404,3405,3406] 13 Jun 1919[3406]. She was born Bet. 01 Mar 1898 - 1899 in Augusta, Richmond Cnty, GA[3407,3408,3409], and died 23 Oct 1977 in Augusta, Richmond Cnty, GA[3410,3411].

Notes for Judson Tannehill VAN HORN:
    In his WWI Draft registration he states that he lives at 614 Spring Street in Scottdale, PA. He works for American Steel and tin Plate Co of Scottdale, PA. He is single tall, medium build, blue eyes and black hair.
    In 1920 he is married and lives on Edwin Ave in Scottdale, PA. He is a renter and works in a rolling mill.
    In 1930 lives on Route 117 New Borge, PA. Works in a home he owns worth $4000 and has a radio.

More About Judson Tannehill VAN HORN:
Burial: Unknown, Augusta, GA[3411]
Occupation: Doubler Sheet Mill, Roller Helper in Rolling Mill, Laborer Sheet Mill

More About Beatrice Elizabeth BARTON:
Burial: Unknown, Augusta, GA

More About Judson VAN HORN and Beatrice BARTON:
Marriage: 13 Jun 1919[3411]

Children of Judson VAN HORN and Beatrice BARTON are:
417.   i.   Judson Tannehill[12] VAN HORN, JR, b. 12 Mar 1920, Scottdale, Westmoreland Cnty, PA; d. Aft. 2008.
418.   ii.   Eunice Matilda VAN HORN, b. 06 Apr 1922, Scottdale, Westmoreland Cnty, PA; d. 18 Dec 2006, Columbia, SC.
419.   iii. Mary Ella VAN HORN, b. 28 Feb 1925, Scottdale, Westmoreland Cnty, PA; d. 10 Jun 2005, Cherokee, NC.

209. John Dick[11] VAN HORN *(Henry D. Foster[10], John Dick[9], Alexander[8], Isaiah[7], Henry B.[6], Henry[5], Christian Barentsen[4] VAN HOORN, Barent Christiansen[3], Christian Barentsen[2], Barent Barents[1])[3412,3413,3414,3415,3416,3417]* was born 19 May 1889 in Scottdale, Westmoreland Cnty, PA[3418], and died 14 Apr 1982 in Meadville, Crawford Cnty, PA[3419]. He married Berdeen Boylan BRAYMER[3420,3421,3422] Abt. 1903 in Scottdale, Westmoreland Cnty, PA, daughter of Charles BRAYMER and Edith BOYLAN. She was born 26 Mar 1889 in Meadville, Crawford Cnty, PA[3423], and died 19 Apr 1984 in Kenmore, Erie Cnty, NY.

Notes for John Dick VAN HORN:
    In his WWI Draft Registration he states he is tall, slender with blue eyes and dark brown hair. He is a minister of the Methodist Episcopal Church in Plumville, PA. He is married.
    In his WW I I Draft registration he is 6' 2" weighs 185 lbs has blue eyes and gray hair. He is a Methodist Minister of the Pittsburgh conference He and his wife life at 729 4th Street in Beaver, PA.

John Dick Van Horn, a minister, had one brother: Judson Tannehill Van Horn and four sisters: Olive Mae, Hazel Foster, Anna Mary and Viola Virginia. He also had two adopted brothers: Gene and Harold Harkcom, sons of his sister Anna Mary Van Horn, who died when Gene and Harold were babies. Gene and Harold were adopter by his John Dick's father Henry Foster Van Horn and his wife Matilda Tannehill Van Horn.

John Dick's brother Judson Tannehill Van Horn, a steel worker, married Beatrice Elizabeth Barton and they had one boy and two girls: Judson Tannehill Van Horn, who married Margaret Alice Anderson, Unice Matilda Van Horn, who married Charles Graves, and later Peter M. Tarpley, and Mary Ella Van Horn, who married Otto William Marshall.

John Dick's sister Olive Mae Van Horn was an accomplished church organist who married Walter Edge, a railroad engineer, and they had one child, Walter Edge.

John Dick's sister Hazel Foster Van Horn married William Presley Donaldson, a grocer in Butler, PA and they had two boys and a girl: Richard Donaldson who married four times and eventually became a landscape contractor, Foster Donaldson who married and became a missionary and Virginia Donaldson who married a military lawyer.

John Dick's sister Anna Mary Van Horn married _____ Harkcom and had two boys. Gene and Harold.

John Dick's sister Viola Virginia Van Horn married William Price, a funeral director and they had a boy and a girl: William Price, Jr. who inherited the funeral business and _____.

More About John Dick VAN HORN:
Burial: Unknown, Scottdale Cemetery Westmoreland Cnty, PA
Lived: 1913, 1225 Arch Street, Pittsburgh, PA[3424]
Military service: 1st Lt US Army WW I
Occupation: Minister Methodist Church

More About John VAN HORN and Berdeen BRAYMER:
Marriage: Abt. 1903, Scottdale, Westmoreland Cnty, PA

Children of John VAN HORN and Berdeen BRAYMER are:
       i.   Chester A.[12] VAN HORN, b. Abt. 1908, PA; d. 1971.
420.   ii. John Foster VAN HORN, b. Private.

210. Viola Virginia[11] VAN HORN *(Henry D. Foster[10], John Dick[9], Alexander[8], Isaiah[7], Henry B.[6], Henry[5], Christian Barentsen[4] VAN HOORN, Barent Christiansen[3], Christian Barentsen[2], Barent Barents[1])*[3425,3426,3427,3428] was born 25 Dec 1890 in Scottdale, Westmoreland Cnty, PA[3429], and died 13 May 1973[3430]. She married William Clark PRICE[3430,3431,3432,3433] Abt. 1914[3434]. He was born 1882 in WV[3435,3436], and died 15 May 1988[3437].

Notes for William Clark PRICE:
    In 1930 he owns his home on Main Street in Meyersdale, PA worth about $15,000 and has a radio. He is a funeral director and an embalmer. His nephew Eugene R. Van Horn is living in the home.

More About William Clark PRICE:
Employment: 1930, Funeral Director and Embalming

More About William PRICE and Viola VAN HORN:
Marriage: Abt. 1914[3438]

Children of Viola VAN HORN and William PRICE are:
       i.   William Rowe[12] PRICE[3438,3439], b. 1915, PA[3440]; d. Unknown.

Notes for William Rowe PRICE:
Inherited the funeral home and became a funeral director.

    ii.   ? PRICE, b. Private.

211. Hazel Foster[11] VAN HORN *(Henry D. Foster[10], John Dick[9], Alexander[8], Isaiah[7], Henry B.[6], Henry[5], Christian Barentsen[4] VAN HOORN, Barent Christiansen[3], Christian Barentsen[2], Barent Barents[1])[3441,3442,3443]* was born 15 Jul 1892 in Scottdale, Westmoreland Cnty, PA[3444], and died 11 Nov 1980[3445]. She married William Presley DONALDSON[3445,3446,3447,3448] 21 Sep 1917, son of William DONALDSON and Agnes SMITH. He was born 16 Apr 1883 in Armstrong Cnty, PA[3449], and died 09 Dec 1956[3449].

Notes for William Presley DONALDSON:
    In 1918 he registers for the civilian draft. He lives at 804 Center in Butler and is self employed as a grocer at 806 Center in butler, PA. His wife is Hazel.
    In 1920 lives at 804 Center next door to his mother and father at 806 Center in Butler, PA. He lists his occupation as a grocery salesman. He owns his house free and clear.
    In 1930 he is living at 804 Center in Butler, PA with his wife Hazel F. and 3 children. Living next door at 806 is his sister Bertha and his mother. He owns his place worth $5500 and has a radio. He is a grocer.
    In 1942 he registers for the civilian draft. He is a self employed grocer at 806 Center Avenue in Butler, Butler Cnty, PA. His telephone is 3757. He lives with his wife Hazel Foster at 804 center Avenue in Butler, PA. He is 5 ft 7 inches tall and weighs 210 lbs. He has brown eyes and hair and a light complexion.

More About William Presley DONALDSON:
Occupation: Groceryman

More About William DONALDSON and Hazel VAN HORN:
Marriage: 21 Sep 1917

Children of Hazel VAN HORN and William DONALDSON are:
    i.   Richard P.[12] DONALDSON, b. Private.
    ii.   Foster V. DONALDSON, b. Private.
    iii.   Virginia M. DONALDSON, b. Private.

212. Olive Mae[11] VAN HORN *(Henry D. Foster[10], John Dick[9], Alexander[8], Isaiah[7], Henry B.[6], Henry[5], Christian Barentsen[4] VAN HOORN, Barent Christiansen[3], Christian Barentsen[2], Barent Barents[1])[3450,3451,3452,3453]* was born 14 Jul 1894 in Scottdale, Westmoreland Cnty, PA[3454], and died 12 Jul 1981 in Greensburg, Westmoreland Cnty, PA[3455]. She married Walter Malcolm EDGE[3455,3456,3457] Abt. 1923[3458], son of Samuel EDGE and Lilly. He was born 02 May 1892 in Lancashire, England[3458,3459], and died Aug 1972 in Pittsburgh, Allegheny Cnty, PA[3460].

Notes for Olive Mae VAN HORN:
    An accomplished church organist.

Notes for Walter Malcolm EDGE:
    In 1920 he is single lodging in Scottdale, PA and working as a railroad fireman.
    In 1930 living on Walnut Avenue in Scottdale, PA. He is a railroad engineer. He and his family live in a rented home that rents for $35/month and they have a radio in the home.

In April 1942 Walter files his draft registration. He is living at 124 Underwood in Greensburg, Westmoreland Cnty, PA. He gives his telephone number as 4171R. He works for Pennsylvania Railroad in Pitcairn, PA. His wife is Olive Mae at the same address. He is 5 ft 7 1/8 inches of height weighs 140 lbs, has a ruddy complexion, blue eyes and brown hair balding. He has a scar on the back of the middle finger of the right hand.

More About Walter Malcolm EDGE:
Employment: Railroad Engineer

More About Walter EDGE and Olive VAN HORN:
Marriage: Abt. 1923[3461]

Child of Olive VAN HORN and Walter EDGE is:
421.   i.   Walter M.[12] EDGE, JR, b. 17 Jun 1925, PA; d. 25 Aug 1999, Greensboro, Guillford Cnty, NC.

213. James Van Horn[11] BALLANTYNE *(Caroline E.[10] VAN HORN, James Wherry[9], Alexander[8], Isaiah[7], Henry B.[6], Henry[5], Christian Barentsen[4] VAN HOORN, Barent Christiansen[3], Christian Barentsen[2], Barent Barents[1])[3462,3463]* was born 13 Oct 1881 in Derry, Westmoreland Cnty, PA[3464,3465], and died 07 Jan 1948 in Edgewood, Allegheny Cnty, PA. He married Lida Carrie RIGG[3466] 13 Oct 1909 in Derry, Westmoreland Cnty, PA, daughter of John RIGG and Ida WEAVER. She was born 06 Aug 1880 in Stonerville, Westmoreland Cnty, PA[3466], and died Unknown.

Notes for James Van Horn BALLANTYNE:
    In the 1900 Census James V is also found in Meadville, Crawford Cnty, PA as a boarder and a student as well as listed with his parents in Derry, PA.
    In his WWI draft registration he states he lives at 820 Wood Street in Wilkinsburg, PA. His occupation is as a Physician. His wife is Lida Rigg Ballantyne and she lives at the same address. His office is in his home.
    In his WWI I draft registration he states he lives at 429 Locust in Edgewood, Allegheny Cnty, PA with his wife Lida Rigg Ballantyne at the dame address. His telephone number is CH0184. He was born in Derry, PA and is self employed working at 901 Wood St Wilkinsburg, PA. He is 5'9" weighs 190# has gray hair and blue eyes with a light complexion.

More About James Van Horn BALLANTYNE:
Burial: 1948, Woodlawn Cemetery, Wilkinsburg, Allegheny Cnty, PA
Occupation: 1930, Physcian

More About James BALLANTYNE and Lida RIGG:
Marriage: 13 Oct 1909, Derry, Westmoreland Cnty, PA
Marriage Place: South Avenue Methodist Church, Derry, PA

Children of James BALLANTYNE and Lida RIGG are:
422.   i.   Dorothy Virginia[12] BALLANTYNE, b. 10 Aug 1910, PA; d. Unknown.
423.   ii.   John Edwin BALLANTYNE, b. 03 Oct 1912, Derry, Westmoreland Cnty, PA; d. 07 Nov 2002, Youngstown, Mahoning Cnty, OH.
424.   iii.   James Van Horn BALLANTYNE, JR, b. 24 Nov 1914, PA; d. 28 Dec 1999, Pittsburgh, Allegheny Cnty, PA.
425.   iv.   Carl Rigg BALLANTYNE, b. 10 Mar 1918, PA; d. 17 Aug 1993, St. Petersburg, Pinnelas Cnty, FL.

214. John Wesley[11] BALLANTYNE *(Caroline E.[10] VAN HORN, James Wherry[9], Alexander[8], Isaiah[7],*

Henry B.[6], Henry[5], Christian Barentsen[4] VAN HOORN, Barent Christiansen[3], Christian Barentsen[2], Barent Barents[1])[3467,3468,3469] was born 21 Jul 1885 in Derry, Westmoreland Cnty, PA[3470,3471], and died Unknown. He married Lattie Mae[3472,3473] Abt. 1908. She was born Abt. 1887 in PA[3474], and died Unknown.

Notes for John Wesley BALLANTYNE:
    In 1910 living on Chestnut Street in Derry, PA. Working as a roofer and plumber.
    In his WWI draft registration he is short, of slender build with grey eyes and black hair. He is a plumber and his wife is Lattie Mae. He lives on N. Chestnut Street in Derry, PA.
    In 1930 he owns his home on 3rd Street in Derry, PA worth $8000 and has a radio. He operates as a plumber for the Ballantyne company.

More About John BALLANTYNE and Lattie Mae:
Marriage: Abt. 1908

Children of John BALLANTYNE and Lattie Mae are:
    i.   Phyllis M.[12] BALLANTYNE[3474,3475], b. Aug 1908, Westmoreland Cnty, PA[3476]; d. Unknown.
    ii.   James C. BALLANTYNE[3477], b. 07 Sep 1912, PA[3477]; d. 30 Jun 1993, St. Petersburg, Pinellas Cnty, FL.

        Notes for James C. BALLANTYNE:
        Enlistment Date: 14 Feb 1942 Enlistment State: Maryland Enlistment City: Fort George G Meade Branch: Branch Immaterial - Warrant Officers, USA Branch Code: Branch Immaterial - Warrant Officers, USA Grade: Private Grade Code: Private Term of Enlistment: Enlistment for the duration of the War or other emergency, plus six months, subject to the discretion of the President or otherwise according to law Component: Selectees (Enlisted Men) Source: Civil Life Education: 4 years of college Civil Occupation: Addressing-Embossing Machine Operator or Clerk, General Marital Status: Single, without dependents Height: 69 Weight: 152

215. James Donald[11] ASHCOM *(Margaret Mary[10] VAN HORN, James Wherry[9], Alexander[8], Isaiah[7], Henry B.[6], Henry[5], Christian Barentsen[4] VAN HOORN, Barent Christiansen[3], Christian Barentsen[2], Barent Barents[1])[3478,3479,3480,3481]* was born 16 Apr 1890 in Conemaugh, Cambria Cnty, PA[3482], and died 03 Mar 1968 in Johnstown, Cambria Cnty, PA. He married Nana Pearl COGLEY[3483,3484] 1913[3485], daughter of John COGLEY and Mary ROWE. She was born 20 Apr 1890 in Dayton, Armstrong Cnty, PA[3486], and died 24 Dec 1967 in New Florence, Westmoreland Cnty, PA.

Notes for James Donald ASHCOM:
    In his 1917 WWI draft registration he lives on Lowry Street in Pittsburgh, PA. He works for the Pennsylvania Railroad. He gives his date and place of birth. He has a wife and 2 children. He says he has brown eyes and brown hair. Nana must have been pregnant with the 3rd child as the registration was 5 June 1917 and May was born in June of 1917.
    In his 1942 WWI I draft registration he gives his birth date and place and his wife's name. He works for High Ridge Water company of Philadelphia, PA in New Florence, PA where he lives. He is 5 ft 8 inches tall and weighs 132 lbs. He has gray eyes, black hair and ruddy complexion.
    In 1930 living on Ninth Street in New Florence, PA in a home he owns worth $1500 and has a radio. His father is also living on Ninth Street in New Florence in 1930.

More About James Donald ASHCOM:
Occupation: Auto Mechanic, Derrick Engineer Railroad

More About James ASHCOM and Nana COGLEY:
Marriage: 1913[3487]

Children of James ASHCOM and Nana COGLEY are:
426.   i.   Frank Martin[12] ASHCOM, b. Abt. 1914, PA; d. Unknown.
      ii.   Thelma Imogene ASHCOM[3488,3489], b. Abt. Dec 1915, PA[3490]; d. Abt. 2003, Akron, Summit Cnty, OH.
427.   iii. Mary Elizabeth ASHCOM, b. 24 Jun 1917, Pittsburgh, Allegheny Cny, PA; d. 24 Aug 2002, Ligonier, Westmoreland Cnty, PA.
      iv. James Donald ASHCOM, JR, b. Private.

216. John Raymond[11] ASHCOM *(Margaret Mary[10] VAN HORN, James Wherry[9], Alexander[8], Isaiah[7], Henry B.[6], Henry[5], Christian Barentsen[4] VAN HOORN, Barent Christiansen[3], Christian Barentsen[2], Barent Barents[1])*[3491,3492,3493] was born 12 Oct 1893 in Huff, Indiana Cnty, PA[3494], and died 14 Jul 1965 in PA[3495]. He married (1) Beulah Vern SHAUL[3496], daughter of Edward SHAUL and Mary PETERS. She was born 29 May 1892, and died Unknown. He married (2) Sylvia M.[3497] Abt. 1914. She was born 1892 in OH[3497], and died Unknown.

Notes for John Raymond ASHCOM:
    In his WWI I registration he is 5ft 10inches has brown eyes and brown hair and has a ruddy complexion. He works for Hollstein Drug Store and lists Mrs. Edward Pardoe of South Fork, PA as one who would always know his address.
    Census shows wife as Sylvia but other records gives name as Buelah.

More About John Raymond ASHCOM:
Lived: 1917, 1506 Wood Street, Wilkinsburg, PA
Occupation: Druggist, Drug Store Proprieter

More About Beulah Vern SHAUL:
Lived: Manorville, PA

More About Sylvia M.:
Occupation: 1930, Pharmicist

More About John ASHCOM and Sylvia M.:
Marriage: Abt. 1914

Children of John ASHCOM and Sylvia M. are:
      i.   Jane S.[12] ASHCOM, b. Private.
      ii.   John Raymond ASHCOM, JR[3497], b. 03 May 1924, Pittsburgh, Allegheny Cnty, PA[3497]; d. 08 Feb 2000, Biloxi, Harrison Cnty, MS.

         More About John Raymond ASHCOM, JR:
         Burial: Unknown, Biloxi National Cemetery Section B Site 273 Biloxi, MS
         Military service: 17 Nov 1947, LCDR US NAVY KOREA

217. Emmett W.[11] CUMMINGS *(Alice Roselia[10] VAN HORN, Henry Coulter[9], Alexander[8], Isaiah[7], Henry B.[6], Henry[5], Christian Barentsen[4] VAN HOORN, Barent Christiansen[3], Christian Barentsen[2], Barent Barents[1])*[3498,3499,3500,3501,3502,3503] was born Feb 1868 in IA[3504], and died Aft. 1920. He married Clara A. DAHL[3505,3506,3507] Abt. 1893[3508], daughter of Hahns DAHL and Jennie. She was born May 1876 in MN*3508*, and died Bef. 1920.

Notes for Emmett W. CUMMINGS:
    In 1920 living with daughter Aura and her family in SD. He is widowed. Working as a common laborer.

More About Emmett W. CUMMINGS:
Occupation: Farmer

Notes for Clara A. DAHL:
    Mother of 5 in 1910 3 living and in the home.

More About Emmett CUMMINGS and Clara DAHL:
Marriage: Abt. 1893*3508*

Children of Emmett CUMMINGS and Clara DAHL are:
      i.   Martin Harry[12] CUMMINGS*3508,3509*, b. 14 Jan 1899, SD*3510,3511*; d. Unknown.

            Notes for Martin Harry CUMMINGS:
            In 1930 he is living with John Moen and his wife. He is a farm laborer.

     ii.   Ruth B. CUMMINGS*3512*, b. Abt. 1904, SD*3512*; d. Unknown.
    iii.   Rhoda A. CUMMINGS*3512*, b. Abt. 1907, SD*3512*; d. Unknown.

218. Thomas Patrick[11] CUMMINGS *(Alice Roselia[10] VAN HORN, Henry Coulter[9], Alexander[8], Isaiah[7], Henry B.[6], Henry[5], Christian Barentsen[4] VAN HOORN, Barent Christiansen[3], Christian Barentsen[2], Barent Barents[1])*3513,3514,3515,3516,3517* was born Bet. 14 Aug 1872 - 1874 in IA*3518,3519*, and died Bet. 1930 - 1940 in Koochiching Cnty, MN. He married Margaret KELLY 1896. She died Unknown.

Notes for Thomas Patrick CUMMINGS:
    In 1920 Thomas is single and living alone on a farm he owns with a mortgage. He is living in Murphy, Koochiching Cnty, MN
    In 1930 he is living in the same area in Section 36 and he owns his farm, is single and living alone.

More About Thomas CUMMINGS and Margaret KELLY:
Marriage: 1896

Child of Thomas CUMMINGS and Margaret KELLY is:
      i.   Alice Irene[12] CUMMINGS, d. Unknown.

219. Charles[11] CUMMINGS *(Alice Roselia[10] VAN HORN, Henry Coulter[9], Alexander[8], Isaiah[7], Henry B.[6], Henry[5], Christian Barentsen[4] VAN HOORN, Barent Christiansen[3], Christian Barentsen[2], Barent Barents[1])*3520,3521,3522,3523,3524* was born 01 May 1879 in Forest City, Winnebago Cnty, IA*3525*, and died Unknown. He married Exenia M. WHITE*3526,3527,3528,3529* 26 Mar 1903, daughter of Edward WHITE and Martha GAST. She was born Jul 1879 in Farmersburg, Clayton Cnty, IA*3530*, and died Unknown.

Notes for Charles CUMMINGS:
    In 1900, 1910 and 1920 Charles is a farmer and in 1930 he is a carpenter and lives in a rented home for $32/month and has a radio.

Isaiah Van Horn Pioneer of Indiana County, Pennsylvania

CUMMINGS
"Past and Present in Allamakee County", by Ellery M. Hancock. 2 vols. Chicago: S. J. Clarke Pub. Co., 1913.

There is no one in Allamakee county who has more truly earned the title of self-made man than Charles Cummings, a prosperous farmer owning one hundred and seventy-four acres in Franklin township and a carpenter by trade, which occupation he followed in earlier years for some time with gratifying success. He was born at Forest City, Iowa, May 1, 1879, and is a son of Thomas and Alice (Van Horn) Cummings, the father a native of Ireland, where he was born in County Meath, September 10, 1832, and the mother of Johnstown, Pennsylvania, where her birth occurred March 21, 1848. Both have passed away, the father's death occurring November 1, 1905, and that of the mother June 17, 1911. The father in early life followed the occupation of a sailor on the Great Lakes and on the Mississippi river. He had come to this country with his father when a boy of but ten years of age, their first location being New Jersey. Later they came to Allamakee county, where Thomas Cummings subsequently married and became a landholder. Still later he went to western Minnesota, there engaging successfully in farming for twenty years, at the end of which period he returned to Franklin township in 1889. Here he settled upon a farm upon which he continued until his death, the mother also remaining there until she passed away. The father was ever interested in the welfare of his locality and prominent and influential with his fellow citizens, although he never aspired to public office.

Charles Cummings was the sixth of a family of seven children. He attended school at Walnut Grove in Monona township, Clayton county, and remained with his mother until 1903, when he moved to Monona, having previously learned the carpenter's trade. He worked at that occupation there for three years and then rented his mother's farm for seven years. In 19?? he bought the farm upon which he now resides. It comprises one hundred and seventy-four acres of fertile land, devoted to general farming and stock-raising. His buildings are kept in good repair and his land brings him rich harvests. He is modern and progressive and follows the latest methods, having installed up-to-date machinery and equipment upon his place. Mr. Cummings is also a stockholder in the Farmers Cooperative Creamery at Monona and in the Farmers Commission Company of that place, both of which organizations were founded in order to facilitate a more profitable disposal of farm products.

On March 26, 1903, Mr. Cummings was married to Miss Exa White, a native of Farmersburg, Clayton county, where she was born July 27, 1879, a daughter of Edward and Martha (Gast) White. The father was born in New Jersey, December 28, 1843, and died August 9, 1891, and the mother was a native of Indiana, her day of birth being August 2, 1841, and her death occurring April 30, 1913. The father came with his parents to Iowa, where they made settlement near Farmersburg, In Clayton county. There he grew to manhood, learning the carpenter's trade ,which he followed all his life. He died in that vicinity and the mother subsequently moved to Monona, where she made her home until her demise. Mrs. Cummings was the sixth in their family of seven children. Mr. and Mrs. Cummings have become the parents of two children: Evelyn Maxine, born May 15, 1904; and Thomas Edward, born February 7, 1906.

Politically Mr. Cummings is a democrat, taking an intelligent interest in all matters that affect the government. He has never aspired to official honors, however, preferring to give his support to worthy public measures as a private citizen. He is a member of the Modern Brotherhood of America but has no other fraternal associations. Such prosperity as has come to him is well merited, as it is but the outcome of intelligently applied efforts and what he has achieved is not only a source of satisfaction to him, but as part of the agricultural development which has taken place in Allamakee county, is a factor in the growth and progress that makes up this rich district in the middle west.

More About Charles CUMMINGS:
Fraternal Organization: Modern Brotherhood of America
Politics: Democrat

More About Charles CUMMINGS and Exenia WHITE:

Marriage: 26 Mar 1903

Children of Charles CUMMINGS and Exenia WHITE are:
- i. Evelyn Maxine[12] CUMMINGS[3530,3531], b. 15 May 1904, IA[3532]; d. Unknown.
- ii. Thomas E. CUMMINGS[3532,3533], b. 07 Feb 1906, IA[3534]; d. Unknown.

220. John A.[11] BOWSER *(Mary Agnes[10] VAN HORN, Henry Coulter[9], Alexander[8], Isaiah[7], Henry B.[6], Henry[5], Christian Barentsen[4] VAN HOORN, Barent Christiansen[3], Christian Barentsen[2], Barent Barents[1])[3535,3536,3537]* was born 07 Aug 1877 in PA[3538], and died 10 Feb 1951 in Dickey Cnty, ND[3539]. He married Sarah Viola TRAVER[3540,3541,3542] Abt. 1898. She was born 24 Mar 1871 in Deer Creek, MN[3543], and died 10 Mar 1938 in Milnor, Sargent Cnty, ND[3544].

Notes for John A. BOWSER:
   Owns his home worth $1500 and has a radio. He is working as a janitor for a Coach House.
   BLM Land listing in Sargent Cnty, ND BOWSER JOHN A 05 131 N 055 W 02 160
251101 PA 11727 12/27/1905

More About John A. BOWSER:
Burial: 1951, Forman Cemetery, Forman, Sargent Cnty, ND
Employment: 1920, Farm Manager

Notes for Sarah Viola TRAVER:
   BOWSER, VIOLA TRAVER
   Mrs. John Bowser of Forman Dies.
   Mrs. John Bowser, age 67, passed away at her home in Forman Friday evening following a paralytic stroke. Funeral services were conducted from the Congregational church Monday afternoon and burial made in the Forman cemetery. Out of town mourners present at the funeral were James Traver and Annie Traver, brother and sister of the deceased, both of Frederick, Oklahoma, and Mary Siring Staff, a sister-in-law, of Baker , Mont.
   Viola Traver was born in Deer Creek, Minn., in 1871 and at the age of 16 years came with her parents to Milnor, N. Dak., where she attended school, on May 25th, 1897 she was united in marriage to John Bowser to which union four children were born, namely: Roy, Lillie and Frank and a deceased son, Ralph. She has lived continuously in Sargent county since coming to the state and for many years has resided in Forman.
   Besides her husband and three children she leaves many other relatives and fiends to mourn her passing.
   Source: Sargent County Teller, March 10, 1938
   Submitted by Jerry McQuay Pierre, SD (Feb 2006) csk

More About Sarah Viola TRAVER:
Burial: Unknown, Forman Cemetery, Forman, Sargent Cnty, ND

More About John BOWSER and Sarah TRAVER:
Marriage: Abt. 1898

Children of John BOWSER and Sarah TRAVER are:
- i. Roy H.[12] BOWSER[3545], b. Abt. 1899, Sargent Cnty, ND[3545]; d. Aft. 1938.
- ii. Ralph R. BOWSER[3546], b. 29 Nov 1900, Sargent Cnty, ND[3546,3547]; d. 10 Mar 1929, Sargent Cnty, ND[3547].
- iii. Lillie V. BOWSER[3548,3549], b. Abt. 1907, Sargent Cnty, ND[3550]; d. Aft. 1938; m. ROWSE; d. Unknown.

iv.   Frank A. BOWSER[3550,3551], b. Abt. 1910, Sargent Cnty, ND[3552]; d. Aft. 1938.

221. Henry Coulter[11] VAN HORN *(Samuel Cornelius[10], Henry Coulter[9], Alexander[8], Isaiah[7], Henry B.[6], Henry[5], Christian Barentsen[4] VAN HOORN, Barent Christiansen[3], Christian Barentsen[2], Barent Barents[1])*[3553,3554,3555,3556,3557] was born Bet. 07 Sep 1884 - 1885 in Warren, Waynesville Cnty, OH[3558,3559], and died 27 Jul 1960 in Dalhart, Dallam Cnty, TX[3560]. He married Ethel Mae[3561] 1921 in Roy, NM. She was born 20 May 1902 in Des Moines, Polk Cnty, IA[3561], and died 08 Oct 1973 in Dalhart, Dallam Cnty, TX[3562,3563].

Notes for Henry Coulter VAN HORN:
    17 April 1907 the Indiana Progress(Indiana, PA) reports that Coulter Van Horn was in the play "Merchant of Venice" playing the part of Portia. The play was in Seward before a large audience.
    26 August 1920 Indiana Weekly Messenger (Indiana, PA) H. C. Van Horn to Alphonse Cunningham 2 lots in East Wheatfield $50.
    In 1930 Harry, wife Ethel and son Harry, Jr. are living on East 4th Street in a rented home. They pay $15/month rent. Harry is a yard man in a tile factory. Prior to moving to Dalhart and working for West Texas Utilities Harry operated a General Store at Roy, New Mexico.

More About Henry Coulter VAN HORN:
Burial: 29 Jul 1960, Memorial Park Cemetery
Lived: 209 E. 4th St. Box 1365 Dalhart, TX
Occupation: West Texas Utilities and SW Public Servic
Veteran: WW I

More About Ethel Mae:
Lived: 209 E. 4th St, Dalhart, TX

More About Henry VAN HORN and Ethel Mae:
Marriage: 1921, Roy, NM

Child of Henry VAN HORN and Ethel Mae is:
    i.   Henry Coulter[12] VAN HORN, JR, b. Private.

222. Leafy Fern[11] VAN HORN *(Samuel Cornelius[10], Henry Coulter[9], Alexander[8], Isaiah[7], Henry B.[6], Henry[5], Christian Barentsen[4] VAN HOORN, Barent Christiansen[3], Christian Barentsen[2], Barent Barents[1])*[3564,3565,3566,3567,3568] was born Bet. 17 Dec 1885 - 1886 in Bettsville, Liberty Twp., Seneca Cnty, OH[3569,3570], and died 18 Nov 1969 in Dayton, Montgomery Cnty, OH. She married Davis Macy WOLF[3571] 21 Dec 1910 in Dalhart, TX, son of John WOLF and Anna MACY. He was born 02 May 1886 in Dayton, Montgomery Cnty, OH[3572,3573], and died 14 Dec 1973 in Walters, Cotton Cnty, OK[3574,3575,3576,3577].

Notes for Leafy Fern VAN HORN:
    Seneca County Ohio birth records, Probate court Book 3 page 227 Leafie E VanHorn Born Dec 17, 1885 in Liberty Twp., Seneca Cnty, OH. Father: Samuel C VanHorn Mother: Emma E Hummel
    1 August 1900 Indiana Progress(Indiana, PA) Leafy and Nellie spend Saturday in Armagh.
    29 March 1905 Indiana Progress(Indiana, PA) reported that Misses Laura and Cordill Tomb of Armagh were the guests of Leafie Van Horn on Saturday and the Sabbath.
    28 Nov. 1906 Indiana Progress(Indiana, PA) reports that Leafy and Nellie spent the Sabbath at Seward and that Nellie Van Horn their aunt and mother was in Harrisburg seeing the Capitol.
    27 November 1907 the Indiana Progress(Indiana, PA) reports that Leafy Van Horn of East

Wheatfield will spend a month in Pittsburgh with friends and from there will go to Fremont, OH for the winter.

2 Nov 1908 the Indiana Evening Gazette reports that Leafy Van Horn of West Wheatfield Twp. has spent the day in town. (It is assumed that this means Indiana, PA)

11 November 1908 the Indiana Weekly Messenger (Indiana, PA) reports the first and final account of Hugh Mack guardian of Leafy Van Horn minor child of Mrs. S. C. Van Horn, late of Xenia, OH.

More About Leafy Fern VAN HORN:
Burial: 21 Nov 1969, Miami Valley Memorial Gardens, Centerville,OH
Social Security Number: 288-07-4824

More About Davis Macy WOLF:
Burial: Unknown, Miami Valley Memorial Gardens, Centerville,OH[3578]
Social Security Number: 302-07-3970

More About Davis WOLF and Leafy VAN HORN:
Marriage: 21 Dec 1910, Dalhart, TX
Marriage Place: Home of Parents Mr. and Mrs. S. C. Van Horn

Children of Leafy VAN HORN and Davis WOLF are:
428.   i.   Emma Elizabeth[12] WOLF, b. 25 Sep 1911, Dalhart, Dallam Cnty, TX; d. 13 May 1982, Murphy, NC.
429.   ii.   Marianna WOLF, b. Bet. 08 Feb 1916 - 1917, Dayton, Montgomery Cnty, OH; d. 13 Feb 1974, Dayton, Montgomery Cnty, OH.
430.   iii. Avis Ruth WOLF, b. 21 Sep 1919, Dayton, Montgomery Cnty, OH; d. 04 Oct 1980, Rolla, Phelps Cnty, MO.
431.   iv.   Thelma Louise WOLF, b. 24 Sep 1921, Dayton, Montgomery Cnty, OH; d. 14 Mar 2006, Dayton, Montgomery Cnty, OH.

223. Nellie Vidella[11] VAN HORN *(Samuel Cornelius[10], Henry Coulter[9], Alexander[8], Isaiah[7], Henry B.[6], Henry[5], Christian Barentsen[4] VAN HOORN, Barent Christiansen[3], Christian Barentsen[2], Barent Barents[1])*[3579,3580,3581,3582,3583] was born Nov 1893 in OH[3584], and died Unknown. She married James Overton SMITH[3585,3586,3587,3588,3589,3590] Jan 1915[3591], son of James SMITH and Matilda. He was born 29 May 1893 in Clinton, Vermillion Cnty, IN[3592,3593], and died Unknown.

Notes for Nellie Vidella VAN HORN:
Notice that Jennie named her daughter after her sister Nellie who was 1 year older than Jennie.
According to Samuel C. Van Horns obituary in the Indiana Progress of Indiana, PA Nellie and James live in Guymon, OK in 1937.

More About Nellie Vidella VAN HORN:
Lived: 1937 Guymon, OK later in Bloomingdale, IN

Notes for James Overton SMITH:
In 1910 the Smith family is living a few farms or ranches from the Van Horn family in Dallam Cnty, TX.
In 1920 living on Omaha Street in Dalhart, TX in a home he owns free and clear.
June 5, 1917 in his WWI Draft Registration he states he has only one arm having lost the other. He was living in Roy, Mora Cnty, NM. He is medium build and medium height with brown hair and eyes. He is married on this date to Nellie.

More About James Overton SMITH:
Occupation: Farmer

More About James SMITH and Nellie VAN HORN:
Marriage: Jan 1915*3594*

Children of Nellie VAN HORN and James SMITH are:
     i.   ?[12] SMITH, b. Abt. Dec 1917, Dalhart, Dallam Cnty, TX; d. Abt. Aug 1919, Dalhart.
          Dallam Cnty, TX*3595*.
    ii.   Doris SMITH, b. Private; m. ? MANNING, Private; b. Private.

        More About ? MANNING and Doris SMITH:
        Private-Begin: Private

   iii. James Overton SMITH, JR, b. Private.

224. Charles[11] VAN HORN *(Hubert Earl[10], Henry Coulter[9], Alexander[8], Isaiah[7], Henry B.[6], Henry[5],
Christian Barentsen[4] VAN HOORN, Barent Christiansen[3], Christian Barentsen[2], Barent Barents[1])*3596,3597*
was born Abt. 1901 in PA*3598*, and died Unknown. He married Argie CONCETTA*3599* Abt. 1921.
She was born Abt. 1902 in Italy*3599*, and died Unknown.

Notes for Charles VAN HORN:
    Concetta Genovese age 11 born PA and a Neice is living in the home.

More About Charles VAN HORN:
Occupation: Salesman Coffee House

More About Charles VAN HORN and Argie CONCETTA:
Marriage: Abt. 1921

Children of Charles VAN HORN and Argie CONCETTA are:
     i.   Marie[12] VAN HORN, b. Private.
432.   ii.   Hubert VAN HORN, b. 09 May 1925, PA; d. 16 Nov 2002, Bradenville,
          Westmoreland, PA.
   iii. Charles VAN HORN, JR, b. Private.

225. Mary Gladys[11] VAN HORN *(Frank[10], William[9], Alexander[8], Isaiah[7], Henry B.[6], Henry[5], Christian
Barentsen[4] VAN HOORN, Barent Christiansen[3], Christian Barentsen[2], Barent Barents[1])* was born 30 Apr
1910 in Buffalo, Harding Cnty, SD, and died 15 Aug 1985 in Bozeman, MT. She married Charles W.
MELANEY 07 Mar 1934 in Buffalo, Harding Cnty, SD. He was born 1909, and died 1981.

More About Charles MELANEY and Mary VAN HORN:
Marriage: 07 Mar 1934, Buffalo, Harding Cnty, SD

Children of Mary VAN HORN and Charles MELANEY are:
     i.   Charles[12] MELANEY, b. Private.
    ii.   Jone MELANEY, b. Private.
   iii. ? MELANEY, b. Private.

226. Joseph M.[11] COLLINS *(Jane[10] MCELHOES, Isaiah[9], Jane[8] VAN HORN, Isaiah[7], Henry B.[6],
Henry[5], Christian Barentsen[4] VAN HOORN, Barent Christiansen[3], Christian Barentsen[2], Barent*

Barents[1])[3600,3601] was born Feb 1882 in PA*[3602]*, and died Unknown. He married ? Abt. 1906. She died Abt. 1908.

More About Joseph COLLINS and ?:
Marriage: Abt. 1906

Child of Joseph COLLINS and ? is:
      i.   Merl F.[12] COLLINS*[3603]*, b. Feb 1908, PA*[3603]*; d. Unknown.

227. Gertrude[11] MCELHOES *(John Kinter[10], Isaiah[9], Jane[8] VAN HORN, Isaiah[7], Henry B.[6], Henry[5], Christian Barentsen[4] VAN HOORN, Barent Christiansen[3], Christian Barentsen[2], Barent Barents[1])[3604,3605,3606]* was born 24 Mar 1869 in Indiana Cnty, PA*[3607]*, and died 26 Mar 1907 in West Hickory, PA. She married William Gillespie MORROW, MD*[3608,3609]* 24 Dec 1896, son of John MORROW and Rebecca MCFARLAND. He was born 20 Dec 1868 in Armstrong Cnty, PA*[3610]*, and died 01 Feb 1932 in Warren, PA.

Notes for Gertrude MCELHOES:
    There is a relatively good chance that Mary and William are children of William's second marriage.
    In 1895 living with her brother Frank in MN and working as a public school teacher.

Notes for William Gillespie MORROW, MD:
    In 1910 William is widowed his children Margaret and John K. as well as his sister Martha Morrow are of the home. He is a practicing general physician.
    In 1920 William is remarried and has two children by his new wife. Margaret is no longer in the family but John K is of the home.

More About William Gillespie MORROW, MD:
Occupation: Physician General Practice

More About William MORROW and Gertrude MCELHOES:
Marriage: 24 Dec 1896

Children of Gertrude MCELHOES and William MORROW are:
433.   i.   Margaret[12] MORROW, b. 06 Jun 1899, PA; d. Unknown.
434.   ii. John K. McElhoes MORROW, b. Abt. 1902, PA; d. Aft. 1942.
       iii. Dorothy MORROW, b. Bet. 12 Feb - 23 Mar 1905, PA; d. Bet. 29 Aug - 01 Sep 1906, Green Twp., Indiana Cnty, PA.

          More About Dorothy MORROW:
          Burial: Unknown, Washington Church Cemetery, Rayne Twp., Indiana Cnty, PA

228. Frank Thomas[11] MCELHOES *(John Kinter[10], Isaiah[9], Jane[8] VAN HORN, Isaiah[7], Henry B.[6], Henry[5], Christian Barentsen[4] VAN HOORN, Barent Christiansen[3], Christian Barentsen[2], Barent Barents[1])[3611,3612,3613,3614]* was born Bet. 06 - 16 Sep 1872 in Rayne Twp., Indiana Cnty, PA*[3615]*, and died 22 May 1946 in Vancover, BC, Canada*[3616]*. He married Patience Ann ANDERSON*[3617,3618]* 15 Jan 1901 in Whapeton, ND. She was born 29 Oct 1876 in St. John, NB, Canada*[3619]*, and died 10 Jan 1947 in Vancover, BC, Canada*[3620]*.

More About Frank Thomas MCELHOES:
Burial: 27 May 1946, Ocean View, Burnaby, BC Canada

Lived: 1908, Otter Tail, MN and Vancover, BC
Occupation: Farmer and Real Estate

More About Patience Ann ANDERSON:
Burial: 13 Jan 1947, Ocean View, Burnaby, BC Canada

More About Frank MCELHOES and Patience ANDERSON:
Marriage: 15 Jan 1901, Whapeton, ND

Children of Frank MCELHOES and Patience ANDERSON are:
435.　　i.　Charles Merle[12] MCELHOES, b. 22 Jan 1902, Ottertail, MN; d. 03 Feb 1970, Calimesa, Riverside Cnty, CA.
436.　　ii.　Waldo Steele MCELHOES, b. 15 Jan 1905, Ottertail, Ottertail Cnty, MN; d. 16 Jul 1979, Winnipeg, MB, Canada.
437.　　iii.　John Gordon MCELHOES, b. 16 Sep 1906, Ottertail, MN; d. 19 Jul 1984, Matsqui, BC Canada.
438.　　iv.　Robert Allan MCELHOES, b. Bet. 21 Jun 1907 - 1908, Strathmore, AB, Canada/MN; d. 26 Feb 1974, Vancover, BC, Canada.
439.　　v.　Spencer Kay MCELHOES, b. 10 Jun 1913, Strathmore, AB, Canada; d. 21 Jul 1943, Sicily, Itlay WWII.
440.　　vi.　Lowell Gladstone MCELHOES, b. 02 Sep 1914, Strathmore, AB, Canada; d. 24 May 1998, Vancover, BC, Canada.
441.　　vii.　Murray Thompson MCELHOES, b. 27 Dec 1916, Strathmore, AB, Canada; d. 05 Dec 2000, Abbotsford, BC, Canada.

229. Mary Lucetta[11] MCELHOES *(John Kinter[10], Isaiah[9], Jane[8] VAN HORN, Isaiah[7], Henry B.[6], Henry[5], Christian Barentsen[4] VAN HOORN, Barent Christiansen[3], Christian Barentsen[2], Barent Barents[1])*[3621,3622,3623,3624,3625] was born 01 Dec 1874 in PA[3626], and died Unknown. She married John GRIFFITH[3627,3628,3629] 28 Dec 1903 in Indiana Cnty, PA[3630]. He was born Dec 1867 in PA[3631], and died Unknown.

Notes for John GRIFFITH:
　　In 1930 he owns his place worth $2,000 and is a retail merchant selling groceries. They live on E Street in Bellingham, WA and do not have a radio.

More About John GRIFFITH:
Occupation: Lumber Mill Laborer;Retail Merchant Grocery

More About John GRIFFITH and Mary MCELHOES:
Marriage: 28 Dec 1903, Indiana Cnty, PA[3632]

Children of Mary MCELHOES and John GRIFFITH are:
　　i.　Grace[12] GRIFFITH[3633,3634], b. 01 Feb 1905, Randolph, WV[3635]; d. Unknown.
　　ii.　Eleanor GRIFFITH[3635,3636], b. Jun 1908, PA[3637]; d. Unknown.
　　iii.　Gertrude GRIFFITH[3637,3638], b. Feb 1911, Canada[3639]; d. Unknown.
　　iv.　Marthabell GRIFFITH, b. Private.

230. Robert Roy[11] MCELHOES *(John Kinter[10], Isaiah[9], Jane[8] VAN HORN, Isaiah[7], Henry B.[6], Henry[5], Christian Barentsen[4] VAN HOORN, Barent Christiansen[3], Christian Barentsen[2], Barent Barents[1])*[3640,3641,3642] was born 13 Jul 1876 in Rayne Twp., Indiana Cnty, PA[3643,3644], and died 25 Feb 1958 in Indiana Cnty, PA. He married Euena Margaretta CRAIG[3645] Abt. 1909. She was born 07 Apr 1881 in

PA[3645], and died Unknown.

Notes for Robert Roy MCELHOES:
    18 March 1908 Indiana Weekly Messenger (Indiana, PA) states that Roy lives in Alberta, Canada and came home for his fathers funeral. Also it is said that his brother Frank lives in Ottertail, MN.
    In his WWI draft registration he is a farmer living on Rt #1 Home, PA. He is tall of medium build and has blue eyes and brown hair. His next of kin is Eugena McElhoes also living at Rt #1 Home, PA

More About Robert Roy MCELHOES:
Lived: 1908, Alberta, Canada

More About Robert MCELHOES and Euena CRAIG:
Marriage: Abt. 1909

Children of Robert MCELHOES and Euena CRAIG are:
            i.   Margaret Agnes[12] MCELHOES[3645], b. Abt. 1910, Canada[3645]; d. Unknown.
442.   ii.   Mary Kathleen MCELHOES, b. 20 Aug 1913, Canada; d. 09 Jun 1977.
            iii. Dorothy Alice MCELHOES, b. Private.

231. Joseph Isaiah[11] MCELHOES *(John Kinter[10], Isaiah[9], Jane[8] VAN HORN, Isaiah[7], Henry B.[6], Henry[5], Christian Barentsen[4] VAN HOORN, Barent Christiansen[3], Christian Barentsen[2], Barent Barents[1])[3646,3647,3648]* was born 18 May 1879 in Rayne Twp., Indiana Cnty, PA[3649], and died 06 Sep 1974 in Rayne Twp., Indiana Cnty, PA. He married Emma Evans WYNCOOP[3650] 1908. She was born 21 Jan 1882 in Green Twp., Indiana Cnty, PA[3650], and died 02 Jun 1965 in Green Twp., Indiana Cnty, PA.

Notes for Joseph Isaiah MCELHOES:
    In 1930 owns his home and has a radio.

More About Joseph Isaiah MCELHOES:
Burial: Unknown, Washington Church Cemetery, Rayne Twp., Indiana Cnty, PA
Occupation: US Postal Service Mail Man

More About Emma Evans WYNCOOP:
Burial: Unknown, Washington Church Cemetery, Rayne Twp., Indiana Cnty, PA

More About Joseph MCELHOES and Emma WYNCOOP:
Marriage: 1908

Children of Joseph MCELHOES and Emma WYNCOOP are:
443.   i.   James K.[12] MCELHOES, b. 02 Oct 1909, PA; d. Unknown.
            ii.   Gertrude Wilhelmina MCELHOES, b. Private.

232. Martha Belle[11] MCELHOES *(John Kinter[10], Isaiah[9], Jane[8] VAN HORN, Isaiah[7], Henry B.[6], Henry[5], Christian Barentsen[4] VAN HOORN, Barent Christiansen[3], Christian Barentsen[2], Barent Barents[1])[3651]* was born Bet. 31 Oct - 01 Nov 1882 in Home, Indiana Cnty, PA[3651], and died 28 Jul 1977 in Burnaby, BC Canada. She married Mansel James GRIFFITH[3652] 03 May 1921 in Vancouver, BC Canada[3652]. He was born 29 Dec 1888 in Lansdowne, Leeds Cnty, ON Canada, and died 19 Jan 1952 in Vancouver, BC, Canada.

Notes for Martha Belle MCELHOES:
    Served in Canadian Expeditionary Force during WWI as a nurse.

More About Martha Belle MCELHOES:
Burial: Unknown, Vancover, BC, Canada Crematoriun
Lived: Vancover, BS, Canada
Occupation: WWI Nurse and Nurse after war
Religion: Presbyterian

Notes for Mansel James GRIFFITH:
Enlisted in the Canadian Expeditionary Force on 10 Sept 1914 at the age of 25 yrs and 9 months.

More About Mansel James GRIFFITH:
Burial: Unknown, Prince George, Canada
Occupation: Stationary Engineer Prince George Hospital
Religion: Presbyterian

More About Mansel GRIFFITH and Martha MCELHOES:
Divorce: 15 Oct 1950, New Westminister, BC Canada
Marriage: 03 May 1921, Vancover, BC Canada[3652]

Child of Martha MCELHOES and Mansel GRIFFITH is:
        i.   Robert Mansell[12] GRIFFITH, b. 19 May 1923, Hazelton, BC Canada; d. 22 May
              1923, Hazelton, BC Canada.

233. George Allen[11] MCELHOES *(James Steele[10], Isaiah[9], Jane[8] VAN HORN, Isaiah[7], Henry B.[6], Henry[5], Christian Barentsen[4] VAN HOORN, Barent Christiansen[3], Christian Barentsen[2], Barent Barents[1])[3653]* was born 15 Oct 1895 in White Twp., Indiana Cnty, PA[3653], and died Unknown. He married Martha SCHURR. She died Unknown.

Notes for George Allen MCELHOES:
    GEORGE ALLEN McELHOES
    File: #2148; Issued: 27 Aug. 1952
Residence: Punxsutawney, Jefferson County, Pennsylvania
Born: 15 Oct. 1895, Indiana, Indiana County, Pennsylvania
Father: JAMES STEELE McELHOES
Race, Age & Occupation: White, 45, Woolen Mill Superintendent
Born: Elderton, Armstrong County, Pennsylvania
Mother: ORPHA McELHOES
Race, Age & Occupation: White, 29
Born: Elderton, Armstrong County, Pennsylvania
Residence: Punxsutawney, Jefferson County, Pennsylvania
Children: 1
        Affidavits:
ORPHA McELHOES -Mother - 15 Nov. 1942
Residence: Punxsutawney, Jefferson County, Pennsylvania CARRIE L. SHARP
Residence: Shelocta, Indiana County, Pennsylvania - 24 Jul. 1942
WILLIAM R. SHARP
Residence: 1058 8th Avenue, Brackenridge, Allegheny County, Pennsylvania- 24 Jul. 1942
        Other: Statement of Minister or Priest: [Record of birth date in church records]: Harry Burton
Boyd, Minister; First Presbyterian Church, Indiana, Pennsylvania

More About George Allen MCELHOES:
Occupation: Woolen Mill Superintendent

Child of George MCELHOES and Martha SCHURR is:
     i.   Jay[12] MCELHOES, b. 1913, Green Twp., Indiana Cnty, PA; d. Unknown.

234. Elva Floid[11] DILTS *(Henry Milton[10], Nancy[9] MCELHOES, Jane[8] VAN HORN, Isaiah[7], Henry B.[6], Henry[5], Christian Barentsen[4] VAN HOORN, Barent Christiansen[3], Christian Barentsen[2], Barent Barents[1])[3654,3655,3656,3657]* was born 01 Mar 1886 in Kellysburg, Indiana Cnty, PA[3658,3659], and died Aft. 1930. She married Charles Franklin REDPATH[3660,3661,3662,3662] 16 Apr 1907[3663]. He was born 25 Sep 1883 in Fairbanks, Westmoreland Cnty, PA[3664], and died Aft. 1930.

Notes for Charles Franklin REDPATH:
    In 1910 living on Market Street in Blairsville, PA with wife and child. They have been married for 3 years and he is an engineer at the water works.
    In 1920 renting at the College Apartments on N. Walnut in Blairsville, PA. He is an Insurance Agent.
    In 1930 renting on Morewood Avenue for $30/month with no radio and they do not live on a farm. He works hanging blocks in a glass works. The 2 older sons Edwin and Paul are listed but are indicated as absent from the family.

More About Charles REDPATH and Elva DILTS:
Marriage: 16 Apr 1907[3665]

Children of Elva DILTS and Charles REDPATH are:
     i.   Edward L.[12] REDPATH[3666,3667], b. Abt. 1907, PA; d. Aft. 1930.
    ii.   Paul R. REDPATH[3668], b. Abt. 1910, PA; d. Aft. 1930.
   iii.   Charlotte Elizabeth REDPATH[3668,3669,3670], b. Abt. 1914, PA; d. Aft. 1930; m. PENSOM[3670]; d. Unknown.
   iv.   Martha E. REDPATH[3671], b. Abt. 1919, PA; d. Aft. 1930.
    v.   James N. REDPATH[3671], b. Abt. 1923, PA; d. Aft. 1930.

235. Martha Elizabeth[11] DILTS *(Henry Milton[10], Nancy[9] MCELHOES, Jane[8] VAN HORN, Isaiah[7], Henry B.[6], Henry[5], Christian Barentsen[4] VAN HOORN, Barent Christiansen[3], Christian Barentsen[2], Barent Barents[1])[3672,3673,3674,3675]* was born Abt. 1887 in PA, and died Unknown. She married Cliford J. KEIL[3676,3677] Aft. 1920, son of Henry KEIL and Louisa VANDERLIN. He was born 17 Jun 1894 in Butler, PA[3678], and died 20 Feb 1972 in Indiana, Indiana Cnty, PA[3678].

More About Cliford J. KEIL:
Burial: Unknown, Blairsville Cemetery, Blairsville, Indiana Cnty, PA
Employment: Purchasing Department Torrance State Hospital
Military service: WWI and Commander of Company L, 110th Pennsylvania Nationa Guard
Professional: Kiwanis and Last Squad Clubs
Religion: Presbyterian Deacon and Session Board Blairsville Church

More About Cliford KEIL and Martha DILTS:
Marriage: Aft. 1920

Children of Martha DILTS and Cliford KEIL are:
     i.   Marilyn L.[12] KEIL, b. Private.

ii. Robert KEIL*3678*, d. 1937.

236. William B.[11] LIGHTCAP *(John Scott[10], Susan[9] MCELHOES, Jane[8] VAN HORN, Isaiah[7], Henry B.[6], Henry[5], Christian Barentsen[4] VAN HOORN, Barent Christiansen[3], Christian Barentsen[2], Barent Barents[1])3679* was born 18 Jan 1878 in PA, and died Sep 1965. He married Laura KONSER Abt. 1904. She was born Abt. 1885 in PA, and died Unknown.

More About William LIGHTCAP and Laura KONSER:
Marriage: Abt. 1904

Children of William LIGHTCAP and Laura KONSER are:
  i. Eva Grace[12] LIGHTCAP, b. Abt. 1907, PA; d. Unknown.
  ii. Arthur Konser LIGHTCAP, b. Private.

237. Susana[11] LIGHTCAP *(John Scott[10], Susan[9] MCELHOES, Jane[8] VAN HORN, Isaiah[7], Henry B.[6], Henry[5], Christian Barentsen[4] VAN HOORN, Barent Christiansen[3], Christian Barentsen[2], Barent Barents[1])3679,3680* was born 05 Nov 1879 in PA, and died Unknown. She married James Harold BEATTY*3680*, son of Joshua BEATTY and Sarah LOWERY. He was born Abt. 1864 in PA*3680*, and died Unknown.

Children of Susana LIGHTCAP and James BEATTY are:
  i. Alma Gertrude[12] BEATTY*3680*, b. Abt. 1908, PA*3680*; d. Unknown.
  ii. Wilber Lightcap BEATTY*3680*, b. Abt. 1910, PA*3680*; d. Unknown.
  iii. Lois Mildred BEATTY*3680*, b. Abt. 1912, PA*3680*; d. Unknown.
  iv. James Harold BEATTY*3680*, b. Abt. 1914, PA*3680*; d. Unknown.

238. Silas Edgar[11] LIGHTCAP *(John Scott[10], Susan[9] MCELHOES, Jane[8] VAN HORN, Isaiah[7], Henry B.[6], Henry[5], Christian Barentsen[4] VAN HOORN, Barent Christiansen[3], Christian Barentsen[2], Barent Barents[1])3681* was born Bet. 1884 - 16 Dec 1885 in East Mahoning, Indiana Cnty, PA, and died 16 Jul 1918. He married Laura Elizabeth MABON. She was born 1884, and died 1962.

Child of Silas LIGHTCAP and Laura MABON is:
  i. John Leonard[12] LIGHTCAP, d. Unknown.

239. George Clair[11] MABON *(Nancy Ann[10] LIGHTCAP, Susan[9] MCELHOES, Jane[8] VAN HORN, Isaiah[7], Henry B.[6], Henry[5], Christian Barentsen[4] VAN HOORN, Barent Christiansen[3], Christian Barentsen[2], Barent Barents[1])3682,3683,3684* was born Aug 1888 in PA*3685*, and died 03 Dec 1967 in Indiana Cnty, PA. He married Virginia C. MCHENRY*3686,3687* 25 Mar 1908 in Indiana Cnty, PA*3688,3689*. She was born Abt. 1884 in PA*3690*, and died Aft. 1967.

More About George MABON and Virginia MCHENRY:
Marriage: 25 Mar 1908, Indiana Cnty, PA*3690,3691*

Children of George MABON and Virginia MCHENRY are:
  i. Robert G.[12] MABON*3692,3693*, b. Abt. 1908, PA*3694*; d. Unknown.

  Notes for Robert G. MABON:
  The Indiana Evening Gazette 3 July 1976 carried a story of the 4 Mabon boys buying a local hardware store in 1939.

293

444.   ii.   Blaine MABON, b. Abt. 1910, PA; d. Unknown.
         iii. Wilmer C. MABON*3695*, b. Abt. 1913, PA*3695*; d. Unknown.
         iv.   Bert M. MABON*3695*, b. Abt. 1915, PA*3695*; d. Unknown.

240. Claude Duval[11] VAN HORN *(John Neff[10], Benjamin Briggs[9], Joshua[8], Isaiah[7], Henry B.[6], Henry[5], Christian Barentsen[4] VAN HOORN, Barent Christiansen[3], Christian Barentsen[2], Barent Barents[1])[3696,3697,3698,3699,3700,3701]* was born 21 Feb 1869 in Indiana Cnty, PA*3702,3703*, and died 23 Jun 1937 in Lyman Cnty, SD*3704*. He married Sophia Christina HELLEKSON*3705,3706,3707* Abt. 1891. She was born Nov 1871 in WI*3708*, and died Aft. 1930.

Notes for Claude Duval VAN HORN:
    In 1930 living in Presho, SD in a rented place that he rents for $15/month. He does not have a radio.

More About Claude Duval VAN HORN:
Occupation: Proprieter Saloon, Race Horse Man Fairs, Mail Carrier Rural Route

More About Claude VAN HORN and Sophia HELLEKSON:
Marriage: Abt. 1891

Children of Claude VAN HORN and Sophia HELLEKSON are:
445.   i.   Walter Duval[12] VAN HORN, b. 06 Jan 1893, Presho, SD; d. Apr 1965, Elkton, Brookings Cnty, SD.
         ii.   Jeannette M. VAN HORN*3708*, b. Jul 1894, SD*3708*; d. Unknown.
         iii. Susan Nova VAN HORN*3708,3709*, b. 06 Mar 1897, Lyman Cnty, SD*3710,3711*; d. Unknown.
         iv.   ? VAN HORN, d. Unknown.

241. William Burton[11] VAN HORN *(John Neff[10], Benjamin Briggs[9], Joshua[8], Isaiah[7], Henry B.[6], Henry[5], Christian Barentsen[4] VAN HOORN, Barent Christiansen[3], Christian Barentsen[2], Barent Barents[1])[3712,3713,3714,3715,3716]* was born 20 Nov 1871 in Indiana Cnty, PA*3717*, and died 12 Oct 1924 in Chamberlain, Brule Cnty, SD. He married Jennie Elizabeth BAIREY*3717,3718,3719* 25 Nov 1895 in Brule Cnty, SD, daughter of George BAIREY and Jane GUPTIL. She was born 17 Dec 1867 in Millville, Wabash Cnty, MN*3720*, and died 29 Dec 1953 in Philadelphia, Philadelphia Cnty, PA.

Notes for William Burton VAN HORN:
    23 November 1910 the Indiana Progress(Indiana, PA) reports the W. B. Van Horn is elected Treasurer of Brule Cnty, SD and that he is the son of the late John N. Van Horn of Georgeville.

More About William VAN HORN and Jennie BAIREY:
Marriage: 25 Nov 1895, Brule Cnty, SD

Children of William VAN HORN and Jennie BAIREY are:
         i.   Jesse Garrett[12] VAN HORN*3720,3721,3722*, b. 03 Oct 1896, Ola, Brule Cnty, SD*3723*; d. Bet. 02 Sep - 12 Nov 1967, Minneapolis, Hennepin Cnty, MN*3724*; m. (1) Clara R.*3725*, Abt. 1925; b. Abt. 1901, IL*3725*; d. Unknown; m. (2) Mariam F. PUGSLEY, Private; b. Private.

         Notes for Jesse Garrett VAN HORN:
             In 1930 lives on Lyndale Ave. south in Minneapolis, MN where he rents for

$62/month and is living with his wife Clara.
Also know as Garrett J. Van Horn.

More About Jesse Garrett VAN HORN:
Occupation: Automobile Insurance Salesman

More About Clara R.:
Occupation: Department Store Saleswoman

More About Jesse VAN HORN and Clara R.:
Marriage: Abt. 1925

More About Jesse VAN HORN and Mariam PUGSLEY:
Private-Begin: Private

      ii.   Joy Avis VAN HORN[3726,3727], b. 29 Jan 1898, Ola, Brule Cnty, SD[3728,3729]; d. Unknown, SD.

446.   iii.   Henry Logan VAN HORN, b. 09 Sep 1901, Ola, Brule Cnty, SD; d. 1981, Baltimore, Baltimore Cnty, MD.

447.   iv.   Jennie Elizabeth VAN HORN, b. 29 Sep 1903, Ola, Brule Cnty, SD; d. 01 Apr 1952, Washington DC.

242. Robert Campbell[11] VAN HORN *(John Neff[10], Benjamin Briggs[9], Joshua[8], Isaiah[7], Henry B.[6], Henry[5], Christian Barentsen[4] VAN HOORN, Barent Christiansen[3], Christian Barentsen[2], Barent Barents[1])*[3730,3731,3732,3733,3734,3735] was born 03 Feb 1875 in Banks Twp., Indiana Cnty, PA[3736], and died 05 Apr 1943 in Kennebec Cnty, SD[3737]. He married Elmira Solle ARMSTRONG[3738,3739,3740,3741,3742] 21 Nov 1899[3743,3744], daughter of Gabriel ARMSTRONG and Mary BIGELOW. She was born 27 Aug 1878 in IL/Ridgeway, IA[3745], and died 18 Jan 1956 in Yankton, SD.

Notes for Robert Campbell VAN HORN:
    His name may be Richard Campbell after his mothers maiden name. He is variously called Richard Clarence and R. Cam Van Horn.

More About Robert Campbell VAN HORN:
Occupation: Farmer, Farmer of Stock Farm and Post Master, Stock Farmer

More About Elmira Solle ARMSTRONG:
Occupation: Assistant Postmaster

More About Robert VAN HORN and Elmira ARMSTRONG:
Marriage: 21 Nov 1899[3746,3747]

Children of Robert VAN HORN and Elmira ARMSTRONG are:
      i.   Florence Loretta[12] VAN HORN[3748,3749,3750], b. 02 Aug 1900, Lyman Cnty, SD[3751]; d. Unknown, Sun City, AZ.

      ii.   Iva Verone VAN HORN[3751,3752,3753], b. Abt. 1904, SD[3754]; d. Unknown.

More About Iva Verone VAN HORN:
Occupation: School Teacher

448.   iii.   Inez Vernal VAN HORN, b. 06 Apr 1905, SD; d. 21 Oct 1985, Pierre, SD.

449.   iv.   Mildred D. VAN HORN, b. Abt. 1907, SD; d. Unknown.

v. Opal Leone VAN HORN*3755,3756*, b. Abt. 1910, SD*3757*; d. Unknown.

243. Myrreel[11] VAN HORN *(John Neff[10], Benjamin Briggs[9], Joshua[8], Isaiah[7], Henry B.[6], Henry[5], Christian Barentsen[4] VAN HOORN, Barent Christiansen[3], Christian Barentsen[2], Barent Barents[1])*3758,3759,3760,3761,3762,3763,3764* was born Jun 1877 in Indiana Cnty, PA*3765*, and died Aft. 1907 in NY, NY. She married Ralph W. GOULD*3766,3767* Abt. 1900, son of Matilda E. WIXSON. He was born Abt. 1866 in NY*3767*, and died Bet. 1910 - 1920.

Notes for Myrreel VAN HORN:
    In 1930 she is widowed living on Corning Rd in Dix, NY, with her son Robert, in a home she owns worth $2500. She has a radio.

More About Myrreel VAN HORN:
Occupation: Farmer, Saleslady General Store

More About Ralph GOULD and Myrreel VAN HORN:
Marriage: Abt. 1900

Children of Myrreel VAN HORN and Ralph GOULD are:
    i.   Florence[12] GOULD*3767*, b. Abt. 1902, NY*3767*; d. Unknown.
    ii.   Helen J. GOULD*3767,3768*, b. Abt. 1906, NY*3769*; d. Unknown.
    iii. John D. GOULD*3770*, b. Abt. 1911, NY*3770*; d. Unknown.
    iv.   Robert C. GOULD*3771,3772*, b. Abt. 1915, NY*3773*; d. Unknown.

244. Nora[11] VAN HORN *(John Neff[10], Benjamin Briggs[9], Joshua[8], Isaiah[7], Henry B.[6], Henry[5], Christian Barentsen[4] VAN HOORN, Barent Christiansen[3], Christian Barentsen[2], Barent Barents[1])*3774,3775,3776,3777,3778,3779,3780* was born 03 Aug 1879 in Indiana Cnty, PA*3781*, and died Aft. 1930 in SD. She married Gustave N. ANDERSON*3782,3783,3784,3785* Abt. 1897 in SD. He was born Sep 1865 in IA/Sweden*3786*, and died Bef. 1930.

Notes for Nora VAN HORN:
    In 1900 she is the mother of 2 neither of which are living at the time of the census.
    In 1910 she is the mother of 3 of which two are living.
    In 1930 she is a widow and lives in Presho, SD alone. She rents for $10/month.

Notes for Gustave N. ANDERSON:
    In 1920 he owns his place with a mortgage and is a farmer.

More About Gustave N. ANDERSON:
Occupation: Farmer

More About Gustave ANDERSON and Nora VAN HORN:
Marriage: Abt. 1897, SD

Children of Nora VAN HORN and Gustave ANDERSON are:
    i.   ?[12] ANDERSON, b. Bef. 1900; d. Bef. 1900.
    ii.   ? ANDERSON, b. Bef. 1900; d. Bef. 1900.
    iii. Neva Emma ANDERSON*3787,3788*, b. 18 Dec 1902, SD*3789,3790*; d. 14 Jan 1998, Clara City, Chippewa Cnty, MN*3791*; m. Theodore WAGNER*3792*, 22 Dec 1922, Fort Pierre, Stanley Cnty, SD*3792*; b. Abt. 1899, Stanley Cnty, SD; d. Unknown.

Isaiah Van Horn Pioneer of Indiana County, Pennsylvania

More About Theodore WAGNER and Neva ANDERSON:
Marriage: 22 Dec 1922, Fort Pierre, Stanley Cnty, SD[3792]

    iv.   J. Alfred ANDERSON[3793,3794], b. Abt. 1906, SD[3795]; d. Unknown.

245. Orin Denton[11] VAN HORN *(James Harvey[10], Benjamin Briggs[9], Joshua[8], Isaiah[7], Henry B.[6], Henry[5], Christian Barentsen[4] VAN HOORN, Barent Christiansen[3], Christian Barentsen[2], Barent Barents[1])*[3796,3797,3798,3799,3800,3801,3802,3803,3804] was born 11 Aug 1874 in South Mahoning Twp., Indiana Cnty, PA[3805], and died 11 Mar 1949 in Marion Center, Indiana Cnty, PA. He married Mary Elizabeth JUART[3806,3807,3808,3809,3810,3811,3812] Abt. 1893, daughter of Charles JEWART and Catherine MCMILLIAN. She was born 08 Sep 1867 in Marion Center, Indiana Cnty, PA[3813], and died 27 Oct 1947 in Indiana, Indiana Cnty, PA.

Notes for Orin Denton VAN HORN:
    In his WWI Draft Registration he states his name as Orin Denton Van Horn. He is a farmer living at Home, Indiana Cnty, PA. He is tall of medium build and has gray eyes and brown hair. His wife is named Mary.
    In 1900 Dent and Mary are living with her father and one brother. She is the mother of 5 children of which 4 are living. One daughter by a previous marriage Charlotte Whitacre is living with the family, Dent is a farm laborer.
    In 1910 name is given as Denton O. He is a teamster and has been married for 16 years. Mary states she is mother of 5 children of which 4 are living. It could be that the person I have as Charles B. is the Asbury Boyd Van Horn.
    25 March 1910 the Indiana Evening Gazette (Indiana, PA) reports that Denton Van Horn was hit with a pane of glass and severed several leaders in his hand while he was fighting a fire at the Rowland home farm.
    In many references the name is given as Denton. His father died at his home according to the 24 Aug. 1921 Indiana Progress(Indiana, PA).
    In 1930 he and Mary are living alone in Wayne Twp., Indiana Cnty, PA. They rent and Dent works at odd jobs as a laborer.
    31 January 1933 the Indiana Evening Gazette (Indiana, PA) reported that the horse that Dent Van Horn used to carry the mail from Marion Center to Glenn Campbell laid down and died in front of the Rochester Mills Post Office on the return trip.

More About Orin Denton VAN HORN:
Burial: Unknown, Barachea Cemetery, Plumville, PA
Occupation: Farmer

More About Mary Elizabeth JUART:
Burial: Unknown, Berachea Cemetery, Plumville, PA
Lived: Dayton, PA

More About Orin VAN HORN and Mary JUART:
Marriage: Abt. 1893

Children of Orin VAN HORN and Mary JUART are:
        i.   Charlotte[12] WHITACRE[3813], b. Feb 1890, PA[3813]; d. Unknown; Stepchild.
450.   ii.   Andrew Glenn VAN HORN, b. 24 Aug 1894, Plumville, Indiana Cnty, PA; d. 07 Oct 1969, Punxsutawney, Jefferson Cnty, PA.
451.   iii. Catherine Isabelle VAN HORN, b. 25 Apr 1896, Plumville, Indiana Cnty, PA; d. 09 Aug 1976, Punxsutwaney, Jefferson Cnty, PA.
      iv.   ? VAN HORN, b. 28 May 1898, Plumville, Indiana Cnty, PA; d. 31 May 1898, Indiana Cnty, PA.

452.   v.   Charles Boyd VAN HORN, b. 09 Jul 1899, Indiana Cnty, PA; d. Aft. 1949.
      vi.   Eugene H. VAN HORN*3814,3815,3816,3817,3818*, b. 16 Sep 1909, Plumville, Indiana Cnty, PA*3819,3820*; d. 02 Jun 1974; m. Rena L., Private; b. Private.

Notes for Eugene H. VAN HORN:
In 1930 Eugene R. Van Horn is living with his aunt and uncle William C. and Viola V. Price age 47 and 35. They are living on Main Street in Meyersdale, PA. William Price is a funeral director and Eugene is an Embalmer.
In the 1953 Scottdale High School Yearbook there is a special page titled Service Roll. This page lists all of the graduates of the High School and Teachers who are fighting to preserve the four freedoms. Eugene Van Horn is listed as a 1937 graduate indicating that he is in the military at that time.

More About Eugene H. VAN HORN:
Burial: Unknown, Greenwood Cemetery, Lower Burrell, Westmoreland Cnty, PA*3821*
Military service: Bet. 1944 - 1945, US Navy WWII MoMM/2/c*3821*

More About Eugene VAN HORN and Rena L.:
Private-Begin: Private

246. Charles Blaine[11] VAN HORN *(James Harvey[10], Benjamin Briggs[9], Joshua[8], Isaiah[7], Henry B.[6], Henry[5], Christian Barentsen[4] VAN HOORN, Barent Christiansen[3], Christian Barentsen[2], Barent Barents[1])3822,3823,3824,3825,3826,3827* was born Bet. 01 - 02 Aug 1890 in Rayne Twp., Indiana Cnty, PA*3828,3829*, and died 01 Nov 1965 in Indiana, Indiana Cnty, PA. He married Laura*3830*. She was born Abt. 1901 in PA*3830*, and died Bet. 1925 - 1930.

Notes for Charles Blaine VAN HORN:
In his WWI Draft Registration he indicates he is of fair completion, medium build, blue eyes and light brown hair.
In 1930 he gives his age as 39 and married at 28. He lives on Ridge Avenue in Marion Center, PA near his brother Park. He is living with his daughter Imogene in a home he owns worth $400.

More About Charles Blaine VAN HORN:
Burial: Unknown, Marion Center Cemetery, Indiana Cnty, PA
Lived: Marion Center, Indiana Cnty, PA
Occupation: Draying, Coal Mine Laborer, Laborer Digging Cellars

Child of Charles VAN HORN and Laura is:
      i.   Imogene[12] VAN HORN, b. Private.

247. Mary Ada[11] VAN HORN *(James Harvey[10], Benjamin Briggs[9], Joshua[8], Isaiah[7], Henry B.[6], Henry[5], Christian Barentsen[4] VAN HOORN, Barent Christiansen[3], Christian Barentsen[2], Barent Barents[1])3831,3832,3833,3834,3835* was born Sep 1894 in Indiana Cnty, PA*3836*, and died Bet. 1969 - 1976. She married Phillip Lisle BLYSTONE*3837,3838,3839* Abt. 1910, son of John BLYSTONE and Mary Ann. He was born Abt. 1880 in PA*3840,3841*, and died Aft. 1930.

Notes for Mary Ada VAN HORN:
In 1930 has her daughter Velma and Velma's husband Lysle Short living in the family. She and her husband live on Fulton T. Pescal Rd, WhiteTwp., Indiana Cnty, PA in a home they own worth $1000. They do not have a radio.

More About Mary Ada VAN HORN:
Lived: Marion Center, Indiana Cnty, PA

More About Phillip Lisle BLYSTONE:
Lived: Locust, PA
Occupation: Railroad Laborer, Farm Laborer, Coal Miner

More About Phillip BLYSTONE and Mary VAN HORN:
Marriage: Abt. 1910

Children of Mary VAN HORN and Phillip BLYSTONE are:
     i.   Velma P.[12] BLYSTONE, b. Private; m. Lysle SHORT[3841], Private; b. Abt. 1908,
         PA[3841]; d. Unknown.

         More About Lysle SHORT:
         Occupation: Railroad Laborer

         More About Lysle SHORT and Velma BLYSTONE:
         Private-Begin: Private

     ii. Elizabeth BLYSTONE, b. Private.

248. Alice Elsie[11] VAN HORN *(James Harvey[10], Benjamin Briggs[9], Joshua[8], Isaiah[7], Henry B.[6], Henry[5], Christian Barentsen[4] VAN HOORN, Barent Christiansen[3], Christian Barentsen[2], Barent Barents[1])*[3842,3843,3844,3845,3846,3847,3848] was born Jun 1896 in Indiana Cnty, PA[3849], and died Aft. 1976. She married Homer N. MONTGOMERY[3850,3851,3852] 19 Jun 1919 in Indiana Cnty, PA[3853], son of Carter MONTGOMERY and Sara M.. He was born Abt. 1893 in PA[3854], and died Unknown.

Notes for Alice Elsie VAN HORN:
    In 1930 her name is given as Elsie L. in the census.

More About Alice Elsie VAN HORN:
Lived: Lower Burrell and New Kensington, PA

Notes for Homer N. MONTGOMERY:
    In 1920 living with parents and helping on the farm.
    In 1930 owns his place worth about $1500 and has a radio.

More About Homer N. MONTGOMERY:
Occupation: Railroad Car Inspector

More About Homer MONTGOMERY and Alice VAN HORN:
Marriage: 19 Jun 1919, Indiana Cnty, PA[3855]

Children of Alice VAN HORN and Homer MONTGOMERY are:
     i.   Howard C.[12] MONTGOMERY, b. Private.
     ii. Grace E. MONTGOMERY, b. Private.

249. LeRoy Kerns[11] VAN HORN *(Alexander Milton[10], Benjamin Briggs[9], Joshua[8], Isaiah[7], Henry B.[6], Henry[5], Christian Barentsen[4] VAN HOORN, Barent Christiansen[3], Christian Barentsen[2], Barent Barents[1])*[3856,3857,3858,3859] was born 08 Jul 1878 in Indiana Cnty, PA[3860,3861], and died 16 Feb 1954 in

Youngstown, Mahoning Cnty, OH[3862,3863,3864]. He married Tirzah Theresa WADDING[3865,3866,3867] 25 Jun 1902. She was born 14 Dec 1882 in Armstrong Cnty, PA[3868], and died 11 Feb 1967 in Youngstown, Mahoning Cnty, OH[3868].

Notes for LeRoy Kerns VAN HORN:
27 Nov. 1901 Indiana Progress (Indiana, PA) LeRoy Van Horn of Sharon and Miss Tuza Wadding visit the A. M. Van Horn's
In 1930 he lives on West Chalmers Avenue in Youngstown, OH in a home he owns worth $8500 and has a radio.

More About LeRoy Kerns VAN HORN:
Lived: New Castle and Alquippa, PA
Occupation: Plaster Contractor

More About LeRoy VAN HORN and Tirzah WADDING:
Marriage: 25 Jun 1902

Children of LeRoy VAN HORN and Tirzah WADDING are:
453.   i.   LeRoy Wadding[12] VAN HORN, b. 20 May 1903, New Castle, PA; d. 03 Mar 1987, Youngstown, Mahoning Cnty, OH.
           ii. Eleanor VAN HORN, b. Private; m. Harry WARNOCK, Private; d. Unknown.

               More About Harry WARNOCK and Eleanor VAN HORN:
               Private-Begin: Private

250. Sprague L.[11] VAN HORN *(Alexander Milton[10], Benjamin Briggs[9], Joshua[8], Isaiah[7], Henry B.[6], Henry[5], Christian Barentsen[4] VAN HOORN, Barent Christiansen[3], Christian Barentsen[2], Barent Barents[1])[3869,3870,3871,3872]* was born 23 Sep 1879 in Plumville, Indiana Cnty, PA[3873,3874], and died 30 Mar 1951 in Ambridge, PA. He married Hattie STOFFLE[3875] 25 Jan 1911 in Economy, PA[3876]. She was born Abt. 1882 in PA[3877], and died Aft. 1951.

Notes for Sprague L. VAN HORN:
Served 25 years on the Ambridge City Council and as the Council's President for 3 years. He was a member of the Presbyterian Church, the Masonic Lodge, Consistory of New Castle, life member of Syria Shrine, Pittsburgh, Elks of Ambridge, charter member of Ambridge Odd Fellows, charter member of the Ambridge Country Club and President of First Federal Saving and Loan of Ambridge.
4 December 1907 it is reported in the Indiana Progress(Indiana, PA) that Sprague Van Horn accompanied by Miss Hattie Schofield of Ambridge, PA spent a few days at the home of his parents Mr. and Mrs. A. M. Van Horn returning home on Sunday.
He was a plastering contractor in 1930 and owned his home worth $12,000 and had a radio in the home. There was a Servant in the home in 1930.
17 Nov. 1938 the Indiana Progress (Indiana, PA) reports that S. L. Van Horn of Ambridge has spent a few days hunting on his father's farm in Rossmoyne.

More About Sprague L. VAN HORN:
Burial: Unknown, Economy Cemetery
Lived: Economy, PA; Alquippa and Ambridge, PA

More About Sprague VAN HORN and Hattie STOFFLE:
Marriage: 25 Jan 1911, Economy, PA[3878]
Marriage date: Rev. W. A. Kinter
Marriage Place: Home of the Bride

Child of Sprague VAN HORN and Hattie STOFFLE is:
454.   i.   Betty J.[12] VAN HORN, b. Private.

251. Mary Mae[11] VAN HORN *(Alexander Milton[10], Benjamin Briggs[9], Joshua[8], Isaiah[7], Henry B.[6], Henry[5], Christian Barentsen[4] VAN HOORN, Barent Christiansen[3], Christian Barentsen[2], Barent Barents[1])[3879,3880]* was born 12 Sep 1882 in Indiana Cnty, PA[3881], and died 31 Oct 1967 in Meadville, PA. She married Harry S. KUEHNER[3882,3883,3884] 19 Aug 1906 in Plumville, Indiana Cnty, PA[3885]. He was born Abt. 1881 in PA, and died Unknown.

More About Mary Mae VAN HORN:
Lived: Meadville and Plumville, PA

Notes for Harry S. KUEHNER:
Also known as Harry Kirshner according to the marriage license listing in the 22 August 1906 Indiana Weekly Messenger (Indiana, PA).

More About Harry S. KUEHNER:
Occupation: Barber in his own shop

More About Harry KUEHNER and Mary VAN HORN:
Marriage: 19 Aug 1906, Plumville, Indiana Cnty, PA[3885]
Marriage date: Rev. M. V. S. Gold
Marriage Place: Baptist Church Parsonage

Children of Mary VAN HORN and Harry KUEHNER are:
     i.   H.[12] Van KUEHNER[3886], b. Abt. 1907, PA[3886]; d. Unknown.
455.   ii. George Kenneth KUEHNER, b. Bet. Jun - 04 Oct 1909, PA; d. 14 Jul 1987, Hartsville, Darlington Cnty, SC.
    iii. Richard Louis KUEHNER, b. Private.

252. George Percy[11] VAN HORN *(Alexander Milton[10], Benjamin Briggs[9], Joshua[8], Isaiah[7], Henry B.[6], Henry[5], Christian Barentsen[4] VAN HOORN, Barent Christiansen[3], Christian Barentsen[2], Barent Barents[1])[3887,3888,3889,3890,3891]* was born Bet. 06 Sep 1883 - 1884 in South Mahoning Twp., Indiana Cnty, PA[3892,3893,3894], and died 12 Jan 1965 in Blairsville, Indiana Cnty, PA[3895]. He married Lulu L. BREZGER[3896,3897] Abt. 1911, daughter of John BREZGER and Margaretta J.. She was born Abt. 1896 in PA, and died Unknown.

Notes for George Percy VAN HORN:
    29 May 1907 the Indiana Progress (Indiana, PA) reports that Percy Van Horn who has been confined at home with rheumatism for the past week is able to be out again.
    In his WWI Draft Registration he lives in Aliquippa, PA at 319 Beaver. He gives his wife Lulu Van Horn as his nearest relative and she lives in Aliquippa at the same address. He is of medium height, slender build and had brown eyes and hair. He is a plasterer and is self employed.
    In 1920 living with wife and 3 children in Aliquippa, PA. He owns his home at 415 Beaver Ave with a mortgage and is a plaster contractor.
    In 1930 Percy is living at 301 Main in Aliquippa, PA. He is divorced age 46 and is a plasterer.
    In his WWII Draft Registration he lives at 658 Maple Avenue, Ambridge, Beaver Cnty, PA. He lists S. L. Van Horn as the relative who should know where to contact him. His address is the same as S. L. Van Horn's. This is likely his brother Sprague L. Van Horn. His work address is also the same and since before he was a self employed plasterer but he lists S. L. Van Horn as his employer. He is white is 5'41/2" weighs 130 lbs has gray hair and a ruddy complexion.

301

Some sources say his name is Percival.

More About George Percy VAN HORN:
Burial: Unknown, Berachea Cemetery, Plumville, Indiana Cnty, PA
Lived: Indiana, Ambidge and Blairsville, Indiana Cnty, PA; 1914 in CA
Religion: Baptist

More About George VAN HORN and Lulu BREZGER:
Divorce: Bef. 1930
Marriage: Abt. 1911

Children of George VAN HORN and Lulu BREZGER are:
456.   i.   Vincent[12] VAN HORN, b. Abt. 1913, CA; d. 1977, New Castle, Lawrence Cnty, PA.
          ii. June VAN HORN, b. Private; m. HUDSON, Private; b. Private.

> More About HUDSON and June VAN HORN:
> Private-Begin: Private

457.   iii. Dale VAN HORN, b. 26 Jun 1917, PA; d. 10 Jun 1992, San Bernardino Cnty, CA.

253. Nellie Gertrude[11] VAN HORN *(Alexander Milton[10], Benjamin Briggs[9], Joshua[8], Isaiah[7], Henry B.[6], Henry[5], Christian Barentsen[4] VAN HOORN, Barent Christiansen[3], Christian Barentsen[2], Barent Barents[1])*[3898,3899,3900,3901,3902,3903] was born 06 Nov 1885 in PA[3904], and died 22 Aug 1964 in Indiana, Indiana Cnty, PA. She married James Buckley RANKIN[3905,3906,3907,3908] 27 Feb 1913 in Indiana Cnty, PA[3909], son of George RANKIN and Mary WYNKOOP. He was born 07 Sep 1888 in Beyer, Indiana Cnty, PA[3910], and died 24 Sep 1966 in Indiana, Indiana Cnty, PA.

Notes for Nellie Gertrude VAN HORN:
    10 June 1908 Indiana Progress (Indiana, PA) reports that Nellie spent the weekend with friends in Plumville.

More About Nellie Gertrude VAN HORN:
Lived: Homer City, PA
Occupation: Trimmer Millenry Store

Notes for James Buckley RANKIN:
    In 1920 owns home with a mortgage.
    In 1930 owns home in Homer, PA on Elm Street worth $3,000 and has a radio. James is a repairman in a power house. They have been married for 16 years as Nellie says she married at age 26 and she is now 42.

More About James Buckley RANKIN:
Occupation: Repairman Coal Mine Power

More About James RANKIN and Nellie VAN HORN:
Marriage: 27 Feb 1913, Indiana Cnty, PA[3911]
Marriage date: Rev. W. S. Sturgeon
Marriage Place: West Indiana House

Children of Nellie VAN HORN and James RANKIN are:
         i. Marjorie May[12] RANKIN, b. 1914, PA; d. 1914, PA.
458.   ii. James Rogers RANKIN, b. 21 Nov 1915, Homer, Indiana Cnty, PA; d. 25 Mar

459.   iii.   Rosemary RANKIN, b. 01 Apr 1920, PA; d. Jun 1992, New Kensington, Westmoreland Cnty, PA.

254. Zula L.[11] VAN HORN *(Alexander Milton[10], Benjamin Briggs[9], Joshua[8], Isaiah[7], Henry B.[6], Henry[5], Christian Barentsen[4] VAN HOORN, Barent Christiansen[3], Christian Barentsen[2], Barent Barents[1])[3912,3913,3914,3915,3916]* was born Mar 1887 in Plumville, PA[3917], and died Aft. 1944. She married Wilmer Todd DIXSON[3918,3919,3920] 25 Dec 1915 in Akron, Summit Cnty, OH[3921], son of DIXSON and Anthra. He was born Bet. 1879 - 1887 in Homer, PA[3922], and died Unknown.

Notes for Zula L. VAN HORN:
    17 July 1907 the Indiana Progress (Indiana, PA) reports that Zula Van Horn has been selected as a South Mahoning teacher.
    15 July 1909 Zula Van Horn was selected as a teacher at South Mahoning.
    24 July 1912 the Indiana County Gazette (Indiana, PA) reports that Zula is to receive her permanent state teaching certificate.

More About Zula L. VAN HORN:
Lived: Dearborn, MI
Occupation: Public School Instructor

Notes for Wilmer Todd DIXSON:
    In 1930 living on East Buchtel in Akron, OH in a home he owns worth $7,500. He is a lumber foreman.

More About Wilmer Todd DIXSON:
Occupation: Bet. 1920 - 1930, Tire Builder for a Rubber Company, Lumber Foreman

More About Wilmer DIXSON and Zula VAN HORN:
Marriage: 25 Dec 1915, Akron, Summit Cnty, OH[3923]

Children of Zula VAN HORN and Wilmer DIXSON are:
        i.   Mildred E.[12] DIXSON, b. Private.
        ii.   Clifford T. DIXSON, b. Private.

255. Russell E.[11] VAN HORN *(Alexander Milton[10], Benjamin Briggs[9], Joshua[8], Isaiah[7], Henry B.[6], Henry[5], Christian Barentsen[4] VAN HOORN, Barent Christiansen[3], Christian Barentsen[2], Barent Barents[1])[3924,3925,3926,3927,3928]* was born Oct 1899 in PA[3929], and died Aft. 1944. He married Mary ROHAN[3930] Abt. 1926[3930], daughter of ROHAN and Ellen. She was born Abt. 1901 in PA[3930], and died Unknown.

Notes for Russell E. VAN HORN:
    In 1920 living with his sister Zula and her family in Akron, OH. He is a tire builder in a rubber company as is his brother in law.
    In 1930 living with wife and daughter in the home of his mother in law. He is a plasterer, contractor and builder.

More About Russell E. VAN HORN:
Lived: Ambridge and Alliquippi, PA

More About Russell VAN HORN and Mary ROHAN:
Marriage: Abt. 1926[3930]

Child of Russell VAN HORN and Mary ROHAN is:
    i.   Mary J.[12] VAN HORN, b. Private.

256. Luther Merle[11] LUKEHART *(Sarah S.[10] VAN HORN, Benjamin Briggs[9], Joshua[8], Isaiah[7], Henry B.[6], Henry[5], Christian Barentsen[4] VAN HOORN, Barent Christiansen[3], Christian Barentsen[2], Barent Barents[1])[3931,3932]* was born 21 Nov 1877 in Armstrong Cnty, PA[3933], and died 18 Oct 1938. He married Alice Leone NEAL[3934]. She was born 18 Jul 1878 in Armstrong Cnty, PA[3934], and died Unknown.

Notes for Luther Merle LUKEHART:
    In 1930 living with wife and 4 children. He is renting for $30/month and does not have a radio. He is a foreman in a fruit cannery in Chino, CA.

More About Luther Merle LUKEHART:
Employment: 1930, Foreman Fruit Cannery

Children of Luther LUKEHART and Alice NEAL are:
    i.   Leola[12] M.LUKEHART[3934], b. Abt. 1912, PA[3934]; d. Unknown.
    ii.   Cleone I. LUKEHART[3934], b. 1905, PA[3934]; d. Unknown.
    iii. Ralph B. LUKEHART[3934], b. Abt. 1907, CA[3934]; d. Unknown.
    iv.   Mary B. LUKEHART[3934], b. Abt. 1909, CA[3934]; d. Unknown.

257. Bertha Agnes[11] LUKEHART *(Sarah S.[10] VAN HORN, Benjamin Briggs[9], Joshua[8], Isaiah[7], Henry B.[6], Henry[5], Christian Barentsen[4] VAN HOORN, Barent Christiansen[3], Christian Barentsen[2], Barent Barents[1])[3935,3936,3937,3938,3939]* was born Bet. 02 - 12 Aug 1880 in Barnard, Armstrong Cnty, PA[3940,3941], and died 01 Apr 1960 in Dayton, Armstrong Cnty, PA[3942]. She married Robert Enos NEAL[3943,3944,3945] Abt. 1900, son of NEAL and Caroline. He was born 28 Nov 1869 in Armstrong Cnty, PA[3946], and died 13 Jan 1953 in Dayton, Armstrong Cnty, PA[3947].

Notes for Bertha Agnes LUKEHART:
    In 1910 living 2 doors from her widowed mother and brother.

More About Bertha Agnes LUKEHART:
Burial: Unknown, United Presbyterian Cemetery, Dayton, PA[3948]
Medical Information: Died at home a a lingering illness
Organizations: Rural Valley Grange 1750
Religion: Dayton, PA United Presbyterian Church

Notes for Robert Enos NEAL:
    In 1930 owns his farm and has a radio. There are his wife and 3 children of the home. His son Robert lives next door with his wife and your daughter.

More About Robert Enos NEAL:
Occupation: Farmer

More About Robert NEAL and Bertha LUKEHART:
Marriage: Abt. 1900

Children of Bertha LUKEHART and Robert NEAL are:
460.   i.   Robert Merle[12] NEAL, b. 10 Nov 1902, Dayton, Armstrong Cnty, PA; d. Unknown.

ii. Lena V. NEAL*3949,3950,3951*, b. Abt. 1904, PA*3952*; d. Unknown; m. MCMEANS*3953*; d. Unknown.

More About Lena V. NEAL:
Lived: Pittsburgh, PA

iii. Harold L. NEAL*3954,3955,3956*, b. Feb 1910, PA*3957*; d. Unknown.

More About Harold L. NEAL:
Lived: Hicksville, Long Island, NY

iv. Dorothy I NEAL, b. Private; m. MCILWAIN*3958*, Private; d. Unknown.

More About MCILWAIN and Dorothy NEAL:
Private-Begin: Private

v. Sarah D. NEAL, b. Private; m. WILSON*3958*, Private; d. Unknown.

More About WILSON and Sarah NEAL:
Private-Begin: Private

258. Homer Boyd[11] LUKEHART *(Sarah S.[10] VAN HORN, Benjamin Briggs[9], Joshua[8], Isaiah[7], Henry B.[6], Henry[5], Christian Barentsen[4] VAN HOORN, Barent Christiansen[3], Christian Barentsen[2], Barent Barents[1])3959,3960,3961* was born 17 Sep 1888 in Armstrong Cnty, PA*3962*, and died 19 Feb 1956 in Dayton, Armstrong Cnty, PA. He married Maude U. STEFFY*3963* Abt. 1912. She was born 06 Mar 1892 in Smicksburg, Indiana Cnty, PA*3963*, and died Unknown.

Notes for Homer Boyd LUKEHART:
    WW I Draft Registration married with child and is a fireman.
    WW II Draft Registration works for the Summit Coal Company

More About Homer Boyd LUKEHART:
Employment: 1930, Painter

More About Homer LUKEHART and Maude STEFFY:
Marriage: Abt. 1912

Children of Homer LUKEHART and Maude STEFFY are:
    i. Leone M.[12] LUKEHART, b. Private.
    ii. Helen R. LUKEHART, b. Private.
    iii. Clifford J. LUKEHART, b. Private.

259. Samuel A.[11] VAN HORN *(John Miles[10], Christian[9], Joshua[8], Isaiah[7], Henry B.[6], Henry[5], Christian Barentsen[4] VAN HOORN, Barent Christiansen[3], Christian Barentsen[2], Barent Barents[1])3964,3965,3966,3967,3968,3969* was born Aug 1866 in PA*3970*, and died Bet. 1920 - 1930*3971*. He married Frances F. HAAS*3972,3973,3974,3975,3976* Abt. 1885. She was born Aug 1853 in PA*3977*, and died Aft. 1930.

Notes for Samuel A. VAN HORN:
    In 1910 lives on Brookville Street in Hawthorn, PA. He and Frances have 3 children all of them living. Rubin is not in the home on this date.

In 1920 lives on Brookville Street in a home he owns with a mortgage in Hawthorn, PA. Also living in the family is a cousin Catherine Hilliard age 72 and widowed. He is a carpenter with his own shop.

More About Samuel A. VAN HORN:
Occupation: Carpenter

Notes for Frances F. HAAS:
In 1930 Frances is a widow. Her son Tallie is living with her, he is single. She owns her home worth $1200 and lives in Hawthorn, PA.

More About Samuel VAN HORN and Frances HAAS:
Marriage: Abt. 1885

Children of Samuel VAN HORN and Frances HAAS are:

    i.   Urbin Melvin[12] VAN HORN[3977,3978], b. Bet. 17 Aug 1885 - 1886, PA[3979,3980]; d. Bef. 1976[3981]; m. Bertha Mae[3982], Abt. 1908[3982]; b. Abt. 1891, PA[3982]; d. Unknown.

       Notes for Urbin Melvin VAN HORN:
       In 1910 living on Maple Street in Hawthorn, Pa in a rental house with his wife of 1 year. He is a carpenter who was not out of work on April 1st. Both he and his wife can read and write.
       In his WWI Draft Registration he gives his name as Urbin Melvin Van Horn. He is a jointer for the C E Andrews Lumber company in New Bethlehem, PA. He is married and lives in New Bethlehem, PA. He is short of medium build with grey eyes and sandy hair.
       He has variously been know in the census as Rubin, Herbin and Kerbin.
       In his WWII Draft Registration he lives on Penn St. in New Bethlehem, PA. He is self employed. He gives his wife's name as Mae. He is white, 5'4", 130 lbs with blue eyes, brown hair and a ruddy complexion.
       2 April 1970 The Oil City Derrick (Oil City, PA) an Urbine Van Horn was admitted to the Brookville Hospital

       More About Urbin Melvin VAN HORN:
       Occupation: Ice Wagon Driver

       More About Urbin VAN HORN and Bertha Mae:
       Marriage: Abt. 1908[3982]

461.   ii.   Lulu V. VAN HORN, b. 29 Jul 1889, PA; d. 18 Jun 1976, Brookville, PA.
       iii.   Tallie Amberson VAN HORN[3983,3984,3985,3986], b. Bet. 19 Jul 1892 - 1893, New Bethlehem, PA[3987,3988]; d. Bet. 1930 - 1976[3989]; m. ?, Bet. 1930 - 1934; d. Unknown.

       Notes for Tallie Amberson VAN HORN:
       The 1900 census has his as a daughter but later censuses list him as a son.
       In his WWI Draft Registration he is single and is a laborer at the Crescent Bottle company in Hawthorn, PA. He is medium build and height and had brown hair and eyes.
       In 1930 single and living with his mother in her home in Hawthorn, PA.

       More About Tallie Amberson VAN HORN:
       Lived: Hawthorn, Clarion Cnty, PA
       Occupation: Electrician Odd Jobs

More About Tallie VAN HORN and ?:
Marriage: Bet. 1930 - 1934

260. Dessia A.[11] VAN HORN *(John Miles[10], Christian[9], Joshua[8], Isaiah[7], Henry B.[6], Henry[5], Christian Barentsen[4] VAN HOORN, Barent Christiansen[3], Christian Barentsen[2], Barent Barents[1])*[3990,3991,3992] was born Oct 1875 in PA[3993,3994,3995], and died Unknown. She married William Tyne SHEPHARD[3996,3997] Abt. 1890, son of William SHEPHARD and Eliza HOLVEY. He was born Bet. Jan 1868 - 08 Apr 1871 in NY or PA[3998,3999], and died Unknown.

Notes for Dessia A. VAN HORN:
Mother of 5 with 4 living in 1900.
In the 1910 Census her name is spelled Adessise. There is a daughter Adessa age 7 of the age of the Dessa found living with her sister Mable in 1920 and aged 17. She has been married for 19 years and has 11 children of which 10 are living.

Notes for William Tyne SHEPHARD.
In 1900 living in McKean Cnty, Pa renting a home. No employment is given but the record shows that he has not been any months without work.
In 1910 he is a sawmill laborer.
Some sources indicate that he was born in Wales but the 1910 census listed PA as birthplace and parents as born in the US.

More About William SHEPHARD and Dessia VAN HORN:
Marriage: Abt. 1890

Children of Dessia VAN HORN and William SHEPHARD are:
462.   i.   George H.[12] SHEPHARD, b. 14 Feb 1893, Kane, PA; d. 17 Mar 1973, Wellsville, NY.
       ii.   Anna V. SHEPHARD[4000,4001], b. Mar 1894, PA[4002,4003]; d. Unknown.
      iii.   Cecile H. SHEPHARD[4004,4005], b. Nov 1896, PA[4006,4007]; d. Unknown.
463.   iv.   Mabel J. SHEPHARD, b. Jun 1898, PA; d. Aft. 1930.
       v.   William T. SHEPHARD[4008], b. Abt. 1900, PA[4008]; d. Unknown.
      vi.   Adessa M. SHEPHARD[4008], b. Abt. 1902, PA[4008]; d. Unknown.
     vii.   Loretta E. SHEPHARD[4008], b. Abt. 1903, PA[4008]; d. Unknown.
    viii.   Walter C. SHEPHARD[4008], b. Abt. 1904, PA[4008]; d. Unknown.
      ix.   Loyd N. SHEPHARD[4008], b. Abt. 1907, PA[4008]; d. Unknown.
      x.   Bella E. SHEPHARD[4008], b. Abt. Feb 1910, PA[4008]; d. Unknown.

261. Emma H.[11] VAN HORN *(John Miles[10], Christian[9], Joshua[8], Isaiah[7], Henry B.[6], Henry[5], Christian Barentsen[4] VAN HOORN, Barent Christiansen[3], Christian Barentsen[2], Barent Barents[1])*[4009,4010,4011,4012] was born Nov 1880 in PA[4013], and died Unknown. She married Richard E. BARKER[4014,4015,4016,4017] Abt. 1897[4018], son of Samuel BARKER and Hannah J.. He was born Mar 1877 in PA[4019], and died Unknown.

Notes for Emma H. VAN HORN:
In 1900 Emma is living in the same Twp. with John M. Van Horn. I have placed her as a child of John M. Van Horn. Additional support for this is that Rachael says in 1900 she is the other of 8 living children with only 7 in the household.
In 1910 living two families from her father and mother. She has been married for 12 years and she has 6 children all of which are living. She and her husband are living with his father.
In 1920 living near her father and his new wife as well as her brother Lester in Falls Creek, PA.

In 1930 Emma and her husband are living on Falls Creek Rd, Sandy, Clearfield Cnty, PA is a home they rent for $12/month. Richard is a painter and does odd jobs. They have living with them her mother Rachel Van Horn, His father Samuel Barker and a niece Emma Van Horn.

Notes for Richard E. BARKER:
In 1900 he is living next door to his parents and he is a teamster.
In 1910 living with his father. He works on a railroad. He and Emma have 6 children.
In 1920 has his father living with him. Also his daughter Lois and her new husband John Wolfe. He is a glass cutter in a glass factory. Living on West Main in Falls Creek, PA in a house they rent.

More About Richard BARKER and Emma VAN HORN:
Marriage: Abt. 1897[4020]

Children of Emma VAN HORN and Richard BARKER are:
    i.   Eva M.[12] BARKER[4021,4022], b. May 1898, PA[4023]; d. Unknown.
    ii.   Samuel S. BARKER[4024,4025], b. Abt. 1900, PA[4026]; d. Unknown.
    iii.   Lois I. BARKER[4026,4027], b. Abt. 1902, PA[4028]; d. Unknown; m. John M. WOLFE[4029]; b. Abt. 1900, PA[4030]; d. Unknown.

        Notes for John M. WOLFE:
        Living with his father in law and working as a laborer in a glass factory.

    iv.   Muriel Ruth BARKER[4031,4032], b. Abt. 1904, PA[4033]; d. Unknown.
    v.   Ellis V. BARKER[4033,4034], b. Abt. 1907, PA[4035]; d. Unknown.
    vi.   Ernest P. BARKER[4035,4036], b. Abt. Aug 1909, PA[4037]; d. Unknown.

262. Stella Marilla[11] VAN HORN *(John Miles[10], Christian[9], Joshua[8], Isaiah[7], Henry B.[6], Henry[5], Christian Barentsen[4] VAN HOORN, Barent Christiansen[3], Christian Barentsen[2], Barent Barents[1])*[4038,4039,4040,4041] was born May 1882 in PA[4042,4043], and died Aft. 1930. She married William Washington GEARHART[4044,4045,4046,4047,4048] Abt. 1904[4049], son of Abraham GEARHART and Caroline RICHNER. He was born Bet. 10 Mar 1876 - 1877 in Jefferson Cnty, PA[4050,4051,4052], and died 08 Feb 1945 in Akron, Summit Cnty, OH.

Notes for Stella Marilla VAN HORN:
The 1910 Census lists 2 children living but neither are enumerated in the census. She and William have been married for 5 years and rent. He is a miner. In 1910 William and Stella are married for 5 years she had 2 children both living but they are not listed.

Notes for William Washington GEARHART:
In his 1915 WWI Draft Registration he works for Summit Coal, Dayton, Armstrong Cnty, PA. He is married and lists Stella Van Horn Gearhart as his nearest relative and living in Dayton, PA. He is medium build of medium height and has blue eyes and light hair.
In 1920 owns home free and clear.
In 1930 lives on Main Street in Dayton, PA in a home he owns worth $1000.

More About William Washington GEARHART:
Occupation: Coal Miner

More About William GEARHART and Stella VAN HORN:
Marriage: Abt. 1904[4052]

Children of Stella VAN HORN and William GEARHART are:
    i.   Lila[12] GEARHART, b. Bef. 1910, PA; d. Unknown.
    ii.   Gertrude GEARHART[4053], b. Abt. 1910, PA[4053]; d. Unknown.
    iii.   Lottie Mae GEARHART[4053,4054,4055,4056], b. 05 Feb 1913, Smicksburg, Indiana Cnty, PA[4057]; d. 1946; m. A. J. DEHAVEN[4058], 24 Dec 1937, Dayton, Armstrong Cnty, PA[4058]; d. Unknown.

        More About A. DEHAVEN and Lottie GEARHART:
        Marriage: 24 Dec 1937, Dayton, Armstrong Cnty, PA[4058]
        Marriage date: Rev G. W. McIntyre
        Marriage Place: Parsonage of the minister

464.   iv.   Lois Fae GEARHART, b. 05 Feb 1913, Smicksburg, Indiana Cnty, PA; d. 18 May 1995, Kittanning, Armstrong Cnty, PA.
    v.   Francis GEARHART, b. Private.
    vi.   Annabelle GEARHART, b. Private.
    vii.   Lester M. GEARHART[4059], b. 19 May 1920, Dayton, Armstrong Cnty, PA[4059,4060]; d. 17 Mar 1982, Niles, Trumbull Cnty, OH[4060]; m. (1) COGLEY, Private; b. Private; m. (2) WALTERS, Private; b. Private.

        More About Lester GEARHART and COGLEY:
        Private-Begin: Private

        More About Lester GEARHART and WALTERS:
        Private-Begin: Private

    viii.   Clara M. GEARHART, b. Private.
    ix.   William GEARHART, JR, b. Private.

263. Lilla L.[11] VAN HORN *(John Miles[10], Christian[9], Joshua[8], Isaiah[7], Henry B.[6], Henry[5], Christian Barentsen[4] VAN HOORN, Barent Christiansen[3], Christian Barentsen[2], Barent Barents[1])*[4061,4062,4063,4064] was born May 1891 in PA[4065], and died Unknown. She married Boyd A. HOOVER[4066,4067] 1909[4068,4069], son of Eury HOOVER and Clara. He was born Jun 1883 in PA[4070], and died Unknown.

Notes for Lilla L. VAN HORN:
    In 1910 Lilla is living with hr parents. She is married with one child of 5 months having been married for 1 year. Her husband is not in the household.

Notes for Boyd A. HOOVER:
    In 1920 rents a home on Main Street in DuBois, PA. He is a truck driver for a grocery store.
    In 1930 owns his home in DuBois, PA worth $4,000 and has a radio. He is a truck driver of a wholesale grocery store.

More About Boyd HOOVER and Lilla VAN HORN:
Marriage: 1909[4071,4072]

Children of Lilla VAN HORN and Boyd HOOVER are:
    i.   Clyde Burnell[12] HOOVER[4073,4074,4075], b. Dec 1910, PA[4076]; d. Unknown.

        More About Clyde Burnell HOOVER:
        Employment: 1930, Machinist in a Silk Factory

    ii.   Florence E. HOOVER, b. Private.
   iii.   Lloyd E. HOOVER*4077,4078*, b. Abt. 1914, PA*4079*; d. Unknown.
   iv.   Jean W. HOOVER, b. Private.
    v.   William W. HOOVER, b. Private.
   vi.   Glenn A. HOOVER, b. Private.

264. Lester Leona[11] VAN HORN *(John Miles[10], Christian[9], Joshua[8], Isaiah[7], Henry B.[6], Henry[5], Christian Barentsen[4] VAN HOORN, Barent Christiansen[3], Christian Barentsen[2], Barent Barents[1])4080,4081,4082,4083* was born 05 Apr 1895 in DuBois, Clearfield Cnty, PA*4084,4085,4086*, and died Aft. 1930. He married Edna MARSH*4087,4088,4089* Abt. 1911, daughter of Zacariah MARSH and Clara. She was born Abt. 1893 in PA*4090*, and died Aft. 1930.

Notes for Lester Leona VAN HORN:
    In his WWI he says he is of medium height, medium build with gray eyes and brown hair. He is married and has 3 children. He lives in Falls Creek, PA and is a laborer for Wolf Bros. Coal Company.
    In 1920 Lester is living next door to John M and his second wife
    In 1930 living next to Donald VanHorn and renting for $7.55 and has a radio.

More About Lester Leona VAN HORN:
Occupation: Foreman Glass Factory, Loader Coal Mine

More About Lester VAN HORN and Edna MARSH:
Marriage: Abt. 1911

Children of Lester VAN HORN and Edna MARSH are:
          i.   Hazel M.[12] VAN HORN*4090,4091*, b. Abt. 1912, PA*4092*; d. Unknown.
         ii.   Elnora VAN HORN, b. Private.
465.   iii.   Emery Ernest VAN HORN, b. Bet. 08 Jan - Feb 1915, Falls Creek, Jefferson Cnty, PA; d. 02 Sep 1996, St. Marys, Elk Cnty, PA.
         iv.   John W. VAN HORN, b. Private.
          v.   Clara Emmagina VAN HORN, b. Private.

265. Donald Michael[11] VAN HORN *(John Miles[10], Christian[9], Joshua[8], Isaiah[7], Henry B.[6], Henry[5], Christian Barentsen[4] VAN HOORN, Barent Christiansen[3], Christian Barentsen[2], Barent Barents[1])4093,4094,4095,4096,4097* was born 28 Nov 1897 in PA*4098,4099*, and died 1970 in PA. He married Hazel V. HENRY*4100,4101* Abt. 1913. She was born 1895 in PA*4101*, and died 1985 in PA.

Notes for Donald Michael VAN HORN:
    In his WWI Draft Registration he states he is a miner for the William Herringer Co in Dubois, Clearfield, PA. His wife is Hazel Henry Van Horn and they live in Falls Creek, PA He is medium height, stout build has gray eyes and brown hair.
    In 1920 his brother in law John H. Henry is living with him.
    In 1930 he is renting for $7.55 and has a radio. He is living next door to Lester Van Horn, his brother, on Clinton Street.
    In the 1948 Dubois City Directory there is a listing that Winfred E. Murphy is a steward at the residence of Don M. Van Horn.

More About Donald Michael VAN HORN:
Burial: 1970, Salem Methodist Church, DuBois, Cleafield Cnty, PA
Occupation: Coal Mine Loader, Miner

More About Hazel V. HENRY:
Burial: 1985, Salem Methodist Church, DuBois, Cleafield Cnty, PA

More About Donald VAN HORN and Hazel HENRY:
Marriage: Abt. 1913

Children of Donald VAN HORN and Hazel HENRY are:
    i.   Mildred A.[12] VAN HORN, b. Private.
    ii. Dorothy L. VAN HORN, b. Private.
    iii. Donald Michael VAN HORN, JR, b. Private.

266. Norman Ernest[11] VAN HORN *(John Miles[10], Christian[9], Joshua[8], Isaiah[7], Henry B.[6], Henry[5], Christian Barentsen[4] VAN HOORN, Barent Christiansen[3], Christian Barentsen[2], Barent Barents[1])*[4102,4103,4104,4105,4106] was born 16 Oct 1899 in PA[4107,4108], and died Unknown. He married Fae WOODWARD[4109,4110] May 1917 in Clearfield Cnty, PA[4110]. She died Unknown.

Notes for Norman Ernest VAN HORN:
    In his 1918 WWI Civilian draft Registration he is of medium build, medium height, brown eyes and black hair. He is a miner and his closest relative is Faie Van Horn. He gives his whole name as Norman Earnest Van Horn.

More About Norman Ernest VAN HORN:
Occupation: B&S Railroad

More About Norman VAN HORN and Fae WOODWARD:
Marriage: May 1917, Clearfield Cnty, PA[4110]

Child of Norman VAN HORN and Fae WOODWARD is:
    i.   Margaret Emma[12] VAN HORN, b. Private.

267. Harvey S.[11] BOSSARD *(Adessa Levina[10] VAN HORN, Christian[9], Joshua[8], Isaiah[7], Henry B.[6], Henry[5], Christian Barentsen[4] VAN HOORN, Barent Christiansen[3], Christian Barentsen[2], Barent Barents[1])*[4111,4112,4113] was born Mar 1893 in PA[4114], and died Unknown. He married Elma[4115]. She was born Abt. 1898 in PA[4115], and died Unknown.

Notes for Harvey S. BOSSARD:
    In 1920 renting in North Point District of West Mahoning Twp. ,Indiana Cnty, PA. Living in the home is his wife and daughter and brother Lee Bossard age 16.

More About Harvey S. BOSSARD:
Employment: 1920, Section Hand Steam Railroad

Child of Harvey BOSSARD and Elma is:
    i.   Monabelle[12] BOSSARD, b. Private.

268. Henry Oliver[11] CARLTON *(Mazella I.[10] VAN HORN, Henry[9], Joshua[8], Isaiah[7], Henry B.[6], Henry[5], Christian Barentsen[4] VAN HOORN, Barent Christiansen[3], Christian Barentsen[2], Barent Barents[1])*[4116] was born 03 Feb 1882 in Northern Twp., Franklin Cnty, IL[4116], and died 21 Aug 1966 in Benton, Franklin Cnty, IL[4116]. He married Golda May DIXON[4116] 20 Sep 1905[4116]. She was born 18 Aug 1888 in Posey Cnty, IN[4116], and died 25 May 1975 in Benton, Franklin Cnty, IL[4116].

More About Henry CARLTON and Golda DIXON:
Marriage: 20 Sep 1905[4116]

Child of Henry CARLTON and Golda DIXON is:
    i.   Wilma[12] CARLTON, b. Private; m. CHILDERS, Private; b. Private.

          More About CHILDERS and Wilma CARLTON:
          Private-Begin: Private

269. Earl Donovan[11] KECK *(Lynn McKee[10], Tabitha Dorcas[9] VAN HORN, Joshua[8], Isaiah[7], Henry B.[6], Henry[5], Christian Barentsen[4] VAN HOORN, Barent Christiansen[3], Christian Barentsen[2], Barent Barents[1])*[4117,4118] was born 08 Apr 1896 in Elk Run, Jefferson Cnty, PA[4119], and died 25 Feb 1966 in Punxsutawney, Jefferson Cnty, PA. He married Louise Ernestine YANHKE[4120] 25 Oct 1916, daughter of Charles YANHKE and Sophia ALLENBAUGH. She was born 1897 in PA[4120], and died 1989.

Notes for Earl Donovan KECK:
    In 1930 he rents for $20/month.

More About Earl Donovan KECK:
Occupation: Bricklayer

More About Earl KECK and Louise YANHKE:
Marriage: 25 Oct 1916

Children of Earl KECK and Louise YANHKE are:
    i.   ?[12] KECK, b. Private.
    ii. ? KECK, b. Private.
    iii. Edith Marie KECK[4120], b. 1917, PA[4120]; d. 1978.
    iv. Alfred Earl KECK, b. Private.
    v. Donald Lloyd KECK[4120], b. 1920, PA[4120]; d. 2002.
    vi. Wanda Louise KECK[4120], b. 1921, PA[4120]; d. 1981.
    vii. Theodore Blaine KECK[4120], b. 1925, PA[4120]; d. 1972.
    viii. Lois W.KECK, b. Private.
    ix. Emogene H. KECK, b. Private.
    x. Joyce Eleanor KECK, b. 1934, PA; d. 2004.
    xi. Clara Jane KECK, b. 1935, PA; d. 1997; m. DEMPSEY, Private; b. Private.

          More About DEMPSEY and Clara KECK:
          Private-Begin: Private

270. Albert Hugh[11] MCAFOOS *(Sarah Dorcas[10] SINK, Sarah[9] VAN HORN, Joshua[8], Isaiah[7], Henry B.[6], Henry[5], Christian Barentsen[4] VAN HOORN, Barent Christiansen[3], Christian Barentsen[2], Barent Barents[1])*[4121,4122,4123] was born 17 Nov 1873 in Franklin Cnty, IL[4124], and died Unknown. He married Nellie B.[4125] Abt. 1900[4125]. She was born 1882 in IA[4125], and died Unknown.

Notes for Albert Hugh MCAFOOS:
    In 1930 married and has a home he owns worth about $500. He does not have a radio. His employment is odd jobs. He is living next door to his sister Ella Mary Hines and her family.

More About Albert MCAFOOS and Nellie B.:
Marriage: Abt. 1900[4125]

Children of Albert MCAFOOS and Nellie B. are:
  i. Ira[12] MCAFOOS[4125], b. Abt. 1911, KS[4125]; d. Unknown.
  ii. Clyde MCAFOOS, b. Private.
  iii. Elmer MCAFOOS[4125], b. Abt. 1902, KS[4125]; d. Unknown.

271. Charles Austin[11] MCAFOOS *(Sarah Dorcas[10] SINK, Sarah[9] VAN HORN, Joshua[8], Isaiah[7], Henry B.[6], Henry[5], Christian Barentsen[4] VAN HOORN, Barent Christiansen[3], Christian Barentsen[2], Barent Barents[1])[4126,4127,4128]* was born 07 May 1876 in Nortern, Franklin Cnty, IL[4129], and died 29 Jan 1962 in Holton, Jackson Cnty, KS. He married (1) Nora E. WAIDELY 1904 in Crab Orchard, KS. She died Unknown. He married (2) Clara Estella HOFFMAN[4129,4130] Abt. 1910. She was born Abt. 1889 in KS[4131], and died Unknown.

Notes for Charles Austin MCAFOOS:
    John WAIDELY m. Jennie MOREHEAD, had dau. Nora E. WAIDELY. Charles A. McAFOOS m. Nora E. WAIDELY 9 Mar 1904 at Crab Orchard. Divorced in 1910. Their 17 year old daughter, Iva W. McAFOOS
    In his WWI draft registration he states he is married to Clara and is a blacksmith for Paul Rhoten in Rexford, KS. He states he is tall of medium build with brown eyes and black hair.
    In 1920 he owns his place free and clear. He lives on Spruce Street in Rexford, KS and is a carpenter.
    In 1930 living in a home he rents for $5/month on South Street in Rexford, KS and is a carpenter.

More About Charles Austin MCAFOOS:
Occupation: Carpenter

More About Charles MCAFOOS and Nora WAIDELY:
Divorce: 1910
Marriage: 1904, Crab Orchard, KS

More About Charles MCAFOOS and Clara HOFFMAN:
Marriage: Abt. 1910

Child of Charles MCAFOOS and Nora WAIDELY is:
  i. Iva W.[12] MCAFOOS, b. Private.

Children of Charles MCAFOOS and Clara HOFFMAN are:
  ii. Charles Raymond[12] MCAFOOS[4131,4132,4133], b. Abt. 1912, KS[4134]; d. Bef. 2010.
  iii. Gertie E. MCAFOOS, b. Private; m. COON, Private; b. Private.

     More About COON and Gertie MCAFOOS:
     Private-Begin: Private

  iv. George E. MCAFOOS[4134,4134,4135], b. Abt. 1915, KS[4136]; d. Bef. 2010.
  v. Harold A. MCAFOOS[4136,4137,4138], b. Abt. 1919, KS[4139]; d. Bef. 2010.
466. vi. Dorothy M. MCAFOOS, b. 01 Feb 1922, St Marys, Pottawatomie Cnty, KS; d. 01 Jan 2010, St Marys, Pottawatomie Cnty, KS.
  vii. Clarence A. MCAFOOS[4140,4141], b. Abt. 1924, KS[4142]; d. Bef. 2010.

    viii.   Cleo H. MCAFOOS[4142,4143], b. Abt. 1927, KS[4144]; d. Aft. 2010.

    ix.   Perry MCAFOOS[4145], d. 1927.

        More About Perry MCAFOOS:
        Burial: Unknown, Hawkeye Cemetery, Decatur Cnty, KS

    x.   Ethel MCAFOOS[4145], d. Aft. 2010; m. ANDERSON, Private; b. Private.

        More About ANDERSON and Ethel MCAFOOS:
        Private-Begin: Private

272. Elsie Estelle[11] MCAFOOS *(Sarah Dorcas*[10] *SINK, Sarah*[9] *VAN HORN, Joshua*[8]*, Isaiah*[7]*, Henry B.*[6]*, Henry*[5]*, Christian Barentsen*[4] *VAN HOORN, Barent Christiansen*[3]*, Christian Barentsen*[2]*, Barent Barents*[1]*)*[4146,4147,4148,4149] was born 03 Sep 1878 in Franklin Cnty, IL[4150], and died 08 Apr 1940 in Rexford, Thomas Cnty, KS or Goodland, KS. She married Samuel Fred POINTER[4151,4152,4153] Abt. 1896, son of Noah POINTER and Hannah ROUSH. He was born 24 Aug 1873 in Monroe Cnty, IA[4154], and died 12 Oct 1940 in Goodland, Sherman Cnty, KS.

Notes for Samuel Fred POINTER:
    In 1930 he is renting for $12/month and as a radio. He is a laborer doing odd jobs.

More About Samuel Fred POINTER:
Occupation: Bet. 1910 - 1920, Farmer

More About Samuel POINTER and Elsie MCAFOOS:
Marriage: Abt. 1896

Children of Elsie MCAFOOS and Samuel POINTER are:
467.   i.   Homer Vernon[12] POINTER, b. 17 Mar 1895, Rexford, Thomas Cnty, KS; d. 13 Feb 1948, Potter, TX.

       ii.   Alvin Everett POINTER[4154,4155], b. 04 May 1900, KS[4156,4157]; d. 20 Feb 1959, Potter, TX; m. Christa; b. 1901; d. Unknown.

           More About Alvin Everett POINTER:
           Employment: 1930, Repairman in Auto Repair Shop

       iii.   Virgie Bernice POINTER[4158,4159], b. Abt. 1901, KS[4160]; d. Unknown.
       iv.   Perry Amos POINTER[4160,4161], b. Abt. 1904, KS[4162]; d. Unknown.
468.   v.   Gladys Mabel POINTER, b. 11 Aug 1906, Oberlin, KS; d. 20 Apr 1996, Fresno, Fresno Cnty, CA.
       vi.   Ferma Dorcas POINTER[4162,4163], b. Abt. 1909, KS[4164]; d. Unknown.
       vii.   Delphia Mae POINTER[4165], b. Abt. 1911, KS[4165]; d. Unknown.
       viii.   Evelyn Ella POINTER, b. Private.

273. Oscar Alvin[11] MCAFOOS *(Sarah Dorcas*[10] *SINK, Sarah*[9] *VAN HORN, Joshua*[8]*, Isaiah*[7]*, Henry B.*[6]*, Henry*[5]*, Christian Barentsen*[4] *VAN HOORN, Barent Christiansen*[3]*, Christian Barentsen*[2]*, Barent Barents*[1]*)*[4166,4167,4168] was born 27 Jun 1887 in Thomas Cnty, KS[4169], and died Sep 1974 in Santa Fe, Santa Fe Cnty, NM. He married Eva[4170] Abt. 1912[4170]. She was born Abt. 1889 in KS[4170], and died Unknown.

Notes for Oscar Alvin MCAFOOS:

His WWI Record shows him as of medium height, medium build, brown eyes and black hair. He is a farmer in Rexford, KS married and has a child in 1917.

In 1930 he owns his place and has a radio. He is a farmer and has a wife and 4 children of the home.

More About Oscar MCAFOOS and Eva:
Marriage: Abt. 1912[4170]

Children of Oscar MCAFOOS and Eva are:
    i.   Evelyn[12] MCAFOOS, b. Private.
    ii.   Walter MCAFOOS, b. Private.
    iii. Velma MCAFOOS, b. Private.
    iv. Ralph MCAFOOS, b. Private.

274. Ella Mary[11] MCAFOOS (*Sarah Dorcas*[10] *SINK, Sarah*[9] *VAN HORN, Joshua*[8], *Isaiah*[7], *Henry B.*[6], *Henry*[5], *Christian Barentsen*[4] *VAN HOORN, Barent Christiansen*[3], *Christian Barentsen*[2], *Barent Barents*[1])[4171,4172,4173] was born Bet. 19 Aug 1893 - 1896 in Thomas Cnty, KS[4174,4175], and died 14 Dec 1955 in Amarillo, Potter Cnty, TX. She married Wallace Logan HINES[4175] 26 May 1914[4175], son of James HINES and Mary ELLIOT. He was born 28 Dec 1887 in Haddam, Washington Cnty, KS[4175], and died 03 Sep 1955 in Denver, Denver Cnty, CO.

Notes for Wallace Logan HINES:
In 1930 owns his home worth about $2,000 and does not have a radio. He works as a school bus repairman.

More About Wallace HINES and Ella MCAFOOS:
Marriage: 26 May 1914[4175]

Children of Ella MCAFOOS and Wallace HINES are:
    i.   ?[12] HINES, b. Private.
    ii.   Mildred Vesta HINES, b. 1917; d. 1917.
    iii. Noran Evelyn HINES, b. 1915; d. 1915.
    iv. Clifford Austin HINES[4176], b. 1916, KS[4176]; d. 24 Apr 1985, Hastings, Adams Cnty, NE[4177].
    v.   Clyde Wallace HINES[4178], b. 1919, KS[4178]; d. 27 Aug 1971, Breezewood, Bedford Cnty, PA.
    vi. Jane T. HINES, b. Private.

275. Calvin[11] SINK (*Austin Addison*[10], *Sarah*[9] *VAN HORN, Joshua*[8], *Isaiah*[7], *Henry B.*[6], *Henry*[5], *Christian Barentsen*[4] *VAN HOORN, Barent Christiansen*[3], *Christian Barentsen*[2], *Barent Barents*[1])[4179,4180,4181,4182] was born Sep 1879 in IL[4183], and died Unknown. He married Lucy[4184,4185] Abt. 1904[4185]. She was born Abt. 1885 in IL[4186], and died Unknown.

Notes for Calvin SINK:
In 1920 owns his place free and clear. He is a farmer. There is a R. Newton Van Horn age 75 born PA and wife L. S. living next door.

More About Calvin SINK and Lucy:
Marriage: Abt. 1904[4187]

Children of Calvin SINK and Lucy are:

    i.   Ora[12] SINK[4188], b. Abt. 1905, IL; d. Unknown.
    ii.   Ethel SINK[4188], b. Abt. 1906, IL; d. Unknown.
   iii. Omar SINK[4188,4189], b. Abt. 1908, IL; d. Unknown.
   iv. Roy SINK[4190,4191], b. Abt. 1910, IL; d. Unknown.
    v.   William SINK[4192,4193], b. Abt. 1911, IL; d. Unknown.
   vi. Edith SINK, b. Private.
  vii. Nellie SINK, b. Private.
 viii. Wilma SINK, b. Private.
   ix. Alice SINK, b. Private.
    x.   Robert SINK, b. Private.

276. Althia[11] SINK *(Austin Addison[10], Sarah[9] VAN HORN, Joshua[8], Isaiah[7], Henry B.[6], Henry[5], Christian Barentsen[4] VAN HOORN, Barent Christiansen[3], Christian Barentsen[2], Barent Barents[1])*[4194,4195] was born Nov 1883 in IL[4196], and died Unknown. She married JOHNSON Abt. 1904. He died Unknown.

Notes for JOHNSON:
    In 1910 is listed as head of the household with her mother living with her. She is married for 5 years and has had 1 child but it is not living in 1910.

More About JOHNSON and Althia SINK:
Marriage: Abt. 1904

Child of Althia SINK and JOHNSON is:
    i.   ?[12] JOHNSON, b. Bef. 1910; d. Bef. 1910.

277. Stella[11] SINK *(Elmer E.[10], Sarah[9] VAN HORN, Joshua[8], Isaiah[7], Henry B.[6], Henry[5], Christian Barentsen[4] VAN HOORN, Barent Christiansen[3], Christian Barentsen[2], Barent Barents[1])*[4197,4198,4199] was born Jan 1890 in IL[4200], and died Unknown. She married (1) Charles LOWERY. He died Unknown. She married (2) John Wesley WITTERS[4201]. He was born Abt. 1880 in IL[4201], and died 1967.

Notes for Stella SINK:
In 1910 Stella is widowed having married a man by the name of Lowery and now living with her step father and mother.

Notes for John Wesley WITTERS:
    In 1920 owns his place free and clear. He is a farmer.

Children of Stella SINK and John WITTERS are:
    i.   Irene V.[12] WITTERS, b. Private.
   ii. Genevieve L. WITTERS, b. Private.
  iii. Charles B. WITTERS, b. Private.
  iv. I. Nadine WITTERS, b. Private.

278. Loren Wilson[11] SINK *(Elmer E.[10], Sarah[9] VAN HORN, Joshua[8], Isaiah[7], Henry B.[6], Henry[5], Christian Barentsen[4] VAN HOORN, Barent Christiansen[3], Christian Barentsen[2], Barent Barents[1])*[4202,4203,4204,4205] was born Bet. Nov 1891 - 11 Aug 1893 in Franklin Cnty, IL[4206], and died 10 Jan 1974 in Ewing, Franklin Cnty, IL[4207]. He married Alice Allie WITTERS[4208,4209] 31 Aug 1913 in Hamilton Cnty, IL. She was born 21 Aug 1894 in Hamilton Cnty, IL[4210], and died 18 Jan 1981.

Notes for Loren Wilson SINK:
    In 1900 and 1910 living with his se\stepfather and mother. By 1910 he is working on the farm. He registers for the WWI Draft and states his birth date is July 11, 1983. He is medium height, slender build and had gray eyes and light hair. He lives in Snowflake, IL is a farmer and has a wife and 2 children on June 5, 1917.
    In 1920 owns his place with a mortgage and is a farmer.

More About Loren Wilson SINK:
Occupation: Public School Teacher

More About Loren SINK and Alice WITTERS:
Marriage: 31 Aug 1913, Hamilton Cnty, IL

Children of Loren SINK and Alice WITTERS are:
    i.   Mildred C.[12] SINK, b. Private.
    ii.   Eugene D. SINK, b. Private.
    iii. Elmer H. SINK, b. Private.
    iv. Dwight E. SINK, b. Private.

279. William Jacob[11] SINK *(Elmer E.[10], Sarah[9] VAN HORN, Joshua[8], Isaiah[7], Henry B.[6], Henry[5], Christian Barentsen[4] VAN HOORN, Barent Christiansen[3], Christian Barentsen[2], Barent Barents[1])*[4211,4212,4213] was born Jun 1894 in IL[4214], and died Unknown. He married Coral Opal BOYER[4215] Abt. 1916. She was born Abt. 1900 in IL[4215], and died Unknown.

Notes for William Jacob SINK:
    In 1930 owns his farm and is a general farmer.

More About William SINK and Coral BOYER:
Marriage: Abt. 1916

Children of William SINK and Coral BOYER are:
    i.   Lucian[12] SINK, b. Private.
    ii.   Maxine SINK, b. Private.
    iii. Frieda SINK, b. Private.
    iv. Rodney SINK, b. Private.

280. Samuel Clyde[11] VAN HORN *(Anderson T.[10], Samuel H.[9], Joshua[8], Isaiah[7], Henry B.[6], Henry[5], Christian Barentsen[4] VAN HOORN, Barent Christiansen[3], Christian Barentsen[2], Barent Barents[1])*[4216,4217] was born Feb 1896 in Punxsutawney, Jefferson Cnty, PA, and died Aft. 1966. He married Anna STAFFORD[4217] 1917. She was born 1891 in Tioga Cnty, PA[4217], and died 17 Apr 1966 in St. Cloud, FL[4217].

More About Samuel VAN HORN and Anna STAFFORD:
Marriage: 1917

Children of Samuel VAN HORN and Anna STAFFORD are:
    i.   Herbert[12] VAN HORN, b. Private.
    ii.   LeRoy VAN HORN, b. Private.

281. Harry V.[11] VAN HORN, JR *(Harry V.[10], John Hastings[9], John[8], Isaiah[7], Henry B.[6], Henry[5],*

Christian Barentsen[4] *VAN HOORN, Barent Christiansen*[3], *Christian Barentsen*[2], *Barent Barents*[1])[4218,4219,4220] was born 15 Oct 1894 in PA[4221], and died 28 Jan 1942. He married Elizabeth B. WALDER[4222,4223] Abt. 1914, daughter of Christ WALDER and Margaret. She was born 08 Feb 1897 in PA[4224], and died Mar 1991 in PA[4225].

Notes for Harry V. VAN HORN, JR:
        WWI Draft Registration married with one child. Living on Church Street in Tuttle Creek, PA. Works for Westinghouse electric as a skilled mechanic. He is medium height, medium build with blue eyes and bond hair.
        Living 2 doors from father and mother and brothers and sisters in 1920. He is listed as Harry Z. Van Horn.
        In 1930 living next door to his parents. He owns his house on Cofford Ave near Oxford Street worth $4000 and has a radio. He is a machinist for a construction steel company.
        Also known as Harry Zerney Van Horn.
.

More About Harry V. VAN HORN, JR:
Occupation: Machinist Steel Mill, Machinist Construction Steel

More About Harry VAN HORN and Elizabeth WALDER:
Marriage: Abt. 1914

Children of Harry VAN HORN and Elizabeth WALDER are:
         i.   Harry W.[12] VAN HORN[4226,4227], b. 14 Jan 1916, PA[4228]; d. 24 Sep 1992, Toms
               River, Ocean Cnty, NJ[4229]; m. Marion L. EGGERS[4230]; b. 10 Jul 1919, PA[4231]; d. 25
               Sep 1990, Toms River, Ocean Cnty, NJ[4231].
469.   ii.   LeRoy VAN HORN, b. Private.
        iii.   Margaret Eliabeth VAN HORN[4232], b. 02 Feb 1921, PA[4232]; d. 1988, CA; m.
               DELONG, Private; b. Private.

               More About DELONG and Margaret VAN HORN:
               Private-Begin: Private

         iv.   Helen A. VAN HORN, b. Private.

282. Ralph Hastings[11] VAN HORN *(Harry V.*[10], *John Hastings*[9], *John*[8], *Isaiah*[7], *Henry B.*[6], *Henry*[5], *Christian Barentsen*[4] *VAN HOORN, Barent Christiansen*[3], *Christian Barentsen*[2], *Barent Barents*[1])[4233,4234,4235] was born 14 Aug 1900 in PA[4236], and died 06 Apr 1997 in Pittsburgh, Alleghney Cnty, PA[4237]. He married Anna SCHIRRA[4238] Abt. 1920. She was born 10 Oct 1898 in PA[4238], and died 03 Dec 1993 in PA.

Notes for Ralph Hastings VAN HORN:
        In 1930 owns house on W. 6th Street in Aspinwall, PA worth $6000 and has a radio. His brother in law August Schirra is living in the home.

More About Ralph Hastings VAN HORN:
Burial: Unknown, Greenwood Cemetery, Sharpsburg, Allegheny Cnty, PA
Occupation: Contract Machinist, Laborer Structural Steel

More About Anna SCHIRRA:
Burial: Unknown, Greenwood Cemetery, Sharpsburg, Allegheny Cnty, PA

More About Ralph VAN HORN and Anna SCHIRRA:

Marriage: Abt. 1920

Children of Ralph VAN HORN and Anna SCHIRRA are:
    i.   Robert E.[12] VAN HORN[4238], b. 28 Jan 1922, PA[4238]; d. 30 May 1995, PA.

          More About Robert E. VAN HORN:
          Burial: Unknown, Greenwood Cemetery, Sharpsburg, Allegheny Cnty, PA
          Military service: Sgt US Army Air Corps - World War II

    ii.   Ruth VAN HORN, b. Private.
    iii. Dorothy VAN HORN, b. Private.

283. Sarah Isabel[11] VAN HORN *(John Hastings[10], James Devin[9], John[8], Isaiah[7], Henry B.[6], Henry[5], Christian Barentsen[4] VAN HOORN, Barent Christiansen[3], Christian Barentsen[2], Barent Barents[1])*[4239,4240,4241,4242] was born Aug 1891 in PA[4243], and died Unknown. She married Garrett DEAN[4244,4245,4246] 1919, He was born 08 Jul 1892 in Evansville, IN[4247,4248], and died Unknown.

Notes for Garrett DEAN:
    In his WWI Civilian Draft Registration he is a Chef at a cafe in Ft. Bliss, TX. He is single, born in Evansville, IN, tall, slender with brown eyes and hair.
    In 1920 he is doing farm labor in Jim Wells Cnty, TX. He lives near his father in law.
    In 1930 living next door to his wife's father John H. VanHorn and brother Arthur P. VanHorn. They are renting for $15/month

More About Garrett DEAN:
Occupation: Postal Clerk

More About Garrett DEAN and Sarah VAN HORN:
Marriage: 1919

Child of Sarah VAN HORN and Garrett DEAN is:
    i.   Dorothy E.[12] DEAN, b. Private.

284. William D.[11] LYDICK *(John Albert[10], Jane Elizabeth[9] VAN HORN, Isaiah[8], Isaiah[7], Henry B.[6], Henry[5], Christian Barentsen[4] VAN HOORN, Barent Christiansen[3], Christian Barentsen[2], Barent Barents[1])*[4249,4250,4251,4252,4252] was born 06 Mar 1884 in Indiana Cnty, PA[4253], and died 1937 in PA. He married Laura HOFFMAN[4254] Abt. 1908. She was born Abt. 1875 in PA[4254], and died Bet. 1916 - 1920.

Notes for William D. LYDICK:
    In 1920 he is a widow living with his brother and widowed mother. He has 2 children who are also in the home at this time.
    In 1930 he is a coal miner listed in the census as an uncle. He is widowed age of 46. He is the uncle of Herman Hadden son of his sister Alice.

More About William D. LYDICK:
Occupation: Coal Miner

Notes for Laura HOFFMAN:
    In 1910 Laura is the wife of William Lydick. This is her second marriage and Williams first. They have been married for 2 years. Laura is the mother of 2 and only Blaine is living. William is a coal miner.

More About William LYDICK and Laura HOFFMAN:
Marriage: Abt. 1908

Children of William LYDICK and Laura HOFFMAN are:
    i.   Blaine A.[12] LYDICK[4255,4256,4257], b. Abt. Aug 1908, PA[4258]; d. Unknown.

          Notes for Blaine A. LYDICK:
          In 1930 living as a lodger on Lincoln Ave. in Youngstown, OH. He is a general
          laborer. He is 23 born PA and parents born PA.

    ii.   Gay L. LYDICK, b. Private.

285. Alice M.[11] LYDICK *(John Albert[10], Jane Elizabeth[9] VAN HORN, Isaiah[8], Isaiah[7], Henry B.[6], Henry[5], Christian Barentsen[4] VAN HOORN, Barent Christiansen[3], Christian Barentsen[2], Barent Barents[1])*[4259,4260,4261] was born Mar 1887 in PA[4262], and died Unknown. She married Isaac M. HADDEN[4263,4264] 1904 in Indiana Cnty, PA[4265,4266]. He was born Abt. 1883 in PA[4267], and died Unknown.

More About Isaac M. HADDEN:
Occupation: Farmer and Brick Yard Laborer

More About Isaac HADDEN and Alice LYDICK:
Marriage: 1904, Indiana Cnty, PA[4267,4268]

Children of Alice LYDICK and Isaac HADDEN are:
    i.   Edna[12] HADDEN[4269,4270], b. Abt. 1904, PA[4271]; d. Unknown.
    ii.   Nova HADDEN[4272], b. Abt. 1906, PA[4272]; d. Unknown.
   iii.   Herman HADDEN[4272,4273], b. Abt. 1908, PA[4274]; d. Unknown; m. Sylvada[4275], Abt. 1929; b. Abt. 1908, PA[4275]; d. Unknown.

          Notes for Herman HADDEN:
          In 1930 renting for $12.50/month married and has his uncle William D. Lydick
          living with him.

          More About Herman HADDEN:
          Occupation: Laborer Brick Yard

          More About Herman HADDEN and Sylvada:
          Marriage: Abt. 1929

    iv.   Helen HADDEN[4276], b. Abt. 1910, PA[4276]; d. Unknown.
    v.   Genavive HADDEN, b. Private.
    vi.   Torrence HADDEN, b. Private.
   vii.   Thelma HADDEN, b. Private.
  viii.   Raymond HADDEN, b. Private.

286. John Torrence[11] LYDICK *(John Albert[10], Jane Elizabeth[9] VAN HORN, Isaiah[8], Isaiah[7], Henry B.[6], Henry[5], Christian Barentsen[4] VAN HOORN, Barent Christiansen[3], Christian Barentsen[2], Barent Barents[1])*[4277,4278,4279] was born Feb 1890 in PA[4280,4281], and died Dec 1975 in Clymer, Indiana Cnty, PA[4282,4283]. He married Sylvia Bell HARMON[4284] Aft. 1920, daughter of Edward HARMON and

Maggie. She was born 31 Oct 1902 in Brush Valley, Indiana Cnty, PA[4284], and died 06 Jan 1998 in Indiana, Indiana Cnty, PA[4284].

Notes for John Torrence LYDICK:
        In his WWI civilian draft registration he gives his birth and employment as a laborer for a company that is not legible. He is tall slender with light blue eyes and dark brown hair. He says he is supporting his mother. Gives full name as James Torrence Lydick.
        In 1920 Todd J. Lydick has living with him his mother, his brother, William D., Williams 2 children Blaine and Gay and a boarder. William is listed twice in the census as also living with his nephew. Both Todd and William are coal miners. Todd is renting the place where they all live.

More About John Torrence LYDICK:
Occupation: Coal Miner

More About Sylvia Bell HARMON:
Burial: Unknown, Greenwood Cemetery, Indiana Cnty, PA
Religion: Shiloh Baptist Church, Deckers Point, PA

More About John LYDICK and Sylvia HARMON:
Marriage: Aft. 1920

Children of John LYDICK and Sylvia HARMON are:
　　　　i.　Viola[12] LYDICK[4284], d. Bef. 1998.
470.　　ii.　Arthur James LYDICK, b. 13 Jul 1938, Clymer, Indiana Cnty, PA; d. 17 Jul 1977, Indiana, Indiana Cnty, PA.
　　　　iii.　Ruby LYDICK[4284], d. Aft. 1998; m. STILES, Private; b. Private.

　　　　　　More About STILES and Ruby LYDICK:
　　　　　　Private-Begin: Private

　　　　iv.　Marie LYDICK[4284], b. 1926; d. Aft. 1998; m. Lloyd BUTTERBAUGH, Private; b. Private.

　　　　　　More About Lloyd BUTTERBAUGH and Marie LYDICK:
　　　　　　Private-Begin: Private

　　　　v.　Ann LYDICK[4284], d. Aft. 1998; m. UNCAPHER, Private; b. Private.

　　　　　　More About UNCAPHER and Ann LYDICK:
　　　　　　Private-Begin: Private

　　　　vi.　Donald LYDICK[4284], d. Aft. 1998; m. Christine, Private; b. Private.

　　　　　　More About Donald LYDICK and Christine:
　　　　　　Private-Begin: Private

287. Elizabeth Pearl[11] PALMER *(Mary A.[10] LYDICK, Jane Elizabeth[9] VAN HORN, Isaiah[8], Isaiah[7], Henry B.[6], Henry[5], Christian Barentsen[4] VAN HOORN, Barent Christiansen[3], Christian Barentsen[2], Barent Barents[1])[4285,4286,4287]* was born Jan 1882 in PA[4288], and died 23 Jul 1966 in Clymer, Indiana Cnty, PA. She married Lorenzo Peter LAMBING[4288,4289] 11 Jun 1898. He was born 07 Jun 1879 in White Twp., Indiana Cnty, PA[4290], and died 27 Sep 1953 in Indiana, Indiana Cnty, PA.

More About Lorenzo Peter LAMBING:

Occupation: Day Laborer; Railroad Laborer

More About Lorenzo LAMBING and Elizabeth PALMER:
Marriage: 11 Jun 1898

Children of Elizabeth PALMER and Lorenzo LAMBING are:
471.   i.   James Robert[12] LAMBING, b. 02 Sep 1898, PA; d. 07 May 1969, Indiana, Indiana Cnty, PA.
      ii.   Norris Glenn LAMBING[4290,4291], b. Sep 1899, PA[4292]; d. Unknown.
     iii.   Annie LAMBING[4293], b. Abt. 1900, PA[4293]; d. Unknown.
472.   iv.   Emma Mable LAMBING, b. 15 Dec 1902, Indiana, Indiana Cnty, PA; d. 08 Feb 1976, Indiana, Indiana Cnty, PA.
      v.   Olive LAMBING[4293], b. Abt. 1905, PA[4293]; d. Unknown.

288. Harry Irvin[11] MYERS *(Martha Jane[10] LYDICK, Jane Elizabeth[9] VAN HORN, Isaiah[8], Isaiah[7], Henry B.[6], Henry[5], Christian Barentsen[4] VAN HOORN, Barent Christiansen[3], Christian Barentsen[2], Barent Barents[1])*[4294,4295] was born 06 Feb 1894 in PA[4296], and died 31 Jan 1970 in Indiana, Indiana Cnty, PA[4296]. He married Wilda BURKETT[4296] Apr 1919[4296]. She died Unknown.

Notes for Harry Irvin MYERS:
2 Feb 1970 Indiana Evening Gazette (Indiana, PA) in his obit it states his birth and death dates, his marriage to Wilda Burkett and the date. He started teaching in 1914 but entered the military in 1917 with the 102nd Engineers NY 28th Division. He taught in the public schools for 37 years. He has a son Harry I and daughter Meridith Langham and a foster child, two brothers and a sister are still living.

More About Harry Irvin MYERS:
Burial: 1970, Oakland Cemetery

More About Harry MYERS and Wilda BURKETT:
Marriage: Apr 1919[4296]

Children of Harry MYERS and Wilda BURKETT are:
      i.   Harry I.[12] MYERS, JR, b. Private.
     ii.   Meredith MYERS, b. Private; m. Nicholas W. LANGHAM, Private; b. Private.

        More About Nicholas LANGHAM and Meredith MYERS:
        Private-Begin: Private

289. Joseph Lucas[11] MYERS *(Martha Jane[10] LYDICK, Jane Elizabeth[9] VAN HORN, Isaiah[8], Isaiah[7], Henry B.[6], Henry[5], Christian Barentsen[4] VAN HOORN, Barent Christiansen[3], Christian Barentsen[2], Barent Barents[1])*[4297,4298,4299] was born 14 Mar 1898 in PA[4299], and died 19 Apr 1975 in Tacoma Park, Montgomery Cnty, MD. He married Pearl SPICHER[4299] 14 Apr 1919[4299], daughter of Geary SPICHER and Martha ROWLEY. She was born Abt. 1898 in PA[4299], and died 31 May 1956 in Tacoma Park, Montgomery Cnty, MD.

More About Joseph MYERS and Pearl SPICHER:
Marriage: 14 Apr 1919[4299]

Children of Joseph MYERS and Pearl SPICHER are:
      i.   Dorothy[12] MYERS, b. Private.

ii.   Arthur Eugene MYERS, b. 17 Jul 1930; d. 18 Feb 1976.

290. Clarence R.[11] MYERS *(Martha Jane[10] LYDICK, Jane Elizabeth[9] VAN HORN, Isaiah[8], Isaiah[7], Henry B.[6], Henry[5], Christian Barentsen[4] VAN HOORN, Barent Christiansen[3], Christian Barentsen[2], Barent Barents[1])[4300,4301]* was born Abt. 1902 in PA[4301], and died Bef. 1970. He married Sadie MCHANNA[4301] Abt. 1920[4301]. She was born Abt. 1901 in PA[4301], and died Unknown.

Notes for Clarence R. MYERS:
   In 1930 renting for $15/month and working as a farm laborer. He and his family live next to his mother and his brother Arthur.

More About Clarence MYERS and Sadie MCHANNA:
Marriage: Abt. 1920[4301]

Children of Clarence MYERS and Sadie MCHANNA are:
   i.   David[12] MYERS, b. Private.
   ii.   Gaynell MYERS, b. Private.
   iii.   Evanell MYERS, b. Private.
   iv.   Vivian MYERS, b. Private.
   v.   Lolabelle MYERS, b. Private.
   vi.   Baby MYERS, b. Private.

291. Albert Dennis[11] MYERS *(Martha Jane[10] LYDICK, Jane Elizabeth[9] VAN HORN, Isaiah[8], Isaiah[7], Henry B.[6], Henry[5], Christian Barentsen[4] VAN HOORN, Barent Christiansen[3], Christian Barentsen[2], Barent Barents[1])[4302,4303,4304,4305]* was born Oct 1899 in Grant Twp., Indiana Cnty, PA[4306,4307], and died Aft. 1970. He married (1) Vera MUMAN[4308] Abt. 1917, daughter of Hervy MUMAN and Mallie. She was born Abt. 1901 in PA[4308], and died Unknown. He married (2) Delsa Joan SHANKLE[4309,4310,4311] 02 Jun 1924, daughter of Wallace SHANKLE and Ida LYDICK. She was born 31 Jul 1896 in Grant Twp., Indiana Cnty, PA[4312], and died 14 Feb 1968 in PA.

Notes for Albert Dennis MYERS:
   25 Feb 1956 Indiana Evening Gazette (Indiana, PA) reports that Dennis Albert and Mrs Myers have been selected by the county commissioners as Superintendent and Matron of the Indiana County Home. They are to receive salaries of $175/month for the Superintendent and $140 for the Matron. Mr. Myers served as Dairy Herdsman for the St. Vincent college and farm manger for the Benedictine Sisters farm and has operated his own farm. In 1930 farming in White Twp. Indiana. He was first married when he was 19 and Delsa when she was 27 so there is a second marriage for him.

More About Albert Dennis MYERS:
Occupation: Farmer

More About Albert MYERS and Vera MUMAN:
Marriage: Abt. 1917

More About Albert MYERS and Delsa SHANKLE:
Marriage: 02 Jun 1924

Child of Albert MYERS and Delsa SHANKLE is:
   i.   Dennis Albert[12] MYERS, JR, b. Private; m. Betty Lou RAINEY, Private; b. Private.

      More About Dennis MYERS and Betty RAINEY:

Private-Begin: Private

292. Thomas Roy[11] SHANKLE *(Ida Mae*[10] *LYDICK, Jane Elizabeth*[9] *VAN HORN, Isaiah*[8]*, Isaiah*[7]*, Henry B.*[6]*, Henry*[5]*, Christian Barentsen*[4] *VAN HOORN, Barent Christiansen*[3]*, Christian Barentsen*[2]*, Barent Barents*[1]*)*[4312,4313,4314,4315] was born 25 Dec 1887 in Grant Twp., Indiana Cnty, PA[4316], and died 07 Jan 1974 in Indiana, Indiana Cnty, PA. He married Grace C. RADKEY[4317] 06 Jul 1915 in Hillsdale, Indiana Cnty, PA, daughter of Jacob RODKEY and Margert WASSAM. She was born 27 Apr 1898 in Grant Twp., Indiana Cnty, PA[4317], and died 05 Dec 1944.

Notes for Thomas Roy SHANKLE:

More About Thomas Roy SHANKLE:
Employment: Mine Loader

More About Thomas SHANKLE and Grace RADKEY:
Marriage: 06 Jul 1915, Hillsdale, Indiana Cnty, PA

Children of Thomas SHANKLE and Grace RADKEY are:
473.   i.   Gerald Clair[12] SHANKLE, b. Private.
474.   ii. Margaret Ida SHANKLE, b. Private.
       iii. Lester Roy SHANKLE[4317], b. Bet. 07 Dec 1917 - 1919, Cherry Hill Twp., Indiana
            Cnty, PA[4317]; d. 05 Jul 1988, Latrobe, Westmoreland Cnty, PA; m. Violet Esther
            GUNTER, Private; b. Private.

            More About Lester SHANKLE and Violet GUNTER:
            Private-Begin: Private

       iv. Ord Paul SHANKLE[4317], b. 20 Jul 1920, Grant Twp., Indiana Cnty, PA[4317]; d. 30
            Sep 1983, Grant Twp., Indiana Cnty, PA; m. (1) Nancy DEVERS, Private; b.
            Private; m. (2) Sarah Mae FITZGERALD, Private; b. Private; m. (3) Ann Blanche
            STINSON, Private; b. Private.

            More About Ord SHANKLE and Nancy DEVERS:
            Private-Begin: Private

            More About Ord SHANKLE and Sarah FITZGERALD:
            Private-Begin: Private

            More About Ord SHANKLE and Ann STINSON:
            Private-Begin: Private

       v.   Kenneth J. SHANKLE, b. Private.
475.   vi. Athelia Grace SHANKLE, b. 1925, PA; d. 2006.

293. Elizabeth Mabel[11] SHANKLE *(Ida Mae*[10] *LYDICK, Jane Elizabeth*[9] *VAN HORN, Isaiah*[8]*, Isaiah*[7]*, Henry B.*[6]*, Henry*[5]*, Christian Barentsen*[4] *VAN HOORN, Barent Christiansen*[3]*, Christian Barentsen*[2]*, Barent Barents*[1]*)*[4318,4319,4320] was born Bet. 13 Feb 1889 - 1890 in Grant Twp., Indiana Cnty, PA[4321], and died 04 Dec 1969 in Indiana Cnty, PA[4322]. She married David WYLAND[4323,4324,4325] 13 Sep 1907. He was born Abt. 1874 in PA[4326], and died 1964 in Indiana Cnty, PA[4327].

More About Elizabeth Mabel SHANKLE:
Burial: Unknown, Taylorsville Cemetery

Notes for David WYLAND:
   In 1930 owns his own home worth $1000 and has a radio. Thier home is on the road from Indiana to Buck Run. He is an odd job laborer. Two children of the age of being in the home are missing in the census. They are Freda and Frances who may have died between 1920 and 1930 or married or working out.

More About David WYLAND:
Employment: Coal Mine

More About David WYLAND and Elizabeth SHANKLE:
Marriage: 13 Sep 1907

Children of Elizabeth SHANKLE and David WYLAND are:
   i.   Mary[12] WYLAND[4328,4329], b. Abt. 1907, PA[4330]; d. Aft. 1969; m. Gilbert MINTO[4331]; d. Unknown.
   ii. Albert J. WYLAND[4332,4333], b. Abt. 1911, PA[4333]; d. Aft. 1969.
   iii. Freda WYLAND[4334], b. 13 Feb 1913, Clymer, Indiana Cnty, PA; d. Bef. 06 Dec 1969.
   iv. Frances WYLAND[4334], b. Abt. 1914, PA; d. Bef. 06 Dec 1969.
   v.   Lisa WYLAND[4334,4335,4336], b. Abt. Mar 1916, PA[4337]; d. Aft. 1969; m. Owen DUFFY, Private; b. Private.

        More About Owen DUFFY and Lisa WYLAND:
        Private-Begin: Private

   vi. Helen WYLAND[4338,4339], b. Jan 1919, PA[4339]; d. Aft. 1969; m. GALESOWSKI, Private; b. Private.

        More About GALESOWSKI and Helen WYLAND:
        Private-Begin: Private

   vii. Edna Faye WYLAND[4339,4340], b. Abt. 1921, PA[4341]; d. Aft. 1969; m. Carl JOHNS, Private; b. Private.

        More About Carl JOHNS and Edna WYLAND:
        Private-Begin: Private

   viii. Oliver WYLAND[4341], b. Abt. 1924, PA[4341]; d. Aft. 1969.
   ix. Richard WYLAND[4341], b. Abt. Jul 1929, PA[4341]; d. Aft. 1969.

294. Myrtle Mae[11] SHANKLE *(Ida Mae[10] LYDICK, Jane Elizabeth[9] VAN HORN, Isaiah[8], Isaiah[7], Henry B.[6], Henry[5], Christian Barentsen[4] VAN HOORN, Barent Christiansen[3], Christian Barentsen[2], Barent Barents[1])[4342,4343,4344,4345]* was born 10 Aug 1892 in Grant Twp., Indiana Cnty, PA[4346,4347], and died 06 Aug 1964 in Indiana, Indiana Cnty, PA[4347]. She married William Carl MOCK[4347,4348,4349,4350] 19 Sep 1912, son of Jacob MOCK and Julian. He was born Abt. 1876 in PA[4351], and died 1941[4352].

More About Myrtle Mae SHANKLE:
Burial: Unknown, Brush Creek Cemetery, Indiana Cnty, PA

Notes for William Carl MOCK:
  In 1920 There are 3 children of the home that are too old to be the children of Myrtle as she would have had to have been 10 when the oldest was born. The younger children are likely Myrtle's beginning with Emerson.
  In 1930 renting for $20/month and does not have a radio. He is a house painter and there are 6 children and wife in the home.

More About William Carl MOCK:
Occupation: Stock Clerk, House Painter

More About William MOCK and Myrtle SHANKLE:
Marriage: 19 Sep 1912

Children of Myrtle SHANKLE and William MOCK are:
  i.   Emerson[12] MOCK[4352,4353,4354], b. Abt. 1913, PA[4355]; d. Aft. 1964.
  ii.   Thomas MOCK[4356,4357,4358], b. Abt. 1914, PA[4359]; d. Aft. 1964.
  iii. Naomi MOCK[4360,4361,4362], b. Abt. 1918, PA[4363]; d. Aft. 1964; m. HEMENWAY, Private; b. Private.

        More About HEMENWAY and Naomi MOCK:
        Private-Begin: Private

  iv.   Jesse MOCK[4364], b. Abt. 1920, PA; d. Aft. 1964.
  v.   Charles MOCK[4364,4365], b. Abt. 1923, PA[4365]; d. Aft. 1964.
  vi.   Harry MOCK[4366,4367], b. Feb 1930, PA[4367]; d. Aft. 1964.
  vii. Richard MOCK[4368], b. Aft. 1930, PA; d. Aft. 1964.
  viii. William Carl MOCK, JR, d. Bef. 1964.

295. Eva Jane[11] SHANKLE *(Ida Mae[10] LYDICK, Jane Elizabeth[9] VAN HORN, Isaiah[8], Isaiah[7], Henry B.[6], Henry[5], Christian Barentsen[4] VAN HOORN, Barent Christiansen[3], Christian Barentsen[2], Barent Barents[1])*[4369,4370,4371,4372,4373] was born 06 Sep 1894 in Grant Twp., Indiana Cnty, PA[4374], and died 03 Jul 1992 in Indiana, Indiana Cnty, PA. She married Jesse Clark MCMANUS[4375,4376,4377] 02 Apr 1913 in Clymer, Indiana Cnty, PA, son of George MCMANUS and Mary HOPKINS. He was born Abt. 1888[4378], and died Unknown.

More About Jesse Clark MCMANUS:
Employment: Miner in Clay Mine

More About Jesse MCMANUS and Eva SHANKLE:
Marriage: 02 Apr 1913, Clymer, Indiana Cnty, PA

Children of Eva SHANKLE and Jesse MCMANUS are:
476.   i.   Theda Agnes[12] MCMANUS, b. 21 May 1918, Kittanning, Armstong Cnty, PA; d. 17 Aug 2007, Plumcreek Twp., Indiana Cnty, PA.
477.   ii. Betty Jane MCMANUS, b. 29 Aug 1922, Chevy Chase, Indiana Cnty, PA; d. 19 Jun 1993.
        iii. Alice May MCMANUS[4379], b. 18 Jan 1929, Aultman, Indiana Cnty, PA[4379]; d. 09 Jan 1933.
        iv. Thomas Dale MCMANUS, d. Aft. 2007; m. Sylvia WILLIAMEE, Private; b. Private.

        More About Thomas MCMANUS and Sylvia WILLIAMEE:
        Private-Begin: Private

296. Delsa Joan[11] SHANKLE *(Ida Mae[10] LYDICK, Jane Elizabeth[9] VAN HORN, Isaiah[8], Isaiah[7], Henry B.[6], Henry[5], Christian Barentsen[4] VAN HOORN, Barent Christiansen[3], Christian Barentsen[2], Barent Barents[1])[4380,4381,4382]* was born 31 Jul 1896 in Grant Twp., Indiana Cnty, PA[4383], and died 14 Feb 1968 in PA. She married Albert Dennis MYERS[4384,4385,4386,4387] 02 Jun 1924, son of John MYERS and Martha LYDICK. He was born Oct 1899 in Grant Twp., Indiana Cnty, PA[4388,4389], and died Aft. 1970.

Notes for Albert Dennis MYERS:
    25 Feb 1956 Indiana Evening Gazette (Indiana, PA) reports that Dennis Albert and Mrs Myers have been selected by the county commissioners as Superintendent and Matron of the Indiana County Home. They are to receive salaries of $175/month for the Superintendent and $140 for the Matron. Mr. Myers served as Dairy Herdsman for the St. Vincent college and farm manger for the Benedictine Sisters farm and has operated his own farm. In 1930 farming in White Twp. Indiana. He was first married when he was 19 and Delsa when she was 27 so there is a second marriage for him.

More About Albert Dennis MYERS:
Occupation: Farmer

More About Albert MYERS and Delsa SHANKLE:
Marriage: 02 Jun 1924

Child is listed above under (291) Albert Dennis MYERS.

297. Ford Russell[11] SHANKLE *(Ida Mae[10] LYDICK, Jane Elizabeth[9] VAN HORN, Isaiah[8], Isaiah[7], Henry B.[6], Henry[5], Christian Barentsen[4] VAN HOORN, Barent Christiansen[3], Christian Barentsen[2], Barent Barents[1])[4390,4391,4392,4393,4394,4395,4396,4397]* was born 09 Apr 1898 in Grant Twp., Indiana Cnty, PA[4397,4398], and died 07 Mar 1987 in Indiana, Indiana Cnty, PA. He married Mildred Grace LAMBING[4399,4400,4401,4402] 19 Jul 1921 in Indiana Cnty, PA[4403], daughter of Thomas LAMBING and Jennie LYDICK. She was born 03 Jun 1900 in Rochester Mills, Indiana Cnty, PA[4404], and died 22 Jan 1987 in White Twp., Indiana Cnty, PA.

Notes for Ford Russell SHANKLE:
    In 1930 renting in Plumville, PA for $13month. There is no radio in the home. Ford is a cutter in a coal mine.

More About Ford Russell SHANKLE:
Occupation: Coal Mine Cutter

More About Ford SHANKLE and Mildred LAMBING:
Marriage: 19 Jul 1921, Indiana Cnty, PA[4405]

Children of Ford SHANKLE and Mildred LAMBING are:
      i.   Mildred Ann[12] SHANKLE[4406,4407], b. 29 Aug 1922, Indiana Cnty, PA[4408]; d. 25 Mar 1995, Mexico Beach Bay, FL[4408]; m. Joseph ORESIK[4409]; b. Abt. 1929, Green Twp., Indiana Cnty, PA; d. Abt. 2001, FL.
478.   ii.   Ford Russell SHANKLE, JR, b. Private.
     iii.   Alvin SHANKLE, b. Private.
     iv.   Jane SHANKLE, b. Private.

298. Rosaline[11] LYDICK *(Ira[10] Van LYDICK, Jane Elizabeth[9] VAN HORN, Isaiah[8], Isaiah[7], Henry*

B.[6], Henry[5], Christian Barentsen[4] VAN HOORN, Barent Christiansen[3], Christian Barentsen[2], Barent Barents[1])[4410] was born Abt. 09 Jul 1899 in PA[4411], and died 26 Mar 1929 in Indiana, Indiana Cnty, PA[4411]. She married Clark W. MILLER[4412,4413]. He was born Abt. 1891 in PA[4414], and died Unknown.

More About Rosaline LYDICK:
Burial: 1929, Greenwood Cemetery, Indiana, PA

Notes for Clark W. MILLER:
    In 1930 barely a year after the death of his wife his infant daughter born in1929 is not of the home. He rents for $20/month and has a radio.

More About Clark W. MILLER:
Employment: 1930, Dairy teamster

Children of Rosaline LYDICK and Clark MILLER are:
    i.   Blane C.[12] MILLER[4414], b. Abt. 1914, Indiana Cnty, PA[4414]; d. Unknown.
    ii.   Howard V. MILLER, b. Private.
    iii. Thelma MILLER, b. Private.
    iv.   Infant MILLER, b. 12 Mar 1929, Indiana Cnty, PA; d. Bef. 1930, Indiana Cnty, PA.

299. Frayne C.[11] LYDICK *(Ira[10] Van LYDICK, Jane Elizabeth[9] VAN HORN, Isaiah[8], Isaiah[7], Henry B.[6], Henry[5], Christian Barentsen[4] VAN HOORN, Barent Christiansen[3], Christian Barentsen[2], Barent Barents[1])[4415,4416,4417]* was born Abt. 1907 in PA[4418], and died Aft. 1929. He married Margaret. She died Unknown.

Notes for Frayne C. LYDICK:
    Frayne Lydick, Maryland, formerly of Indiana, died Saturday, July 15, 1972, in Maryland. He was a son of Van and Myrtle Moore Lydick. Surviving are his widow, Margaret; five sons: George, Gordon, Harry, Frayne, Jr. and Rev. Donald; 24 grandchildren; a sister, Mrs. Audrew Cunningham, Indiana; a brother, Oliver, Indianapolis, Ind.; and several nieces and nephews. Services were held at the Gasch Funeral Home, Hyattsville, Md. with military rites at the Gettysburg National Cemetery on Thursday, July 20.

Children of Frayne LYDICK and Margaret are:
    i.   George[12] LYDICK, b. Private.
    ii.   Gordon LYDICK, b. Private.
    iii. Harry LYDICK, b. Private.
    iv.   Frayne C. LYDICK, JR, b. Private.
    v.   Rev. Donald LYDICK, b. Private.

300. Ira Paul[11] WILT *(Ruth E.[10] LYDICK, Jane Elizabeth[9] VAN HORN, Isaiah[8], Isaiah[7], Henry B.[6], Henry[5], Christian Barentsen[4] VAN HOORN, Barent Christiansen[3], Christian Barentsen[2], Barent Barents[1])[4419]* was born Apr 1895 in PA[4419], and died 15 May 1982 in Indiana Cnty, PA. He married Gaynell WIDDOWSON[4420]. She died Bef. 1982[4420].

Notes for Ira Paul WILT:
    I. PAUL WILT, 87, of Clymer RD 1, died Friday, May 15, 1982, at the Indiana Hospital. A son of Harry N. and Ruth Lydick Wilt, he was born April 23, 1895 in Pleasant Valley, Green Township, Indiana County. Mr. Wilt was a charter member of the Calvary Baptist Church of Clymer where he served as Sunday School superintendent, Sunday School teacher and was a member of the board of trustees and board of deacons. He was a charter member of the Two Lick Valley Rod and Gun Club

where he served as president and secretary-treasurer. Mr. Wilt was a member of the County State and National Rural Letter Carriers Association and has served as the president of the County Rural Letter Carriers' Association. He had lived his entire life in the Indiana County area where he had owned Wilt's Service Station and Grocery Store in Buck Run for many years. He also served in the U.S. Army during World War II. Surviving are four sons: Dr. Lloyd P. of Houghton, N. Y.; Rev. Edmund H. of Dayton, Georgia; William B. of Largo, Fla.; Donald B. of Lawton, Ok.; five daughters: Mrs. Richard (Vivian) Foster of Boynton Beach, Fla.; Mrs. George (Ruth) Knight of Mansfield, Ohio; Mrs. Bill (Joan) Hill of Vaughnsville, Ohio; Mrs. John (Dorothy) Kelbaugh of Baltimore, Md.; Mrs. William (Meredith) Beck of Indiana; a brother, Benjamin O. Wilt of Lantana, Fla.: 30 grandchildren and 20 great grandchildren. He was preceded in death by his wife, Gaynell Widdowson Wilt in 1978; and by three brothers: Frank, Joseph and Calvin. Friends will be received from 7-9 p.m. today, (Saturday) and from 2-4 and 7-9 p.m. Sunday at Robinson-Lytle's, Indiana and one hour prior to service at the Calvary Baptist Church, Clymer, where services will be held Monday, May 17, at 11 a.m. Dr. Ralph Wingate will officiate and interment will be in Ruffner Cemetery.

Children of Ira WILT and Gaynell WIDDOWSON are:

    i.   Dr. Lloyd P.[12] WILT, b. Private.
    ii.   Rev. Edmond H. WILT, b. Private.
   iii.   William B. WILT, b. Private.
   iv.   Donald B. WILT, b. Private.
   v.   Vivian WILT, b. Private; m. Richard FOSTER, Private; b. Private.

       More About Richard FOSTER and Vivian WILT:
       Private-Begin: Private

   vi.   Ruth WILT, b. Private; m. George KNIGHT, Private; b. Private.

       More About George KNIGHT and Ruth WILT:
       Private-Begin: Private

   vii.   Joan WILT, b. Private; m. Bill HILL, Private; b. Private.

       More About Bill HILL and Joan WILT:
       Private-Begin: Private

   viii.   Dorothy WILT, b. Private; m. John KELBAUGH, Private; b. Private.

       More About John KELBAUGH and Dorothy WILT:
       Private-Begin: Private

   ix.   Meredith WILT, b. Private; m. William BECK, Private; b. Private.

       More About William BECK and Meredith WILT:
       Private-Begin: Private

301. Mildred Grace[11] LAMBING *(Jennie B.[10] LYDICK, Jane Elizabeth[9] VAN HORN, Isaiah[8], Isaiah[7], Henry B.[6], Henry[5], Christian Barentsen[4] VAN HOORN, Barent Christiansen[3], Christian Barentsen[2], Barent Barents[1])*[4421,4422,4423,4424] was born 03 Jun 1900 in Rochester Mills, Indiana Cnty, PA[4424], and died 22 Jan 1987 in White Twp., Indiana Cnty, PA. She married Ford Russell SHANKLE[4424,4425,4426,4427,4428,4429,4430,4431] 19 Jul 1921 in Indiana Cnty, PA[4432], son of Wallace SHANKLE and Ida LYDICK. He was born 09 Apr 1898 in Grant Twp., Indiana Cnty, PA[4433,4434], and died 07 Mar 1987 in Indiana, Indiana Cnty, PA.

Notes for Ford Russell SHANKLE:
In 1930 renting in Plumville, PA for $13month. There is no radio in the home. Ford is a cutter in a coal mine.

More About Ford Russell SHANKLE:
Occupation: Coal Mine Cutter

More About Ford SHANKLE and Mildred LAMBING:
Marriage: 19 Jul 1921, Indiana Cnty, PA*4435*

Children are listed above under (297) Ford Russell SHANKLE.

302. Charles A.[11] LAMBING *(Jennie B.[10] LYDICK, Jane Elizabeth[9] VAN HORN, Isaiah[8], Isaiah[7], Henry B.[6], Henry[5], Christian Barentsen[4] VAN HOORN, Barent Christiansen[3], Christian Barentsen[2], Barent Barents[1])[4436]* was born 14 Oct 1904 in Green Twp., Indiana Cnty, PA*4436*, and died 17 Jan 1979 in Natrona Heights, Allegheny Cnty, PA*4437*. He married Aurelia EMMERT Private. She was born Private.

Notes for Charles A. LAMBING:
CHARLES A. LAMBING--Indiana Evening Gazette (Indiana, PA), Thursday, January 18, 1979 "Charles A. Lambing, 74, 2298 Seventh St., New Kensington, died Wednesday, Jan. 17,. 1979, in Allegheny Valley Hospital, Natrona Heights,following a short illness. The son of Thomas A. and Gennie Lydic Lambing, he was born Oct. 14, 1904, in Indiana County. Mr. Lambing was a member of Pentecostal Holiness Church, Truxall. He had been a resident of New Kensington since 1942 moving there from Indiana County. He retired from Union Spring and Manufacturing Corporation in 1969. His employment there began in 1942. Surviving are his wife, Aurelia Emmert Lambing; one daughter, Mrs. Frank (Linda) Marin, Pittsburgh; two brothers,Paul, Marion Center, Cloyd, Bridgeport, Conn.; four sisters: Mrs. Ford (Grace) Shankle, Penn Run; Mrs. Thomas (Ethel) Wadding, Spring Church; Mrs. Zella Myers, Bridgeport, Conn.; Mrs. William (Bernice) Jones,Philadelphia. Friends will be received from 7-9 p.m. today and 2-4 and 7-9 Friday in the Richard J. Churchfield Funeral Home, 501 Fifth Ave., New Kensington, where a service will be held at 11 a.m. Saturday, Jan. 20, with his pastors, the Rev. Joseph Wicker and the Rev. William Hamilton officiating. Interment will follow in Plum Creek Cemetery, Plum Borough."

More About Charles A. LAMBING:
Burial: Unknown, Plum Creek Cemetery, Indiana Cnty, PA
Employment: Bet. 1942 - 1969, Union Spring and Manufacturing
Religion: Pentecostal Holiness Church

More About Charles LAMBING and Aurelia EMMERT:
Private-Begin: Private

Child of Charles LAMBING and Aurelia EMMERT is:
      i.   Linda[12] LAMBING, b. Private; m. Frank MARIN, Private; b. Private.

          More About Frank MARIN and Linda LAMBING:
          Private-Begin: Private

303. John Crawford[11] LYDICK *(Milton Crawford[10], Mary P.[9] VAN HORN, Isaiah[8], Isaiah[7], Henry B.[6], Henry[5], Christian Barentsen[4] VAN HOORN, Barent Christiansen[3], Christian Barentsen[2], Barent Barents[1])[4438]* was born 08 Oct 1906 in Green Twp., Indiana Cnty, PA, and died Unknown. He married Elsie

RUSSELL Private. She was born Private.

More About John LYDICK and Elsie RUSSELL:
Private-Begin: Private

Children of John LYDICK and Elsie RUSSELL are:
   i. ?[12] LYDICK, b. Private.
   ii. ? LYDICK, b. Private.

304. Blair James[11] LYDICK *(Joseph Bell[10], Mary P.[9] VAN HORN, Isaiah[8], Isaiah[7], Henry B.[6], Henry[5], Christian Barentsen[4] VAN HOORN, Barent Christiansen[3], Christian Barentsen[2], Barent Barents[1])[4439]* was born 15 Nov 1896 in Cherryhill Twp., Indiana Cnty., PA[4439], and died 17 Sep 1970 in Cherryhill Twp., Indiana Cnty, PA. He married (1) Grace Sylvia LIVINGSTON. She was born 17 Mar 1907 in Rayne Twp., Indiana Cnty, PA, and died 01 May 1948 in Indiana Cnty, PA. He married (2) Carrie Emma CARNAHAN 23 Aug 1952 in Indiana Cnty, PA. She was born 1882 in PA, and died Unknown. He married (3) Agnez Florence BOLLINGER Private. She was born Private.

Notes for Blair James LYDICK:
  Blair's marriage to Carrie Emma Carnahan Reed is his second marriage. His first wife, Grace Livingston died May 1, 1948. Both of his parents were deceased when he married Carrie Emma Carnahan Reed on August 23, 1952. Blair's obituary lists him as the husband of Agnes Florence Bollinger and states that he was preceded in death by his 1st wife, Grace Livingston, and a son, Clyde E., but does not mention Carrie Emma Carnahan Reed. Blair was a retired miner, employed by the R & P Coal Company for 19 years and a veteran of World War l. He was a member of the Pentecostal Holiness Church in Indiana, where services were held for Blair. This information was from his Obituary. Blair's obit also states that he has a half brother, Leroy Lydick of Johnstown, besides his brother Fero and his sister Della.

More About Blair LYDICK and Carrie CARNAHAN:
Marriage: 23 Aug 1952, Indiana Cnty, PA

More About Blair LYDICK and Agnez BOLLINGER:
Private-Begin: Private

Children of Blair LYDICK and Grace LIVINGSTON are:
479. i. Clyde Emory[12] LYDICK, b. 02 Aug 1924, White Twp., Indiana Cnty, PA; d. 11 Nov 1950.
480. ii. Blair James LYDICK, JR, b. 06 Mar 1937, Cherryhill Twp., Indiana Cnty, PA; d. 15 Sep 1991, Malborough, Indiana Cnty, PA.
   iii. Dora LYDICK, b. Private.
   iv. ? LYDICK, b. Private.
   v. ? LYDICK, b. Private.
   vi. ? LYDICK, b. Private.

305. Della Gloria[11] LYDICK *(Joseph Bell[10], Mary P.[9] VAN HORN, Isaiah[8], Isaiah[7], Henry B.[6], Henry[5], Christian Barentsen[4] VAN HOORN, Barent Christiansen[3], Christian Barentsen[2], Barent Barents[1])[4439]* was born 27 Jul 1897 in Mitchell Mills, Indiana Cnty, PA[4439], and died Unknown. She married (1) Edward Patrick DALY 17 Oct 1915 in Indiana Cnty, PA. He was born 05 Apr 1889 in Snowshoe, Centre Cnty, PA, and died Unknown. She married (2) Howard G. NORRIS Private. He was born Private.

Notes for Della Gloria LYDICK:

Della Gloria Lydick was born in 1897 in Mitchell Mills, Indiana County, Pennsylvania.
In 1900 she lived in Cherry Hill Township, population of 100, Indiana Cnty, PA
In 1910 she lived on Hancock St in Clymer Boro (Clymer is also Cherryhill), PA
In 1920 she lived on 2nd St in Ernest, PA.

Della's first husband, Edward Patrick Daly, died Sept 14, 1944. She married Howard G. Norris on June 5, 1969 at the age of 71. Della lived at Fairwinds Manor Nursing Home 126 Iron bridge Road in Sarver, Pennsylvania at the time of her death. Services were held at Krynicki Funeral Home.

Notes for Edward Patrick DALY:
Edward & Della were married twice, once by a Justice of the Peace, J. A. Crossman on Oct 7, 1915 and once in church. Their marriage application was in Indiana County on Oct 7, 1915 and shows him as 27 years of age in Oct of 1915. Della was 17 years old at the time of her marriage it shows Della's mother, Maggie J Fulmer, with an Indiana residence and her father, Joseph Lydick, at a Clymer
residence.

More About Edward DALY and Della LYDICK:
Marriage: 17 Oct 1915, Indiana Cnty, PA

More About Howard NORRIS and Della LYDICK:
Private-Begin: Private

Children of Della LYDICK and Edward DALY are:
    i.   Clair[12] DALY, b. Private.
    ii.   June Marie DALY, b. Private.
    iii.   Wiliam Wilson DALY, b. Private.
    iv.   ? DALY, b. Private.
    v.   Virginia M. DALY, b. Private.
    vi.   Edward Patrick DALY, JR, b. Private.
    vii.   ? DALY, b. Private.
    viii.   ? DALY, b. Private.
    ix.   ? DALY, b. Private.
    x.   Thomas L. DALY, b. Private.
    xi.   Daniel L. DALY, b. Private.

306. Tero Fulmer[11] LYDICK *(Joseph Bell[10], Mary P.[9] VAN HORN, Isaiah[8], Isaiah[7], Henry B.[6], Henry[5], Christian Barentsen[4] VAN HOORN, Barent Christiansen[3], Christian Barentsen[2], Barent Barents[1])[4439]* was born 03 Mar 1899 in Diamondville, Indiana Cnty, PA[4439], and died Unknown. He married Lillian E. LYDICK Private. She was born Private.

More About Tero LYDICK and Lillian LYDICK:
Private-Begin: Private

Children of Tero LYDICK and Lillian LYDICK are:
    i.   ?[12] LYDICK, b. Private.
    ii.   ? LYDICK, b. Private.
    iii.   ? LYDICK, b. Private.
    iv.   Eleanor Jane LYDICK, b. Private.
    v.   ? LYDICK, b. Private.
    vi.   ? LYDICK, b. Private.
    vii.   ? LYDICK, b. Private.

viii.   ? LYDICK, b. Private.

307. John Wesley[11] VAN HORN *(William[10], John A.[9], Isaiah[8], Isaiah[7], Henry B.[6], Henry[5], Christian Barentsen[4] VAN HOORN, Barent Christiansen[3], Christian Barentsen[2], Barent Barents[1])*[4440,4441,4442] was born 07 Oct 1893 in Berkeley Cnty, WV[4443], and died Unknown. He married Vallie V.[4444,4445] Abt. 1914. She was born Abt. 1893 in WV[4446], and died Unknown.

Notes for John Wesley VAN HORN:
     In 1930 John's 3 children are with his wife and her new husband John Stanley. Either John has died or they are divorced. If John is deceased he died between 1920 and 1925.

More About John Wesley VAN HORN:
Occupation: Farm Laborer

More About John VAN HORN and Vallie V.:
Marriage: Abt. 1914

Children of John VAN HORN and Vallie V. are:
     i.   Russell L.[12] VAN HORN, b. Private.
     ii.   Thelma L. VAN HORN, b. Private.
     iii. Evelyn I. VAN HORN[4447], b. Abt. 1910, WV[4447]; d. Unknown.

308. Daniel H.[11] VAN HORN *(William[10], John A.[9], Isaiah[8], Isaiah[7], Henry B.[6], Henry[5], Christian Barentsen[4] VAN HOORN, Barent Christiansen[3], Christian Barentsen[2], Barent Barents[1])*[4448,4449,4450,4451] was born Sep 1895 in WV[4452], and died Unknown. He married Hazel G.[4453,4454] Abt. 1919 in WV. She was born Abt. 1897 in WV[4455], and died Unknown.

Notes for Daniel H. VAN HORN:
     In 1920 Dan and his brother John are living next to each other in Falling Waters, WV.

More About Daniel H. VAN HORN:
Occupation: Farm Laborer

More About Daniel VAN HORN and Hazel G.:
Marriage: Abt. 1919, WV

Children of Daniel VAN HORN and Hazel G. are:
     i.   Amos C.[12] VAN HORN, b. Private.
     ii.   Ruby F. VAN HORN, b. Private.
     iii. Genevieve M. VAN HORN, b. Private.
     iv.   Bernard VAN HORN, b. Private.

309. James Allen[11] GAGEBY *(Nora Mary Agnes[10] VAN HORN, John A.[9], Isaiah[8], Isaiah[7], Henry B.[6], Henry[5], Christian Barentsen[4] VAN HOORN, Barent Christiansen[3], Christian Barentsen[2], Barent Barents[1])*[4456,4457,4458] was born Feb 1900 in Bunker Hill, Berkeley Cnty, WV[4458], and died 08 Aug 1966 in Martinsburg, Berkeley Cnty, WV. He married Martha Virginia MOLER, daughter of Eugene MOLER and Mary ENGLE. She was born 05 Mar 1900 in Harpers Ferry, Jefferson Cnty, WV, and died 16 Mar 1959 in Martinsburg, Berkeley Cnty, WV.

More About James Allen GAGEBY:

Isaiah Van Horn Pioneer of Indiana County, Pennsylvania

Burial: Unknown, Morgan Chapel Cemetery, Bunker Hill, WV

More About Martha Virginia MOLER:
Burial: Unknown, Morgan Chapel Cemetery, Bunker Hill, WV

Children of James GAGEBY and Martha MOLER are:
      i.   Alan Porterfield[12] GAGEBY, b. 08 Mar 1921, Berkeley Cnty, WV; d. 07 Mar 1925, Berkeley Cnty, WV.

          More About Alan Porterfield GAGEBY:
          Burial: Unknown, Morgan Chapel Cemetery, Bunker Hill, WV

481.   ii.   Naomi Jane GAGEBY, b. 25 Oct 1924, Martinsburg, Berkeley Cnty, WV; d. 25 Nov 1979, Winchester, Frederick Cnty, MD.
    iii.   Mildred Genevieve GAGEBY, b. Private; m. Marvin L. BROWN, Private; b. Private.

          More About Marvin BROWN and Mildred GAGEBY:
          Private-Begin: Private

    iv.   Imogene Elaine GAGEBY, b. Private.

310. John Henry[11] GAGEBY *(Nora Mary Agnes[10] VAN HORN, John A.[9], Isaiah[8], Isaiah[7], Henry B.[6], Henry[5], Christian Barentsen[4] VAN HOORN, Barent Christiansen[3], Christian Barentsen[2], Barent Barents[1])*[4459,4460] was born 01 Jun 1913 in Berkeley Cnty, WV[4461], and died 19 Sep 1981 in Biglerville, Adams Cnty, PA. He married Lila Mae BILLMYER 08 Dec 1945 in Gerrardstown, Berkeley Cnty, WV, daughter of Archie and Rosetta SHIRLEY. She was born 02 Aug 1920 in Beddington, VA, and died 03 Nov 1989 in Biglerville, Adams Cnty, PA.

More About John Henry GAGEBY:
Employment: 1930, Salesman Retail Grocery

More About John GAGEBY and Lila BILLMYER:
Marriage: 08 Dec 1945, Gerrardstown, Berkeley Cnty, WV

Children of John GAGEBY and Lila BILLMYER are:
      i.   ?[12] GAGEBY, b. Private.
     ii.   ? GAGEBY, b. Private.

311. Ida May[11] GAGEBY *(Nora Mary Agnes[10] VAN HORN, John A.[9], Isaiah[8], Isaiah[7], Henry B.[6], Henry[5], Christian Barentsen[4] VAN HOORN, Barent Christiansen[3], Christian Barentsen[2], Barent Barents[1])*[4462,4463] was born 08 Jul 1904 in Berkeley Cnty, WV[4463], and died 14 Nov 1983 in Martinsburg, Berkeley Cnty, WV. She married Jame Link COFFINBERGER 20 Dec 1924 in Winchester, Frederick Cnty, VA. He was born 21 Feb 1905 in Martinsburg, Berkeley Cnty, WV, and died 11 Dec 1982 in Martinsburg, Berkeley Cnty, WV.

More About Ida May GAGEBY:
Burial: Unknown, Morgan Chapel Cemetery, Bunker Hill, WV
Religion: Luthern

More About Jame Link COFFINBERGER:
Burial: Unknown, Morgan Chapel Cemetery, Bunker Hill, WV

More About Jame COFFINBERGER and Ida GAGEBY:
Marriage: 20 Dec 1924, Winchester, Frederick Cnty, VA

Children of Ida GAGEBY and Jame COFFINBERGER are:
     i. David[12] COFFINBERGER, b. Private.
    ii. Ann V. COFFINBERGER, b. Private.

312. William Brown[11] GAGEBY *(Nora Mary Agnes*[10] *VAN HORN, John A.*[9]*, Isaiah*[8]*, Isaiah*[7]*, Henry B.*[6]*, Henry*[5]*, Christian Barentsen*[4] *VAN HOORN, Barent Christiansen*[3]*, Christian Barentsen*[2]*, Barent Barents*[1]*)*[4464,4465] was born 03 Oct 1909 in Bunker Hill, Berkeley Cnty, WV[4466], and died 31 Dec 1974 in Martinsburg, Berkeley Cnty, WV. He married Phylis WIDMEYER. She was born Abt. 1909, and died Unknown.

More About William Brown GAGEBY:
Burial: Unknown, Morgan Chapel Cemetery, Bunker Hill, WV
Employment: 1930, Laborer Woolen Mill in Finishing Department

Child of William GAGEBY and Phylis WIDMEYER is:
     i. ?[12] GAGEBY, b. Private.

313. Margaret Picolla Van Horn[11] GAGEBY *(Florida Anna Virginia*[10] *VAN HORN, John A.*[9]*, Isaiah*[8]*, Isaiah*[7]*, Henry B.*[6]*, Henry*[5]*, Christian Barentsen*[4] *VAN HOORN, Barent Christiansen*[3]*, Christian Barentsen*[2]*, Barent Barents*[1]*)*[4467,4468] was born Abt. 1894 in WV[4469], and died Unknown. She married Carl Pitkin SCHULTZ Abt. 1920 in Berkeley Cnty, WV. He died Unknown.

Notes for Margaret Picolla Van Horn GAGEBY:
    In 1920 she is living with her parents and she is widowed with a daughter age 5. The last names are unknown as they are listed after Jennie VanHorn a widow and age 72. She is listed as an aunt but this must be Florida's mother.
    In Margery's obituary it doesn't list her parents which is unusual. She was also born in 1895, seven year's before Charles and Florida were married. It is reported that Margery was a Van Horn. In a couple of the siblings obituaries it lists her as a half sister and in Mary's and Florida's it lists her as a sister. From this it possible that she is the daughter of Jane Narcissa and John A. Van Horn.

More About Carl SCHULTZ and Margaret GAGEBY:
Marriage: Abt. 1920, Berkeley Cnty, WV

Child of Margaret GAGEBY and Carl SCHULTZ is:
     i. Margie[12] GAGEBY, b. Private.

314. Mary Edith[11] CATLETT *(Mary Pearl*[10] *HUTZLER, Roseannah*[9] *VAN HORN, Isaiah*[8]*, Isaiah*[7]*, Henry B.*[6]*, Henry*[5]*, Christian Barentsen*[4] *VAN HOORN, Barent Christiansen*[3]*, Christian Barentsen*[2]*, Barent Barents*[1]*)*[4470,4471,4472] was born Abt. 1898 in MD[4473], and died 11 Sep 1954 in Brunswick, Frederick Cnty, MD[4474,4475]. She married George Grayson KOOGLE[4476,4477] Abt. 1919. He was born Abt. 1897 in MD[4478], and died Aft. 1954[4479].

More About George KOOGLE and Mary CATLETT:
Marriage: Abt. 1919

Children of Mary CATLETT and George KOOGLE are:
    i.   George Grayson[12] KOOGLE, JR, b. Private.
    ii. Virgina Lee KOOGLE, b. Private; m. BURKE, Private; b. Private.

          More About BURKE and Virgina KOOGLE:
          Private-Begin: Private

    iii. Mary Pearl KOOGLE, b. Private; m. SLAGLE, Private; b. Private.

          More About SLAGLE and Mary KOOGLE:
          Private-Begin: Private

    iv. Ernest William KOOGLE, b. Private.

315. Forest W.[11] MCBEE *(Nannie Mae[10] HUTZLER, Roseannah[9] VAN HORN, Isaiah[8], Isaiah[7], Henry B.[6], Henry[5], Christian Barentsen[4] VAN HOORN, Barent Christiansen[3], Christian Barentsen[2], Barent Barents[1])[4480,4481,4482]* was born Mar 1898 in WV[4483], and died Unknown. He married Nellie[4484] Abt. 1921[4484]. She was born 1900 in WV, and died Unknown.

Notes for Forest W. MCBEE:
    In 1930 he and Nellie have been married for 8 years. He is renting for $25/month at 206 North Raleigh Street in Martinsburg, WV. He has two children that are likely from a previous marriage.

More About Forest W. MCBEE:
Employment: 1930, Railroad Brakeman

More About Forest MCBEE and Nellie:
Marriage: Abt. 1921[4484]

Children of Forest MCBEE and Nellie are:
    i.   Dora[12] MCBEE, b. Private.
    ii. Gladys MCBEE, b. Private.
    iii. Helen MCBEE, b. Private.

316. John Harland[11] HUTZLER *(Ernest Irvin[10], Roseannah[9] VAN HORN, Isaiah[8], Isaiah[7], Henry B.[6], Henry[5], Christian Barentsen[4] VAN HOORN, Barent Christiansen[3], Christian Barentsen[2], Barent Barents[1])[4485]* was born 03 May 1905 in Gerrardstown, Berkeley Cnty, WV[4485], and died 29 Apr 1975 in Inwood, Berkeley Cnty, WV. He married Marion Beatrice BAKER 30 Jun 1923 in Martinsburg, Berkeley Cnty, WV, daughter of Edgar BAKER and Ethel MAITLAND. She was born 14 May 1908 in Baltimore, MD, and died 19 Aug 1987 in Martinsburg, Berkeley Cnty, WV.

More About John HUTZLER and Marion BAKER:
Marriage: 30 Jun 1923, Martinsburg, Berkeley Cnty, WV

Children of John HUTZLER and Marion BAKER are:
    i.   Rebekah[12] HUTZLER, b. Private; m. MALATT, Private; b. Private.

          More About MALATT and Rebekah HUTZLER:
          Private-Begin: Private

    ii. Thomas Lowell HUTZLER, b. Private.
    iii. James Stewart HUTZLER, b. Private.

iv.   Richard Ernest HUTZLER, b. Private.

317. Harwood Trammell[11] HUTZLER *(Harwood Chapman[10], Roseannah[9] VAN HORN, Isaiah[8], Isaiah[7], Henry B.[6], Henry[5], Christian Barentsen[4] VAN HOORN, Barent Christiansen[3], Christian Barentsen[2], Barent Barents[1])[4486,4487]* was born 17 Nov 1918 in Jefferson Cnty, WV[4487], and died 08 Jul 1993 in Martinsburg, Berkeley Cnty, WV[4488]. He married ? Private. She was born Private.

More About Harwood HUTZLER and ?:
Private-Begin: Private

Children of Harwood HUTZLER and ? are:
     i.   ?[12] HUTZLER, b. Private; m. OWENS, Private; b. Private.

           More About OWENS and ? HUTZLER:
           Private-Begin: Private

    ii.   ? HUTZLER, b. Private; m. SHAFFER, Private; b. Private.

           More About SHAFFER and ? HUTZLER:
           Private-Begin: Private

   iii.   ? HUTZLER, b. Private.

318. William R.[11] DILTS *(Caroline Widmina[10] STEAR, Margaret J.[9] VAN HORN, William G.[8], Isaiah[7], Henry B.[6], Henry[5], Christian Barentsen[4] VAN HOORN, Barent Christiansen[3], Christian Barentsen[2], Barent Barents[1])[4489,4490,4491]* was born 12 Jul 1875 in PA[4492], and died Unknown. He married Mae B.[4493,4494]. She was born Abt. 1875 in KS[4495], and died Unknown.

More About William R. DILTS:
Employment: 1920, Driller Oil Field
Occupation: 1930, Pharmacist Drug Store

Child of William DILTS and Mae B. is:
     i.   Lawrence M.[12] DILTS[4496,4497], b. Abt. 1906, KS[4498]; d. Unknown.

319. Frederick[11] DILTS *(Caroline Widmina[10] STEAR, Margaret J.[9] VAN HORN, William G.[8], Isaiah[7], Henry B.[6], Henry[5], Christian Barentsen[4] VAN HOORN, Barent Christiansen[3], Christian Barentsen[2], Barent Barents[1])[4499,4500]* was born 17 Aug 1893 in OK[4501], and died Aft. 1930. He married Florence[4502]. She was born Abt. 1901 in MO[4502], and died Unknown.

Child of Frederick DILTS and Florence is:
     i.   John Frederick[12] DILTS, b. Private.

320. Daniel W.[11] DILTS *(Caroline Widmina[10] STEAR, Margaret J.[9] VAN HORN, William G.[8], Isaiah[7], Henry B.[6], Henry[5], Christian Barentsen[4] VAN HOORN, Barent Christiansen[3], Christian Barentsen[2], Barent Barents[1])[4503,4504]* was born 10 Jul 1896 in OK[4505], and died Aft. 1930. He married Viola[4506] Abt. 1923. She was born Abt. 1904 in KS[4506], and died Unknown.

Notes for Daniel W. DILTS:

In 1930 living next door to brothers Tom and Fred and farming in Pueblo Cnty, CO.

More About Daniel DILTS and Viola:
Marriage: Abt. 1923

Children of Daniel DILTS and Viola are:
    i.   Novell B.[12] DILTS, b. Private.
    ii.   Deloris Louise DILTS, b. Private.
    iii.   Lola Fern DILTS, b. Private.
    iv.   J. LaRetta DILTS, b. Private.

321. Inez Ethel[11] STEAR *(David Blanchard[10], Margaret J.[9] VAN HORN, William G.[8], Isaiah[7], Henry B.[6], Henry[5], Christian Barentsen[4] VAN HOORN, Barent Christiansen[3], Christian Barentsen[2], Barent Barents[1])[4507,4508,4509]* was born Abt. 1890 in PA[4510,4511], and died Mar 1975 in Smicksburg, Indiana Cnty, PA. She married (1) William Marshall LIAS 02 Nov 1910 in Indiana Cnty, PA, son of John LIAS. He was born 1888, and died 1952. She married (2) Raymond Merle NEVILLE[4512,4513] Jul 1921. He was born Abt. 1895 in PA[4513], and died Aft. 1965.

Notes for Inez Ethel STEAR:
    Wednesday, November 2, 1910 Indiana Evening Gazette (Indiana, PA) Weddings--Lias--Stear In the presence of about fifty relatives, Mr William M. Lias, of Vandergrift, and Miss Inez Ethel Stear, daughter of D.B. Stear, of Trade City, were married at the home of the bride's parents last evening at 8 o'clock. The ceremony was performed by Rev. J.F. Stabley of Smicksburg, pastor of Trade City Lutheran Church. The couple was attended by Mr Walter Neal and Miss Emma Smith, both of Trade City. An elaborate supper was served to the guests immediately after the ceremony. The bride is one of the prominent young women of that section of the county, and Mr. Lias, who was born and raised at Dayton, Armstrong county is a son of Mr. John Lias, a prominent travelling salesman. After a wedding trip the couple will reside in Vandergrift where Mr. Lias is employed in the Steel Mill.
    1920 Census Inez Lias was "partner" to the head of household who was Anna Bair(Boris) age; 32. Inez Lias was divorced; age 28 & living with her daughter, Leonore Lias, age;8 who was listed as a boarder
    28 Jul 1921 Indiana Weekly Messenger (Indiana, PA) Mrs Inez Lias, daughter of Mr and Mrs D.B. Stear, of Trade City, and R. Merle Neville, son of Mrs William Neville, of Punxsutawney were quietly married at First Presbyterian parsonage on Thursday. Rev. C.B. Wible performed the ceremony.
    7 October 1921 & 7 October 1924 Indiana Evening Gazette (Indiana, PA) reports that Mr. and Mrs Merle Neville were the Sabbath guests of Mr. and Mrs D. B. STEAR along with Mr and Mrs Jones both of Punxsutawney.
    14 Sept 1924 Indiana Evening Gazette (Indiana, PA) reports that the Nevilles visited the Stears

More About William LIAS and Inez STEAR:
Divorce: Bef. 1920
Marriage: 02 Nov 1910, Indiana Cnty, PA

Notes for Raymond Merle NEVILLE:
    11 Sept 1942 the Indiana Evening Gazette (Indiana, PA) reports that Merl is home from NY where he is working.
    26 Sept 1943 the Indiana Evening Gazette (Indiana, PA) reports that Merl who works in Pittsburgh spent the weekend at home.
    31 March 1956 the Indiana Evening Gazette (Indiana, PA) publishes an add offering the Merle Neville farm of 85 acres and a 6 room house near North Point, PA for sale. He is accepting $4000 if

sold in 60 days. The farm has gas and electricity available and also has small and large game.

More About Raymond NEVILLE and Inez STEAR:
Marriage: Jul 1921

Child of Inez STEAR and William LIAS is:
     i.   Lenore B.[12] LIAS[4514,4515], b. Abt. 1911, PA[4515]; d. Unknown.

Child of Inez STEAR and Raymond NEVILLE is:
     ii.   Raymond Merle[12] NEVILLE, JR, b. Private.

322. Ermond Lester[11] STEAR *(Ambrose Kelly[10], Margaret J.[9] VAN HORN, William G.[8], Isaiah[7], Henry B.[6], Henry[5], Christian Barentsen[4] VAN HOORN, Barent Christiansen[3], Christian Barentsen[2], Barent Barents[1])* was born Private. He married Ellen Marie BAIR Private. She was born Private.

More About Ermond STEAR and Ellen BAIR:
Private-Begin: Private

Child of Ermond STEAR and Ellen BAIR is:
     i.   Darlene Ellen[12] STEAR, b. Private; m. Lee George BORTS, Private; b. Private.

            More About Lee BORTS and Darlene STEAR:
            Private-Begin: Private

323. Byron L.[11] STEAR *(Enoch Blair[10], Margaret J.[9] VAN HORN, William G.[8], Isaiah[7], Henry B.[6], Henry[5], Christian Barentsen[4] VAN HOORN, Barent Christiansen[3], Christian Barentsen[2], Barent Barents[1])[4516,4517,4518]* was born Mar 1898 in PA[4519], and died Unknown.

Child of Byron L. STEAR is:
     i.   Frank N.[12] STEAR, b. Private.

324. Homer[11] LAFFERTY *(Alice Melissa[10] COON, Catherine[9] VAN HORN, William G.[8], Isaiah[7], Henry B.[6], Henry[5], Christian Barentsen[4] VAN HOORN, Barent Christiansen[3], Christian Barentsen[2], Barent Barents[1])* was born 18 Sep 1876 in PA, and died 1950. He married Bertha L. REISH. She was born 1881 in PA, and died Unknown.

Child of Homer LAFFERTY and Bertha REISH is:
     i.   Ruth Mildred[12] LAFFERTY, b. Private.

325. Mabel[11] COON *(Charles Barclay[10], Catherine[9] VAN HORN, William G.[8], Isaiah[7], Henry B.[6], Henry[5], Christian Barentsen[4] VAN HOORN, Barent Christiansen[3], Christian Barentsen[2], Barent Barents[1])* was born Abt. 1901, and died Unknown. She married Walter LEACH. He died Unknown.

Children of Mabel COON and Walter LEACH are:
     i.   ?[12] LEACH, b. Private.
     ii.   ? LEACH, b. Private.

326. Don Mitchell[11] COON *(Wade Blair[10], Catherine[9] VAN HORN, William G.[8], Isaiah[7], Henry B.[6], Henry[5], Christian Barentsen[4] VAN HOORN, Barent Christiansen[3], Christian Barentsen[2], Barent Barents[1])[4520,4521,4522]* was born 21 Jan 1896 in Punxsutawney, Jefferson Cnty, PA[4523,4524], and died Mar 1962 in Compton, Los Angeles Cnty, CA. He married Myrtle Irene HARDY[4525,4526] Bef. 1920 in UT[4526]. She was born 28 Jun 1896 in Marysville, Piute Cnty, UT[4527], and died Mar 1962 in Los Angeles Cnty, CA.

Notes for Don Mitchell COON:
In 1930 living on Spring Street in Compton, CA in a rented home and they have a radio. He lists no employment.

More About Don Mitchell COON:
Employment: 1920, Railroad Check Clerk

More About Don COON and Myrtle HARDY:
Marriage: Bef. 1920, UT[4528]

Children of Don COON and Myrtle HARDY are:
    i.   William K.[12] COON, b. Private.
   ii.   Grace M. COON, b. Private.

327. Harry L.[11] COON *(Wade Blair[10], Catherine[9] VAN HORN, William G.[8], Isaiah[7], Henry B.[6], Henry[5], Christian Barentsen[4] VAN HOORN, Barent Christiansen[3], Christian Barentsen[2], Barent Barents[1])[4528,4529,4530]* was born Jun 1898 in PA[4531,4532], and died Unknown. He married Idonna[4533]. She was born Abt. 1899 in UT[4533], and died Unknown.

Notes for Harry L. COON:
In 1930 he lives on South Canada in Santa Barbara, CA in a rented home at $50/month. they have a radio in the home. Harry is a manager of general trucking.

Children of Harry COON and Idonna are:
    i.   Wade R.[12] COON, b. Private.
   ii.   Helen COON, b. Private.

328. Kimmel B.[11] COON *(Wade Blair[10], Catherine[9] VAN HORN, William G.[8], Isaiah[7], Henry B.[6], Henry[5], Christian Barentsen[4] VAN HOORN, Barent Christiansen[3], Christian Barentsen[2], Barent Barents[1])[4534,4535]* was born Abt. 1901 in PA[4536], and died Aft. 1971[4537]. He married (1) Mildred Agnes MARTIN[4538] Abt. 1925 in UT. She was born Abt. 1904 in UT[4538], and died Bef. 1971. He married (2) Myrtle HORTON TANNER[4539] 02 Jul 1971 in Los Angeles Cnty, CA[4539]. She was born Abt. 1900[4539], and died Unknown.

Notes for Kimmel B. COON:
In 1910 Kimmel is living with his grandfather Eden Mitchell in Jefferson Cnty, PA

More About Kimmel B. COON:
Employment: 1930, Railroad Locomotive Fireman

More About Kimmel COON and Mildred MARTIN:
Marriage: Abt. 1925, UT

More About Kimmel COON and Myrtle TANNER:

Marriage: 02 Jul 1971, Los Angeles Cnty, CA[4539]

Children of Kimmel COON and Mildred MARTIN are:
  i.   Daniel B.[12] COON, b. Private; m. Joyce Eileen SCOTT, Private; b. Private.

       More About Daniel COON and Joyce SCOTT:
       Private-Begin: Private

  ii. Herbert Lex COON, b. 09 Feb 1931, Milford, Beaver Cnty, PA; d. 06 May 1991; m.
       MERRYWEATHER, Private; b. Private.

       More About Herbert COON and MERRYWEATHER:
       Private-Begin: Private

329. Dollie Irene[11] CONDRON *(William Madison[10], Dorcas[9] VAN HORN, William G.[8], Isaiah[7], Henry B.[6], Henry[5], Christian Barentsen[4] VAN HOORN, Barent Christiansen[3], Christian Barentsen[2], Barent Barents[1])*[4540,4541,4542] was born Apr 1890 in PA[4543], and died 1958. She married William Francis LUKEHART[4544,4545]. He was born 19 Oct 1888 in Tyrone, PA[4546], and died Jan 1935 in Ernest, Indiana Cnty, PA.

More About William Francis LUKEHART:
Employment: 1920, Railroad Boilermaker

Children of Dollie CONDRON and William LUKEHART are:
482.   i.   William Thomas[12] LUKEHART, b. 07 Nov 1908, PA; d. 26 Jun 1958, Indiana Cnty,
             PA.
        ii. Ira M. LUKEHART[4546,4547], b. Abt. 1914, PA[4548]; d. Unknown.
        iii. Jane M. LUKEHART, b. Private.
        iv. Roy R. LUKEHART, b. Private.

330. Ira Sloan[11] CONDRON *(William Madison[10], Dorcas[9] VAN HORN, William G.[8], Isaiah[7], Henry B.[6], Henry[5], Christian Barentsen[4] VAN HOORN, Barent Christiansen[3], Christian Barentsen[2], Barent Barents[1])*[4549,4550,4551,4552] was born 05 Jul 1893 in Home, PA[4553,4554,4555], and died 29 Apr 1958. He married (1) Agnes M.[4556,4557] Bef. 1920. She was born Abt. 1896 in PA[4558], and died Unknown. He married (2) Gertrude Elise LNU 1936. She was born 1912, and died 1946.

Notes for Ira Sloan CONDRON:
    In his WWI draft registration he is of medium height, medium build, blue eyes and black hair.
    In 1920 living on Freeport Rd in O'Hara Twp., Allegheny Cnty, PA renting and employed as a machinist in a steel mill.
    In 1930 living in the same location as in 1920 renting for $40/month and does not have a radio. He is a machinist with a steel mill. There are 2 lodgers living in the home.

More About Ira CONDRON and Agnes M.:
Marriage: Bef. 1920

More About Ira CONDRON and Gertrude LNU:
Marriage: 1936

Child of Ira CONDRON and Gertrude LNU is:
  i.   Robert[12] CONDRON, b. Private.

331. Olive Florence[11] CONDRON *(Charles Gillis[10], Dorcas[9] VAN HORN, William G.[8], Isaiah[7], Henry B.[6], Henry[5], Christian Barentsen[4] VAN HOORN, Barent Christiansen[3], Christian Barentsen[2], Barent Barents[1])[4559,4560]* was born 25 Aug 1892 in Verona, Allegheny Cnty, PA[4561], and died 09 Jul 1977 in Oakmont, Allegheny Cnty, PA. She married Arthur James YOUNG[4562,4563,4564] Abt. 1916, son of Reuben YOUNG and Sarah GREEN. He was born 24 May 1891 in Punxsutawney, Jefferson Cnty, PA[4565], and died 29 Dec 1987 in Lewes, Sussex Cnty, DE.

Notes for Arthur James YOUNG:
His WWI Draft Registration states he is short of medium build with gray eyes and dark brown hair. He is a moulder in Edgewater Steel and lives in Verona, PA at #459 Union Street. He is married with a child on June 15, 1917.
In 1920 living on North Ave near Union Street and near Olive's parents.
In 1930 living 459 Union Street in a house he owns worth $3000 works in a spring Mill and living a short distance from Olive's widowed mother.

More About Arthur James YOUNG:
Occupation: Moulder Steel Plant

More About Arthur YOUNG and Olive CONDRON:
Marriage: Abt. 1916

Children of Olive CONDRON and Arthur YOUNG are:
     i.   Sarah Jane[12] YOUNG, b. Private.
    ii.   Florence YOUNG, b. Private.
   iii.   George YOUNG, b. Private.

332. Owen Meridith[11] SERENE *(Stella M.[10] VAN HORN, George Logan[9], William G.[8], Isaiah[7], Henry B.[6], Henry[5], Christian Barentsen[4] VAN HOORN, Barent Christiansen[3], Christian Barentsen[2], Barent Barents[1])[4566,4567,4568,4569,4570]* was born 15 Jul 1899 in North Point or Saltsburg, Indiana Cnty, PA[4571], and died 14 Jan 1951 in Saltsburg, Indiana Cnty, PA[4572]. He married Ruth Margaret JOHNSTON[4573] 1925, daughter of Thomas JOHNSTON and Anna BAKER. She was born 10 May 1903 in Saltsburg, Indiana Cnty, PA[4574], and died 28 May 1981 in Venice, Sarasota Cnty, FL[4575].

Notes for Owen Meridith SERENE:
In 1920 living with parents and working in his father's meat market.
In 1930 married for 4 years, owns his own home in High Street in Saltsburg, PA worth $5,000 and has a radio. He is a bank clerk.
He later became the Cashier of the First National Bank of Saltsburg, PA.

More About Owen Meridith SERENE:
Burial: Unknown, Edgewood Cemetery, Saltsburg, PA
Cause of Death: Heart Attack
Employment: Salesman Meat Market, Bank Clerk
Fraternal Organization: Elks and Odd Fellows
Military service: 30 Jul 1918, WWI wounded and gassed in France and received the Purple Heart
Occupation: 1940, Cashier and Vice President of 1st National Bank of Saltsburg
Professional: American Legion and Veterans of Foreign Wars
Religion: St. Johns Luthern Church of Saltsburg, PA

More About Owen SERENE and Ruth JOHNSTON:
Marriage: 1925

Child of Owen SERENE and Ruth JOHNSTON is:
483.   i.   Mary Lou[12] SERENE, b. 30 Jan 1934; d. Aft. 1951.

333. Mary Isabel[11] VAN HORN *(Elmer Monroe[10], George Logan[9], William G.[8], Isaiah[7], Henry B.[6], Henry[5], Christian Barentsen[4] VAN HOORN, Barent Christiansen[3], Christian Barentsen[2], Barent Barents[1])[4576,4577]* was born Abt. 1905 in PA[4578], and died Unknown. She married William DOLBY[4578] Abt. 1922. He was born Abt. 1904 in PA[4578], and died Unknown.

More About William DOLBY:
Occupation: Coal Miner

More About William DOLBY and Mary VAN HORN:
Marriage: Abt. 1922

Child of Mary VAN HORN and William DOLBY is:
       i.   William[12] DOLBY, JR, b. Private

334. Homer E.[11] VAN HORN *(Arnold Wilton[10], George Logan[9], William G.[8], Isaiah[7], Henry B.[6], Henry[5], Christian Barentsen[4] VAN HOORN, Barent Christiansen[3], Christian Barentsen[2], Barent Barents[1])[4579,4580,4581]* was born Abt. 1903 in PA[4581], and died Aft. 1973. He married Elizabeth[4581] Abt. 1927[4581]. She was born Abt. 1908 in OH[4581], and died Unknown.

Notes for Homer E. VAN HORN:
       In 1930 living in a rented home and does not have a radio. He is a matcher in a steel mill. He and Elizabeth have a daughter Harriett who is 3 months old.

More About Homer E. VAN HORN:
Employment: 1930, Steel Mill Matcher
Lived: Warren, OH

More About Homer VAN HORN and Elizabeth:
Marriage: Abt. 1927[4581]

Child of Homer VAN HORN and Elizabeth is:
       i.   Harriett[12] VAN HORN, b. Private.

335. Nelson Blair[11] VAN HORN *(Arnold Wilton[10], George Logan[9], William G.[8], Isaiah[7], Henry B.[6], Henry[5], Christian Barentsen[4] VAN HOORN, Barent Christiansen[3], Christian Barentsen[2], Barent Barents[1])[4582]* was born 13 Aug 1913 in NuMine, Armstrong Cnty, PA, and died 02 Feb 1993 in Willoughby, OH. He married Ester BOWSER Private. She was born Private.

More About Nelson Blair VAN HORN:
Burial: Unknown, Rural Valley Cemetery, Indiana Cnty, PA
Lived: Wickliffe, OH
Occupation: Ajax for 30 years

More About Nelson VAN HORN and Ester BOWSER:
Private-Begin: Private

Children of Nelson VAN HORN and Ester BOWSER are:

i.   Wilton Blair[12] VAN HORN, b. Private.
ii. Rose Marie VAN HORN, b. Private; m. John SVEDEK, Private; b. Private.

More About John SVEDEK and Rose VAN HORN:
Private-Begin: Private

iii. Judy VAN HORN, b. Private; m. Sam TIRABASSI, Private; b. Private.

More About Sam TIRABASSI and Judy VAN HORN:
Private-Begin: Private

336. Owen DeLone[11] VAN HORNE *(Arnold Wilton[10] VAN HORN, George Logan[9], William G.[8], Isaiah[7], Henry B.[6], Henry[5], Christian Barentsen[4] VAN HOORN, Barent Christiansen[3], Christian Barentsen[2], Barent Barents[1])[4582,4583,4584]* was born 06 Mar 1916 in Cowansannock Twp., Armstong Cnty, PA[4584,4585], and died 26 Mar 1964 in NuMine, Armstrong Cnty, PA[4585]. He married Mae V. REEFER[4586,4587], daughter of Artie REEFER and Irene JEWART. She was born 05 Jun 1919 in Plumcreek, Armstrong Cnty, PA[4588], and died 06 Mar 1998 in Rural Valley, Armstrong Cnty, PA[4588].

Notes for Owen DeLone VAN HORNE:
    In 1930 Owen Delone is boarding with the Verner Shields family his father having died in 1929.

Notes for Mae V. REEFER:
    9 April 1959 Simpson's Leader-Times (Kittanning, PA) Mrs. Mae Van Horn elected treasurer of the NuMine PTA.

Children of Owen VAN HORNE and Mae REEFER are:
        i.   Ronald Owen[12] VAN HORNE, b. Private; m. Sherri Lynn PATTERSON, Private; b. Private.

        More About Ronald VAN HORNE and Sherri PATTERSON:
        Private-Begin: Private

        ii. Donna Lee VAN HORNE, b. Private.
        iii. DeLone W. VAN HORNE, b. Private; m. Marianne S. CLAYPOOLE, Private; b. Private.

        More About DeLone VAN HORNE and Marianne CLAYPOOLE:
        Private-Begin: Private

337. Ida[11] VAN HORN *(Arnold Wilton[10], George Logan[9], William G.[8], Isaiah[7], Henry B.[6], Henry[5], Christian Barentsen[4] VAN HOORN, Barent Christiansen[3], Christian Barentsen[2], Barent Barents[1])[4589]* was born Abt. 1919 in PA, and died Aft. 1993. She married Harold ISAACSON Private. He was born Private.

More About Harold ISAACSON and Ida VAN HORN:
Private-Begin: Private

Child of Ida VAN HORN and Harold ISAACSON is:
        i.   Myrna[12] ISAACSON, b. Private.

338. Mary Emma[11] VAN HORN *(Edward Harry[10], Samuel Redding[9], William G.[8], Isaiah[7], Henry B.[6], Henry[5], Christian Barentsen[4] VAN HOORN, Barent Christiansen[3], Christian Barentsen[2], Barent Barents[1])[4590,4591,4592]* was born Abt. 1907 in PA[4593], and died Unknown. She married Ralph E. DURBIN[4594] Abt. 1927, son of Edward DURBIN and Rose C.. He was born Abt. 1904 in PA[4594], and died Unknown.

More About Mary Emma VAN HORN:
Lived: Brockway, Jefferson Cnty, PA

Notes for Ralph E. DURBIN:
 In 1930 he owns his place worth $6,000 and has a radio. Living next door to his parents. Working as a typesetter in his father's newspaper. His father is editor and his mother is a reporter.

More About Ralph E. DURBIN:
Occupation: Newspaper Typesetter

More About Ralph DURBIN and Mary VAN HORN:
Marriage: Abt. 1927

Child of Mary VAN HORN and Ralph DURBIN is:
 i. Keith E.[12] DURBIN, b. Private.

339. Walter Edward[11] VAN HORN *(Edward Harry[10], Samuel Redding[9], William G.[8], Isaiah[7], Henry B.[6], Henry[5], Christian Barentsen[4] VAN HOORN, Barent Christiansen[3], Christian Barentsen[2], Barent Barents[1])[4595,4596,4597]* was born 02 Mar 1909 in Punxsutawney, Jefferson Cnty, PA[4598], and died 14 Sep 1994 in Jamestown, NY[4599]. He married Marion Isabelle CREE[4599] 25 Jan 1931[4599], daughter of Axel CREE and Cristina JOHNSON. She was born 22 Jul 1911 in Busti, NY[4599], and died 02 Mar 2001 in Jamestown, Chautauqua Cnty, NY[4599].

Notes for Walter Edward VAN HORN:
 11 June 1919 the Indiana Progress (Indiana, PA) reported that Walter the young son of Mrs. Harry Van Horn fell and broke his collarbone while playing.
 Not living with parents in 1920.

More About Walter Edward VAN HORN:
Lived: Haines City, FL

More About Walter VAN HORN and Marion CREE:
Marriage: 25 Jan 1931[4599]

Child of Walter VAN HORN and Marion CREE is:
484. i. Joyce Ann[12] VAN HORN, b. Private.

340. Clark Lewis[11] STEELE *(Elijah Work[10], Dorcas[9] HAMILTON, Nancy[8] VAN HORN, Isaiah[7], Henry B.[6], Henry[5], Christian Barentsen[4] VAN HOORN, Barent Christiansen[3], Christian Barentsen[2], Barent Barents[1])[4600,4601,4602]* was born 08 Oct 1879 in East Mahoning Twp.,Indiana Cnty, PA[4603,4604], and died May 1963. He married Charissa B. CALDWELL[4605]. She was born Abt. 1882 in PA[4605], and died Unknown.

Children of Clark STEELE and Charissa CALDWELL are:
485. i. Arveta T.[12] STEELE, b. Abt. 1902, PA; d. Unknown.

    ii. Helen N. STEELE*4605*, b. Abt. 1905, Limestone Twp., Clarion Cnty, PA*4605*; d. Unknown.

    iii. Harold C. STEELE*4605*, b. 25 Apr 1908, Limestone Twp., Clarion Cnty, PA*4605*; d. Apr 1985, Strattanville, Clarion Cnty, PA.

486. iv. Bertha Olive STEELE, b. 29 Mar 1912, Limestone Twp., Clarion Cnty, PA; d. 14 Oct 1991, Strattanville, Clarion Cnty, PA.

487. v. Clair W. STEELE, b. 12 Oct 1923, Limestone Twp., Clarion Cnty, PA; d. 07 Nov 2007, Brookville, Jefferson Cnty, PA.

341. Clare Clawson[11] STEELE *(Elijah Work[10], Dorcas[9] HAMILTON, Nancy[8] VAN HORN, Isaiah[7], Henry B.[6], Henry[5], Christian Barentsen[4] VAN HOORN, Barent Christiansen[3], Christian Barentsen[2], Barent Barents[1])[4606,4607]* was born 18 Oct 1888 in East Mahoning Twp.,Indiana Cnty, PA*4608*, and died 10 Nov 1964 in Punxsutawney, Jefferson Cnty, PA*4609*. He married Viola Sophia LODING*4610* Abt. 1908*4610*. She was born 1888 in PA*4610*, and died 1970.

Notes for Clare Clawson STEELE:
   In 1930 he is a farmer and owns his place worth about $4,000. He has a radio in the home. His name is spelled Clair or Clare.
   In his WWII Draft Registration he is 5ft 11 inches and weighs 190 pounds. He is self employed and his wife is Viola. He spells his name as Clare C. Steele.

More About Clare STEELE and Viola LODING:
Marriage: Abt. 1908*4610*

Children of Clare STEELE and Viola LODING are:
    i. Charles[12] STEELE*4610*, b. Abt. 1910, PA; d. Unknown.
    ii. Mary STEELE*4610*, b. Abt. 1912, PA; d. Unknown.
    iii. Ethel STEELE, b. Private.
    iv. Mildred STEELE, b. Private.
    v. Thelma STEELE, b. Private.

488. vi. Martha Elizabeth STEELE, b. 14 Dec 1920, Rochester Mills, Indiana Cnty, PA; d. 18 Aug 1997, Jefferson Cnty, PA.

342. Hazel B.[11] MCADOO *(Ada Myrtle[10] VAN HORN, Bennett Work[9], George Logan[8], Isaiah[7], Henry B.[6], Henry[5], Christian Barentsen[4] VAN HOORN, Barent Christiansen[3], Christian Barentsen[2], Barent Barents[1])[4611,4612,4613,4614]* was born 02 Nov 1895 in Indiana Cnty, PA*4615*, and died 07 Sep 1985 in Monroeville, Allegheny Cty, PA. She married Paul BUTTERBAUGH*4616,4617* Abt. 1920*4617*, son of Sloan BUTTERBAUGH and Sarah GALLAGHER. He was born 25 Jul 1894 in Green Twp., Indiana Cnty, PA, and died 18 Aug 1980 in Pittsburgh, Allegheny Cnty, PA.

More About Hazel B. MCADOO:
Occupation: Stenographer Glass Factory

Notes for Paul BUTTERBAUGH:
   In 1920 living with his parents in Green Twp., Indiana Cnty, PA. He is a battery man at the Exide Battery station.
   In 1930 living on Locust Street in Indiana, PA in a home he rents for $30/month and has a radio. He is married with a wife and 2 sons living in the home.
   10 and 21 June 1919 Indiana Evening Gazette (Indiana, PA) Paul Butterbaugh is in charge of the Exide battery station at Utility Electric Co.

More About Paul BUTTERBAUGH:
Occupation: Garage Batteryman

More About Paul BUTTERBAUGH and Hazel MCADOO:
Marriage: Abt. 1920[4617]

Children of Hazel MCADOO and Paul BUTTERBAUGH are:
    i.   Donald Paul[12] BUTTERBAUGH[4617], b. 26 Oct 1924, PA[4617]; d. 01 Dec 1943, Mt Pantano, Italy.
   ii.   William S. BUTTERBAUGH[4617], b. Abt. 1927, PA[4617]; d. Aft. 1985.

343. Esther M.[11] MCADOO *(Ada Myrtle[10] VAN HORN, Bennett Work[9], George Logan[8], Isaiah[7], Henry B.[6], Henry[5], Christian Barentsen[4] VAN HOORN, Barent Christiansen[3], Christian Barentsen[2], Barent Barents[1])*[4618,4619,4620,4621,4622] was born 20 May 1897 in Indiana Cnty, PA[4623], and died 28 Mar 1998 in St. Andrew's Village, Indiana, Indiana Cnty, PA[4623]. She married Charles Andrew FERRIER[4624,4625,4626,4627,4628] 18 Sep 1922 in PA[4629], son of Andrew FERRIER and Sarah SHEARER. He was born 05 May 1896 in Indiana, Indiana Cnty, Pa[4630,4631], and died 07 Apr 1987 in Indiana, Indiana Cnty, PA[4632].

Notes for Esther M. MCADOO:
    1 Nov 1916 Indiana Evening Gazette (Indiana, PA) Esther McAdoo daughter of Mr. and Mrs William McAdoo of Philadelphia Street has left by train for Pittsburgh to study nursing at the South Side Hospital Training school for nurses. Mrs McAdoo accompanied her daughter.

More About Esther M. MCADOO:
Burial: Unknown, Oakland Cemetery, Indiana, PA
Degree: Indiana High School and Indiana Normal School, Indiana, PA
Fraternal Organization: Eastern Star
Religion: Zion Luthern Church, Indiana, PA

Notes for Charles Andrew FERRIER:
    In 1900 lives on South 7th Street in Indiana, PA with his parents. His father is Street Commissioner.
    In 1930 owns his home on South 6th Street in Indiana, PA. The home is worth $7,000 and he has a radio. He is working as an engineer in a power plant. He and Ester have been married about 7 years and they have one child Mary Jane who is 4 years and 5 months.
    From a newspaper article source unknown:
    Charles A. Ferrier, a son of Mr. and Mrs. A. C. Ferrier was born May 5, 896. He enlisted in the Coast Artillery corps December 8, 1917, and was assigned to Battery D, 1st Battalion French Artillery, 1st Army Corps. Was located at Fort Crockett, Tex., for training and while there was transferred fro Coast to Trench Artillery. Sailed for France March 1918. Promoted to Corporal June, 1918. Participated in the battles of the Aisne-Marne Offensive; St.Mihiel Offensive and Meuse-Argonne Offensive. Arrived in the U. S. February 28, 1919, and received his honorable discharge, March 15, 119, at Camp Dix, N. J.
    From Indiana Gazette 4-9-1987 Charles A. Ferrier, 90, Indiana, died Tuesday, April 7, 1987, in Scenery Hill Manor, Indiana.
    A son of Andrew Charels and Sarah Jane Shearer Ferrier, he was born May 5, 1896, in Indiana.
    Mr Ferrier was a member of the Zion Lutheran Church of Indiana; Benjamin Franklin F &AM lodge 753 and the Coudersport Consistory.
    He had been a lifelong resident of Indiana and retired in 1961 as chief operating engineer at the IUP power plant after 44 years of service. He was a veteran of World War I service. having served overseas with the U S Army.
    Surviving are his wife, Esther McAdoo Ferrier; a daughter, Mrs Charles (Mary Jane) Duncan,

Ypsilanti, Mich; two grandchildren.

He was preceded in death by a sister, Mrs May L. Freedline.

Friends will be received from 3-5 and 7-9 pm Thursday at Robinson-Lytle's Indiana, where services will be held at 11 a m. Friday. Pastor Bernhard a Bischoff will officiate with interment to follow in the Oakland Cemetery, Indiana.

More About Charles Andrew FERRIER:
Burial: 10 Apr 1987, Oakland Cemetery, Indiana, PA
Lived: 1947, 462 South Eleventh Indiana, PA
Occupation: Power Plant Engineer or electrical Engineer at Indiana Normal School

More About Charles FERRIER and Esther MCADOO:
Marriage: 18 Sep 1922, PA[4633]
Marriage date: Rev. Dr. J. H. Baker of Zion Luthern Church Indiana, PA
Marriage Place: Zion Luthern Church Indiana, PA

Child of Esther MCADOO and Charles FERRIER is:
489.   i.   Mary Jane[12] FERRIER, b. Abt. Nov 1925, PA; d. Aft. 1998.

344. Nellie E.[11] MCADOO *(Ada Myrtle[10] VAN HORN, Bennett Work[9], George Logan[8], Isaiah[7], Henry B.[6], Henry[5], Christian Barentsen[4] VAN HOORN, Barent Christiansen[3], Christian Barentsen[2], Barent Barents[1])*[4634,4635,4636,4637,4638,4639] was born Abt. 1900 in PA, and died Aft. 1998. She married John Chester TRAINER[4640,4641,4642,4643] 06 Jun 1924 in Indiana, Indiana Cnty, PA[4644], son of Winfred TRAINER and Caroline STRATTON. He was born 15 May 1894 in Brookville, Jefferson Cnty, PA[4645,4646], and died 07 Sep 1954 in Indiana, Indiana Cnty, PA[4647].

Notes for Nellie E. MCADOO:
In a news article in the Indiana Evening Gazette (Indiana, PA) Nellie a daughter of Willima McAdoo of 350 Chestnut held a lawn fete of ice cream and cake to raise funds for the Christian Endeavor of the UP Church.

14 Sept 1921 Indiana Evening Gazette (Indiana, PA) Nell McAddo left for New Brighton where she will be an instructor in the Public Schools. Other articles indicate she taught in the Commercial Department of Brighton High School

28 Nov 1930 Indiana Evening Gazette (Indiana, PA) announces the Thanksgiving birth of a son to Mr. and Mrs Trainer of North 6th Street Indiana, PA

15 Sept. 1942 Indiana Evening Gazette (Indiana, PA) reports that Mrs John Trainer is the 2nd grade teacher at the First United Presbyterian Church

Notes for John Chester TRAINER:
Played for the Collegians in 1912 billed as one of the best semipro teams to exist. A photo of the team including John is printed in the 8 Aug 1966 Indiana Evening Gazette (Indiana, PA).

8 July 925 Indiana Evening Gazette (Indiana, PA) reports that John Trainer short stop and one of the best players on the Normal team for the past several seasons has signed with the Dubois team for the next season.

Coached baseball for the Johnstown Johnnies Independents in the 1924 season.

Active in the Indiana Kennel club and Dog Show. He and Nell loved to roller skate.

2 Dec 1931 Indiana Evening Gazette (Indiana, PA) repots John getting 11 point Buck that weighed 185 lbs dressed shot near Nolo.

The 9 Dec, 1931 edition reports the fireman being served venison a al Trainer at a meal for the firemen with the venison supplied from the 11 point buck shot by John Trainer earlier.

Numerous articles report on Trany being needed as coach for the local team and attempts to get him a job with the highway department so he can lead and coach the baseball team.

8 Jan 1946 Indiana Evening Gazette (Indiana, PA) John C. Trainer was elected to the Indiana

Isaiah Van Horn Pioneer of Indiana County, Pennsylvania

Burrough council from the 2nd Ward

According to his WWI I Draft registration he is 5 ft 71/2 inches and weighs 135 pounds. He is bald and has brown eyes. He works for the Department of Highways and lives 495 S. 6th Street in Indiana, PA.

Numerous articles in the early 1930s discuss Trainey as being needed to have a good town baseball team. He is willing to help but insists that full cooperation of all the team members and the team will be needed. In 1936 it is reported that the town was unsuccessful in getting the highway department to transfer him to Indiana to help the town with their baseball team.

More About John Chester TRAINER:
Burial: Unknown, Brookville Cemetery, Brookville, Jefferson Cnty, PA
Elected: Borrough Councilman
Lived: Bet. 1900 - 1954, Indiana, Indiana Cnty, PA
Occupation: Pennsylvania Highway Department[4648]
Religion: United Presbyterian Church

More About John TRAINER and Nellie MCADOO:
Marriage: 06 Jun 1924, Indiana, Indiana Cnty, PA[4649]
Marriage date: J. C. Pinkerton, DD
Marriage Place: 06 Jun 1924, Manse of the First Presbyterian Church

Children of Nellie MCADOO and John TRAINER are:
    i.   John Chester[12] TRAINER, JR, b. Private; m. Dorothy HUNT, Private; b. Private.

        More About John TRAINER and Dorothy HUNT:
        Private-Begin: Private

    ii.   Daniel T. TRAINER, b. Private.

345. Jane E.[11] MCADOO *(Ada Myrtle[10] VAN HORN, Bennett Work[9], George Logan[8], Isaiah[7], Henry B.[6], Henry[5], Christian Barentsen[4] VAN HOORN, Barent Christiansen[3], Christian Barentsen[2], Barent Barents[1])[4650,4651,4652,4653]* was born Abt. 1905 in PA[4653], and died Bef. 1998. She married Jesse C. JACKSON[4654,4655] Aft. 1920, son of Horace JACKSON and Bertha J.. He was born Abt. 1902 in PA[4656], and died Unknown.

Notes for Jane E. MCADOO:
29 April 1918 Indiana Evening gazette lists all four McAdoo sisters as being on the honor roll of the Indiana Normal School.

Notes for Jesse C. JACKSON:
In 1930 lives on the North side of 1st Street in Apollo, PA in a home he owns Worth $4500 and has a radio. He is a salesman in a Gents Furnishings store. He lives there with a wife of 2 years and a daughter Jessie who is 11 months.

More About Jesse JACKSON and Jane MCADOO:
Marriage: Aft. 1920

Child of Jane MCADOO and Jesse JACKSON is:
    i.   Jessie J.[12] JACKSON, b. Private.

346. Herbert Riggle[11] AUL *(Mary Caroline[10] VAN HORN, Bennett Work[9], George Logan[8], Isaiah[7], Henry B.[6], Henry[5], Christian Barentsen[4] VAN HOORN, Barent Christiansen[3], Christian Barentsen[2], Barent*

Barents[1][4657,4658,4659,4660,4661] was born 22 Feb 1896 in Georgeville, Indiana Cnty, PA[4662,4663], and died 22 Apr 1974 in Indiana, Indiana Cnty, PA[4664]. He married Margaret BECK[4665,4666] Abt. 1918. She was born Abt. 1898 in Elinora, PA[4667], and died Unknown.

Notes for Herbert Riggle AUL:
    28 August 1912 the Indiana Progress (Indiana, PA) reported that he was the guest of his grandparents Mr and Mrs B. W. Van Horn on Sunday
    In 1930 he is renting for $8.00/month as are most of his neighbors. He is a motor man in a coal mine,

More About Herbert Riggle AUL:
Lived: Sagamore, PA and Niagra Falls, Niagra Cnty, NY
Military service: Vetern of WWI
Occupation: Coal Miner

More About Herbert AUL and Margaret BECK:
Marriage: Abt. 1918

Children of Herbert AUL and Margaret BECK are:
    i.   James E.[12] AUL, b. Private.
    ii.   Arthur Melvin AUL[4668,4669], b. Abt. 1924, PA[4670]; d. Sep 1987.

          More About Arthur Melvin AUL:
          Lived: Niagra Falls, Niagra Cnty, NY

    iii. Imogene Mildred AUL[4670,4671], b. Abt. May 1929, Numine, Armstrong Cnty, PA; d. Oct 1986; m. (1) ZANOTTI, Private; b. Private; m. (2) Tony FERRARO, Private; b. Private.

          More About ZANOTTI and Imogene AUL:
          Private-Begin: Private

          More About Tony FERRARO and Imogene AUL:
          Private-Begin: Private

    iv.   William L. AUL, b. Private.
    v.   Robert AUL, b. Private.

347. Curtis Edwin[11] AUL *(Mary Caroline*[10] *VAN HORN, Bennett Work*[9]*, George Logan*[8]*, Isaiah*[7]*, Henry B.*[6]*, Henry*[5]*, Christian Barentsen*[4] *VAN HOORN, Barent Christiansen*[3]*, Christian Barentsen*[2]*, Barent Barents*[1]*)*[4672,4673,4674,4675,4676,4677,4678] was born Bet. Nov 1897 - 21 Sep 1898 in PA[4679,4680], and died 13 Apr 1972. He married Pearl June HALL[4681]. She was born 1897 in PA[4681], and died Unknown.

Notes for Curtis Edwin AUL:
    24 Dec 1919 Indiana Progress (Indiana, PA) notes that Curt Aul spent the Sabbath with his grand parents Mr. and Mrs. Bennett VanHorne.
    In his WWI Draft Registration he is living with his parents at 19 Harvey, Sagamore, PA. He is a miner for Sagamore Coal and Coke, He is of medium height and build with gray eyes and brown hair.
    In 1930 renting for $12/month and has a wife and 2 children. There is no radio in the home.

More About Curtis Edwin AUL:
Lived: DuBoise, PA

Occupation: Tipple Laborer, Laborer Coal Mine

Children of Curtis AUL and Pearl HALL are:
490.   i.   Larue Bernadine[12] AUL, b. Private.
        ii.   Merle AUL, b. Private; m. Gladys Viola HAYS, Private; b. Private.

           More About Merle AUL and Gladys HAYS:
           Private-Begin: Private

348. Bertha Della[11] AUL *(Mary Caroline*[10] *VAN HORN, Bennett Work*[9]*, George Logan*[8]*, Isaiah*[7]*, Henry B.*[6]*, Henry*[5]*, Christian Barentsen*[4] *VAN HOORN, Barent Christiansen*[3]*, Christian Barentsen*[2]*, Barent Barents*[1]*)*[4682,4683,4684,4685,4686,4687] was born 06 Aug 1899 in PA[4688], and died Bet. Jun 1986 - 24 Jun 1988. She married John Reid MCCAUSLAND[4689,4690,4691,4692,4693] Abt. 1916, son of Campbell MCCAUSLAND and Jane JEWART. He was born Jul 1898 in PA[4694,4695], and died 03 May 1983.

More About Bertha Della AUL:
Religion: Presbyterian

Notes for John Reid MCCAUSLAND:
    In 1930 living on Church Street in Sagamore, PA in a home he rents for $9/month.
    16 May 1955 Indiana Evening Gazette (Indiana, PA) lists John R. McCausland as a Republican Candidate for County Supervisor.

More About John Reid MCCAUSLAND:
Lived: Sagamore, PA
Occupation: Laborer Coal Mine

More About John MCCAUSLAND and Bertha AUL:
Marriage: Abt. 1916

Children of Bertha AUL and John MCCAUSLAND are:
        i.   Ruby Mae[12] MCCAUSLAND, b. 15 Feb 1919, Sagamore, Armstrong Cnty, PA; d. 15 Feb 1919.
491.   ii.   Robert Clark MCCAUSLAND, b. 12 Jul 1920, Sagamore, Armstrong Cnty, PA; d. 11 Mar 1992, Pittsburgh, PA.
492.   iii.   Florence Jane MCCAUSLAND, b. 26 Dec 1921, PA; d. Aft. 1992.
493.   iv.   Donald Reid MCCAUSLAND, b. 14 May 1924, PA; d. 22 Nov 2003, Rural Valley, Armstrong Cnty, PA.
494.   v.   Clair Eugene MCCAUSLAND, b. 27 Jun 1926, Sagamore, Armstrong Cnty, PA; d. Aft. 1992.
495.   vi.   Grace Lucille MCCAUSLAND, b. 08 Aug 1930, PA; d. Aft. 1992.
496.   vii.   Dorothy Jean MCCAUSLAND, b. 10 Sep 1934, PA; d. Aft. 1992.
497.   viii.   Shirley Ann MCCAUSLAND, b. 16 Sep 1936, PA; d. Aft. 1992.

349. Iva Bell[11] AUL *(Mary Caroline*[10] *VAN HORN, Bennett Work*[9]*, George Logan*[8]*, Isaiah*[7]*, Henry B.*[6]*, Henry*[5]*, Christian Barentsen*[4] *VAN HOORN, Barent Christiansen*[3]*, Christian Barentsen*[2]*, Barent Barents*[1]*)*[4696,4697,4698,4699] was born Bet. 11 - 12 Nov 1901 in Georgeville, Indiana Cnty, PA[4700,4701], and died 09 Apr 1951 in Clearfield, Clearfield Cnty, PA[4701]. She married James Oliver HOPKINS[4702,4703]. He died Unknown.

More About Iva Bell AUL:
Burial: Unknown, Croyle Cemetery, Utahville, PA

Cause of Death: Pneumonia

Children of Iva AUL and James HOPKINS are:
  i.   Betty[12] HOPKINS[4703], d. 2002.
  ii. James HOPKINS[4703], d. 2003.
  iii. Loriane HOPKINS, b. Private.

350. Alma Florence[11] AUL *(Mary Caroline[10] VAN HORN, Bennett Work[9], George Logan[8], Isaiah[7], Henry B.[6], Henry[5], Christian Barentsen[4] VAN HOORN, Barent Christiansen[3], Christian Barentsen[2], Barent Barents[1])[4704,4705,4706,4707,4708]* was born 14 Apr 1903 in Georgeville, Indiana Cnty, PA[4709], and died 03 Sep 1957 in Indiana, Indiana Cnty, PA[4710]. She married Delbert O. SHAFFER[4711,4712,4713]. He died Aft. Sep 1957[4713].

Notes for Alma Florence AUL:
1 March 1922 Indiana Progress (Indiana, PA) Alma Aul of near Atwood visits her cousin Irene Johnson of Smyrna

More About Alma Florence AUL:
Burial: Unknown, Atwood Cemetery
Lived: Sagamore, PA
Religion: Sagamore Presbyterian Church, Sagamore, PA

Children of Alma AUL and Delbert SHAFFER are:
  i.   Harold L.[12] SHAFFER, b. Private.
  ii. Lewis SHAFFER[4713], d. Bef. Sep 1957.
  iii. Donald SHAFFER[4713], d. Bef. Sep 1957.

351. Mary Jane[11] AUL *(Mary Caroline[10] VAN HORN, Bennett Work[9], George Logan[8], Isaiah[7], Henry B.[6], Henry[5], Christian Barentsen[4] VAN HOORN, Barent Christiansen[3], Christian Barentsen[2], Barent Barents[1])[4714,4715,4716,4717,4718,4719]* was born 04 Sep 1905 in Rossmoyne, Indiana Cnty, PA[4720], and died 24 Apr 1978. She married (1) Earl RUPERT[4721,4722,4723] Abt. 1930. He died Unknown. She married (2) George KELLY Private. He was born Private.

More About Mary Jane AUL:
Lived: Marion Center, PA

More About Earl RUPERT and Mary AUL:
Marriage: Abt. 1930

More About George KELLY and Mary AUL:
Private-Begin: Private

Child of Mary AUL and Earl RUPERT is:
  i.   Sara[12] RUPERT, b. Private.

352. Myrtle Linda[11] AUL *(Mary Caroline[10] VAN HORN, Bennett Work[9], George Logan[8], Isaiah[7], Henry B.[6], Henry[5], Christian Barentsen[4] VAN HOORN, Barent Christiansen[3], Christian Barentsen[2], Barent Barents[1])[4724,4725,4726]* was born Bet. 03 Nov - Dec 1909 in PA[4727], and died 13 Feb 1950 in Niagra Falls, Niagra Cnty, NY[4728]. She married John Edward WAGNER[4728,4729]. He was born 1904, and died Aft. 1950.

Notes for Myrtle Linda AUL:
    31 March 1921 Indiana Progress (Indiana, PA Myrtle is the guest of her cousin Vela Johnson of Smyrna on the Sabbath.

Children of Myrtle AUL and John WAGNER are:
    i. Eugene Monroe[12] WAGNER[4729], b. 14 Apr 1931, Sagamore, Armstrong Cnty, PA; d. 27 Oct 1967, Baltimore, Baltimore Cnty, MD; m. HUMPTON, Private; b. Private.

        More About Eugene Monroe WAGNER:
        Burial: Unknown, Niagra Falls Memorial Park, Lewiston, NY
        Cause of Death: delerium tremems, acute and chronic alcoholism, severe bilateral tuberculosis

        More About Eugene WAGNER and HUMPTON:
        Private-Begin: Private

    ii. Helen WAGNER[4729], d. Aft. 1950.
    iii. Romaine WAGNER[4729], d. Aft. 1950.
    iv. Robert WAGNER[4729], d. Aft. 1950.
    v. Donald WAGNER[4729], d. Aft. 1950.
    vi. Burldine WAGNER[4729], d. Aft. 1950.
    vii. John Edward WAGNER, JR[4729], d. Aft. 1950.

353. Lawrence David[11] AUL *(Mary Caroline[10] VAN HORN, Bennett Work[9], George Logan[8], Isaiah[7], Henry B.[6], Henry[5], Christian Barentsen[4] VAN HOORN, Barent Christiansen[3], Christian Barentsen[2], Barent Barents[1])*[4730,4731,4732,4733,4734] was born 27 Jul 1912 in Sagamore, Armstrong Cnty, PA[4735], and died 07 Jan 1984 in Niagra Falls, Niagra Cnty, NY. He married (1) Gwendolyn E. REARICH 21 Feb 1936. She was born 1915 in Yalesboro, PA, and died 13 Jun 1939. He married (2) Nova Jane MINSER[4736] 08 Aug 1941 in Rochester Mills, PA[4736], daughter of Clair MINSER and Mary KUNTZ. She was born 19 Dec 1923 in Marion Center, Indiana Cnty, PA, and died 24 Oct 1999.

Notes for Lawrence David AUL:
    26 April 1950 Indiana Evening gazette Lawrence Aul selling a pair of gray mares weighing 3000 pounds and a black horse weight 1200 pounds along with a set of double work harness. Located Marion Center about 1/2 mile from Oak Tree Station..

More About Lawrence David AUL:
Employment: Niagra Alkali Works, Niagra Fall, NY
Lived: Bef. 1941, Niagra Falls, Niagra Cnty, NY
Medical Information: Had a heart attack on 22 Dec. 1960

More About Gwendolyn E. REARICH:
Cause of Death: Died in Childbirth

More About Lawrence AUL and Gwendolyn REARICH:
Marriage: 21 Feb 1936

More About Lawrence AUL and Nova MINSER:
Marriage: 08 Aug 1941, Rochester Mills, PA[4736]
Marriage date: Rev H. F. Given

Children of Lawrence AUL and Nova MINSER are:

    i.   Charles K.[12] AUL, b. Private.
   ii.   Larry Arthur AUL, b. Private.
  iii.   Norman L. AUL, b. Private.
  iv.   Raymond Curtis AUL, b. Private.
   v.   ? AUL, b. Private.

354. Floyd William[11] AUL *(Mary Caroline[10] VAN HORN, Bennett Work[9], George Logan[8], Isaiah[7], Henry B.[6], Henry[5], Christian Barentsen[4] VAN HOORN, Barent Christiansen[3], Christian Barentsen[2], Barent Barents[1])[4737,4738,4739,4740,4741,4742]* was born Abt. 1914 in Sagamore, Armstrong Cnty, PA[4743], and died 02 Dec 1977 in Tucson, AZ. He married Violet Mae GAMBEL[4744,4745] 04 Dec 1937[4746], daughter of Samuel GAMBEL and Lillie POSTLEWEIT. She was born 1915 in North Mahoning, Indiana Cnty, PA, and died 10 Sep 1979 in Tucson, AZ.

More About Floyd William AUL:
Lived: Niagra Falls, Niagra Cnty, NY

More About Violet Mae GAMBEL:
Lived: 1969, Niagra Falls, Niagra Cnty, NY

More About Floyd AUL and Violet GAMBEL:
Marriage: 04 Dec 1937[4746]

Children of Floyd AUL and Violet GAMBEL are:
    i.   Liola[12] AUL, b. Private.
   ii.   Ronals AUL, b. Private.
  iii.   Ruth Ann AUL, b. Private.

355. Nelson Ernest[11] SHAFFER *(Cora Belle[10] VAN HORN, Bennett Work[9], George Logan[8], Isaiah[7], Henry B.[6], Henry[5], Christian Barentsen[4] VAN HOORN, Barent Christiansen[3], Christian Barentsen[2], Barent Barents[1])[4747,4748,4749,4750]* was born 26 Feb 1901 in Indiana Cnty, PA or Dubois. Clearfield Cnty, PA[4751], and died 12 Jan 1959 in Kittanning, Armstrong Cnty, PA. He married Margaret E. DOUDS[4752,4753] Feb 1923 in Indiana Cnty, PA[4754], daughter of DOUDS and Vernie. She was born 27 Aug 1902 in PA[4755], and died Sep 1978 in Plumville, Indiana Cnty, PA[4756].

Notes for Nelson Ernest SHAFFER:
    3 Oct 1935 Indiana Evening Gazette (Indiana, PA) Nelson wins the Democratic Nomination for Constable in Plumville, PA.
    9 Sept 1949 Indiana Evening Gazette (Indiana, PA) Nelson elected as Plumville Constable as a Republican. In the same paper is is reported that Nelson is elected as a Burgess for Plumville as a Republican.
    26 May 1953 Indiana Evening Gazette (Indiana, PA) reports that Nelson is recognized for his parts sales with the Belt of Champions by the Pontiac Motor Division.

More About Nelson Ernest SHAFFER:
Lived: Plumville, PA

Marriage Notes for Nelson SHAFFER and Margaret DOUDS:
    15 Feb 1923 the Indiana Weekly Messenger (Indiana, PA) reported a license issued between Nelson E. Shaffer and Margaret E. Douds both of Plumville, PA

More About Nelson SHAFFER and Margaret DOUDS:

Marriage: Feb 1923, Indiana Cnty, PA[4757]

Children of Nelson SHAFFER and Margaret DOUDS are:

| 498. | i. | Helen[12] SHAFFER, b. Private. |
| | ii. | Nelson Earnest SHAFFER, JR[4758], b. 21 Sep 1924; d. 15 Oct 1999, Yatesboro, Armstrong Cnty, PA; m. ?, Private; b. Private. |

Notes for Nelson Earnest SHAFFER, JR:
12 Nov 1948 Indiana Weekly Messenger (Indiana, PA) reports that Nelson Earnest Shaffer of Plumville is called for a draft physical.
24 April 1950 reported in the Indiana Evening Gazette (Indiana, PA) that Pfc. Nelson Shaffer, Jr assisted in the army maneuvers as a runner

More About Nelson SHAFFER and ?:
Private-Begin: Private

| 499. | iii. | Jane SHAFFER, b. Private. |
| 500. | iv. | Verna M. SHAFFER, b. 07 Oct 1927, Plumville, Indiana Cnty, PA; d. 12 Dec 1994, Cleveland, OH. |

356. Dorothy Bell[11] SHAFFER *(Cora Belle[10] VAN HORN, Bennett Work[9], George Logan[8], Isaiah[7], Henry B.[6], Henry[5], Christian Barentsen[4] VAN HOORN, Barent Christiansen[3], Christian Barentsen[2], Barent Barents[1])*[4759,4760,4761] was born 13 Nov 1903 in DuBois, Indiana Cnty, PA[4762,4763], and died 13 May 1945 in Johnstown, Cambria Cnty, PA[4763]. She married Charles R. WEAVER[4764] Abt. 1920. He was born Abt. 1901 in PA[4764], and died Aft. 1945[4765].

More About Dorothy Bell SHAFFER:
Burial: Unknown, Oakland Cemetery, Indiana Cnty, PA
Fraternal Organization: F. O. E. Ladies Auxillary
Lived: Indiana, Indiana Cnty, PA
Religion: United Presbyterian Church

Notes for Charles R. WEAVER:
In 1930 renting on North Ninth Street in Indiana, PA for $15/month and has a radio. He is a meat truck driver.

More About Charles WEAVER and Dorothy SHAFFER:
Marriage: Abt. 1920

Children of Dorothy SHAFFER and Charles WEAVER are:

	i.	Albert Dean[12] WEAVER, b. Private.
	ii.	Donna Belle WEAVER, b. Private.
	iii.	Vernard Leroy WEAVER, b. Private.

357. Agnes Marie[11] SHAFFER *(Cora Belle[10] VAN HORN, Bennett Work[9], George Logan[8], Isaiah[7], Henry B.[6], Henry[5], Christian Barentsen[4] VAN HOORN, Barent Christiansen[3], Christian Barentsen[2], Barent Barents[1])*[4766,4767,4768,4769,4770] was born 02 Jan 1906 in Ernest, Indiana Cnty, PA[4771], and died 26 May 1994 in Indiana, Indiana Cnty, PA. She married Thomas BANKS[4772,4773] Aft. 1923. He was born 01 May 1901 in Glenn, Camppbell Cnty, PA[4773], and died 22 Jun 1989 in Indiana Cnty, PA.

Notes for Agnes Marie SHAFFER:

27 Sept. 1926 Mrs Banks of Chambersville is called home to care for her mother Mrs. Albert Shaffer due to illness and recent surgery at Indiana Hospital.

19 Jan 1938 Mrs Banks of Chambersville is recuperating from surgery in the Indiana Hospital Her brother Claude Shaffer was also in the hospital after a surgery on Friday January 7, 1938.

More About Agnes Marie SHAFFER:
Lived: Homer City, PA

Notes for Thomas BANKS:
In 1930 has been married for 6 years. He is a coal miner and rents for $6/month. They do not have a radio.

More About Thomas BANKS:
Occupation: 1930, Coal Miner

More About Thomas BANKS and Agnes SHAFFER:
Marriage: Aft. 1923

Children of Agnes SHAFFER and Thomas BANKS are:
      i.   Louise[12] BANKS, b. Private; m. Edward W. GREESLEY, Private; b. Private.

          More About Edward GREESLEY and Louise BANKS:
          Private-Begin: Private

501.   ii.   Helen BANKS, b. Private.
        iii.   Rosemary BANKS, b. Private.

358. Claude Ellsworth[11] SHAFFER *(Cora Belle[10] VAN HORN, Bennett Work[9], George Logan[8], Isaiah[7], Henry B.[6], Henry[5], Christian Barentsen[4] VAN HOORN, Barent Christiansen[3], Christian Barentsen[2], Barent Barents[1])[4774,4775,4776,4777]* was born 21 Jun 1910 in Indiana Cnty, PA[4778], and died 30 Jun 1981. He married (1) Almeda HENNEMAN Private. She was born Private. He married (2) Lilla Elizabeth BOTHELL Aft. 1930. She died Bef. 2005.

Notes for Claude Ellsworth SHAFFER:
25 July 1945 Claude advertises roofs to repair, paint or shingle by the hour or contract.

20 Sept 1949 Claude Shaffer places an ad indicating that his wife Lilla Bothel Shaffer has left his bed and board without cause and notifies all that they are not to harbor her on his account and that he is not responsible for any of her bills or debts.

29 March 1961 Indiana Evening Gazette (Indiana, PA) Shaffers Lake is opening on March 31 for fishing Rt 1 Home, PA.

More About Claude Ellsworth SHAFFER:
Lived: Indiana, Indiana Cnty, PA

More About Claude SHAFFER and Almeda HENNEMAN:
Private-Begin: Private

More About Claude SHAFFER and Lilla BOTHELL:
Marriage: Aft. 1930

Children of Claude SHAFFER and Lilla BOTHELL are:
      i.   Leona[12] SHAFFER, b. Private.
502.   ii.   John William SHAFFER, b. 07 Dec 1942, Indiana Cnty, PA; d. 26 Jun 2006,

Indiana, Indiana Cnty, PA.
iii.   Claire SHAFFER, d. Aft. 2006; m. Anita; d. Aft. 2006.
iv.   James SHAFFER, d. Aft. 2006; m. Mary Lou; d. Aft. 2006.
v.   Dorothy SHAFFER, b. Private; m. GIMA, Private; b. Private.

More About GIMA and Dorothy SHAFFER:
Private-Begin: Private

vi.   Mary SHAFFER, b. Private; m. LAZOR, Private; b. Private.

More About LAZOR and Mary SHAFFER:
Private-Begin: Private

vii.   Jean SHAFFER, b. Private; m. UHER, Private; b. Private.

More About UHER and Jean SHAFFER:
Private-Begin: Private

viii.   Sally SHAFFER, b. 28 Sep 1940; d. Aft. 2002; m. Beryl Crea LYDIC, 14 Feb; b. 21
Mar 1932; d. Aft. 2006.

More About Beryl LYDIC and Sally SHAFFER:
Marriage: 14 Feb

ix.   Thomas SHAFFER, b. Private.
x.   Clarence E. SHAFFER, d. 14 May 2005.

359. Gladys Rossett[11] SHAFFER *(Cora Belle[10] VAN HORN, Bennett Work[9], George Logan[8], Isaiah[7], Henry B.[6], Henry[5], Christian Barentsen[4] VAN HOORN, Barent Christiansen[3], Christian Barentsen[2], Barent Barents[1])[4778]* was born Bet. 07 Jan - 26 Feb 1913 in Indiana Cnty, PA[4778], and died 17 Mar 1933 in Indiana, Indiana Cnty, PA[4779]. She married Ralph MARSHALL[4779]. He died Unknown.

More About Gladys Rossett SHAFFER:
Burial: Mar 1933, Plumville, Indiana Cnty, PA

Child of Gladys SHAFFER and Ralph MARSHALL is:
i.   Shirley Irene[12] MARSHALL, b. Private.

360. Staff Sgt Clyde Sylvester[11] SHAFFER *(Cora Belle[10] VAN HORN, Bennett Work[9], George Logan[8], Isaiah[7], Henry B.[6], Henry[5], Christian Barentsen[4] VAN HOORN, Barent Christiansen[3], Christian Barentsen[2], Barent Barents[1])[4780,4781,4782,4783,4784]* was born Bet. 07 Dec 1918 - Jan 1919 in Plumvile, Indiana Cnty, PA[4785], and died 06 Mar 1998 in Dixonville, Indiana Cnty, PA[4786]. He married Ferne Ellen AIRGOOD[4787] May 1950 in Indiana, Indiana Cnty, PA[4787], daughter of Kepple AIRGOOD and Mary PEOPLES. She was born 26 Sep 1925 in Big Run, PA, and died 03 Jul 1992 in Indiana Cnty, PA[4788].

Notes for Staff Sgt Clyde Sylvester SHAFFER:
30 Jun 1943 Indiana Evening Gazette (Indiana, PA) Pfc Clyde S. Shaffer has been stationed in Nashville, TN is now transferred to Camp Gordon in GA after spending a 10 day furlough with his mother Cora Shaffer of Indiana.
6 June 1945 Indiana Evening Gazette (Indiana, PA) Staff Sergeant Clyde S. Shaffer is awarded the Bronze Star for his heroic service in Italy and his commendation is signed by General Mark

Clark. He is the son of Cora Shaffer of Indiana and he is currently serving in the Austrian Alps. His brother Paul is with the Company A 82nd Engineers in Germany at this time.

More About Staff Sgt Clyde Sylvester SHAFFER:
Military service: Army stationed at Camp Shelby and in France

More About Clyde SHAFFER and Ferne AIRGOOD:
Marriage: May 1950, Indiana, Indiana Cnty, PA[4789]

Children of Clyde SHAFFER and Ferne AIRGOOD are:
503.   i.   Judy Lynn[12] SHAFFER, b. Private.
        ii. Beryl Emerson SHAFFER, b. 01 Dec 1950, Indiana, Indiana Cnty, PA; d. Aft. 2006; m. Deborah May GALENTINE, 03 Sep 1983; b. 06 Aug 1952; d. Aft. 2006.

            More About Beryl SHAFFER and Deborah GALENTINE:
            Marriage: 03 Sep 1983

504.   iii. Connie May SHAFFER, b. Private.
505.   iv. Gary Lee SHAFFER, b. Private.
506.   v.   Edgar Dean SHAFFER, b. Private.
507.   vi. Lois Jean SHAFFER, b. Private.
       vii. Kevin Jon SHAFFER, b. Private.
     viii. Ruth Ann SHAFFER, b. Private.
       ix. Lisa Jo SHAFFER, b. Private.

361. William Clair[11] JOHNSTON (*Anna Florence[10] VAN HORN, Bennett Work[9], George Logan[8], Isaiah[7], Henry B.[6], Henry[5], Christian Barentsen[4] VAN HOORN, Barent Christiansen[3], Christian Barentsen[2], Barent Barents[1]*)[4790,4791] was born 28 Apr 1901 in Rossmoyne, Indiana Cnty, PA[4792], and died 19 Oct 1986 in Rochester Mills, PA. He married Pansy BRILHART 06 Sep 1922. She died 16 Nov 1985.

Notes for William Clair JOHNSTON:
    Nominated by the Republican Party for Supervisor East Mahoning Twp in 1961.

More About William JOHNSTON and Pansy BRILHART:
Marriage: 06 Sep 1922

Children of William JOHNSTON and Pansy BRILHART are:
508.   i.   William L.[12] JOHNSTON, b. 21 Sep 1928, Homer City, PA; d. 10 Jul 1996, Punxsutawney, PA.
        ii. Hazel JOHNSTON, b. Private; m. SNYDER, Private; b. Private.

            More About SNYDER and Hazel JOHNSTON:
            Private-Begin: Private

362. Irene Mae[11] JOHNSTON (*Anna Florence[10] VAN HORN, Bennett Work[9], George Logan[8], Isaiah[7], Henry B.[6], Henry[5], Christian Barentsen[4] VAN HOORN, Barent Christiansen[3], Christian Barentsen[2], Barent Barents[1]*)[4792,4793] was born 21 Oct 1904 in Georgeville, Indiana Cnty, PA[4794], and died 29 Sep 1969 in Punzsutawney, Jefferson Cnty, PA[4795]. She married Alvord Boyd STEELE[4796,4797,4798] Abt. 1923. He was born 1898 in PA, and died 1962[4798].

More About Irene Mae JOHNSTON:
Burial: Unknown, Mahoning Cemetery, Marion Center, PA

Cause of Death: Injuries sustained in an auto accident
Religion: United Presbyterian Church

More About Alvord STEELE and Irene JOHNSTON:
Marriage: Abt. 1923

Children of Irene JOHNSTON and Alvord STEELE are:

509.	i.	Raymond[12] STEELE, b. Private.
510.	ii.	Myrna J. STEELE, b. Private.
511.	iii.	Evelyn Jane STEELE, b. 23 Mar 1928, South Mahoning Twp., Indiana Cnty, PA; d. 14 Nov 2004, Indiana, Indiana Cnty, PA.
512.	iv.	Lulu A. STEELE, b. 09 Dec 1929, South Mahoning Twp., Indiana Cnty, PA; d. 02 Jun 1999, Indiana Cnty, PA.
	v.	Melvin Dean STEELE, b. Private.
	vi.	Rodger Lyle STEELE, b. Private.
513.	vii.	Bruce STEELE, b. Private.
514.	viii.	Harold Blaine STEELE, b. Private.
515.	ix.	Martha STEELE, b. Private.
516.	x.	Donna STEELE, b. Private.
517.	xi.	Earl Clark STEELE, b. 25 Feb 1935, Plumville, Indiana Cnty, PA; d. 01 Apr 2002, Indian Haven, Indiana, Indiana Cnty, PA.
	xii.	Infant STEELE, b. Private.

363. Velma A.[11] JOHNSTON *(Anna Florence[10] VAN HORN, Bennett Work[9], George Logan[8], Isaiah[7], Henry B.[6], Henry[5], Christian Barentsen[4] VAN HOORN, Barent Christiansen[3], Christian Barentsen[2], Barent Barents[1])[4799,4800,4801]* was born Abt. 1906 in Indiana Cnty, PA[4802], and died Aft. 1971. She married Ronald SKINNER[4803,4804]. He died Unknown.

Child of Velma JOHNSTON and Ronald SKINNER is:
    i.   Cathy[12] SKINNER, b. Private.

364. Lester Carl[11] JOHNSTON *(Anna Florence[10] VAN HORN, Bennett Work[9], George Logan[8], Isaiah[7], Henry B.[6], Henry[5], Christian Barentsen[4] VAN HOORN, Barent Christiansen[3], Christian Barentsen[2], Barent Barents[1])[4805,4806,4807,4808]* was born 23 Nov 1911 in South Mahoning Twp., Indiana Cnty, PA[4809], and died 17 Sep 1975 in Home, PA. He married Princess Mary Virginia LUTZ[4810] Abt. 1933. She died 14 Jul 1978.

Notes for Lester Carl JOHNSTON:
    2 Oct 1948 Indiana Evening Gazette (Indiana, PA) Lester advertises 2 registered male beagles for sale or will trade for 410 or 20 gage shotgun also a 2 year running treeing coon dog with a beautiful voice. Home, PA one mile west of Ambrose.
    29 June 1955 Lester Carl Johnston places a notice that his wife Mary Virginia Lutz Johnston has left his bed and board w/o cause and he is not responsible for any debts contracted by or for her. He lives in Home, PA
    In 1961 Lester was seeking the Democratic Nomination for supervisor Rayne Twp.

More About Lester Carl JOHNSTON:
Lived: 1928, Kellysburg, Indiana Cnty, PA

More About Lester JOHNSTON and Princess LUTZ:
Marriage: Abt. 1933
Separation: 1955, Mary Lutz left w/o cause

Children of Lester JOHNSTON and Princess LUTZ are:
     i. Carl Eugene[12] JOHNSTON[4811], b. 28 Nov 1935, Indiana Cnty, PA; d. 08 Nov 1965, Orchard Park, NY[4811]; m. Glennabelle DILTS, Private; b. Private.

        More About Carl Eugene JOHNSTON:
        Burial: Unknown, Armor Cemetery, Orchard Park, NY
        Cause of Death: Auto Accident
        Medical Information: Thrown from auto and crushed beneath the auto when his auto skidded while returning home from work in Buffalo, NY

        More About Carl JOHNSTON and Glennabelle DILTS:
        Private-Begin: Private

518.   ii. Russell Paul JOHNSTON, b. Private.

365. Walter R.[11] JOHNSTON *(Anna Florence[10] VAN HORN, Bennett Work[9], George Logan[8], Isaiah[7], Henry B.[6], Henry[5], Christian Barentsen[4] VAN HOORN, Barent Christiansen[3], Christian Barentsen[2], Barent Barents[1])[4812,4813,4814]* was born 27 Sep 1918 in South Mahoning Twp., Indiana Cnty, PA[4815], and died 05 Jul 1994 in Indiana Cnty, PA. He married Gail MILLER 14 Nov 1942 in Smicksburg, Indiana Cnty, PA. She died 1994.

Notes for Walter R. JOHNSTON:
    6 Aug 1963 Indiana Evening Gazette (Indiana, PA) Walter works for McGill Motors and has been with them for 2 years.

More About Walter JOHNSTON and Gail MILLER:
Marriage: 14 Nov 1942, Smicksburg, Indiana Cnty, PA
Marriage date: Rev. Jacob Troutman
Marriage Place: Parsonage

Children of Walter JOHNSTON and Gail MILLER are:
519.   i. Larry R.[12] JOHNSTON, b. Private.
520.   ii. Bernice JOHNSTON, b. Private.
521.   iii. James B. JOHNSTON, b. Private.

366. Floyd Albert[11] VAN HORN *(Robert Lee Claire[10], Bennett Work[9], George Logan[8], Isaiah[7], Henry B.[6], Henry[5], Christian Barentsen[4] VAN HOORN, Barent Christiansen[3], Christian Barentsen[2], Barent Barents[1])[4816,4817,4818,4819,4820,4821,4822]* was born 08 Oct 1908 in Plumville, Indiana Cnty, PA[4823,4824], and died 24 Jul 1987 in Youngstown, Mahoning Cnty, OH[4825,4826]. He married Katherine Belle JUART[4827] 1933, daughter of Andrew JUART and Susanna MCMAUS. She was born 12 Jul 1914 in Home, Indiana Cnty, PA[4828], and died 13 Apr 2001 in Niles, Trumbull Cnty, OH[4828].

Notes for Floyd Albert VAN HORN:
    31 March 1937 the Indiana Progress (Indiana, PA) reports that Floyd A. Van Horn purchased a lot from J. W. Weaver in South Mahoning Twp. for $35.

More About Floyd Albert VAN HORN:
Occupation: Coal Miner

More About Katherine Belle JUART:
Burial: Unknown, Greenhaven Cemetery, Canfield, OH

Hobies: Bingo, Needlework, Sewing and Crocheting
Occupation: Cook at Fogerty's Restaurant at Niles, OH, Rudy's Snack Shack and Alberinis Restaurant
Religion: First Church of God Mineral Ridge, PA

More About Floyd VAN HORN and Katherine JUART:
Marriage: 1933

Children of Floyd VAN HORN and Katherine JUART are:
522.	i.	Charles Lee[12] VAN HORN, b. Private.
523.	ii.	Howard Eugene VAN HORN, b. Private.
	iii.	Gary VAN HORN, b. Private; m. Janet HORN, Private; b. Private.

        More About Gary VAN HORN and Janet HORN:
        Private-Begin: Private

| | iv. | James VAN HORN, b. Private. |

367. Wilbur Bennett[11] VAN HORN *(Robert Lee Claire[10], Bennett Work[9], George Logan[8], Isaiah[7], Henry B.[6], Henry[5], Christian Barentsen[4] VAN HOORN, Barent Christiansen[3], Christian Barentsen[2], Barent Barents[1])*[4829,4830,4831,4832,4833,4834,4835] was born 24 Feb 1910 in Plumville, Indiana Cnty, PA[4836,4837], and died 11 Jul 1998 in Indiana, Indiana Cnty, PA[4838]. He married (1) Florence KIRKPATRICK[4838], daughter of Arthur KIRKPATRICK and Mamie ANDERSON. She was born 08 Feb 1920 in Dayton, PA, and died 22 Mar 1990 in Indiana, Indiana Cnty, PA[4838,4839]. He married (2) Mildred Wenona ADAMSON[4840,4841] 16 Nov 1933 in Plumville, PA[4841], daughter of Joseph Sylvester ADAMSON. She died Aft. 1986.

Notes for Wilbur Bennett VAN HORN:
    30 October 1970 Edition of the Indiana Evening Gazette (Indiana, PA) in Ridge Lanes Tenpin as having the high single score of 247 and the high triple score of 650.

More About Wilbur Bennett VAN HORN:
Burial: Unknown, Smicksburh Cemetery, Smicksburg, PA
Hobies: Bowling and Hunting
Occupation: Coal Miner, FMC
Religion: Harmony Grove Luthern Church of Willet, PA

More About Florence KIRKPATRICK:
Burial: Unknown, Smicksburg Cemetery, Smicksburg, PA

More About Wilbur VAN HORN and Mildred ADAMSON:
Marriage: 16 Nov 1933, Plumville, PA[4841]
Marriage date: J. E. McCall

Children of Wilbur VAN HORN and Mildred ADAMSON are:
| 524. | i. | Joseph Lee[12] VAN HORN, b. 04 Apr 1934, Plumville, Indiana Cnty, PA; d. 31 Mar 1985, Creekside, Indiana Cnty, PA. |
| | ii. | Harold Barney VAN HORN[4842,4843], b. Bet. 1934 - 1942, Denver, Denver Cnty, CO; d. Aft. 1998; m. Patricia Lee SKINNER, Private; b. Private. |

        More About Harold Barney VAN HORN:
        Lived: Pleasant Hills, CA
        Occupation: Allyn and Bacon Publishers, Wenger Theatrical supplies

More About Harold VAN HORN and Patricia SKINNER:
Private-Begin: Private

525.   iii.   William James VAN HORN, b. Abt. 1942, Indiana Cnty, PA; d. Aft. 1998.
526.   iv.   Lyle Bennett VAN HORN, b. 16 Feb 1943, Niagra Falls, Niagra Cnty, NY; d. 20 Apr 1986, Ravenna, OH.

368. Olive Marion[11] VAN HORN *(Robert Lee Claire[10], Bennett Work[9], George Logan[8], Isaiah[7], Henry B.[6], Henry[5], Christian Barentsen[4] VAN HOORN, Barent Christiansen[3], Christian Barentsen[2], Barent Barents[1])[4844,4845,4846,4847,4848]* was born 24 Dec 1911 in Plumville, Indiana Cnty, PA[4848], and died 19 Mar 2000 in Portsmouth, VA. She married Laurence Robert FREDERICK[4849,4850,4851] 25 May 1932 in Dayton, Armstrong Cnty, PA, son of S. FREDERICK and M. HEITZENRATER. He was born 09 Dec 1908 in Port Huron, MI, and died 14 Feb 1999 in Kane, PA.

More About Laurence FREDERICK and Olive VAN HORN:
Marriage: 25 May 1932, Dayton, Armstrong Cnty, PA

Children of Olive VAN HORN and Laurence FREDERICK are:
    i.   Nancy Lee[12] FREDERICK, b. Private; m. William BARR, Private; b. Private.

        More About William BARR and Nancy FREDERICK:
        Private-Begin: Private

    ii.   Samuel Laurence FREDERICK, b. Private; m. Vonnie, Private; b. Private.

        More About Samuel FREDERICK and Vonnie:
        Private-Begin: Private

    iii.   Alice Elaine FREDERICK, b. Private; m. Ted HESS, Private; b. Private.

        More About Ted HESS and Alice FREDERICK:
        Private-Begin: Private

369. Robert[11] VAN HORN *(Robert Lee Claire[10], Bennett Work[9], George Logan[8], Isaiah[7], Henry B.[6], Henry[5], Christian Barentsen[4] VAN HOORN, Barent Christiansen[3], Christian Barentsen[2], Barent Barents[1])[4852,4853,4854,4855,4856]* was born 29 Sep 1913 in Plumville, Indiana Cnty, PA[4857], and died Aft. 1987. He married Mary SAHYONNE Private. She was born Private.

Notes for Robert VAN HORN:
    In 1920 Robert is living with his grandparents.
    In 1930 he is living with his widowed grandmother.

More About Robert VAN HORN:
Lived: Wallkill, NY

More About Robert VAN HORN and Mary SAHYONNE:
Private-Begin: Private

Child of Robert VAN HORN and Mary SAHYONNE is:
    i.   Shirley[12] VAN HORN, b. Private; m. BARDIN, Private; b. Private.

More About BARDIN and Shirley VAN HORN:
Private-Begin: Private

370. June Louise[11] VAN HORN *(Robert Lee Claire[10], Bennett Work[9], George Logan[8], Isaiah[7], Henry B.[6], Henry[5], Christian Barentsen[4] VAN HOORN, Barent Christiansen[3], Christian Barentsen[2], Barent Barents[1])*[4858,4859,4860,4861,4862,4863,4864] was born 08 Jun 1915 in Plumville, Indiana Cnty, PA[4865], and died Aft. 1989. She married James COON[4866,4867] 1934 in Indiana Cnty, PA. He died Unknown.

Notes for June Louise VAN HORN:
31 May 1941 Indiana Evening Progress (Indiana, PA) Mr and Mrs James Coon and family visited her parents Mr and Mrs Lee Van Horn of Plumville.

More About James COON and June VAN HORN:
Marriage: 1934, Indiana Cnty, PA

Children of June VAN HORN and James COON are:
    i.   Robert[12] COON, b. Private.
    ii. Ronald COON, b. Private.
   iii. Margaret COON, b. Private.
   iv. Allan COON, b. Private.
    v. Cynthia COON, b. Private.
   vi. Carol Sue COON, b. Private.
  vii. William COON, b. Private.

371. Alice Belle[11] VAN HORN *(Robert Lee Claire[10], Bennett Work[9], George Logan[8], Isaiah[7], Henry B.[6], Henry[5], Christian Barentsen[4] VAN HOORN, Barent Christiansen[3], Christian Barentsen[2], Barent Barents[1])*[4868,4869,4870,4871] was born 24 Oct 1917 in Plumville, Indiana Cnty, PA[4872], and died Bet. 1951 - 1989. She married Andrew PETRUNEY Private. He was born Private.

Notes for Alice Belle VAN HORN:
Graduated from Plumville High school on May 22, 1935 according to the Indiana Progress (Indiana, PA) of May 29, 1935.

More About Alice Belle VAN HORN:
Lived: Kane, PA

More About Andrew PETRUNEY and Alice VAN HORN:
Private-Begin: Private

Children of Alice VAN HORN and Andrew PETRUNEY are:
527.   i. Marianne[12] PETRUNEY, b. Private.
       ii. Terri Lynn PETRUNEY, b. Private.

372. Howard Lee[11] VAN HORN *(Robert Lee Claire[10], Bennett Work[9], George Logan[8], Isaiah[7], Henry B.[6], Henry[5], Christian Barentsen[4] VAN HOORN, Barent Christiansen[3], Christian Barentsen[2], Barent Barents[1])*[4873,4874,4875,4876,4877] was born 14 Dec 1919 in Plumville, Indiana Cnty, PA[4878], and died Jan 1984 in Tanawanda, Erie Cnty, NY[4879]. He married (1) Julia Private. She was born Private. He married (2) Shirley PARSELL Private, daughter of PARSELL and Olive. She was born Private.

Notes for Howard Lee VAN HORN:
28 Jan 1932 Indiana Evening Gazette (Indiana, PA) lists the members of the IOOF Scout

Troop of Plumville including 26 boys one of whom was Howard Van Horn,
9 Dec 1932 Indiana Evening Gazette (Indiana, PA) Howard Van Horn of Plumville received his second class BSA badge along with others mentioned.
3 July 1941 the Indiana Evening Gazette (Indiana, PA) lists Howard Lee Van Horn of Plumville among the Registrants that are eligible for the July 1, 1941 draft that lowered the age from 35 to 28.

More About Howard Lee VAN HORN:
Lived: Niagra Falls, Niagra Cnty, NY
Military service: WWI Veteran of the US Army 15th Evac Hospital

More About Howard VAN HORN and Julia:
Private-Begin: Private

More About Howard VAN HORN and Shirley PARSELL:
Private-Begin: Private

Children of Howard VAN HORN and Shirley PARSELL are:
     i. Randall[12] VAN HORN, b. Private.
    ii. Patricia VAN HORN, b. Private.

373. William Clyde[11] VAN HORN *(Robert Lee Claire[10], Bennett Work[9], George Logan[8], Isaiah[7], Henry B.[6], Henry[5], Christian Barentsen[4] VAN HOORN, Barent Christiansen[3], Christian Barentsen[2], Barent Barents[1])[4880,4881,4882,4883,4884]* was born 24 Jan 1922 in Plumville, Indiana Cnty, PA[4885], and died Aft. 1998. He married Helen KROFT Private. She was born Private.

More About William Clyde VAN HORN:
Lived: NY
Military service: 01 Jun 1939, WW II Army Air Corp Hawaii, South Pacific and France

More About William VAN HORN and Helen KROFT:
Private-Begin: Private

Children of William VAN HORN and Helen KROFT are:
528.   i. William[12] VAN HORN, b. Private.
529.   ii. Sharon VAN HORN, b. Private.
    iii. Dennis VAN HORN, b. Private.
    iv. Debra VAN HORN, b. Private.
    v. Rodney VAN HORN, b. Private.

374. Hillary Leroy[11] VAN HORN *(Robert Lee Claire[10], Bennett Work[9], George Logan[8], Isaiah[7], Henry B.[6], Henry[5], Christian Barentsen[4] VAN HOORN, Barent Christiansen[3], Christian Barentsen[2], Barent Barents[1])[4886,4887,4888]* was born 10 Oct 1924 in Plumville, Indiana Cnty, PA[4889], and died 24 Oct 1973 in Niagra Falls, Niagra Cnty, NY. He married Ann CONNELL Private. She was born Private.

Notes for Hillary Leroy VAN HORN:
Hillary entered the service in April 1943 and was wounded in action in Belgium.

More About Hillary Leroy VAN HORN:
Military service: Paratrooper WW II

More About Hillary VAN HORN and Ann CONNELL:

Private-Begin: Private

Children of Hillary VAN HORN and Ann CONNELL are:
   i.   Gloria Jean[12] VAN HORN, b. Private.
   ii. Raymond Lee VAN HORN, b. Private.

375. Donald Charles[11] VAN HORN *(Robert Lee Claire[10], Bennett Work[9], George Logan[8], Isaiah[7], Henry B.[6], Henry[5], Christian Barentsen[4] VAN HOORN, Barent Christiansen[3], Christian Barentsen[2], Barent Barents[1])*[4890,4891,4892,4893,4894,4895] was born 21 Feb 1927 in Plumville, Indiana Cnty, PA[4896], and died 2000[4897]. He married Margaret Ann SLONINGER[4897,4898] 29 Jun 1949 in Indiana Cnty, PA[4898], daughter of John SLONINGER and Vernie LEWIS. She was born 30 Jul 1931 in Dayton, PA[4899], and died 20 Feb 2005 in Indiana, Indiana Cnty, PA[4899].

Notes for Donald Charles VAN HORN:
   Donald joined the Navy in May 1944 and served in the South Pacific from August 1944.

More About Donald Charles VAN HORN:
Lived: NY
Military service: Navy WW II

More About Margaret Ann SLONINGER:
Burial: Unknown, Acasia Cemetery, North Tonawanda, NY

Marriage Notes for Donald VAN HORN and Margaret SLONINGER:
   Marriage license is listed in the 29 June 1949 Indiana Evening Gazette (Indiana, PA)

More About Donald VAN HORN and Margaret SLONINGER:
Marriage: 29 Jun 1949, Indiana Cnty, PA[4900]

Children of Donald VAN HORN and Margaret SLONINGER are:
530.   i.   Thomas M.[12] VAN HORN, b. Private.
531.   ii. Donna Lynn VAN HORN, b. 1957; d. 1992.

376. Richard Max[11] VAN HORN *(Robert Lee Claire[10], Bennett Work[9], George Logan[8], Isaiah[7], Henry B.[6], Henry[5], Christian Barentsen[4] VAN HOORN, Barent Christiansen[3], Christian Barentsen[2], Barent Barents[1])*[4901,4902,4903,4904] was born 12 Nov 1929 in Plumville, Indiana Cnty, PA[4905], and died Bef. 1989. He married (1) Shirley STITELER Private. She was born Private. He married (2) Dixie LEE Private. She was born Private. He married (3) Ruth KUNCYTES Private. She was born Private.

More About Richard Max VAN HORN:
Lived: OH
Military service: Army in Japan and Korea

More About Richard VAN HORN and Shirley STITELER:
Private-Begin: Private

More About Richard VAN HORN and Dixie LEE:
Private-Begin: Private

More About Richard VAN HORN and Ruth KUNCYTES:
Private-Begin: Private

Children of Richard VAN HORN and Ruth KUNCYTES are:
  i. Richard[12] VAN HORN, b. Private.
  ii. Sandra VAN HORN, b. Private.

377. George Eugene[11] VAN HORN *(Robert Lee Claire[10], Bennett Work[9], George Logan[8], Isaiah[7], Henry B.[6], Henry[5], Christian Barentsen[4] VAN HOORN, Barent Christiansen[3], Christian Barentsen[2], Barent Barents[1])[4906,4907,4908]* was born 02 Sep 1931 in Plumville, Indiana Cnty, PA, and died Aft. 1998. He married Dorothy KAMENSKY Private. She was born Private.

More About George Eugene VAN HORN:
Lived: Plumville, PA and Warren, OH
Military service: Army

More About George VAN HORN and Dorothy KAMENSKY:
Private-Begin: Private

Child of George VAN HORN and Dorothy KAMENSKY is:
  i. Stephen[12] VAN HORN, b. Private.

378. Carrie Etta[11] VAN HORN *(James Ira[10], Bennett Work[9], George Logan[8], Isaiah[7], Henry B.[6], Henry[5], Christian Barentsen[4] VAN HOORN, Barent Christiansen[3], Christian Barentsen[2], Barent Barents[1])[4909,4910,4911]* was born Abt. 1914 in PA[4912], and died 03 Dec 1968 in Dixonville, PA[4913]. She married Alexander Thomas LAMBING[4914] Abt. 1927, son of Simona LAMBING and Martha CONNER. He was born 18 May 1892 in Bush Valley Twp., Indiana Cnty, PA[4914], and died 30 Aug 1970 in Indiana, Indiana Cnty, PA[4915].

Notes for Carrie Etta VAN HORN:
  Died at the home of Mrs Mildred Smith.

Notes for Alexander Thomas LAMBING:
  His sister in law Arlene is living in the family.

More About Alexander Thomas LAMBING:
Burial: Unknown, Ruffner Cemetery, Tanoma, PA
Occupation: Railroad section laborer Penn Central for 40 years

More About Alexander LAMBING and Carrie VAN HORN:
Marriage: Abt. 1927

Children of Carrie VAN HORN and Alexander LAMBING are:
    i. James Alexander[12] LAMBING, b. Private.
532. ii. Donald H. LAMBING, b. Private.
    iii. Mildred LAMBING, b. Private; m. SMITH, Private; b. Private.

      More About SMITH and Mildred LAMBING:
      Private-Begin: Private

    iv. Nancy Mary LAMBING[4915], b. 03 Apr 1943, Indiana Cnty, PA; d. Sep 1989, Indiana Cnty, PA; m. Charles LEE, Private; b. Private.

      More About Charles LEE and Nancy LAMBING:
      Private-Begin: Private

      v.   Ronald E. LAMBING, b. Private.

     vi.   Richard S. LAMBING[4915], b. 25 May 1931, Marion Center, Indiana Cnty, PA; d. 05 Jun 2000, Williamstown, Wood Cnty, WV; m. LONG, Private; b. Private.

         More About Richard LAMBING and LONG:
         Private-Begin: Private

533.   vii.   Dale Robert LAMBING, b. 05 Jun 1934, Indiana Cnty, PA; d. 16 Sep 1967, Armstrong Cnty, PA.

379. Deloris Belle[11] VAN HORN *(James Ira[10], Bennett Work[9], George Logan[8], Isaiah[7], Henry B.[6], Henry[5], Christian Barentsen[4] VAN HOORN, Barent Christiansen[3], Christian Barentsen[2], Barent Barents[1])*[4916,4917] was born 04 Sep 1915 in East Mahoning Twp., Indiana Cnty, PA[4918,4919], and died 21 Jul 1971 in Kittanning, Armstrong Cnty, PA[4919]. She married John Ray WEAVER[4919] 11 Sep 1931 in Indiana Cnty, PA[4919], son of Solomon WEAVER and Rose LITTLE. He was born 10 Jul 1904, and died 22 Nov 1976.

Notes for Deloris Belle VAN HORN:
    In 1930 Delores is boarding with the Vernon Shields family.

More About Deloris Belle VAN HORN:
Burial: Unknown, Gilgal Cemetery, Indiana Cnty, PA
Religion: Baptist

More About John WEAVER and Deloris VAN HORN:
Marriage: 11 Sep 1931, Indiana Cnty, PA[4919]

Children of Deloris VAN HORN and John WEAVER are:
534.   i.   Betty M.[12] WEAVER, b. 04 Aug 1932, South Mahoning Twp., Indiana Cnty, PA; d. 30 Jul 1999, Kittanning, Armstrong Cnty, PA.
535.   ii.   Annabelle WEAVER, b. 06 Sep 1934, Plumville, Indiana Cnty, PA; d. 22 Jul 1996, Pittsburgh, Allegheny Cnty, PA.
     iii.   Margaret WEAVER, b. Private; m. Reed CRAMER, Private; b. Private.

         More About Reed CRAMER and Margaret WEAVER:
         Private-Begin: Private

     iv.   Mary WEAVER, b. Private; m. Clair LEWIS, Private; b. Private.

         More About Clair LEWIS and Mary WEAVER:
         Private-Begin: Private

     v.   Shirley WEAVER, b. Private; m. Waldo CRAIG, Private; b. Private.

         More About Waldo CRAIG and Shirley WEAVER:
         Private-Begin: Private

     vi.   John Ray WEAVER, JR, b. Private.
     vii.   James WEAVER, b. Private.
536.   viii.   Vernie M. WEAVER, d. 1989.

380. Arlene May[11] VAN HORN *(James Ira[10], Bennett Work[9], George Logan[8], Isaiah[7], Henry B.[6], Henry[5], Christian Barentsen[4] VAN HOORN, Barent Christiansen[3], Christian Barentsen[2], Barent Barents[1])[4920,4921,4922,4923]* was born 29 Mar 1918 in South Mahoning Twp., Indiana Cnty, PA[4924], and died 19 Dec 1975 in Indiana, Indiana Cnty, PA. She married William M. STEWART[4925,4926] Abt. 1938. He was born 1909, and died 1996.

Notes for Arlene May VAN HORN:
    In 1930 living with her sister Carre and her husband.

More About Arlene May VAN HORN:
Burial: Unknown, Gilgal Cemetery Gilgal UP Church Indiana Cnty, PA

More About William M. STEWART:
Burial: Unknown, Gilgal Cemetery Gilgal UP Church Indiana Cnty, PA

More About William STEWART and Arlene VAN HORN:
Marriage: Abt. 1938

Children of Arlene VAN HORN and William STEWART are:
    i.   William M.[12] STEWART, JR, b. Private.
    ii.   Jeanne STEWART, b. Private; m. (1) Lloyd HEBERLING, Private; b. Private; m. (2) Lysle MCAFOOSE, Private; b. Private.

        More About Lloyd HEBERLING and Jeanne STEWART:
        Private-Begin: Private

        More About Lysle MCAFOOSE and Jeanne STEWART:
        Private-Begin: Private

    iii.   Gary Lee STEWART[4926], b. 24 Dec 1948, East Mahoning, Indiana Cnty, PA[4926]; d. 08 Jul 1964, Punxsutawney, PA[4926].

        More About Gary Lee STEWART:
        Boy Scouts of America: Troop 52 Rochester Mills, PA
        Burial: Unknown, Gilgal Cemetery, Indiana Cnty, PA
        Cause of Death: Farm Accident
        Religion: Methodist

381. John Simpson[11] VAN HORN *(Harry Bennett[10], Bennett Work[9], George Logan[8], Isaiah[7], Henry B.[6], Henry[5], Christian Barentsen[4] VAN HOORN, Barent Christiansen[3], Christian Barentsen[2], Barent Barents[1])[4927,4928,4929,4930,4931]* was born 24 Feb 1914 in Georgeville, Indiana Cnty, PA[4932,4933], and died 06 Jun 1993 in Monroeville or Export, PA[4933]. He married Marion Catherine LEARN[4934,4935] 21 Aug 1937 in Indiana Cnty, PA, daughter of William LEARN. She was born 09 Jul 1916 in Indiana Cnty, PA[4936], and died 31 Jan 2000 in Export, PA[4936].

More About John Simpson VAN HORN:
Burial: Unknown, Twin Valley Memorial Park, Delmont, PA
Occupation: Machinist Westinghouse Electric East Pittsburgh, PA
Religion: Emanuel Luthern Church of Export, PA

Notes for Marion Catherine LEARN:
    Marion Learn Van Horn, 83, of Export, died Monday, Jan. 31, 2000. She was born July 9, 1916, in Indiana, Pa., a daughter of the late Mr. and Mrs. William Learn. She was also preceded in death by

her husband, John S. Van Horn. Mrs. Van Horn was a member of the Emmanuel Lutheran Church in Export. She is survived by a son, Donald Van Horn and wife, Nora, of Murrysville; three daughters, Mrs. Frank (Ellen) Ruzbarsky of Murrysville, Mrs. Paul (Carol) Graf and Mrs. Carl (Sandra) Barone, both of Penn Hills; two sisters, Mrs. Walter (Ruth) Van Horn of Plum Borough and Rosella Hill of Indiana, Pa.; 12 grandchildren; and 21 great-grandchildren. Friends will be received at the EDWIN N. WOLFE FUNERAL HOME INC., Export, Wednesday from 2 to 4 and 7 to 9 p.m., where services will be held Thursday at 11 a.m. with the Rev. Gregory B. Held officiating. Interment Twin Valley Memorial Park, Delmont.

More About Marion Catherine LEARN:
Burial: Unknown, Twin Valley Memorial Park, Delmont, PA

Marriage Notes for John VAN HORN and Marion LEARN:
    The Indiana Progress(Indiana, PA) of August 8, 1937 reports that a marriage license was issued to John Van Horn of W. Mahoning Twp and Marion Learn of Grant Twp.

More About John VAN HORN and Marion LEARN:
Marriage: 21 Aug 1937, Indiana Cnty, PA

Children of John VAN HORN and Marion LEARN are:
      i.   Donald[12] VAN HORN, b. Private; m. Nora, Private; b. Private.

            More About Donald VAN HORN and Nora:
            Private-Begin: Private

      ii.   Ellen VAN HORN, b. Private; m. Frank RUZBARSKY, Private; b. Private.

            More About Frank RUZBARSKY and Ellen VAN HORN:
            Private-Begin: Private

      iii. Carol VAN HORN, b. Private; m. Paul GRAF, Private; b. Private.

            More About Paul GRAF and Carol VAN HORN:
            Private-Begin: Private

      iv. Sandra VAN HORN, b. Private; m. Carl BARONE, Private; b. Private.

            More About Carl BARONE and Sandra VAN HORN:
            Private-Begin: Private

382. Walter L.[11] VAN HORN *(Harry Bennett*[10]*, Bennett Work*[9]*, George Logan*[8]*, Isaiah*[7]*, Henry B.*[6]*, Henry*[5]*, Christian Barentsen*[4] *VAN HOORN, Barent Christiansen*[3]*, Christian Barentsen*[2]*, Barent Barents*[1]*)*[4937,4938,4939] was born 14 Mar 1917 in Smicksburg, Indiana Cnty, PA[4940], and died 21 Feb 2008 in Murrysville, Westmoreland Cnty or Smicksburg, Indiana Cnty, PA[4941]. He married Hazel Ruth LEARN Bef. 1955, daughter of William LEARN. She died Aft. 2008.

Notes for Walter L. VAN HORN:
    Walter L. Van Horn, 90, of Murrysville, died Thursday, Feb. 21, 2008. He was born March 14, 1917, in Smicksburg to the late Harry and Irene Bertha Simpson Van Horn and also was predeceased by a son, Thomas K. Van Horn, five brothers and a sister. Walter was a member of Operating Engineers Local 66 and Christ's Lutheran Church, Murrysville. Surviving are his wife, Hazel Learn

Van Horn; daughter, Janet Schoffstall, of Export; grandchildren, Ruth Ann Karcher and Tracy Battaglia; great-grandchildren, Vanessa and James; sisters, Mary Qualey, of Apollo, and Twila Rupert, of Shelocta, and brother, Blaine Van Horn, of Apollo. Visitation from 7 to 9 p.m. Saturday and 2 to 4 and 7 to 9 p.m. Sunday at the HART FUNERAL HOME INC., Murrysville, where a service will be at 10:30 a.m. Monday with Pastor Edward F. Sheehan officiating. Interment will follow in Hankey Church Cemetery, Murrysville.
(Obituary from The Valley News Dispatch, Tarentum, Pa.)

More About Walter L. VAN HORN:
Burial: Unknown, Hankey's Cemetery, Murrysville, Westmoreland Cnty, PA

More About Walter VAN HORN and Hazel LEARN:
Marriage: Bef. 1955

Children of Walter VAN HORN and Hazel LEARN are:
     i.   Janet[12] VAN HORN, b. Private; m. SCHOFFSTALL, Private; b. Private.

          More About SCHOFFSTALL and Janet VAN HORN:
          Private-Begin: Private

    ii.   Thomas K. VAN HORN, d. Bef. 2008.

383. Merle Wayne[11] VAN HORN *(Harry Bennett[10], Bennett Work[9], George Logan[8], Isaiah[7], Henry B.[6], Henry[5], Christian Barentsen[4] VAN HOORN, Barent Christiansen[3], Christian Barentsen[2], Barent Barents[1])[4942,4943,4944,4945]* was born 24 Feb 1919 in Indiana Cnty, PA[4946], and died 28 Aug 1948 in Tarentum, PA[4947]. He married Glennetta M. WHITE[4948] 21 Aug 1941, daughter of Clarence WHITE and Gertrude CAMPBELL. She was born 19 Jun 1924 in Punxsutawney, Jefferson Cnty, PA[4948], and died 04 Feb 1994 in Punxsutawney, Jefferson Cnty, PA[4948].

Notes for Merle Wayne VAN HORN:
      6 October 1922 Indiana Evening Gazette (Indiana, PA) reports that Merle Van Horn was injured when he was run over my his father as he was backing the automobile.

More About Merle Wayne VAN HORN:
Burial: Unknown, Gilgal Cemetery, Indiana Cnty, PA
Cause of Death: Auto Accident

More About Glennetta M. WHITE:
Burial: Unknown, Gilgal Cemetery Gilgal UP Church Indiana Cnty, PA
Lived: 441 S. Main, Punxsutawney, PA
Occupation: Punxsutawney Sportswear Company, Punxsutawney, Jefferson Cnty, PA
Religion: Christian Missionary Alliance

More About Merle VAN HORN and Glennetta WHITE:
Marriage: 21 Aug 1941

Children of Merle VAN HORN and Glennetta WHITE are:
     i.   Shirley Jean[12] VAN HORN, b. Private; m. Lionel BERRY, Private; b. Private.

          More About Lionel BERRY and Shirley VAN HORN:
          Private-Begin: Private

ii.   Merle Raymond VAN HORN, b. Private.
iii. Nancy Arlene VAN HORN, b. Private; m. Donald Dee FORREST, Private; b. Private.

More About Donald FORREST and Nancy VAN HORN:
Private-Begin: Private

384. Mary Belle[11] VAN HORN *(Harry Bennett[10], Bennett Work[9], George Logan[8], Isaiah[7], Henry B.[6], Henry[5], Christian Barentsen[4] VAN HOORN, Barent Christiansen[3], Christian Barentsen[2], Barent Barents[1])[4949,4950,4951]* was born Abt. 1920 in Indiana Cnty, PA[4952], and died Aft. 1988. She married (1) Gordon BROWN Private. He was born Private. She married (2) William QUALEY Private. He was born Private.

More About Mary Belle VAN HORN:
Lived: 1955, Courtland, OH

More About Gordon BROWN and Mary VAN HORN:
Private-Begin: Private

More About William QUALEY and Mary VAN HORN:
Private-Begin: Private

Children of Mary VAN HORN and Gordon BROWN are:
i.   ?[12] BROWN, b. Private.
ii. ? BROWN, b. Private.

385. Helen Louise[11] VAN HORN *(Harry Bennett[10], Bennett Work[9], George Logan[8], Isaiah[7], Henry B.[6], Henry[5], Christian Barentsen[4] VAN HOORN, Barent Christiansen[3], Christian Barentsen[2], Barent Barents[1])[4952,4953,4954]* was born Bet. 13 Jun - Jul 1926 in Indiana Cnty, PA[4955], and died 08 Sep 1990 in PA[4956]. She married (1) Herbert BOWSER[4957]. He was born 04 Mar 1929 in PA, and died 12 Feb 2004 in Cadoga, Armstrong Cnty, PA[4958]. She married (2) Albert Anthony LUKEHART Private, son of Clayton LUKEHART and Anna FISHER. He was born Private.

More About Helen Louise VAN HORN:
Lived: Cortland, OH

More About Albert LUKEHART and Helen VAN HORN:
Private-Begin: Private

Children of Helen VAN HORN and Albert LUKEHART are:
i.   Gloria Jane[12] LUKEHART, b. 17 Jan 1946; d. 17 Jan 1946.

Notes for Gloria Jane LUKEHART:
Born and died at the home the grandparents Clayton Lukehart.

ii. Donna LUKEHART, b. Private.
iii. Linda Lee LUKEHART, b. 01 Apr 1949; d. 12 Jul 1957.
iv. James Albert LUKEHART, b. Private.
v.   Dianne Lynne LUKEHART, b. Private.

386. Blaine W.[11] VAN HORN *(Harry Bennett[10], Bennett Work[9], George Logan[8], Isaiah[7], Henry B.[6],*

Henry[5], Christian Barentsen[4] VAN HOORN, Barent Christiansen[3], Christian Barentsen[2], Barent Barents[1])[4959,4960,4961,4962] was born 26 Jan 1928 in Indiana Cnty, PA[4963], and died Aft. 2008. He married Ruth WALTZ[4964,4965,4966] 25 Dec 1947 in Punsutawney, PA[4967,4968], daughter of Lloyd WALTZ. She was born 15 Sep 1930, and died Aft. 2006.

Notes for Blaine W. VAN HORN:
   In WWI I Enlistment documents he is born in 1928 and has a Grammer school education. He is single with no dependents.

More About Blaine W. VAN HORN:
Lived: Apollo,PA
Military service: US Army in Japan

More About Blaine VAN HORN and Ruth WALTZ:
Marriage: 25 Dec 1947, Punsutawney, PA[4969,4970]
Marriage date: Rev. Clark Wilson
Marriage Place: Rev. and Mrs. Wilson's home in Punxsutwaney, PA

Children of Blaine VAN HORN and Ruth WALTZ are:
    i.   Karen[12] VAN HORN, b. Private.
    ii. Blaine W. VAN HORN, JR, b. Private.
    iii. Melinda VAN HORN[4971], b. 30 Oct 1953, PA; d. 30 Oct 1953, New Kensington, PA.

        More About Melinda VAN HORN:
        Burial: Unknown, Gilgal Cemetery, Indiana County, PA

    iv. Kenneth Allan VAN HORN[4972], b. 05 Apr 1955, PA; d. 06 Apr 1955, PA.

        More About Kenneth Allan VAN HORN:
        Burial: Unknown, Gilgal Cemetery, Indiana County, PA

387. Twila May[11] VAN HORN *(Harry Bennett[10], Bennett Work[9], George Logan[8], Isaiah[7], Henry B.[6], Henry[5], Christian Barentsen[4] VAN HOORN, Barent Christiansen[3], Christian Barentsen[2], Barent Barents[1])[4973,4974]* was born Aft. 1930, and died Aft. 2008. She married Theadore RUPERT[4975], son of H. RUPERT and Mary B.. He was born Abt. 1930 in Schelocta, Indiana Cnty, PA, and died Aft. 2006.

Notes for Twila May VAN HORN:
   10 July 1941 the Indiana Evening Gazette (Indiana, PA) reports that Twila Van Horn is a member of the Willing Workers 4H Club of Georgeville.

More About Twila May VAN HORN:
Lived: Schelocta, Indiana Cnty, PA

More About Theadore RUPERT:
Lived: 1955, South Bend, Armstrong Cnty, PA

Children of Twila VAN HORN and Theadore RUPERT are:
537.   i.   Larry A.[12] RUPERT, b. Private.
538.   ii. Beverly Jean RUPERT, b. Private.
539.   iii. Patricia Ann RUPERT, b. 18 Nov 1959, Indiana, Indiana Cnty, PA; d. Aft. 2002.
        iv. Connie RUPERT, b. Private.

v. Kathy Lynn RUPERT, b. Private; m. Jeffery David CURRY, Private; b. Private.

More About Jeffery CURRY and Kathy RUPERT:
Private-Begin: Private

vi. Jeffery Allen RUPERT, b. Private.
vii. Lisa Kaye RUPERT, b. Private.

388. Lawrence Kenneth[11] GOOD *(Pearl Agnes[10] VAN HORN, Bennett Work[9], George Logan[8], Isaiah[7], Henry B.[6], Henry[5], Christian Barentsen[4] VAN HOORN, Barent Christiansen[3], Christian Barentsen[2], Barent Barents[1])[4976,4977]* was born Abt. 29 Jan 1914 in South Mahoning Twp., Indiana Cnty, PA[4978], and died 20 Jan 1968 in New Castle, PA. He married Elsie HINTON Private. She was born Private.

Notes for Lawrence Kenneth GOOD:
In 1930 filed a petition to run for supervisor Pine Twp., Indiana Cnty, PA.

More About Lawrence GOOD and Elsie HINTON:
Private-Begin: Private

Children of Lawrence GOOD and Elsie HINTON are:
540.   i. Lawrence Carl[12] GOOD, b. Private.
541.   ii. Jack Nelson GOOD, b. Private.
       iii. Darlene Bertha GOOD, b. Private.
       iv. Lorraine Ruth GOOD, b. Private; m. Vincent ENGLISH, Private; b. Private.

       More About Vincent ENGLISH and Lorraine GOOD:
       Private-Begin: Private

389. Wilbur Dale[11] GOOD *(Pearl Agnes[10] VAN HORN, Bennett Work[9], George Logan[8], Isaiah[7], Henry B.[6], Henry[5], Christian Barentsen[4] VAN HOORN, Barent Christiansen[3], Christian Barentsen[2], Barent Barents[1])[4978,4979]* was born 16 Jul 1916 in South Mahoning Twp., Indiana Cnty, PA[4980], and died 15 Sep 1991 in Indiana, Indiana Cnty, PA. He married Delsie Pearl HEBERLING 10 Nov 1937 in Plumville, Indiana Cnty, PA, daughter of John HEBERLING and Effie LUKEHART. She was born 08 Nov 1917 in South Mahoning Twp., Indiana Cnty, PA, and died 06 Feb 2001 in St. Andrews Village, Indiana Cnty, PA.

More About Wilbur GOOD and Delsie HEBERLING:
Marriage: 10 Nov 1937, Plumville, Indiana Cnty, PA
Marriage date: Rev. J. Edwin Giffen
Marriage Place: Presbyterian Manse

Children of Wilbur GOOD and Delsie HEBERLING are:
       i. Donna Jean[12] GOOD, b. 08 Feb 1939, South Mahoning Twp., Indiana Cnty, PA; d. 03 Jan 1946, Johnstown, Cambria Cnty, PA.
       ii. Senita Doris GOOD, b. 16 Jun 1940, South Mahoning Twp., Indiana Cnty, PA; d. Bet. 16 Jun 1940 - 1941, South Mahoning Twp., Indiana Cnty, PA.
       iii. Infant GOOD, b. 14 Mar 1941, South Mahoning Twp., Indiana Cnty, PA; d. 14 Mar 1941, South Mahoning Twp., Indiana Cnty, PA.
       iv. Harold Wilbur GOOD, b. 19 Mar 1944, South Mahoning Twp., Indiana Cnty, PA; d. 21 Mar 1944, South Mahoning Twp., Indiana Cnty, PA.
       v. Infant GOOD, b. 22 Oct 1945, South Mahoning Twp., Indiana Cnty, PA; d. 22 Oct 1945, South Mahoning Twp., Indiana Cnty, PA.

vi. Raymond GOOD, b. 12 Jan 1948; d. 12 Jan 1948.
vii. Max Glenn GOOD, b. 23 Oct 1950; d. 23 Oct 1950.

390. Ernest Glenn[11] GOOD *(Pearl Agnes[10] VAN HORN, Bennett Work[9], George Logan[8], Isaiah[7], Henry B.[6], Henry[5], Christian Barentsen[4] VAN HOORN, Barent Christiansen[3], Christian Barentsen[2], Barent Barents[1])[4980,4981]* was born 11 Dec 1920 in Sagamore, Armstrong Cnty, PA[4982], and died Aft. 2008. He married (1) Louise STENMAN Abt. 1941, daughter of Carl STENMAN and Agnes ANDERSON. She was born 01 Oct 1921, and died Aft. 2004. He married (2) Betty Bef. 2008. She died Aft. 2008.

More About Ernest GOOD and Louise STENMAN:
Marriage: Abt. 1941

More About Ernest GOOD and Betty:
Marriage: Bef. 2008

Children of Ernest GOOD and Louise STENMAN are:
    i. Donald Eugene[12] GOOD, b. Private; m. Helen Kathleen IRWIN, Private; b. Private.

       More About Donald GOOD and Helen IRWIN:
       Private-Begin: Private

542.   ii. Richard Ernest GOOD, b. Private.
    iii. Margaret Joanne GOOD, b. Private; m. Charles CONDRON, Private; b. Private.

       More About Charles CONDRON and Margaret GOOD:
       Private-Begin: Private

    iv. Glenda Lee GOOD, b. Private; m. Joseph BUREAU, Private; b. Private.

       More About Joseph BUREAU and Glenda GOOD:
       Private-Begin: Private

    v.   Lois Arlene GOOD, b. Private.
    vi. Michael Glenn GOOD, b. Private.

391. Alice Belle[11] GOOD *(Pearl Agnes[10] VAN HORN, Bennett Work[9], George Logan[8], Isaiah[7], Henry B.[6], Henry[5], Christian Barentsen[4] VAN HOORN, Barent Christiansen[3], Christian Barentsen[2], Barent Barents[1])[4982,4983]* was born 14 Apr 1923 in Plumville, Indiana Cnty, PA[4984], and died 14 Feb 2008 in Felt Manor, Emporium, Indiana Cnty, PA. She married (1) ? Private. He was born Private. She married (2) Melvin P. HAYES Private. He was born Private.

More About ? and Alice GOOD:
Private-Begin: Private

More About Melvin HAYES and Alice GOOD:
Private-Begin: Private

Children of Alice GOOD and Melvin HAYES are:
    i. Virginia Marie[12] HAYES, b. Private; m. (1) Charles CHMELAR, Private; b. Private; m. (2) William SZMANSKI, Private; b. Private.

More About Charles CHMELAR and Virginia HAYES:
Private-Begin: Private

More About William SZMANSKI and Virginia HAYES:
Private-Begin: Private

543.   ii.   Arnold Clarence HAYES, b. Private.
       iii. Janice Ann HAYES, b. Private; m. Bud MCCURLEY, Private; b. Private.

More About Bud MCCURLEY and Janice HAYES:
Private-Begin: Private

544.   iv. Rheta HAYES, b. Private.
545.   v.   Barbara Elaine HAYES, b. Private.

392. Lola Stella[11] GOOD *(Pearl Agnes[10] VAN HORN, Bennett Work[9], George Logan[8], Isaiah[7], Henry B.[6], Henry[5], Christian Barentsen[4] VAN HOORN, Barent Christiansen[3], Christian Barentsen[2], Barent Barents[1])[4984,4985,4986]* was born 17 Oct 1925 in Indiana Cnty, PA[4987], and died Aft. 2008. She married (1) Clair LUCE[4988] Abt. 1947. He was born 18 May 1921, and died 27 Aug 1975 in Clearfield, PA. She married (2) Andrew SMITH Bef. 1970. He was born 11 Sep, and died Aft. 1977.

More About Clair LUCE and Lola GOOD:
Marriage: Abt. 1947

More About Andrew SMITH and Lola GOOD:
Marriage: Bef. 1970

Children of Lola GOOD and Clair LUCE are:
546.   i.   Terry Lee[12] LUCE, b. Private.
547.   ii. Connie Eileen LUCE, b. Private.

Child of Lola GOOD and Andrew SMITH is:
       iii. Sharon[12] SMITH, b. Private.

393. Geraldine[11] VAN HORN *(Norman Clarence[10], Bennett Work[9], George Logan[8], Isaiah[7], Henry B.[6], Henry[5], Christian Barentsen[4] VAN HOORN, Barent Christiansen[3], Christian Barentsen[2], Barent Barents[1])[4989,4990]* was born in Marion Center, Indiana Cnty, PA, and died Aft. 1997. She married (1) William FRYE Private. He was born Private. She married (2) William Dale MCKEE Private, son of G. B. MCKEE. He was born Private.

More About William FRYE and Geraldine VAN HORN:
Private-Begin: Private

More About William MCKEE and Geraldine VAN HORN:
Private-Begin: Private

Children of Geraldine VAN HORN and William MCKEE are:
548.   i.   William Dale[12] MCKEE, JR, b. Private.
       ii. Norman Richard MCKEE, b. Private.

394. Lavona[11] VAN HORN *(Norman Clarence[10], Bennett Work[9], George Logan[8], Isaiah[7], Henry B.[6], Henry[5], Christian Barentsen[4] VAN HOORN, Barent Christiansen[3], Christian Barentsen[2], Barent Barents[1])[4991,4992]* was born in Smicksburg, PA, and died 1992. She married Charles BROOKS Private, son of Janet. He was born Private.

Notes for Lavona VAN HORN:
　　At the Ox Hill Grange Hall Flag Day Program reported in the 5 June 1954 edition of the Indiana Evening Gazette (Indiana, PA) Lavona Van Horn gave a reading.
　　It is also reported on 19 June 1954 in the Indiana Evening Gazette (Indiana, PA) paper that Lavona will be the flower girl in a mock wedding at the Grange Hall.

More About Lavona VAN HORN:
Occupation: Cameron Manufacturing of Reynoldsville, PA

More About Charles BROOKS and Lavona VAN HORN:
Private-Begin: Private

Children of Lavona VAN HORN and Charles BROOKS are:
　　　　i.　Crystal Ellen[12] BROOKS, b. Private.
549.　　ii.　Charles Scott BROOKS, b. Private.

395. Norma Jean[11] VAN HORN *(Norman Clarence[10], Bennett Work[9], George Logan[8], Isaiah[7], Henry B.[6], Henry[5], Christian Barentsen[4] VAN HOORN, Barent Christiansen[3], Christian Barentsen[2], Barent Barents[1])* was born Private. She married (1) Gerald LEE Private. He was born Private. She married (2) CAMPBELL Private. He was born Private.

More About Gerald LEE and Norma VAN HORN:
Private-Begin: Private

More About CAMPBELL and Norma VAN HORN:
Private-Begin: Private

Child of Norma VAN HORN and Gerald LEE is:
　　　　i.　Sherry Christine[12] LEE, b. Private.

396. Virginia E.[11] VAN HORN *(Norman Clarence[10], Bennett Work[9], George Logan[8], Isaiah[7], Henry B.[6], Henry[5], Christian Barentsen[4] VAN HOORN, Barent Christiansen[3], Christian Barentsen[2], Barent Barents[1])[4993,4994,4995]* was born 10 Aug 1926 in PA[4995], and died Bef. 2005. She married (1) Vernon SMITH Private. He was born Private. She married (2) Edgar D. TALLEY Private. He was born Private.

More About Vernon SMITH and Virginia VAN HORN:
Private-Begin: Private

More About Edgar TALLEY and Virginia VAN HORN:
Private-Begin: Private

Children of Virginia VAN HORN and Edgar TALLEY are:
550.　　i.　?[12] TALLEY, b. Private.
　　　　ii.　Edgar TALLEY, b. Private; m. Virginia SMITH, Private; b. Private.

More About Edgar TALLEY and Virginia SMITH:
Private-Begin: Private

397. Glenn LeRoy[11] VAN HORN *(Norman Clarence[10], Bennett Work[9], George Logan[8], Isaiah[7], Henry B.[6], Henry[5], Christian Barentsen[4] VAN HOORN, Barent Christiansen[3], Christian Barentsen[2], Barent Barents[1])[4996,4997,4998]* was born 20 Aug 1933 in Smicksburg, PA[4999], and died 31 Jan 1988 in Kensington, PA[4999,5000]. He married (1) Linda BLACKBURN Private. She was born Private. He married (2) Elizabeth MILLER Private, daughter of Carl MILLER. She was born Private.

Notes for Glenn LeRoy VAN HORN:
     22 July 1953 Indiana Evening Gazette reports that Glenn Leroy Van Horn has been inducted into the army and will leave on the 28th of July for Pittsburgh where they will be assigned.
     10 December 1953 it is reported that Glenn's parents, his sister Geraldine and her husband visited him at Ft. Pickett, VA and his wife returned to Marion Center with them.

More About Glenn LeRoy VAN HORN:
Lived: Vandergrift, Westmoreland Cnty, PA
Military service: 1201st Medical Detachment at Fort Jay, NY Rank of Pvt. on 2/3/1954 Koean War Veteran
Occupation: Packard Electric Warren OH, Don Martin Trucking of Sarver, PA

More About Glenn VAN HORN and Linda BLACKBURN:
Private-Begin: Private

More About Glenn VAN HORN and Elizabeth MILLER:
Private-Begin: Private

Children of Glenn VAN HORN and Elizabeth MILLER are:
      i.   Kenneth Lee[12] VAN HORN, b. Private.
     ii.   Robert VAN HORN, b. Private.
    iii.   Charles Kuras VAN HORN, b. Private.
    iv.   John Kuras VAN HORN, b. Private.
     v.   Lexey VAN HORN, b. Private.
    vi.   Peggy VAN HORN, b. Private; m. WILMAN, Private; b. Private.

        More About WILMAN and Peggy VAN HORN:
        Private-Begin: Private

    vii.   Linda VAN HORN, b. Private; m. MCMUNN, Private; b. Private.

        More About MCMUNN and Linda VAN HORN:
        Private-Begin: Private

398. Martin W.[11] FETTERHOFF *(Dollie Ethel[10] VAN HORN, Bennett Work[9], George Logan[8], Isaiah[7], Henry B.[6], Henry[5], Christian Barentsen[4] VAN HOORN, Barent Christiansen[3], Christian Barentsen[2], Barent Barents[1])[5001]* was born 26 May 1916 in North Mahoning, Indiana Cnty, PA[5001], and died 05 Nov 1993 in Indiana, Indiana Cnty, PA. He married (1) Martha GASTON Private. She was born Private. He married (2) Ethel May SMITH Private. She was born Private.

More About Martin FETTERHOFF and Martha GASTON:
Private-Begin: Private

More About Martin FETTERHOFF and Ethel SMITH:
Private-Begin: Private

Children of Martin FETTERHOFF and Ethel SMITH are:
     i.   Susan[12] FETTERHOFF, b. Private; m. WOLOSZYN, Private; b. Private.

          More About WOLOSZYN and Susan FETTERHOFF:
          Private-Begin: Private

    ii.   Cecilia FETTERHOFF, b. Private; m. SLACK, Private; b. Private.

          More About SLACK and Cecilia FETTERHOFF:
          Private-Begin: Private

   iii.   David FETTERHOFF, b. Private.
   iv.   Norman Eugene FETTERHOFF, b. Private.
    v.   Jay FETTERHOFF, d. Aft. 1993.
   vi.   Darrell FETTERHOFF, d. Bef. 1993.

399. Ruby L.[11] FETTERHOFF *(Dollie Ethel[10] VAN HORN, Bennett Work[9], George Logan[8], Isaiah[7], Henry B.[6], Henry[5], Christian Barentsen[4] VAN HOORN, Barent Christiansen[3], Christian Barentsen[2], Barent Barents[1])[5001]* was born 27 Mar 1918 in Trade City, PA[5001], and died 12 Jan 2007 in Mulberry Square. She married Clarence Eugene SWARMER[5002] 09 Sep 1939. He died 19 Sep 1992.

More About Clarence SWARMER and Ruby FETTERHOFF:
Marriage: 09 Sep 1939

Children of Ruby FETTERHOFF and Clarence SWARMER are:
     i.   Barbara[12] SWARMER, b. Private; m. William POSTLEWAITE, Private; b. Private.

          More About William POSTLEWAITE and Barbara SWARMER:
          Private-Begin: Private

    ii.   Joseph SWARMER, b. Private; m. Doris, Private; b. Private.

          More About Joseph SWARMER and Doris:
          Private-Begin: Private

   iii.   John Francis SWARMER, b. Private.

400. Anna Belle[11] FETTERHOFF *(Dollie Ethel[10] VAN HORN, Bennett Work[9], George Logan[8], Isaiah[7], Henry B.[6], Henry[5], Christian Barentsen[4] VAN HOORN, Barent Christiansen[3], Christian Barentsen[2], Barent Barents[1])* was born Private. She married Harold Wallace SCHURR Private. He was born Private.

More About Harold SCHURR and Anna FETTERHOFF:
Private-Begin: Private

Child of Anna FETTERHOFF and Harold SCHURR is:
     i.   ?[12] SCHURR, b. Private.

401. Pearl M.[11] FETTERHOFF *(Dollie Ethel[10] VAN HORN, Bennett Work[9], George Logan[8], Isaiah[7],*

Henry B.[6], Henry[5], Christian Barentsen[4] VAN HOORN, Barent Christiansen[3], Christian Barentsen[2], Barent Barents[1])[5003,5004,5005] was born Abt. 1924 in PA[5006], and died Aft. 2007. She married (1) Marion Earl MAUK[5007] 1943, son of James MAUK and Inez. He was born in Plumville, Indiana Cnty, PA, and died 23 Sep 1949 in Battle Creek, MI. She married (2) John FERN Private. He was born Private.

Notes for Pearl M. FETTERHOFF:
June 1953 chosen as Sesqui Queen. Married Marion Earl MAUK in 1943 and moved to Battle Creek, MI where she worked in the Kellog factory. The early death of her husband after a long illness brought her back to Plumville where she sells Avon and is the regional sale representative, serves as a Cub Scout Den leader is active in the Plumville Presbyterian Chruch. She is a graduate of Plumville High she married right after graduation.

More About Marion MAUK and Pearl FETTERHOFF:
Marriage: 1943

More About John FERN and Pearl FETTERHOFF:
Private-Begin: Private

Children of Pearl FETTERHOFF and Marion MAUK are:
    i.   Kenneth[12] MAUK, b. Private.
    ii.   Darlene MAUK, b. Private.
    iii.   Donald MAUK, b. Private.

402. Marjorie[11] DILTS *(Edna Gertude[10] VAN HORN, Bennett Work[9], George Logan[8], Isaiah[7], Henry B.[6], Henry[5], Christian Barentsen[4] VAN HOORN, Barent Christiansen[3], Christian Barentsen[2], Barent Barents[1])* was born Private. She married Stephen DEDON Private. He was born 23 Sep 1927 in Cleveland, OH, and died 18 May 1969.

More About Stephen DEDON and Marjorie DILTS:
Private-Begin: Private

Children of Marjorie DILTS and Stephen DEDON are:
    i.   Randa[12] DEDON, b. Private.
    ii.   Marna DEDON, b. Private.
    iii.   Trudy DEDON, b. Private.
    iv.   Stephen DEDON, JR, b. Private.
    v.   Barry DEDON, b. Private.

403. Samuel Andrew[11] OLSON, JR *(Verna Viola[10] VAN HORN, Bennett Work[9], George Logan[8], Isaiah[7], Henry B.[6], Henry[5], Christian Barentsen[4] VAN HOORN, Barent Christiansen[3], Christian Barentsen[2], Barent Barents[1])* was born 17 Aug, and died Aft. 1962. He married ? Private. She was born Private.

More About Samuel Andrew OLSON, JR:
Military service: Bet. 1951 - 1953, Rank of Cpl Army served in Germany

More About Samuel OLSON and ?:
Private-Begin: Private

Children of Samuel OLSON and ? are:
    i.   John Thomas[12] OLSON, b. Private.
    ii.   Rose Ann OLSON, b. Private.
    iii.   Debra Ann OLSON, b. Private.

Generation No. 6

404. Winifred[12] BARR *(Carleton Van Horn[11], Mary C[10] VAN HORN, James Thompson[9], Henry[8], Isaiah[7], Henry B.[6], Henry[5], Christian Barentsen[4] VAN HOORN, Barent Christiansen[3], Christian Barentsen[2], Barent Barents[1])* was born Private. She married Lees S. ELLSWORTH Private. He was born Private.

More About Lees ELLSWORTH and Winifred BARR:
Private-Begin: Private

Children of Winifred BARR and Lees ELLSWORTH are:
     i.   Cheryl[13] ELLSWORTH, b. Private.
    ii.   Kathy ELLSWORTH, b. Private.
   iii.   Cynthia ELLSWORTH, b. Private.

405. Carleton Van Horn[12] BARR *(Carleton Van Horn[11], Mary C[10] VAN HORN, James Thompson[9], Henry[8], Isaiah[7], Henry B.[6], Henry[5], Christian Barentsen[4] VAN HOORN, Barent Christiansen[3], Christian Barentsen[2], Barent Barents[1])* was born Private. He married Romayne MCLAUGHLIN Private, daughter of Charles T. MCLAUGHLIN. She was born Private.

More About Carleton BARR and Romayne MCLAUGHLIN:
Private-Begin: Private

Children of Carleton BARR and Romayne MCLAUGHLIN are:
     i.   Ronald[13] BARR, b. Private.
    ii.   Richard BARR, b. Private.

406. Lois Isabell[12] ALLISON *(Helen C.[11] BARR, Mary C[10] VAN HORN, James Thompson[9], Henry[8], Isaiah[7], Henry B.[6], Henry[5], Christian Barentsen[4] VAN HOORN, Barent Christiansen[3], Christian Barentsen[2], Barent Barents[1])* was born Private. She married Lawrence J. REITHMILLER Private, son of Ira REITHMILLER and Pearl SIVERD. He was born Private.

More About Lawrence REITHMILLER and Lois ALLISON:
Private-Begin: Private

Child of Lois ALLISON and Lawrence REITHMILLER is:
     i.   ?[13] REITHMILLER, b. Private.

407. Sarah[12] WORK *(Phillip[11], Hubert Robert[10], Tabitha Logan[9] VAN HORN, Henry[8], Isaiah[7], Henry B.[6], Henry[5], Christian Barentsen[4] VAN HOORN, Barent Christiansen[3], Christian Barentsen[2], Barent Barents[1])* was born Private. She married John Edrington SMITH III Private. He was born Private.

More About John SMITH and Sarah WORK:
Private-Begin: Private

Children of Sarah WORK and John SMITH are:
     i.   Sandra Lee[13] SMITH, b. Private.
    ii.   John Edrington SMITH IV, b. Private.
   iii.   Ann Carolyn SMITH, b. Private.

408. Laura May[12] WORK *(Phillip[11], Hubert Robert[10], Tabitha Logan[9] VAN HORN, Henry[8], Isaiah[7], Henry B.[6], Henry[5], Christian Barentsen[4] VAN HOORN, Barent Christiansen[3], Christian Barentsen[2], Barent Barents[1])* was born Private. She married Edward Churchill THOMAS[5008] Private. He was born 07 May 1909 in Milwaukee, WI[5008], and died Unknown.

More About Edward Churchill THOMAS:
Occupation: Newpaper Publisher

More About Edward THOMAS and Laura WORK:
Private-Begin: Private

Child of Laura WORK and Edward THOMAS is:
      i.   Brent Allan[13] THOMAS, b. Private.

409. Elizabeth[12] WORK *(Phillip[11], Hubert Robert[10], Tabitha Logan[9] VAN HORN, Henry[8], Isaiah[7], Henry B.[6], Henry[5], Christian Barentsen[4] VAN HOORN, Barent Christiansen[3], Christian Barentsen[2], Barent Barents[1])* was born Private. She married (1) Kenneth JACKSON Private. He was born Private. She married (2) Robert Grier PARKS Private. He was born Private.

More About Kenneth JACKSON and Elizabeth WORK:
Private-Begin: Private

More About Robert PARKS and Elizabeth WORK:
Private-Begin: Private

Child of Elizabeth WORK and Kenneth JACKSON is:
      i.   ?[13] JACKSON, b. Private.

410. Julia Machold[12] BISSELL *(Dorcas Logan[11] WORK, Hubert Robert[10], Tabitha Logan[9] VAN HORN, Henry[8], Isaiah[7], Henry B.[6], Henry[5], Christian Barentsen[4] VAN HOORN, Barent Christiansen[3], Christian Barentsen[2], Barent Barents[1])* was born Private. She married James Dwight BAILETT Private, son of Francis BAILETT and Gladys BRANNON. He was born Private.

More About James BAILETT and Julia BISSELL:
Private-Begin: Private

Children of Julia BISSELL and James BAILETT are:
      i.   Catherine Work[13] BAILETT, b. Private.
     ii.   Susan Dwight BAILETT, b. Private.

411. Hubert Van Horn[12] WORK III *(Robert Van Horn[11], Hubert Robert[10], Tabitha Logan[9] VAN HORN, Henry[8], Isaiah[7], Henry B.[6], Henry[5], Christian Barentsen[4] VAN HOORN, Barent Christiansen[3], Christian Barentsen[2], Barent Barents[1])[5009]* was born 01 Sep 1928 in Denver, Denver Cnty, CO[5009], and died 04 Aug 2007 in Denver, Denver Cnty, CO or Englewood, Arapahoe Cnty, CO. He married Shirley Louise CHRISTIANSEN. She was born 29 Jan 1930 in IL, and died 29 Jan 2005 in Colorado Springs, CO.

More About Hubert Van Horn WORK III:

Employment: Executive Vice President Weicker Transfer & Storage and Chairman of the Board of Allied Van Lines

Child of Hubert WORK and Shirley CHRISTIANSEN is:
      i.   ?[13] WORK, b. Private.

412. Minnie[12] VAN HORN *(Harry Burk[11], William Alexander[10], Henry Coulter[9], Alexander[8], Isaiah[7], Henry B.[6], Henry[5], Christian Barentsen[4] VAN HOORN, Barent Christiansen[3], Christian Barentsen[2], Barent Barents[1])[5010,5011,5012]* was born Abt. 1903 in PA[5013], and died Unknown. She married Ralph P. JELLISON[5014] Abt. 1922[5014]. He was born Abt. 1889, and died Unknown.

Notes for Minnie VAN HORN:
    In 1930 living on Holmes St. in Pittsburgh, PA in a home they rent for $40/month, They have a radio. Minnie's sister Hazel is living with them. Ralp is a brick mason who does contract work. They have been married for about 7 years.

More About Minnie VAN HORN:
Employment: 1920, Can Inspector

More About Ralph JELLISON and Minnie VAN HORN:
Marriage: Abt. 1922[5014]

Child of Minnie VAN HORN and Ralph JELLISON is:
      i.   Mary P.[13] JELLISON, b. Private.

413. Gretchen[12] BROOKS *(Clarence Wilbur[11], Sarah Jane[10] VAN HORN, John Dick[9], Alexander[8], Isaiah[7], Henry B.[6], Henry[5], Christian Barentsen[4] VAN HOORN, Barent Christiansen[3], Christian Barentsen[2], Barent Barents[1])[5015,5016,5017]* was born Abt. Jan 1910 in PA[5018], and died Unknown. She married Rober Albert BITNER. He died Unknown.

Child of Gretchen BROOKS and Rober BITNER is:
      i.   ?[13] BITNER, b. Private.

414. William Lynn[12] BROOKS *(Clarence Wilbur[11], Sarah Jane[10] VAN HORN, John Dick[9], Alexander[8], Isaiah[7], Henry B.[6], Henry[5], Christian Barentsen[4] VAN HOORN, Barent Christiansen[3], Christian Barentsen[2], Barent Barents[1])[5019]* was born 26 Apr 1922 in Crafton, Allegheny Cnty, PA[5019], and died 03 Mar 1993 in Terra Haute, Vigo Cnty, IN. He married ROMANO Private. She was born Private.

More About William BROOKS and ROMANO:
Private-Begin: Private

Child of William BROOKS and ROMANO is:
      i.   ?[13] BROOKS, b. Private.

415. Eugene R. HARKCOM[12] VAN HORN *(Annie[11], Henry D. Foster[10], John Dick[9], Alexander[8], Isaiah[7], Henry B.[6], Henry[5], Christian Barentsen[4] VAN HOORN, Barent Christiansen[3], Christian Barentsen[2], Barent Barents[1])[5020,5021]* was born 17 Dec 1908 in Scottdale, Westmoreland Cnty, PA[5022], and died 10 Mar 2007 in Altoona, Blair Cnty, PA. He married Mildred STEWART. She died 1996.

Notes for Eugene R. HARKCOM VAN HORN:
    Adopted by his Van Horn grandparents after the death of his mother.
    1930 living with his aunt Viola Price. He is an embalmer for an undertaker.
    14 September 1970 The Progress (Clearfield, PA) notes that friends may call at the Eugene R. Van Horn Funeral Home in Monroeville, PA.

More About Eugene R. HARKCOM VAN HORN:
Employment: 1930, Embalmer and Undertaker

Child of Eugene VAN HORN and Mildred STEWART is:
    i.   Lloyd[13] HARKCOM, b. Private.

416. Harold V. HARKCOM[12] VAN HORN *(Annie[11], Henry D. Foster[10], John Dick[9], Alexander[8], Isaiah[7], Henry B.[6], Henry[5], Christian Barentsen[4] VAN HOORN, Barent Christiansen[3], Christian Barentsen[2], Barent Barents[1])[5023,5024,5025]* was born Abt. 1906 in Scottdale, Westmoreland Cnty, PA[5025,5026], and died Abt. 1958 in PA. He married (1) Ruth Loraine BERRY, daughter of Thomas BERRY and Mary WILLIAMS. She was born 24 Oct 1913 in Scottdale, Westmoreland Cnty, PA, and died 12 Feb 2001 in Pinellas Park, Pinellas Cnty, FL. He married (2) Lenora E. BOSH[5027] Abt. 1924, daughter of Charles BOSH and Daisy M.. She was born Abt. 1908 in PA[5027], and died Unknown.

Notes for Harold V. HARKCOM VAN HORN:
    Adopted by his Van Horn grandparents after the death of his mother.
    In 1930 Harold and his wife of about 6 years are living with her parents. The have a small daughter. They live on Market Street in Scottdale, PA. He is a clerk in the Post Office.

More About Harold V. HARKCOM VAN HORN:
Employment: 1930, Post Office Clerk

More About Harold VAN HORN and Lenora BOSH:
Marriage: Abt. 1924

Child of Harold VAN HORN and Lenora BOSH is:
    i.   Shirley E.[13] VAN HORN, b. Private.

417. Judson Tannehill[12] VAN HORN, JR *(Judson Tannehill[11], Henry D. Foster[10], John Dick[9], Alexander[8], Isaiah[7], Henry B.[6], Henry[5], Christian Barentsen[4] VAN HOORN, Barent Christiansen[3], Christian Barentsen[2], Barent Barents[1])[5028]* was born 12 Mar 1920 in Scottdale, Westmoreland Cnty, PA[5028], and died Aft. 2008. He married Margaret Alice ANDERSON[5029] 03 Aug 1946, daughter of Guy ANDERSON and Lena. She was born 08 Apr 1922 in Wabash, IN[5029], and died Aft. 2007.

Notes for Judson Tannehill VAN HORN, JR:
    Enlisted on 6 October 1941 at Ft McPherson Atlanta, GA he was single at the time of enlistment as a private.

More About Judson VAN HORN and Margaret ANDERSON:
Marriage: 03 Aug 1946

Children of Judson VAN HORN and Margaret ANDERSON are:
    i.   Marjorie[13] VAN HORN, b. Private; m. Joel BLACKWELL, Private; b. Private.

        More About Joel BLACKWELL and Marjorie VAN HORN:
        Private-Begin: Private

ii.   Charlotte Ann VAN HORN, b. Private.
551.   iii.   Mary Elizabeth VAN HORN, b. Private.
552.   iv.   Patricia Louise VAN HORN, b. Private.

418. Eunice Matilda[12] VAN HORN *(Judson Tannehill[11], Henry D. Foster[10], John Dick[9], Alexander[8], Isaiah[7], Henry B.[6], Henry[5], Christian Barentsen[4] VAN HOORN, Barent Christiansen[3], Christian Barentsen[2], Barent Barents[1])[5030]* was born 06 Apr 1922 in Scottdale, Westmoreland Cnty, PA[5030], and died 18 Dec 2006 in Columbia, SC[5031]. She married (1) Charles Lee GRAVES[5031] 1939 in Winchester, VA. He was born 1918 in Winchester, VA[5031], and died Abt. 1942 in Augusta, GA[5031]. She married (2) Marvin Harold TARPLEY[5031] 31 Aug 1951 in Aiken, SC. He was born 26 Oct 1912 in GA[5031], and died 07 Jun 1991 in Columbia, SC[5031].

More About Charles GRAVES and Eunice VAN HORN:
Marriage: 1939, Winchester, VA

More About Marvin TARPLEY and Eunice VAN HORN:
Marriage: 31 Aug 1951, Aiken, SC

Child of Eunice VAN HORN and Charles GRAVES is:
553.   i.   Charles Lee (GRAVES)[13] TARPLEY, JR, b. Private.

Child of Eunice VAN HORN and Marvin TARPLEY is:
554.   ii.   Peter Harold[13] TARPLEY, b. Private.

419. Mary Ella[12] VAN HORN *(Judson Tannehill[11], Henry D. Foster[10], John Dick[9], Alexander[8], Isaiah[7], Henry B.[6], Henry[5], Christian Barentsen[4] VAN HOORN, Barent Christiansen[3], Christian Barentsen[2], Barent Barents[1])[5032,5033]* was born 28 Feb 1925 in Scottdale, Westmoreland Cnty, PA[5034], and died 10 Jun 2005 in Cherokee, NC[5035]. She married Otto William MARSHALL, JR[5035] 19 Sep 1941 in Aiken, SC[5035], son of Otto MARSHALL and Margaret REYNOLDS. He was born 08 Feb 1923 in Augusta, GA[5035], and died 08 Nov 1980 in Augusta, GA[5035].

More About Otto William MARSHALL, JR:
Burial: 11 Nov 1980, Westover Memorial Park, Augusta, GA

More About Otto MARSHALL and Mary VAN HORN:
Marriage: 19 Sep 1941, Aiken, SC[5035]

Children of Mary VAN HORN and Otto MARSHALL are:
555.   i.   Jacqueline Ann[13] MARSHALL, b. Private.
ii.   Otto William MARSHALL III, b. Private; m. Barbara HOLZER, Private; b. Private.

More About Otto MARSHALL and Barbara HOLZER:
Private-Begin: Private

420. John Foster[12] VAN HORN *(John Dick[11], Henry D. Foster[10], John Dick[9], Alexander[8], Isaiah[7], Henry B.[6], Henry[5], Christian Barentsen[4] VAN HOORN, Barent Christiansen[3], Christian Barentsen[2], Barent Barents[1])* was born Private. He married Victoria Joyce HANSEN Private. She was born Private.

More About John VAN HORN and Victoria HANSEN:
Private-Begin: Private

Children of John VAN HORN and Victoria HANSEN are:
     i.   Isabel Berdeen[13] VAN HORN, b. Private.
    ii. John Edwin VAN HORN, b. Private; m. Judith A. THEIS, Private; b. Private.

        More About John VAN HORN and Judith THEIS:
        Private-Begin: Private

421. Walter M.[12] EDGE, JR *(Olive Mae[11] VAN HORN, Henry D. Foster[10], John Dick[9], Alexander[8], Isaiah[7], Henry B.[6], Henry[5], Christian Barentsen[4] VAN HOORN, Barent Christiansen[3], Christian Barentsen[2], Barent Barents[1])[5036]* was born 17 Jun 1925 in PA[5036,5037], and died 25 Aug 1999 in Greensboro, Guillford Cnty, NC[5037].

Notes for Walter M. EDGE, JR:
    Children listed are named in obituary.

More About Walter M. EDGE, JR:
Enlisted: Sales Represenative mining and manufactureing blast furnaces and steel works

Children of Walter M. EDGE, JR are:
     i.   Judy[13] EDGE, b. Private; m. HUNT, Private; b. Private.

        More About HUNT and Judy EDGE:
        Private-Begin: Private

     ii. Kimberly EDGE, b. Private.
   iii. Moses H. EDGE, b. Private.
   iv. Mary EDGE, b. Private; m. PATRICIA, Private; b. Private.

        More About PATRICIA and Mary EDGE:
        Private-Begin: Private

422. Dorothy Virginia[12] BALLANTYNE *(James Van Horn[11], Caroline E.[10] VAN HORN, James Wherry[9], Alexander[8], Isaiah[7], Henry B.[6], Henry[5], Christian Barentsen[4] VAN HOORN, Barent Christiansen[3], Christian Barentsen[2], Barent Barents[1])[5038]* was born 10 Aug 1910 in PA[5038], and died Unknown. She married George Edward MILLIKEN 13 Oct 1934 in Derry, Westmoreland Cnty, PA. He was born 13 Jul 1910 in Swissvale, Allegheny Cnty, PA, and died Unknown.

More About George MILLIKEN and Dorothy BALLANTYNE:
Marriage: 13 Oct 1934, Derry, Westmoreland Cnty, PA
Marriage Place: South Avenue Methodist Church, Derry, PA

Children of Dorothy BALLANTYNE and George MILLIKEN are:
     i.   ?[13] MILLIKEN, b. Private.
    ii. ? MILLIKEN, b. Private.
   iii. ? MILLIKEN, b. Private.

423. John Edwin[12] BALLANTYNE *(James Van Horn[11], Caroline E.[10] VAN HORN, James Wherry[9], Alexander[8], Isaiah[7], Henry B.[6], Henry[5], Christian Barentsen[4] VAN HOORN, Barent Christiansen[3], Christian*

Barentsen², *Barent Barents¹)⁵⁰³⁸* was born 03 Oct 1912 in Derry, Westmoreland Cnty, PA⁵⁰³⁸, and died 07 Nov 2002 in Youngstown, Mahoning Cnty, OH. He married Elizabeth Jane GILLESPIE 16 Apr 1942. She was born 15 May 1910 in Wilkinsburg, Allegheny Cnty, PA, and died Unknown.

More About John BALLANTYNE and Elizabeth GILLESPIE:
Marriage: 16 Apr 1942

Children of John BALLANTYNE and Elizabeth GILLESPIE are:
    i.   ?¹³ BALLANTYNE, b. Private.
    ii. ? BALLANTYNE, b. Private.

424. James Van Horn¹² BALLANTYNE, JR *(James Van Horn¹¹, Caroline E.¹⁰ VAN HORN, James Wherry⁹, Alexander⁸, Isaiah⁷, Henry B.⁶, Henry⁵, Christian Barentsen⁴ VAN HOORN, Barent Christiansen³, Christian Barentsen², Barent Barents¹)⁵⁰³⁸* was born 24 Nov 1914 in PA⁵⁰³⁸, and died 28 Dec 1999 in Pittsburgh, Allegheny Cnty, PA. He married ? Private. She was born Private.

More About James BALLANTYNE and ?:
Private-Begin: Private

Children of James BALLANTYNE and ? are:
    i.   ?¹³ BALLANTYNE, b. Private.
    ii. ? BALLANTYNE, b. Private.
    iii. ? BALLANTYNE, b. Private.
    iv. ? BALLANTYNE, b. Private.

425. Carl Rigg¹² BALLANTYNE *(James Van Horn¹¹, Caroline E.¹⁰ VAN HORN, James Wherry⁹, Alexander⁸, Isaiah⁷, Henry B.⁶, Henry⁵, Christian Barentsen⁴ VAN HOORN, Barent Christiansen³, Christian Barentsen², Barent Barents¹)⁵⁰³⁸* was born 10 Mar 1918 in PA⁵⁰³⁸, and died 17 Aug 1993 in St. Petersburg, Pinnelas Cnty, FL. He married ? Private. She was born Private.

More About Carl BALLANTYNE and ?:
Private-Begin: Private

Children of Carl BALLANTYNE and ? are:
    i.   ?¹³ BALLANTYNE, b. Private.
    ii. ? BALLANTYNE, b. Private.
    iii. ? BALLANTYNE, b. Private.

426. Frank Martin¹² ASHCOM *(James Donald¹¹, Margaret Mary¹⁰ VAN HORN, James Wherry⁹, Alexander⁸, Isaiah⁷, Henry B.⁶, Henry⁵, Christian Barentsen⁴ VAN HOORN, Barent Christiansen³, Christian Barentsen², Barent Barents¹)⁵⁰³⁹,⁵⁰⁴⁰* was born Abt. 1914 in PA⁵⁰⁴¹, and died Unknown. He married Susanna FLETCHER Private. She was born Private.

More About Frank ASHCOM and Susanna FLETCHER:
Private-Begin: Private

Children of Frank ASHCOM and Susanna FLETCHER are:
556.   i.   Frank Martin¹³ ASHCOM, JR, b. Private.
557.   ii. Sandra Lee ASHCOM, b. Private.

427. Mary Elizabeth[12] ASHCOM *(James Donald[11], Margaret Mary[10] VAN HORN, James Wherry[9], Alexander[8], Isaiah[7], Henry B.[6], Henry[5], Christian Barentsen[4] VAN HOORN, Barent Christiansen[3], Christian Barentsen[2], Barent Barents[1])[5041,5042]* was born 24 Jun 1917 in Pittsburgh, Allegheny Cny, PA[5043], and died 24 Aug 2002 in Ligonier, Westmoreland Cnty, PA[5044]. She married William WINEBRENNER Aft. 1930, son of Joseph WINEBRENNER and Mabel WINKELMAN. He was born 16 Sep 1910 in New Florence, Westmoreland Cnty, PA, and died 09 Aug 1986 in Johnstown, Cambria Cnty, PA[5044].

More About William WINEBRENNER and Mary ASHCOM:
Marriage: Aft. 1930

Children of Mary ASHCOM and William WINEBRENNER are:
      i.   Anna Jane[13] WINEBRENNER, b. Private; m. Tim NIXON, Private; b. Private.

          More About Tim NIXON and Anna WINEBRENNER:
          Private-Begin: Private

      ii. Diana WINEBRENNER, b. Private; m. Bruce WILLIAMS, Private; b. Private.

          More About Bruce WILLIAMS and Diana WINEBRENNER:
          Private-Begin: Private

      iii. Linda WINEBRENNER, b. Private; m. Lynn FARRARO, Private; b. Private.

          More About Lynn FARRARO and Linda WINEBRENNER:
          Private-Begin: Private

558.   iv. Nana Pearl WINEBRENNER, b. Private.

428. Emma Elizabeth[12] WOLF *(Leafy Fern[11] VAN HORN, Samuel Cornelius[10], Henry Coulter[9], Alexander[8], Isaiah[7], Henry B.[6], Henry[5], Christian Barentsen[4] VAN HOORN, Barent Christiansen[3], Christian Barentsen[2], Barent Barents[1])[5045]* was born 25 Sep 1911 in Dalhart, Dallam Cnty, TX, and died 13 May 1982 in Murphy, NC[5046]. She married (1) Samuel H. HUDSON Oct 1928. He died Unknown. She married (2) Lester George HAAS 30 Mar 1935. He was born 06 Oct 1908 in Middletown, OH, and died 17 Sep 1984 in Murphy, NC[5047,5048,5049,5050].

More About Emma Elizabeth WOLF:
Burial: Unknown, Miami Valley Memorial Gardens Centerville, OH[5051]

More About Samuel HUDSON and Emma WOLF:
Marriage: Oct 1928

More About Lester George HAAS:
Burial: Unknown, Miami Valley Memorial Gardens Centerville, OH[5051]
Lived: Last residence: NC 28906[5052]

More About Lester HAAS and Emma WOLF:
Marriage: 30 Mar 1935

Child of Emma WOLF and Samuel HUDSON is:
559.   i.   Norma Davene[13] HUDSON, b. 23 Jul 1929, Dayton, Montgomery Cnty, OH; d. 27

May 2007, Toledo, Lucas Cnty, OH.

Children of Emma WOLF and Lester HAAS are:
560.   ii.   Beverly Ann[13] HAAS, b. Private.
561.   iii.   Rodney Albert HAAS, b. Private.
562.   iv.   Marcia Kay HAAS, b. Private.

429. Marianna[12] WOLF *(Leafy Fern[11] VAN HORN, Samuel Cornelius[10], Henry Coulter[9], Alexander[8], Isaiah[7], Henry B.[6], Henry[5], Christian Barentsen[4] VAN HOORN, Barent Christiansen[3], Christian Barentsen[2], Barent Barents[1])* was born Bet. 08 Feb 1916 - 1917 in Dayton, Montgomery Cnty, OH, and died 13 Feb 1974 in Dayton, Montgomery Cnty, OH. She married Malcolm Berger FRANK 05 Jul 1937 in Warsaw, KY. He was born 01 Oct 1910 in Dayton, Montgomery Cnty, OH, and died 30 Jul 2001 in Dayton, Montgomery Cnty, OH.

More About Marianna WOLF:
Burial: 16 Feb 1974, Zion Shoup Cemetery, Beaver Creek, OH

Notes for Malcolm Berger FRANK:
    Mal returned from service in WWII with little or no opportunity for employment. He and his brother decided that, due to the fact that people did not like to be seen in a liquor store, that a home delivery service for various forms of liquor might be a way to go into business. The concept was well accepted and soon they had a number of unmarked panel trucks making home deliveries. The state of Ohio decided that all liquor above 14 proof would be sold in state liquor stores. This opened another opportunity for Mall and his enterprising brothers. The purchased or rented locations adjacent to or near state liquor stores. They formed Arrow Wines. They focused on the idea of providing all the wines, mixes and party favors for those who purchased their liquor from the state store. This business provided a comfortable living for the brothers and their families for many years. In fact some of the children of the original founders of Arrow wines still operate and work in the various stores that are located in Dayton, OH.
    The author would work for his Uncle Mal when he was in college and the family was in OH for Christmas.

More About Malcolm Berger FRANK:
Burial: Unknown, Zion Shoup Cemetery Greene Cnty, OH
Lived: Grangehall Rd, Beaver Creek, Greene Cnty, OH
Occupation: Owner and Founder of Arrow Wine Stores in Dayton, Montgomery Cnty, OH

More About Malcolm FRANK and Marianna WOLF:
Marriage: 05 Jul 1937, Warsaw, KY

Children of Marianna WOLF and Malcolm FRANK are:
        i.   Sally Ann[13] FRANK, b. Private; m. James Anthony HALLER, Private; b. Private.

              More About James HALLER and Sally FRANK:
              Private-Begin: Private

563.   ii.   Malcolm David FRANK, b. Private.
        iii. Melissa Lee FRANK, b. Private; m. BARR, Private; b. Private.

              More About BARR and Melissa FRANK:
              Private-Begin: Private

  iv. Stephen Alan FRANK, b. Private.

430. Avis Ruth[12] WOLF *(Leafy Fern[11] VAN HORN, Samuel Cornelius[10], Henry Coulter[9], Alexander[8], Isaiah[7], Henry B.[6], Henry[5], Christian Barentsen[4] VAN HOORN, Barent Christiansen[3], Christian Barentsen[2], Barent Barents[1])[5053]* was born 21 Sep 1919 in Dayton, Montgomery Cnty, OH, and died 04 Oct 1980 in Rolla, Phelps Cnty, MO[5054,5054]. She married Reverend, Dr. John Baber MORGAN Private, son of Walter MORGAN and Sarah BABER. He was born Private.

More About Avis Ruth WOLF:
Burial: Unknown, Miami Valley Memorial Gardens Centerville, OH

More About John MORGAN and Avis WOLF:
Private-Begin: Private

Children of Avis WOLF and John MORGAN are:
564. i. Dr. Johnie Derald[13] MORGAN, SR , b. Private.
565. ii. Ruth Fern MORGAN, b. Private.
566. iii. Michael Melvin MORGAN, b. Private.

431. Thelma Louise[12] WOLF *(Leafy Fern[11] VAN HORN, Samuel Cornelius[10], Henry Coulter[9], Alexander[8], Isaiah[7], Henry B.[6], Henry[5], Christian Barentsen[4] VAN HOORN, Barent Christiansen[3], Christian Barentsen[2], Barent Barents[1])* was born 24 Sep 1921 in Dayton, Montgomery Cnty, OH[5055], and died 14 Mar 2006 in Dayton, Montgomery Cnty, OH. She married Walter Clarence CECIL, JR 14 Oct 1944. He was born 19 Feb 1922, and died 31 Dec 1987 in Dayton, Montgomery Cnty, OH[5056,5056].

More About Walter CECIL and Thelma WOLF:
Marriage: 14 Oct 1944

Children of Thelma WOLF and Walter CECIL are:
567. i. Larry[13] CECIL, b. Private.
568. ii. Judy CECIL, b. Private.

432. Hubert[12] VAN HORN *(Charles[11], Hubert Earl[10], Henry Coulter[9], Alexander[8], Isaiah[7], Henry B.[6], Henry[5], Christian Barentsen[4] VAN HOORN, Barent Christiansen[3], Christian Barentsen[2], Barent Barents[1])[5057]* was born 09 May 1925 in PA[5057], and died 16 Nov 2002 in Bradenville, Westmoreland, PA. He married Olive THOMAS? Private. She was born Private.

More About Hubert VAN HORN and Olive THOMAS?:
Private-Begin: Private

Child of Hubert VAN HORN and Olive THOMAS? is:
  i. Hubert[13] VAN HORN, JR, b. Private; m. Lyia Louise SHIELDS, Private; b. Private.

   More About Hubert VAN HORN and Lyia SHIELDS:
   Private-Begin: Private

433. Margaret[12] MORROW *(Gertrude[11] MCELHOES, John Kinter[10], Isaiah[9], Jane[8] VAN HORN, Isaiah[7], Henry B.[6], Henry[5], Christian Barentsen[4] VAN HOORN, Barent Christiansen[3], Christian Barentsen[2], Barent Barents[1])[5058,5059,5060]* was born 06 Jun 1899 in PA[5061], and died Unknown. She married William

ORR[5061] Abt. 1926. He was born Abt. 1897 in NY[5061], and died Unknown.

Notes for Margaret MORROW:
Her sister Mary R. is living with her and her husband.

More About Margaret MORROW:
Occupation: Nurse

More About William ORR:
Occupation: Physician

More About William ORR and Margaret MORROW:
Marriage: Abt. 1926

Children of Margaret MORROW and William ORR are:
    i.   James M.[13] ORR, b. Private.
    ii.   John ORR, b. Private.
    iii. Marla ORR, b. Private.
    iv. William ORR, b. Private.

434. John K. McElhoes[12] MORROW *(Gertrude[11] MCELHOES, John Kinter[10], Isaiah[9], Jane[8] VAN HORN, Isaiah[7], Henry B.[6], Henry[5], Christian Barentsen[4] VAN HOORN, Barent Christiansen[3], Christian Barentsen[2], Barent Barents[1])*[5062,5063,5064] was born Abt. 1902 in PA[5065], and died Aft. 1942. He married Agnes Culshaw COOLEY[5066] Abt. 1925[5066]. She was born Abt. 1900 in PA[5066], and died Aft. 1942.

Notes for John K. McElhoes MORROW:
    In 1930 lives on Emerald Street in Pittsburgh, PA in a home he rents for 449/month. He is married has a daughter and is a newspaper reporter. Ruth may be a step daughter as Agnes was married for the first time at 18 and John at 24. This would mean that Ruth was born a couple of years before John and Agnes married.
    Name: John K Morrow Birth Year: 1902 Race: White, citizen (White) Nativity State or Country: Pennsylvania State of Residence: Pennsylvania Enlistment Date: 5 Oct 1942 Enlistment State: Pennsylvania Enlistment City: Pittsburgh Branch: Branch Immaterial Warrant Officers, USA Branch Code: Branch Immaterial - Warrant Officers, USA Grade: Private Grade Code: Private Term of Enlistment: Enlistment for the duration of the War or other emergency, plus six months, subject to the discretion of the President or otherwise according to law
Component: Selectees (Enlisted Men) Source: Civil Life Education: 4 years of college Civil Occupation: Semiskilled filers, grinders, buffers, and polishers (metal) Marital Status: Married Height: 66 Weight: 152

More About John K. McElhoes MORROW:
Occupation: Newspaper Reporter

More About John MORROW and Agnes COOLEY:
Marriage: Abt. 1925[5066]

Children of John MORROW and Agnes COOLEY are:
    i.   Ruth[13] MORROW, b. Private.
    ii.   William MORROW, b. Private.

435. Charles Merle[12] MCELHOES *(Frank Thomas[11], John Kinter[10], Isaiah[9], Jane[8] VAN HORN,*

Isaiah[7], Henry B.[6], Henry[5], Christian Barentsen[4] VAN HOORN, Barent Christiansen[3], Christian Barentsen[2], Barent Barents[1])[5067,5068,5069] was born 22 Jan 1902 in Ottertail, MN[5070], and died 03 Feb 1970 in Calimesa, Riverside Cnty, CA[5071,5072]. He married (1) Margaret I. JACK. She died Unknown. He married (2) Anna Sampson BENT[5073,5074] Mar 1924 in CA, daughter of Charles BENT and Margarita CARRILLO. She was born 04 Oct 1901 in AZ[5075], and died 04 Nov 1977 in Inglewood, Los Angeles Cnty, CA.

Notes for Charles Merle MCELHOES:
In 1924 C. Merle is registered to vote as a Republican at the address of 4320 Moneta Ave, Los Angeles, CA
In 1930 he is rooming in Los Angeles, CA and working as a Bakery salesman. He is divorced as of this date from Anna.
In 1934 CA voter rolls finds him at 2131 S. Hoover St. Los Angeles, CA living with Mrs Mildred McElhoes. He is registered as a Republican and she as a Democrat.
In 1936 living at 704 S. Ward St. Los Angeles with Mrs. Mildred McElhoes he is registered as a DS she as a D and he is a salesman and she a housewife.
In 1938 registered at 833 W 68th St with Mrs. Mildred J. McElhoes and he is a salesman she a housewife and both are Democrats.
In 1941 and 1944 at 2141 W. 80th Street in Los Angeles apparently by himself on the voter rolls as a DS. He is listed in 1944 as a salesman.
In 1948 and 1950 Frank C. and his father Charles M are living on 2141 W 80th as registered voters. Both as DS.
In 1952 he shows up on the voter rolls in Los Angeles at 2141 W. 80th with Mrs Anna S. McElhoes at the same address. This is the mother of his child so the story is interesting as they must have gotten back together after a divorce and another marriage in between. She is registered as a republican and he as a DS.

Notes for Anna Sampson BENT:
In 1920 Annie is living with her married sister Mabel J. Manke in Los Angles, CA on South Main Street. She is working as a stenographer in an office.
In 1930 she is living with her sister Mabel and is divorced renting for $27.50 a month and has a radio. Her sister is widowed. She is working in a Dry Goods store as a stenographer.

More About Charles MCELHOES and Anna BENT:
Divorce: Bef. 1930
Marriage: Mar 1924, CA

Child of Charles MCELHOES and Anna BENT is:
      i.   Frank Charles[13] MCELHOES, b. Private; m. (1) Sheila M. GREEN, Private; b. Private; m. (2) Dorothy L. WATTS, Private; b. Private.

           More About Frank MCELHOES and Sheila GREEN:
           Private-Begin: Private

           More About Frank MCELHOES and Dorothy WATTS:
           Private-Begin: Private

436. Waldo Steele[12] MCELHOES *(Frank Thomas[11], John Kinter[10], Isaiah[9], Jane[8] VAN HORN, Isaiah[7], Henry B.[6], Henry[5], Christian Barentsen[4] VAN HOORN, Barent Christiansen[3], Christian Barentsen[2], Barent Barents[1])[5076,5077]* was born 15 Jan 1905 in Ottertail, Ottertail Cnty, MN[5078], and died 16 Jul 1979 in Winnipeg, MB, Canada. He married Grace MCCONNELL 23 Mar 1929 in Winnipeg, MB, Canada, daughter of Alfred MCCONNELL and Jane CHRISTIE. She was born 29 Aug 1902 in Guelph, ON, Canada, and died 26 Apr 1993 in Winnipeg, Manitoba, Canada.

Notes for Waldo Steele MCELHOES:
   Migrated from Ottertail, MN in 1908 first to Strathmore, AB, Canada then in 1920 to Vancouver, BC, Canada.
   In the late 1920s migrated to Winnipeg, MB, Canada looking for work where he met and married Grace Mcconnell. Having found work and a wife he settled there and raises his family in Winnipeg where all his children and grandchildren were born.

More About Waldo Steele MCELHOES:
Burial: 20 Jul 1979, Winnipeg, Manitoba, Canada
Occupation: Self Employed Real Estate and Insurance Agent

Notes for Grace MCCONNELL:
   Migrated from Guelph, ON, Canada in the late 1920s to attend for an infirm aunt Margaret Sydney Chirstie.
   She obtained employment in Winnipeg where she met Waldo McElhoes, married and reared her family.

More About Grace MCCONNELL:
Burial: 29 Apr 1993, Winnipeg, Manitoba, Canada

More About Waldo MCELHOES and Grace MCCONNELL:
Marriage: 23 Mar 1929, Winnipeg, MB, Canada

Children of Waldo MCELHOES and Grace MCCONNELL are:
   i.   Frederick Waldo[13] MCELHOES, b. Private; m. Elizabeth Kathleen MCKENZIE, Private; b. Private.

        More About Frederick MCELHOES and Elizabeth MCKENZIE:
        Private-Begin: Private

569.   ii. Richard Alan MCELHOES, b. Private.
        iii. Mary Jane MCELHOES, b. Private; m. James Ronald CORRIGAL, Private; b. Private.

        More About James CORRIGAL and Mary MCELHOES:
        Private-Begin: Private

437. John Gordon[12] MCELHOES *(Frank Thomas[11], John Kinter[10], Isaiah[9], Jane[8] VAN HORN, Isaiah[7], Henry B.[6], Henry[5], Christian Barentsen[4] VAN HOORN, Barent Christiansen[3], Christian Barentsen[2], Barent Barents[1])[5079]* was born 16 Sep 1906 in Ottertail, MN[5079], and died 19 Jul 1984 in Matsqui, BC Canada. He married Eileen Hazel GOFFIN Private. She was born Private.

More About John MCELHOES and Eileen GOFFIN:
Private-Begin: Private

Child of John MCELHOES and Eileen GOFFIN is:
   i.   Elizabeth Ann[13] MCELHOES, b. Private; m. Ted PARKER, Private; b. Private.

        More About Ted PARKER and Elizabeth MCELHOES:
        Private-Begin: Private

438. Robert Allan[12] MCELHOES *(Frank Thomas*[11]*, John Kinter*[10]*, Isaiah*[9]*, Jane*[8] *VAN HORN, Isaiah*[7]*, Henry B.*[6]*, Henry*[5]*, Christian Barentsen*[4] *VAN HOORN, Barent Christiansen*[3]*, Christian Barentsen*[2]*, Barent Barents*[1]*)*[5079] was born Bet. 21 Jun 1907 - 1908 in Strathmore, AB, Canada/MN[5079], and died 26 Feb 1974 in Vancouver, BC, Canada[5080]. He married Adrianna TWISK Private. She was born Private.

More About Robert MCELHOES and Adrianna TWISK:
Private-Begin: Private

Children of Robert MCELHOES and Adrianna TWISK are:
      i.   Faye Adrienne[13] MCELHOES, b. Private; m. Thomas Richard HOLLGATE, Private; b. Private.

          More About Thomas HOLLGATE and Faye MCELHOES:
          Private-Begin: Private

     ii.   Roberta Ann MCELHOES, b. Private.
    iii.   Brian Lorne MCELHOES, b. Private; m. Emma DICK, Private; b. Private.

          More About Brian MCELHOES and Emma DICK:
          Private-Begin: Private

    iv.   Roy Allan MCELHOES, b. Private; m. Judith Joanna SMITH, Private; b. Private.

          More About Roy MCELHOES and Judith SMITH:
          Private-Begin: Private

439. Spencer Kay[12] MCELHOES *(Frank Thomas*[11]*, John Kinter*[10]*, Isaiah*[9]*, Jane*[8] *VAN HORN, Isaiah*[7]*, Henry B.*[6]*, Henry*[5]*, Christian Barentsen*[4] *VAN HOORN, Barent Christiansen*[3]*, Christian Barentsen*[2]*, Barent Barents*[1]*)* was born 10 Jun 1913 in Strathmore, AB, Canada, and died 21 Jul 1943 in Sicily, Itlay WWII. He married Constance Viola MENDES Private. She was born Private.

Notes for Spencer Kay MCELHOES:
    Killed in the line of action with the Canadian Army. He was a Lance Corporal with the Seaforth Highlanders of Canada.

More About Spencer MCELHOES and Constance MENDES:
Private-Begin: Private

Child of Spencer MCELHOES and Constance MENDES is:
      i.   John Spencer[13] MCELHOES, b. Private; m. Gloria GREEN, Private; b. Private.

          More About John MCELHOES and Gloria GREEN:
          Private-Begin: Private

440. Lowell Gladstone[12] MCELHOES *(Frank Thomas*[11]*, John Kinter*[10]*, Isaiah*[9]*, Jane*[8] *VAN HORN, Isaiah*[7]*, Henry B.*[6]*, Henry*[5]*, Christian Barentsen*[4] *VAN HOORN, Barent Christiansen*[3]*, Christian Barentsen*[2]*, Barent Barents*[1]*)* was born 02 Sep 1914 in Strathmore, AB, Canada, and died 24 May 1998 in Vancouver, BC, Canada. He married Phyllis MCCARTNEY 03 Jul 1943. She died 25 Dec 1987.

More About Lowell MCELHOES and Phyllis MCCARTNEY:
Marriage: 03 Jul 1943

Children of Lowell MCELHOES and Phyllis MCCARTNEY are:
    i.   Janet Elizabeth[13] MCELHOES, b. Private; m. Preston MEDD, Private; b. Private.

        More About Preston MEDD and Janet MCELHOES:
        Private-Begin: Private

    ii. Kenneth Robert MCELHOES, b. Private; m. Valarie HARRISON, Private; b. Private.

        More About Kenneth MCELHOES and Valarie HARRISON:
        Private-Begin: Private

441. Murray Thompson[12] MCELHOES *(Frank Thomas[11], John Kinter[10], Isaiah[9], Jane[8] VAN HORN, Isaiah[7], Henry B.[6], Henry[5], Christian Barentsen[4] VAN HOORN, Barent Christiansen[3], Christian Barentsen[2], Barent Barents[1])* was born 27 Dec 1916 in Strathmore, AB, Canada, and died 05 Dec 2000 in Abbotsford, BC, Canada. He married Lorraine CLARK Private. She was born Private.

More About Murray Thompson MCELHOES:
Naturalization: 17 Oct 1910, Aberta, Canada

More About Murray MCELHOES and Lorraine CLARK:
Private-Begin: Private

Children of Murray MCELHOES and Lorraine CLARK are:
    i.   David Allan[13] MCELHOES, b. Private; m. Lavina MCPEEK, Private; b. Private.

        More About David MCELHOES and Lavina MCPEEK:
        Private-Begin: Private

    ii. Patricia MCELHOES, b. Private; m. Benjamin ADAMS, Private; b. Private.

        More About Benjamin ADAMS and Patricia MCELHOES:
        Private-Begin: Private

442. Mary Kathleen[12] MCELHOES *(Robert Roy[11], John Kinter[10], Isaiah[9], Jane[8] VAN HORN, Isaiah[7], Henry B.[6], Henry[5], Christian Barentsen[4] VAN HOORN, Barent Christiansen[3], Christian Barentsen[2], Barent Barents[1])[5081]* was born 20 Aug 1913 in Canada[5081], and died 09 Jun 1977. She married (1) Andrew Jackson STATES. He was born in Grant Twp., Indiana Cnty, PA, and died Unknown. She married (2) Vernon SMITH. He died Unknown.

Children of Mary MCELHOES and Andrew STATES are:
    i.   Linda[13] STATES, b. Private.
    ii. Diane STATES, b. Private.
    iii. Pamela STATES, b. Private.

443. James K.[12] MCELHOES *(Joseph Isaiah[11], John Kinter[10], Isaiah[9], Jane[8] VAN HORN, Isaiah[7], Henry B.[6], Henry[5], Christian Barentsen[4] VAN HOORN, Barent Christiansen[3], Christian Barentsen[2], Barent Barents[1])[5081]* was born 02 Oct 1909 in PA[5081], and died Unknown. He married Isabell MILLIGAN Private. She was born Private.

More About James K. MCELHOES:

Burial: Unknown, Washington Church Cemetery, Rayne Twp., Indiana Cnty, PA

More About James MCELHOES and Isabell MILLIGAN:
Private-Begin: Private

Children of James MCELHOES and Isabell MILLIGAN are:
     i.   Ann[13] MCELHOES, b. Private.
    ii.   Patty MCELHOES, b. Private.

444. Blaine[12] MABON *(George Clair[11], Nancy Ann[10] LIGHTCAP, Susan[9] MCELHOES, Jane[8] VAN HORN, Isaiah[7], Henry B.[6], Henry[5], Christian Barentsen[4] VAN HOORN, Barent Christiansen[3], Christian Barentsen[2], Barent Barents[1])[5082]* was born Abt. 1910 in PA[5082], and died Unknown.

Child of Blaine MABON is:
     i.   ?[13] MABON, b. Private; m. Francis X. COOPER, Private; b. Private.

        More About Francis COOPER and ? MABON:
        Private-Begin: Private

445. Walter Duval[12] VAN HORN *(Claude Duval[11], John Neff[10], Benjamin Briggs[9], Joshua[8], Isaiah[7], Henry B.[6], Henry[5], Christian Barentsen[4] VAN HOORN, Barent Christiansen[3], Christian Barentsen[2], Barent Barents[1])[5083,5084]* was born 06 Jan 1893 in Presho, SD[5085], and died Apr 1965 in Elkton, Brookings Cnty, SD[5086]. He married Nan C. CORCORAN[5087] 01 Jun 1926 in Presho, Lyman Cnty SD. She was born 19 Feb 1893 in NE[5087], and died Jun 1975 in Elkton, Brookings Cnty, SD.

Notes for Walter Duval VAN HORN:
    In 1920 living with parents and farming.
    In 1930 owns his place in Presho, SD worth $1000 and has a radio.

More About Walter Duval VAN HORN:
Occupation: Proprietor Pool Hall

More About Walter VAN HORN and Nan CORCORAN:
Marriage: 01 Jun 1926, Presho, Lyman Cnty SD
Marriage date: John Frei
Marriage Place: Holy Angels Church, Presho, SD

Child of Walter VAN HORN and Nan CORCORAN is:
     i.   Merna V.[13] VAN HORN, b. Private.

446. Henry Logan[12] VAN HORN *(William Burton[11], John Neff[10], Benjamin Briggs[9], Joshua[8], Isaiah[7], Henry B.[6], Henry[5], Christian Barentsen[4] VAN HOORN, Barent Christiansen[3], Christian Barentsen[2], Barent Barents[1])[5088,5089,5090]* was born 09 Sep 1901 in Ola, Brule Cnty, SD[5091], and died 1981 in Baltimore, Baltimore Cnty, MD. He married Elsie A. FRICK[5092] Abt. 1927[5092]. She was born Abt. 1901 in IA[5092], and died Unknown.

Notes for Henry Logan VAN HORN:
    In 1930 living on 96th Street in Queens, NY with wife daughter and sister in law in a rented place for which they pay $65/month. They have a radio.

More About Henry Logan VAN HORN:
Occupation: Accountant Auditing Firm

More About Henry VAN HORN and Elsie FRICK:
Marriage: Abt. 1927[5092]

Child of Henry VAN HORN and Elsie FRICK is:
    i.   Phylis R.[13] VAN HORN, b. Private.

447. Jennie Elizabeth[12] VAN HORN *(William Burton[11], John Neff[10], Benjamin Briggs[9], Joshua[8], Isaiah[7], Henry B.[6], Henry[5], Christian Barentsen[4] VAN HOORN, Barent Christiansen[3], Christian Barentsen[2], Barent Barents[1])*[5093,5094,5095] was born 29 Sep 1903 in Ola, Brule Cnty, SD[5096], and died 01 Apr 1952 in Washington DC. She married (1) Carleton George ALBRIGHT[5097], son of George ALBRIGHT and Minnie SCHEUCH. He was born 08 Jan 1903 in Elsworth, Elsworth Cnty, KS/IL[5097], and died 02 May 1962 in Wichita, Sedgewick Cnty, KS/Wichita, Sedgwick Co., KS. She married (2) Paul GOODMAN. He died Unknown.

Notes for Jennie Elizabeth VAN HORN:
    It is alleged that she had an affair with Carleton George Albright in 1928 in Tyndall, SD which resulted in her taking the name O'Rourke for her daughter. She later married Paul Goodman and had 2 children by him Paul and Aileen.
    In 1930 divorced with a small daughter and her widowed mother living with her on 13th Street in Sioux Falls, SD. She is renting for $65/month and has two lodgers in the home.

More About Jennie Elizabeth VAN HORN:
Occupation: Teacher Public School

Child of Jennie VAN HORN and Carleton ALBRIGHT is:
570.   i.   Betty Jane[13] O'ROURKE, b. 06 Oct 1928, Omaha, Douglas Cnty, NE; d. 23 May 1980, Dallas, Dallas Cnty, TX.

Children of Jennie VAN HORN and Paul GOODMAN are:
    ii.   Paul[13] GOODMAN, b. Private.
    iii.   Aileen GOODMAN, b. Private.

448. Inez Vernal[12] VAN HORN *(Robert Campbell[11], John Neff[10], Benjamin Briggs[9], Joshua[8], Isaiah[7], Henry B.[6], Henry[5], Christian Barentsen[4] VAN HOORN, Barent Christiansen[3], Christian Barentsen[2], Barent Barents[1])*[5098,5099,5100,5101] was born 06 Apr 1905 in SD[5102], and died 21 Oct 1985 in Pierre, SD. She married (1) Fred William BENISH 05 Jul 1938 in Kennebec, Lyman Cnty, SD, son of Frank BENES and Margaret BAYLOR. He was born 18 Apr 1886 in Mt. Vernon, IA, and died 1950 in Herlong, CA. She married (2) Carl S. KITTLESON[5103] 1952 in Pierre, SD. He was born 1904 in Presho, SD, and died 31 Mar 1996 in Pierre, SD.

More About Inez Vernal VAN HORN:
Occupation: Stenographer Lawyers Office.

More About Fred BENISH and Inez VAN HORN:
Marriage: 05 Jul 1938, Kennebec, Lyman Cnty, SD
Marriage date: John S. Palmer Methodist Minister

More About Carl KITTLESON and Inez VAN HORN:

Marriage: 1952, Pierre, SD

Child of Inez VAN HORN and Carl KITTLESON is:
571.   i.   Robert William[13] BENISH, b. Private.

449. Mildred D.[12] VAN HORN *(Robert Campbell*[11]*, John Neff*[10]*, Benjamin Briggs*[9]*, Joshua*[8]*, Isaiah*[7]*, Henry B.*[6]*, Henry*[5]*, Christian Barentsen*[4] *VAN HOORN, Barent Christiansen*[3]*, Christian Barentsen*[2]*, Barent Barents*[1]*)*[5104,5105,5106,5107] was born Abt. 1907 in SD[5108,5109], and died Unknown. She married Ralph MITCHELL[5110] Abt. 1925. He was born Abt. 1905 in SD[5110], and died Unknown.

Notes for Mildred D. VAN HORN:
    Mildred and her husband are living in her parents home in 1930.

More About Ralph MITCHELL:
Occupation: Linotype Operator

More About Ralph MITCHELL and Mildred VAN HORN:
Marriage: Abt. 1925

Child of Mildred VAN HORN and Ralph MITCHELL is:
        i.   Norma G.[13] MITCHELL, b. Private.

450. Andrew Glenn[12] VAN HORN *(Orin Denton*[11]*, James Harvey*[10]*, Benjamin Briggs*[9]*, Joshua*[8]*, Isaiah*[7]*, Henry B.*[6]*, Henry*[5]*, Christian Barentsen*[4] *VAN HOORN, Barent Christiansen*[3]*, Christian Barentsen*[2]*, Barent Barents*[1]*)*[5111,5112,5113,5114,5115,5116,5117,5118,5119] was born 24 Aug 1894 in Plumville, Indiana Cnty, PA[5120,5121], and died 07 Oct 1969 in Punxsutawney, Jefferson Cnty, PA. He married Nellie Mae CLOWER[5122,5123,5124,5125,5126] 01 Jan 1917 in Wellsburg, WV, daughter of Frank CLOWER and Rose HENDERSON. She was born 19 Apr 1900 in Creekside, PA[5127], and died 06 Dec 1984 in Punxsutawney, Jefferson Cnty, PA[5127].

Notes for Andrew Glenn VAN HORN:
    In his WWI Draft Registration he says he is of medium height, slender build with blue eyes and light hair. He is a railroad trainman and lives in Clarksdale, PA. He is married and was born in Dayton, PA.
    In 1930 had a radio and was a renter at $15/month.
    In 1947 the Punxsutawney City Directory Andrew G. Van Horn lives at 222 Pine with his wife Nelly M. he is a conductor for the B&O Railroad and his telephone number is 228M. Apparently there are also living at this address Pete Skoff and R. J. Weltner with the same phone number.
    In the 1951 Punxsutawney Con Survey Directory his phone is 228M.

More About Andrew Glenn VAN HORN:
Burial: Unknown, Greenwood Cemetery, Indiana, PA
Lived: Creekside, PA
Occupation: Steam Railrad Brakeman, B&O Conductor
Organizations: Punxsutawney, Jefferson Cnty, PA Moose Lodge Charter Member and Brotherhood of Railroad Trainmen
Religion: Evangelical United Church and Creekside Methodist Church

Notes for Nellie Mae CLOWER:
    From a newspaper article on the occasion of the golden wedding anniversary we learn that Nellie enjoys embroidering and crocheting while Andrew is hunter and fisherman. They vacation in Florida and take their trailer to Harrington, DE where Andrew loves to fish in the Delaware Bay.

More that 200 people attending the event at Bucks Restaurant. Children listed were Eber, Richard, Frank and William. The Horace listed in Nellie's obituary may be Horace Albert Van Horn.

More About Nellie Mae CLOWER:
Religion: Woodland Ave. United Methodist Church and Evangelical United church

More About Andrew VAN HORN and Nellie CLOWER:
Marriage: 01 Jan 1917, Wellsburg, WV
Marriage date: Rev. G. A. Allison a Methodist Minister

Children of Andrew VAN HORN and Nellie CLOWER are:

      i.   Herman Eber[13] VAN HORN[5128,5129], b. 12 Dec 1917, Punxsutawney, Jefferson Cnty, PA[5130]; d. May 1980, New Kensington, Westmoreland Cnty, PA.

           More About Herman Eber VAN HORN:
           Lived: Herminie, PA

      ii. Emma Mary VAN HORN[5130], b. Dec 1919, Punxsutawney, Jefferson Cnty, PA[5130]; d. 17 Jan 1921, Punxsutawney, Jefferson Cnty, PA.

           Notes for Emma Mary VAN HORN:
           She is not listed in the 1930 Census so she may have died before 1930.

      iii. Horace Albert VAN HORN[5131], b. 1921, Punxsutawney, Jefferson Cnty, PA; d. 12 Sep 1922, Punxsutawney, Jefferson Cnty, PA.

572.   iv. Richard Glenn VAN HORN, b. 08 Jan 1923, Creekside, PA; d. 20 Nov 1967, Punxsutawney, Jefferson Cnty, PA.

573.   v.   Frank O. VAN HORN, b. 15 Nov 1924, Punxsutawney, Jefferson Cnty, PA; d. 08 Jul 1971, Tonawanda, Erie Cnty, NY.

      vi. Raymond E. VAN HORN[5131,5132], b. Apr 1926, PA[5132]; d. Aft. 06 Dec 1984.

           Notes for Raymond E. VAN HORN:
           The 1947 Punxsutawney City directory has him living at 222 Pine with parents and that he is a driver for Mahoning Ice Cream.

      vii. William H. VAN HORN[5133,5134], b. Feb 1930, PA[5134]; d. Aft. 06 Dec 1984.

           Notes for William H. VAN HORN:
           16 June 1943 the Indiana Evening Gazette (Indiana, PA) lists William Van Horn as having passed the 8th grade test.

           More About William H. VAN HORN:
           Lived: North Tonawanda, NY

451. Catherine Isabelle[12] VAN HORN *(Orin Denton[11], James Harvey[10], Benjamin Briggs[9], Joshua[8], Isaiah[7], Henry B.[6], Henry[5], Christian Barentsen[4] VAN HOORN, Barent Christiansen[3], Christian Barentsen[2], Barent Barents[1])*[5135,5136,5137,5138,5139,5140,5141] was born 25 Apr 1896 in Plumville, Indiana Cnty, PA[5142], and died 09 Aug 1976 in Punxsutwaney, Jefferson Cnty, PA. She married Oran E. BREWER[5143,5144,5145,5146] 05 Jan 1916 in Indiana, Indiana Cnty, PA[5147,5148], son of William BREWER and Martha ROOF. He was born 23 Sep 1893 in Washington, Indiana Cnty, PA[5149], and died 27 Feb 1982 in Creekside, Indiana Cnty, PA[5150].

Notes for Oran E. BREWER:

In his WW I Draft Registration he gives his birthday, has a wife and 1 child. He lives in Creekside, Washington Twp., PA and works as a locomotive fireman for the BRP Railroad in Creekside, PA. He is medium height and build. He has blue eyes and and light hair.

In 1920 his name is Oran E. Brewer. He lives in Creekside, PA in a home he owns free and clear. He is a railroad fireman.

In 1930 name is also spelled Oren, He lives on Creek Rd, Washington, Indiana Cnty, PA in a home he owns worth $1300. He is a miner.

In his WW II Draft Registration he lives on RFD #1 Creekside, Washington Twp., Indiana Cnty, PA. His wife is Catherine Brewer. He works for R&P Coal company in Ernest, PA. He signs his name Oran and gives his birthday. Oran is white, 5'8", weighs 120 pounds and has brown eyes and hair,

More About Oran BREWER and Catherine VAN HORN:
Marriage: 05 Jan 1916, Indiana, Indiana Cnty, PA[5151,5152]
Marriage date: Rev W. J. Wilson
Marriage Place: Ministers Residence Oakland Ave Indiana, PA

Children of Catherine VAN HORN and Oran BREWER are:
  i. Madeline M.[13] BREWER, b. Private.
  ii. Donald J. BREWER[5153], b. 22 Jul 1919, Creekside, Indiana Cnty, PA[5153]; d. 20 Jan 1921, Creekside, Indiana Cnty, PA.
574. iii. Ronald J. BREWER, b. 22 Jul 1919, Creekside, Indiana Cnty, PA; d. 11 May 2002, Creekside, Indiana Cnty, PA.
  iv. Dwite BREWER, b. Private.

452. Charles Boyd[12] VAN HORN *(Orin Denton[11], James Harvey[10], Benjamin Briggs[9], Joshua[8], Isaiah[7], Henry B.[6], Henry[5], Christian Barentsen[4] VAN HOORN, Barent Christiansen[3], Christian Barentsen[2], Barent Barents[1])*[5154,5155,5156,5157,5158,5159] was born 09 Jul 1899 in Indiana Cnty, PA[5159,5160,5161], and died Aft. 1949. He married Sara Elizabeth HEITZENRATER[5162,5163,5164] 30 Aug 1918[5165], daughter of Samuel HEITZENRATER and Rose LOVE. She was born Bet. 1896 - 1902 in Marion Center, Indiana Cnty, PA[5166], and died Unknown.

Notes for Charles Boyd VAN HORN:
20 September 1918 Indiana Evening Gazette (Indiana, PA) lists Charles Boyd Van Horn of Creekside, PA as receiving a draft registrant questionnaire.

His civilian draft registration indicated he is of medium height, medium build and has brown hair and eyes.

In 1930 rents for $15/month and has a radio.

May be Asbury or Eugene Van Horn rather than Charles in some sources.

More About Charles Boyd VAN HORN:
Occupation: Brakeman, Borrough Laborer

More About Charles VAN HORN and Sara HEITZENRATER:
Marriage: 30 Aug 1918[5167]

Children of Charles VAN HORN and Sara HEITZENRATER are:
  i. Dorothy May[13] VAN HORN, b. Private.
  ii. Ralph E. VAN HORN, b. Private.
  iii. M. Evelyn VAN HORN, b. Private.

453. LeRoy Wadding[12] VAN HORN *(LeRoy Kerns[11], Alexander Milton[10], Benjamin Briggs[9], Joshua[8],*

Isaiah[7], Henry B.[6], Henry[5], Christian Barentsen[4] VAN HOORN, Barent Christiansen[3], Christian Barentsen[2], Barent Barents[1])[5168,5169,5170,5171] was born 20 May 1903 in New Castle, PA[5172], and died 03 Mar 1987 in Youngstown, Mahoning Cnty, OH[5173]. He married Evelyn STEWART[5174] 16 Jan 1937. She was born 06 Jan 1916 in Butler, PA[5174], and died 26 Sep 1988 in Youngstown, Mahoning Cnty, OH[5175].

More About LeRoy Wadding VAN HORN:
Lived: Canfield, OH
Occupation: House Plasterer

More About LeRoy VAN HORN and Evelyn STEWART:
Marriage: 16 Jan 1937

Child of LeRoy VAN HORN and Evelyn STEWART is:
575.   i.   Gretchen Ann[13] VAN HORN, b. Private.

454. Betty J.[12] VAN HORN *(Sprague L.[11], Alexander Milton[10], Benjamin Briggs[9], Joshua[8], Isaiah[7], Henry B.[6], Henry[5], Christian Barentsen[4] VAN HOORN, Barent Christiansen[3], Christian Barentsen[2], Barent Barents[1])* was born Private. She married Arthur POST[5176] Private. He died Unknown.

More About Arthur POST and Betty VAN HORN:
Private-Begin: Private

Children of Betty VAN HORN and Arthur POST are:
        i.   ?[13] POST, b. Private.
        ii.   ? POST, b. Private.
        iii. ? POST, b. Private.

455. George Kenneth[12] KUEHNER *(Mary Mae[11] VAN HORN, Alexander Milton[10], Benjamin Briggs[9], Joshua[8], Isaiah[7], Henry B.[6], Henry[5], Christian Barentsen[4] VAN HOORN, Barent Christiansen[3], Christian Barentsen[2], Barent Barents[1])[5177,5178]* was born Bet. Jun - 04 Oct 1909 in PA[5179], and died 14 Jul 1987 in Hartsville, Darlington Cnty, SC[5180]. He married Mildred Heavlyn BOBBITT[5180] 18 Aug 1939[5180]. She was born 20 Apr 1917 in Durham, NC, and died 19 Oct 2000 in Columbis, Richland Cnty, SC.

More About George Kenneth KUEHNER:
Lived: Meadville, PA

More About George KUEHNER and Mildred BOBBITT:
Marriage: 18 Aug 1939[5180]

Child of George KUEHNER and Mildred BOBBITT is:
576.   i.   Karen Mildred[13] KUEHNER, b. Private.

456. Vincent[12] VAN HORN *(George Percy[11], Alexander Milton[10], Benjamin Briggs[9], Joshua[8], Isaiah[7], Henry B.[6], Henry[5], Christian Barentsen[4] VAN HOORN, Barent Christiansen[3], Christian Barentsen[2], Barent Barents[1])[5181,5182,5183]* was born Abt. 1913 in CA[5184], and died 1977 in New Castle, Lawrence Cnty, PA. He married Helen HILL, daughter of Ira HILL and Cora GLASSER. She was born 1913 in PA, and died 1996 in New Brighton, Beaver Cnty, PA.

Notes for Vincent VAN HORN:
    In 1930 living with his mother and her second husband Rudolph Nye. The 3 children are living

together with their mother.

Child of Vincent VAN HORN and Helen HILL is:
    i.   ?[13] VAN HORN, b. Private.

457. Dale[12] VAN HORN *(George Percy[11], Alexander Milton[10], Benjamin Briggs[9], Joshua[8], Isaiah[7], Henry B.[6], Henry[5], Christian Barentsen[4] VAN HOORN, Barent Christiansen[3], Christian Barentsen[2], Barent Barents[1])[5185,5186,5187]* was born 26 Jun 1917 in PA[5188,5189], and died 10 Jun 1992 in San Bernardino Cnty, CA[5189]. He married (1) Edna SWIFT Private. She was born Private. He married (2) Evelyn M. KASTEN Private. She was born Private.

Notes for Dale VAN HORN:
    In 1920 Dale is shown as a son and in 1930 as a step daughter.
    The California Death Index has his mothers name as Drezger which means that this is very likely this dale as his mother's last name was Brezger and he was born in June, 1917 to Lulu Brezger and Percy Van Horn,

More About Dale VAN HORN and Edna SWIFT:
Private-Begin: Private

More About Dale VAN HORN and Evelyn KASTEN:
Private-Begin: Private

Child of Dale VAN HORN and Edna SWIFT is:
577.   i.   Edward Dale[13] VAN HORN, b. Apr 1940, Aliquippa, Beaver Cnty, PA; d. Sep 2002, CA.

Child of Dale VAN HORN and Evelyn KASTEN is:
    ii.   ?[13] VAN HORN, b. Private; m. ALBERGO, Private; b. Private.

        More About ALBERGO and ? VAN HORN:
        Private-Begin: Private

458. James Rogers[12] RANKIN *(Nellie Gertrude[11] VAN HORN, Alexander Milton[10], Benjamin Briggs[9], Joshua[8], Isaiah[7], Henry B.[6], Henry[5], Christian Barentsen[4] VAN HOORN, Barent Christiansen[3], Christian Barentsen[2], Barent Barents[1])[5190,5191]* was born 21 Nov 1915 in Homer, Indiana Cnty, PA[5192], and died 25 Mar 1995 in White Twp., Indiana Cnty, PA[5193]. He married Mildred RUDDOCK. She was born 26 May 1917 in West Lebanon, Indiana Cnty, PA, and died 20 Mar 2000 in Indiana Cnty, PA.

Notes for James Rogers RANKIN:
    20 Jan 1933 Indiana Evening Gazette (Indiana, PA) visited with his grandfather A. M. Van Horn in the previous week.

Children of James RANKIN and Mildred RUDDOCK are:
    i.   Rosemary[13] RANKIN, b. Private; m. Dave JOHNSTON, Private; b. Private.

        More About Dave JOHNSTON and Rosemary RANKIN:
        Private-Begin: Private

    ii.   Marjorie Nell RANKIN, b. Private; m. Jeffery KIMBLE, Private; b. Private.

More About Jeffery KIMBLE and Marjorie RANKIN:
Private-Begin: Private

578.   iii.   Janice Louise RANKIN, b. 22 May 1943, White Twp., Indiana Cnty, PA; d. 09 Jun 2004, Blairsville, Indiana Cnty, PA.

459. Rosemary[12] RANKIN *(Nellie Gertrude[11] VAN HORN, Alexander Milton[10], Benjamin Briggs[9], Joshua[8], Isaiah[7], Henry B.[6], Henry[5], Christian Barentsen[4] VAN HOORN, Barent Christiansen[3], Christian Barentsen[2], Barent Barents[1])[5194]* was born 01 Apr 1920 in PA[5194], and died Jun 1992 in New Kensington, Westmoreland Cnty, PA. She married Vernon W. RIEKE. He was born 25 Oct 1915 in MO, and died 29 Apr 2003 in New Kensington, Westmoreland Cnty, PA[5195].

Child of Rosemary RANKIN and Vernon RIEKE is:
    i.   ?[13] RIEKE, b. Private.

460. Robert Merle[12] NEAL *(Bertha Agnes[11] LUKEHART, Sarah S.[10] VAN HORN, Benjamin Briggs[9], Joshua[8], Isaiah[7], Henry B.[6], Henry[5], Christian Barentsen[4] VAN HOORN, Barent Christiansen[3], Christian Barentsen[2], Barent Barents[1])[5196,5197,5198,5199]* was born 10 Nov 1902 in Dayton, Armstrong Cnty, PA[5200], and died Unknown. He married Anna Pearl DILL[5201,5202] Abt. 1927[5203], daughter of William DILL and Eliza MARSHALL. She was born 1908 in PA, and died Unknown.

Notes for Robert Merle NEAL:
    In 1930 living next door to his father and mother. He rents for $5/month and works the home farm.

More About Robert Merle NEAL:
Lived: Dayton, PA

More About Robert NEAL and Anna DILL:
Marriage: Abt. 1927[5203]

Children of Robert NEAL and Anna DILL are:
579.   i.   Shirley Mae[13] NEAL, b. 01 Dec 1930, Cowanshannock Twp., Armstrong Cnty, PA; d. 24 Jan 2005, Sebring, FL.
    ii.   Kenneth NEAL, b. Private; m. Donna, Private; b. Private.

More About Kenneth NEAL and Donna:
Private-Begin: Private

    iii.   Lois Jean NEAL, b. Private; m. Donald WINDOWS, Private; b. Private.

More About Donald WINDOWS and Lois NEAL:
Private-Begin: Private

461. Lulu V.[12] VAN HORN *(Samuel A.[11], John Miles[10], Christian[9], Joshua[8], Isaiah[7], Henry B.[6], Henry[5], Christian Barentsen[4] VAN HOORN, Barent Christiansen[3], Christian Barentsen[2], Barent Barents[1])[5204,5205,5206]* was born 29 Jul 1889 in PA[5207], and died 18 Jun 1976 in Brookville, PA[5208]. She married Frank FERGUSON[5208,5209] 16 Nov 1910[5210]. He was born Abt. 1888 in PA[5211], and died Bef. 1976[5212].

More About Lulu V. VAN HORN:

Burial: Unknown, New Bethlehem Cemetery, New Bethlehem, PA

Notes for Frank FERGUSON:
In 1930 renting a home that is worth $5,000 and they have a radio. They have been married for 19 years and Frank is an Assistant Cashier at a bank.

More About Frank FERGUSON and Lulu VAN HORN:
Marriage: 16 Nov 1910[5212]

Child of Lulu VAN HORN and Frank FERGUSON is:
580.   i.   Jean E.[13] FERGUSON, b. Private.

462. George H.[12] SHEPHARD *(Dessia A.[11] VAN HORN, John Miles[10], Christian[9], Joshua[8], Isaiah[7], Henry B.[6], Henry[5], Christian Barentsen[4] VAN HOORN, Barent Christiansen[3], Christian Barentsen[2], Barent Barents[1])*[5213,5214,5215] was born 14 Feb 1893 in Kane, PA[5216,5217], and died 17 Mar 1973 in Wellsville, NY. He married Eunice W. KIFFER[5218] Abt. 1910[5218]. She was born 19 Jan 1894 in Endeavor, PA[5218], and died 01 Jun 1983 in Wellsville, NY.

Notes for George H. SHEPHARD:
In 1930 living in the Allegheny National Forest and renting for $5/month. He is an oil foreman. They have a radio.

More About George SHEPHARD and Eunice KIFFER:
Marriage: Abt. 1910[5218]

Children of George SHEPHARD and Eunice KIFFER are:
581.   i.   Delores Ariel[13] SHEPHARD, b. Abt. 1915, PA; d. Aft. 1993.
         ii.   Pearl E. SHEPHARD, b. Private.
         iii. Virginia A. SHEPHARD, b. Private.
         iv.   Ruth A. SHEPHARD, b. Private.

463. Mabel J.[12] SHEPHARD *(Dessia A.[11] VAN HORN, John Miles[10], Christian[9], Joshua[8], Isaiah[7], Henry B.[6], Henry[5], Christian Barentsen[4] VAN HOORN, Barent Christiansen[3], Christian Barentsen[2], Barent Barents[1])*[5219,5220,5221,5222] was born Jun 1898 in PA[5223,5224,5225], and died Aft. 1930. She married Edwin Harold STANTON[5226,5227]. He was born Abt. 1896[5228], and died Aft. 1930.

Notes for Edwin Harold STANTON:
In 1920 renting on Cascade Street in Erie, PA. He is a factory laborer. There is a Dessa Shepard age 17 living in the family and listed as a lodger. She is likely related to Mabel as a sister or niece.
In 1930 living on Raspberry Street in Millcreek Twp., Erie Cnty, PA in a home they rent for $35/month. He is a brass polisher in a brass manufacturing operation. There is no radio in the home.

Children of Mabel SHEPHARD and Edwin STANTON are:
         i.   Roberta[13] STANTON[5228,5229], b. Abt. 1915[5230]; d. Aft. 2008.
582.   ii.   Raymond Walter STANTON, b. 28 Aug 1918, PA; d. 08 May 1971, Erie, Erie Cnty, PA.
583.   iii. Margaret STANTON, b. 14 Oct 1919, PA; d. 02 Dec 2002, Erie, Erie Cnty, PA.
584.   iv.   Geraldine STANTON, b. 21 May 1921, Erie, Erie Cnty, PA; d. 21 May 2008, Portland, OR.

464. Lois Fae[12] GEARHART *(Stella Marilla[11] VAN HORN, John Miles[10], Christian[9], Joshua[8], Isaiah[7], Henry B.[6], Henry[5], Christian Barentsen[4] VAN HOORN, Barent Christiansen[3], Christian Barentsen[2], Barent Barents[1])*[5231,5232,5233] was born 05 Feb 1913 in Smicksburg, Indiana Cnty, PA[5234], and died 18 May 1995 in Kittanning, Armstrong Cnty, PA. She married Delbert Clair HARTZELL. He was born 16 Nov 1910 in PA[5235], and died 21 Jan 2006 in Rural Valley, Armstrong Cnty, PA[5235].

Children of Lois GEARHART and Delbert HARTZELL are:

585. i.   Stella[13] HARTZELL, b. Private.
       ii.   Sarah Jane HARTZELL, b. 09 Jan 1936; d. 04 Feb 1986.
       iii. James Edward HARTZELL[5236], b. 19 Jun 1943, Cowanshannock Twp., Armstrong Cnty, PA; d. 19 Feb 1988, Kittanning, Armstrong Cnty, PA.
       iv.   Raymond HARTZELL, b. Private.
       v.   Louis HARTZELL, b. Private.
       vi.   William HARTZELL, b. Private.
       vii. ? HARTZELL, b. Private.
586. viii. Virginia HARTZELL, b. Private.
       ix.   Sarah HARTZELL, b. Private; m. Carl Leroy BORTZ, Private; b. Private.

             More About Carl BORTZ and Sarah HARTZELL:
             Private-Begin: Private

       x.   Edith Frances HARTZELL, b. Private; m. Wayne Lee DEVAUGHN, Private; b. Private.

             More About Wayne DEVAUGHN and Edith HARTZELL:
             Private-Begin: Private

       xi.   Hazel HARTZELL, b. Private.

465. Emery Ernest[12] VAN HORN *(Lester Leona[11], John Miles[10], Christian[9], Joshua[8], Isaiah[7], Henry B.[6], Henry[5], Christian Barentsen[4] VAN HOORN, Barent Christiansen[3], Christian Barentsen[2], Barent Barents[1])*[5237,5238] was born Bet. 08 Jan - Feb 1915 in Falls Creek, Jefferson Cnty, PA[5239], and died 02 Sep 1996 in St. Marys, Elk Cnty, PA. He married Francis BENTON Private. She was born Private.

More About Emery VAN HORN and Francis BENTON:
Private-Begin: Private

Children of Emery VAN HORN and Francis BENTON are:
       i.   Carol[13] VAN HORN, b. Private.
       ii.   Emery Ernest VAN HORN, JR, b. Private.
       iii. Laverne C. VAN HORN, b. Private.
       iv.   Lesley VAN HORN, b. Private.
       v.   ? VAN HORN, b. Private.
       vi.   Marion Ives VAN HORN, b. Private.

466. Dorothy M.[12] MCAFOOS *(Charles Austin[11], Sarah Dorcas[10] SINK, Sarah[9] VAN HORN, Joshua[8], Isaiah[7], Henry B.[6], Henry[5], Christian Barentsen[4] VAN HOORN, Barent Christiansen[3], Christian Barentsen[2], Barent Barents[1])*[5240,5241] was born 01 Feb 1922 in St Marys, Pottawatomie Cnty, KS[5242], and died 01 Jan 2010 in St Marys, Pottawatomie Cnty, KS[5243]. She married Warren Alfred MILLER[5244,5245] 14 Sep 1940 in Alma, KS[5245], son of Dennis MILLER and Aseneth F.. He was born 04 Dec 1917 in

Lawrence, Cloud Cnty, KS[5246], and died 14 Apr 2003 in St Marys, Pottawatomie Cnty, KS[5247].

Notes for Dorothy M. MCAFOOS:
    Dorothy M. Miller, 87, passed away, Friday, January 1, 2010 at
the St. Marys Manor.
    She was born February 1, 1922 at St. Marys, the daughter of Charles and Clara Hoffman
McAfoos. She attended grade school
at Rexford Kansas and graduated from St. Marys High School. Mrs. Miller had worked at Wehner's
Variety Store and later in the lunchroom at St. Marys Grade School. She was a member of the St.
Marys United Methodist Church and the Sunflower Club. On September 14, 1940, she was united in
marriage to Warren A. Miller at Alma. He preceded her in death on April 14, 2004. Mrs. Miller was
also preceded in death by brothers, Charles, George, Harold, Clarence and Perry McAfoos. She was
also preceded in death by her sister, Gertrude Coon. Survivors include a son, Dennis (Mary) Miller,
St. Marys; a daughter, Karen Schoemann, rural Belvue; her brother Cleo H. McAfoos, Kansas City,
MO; her sister, Ethel Anderson in Colorado; 6 grandchildren and 16 great-grandchildren. Funeral
services will be 10:30 A.M. Tuesday, January, 5, 2010 at the St. Marys United Methodist Church.
Interment will be in Valley View Cemetery, St. Marys. Mrs. Miller will lie in state after 2:00 P.M.
Monday, January 4, 2010 at Piper Funeral Home in St. Marys where the family will receive friends
from 6:00 until 7:30 P.M. Memorial contributions may be made to the St. Marys United Methodist
Church and sent in care of the funeral home.

More About Warren MILLER and Dorothy MCAFOOS:
Marriage: 14 Sep 1940, Alma, KS[5248]

Children of Dorothy MCAFOOS and Warren MILLER are:
    i.   Dennis Leroy[13] MILLER, b. Private; m. Mary, Private; b. Private.

        More About Dennis MILLER and Mary:
        Private-Begin: Private

    ii.   Karen MILLER, b. Private; m. SCHOEMANN, Private; b. Private.

        More About SCHOEMANN and Karen MILLER:
        Private-Begin: Private

467. Homer Vernon[12] POINTER *(Elsie Estelle*[11] *MCAFOOS, Sarah Dorcas*[10] *SINK, Sarah*[9] *VAN HORN, Joshua*[8], *Isaiah*[7], *Henry B.*[6], *Henry*[5], *Christian Barentsen*[4] *VAN HOORN, Barent Christiansen*[3], *Christian Barentsen*[2], *Barent Barents*[1])[5249,5250,5251] was born 17 Mar 1895 in Rexford, Thomas Cnty,
KS[5252], and died 13 Feb 1948 in Potter, TX[5253]. He married Grace GOODLOE[5254,5255], daughter
of Robert GOODLOE and Martha THRAILKILL. She was born Bet. 1890 - 1892 in KS, and died
23 Oct 1965 in Abilene, Taylor Cnty, TX[5256].

Notes for Homer Vernon POINTER:
    In 1920 owns his place in Guymon, OK free and clear. He is a garage proprietor
    In 1930 listed as Herbert or Hubert Pointer. He is renting for $35/month on East 4th Street in
Dalhart, TX. He is an implement salesman. As his wife and first son are the same names this is our
Homer Pointer.

Children of Homer POINTER and Grace GOODLOE are:
    i.   Robert Earl[13] POINTER, b. Private.
    ii. Ferma R. POINTER, b. Private.
    iii. Virginia R. POINTER, b. Private.
    iv. Harry Vernon POINTER[5257], b. Abt. 1925, OK[5257]; d. 24 Dec 1995, Navasota,

Grimes Cnty, TX*5258*; m. Lola M. MCMURTRIE, Private; b. Private.

More About Harry POINTER and Lola MCMURTRIE:
Private-Begin: Private

468. Gladys Mabel[12] POINTER *(Elsie Estelle[11] MCAFOOS, Sarah Dorcas[10] SINK, Sarah[9] VAN HORN, Joshua[8], Isaiah[7], Henry B.[6], Henry[5], Christian Barentsen[4] VAN HOORN, Barent Christiansen[3], Christian Barentsen[2], Barent Barents[1])[5259,5260]* was born 11 Aug 1906 in Oberlin, KS[5261], and died 20 Apr 1996 in Fresno, Fresno Cnty, CA. She married Edwin Gilmore ANTHONY. He was born 1901, and died 1987.

Children of Gladys POINTER and Edwin ANTHONY are:
  i.   ?[13] ANTHONY, b. Private.
  ii. ? ANTHONY, b. Private.
  iii. ? ANTHONY, b. Private.

469. LeRoy[12] VAN HORN *(Harry V.[11], Harry V.[10], John Hastings[9], John[8], Isaiah[7], Henry B.[6], Henry[5], Christian Barentsen[4] VAN HOORN, Barent Christiansen[3], Christian Barentsen[2], Barent Barents[1])* was born Private.

Child of LeRoy VAN HORN is:
  i.   Barbara[13] VAN HORN, b. Private.

470. Arthur James[12] LYDICK *(John Torrence[11], John Albert[10], Jane Elizabeth[9] VAN HORN, Isaiah[8], Isaiah[7], Henry B.[6], Henry[5], Christian Barentsen[4] VAN HOORN, Barent Christiansen[3], Christian Barentsen[2], Barent Barents[1])[5262]* was born 13 Jul 1938 in Clymer, Indiana Cnty, PA, and died 17 Jul 1977 in Indiana, Indiana Cnty, PA. He married Kathy BRAUGHLER Private. She was born Private.

Notes for Arthur James LYDICK:
    Arthur James Lydick Sr., 59, of Clymer RD1 died Thursday, July 17, 1997, at the Indiana Hospital.
    The son of Todd and Sylvia Baines Lydick, he was born Jan. 13, 1938, in Clymer. Mr. Lydick was a truck driver and a social member of the Clymer American Legion Post No. 222 and the Clymer LOOM Lodge NO. 670.
    Surviving are his wife, Kathy Braughler, Clymer RD1; his mother of Clymer; three children; Arthur Jr., Frankville; Shawn and Chris, both at home; two sisters: Marie Buterbaugh, Cookport; Ruby Stiles, Strongstown; and two grandchildren: Kayla and Eric Harris. Indiana Gazette Jul 19, 1997

More About Arthur LYDICK and Kathy BRAUGHLER:
Private-Begin: Private

Children of Arthur LYDICK and Kathy BRAUGHLER are:
  i.   Arthur James[13] LYDICK, JR, b. Private.
  ii. Shawn LYDICK, b. Private.
  iii. Chris LYDICK, b. Private.

471. James Robert[12] LAMBING *(Elizabeth Pearl[11] PALMER, Mary A.[10] LYDICK, Jane Elizabeth[9]*

Isaiah Van Horn Pioneer of Indiana County, Pennsylvania

VAN HORN, Isaiah[8], Isaiah[7], Henry B.[6], Henry[5], Christian Barentsen[4] VAN HOORN, Barent Christiansen[3], Christian Barentsen[2], Barent Barents[1])[5263,5264,5265,5266] was born 02 Sep 1898 in PA[5267,5268], and died 07 May 1969 in Indiana, Indiana Cnty, PA[5269]. He married Francis Martha MANNING[5270] Abt. 1918. She was born 13 Feb 1900 in Croyle, Cambria Cnty, PA[5270], and died 25 Feb 1978 in Indiana, Indiana Cnty, PA[5271].

Notes for James Robert LAMBING:
In his WWI Draft Registration he states he is of medium build, medium height and has blue eyes and brown hair. He lists his mother of Homer City, PA as his next of kin.

More About James Robert LAMBING:
Burial: 10 May 1969, Oakland, Indiana Cnty, PA
Lived: Homer City, Indiana Cnty, PA
Occupation: Laborer Lucerne Mines

More About Francis Martha MANNING:
Burial: 28 Feb 1978, Oakland, Indiana Cnty, PA

More About James LAMBING and Francis MANNING:
Marriage: Abt. 1918

Children of James LAMBING and Francis MANNING are:
  i.   George Robert[13] LAMBING[5272,5273], b. 28 Nov 1919, Homer City, Indiana Cnty, PA[5274]; d. 08 Dec 1986, West Lake, Cuyahoga Cnty, OH[5275]; m. Stella KOLISH, Private; b. Private.

       More About George Robert LAMBING:
       Burial: 11 Dec 1986, Greenwood Cemetery, Indiana, PA
       Lived: 441 S. Main Homer City, PA
       Military service: Bet. 06 Jun 1944 - 11 Dec 1945, US Navy

       More About George LAMBING and Stella KOLISH:
       Private-Begin: Private

587.   ii. Myrtle Olive LAMBING, b. 23 Sep 1922, Homer City, Indiana Cnty, PA; d. 25 Jun 1984, Akron, Summit Cnty, OH.
       iii. Betty M. LAMBING, b. Private.
       iv. Isabelle LAMBING, b. Private.
       v.   James M. LAMBING, b. 27 May 1929, PA; d. 17 Jan 1994, Clymer, Indiana Cnty, PA[5276]; m. Ruth Virginia Madaline DOWDEN, Private; b. Private.

       More About James LAMBING and Ruth DOWDEN:
       Private-Begin: Private

472. Emma Mable[12] LAMBING *(Elizabeth Pearl[11] PALMER, Mary A.[10] LYDICK, Jane Elizabeth[9] VAN HORN, Isaiah[8], Isaiah[7], Henry B.[6], Henry[5], Christian Barentsen[4] VAN HOORN, Barent Christiansen[3], Christian Barentsen[2], Barent Barents[1])[5277]* was born 15 Dec 1902 in Indiana, Indiana Cnty, PA[5277], and died 08 Feb 1976 in Indiana, Indiana Cnty, PA. She married William J. LIVINGSTON. He was born 25 Nov 1901 in White Twp., Indiana Cnty, PA, and died 27 Nov 1944 in Indiana, Indiana Cnty, PA.

Child of Emma LAMBING and William LIVINGSTON is:
  i.   ?[13] LIVINGSTON, b. Private; m. ? SKINNER, Private; b. Private.

More About ? LIVINGSTON and ? SKINNER:
Private-Begin: Private

473. Gerald Clair[12] SHANKLE *(Thomas Roy[11], Ida Mae[10] LYDICK, Jane Elizabeth[9] VAN HORN, Isaiah[8], Isaiah[7], Henry B.[6], Henry[5], Christian Barentsen[4] VAN HOORN, Barent Christiansen[3], Christian Barentsen[2], Barent Barents[1])* was born Private. He married Elizabeth P. ONDO Private. She was born Private.

More About Gerald SHANKLE and Elizabeth ONDO:
Private-Begin: Private

Children of Gerald SHANKLE and Elizabeth ONDO are:
588.   i.   Patricia Ann[13] SHANKLE, b. Private.
         ii.   Julia SHANKLE, b. Private.
        iii.   Gerald Clair SHANKLE, JR, b. Private.

474. Margaret Ida[12] SHANKLE *(Thomas Roy[11], Ida Mae[10] LYDICK, Jane Elizabeth[9] VAN HORN, Isaiah[8], Isaiah[7], Henry B.[6], Henry[5], Christian Barentsen[4] VAN HOORN, Barent Christiansen[3], Christian Barentsen[2], Barent Barents[1])* was born Private. She married Walter Arnold SEXTON Private. He was born 24 Jun 1914, and died Unknown.

More About Walter SEXTON and Margaret SHANKLE:
Private-Begin: Private

Children of Margaret SHANKLE and Walter SEXTON are:
589.   i.   Charlotte Lou[13] SEXTON, b. Private.
590.   ii.   Esther Jean SEXTON, b. Private.
591.   iii.   Robert LeRoy SEXTON, b. Private.
592.   iv.   James Arnold SEXTON, b. Private.
593.   v.   John Franklin SEXTON, b. Private.

475. Athelia Grace[12] SHANKLE *(Thomas Roy[11], Ida Mae[10] LYDICK, Jane Elizabeth[9] VAN HORN, Isaiah[8], Isaiah[7], Henry B.[6], Henry[5], Christian Barentsen[4] VAN HOORN, Barent Christiansen[3], Christian Barentsen[2], Barent Barents[1])[5278]* was born 1925 in PA[5278], and died 2006. She married Edgar Gene FITZGERALD. He was born 1923, and died 2004.

Child of Athelia SHANKLE and Edgar FITZGERALD is:
         i.   Sally Ann[13] FITZGERALD, b. Private.

476. Theda Agnes[12] MCMANUS *(Eva Jane[11] SHANKLE, Ida Mae[10] LYDICK, Jane Elizabeth[9] VAN HORN, Isaiah[8], Isaiah[7], Henry B.[6], Henry[5], Christian Barentsen[4] VAN HOORN, Barent Christiansen[3], Christian Barentsen[2], Barent Barents[1])[5279,5280]* was born 21 May 1918 in Kittanning, Armstong Cnty, PA[5281], and died 17 Aug 2007 in Plumcreek Twp., Indiana Cnty, PA[5282]. She married Arthur Glenn BLACK 06 Jul 1938 in Indiana Cnty, PA, son of Walter BLACK and Ruth KING. He was born 20 Apr 1919 in Parkwood, Indiana Cnty, PA, and died 03 Jan 1990 in East Franklin Twp., Armstrong Cnty, PA[5282].

More About Arthur BLACK and Theda MCMANUS:

Marriage: 06 Jul 1938, Indiana Cnty, PA

Children of Theda MCMANUS and Arthur BLACK are:
    i.   ?[13] BLACK, b. Private.
    ii. ? BLACK, b. Private.
    iii. ? BLACK, b. Private.
    iv. ? BLACK, b. Private.
    v.   ? BLACK, b. Private.
    vi. ? BLACK, b. Private.
    vii. ? BLACK, b. Private.
    viii. ? BLACK, b. Private.
    ix. Howard Paul BLACK, b. 30 Apr 1955, Armstrong Cnty, PA; d. 09 Dec 2003,
         Kittanning, Armstong Cnty, PA; m. (1) Marlene Gail BISH, Private; b. Private; m.
         (2) Diane KAMMERDINER, Private; b. Private.

         More About Howard BLACK and Marlene BISH:
         Private-Begin: Private

         More About Howard BLACK and Diane KAMMERDINER:
         Private-Begin: Private

477. Betty Jane[12] MCMANUS *(Eva Jane[11] SHANKLE, Ida Mae[10] LYDICK, Jane Elizabeth[9] VAN HORN, Isaiah[8], Isaiah[7], Henry B.[6], Henry[5], Christian Barentsen[4] VAN HOORN, Barent Christiansen[3], Christian Barentsen[2], Barent Barents[1])[5283,5284]* was born 29 Aug 1922 in Chevy Chase, Indiana Cnty, PA[5285], and died 19 Jun 1993. She married Earl E. SCOTT Private, son of Howard L. SCOTT. He was born Private.

More About Betty Jane MCMANUS:
Lived: Bet. 1943 - 1947, 559 E. College, Indiana, PA

More About Earl SCOTT and Betty MCMANUS:
Private-Begin: Private

Children of Betty MCMANUS and Earl SCOTT are:
    i.   Earl Eugene[13] SCOTT, b. Indiana Cnty, PA; d. 22 Jan 1943, Indiana Cnty, PA.
    ii. Robert Clair SCOTT, b. Private.

478. Ford Russell[12] SHANKLE, JR *(Ford Russell[11], Ida Mae[10] LYDICK, Jane Elizabeth[9] VAN HORN, Isaiah[8], Isaiah[7], Henry B.[6], Henry[5], Christian Barentsen[4] VAN HOORN, Barent Christiansen[3], Christian Barentsen[2], Barent Barents[1])* was born Private.

Child of Ford Russell SHANKLE, JR is:
    i.   Evan Wallace[13] SHANKLE, b. Private.

479. Clyde Emory[12] LYDICK *(Blair James[11], Joseph Bell[10], Mary P.[9] VAN HORN, Isaiah[8], Isaiah[7], Henry B.[6], Henry[5], Christian Barentsen[4] VAN HOORN, Barent Christiansen[3], Christian Barentsen[2], Barent Barents[1])* was born 02 Aug 1924 in White Twp., Indiana Cnty, PA, and died 11 Nov 1950. He married Agnes Goldie MIHALICH Private. She was born Private.

Notes for Clyde Emory LYDICK:
    Clyde Emory was 26 years old when he was killed in an automobile accident. He served in

World War ll in A-T Co. 26th Infantry Regiment, 1st Division. He operated shuttle cars in the Ernst Mine of the Rochester and Pittsburgh Coal Co. He was a member of the Ernest Local No. 599, U.M.W. of A. and Clymer Post No. 22 American Legion. This information came from his obituary

More About Clyde LYDICK and Agnes MIHALICH:
Private-Begin: Private

Children of Clyde LYDICK and Agnes MIHALICH are:
  i.   ?[13] LYDICK, b. Private.
  ii. ? LYDICK, b. Private.

480. Blair James[12] LYDICK, JR *(Blair James[11], Joseph Bell[10], Mary P.[9] VAN HORN, Isaiah[8], Isaiah[7], Henry B.[6], Henry[5], Christian Barentsen[4] VAN HOORN, Barent Christiansen[3], Christian Barentsen[2], Barent Barents[1])* was born 06 Mar 1937 in Cherryhill Twp., Indiana Cnty, PA, and died 15 Sep 1991 in Malborough, Indiana Cnty, PA. He married ? Private. She was born Private.

More About Blair LYDICK and ?:
Private-Begin: Private

Children of Blair LYDICK and ? are:
  i.   ?[13] LYDICK, b. Private.
  ii.   ? LYDICK, b. Private.
  iii. ? LYDICK, b. Private.

481. Naomi Jane[12] GAGEBY *(James Allen[11], Nora Mary Agnes[10] VAN HORN, John A.[9], Isaiah[8], Isaiah[7], Henry B.[6], Henry[5], Christian Barentsen[4] VAN HOORN, Barent Christiansen[3], Christian Barentsen[2], Barent Barents[1])* was born 25 Oct 1924 in Martinsburg, Berkeley Cnty, WV, and died 25 Nov 1979 in Winchester, Frederick Cnty, MD. She married Charles William GRUBB. He was born 23 Jun 1923 in Martinsburg, Berkeley Cnty, WV, and died 16 Aug 1977 in Winchester, Frederick Cnty, MD.

More About Naomi Jane GAGEBY:
Burial: Unknown, Pleasant View Cemetery, Martinsburg, WV

Child of Naomi GAGEBY and Charles GRUBB is:
  i.   ?[13] GRUBB, b. Private.

482. William Thomas[12] LUKEHART *(Dollie Irene[11] CONDRON, William Madison[10], Dorcas[9] VAN HORN, William G.[8], Isaiah[7], Henry B.[6], Henry[5], Christian Barentsen[4] VAN HOORN, Barent Christiansen[3], Christian Barentsen[2], Barent Barents[1])*[5286,5287] was born 07 Nov 1908 in PA[5288], and died 26 Jun 1958 in Indiana Cnty, PA. He married Mildred Minne WASSAM Private. She was born Private.

More About William Thomas LUKEHART:
Burial: Unknown, Oakland Cemetery, Indiana Cnty, PA

More About William LUKEHART and Mildred WASSAM:
Private-Begin: Private

Children of William LUKEHART and Mildred WASSAM are:
  i.   Richard M[13] LUKEHART, b. Private.
  ii. James Francis LUKEHART, b. Private.

483. Mary Lou[12] SERENE *(Owen Meridith[11], Stella M.[10] VAN HORN, George Logan[9], William G.[8], Isaiah[7], Henry B.[6], Henry[5], Christian Barentsen[4] VAN HOORN, Barent Christiansen[3], Christian Barentsen[2], Barent Barents[1])* was born 30 Jan 1934, and died Aft. 1951. She married David Daniel MEYER Private, son of John MEYER and Viola BROWN. He was born Private.

More About David MEYER and Mary SERENE:
Private-Begin: Private

Children of Mary SERENE and David MEYER are:
594.　　i.　Rebecca Katherine[13] MEYER, b. Private.
　　　　ii.　Suzanne Ruth MEYER, b. Private.

484. Joyce Ann[12] VAN HORN *(Walter Edward[11], Edward Harry[10], Samuel Redding[9], William G.[8], Isaiah[7], Henry B.[6], Henry[5], Christian Barentsen[4] VAN HOORN, Barent Christiansen[3], Christian Barentsen[2], Barent Barents[1])* was born Private. She married David Gilbert BURGESON Private. He was born Private.

More About David BURGESON and Joyce VAN HORN:
Private-Begin: Private

Child of Joyce VAN HORN and David BURGESON is:
　　　　i.　Joyce Ann Van Horn[13] BURGESON, b. Private.

485. Arveta T.[12] STEELE *(Clark Lewis[11], Elijah Work[10], Dorcas[9] HAMILTON, Nancy[8] VAN HORN, Isaiah[7], Henry B.[6], Henry[5], Christian Barentsen[4] VAN HOORN, Barent Christiansen[3], Christian Barentsen[2], Barent Barents[1])[5289]* was born Abt. 1902 in PA[5289], and died Unknown. She married Archie Merle SMITH. He died Unknown.

Children of Arveta STEELE and Archie SMITH are:
　　　　i.　Eleanor[13] SMITH, b. 04 Mar 1923, Limestone Twp., Clarion Cnty, PA; d. Oct 1980, Shippenville, Clarion Cnty, PA.
　　　　ii.　Dorothy Marie SMITH, b. 10 Apr 1921, Limestone Twp., Clarion Cnty, PA; d. 05 Feb 2008, Clarion, Clarion Cnty, PA.
　　　　iii.　? SMITH, b. Private.
　　　　iv.　? SMITH, b. Private.

486. Bertha Olive[12] STEELE *(Clark Lewis[11], Elijah Work[10], Dorcas[9] HAMILTON, Nancy[8] VAN HORN, Isaiah[7], Henry B.[6], Henry[5], Christian Barentsen[4] VAN HOORN, Barent Christiansen[3], Christian Barentsen[2], Barent Barents[1])* was born 29 Mar 1912 in Limestone Twp., Clarion Cnty, PA, and died 14 Oct 1991 in Strattanville, Clarion Cnty, PA. She married Rosco Thomas SMITH. He was born 1906, and died 25 Mar 1975 in Strattanville, Clarion Cnty, PA.

Children of Bertha STEELE and Rosco SMITH are:
　　　　i.　?[13] SMITH, b. Private.
　　　　ii.　? SMITH, b. Private.
　　　　iii.　? SMITH, b. Private.
　　　　iv.　? SMITH, b. Private.

487. Clair W.[12] STEELE *(Clark Lewis[11], Elijah Work[10], Dorcas[9] HAMILTON, Nancy[8] VAN HORN, Isaiah[7], Henry B.[6], Henry[5], Christian Barentsen[4] VAN HOORN, Barent Christiansen[3], Christian Barentsen[2], Barent Barents[1])* was born 12 Oct 1923 in Limestone Twp., Clarion Cnty, PA, and died 07 Nov 2007 in Brookville, Jefferson Cnty, PA. He married ? DAVIS Private. She was born Private.

More About Clair W. STEELE:
Burial: Unknown, Pisque Cemetery, Clarion Cnty, PA

More About Clair STEELE and ? DAVIS:
Private-Begin: Private

Children of Clair STEELE and ? DAVIS are:
     i.   ?[13] STEELE, b. Private.
    ii.   ? STEELE, b. Private.
   iii.   ? STEELE, b. Private.
   iv.   ? STEELE, b. Private.
    v.   Larry STEELE, b. 01 Aug 1955; d. Oct 1978.
595.   vi.   Michael W. STEELE, b. 23 Feb 1957, Brookville, Jefferson Cnty, PA; d. 04 Jul 2005, Clarion Cnty, PA.

488. Martha Elizabeth[12] STEELE *(Clare Clawson[11], Elijah Work[10], Dorcas[9] HAMILTON, Nancy[8] VAN HORN, Isaiah[7], Henry B.[6], Henry[5], Christian Barentsen[4] VAN HOORN, Barent Christiansen[3], Christian Barentsen[2], Barent Barents[1])[5290]* was born 14 Dec 1920 in Rochester Mills, Indiana Cnty, PA, and died 18 Aug 1997 in Jefferson Cnty, PA[5291]. She married Wayne Dwenard WHITE. He was born 1918, and died 1999.

Children of Martha STEELE and Wayne WHITE are:
     i.   ?[13] WHITE, b. Private.
    ii.   ? WHITE, b. Private.
   iii.   ? WHITE, b. Private.
   iv.   ? WHITE, b. Private.

489. Mary Jane[12] FERRIER *(Esther M.[11] MCADOO, Ada Myrtle[10] VAN HORN, Bennett Work[9], George Logan[8], Isaiah[7], Henry B.[6], Henry[5], Christian Barentsen[4] VAN HOORN, Barent Christiansen[3], Christian Barentsen[2], Barent Barents[1])[5292,5293,5294,5295,5296]* was born Abt. Nov 1925 in PA[5297], and died Aft. 1998. She married (1) E. H. HOLBEN, JR Private, son of E. H. HOLBEN. He was born Private. She married (2) Charles H. DUNCAN Private. He was born Private.

Notes for Mary Jane FERRIER:
    Her mother died in her home in 1998.
    Member of the Girl Scout Troop III and was a patrol leader. 21 Oct 1939 and 24 August 1943 Indiana Evening Gazette (Indiana, PA)

More About Mary Jane FERRIER:
Degree: Indiana State Teachers College
Lived: 1960, 495 S. 6th Indiana, PA

More About E. HOLBEN and Mary FERRIER:
Private-Begin: Private

More About Charles DUNCAN and Mary FERRIER:
Private-Begin: Private

Children of Mary FERRIER and Charles DUNCAN are:
      i.   Bonnie Lu[13] DUNCAN[5298], b. 02 Dec 1960, Indiana, Indiana Cnty, PA[5298]; d. 04 Dec 1960, Indiana, Indiana Cnty, PA[5298].

             More About Bonnie Lu DUNCAN:
             Burial: Unknown, Oakland Cemetery, Indiana, PA

596.   ii.   Laurel DUNCAN, b. Private.
        iii. Betsy DUNCAN, b. Private; m. YORKE, Private; b. Private.

             More About YORKE and Betsy DUNCAN:
             Private-Begin: Private

490. Larue Bernadine[12] AUL *(Curtis Edwin[11], Mary Caroline[10] VAN HORN, Bennett Work[9], George Logan[8], Isaiah[7], Henry B.[6], Henry[5], Christian Barentsen[4] VAN HOORN, Barent Christiansen[3], Christian Barentsen[2], Barent Barents[1])* was born Private. She married (1) Edwin MULBERGER Private. He was born Private. She married (2) Lyle SHELLHAMMER Private. He was born Private.

More About Edwin MULBERGER and Larue AUL:
Private-Begin: Private

More About Lyle SHELLHAMMER and Larue AUL:
Private-Begin: Private

Children of Larue AUL and Lyle SHELLHAMMER are:
      i.   Matthew[13] SHELLHAMMER, b. Private.
      ii.   ? SHELLHAMMER, b. Private.

491. Robert Clark[12] MCCAUSLAND *(Bertha Della[11] AUL, Mary Caroline[10] VAN HORN, Bennett Work[9], George Logan[8], Isaiah[7], Henry B.[6], Henry[5], Christian Barentsen[4] VAN HOORN, Barent Christiansen[3], Christian Barentsen[2], Barent Barents[1])[5299,5300]* was born 12 Jul 1920 in Sagamore, Armstrong Cnty, PA[5301], and died 11 Mar 1992 in Pittsburgh, PA. He married Helen Arlene ADAMSON Private, daughter of John ADAMSON. She was born Private.

Notes for Robert Clark MCCAUSLAND:
     13 March 1947 Indiana Evening Gazette (Indiana, PA) reports a sale of a lot in Plumville, Pa by Robert McCausland to Elsie I. Edwards and husband.

More About Robert Clark MCCAUSLAND:
Employment: Copperweld Steel
Lived: Dayton, PA, Levittsburg and Warren, OH

More About Robert MCCAUSLAND and Helen ADAMSON:
Private-Begin: Private

Children of Robert MCCAUSLAND and Helen ADAMSON are:
      i.   Donald Reid[13] MCCAUSLAND, b. Private.
      ii.   Florence J. MCCAUSLAND, b. Private.
597.   iii. Helen Arlene MCCAUSLAND, b. Private.
598.   iv. Linda Jean MCCAUSLAND, b. Private.

492. Florence Jane[12] MCCAUSLAND *(Bertha Della[11] AUL, Mary Caroline[10] VAN HORN, Bennett Work[9], George Logan[8], Isaiah[7], Henry B.[6], Henry[5], Christian Barentsen[4] VAN HOORN, Barent Christiansen[3], Christian Barentsen[2], Barent Barents[1])[5301,5302]* was born 26 Dec 1921 in PA[5303], and died Aft. 1992. She married James Clarence COOPER Private. He was born Private.

More About James COOPER and Florence MCCAUSLAND:
Private-Begin: Private

Children of Florence MCCAUSLAND and James COOPER are:
599.   i.   James Clarence[13] COOPER, JR, b. Private.
600.   ii. Sally Ann COOPER, b. Private.
601.   iii. John Ronald COOPER, b. Private.
602.   iv. Cathy Ann COOPER, b. Private.

493. Donald Reid[12] MCCAUSLAND *(Bertha Della[11] AUL, Mary Caroline[10] VAN HORN, Bennett Work[9], George Logan[8], Isaiah[7], Henry B.[6], Henry[5], Christian Barentsen[4] VAN HOORN, Barent Christiansen[3], Christian Barentsen[2], Barent Barents[1])[5303]* was born 14 May 1924 in PA[5303], and died 22 Nov 2003 in Rural Valley, Armstrong Cnty, PA[5304]. He married Charlotte Marie MCMASTERS 24 Sep 1944, daughter of John MCMASTERS and Sarah STEVENS. She was born 07 Sep 1926 in Centre Twp., Indiana Cnty, PA, and died 11 May 1996 in Kittanning, Armstrong Cnty, PA.

More About Donald Reid MCCAUSLAND:
Lived: Rural Valley, PA

More About Donald MCCAUSLAND and Charlotte MCMASTERS:
Marriage: 24 Sep 1944

Children of Donald MCCAUSLAND and Charlotte MCMASTERS are:
603.   i.   Charlene Marie[13] MCCAUSLAND, b. Private.
604.   ii. Donald Reid MCCAUSLAND, JR, b. Private.
605.   iii. Larry John MCCAUSLAND, b. Private.
606.   iv. Dennis Lee MCCAUSLAND, b. Private.
607.   v.   Maxine Dee MCCAUSLAND, b. Private.
608.   vi. Kathleen Joy MCCAUSLAND, b. Private.

494. Clair Eugene[12] MCCAUSLAND *(Bertha Della[11] AUL, Mary Caroline[10] VAN HORN, Bennett Work[9], George Logan[8], Isaiah[7], Henry B.[6], Henry[5], Christian Barentsen[4] VAN HOORN, Barent Christiansen[3], Christian Barentsen[2], Barent Barents[1])[5305]* was born 27 Jun 1926 in Sagamore, Armstrong Cnty, PA[5305], and died Aft. 1992. He married Sara Marie WHITACRE Private, daughter of Gilbert WHITACRE and Sarah UMBAUGH. She was born Private.

More About Clair Eugene MCCAUSLAND:
Lived: Warren & Windam, OH

More About Clair MCCAUSLAND and Sara WHITACRE:
Private-Begin: Private

Children of Clair MCCAUSLAND and Sara WHITACRE are:
          i.   John Clark[13] MCCAUSLAND, b. 20 Feb 1948; d. 20 Feb 1948.
609.   ii. Robert Clair MCCAUSLAND, b. Private.

610.　iii.　Thomas Lee MCCAUSLAND, b. Private.
611.　iv.　Gary Lynn MCCAUSLAND, b. Private.

495. Grace Lucille[12] MCCAUSLAND *(Bertha Della[11] AUL, Mary Caroline[10] VAN HORN, Bennett Work[9], George Logan[8], Isaiah[7], Henry B.[6], Henry[5], Christian Barentsen[4] VAN HOORN, Barent Christiansen[3], Christian Barentsen[2], Barent Barents[1])[5306]* was born 08 Aug 1930 in PA, and died Aft. 1992. She married Merrill Ward LARGE Private, son of Rev. P. W. LARGE. He was born Private.

More About Grace Lucille MCCAUSLAND:
Employment: G. C. Murray Co., Indiana, PA
Lived: Sharpsville, PA

More About Merrill LARGE and Grace MCCAUSLAND:
Private-Begin: Private

Children of Grace MCCAUSLAND and Merrill LARGE are:
612.　i.　David Bruce[13] LARGE, b. Private.
613.　ii.　Richard Ward LARGE, b. Private.
614.　iii.　Diane Lee LARGE, b. Private.
　　　iv.　Patricia Ann LARGE, b. Private.
615.　v.　Deborah Sue LARGE, b. Private.

496. Dorothy Jean[12] MCCAUSLAND *(Bertha Della[11] AUL, Mary Caroline[10] VAN HORN, Bennett Work[9], George Logan[8], Isaiah[7], Henry B.[6], Henry[5], Christian Barentsen[4] VAN HOORN, Barent Christiansen[3], Christian Barentsen[2], Barent Barents[1])[5307,5308]* was born 10 Sep 1934 in PA, and died Aft. 1992. She married Murray Lynn SHOTTS Private. He was born Private.

More About Dorothy Jean MCCAUSLAND:
Lived: Dayton, PA & Bedford Heights, OH

More About Murray SHOTTS and Dorothy MCCAUSLAND:
Private-Begin: Private

Children of Dorothy MCCAUSLAND and Murray SHOTTS are:
616.　i.　Edward Bruce[13] SHOTTS, b. Private.
617.　ii.　John Murray SHOTTS, b. Private.
618.　iii.　Richard Earl SHOTTS, b. Private.
619.　iv.　Terry Lynn SHOTTS, b. Private.
　　　v.　Jeffery Scott SHOTTS, b. Private.
620.　vi.　Donald Lee SHOTTS, b. Private.
621.　vii.　Norma Jean SHOTTS, b. Private.

497. Shirley Ann[12] MCCAUSLAND *(Bertha Della[11] AUL, Mary Caroline[10] VAN HORN, Bennett Work[9], George Logan[8], Isaiah[7], Henry B.[6], Henry[5], Christian Barentsen[4] VAN HOORN, Barent Christiansen[3], Christian Barentsen[2], Barent Barents[1])[5309]* was born 16 Sep 1936 in PA, and died Aft. 1992. She married Conrad Joseph SHEMO Private, son of SHEMO and Elizabeth. He was born Private.

More About Shirley Ann MCCAUSLAND:
Lived: Clymer, PA

More About Conrad SHEMO and Shirley MCCAUSLAND:

Private-Begin: Private

Child of Shirley MCCAUSLAND and Conrad SHEMO is:
  i.   Rodney Alan[13] SHEMO, b. Private; m. Carolyn Faye Schurr MCMILLEN, Private; b. Private.

       More About Rodney SHEMO and Carolyn MCMILLEN:
       Private-Begin: Private

498. Helen[12] SHAFFER *(Nelson Ernest[11], Cora Belle[10] VAN HORN, Bennett Work[9], George Logan[8], Isaiah[7], Henry B.[6], Henry[5], Christian Barentsen[4] VAN HOORN, Barent Christiansen[3], Christian Barentsen[2], Barent Barents[1])* was born Private. She married Samuel GETT Private. He was born Private.

More About Samuel GETT and Helen SHAFFER:
Private-Begin: Private

Child of Helen SHAFFER and Samuel GETT is:
  i.   ?[13] GETT, b. Private.

499. Jane[12] SHAFFER *(Nelson Ernest[11], Cora Belle[10] VAN HORN, Bennett Work[9], George Logan[8], Isaiah[7], Henry B.[6], Henry[5], Christian Barentsen[4] VAN HOORN, Barent Christiansen[3], Christian Barentsen[2], Barent Barents[1])* was born Private. She married Michael RUSNICA[5310] Private, son of Thomas RUSNICA and Nellie TRACZ. He was born 29 Jun 1924 in Numine, Cowshannock Cnty, PA, and died 11 Apr 2007 in Numine, Cowshannock Cnty, PA.

More About Michael RUSNICA and Jane SHAFFER:
Private-Begin: Private

Children of Jane SHAFFER and Michael RUSNICA are:
  i.   Tom[13] RUSNICA, b. Private; m. Arlene, Private; b. Private.

       More About Tom RUSNICA and Arlene:
       Private-Begin: Private

  ii. Carol RUSNICA, b. Private; m. Jim DICKEY, Private; b. Private.

       More About Jim DICKEY and Carol RUSNICA:
       Private-Begin: Private

500. Verna M.[12] SHAFFER *(Nelson Ernest[11], Cora Belle[10] VAN HORN, Bennett Work[9], George Logan[8], Isaiah[7], Henry B.[6], Henry[5], Christian Barentsen[4] VAN HOORN, Barent Christiansen[3], Christian Barentsen[2], Barent Barents[1])[5310]* was born 07 Oct 1927 in Plumville, Indiana Cnty, PA, and died 12 Dec 1994 in Cleveland, OH. She married Donald POMPELIA Private. He was born Private.

More About Donald POMPELIA and Verna SHAFFER:
Private-Begin: Private

Children of Verna SHAFFER and Donald POMPELIA are:
  i.   Terry[13] POMPELIA, b. Private.
  ii. Mick POMPELIA, b. Private.
  iii. Shawn POMPELIA, b. Private.

416

501. Helen[12] BANKS *(Agnes Marie[11] SHAFFER, Cora Belle[10] VAN HORN, Bennett Work[9], George Logan[8], Isaiah[7], Henry B.[6], Henry[5], Christian Barentsen[4] VAN HOORN, Barent Christiansen[3], Christian Barentsen[2], Barent Barents[1])* was born Private. She married Alfred ANDERSON Private, son of Arthur ANDERSON. He was born Private.

More About Alfred ANDERSON and Helen BANKS:
Private-Begin: Private

Children of Helen BANKS and Alfred ANDERSON are:
    i.   Thomas[13] ANDERSON, b. Private.
    ii.   Edward W. ANDERSON, b. Private.
    iii.   Timothy Alan ANDERSON, b. Private.
    iv.   Ann ANDERSON, b. Private; m. Denny PARK, Private; b. Private.

        More About Denny PARK and Ann ANDERSON:
        Private-Begin: Private

502. John William[12] SHAFFER *(Claude Ellsworth[11], Cora Belle[10] VAN HORN, Bennett Work[9], George Logan[8], Isaiah[7], Henry B.[6], Henry[5], Christian Barentsen[4] VAN HOORN, Barent Christiansen[3], Christian Barentsen[2], Barent Barents[1])* was born 07 Dec 1942 in Indiana Cnty, PA, and died 26 Jun 2006 in Indiana, Indiana Cnty, PA. He married Betty Jane BENAMATI Private. She was born Private.

More About John SHAFFER and Betty BENAMATI:
Private-Begin: Private

Children of John SHAFFER and Betty BENAMATI are:
622.   i.   Shay Linda[13] SHAFFER, b. Private.
      ii.   Terry SHAFFER, b. Private.
      iii.   John William SHAFFER, JR, b. Private.

503. Judy Lynn[12] SHAFFER *(Clyde Sylvester[11], Cora Belle[10] VAN HORN, Bennett Work[9], George Logan[8], Isaiah[7], Henry[5], Christian Barentsen[4] VAN HOORN, Barent Christiansen[3], Christian Barentsen[2], Barent Barents[1])* was born Private. She married (1) Dennis MCCARTNEY Private. He was born Private. She married (2) Albert Blaine CUNNINGHAM Private, son of Delose CUNNINGHAM and Bertha BREWER. He was born Private. She married (3) George Joseph CLARK Private. He was born Private. She married (4) ? Private. He was born Private.

More About Dennis MCCARTNEY and Judy SHAFFER:
Private-Begin: Private

More About Albert CUNNINGHAM and Judy SHAFFER:
Private-Begin: Private

More About George CLARK and Judy SHAFFER:
Private-Begin: Private

More About ? and Judy SHAFFER:
Private-Begin: Private

Child of Judy SHAFFER and Albert CUNNINGHAM is:

    i.   Jeffery Alan[13] CUNNINGHAM, b. Private.

Child of Judy SHAFFER and George CLARK is:
    ii.   Joseph CLARK[13] SHAFFER, b. Private.

Child of Judy SHAFFER and ? is:
    iii.   Sean Daniel ?[13] SHAFFER, b. Private.

504. Connie May[12] SHAFFER *(Clyde Sylvester[11], Cora Belle[10] VAN HORN, Bennett Work[9], George Logan[8], Isaiah[7], Henry B.[6], Henry[5], Christian Barentsen[4] VAN HOORN, Barent Christiansen[3], Christian Barentsen[2], Barent Barents[1])* was born Private. She married Edward Wayne MILLER Private, son of H. MILLER and Anna BREWER. He was born Private.

More About Edward MILLER and Connie SHAFFER:
Private-Begin: Private

Children of Connie SHAFFER and Edward MILLER are:
    i.   Edward Wayne[13] MILLER, JR, b. Private.
    ii.   Mark Anthony MILLER, b. Private.
    iii.   Steven Michael MILLER, b. Private.
    iv.   David Scott MILLER, b. Private.
    v.   Kimberly Mae MILLER, b. Private.
    vi.   Sonya Fae MILLER, b. Private.
    vii.   Heather Kay MILLER, b. Private.

505. Gary Lee[12] SHAFFER *(Clyde Sylvester[11], Cora Belle[10] VAN HORN, Bennett Work[9], George Logan[8], Isaiah[7], Henry B.[6], Henry[5], Christian Barentsen[4] VAN HOORN, Barent Christiansen[3], Christian Barentsen[2], Barent Barents[1])* was born Private. He married Donna Kay ERB Private, daughter of Robert ERB and Denise ORR. She was born Private.

More About Gary SHAFFER and Donna ERB:
Private-Begin: Private

Children of Gary SHAFFER and Donna ERB are:
    i.   Gary Lee[13] SHAFFER, JR, b. Private.
    ii.   Heather Lynn SHAFFER, b. Private.

506. Edgar Dean[12] SHAFFER *(Clyde Sylvester[11], Cora Belle[10] VAN HORN, Bennett Work[9], George Logan[8], Isaiah[7], Henry B.[6], Henry[5], Christian Barentsen[4] VAN HOORN, Barent Christiansen[3], Christian Barentsen[2], Barent Barents[1])* was born Private. He married Audrey Juanita PEARCE Private, daughter of Norman PEARCE and Lois ARMSTRONG. She was born Private.

More About Edgar SHAFFER and Audrey PEARCE:
Private-Begin: Private

Child of Edgar SHAFFER and Audrey PEARCE is:
    i.   Richard Clyde[13] SHAFFER, b. Private.

507. Lois Jean[12] SHAFFER *(Clyde Sylvester[11], Cora Belle[10] VAN HORN, Bennett Work[9], George Logan[8], Isaiah[7], Henry B.[6], Henry[5], Christian Barentsen[4] VAN HOORN, Barent Christiansen[3], Christian Barentsen[2], Barent Barents[1])* was born Private. She married Doug Raymond BIGLER Private. He was born Private.

More About Doug BIGLER and Lois SHAFFER:
Private-Begin: Private

Child of Lois SHAFFER and Doug BIGLER is:
     i.   Stephanie[13] BIGLER, b. Private.

508. William L.[12] JOHNSTON *(William Clair[11], Anna Florence[10] VAN HORN, Bennett Work[9], George Logan[8], Isaiah[7], Henry B.[6], Henry[5], Christian Barentsen[4] VAN HOORN, Barent Christiansen[3], Christian Barentsen[2], Barent Barents[1])* was born 21 Sep 1928 in Homer City, PA, and died 10 Jul 1996 in Punxsutawney, PA. He married Betty Lou REED Private. She was born Private.

More About William JOHNSTON and Betty REED:
Private-Begin: Private

Child of William JOHNSTON and Betty REED is:
623.   i.   Luanna[13] JOHNSTON, b. Private.

509. Raymond[12] STEELE *(Irene Mae[11] JOHNSTON, Anna Florence[10] VAN HORN, Bennett Work[9], George Logan[8], Isaiah[7], Henry B.[6], Henry[5], Christian Barentsen[4] VAN HOORN, Barent Christiansen[3], Christian Barentsen[2], Barent Barents[1])* was born Private.

Children of Raymond STEELE are:
     i.   Diane[13] STEELE, b. Private.
    ii.   Carol STEELE, b. Private.

510. Myrna J.[12] STEELE *(Irene Mae[11] JOHNSTON, Anna Florence[10] VAN HORN, Bennett Work[9], George Logan[8], Isaiah[7], Henry B.[6], Henry[5], Christian Barentsen[4] VAN HOORN, Barent Christiansen[3], Christian Barentsen[2], Barent Barents[1])* was born Private. She married Harold MARSHALL Private. He was born Private.

More About Harold MARSHALL and Myrna STEELE:
Private-Begin: Private

Children of Myrna STEELE and Harold MARSHALL are:
     i.   Lois[13] MARSHALL, b. Private.
    ii.   Gary Eugene MARSHALL, b. Private.
   iii.   Doris MARSHALL, b. Private.
   iv.   Larry MARSHALL, b. Private.
    v.   Terry MARSHALL, b. Private.

511. Evelyn Jane[12] STEELE *(Irene Mae[11] JOHNSTON, Anna Florence[10] VAN HORN, Bennett Work[9], George Logan[8], Isaiah[7], Henry B.[6], Henry[5], Christian Barentsen[4] VAN HOORN, Barent Christiansen[3], Christian Barentsen[2], Barent Barents[1])[5311]* was born 23 Mar 1928 in South Mahoning Twp., Indiana Cnty,

PA, and died 14 Nov 2004 in Indiana, Indiana Cnty, PA. She married (1) Roy VINTON[5311,5312]. He died 1986. She married (2) William C. LUNDSTROM, SR Private. He was born Private.

More About William LUNDSTROM and Evelyn STEELE:
Private-Begin: Private

Children of Evelyn STEELE and Roy VINTON are:
    i.   Kenneth[13] VINTON, b. Private; m. Mary Ann, Private; b. Private.

        More About Kenneth VINTON and Mary Ann:
        Private-Begin: Private

    ii. Harry VINTON, b. Private; m. Debbie, Private; b. Private.

        More About Harry VINTON and Debbie:
        Private-Begin: Private

    iii. David VINTON, b. Private; m. Brenda, Private; b. Private.

        More About David VINTON and Brenda:
        Private-Begin: Private

512. Lulu A.[12] STEELE *(Irene Mae*[11] *JOHNSTON, Anna Florence*[10] *VAN HORN, Bennett Work*[9], *George Logan*[8], *Isaiah*[7], *Henry B.*[6], *Henry*[5], *Christian Barentsen*[4] *VAN HOORN, Barent Christiansen*[3], *Christian Barentsen*[2], *Barent Barents*[1])[5313] was born 09 Dec 1929 in South Mahoning Twp., Indiana Cnty, PA, and died 02 Jun 1999 in Indiana Cnty, PA. She married Richard MALCOLM Private. He was born Private.

More About Richard MALCOLM and Lulu STEELE:
Private-Begin: Private

Children of Lulu STEELE and Richard MALCOLM are:
    i.   Dennis R.[13] MALCOLM, b. Private; m. Sandra, Private; b. Private.

        More About Dennis MALCOLM and Sandra:
        Private-Begin: Private

    ii. Gregory N. MALCOLM, b. Private.
    iii. Patricia E. MALCOLM, b. Private; m. John MYERS, Private; b. Private.

        More About John MYERS and Patricia MALCOLM:
        Private-Begin: Private

513. Bruce[12] STEELE *(Irene Mae*[11] *JOHNSTON, Anna Florence*[10] *VAN HORN, Bennett Work*[9], *George Logan*[8], *Isaiah*[7], *Henry B.*[6], *Henry*[5], *Christian Barentsen*[4] *VAN HOORN, Barent Christiansen*[3], *Christian Barentsen*[2], *Barent Barents*[1])* was born Private.

Children of Bruce STEELE are:
    i.   Danny[13] STEELE, b. Private.
    ii. Janet STEELE, b. Private.
    iii. Bonnie STEELE, b. Private.

514. Harold Blaine[12] STEELE *(Irene Mae[11] JOHNSTON, Anna Florence[10] VAN HORN, Bennett Work[9], George Logan[8], Isaiah[7], Henry B.[6], Henry[5], Christian Barentsen[4] VAN HOORN, Barent Christiansen[3], Christian Barentsen[2], Barent Barents[1])* was born Private.

Children of Harold Blaine STEELE are:
    i.   Sandra[13] STEELE, b. Private.
    ii. Cynthia STEELE, b. Private.

515. Martha[12] STEELE *(Irene Mae[11] JOHNSTON, Anna Florence[10] VAN HORN, Bennett Work[9], George Logan[8], Isaiah[7], Henry B.[6], Henry[5], Christian Barentsen[4] VAN HOORN, Barent Christiansen[3], Christian Barentsen[2], Barent Barents[1])* was born Private. She married Thomas ANDERSON Private. He was born Private.

More About Thomas ANDERSON and Martha STEELE:
Private-Begin: Private

Child of Martha STEELE and Thomas ANDERSON is:
    i.   Brian[13] ANDERSON, b. Private.

516. Donna[12] STEELE *(Irene Mae[11] JOHNSTON, Anna Florence[10] VAN HORN, Bennett Work[9], George Logan[8], Isaiah[7], Henry B.[6], Henry[5], Christian Barentsen[4] VAN HOORN, Barent Christiansen[3], Christian Barentsen[2], Barent Barents[1])* was born Private. She married Eugene DAUGHERTY Private. He was born Private.

More About Eugene DAUGHERTY and Donna STEELE:
Private-Begin: Private

Child of Donna STEELE and Eugene DAUGHERTY is:
    i.   Karen[13] DAUGHERTY, b. Private.

517. Earl Clark[12] STEELE *(Irene Mae[11] JOHNSTON, Anna Florence[10] VAN HORN, Bennett Work[9], George Logan[8], Isaiah[7], Henry B.[6], Henry[5], Christian Barentsen[4] VAN HOORN, Barent Christiansen[3], Christian Barentsen[2], Barent Barents[1])[5313]* was born 25 Feb 1935 in Plumville, Indiana Cnty, PA, and died 01 Apr 2002 in Indian Haven, Indiana, Indiana Cnty, PA. He married Floy L. KUNSELMAN Private. She was born Private.

More About Earl STEELE and Floy KUNSELMAN:
Private-Begin: Private

Children of Earl STEELE and Floy KUNSELMAN are:
    i.   Cathy[13] STEELE, b. Private; m. Gerald COSTIN, Private; b. Private.

          More About Gerald COSTIN and Cathy STEELE:
          Private-Begin: Private

    ii. Carla STEELE, b. Private.
    iii. Frank STEELE, b. Private; m. Tammy, Private; b. Private.

          More About Frank STEELE and Tammy:

Private-Begin: Private

iv.   Sonya Rae STEELE, d. 1969.

518. Russell Paul[12] JOHNSTON *(Lester Carl[11], Anna Florence[10] VAN HORN, Bennett Work[9], George Logan[8], Isaiah[7], Henry B.[6], Henry[5], Christian Barentsen[4] VAN HOORN, Barent Christiansen[3], Christian Barentsen[2], Barent Barents[1])* was born Private. He married ? Private. She was born Private.

More About Russell JOHNSTON and ?:
Private-Begin: Private

Child of Russell JOHNSTON and ? is:
i.   Princess Paula Ann[13] JOHNSTON, b. Private.

519. Larry R.[12] JOHNSTON *(Walter R.[11], Anna Florence[10] VAN HORN, Bennett Work[9], George Logan[8], Isaiah[7], Henry B.[6], Henry[5], Christian Barentsen[4] VAN HOORN, Barent Christiansen[3], Christian Barentsen[2], Barent Barents[1])* was born Private. He married Sharon RIDDLE Private. She was born Private.

More About Larry JOHNSTON and Sharon RIDDLE:
Private-Begin: Private

Children of Larry JOHNSTON and Sharon RIDDLE are:
i.   Charles Robert[13] JOHNSTON, b. Private.
ii.   Wayne Raymond JOHNSTON, b. Private.

520. Bernice[12] JOHNSTON *(Walter R.[11], Anna Florence[10] VAN HORN, Bennett Work[9], George Logan[8], Isaiah[7], Henry B.[6], Henry[5], Christian Barentsen[4] VAN HOORN, Barent Christiansen[3], Christian Barentsen[2], Barent Barents[1])* was born Private. She married SMITH Private. He was born Private.

More About SMITH and Bernice JOHNSTON:
Private-Begin: Private

Children of Bernice JOHNSTON and SMITH are:
i.   Vickie[13] SMITH, b. Private.
ii.   Shane SMITH, b. Private.

521. James B.[12] JOHNSTON *(Walter R.[11], Anna Florence[10] VAN HORN, Bennett Work[9], George Logan[8], Isaiah[7], Henry B.[6], Henry[5], Christian Barentsen[4] VAN HOORN, Barent Christiansen[3], Christian Barentsen[2], Barent Barents[1])* was born Private. He married Denise BENAMATI Private. She was born Private.

More About James JOHNSTON and Denise BENAMATI:
Private-Begin: Private

Child of James JOHNSTON and Denise BENAMATI is:
i.   Christie[13] JOHNSTON, b. Private.

522. Charles Lee[12] VAN HORN *(Floyd Albert*[11]*, Robert Lee Claire*[10]*, Bennett Work*[9]*, George Logan*[8]*, Isaiah*[7]*, Henry B.*[6]*, Henry*[5]*, Christian Barentsen*[4] *VAN HOORN, Barent Christiansen*[3]*, Christian Barentsen*[2]*, Barent Barents*[1]*)* was born Private. He married Frances Evelyn SCHRECKENGOST Private. She was born Private.

More About Charles VAN HORN and Frances SCHRECKENGOST:
Private-Begin: Private

Children of Charles VAN HORN and Frances SCHRECKENGOST are:
     i.   Sandra[13] VAN HORN, b. Private.
    ii.   Charles VAN HORN, b. Private.
   iii.   Susan VAN HORN, b. Private.

523. Howard Eugene[12] VAN HORN *(Floyd Albert*[11]*, Robert Lee Claire*[10]*, Bennett Work*[9]*, George Logan*[8]*, Isaiah*[7]*, Henry B.*[6]*, Henry*[5]*, Christian Barentsen*[4] *VAN HOORN, Barent Christiansen*[3]*, Christian Barentsen*[2]*, Barent Barents*[1]*)* was born Private. He married Patricia HEITMAN Private. She was born Private.

More About Howard VAN HORN and Patricia HEITMAN:
Private-Begin: Private

Children of Howard VAN HORN and Patricia HEITMAN are:
     i.   Wayne[13] VAN HORN, b. Private.
    ii.   Allan VAN HORN, b. Private.

524. Joseph Lee[12] VAN HORN *(Wilbur Bennett*[11]*, Robert Lee Claire*[10]*, Bennett Work*[9]*, George Logan*[8]*, Isaiah*[7]*, Henry B.*[6]*, Henry*[5]*, Christian Barentsen*[4] *VAN HOORN, Barent Christiansen*[3]*, Christian Barentsen*[2]*, Barent Barents*[1]*)*[5314,5315,5316] was born 04 Apr 1934 in Plumville, Indiana Cnty, PA, and died 31 Mar 1985 in Creekside, Indiana Cnty, PA. He married Kathleen NESBIT[5317,5318], daughter of John NESBIT and Florence WISSINGER. She died 06 Nov 2001 in Creekside, Indiana Cnty, PA[5319].

Notes for Joseph Lee VAN HORN:
    15 May 1961 Indiana Evening Gazette (Indiana, PA) Joseph L. Van Horn of Indiana age 27 was involved in a motorcycle auto accident at 4th and Philadelphia Streets. He was treated for abrasions and released. He lived at 252 Olive Street, Indiana, PA.

More About Joseph Lee VAN HORN:
Fraternal Organization: Benjamin Franklin F&AM Lodge 753
Occupation: FMC for 29 years
Organizations: Coudersport Consistory, National Rifelman's Association
Religion: Creekside, PA United Methodist Church

More About Kathleen NESBIT:
Occupation: Local Tax Collector for 25 years[5320]
Religion: Creekside, PA United Methodist Church

Children of Joseph VAN HORN and Kathleen NESBIT are:
     i.   Gregg[13] VAN HORN[5321,5322,5323], d. Aft. 2010; m. Kathie MCINTIRE, Private; b. Private.

        Notes for Gregg VAN HORN:
        Gregg Van Horn operates a Christmas tree farm at 5601 Hwy 954 N Creekside PA

Isaiah Van Horn Pioneer of Indiana County, Pennsylvania

15732 he wrote the following article while President of the Christmas Tree Growers Association:

History of Indiana County Christmas Tree Growers' Association

Growing Christmas Trees as a farm crop seems to have started in Indiana County, PA in the years following 1918. Murray C. Stewart, Sam Dible, Walter Schroth, Silas Streams, Fred Musser, and others were first to plant various pines and spruces for the purpose of Christmas Trees.

In 1944 a group of Christmas Tree Growers had organized the Pennsylvania Christmas Tree Growers Association. Murray C. Stewart of Homer City was its first president.

In 1957 a National Christmas Tree Association was founded and Murray C. Stewart served as its first president.

On March 5, 1956 the Indiana Christmas Tree Growers Association was organized in Indiana with 178 attending the meeting. Douglas A. Malcolm served as the first president. The by-laws were written by the following: Clair Wassau, Sam Dible, Roy Orr, Roy Fleming, Bill Stevens, Doug Malcolm, Beryl Johnston, Percial Park, Regis McKnight and Louis Long. This organization has been active for more than 52 years promoting the production of high quality Christmas Trees, marketing them at fair profit and having them reach the consumer at prices as reasonable as possible.

Also in 1956 the idea for a motorized Christmas Tree Baler was started in a service station in Creekside, Indiana County. The idea was that of Beryl Johnston, Board Member and his father Clair. During the Winter of 1956 work began, experimenting through trial and error. It was not until 1959 that the first baler was used in the field. The Balers were produced and sold beginning in 1960. Somewhere between 100 and 200 Balers were made. The last baler was made around 1968. The first "Johnston Baler" produced in 1959 is still in use at Johnston's Nursery.

Although the County Association is not officially affiliated with the PA Christmas Tree Grower Association, a warm fraternal and cooperative relationship exists. Many members of the County Association are also member of the State Association. Exchange of information through Association meetings helps to maintain a high level of culture.

Christmas Trees from 1918-1944 were naturally grown. Shearing trees did not really start till around 1944. In 1945 County Agent Jack Warner gave a tree shearing demonstration. Hedge shears or a sharp pocket knife were the first tools of choice. Trees were only sheared every 2 years.

On June 8, 1954 another tree shearing demonstration was held in Aultman. The second one that month was held on Beryl Johnston's Farm by Sam Dible using a hand-held grass sickles. Today most all Christmas Trees are sheared every year.

In 1957 the Indiana County Tree Growers cut a 53 year old Norway Spruce 71 feet high in early December on the farm of Robert S. Uncapher and sent it to be used as a Christmas Tree at the Gateway Center, Pittsburgh. In 1958 and 1959 The Gateway trees were cut at the Cyrus Pershing Wissingers Farm in Willet.

In 1961 The Candle Stick Tours began in late May. The event comes at a time when the light green new growth of the Christmas Trees (mainly pines) stands out like a candle at the end of each branch. Bus and car loads of visitors tour various tree plantations.

In 1963 Christmas Trees were sent to decorate the halls of Congress.

In 1964 the first Indiana County Christmas Tree Festival was held during the Candle Stick tour. Visitors had the opportunity not only to enjoy a Tree Farm Tour, but also view Antique Autos, attend a Gun and Coin Show, a Corn Planter Indiana Show, Square Dancing, Coronation of Queen Evergreen, and a host of other activities to make the festival a memorable weekend for every one who attended.

Isaiah Van Horn Pioneer of Indiana County, Pennsylvania

In 1966 a letter to the Indiana Gazette dated November 29, from an Indiana County soldier stationed in Saigon Vietnam, inquired if it would be possible for his unit to have a Christmas Tree for the Holidays. Roy Fleming brought a 5' tree, well wrapped for shipment, on behalf of the Indiana County Tree Growers. The Gazette underwrote the cost of shipping the tree by air to the base and followed up by asking the Associated Press to keep an eye on the trees arrival so the paper could receive pictures of the men and their tree. The tree arrived on time. The Indiana County Christmas Tree Growers have also sent trees to New York firemen families, after 911, and donated trees for troops of the Iraq War and their families.

In August of 1968 over 1000 Christmas Tree Growers met in Indiana for the Convention of the National Christmas Tree Growers Association.

Another achievement of the Association is promoting and sponsoring the Christmas Tree Competitive exhibit of the Christmas Trees at the Indiana County Fair, on the week before Labor Day. In 2007 we also started a Christmas Tree Decorating Contest at the fair to promote the "real tree".

2004 was the first year of Christmas in July at Idlewild Park in Ligonier, PA. The Association decorated 20 to 30 Christmas Trees. Some are traditional, while others are themed. Area businesses and groups also decorate trees to promote their business. The trees are in a pavilion for a week. The public can walk through and vote on their favorite tree. The winner receives a plaque and money prize.

In 2007 we moved to Story Book Forest at Idlewild Park for a Story Book Christmas. We feel this is a great way to promote the "real tree" to children of all ages.

Every Spring we help with a Christmas Tree Seminar put on by our County Agent Bob Pollock, around 70-100 people attend.

Now in 2008 there are not as many tree growers as in years past. But Indiana Growers still grow and sell a large quantity of trees. When it all started in 1918 till the late 80's the Scotch Pine was King. The Fraser Fir moved into first place in the 90's with Douglas Fir into second. The Firs are King now. What will it be in 20 years? You can bet the Indiana county Christmas Tree Growers will be growing it.

President
Gregg A. VanHorn

How We Became the Capital

In 1956 an estimated 700,000 trees in Indiana County were cut that year. Some time during this period Indiana County began to be touted as the "Christmas Tree Capital of the World", according to an Associated Press Dispatch. About 1958 Shelton, Washington laid claim to the Christmas Tree Capital title but was repulsed when Walter Schroth one of Indiana County's nurserymen revealed he had an order for 15,000 trees to be shipped to Tacoma, Washington. Other states may produce more now, but we were the first. A newspaper reporter doing a story on the other capitals, reported we were the only ones with the signs up along the road that say, "Indiana County Christmas Tree Capital of the World.

More About Gregg VAN HORN and Kathie MCINTIRE:
Private-Begin: Private

624.	ii.	Tracy Dawn VAN HORN, b. 21 Mar 1966; d. Aft. 2010.
625.	iii.	Lori Jo VAN HORN, b. Marion Center, Indiana Cnty, PA; d. Aft. 2010.
626.	iv.	Luke VAN HORN, d. Aft. 2010.

525. William James[12] VAN HORN *(Wilbur Bennett[11], Robert Lee Claire[10], Bennett Work[9], George Logan[8], Isaiah[7], Henry B.[6], Henry[5], Christian Barentsen[4] VAN HOORN, Barent Christiansen[3], Christian Barentsen[2], Barent Barents[1])[5324,5325]* was born Abt. 1942 in Indiana Cnty, PA, and died Aft. 1998. He married (1) Patricia A. MARI Private. She was born Private. He married (2) Terry MOORE Private. She was born Private.

More About William James VAN HORN:
Military service: 1960, US Marine Corp

More About William VAN HORN and Patricia MARI:
Private-Begin: Private

More About William VAN HORN and Terry MOORE:
Private-Begin: Private

Child of William VAN HORN and Patricia MARI is:
      i.   Gina Mari[13] VAN HORN, b. Private; m. Gregory Gerald STOKES, Private; b. Private.

           More About Gregory STOKES and Gina VAN HORN:
           Private-Begin: Private

Children of William VAN HORN and Terry MOORE are:
     ii.   Christy Lynn[13] VAN HORN, b. Private.
    iii.   Jamie Lee VAN HORN, b. Private.

526. Lyle Bennett[12] VAN HORN *(Wilbur Bennett[11], Robert Lee Claire[10], Bennett Work[9], George Logan[8], Isaiah[7], Henry B.[6], Henry[5], Christian Barentsen[4] VAN HOORN, Barent Christiansen[3], Christian Barentsen[2], Barent Barents[1])[5326,5327,5328]* was born 16 Feb 1943 in Niagra Falls, Niagra Cnty, NY, and died 20 Apr 1986 in Ravenna, OH. He married Virginia SHIELDS Private. She was born Private.

Notes for Lyle Bennett VAN HORN:
    13 May 1955 the Indiana Evening Gazette (Indiana, PA) reports that Lyle Van Horn is accepted into membership of the local United Presbyterian Church.
    5 June 1961 the Indiana Evening Gazette (Indiana, PA) lists Lyle Bennett Van Horn as Indiana High School graduate in the special program of Machine Tool Operations.
    1961 School Yearbook for Indiana High School Lyle Bennet Van Horn is listed on p. 55. He was Homeroom President 11, 12; Homeroom Secretary 12. Lyle enjoys swimming and cars. He plans to join some branch of the service after he graduates.

More About Lyle Bennett VAN HORN:
Military service: Vietnam War
Occupation: Filmco in Streetsboro, OH
Religion: Indiana, PA United Presbyterian Church; Frostroad Chapel

More About Lyle VAN HORN and Virginia SHIELDS:
Private-Begin: Private

Children of Lyle VAN HORN and Virginia SHIELDS are:
     i.   Billy Joe[13] VAN HORN, b. Private.
    ii.   Melinda VAN HORN, b. Private; m. FRONEK, Private; b. Private.

More About FRONEK and Melinda VAN HORN:
Private-Begin: Private

 iii. Bonnie VAN HORN, b. Private; m. STUCZYNSKI, Private; b. Private.

More About STUCZYNSKI and Bonnie VAN HORN:
Private-Begin: Private

 iv. Krystal VAN HORN, b. Private.

527. Marianne[12] PETRUNEY *(Alice Belle[11] VAN HORN, Robert Lee Claire[10], Bennett Work[9], George Logan[8], Isaiah[7], Henry B.[6], Henry[5], Christian Barentsen[4] VAN HOORN, Barent Christiansen[3], Christian Barentsen[2], Barent Barents[1])* was born Private. She married Thomas JOHNSTON Private. He was born Private.

More About Thomas JOHNSTON and Marianne PETRUNEY:
Private-Begin: Private

Children of Marianne PETRUNEY and Thomas JOHNSTON are:
 i. Kelle Rae[13] JOHNSTON, b. Private.
 ii. Shelle Ann JOHNSTON, b. Private.

528. William[12] VAN HORN *(William Clyde[11], Robert Lee Claire[10], Bennett Work[9], George Logan[8], Isaiah[7], Henry B.[6], Henry[5], Christian Barentsen[4] VAN HOORN, Barent Christiansen[3], Christian Barentsen[2], Barent Barents[1])* was born Private.

Child of William VAN HORN is:
 i. Brian Edward[13] VAN HORN, b. Private.

529. Sharon[12] VAN HORN *(William Clyde[11], Robert Lee Claire[10], Bennett Work[9], George Logan[8], Isaiah[7], Henry B.[6], Henry[5], Christian Barentsen[4] VAN HOORN, Barent Christiansen[3], Christian Barentsen[2], Barent Barents[1])* was born Private. She married Gordon HASELY Private. He was born Private.

More About Gordon HASELY and Sharon VAN HORN:
Private-Begin: Private

Child of Sharon VAN HORN and Gordon HASELY is:
 i. Gordon[13] HASELY, JR, b. Private.

530. Thomas M.[12] VAN HORN *(Donald Charles[11], Robert Lee Claire[10], Bennett Work[9], George Logan[8], Isaiah[7], Henry B.[6], Henry[5], Christian Barentsen[4] VAN HOORN, Barent Christiansen[3], Christian Barentsen[2], Barent Barents[1])* was born Private.

Child of Thomas M. VAN HORN is:
 i. Julie[13] VAN HORN, b. Private.

531. Donna Lynn[12] VAN HORN *(Donald Charles[11], Robert Lee Claire[10], Bennett Work[9], George Logan[8], Isaiah[7], Henry B.[6], Henry[5], Christian Barentsen[4] VAN HOORN, Barent Christiansen[3], Christian Barentsen[2],*

Barent Barents[1])[5329] was born 1957, and died 1992. She married George BOLVIN Private. He was born Private.

More About George BOLVIN and Donna VAN HORN:
Private-Begin: Private

Children of Donna VAN HORN and George BOLVIN are:
    i.   Donald[13] BOLVIN, b. Private.
   ii.   Jeremy BOLVIN, b. Private.

532. Donald H.[12] LAMBING *(Carrie Etta[11] VAN HORN, James Ira[10], Bennett Work[9], George Logan[8], Isaiah[7], Henry B.[6], Henry[5], Christian Barentsen[4] VAN HOORN, Barent Christiansen[3], Christian Barentsen[2], Barent Barents[1])* was born Private. He married ? LOWMAN Private, daughter of Worth LOWMAN. She was born Private.

More About Donald LAMBING and ? LOWMAN:
Private-Begin: Private

Child of Donald LAMBING and ? LOWMAN is:
    i.   Donald[13] LAMBING, b. Private.

533. Dale Robert[12] LAMBING *(Carrie Etta[11] VAN HORN, James Ira[10], Bennett Work[9], George Logan[8], Isaiah[7], Henry B.[6], Henry[5], Christian Barentsen[4] VAN HOORN, Barent Christiansen[3], Christian Barentsen[2], Barent Barents[1])[5330,5331,5332]* was born 05 Jun 1934 in Indiana Cnty, PA, and died 16 Sep 1967 in Armstrong Cnty, PA[5332]. He married (1) Margaret HARDY Private. She was born Private. He married (2) Louella Madge LONG Private, daughter of Elmer LONG. She was born Private.

More About Dale Robert LAMBING:
Military service: US Marine Corp
Occupation: United Door

More About Dale LAMBING and Margaret HARDY:
Private-Begin: Private

More About Dale LAMBING and Louella LONG:
Private-Begin: Private

Child of Dale LAMBING and Margaret HARDY is:
    i.   Dale Robert[13] LAMBING, JR, b. 22 Dec 1956, NC; d. 16 Sep 1967.

Children of Dale LAMBING and Louella LONG are:
   ii.   Sharon Irene[13] LAMBING, b. Private.
  iii.   Linda LAMBING, b. Private.

534. Betty M.[12] WEAVER *(Deloris Belle[11] VAN HORN, James Ira[10], Bennett Work[9], George Logan[8], Isaiah[7], Henry B.[6], Henry[5], Christian Barentsen[4] VAN HOORN, Barent Christiansen[3], Christian Barentsen[2], Barent Barents[1])[5333]* was born 04 Aug 1932 in South Mahoning Twp., Indiana Cnty, PA, and died 30 Jul 1999 in Kittanning, Armstrong Cnty, PA. She married Clair PEFFER[5333]. He was born 03 Aug 1924, and died 25 Jul 2005.

Children of Betty WEAVER and Clair PEFFER are:

    i.   Ronald C.[13] PEFFER, b. Private.

    ii.   Ella Mae PEFFER, b. Private; m. DOWN, Private; b. Private.

            More About DOWN and Ella PEFFER:
            Private-Begin: Private

    iii.   Jane PEFFER, b. Private; m. COCHRAN, Private; b. Private.

            More About COCHRAN and Jane PEFFER:
            Private-Begin: Private

    iv.   Connie L. PEFFER, b. Private.

535. Annabelle[12] WEAVER *(Deloris Belle[11] VAN HORN, James Ira[10], Bennett Work[9], George Logan[8], Isaiah[7], Henry B.[6], Henry[5], Christian Barentsen[4] VAN HOORN, Barent Christiansen[3], Christian Barentsen[2], Barent Barents[1])[5333]* was born 06 Sep 1934 in Plumville, Indiana Cnty, PA, and died 22 Jul 1996 in Pittsburgh, Allegheny Cnty, PA. She married William Robert WEAVER, JR[5333], son of William Robert WEAVER. He died 1977.

Children of Annabelle WEAVER and William WEAVER are:

    i.   Carol[13] WEAVER, b. Private; m. ELKIN, Private; b. Private.

            More About ELKIN and Carol WEAVER:
            Private-Begin: Private

    ii.   Bonnie WEAVER, b. Private; m. DEAN, Private; b. Private.

            More About DEAN and Bonnie WEAVER:
            Private-Begin: Private

    iii.   Bobbie WEAVER, b. Private; m. SUTTER, Private; b. Private.

            More About SUTTER and Bobbie WEAVER:
            Private-Begin: Private

    iv.   Willam Robert WEAVER III, b. Private.
    v.   Larry WEAVER, b. Private.
    vi.   Glenn WEAVER, b. Private.
    vii.   Dan WEAVER, b. Private.
    viii.   Delphis WEAVER, b. Private.
    ix.   Dennis WEAVER, b. Private.

536. Vernie M.[12] WEAVER *(Deloris Belle[11] VAN HORN, James Ira[10], Bennett Work[9], George Logan[8], Isaiah[7], Henry B.[6], Henry[5], Christian Barentsen[4] VAN HOORN, Barent Christiansen[3], Christian Barentsen[2], Barent Barents[1])[5333]* died 1989. She married Blair I. SHANK, JR[5333], son of Blair SHANK and Wilda HICKS. He was born 28 Mar 1933 in Indiana Cnty, PA, and died 05 Apr 2003 in Punxsutawney, PA.

Children of Vernie WEAVER and Blair SHANK are:

627.   i.   Thomas Wayne[13] SHANK, b. Private.

ii.   Richard L. SHANK, b. Private; m. Sandra, Private; b. Private.

More About Richard SHANK and Sandra:
Private-Begin: Private

537. Larry A.[12] RUPERT *(Twila May[11] VAN HORN, Harry Bennett[10], Bennett Work[9], George Logan[8], Isaiah[7], Henry B.[6], Henry[5], Christian Barentsen[4] VAN HOORN, Barent Christiansen[3], Christian Barentsen[2], Barent Barents[1])* was born Private. He married Audrey Darlene NEWSOM Private, daughter of Robert E. NEWSOM. She was born Private.

More About Larry RUPERT and Audrey NEWSOM:
Private-Begin: Private

Child of Larry RUPERT and Audrey NEWSOM is:
    i.   Michael Shawn[13] RUPERT, b. Private.

538. Beverly Jean[12] RUPERT *(Twila May[11] VAN HORN, Harry Bennett[10], Bennett Work[9], George Logan[8], Isaiah[7], Henry B.[6], Henry[5], Christian Barentsen[4] VAN HOORN, Barent Christiansen[3], Christian Barentsen[2], Barent Barents[1])* was born Private. She married Keith Edward WELTEROTH Private, son of Edward WELTEROTH. He was born Private.

More About Keith WELTEROTH and Beverly RUPERT:
Private-Begin: Private

Child of Beverly RUPERT and Keith WELTEROTH is:
    i.   Matthew[13] WELTEROTH, b. Private.

539. Patricia Ann[12] RUPERT *(Twila May[11] VAN HORN, Harry Bennett[10], Bennett Work[9], George Logan[8], Isaiah[7], Henry B.[6], Henry[5], Christian Barentsen[4] VAN HOORN, Barent Christiansen[3], Christian Barentsen[2], Barent Barents[1])[5334]* was born 18 Nov 1959 in Indiana, Indiana Cnty, PA[5334], and died Aft. 2002. She married Leo Burnell JEWART, JR Private, son of Leo JEWART and Isabelle SCARRY. He was born Private.

More About Leo JEWART and Patricia RUPERT:
Private-Begin: Private

Child of Patricia RUPERT and Leo JEWART is:
628.   i.   Jody Lynn[13] JEWART, b. Private.

540. Lawrence Carl[12] GOOD *(Lawrence Kenneth[11], Pearl Agnes[10] VAN HORN, Bennett Work[9], George Logan[8], Isaiah[7], Henry B.[6], Henry[5], Christian Barentsen[4] VAN HOORN, Barent Christiansen[3], Christian Barentsen[2], Barent Barents[1])* was born Private. He married Charlene WILSON Private. She was born Private.

More About Lawrence GOOD and Charlene WILSON:
Private-Begin: Private

Children of Lawrence GOOD and Charlene WILSON are:
    i.   Leonard Carl[13] GOOD, b. Private.

     ii.   Steven Michael GOOD, b. Private.
    iii.   Barbara GOOD, b. Private.

541. Jack Nelson[12] GOOD *(Lawrence Kenneth[11], Pearl Agnes[10] VAN HORN, Bennett Work[9], George Logan[8], Isaiah[7], Henry B.[6], Henry[5], Christian Barentsen[4] VAN HOORN, Barent Christiansen[3], Christian Barentsen[2], Barent Barents[1])* was born Private. He married Barbara STEWART Private. She was born Private.

More About Jack GOOD and Barbara STEWART:
Private-Begin: Private

Child of Jack GOOD and Barbara STEWART is:
     i.   Randy[13] GOOD, b. Private.

542. Richard Ernest[12] GOOD *(Ernest Glenn[11], Pearl Agnes[10] VAN HORN, Bennett Work[9], George Logan[8], Isaiah[7], Henry B.[6], Henry[5], Christian Barentsen[4] VAN HOORN, Barent Christiansen[3], Christian Barentsen[2], Barent Barents[1])* was born Private. He married Isabelle Mae ALABRAN Private, daughter of Frank ALABRAN and Martha. She was born Private.

More About Richard GOOD and Isabelle ALABRAN:
Private-Begin: Private

Children of Richard GOOD and Isabelle ALABRAN are:
     i.   Lois Arlene[13] GOOD, b. Private.
    ii.   Michael Glenn GOOD, b. Private.

543. Arnold Clarence[12] HAYES *(Alice Belle[11] GOOD, Pearl Agnes[10] VAN HORN, Bennett Work[9], George Logan[8], Isaiah[7], Henry B.[6], Henry[5], Christian Barentsen[4] VAN HOORN, Barent Christiansen[3], Christian Barentsen[2], Barent Barents[1])* was born Private. He married (1) Linda M. VANDIVNER Private. She was born Private. He married (2) Linda Kathleen METZ Private, daughter of Albert METZ. She was born Private. He married (3) Gloria Private. She was born Private.

More About Arnold HAYES and Linda VANDIVNER:
Private-Begin: Private

More About Arnold HAYES and Linda METZ:
Private-Begin: Private

More About Arnold HAYES and Gloria:
Private-Begin: Private

Child of Arnold HAYES and Linda VANDIVNER is:
     i.   Matthew[13] HAYES, d. 10 Nov 1973.

544. Rheta[12] HAYES *(Alice Belle[11] GOOD, Pearl Agnes[10] VAN HORN, Bennett Work[9], George Logan[8], Isaiah[7], Henry B.[6], Henry[5], Christian Barentsen[4] VAN HOORN, Barent Christiansen[3], Christian Barentsen[2], Barent Barents[1])* was born Private. She married Daniel Alan REED Private. He was born Private.

More About Daniel REED and Rheta HAYES:

Private-Begin: Private

Child of Rheta HAYES and Daniel REED is:
     i.   Timothy[13] REED, d. 12 Dec 1993.

545. Barbara Elaine[12] HAYES *(Alice Belle[11] GOOD, Pearl Agnes[10] VAN HORN, Bennett Work[9], George Logan[8], Isaiah[7], Henry B.[6], Henry[5], Christian Barentsen[4] VAN HOORN, Barent Christiansen[3], Christian Barentsen[2], Barent Barents[1])* was born Private. She married Gene Robert MASTELLER Private. He was born Private.

More About Gene MASTELLER and Barbara HAYES:
Private-Begin: Private

Child of Barbara HAYES and Gene MASTELLER is:
     i.   John E.[13] MASTELLER, b. Private.

546. Terry Lee[12] LUCE *(Lola Stella[11] GOOD, Pearl Agnes[10] VAN HORN, Bennett Work[9], George Logan[8], Isaiah[7], Henry B.[6], Henry[5], Christian Barentsen[4] VAN HOORN, Barent Christiansen[3], Christian Barentsen[2], Barent Barents[1])* was born Private. He married Doris Marie SMITH Private, daughter of Albert E. SMITH. She was born Private.

More About Terry LUCE and Doris SMITH:
Private-Begin: Private

Children of Terry LUCE and Doris SMITH are:
     i.   Tina Diane[13] LUCE, b. Private; m. Daniel Edward DONAHUE, Private; b. Private.

            More About Daniel DONAHUE and Tina LUCE:
            Private-Begin: Private

    ii.   Denis Renee LUCE, b. Private; m. David J. THOMAS, Private; b. Private.

            More About David THOMAS and Denis LUCE:
            Private-Begin: Private

    iii.   Tracy Autumn LUCE, b. Private.

547. Connie Eileen[12] LUCE *(Lola Stella[11] GOOD, Pearl Agnes[10] VAN HORN, Bennett Work[9], George Logan[8], Isaiah[7], Henry B.[6], Henry[5], Christian Barentsen[4] VAN HOORN, Barent Christiansen[3], Christian Barentsen[2], Barent Barents[1])* was born Private. She married Edward Daniel BODENHORN Private, son of Glenn BODENHORN. He was born Private.

More About Edward BODENHORN and Connie LUCE:
Private-Begin: Private

Children of Connie LUCE and Edward BODENHORN are:
     i.   Amy Suzanne[13] BODENHORN, b. Private.
    ii.   Bridget Marie BODENHORN, b. Private.
    iii.   Edward Glenn BODENHORN, b. Private.

548. William Dale[12] MCKEE, JR *(Geraldine[11] VAN HORN, Norman Clarence[10], Bennett Work[9], George Logan[8], Isaiah[7], Henry B.[6], Henry[5], Christian Barentsen[4] VAN HOORN, Barent Christiansen[3], Christian Barentsen[2], Barent Barents[1])* was born Private.

Child of William Dale MCKEE, JR is:
      i. Emily Lynn[13] MCKEE, b. Private.

549. Charles Scott[12] BROOKS *(Lavona[11] VAN HORN, Norman Clarence[10], Bennett Work[9], George Logan[8], Isaiah[7], Henry B.[6], Henry[5], Christian Barentsen[4] VAN HOORN, Barent Christiansen[3], Christian Barentsen[2], Barent Barents[1])* was born Private. He married Roxane MARSHALL Private, daughter of Robert MARSHALL and Dorothy REEFER. She was born Private.

More About Charles BROOKS and Roxane MARSHALL:
Private-Begin: Private

Children of Charles BROOKS and Roxane MARSHALL are:
      i. Charles[13] BROOKS, b. Private.
     ii. Cari Michelle BROOKS, b. Private.

550. ?[12] TALLEY *(Virginia E.[11] VAN HORN, Norman Clarence[10], Bennett Work[9], George Logan[8], Isaiah[7], Henry B.[6], Henry[5], Christian Barentsen[4] VAN HOORN, Barent Christiansen[3], Christian Barentsen[2], Barent Barents[1])* was born Private. She married Thomas L. STREAMS Private. He was born Private.

More About Thomas STREAMS and ? TALLEY:
Private-Begin: Private

Child of ? TALLEY and Thomas STREAMS is:
      i. Stacie Lynn[13] STREAMS, b. Private.

Generation No. 7

551. Mary Elizabeth[13] VAN HORN *(Judson Tannehill[12], Judson Tannehill[11], Henry D. Foster[10], John Dick[9], Alexander[8], Isaiah[7], Henry B.[6], Henry[5], Christian Barentsen[4] VAN HOORN, Barent Christiansen[3], Christian Barentsen[2], Barent Barents[1])* was born Private. She married Steven LARISCY Private. He was born Private.

More About Steven LARISCY and Mary VAN HORN:
Private-Begin: Private

Children of Mary VAN HORN and Steven LARISCY are:
629.   i. Angela[14] LARISCY, b. Private.
        ii. Dianne LARISCY, b. Private.
      iii. Michael LARISCY, b. Private.
      iv. Christina LARISCY, b. Private.

552. Patricia Louise[13] VAN HORN *(Judson Tannehill[12], Judson Tannehill[11], Henry D. Foster[10], John Dick[9], Alexander[8], Isaiah[7], Henry B.[6], Henry[5], Christian Barentsen[4] VAN HOORN, Barent Christiansen[3], Christian Barentsen[2], Barent Barents[1])* was born Private. She married PRESSLEY Private. He was born Private.

More About PRESSLEY and Patricia VAN HORN:
Private-Begin: Private

Children of Patricia VAN HORN and PRESSLEY are:
      i.   Adrian[14] PRESSLEY, b. Private.
630.   ii. Margaret PRESSLEY, b. Private.

553. Charles Lee (GRAVES)[13] TARPLEY, JR *(Eunice Matilda[12] VAN HORN, Judson Tannehill[11], Henry D. Foster[10], John Dick[9], Alexander[8], Isaiah[7], Henry B.[6], Henry[5], Christian Barentsen[4] VAN HOORN, Barent Christiansen[3], Christian Barentsen[2], Barent Barents[1])* was born Private. He married Margaret Jeane BROYLES[5335] Private, daughter of Charles BROYLES and Margaret JOHNSON. She was born 24 Jul 1943 in Valdosta, GA[5335], and died 15 Jul 2006 in Valdosta, GA[5335].

More About Charles TARPLEY and Margaret BROYLES:
Private-Begin: Private

Children of Charles TARPLEY and Margaret BROYLES are:
      i.   Bradley Christopher (GRAVES)[14] TARPLEY, b. Private; m. Mary Clare DIPLANTIS, Private; b. Private.

          More About Bradley TARPLEY and Mary DIPLANTIS:
          Private-Begin: Private

     ii. Lee Edward (GRAVES) TARPLEY, b. Private; m. Maurie Carol HINSON, Private; b. Private.

          More About Lee TARPLEY and Maurie HINSON:
          Private-Begin: Private

554. Peter Harold[13] TARPLEY *(Eunice Matilda[12] VAN HORN, Judson Tannehill[11], Henry D. Foster[10], John Dick[9], Alexander[8], Isaiah[7], Henry B.[6], Henry[5], Christian Barentsen[4] VAN HOORN, Barent Christiansen[3], Christian Barentsen[2], Barent Barents[1])* was born Private. He married Raven Simkins GRAYDON Private, daughter of Augustus GRAYDON and Marion HUNT. She was born Private.

More About Peter TARPLEY and Raven GRAYDON:
Private-Begin: Private

Child of Peter TARPLEY and Raven GRAYDON is:
      i.   Raven Lewis[14] TARPLEY, b. Private.

555. Jacqueline Ann[13] MARSHALL *(Mary Ella[12] VAN HORN, Judson Tannehill[11], Henry D. Foster[10], John Dick[9], Alexander[8], Isaiah[7], Henry B.[6], Henry[5], Christian Barentsen[4] VAN HOORN, Barent Christiansen[3], Christian Barentsen[2], Barent Barents[1])* was born Private. She married (1) Herbert Fargo CLARK Private. He was born Private. She married (2) Frank Gordon WILLEY, JR Private, son of Frank WILLEY and Jennie GRIVE. He was born Private.

More About Herbert CLARK and Jacqueline MARSHALL:
Private-Begin: Private

More About Frank WILLEY and Jacqueline MARSHALL:
Private-Begin: Private

Child of Jacqueline MARSHALL and Frank WILLEY is:
631.   i.   Melody Frances[14] WILLEY, b. Private.

556. Frank Martin[13] ASHCOM, JR *(Frank Martin[12], James Donald[11], Margaret Mary[10] VAN HORN, James Wherry[9], Alexander[8], Isaiah[7], Henry B.[6], Henry[5], Christian Barentsen[4] VAN HOORN, Barent Christiansen[3], Christian Barentsen[2], Barent Barents[1])* was born Private. He married Sandra Lee BERKLEY Private. She was born Private.

More About Frank ASHCOM and Sandra BERKLEY:
Private-Begin: Private

Children of Frank ASHCOM and Sandra BERKLEY are:
632.   i.   Kelly Ann[14] ASHCOM, b. Private.
633.   ii.   Tina Marie ASHCOM, b. Private.
        iii.   Vickie Lynn ASHCOM, b. Private.

557. Sandra Lee[13] ASHCOM *(Frank Martin[12], James Donald[11], Margaret Mary[10] VAN HORN, James Wherry[9], Alexander[8], Isaiah[7], Henry B.[6], Henry[5], Christian Barentsen[4] VAN HOORN, Barent Christiansen[3], Christian Barentsen[2], Barent Barents[1])* was born Private. She married William TINCKER Private. He was born Private.

More About William TINCKER and Sandra ASHCOM:
Private-Begin: Private

Child of Sandra ASHCOM and William TINCKER is:
        i.   Susanne Marie[14] TINCKER, b. Private.

558. Nana Pearl[13] WINEBRENNER *(Mary Elizabeth[12] ASHCOM, James Donald[11], Margaret Mary[10] VAN HORN, James Wherry[9], Alexander[8], Isaiah[7], Henry B.[6], Henry[5], Christian Barentsen[4] VAN HOORN, Barent Christiansen[3], Christian Barentsen[2], Barent Barents[1])* was born Private. She married Charles SEIRING, JR Private, son of Charles SEIRING. He was born Private.

More About Charles SEIRING and Nana WINEBRENNER:
Private-Begin: Private

Child of Nana WINEBRENNER and Charles SEIRING is:
        i.   Charles[14] SEIRING III, b. Private.

559. Norma Davene[13] HUDSON *(Emma Elizabeth[12] WOLF, Leafy Fern[11] VAN HORN, Samuel Cornelius[10], Henry Coulter[9], Alexander[8], Isaiah[7], Henry B.[6], Henry[5], Christian Barentsen[4] VAN HOORN, Barent Christiansen[3], Christian Barentsen[2], Barent Barents[1])* was born 23 Jul 1929 in Dayton, Montgomery Cnty, OH, and died 27 May 2007 in Toledo, Lucas Cnty, OH. She married Sheldon Henry SCHIMMEL 31 Dec 1949 in Beavercreek, OH. He was born 12 Mar 1928 in Rockyridge, OH, and died 05 Oct 2001 in Toledo, Lucas Cnty, OH.

Notes for Norma Davene HUDSON:

Davene Schimmel 1929-2007
SCHIMMEL N. Davene "Davene" Davene Schimmel, 77, of West Toledo, passed away May 27, 2007, in The Toledo Hospital due to complications after a recent heart attack. She was born July 23, 1929, in Dayton, Ohio to Samuel and Elizabeth (Wolf) Hudson. She graduated from Hillsboro High School in 1947. She was a United Methodist Lay Minister, Volunteer Chaplain at Flower Hospital and an active member and leader of Hope United Methodist Church. She was involved in numerous charities and organizations including the Red Cross, Interfaith Blood Drive for the last 18 years, most recently the President of the Flower Hospital Guild and as a member of the board of the Flower Hospital, just to name a few. Davene was preceded in death by her husband, Rusty and son, Bruce. She is survived by her daughters, Melanee (David Wagner) and Shelda Schimmel; grandson, Bruce Schimmel II; granddaughter, Kody Turner-Schimmel; brother, Rod (Cleta) Haas; sisters, Bev (Paul) Lucas and Marcia (Gerald) Boyd; many nieces, nephews, cousins and special friends. Remember Me A child of God, daughter, granddaughter, wife, mother, grandmother, sister, aunt, niece, cousin and friend. That is what my life has been. One single rose is all I ask to remember me. "I request that no flowers but a single rose be sent by anyone who wishes to express from their heart who remembers me. Those who want to do more please consider giving a contribution to one of the following: Hope United Methodist Church, Friendly Center, Cherry Street Mission, Harbor House on Cherry Street (all located in Toledo) or the Home of Mercy in Williston, Ohio." The family would like to express their deepest gratitude to all those who were part of the wonderful care received during her stay in the Cardiac Recovery Unit at The Toledo Hospital. Services will be 10:00 a.m. Wednesday in the Ansberg-West Funeral Home with Rev. John Richards officiating, where friends are invited to visit from 5:00 to 9:00 p.m. Tuesday. Interment in Willow Cemetery. Online condolences may be sent to www.ansberg-west.com
Published in the Toledo Blade from 5/28/2007 - 5/29/2007

More About Norma Davene HUDSON:
Burial: 30 May 2007, Willow Cemetery, Pickle Rd, Oregon, Lucas Cnty, OH

More About Sheldon Henry SCHIMMEL:
Burial: 08 Oct 2001, Willow Cemetery, Oregon, Lucas Cnty, OH[5336]
Military service: WW II Merchant Marines
Occupation: Sheet Metal Worker Local6/33 Union and Master Engraver
Religion: Hope United Methodist Church, Toledo, OH

More About Sheldon SCHIMMEL and Norma HUDSON:
Marriage: 31 Dec 1949, Beavercreek, OH
Marriage date: Married in the home of Marriana and Mal Frank[5337]

Children of Norma HUDSON and Sheldon SCHIMMEL are:
      i.   Bruce Douglas[14] SCHIMMEL, b. 20 Dec 1956, Toledo, Lucas Cnty, OH; d. Bet. 29 - 30 Jan 1958, Toledo, OH.
634.   ii. Melanee Sue SCHIMMEL, b. Private.
635.   iii. Shelda Lynn SCHIMMEL, b. Private.

560. Beverly Ann[13] HAAS *(Emma Elizabeth[12] WOLF, Leafy Fern[11] VAN HORN, Samuel Cornelius[10], Henry Coulter[9], Alexander[8], Isaiah[7], Henry B.[6], Henry[5], Christian Barentsen[4] VAN HOORN, Barent Christiansen[3], Christian Barentsen[2], Barent Barents[1])* was born Private. She married Paul Ray LUCAS Private. He was born Private.

More About Paul LUCAS and Beverly HAAS:
Private-Begin: Private

Child of Beverly HAAS and Paul LUCAS is:
636.   i.   Paula Diane[14] LUCUS, b. Private.

561. Rodney Albert[13] HAAS *(Emma Elizabeth[12] WOLF, Leafy Fern[11] VAN HORN, Samuel Cornelius[10], Henry Coulter[9], Alexander[8], Isaiah[7], Henry B.[6], Henry[5], Christian Barentsen[4] VAN HOORN, Barent Christiansen[3], Christian Barentsen[2], Barent Barents[1])* was born Private. He married Cleta STUBBLEFIELD Private. She was born Private.

More About Rodney HAAS and Cleta STUBBLEFIELD:
Private-Begin: Private

Children of Rodney HAAS and Cleta STUBBLEFIELD are:
637.   i.   Vicki Lynn[14] HAAS, b. Private.
        ii.   Lisa Carol HAAS, b. Private.

562. Marcia Kay[13] HAAS *(Emma Elizabeth[12] WOLF, Leafy Fern[11] VAN HORN, Samuel Cornelius[10], Henry Coulter[9], Alexander[8], Isaiah[7], Henry B.[6], Henry[5], Christian Barentsen[4] VAN HOORN, Barent Christiansen[3], Christian Barentsen[2], Barent Barents[1])* was born Private. She married Gerald BOYD Private. He was born Private.

More About Gerald BOYD and Marcia HAAS:
Private-Begin: Private

Child of Marcia HAAS and Gerald BOYD is:
        i.   Julie Ann[14] BOYD, b. Private.

563. Malcolm David[13] FRANK *(Marianna[12] WOLF, Leafy Fern[11] VAN HORN, Samuel Cornelius[10], Henry Coulter[9], Alexander[8], Isaiah[7], Henry B.[6], Henry[5], Christian Barentsen[4] VAN HOORN, Barent Christiansen[3], Christian Barentsen[2], Barent Barents[1])* was born Private. He married Patti SWINK Private. She was born Private.

More About Malcolm FRANK and Patti SWINK:
Private-Begin: Private

Children of Malcolm FRANK and Patti SWINK are:
638.   i.   Rise" Ka[14] FRANK, b. Private.
639.   ii.   Jennifer FRANK, b. Private.

564. Dr. Johnie Derald[13] MORGAN, SR. *(Avis Ruth[12] WOLF, Leafy Fern[11] VAN HORN, Samuel Cornelius[10], Henry Coulter[9], Alexander[8], Isaiah[7], Henry B.[6], Henry[5], Christian Barentsen[4] VAN HOORN, Barent Christiansen[3], Christian Barentsen[2], Barent Barents[1])* was born Private. He married Elizabeth June MCKNEELY Private, daughter of Eldridge MCKNEELY and Lucile JACKSON. She was born Private.

More About Johnie MORGAN and Elizabeth MCKNEELY:
Private-Begin: Private

Children of Johnie MORGAN and Elizabeth MCKNEELY are:
640.   i.   Laura Elizabeth[14] MORGAN, b. Private.

641.   ii.   Kimberly Ann MORGAN, b. Private.
642.   iii. Rebecca Ruth MORGAN, b. Private.
643.   iv. Johnie Derald MORGAN, JR, b. Private.

565. Ruth Fern[13] MORGAN *(Avis Ruth[12] WOLF, Leafy Fern[11] VAN HORN, Samuel Cornelius[10], Henry Coulter[9], Alexander[8], Isaiah[7], Henry B.[6], Henry[5], Christian Barentsen[4] VAN HOORN, Barent Christiansen[3], Christian Barentsen[2], Barent Barents[1])* was born Private. She married Alvin Albert HAGG Private. He was born Private.

More About Alvin HAGG and Ruth MORGAN:
Private-Begin: Private

Children of Ruth MORGAN and Alvin HAGG are:
644.   i.   Sheryl Ann[14] HAGG, b. Private.
645.   ii. Jeffrey Alvin HAGG, b. Private.
646.   iii. Deborah Ruth HAGG, b. Private.
        iv. Deanna Elizabeth HAGG, b. Private.

566. Michael Melvin[13] MORGAN *(Avis Ruth[12] WOLF, Leafy Fern[11] VAN HORN, Samuel Cornelius[10], Henry Coulter[9], Alexander[8], Isaiah[7], Henry B.[6], Henry[5], Christian Barentsen[4] VAN HOORN, Barent Christiansen[3], Christian Barentsen[2], Barent Barents[1])* was born Private. He married Cynthia Ann SMITH Private. She was born Private.

More About Michael MORGAN and Cynthia SMITH:
Private-Begin: Private

Children of Michael MORGAN and Cynthia SMITH are:
        i.   James Michael[14] MORGAN, b. Private.
        ii. Ashley Nicole MORGAN, b. Private.

567. Larry[13] CECIL *(Thelma Louise[12] WOLF, Leafy Fern[11] VAN HORN, Samuel Cornelius[10], Henry Coulter[9], Alexander[8], Isaiah[7], Henry B.[6], Henry[5], Christian Barentsen[4] VAN HOORN, Barent Christiansen[3], Christian Barentsen[2], Barent Barents[1])* was born Private. He married (1) Carol ? Private. She was born Private. He married (2) Pamela SCHALTZ Private. She was born Private.

More About Larry CECIL and Carol ?:
Private-Begin: Private

More About Larry CECIL and Pamela SCHALTZ:
Private-Begin: Private

Child of Larry CECIL and Carol ? is:
        i.   Katy[14] CECIL, b. Private.

Child of Larry CECIL and Pamela SCHALTZ is:
        ii. Tony Anthony[14] CECIL, b. Private.

568. Judy[13] CECIL *(Thelma Louise[12] WOLF, Leafy Fern[11] VAN HORN, Samuel Cornelius[10], Henry*

Coulter⁹, Alexander⁸, Isaiah⁷, Henry B.⁶, Henry⁵, Christian Barentsen⁴ VAN HOORN, Barent Christiansen³, Christian Barentsen², Barent Barents¹) was born Private. She married Ronnie D. LINDSEY Private. He was born Private.

More About Ronnie LINDSEY and Judy CECIL:
Private-Begin: Private

Children of Judy CECIL and Ronnie LINDSEY are:
    i.   Chad Michael¹⁴ LINDSEY, b. 22 Nov 1977, Dayton, Montgomery Cnty, OH; d. 14 Nov 2007, Dayton, Montgomery Cnty, OH.
   ii.   Matthew Dawson LINDSEY, b. Private.

569. Richard Alan¹³ MCELHOES *(Waldo Steele¹², Frank Thomas¹¹, John Kinter¹⁰, Isaiah⁹, Jane⁸ VAN HORN, Isaiah⁷, Henry B.⁶, Henry⁵, Christian Barentsen⁴ VAN HOORN, Barent Christiansen³, Christian Barentsen², Barent Barents¹)* was born Private. He married (1) Phyllis Rose WITWICKI Private, daughter of Frank WITWICKI and Josephine WASIO. She was born Private. He married (2) Gertude Genowefa DUDZINSKI Private, daughter of Joseph DUDZINSKI and Wanda JAKUBOWSKI. She was born Private.

More About Richard MCELHOES and Phyllis WITWICKI:
Private-Begin: Private

More About Richard MCELHOES and Gertude DUDZINSKI:
Private-Begin: Private

Children of Richard MCELHOES and Phyllis WITWICKI are:
    i.   Carol Anne¹⁴ MCELHOES, b. Private; m. Benjamin ZAJAC, Private; b. Private.

       More About Benjamin ZAJAC and Carol MCELHOES:
       Private-Begin: Private

   ii.   Leslie Margaret MCELHOES, b. Private; m. David KEEFE, Private; b. Private.

       More About David KEEFE and Leslie MCELHOES:
       Private-Begin: Private

Child of Richard MCELHOES and Gertude DUDZINSKI is:
   iii.   David M.¹⁴ MCELHOES, b. Private.

570. Betty Jane¹³ O'ROURKE *(Jennie Elizabeth¹² VAN HORN, William Burton¹¹, John Neff¹⁰, Benjamin Briggs⁹, Joshua⁸, Isaiah⁷, Henry B.⁶, Henry⁵, Christian Barentsen⁴ VAN HOORN, Barent Christiansen³, Christian Barentsen², Barent Barents¹)⁵³³⁸* was born 06 Oct 1928 in Omaha, Douglas Cnty, NE⁵³³⁸, and died 23 May 1980 in Dallas, Dallas Cnty, TX. She married John Dwight WEEKS 10 Jan 1948 in Annapolis, Ann Arundel, MD. He was born 06 Oct 1928 in Omaha, Douglas Cnty, NE, and died 15 Oct 1991 in Richardson, Dallas Cnty, TX.

More About John WEEKS and Betty O'ROURKE:
Marriage: 10 Jan 1948, Annapolis, Ann Arundel, MD

Child of Betty O'ROURKE and John WEEKS is:
    i.   ?¹⁴ WEEKS, b. Private.

571. Robert William[13] BENISH *(Inez Vernal[12] VAN HORN, Robert Campbell[11], John Neff[10], Benjamin Briggs[9], Joshua[8], Isaiah[7], Henry B.[6], Henry[5], Christian Barentsen[4] VAN HOORN, Barent Christiansen[3], Christian Barentsen[2], Barent Barents[1])* was born Private. He married (1) Marian Adell TUPPER Private, daughter of Edward TUPPER and Delores BERGLUND. She was born Private. He married (2) Lois Jean LOKSTAD Private. She was born Private.

More About Robert BENISH and Marian TUPPER:
Private-Begin: Private

More About Robert BENISH and Lois LOKSTAD:
Private-Begin: Private

Children of Robert BENISH and Marian TUPPER are:
        i.   William Carl[14] BENISH, b. Private; m. Robin Amiee PUFFENBARGER, Private; b. Private.

          More About William BENISH and Robin PUFFENBARGER:
          Private-Begin: Private

647.   ii. Billie Burnetta DESPAIN, b. Private.
       iii. Robert Edward DESPAIN, b. Private.
       iv. Ronald Wendell DESPAIN, b. Private.
       v. Bonnie Christine DESPAIN, b. Private; m. Roger Larry SWANSON, Private; b. Private.

          More About Roger SWANSON and Bonnie DESPAIN:
          Private-Begin: Private

572. Richard Glenn[13] VAN HORN *(Andrew Glenn[12], Orin Denton[11], James Harvey[10], Benjamin Briggs[9], Joshua[8], Isaiah[7], Henry B.[6], Henry[5], Christian Barentsen[4] VAN HOORN, Barent Christiansen[3], Christian Barentsen[2], Barent Barents[1])[5339,5340,5341,5342]* was born 08 Jan 1923 in Creekside, PA[5343,5344], and died 20 Nov 1967 in Punxsutawney, Jefferson Cnty, PA[5345]. He married Louise HODGE[5345,5346,5347] 28 Oct 1950. She died Aft. 1994.

Notes for Richard Glenn VAN HORN:
    The 1947 Punxsutawney City directory has him living at 222 Pine with parents and that he is a freight checker for the B&O Railroad.
    The 1951 Punxsutawney Con Survey lists him living at 104 Ridge Ave in the home of M. E. Haney.

More About Richard Glenn VAN HORN:
Burial: Unknown, Lakelawn Memorial Park near Reynoldsville, PA[5347]
Cause of Death: Heart Attack
Lived: Punxsutawney, Jefferson Cnty, PA
Military service: WW II Navy Boatswain Mate 2/c[5347]
Occupation: Clerk Riker Yards of the B&O Railroad
Organizations: Coudersport Consistory, VFW, Mason
Religion: Methodist

More About Richard VAN HORN and Louise HODGE:

Marriage: 28 Oct 1950

Children of Richard VAN HORN and Louise HODGE are:
648.   i.   Richard Glenn[14] VAN HORN, JR, b. Bet. 1951 - 1967; d. Aft. 2005.
            ii.   Tammy VAN HORN, b. Private.

573. Frank O.[13] VAN HORN *(Andrew Glenn[12], Orin Denton[11], James Harvey[10], Benjamin Briggs[9], Joshua[8], Isaiah[7], Henry B.[6], Henry[5], Christian Barentsen[4] VAN HOORN, Barent Christiansen[3], Christian Barentsen[2], Barent Barents[1])[5348,5349,5350]* was born 15 Nov 1924 in Punxsutawney, Jefferson Cnty, PA[5350], and died 08 Jul 1971 in Tonawanda, Erie Cnty, NY. He married Antoinette SALVAGGIO[5351]. She died Aft. 1971.

Notes for Frank O. VAN HORN:
        The 1947 Punxsutawney City Directory lists Frank and wife Antoinette living at 346 Pine with no employment listed.
        The 1951 Punxsutawney con Survey Directory list Frank Van Horn at the home of Serian Dominick at the address of 111 Chestnut South.

More About Frank O. VAN HORN:
Lived: North Tonawanda, NY
Military service: WW II Navy

Children of Frank VAN HORN and Antoinette SALVAGGIO are:
            i.   James[14] VAN HORN, b. Private.
           ii.   William VAN HORN, b. Private.
          iii.   Michael VAN HORN, b. Private.
           iv.   Mary VAN HORN, b. Private.
            v.   Deborah VAN HORN, b. Private.
           vi.   Allison VAN HORN, b. Private.

574. Ronald J.[13] BREWER *(Catherine Isabelle[12] VAN HORN, Orin Denton[11], James Harvey[10], Benjamin Briggs[9], Joshua[8], Isaiah[7], Henry B.[6], Henry[5], Christian Barentsen[4] VAN HOORN, Barent Christiansen[3], Christian Barentsen[2], Barent Barents[1])[5352,5353]* was born 22 Jul 1919 in Creekside, Indiana Cnty, PA[5354,5355], and died 11 May 2002 in Creekside, Indiana Cnty, PA[5356]. He married Effie V. BARNETT. She was born 26 Mar 1923 in Smicksburg, Indiana Cnty, PA, and died 11 Jul 2000 in Pittsburgh, Allegheny Cnty, PA.

Children of Ronald BREWER and Effie BARNETT are:
            i.   ?[14] BREWER, b. Private.
           ii.   ? BREWER, b. Private.

575. Gretchen Ann[13] VAN HORN *(LeRoy Wadding[12], LeRoy Kerns[11], Alexander Milton[10], Benjamin Briggs[9], Joshua[8], Isaiah[7], Henry B.[6], Henry[5], Christian Barentsen[4] VAN HOORN, Barent Christiansen[3], Christian Barentsen[2], Barent Barents[1])* was born Private. She married George Webber MCGRAW Private. He was born Private.

More About George MCGRAW and Gretchen VAN HORN:
Private-Begin: Private

Child of Gretchen VAN HORN and George MCGRAW is:

    i.   D. Scott Van Horn[14] MCGRAW, b. Private.

576. Karen Mildred[13] KUEHNER *(George Kenneth[12], Mary Mae[11] VAN HORN, Alexander Milton[10], Benjamin Briggs[9], Joshua[8], Isaiah[7], Henry B.[6], Henry[5], Christian Barentsen[4] VAN HOORN, Barent Christiansen[3], Christian Barentsen[2], Barent Barents[1])* was born Private. She married William Malcolm HOPKINS Private. He was born Private.

More About William HOPKINS and Karen KUEHNER:
Private-Begin: Private

Child of Karen KUEHNER and William HOPKINS is:
    i.   Karen Mildred Kuehner[14] HOPKINS, b. Private.

577. Edward Dale[13] VAN HORN *(Dale[12], George Percy[11], Alexander Milton[10], Benjamin Briggs[9], Joshua[8], Isaiah[7], Henry B.[6], Henry[5], Christian Barentsen[4] VAN HOORN, Barent Christiansen[3], Christian Barentsen[2], Barent Barents[1])* was born Apr 1940 in Aliquippa, Beaver Cnty, PA, and died Sep 2002 in CA. He married PETTY Private, daughter of Theo PETTY and Lucy AZEVEDO. She was born Private.

More About Edward VAN HORN and PETTY:
Private-Begin: Private

Children of Edward VAN HORN and PETTY are:
    i.   Joseph[14] VAN HORN, b. 1964; d. 1964.
    ii.   Roseann VAN HORN, b. 1964; d. 1964.
    iii.   Dale VAN HORN, b. 1964; d. 1964.
    iv.   ? VAN HORN, b. Private.

578. Janice Louise[13] RANKIN *(James Rogers[12], Nellie Gertrude[11] VAN HORN, Alexander Milton[10], Benjamin Briggs[9], Joshua[8], Isaiah[7], Henry B.[6], Henry[5], Christian Barentsen[4] VAN HOORN, Barent Christiansen[3], Christian Barentsen[2], Barent Barents[1])[5357]* was born 22 May 1943 in White Twp., Indiana Cnty, PA[5357], and died 09 Jun 2004 in Blairsville, Indiana Cnty, PA[5357]. She married (1) Edward George MARINKO Private. He was born Private. She married (2) Gilbert D. BRIGHTBILL[5357]. He was born 25 Jan 1953[5358], and died 10 Oct 2005 in Indiana Cnty, PA[5358].

Notes for Janice Louise RANKIN:
    Janice R. Louise Brightbill, Blairsville
    Insurance worker in California, member of Blair. Garden Club, Women of Moose
    Janice Louise Rankin Brightbill, 61, of Blairsville, died Wednesday, June 9, 2004, at her home. She was born May 22, 1943, in Indiana, the daughter of James Rogers and Mildred Ruddock Rankin.
    She lived most of her life in California and was an escrow officer for Fidelity Title Insurance before moving back to Indiana where she was a bookkeeper for Indiana Free Library. She was a member of the Blairsville Garden Club and Women of the Moose, Sonora, Calif.
    Mrs. Brightbill was also a former member of the New Century Club and the Blairsville Book Club. She was an avid gardener, reader and cook and was a loving wife, mother, grandmother and sister.
    Surviving are her husband, Gilbert; Also two sons: Eric Marinko, Blairsville; James Marinko and wife Maria, North Huntingdon: stepchildren Jeannette and Joel Brightbill, Blairsville; Timothy and Joshua Brightbill; Also sisters: Marjorie Nell Kimble and husband Jeffrey, Westminster, Md.; Rosemary Johnston and husband Dave, Creekside; grandchildren: Stephen and Jessica Marinko; Sarah and Madison Brightbill;her mother-in-law, E. Jeannette Brightbill, Lebanon; Also an aunt,

Mary Catherine Ruddock, of Johnstown, and a number of nieces and nephews.
She was preceded in death by her parents and a son, Steven Edward Marinko.
Funeral services were held Saturday at Robinson-Lytle, Indiana with the Rev. Paul Carter officiating. Interment was in the Greenwood Cemetery, in Indiana.
Memorial contributions may be made to the VNA/Hospice Foundation, 850 Hospital Drive, suite 3000, Indiana, Pa. 15701.
Daily Courier (Pittsburgh, PA) - (Jun/11/2004)

More About Edward MARINKO and Janice RANKIN:
Private-Begin: Private

Notes for Gilbert D. BRIGHTBILL:
US Public Records Index Gilbert D Brightbill Birth Date: 25 Jan 1953 Address: 48 W Campbell, Blairsville, PA, 15717 (1994)
[427 Old Airport Rd, Blairsville, PA, 15717 (1994)] [21943 Fallview Dr, Sonora, CA, 95370]

Gilbert D. Brightbill, 52, of Blairsville, died Monday, Oct. 10, 2005, at Indiana Regional Medical Center. A son of Guy W. and E. Jean-.
nette Hartman Brightbill, he was born Jan. 25,1953, in Lebanon. Before moving back to the Blairsville area 12 years ago, he lived in California. He was an avid country line dance and reader.
His passion for automobiles led him to be certified as a master mechanic.
Surviving are his mother of Lebanon; four children: Timothy J. Brightbill, Joshua D. Brightbill, Jeannette Faye Brightbill of Blairsville and Joel W. Brightbill of Blairsville ; two stepchildren: Eric Marinko of Blairsville and James Marinko and his wife, Maria, of North Huntingdon; the following brothers and sisters: Gary Brightbill of Crossroads, VV.Va.; Karen Brightbill of Reading; Jerry Brightbill ofYork; Brian Brightbill of Lebanon; and Marietta Brightbill of California; four grandchildren: Sarah Faye and Madison Louise Brightbill and James Stephen and Jessica Taylor Marinko; and numerous nieces and nephews.
He was preceded in death by his father; his wife, Janice Louise Rankin Brightbill, in 2004; and a stepson Steven Marinko.
Friends will be received from 7 to 9 p.m. today at Robinson-Lytle Inc., Indiana, where a funeral service will be held at 1 p.m. Friday
with the Rev. Paul Carter officiating. Interment will be in Greenwood Cemetery.
Memorial contributions may be made to the American Heart Association, 400 Luray Ave.,Johnstown, PA 15904.

Children of Janice RANKIN and Edward MARINKO are:
      i.   Steven Edward[14] MARINKO[5359], b. 10 Dec 1967, CA; d. 27 Jul 1990, Stanislaus, CA[5360].
      ii.   Eric MARINKO, b. Private.
649.   iii.   James MARINKO, b. Private.

579. Shirley Mae[13] NEAL *(Robert Merle[12], Bertha Agnes[11] LUKEHART, Sarah S.[10] VAN HORN, Benjamin Briggs[9], Joshua[8], Isaiah[7], Henry B.[6], Henry[5], Christian Barentsen[4] VAN HOORN, Barent Christiansen[3], Christian Barentsen[2], Barent Barents[1])[5361]* was born 01 Dec 1930 in Cowanshannock Twp., Armstrong Cnty, PA[5361], and died 24 Jan 2005 in Sebring, FL[5361]. She married William E. BARRETT Private. He was born Private.

Notes for Shirley Mae NEAL:

Obituaries For Thursday, January 27, 2005
Shirley Mae Barrett, Smicksburg
Shirley Mae (Neal) Barrett, 74, of 229 Dayton-Smicksburg Road, Smicksburg, West Mahoning Township (Indiana County), died Monday, Jan. 24, 2005 in Florida Hospital Heartland Medical Center, Sebring, Fla.

She was born Dec. 1, 1930 in Cowanshannock Township to R. Mearle and A. Pearle (Dill) Neal.

For 30 years, Mrs. Barrett along with her husband, owned and operated Barrett Equipment, dealing in John Deere equipment. She also was a homemaker.

She was a member of the Dayton Glade Run Presbyterian Church.

She was a member of the Dayton Valley Campers.

Survivors include her husband of 54 years, William E. Barrett, whom she married April 12, 1950; one son, Gerald W. Barrett of Smicksburg; three daughters, Nancy D. Foote and husband Herb of Bethel Park, Mrs. Robert (Jennifer D.) Barrett-Johnston of Sunbury, Ohio and Michelle L. Peterson and husband David of Smicksburg; eight grandchildren; one brother, Kenneth Neal and wife Donna of Dayton RD2; and one sister, Jean Windows and husband Donald of Rural Valley RD1.

She was preceded in death by her parents.

Friends will be received from 2 to 4 and 7 to 9 p.m. Thursday at the Carson/Boyer Funeral Home, Inc., 724 Main St., Rural Valley. Additional visitation will be held from 10 a.m. Friday at the Dayton Glade Run Presbyterian Church until funeral services at 11 a.m. with her pastor, the Rev. Dr. Donald M. Rising, officiating. Burial will be in the Dayton Glade Run Cemetery, Wayne Township.

More About William BARRETT and Shirley NEAL:
Private-Begin: Private

Children of Shirley NEAL and William BARRETT are:
      i.   Nancy D.[14] BARRETT, b. Private; m. Herb FOOTE, Private; b. Private.

          More About Herb FOOTE and Nancy BARRETT:
          Private-Begin: Private

      ii. Gerald W. BARRETT, b. Private.
     iii. Jennifer D. BARRETT, b. Private; m. Robert JOHNSTON, Private; b. Private.

          More About Robert JOHNSTON and Jennifer BARRETT:
          Private-Begin: Private

     iv. Michelle L. BARRETT, b. Private; m. David PETERSON, Private; b. Private.

          More About David PETERSON and Michelle BARRETT:
          Private-Begin: Private

580. Jean E.[13] FERGUSON *(Lulu V.[12] VAN HORN, Samuel A.[11], John Miles[10], Christian[9], Joshua[8], Isaiah[7], Henry B.[6], Henry[5], Christian Barentsen[4] VAN HOORN, Barent Christiansen[3], Christian Barentsen[2], Barent Barents[1])* was born Private. She married J. E. NEWLLN Private. He was born Private.

More About J. NEWLLN and Jean FERGUSON:
Private-Begin: Private

Child of Jean FERGUSON and J. NEWLLN is:

650.   i.   ?[14] NEWLLN, b. Private.

581. Delores Ariel[13] SHEPHARD *(George H.[12], Dessia A.[11] VAN HORN, John Miles[10], Christian[9], Joshua[8], Isaiah[7], Henry B.[6], Henry[5], Christian Barentsen[4] VAN HOORN, Barent Christiansen[3], Christian Barentsen[2], Barent Barents[1])[5362]* was born Abt. 1915 in PA[5362], and died Aft. 1993. She married Clyde Daniel SIBBLE. He was born 29 Sep 1911, and died 30 Dec 1993.

Child of Delores SHEPHARD and Clyde SIBBLE is:
     i.   ?[14] SIBBLE, b. Private.

582. Raymond Walter[13] STANTON *(Mabel J.[12] SHEPHARD, Dessia A.[11] VAN HORN, John Miles[10], Christian[9], Joshua[8], Isaiah[7], Henry B.[6], Henry[5], Christian Barentsen[4] VAN HOORN, Barent Christiansen[3], Christian Barentsen[2], Barent Barents[1])[5363,5364]* was born 28 Aug 1918 in PA[5365], and died 08 May 1971 in Erie, Erie Cnty, PA. He married (1) Hilda MILLER. She was born 12 Apr 1917 in Olean, NY, and died 21 Mar 2006 in Erie, Erie Cnty, PA. He married (2) MUSSETT Private. She was born Private.

More About Raymond STANTON and MUSSETT:
Private-Begin: Private

Children of Raymond STANTON and Hilda MILLER are:
     i.   ?[14] STANTON, b. Private.
     ii.   ? STANTON, b. Private.
     iii.   ? STANTON, b. Private.
     iv.   ? STANTON, b. Private.
     v.   Raymond Walter STANTON. JR[5366], b. 03 Jul 1952, Erie, Erie Cnty, PA[5366]; d. 31 Jul 2007, Erie, Erie Cnty, PA[5366].

Children of Raymond STANTON and MUSSETT are:
651.   vi.   ?[14] STANTON, b. Private.
     vii.   ? STANTON, b. Private; m. (1) ELLETSON, Private; b. Private; m. (2) HEADLEY, Private; b. Private.

         More About ELLETSON and ? STANTON:
         Private-Begin: Private

         More About HEADLEY and ? STANTON:
         Private-Begin: Private

652.   viii.   Beverly STANTON, b. 11 Dec 1941, Erie, Erie Cnty, PA; d. 08 Dec 2000, Erie, Erie Cnty, PA.

583. Margaret[13] STANTON *(Mabel J.[12] SHEPHARD, Dessia A.[11] VAN HORN, John Miles[10], Christian[9], Joshua[8], Isaiah[7], Henry B.[6], Henry[5], Christian Barentsen[4] VAN HOORN, Barent Christiansen[3], Christian Barentsen[2], Barent Barents[1])[5367,5368]* was born 14 Oct 1919 in PA[5369], and died 02 Dec 2002 in Erie, Erie Cnty, PA. She married KEPHART Private. He was born Private.

More About KEPHART and Margaret STANTON:
Private-Begin: Private

Children of Margaret STANTON and KEPHART are:
 i. ?[14] KEPHART, b. Private.
 ii. ? KEPHART, b. Private.
 iii. ? KEPHART, b. Private.
 iv. ? KEPHART, b. Private.

584. Geraldine[13] STANTON *(Mabel J.[12] SHEPHARD, Dessia A.[11] VAN HORN, John Miles[10], Christian[9], Joshua[8], Isaiah[7], Henry B.[6], Henry[5], Christian Barentsen[4] VAN HOORN, Barent Christiansen[3], Christian Barentsen[2], Barent Barents[1])[5369]* was born 21 May 1921 in Erie, Erie Cnty, PA[5369], and died 21 May 2008 in Portland, OR. She married Nicholas George LUCAS Private. He was born Private.

More About Nicholas LUCAS and Geraldine STANTON:
Private-Begin: Private

Children of Geraldine STANTON and Nicholas LUCAS are:
 i. ?[14] LUCAS, b. Private.
 ii. ? LUCAS, b. Private.
 iii. ? LUCAS, b. Private.
 iv. ? LUCAS, b. Private.
 v. ? LUCAS, b. Private.
 vi. ? LUCAS, b. Private.
 vii. ? LUCAS, b. Private.
 viii. ? LUCAS, b. Private.
 ix. ? LUCAS, b. Private.
 x. ? LUCAS, b. Private.
 xi. ? LUCAS, b. Private.
 xii. ? LUCAS, b. Private.

585. Stella[13] HARTZELL *(Lois Fae[12] GEARHART, Stella Marilla[11] VAN HORN, John Miles[10], Christian[9], Joshua[8], Isaiah[7], Henry B.[6], Henry[5], Christian Barentsen[4] VAN HOORN, Barent Christiansen[3], Christian Barentsen[2], Barent Barents[1])* was born Private. She married Ron MONOSKEY Private. He was born Private.

More About Ron MONOSKEY and Stella HARTZELL:
Private-Begin: Private

Child of Stella HARTZELL and Ron MONOSKEY is:
 i. Jenn[14] MONOSKEY, b. Private; m. RANKIN, Private; b. Private.

  More About RANKIN and Jenn MONOSKEY:
  Private-Begin: Private

586. Virginia[13] HARTZELL *(Lois Fae[12] GEARHART, Stella Marilla[11] VAN HORN, John Miles[10], Christian[9], Joshua[8], Isaiah[7], Henry B.[6], Henry[5], Christian Barentsen[4] VAN HOORN, Barent Christiansen[3], Christian Barentsen[2], Barent Barents[1])* was born Private. She married Gerald RIFFLE Private. He was born Private.

More About Gerald RIFFLE and Virginia HARTZELL:
Private-Begin: Private

Children of Virginia HARTZELL and Gerald RIFFLE are:
    i.   Gary Lee[14] RIFFLE, b. Private.
   ii.   Jerry RIFFLE, b. Private.

587. Myrtle Olive[13] LAMBING *(James Robert[12], Elizabeth Pearl[11] PALMER, Mary A.[10] LYDICK, Jane Elizabeth[9] VAN HORN, Isaiah[8], Isaiah[7], Henry B.[6], Henry[5], Christian Barentsen[4] VAN HOORN, Barent Christiansen[3], Christian Barentsen[2], Barent Barents[1])* was born 23 Sep 1922 in Homer City, Indiana Cnty, PA, and died 25 Jun 1984 in Akron, Summit Cnty, OH[5370,5371]. She married (1) Robert CARPENTER. He died 1986. She married (2) Robert CAYSENTER Private. He was born Private.

More About Robert CAYSENTER and Myrtle LAMBING:
Private-Begin: Private

Child of Myrtle LAMBING and Robert CARPENTER is:
    i.   Robert[14] CARPENTER, b. Private.

588. Patricia Ann[13] SHANKLE *(Gerald Clair[12], Thomas Roy[11], Ida Mae[10] LYDICK, Jane Elizabeth[9] VAN HORN, Isaiah[8], Isaiah[7], Henry B.[6], Henry[5], Christian Barentsen[4] VAN HOORN, Barent Christiansen[3], Christian Barentsen[2], Barent Barents[1])* was born Private. She married Richard M. COALMER Private. He was born Private.

More About Richard COALMER and Patricia SHANKLE:
Private-Begin: Private

Children of Patricia SHANKLE and Richard COALMER are:
    i.   Ryan P.[14] COALMER, b. Private.
   ii.   Amanda G. COALMER, b. Private.

589. Charlotte Lou[13] SEXTON *(Margaret Ida[12] SHANKLE, Thomas Roy[11], Ida Mae[10] LYDICK, Jane Elizabeth[9] VAN HORN, Isaiah[8], Isaiah[7], Henry B.[6], Henry[5], Christian Barentsen[4] VAN HOORN, Barent Christiansen[3], Christian Barentsen[2], Barent Barents[1])* was born Private. She married Calvin G. OVERMAN Private. He was born Private.

More About Calvin OVERMAN and Charlotte SEXTON:
Private-Begin: Private

Child of Charlotte SEXTON and Calvin OVERMAN is:
    i.   Ricky I.[14] OVERMAN, b. Private.

590. Esther Jean[13] SEXTON *(Margaret Ida[12] SHANKLE, Thomas Roy[11], Ida Mae[10] LYDICK, Jane Elizabeth[9] VAN HORN, Isaiah[8], Isaiah[7], Henry B.[6], Henry[5], Christian Barentsen[4] VAN HOORN, Barent Christiansen[3], Christian Barentsen[2], Barent Barents[1])* was born Private. She married Kenneth Harold SHIELDS Private. He was born Private.

More About Kenneth SHIELDS and Esther SEXTON:
Private-Begin: Private

Child of Esther SEXTON and Kenneth SHIELDS is:

        i.   Pamela J.[14] SHIELDS, b. Private.

591. Robert LeRoy[13] SEXTON *(Margaret Ida[12] SHANKLE, Thomas Roy[11], Ida Mae[10] LYDICK, Jane Elizabeth[9] VAN HORN, Isaiah[8], Isaiah[7], Henry B.[6], Henry[5], Christian Barentsen[4] VAN HOORN, Barent Christiansen[3], Christian Barentsen[2], Barent Barents[1])* was born Private. He married (1) Cheryl Lee VANDALEN Private. She was born Private. He married (2) Grace Elizabeth DUFF Private. She was born Private.

More About Robert SEXTON and Cheryl VANDALEN:
Private-Begin: Private

More About Robert SEXTON and Grace DUFF:
Private-Begin: Private

Child of Robert SEXTON and Cheryl VANDALEN is:
        i.   Maureen Ruben[14] SEXTON, b. Private.

Child of Robert SEXTON and Grace DUFF is:
        ii. Jennifer Elizabeth[14] SEXTON, b. Private.

592. James Arnold[13] SEXTON *(Margaret Ida[12] SHANKLE, Thomas Roy[11], Ida Mae[10] LYDICK, Jane Elizabeth[9] VAN HORN, Isaiah[8], Isaiah[7], Henry B.[6], Henry[5], Christian Barentsen[4] VAN HOORN, Barent Christiansen[3], Christian Barentsen[2], Barent Barents[1])* was born Private. He married Linda COLEMAN Private. She was born Private.

More About James SEXTON and Linda COLEMAN:
Private-Begin: Private

Child of James SEXTON and Linda COLEMAN is:
        i.   Amy Christine[14] SEXTON, b. Private.

593. John Franklin[13] SEXTON *(Margaret Ida[12] SHANKLE, Thomas Roy[11], Ida Mae[10] LYDICK, Jane Elizabeth[9] VAN HORN, Isaiah[8], Isaiah[7], Henry B.[6], Henry[5], Christian Barentsen[4] VAN HOORN, Barent Christiansen[3], Christian Barentsen[2], Barent Barents[1])* was born Private. He married Paulette KOWECHUCK Private. She was born Private.

More About John SEXTON and Paulette KOWECHUCK:
Private-Begin: Private

Child of John SEXTON and Paulette KOWECHUCK is:
        i.   John Franklin[14] SEXTON, JR, b. Private.

594. Rebecca Katherine[13] MEYER *(Mary Lou[12] SERENE, Owen Meridith[11], Stella M.[10] VAN HORN, George Logan[9], William G.[8], Isaiah[7], Henry B.[6], Henry[5], Christian Barentsen[4] VAN HOORN, Barent Christiansen[3], Christian Barentsen[2], Barent Barents[1])* was born Private. She married Edward John GOTTLIEB Private, son of Joseph GOTTLIEB and Ruth KELSKY. He was born Private.

More About Edward GOTTLIEB and Rebecca MEYER:

Private-Begin: Private

Children of Rebecca MEYER and Edward GOTTLIEB are:
- i. Emily Sarah[14] GOTTLIEB, b. Private.
- ii. Vanessa Morgan GOTTLIEB, b. Private.
- iii. Oliver Sidney GOTTLIEB, b. 08 Jul 2004, Los Angeles, Los Angeles Cnty, CA; d. 11 Jul 2004, Los Angeles, Los Angeles Cnty, CA.
- iv. Audrey Katherine GOTTLIEB, b. Private.

595. Michael W.[13] STEELE *(Clair W.[12], Clark Lewis[11], Elijah Work[10], Dorcas[9] HAMILTON, Nancy[8] VAN HORN, Isaiah[7], Henry B.[6], Henry[5], Christian Barentsen[4] VAN HOORN, Barent Christiansen[3], Christian Barentsen[2], Barent Barents[1])* was born 23 Feb 1957 in Brookville, Jefferson Cnty, PA, and died 04 Jul 2005 in Clarion Cnty, PA. He married HEASLEY Private. She was born Private.

More About Michael W. STEELE:
Burial: Unknown, Cedarview Memorial Park, Clarion Cnty, PA

More About Michael STEELE and HEASLEY:
Private-Begin: Private

Children of Michael STEELE and HEASLEY are:
- i. ?[14] STEELE, b. Private.
- ii. ? STEELE, b. Private.
- iii. ? STEELE, b. Private.

596. Laurel[13] DUNCAN *(Mary Jane[12] FERRIER, Esther M.[11] MCADOO, Ada Myrtle[10] VAN HORN, Bennett Work[9], George Logan[8], Isaiah[7], Henry B.[6], Henry[5], Christian Barentsen[4] VAN HOORN, Barent Christiansen[3], Christian Barentsen[2], Barent Barents[1])* was born Private. She married BEDORE Private. He was born Private.

More About BEDORE and Laurel DUNCAN:
Private-Begin: Private

Children of Laurel DUNCAN and BEDORE are:
- i. Jared[14] BEDORE, b. Private.
- ii. Elizabeth BEDORE, b. Private.

597. Helen Arlene[13] MCCAUSLAND *(Robert Clark[12], Bertha Della[11] AUL, Mary Caroline[10] VAN HORN, Bennett Work[9], George Logan[8], Isaiah[7], Henry B.[6], Henry[5], Christian Barentsen[4] VAN HOORN, Barent Christiansen[3], Christian Barentsen[2], Barent Barents[1])* was born Private. She married Fairman Fred FULTON Private, son of F. F. FULTON. He was born Private.

More About Fairman FULTON and Helen MCCAUSLAND:
Private-Begin: Private

Children of Helen MCCAUSLAND and Fairman FULTON are:
- i. Bonnie Lynn[14] FULTON, b. Private; m. John VALKOSKY, Private; b. Private.

    More About John VALKOSKY and Bonnie FULTON:
    Private-Begin: Private

    ii.   Robert Guy FULTON, b. Private; m. Deena Renee HARKLEROAD, Private; b. Private.

        More About Robert FULTON and Deena HARKLEROAD:
        Private-Begin: Private

    iii.   David James FULTON, b. Private; m. Christine Ann MECKLEY, Private; b. Private.

        More About David FULTON and Christine MECKLEY:
        Private-Begin: Private

598. Linda Jean[13] MCCAUSLAND *(Robert Clark[12], Bertha Della[11] AUL, Mary Caroline[10] VAN HORN, Bennett Work[9], George Logan[8], Isaiah[7], Henry B.[6], Henry[5], Christian Barentsen[4] VAN HOORN, Barent Christiansen[3], Christian Barentsen[2], Barent Barents[1])* was born Private. She married William Roy LEWIS Private. He was born Private.

More About William LEWIS and Linda MCCAUSLAND:
Private-Begin: Private

Children of Linda MCCAUSLAND and William LEWIS are:
653.   i.   William Roy[14] LEWIS, JR, b. Private.
654.   ii.   Pamela Jean LEWIS, b. Private.
       iii.   Michael James LEWIS, b. Private.

599. James Clarence[13] COOPER, JR *(Florence Jane[12] MCCAUSLAND, Bertha Della[11] AUL, Mary Caroline[10] VAN HORN, Bennett Work[9], George Logan[8], Isaiah[7], Henry B.[6], Henry[5], Christian Barentsen[4] VAN HOORN, Barent Christiansen[3], Christian Barentsen[2], Barent Barents[1])* was born Private. He married Barbara HARPSTER Private. She was born Private.

More About James COOPER and Barbara HARPSTER:
Private-Begin: Private

Children of James COOPER and Barbara HARPSTER are:
655.   i.   James Lloyd[14] COOPER, b. Private.
656.   ii.   Melissa Ann COOPER, b. Private.

600. Sally Ann[13] COOPER *(Florence Jane[12] MCCAUSLAND, Bertha Della[11] AUL, Mary Caroline[10] VAN HORN, Bennett Work[9], George Logan[8], Isaiah[7], Henry B.[6], Henry[5], Christian Barentsen[4] VAN HOORN, Barent Christiansen[3], Christian Barentsen[2], Barent Barents[1])* was born Private. She married David Bruce HECKMAN Private. He was born Private.

More About David HECKMAN and Sally COOPER:
Private-Begin: Private

Children of Sally COOPER and David HECKMAN are:
657.   i.   David James[14] HECKMAN, b. Private.
658.   ii.   Kevin Lee HECKMAN, b. Private.
      iii.   Chadwick Arron HECKMAN, b. Private; m. Crystal Lynn, Private; b. Private.

        More About Chadwick HECKMAN and Crystal Lynn:

Private-Begin: Private

    iv.   Bruce Eugene HECKMAN, b. Private; m. Janet S. HALLWORK, Private; b. Private.

          More About Bruce HECKMAN and Janet HALLWORK:
          Private-Begin: Private

    v.   Jennie Lynn HECKMAN, b. Private.

601. John Ronald[13] COOPER *(Florence Jane[12] MCCAUSLAND, Bertha Della[11] AUL, Mary Caroline[10] VAN HORN, Bennett Work[9], George Logan[8], Isaiah[7], Henry B.[6], Henry[5], Christian Barentsen[4] VAN HOORN, Barent Christiansen[3], Christian Barentsen[2], Barent Barents[1])* was born Private. He married Donna Jean MCINTIRE Private, daughter of Gerald MCINTIRE and Ann. She was born Private.

More About John COOPER and Donna MCINTIRE:
Private-Begin: Private

Children of John COOPER and Donna MCINTIRE are:
    i.   Brian John[14] COOPER, b. Private.
    ii.   Allen Lee COOPER, b. Private.

602. Cathy Ann[13] COOPER *(Florence Jane[12] MCCAUSLAND, Bertha Della[11] AUL, Mary Caroline[10] VAN HORN, Bennett Work[9], George Logan[8], Isaiah[7], Henry B.[6], Henry[5], Christian Barentsen[4] VAN HOORN, Barent Christiansen[3], Christian Barentsen[2], Barent Barents[1])* was born Private. She married Robert Glenn HILLIARD Private. He was born Private.

More About Robert HILLIARD and Cathy COOPER:
Private-Begin: Private

Child of Cathy COOPER and Robert HILLIARD is:
    i.   Robert Glenn[14] HILLIARD, JR, b. Private.

603. Charlene Marie[13] MCCAUSLAND *(Donald Reid[12], Bertha Della[11] AUL, Mary Caroline[10] VAN HORN, Bennett Work[9], George Logan[8], Isaiah[7], Henry B.[6], Henry[5], Christian Barentsen[4] VAN HOORN, Barent Christiansen[3], Christian Barentsen[2], Barent Barents[1])* was born Private. She married Arthur Wayne RUPP Private. He was born Private.

More About Arthur RUPP and Charlene MCCAUSLAND:
Private-Begin: Private

Children of Charlene MCCAUSLAND and Arthur RUPP are:
659.	i.	Christine Marie[14] RUPP, b. Private.
660.	ii.	Cynthia Mae RUPP, b. Private.
661.	iii.	Beverly Sue RUPP, b. Private.
662.	iv.	Annette Carol RUPP, b. Private.
663.	v.	Kelvin Arthur RUPP, b. Private.
	vi.	Kevin Wayne RUPP, b. Private; m. Melissa Lynn SHNYDER, Private; b. Private.

          More About Kevin RUPP and Melissa SHNYDER:
          Private-Begin: Private

604. Donald Reid[13] MCCAUSLAND, JR *(Donald Reid[12], Bertha Della[11] AUL, Mary Caroline[10] VAN HORN, Bennett Work[9], George Logan[8], Isaiah[7], Henry B.[6], Henry[5], Christian Barentsen[4] VAN HOORN, Barent Christiansen[3], Christian Barentsen[2], Barent Barents[1])* was born Private. He married Ethel Eileen JOHNSTON Private. She was born Private.

More About Donald MCCAUSLAND and Ethel JOHNSTON:
Private-Begin: Private

Children of Donald MCCAUSLAND and Ethel JOHNSTON are:
664.   i.   Julie Ann[14] MCCAUSLAND, b. Private.
        ii. Joseph Reid MCCAUSLAND, b. Private.

605. Larry John[13] MCCAUSLAND *(Donald Reid[12], Bertha Della[11] AUL, Mary Caroline[10] VAN HORN, Bennett Work[9], George Logan[8], Isaiah[7], Henry B.[6], Henry[5], Christian Barentsen[4] VAN HOORN, Barent Christiansen[3], Christian Barentsen[2], Barent Barents[1])* was born Private. He married Lou Ann SPENCER Private. She was born Private.

More About Larry MCCAUSLAND and Lou SPENCER:
Private-Begin: Private

Children of Larry MCCAUSLAND and Lou SPENCER are:
665.   i.   Larry John[14] MCCAUSLAND, JR, b. Private.
666.   ii. Terry Lee MCCAUSLAND, b. Private.

606. Dennis Lee[13] MCCAUSLAND *(Donald Reid[12], Bertha Della[11] AUL, Mary Caroline[10] VAN HORN, Bennett Work[9], George Logan[8], Isaiah[7], Henry B.[6], Henry[5], Christian Barentsen[4] VAN HOORN, Barent Christiansen[3], Christian Barentsen[2], Barent Barents[1])* was born Private. He married (1) Karen Louise STIVANSICK Private. She was born 24 Feb 1958, and died 04 May 1996. He married (2) Candie Kay MCQUISTON Private. She was born Private.

More About Dennis MCCAUSLAND and Karen STIVANSICK:
Private-Begin: Private

More About Dennis MCCAUSLAND and Candie MCQUISTON:
Private-Begin: Private

Children of Dennis MCCAUSLAND and Karen STIVANSICK are:
        i.   Nicholas John[14] MCCAUSLAND, b. Private.
        ii. Douglas Reid MCCAUSLAND, b. Private.
        iii. Suzanne Marie MCCAUSLAND, b. Private.

607. Maxine Dee[13] MCCAUSLAND *(Donald Reid[12], Bertha Della[11] AUL, Mary Caroline[10] VAN HORN, Bennett Work[9], George Logan[8], Isaiah[7], Henry B.[6], Henry[5], Christian Barentsen[4] VAN HOORN, Barent Christiansen[3], Christian Barentsen[2], Barent Barents[1])* was born Private. She married (1) Jeffery Allen FAIRMAN Private. He was born Private. She married (2) Kenneth Barry ISENBURG Private. He was born 12 May 1950, and died Nov 1983.

More About Jeffery FAIRMAN and Maxine MCCAUSLAND:

Private-Begin: Private

More About Kenneth ISENBURG and Maxine MCCAUSLAND:
Private-Begin: Private

Children of Maxine MCCAUSLAND and Jeffery FAIRMAN are:
    i.   Jeffery Allen[14] FAIRMAN, JR, b. Private.
   ii.   Jeremy Carl FAIRMAN, b. Private.

608. Kathleen Joy[13] MCCAUSLAND *(Donald Reid*[12]*, Bertha Della*[11] *AUL, Mary Caroline*[10] *VAN HORN, Bennett Work*[9]*, George Logan*[8]*, Isaiah*[7]*, Henry B.*[6]*, Henry*[5]*, Christian Barentsen*[4] *VAN HOORN, Barent Christiansen*[3]*, Christian Barentsen*[2]*, Barent Barents*[1]*)* was born Private. She married Johnny Brett KEELER Private. He was born Private.

More About Johnny KEELER and Kathleen MCCAUSLAND:
Private-Begin: Private

Child of Kathleen MCCAUSLAND and Johnny KEELER is:
    i.   Clayton Brett[14] KEELER, b. Private.

609. Robert Clair[13] MCCAUSLAND *(Clair Eugene*[12]*, Bertha Della*[11] *AUL, Mary Caroline*[10] *VAN HORN, Bennett Work*[9]*, George Logan*[8]*, Isaiah*[7]*, Henry B.*[6]*, Henry*[5]*, Christian Barentsen*[4] *VAN HOORN, Barent Christiansen*[3]*, Christian Barentsen*[2]*, Barent Barents*[1]*)* was born Private. He married Diane Jean GIFFITH Private. She was born Private.

More About Robert MCCAUSLAND and Diane GIFFITH:
Private-Begin: Private

Child of Robert MCCAUSLAND and Diane GIFFITH is:
    i.   Nancy Elizabeth[14] MCCAUSLAND, b. Private.

610. Thomas Lee[13] MCCAUSLAND *(Clair Eugene*[12]*, Bertha Della*[11] *AUL, Mary Caroline*[10] *VAN HORN, Bennett Work*[9]*, George Logan*[8]*, Isaiah*[7]*, Henry B.*[6]*, Henry*[5]*, Christian Barentsen*[4] *VAN HOORN, Barent Christiansen*[3]*, Christian Barentsen*[2]*, Barent Barents*[1]*)* was born Private. He married Mary Jean DOLLISON Private. She was born Private.

More About Thomas MCCAUSLAND and Mary DOLLISON:
Private-Begin: Private

Children of Thomas MCCAUSLAND and Mary DOLLISON are:
    i.   Thomas Lee[14] MCCAUSLAND, JR, b. Private.
   ii.   Steven Robert MCCAUSLAND, b. Private.

611. Gary Lynn[13] MCCAUSLAND *(Clair Eugene*[12]*, Bertha Della*[11] *AUL, Mary Caroline*[10] *VAN HORN, Bennett Work*[9]*, George Logan*[8]*, Isaiah*[7]*, Henry B.*[6]*, Henry*[5]*, Christian Barentsen*[4] *VAN HOORN, Barent Christiansen*[3]*, Christian Barentsen*[2]*, Barent Barents*[1]*)* was born Private. He married Manda NECO Private. She was born Private.

More About Gary MCCAUSLAND and Manda NECO:

Private-Begin: Private

Child of Gary MCCAUSLAND and Manda NECO is:
   i.   Nicole Marie[14] MCCAUSLAND, b. Private.

612. David Bruce[13] LARGE *(Grace Lucille[12] MCCAUSLAND, Bertha Della[11] AUL, Mary Caroline[10] VAN HORN, Bennett Work[9], George Logan[8], Isaiah[7], Henry B.[6], Henry[5], Christian Barentsen[4] VAN HOORN, Barent Christiansen[3], Christian Barentsen[2], Barent Barents[1])* was born Private. He married Janet WEBER Private. She was born Private.

More About David LARGE and Janet WEBER:
Private-Begin: Private

Children of David LARGE and Janet WEBER are:
   i.   Justin Matthew[14] LARGE, b. Private.
   ii. Jenneifer Leah LARGE, b. Private.

613. Richard Ward[13] LARGE *(Grace Lucille[12] MCCAUSLAND, Bertha Della[11] AUL, Mary Caroline[10] VAN HORN, Bennett Work[9], George Logan[8], Isaiah[7], Henry B.[6], Henry[5], Christian Barentsen[4] VAN HOORN, Barent Christiansen[3], Christian Barentsen[2], Barent Barents[1])* was born Private. He married Susan THOMAS Private. She was born Private.

More About Richard LARGE and Susan THOMAS:
Private-Begin: Private

Children of Richard LARGE and Susan THOMAS are:
   i.   Mark Richard[14] LARGE, b. Private.
   ii.   Pamela Sue LARGE, b. Private.
   iii. Matthew Ward LARGE, b. Private.

614. Diane Lee[13] LARGE *(Grace Lucille[12] MCCAUSLAND, Bertha Della[11] AUL, Mary Caroline[10] VAN HORN, Bennett Work[9], George Logan[8], Isaiah[7], Henry B.[6], Henry[5], Christian Barentsen[4] VAN HOORN, Barent Christiansen[3], Christian Barentsen[2], Barent Barents[1])* was born Private. She married Joseph Edward CLAWSON Private. He was born Private.

More About Joseph CLAWSON and Diane LARGE:
Private-Begin: Private

Children of Diane LARGE and Joseph CLAWSON are:
   i.   Donald Ward[14] CLAWSON, b. Private.
   ii.   Daniell Renee CLAWSON, b. Private.
   iii. Nicole Susette CLAWSON, b. Private.

615. Deborah Sue[13] LARGE *(Grace Lucille[12] MCCAUSLAND, Bertha Della[11] AUL, Mary Caroline[10] VAN HORN, Bennett Work[9], George Logan[8], Isaiah[7], Henry B.[6], Henry[5], Christian Barentsen[4] VAN HOORN, Barent Christiansen[3], Christian Barentsen[2], Barent Barents[1])* was born Private. She married Roger Albert LYNCH Private. He was born Private.

More About Roger LYNCH and Deborah LARGE:

Private-Begin: Private

Children of Deborah LARGE and Roger LYNCH are:
  i. Shawn Michael[14] LYNCH, b. Private.
  ii. Jennifer Erin LYNCH, b. Private.
  iii. Kelly Lynn LYNCH, b. Private.

616. Edward Bruce[13] SHOTTS *(Dorothy Jean[12] MCCAUSLAND, Bertha Della[11] AUL, Mary Caroline[10] VAN HORN, Bennett Work[9], George Logan[8], Isaiah[7], Henry B.[6], Henry[5], Christian Barentsen[4] VAN HOORN, Barent Christiansen[3], Christian Barentsen[2], Barent Barents[1])* was born Private. He married Connie Ann STEFFY Private. She was born Private.

More About Edward SHOTTS and Connie STEFFY:
Private-Begin: Private

Children of Edward SHOTTS and Connie STEFFY are:
  i. Nathan Edward[14] SHOTTS, b. Private.
  ii. Eric Lynn SHOTTS, b. Private.

617. John Murray[13] SHOTTS *(Dorothy Jean[12] MCCAUSLAND, Bertha Della[11] AUL, Mary Caroline[10] VAN HORN, Bennett Work[9], George Logan[8], Isaiah[7], Henry B.[6], Henry[5], Christian Barentsen[4] VAN HOORN, Barent Christiansen[3], Christian Barentsen[2], Barent Barents[1])* was born Private. He married Ora Geraldine WOOLSY Private. She was born Private.

More About John SHOTTS and Ora WOOLSY:
Private-Begin: Private

Children of John SHOTTS and Ora WOOLSY are:
  i. Stephen Murray[14] SHOTTS, b. Private; m. Sandra Gina ELROD, Private; b. Private.

     More About Stephen SHOTTS and Sandra ELROD:
     Private-Begin: Private

  ii. Gary Reid SHOTTS, b. Private.

618. Richard Earl[13] SHOTTS *(Dorothy Jean[12] MCCAUSLAND, Bertha Della[11] AUL, Mary Caroline[10] VAN HORN, Bennett Work[9], George Logan[8], Isaiah[7], Henry B.[6], Henry[5], Christian Barentsen[4] VAN HOORN, Barent Christiansen[3], Christian Barentsen[2], Barent Barents[1])* was born Private. He married Candice Lee COOPER Private. She was born Private.

More About Richard SHOTTS and Candice COOPER:
Private-Begin: Private

Children of Richard SHOTTS and Candice COOPER are:
  i. Richard Michael[14] SHOTTS, b. Private.
  ii. Jessica Lynn SHOTTS, b. Private.

619. Terry Lynn[13] SHOTTS *(Dorothy Jean[12] MCCAUSLAND, Bertha Della[11] AUL, Mary Caroline[10] VAN HORN, Bennett Work[9], George Logan[8], Isaiah[7], Henry B.[6], Henry[5], Christian Barentsen[4] VAN*

HOORN, *Barent Christiansen³, Christian Barentsen², Barent Barents¹)* was born Private. She married Gerald David BAKER Private. He was born Private.

More About Gerald BAKER and Terry SHOTTS:
Private-Begin: Private

Children of Terry SHOTTS and Gerald BAKER are:
    i.   David Paul¹⁴ BAKER, b. Private.
    ii. Michael Scott BAKER, b. Private.
    iii. Lindsay Marie BAKER, b. Private.

620. Donald Lee¹³ SHOTTS *(Dorothy Jean¹² MCCAUSLAND, Bertha Della¹¹ AUL, Mary Caroline¹⁰ VAN HORN, Bennett Work⁹, George Logan⁸, Isaiah⁷, Henry B.⁶, Henry⁵, Christian Barentsen⁴ VAN HOORN, Barent Christiansen³, Christian Barentsen², Barent Barents¹)* was born Private. He married Marlene PIFER Private. She was born Private.

More About Donald SHOTTS and Marlene PIFER:
Private-Begin: Private

Children of Donald SHOTTS and Marlene PIFER are:
    i. James Edward¹⁴ SHOTTS, b. Private.
    ii. Ryan Lee SHOTTS, b. Private.

621. Norma Jean¹³ SHOTTS *(Dorothy Jean¹² MCCAUSLAND, Bertha Della¹¹ AUL, Mary Caroline¹⁰ VAN HORN, Bennett Work⁹, George Logan⁸, Isaiah⁷, Henry B.⁶, Henry⁵, Christian Barentsen⁴ VAN HOORN, Barent Christiansen³, Christian Barentsen², Barent Barents¹)* was born Private. She married (1) James Patrick CURRLL Private. He was born Private. She married (2) Lewis George HUNTER Private. He was born Private.

More About James CURRLL and Norma SHOTTS:
Private-Begin: Private

More About Lewis HUNTER and Norma SHOTTS:
Private-Begin: Private

Children of Norma SHOTTS and Lewis HUNTER are:
    i. Cody James¹⁴ HUNTER, b. Private.
    ii. Tyler Andrew HUNTER, b. Private.

622. Shay Linda¹³ SHAFFER *(John William¹², Claude Ellsworth¹¹, Cora Belle¹⁰ VAN HORN, Bennett Work⁹, George Logan⁸, Isaiah⁷, Henry B.⁶, Henry⁵, Christian Barentsen⁴ VAN HOORN, Barent Christiansen³, Christian Barentsen², Barent Barents¹)* was born Private. She married ROBINSON Private. He was born Private.

More About ROBINSON and Shay SHAFFER:
Private-Begin: Private

Children of Shay SHAFFER and ROBINSON are:
    i. Junior¹⁴ ROBINSON, b. Private.
    ii. Evin ROBINSON, b. Private; m. PAGE, Private; b. Private.

More About Evin ROBINSON and PAGE:
Private-Begin: Private

623. Luanna[13] JOHNSTON *(William L.[12], William Clair[11], Anna Florence[10] VAN HORN, Bennett Work[9], George Logan[8], Isaiah[7], Henry B.[6], Henry[5], Christian Barentsen[4] VAN HOORN, Barent Christiansen[3], Christian Barentsen[2], Barent Barents[1])* was born Private. She married Roger DINGER Private. He was born Private.

More About Roger DINGER and Luanna JOHNSTON:
Private-Begin: Private

Children of Luanna JOHNSTON and Roger DINGER are:
    i.   Mysti[14] DINGER, b. Private.
    ii. Melanie DINGER, b. Private.
    iii. Mindi DINGER, b. Private.

624. Tracy Dawn[13] VAN HORN *(Joseph Lee[12], Wilbur Bennett[11], Robert Lee Claire[10], Bennett Work[9], George Logan[8], Isaiah[7], Henry B.[6], Henry[5], Christian Barentsen[4] VAN HOORN, Barent Christiansen[3], Christian Barentsen[2], Barent Barents[1])[5372,5373]* was born 21 Mar 1966, and died Aft. 2010. She married David JUART Private, son of Theodore JUART and Stella PLUTO. He was born Private.

More About Tracy Dawn VAN HORN:
Degree: BS Education in Business Education
Occupation: Secretary Indiana University of PA, Indiana, PA

More About David JUART and Tracy VAN HORN:
Private-Begin: Private

Children of Tracy VAN HORN and David JUART are:
    i.   Sadie Kathleen[14] JUART, b. Private.
    ii. Isaac David JUART, b. Private.

625. Lori Jo[13] VAN HORN *(Joseph Lee[12], Wilbur Bennett[11], Robert Lee Claire[10], Bennett Work[9], George Logan[8], Isaiah[7], Henry B.[6], Henry[5], Christian Barentsen[4] VAN HOORN, Barent Christiansen[3], Christian Barentsen[2], Barent Barents[1])[5374,5375]* was born in Marion Center, Indiana Cnty, PA[5376], and died Aft. 2010. She married Kenneth Wade MARSHALL Private[5377], son of Thomas MARSHALL and Carol. He was born Private.

Notes for Lori Jo VAN HORN:
Lori Jo Van Horn Marshall is employed in the Office of Graduate Studies and Research at Indiana University of Pennsylvania.

More About Kenneth MARSHALL and Lori VAN HORN:
Private-Begin: Private[5377]

Children of Lori VAN HORN and Kenneth MARSHALL are:
    i.   Joseph Wade[14] MARSHALL, b. Private.
    ii. Jared MARSHALL, b. Private.
    iii. Trenton MARSHALL, b. Private.

626. Luke[13] VAN HORN *(Joseph Lee[12], Wilbur Bennett[11], Robert Lee Claire[10], Bennett Work[9], George Logan[8], Isaiah[7], Henry B.[6], Henry[5], Christian Barentsen[4] VAN HOORN, Barent Christiansen[3], Christian Barentsen[2], Barent Barents[1])[5378,5379,5380]* died Aft. 2010. He married Kimberly Dawn FRAILEY[5381] 28 Nov 1992 in South Bend, PA, daughter of Ron FRAILEY and Sandra. She died Aft. 2010.

More About Luke VAN HORN:
Occupation: Walter L. Houser Coal Company Kittanning, PA, Dalla Morris Drilling

More About Kimberly Dawn FRAILEY:
Occupation: Secretary Indiana Hospital, Indiana, PA, Homemaker

More About Luke VAN HORN and Kimberly FRAILEY:
Marriage: 28 Nov 1992, South Bend, PA
Marriage date: St. Jacobs Church of Christ South Bend, PA

Children of Luke VAN HORN and Kimberly FRAILEY are:
      i.   Kaleb Luke[14] VAN HORN, b. Private.
     ii.   Kolton VAN HORN, b. Private.

627. Thomas Wayne[13] SHANK *(Vernie M.[12] WEAVER, Deloris Belle[11] VAN HORN, James Ira[10], Bennett Work[9], George Logan[8], Isaiah[7], Henry B.[6], Henry[5], Christian Barentsen[4] VAN HOORN, Barent Christiansen[3], Christian Barentsen[2], Barent Barents[1])* was born Private. He married Theresa Anne LOCKHART Private, daughter of Charles LOCKHART and Jacqueline SNYDER. She was born Private.

More About Thomas SHANK and Theresa LOCKHART:
Private-Begin: Private

Child of Thomas SHANK and Theresa LOCKHART is:
      i.   Jacob[14] SHANK, b. Private.

628. Jody Lynn[13] JEWART *(Patricia Ann[12] RUPERT, Twila May[11] VAN HORN, Harry Bennett[10], Bennett Work[9], George Logan[8], Isaiah[7], Henry B.[6], Henry[5], Christian Barentsen[4] VAN HOORN, Barent Christiansen[3], Christian Barentsen[2], Barent Barents[1])* was born Private. She married Lee GRAHAM Private, son of Monty GRAHAM and Kate. He was born Private.

More About Lee GRAHAM and Jody JEWART:
Private-Begin: Private

Child of Jody JEWART and Lee GRAHAM is:
      i.   Ashlee Nicole[14] GRAHAM, b. Private.

Generation No. 8

629. Angela[14] LARISCY *(Mary Elizabeth[13] VAN HORN, Judson Tannehill[12], Judson Tannehill[11], Henry D. Foster[10], John Dick[9], Alexander[8], Isaiah[7], Henry B.[6], Henry[5], Christian Barentsen[4] VAN HOORN, Barent Christiansen[3], Christian Barentsen[2], Barent Barents[1])* was born Private. She married Donald NORTENSTINE Private. He was born Private.

More About Donald NORTENSTINE and Angela LARISCY:
Private-Begin: Private

Child of Angela LARISCY and Donald NORTENSTINE is:
  i. Angela[15] NORTENSTINE, b. Private.

630. Margaret[14] PRESSLEY *(Patricia Louise[13] VAN HORN, Judson Tannehill[12], Judson Tannehill[11], Henry D. Foster[10], John Dick[9], Alexander[8], Isaiah[7], Henry B.[6], Henry[5], Christian Barentsen[4] VAN HOORN, Barent Christiansen[3], Christian Barentsen[2], Barent Barents[1])* was born Private. She married Clayton MCCLANAHAN Private. He was born Private.

More About Clayton MCCLANAHAN and Margaret PRESSLEY:
Private-Begin: Private

Children of Margaret PRESSLEY and Clayton MCCLANAHAN are:
  i. Amber[15] MCCLANAHAN, b. Private.
  ii. Faith MCCLANAHAN, b. Private.
  iii. Lindsay MCCLANAHAN, b. Private.

631. Melody Frances[14] WILLEY *(Jacqueline Ann[13] MARSHALL, Mary Ella[12] VAN HORN, Judson Tannehill[11], Henry D. Foster[10], John Dick[9], Alexander[8], Isaiah[7], Henry B.[6], Henry[5], Christian Barentsen[4] VAN HOORN, Barent Christiansen[3], Christian Barentsen[2], Barent Barents[1])* was born Private. She married William HUDDLESTON Private, son of Thomas HUDDLESTON and Sally PRIDGEN. He was born Private.

More About William HUDDLESTON and Melody WILLEY:
Private-Begin: Private

Children of Melody WILLEY and William HUDDLESTON are:
  i. Nyah Marie[15] HUDDLESTON, b. Private.
  ii. Hannah Renee HUDDLESTON, b. Private.

632. Kelly Ann[14] ASHCOM *(Frank Martin[13], Frank Martin[12], James Donald[11], Margaret Mary[10] VAN HORN, James Wherry[9], Alexander[8], Isaiah[7], Henry B.[6], Henry[5], Christian Barentsen[4] VAN HOORN, Barent Christiansen[3], Christian Barentsen[2], Barent Barents[1])* was born Private. She married SCHUETTE Private. He was born Private.

More About SCHUETTE and Kelly ASHCOM:
Private-Begin: Private

Child of Kelly ASHCOM and SCHUETTE is:
  i. Alysa Janell[15] SCHUETTE, b. Private.

633. Tina Marie[14] ASHCOM *(Frank Martin[13], Frank Martin[12], James Donald[11], Margaret Mary[10] VAN HORN, James Wherry[9], Alexander[8], Isaiah[7], Henry B.[6], Henry[5], Christian Barentsen[4] VAN HOORN, Barent Christiansen[3], Christian Barentsen[2], Barent Barents[1])* was born Private. She married Bryan VERZAL Private, son of VERZAL. He was born Private.

More About Bryan VERZAL and Tina ASHCOM:
Private-Begin: Private

Children of Tina ASHCOM and Bryan VERZAL are:
    i.   Aaron[15] VERZAL, b. Private.
    ii. Kayla VERZAL, b. Private.
    iii. Tyler VERZAL, b. Private.

634. Melanee Sue[14] SCHIMMEL *(Norma Davene[13] HUDSON, Emma Elizabeth[12] WOLF, Leafy Fern[11] VAN HORN, Samuel Cornelius[10], Henry Coulter[9], Alexander[8], Isaiah[7], Henry B.[6], Henry[5], Christian Barentsen[4] VAN HOORN, Barent Christiansen[3], Christian Barentsen[2], Barent Barents[1])* was born Private. She married (1) David WAGNER Private. He was born Private. She married (2) Joe SMITH Private. He was born Private.

More About David WAGNER and Melanee SCHIMMEL:
Private-Begin: Private

More About Joe SMITH and Melanee SCHIMMEL:
Private-Begin: Private

Child of Melanee SCHIMMEL and Joe SMITH is:
    i.   Kody Lou[15] TURNER-SCHIMMEL, b. Private.

635. Shelda Lynn[14] SCHIMMEL *(Norma Davene[13] HUDSON, Emma Elizabeth[12] WOLF, Leafy Fern[11] VAN HORN, Samuel Cornelius[10], Henry Coulter[9], Alexander[8], Isaiah[7], Henry B.[6], Henry[5], Christian Barentsen[4] VAN HOORN, Barent Christiansen[3], Christian Barentsen[2], Barent Barents[1])* was born Private. She married Dennis WEIRICH Private. He was born Private.

More About Dennis WEIRICH and Shelda SCHIMMEL:
Private-Begin: Private

Child of Shelda SCHIMMEL and Dennis WEIRICH is:
    i.   Bruce Douglas[15] SCHIMMEL II, b. Private.

636. Paula Diane[14] LUCUS *(Beverly Ann[13] HAAS, Emma Elizabeth[12] WOLF, Leafy Fern[11] VAN HORN, Samuel Cornelius[10], Henry Coulter[9], Alexander[8], Isaiah[7], Henry B.[6], Henry[5], Christian Barentsen[4] VAN HOORN, Barent Christiansen[3], Christian Barentsen[2], Barent Barents[1])* was born Private. She married Doug BROOKS Private. He was born Private.

More About Doug BROOKS and Paula LUCUS:
Private-Begin: Private

Child of Paula LUCUS and Doug BROOKS is:
    i.   Lucas[15] BROOKS, b. Private.

637. Vicki Lynn[14] HAAS *(Rodney Albert[13], Emma Elizabeth[12] WOLF, Leafy Fern[11] VAN HORN, Samuel Cornelius[10], Henry Coulter[9], Alexander[8], Isaiah[7], Henry B.[6], Henry[5], Christian Barentsen[4] VAN HOORN, Barent Christiansen[3], Christian Barentsen[2], Barent Barents[1])* was born Private. She married Robert Charles WISSEL Private. He was born Private.

More About Robert WISSEL and Vicki HAAS:
Private-Begin: Private

Children of Vicki HAAS and Robert WISSEL are:
  i.   Ashley Elizabeth[15] WISSEL, b. Private.
  ii.   Sarah Michelle WISSEL, b. Private.

638. Rise" Ka[14] FRANK *(Malcolm David[13], Marianna[12] WOLF, Leafy Fern[11] VAN HORN, Samuel Cornelius[10], Henry Coulter[9], Alexander[8], Isaiah[7], Henry B.[6], Henry[5], Christian Barentsen[4] VAN HOORN, Barent Christiansen[3], Christian Barentsen[2], Barent Barents[1])* was born Private. She married Kenneth Dean STRASSER Private. He was born Private.

More About Kenneth STRASSER and Rise" FRANK:
Private-Begin: Private

Children of Rise" FRANK and Kenneth STRASSER are:
  i.   Joshua Tate[15] STRASSER, b. Private.
  ii.   Ashley Nichole STRASSER, b. Private.

639. Jennifer[14] FRANK *(Malcolm David[13], Marianna[12] WOLF, Leafy Fern[11] VAN HORN, Samuel Cornelius[10], Henry Coulter[9], Alexander[8], Isaiah[7], Henry B.[6], Henry[5], Christian Barentsen[4] VAN HOORN, Barent Christiansen[3], Christian Barentsen[2], Barent Barents[1])* was born Private. She married Gerald Lee JACOBS, JR Private. He was born Private.

More About Gerald JACOBS and Jennifer FRANK:
Private-Begin: Private

Child of Jennifer FRANK and Gerald JACOBS is:
  i.   Robin Andrew[15] JACOBS, b. Private.

640. Laura Elizabeth[14] MORGAN *(Johnie Derald[13], Avis Ruth[12] WOLF, Leafy Fern[11] VAN HORN, Samuel Cornelius[10], Henry Coulter[9], Alexander[8], Isaiah[7], Henry B.[6], Henry[5], Christian Barentsen[4] VAN HOORN, Barent Christiansen[3], Christian Barentsen[2], Barent Barents[1])* was born Private. She married Charles Tracy NAFF Private, son of Harold NAFF and Kay NORRIS. He was born Private.

More About Charles NAFF and Laura MORGAN:
Private-Begin: Private

Children of Laura MORGAN and Charles NAFF are:
  i.   Harrison Ford[15] NAFF, b. Private.
  ii.   Hannah Elizabeth NAFF, b. Private.
  iii. Hayley Morgan NAFF, b. Private.

641. Kimberly Ann[14] MORGAN *(Johnie Derald[13], Avis Ruth[12] WOLF, Leafy Fern[11] VAN HORN, Samuel Cornelius[10], Henry Coulter[9], Alexander[8], Isaiah[7], Henry B.[6], Henry[5], Christian Barentsen[4] VAN HOORN, Barent Christiansen[3], Christian Barentsen[2], Barent Barents[1])* was born Private. She married (1) Phillip Michael BORTHACYRE Private, son of Mary. He was born Private. She married (2) Micheal Roy WEBB Private, son of Harold WEBB and Christine BECKER. He was born Private.

More About Phillip BORTHACYRE and Kimberly MORGAN:
Private-Begin: Private

More About Micheal WEBB and Kimberly MORGAN:
Private-Begin: Private

Children of Kimberly MORGAN and Phillip BORTHACYRE are:
    i.   Mary-Anne Elizabeth[15] BORTHACYRE, b. Private.
    ii. Phillip Michael BORTHACYRE II, b. 17 Apr 1987, Rolla, Phelps Cnty, MO; d. 15 Mar 2006, Rolla, Phelps Cnty, MO.

> More About Phillip Michael BORTHACYRE II:
> Burial: Unknown, Rolla Cemetery, Rolla, Phelps Cnty, MO
> Cause of Death: Died of a disease that was not clearly diagnosed.
> Medical Information: Phillip suffered severly from the time he was a junior in High School until his death with showers of blood clots that started in his lower leg and moved to other locations in his body.

642. Rebecca Ruth[14] MORGAN *(Johnie Derald[13], Avis Ruth[12] WOLF, Leafy Fern[11] VAN HORN, Samuel Cornelius[10], Henry Coulter[9], Alexander[8], Isaiah[7], Henry B.[6], Henry[5], Christian Barentsen[4] VAN HOORN, Barent Christiansen[3], Christian Barentsen[2], Barent Barents[1])* was born Private. She married William Alan WARE Private, son of Harold WARE and Ramona. He was born Private.

More About William WARE and Rebecca MORGAN:
Private-Begin: Private

Children of Rebecca MORGAN and William WARE are:
    i.   William Braden[15] WARE, b. Private.
    ii. Macy Ruth WARE, b. Private.
    iii. Lucas Jackson WARE, b. Private.

643. Johnie Derald[14] MORGAN, JR *(Johnie Derald[13], Avis Ruth[12] WOLF, Leafy Fern[11] VAN HORN, Samuel Cornelius[10], Henry Coulter[9], Alexander[8], Isaiah[7], Henry B.[6], Henry[5], Christian Barentsen[4] VAN HOORN, Barent Christiansen[3], Christian Barentsen[2], Barent Barents[1])* was born Private. He married Carolina ESTRADA Private. She was born Private.

More About Johnie MORGAN and Carolina ESTRADA:
Private-Begin: Private

Child of Johnie MORGAN and Carolina ESTRADA is:
    i.   Johnie Derald[15] MORGAN III, b. Private.

644. Sheryl Ann[14] HAGG *(Ruth Fern[13] MORGAN, Avis Ruth[12] WOLF, Leafy Fern[11] VAN HORN, Samuel Cornelius[10], Henry Coulter[9], Alexander[8], Isaiah[7], Henry B.[6], Henry[5], Christian Barentsen[4] VAN HOORN, Barent Christiansen[3], Christian Barentsen[2], Barent Barents[1])* was born Private. She married Nickey Shawn MARTINO Private. He was born Private.

More About Nickey MARTINO and Sheryl HAGG:
Private-Begin: Private

Children of Sheryl HAGG and Nickey MARTINO are:
    i.   Isabella Morgan[15] MARTINO, b. Private.
    ii. Braden Reid MARTINO, b. Private.

645. Jeffrey Alvin[14] HAGG *(Ruth Fern[13] MORGAN, Avis Ruth[12] WOLF, Leafy Fern[11] VAN HORN, Samuel Cornelius[10], Henry Coulter[9], Alexander[8], Isaiah[7], Henry B.[6], Henry[5], Christian Barentsen[4] VAN HOORN, Barent Christiansen[3], Christian Barentsen[2], Barent Barents[1])* was born Private. He married Theresa Jo ABELL Private. She was born Private.

More About Jeffrey HAGG and Theresa ABELL:
Private-Begin: Private

Child of Jeffrey HAGG and Theresa ABELL is:
    i.   Joshua Jeffrey[15] HAGG, b. Private.

646. Deborah Ruth[14] HAGG *(Ruth Fern[13] MORGAN, Avis Ruth[12] WOLF, Leafy Fern[11] VAN HORN, Samuel Cornelius[10], Henry Coulter[9], Alexander[8], Isaiah[7], Henry B.[6], Henry[5], Christian Barentsen[4] VAN HOORN, Barent Christiansen[3], Christian Barentsen[2], Barent Barents[1])* was born Private. She married James FREY Private. He was born Private.

More About James FREY and Deborah HAGG:
Private-Begin: Private

Children of Deborah HAGG and James FREY are:
    i.   Zoe Autumn[15] FREY, b. Private.
    ii. Noa James FREY, b. Private.

647. Billie Burnetta[14] DESPAIN *(Robert William[13] BENISH, Inez Vernal[12] VAN HORN, Robert Campbell[11], John Neff[10], Benjamin Briggs[9], Joshua[8], Isaiah[7], Henry B.[6], Henry[5], Christian Barentsen[4] VAN HOORN, Barent Christiansen[3], Christian Barentsen[2], Barent Barents[1])* was born Private. She married Robert Douglas AMMENS Private. He was born Private.

More About Robert AMMENS and Billie DESPAIN:
Private-Begin: Private

Child of Billie DESPAIN and Robert AMMENS is:
    i.   Samantha Lynette[15] AMMENS, b. Private; m. Kermit Edwin DAVIS, JR, Private; b. Private.

        More About Kermit DAVIS and Samantha AMMENS:
        Private-Begin: Private

648. Richard Glenn[14] VAN HORN, JR *(Richard Glenn[13], Andrew Glenn[12], Orin Denton[11], James Harvey[10], Benjamin Briggs[9], Joshua[8], Isaiah[7], Henry B.[6], Henry[5], Christian Barentsen[4] VAN HOORN, Barent Christiansen[3], Christian Barentsen[2], Barent Barents[1])[5382,5383,5384]* was born Bet. 1951 - 1967, and died Aft. 2005. He married (1) Barbara Ann ALBERTI[5384], daughter of John ALBERTI and Ramona. She was born 12 Apr 1967 in Kittanning, PA[5384], and died 02 Apr 2005 in Kittanning, PA[5384]. He married (2) Joyce SHIOCK[5385] Abt. 1976, daughter of John SHIOCK and Jean. She was born 28 Mar 1958 in Punxsutawney, Jefferson Cnty, PA, and died 02 Nov 1980 in Punxsutawney, Jefferson

Cnty, PA.

More About Richard Glenn VAN HORN, JR:
Lived: Dayton, PA

More About Barbara Ann ALBERTI:
Burial: Unknown, St. John's Cemetry Sagamore, PA
Occupation: Care Giver at Royal Oak Manor in Rural Valley, PA

More About Joyce SHIOCK:
Burial: Unknown, St. Adrian Cemetery Jefferson Cnty, PA

More About Richard VAN HORN and Joyce SHIOCK:
Marriage: Abt. 1976

Children of Richard VAN HORN and Barbara ALBERTI are:
      i.   Eric[15] VAN HORN, b. Private.
     ii.   Matthew VAN HORN, b. Private.

Children of Richard VAN HORN and Joyce SHIOCK are:
    iii.   Richard G.[15] VAN HORN III[5385], b. 21 Nov 1978, Punxsutawney, Indiana Cnty, PA[5385]; d. 21 Jun 1994, Valier, Jefferson Cnty, PA[5385].

          More About Richard G. VAN HORN III:
          Burial: Unknown, Valier Cemetery, Valier, Jefferson Cnty, PA

     iv.   Samuel VAN HORN, b. Private.
      v.   Ashley VAN HORN, b. Private.

649. James[14] MARINKO *(Janice Louise[13] RANKIN, James Rogers[12], Nellie Gertrude[11] VAN HORN, Alexander Milton[10], Benjamin Briggs[9], Joshua[8], Isaiah[7], Henry B.[6], Henry[5], Christian Barentsen[4] VAN HOORN, Barent Christiansen[3], Christian Barentsen[2], Barent Barents[1])* was born Private. He married Maria TORRES Private. She was born Private.

More About James MARINKO and Maria TORRES:
Private-Begin: Private

Children of James MARINKO and Maria TORRES are:
      i.   Stephen[15] MARINKO, b. Private.
     ii.   Jessica MARINKO, b. Private.

650. ?[14] NEWLLN *(Jean E.[13] FERGUSON, Lulu V.[12] VAN HORN, Samuel A.[11], John Miles[10], Christian[9], Joshua[8], Isaiah[7], Henry B.[6], Henry[5], Christian Barentsen[4] VAN HOORN, Barent Christiansen[3], Christian Barentsen[2], Barent Barents[1])* was born Private. She married Fred SNYDER Private. He was born Private.

More About Fred SNYDER and ? NEWLLN:
Private-Begin: Private

Children of ? NEWLLN and Fred SNYDER are:
      i.   ?[15] SNYDER, b. Private.

       ii.   ? SNYDER, b. Private.

651. ?[14] STANTON *(Raymond Walter[13], Mabel J.[12] SHEPHARD, Dessia A.[11] VAN HORN, John Miles[10], Christian[9], Joshua[8], Isaiah[7], Henry B.[6], Henry[5], Christian Barentsen[4] VAN HOORN, Barent Christiansen[3], Christian Barentsen[2], Barent Barents[1])* was born Private. She married BALCZUM Private. He was born Private.

More About BALCZUM and ? STANTON:
Private-Begin: Private

Children of ? STANTON and BALCZUM are:
      i.   ?[15] BALCZUM, b. Private.
     ii.   ? BALCZUM, b. Private.
   iii.   ? BALCZUM, b. Private.
   iv.   ? BALCZUM, b. Private.

652. Beverly[14] STANTON *(Raymond Walter[13], Mabel J.[12] SHEPHARD, Dessia A.[11] VAN HORN, John Miles[10], Christian[9], Joshua[8], Isaiah[7], Henry B.[6], Henry[5], Christian Barentsen[4] VAN HOORN, Barent Christiansen[3], Christian Barentsen[2], Barent Barents[1])* was born 11 Dec 1941 in Erie, Erie Cnty, PA, and died 08 Dec 2000 in Erie, Erie Cnty, PA. She married TANNER Private. He was born Private.

More About TANNER and Beverly STANTON:
Private-Begin: Private

Children of Beverly STANTON and TANNER are:
      i.   ?[15] TANNER, b. Private.
     ii.   ? TANNER, b. Private.
   iii.   ? TANNER, b. Private.

653. William Roy[14] LEWIS, JR *(Linda Jean[13] MCCAUSLAND, Robert Clark[12], Bertha Della[11] AUL, Mary Caroline[10] VAN HORN, Bennett Work[9], George Logan[8], Isaiah[7], Henry B.[6], Henry[5], Christian Barentsen[4] VAN HOORN, Barent Christiansen[3], Christian Barentsen[2], Barent Barents[1])* was born Private. He married Josie Maire SUMMERS Private. She was born Private.

More About William LEWIS and Josie SUMMERS:
Private-Begin: Private

Child of William LEWIS and Josie SUMMERS is:
      i.   Robert Allen[15] LEWIS, b. Private.

654. Pamela Jean[14] LEWIS *(Linda Jean[13] MCCAUSLAND, Robert Clark[12], Bertha Della[11] AUL, Mary Caroline[10] VAN HORN, Bennett Work[9], George Logan[8], Isaiah[7], Henry B.[6], Henry[5], Christian Barentsen[4] VAN HOORN, Barent Christiansen[3], Christian Barentsen[2], Barent Barents[1])* was born Private. She married Mike GEARHART Private. He was born Private.

More About Mike GEARHART and Pamela LEWIS:
Private-Begin: Private

Children of Pamela LEWIS and Mike GEARHART are:

    i.   Amber Marie[15] GEARHART, b. Private.
   ii.   Kristina Michelle GEARHART, b. Private.

655. James Lloyd[14] COOPER *(James Clarence[13], Florence Jane[12] MCCAUSLAND, Bertha Della[11] AUL, Mary Caroline[10] VAN HORN, Bennett Work[9], George Logan[8], Isaiah[7], Henry B.[6], Henry[5], Christian Barentsen[4] VAN HOORN, Barent Christiansen[3], Christian Barentsen[2], Barent Barents[1])* was born Private. He married Dawn Michelle SHRA Private. She was born Private.

More About James COOPER and Dawn SHRA:
Private-Begin: Private

Child of James COOPER and Dawn SHRA is:
    i.   James Ryan[15] COOPER, b. Private.

656. Melissa Ann[14] COOPER *(James Clarence[13], Florence Jane[12] MCCAUSLAND, Bertha Della[11] AUL, Mary Caroline[10] VAN HORN, Bennett Work[9], George Logan[8], Isaiah[7], Henry B.[6], Henry[5], Christian Barentsen[4] VAN HOORN, Barent Christiansen[3], Christian Barentsen[2], Barent Barents[1])* was born Private. She married Jerry Wade HUGHES Private. He was born Private.

More About Jerry HUGHES and Melissa COOPER:
Private-Begin: Private

Child of Melissa COOPER and Jerry HUGHES is:
    i.   Morgan Eliabeth[15] HUGHES, b. Private.

657. David James[14] HECKMAN *(Sally Ann[13] COOPER, Florence Jane[12] MCCAUSLAND, Bertha Della[11] AUL, Mary Caroline[10] VAN HORN, Bennett Work[9], George Logan[8], Isaiah[7], Henry B.[6], Henry[5], Christian Barentsen[4] VAN HOORN, Barent Christiansen[3], Christian Barentsen[2], Barent Barents[1])* was born Private. He married Pamela Eline MOSKY Private. She was born Private.

More About David HECKMAN and Pamela MOSKY:
Private-Begin: Private

Child of David HECKMAN and Pamela MOSKY is:
    i.   David James[15] HECKMAN, JR, b. Private.

658. Kevin Lee[14] HECKMAN *(Sally Ann[13] COOPER, Florence Jane[12] MCCAUSLAND, Bertha Della[11] AUL, Mary Caroline[10] VAN HORN, Bennett Work[9], George Logan[8], Isaiah[7], Henry B.[6], Henry[5], Christian Barentsen[4] VAN HOORN, Barent Christiansen[3], Christian Barentsen[2], Barent Barents[1])* was born Private. He married Shelly FOX Private. She was born Private.

More About Kevin HECKMAN and Shelly FOX:
Private-Begin: Private

Child of Kevin HECKMAN and Shelly FOX is:
    i.   Kory Lee[15] HECKMAN, b. Private.

659. Christine Marie[14] RUPP *(Charlene Marie[13] MCCAUSLAND, Donald Reid[12], Bertha Della[11] AUL,*

Mary Caroline[10] *VAN HORN, Bennett Work*[9], *George Logan*[8], *Isaiah*[7], *Henry B.*[6], *Henry*[5], *Christian Barentsen*[4] *VAN HOORN, Barent Christiansen*[3], *Christian Barentsen*[2], *Barent Barents*[1]*)* was born Private. She married John Edward STIVASON Private. He was born Private.

More About John STIVASON and Christine RUPP:
Private-Begin: Private

Children of Christine RUPP and John STIVASON are:
    i.   Curtis John[15] STIVASON, b. Private.
    ii.   Cory Wayne STIVASON, b. Private.
    iii.   Candice Marie STIVASON, b. Private.

660. Cynthia Mae[14] RUPP *(Charlene Marie*[13] *MCCAUSLAND, Donald Reid*[12], *Bertha Della*[11] *AUL, Mary Caroline*[10] *VAN HORN, Bennett Work*[9], *George Logan*[8], *Isaiah*[7], *Henry B.*[6], *Henry*[5], *Christian Barentsen*[4] *VAN HOORN, Barent Christiansen*[3], *Christian Barentsen*[2], *Barent Barents*[1]*)* was born Private. She married Robert Kenneth MOORE Private. He was born Private.

More About Robert MOORE and Cynthia RUPP:
Private-Begin: Private

Children of Cynthia RUPP and Robert MOORE are:
    i.   Natalie Lynn[15] MOORE, b. Private.
    ii.   Brett Robert MOORE, b. Private.
    iii.   Brandon James MOORE, b. Private.

661. Beverly Sue[14] RUPP *(Charlene Marie*[13] *MCCAUSLAND, Donald Reid*[12], *Bertha Della*[11] *AUL, Mary Caroline*[10] *VAN HORN, Bennett Work*[9], *George Logan*[8], *Isaiah*[7], *Henry B.*[6], *Henry*[5], *Christian Barentsen*[4] *VAN HOORN, Barent Christiansen*[3], *Christian Barentsen*[2], *Barent Barents*[1]*)* was born Private. She married Anthony DIMAIO Private. He was born Private.

More About Anthony DIMAIO and Beverly RUPP:
Private-Begin: Private

Children of Beverly RUPP and Anthony DIMAIO are:
    i.   Manda Sue[15] DIMAIO, b. Private.
    ii.   Chelsea Marie DIMAIO, b. Private.

662. Annette Carol[14] RUPP *(Charlene Marie*[13] *MCCAUSLAND, Donald Reid*[12], *Bertha Della*[11] *AUL, Mary Caroline*[10] *VAN HORN, Bennett Work*[9], *George Logan*[8], *Isaiah*[7], *Henry B.*[6], *Henry*[5], *Christian Barentsen*[4] *VAN HOORN, Barent Christiansen*[3], *Christian Barentsen*[2], *Barent Barents*[1]*)* was born Private. She married Shawn Michael MURRAY Private. He was born Private.

More About Shawn MURRAY and Annette RUPP:
Private-Begin: Private

Children of Annette RUPP and Shawn MURRAY are:
    i.   Dana Anette[15] MURRAY, b. Private.
    ii.   Alexa Ann MURRAY, b. Private.

663. Kelvin Arthur[14] RUPP *(Charlene Marie[13] MCCAUSLAND, Donald Reid[12], Bertha Della[11] AUL, Mary Caroline[10] VAN HORN, Bennett Work[9], George Logan[8], Isaiah[7], Henry B.[6], Henry[5], Christian Barentsen[4] VAN HOORN, Barent Christiansen[3], Christian Barentsen[2], Barent Barents[1])* was born Private. He married Erica Jennifer SMITH Private. She was born Private.

More About Kelvin RUPP and Erica SMITH:
Private-Begin: Private

Child of Kelvin RUPP and Erica SMITH is:
      i.   Taylor Cathline[15] RUPP, b. Private.

664. Julie Ann[14] MCCAUSLAND *(Donald Reid[13], Donald Reid[12], Bertha Della[11] AUL, Mary Caroline[10] VAN HORN, Bennett Work[9], George Logan[8], Isaiah[7], Henry B.[6], Henry[5], Christian Barentsen[4] VAN HOORN, Barent Christiansen[3], Christian Barentsen[2], Barent Barents[1])* was born Private.

Child of Julie Ann MCCAUSLAND is:
      i.   Josie Marie[15] MCCAUSLAND, b. Private.

665. Larry John[14] MCCAUSLAND, JR *(Larry John[13], Donald Reid[12], Bertha Della[11] AUL, Mary Caroline[10] VAN HORN, Bennett Work[9], George Logan[8], Isaiah[7], Henry B.[6], Henry[5], Christian Barentsen[4] VAN HOORN, Barent Christiansen[3], Christian Barentsen[2], Barent Barents[1])* was born Private. He married Tonia Marie JOHNS Private. She was born Private.

More About Larry MCCAUSLAND and Tonia JOHNS:
Private-Begin: Private

Children of Larry MCCAUSLAND and Tonia JOHNS are:
      i.   Larry Tyler[15] MCCAUSLAND, b. Private.
     ii.   Haley Gabrial MCCAUSLAND, b. Private.

666. Terry Lee[14] MCCAUSLAND *(Larry John[13], Donald Reid[12], Bertha Della[11] AUL, Mary Caroline[10] VAN HORN, Bennett Work[9], George Logan[8], Isaiah[7], Henry B.[6], Henry[5], Christian Barentsen[4] VAN HOORN, Barent Christiansen[3], Christian Barentsen[2], Barent Barents[1])* was born Private. He married Bridgett FERICOLY Private. She was born Private.

More About Terry MCCAUSLAND and Bridgett FERICOLY:
Private-Begin: Private

Child of Terry MCCAUSLAND and Bridgett FERICOLY is:
      i.   Megan Renee[15] MCCAUSLAND, b. Private.

Endnotes

1. *Isaiah Van Horn Will 27 April, 1839 Indiana Cnty, PA.*
2. *Interments of the Gilgal Cemetery, Gilgal Church, Indiana Cnty, PA.*
3. *Mahoning, Indiana Cnty, PA 1840 Census p. 122.*
4. *DAR Lineage Book 149 (56430).*
5. DAR National Record Copy of Member Application# 448771.

6. Hamilton, Von Gail, *Work Family History: Twelve Generations of Work in America 1690-1969,* Park City, Utah, (Park City, Utah: Publishers Press, 1969, 614 pgs.).
7. *Interments of the Gilgal Cemetery, Gilgal Church, Indiana Cnty, PA.*
8. *Abstract of Graves of Revolutionary Patriots, Vol.4, Serial: 11831.*
9. *DAR Lineage Book 149 (56430).*
10. *East Mahoning Twp., Indiana Cnty, PA 1850 Census p. 247.*
11. DAR National Record Copy of Member Application # 800118.
12. *East Mahoning Twp., Indiana Cnty, PA 1850 Census p. 247.*
13. DAR National Certificate Record Copy of Member Application , #451294.
14. Pennsylvania Archives, 2nd Series, Volume 14.
15. *Pennsylvania Archives Series: Series 5 Volume: V Chapter: Muster Rolls and Papers Relating to the Associators and Militia of the County of Bucks. .*
16. DAR National Record Copy of Member Application # 800118.
17. *Isaiah Van Horn Will 27 April, 1839 Indiana Cnty, PA.*
18. *DAR Lineage Book 149 (56430).*
19. *The National Society of the Daughters of the American Revolution Volume 57.*
20. *East Mahoning Twp., Indiana Cnty, PA 1870 Census p. 201B.*
21. *East Mahoning Twp., Indiana Cnty, PA 1850 Census p. 247.*
22. *East Mahoning Twp., Indiana Cnty, PA 1860 Census p. 308.*
23. DAR National Record Copy of Member Application# 446865.
24. *Interments of the Gilgal Cemetery, Gilgal Church, Indiana Cnty, PA.*
25. *The National Society of the Daughters of the American Revolution Volume 57.*
26. *DAR Lineage Book 149 (56430).*
27. *East Mahoning Twp., Indiana Cnty, PA 1850 Census p. 247.*
28. *Robert Thompson Will Indiana County Will Book Volume 1 No 19 p. 14.*
29. DAR National Record Copy of Member Application# 446865.
30. *Interments of the Gilgal Cemetery, Gilgal Church, Indiana Cnty, PA.*
31. DAR National Record Copy of Member Application# 446865.
32. *Isaiah Van Horn Will 27 April, 1839 Indiana Cnty, PA,* No 763, Vol 1, p 493.
33. *West Wheatfield Twp., Indiana Cnty, PA 1870 Census p. 401B.*
34. *St. Clair Twp., Westmoreland Cnty, PA 1860 Census p. 936.*
35. *Fairfield, Westmoreland Cnty, PA 1850 Census p. 125 B & 126.*
36. "9 September 1891 Indiana County Gazette (Indiana, PA) Article on 5 generations of Van Horn in one family."
37. *West Wheatfield Twp., Indiana Cnty, PA 1870 Census p. 401B.*
38. "Indiana Progress (Indiana Cnty, PA) 24 August 1871."
39. *Alexander Van Horn Will 4 May 1869 Indiana Cnty, PA, Vol 3, p. 576 proved 1871.*
40. *West Wheatfield Twp., Indiana Cnty, PA 1870 Census p. 401B.*
41. *West Wheatfield Twp., Indiana Cnty, PA 1880 Census ED 244 Sh 440C.*
42. *St. Clair Twp., Westmoreland Cnty, PA 1860 Census p. 936.*
43. *Fairfield, Westmoreland Cnty, PA 1850 Census p. 125 B & 126.*
44. "9 September 1891 Indiana County Gazette (Indiana, PA) Article on 5 generations of Van Horn in one family."
45. *West Wheatfield Twp., Indiana Cnty, PA 1870 Census p. 401B.*
46. *Will of Mary Van Horn Indiana Cnty, PA #5362, p. 131.*
47. *Cemetery Listing Indiana Cnty, PA.*
48. *Pennsylvania Veterans Burial Cards 1777-1999,* "Electronic."
49. *Cemetery Listing Indiana Cnty, PA.*
50. *Alexander Van Horn Will 4 May 1869 Indiana Cnty, PA, Vol 3, p. 576 proved 1871.*
51. *Will of Mary Van Horn Indiana Cnty, PA #5362, p. 131.*
52. *West Wheatfield Twp., Indiana Cnty, PA 1880 Census ED 244 Sh 440C.*
53. *Will of Mary Van Horn Indiana Cnty, PA #5362, p. 131.*
54. "March 6, 1895 Indiana Progress (Indiana, PA) ."
55. *Pennsylvania Veterans Burial Cards 1777-1999,* "Electronic."

56. *St. Clair Twp., Westmoreland Cnty, PA 1860 Census p. 936.*
57. *Fairfield, Westmoreland Cnty, PA 1850 Census p. 125 B & 126.*
58. *Isaiah Van Horn Will 27 April, 1839 Indiana Cnty, PA.*
59. Dick McElhoes, Rootsweb Posting McElhoes Mixup.
60. *Rayne Twp., Indiana Cnty, PA 1860 Census p. 171.*
61. Clarence D. Stephenson, Indiana County 175th Anniversary History, (Vol IV p. 433).
62. DAR National Record Copy of Member Application# 448771.
63. Dick McElhoes, Rootsweb Posting McElhoes Mixup.
64. DAR National Record Copy of Member Application# 448771.
65. Clarence D. Stephenson, Indiana County 175th Anniversary History, (Vol IV p. 433).
66. DAR National Record Copy of Member Application# 448771.
67. *Isaiah Van Horn Will 27 April, 1839 Indiana Cnty, PA.*
68. *Family Sheet from David and Donna King of Benicia, CA.*
69. *South Mahoning Twp., Indiana Cnty, PA 1860 Census p. 333.*
70. *South Mahoning Twp., Indiana Cnty, PA 1870 Census p. 354B.*
71. *Mahoning Twp., Indiana Cnty, PA 1840 Census p. 128.*
72. DAR National Record Copy of Member Application # 614578.
73. *Family Sheet from David and Donna King of Benicia, CA.*
74. D. Scott Van Horn Family Group Sheet, August 8, 1983.
75. *South Mahoning Twp., Indiana Cnty, PA 1860 Census p. 333.*
76. *Mahoning Twp., Indiana Cnty, PA 1840 Census p. 128.*
77. DAR National Record Copy of Member Application # 614578.
78. *South Mahoning Twp., Indiana Cnty, PA 1860 Census p. 248.*
79. DAR National Record Copy of Member Application # 614578.
80. *Mahoning Twp., Indiana Cnty, PA 1840 Census p. 128.*
81. *South Mahoning Twp., Indiana Cnty, PA 1860 Census p. 333.*
82. *Mahoning Twp., Indiana Cnty, PA 1840 Census p. 128.*
83. *Isaiah Van Horn Will 27 April, 1839 Indiana Cnty, PA.*
84. *Allegheny Ward 1, Allegheny Cnty, PA 1850 Census p. 20B.*
85. *Allegheny Ward 2, Allegheny Cnty, PA 1860 Census p. 892.*
86. *Allegheny, Allegheny Cnty, PA 1880 Census ED 7 Sh 26.*
87. *Allegheny Ward 1, Allegheny Cnty, PA 1850 Census p. 20B.*
88. The Abridged Compendium of American Genealogy, p 236.
89. *Allegheny Ward 1, Allegheny Cnty, PA 1850 Census p. 20B.*
90. *Allegheny Ward 2, Allegheny Cnty, PA 1860 Census p. 892.*
91. The Abridged Compendium of American Genealogy, p 236.
92. The Abridged Compendium of American Genealogy.
93. *Allegheny Ward 1, Allegheny Cnty, PA 1850 Census p. 20B.*
94. The Abridged Compendium of American Genealogy, p 236.
95. *Allegheny Ward 1, Allegheny Cnty, PA 1850 Census p. 20B.*
96. "2 March 1898 Indiana Progress (Indiana, PA) Mary A. Van Horn Obituary."
97. *Isaiah Van Horn Will 27 April, 1839 Indiana Cnty, PA.*
98. *South Mahoning Twp., Indiana Cnty, PA 1860 Census p. 330B.*
99. *South Mahoning Twp., Indiana Cnty, PA 1850 Census p. 198B.*
100. *Gerrardstown, Berkeley Cnty, WV 1870 Census p. 177.*
101. *Green Twp., Indiana Cnty, PA 1880 Census ED 140 Sh 14 & 15.*
102. *South Mahoning Twp., Indiana Cnty, PA 1860 Census p. 330B.*
103. *Gerrardstown, Berkeley Cnty, WV 1870 Census p. 177.*
104. "Indiana Progress (Indiana Cnty, PA) March 2, 1898."
105. *South Mahoning Twp., Indiana Cnty, PA 1860 Census p. 330B.*
106. "2 March 1898 Indiana Progress (Indiana, PA) Mary A. Van Horn Obituary."
107. *South Mahoning Twp., Indiana Cnty, PA 1850 Census p. 198B.*
108. *Gerrardstown, Berkeley Cnty, WV 1870 Census p. 177.*
109. *Green Twp., Indiana Cnty, PA 1880 Census ED 140 Sh 14 & 15.*

110. *South Mahoning Twp., Indiana Cnty, PA 1860 Census p. 330B.*
111. *Gerrardstown, Berkeley Cnty, WV 1870 Census p. 177.*
112. "Indiana Progress (Indiana Cnty, PA) March 2, 1898."
113. *Isaiah Van Horn Will 27 April, 1839 Indiana Cnty, PA.*
114. *Interments of the Gilgal Cemetery, Gilgal Church, Indiana Cnty, PA.*
115. Wetzel.ged.
116. *East Mahoning Twp., Indiana Cnty, PA 1860 Census p. 306.*
117. *West Mahoning Twp., Indiana Cnty, PA 1870 Census p. 390.*
118. *West Mahoning Twp., Indiana Cnty, PA 1880 Census ED 144 Sh 325C.*
119. *West Mahoning Twp., Indiana Cnty, PA 1850 Census p. 174B.*
120. DAR National Record Copy of Member Application # 800118.
121. *Interments of the Gilgal Cemetery, Gilgal Church, Indiana Cnty, PA.*
122. *West Mahoning Twp., Indiana Cnty, PA 1850 Census p. 174B.*
123. *East Mahoning Twp., Indiana Cnty, PA 1860 Census p. 306.*
124. *West Mahoning Twp., Indiana Cnty, PA 1870 Census p. 390.*
125. *West Mahoning Twp., Indiana Cnty, PA 1880 Census ED 144 Sh 325C.*
126. *Interments of the Gilgal Cemetery, Gilgal Church, Indiana Cnty, PA.*
127. *West Mahoning Twp., Indiana Cnty, PA 1850 Census p. 174B.*
128. *West Mahoning Twp., Indiana Cnty, PA 1870 Census p. 390.*
129. *West Mahoning Twp., Indiana Cnty, PA 1850 Census p. 174B.*
130. *Isaiah Van Horn Will 27 April, 1839 Indiana Cnty, PA.*
131. *East Mahoning Twp., Indiana Cnty, PA 1860 Census p. 170B.*
132. *East Mahoning Twp., Indiana Cnty, PA 1850 Census p. 247.*
133. Hamilton, Von Gail, *Work Family History: Twelve Generations of Work in America 1690-1969, Park City, Utah,* (Park City, Utah: Publishers Press, 1969, 614 pgs.).
134. *East Mahoning Twp., Indiana Cnty, PA 1860 Census p. 170B.*
135. *East Mahoning Twp., Indiana Cnty, PA 1850 Census p. 247.*
136. Hamilton, Von Gail, *Work Family History: Twelve Generations of Work in America 1690-1969, Park City, Utah,* (Park City, Utah: Publishers Press, 1969, 614 pgs.).
137. *East Mahoning Twp., Indiana Cnty, PA 1860 Census p. 170B.*
138. *East Mahoning Twp., Indiana Cnty, PA 1850 Census p. 247.*
139. *East Mahoning Twp., Indiana Cnty, PA 1860 Census p. 170B.*
140. *East Mahoning Twp., Indiana Cnty, PA 1850 Census p. 247.*
141. *East Mahoning Twp., Indiana Cnty, PA 1860 Census p. 170B.*
142. *Isaiah Van Horn Will 27 April, 1839 Indiana Cnty, PA.*
143. *South Mahoning Twp., Indiana Cnty, PA 1860 Census p. 330B.*
144. *Interments of the Gilgal Cemetery, Gilgal Church, Indiana Cnty, PA.*
145. *Isaiah Van Horn Will 27 April, 1839 Indiana Cnty, PA.*
146. *South Mahoning Twp., Indiana Cnty, PA 1860 Census p. 330B.*
147. *South Mahoning Twp., Indiana Cnty, PA 1870 Census p. 351B.*
148. *South Mahoning Twp., Indiana Cnty, PA 1880 Census ED 143 Sh 26.*
149. *South Mahoning Twp., Indiana Cnty, PA 1900 Census ED 64 Sh 2B .*
150. *East Mahoning Twp., Indiana Cnty, PA 1850 Census p. 247.*
151. Hamilton, Von Gail, *Work Family History: Twelve Generations of Work in America 1690-1969, Park City, Utah,* (Park City, Utah: Publishers Press, 1969, 614 pgs.).
152. *Interments of the Gilgal Cemetery, Gilgal Church, Indiana Cnty, PA.*
153. *Cemetery Listing Indiana Cnty, PA.*
154. "6 March 1901 Indiana County Gazette (Indiana, PA)."
155. *Interments of the Gilgal Cemetery, Gilgal Church, Indiana Cnty, PA.*
156. *South Mahoning Twp., Indiana Cnty, PA 1860 Census p. 330B.*
157. *South Mahoning Twp., Indiana Cnty, PA 1870 Census p. 351B.*
158. *South Mahoning Twp., Indiana Cnty, PA 1880 Census ED 143 Sh 26.*
159. *East Mahoning Twp., Indiana Cnty, PA 1850 Census p. 247.*
160. Hamilton, Von Gail, *Work Family History: Twelve Generations of Work in America 1690-1969, Park*

City, Utah, (Park City, Utah: Publishers Press, 1969, 614 pgs.).

161. *Interments of the Gilgal Cemetery, Gilgal Church, Indiana Cnty, PA.*

162. *South Mahoning Twp., Indiana Cnty, PA 1860 Census p. 330B.*

163. Hamilton, Von Gail, *Work Family History: Twelve Generations of Work in America 1690-1969,* Park *City, Utah,* (Park City, Utah: Publishers Press, 1969, 614 pgs.).

164. *Interments of the Gilgal Cemetery, Gilgal Church, Indiana Cnty, PA.*

165. Hamilton, Von Gail, *Work Family History: Twelve Generations of Work in America 1690-1969,* Park *City, Utah,* (Park City, Utah: Publishers Press, 1969, 614 pgs.).

166. *Interments of the Gilgal Cemetery, Gilgal Church, Indiana Cnty, PA.*

167. *East Mahoning Twp., Indiana Cnty, PA 1850 Census p. 247.*

168. Hamilton, Von Gail, *Work Family History: Twelve Generations of Work in America 1690-1969,* Park *City, Utah,* (Park City, Utah: Publishers Press, 1969, 614 pgs.).

169. *East Mahoning Twp., Indiana Cnty, PA 1850 Census p. 247.*

170. *US Federal Census Mortality Schedules Index 1860 ID # MRT317_1600.*

171. Hamilton, Von Gail, *Work Family History: Twelve Generations of Work in America 1690-1969,* Park *City, Utah,* (Park City, Utah: Publishers Press, 1969, 614 pgs.).

172. *US Federal Census Mortality Index 1860.*

173. Indiana Cnty, PA Birth Records 1852-1856.

174. Hamilton, Von Gail, *Work Family History: Twelve Generations of Work in America 1690-1969,* Park *City, Utah,* (Park City, Utah: Publishers Press, 1969, 614 pgs.).

175. *US Federal Census Mortality Index 1860.*

176. "Indiana Weekly Messenger (Indiana, PA) 11 January 1899."

177. *Armagh, Indiana Cnty, PA 1850 Census p. 128B.*

178. "Indiana Weekly Messenger (Indiana, PA) 11 January 1899."

179. *Armagh, Indiana Cnty, PA 1850 Census p. 128B.*

180. *East Mahoning Twp., Indiana Cnty, PA 1860 Census p. 179 A&B.*

181. *East Mahoning Twp., Indiana Cnty, PA 1870 Census p. 199 & 200.*

182. *East Mahoning Twp., Indiana Cnty, PA 1880 Census ED 145 Sh 10B.*

183. *Armagh, Indiana Cnty, PA 1850 Census p. 128B.*

184. "Indiana Weekly Messenger (Indiana, PA) 11 January 1899."

185. *Armagh, Indiana Cnty, PA 1850 Census p. 128B.*

186. *East Mahoning Twp., Indiana Cnty, PA 1860 Census p. 179 A&B.*

187. *Armagh, Indiana Cnty, PA 1850 Census p. 128B.*

188. *East Mahoning Twp., Indiana Cnty, PA 1860 Census p. 179 A&B.*

189. "Indiana Weekly Messenger (Indiana, PA) 11 January 1899."

190. *East Mahoning Twp., Indiana Cnty, PA 1860 Census p. 179 A&B.*

191. *East Mahoning Twp., Indiana Cnty, PA 1880 Census ED 145 Sh 10B.*

192. "Elizabeth Van Horn Obituary Indiana County Genealogical and Historical Society Newspaper Clippings."

193. *1860 Census Rayne Twp., Indiana Cnty, PA p. 307.*

194. *Rayne, Indiana Cnty, PA 1870 Census p. 346B.*

195. *Marion Center, East Mahoning Twp., Indiana Cnty, PA 1900 Census ED 53 Sh 9A.*

196. "James T. Van Horn Obituary Indiana County Genealogical and Historical Society Newspaper Clippings."

197. *1860 Census Rayne Twp., Indiana Cnty, PA p. 307.*

198. "James T. Van Horn Obituary Indiana County Genealogical and Historical Society Newspaper Clippings."

199. *1860 Census Rayne Twp., Indiana Cnty, PA p. 307.*

200. *Rayne, Indiana Cnty, PA 1870 Census p. 346B.*

201. "Elizabeth Van Horn Obituary Indiana County Genealogical and Historical Society Newspaper Clippings."

202. *Marion Center, East Mahoning Twp., Indiana Cnty, PA 1900 Census ED 53 Sh 9A.*

203. *East Mahoning Twp., Indiana Cnty, PA 1910 Census ED 73 Sh 9A.*

204. DAR National Record Copy of Member Application # 684102.

205. *1860 Census Rayne Twp., Indiana Cnty, PA p. 307.*
206. "Ellen H. Meanor Van Horn Obituary Indiana County Genealogical and Historical Society Newspaper Clippings."
207. DAR National Record Copy of Member Application # 684102.
208. "Ellen H. Meanor Van Horn Obituary Indiana County Genealogical and Historical Society Newspaper Clippings."
209. "Indiana Weekly Messenger (Indiana, PA) 20 November 1919."
210. *Rayne, Indiana Cnty, PA 1870 Census p. 346B.*
211. *1860 Census Rayne Twp., Indiana Cnty, PA p. 307.*
212. "8 Feb 1883 Indiana Progress (Indiana, PA)."
213. "Elizabeth Van Horn Obituary Indiana County Genealogical and Historical Society Newspaper Clippings."
214. *1860 Census Rayne Twp., Indiana Cnty, PA p. 307.*
215. *Rayne, Indiana Cnty, PA 1870 Census p. 346B.*
216. "James T. Van Horn Obituary Indiana County Genealogical and Historical Society Newspaper Clippings."
217. *Marion Center, East Mahoning Twp., Indiana Cnty, PA 1900 Census ED 53 Sh 9A.*
218. *East Mahoning Twp., Indiana Cnty, PA 1910 Census ED 73 Sh 1A.*
219. *Indiana, Indiana Cnty, PA 1930 Census ED 34 Sh 6A.*
220. *Rayne, Indiana Cnty, PA 1870 Census p. 346B.*
221. "Elizabeth Van Horn Obituary Indiana County Genealogical and Historical Society Newspaper Clippings."
222. "8 Sept 1881 Indiana Progress (Indiana, PA)."
223. "Indiana Progress (Indiana Cnty, PA)."
224. "8 Sept 1881 Indiana Progress (Indiana, PA)."
225. Hamilton, Von Gail, *Work Family History: Twelve Generations of Work in America 1690-1969,* Park City, Utah, (Park City, Utah: Publishers Press, 1969, 614 pgs.).
226. Indiana Cnty, PA Birth Records 1852-1856.
227. *DAR Lineage Book 80 (69218).*
228. *East Mahoning Twp., Indiana Cnty, PA 1860 Census p. 170.*
229. *East Mahoning Twp., Indiana Cnty, PA 1870 Census p. 201B.*
230. Hamilton, Von Gail, *Work Family History: Twelve Generations of Work in America 1690-1969,* Park City, Utah, (Park City, Utah: Publishers Press, 1969, 614 pgs.).
231. *DAR Lineage Book 80 (69218).*
232. *East Mahoning Twp., Indiana Cnty, PA 1860 Census p. 170.*
233. *East Mahoning Twp., Indiana Cnty, PA 1870 Census p. 201B.*
234. Hamilton, Von Gail, *Work Family History: Twelve Generations of Work in America 1690-1969,* Park City, Utah, (Park City, Utah: Publishers Press, 1969, 614 pgs.).
235. *East Mahoning Twp., Indiana Cnty, PA 1860 Census p. 170.*
236. *DAR Lineage Book 80 (69218).*
237. *East Mahoning Twp., Indiana Cnty, PA 1860 Census p. 170.*
238. *East Mahoning Twp., Indiana Cnty, PA 1870 Census p. 201B.*
239. "10 Aug. 1922 Indiana Weekly Messenger (Indiana, PA) Aaron Steele Obituary."
240. *Indiana, Indiana Cnty, PA 1910 Census ED 82 Sh 3B.*
241. *East Mahoning Twp., Indiana Cnty, PA 1860 Census p. 170.*
242. *East Mahoning Twp., Indiana Cnty, PA 1850 Census p. 247.*
243. "10 Aug. 1922 Indiana Weekly Messenger (Indiana, PA) Aaron Steele Obituary."
244. *Indiana, Indiana Cnty, PA 1910 Census ED 82 Sh 3B.*
245. "8 July 1908 Indiana Evening Gazette (Indiana, PA) Miriam Work Van Horn Obiturary."
246. *Indiana, Indiana Cnty, PA 1910 Census ED 82 Sh 3B.*
247. *East Mahoning Twp., Indiana Cnty, PA 1850 Census p. 247.*
248. "10 Aug. 1922 Indiana Weekly Messenger (Indiana, PA) Aaron Steele Obituary."
249. *Indiana, Indiana Cnty, PA 1910 Census ED 82 Sh 3B.*
250. *East Mahoning Twp., Indiana Cnty, PA 1870 Census p. 201B.*

251. *The National Society of the Daughters of the American Revolution Volume 57.*
252. *Pomeroy, Meigs Cnty, OH 1850 Census p. 110.*
253. *Kansas City, Jackson Cnty, MO 1860 Census p. 101.*
254. *Kansas City, Jackson Cnty, MO 1870 Census p. 503.*
255. *Kansas City, Jackson Cnty, MO 1880 Census ED 7 Sh 199C.*
256. *Blue Twp., Jackson Cnty, MO 1900 Census ED 2 Sh 7B.*
257. *Blue Twp., Jackson Cnty, MO 1910 Census ED 5 Sh 12A.*
258. *DAR Lineage Book 251 (71704).*
259. *Pomeroy, Meigs Cnty, OH 1850 Census p. 110.*
260. *The National Society of the Daughters of the American Revolution Volume 57.*
261. *Pomeroy, Meigs Cnty, OH 1850 Census p. 110.*
262. *Kansas City, Jackson Cnty, MO 1860 Census p. 101.*
263. *Kansas City, Jackson Cnty, MO 1870 Census p. 503.*
264. *Kansas City, Jackson Cnty, MO 1880 Census ED 7 Sh 199C.*
265. *Blue Twp., Jackson Cnty, MO 1900 Census ED 2 Sh 7B.*
266. *Blue Twp., Jackson Cnty, MO 1910 Census ED 5 Sh 12A.*
267. *DAR Lineage Book 149 (56430).*
268. *Pomeroy, Meigs Cnty, OH 1850 Census p. 110.*
269. "Indiana Progress (Indiana Cnty, PA) 3 August 1910."
270. *Pomeroy, Meigs Cnty, OH 1850 Census p. 110.*
271. *Kansas City, Jackson Cnty, MO 1860 Census p. 101.*
272. *Kansas City, Jackson Cnty, MO 1870 Census p. 503.*
273. *Kansas City, Jackson Cnty, MO 1880 Census ED 2 Sh 55A.*
274. *Kansas City, Jackson Cnty, MO 1860 Census p. 101.*
275. *Kansas City, Jackson Cnty, MO 1880 Census ED 2 Sh 55A.*
276. "Indiana Weekly Messenger (Indiana, PA) 21 November 1918."
277. *Kansas City, Jackson Cnty, MO 1880 Census ED 2 Sh 55A.*
278. C. S. Williams, *Christian Barentsen Van Horn and His Descendants* , (1911 NY).
279. *Kansas City, Jackson Cnty, MO 1870 Census p. 503.*
280. *Kansas City, Jackson Cnty, MO 1880 Census ED 7 Sh 199C.*
281. *Kansas City, Jackson Cnty, MO 1870 Census p. 503.*
282. *Kansas City, Jackson Cnty, MO 1880 Census ED 7 Sh 199C.*
283. C. S. Williams, Christian Barentsen Van Horn and His Descendants, 1911 NY.
284. *East Mahoning Twp., Indiana Cnty, PA1870 Census p. 205B.*
285. *East Mahoning Twp., Indiana Cnty, PA 1860 Census p. 308.*
286. *East Mahoning Twp., Indiana Cnty, PA 1880 Census ED 145 Sh 338C.*
287. *East Mahoning Twp., Indiana Cnty, PA 1850 Census p. 247.*
288. "25 Aug 1941 Indiana Evening Gazette (Indiana, PA) Edith Lee Van Horn Shields Obituary."
289. *East Mahoning Twp., Indiana Cnty, PA1870 Census p. 205B.*
290. *East Mahoning Twp., Indiana Cnty, PA 1860 Census p. 172B.*
291. "Indiana Progress (Indiana Cnty, PA) May 5, 1887."
292. "Indiana Weekly Messenger (Indiana, PA) 4 May 1887."
293. *East Mahoning Twp., Indiana Cnty, PA 1860 Census p. 172B, 172B.*
294. *East Mahoning Twp., Indiana Cnty, PA1870 Census p. 205B.*
295. *East Mahoning Twp., Indiana Cnty, PA 1860 Census p. 172B, 172B.*
296. *East Mahoning Twp., Indiana Cnty, PA1870 Census p. 205B.*
297. *East Mahoning Twp., Indiana Cnty, PA 1860 Census p. 172B, 172B.*
298. *East Mahoning Twp., Indiana Cnty, PA1870 Census p. 205B.*
299. *Lower Turkeyfoot, Somerset Cnty, PA 1870 Census p. 363B.*
300. *Springfiield, Fayette Cnty, PA 1880 Census ED 55 Sh 457C.*
301. *St. Clair Twp., Westmoreland Cnty, PA 1860 Census p. 934.*
302. *Will of Mary Van Horn Indiana Cnty, PA #5362, p. 131.*
303. *Mt. Pleasant, Westmoreland Cnty, PA 1900 Census ED 119 Sh 12B.*
304. *Lower Turkeyfoot, Somerset Cnty, PA 1870 Census p. 363B.*

305. Willey, Gordon (Van Horn TREE) Husband of Jacqueline Marshal Granddaughter of Judson Van Horn.
306. *Lower Turkeyfoot, Somerset Cnty, PA 1870 Census p. 363B.*
307. *Springfiield, Fayette Cnty, PA 1880 Census ED 55 Sh 457C.*
308. *St. Clair Twp., Westmoreland Cnty, PA 1860 Census p. 934.*
309. *Mt. Pleasant, Westmoreland Cnty, PA 1900 Census ED 119 Sh 12B.*
310. Willey, Gordon (Van Horn TREE) Husband of Jacqueline Marshal Granddaughter of Judson Van Horn.
311. *Springfield Twp., Fayette Cnty, PA 1910 Census ED 74 Sh 7B.*
312. *Lower Turkeyfoot, Somerset Cnty, PA 1870 Census p. 363B.*
313. *St. Clair Twp., Westmoreland Cnty, PA 1860 Census p. 934.*
314. *Lower Turkeyfoot, Somerset Cnty, PA 1870 Census p. 363B.*
315. *Springfiield, Fayette Cnty, PA 1880 Census ED 55 Sh 457C.*
316. *Lower Turkeyfoot, Somerset Cnty, PA 1870 Census p. 363B.*
317. *Springfiield, Fayette Cnty, PA 1880 Census ED 55 Sh 457C.*
318. *Mt. Pleasant, Westmoreland Cnty, PA 1900 Census ED 119 Sh 12B.*
319. *Springfiield, Fayette Cnty, PA 1880 Census ED 55 Sh 457C.*
320. *Alexander Van Horn Will 4 May 1869 Indiana Cnty, PA, Vol 3, p. 576 proved 1871.*
321. James W. Van Horn Will, Indiana Cnty, PA, Vol 8, p 251.
322. *Will of Mary Van Horn Indiana Cnty, PA #5362, p. 131.*
323. *West Mahoning Twp., Indiana Cnty, PA 1860 Census p. 390.*
324. *West Wheatfield Twp., Indiana Cnty, PA 1880 Census ED 244 Sh 440C.*
325. *Williamsport Ward 3, Lycoming Cnty, PA 1870 Census p. 476B.*
326. "9 September 1891 Indiana County Gazette (Indiana, PA) Article on 5 generations of Van Horn in one family."
327. *West Mahoning Twp., Indiana Cnty, PA 1860 Census p. 390.*
328. Will of J. W. Van Horn #5483 Indiana Cnty, PA.
329. "6 June 1894 Indiana County Gazette (Indiana, PA) James Wherry Van Horn Obituary."
330. *West Wheatfield Twp., Indiana Cnty, PA 1860 Census p. 390 A and B.*
331. *Williamsport Ward 3, Lycoming Cnty, PA 1870 Census p. 476B.*
332. "6 June 1894 Indiana County Gazette (Indiana, PA) James Wherry Van Horn Obituary."
333. *West Wheatfield Twp., Indiana Cnty, PA 1860 Census p. 390 A and B.*
334. "6 June 1894 Indiana County Gazette (Indiana, PA) James Wherry Van Horn Obituary."
335. Will of J. W. Van Horn #5483 Indiana Cnty, PA.
336. *West Wheatfield Twp., Indiana Cnty, PA 1860 Census p. 390 A and B.*
337. *Williamsport Ward 3, Lycoming Cnty, PA 1870 Census p. 476B.*
338. *Williamsport, Ward 4, Lycoming Cnty, PA 1910 Census ED 81 Sh 4B.*
339. *Williamsport Ward 4, Lycoming Cnty, PA 1900 Census ED 82 Sh 10A.*
340. "6 June 1894 Indiana County Gazette (Indiana, PA) James Wherry Van Horn Obituary."
341. *West Mahoning Twp., Indiana Cnty, PA 1860 Census p. 390.*
342. *Williamsport Ward 4, Lycoming Cnty, PA 1900 Census ED 82 Sh 10A.*
343. Will of J. W. Van Horn #5483 Indiana Cnty, PA.
344. *Williamsport, Ward 4, Lycoming Cnty, PA 1910 Census ED 81 Sh 4B.*
345. *Plunketts Creek, Lycoming Cnty, PA 1860 Census p.685.*
346. *Williamsport Ward 4, Lycoming Cnty, PA 1900 Census ED 82 Sh 10A.*
347. *Williamsport, Lycoming Cnty, PA 1880 Census ED 70 Sh 508C.*
348. *Williamsport Ward 4, Lycoming Cnty, PA 1900 Census ED 82 Sh 10A.*
349. "26 and 27 January 1915 Gazette and Bulletin (Williamsport, PA)."
350. *Williamsport, Ward 4, Lycoming Cnty, PA 1910 Census ED 81 Sh 4B.*
351. *Plunketts Creek, Lycoming Cnty, PA 1860 Census p.685.*
352. *Williamsport Ward 4, Lycoming Cnty, PA 1900 Census ED 82 Sh 10A.*
353. "26 and 27 January 1915 Gazette and Bulletin (Williamsport, PA)."
354. *Williamsport Ward 4, Lycoming Cnty, PA 1900 Census ED 82 Sh 10A.*
355. Will of J. W. Van Horn #5483 Indiana Cnty, PA.

356. *West Wheatfield Twp., Indiana Cnty, PA 1860 Census p. 390 A and B.*
357. *West Mahoning Twp., Indiana Cnty, PA 1880 Census ED 144 Sh 325C.*
358. *West Wheatfield Twp., Indiana Cnty, PA 1910 Census ED 97 Sh 7A.*
359. *Williamsport Ward 3, Lycoming Cnty, PA 1870 Census p. 476B.*
360. *West Wheatfield Twp., Indiana Cnty, PA 1900 Census ED 66 Sh 15A.*
361. *Will of Mary Van Horn Indiana Cnty, PA #5362, p. 131.*
362. *New Florence, Westmoreland Cnty, PA 1930 Census ED 114 Sh 3A.*
363. *New Florence, Westmoreland Cnty, PA 1920 Census ED 171 Sh 7B.*
364. "9 September 1891 Indiana County Gazette (Indiana, PA) Article on 5 generations of Van Horn in one family."
365. "6 June 1894 Indiana County Gazette (Indiana, PA) James Wherry Van Horn Obituary."
366. *West Wheatfield Twp., Indiana Cnty, PA 1860 Census p. 390 A and B.*
367. Handwritten Notes of Leafy Fern Van Horn Wolf.
368. *Alexander Van Horn Will 4 May 1869 Indiana Cnty, PA, Vol 3, p. 576 proved 1871.*
369. *Will of Mary Van Horn Indiana Cnty, PA #5362, p. 131.*
370. *East Wheatfield Twp., Indiana Cnty, PA 1870 Census p. 22B, p. 228.*
371. *East Wheatfield Twp., Indiana Cnty, PA 1860 Census p. 374.*
372. "23 Oct 1907 Indiana Evening Gazette (Indiana, PA) Van Horn, John N. Obituary ."
373. *East Wheatfield Twp., Indiana Cnty, PA 1880 Census ED 135 Sh 146C.*
374. Professor J. T. Stewart, *History of Indiana County, Pennsylvania Her People, Past and Present Vol II,* (J. H. Beers & Co, 1913 Chicago).
375. DAR National Record Copy of Member Application # 184963.
376. *East Wheatfield Twp., Indiana Cnty, PA 1870 Census p. 22B, p. 228.*
377. *East Wheatfield Twp., Indiana Cnty, PA 1860 Census p. 374.*
378. *Will of Mary Van Horn Indiana Cnty, PA #5362, p. 131.*
379. "Van Horn, Henry Coulter Obituary Indiana County Genealogical and Historical Society Newspaper Clippings."
380. "20 July 1898 Indiana Weekly Messenger (Indiana, PA) H. C. Van Horn Notice of Death."
381. Handwritten Notes of Leafy Fern Van Horn Wolf.
382. *East Wheatfield Twp., Indiana Cnty, PA 1860 Census p. 374.*
383. Professor J. T. Stewart, *History of Indiana County, Pennsylvania Her People, Past and Present Vol II,* (J. H. Beers & Co, 1913 Chicago).
384. DAR National Record Copy of Member Application # 184963.
385. *East Wheatfield Twp., Indiana Cnty, PA 1870 Census p. 22B.*
386. *East Wheatfield Twp., Indiana Cnty, PA 1860 Census p. 374.*
387. *Cemetery Listing Indiana Cnty, PA.*
388. *Pennsylvania Veterans Burial Cards 1777-1999,* "Electronic."
389. *Cemetery Listing Indiana Cnty, PA.*
390. *East Wheatfield Twp., Indiana Cnty, PA 1870 Census p. 22B.*
391. *East Wheatfield Twp., Indiana Cnty, PA 1860 Census p. 374.*
392. *East Wheatfield Twp., Indiana Cnty, PA 1870 Census p. 22B.*
393. "Indiana Weekly Messenger (Indiana, PA) 29 June 1922."
394. *East Wheatfield Twp., Indiana Cnty, PA 1870 Census p. 22B.*
395. *Alexander Van Horn Will 4 May 1869 Indiana Cnty, PA, Vol 3, p. 576 proved 1871,* Vol. 3, p 576 1871.
396. *West Wheatfield Twp., Indiana Cnty, PA 1860 Census p. 390B.*
397. *Fairfield, Westmoreland Cnty, PA 1850 Census p. 125 B & 126.*
398. *West Wheatfield Twp., Indiana Cnty, PA 1860 Census p. 390B.*
399. *Alexander Van Horn Will 4 May 1869 Indiana Cnty, PA, Vol 3, p. 576 proved 1871.*
400. *West Wheatfield Twp., Indiana Cnty, PA 1860 Census p. 390 A and B.*
401. *Alexander Van Horn Will 4 May 1869 Indiana Cnty, PA, Vol 3, p. 576 proved 1871.*
402. *West Wheatfield Twp., Indiana Cnty, PA 1860 Census p. 390 A and B.*
403. *Jefferson Twp., Allamamkee Cnty, IA 1860 Census p. 259.*
404. *Jefferson Twp., Allamamkee Cnty, IA 1880 Census ED 7 Sh 6B.*

405. *Jefferson Twp., Allamamkee Cnty, IA 1860 Census p. 259.*
406. *Rossville Cemetery Records, Allamakee Cnty, IA Genelogy Records,* "Electronic."
407. *Jefferson Twp., Allamamkee Cnty, IA 1860 Census p. 259.*
408. *Jefferson Twp., Allamamkee Cnty, IA 1880 Census ED 7 Sh 6B.*
409. *Jefferson Twp., Allamakee Cnty, IA 1900 Census ED 6 Sh 3B.*
410. *Jefferson Twp., Allamamkee Cnty, IA 1860 Census p. 259.*
411. *Rossville Cemetery Records, Allamakee Cnty, IA Genelogy Records,* "Electronic."
412. *Jefferson Twp., Allamamkee Cnty, IA 1860 Census p. 259.*
413. *Jefferson Twp., Allamamkee Cnty, IA 1880 Census ED 7 Sh 6B.*
414. *Jefferson Twp., Allamakee Cnty, IA 1900 Census ED 6 Sh 3B.*
415. *Jefferson Twp., Allamamkee Cnty, IA 1860 Census p. 259.*
416. *Rossville Cemetery Records, Allamakee Cnty, IA Genelogy Records,* "Electronic."
417. *Jefferson Twp., Allamamkee Cnty, IA 1860 Census p. 259.*
418. *Rossville Cemetery Records, Allamakee Cnty, IA Genelogy Records,* "Electronic."
419. *Jefferson Twp., Allamamkee Cnty, IA 1880 Census ED 7 Sh 6B.*
420. *Sanborn, O'Brien Cnty, IA 1925 Census p. 130/138.*
421. *Jefferson Twp., Allamakee Cnty, IA 1900 Census ED 6 Sh 3B.*
422. *Jefferson Twp., Allamamkee Cnty, IA 1880 Census ED 7 Sh 6B.*
423. *Sanborn, O'Brien Cnty, IA 1925 Census p. 130/138.*
424. *Alexander Van Horn Will 4 May 1869 Indiana Cnty, PA, Vol 3, p. 576 proved 1871.*
425. "Indiana Evening Gazette (Indiana, PA) May 3, 1909 David Wakefield Obituary."
426. *Fairfield, Westmoreland Cnty, PA 1850 Census p. 125 B & 126.*
427. *St. Clair Twp., Westmoreland Cnty, PA 1860 Census p. 934.*
428. *St. Clair Twp., Westmoreland Cnty, PA 1860 Census p. 936.*
429. *Alexander Van Horn Will 4 May 1869 Indiana Cnty, PA, Vol 3, p. 576 proved 1871.*
430. *St. Clair Twp., Westmoreland Cnty, PA 1860 Census p. 934.*
431. *East Whestfield Twp., Indiana Cnty, PA 1900 Census ED 37 Sh 3B.*
432. *East Wheatfield Twp., Indiana Cnty, PA 1880 Census ED 135 Sh 13B.*
433. *St. Clair Twp., Westmoreland Cnty, PA 1860 Census p. 936.*
434. "Indiana Evening Gazette (Indiana, PA) May 3, 1909 David Wakefield Obituary."
435. *Alexander Van Horn Will 4 May 1869 Indiana Cnty, PA, Vol 3, p. 576 proved 1871.*
436. *East Wheatfield Twp., Indiana Cnty, PA 1880 Census ED 135 Sh 146C.*
437. *St. Clair Twp., Westmoreland Cnty, PA 1860 Census p. 936.*
438. *East Wheatfield Twp., Indiana Cnty, PA 1880 Census ED 135 Sh 146C.*
439. *St. Clair Twp., Westmoreland Cnty, PA 1860 Census p. 936.*
440. *Alexander Van Horn Will 4 May 1869 Indiana Cnty, PA, Vol 3, p. 576 proved 1871.*
441. *St. Clair Twp., Westmoreland Cnty, PA 1860 Census p. 936.*
442. *Alexander Van Horn Will 4 May 1869 Indiana Cnty, PA, Vol 3, p. 576 proved 1871.*
443. *St. Clair Twp., Westmoreland Cnty, PA 1860 Census p. 936.*
444. *Alexander Van Horn Will 4 May 1869 Indiana Cnty, PA, Vol 3, p. 576 proved 1871.*
445. *St. Clair Twp., Westmoreland Cnty, PA 1860 Census p. 936.*
446. *Alexander Van Horn Will 4 May 1869 Indiana Cnty, PA, Vol 3, p. 576 proved 1871.*
447. *East Wheatfield Twp., Indiana Cnty, PA 1880 Census ED 135 Sh 13B.*
448. *West Wheatfield Twp., Indiana Cnty, PA 1870 Census p. 401B.*
449. *Rayne Twp., Indiana Cnty, PA 1850 Census p. 194.*
450. Dick McElhoes, Rootsweb Posting McElhoes Mixup.
451. *Rayne Twp., Indiana Cnty, PA 1880 Census ED 142 Sh 284A.*
452. *Rayne Twp., Indiana Cnty, PA 1870 Census p. 342.*
453. *Rayne Twp., Indiana Cnty, PA 1850 Census p. 194.*
454. *Rayne Twp., Indiana Cnty, PA 1870 Census p. 342.*
455. *Rayne Twp., Indiana Cnty, PA 1850 Census p. 194.*
456. *Rayne Twp., Indiana Cnty, PA 1880 Census ED 142 Sh 284A.*
457. *Rayne Twp., Indiana Cnty, PA 1870 Census p. 342,   .*
458. *Rayne Twp., Indiana Cnty, PA 1880 Census ED 142 Sh 284A.*

459. Dick McElhoes, Rootsweb Posting McElhoes Mixup.
460. *Rayne Twp., Indiana Cnty, PA 1860 Census p. 171.*
461. Clarence D. Stephenson, *Indiana County 175th Anniversary History*, (Vol. IV, p. 37).
462. DAR National Record Copy of Member Application# 448771.
463. *Rayne Twp., Indiana Cnty, PA 1860 Census p. 171.*
464. DAR National Record Copy of Member Application# 448771.
465. Dick McElhoes, Rootsweb Posting McElhoes Mixup.
466. *Rayne Twp., Indiana Cnty, PA 1860 Census p. 171.*
467. Clarence D. Stephenson, *Indiana County 175th Anniversary History*, (Vol. IV, p. 37).
468. DAR National Record Copy of Member Application# 448771.
469. *Rayne Twp., Indiana Cnty, PA 1860 Census p. 171.*
470. DAR National Record Copy of Member Application# 448771.
471. *Rayne Twp., Indiana Cnty, PA 1860 Census p. 171.*
472. Dick McElhoes, Rootsweb Posting McElhoes Mixup.
473. *Cherry Hill Twp., Indiana Cnty, PA 1880 Census ED 139 Sh 220C.*
474. *Green Twp., Indiana Cnty, PA 1860 Census p. 212B.*
475. *Green Twp., Indiana Cnty, PA 1870 Census p. 150B.*
476. *Cherry Hill Twp., Indiana Cnty, PA 1880 Census ED 139 Sh 220C.*
477. Dick McElhoes, Rootsweb Posting McElhoes Mixup.
478. *Green Twp., Indiana Cnty, PA 1860 Census p. 212B.*
479. *Green Twp., Indiana Cnty, PA 1870 Census p. 150B.*
480. *Cherry Hill Twp., Indiana Cnty, PA 1880 Census ED 139 Sh 215A.*
481. *Green Twp., Indiana Cnty, PA 1860 Census p. 212B.*
482. *Green Twp., Indiana Cnty, PA 1870 Census p. 150B.*
483. *Cherry Hill Twp., Indiana Cnty, PA 1880 Census ED 139 Sh 215A.*
484. *Green Twp., Indiana Cnty, PA 1860 Census p. 212B.*
485. Dick McElhoes, Rootsweb Posting McElhoes Mixup.
486. *East Mahoning Twp., Indiana Cnty, PA 1850 Census p. 247B & 248.*
487. *East Mahoning Twp., Indiana Cnty, PA 1900 Census ED 53 Sh 6B.*
488. *East Mahoning Twp., Indiana Cnty, PA 1900 Census ED 53 Sh 3A.*
489. Dick McElhoes, Rootsweb Posting McElhoes Mixup.
490. *East Mahoning Twp., Indiana Cnty, PA 1850 Census p. 247B & 248.*
491. *East Mahoning Twp., Indiana Cnty, PA 1870 Census p. 213.*
492. *East Mahoning Twp., Indiana Cnty, PA 1850 Census p. 247B & 248.*
493. "29 October 1897 Indiana Weekly Messenger (Indiana, PA)."
494. *East Mahoning Twp., Indiana Cnty, PA 1870 Census p. 213.*
495. "29 October 1897 Indiana Weekly Messenger (Indiana, PA)."
496. *East Mahoning Twp., Indiana Cnty, PA 1870 Census p. 213.*
497. *East Mahoning Twp., Indiana Cnty, PA 1900 Census ED 53 Sh 6B.*
498. *East Mahoning Twp., Indiana Cnty, PA 1870 Census p. 213.*
499. *Family Sheet from David and Donna King of Benicia, CA.*
500. *South Mahoning Twp., Indiana Cnty, PA 1860 Census p. 248.*
501. *South Mahoning Twp., Indiana Cnty, PA 1870 Census p. 354B.*
502. *South Mahoning Twp., Indiana Cnty, PA 1880 Census ED 143 Sh 28.*
503. Will of B. B. Van Horn Indiana Cnty, PA.
504. *Mahoning Twp., Indiana Cnty, PA 1840 Census p. 128.*
505. DAR National Record Copy of Member Application # 835192.
506. *Family Sheet from David and Donna King of Benicia, CA.*
507. D. Scott Van Horn Family Group Sheet, August 8, 1983.
508. Will of B. B. Van Horn Indiana Cnty, PA.
509. *Family Sheet from David and Donna King of Benicia, CA.*
510. *South Mahoning Twp., Indiana Cnty, PA 1860 Census p. 248.*
511. *South Mahoning Twp., Indiana Cnty, PA 1870 Census p. 354B.*
512. *South Mahoning Twp., Indiana Cnty, PA 1880 Census ED 143 Sh 28.*

513. *South Mahoning Twp., Indiana Cnty, PA 1900 Census ED 64 Sh 3A.*
514. Will of B. B. Van Horn Indiana Cnty, PA.
515. "Phoebe Neff Van Horn Obituary 9 Feb 1905 Indiana Evening Gazette (Indiana, PA) p. 1."
516. DAR National Record Copy of Member Application # 486836.
517. *Family Sheet from David and Donna King of Benicia, CA.*
518. *South Mahoning Twp., Indiana Cnty, PA 1900 Census ED 64 Sh 3A.*
519. *Family Sheet from David and Donna King of Benicia, CA.*
520. "Phoebe Neff Van Horn Obituary 9 Feb 1905 Indiana Evening Gazette (Indiana, PA) p. 1."
521. DAR National Record Copy of Member Application # 486836.
522. "Indiana Progress (Indiana Cnty, PA) 14 September 1910."
523. *West Mahoning Twp., Indiana Cnty, PA 1860 Census p. 195.*
524. *Wayne Twp., Armstrong Cnty, PA 1870 Census p. 535.*
525. *Wayne Twp., Armstrong Cnty, PA 1900 Census ED 9 Sh 9B&10A.*
526. *Wayne Twp., Armstrong Cnty, PA 1880 Census ED 23 Sh 474C.*
527. *Mahoning Twp., Indiana Cnty, PA 1840 Census p. 128.*
528. *West Mahoning Twp., Indiana Cnty, PA 1860 Census p. 195.*
529. *Wayne Twp., Armstrong Cnty, PA 1870 Census p. 535.*
530. *West Mahoning Twp., Indiana Cnty, PA 1860 Census p. 195.*
531. *Wayne Twp., Armstrong Cnty, PA 1880 Census ED 23 Sh 474C.*
532. *West Mahoning Twp., Indiana Cnty, PA 1860 Census p. 195.*
533. *Wayne Twp., Armstrong Cnty, PA 1870 Census p. 535.*
534. *West Mahoning Twp., Indiana Cnty, PA 1860 Census p. 195.*
535. *Wayne Twp., Armstrong Cnty, PA 1870 Census p. 535.*
536. *West Mahoning Twp., Indiana Cnty, PA 1860 Census p. 195.*
537. Indiana Cnty, PA Marriage Records.
538. *Brookville, Jefferson Cnty, PA 1880 Census ED 186 Sh 30.*
539. *Mahoning Twp., Indiana Cnty, PA 1840 Census p. 128.*
540. *South Mahoning Twp., Indiana Cnty, PA 1860 Census p. 340.*
541. *Brookville, Jefferson Cnty, PA 1880 Census ED 186 Sh 30.*
542. *Brookville, Jefferson Cnty, PA 1870 Census p. 199.*
543. *South Mahoning Twp., Indiana Cnty, PA 1860 Census p. 340.*
544. Indiana Cnty, PA Marriage Records.
545. *Brookville, Jefferson Cnty, PA 1880 Census ED 186 Sh 30.*
546. Indiana Cnty, PA Marriage Records.
547. *"Some Descendants of John Counts of Glade Hollow 1722-1977".*
548. *South Mahoning Twp., Indiana Cnty, PA 1860 Census p. 340.*
549. *Family Sheet from David and Donna King of Benicia, CA.*
550. *South Mahoning Twp., Indiana Cnty, PA 1860 Census p. 331B.*
551. *Mahoning Twp., Indiana Cnty, PA 1840 Census p. 128.*
552. *Franklin Cnty, IL 1870 Census p. 253B.*
553. DAR National Record Copy of Member Application # 614578.
554. *Family Sheet from David and Donna King of Benicia, CA.*
555. DAR National Record Copy of Member Application # 614578.
556. *Family Sheet from David and Donna King of Benicia, CA.*
557. DAR National Record Copy of Member Application # 614578.
558. *South Mahoning Twp., Indiana Cnty, PA 1860 Census p. 331B.*
559. *Franklin Cnty, IL 1870 Census p. 253B.*
560. DAR National Record Copy of Member Application # 614578.
561. *South Mahoning Twp., Indiana Cnty, PA 1860 Census p. 331B.*
562. DAR National Record Copy of Member Application # 614578.
563. *South Mahoning Twp., Indiana Cnty, PA 1860 Census p. 331B.*
564. *Franklin Cnty, IL 1870 Census p. 253B.*
565. *South Mahoning Twp., Indiana Cnty, PA 1860 Census p. 331B.*
566. *Franklin Cnty, IL 1870 Census p. 253B.*

567. *South Mahoning Twp., Indiana Cnty, PA 1860 Census p. 331B.*
568. *Franklin Cnty, IL 1870 Census p. 253B.*
569. *Punxsutwaney, Jefferson Cnty, PA 1850 Census p. 76.*
570. *Punxsutwaney, Jefferson Cnty, PA 1860 Census p. 293B.*
571. *Punxsutwaney, Jefferson Cnty, PA 1870 Census p. 293.*
572. *Punxsutawney, Jefferson Cnty, PA 1920 Census ED 158 Sh 11B.*
573. *Punxsutawney, Jefferson Cnty, PA 1900 Census ED 73 Sh 22B.*
574. *Punxsutawney, Jefferson Cnty, PA 1880 Census ED 203 Sh 317C.*
575. *Mahoning Twp., Indiana Cnty, PA 1840 Census p. 128.*
576. *Punxsutwaney, Jefferson Cnty, PA 1850 Census p. 76.*
577. *Punxsutwaney, Jefferson Cnty, PA 1860 Census p. 293B.*
578. *Punxsutwaney, Jefferson Cnty, PA 1870 Census p. 293.*
579. *Punxsutawney, Jefferson Cnty, PA 1880 Census ED 203 Sh 317C.*
580. *Punxsutwaney, Jefferson Cnty, PA 1850 Census p. 76.*
581. *Punxsutwaney, Jefferson Cnty, PA 1860 Census p. 293B.*
582. *Punxsutwaney, Jefferson Cnty, PA 1870 Census p. 293.*
583. *Punxsutawney, Jefferson Cnty, PA 1880 Census ED 203 Sh 317C.*
584. *Punxsutwaney, Jefferson Cnty, PA 1850 Census p. 76.*
585. *Punxsutwaney, Jefferson Cnty, PA 1860 Census p. 293B.*
586. *Punxsutwaney, Jefferson Cnty, PA 1870 Census p. 293.*
587. *Punxsutawney, Jefferson Cnty, PA 1880 Census ED 203 Sh 317C.*
588. *Punxsutwaney, Jefferson Cnty, PA 1870 Census p. 293.*
589. *Webbs Prairie, Franklin Cnty, IL 1870 Census p. 251.*
590. *South Mahoning Twp., Indiana Cnty, PA 1860 Census p. 334.*
591. *Mahoning Twp., Indiana Cnty, PA 1840 Census p. 128.*
592. *Northern Twp., Franklin Cnty, IL 1880 Censes ED 14 Sh 50/52D.*
593. *Webbs Prairie, Franklin Cnty, IL 1870 Census p. 251.*
594. *South Mahoning Twp., Indiana Cnty, PA 1860 Census p. 334.*
595. *Northern Twp., Franklin Cnty, IL 1880 Censes ED 14 Sh 50/52D.*
596. *Webbs Prairie, Franklin Cnty, IL 1870 Census p. 251.*
597. *South Mahoning Twp., Indiana Cnty, PA 1860 Census p. 334.*
598. *Dahlgren, Franklin Cnty, IL 1900 Census ED 50 Sh 28A.*
599. *South Mahoning Twp., Indiana Cnty, PA 1860 Census p. 334.*
600. *Dahlgren, Franklin Cnty, IL 1900 Census ED 50 Sh 28A.*
601. *South Mahoning Twp., Indiana Cnty, PA 1860 Census p. 334.*
602. *Webbs Prairie, Franklin Cnty, IL 1870 Census p. 251.*
603. *South Mahoning Twp., Indiana Cnty, PA 1860 Census p. 334.*
604. Indiana Cnty, PA Marriage Records.
605. *Greenwood Twp., Clearfield Cnty, PA 1880 Census ED 269 Sh 28.*
606. *South Mahoning Twp., Indiana Cnty, PA 1860 Census p. 333.*
607. *Ferguson Twp., Clearfield Cnty, PA 1870 Census p. 163B.*
608. *Mahoning Twp., Indiana Cnty, PA 1840 Census p. 128.*
609. Hamilton, Von Gail, *Work Family History: Twelve Generations of Work in America 1690-1969, Park City, Utah*, (Park City, Utah: Publishers Press, 1969, 614 pgs.).
610. *South Mahoning Twp., Indiana Cnty, PA 1860 Census p. 333.*
611. *Greenwood Twp., Clearfield Cnty, PA 1880 Census ED 269 Sh 28.*
612. Indiana Cnty, PA Marriage Records.
613. *Ferguson Twp., Clearfield Cnty, PA 1870 Census p. 163B.*
614. *Greenwood Twp., Clearfield Cnty, PA 1880 Census ED 269 Sh 28.*
615. "Indiana Evening Gazette (Indiana, PA) 15 July 1908 Miriam Work Van Horn Obituary."
616. *East Mahoning Twp., Indiana Cnty, PA 1850 Census p. 247.*
617. *South Mahoning Twp., Indiana Cnty, PA 1860 Census p. 333.*
618. Hamilton, Von Gail, *Work Family History: Twelve Generations of Work in America 1690-1969, Park City, Utah*, (Park City, Utah: Publishers Press, 1969, 614 pgs.).

619. "8 July 1908 Indiana Evening Gazette (Indiana, PA) Miriam Work Van Horn Obiturary."
620. Indiana Cnty, PA Marriage Records.
621. *Greenwood Twp., Clearfield Cnty, PA 1880 Census ED 269 Sh 28.*
622. *East Mahoning Twp., Indiana Cnty, PA 1850 Census p. 247.*
623. "Indiana Evening Gazette (Indiana, PA) 15 July 1908 Miriam Work Van Horn Obituary."
624. *Pennsylvania Veterans Burial Cards 1777-1999*, "Electronic."
625. Indiana Cnty, PA Marriage Records.
626. *Allegheny Ward 1, Allegheny Cnty, PA 1850 Census p. 20B.*
627. *Allegheny Ward 5, Allegheny Cnty, PA 1870 Census p. 509.*
628. *Allegheny Ward, Allegheny Cnty, PA 1880 Census ED 14 Sh 472A.*
629. *Allegheny Ward 3, Allegheny Cnty, PA 1860 Census p. 914.*
630. *Allegheny Ward 1, Allegheny Cnty, PA 1850 Census p. 20B.*
631. *Allegheny Ward 5, Allegheny Cnty, PA 1870 Census p. 509.*
632. *Allegheny Ward, Allegheny Cnty, PA 1880 Census ED 14 Sh 472A.*
633. *Allegheny Ward 3, Allegheny Cnty, PA 1860 Census p. 914.*
634. *Allegheny Ward 5, Allegheny Cnty, PA 1870 Census p. 509.*
635. *Allegheny Ward 3, Allegheny Cnty, PA 1860 Census p. 914.*
636. *Allegheny Ward 5, Allegheny Cnty, PA 1870 Census p. 509.*
637. *Allegheny Ward 3, Allegheny Cnty, PA 1860 Census p. 914.*
638. *Allegheny Ward 5, Allegheny Cnty, PA 1870 Census p. 509.*
639. *Allegheny Ward 3, Allegheny Cnty, PA 1860 Census p. 914.*
640. *Allegheny Ward 5, Allegheny Cnty, PA 1870 Census p. 509.*
641. *Allegheny Ward, Allegheny Cnty, PA 1880 Census ED 14 Sh 472A.*
642. *Allegheny Ward 3, Allegheny Cnty, PA 1860 Census p. 914.*
643. *Allegheny Ward 5, Allegheny Cnty, PA 1870 Census p. 509.*
644. *Allegheny Ward, Allegheny Cnty, PA 1880 Census ED 14 Sh 472A.*
645. *Allegheny Ward 5, Allegheny Cnty, PA 1870 Census p. 509.*
646. *Allegheny Ward, Allegheny Cnty, PA 1880 Census ED 14 Sh 472A.*
647. *Allegheny Ward 5, Allegheny Cnty, PA 1870 Census p. 509.*
648. *Allegheny Ward 1, Allegheny Cnty, PA 1850 Census p. 20B.*
649. *Allegheny Ward 3, Allegheny Cnty, PA 1860 Census p. 918.*
650. *Allegheny, Allegheny Cnty, PA 1850 Census ED 7 Sh 26.*
651. *Allegheny, Allegheny Cnty, PA 1880 Census ED 7 Sh 26.*
652. *Allegheny Ward 1, Allegheny Cnty, PA 1850 Census p. 20B.*
653. *Allegheny, Allegheny Cnty, PA 1880 Census ED 7 Sh 26.*
654. *Allegheny, Allegheny Cnty, PA 1880 Census ED 17 Sh 26.*
655. *Allegheny Ward 3, Allegheny Cnty, PA 1860 Census p. 918.*
656. *Allegheny, Allegheny Cnty, PA 1880 Census ED 7 Sh 26.*
657. *Allegheny Ward 3, Allegheny Cnty, PA 1860 Census p. 918.*
658. *Allegheny, Allegheny Cnty, PA 1880 Census ED 17 Sh 26.*
659. *Allegheny Ward 3, Allegheny Cnty, PA 1860 Census p. 918.*
660. *Allegheny, Allegheny Cnty, PA 1880 Census ED 17 Sh 26.*
661. *Allegheny Ward 3, Allegheny Cnty, PA 1860 Census p. 918.*
662. *Allegheny, Allegheny Cnty, PA 1880 Census ED 7 Sh 26.*
663. The Abridged Compendium of American Genealogy, p 236.
664. *Allegheny Ward 1, Allegheny Cnty, PA 1850 Census p. 20B.*
665. *Allegheny Ward 2, Allegheny Cnty, PA 1860 Census p. 892.*
666. The Abridged Compendium of American Genealogy, p 236.
667. *Allegheny Ward 1, Allegheny Cnty, PA 1850 Census p. 20B.*
668. The Abridged Compendium of American Genealogy, p 236.
669. *Allegheny Ward 2, Allegheny Cnty, PA 1860 Census p. 892.*
670. The Abridged Compendium of American Genealogy, p 236.
671. *Allegheny Ward 2, Allegheny Cnty, PA 1860 Census p. 892.*
672. The Abridged Compendium of American Genealogy, p 236.

673. Indiana Cnty, PA Marriage Records.
674. *South Mahoning Twp., Indiana Cnty, PA 1850 Census p. 198B.*
675. *Green Twp., Indiana Cnty, PA 1880 Census ED 140 Sh 14 & 15.*
676. *History of Indiana County, Penn'a,* (J. A. Caldwell, Newark, OH 1880).
677. *Rayne Twp., Indiana Cnty, PA 1900 Census ED 61 Sh 2B.*
678. *East Mahoning Twp., Indiana Cnty, PA 1870 Census p. 210B.*
679. *Green Twp., Indiana Cnty, PA 1860 Census p. 200.*
680. "Indiana Progress (Indiana Cnty, PA) March 2, 1898."
681. *South Mahoning Twp., Indiana Cnty, PA 1850 Census p. 198B.*
682. Indiana Cnty, PA Marriage Records.
683. *Green Twp., Indiana Cnty, PA 1880 Census ED 140 Sh 14 & 15.*
684. *History of Indiana County, Penn'a,* (J. A. Caldwell, Newark, OH 1880).
685. *Rayne Twp., Indiana Cnty, PA 1900 Census ED 61 Sh 2B.*
686. *Grant Twp., Indiana Cnty, PA 1910 Census ED 76 Sh 11B.*
687. *East Mahoning Twp., Indiana Cnty, PA 1870 Census p. 210B.*
688. *Green Twp., Indiana Cnty, PA 1860 Census p. 200.*
689. "Indiana Progress (Indiana Cnty, PA) March 2, 1898."
690. Indiana Cnty, PA Marriage Records.
691. *Green Twp., Indiana Cnty, PA 1880 Census ED 140 Sh 14 & 15.*
692. *Historical & Genealogical Society of Indiana County Cemetery Records of Indiana County, Pennsylvania,* (1939 974.889V3h).
693. Indiana Cnty, PA Marriage Records.
694. *Green Twp., Indiana Cnty, PA 1860 Census p. 200.*
695. *Historical & Genealogical Society of Indiana County Cemetery Records of Indiana County, Pennsylvania,* (1939 974.889V3h).
696. *South Mahoning Twp., Indiana Cnty, PA 1850 Census p. 198B.*
697. *Washington Twp., Indiana Cnty, PA 1870 Census p. 372.*
698. *Washington Twp., Indiana Cnty, PA 1880 Census ED 141 Sh 276A.*
699. *East Mahoning Twp., Indiana Cnty, PA 1900 Census ED 53 Sh 6A.*
700. *Marion Center Boro, Indiana Cnty, PA 1910 Census ED 73 Sh 10A.*
701. "Indiana Progress (Indiana Cnty, PA) March 2, 1898."
702. *South Mahoning Twp., Indiana Cnty, PA 1870 Census p. 351B.*
703. *South Mahoning Twp., Indiana Cnty, PA 1850 Census p. 198B.*
704. "11 Nov 1920 Indiana Evening Gazette (Indiana, PA) Martha Van Horn Obituary."
705. *East Mahoning Twp., Indiana Cnty, PA 1900 Census ED 53 Sh 6A.*
706. "Indiana Progress (Indiana Cnty, PA) March 2, 1898."
707. *Marion Center Boro, Indiana Cnty, PA 1910 Census ED 73 Sh 10A.*
708. "11 Nov 1920 Indiana Evening Gazette (Indiana, PA) Martha Van Horn Obituary."
709. *East Mahoning Twp., Indiana Cnty, PA 1900 Census ED 53 Sh 6A.*
710. "11 Nov 1920 Indiana Evening Gazette (Indiana, PA) Martha Van Horn Obituary."
711. *South Mahoning Twp., Indiana Cnty, PA 1860 Census p. 330B.*
712. "2 March 1898 Indiana Progress (Indiana, PA) Mary A. Van Horn Obituary."
713. *South Mahoning Twp., Indiana Cnty, PA 1850 Census p. 198B.*
714. *History of Indiana County, Penn'a,* (J. A. Caldwell, Newark, OH 1880).
715. *East Mahoning Twp., Indiana Cnty, PA 1870 Census p. 210B.*
716. *East Mahoning Twp., Indiana Cnty, PA 1880 Census ED 145 Sh 14.*
717. "Indiana Progress (Indiana Cnty, PA) March 2, 1898."
718. *South Mahoning Twp., Indiana Cnty, PA 1860 Census p. 330B.*
719. *South Mahoning Twp., Indiana Cnty, PA 1850 Census p. 198B.*
720. "23 October 1914 Indiana Evening Gazette (Indiana, PA) Obituary of Mary Van Horn Lydick."
721. "2 March 1898 Indiana Progress (Indiana, PA) Mary A. Van Horn Obituary."
722. *History of Indiana County, Penn'a,* (J. A. Caldwell, Newark, OH 1880).
723. *East Mahoning Twp., Indiana Cnty, PA 1870 Census p. 210B.*
724. *East Mahoning Twp., Indiana Cnty, PA 1880 Census ED 145 Sh 14.*

725. "Indiana Progress (Indiana Cnty, PA) March 2, 1898."
726. *East Mahoning Twp., Indiana Cnty, PA 1870 Census p. 210B.*
727. *South Mahoning Twp., Indiana Cnty, PA 1860 Census p. 330B.*
728. "2 March 1898 Indiana Progress (Indiana, PA) Mary A. Van Horn Obituary."
729. *South Mahoning Twp., Indiana Cnty, PA 1850 Census p. 198B.*
730. *Gerrardstown, Berkeley Cnty, WV 1870 Census p. 177.*
731. *Jefferson Twp., Montgomery Cnty, OH 1920 Census ED 222 Sh 5B.*
732. "Indiana Progress (Indiana Cnty, PA) March 2, 1898."
733. *South Mahoning Twp., Indiana Cnty, PA 1860 Census p. 330B.*
734. *South Mahoning Twp., Indiana Cnty, PA 1850 Census p. 198B.*
735. *Gerrardstown, Berkeley Cnty, WV 1870 Census p. 177.*
736. *Gerrardstown, Berkeley Cnty, WV 1880 Census ED 14 Sh 22.*
737. *Gerrardstown, Berkeley Cnty, WV 1910 Census ED 16 Sh 6A&B.*
738. *Gerrardstown, Berkeley Cnty, WV 1920 Census ED 22 Sh 10B.*
739. *Gerrardstown, Berkeley Cnty, WV 1900 Census ED 12 Sh 3A.*
740. *Gerrardstown, Berkeley Cnty, WV 1930 Census ED 5 Sh 3A.*
741. *Gerrardstown, Berkeley Cnty, WV 1870 Census p. 177.*
742. *Gerrardstown, Berkeley Cnty, WV 1910 Census ED 16 Sh 6A&B.*
743. *Gerrardstown, Berkeley Cnty, WV 1870 Census p. 177.*
744. *Martinsburg Ward 2, Berkeley Cnty, WV 1920 Census ED 28 Sh 15A.*
745. *Martinsburg Ward 2, Berkeley Cnty, WV 1910 Census ED 20 Sh 7B.*
746. *Martinsburg, Berkeley Cnty, WV 1930 Census ED 14 Sh 7A.*
747. *Gerrardstown, Berkeley Cnty, WV 1870 Census p. 177.*
748. *Martinsburg Ward 2, Berkeley Cnty, WV 1910 Census ED 20 Sh 7B.*
749. *Martinsburg Ward 2, Berkeley Cnty, WV 1920 Census ED 28 Sh 15A.*
750. *Martinsburg, Berkeley Cnty, WV 1930 Census ED 14 Sh 7A.*
751. *Martinsburg Ward 2, Berkeley Cnty, WV 1910 Census ED 20 Sh 7B.*
752. *Gerrardstown, Berkeley Cnty, WV 1880 Census ED 14 Sh 22.*
753. *South Mahoning Twp., Indiana Cnty, PA 1860 Census p. 330B.*
754. "2 March 1898 Indiana Progress (Indiana, PA) Mary A. Van Horn Obituary."
755. *Gerrardstown, Berkeley Cnty, WV 1910 Census ED 15 Sh 8B.*
756. *South Mahoning Twp., Indiana Cnty, PA 1850 Census p. 198B.*
757. *Email Rebekah Hutzler Malatt April 10, 2006, "Electronic."*
758. *Gerrardstown, Berkeley Cnty, WV 1900 Census ED 12 Sh 4B.*
759. "Indiana Progress (Indiana Cnty, PA) March 2, 1898."
760. *Shanghai, Berkeley Cnty, WV 1870 Census p 176.*
761. *South Mahoning Twp., Indiana Cnty, PA 1860 Census p. 330B.*
762. *Gerrardstown, Berkeley Cnty, WV 1910 Census ED 15 Sh 8B.*
763. *South Mahoning Twp., Indiana Cnty, PA 1850 Census p. 198B.*
764. *Gerrardstown, Berkeley Cnty, WV 1910 Census ED 15 Sh 8B.*
765. *Email Rebekah Hutzler Malatt April 10, 2006, "Electronic."*
766. *Gerrardstown, Berkeley Cnty, WV 1900 Census ED 12 Sh 4B.*
767. "Indiana Progress (Indiana Cnty, PA) March 2, 1898."
768. *Shanghai, Berkeley Cnty, WV 1870 Census p 176.*
769. *Gerrardstown, Berkeley Cnty, WV 1910 Census ED 15 Sh 8B.*
770. *Email Rebekah Hutzler Malatt April 10, 2006, "Electronic."*
771. *Gerrardstown, Berkeley Cnty, WV 1900 Census ED 12 Sh 4B.*
772. *Email Rebekah Hutzler Malatt April 10, 2006, "Electronic."*
773. *Gerrardstown, Berkeley Cnty, WV 1900 Census ED 12 Sh 4B.*
774. *Email Rebekah Hutzler Malatt April 10, 2006, "Electronic."*
775. *East Mahoning Twp., Indiana Cnty, PA 1850 Census p. 247.*
776. *East Mahoning Twp., Indiana Cnty, PA 1860 Census p. 170B.*
777. *Liberty Twp., Clarke Cnty, IA 1870 Census p. 61B.*
778. *Liberty Twp., Clarke Cnty, IA 1880 Census ED 40 Sh 8D.*

779. *East Mahoning Twp., Indiana Cnty, PA 1850 Census p. 247.*
780. *East Mahoning Twp., Indiana Cnty, PA 1860 Census p. 170B.*
781. *East Mahoning Twp., Indiana Cnty, PA 1850 Census p. 247.*
782. *East Mahoning Twp., Indiana Cnty, PA 1860 Census p. 170B.*
783. *Liberty Twp., Fairfield Cnty, OH 1870 Census p.61B.*
784. *East Mahoning Twp., Indiana Cnty, PA 1860 Census p. 170B.*
785. *Liberty Twp., Fairfield Cnty, OH 1870 Census p.61B.*
786. *East Mahoning Twp., Indiana Cnty, PA 1860 Census p. 170B.*
787. *West Mahoning Twp., Indiana Cnty, PA 1850 Census p. 174B.*
788. "Indiana Weekly Messenger (Indiana, PA) 8 May 1895," Estate of Enoch Stear.
789. *North Mahoning Twp., Indiana Cnty, PA 1870 Census p. 306B.*
790. *Davidsville, North Mahoning Twp., Indiana Cnty, PA 1880 Census ED 146 Sh 358C.*
791. DAR National Record Copy of Member Application # 800118.
792. *West Mahoning Twp., Indiana Cnty, PA 1850 Census p. 174B.*
793. DAR National Record Copy of Member Application # 800118.
794. "Indiana Weekly Messenger (Indiana, PA) 8 May 1895," Estate of Enoch Stear.
795. *North Mahoning Twp., Indiana Cnty, PA 1870 Census p. 306B.*
796. *Davidsville, North Mahoning Twp., Indiana Cnty, PA 1880 Census ED 146 Sh 358C.*
797. *North Mahoning Twp., Indiana Cnty, PA 1870 Census p. 306B.*
798. DAR National Record Copy of Member Application # 800118.
799. *West Mahoning Twp., Indiana Cnty, PA 1850 Census p. 174B.*
800. *West Mahoning Twp., Indiana Cnty, PA 1860 Census p. 189B.*
801. *Canoe Twp., Indiana Cnty, PA 1880 Census ED 149 Sh 398.*
802. *North Mahoning Twp., Indiana Cnty, PA 1870 Census p. 305.*
803. *West Mahoning Twp., Indiana Cnty, PA 1850 Census p. 174B.*
804. *West Mahoning Twp., Indiana Cnty, PA 1860 Census p. 189B.*
805. *Canoe Twp., Indiana Cnty, PA 1880 Census ED 149 Sh 398.*
806. *North Mahoning Twp., Indiana Cnty, PA 1870 Census p. 305.*
807. *Young Twp., Jefferson Cnty, PA 1910 Census ED 103 Sh 8A.*
808. *West Mahoning Twp., Indiana Cnty, PA 1860 Census p. 189B.*
809. "21 October 1910 Indiana Evening Gazette (Indiana, PA) Jacob Coon Obiturary."
810. *West Mahoning Twp., Indiana Cnty, PA 1860 Census p. 189B.*
811. *Canoe Twp., Indiana Cnty, PA 1880 Census ED 149 Sh 398.*
812. "21 October 1910 Indiana Evening Gazette (Indiana, PA) Jacob Coon Obiturary."
813. *West Mahoning Twp., Indiana Cnty, PA 1860 Census p. 189B.*
814. *North Mahoning Twp., Indiana Cnty, PA 1870 Census p. 305.*
815. *Canoe Twp., Indiana Cnty, PA 1880 Census ED 149 Sh 398.*
816. *North Mahoning Twp., Indiana Cnty, PA 1870 Census p. 305.*
817. *6 Nov 1912 Indiana Progress (Indiana, PA) Frank Coon Death Notice.*
818. *Canoe Twp., Indiana Cnty, PA 1880 Census ED 149 Sh 398.*
819. *West Mahoning Twp., Indiana Cnty, PA 1850 Census p. 174B.*
820. *Smicksburg, Indiana Cnty, PA 1870 Census p. 396A&B.*
821. History of Indiana County, Pennsylvania, p 416.
822. *Smicksburg, Indiana Cnty, PA 1860 Census p 357.*
823. *West Mahoning Twp., Indiana Cnty, PA 1850 Census p. 174B.*
824. *Smicksburg, Indiana Cnty, PA 1880 Census ED 144 Sh 326A.*
825. *Smicksburg, Indiana Cnty, PA 1870 Census p. 396A&B.*
826. History of Indiana County, Pennsylvania, p 416.
827. *Smicksburg, Indiana Cnty, PA 1860 Census p 357.*
828. *Smicksburg, Indiana Cnty, PA 1880 Census ED 144 Sh 326A.*
829. *Smicksburg, Indiana Cnty, PA 1870 Census p. 396A&B.*
830. *West Philomth, Benton Cnty, OR 1910 Census ED 15 Sh 2A.*
831. *Punxsutawney, Jefferson Cnty, PA 1900 Census ED 74 Sh 11B.*
832. *Smicksburg, Indiana Cnty, PA 1930 Census ED 47 Sh 2A.*

833. *Smicksburg, Indiana Cnty, PA 1860 Census p 357.*
834. *Smicksburg, Indiana Cnty, PA 1880 Census ED 144 Sh 326A.*
835. *Punxsutawney, Jefferson Cnty, PA 1900 Census ED 74 Sh 11B.*
836. *West Philomth, Benton Cnty, OR 1910 Census ED 15 Sh 2A.*
837. *Punxsutawney, Jefferson Cnty, PA 1900 Census ED 74 Sh 11B.*
838. *West Philomth, Benton Cnty, OR 1910 Census ED 15 Sh 2A.*
839. *Punxsutawney, Jefferson Cnty, PA 1900 Census ED 74 Sh 11B.*
840. *Smicksburg, Indiana Cnty, PA 1880 Census ED 144 Sh 326A.*
841. *Smicksburg, Indiana Cnty, PA 1870 Census p. 396A&B.*
842. *Smicksburg, Indiana Cnty, PA 1880 Census ED 144 Sh 326A.*
843. *West Mahoning Twp., Indiana Cnty, PA 1850 Census p. 174B.*
844. *Blairsville, Indiana Cnty, PA 1860 Census p. 38.*
845. *Burrell, Westmoreland Cnty, PA 1870 Census p. 49A & B.*
846. *Parnassus, Westmoreland Cnty, PA 1880 Census ED 102 Sh 1 & 2.*
847. "George Logan Van Horn Obituary 21 Sept 1909 Indiana Evening Gazette (Indiana, PA)."
848. *West Mahoning Twp., Indiana Cnty, PA 1850 Census p. 174B.*
849. *Blairsville, Indiana Cnty, PA 1860 Census p. 38.*
850. *Burrell, Westmoreland Cnty, PA 1870 Census p. 49A & B.*
851. *Parmassus, Westmoreland Cnty, PA 1880 Census ED 102 Sh 1 & 2.*
852. "George Logan Van Horn Obituary 21 Sept 1909 Indiana Evening Gazette (Indiana, PA)."
853. *Blairsville, Indiana Cnty, PA 1860 Census p. 38.*
854. *Burrell, Westmoreland Cnty, PA 1870 Census p. 49A & B.*
855. *Parmassus, Westmoreland Cnty, PA 1880 Census ED 102 Sh 1 & 2.*
856. *Blairsville, Indiana Cnty, PA 1860 Census p. 38.*
857. *Burrell, Westmoreland Cnty, PA 1870 Census p. 49A & B.*
858. *Parmassus, Westmoreland Cnty, PA 1880 Census ED 102 Sh 1 & 2.*
859. *Burrell, Westmoreland Cnty, PA 1870 Census p. 49A & B.*
860. *Parmassus, Westmoreland Cnty, PA 1880 Census ED 102 Sh 1 & 2.*
861. *Burrell, Westmoreland Cnty, PA 1870 Census p. 49A & B.*
862. *Parmassus, Westmoreland Cnty, PA 1880 Census ED 102 Sh 1 & 2.*
863. *Burrell, Westmoreland Cnty, PA 1870 Census p. 49A & B.*
864. *Parmassus, Westmoreland Cnty, PA 1880 Census ED 102 Sh 1 & 2.*
865. *Burrell, Westmoreland Cnty, PA 1870 Census p. 49A & B.*
866. *Parmassus, Westmoreland Cnty, PA 1880 Census ED 102 Sh 1 & 2.*
867. "George Logan Van Horn Obituary 21 Sept 1909 Indiana Evening Gazette (Indiana, PA)."
868. *West Mahoning Twp., Indiana Cnty, PA 1850 Census p. 174B.*
869. *East Mahoning Twp., Indiana Cnty, PA 1860 Census p. 306.*
870. *West Mahoning Twp., Indiana Cnty, PA 1870 Census p. 390.*
871. *West Mahoning Twp., Indiana Cnty, PA 1880 Census ED 144 Sh 325C.*
872. *West Mahoning Twp., Indiana Cnty, PA 1900 Census ED 63 Sh 6A.*
873. *East Mahoning Twp., Indiana Cnty, PA 1860 Census p. 172B, 171B.*
874. *West Mahoning Twp., Indiana Cnty, PA 1850 Census p. 174B.*
875. "Indiana Evening Gazette (Indiana, PA) 22 September 1909."
876. "21 Sept 1909 Indiana Evening Gazette (Indiana, PA) Obit of George Logan."
877. *West Mahoning Twp., Indiana Cnty, PA 1870 Census p. 390.*
878. *West Mahoning Twp., Indiana Cnty, PA 1880 Census ED 144 Sh 325C.*
879. *West Mahoning Twp., Indiana Cnty, PA 1900 Census ED 63 Sh 6A.*
880. *Saltsburg, Indiana Cnty, PA 1910 Census ED 91 Sh 4B.*
881. *West Mahoning Twp., Indiana Cnty, PA 1870 Census p. 390.*
882. *West Mahoning Twp., Indiana Cnty, PA 1900 Census ED 63 Sh 6A.*
883. *Cemetery Listing Indiana Cnty, PA.*
884. *Pennsylvania Veterans Burial Cards 1777-1999,* "Electronic."
885. "22 March 1923 Indiana Weekly Messenger (Indiana, PA) Tirzah Van Horn Obituary."
886. "George Logan Van Horn Obituary 21 Sept 1909 Indiana Evening Gazette (Indiana, PA)."

887. *West Mahoning Twp., Indiana Cnty, PA 1880 Census ED 144 Sh 325C.*
888. *Ridgeway, Elk Cnty, PA 1900 Census ED 41 Sh 7A.*
889. *West Mahoning Twp., Indiana Cnty, PA 1870 Census p. 390.*
890. *Ridgeway, Elk Cnty, PA 1910 Census ED 46 Sh 18A.*
891. *Ridgeway, Elk Cnty, PA 1920 Census ED 17 Sh 10B.*
892. "22 March 1923 Indiana Weekly Messenger (Indiana, PA) Tirzah Van Horn Obituary."
893. *Ridgeway, Elk Cnty, PA 1900 Census ED 41 Sh 7A.*
894. "22 March 1923 Indiana Weekly Messenger (Indiana, PA) Tirzah Van Horn Obituary."
895. *West Mahoning Twp., Indiana Cnty, PA 1850 Census p. 174B.*
896. *East Mahoning Twp., Indiana Cnty, PA 1860 Census p. 306.*
897. *History of Indiana County, Penn'a,* (J. A. Caldwell, Newark, OH 1880).
898. *West Mahoning Twp., Indiana Cnty, PA 1880 Census ED 144 Sh 22B.*
899. *West Mahoning Twp., Indiana Cnty, PA 1870 Census p. 389.*
900. *East Mahoning Twp., Indiana Cnty, PA 1860 Census p. 172B, 171B.*
901. *West Mahoning Twp., Indiana Cnty, PA 1850 Census p. 174B.*
902. *History of Indiana County, Penn'a,* (J. A. Caldwell, Newark, OH 1880).
903. *West Mahoning Twp., Indiana Cnty, PA 1870 Census p. 389.*
904. *History of Indiana County, Penn'a,* (J. A. Caldwell, Newark, OH 1880).
905. *West Mahoning Twp., Indiana Cnty, PA 1870 Census p. 389.*
906. *History of Indiana County, Penn'a,* (J. A. Caldwell, Newark, OH 1880).
907. *West Mahoning Twp., Indiana Cnty, PA 1880 Census ED 144 Sh 22B.*
908. *West Mahoning Twp., Indiana Cnty, PA 1870 Census p. 389.*
909. *West Mahoning Twp., Indiana Cnty, PA 1880 Census ED 144 Sh 22B.*
910. *History of Indiana County, Penn'a,* (J. A. Caldwell, Newark, OH 1880).
911. *West Mahoning Twp., Indiana Cnty, PA 1880 Census ED 144 Sh 22B.*
912. *West Mahoning Twp., Indiana Cnty, PA 1870 Census p. 389.*
913. *West Mahoning Twp., Indiana Cnty, PA 1880 Census ED 144 Sh 22B.*
914. *History of Indiana County, Penn'a,* (J. A. Caldwell, Newark, OH 1880).
915. *West Mahoning Twp., Indiana Cnty, PA 1880 Census ED 144 Sh 22B.*
916. *Brockway, Snyder Twp., Jefferson Cnty, PA 1900 Census ED 58 Sh 14A.*
917. *East Mahoning Twp., Indiana Cnty, PA 1860 Census p. 306.*
918. *West Mahoning Twp., Indiana Cnty, PA 1870 Census p. 390.*
919. *East Mahoning Twp., Indiana Cnty, PA 1860 Census p. 172B, 171B.*
920. *Brockway, Snyder Twp., Jefferson Cnty, PA 1900 Census ED 58 Sh 14A.*
921. DAR National Record Copy of Member Application # 862524.
922. *Snyder Twp., Jefferson Cnty, PA 1910 Census ED 90 Sh 15A.*
923. *Brockway, Snyder Twp., Jefferson Cnty, PA 1900 Census ED 58 Sh 14A.*
924. *Snyder Twp., Jefferson Cnty, PA 1910 Census ED 90 Sh 15A.*
925. *Brockway, Snyder Twp., Jefferson Cnty, PA 1900 Census ED 58 Sh 14A.*
926. *East Mahoning Twp., Indiana Cnty, PA 1860 Census p. 170.*
927. *East Mahoning Twp., Indiana Cnty, PA 1850 Census p. 247.*
928. Hamilton, Von Gail, *Work Family History: Twelve Generations of Work in America 1690-1969,* *Park City, Utah,* (Park City, Utah: Publishers Press, 1969, 614 pgs.).
929. *East Mahoning Twp., Indiana Cnty, PA 1860 Census p. 170.*
930. *East Mahoning Twp., Indiana Cnty, PA 1850 Census p. 247.*
931. *East Mahoning Twp., Indiana Cnty, PA 1860 Census p. 170.*
932. Hamilton, Von Gail, *Work Family History: Twelve Generations of Work in America 1690-1969,* *Park City, Utah,* (Park City, Utah: Publishers Press, 1969, 614 pgs.).
933. *East Mahoning Twp., Indiana Cnty, PA 1900 Census ED 53 Sh 6B.*
934. Hamilton, Von Gail, *Work Family History: Twelve Generations of Work in America 1690-1969,* *Park City, Utah,* (Park City, Utah: Publishers Press, 1969, 614 pgs.).
935. *East Mahoning Twp., Indiana Cnty, PA 1850 Census p. 247.*
936. *East Mahoning Twp., Indiana Cnty, PA 1860 Census p. 170.*
937. Hamilton, Von Gail, *Work Family History: Twelve Generations of Work in America 1690-1969,* *Park*

City, Utah, (Park City, Utah: Publishers Press, 1969, 614 pgs.).

938. *East Mahoning Twp., Indiana Cnty, PA 1860 Census p. 170.*

939. Hamilton, Von Gail, *Work Family History: Twelve Generations of Work in America 1690-1969, Park City, Utah,* (Park City, Utah: Publishers Press, 1969, 614 pgs.).

940. *East Mahoning Twp., Indiana Cnty, PA 1860 Census p. 170.*

941. Hamilton, Von Gail, *Work Family History: Twelve Generations of Work in America 1690-1969, Park City, Utah,* (Park City, Utah: Publishers Press, 1969, 614 pgs.).

942. *East Mahoning Twp., Indiana Cnty, PA 1860 Census p. 170.*

943. Hamilton, Von Gail, *Work Family History: Twelve Generations of Work in America 1690-1969, Park City, Utah,* (Park City, Utah: Publishers Press, 1969, 614 pgs.).

944. *East Mahoning Twp., Indiana Cnty, PA 1850 Census p. 247.*

945. *East Mahoning Twp., Indiana Cnty, PA 1860 Census p. 171.*

946. *East Mahoning Twp., Indiana Cnty, PA 1850 Census p. 247.*

947. *Interments of the Gilgal Cemetery, Gilgal Church, Indiana Cnty, PA.*

948. *South Mahoning Twp., Indiana Cnty, PA 1860 Census p. 330B.*

949. "Van Horn, Bennett Work Obituary Indiana County Genealogical and Historical Society Newspaper Clippings."

950. *South Mahoning Twp., Indiana Cnty, PA 1870 Census p. 351B.*

951. *South Mahoning Twp., Indiana Cnty, PA 1880 Census ED 143 Sh 26.*

952. *South Mahoning Twp., Indiana Cnty, PA 1900 Census ED 64 Sh 2B .*

953. "Sprague L. Van Horn Obituary Indiana County Genealogical and Historical Society Newspaper Clippings."

954. *East Mahoning Twp., Indiana Cnty, PA 1860 Census p. 170.*

955. *East Mahoning Twp., Indiana Cnty, PA 1850 Census p. 247.*

956. Hamilton, Von Gail, *Work Family History: Twelve Generations of Work in America 1690-1969, Park City, Utah,* (Park City, Utah: Publishers Press, 1969, 614 pgs.).

957. "22 May 1953 Indiana Evening Gazette (Indiana, PA) Mrs. Adda M. McAdoo Obituary."

958. *South Mahoning Twp., Indiana Cnty, PA 1910 Census ED 93 Sh 3A.*

959. *Interments of the Gilgal Cemetery, Gilgal Church, Indiana Cnty, PA.*

960. *South Mahoning Twp., Indiana Cnty, PA 1860 Census p. 330B.*

961. Hamilton, Von Gail, *Work Family History: Twelve Generations of Work in America 1690-1969, Park City, Utah,* (Park City, Utah: Publishers Press, 1969, 614 pgs.).

962. *Interments of the Gilgal Cemetery, Gilgal Church, Indiana Cnty, PA.*

963. Hamilton, Von Gail, *Work Family History: Twelve Generations of Work in America 1690-1969, Park City, Utah,* (Park City, Utah: Publishers Press, 1969, 614 pgs.).

964. *Interments of the Gilgal Cemetery, Gilgal Church, Indiana Cnty, PA.*

965. "Van Horn, Bennett Work Obituary Indiana County Genealogical and Historical Society Newspaper Clippings."

966. *South Mahoning Twp., Indiana Cnty, PA 1880 Census ED 143 Sh 26.*

967. *South Mahoning Twp., Indiana Cnty, PA 1900 Census ED 64 Sh 2B .*

968. *South Mahoning Twp., Indiana Cnty, PA 1910 Census ED 93 Sh 3A.*

969. *Plumville, South Mahoning Twp., Indiana Cnty, PA 1930 Census ED 42 Sh 5A.*

970. *East Mahoning Twp., Indiana Cnty, PA 1860 Census p. 170.*

971. "22 May 1953 Indiana Evening Gazette (Indiana, PA) Mrs. Adda M. McAdoo Obituary."

972. Indiana Cnty, PA Marriage Records.

973. *Interments of the Gilgal Cemetery, Gilgal Church, Indiana Cnty, PA.*

974. *East Mahoning Twp., Indiana Cnty, PA 1860 Census p. 170.*

975. *Interments of the Gilgal Cemetery, Gilgal Church, Indiana Cnty, PA.*

976. "Mary Belle Nichol Van Horn Obituary Indiana County Genealogical and Historical Society Newspaper Clippings."

977. *Pennsylvania Veterans Burial Cards 1777-1999,* "Electronic."

978. Indiana Cnty, PA Marriage Records.

979. *Interments of the Gilgal Cemetery, Gilgal Church, Indiana Cnty, PA.*

980. *South Mahoning Twp., Indiana Cnty, PA 1880 Census ED 143 Sh 26.*

981. *Interments of the Gilgal Cemetery, Gilgal Church, Indiana Cnty, PA.*

982. *Cemetery Listing Indiana Cnty, PA.*

983. *Pennsylvania Veterans Burial Cards 1777-1999,* "Electronic."

984. "Indiana Weekly Messenger (Indiana, PA) 11 January 1899."

985. *East Mahoning Twp., Indiana Cnty, PA 1880 Census ED 145 Sh 10B.*

986. DAR National Record Copy of Member Application# 446865.

987. *East Mahoning Twp., Indiana Cnty, PA 1880 Census ED 145 Sh 10B.*

988. DAR National Record Copy of Member Application# 446865.

989. "Indiana Weekly Messenger (Indiana, PA) 11 January 1899."

990. *Washington, Distict of Columbia, 1900 Census ED 120 Sh 7A.*

991. *Washington Distict of Columbia, 1930 Census ED 242 Sh 7A.*

992. *Washington, District of Columbia, 1920 Census ED 219 Sh 15A.*

993. *Washington, Distict of Columbia, 1900 Census ED 120 Sh 7A.*

994. DAR National Record Copy of Member Application# 446865.

995. *Washington, Distict of Columbia, 1900 Census ED 120 Sh 7A.*

996. *Washington Distict of Columbia, 1930 Census ED 242 Sh 7A.*

997. *Washington, District of Columbia, 1920 Census ED 219 Sh 15A.*

998. *Washington, Distict of Columbia, 1900 Census ED 120 Sh 7A.*

999. *East Mahoning Twp., Indiana Cnty, PA 1860 Census p. 179 A&B.*

1000. *Hillsboro, Montgomery Cnty, IL 1880 Census ED 148 Sh 18B.*

1001. *East Mahoning Twp., Indiana Cnty, PA 1860 Census p. 179 A&B.*

1002. *Hillsboro, Montgomery Cnty, IL 1880 Census ED 148 Sh 18B.*

1003. *Ohio Cnty, VA 1860 Census p. 485B.*

1004. *Liberty, Ohio Cnty, WV 1870 Census p. 10.*

1005. *St Louis, St Louis Cnty, MO 1900 Census ED 314 Sh 11B.*

1006. *Hillsboro, Montgomery Cnty, IL 1880 Census ED 148 Sh 18B.*

1007. *Rayne Twp., Indiana Cnty, PA 1870 Census p. 339B.*

1008. *Washington Twp., Indiana Cnty, PA 1880 Census ED 141 Sh 273C.*

1009. "11 Feb 1937 Indiana Gazette (indiana, PA) Margaret T. McLaughlin Obit."

1010. *Rayne Twp., Indiana Cnty, PA 1870 Census p. 339B.*

1011. "11 Feb 1937 Indiana Gazettte (indiana, PA) Margaret T. McLaughlin Obit."

1012. *Rayne Twp., Indiana Cnty, PA 1870 Census p. 339B.*

1013. *Washington Twp., Indiana Cnty, PA 1880 Census ED 141 Sh 273C.*

1014. "11 Feb 1937 Indiana Gazettte (indiana, PA) Margaret T. McLaughlin Obit."

1015. *Rayne Twp., Indiana Cnty, PA 1870 Census p. 339B.*

1016. *Washington Twp., Indiana Cnty, PA 1880 Census ED 141 Sh 273C.*

1017. "11 Feb 1937 Indiana Gazettte (indiana, PA) Margaret T. McLaughlin Obit."

1018. *Rayne Twp., Indiana Cnty, PA 1870 Census p. 339B.*

1019. *Washington Twp., Indiana Cnty, PA 1880 Census ED 141 Sh 273C.*

1020. "11 Feb 1937 Indiana Gazettte (indiana, PA) Margaret T. McLaughlin Obit."

1021. *Washington Twp., Indiana Cnty, PA 1880 Census ED 141 Sh 273C.*

1022. "18 March 1908 Indiana Weekly Messenger (Indiana, PA)."

1023. *Washington Twp., Indiana Cnty, PA 1880 Census ED 141 Sh 273C.*

1024. "18 March 1908 Indiana Weekly Messenger (Indiana, PA)."

1025. *Washington Twp., Indiana Cnty, PA 1880 Census ED 141 Sh 273C.*

1026. "18 March 1908 Indiana Weekly Messenger (Indiana, PA)."

1027. *Washington Twp., Indiana Cnty, PA 1900 Census ED 65 Sh 1B.*

1028. "11 Feb 1937 Indiana Gazettte (indiana, PA) Margaret T. McLaughlin Obit."

1029. *Washington Twp., Indiana Cnty, PA 1900 Census ED 65 Sh 1B.*

1030. "18 March 1908 Indiana Weekly Messenger (Indiana, PA)."

1031. *Washington Twp., Indiana Cnty, PA 1900 Census ED 65 Sh 1B.*

1032. "11 Feb 1937 Indiana Gazettte (indiana, PA) Margaret T. McLaughlin Obit."

1033. *Washington Twp., Indiana Cnty, PA 1900 Census ED 65 Sh 1B.*

1034. "18 March 1908 Indiana Weekly Messenger (Indiana, PA)."

1035. *Washington Twp., Indiana Cnty, PA 1900 Census ED 65 Sh 1B.*
1036. "18 March 1908 Indiana Weekly Messenger (Indiana, PA)."
1037. *Washington Twp., Indiana Cnty, PA 1900 Census ED 65 Sh 1B.*
1038. "18 March 1908 Indiana Weekly Messenger (Indiana, PA)."
1039. *Washington Twp., Indiana Cnty, PA 1900 Census ED 65 Sh 1B.*
1040. "18 March 1908 Indiana Weekly Messenger (Indiana, PA)."
1041. *1860 Census Rayne Twp., Indiana Cnty, PA p. 307.*
1042. *Rayne, Indiana Cnty, PA 1870 Census p. 346B.*
1043. "James T. Van Horn Obituary Indiana County Genealogical and Historical Society Newspaper Clippings."
1044. *Indiana, Indiana Cnty, PA 1930 Census ED 32 Sh 1B.*
1045. "Elizabeth Van Horn Obituary Indiana County Genealogical and Historical Society Newspaper Clippings."
1046. *Green Twp., Indiana Cnty, PA 1900 Census ED 55 Sh 9A.*
1047. *Green Twp., Indiana Cnty, PA 1920 Census ED 110 Sh 22A.*
1048. "Indiana Progress (Indiana Cnty, PA) Jan. 1, 1936 Barr- Van Horn Golden Anniversay Announcement."
1049. "27 Oct 1909 Indiana Evening Gazette (Indiana, PA) Obituary of Margaret Douglas."
1050. *1860 Census Rayne Twp., Indiana Cnty, PA p. 307.*
1051. *Indiana, Indiana Cnty, PA 1930 Census ED 32 Sh 1B.*
1052. *Green Twp., Indiana Cnty, PA 1900 Census ED 55 Sh 9A.*
1053. DAR National Record Copy of Member Application # 684102.
1054. "Elizabeth Van Horn Obituary Indiana County Genealogical and Historical Society Newspaper Clippings."
1055. *Indiana, Indiana Cnty, PA 1930 Census ED 32 Sh 1B.*
1056. *Green Twp., Indiana Cnty, PA 1900 Census ED 55 Sh 9A.*
1057. *Green Twp., Indiana Cnty, PA 1920 Census ED 110 Sh 22A.*
1058. "Indiana Progress (Indiana Cnty, PA) Jan. 1, 1936 Barr- Van Horn Golden Anniversay Announcement."
1059. DAR National Record Copy of Member Application # 684102.
1060. *Indiana, Indiana Cnty, PA 1930 Census ED 32 Sh 1B.*
1061. *Green Twp., Indiana Cnty, PA 1900 Census ED 55 Sh 9A.*
1062. DAR National Record Copy of Member Application # 684102.
1063. "Indiana Weekly Messenger (Indiana, PA) 20 November 1919."
1064. DAR National Record Copy of Member Application # 684102.
1065. *Indiana, Indiana Cnty, PA 1930 Census ED 32 Sh 1B.*
1066. *Green Twp., Indiana Cnty, PA 1900 Census ED 55 Sh 9A.*
1067. *Green Twp., Indiana Cnty, PA 1920 Census ED 110 Sh 22A.*
1068. "Indiana Progress (Indiana Cnty, PA) Jan. 1, 1936 Barr- Van Horn Golden Anniversay Announcement."
1069. *Green Twp., Indiana Cnty, PA 1900 Census ED 55 Sh 9A.*
1070. "Elizabeth Van Horn Obituary Indiana County Genealogical and Historical Society Newspaper Clippings."
1071. "James W. Van Horn Obituary Indiana County Genealogical and Historical Society Newspaper Clippings."
1072. *Irwin Ward 2, Westmoreland Cnty, PA 1910 Census ED 140 Sh 14A.*
1073. *Rayne, Indiana Cnty, PA 1870 Census p. 346B.*
1074. "James T. Van Horn Obituary Indiana County Genealogical and Historical Society Newspaper Clippings."
1075. *Marion Center, East Mahoning Twp., Indiana Cnty, PA 1900 Census ED 53 Sh 11B.*
1076. *Indiana, Indiana Cnty, PA 1930 Census ED 34 Sh 6A.*
1077. "27 Oct 1909 Indiana Evening Gazette (Indiana, PA) Obituary of Margaret Douglas."
1078. *White Twp., Indiana Cnty, PA 1920 Census ED 133 Sh 9A.*
1079. "James W. Van Horn Obituary Indiana County Genealogical and Historical Society

Newspaper Clippings."
1080. *Marion Center, East Mahoning Twp., Indiana Cnty, PA 1900 Census ED 53 Sh 11B.*
1081. *Rayne, Indiana Cnty, PA 1870 Census p. 346B.*
1082. "James W. Van Horn Obituary Indiana County Genealogical and Historical Society Newspaper Clippings."
1083. *Irwin Ward 2, Westmoreland Cnty, PA 1910 Census ED 140 Sh 14A.*
1084. "Melissa Allison Van Horn Obituary Indiana County Genealogical and Historical Society Newspaper Clippings."
1085. *Marion Center, East Mahoning Twp., Indiana Cnty, PA 1900 Census ED 53 Sh 11B.*
1086. *Indiana, Indiana Cnty, PA 1930 Census ED 33 Sh 2A.*
1087. *White Twp., Indiana Cnty, PA 1920 Census ED 133 Sh 9A.*
1088. "4 May 1907 Indiana Evening Gazette (Indiana, PA)."
1089. *Irwin Ward 2, Westmoreland Cnty, PA 1910 Census ED 140 Sh 14A.*
1090. *Marion Center, East Mahoning Twp., Indiana Cnty, PA 1900 Census ED 53 Sh 11B.*
1091. "Melissa Allison Van Horn Obituary Indiana County Genealogical and Historical Society Newspaper Clippings."
1092. "James W. Van Horn Obituary Indiana County Genealogical and Historical Society Newspaper Clippings."
1093. *Irwin Ward 2, Westmoreland Cnty, PA 1910 Census ED 140 Sh 14A.*
1094. "Effie G. Van Horn Obituary."
1095. "Melissa Allison Van Horn Obituary Indiana County Genealogical and Historical Society Newspaper Clippings."
1096. *Marion Center, East Mahoning Twp., Indiana Cnty, PA 1900 Census ED 53 Sh 11B.*
1097. *Indiana, Indiana Cnty, PA 1930 Census ED 33 Sh 2A.*
1098. *White Twp., Indiana Cnty, PA 1920 Census ED 133 Sh 9A.*
1099. *Irwin Ward 2, Westmoreland Cnty, PA 1910 Census ED 140 Sh 14A.*
1100. *Marion Center, East Mahoning Twp., Indiana Cnty, PA 1900 Census ED 53 Sh 11B.*
1101. "Effie G. Van Horn Obituary."
1102. *Rayne, Indiana Cnty, PA 1870 Census p. 346B.*
1103. "James T. Van Horn Obituary Indiana County Genealogical and Historical Society Newspaper Clippings."
1104. *Pct. 2, Otero Cnty, CO 1900 Census ED 80 Sh 14A.*
1105. *Rayne, Indiana Cnty, PA 1870 Census p. 346B.*
1106. "27 Oct 1909 Indiana Evening Gazette (Indiana, PA) Obituary of Margaret Douglas."
1107. "Indiana Evening Gazette (Indiana, PA) 19 December 1906."
1108. *Pct. 2, Otero Cnty, CO 1900 Census ED 80 Sh 14A.*
1109. *Twin Falls, Twin Falls Cnty, ID 1910 Census ED 268 Sh 3A.*
1110. "27 Oct 1909 Indiana Evening Gazette (Indiana, PA) Obituary of Margaret Douglas."
1111. *Hollister, Twin Falls Cnty, ID 1920 Census ED 237 Sh 5B.*
1112. *Pct. 2, Otero Cnty, CO 1900 Census ED 80 Sh 14A.*
1113. *Twin Falls, Twin Falls Cnty, ID 1910 Census ED 268 Sh 3A.*
1114. *Pct. 2, Otero Cnty, CO 1900 Census ED 80 Sh 14A.*
1115. *Twin Falls, Twin Falls Cnty, ID 1910 Census ED 268 Sh 3A.*
1116. *Hollister, Twin Falls Cnty, ID 1920 Census ED 237 Sh 5B.*
1117. *Passenger List for the Ship Malolo arriving in San Francisco, CA on 15 Feb. 1929,* "Electronic."
1118. "Indiana Evening Gazette (Indiana, PA) 19 December 1906."
1119. *Twin Falls, Twin Falls Cnty, ID 1930 Census ED 28 Sh 7A.*
1120. *Twin Falls, Twin Falls Cnty, ID 1910 Census ED 268 Sh 3A.*
1121. *Hollister, Twin Falls Cnty, ID 1920 Census ED 237 Sh 5B.*
1122. *Twin Falls, Twin Falls Cnty, ID 1930 Census ED 28 Sh 7A.*
1123. "Elizabeth Van Horn Obituary Indiana County Genealogical and Historical Society Newspaper Clippings."
1124. "James W. Van Horn Obituary Indiana County Genealogical and Historical Society Newspaper Clippings."

1125. *Rayne, Indiana Cnty, PA 1870 Census p. 346B.*
1126. "James T. Van Horn Obituary Indiana County Genealogical and Historical Society Newspaper Clippings."
1127. *Waynesburg, Greene Cnty, PA 1920 Census ED 151 Sh 14A.*
1128. *Waynesburg, Greene Cnty, PA 1930 Census ED 29 Sh 11B.*
1129. "27 Oct 1909 Indiana Evening Gazette (Indiana, PA) Obituary of Margaret Douglas."
1130. *Rayne, Indiana Cnty, PA 1870 Census p. 346B.*
1131. "Elizabeth Van Horn Obituary Indiana County Genealogical and Historical Society Newspaper Clippings."
1132. *Waynesburg, Greene Cnty, PA 1920 Census ED 151 Sh 14A.*
1133. *Waynesburg, Greene Cnty, PA 1930 Census ED 29 Sh 11B.*
1134. *Waynesburg, Greene Cnty, PA 1920 Census ED 151 Sh 14A.*
1135. *Waynesburg, Greene Cnty, PA 1930 Census ED 29 Sh 11B.*
1136. *Waynesburg, Greene Cnty, PA 1920 Census ED 151 Sh 14A.*
1137. *Waynesburg, Greene Cnty, PA 1930 Census ED 29 Sh 11B.*
1138. *Waynesburg, Greene Cnty, PA 1920 Census ED 151 Sh 14A.*
1139. *Waynesburg, Greene Cnty, PA 1930 Census ED 29 Sh 11B.*
1140. *Waynesburg, Greene Cnty, PA 1920 Census ED 151 Sh 14A.*
1141. "Elizabeth Van Horn Obituary Indiana County Genealogical and Historical Society Newspaper Clippings."
1142. "James W. Van Horn Obituary Indiana County Genealogical and Historical Society Newspaper Clippings."
1143. *Walden, Jackson Cnty, CO 1920 Census ED 59 Sh 3A & B.*
1144. "Wedding Announcement dated 1902 George Van Horn and Bell ColemanIndiana County Genealogical and Historical Society Newspaper Clippings."
1145. "27 Oct 1909 Indiana Evening Gazette (Indiana, PA) Obituary of Margaret Douglas."
1146. *Greeley, Weld Cnty, CO 1930 census ED 100 Sh 20A.*
1147. *Walden, Jackson Cnty, CO 1920 Census ED 59 Sh 3A & B.*
1148. "Wedding Announcement dated 1902 George Van Horn and Bell ColemanIndiana County Genealogical and Historical Society Newspaper Clippings."
1149. *Loveland, Larimer Cnty, CO 1930 Census ED 16 Sh 9A.*
1150. "Wedding Announcement dated 1902 George Van Horn and Bell ColemanIndiana County Genealogical and Historical Society Newspaper Clippings."
1151. *Walden, Jackson Cnty, CO 1920 Census ED 59 Sh 3A & B.*
1152. "Wedding Announcement dated 1902 George Van Horn and Bell ColemanIndiana County Genealogical and Historical Society Newspaper Clippings."
1153. *Walden, Jackson Cnty, CO 1920 Census ED 59 Sh 3A & B.*
1154. *Loveland, Larimer Cnty, CO 1930 Census ED 16 Sh 9A.*
1155. *Walden, Jackson Cnty, CO 1920 Census ED 59 Sh 3A & B.*
1156. *East Mahoning Twp., Indiana Cnty, PA 1860 Census p. 170.*
1157. *DAR Lineage Book 80 (69218).*
1158. *East Mahoning Twp., Indiana Cnty, PA 1870 Census p. 201B.*
1159. *West Indiana Borough, Indiana Cnty, PA 1880 Census ED 127 Sh 21A.*
1160. *Des Moines, Ward 1, Polk Cnty, IA 1925 Iowa Census.*
1161. *East Mahoning Twp., Indiana Cnty, PA 1850 Census p. 247B.*
1162. *East Mahoning Twp., Indiana Cnty, PA 1860 Census p. 170.*
1163. *DAR Lineage Book 80 (69218).*
1164. Hamilton, Von Gail, *Work Family History: Twelve Generations of Work in America 1690-1969, Park City, Utah,* (Park City, Utah: Publishers Press, 1969, 614 pgs.).
1165. *West Indiana Borough, Indiana Cnty, PA 1880 Census ED 127 Sh 21A.*
1166. *East Mahoning Twp., Indiana Cnty, PA 1860 Census p. 170.*
1167. *East Mahoning Twp., Indiana Cnty, PA 1870 Census p. 201B.*
1168. *DAR Lineage Book 251 (71704).*
1169. *Ft. Morgan, Morgan Cnty, CO 1910 Census ED 248 29A.*

1170. *Ft. Morgan, Morgan Cnty, CO 1900 Census ED 185 Sh 9A.*
1171. *East Mahoning Twp., Indiana Cnty, PA 1870 Census p. 201B.*
1172. *DAR Lineage Book 251 (71704).*
1173. Hamilton, Von Gail, *Work Family History: Twelve Generations of Work in America 1690-1969, Park City, Utah*, (Park City, Utah: Publishers Press, 1969, 614 pgs.).
1174. *Ft. Morgan, Morgan Cnty, CO 1910 Census ED 248 Sh 29A.*
1175. *Ft. Morgan, Morgan Cnty, CO 1900 Census ED 185 Sh 9A.*
1176. Hamilton, Von Gail, *Work Family History: Twelve Generations of Work in America 1690-1969, Park City, Utah*, (Park City, Utah: Publishers Press, 1969, 614 pgs.).
1177. *Ft. Morgan, Morgan Cnty, CO 1910 Census ED 248 29A.*
1178. Hamilton, Von Gail, *Work Family History: Twelve Generations of Work in America 1690-1969, Park City, Utah*, (Park City, Utah: Publishers Press, 1969, 614 pgs.).
1179. *Oberlin, Loraine Cnty, OH 1930 Census ED 67 Sh 7A.*
1180. "19 May 1954 Indiana Evening Gazette (Indiana, PA) Mary Work Steele Obit."
1181. *Ft. Morgan, Morgan Cnty, CO 1910 Census ED 248 29A.*
1182. *Ft. Morgan, Morgan Cnty, CO 1900 Census ED 185 Sh 9A.*
1183. *Ft. Morgan, Morgan Cnty, CO 1910 Census ED 248 29A.*
1184. *California Death Index 1940-1997,* "Electronic."
1185. Hamilton, Von Gail, *Work Family History: Twelve Generations of Work in America 1690-1969, Park City, Utah*, (Park City, Utah: Publishers Press, 1969, 614 pgs.).
1186. *Oberlin, Loraine Cnty, OH 1930 Census ED 67 Sh 7A.*
1187. "19 May 1954 Indiana Evening Gazette (Indiana, PA) Mary Work Steele Obit."
1188. *Ft. Morgan, Morgan Cnty, CO 1910 Census ED 248 29A.*
1189. *East Mahoning Twp., Indiana Cnty, PA 1860 Census p. 170.*
1190. *East Mahoning Twp., Indiana Cnty, PA 1870 Census p. 201B.*
1191. "19 May 1954 Indiana Evening Gazette (Indiana, PA) Mary Work Steele Obit."
1192. Hamilton, Von Gail, *Work Family History: Twelve Generations of Work in America 1690-1969, Park City, Utah*, (Park City, Utah: Publishers Press, 1969, 614 pgs.).
1193. *Pueblo, Pueblo Cnty, CO 1900 Census ED 98 Sh 1A.*
1194. *East Mahoning Twp., Indiana Cnty, PA 1860 Census p. 170.*
1195. Hubert Work Passport Application 38090 Sept 13, 1910.
1196. Hamilton, Von Gail, *Work Family History: Twelve Generations of Work in America 1690-1969, Park City, Utah*, (Park City, Utah: Publishers Press, 1969, 614 pgs.).
1197. *Pueblo, Pueblo Cnty, CO 1900 Census ED 98 Sh 1A.*
1198. Hubert Work Passport Application 38090 Sept 13, 1910.
1199. Hamilton, Von Gail, *Work Family History: Twelve Generations of Work in America 1690-1969, Park City, Utah*, (Park City, Utah: Publishers Press, 1969, 614 pgs.).
1200. "19 May 1954 Indiana Evening Gazette (Indiana, PA) Mary Work Steele Obit."
1201. Hamilton, Von Gail, *Work Family History: Twelve Generations of Work in America 1690-1969, Park City, Utah*, (Park City, Utah: Publishers Press, 1969, 614 pgs.).
1202. *DAR Lineage Book 149 (56430).*
1203. *The National Society of the Daughters of the American Revolution Volume 57.*
1204. *Kansas City, Jackson Cnty, MO 1860 Census p. 101.*
1205. *Kansas City, Jackson Cnty, MO 1870 Census p. 503.*
1206. *Kansas City, Jackson Cnty, MO 1880 Census ED 7 Sh 30.*
1207. *Blue Twp., Jackson Cnty, MO 1900 Census ED 2 Sh 7B.*
1208. *Blue Twp., Jackson Cnty, MO 1910 Census ED 5 Sh 12A.*
1209. *Blue Twp., Jackson Cnty, MO 1920 Census ED 286 Sh 21A.*
1210. *Blue Twp., Jackson Cnty, MO 1930 Census ED 260 Sh 12A.*
1211. *Kansas City, Jackson Cnty, MO 1860 Census p. 101.*
1212. *Kansas City, Jackson Cnty, MO 1880 Census ED 7 Sh 30.*
1213. *The National Society of the Daughters of the American Revolution Volume 57.*
1214. *DAR Lineage Book 149 (56430).*
1215. "Katheen Nesbit Van Horn Obituary Indiana County Genealogical and Historical Society

Newspaper Clippings."
1216. *Blue Twp., Jackson Cnty, MO 1900 Census ED 2 Sh 7B.*
1217. *Blue Twp., Jackson Cnty, MO 1910 Census ED 5 Sh 12A.*
1218. *Kansas City, Jackson Cnty, MO 1880 Census ED 7 Sh 30.*
1219. *Blue Twp., Jackson Cnty, MO 1920 Census ED 286 Sh 21A.*
1220. *The National Society of the Daughters of the American Revolution Volume 57.*
1221. *DAR Lineage Book 149 (56430).*
1222. *Kansas City, Jackson Cnty, MO 1880 Census ED 7 Sh 30.*
1223. *Blue Twp., Jackson Cnty, MO 1900 Census ED 2 Sh 7B.*
1224. *Blue Twp., Jackson Cnty, MO 1910 Census ED 5 Sh 12A.*
1225. *Blue Twp., Jackson Cnty, MO 1920 Census ED 286 Sh 21A.*
1226. *Blue Twp., Jackson Cnty, MO 1930 Census ED 260 Sh 12A.*
1227. *DAR Lineage Book 149 (56430).*
1228. *Kansas City, Jackson Cnty, MO 1880 Census ED 7 Sh 30.*
1229. *East Mahoning Twp., Indiana Cnty, PA 1870 Census p. 205B.*
1230. *East Mahoning Twp., Indiana Cnty, PA 1860 Census p. 172B, 172B.*
1231. *Brookfield, Jefferson Cnty, PA 1880 Census ED 186 Sh 10C.*
1232. *Barnett Twp., Forest Cnty, PA 1900 Census ED 45 Sh 12A.*
1233. *East Mahoning Twp., Indiana Cnty, PA 1870 Census p. 205B.*
1234. *Brookfield, Jefferson Cnty, PA 1880 Census ED 186 Sh 10C.*
1235. *Punxsutawney, Jefferson Cnty, PA 1860 Census p. 293.*
1236. *East Mahoning Twp., Indiana Cnty, PA 1870 Census p. 205B.*
1237. *Barnett Twp., Forest Cnty, PA 1900 Census ED 45 Sh 12A.*
1238. *Brookfield, Jefferson Cnty, PA 1880 Census ED 186 Sh 10C.*
1239. *Barnett Twp., Forest Cnty, PA 1900 Census ED 45 Sh 12A.*
1240. *East Mahoning Twp., Indiana Cnty, PA 1870 Census p. 205B, 172B.*
1241. *East Mahoning Twp., Indiana Cnty, PA 1860 Census p. 172B.*
1242. *East Mahoning Twp., Indiana Cnty, PA 1880 Census ED 145 Sh 338C.*
1243. *East Mahoning Twp., Indiana Cnty, PA 1870 Census p. 205B.*
1244. *East Wheatfield Twp., Indiana Cnty, PA 1860 Census p. 374.*
1245. *East Mahoning Twp., Indiana Cnty, PA 1880 Census ED 145 Sh 338C.*
1246. *East Wheatfield Twp., Indiana Cnty, PA 1910 Census ED 74 Sh 9A.*
1247. *East Wheatfield Twp., Indiana Cnty, PA 1900 Census ED 37 Sh 1B.*
1248. *East Wheatfield Twp., Indiana Cnty, PA 1860 Census p. 374.*
1249. *East Mahoning Twp., Indiana Cnty, PA 1880 Census ED 145 Sh 338C.*
1250. *East Mahoning Twp., Indiana Cnty, PA 1870 Census p. 205B.*
1251. *East Mahoning Twp., Indiana Cnty, PA 1880 Census ED 145 Sh 338C.*
1252. "25 Aug 1941 Indiana Evening Gazette (Indiana, PA) Edith Lee Van Horn Shields Obituary."
1253. *Barnett, Forest Cnty, PA 1900 Census ED 45 Sh 13B.*
1254. *Barnett, Forest Cnty, PA 1910 Census ED 54 Sh 5B.*
1255. *Brookville, Jefferson Cnty, PA 1920 Census ED 141 Sh 18A.*
1256. *Brookville, Jefferson Cnty, PA 1930 Census ED 6 Sh 26A.*
1257. *East Mahoning Twp., Indiana Cnty, PA 1880 Census ED 145 Sh 338C.*
1258. "25 Aug 1941 Indiana Evening Gazette (Indiana, PA) Edith Lee Van Horn Shields Obituary."
1259. *Barnett, Forest Cnty, PA 1910 Census ED 54 Sh 5B.*
1260. *Barnett, Forest Cnty, PA 1900 Census ED 45 Sh 13B.*
1261. *Brookville, Jefferson Cnty, PA 1920 Census ED 141 Sh 18A.*
1262. *Barnett Twp., Forest Cnty, PA 1900 Census ED 45 Sh 12A.*
1263. "25 Aug 1941 Indiana Evening Gazette (Indiana, PA) Edith Lee Van Horn Shields Obituary."
1264. *Barnett Twp., Forest Cnty, PA 1900 Census ED 45 Sh 12A.*
1265. "25 Aug 1941 Indiana Evening Gazette (Indiana, PA) Edith Lee Van Horn Shields Obituary."
1266. *Barnett, Forest Cnty, PA 1910 Census ED 54 Sh 5B.*
1267. *Barnett, Forest Cnty, PA 1900 Census ED 45 Sh 13B.*
1268. *Brookville, Jefferson Cnty, PA 1920 Census ED 141 Sh 18A.*

1269. *Brookville, Jefferson Cnty, PA 1930 Census ED 6 Sh 26A.*
1270. *Barnett Twp., Forest Cnty, PA 1900 Census ED 45 Sh 12A.*
1271. "25 Aug 1941 Indiana Evening Gazette (Indiana, PA) Edith Lee Van Horn Shields Obituary."
1272. *Brookville, Jefferson Cnty, PA 1920 Census ED 141 Sh 18A.*
1273. Indiana Cnty, PA Marriage Records.
1274. *East Mahoning Twp., Indiana Cnty, PA1870 Census p. 205B.*
1275. *East Mahoning Twp., Indiana Cnty, PA 1880 Census ED 145 Sh 338C.*
1276. *Barnett Twp., Forest Cnty, PA 1900 Census ED 45 Sh 12B.*
1277. *Barnett Twp., Forest Cnty, PA 1910 Census ED 54 Sh 3B.*
1278. *Barnett Twp., Forest Cnty, PA 1920 Census ED 24 Sh 2B.*
1279. "25 Aug 1941 Indiana Evening Gazette (Indiana, PA) Edith Lee Van Horn Shields Obituary."
1280. *East Mahoning Twp., Indiana Cnty, PA1870 Census p. 205B.*
1281. *East Mahoning Twp., Indiana Cnty, PA 1880 Census ED 145 Sh 338C.*
1282. "18 Aug 1953 Indiana Evening gazette (Indiana, PA) Minnie Brewer Obituary."
1283. Indiana Cnty, PA Marriage Records.
1284. *Barnett Twp., Forest Cnty, PA 1900 Census ED 45 Sh 12B.*
1285. *Barnett Twp., Forest Cnty, PA 1910 Census ED 54 Sh 3B.*
1286. *Barnett Twp., Forest Cnty, PA 1920 Census ED 24 Sh 2B.*
1287. Indiana Cnty, PA Marriage Records.
1288. "14 Feb 1933 Indiana Evening Gazette (Indiana, PA) Dr. J. J. Brewer Obituary."
1289. *Barnett Twp., Forest Cnty, PA 1900 Census ED 45 Sh 12B.*
1290. "14 Feb 1933 Indiana Evening Gazette (Indiana, PA) Dr. J. J. Brewer Obituary."
1291. Indiana Cnty, PA Marriage Records.
1292. "14 Feb 1933 Indiana Evening Gazette (Indiana, PA) Dr. J. J. Brewer Obituary."
1293. *Barnett Twp., Forest Cnty, PA 1900 Census ED 45 Sh 12B.*
1294. *Barnett Twp., Forest Cnty, PA 1910 Census ED 54 Sh 3B.*
1295. *Barnett Twp., Forest Cnty, PA 1920 Census ED 24 Sh 2B.*
1296. *Barnett Twp., Forest Cnty, PA 1900 Census ED 45 Sh 12B.*
1297. WWI Civilian Draft Registration Index.
1298. *WWII Civilian Draft Registration,* "Electronic."
1299. *Barnett Twp., Forest Cnty, PA 1900 Census ED 45 Sh 12B.*
1300. *Barnett Twp., Forest Cnty, PA 1910 Census ED 54 Sh 3B.*
1301. *Barnett Twp., Forest Cnty, PA 1920 Census ED 24 Sh 2B.*
1302. *Barnett Twp., Forest Cnty, PA 1900 Census ED 45 Sh 12B.*
1303. *WWII Civilian Draft Registration,* "Electronic."
1304. *Barnett Twp., Forest Cnty, PA 1900 Census ED 45 Sh 12B.*
1305. *Barnett Twp., Forest Cnty, PA 1910 Census ED 54 Sh 3B.*
1306. *Columbus, Franklin Cnty, OH 1930 Census ED 240 Sh 29 B.*
1307. *Barnett Twp., Forest Cnty, PA 1900 Census ED 45 Sh 12B.*
1308. *Columbus, Franklin Cnty, OH 1930 Census ED 240 Sh 29 B.*
1309. *Barnett Twp., Forest Cnty, PA 1900 Census ED 45 Sh 12B.*
1310. *Barnett Twp., Forest Cnty, PA 1910 Census ED 54 Sh 3B.*
1311. *Barnett Twp., Forest Cnty, PA 1920 Census ED 24 Sh 2B.*
1312. *New Bethlehem, Clarion Cnty, PA 1930 ED 22 Sh 5A.*
1313. *Barnett Twp., Forest Cnty, PA 1900 Census ED 45 Sh 12B.*
1314. *New Bethlehem, Clarion Cnty, PA 1930 ED 22 Sh 5A.*
1315. *Barnett Twp., Forest Cnty, PA 1910 Census ED 54 Sh 3B.*
1316. *Barnett Twp., Forest Cnty, PA 1920 Census ED 24 Sh 2B.*
1317. *Otto Twp., McKean Cnty, PA 1930 Census ED 30 Sh 12B.*
1318. *Barnett Twp., Forest Cnty, PA 1910 Census ED 54 Sh 3B.*
1319. *Otto Twp., McKean Cnty, PA 1930 Census ED 30 Sh 12B.*
1320. *Lower Turkeyfoot, Somerset Cnty, PA 1870 Census p. 363B.*
1321. *Springfiield, Fayette Cnty, PA 1880 Census ED 55 Sh 457C.*
1322. *St. Clair Twp., Westmoreland Cnty, PA 1860 Census p. 934.*

1323. *Springfield Twp., Fayette Cnty, PA 1910 Census ED 74 Sh 7B.*
1324. *Springfield Twp., Fayette Cnty, PA 1920 Census ED 91 Sh 9B.*
1325. *Springfield Twp., Fayette Cnty, PA 1930 Census ED 94 Sh 16B.*
1326. *Springfield Twp., Fayette Cnty, PA 1900 Census ED 64 Sh 9B & 10A.*
1327. *Lower Turkeyfoot, Somerset Cnty, PA 1870 Census p. 363B.*
1328. *Springfield Twp., Fayette Cnty, PA 1910 Census ED 74 Sh 7B.*
1329. *Springfield Twp., Fayette Cnty, PA 1920 Census ED 91 Sh 9B.*
1330. *Springfield Twp., Fayette Cnty, PA 1930 Census ED 94 Sh 16B.*
1331. *Springfield Twp., Fayette Cnty, PA 1900 Census ED 64 Sh 9B & 10A.*
1332. *Springfield Twp., Fayette Cnty, PA 1900 Census ED 64 Sh 9B.*
1333. *Springfield Twp., Fayette Cnty, PA 1910 Census ED 74 Sh 7B.*
1334. *Springfield Twp., Fayette Cnty, PA 1900 Census ED 64 Sh 9B.*
1335. *Springfield Twp., Fayette Cnty, PA 1900 Census ED 64 Sh 9B & 10A.*
1336. *Springfield Twp., Fayette Cnty, PA 1900 Census ED 64 Sh 9B.*
1337. *Springfield Twp., Fayette Cnty, PA 1910 Census ED 74 Sh 7B.*
1338. *Springfield Twp., Fayette Cnty, PA 1900 Census ED 64 Sh 9B & 10A.*
1339. *Crafton, Allegheny Cnty, PA 1920 Census ED 74 Sh 20B.*
1340. *Springfield Twp., Fayette Cnty, PA 1910 Census ED 74 Sh 7B.*
1341. *Springfield Twp., Fayette Cnty, PA 1900 Census ED 64 Sh 9B & 10A.*
1342. *Washington, District of Columbia, 1930 Census ED 375 Sh 4B.*
1343. *Springfield Twp., Fayette Cnty, PA 1910 Census ED 74 Sh 7B.*
1344. *Washington, District of Columbia, 1930 Census ED 375 Sh 4B.*
1345. *Scottdale Ward 1, Westmoreland Cnty, PA 1910 Census ED 191 Sh 12A.*
1346. *Scottdale, Westmoreland Cnty, PA 1900 Census ED 132 Sh 1A & B.*
1347. *Lower Turkeyfoot, Somerset Cnty, PA 1870 Census p. 363B.*
1348. *Springfield, Fayette Cnty, PA 1880 Census ED 55 Sh 457C.*
1349. *Scottdale Ward 1, Westmoreland Cnty, PA 1920 Census ED 201 Sh 18B.*
1350. *Scottdale Ward 1, Westmoreland Cnty, PA 1930 Census ED 145 Sh 4A.*
1351. *Scottdale Ward 1, Westmoreland Cnty, PA 1910 Census ED 191 Sh 12A.*
1352. *Scottdale, Westmoreland Cnty, PA 1900 Census ED 132 Sh 1A & B.*
1353. *Scottdale Ward 1, Westmoreland Cnty, PA 1920 Census ED 201 Sh 18B.*
1354. *Scottdale Ward 1, Westmoreland Cnty, PA 1930 Census ED 145 Sh 4A.*
1355. *Scottdale Ward 1, Westmoreland Cnty, PA 1910 Census ED 191 Sh 12A.*
1356. Willey, Gordon (Van Horn TREE) Husband of Jacqueline Marshal Granddaughter of Judson Van Horn.
1357. *Lower Turkeyfoot, Somerset Cnty, PA 1870 Census p. 363B.*
1358. *Springfield, Fayette Cnty, PA 1880 Census ED 55 Sh 457C.*
1359. *Dawson, Fayette Cnty, PA 1900 Census ED 13 Sh 5A.*
1360. *Dawson, Fayette Cnty, PA 1910 Census ED 17 Sh 5B.*
1361. *Dawson, Fayette Cnty, PA 1920 Census ED 20 Sh 3B.*
1362. *Dawson, Fayette Cnty, PA 1930 Census ED 15 Sh 2A.*
1363. *Lower Turkeyfoot, Somerset Cnty, PA 1870 Census p. 363B.*
1364. *Dawson, Fayette Cnty, PA 1900 Census ED 13 Sh 5A.*
1365. *Dawson, Fayette Cnty, PA 1910 Census ED 17 Sh 5B.*
1366. *Dawson, Fayette Cnty, PA 1920 Census ED 20 Sh 3B.*
1367. *Dawson, Fayette Cnty, PA 1900 Census ED 13 Sh 5A.*
1368. *Dawson, Fayette Cnty, PA 1910 Census ED 17 Sh 5B.*
1369. *Dawson, Fayette Cnty, PA 1920 Census ED 20 Sh 3B.*
1370. *Dawson, Fayette Cnty, PA 1930 Census ED 15 Sh 2A.*
1371. *Dawson, Fayette Cnty, PA 1900 Census ED 13 Sh 5A.*
1372. *WWII Civilian Draft Registration,* "Electronic."
1373. *Dawson, Fayette Cnty, PA 1900 Census ED 13 Sh 5A.*
1374. *Dawson, Fayette Cnty, PA 1910 Census ED 17 Sh 5B.*
1375. *Dawson, Fayette Cnty, PA 1920 Census ED 20 Sh 3B.*

1376. *Dawson, Fayette Cnty, PA 1930 Census ED 15 Sh 2A.*
1377. *Dawson, Fayette Cnty, PA 1900 Census ED 13 Sh 5A.*
1378. *Dawson, Fayette Cnty, PA 1910 Census ED 17 Sh 5B.*
1379. *Dawson, Fayette Cnty, PA 1920 Census ED 20 Sh 3B.*
1380. *Dawson, Fayette Cnty, PA 1930 Census ED 15 Sh 2A.*
1381. *Dawson, Fayette Cnty, PA 1900 Census ED 13 Sh 5A.*
1382. *Dawson, Fayette Cnty, PA 1910 Census ED 17 Sh 5B.*
1383. *Dawson, Fayette Cnty, PA 1920 Census ED 20 Sh 3B.*
1384. *Dawson, Fayette Cnty, PA 1900 Census ED 13 Sh 5A.*
1385. *Dawson, Fayette Cnty, PA 1910 Census ED 17 Sh 5B.*
1386. *Dawson, Fayette Cnty, PA 1920 Census ED 20 Sh 3B.*
1387. *Dawson, Fayette Cnty, PA 1930 Census ED 15 Sh 2A.*
1388. *Dawson, Fayette Cnty, PA 1910 Census ED 17 Sh 5B.*
1389. Will of J. W. Van Horn #5483 Indiana Cnty, PA.
1390. *West Wheatfield Twp., Indiana Cnty, PA 1860 Census p. 390 A and B.*
1391. *Derry Station, Westmoreland Cnty, PA 1880 Census ED 115 Sh 148.*
1392. *Niagra Falls Ward 2, Niagra Cnty, NY 1900 Census ED 73 Sh 12A.*
1393. *Niagra Falls Ward 7, Niagra Cnty, NY 1910 Census ED 112 Sh 1B.*
1394. *Williamsport Ward 3, Lycoming Cnty, PA 1870 Census p. 476B.*
1395. *Niagara Falls, Niagara Cnty, NY 1930 Census ED 48 Sh 8B.*
1396. "6 June 1894 Indiana County Gazette (Indiana, PA) James Wherry Van Horn Obituary."
1397. *West Wheatfield Twp., Indiana Cnty, PA 1860 Census p. 390 A and B.*
1398. *Derry Station, Westmoreland Cnty, PA 1880 Census ED 115 Sh 148.*
1399. Will of J. W. Van Horn #5483 Indiana Cnty, PA.
1400. *Derry Station, Westmoreland Cnty, PA 1880 Census ED 115 Sh 148.*
1401. *Niagra Falls Ward 2, Niagra Cnty, NY 1900 Census ED 73 Sh 12A.*
1402. *Niagra Falls Ward 7, Niagra Cnty, NY 1910 Census ED 112 Sh 1B.*
1403. *Derry Station, Westmoreland Cnty, PA 1880 Census ED 115 Sh 148.*
1404. *Niagra Falls Ward 2, Niagra Cnty, NY 1900 Census ED 73 Sh 12A.*
1405. *Niagra Falls Ward 7, Niagra Cnty, NY 1910 Census ED 112 Sh 1B.*
1406. *Niagara Falls, Niagara Cnty, NY 1920 Census ED 10 Sh 10A.*
1407. *Niagara Falls, Niagara Cnty, NY 1930 Census ED 48 Sh 8B.*
1408. *Derry Station, Westmoreland Cnty, PA 1880 Census ED 115 Sh 148.*
1409. *Niagara Falls Ward 2, Niagara Cnty, NY 1900 Census ED 73 Sh 12A.*
1410. *Niagara Falls, Niagara Cnty, NY 1920 Census ED 10 Sh 10A.*
1411. *Niagara Falls, Niagara Cnty, NY 1930 Census ED 48 Sh 8B.*
1412. *Niagara Falls, Niagara Cnty, NY 1920 Census ED 10 Sh 10A.*
1413. *Niagra Falls Ward 2, Niagra Cnty, NY 1900 Census ED 73 Sh 12A.*
1414. *WWII Civilian Draft Registration,* "Electronic."
1415. *Denver, Denver Cnty, CO 1920 Census ED 236 Sh 5B.*
1416. *Niagra Falls Ward 2, Niagra Cnty, NY 1900 Census ED 73 Sh 12A.*
1417. *WWII Civilian Draft Registration,* "Electronic."
1418. *Denver, Denver Cnty, CO 1920 Census ED 236 Sh 5B.*
1419. Will of J. W. Van Horn #5483 Indiana Cnty, PA.
1420. *West Wheatfield Twp., Indiana Cnty, PA 1860 Census p. 390 A and B.*
1421. *Derry, Westmoreland Cnty, PA 1900 Census ED 89 Sh 1B.*
1422. *Williamsport Ward 3, Lycoming Cnty, PA 1870 Census p. 476B.*
1423. *Derry Station, Westmoreland Cnty, PA 1880 Census ED 115 Sh 148.*
1424. *Derry, Westmoreland Cnty, PA 1910 Census ED 109 Sh 11B.*
1425. "6 June 1894 Indiana County Gazette (Indiana, PA) James Wherry Van Horn Obituary."
1426. *West Wheatfield Twp., Indiana Cnty, PA 1860 Census p. 390 A and B.*
1427. Will of J. W. Van Horn #5483 Indiana Cnty, PA.
1428. *Derry, Westmoreland Cnty, PA 1900 Census ED 89 Sh 1B.*
1429. *Derry Station, Westmoreland Cnty, PA 1880 Census ED 115 Sh 148.*

1430. *Derry, Westmoreland Cnty, PA 1910 Census ED 109 Sh 11B.*
1431. *Derry, Westmoreland Cnty, PA 1920 Census ED 79 Sh 1B.*
1432. *Derry, Westmoreland Cnty, PA 1930 Census ED 13 Sh 29A.*
1433. *Derry, Westmoreland Cnty, PA 1900 Census ED 89 Sh 1B.*
1434. *Derry Station, Westmoreland Cnty, PA 1880 Census ED 115 Sh 148.*
1435. *Derry, Westmoreland Cnty, PA 1910 Census ED 109 Sh 11B.*
1436. *Derry, Westmoreland Cnty, PA 1920 Census ED 79 Sh 1B.*
1437. *Derry, Westmoreland Cnty, PA 1900 Census ED 89 Sh 1B.*
1438. *Derry, Westmoreland Cnty, PA 1910 Census ED 109 Sh 11B.*
1439. *Derry, Westmoreland Cnty, PA 1900 Census ED 89 Sh 1B.*
1440. *West Wheatfield Twp., Indiana Cnty, PA 1880 Census ED 244 Sh 440C.*
1441. Will of J. W. Van Horn #5483 Indiana Cnty, PA.
1442. *Williamsport Ward 3, Lycoming Cnty, PA 1870 Census p. 476B.*
1443. *West Wheatfield Twp., Indiana Cnty, PA 1900 Census ED 66 Sh 15A.*
1444. *West Wheatfield Twp., Indiana Cnty, PA 1910 Census ED 97 Sh 6A.*
1445. *New Florence, Westmoreland Cnty, PA 1920 Census ED 171 Sh 7B.*
1446. *West Wheatfield Twp., Indiana Cnty, PA 1880 Census ED 244 Sh 440C.*
1447. *West Wheatfield Twp., Indiana Cnty, PA 1910 Census ED 97 Sh 6A.*
1448. *New Florence, Westmoreland Cnty, PA 1930 Census ED 114 Sh 3A.*
1449. *New Florence, Westmoreland Cnty, PA 1920 Census ED 171 Sh 7B.*
1450. *West Wheatfield Twp., Indiana Cnty, PA 1910 Census ED 97 Sh 6A.*
1451. *West Wheatfield Twp., Indiana Cnty, PA 1900 Census ED 66 Sh 15A.*
1452. *West Wheatfield Twp., Indiana Cnty, PA 1910 Census ED 97 Sh 7A.*
1453. *Dale, Cambria Cnty, PA 1930 Census ED 30 Sh 10A.*
1454. *West Wheatfield Twp., Indiana Cnty, PA 1900 Census ED 66 Sh 15A.*
1455. *Dale, Cambria Cnty, PA 1930 Census ED 30 Sh 10A.*
1456. *West Wheatfield Twp., Indiana Cnty, PA 1900 Census ED 66 Sh 15A.*
1457. *West Wheatfield Twp., Indiana Cnty, PA 1910 Census ED 97 Sh 7A.*
1458. *New Florence, Westmoreland Cnty, PA 1920 Census ED 171 Sh 7B.*
1459. *West Wheatfield Twp., Indiana Cnty, PA 1900 Census ED 66 Sh 15A.*
1460. *West Wheatfield Twp., Indiana Cnty, PA 1910 Census ED 97 Sh 7A.*
1461. *New Florence, Westmoreland Cnty, PA 1920 Census ED 171 Sh 7B.*
1462. *West Wheatfield Twp., Indiana Cnty, PA 1910 Census ED 97 Sh 7A.*
1463. *East Wheatfield Twp., Indiana Cnty, PA 1860 Census p. 374.*
1464. *Franklin Twp., Allamakee Cnty, IA 1900 Census ED 3 Sh 4A&B.*
1465. *Township 160, Koochiching Cnty, MN 1910 Census ED 93 Sh 4A.*
1466. *Kanaranzi, Rock Cnty, MN 1885 MN Census p. 6.*
1467. *Center, Winnebago Cnty, IA 1870 Census p. 8.*
1468. *East Wheatfield Twp., Indiana Cnty, PA 1860 Census p. 374.*
1469. *Franklin Twp., Allamakee Cnty, IA 1900 Census ED 3 Sh 4A&B.*
1470. *Kanaranzi, Rock Cnty, MN 1885 MN Census p. 6.*
1471. *Center, Winnebago Cnty, IA 1870 Census p. 8.*
1472. *Franklin Twp., Allamakee Cnty, IA 1900 Census ED 3 Sh 4A&B.*
1473. *Kanaranzi, Rock Cnty, MN 1885 MN Census p. 6.*
1474. *Center, Winnebago Cnty, IA 1870 Census p. 8.*
1475. *Franklin Twp., Allamakee Cnty, IA 1900 Census ED 3 Sh 4A&B.*
1476. *Center, Winnebago Cnty, IA 1870 Census p. 8.*
1477. *Franklin Twp., Allamakee Cnty, IA 1900 Census ED 3 Sh 4A&B.*
1478. *Township 160, Koochiching Cnty, MN 1910 Census ED 93 Sh 4A.*
1479. *Franklin Twp., Allamakee Cnty, IA 1900 Census ED 3 Sh 4A&B.*
1480. *East Wheatfield Twp., Indiana Cnty, PA 1860 Census p. 374.*
1481. *East Mahoning Twp., Indiana Cnty, PA 1880 Census ED 145 Sh 338C.*
1482. *East Wheatfield Twp., Indiana Cnty, PA 1910 Census ED 74 Sh 9A.*
1483. *East Wheatfield Twp., Indiana Cnty, PA 1900 Census ED 37 Sh 1B.*

1484. *East Wheatfield Twp., Indiana Cnty, PA 1860 Census p. 374.*
1485. *East Mahoning Twp., Indiana Cnty, PA 1880 Census ED 145 Sh 338C.*
1486. *East Mahoning Twp., Indiana Cnty, PA1870 Census p. 205B,* 172B.
1487. *East Mahoning Twp., Indiana Cnty, PA 1860 Census p. 172B.*
1488. *East Mahoning Twp., Indiana Cnty, PA 1880 Census ED 145 Sh 338C.*
1489. *East Mahoning Twp., Indiana Cnty, PA1870 Census p. 205B.*
1490. *East Wheatfield Twp., Indiana Cnty, PA 1910 Census ED 74 Sh 9A.*
1491. *East Wheatfield Twp., Indiana Cnty, PA 1900 Census ED 37 Sh 1B.*
1492. *East Wheatfield Twp., Indiana Cnty, PA 1910 Census ED 74 Sh 9A.*
1493. *East Wheatfield Twp., Indiana Cnty, PA 1900 Census ED 37 Sh 1B.*
1494. *East Wheatfield Twp., Indiana Cnty, PA 1870 Census p. 22B.*
1495. *East Wheatfield Twp., Indiana Cnty, PA 1860 Census p. 374.*
1496. *Millville, Cambria Cnty, PA 1880 Census ED 187 Sh 166C.*
1497. *Milnor Ward 2, Sargent Cnty, ND1910 Census ED 200 Sh 4B.*
1498. *Forman, Sargent Cnty, ND 1920 Census ED 154 Sh 8A.*
1499. *Milnor, Sargent Cnty, ND 1900 Census ED 159 Sh 3A.*
1500. *East Wheatfield Twp., Indiana Cnty, PA 1860 Census p. 374.*
1501. *Millville, Cambria Cnty, PA 1880 Census ED 187 Sh 166C.*
1502. *Milnor Ward 2, Sargent Cnty, ND1910 Census ED 200 Sh 4B.*
1503. *Milnor, Sargent Cnty, ND 1900 Census ED 159 Sh 3A.*
1504. *Forman, Sargent Cnty, ND 1920 Census ED 154 Sh 8A.*
1505. *Millville, Cambria Cnty, PA 1880 Census ED 187 Sh 166C.*
1506. *Milnor, Sargent Cnty, ND 1900 Census ED 159 Sh 3A.*
1507. *Milnor Ward 2, Sargent Cnty, ND1910 Census ED 200 Sh 4B.*
1508. *Milnor, Sargent Cnty, ND 1900 Census ED 159 Sh 3A.*
1509. *Milnor Ward 2, Sargent Cnty, ND1910 Census ED 200 Sh 4B.*
1510. *Milnor, Sargent Cnty, ND 1900 Census ED 159 Sh 3A.*
1511. *Milnor Ward 2, Sargent Cnty, ND1910 Census ED 200 Sh 4B.*
1512. *East Wheatfield Twp., Indiana Cnty, PA 1860 Census p. 374.*
1513. *East Wheatfield Twp., Indiana Cnty, PA 1870 Census p. 22B.*
1514. *East Wheatfield Twp., Indiana Cnty, PA 1860 Census p. 374.*
1515. *East Wheatfield Twp., Indiana Cnty, PA 1870 Census p. 228.*
1516. *East Wheatfield Twp., Indiana Cnty, PA 1870 Census p. 22B.*
1517. *East Wheatfield Twp., Indiana Cnty, PA 1880 Census ED 135 Sh 146C.*
1518. *East Wheatfield Twp., Indiana Cnty, PA 1870 Census p. 22B.*
1519. *East Wheatfield Twp., Indiana Cnty, PA 1860 Census p. 374.*
1520. *Kiona, Yakama Cnty, WA 1900 Census ED 108 Sh 1A.*
1521. *Richland, Benton Cnty, WA 1910 Census ED 22 Sh 9B.*
1522. DAR National Record Copy of Member Application # 184963.
1523. *East Wheatfield Twp., Indiana Cnty, PA 1860 Census p. 374.*
1524. "Indiana Progress (Indiana Cnty, PA) 17 December 1919."
1525. *Kiona, Yakama Cnty, WA 1900 Census ED 108 Sh 1A.*
1526. *Richland, Benton Cnty, WA 1910 Census ED 22 Sh 9B.*
1527. *Seattle, King Cnty, WA 1920 Census ED 222 Sh 2B.*
1528. DAR National Record Copy of Member Application # 184963.
1529. *Kiona, Yakama Cnty, WA 1900 Census ED 108 Sh 1A.*
1530. *Richland, Benton Cnty, WA 1910 Census ED 22 Sh 9B.*
1531. *Horn Rapids, Benton Cnty, WA1920 Census ED 26 Sh 4A.*
1532. *Monrovia, Los Angles Cnty, CA 1930 Census ED 1158 Sh 11B.*
1533. *Kiona, Yakama Cnty, WA 1900 Census ED 108 Sh 1A.*
1534. *California Death Index 1940-1997,* "Electronic."
1535. *Kiona, Yakama Cnty, WA 1900 Census ED 108 Sh 1A.*
1536. *Richland, Benton Cnty, WA 1910 Census ED 22 Sh 9B.*
1537. *Elma, Grays Harbor, WA 1920 Census ED 95 Sh 13A.*

1538. *Kiona, Yakama Cnty, WA 1900 Census ED 108 Sh 1A.*
1539. *Richland, Benton Cnty, WA 1910 Census ED 22 Sh 9B.*
1540. *Seattle, King Cnty, WA 1930 Census ED 53 Sh 1B.*
1541. *Seattle, King Cnty, WA 1920 Census ED 222 Sh 2B.*
1542. DAR National Record Copy of Member Application # 184963.
1543. *Kiona, Yakama Cnty, WA 1900 Census ED 108 Sh 1A.*
1544. *East Wheatfield Twp., Indiana Cnty, PA 1900 Census ED 37 Sh 2B .*
1545. The Van Horn Family History by Francis M. Marvin 1929, The Press Publishing Co., p 373-4.
1546. Social Security Application, Application of daughter Leafy Fern VanHorn.
1547. *East Wheatfield Twp., Indiana Cnty, PA 1860 Census p. 374.*
1548. *Dalhart, Dallam Cnty, TX 1920 Census ED 46 Sh 5A.*
1549. *Justice Pct. 2, Dallam Cnty, TX 1910 Census ED 69 Sh 4B.*
1550. *East Wheatfield Twp., Indiana Cnty, PA 1870 Census p. 22B.*
1551. Handwritten Notes of Leafy Fern Van Horn Wolf.
1552. The Van Horn Family History by Francis M. Marvin 1929, The Press Publishing Co., p 373-4.
1553. *Dalhart, Dallam Cnty, TX 1920 Census ED 46 Sh 5A.*
1554. *East Wheatfield Twp., Indiana Cnty, PA 1860 Census p. 374.*
1555. *Texas Death Index 1903-2000*, "Electronic," Certificate # 1279.
1556. "21 Jan 1937 Indiana Weekly Messenger (Indiana, PA) S. C. Van Horn Obit."
1557. Handwritten Notes of Leafy Fern Van Horn Wolf.
1558. Social Security Application, Application of daughter Leafy Fern Van Horn.
1559. *Jackson Twp., Sandusky Cnty, OH 1860 Census p. 232.*
1560. *Jackson Twp., Sandusky Cnty, OH 1870 Census p. 147.*
1561. *Jackson Twp., Sandusky Cnty, OH 1880 Census ED 75 Sh 95A.*
1562. *Jackson Twp., Sandusky Cnty, OH 1860 Census p. 232.*
1563. *Grave Stone Liberty Cemetery Bettsville, OH*, "fig."
1564. *Dalhart, Dallam Cnty, TX 1920 Census ED 46 Sh 5A.*
1565. *Justice Pct. 2, Dallam Cnty, TX 1910 Census ED 69 Sh 4B.*
1566. *East Wheatfield Twp., Indiana Cnty, PA 1900 Census ED 37 Sh 2B .*
1567. *Jackson Twp., Sandusky Cnty, OH 1860 Census p. 232.*
1568. *Jackson Twp., Sandusky Cnty, OH 1870 Census p. 147.*
1569. *Justice Pct. 2, Dallam Cnty, TX 1910 Census ED 69 Sh 4B.*
1570. *East Wheatfield Twp., Indiana Cnty, PA 1900 Census ED 37 Sh 2B , ED 37, S 2.*
1571. *Dalhart, Dallam Cnty, TX 1920 Census ED 46 Sh 5A.*
1572. *Justice Pct. 2, Dallam Cnty, TX 1910 Census ED 69 Sh 4A.*
1573. *Jackson Twp., Sandusky Cnty, OH 1860 Census p. 232.*
1574. *Texas Death Index 1903-2000*, "Electronic," Certificate # 39246.
1575. "21 Jan 1937 Indiana Weekly Messenger (Indiana, PA) S. C. Van Horn Obit."
1576. *Justice Pct. 2, Dallam Cnty, TX 1910 Census ED 69 Sh 4B.*
1577. "21 Jan 1937 Indiana Weekly Messenger (Indiana, PA) S. C. Van Horn Obit."
1578. *East Wheatfield Twp., Indiana Cnty, PA 1870 Census p. 22B.*
1579. *Wilkinsburg Ward 2, Allegheny Cnty, PA1910 Census ED 273 Sh 8B.*
1580. *Braddock, Allegheny Cnty, PA 1900 Census ED 353 Sh 4B.*
1581. "21 Jan 1937 Indiana Weekly Messenger (Indiana, PA) S. C. Van Horn Obit."
1582. *St. Petersburg, Pinellas Cnty, FL 1920 Census ED 138 Sh 13B.*
1583. *East Wheatfield Twp., Indiana Cnty, PA 1870 Census p. 22B.*
1584. *Florida Death Index 1877-1998*, "Electronic."
1585. *Wilkinsburg Ward 2, Allegheny Cnty, PA1910 Census ED 273 Sh 8B.*
1586. *Braddock, Allegheny Cnty, PA 1900 Census ED 353 Sh 4B.*
1587. "21 Jan 1937 Indiana Weekly Messenger (Indiana, PA) S. C. Van Horn Obit."
1588. *Wilkinsburg Ward 2, Allegheny Cnty, PA1910 Census ED 273 Sh 8B.*
1589. *Braddock, Allegheny Cnty, PA 1900 Census ED 353 Sh 4B.*
1590. *Greensburg, Westmoreland Cnty, PA 1910 Census ED 127 Sh 9A.*
1591. WWI Civilian Draft Registration Index.

1592. *Braddock, Allegheny Cnty, PA 1900 Census ED 353 Sh 4B.*
1593. WWI Civilian Draft Registration Index.
1594. *Greensburg, Westmoreland Cnty, PA 1910 Census ED 127 Sh 9A.*
1595. *Braddock, Allegheny Cnty, PA 1900 Census ED 353 Sh 4B.*
1596. *Wilkinsburg Ward 2, Allegheny Cnty, PA1910 Census ED 273 Sh 8B.*
1597. *Braddock, Allegheny Cnty, PA 1900 Census ED 353 Sh 4B.*
1598. *Wilkinsburg Ward 2, Allegheny Cnty, PA1910 Census ED 273 Sh 8B.*
1599. *Braddock, Allegheny Cnty, PA 1900 Census ED 353 Sh 4B.*
1600. *Soldiers of the Great War Pennsylvania p. 154,* "Electronic."
1601. *Wilkinsburg Ward 2, Allegheny Cnty, PA1910 Census ED 273 Sh 8B.*
1602. *Braddock, Allegheny Cnty, PA 1900 Census ED 353 Sh 4B.*
1603. *St. Petersburg, Pinellas Cnty, FL 1930 Census ED 9 Sh 26B.*
1604. *Braddock, Allegheny Cnty, PA 1900 Census ED 353 Sh 4B.*
1605. *St. Petersburg, Pinellas Cnty, FL 1930 Census ED 9 Sh 26B.*
1606. *East Wheatfield Twp., Indiana Cnty, PA 1870 Census p. 22B.*
1607. *East Wheatfield Twp., Indiana Cnty, PA 1880 Census ED 135 Sh 146C.*
1608. *East Wheatfield Twp., Indiana Cnty, PA 1910 Census ED 74 Sh 6B.*
1609. *Wilkinsburg Ward 2, Allegheny Cnty, PA1900 Census ED 531 Sh 10A.*
1610. *Pittsburgh Ward 24, Allegheny Cnty, PA 1910 Census ED 604 Sh 17B.*
1611. *East Wheatfield Twp., Indiana Cnty, PA 1880 Census ED 135 Sh 146C.*
1612. *East Wheatfield Twp., Indiana Cnty, PA 1910 Census ED 74 Sh 6B.*
1613. *Wilkinsburg Ward 2, Allegheny Cnty, PA1900 Census ED 531 Sh 10A.*
1614. *Pittsburgh Ward 24, Allegheny Cnty, PA 1910 Census ED 604 Sh 17B.*
1615. *Wilkinsburg Ward 2, Allegheny Cnty, PA1900 Census ED 531 Sh 10A.*
1616. *Pittsburgh Ward 24, Allegheny Cnty, PA 1910 Census ED 604 Sh 17B.*
1617. *Wilkinsburg Ward 2, Allegheny Cnty, PA1900 Census ED 531 Sh 10A.*
1618. *Jefferson Twp., Allamamkee Cnty, IA 1880 Census ED 7 Sh 6B.*
1619. *Rayne Twp., Indiana Cnty, PA 1850 Census p. 194.*
1620. *Young Twp., Indiana Cnty, PA 1900 Census ED 69 Sh 2B.*
1621. *Rayne Twp., Indiana Cnty, PA 1880 Census ED 142 Sh 284A.*
1622. *Young Twp., Indiana Cnty, PA 1910 Census ED 100 Sh 2B.*
1623. *Rayne Twp., Indiana Cnty, PA 1870 Census p. 342.*
1624. *Rayne Twp., Indiana Cnty, PA 1850 Census p. 194.*
1625. *Young Twp., Indiana Cnty, PA 1900 Census ED 69 Sh 2B.*
1626. *Young Twp., Indiana Cnty, PA 1910 Census ED 100 Sh 2B.*
1627. *Young Twp., Indiana Cnty, PA 1900 Census ED 69 Sh 2B.*
1628. *Young Twp., Indiana Cnty, PA 1910 Census ED 100 Sh 2B.*
1629. *Young Twp., Indiana Cnty, PA 1900 Census ED 69 Sh 2B.*
1630. *Rayne Twp., Indiana Cnty, PA 1850 Census p. 194.*
1631. *Rayne Twp., Indiana Cnty, PA 1900 Census ED 60 Sh 3B.*
1632. *Rayne, Indiana Cnty, PA 1880 Census ED 142 Sh 248A.*
1633. *Rayne Twp., Indiana Cnty, PA 1900 Census ED 60 Sh 3B.*
1634. *Rayne, Indiana Cnty, PA 1880 Census ED 142 Sh 248A.*
1635. *Rayne Twp., Indiana Cnty, PA 1900 Census ED 60 Sh 3B.*
1636. *Holbrook, Multnomah Cnty, OR 1920 Census ED 204 Sh 3B.*
1637. *Gilman, King Cnty, WA 1910 Census ED 32 Sh 5A.*
1638. *Rayne Twp., Indiana Cnty, PA 1900 Census ED 60 Sh 3B.*
1639. *British Columbia Death Index 1872-1979,* "Electronic."
1640. *Rayne Twp., Indiana Cnty, PA 1850 Census p. 194.*
1641. *Rayne Twp., Indiana Cnty, PA 1880 Census ED 142 Sh 284A.*
1642. *Rayne Twp., Indiana Cnty, PA 1870 Census p. 342.*
1643. *Rayne Twp., Indiana Cnty, PA 1910 Census ED 89 Sh 2B.*
1644. *Rayne Twp., Indiana Cnty, PA 1850 Census p. 194.*
1645. *Rayne Twp., Indiana Cnty, PA 1910 Census ED 89 Sh 2B.*

1646. *Rayne Twp., Indiana Cnty, PA 1860 Census p. 171.*
1647. *Blairsville, Indiana Cnty, PA 1920 Census ED 91 Sh 11A.*
1648. DAR National Record Copy of Member Application # 449599.
1649. *Blairsville, Indiana Cnty, PA 1910 Census ED 57 Sh 19A & B.*
1650. DAR National Record Copy of Member Application# 448771.
1651. DAR National Record Copy of Member Application # 449599.
1652. DAR National Record Copy of Member Application# 448771.
1653. *Blairsville, Indiana Cnty, PA 1920 Census ED 91 Sh 11A.*
1654. *Blairsville, Indiana Cnty, PA 1910 Census ED 57 Sh 19A & B.*
1655. DAR National Record Copy of Member Application # 449599.
1656. *Blairsville, Indiana Cnty, PA 1910 Census ED 57 Sh 19A & B.*
1657. *Blairsville, Indiana Cnty, PA 1920 Census ED 91 Sh 11A.*
1658. *Blairsville, Indiana Cnty, PA 1910 Census ED 57 Sh 19A & B.*
1659. *Green Twp., Indiana Cnty, PA 1860 Census p. 212B.*
1660. *Green Twp., Indiana Cnty, PA 1870 Census p. 150A.*
1661. *Cherry Hill Twp., Indiana Cnty, PA 1880 Census ED 139 Sh 18B.*
1662. *Green Twp., Indiana Cnty, PA 1860 Census p. 212B.*
1663. *Green Twp., Indiana Cnty, PA 1870 Census p. 150A.*
1664. *Cherry Hill Twp., Indiana Cnty, PA 1880 Census ED 139 Sh 18B.*
1665. *Cherry Hill Twp., Indiana Cnty, PA 1900 Census ED 49 Sh 3B.*
1666. *Green Twp., Indiana Cnty, PA 1870 Census p. 150A.*
1667. *Cherry Hill Twp., Indiana Cnty, PA 1880 Census ED 139 Sh 18B.*
1668. *Green Twp., Indiana Cnty, PA 1870 Census p. 150A.*
1669. *Cherry Hill Twp., Indiana Cnty, PA 1880 Census ED 139 Sh 18B.*
1670. *Green Twp., Indiana Cnty, PA 1860 Census p. 212B.*
1671. *Green Twp., Indiana Cnty, PA 1870 Census p. 150B.*
1672. *Cherry Hill Twp., Indiana Cnty, PA 1880 Census ED 139 Sh 215A.*
1673. *Cherry Hill Twp., Indiana Cnty, PA 1900 Census ED 50 Sh 11A.*
1674. *Green Twp., Indiana Cnty, PA 1860 Census p. 212B.*
1675. *Cherry Hill Twp., Indiana Cnty, PA 1900 Census ED 50 Sh 11A.*
1676. *Cherry Hill Twp., Indiana Cnty, PA 1880 Census ED 139 Sh 220C.*
1677. *Green Twp., Indiana Cnty, PA 1860 Census p. 212B.*
1678. *Green Twp., Indiana Cnty, PA 1870 Census p. 150B.*
1679. *Cherry Hill Twp., Indiana Cnty, PA 1880 Census ED 139 Sh 220C.*
1680. *East Mahoning Twp., Indiana Cnty, PA 1850 Census p. 247B & 248.*
1681. "29 October 1897 Indiana Weekly Messenger (Indiana, PA)."
1682. *East Mahoning Twp., Indiana Cnty, PA 1870 Census p. 212.*
1683. *East Mahoning Twp., Indiana Cnty, PA 1880 Census ED 143 Sh 18B.*
1684. *East Mahoning Twp., Indiana Cnty, PA 1850 Census p. 247B & 248.*
1685. "29 October 1897 Indiana Weekly Messenger (Indiana, PA)."
1686. *East Mahoning Twp., Indiana Cnty, PA 1870 Census p. 212.*
1687. *East Mahoning Twp., Indiana Cnty, PA 1880 Census ED 143 Sh 18B.*
1688. "29 October 1897 Indiana Weekly Messenger (Indiana, PA)."
1689. *East Mahoning Twp., Indiana Cnty, PA 1870 Census p. 212.*
1690. *East Mahoning Twp., Indiana Cnty, PA 1880 Census ED 143 Sh 18B.*
1691. *East Mahoning Twp., Indiana Cnty, PA 1870 Census p. 212.*
1692. *East Mahoning Twp., Indiana Cnty, PA 1880 Census ED 143 Sh 18B.*
1693. *East Mahoning Twp., Indiana Cnty, PA 1870 Census p. 213.*
1694. *East Mahoning Twp., Indiana Cnty, PA 1900 Census ED 53 Sh 7A.*
1695. *East Mahoning Twp., Indiana Cnty, PA 1870 Census p. 213.*
1696. *White Twp., Indiana Cnty, PA 1900 Census ED 67 Sh 1A.*
1697. *Indiana, Indiana Cnty, PA 1910 Census ED 83 Sh 7A.*
1698. *East Mahoning Twp., Indiana Cnty, PA 1870 Census p. 213.*
1699. *White Twp., Indiana Cnty, PA 1900 Census ED 67 Sh 1A.*

1700. *Indiana, Indiana Cnty, PA 1910 Census ED 83 Sh 7A.*
1701. *White Twp., Indiana Cnty, PA 1900 Census ED 67 Sh 1A.*
1702. *East Mahoning Twp., Indiana Cnty, PA 1870 Census p. 213.*
1703. *East Mahoning Twp., Indiana Cnty, PA 1910 Census ED 73 Sh 6A.*
1704. *East Mahoning Twp., Indiana Cnty, PA 1900 Census ED 53 Sh 6B.*
1705. *East Mahoning Twp., Indiana Cnty, PA 1910 Census ED 73 Sh 6A.*
1706. *East Mahoning Twp., Indiana Cnty, PA 1900 Census ED 53 Sh 6B.*
1707. *East Mahoning Twp., Indiana Cnty, PA 1910 Census ED 73 Sh 6A.*
1708. *East Mahoning Twp., Indiana Cnty, PA 1900 Census ED 53 Sh 6B.*
1709. *East Mahoning Twp., Indiana Cnty, PA 1910 Census ED 73 Sh 6A.*
1710. *East Mahoning Twp., Indiana Cnty, PA 1900 Census ED 53 Sh 6B.*
1711. *East Mahoning Twp., Indiana Cnty, PA 1910 Census ED 73 Sh 6A.*
1712. "Martha Bell Nichol Van Horn Obituary."
1713. Hamilton, Von Gail, *Work Family History: Twelve Generations of Work in America 1690-1969, Park City, Utah,* (Park City, Utah: Publishers Press, 1969, 614 pgs.).
1714. "Jennie Van Horn Obituary."
1715. "Phoebe Neff Van Horn Obituary 9 Feb 1905 Indiana Evening Gazette (Indiana, PA) p. 1."
1716. "23 Oct 1907 Indiana Evening Gazette (Indiana, PA) Van Horn, John N. Obituary ."
1717. *Banks Twp., Indiana Cnty, PA 1880 Census ED 150 Sh 405 A & B.*
1718. *United States Homestead Certificate 639, Application 1309 signed by Ulysses S. Grant 9/20/1873.*
1719. *Banks Twp., Indiana Cnty, PA 1870 Census p. 22.*
1720. *Interments of the Gilgal Cemetery, Gilgal Church, Indiana Cnty, PA.*
1721. *Banks Twp., Indiana Cnty, PA 1870 Census p. 22.*
1722. *Interments of the Gilgal Cemetery, Gilgal Church, Indiana Cnty, PA.*
1723. "23 Oct 1907 Indiana Evening Gazette (Indiana, PA) Van Horn, John N. Obituary ."
1724. DAR National Record Copy of Member Application # 486836.
1725. "Jennie Van Horn Obituary."
1726. *Banks Twp., Indiana Cnty, PA 1880 Census ED 150 Sh 405 A & B.*
1727. *Banks Twp., Indiana Cnty, PA 1870 Census p. 22.*
1728. "Jennie Van Horn Obituary."
1729. DAR National Record Copy of Member Application # 486836.
1730. "Jennie Van Horn Obituary."
1731. *Banks, Indiana Cnty, PA 1870 Census p. 22.*
1732. "Jennie Van Horn Obituary."
1733. DAR National Record Copy of Member Application # 486836.
1734. "Martha Bell Nichol Van Horn Obituary."
1735. *East Mahoning Twp., Indiana Cnty, PA 1910 Census ED 73 Sh 9A.*
1736. *East Mahoning Twp., Indiana Cnty, PA 1920 Census ED 108 Sh 2A.*
1737. *East Mahoning Twp., Indiana Cnty, PA 1930 Census ED 24 Sh 4A.*
1738. *East Mahoning Twp., Indiana Cnty, PA 1860 Census p. 171.*
1739. "23 Nov 1904 Indiana County Gazette (Indiana, PA) Marriage Announcement."
1740. "Martha Bell Nichol Van Horn Obituary."
1741. *East Mahoning Twp., Indiana Cnty, PA 1860 Census p. 171.*
1742. "Martha Bell Nichol Van Horn Obituary."
1743. "15 August 1942 Indiana Evening Gazette (Indiana, PA) Death Notice of Mrs Belle Van Horn of Plumville."
1744. *Cemetery Listing Indiana Cnty, PA.*
1745. *Pennsylvania Veterans Burial Cards 1777-1999,* "Electronic."
1746. "Jennie Van Horn Obituary."
1747. DAR National Record Copy of Member Application # 486836.
1748. "23 Nov 1904 Indiana County Gazette (Indiana, PA) Marriage Announcement."
1749. "23 Oct 1907 Indiana Evening Gazette (Indiana, PA) Van Horn, John N. Obituary ."
1750. "Jennie Van Horn Obituary."
1751. *Twp. 105, Lyman Cnty, SD 1900 Census ED 43 Sh 1B.*

1752. "Phoebe Neff Van Horn Obituary 9 Feb 1905 Indiana Evening Gazette (Indiana, PA) p. 1."
1753. *South Mahoning Twp., Indiana Cnty, PA 1860 Census p. 248.*
1754. *South Mahoning Twp., Indiana Cnty, PA 1870 Census p. 354B.*
1755. *South Mahoning Twp., Indiana Cnty, PA 1880 Census ED 143 Sh 28.*
1756. *Marion Center, East Mahoning Twp., Indiana Cnty, PA 1910 Census ED 73 Sh 13A.*
1757. *East Mahoning Twp., Indiana Cnty, PA 1920 Census ED 108 Sh 12B.*
1758. *Marion Center, East Mahoning Twp., Indiana Cnty, PA 1900 Census ED 53 Sh 10A.*
1759. "25 Aug, 1921 Indiana Weekly Messenger(Indiana, PA) Harvey Van Horn Obit."
1760. *South Mahoning Twp., Indiana Cnty, PA 1860 Census p. 248.*
1761. "Indiana Progress (Indiana Cnty, PA) 24 August 1921."
1762. *South Mahoning Twp., Indiana Cnty, PA 1880 Census ED 143 Sh 28.*
1763. *Marion Center, East Mahoning Twp., Indiana Cnty, PA 1910 Census ED 73 Sh 13A.*
1764. *Marion Center, East Mahoning Twp., Indiana Cnty, PA 1900 Census ED 53 Sh 10A.*
1765. *South Mahoning Twp., Indiana Cnty, PA 1880 Census ED 143 Sh 28.*
1766. "Indiana Progress (Indiana Cnty, PA) 24 August 1921."
1767. *Marion Center, East Mahoning Twp., Indiana Cnty, PA 1900 Census ED 53 Sh 10A.*
1768. "Oran Dent Van Horn Obituary Indiana County Genealogical and Historical Society Newspaper Clippings."
1769. *South Mahoning Twp., Indiana Cnty, PA 1880 Census ED 143 Sh 28.*
1770. "25 Aug, 1921 Indiana Weekly Messenger(Indiana, PA) Harvey Van Horn Obit."
1771. *South Mahoning Twp., Indiana Cnty, PA 1880 Census ED 143 Sh 28.*
1772. "Park Van Horn Obituary Indiana County Genealogical and Historical Society Newspaper Clippings."
1773. "Charles Blaine Van Horn Obituary Indiana County Genealogical and Historical Society Newspaper Clippings."
1774. "Oran Dent Van Horn Obituary Indiana County Genealogical and Historical Society Newspaper Clippings."
1775. *Marion Center, East Mahoning Twp., Indiana Cnty, PA 1910 Census ED 73 Sh 13A.*
1776. *East Mahoning Twp., Indiana Cnty, PA 1920 Census ED 108 Sh 2A.*
1777. *Marion Center, East Mahoning Twp., Indiana Cnty, PA 1930 Census ED 36 Sh 5A.*
1778. *Marion Center, East Mahoning Twp., Indiana Cnty, PA 1900 Census ED 53 Sh 10A.*
1779. "25 Aug, 1921 Indiana Weekly Messenger(Indiana, PA) Harvey Van Horn Obit."
1780. "Park Van Horn Obituary Indiana County Genealogical and Historical Society Newspaper Clippings."
1781. *WWII Civilian Draft Registration*, "Electronic."
1782. *Marion Center, East Mahoning Twp., Indiana Cnty, PA 1930 Census ED 36 Sh 5A.*
1783. *WWI Draft Registration Card 1917-1918*, "Electronic."
1784. "Park Van Horn Obituary Indiana County Genealogical and Historical Society Newspaper Clippings."
1785. *Marion Center, East Mahoning Twp., Indiana Cnty, PA 1930 Census ED 36 Sh 5A.*
1786. *WWII Civilian Draft Registration*, "Electronic."
1787. *East Mahoning Twp., Indiana Cnty, PA 1920 Census ED 108 Sh 10A.*
1788. "Oran Dent Van Horn Obituary Indiana County Genealogical and Historical Society Newspaper Clippings."
1789. *Marion Center, East Mahoning Twp., Indiana Cnty, PA 1910 Census ED 73 Sh 13A.*
1790. *East Mahoning Twp., Indiana Cnty, PA 1920 Census ED 108 Sh 12B.*
1791. *Marion Center, East Mahoning Twp., Indiana Cnty, PA 1900 Census ED 53 Sh 10A.*
1792. "25 Aug, 1921 Indiana Weekly Messenger(Indiana, PA) Harvey Van Horn Obit."
1793. *Marion Center, East Mahoning Twp., Indiana Cnty, PA 1910 Census ED 73 Sh 13A.*
1794. "Indiana Evening Gazette (Indiana, PA) 8 April 1969 Annie P. Kephart Obituary."
1795. *East Mahoning Twp., Indiana Cnty, PA 1920 Census ED 108 Sh 12B.*
1796. "Indiana Evening Gazette (Indiana, PA) 8 April 1969 Annie P. Kephart Obituary."
1797. "Indiana Weekly Messenger (Indiana, PA) 28 February 1918."
1798. "Indiana Evening Gazette (Indiana, PA) 21 February 1918."

1799. *East Mahoning Twp., Indiana Cnty, PA 1920 Census ED 108 Sh 12B.*
1800. "Indiana Evening Gazette (Indiana, PA) 8 April 1969 Annie P. Kephart Obituary."
1801. "Indiana Weekly Messenger (Indiana, PA) 28 February 1918."
1802. "Indiana Evening Gazette (Indiana, PA) 21 February 1918."
1803. D. Scott Van Horn Family Group Sheet, August 8, 1983.
1804. "Phoebe Neff Van Horn Obituary 9 Feb 1905 Indiana Evening Gazette (Indiana, PA) p. 1."
1805. "LeRoy Van Horn Obituary Indiana County Genealogical and Historical Society Newspaper Clippings."
1806. *South Mahoning Twp., Indiana Cnty, PA 1910 Census ED 93 Sh 2A.*
1807. "A. M. Van Horn Obituary Indiana County Genealogical and Historical Society Newspaper Clippings."
1808. Will of B. B. Van Horn Indiana Cnty, PA.
1809. *South Mahoning Twp., Indiana Cnty, PA 1860 Census p. 248.*
1810. *South Mahoning Twp., Indiana Cnty, PA 1870 Census p. 354B.*
1811. *East Mahoning Twp., Indiana Cnty, PA 1880 Census ED 145 Sh 20.*
1812. *South Mahoning Twp., Indiana Cnty, PA 1900 Census ED 64 Sh 3A.*
1813. *South Mahoning Twp., Indiana Cnty, PA 1920 Census ED 124 Sh 6B.*
1814. DAR National Record Copy of Member Application # 835192.
1815. D. Scott Van Horn Family Group Sheet, August 8, 1983.
1816. *South Mahoning Twp., Indiana Cnty, PA 1910 Census ED 93 Sh 2A.*
1817. "A. M. Van Horn Obituary Indiana County Genealogical and Historical Society Newspaper Clippings."
1818. *East Mahoning Twp., Indiana Cnty, PA 1880 Census ED 145 Sh 20.*
1819. *South Mahoning Twp., Indiana Cnty, PA 1900 Census ED 64 Sh 3A.*
1820. D. Scott Van Horn Family Group Sheet, August 8, 1983.
1821. " 3 Jan 1878 Indiana Progress (Indiana, PA)."
1822. "LeRoy Van Horn Obituary Indiana County Genealogical and Historical Society Newspaper Clippings."
1823. *South Mahoning Twp., Indiana Cnty, PA 1910 Census ED 93 Sh 2A.*
1824. *South Mahoning Twp., Indiana Cnty, PA 1900 Census ED 64 Sh 3A.*
1825. *South Mahoning Twp., Indiana Cnty, PA 1920 Census ED 124 Sh 6B.*
1826. *South Mahoning Twp., Indiana Cnty, PA 1910 Census ED 93 Sh 2A.*
1827. "LeRoy Van Horn Obituary Indiana County Genealogical and Historical Society Newspaper Clippings."
1828.   Floyd G. Hoenstine, *1955 YEAR Book of the Pa Society, Sons of the American Revolution,* (Call # E 202.3 .P46 1955x by Mirror Printing Co., Altoona, Pa).
1829. Rinn, Mrs Samuel, Helmen, Blaine et al, Cemetery Records of Indiana County, Pennsylvania, James LaTort Chapter Daughters of the American Colonists, Connelsville, PA, 1957.
1830. "Phoebe Neff Van Horn Obituary 9 Feb 1905 Indiana Evening Gazette (Indiana, PA) p. 1."
1831. *Cowanshannock Twp., Armstrong Cnty, PA 1900 Census ED 3 Sh 3A.*
1832. Will of B. B. Van Horn Indiana Cnty, PA.
1833. *South Mahoning Twp., Indiana Cnty, PA 1860 Census p. 248.*
1834. *South Mahoning Twp., Indiana Cnty, PA 1870 Census p. 354B.*
1835. *Cowanshannock Twp., Armstrong Cnty, PA 1910 Census ED 9 Sh 7A.*
1836. *Cowanshannock Twp., Armstrong Cnty, PA 1930 Census ED 11 Sh 2A.*
1837. "2 April 1960 Simpson's Leader-Times (Kittanning, PA) Bertha A. Lukehart Neal Obituary."
1838. *South Mahoning Twp., Indiana Cnty, PA 1860 Census p. 248.*
1839. "Phoebe Neff Van Horn Obituary 9 Feb 1905 Indiana Evening Gazette (Indiana, PA) p. 1."
1840. Will of B. B. Van Horn Indiana Cnty, PA.
1841. "2 April 1960 Simpson's Leader-Times (Kittanning, PA) Bertha A. Lukehart Neal Obituary."
1842. "14 October 1874 The Indiana Messenger (Indiana, PA)."
1843. *Cowanshannock Twp., Armstrong Cnty, PA 1900 Census ED 3 Sh 3A.*
1844. "14 October 1874 The Indiana Messenger (Indiana, PA)."
1845. *Cowanshannock Twp., Armstrong Cnty, PA 1930 Census ED 11 Sh 2A.*

1846. *Derry, Westmoreland Cnty, PA 1910 Census ED 112 Sh 6A.*
1847. *West Mahoning Twp., Indiana Cnty, PA 1860 Census p. 195.*
1848. *Wayne Twp., Armstrong Cnty, PA 1870 Census p. 535.*
1849. *Porter Twp., Jefferson Cnty, PA 1880 Census ED 197 Sh 191A.*
1850. *Falls Creek, Jefferson Cnty, PA 1920 Census ED 146 Sh 1A.*
1851. *Troutville Pct., Brady Twp., Clearfield Cnty, PA 1900 Census ED 55 Sh 7B.*
1852. *Luthersburg Pct., Brady Twp., Clearfield Cnty, PA 1910 Census ED 55 Sh 12A.*
1853. *West Mahoning Twp., Indiana Cnty, PA 1860 Census p. 195.*
1854. *Wayne Twp., Armstrong Cnty, PA 1870 Census p. 535.*
1855. *Porter Twp., Jefferson Cnty, PA 1880 Census ED 197 Sh 191A.*
1856. *Porter Twp., Jefferson Cnty, PA 1850 Census p. 73.*
1857. *Wayne Twp., Armstrong Cnty, PA 1870 Census p. 535.*
1858. *Falls Creek, Jefferson Cnty, PA 1920 Census ED 146 Sh 1A.*
1859. *Troutville Pct., Brady Twp., Clearfield Cnty, PA 1900 Census ED 55 Sh 7B.*
1860. *Luthersburg Pct., Brady Twp., Clearfield Cnty, PA 1910 Census ED 55 Sh 12A.*
1861. *Troutville Pct., Brady Twp., Clearfield Cnty, PA 1900 Census ED 55 Sh 7B.*
1862. *Falls Creek, Jefferson Cnty, PA 1920 Census ED 146 Sh 1A.*
1863. *Troutville Pct., Brady Twp., Clearfield Cnty, PA 1900 Census ED 55 Sh 7B.*
1864. *Pennsylvania Veterans Burial Cards 1777-1999,* "Electronic."
1865. *Troutville Pct., Brady Twp., Clearfield Cnty, PA 1900 Census ED 55 Sh 7B.*
1866. *Wayne Twp., Armstrong Cnty, PA 1870 Census p. 535.*
1867. *Porter Twp., Jefferson Cnty, PA 1880 Census ED 197 Sh 191A.*
1868. *Wayne Twp., Armstrong Cnty, PA 1870 Census p. 535.*
1869. *Porter Twp., Jefferson Cnty, PA 1880 Census ED 197 Sh 191A.*
1870. *Troutville Pct., Brady Twp., Clearfield Cnty, PA 1900 Census ED 55 Sh 7B.*
1871. *Luthersburg Pct., Brady Twp., Clearfield Cnty, PA 1910 Census ED 55 Sh 12A.*
1872. *Troutville Pct., Brady Twp., Clearfield Cnty, PA 1900 Census ED 55 Sh 7B.*
1873. *Wayne Twp., Armstrong Cnty, PA 1900 Census ED 9 Sh 9B&10A.*
1874. "29 Jan 1962 Simpson's Leader-Times (Kittanning, PA) Coral Ayers Rupp Obituary."
1875. *Wayne Twp., Armstrong Cnty, PA 1910 Census ED 49 Sh 7B.*
1876. *Wayne Twp., Armstrong Cnty, PA 1900 Census ED 9 Sh 9B&10A.*
1877. "29 Jan 1962 Simpson's Leader-Times (Kittanning, PA) Coral Ayers Rupp Obituary."
1878. *Wayne Twp., Armstrong Cnty, PA 1910 Census ED 49 Sh 7B.*
1879. *Wayne Twp., Armstrong Cnty, PA 1900 Census ED 9 Sh 9B&10A.*
1880. "29 Jan 1962 Simpson's Leader-Times (Kittanning, PA) Coral Ayers Rupp Obituary."
1881. *Wayne Twp., Armstrong Cnty, PA 1900 Census ED 9 Sh 9B&10A.*
1882. "29 Jan 1962 Simpson's Leader-Times (Kittanning, PA) Coral Ayers Rupp Obituary."
1883. *Wayne Twp., Armstrong Cnty, PA 1900 Census ED 9 Sh 9B&10A.*
1884. "29 Jan 1962 Simpson's Leader-Times (Kittanning, PA) Coral Ayers Rupp Obituary."
1885. *Wayne Twp., Armstrong Cnty, PA 1910 Census ED 49 Sh 7B.*
1886. *Wayne Twp., Armstrong Cnty, PA 1900 Census ED 9 Sh 9B&10A.*
1887. "29 Jan 1962 Simpson's Leader-Times (Kittanning, PA) Coral Ayers Rupp Obituary."
1888. *Wayne Twp., Armstrong Cnty, PA 1910 Census ED 49 Sh 7B.*
1889. *West Mahoning Twp., Indiana Cnty, PA 1920 Census ED 128 Sh 5A.*
1890. *Wayne Twp., Armstrong Cnty, PA 1910 Census ED 49 Sh 7B.*
1891. *South Mahoning Twp., Indiana Cnty, PA 1860 Census p. 330B.*
1892. *Beaver Meadow, Banks Twp., Carbon Cnty, PA 1880 Census ED 110 Sh 255.*
1893. *South Mahoning Twp., Indiana Cnty, PA 1860 Census p. 331B.*
1894. *Beaver Meadow, Banks Twp., Carbon Cnty, PA 1880 Census ED 110 Sh 255.*
1895. *South Mahoning Twp., Indiana Cnty, PA 1860 Census p. 331B.*
1896. *Franklin Cnty, IL 1870 Census p. 253B.*
1897. DAR National Record Copy of Member Application # 614578.
1898. *South Mahoning Twp., Indiana Cnty, PA 1860 Census p. 331B.*
1899. DAR National Record Copy of Member Application # 614578.

1900. *Mount Vernon, Jefferson Cnty, IL 1920 Census ED 134 Sh 11A.*
1901. *Franklin Cnty, IL 1870 Census p. 253B.*
1902. *Mount Vernon, Jefferson Cnty, IL 1910 Census ED 107 Sh 10B.*
1903. *Northern Twp., Franklin Cnty, IL 1900 Census ED 33 Sh 7A.*
1904. *Franklin Cnty, IL 1870 Census p. 253B.*
1905. *Mount Vernon, Jefferson Cnty, IL 1910 Census ED 107 Sh 10B.*
1906. *Northern Twp., Franklin Cnty, IL 1900 Census ED 33 Sh 7A.*
1907. *Mount Vernon, Jefferson Cnty, IL 1910 Census ED 107 Sh 10B.*
1908. *Northern Twp., Franklin Cnty, IL 1900 Census ED 33 Sh 7A.*
1909. *Mount Vernon, Jefferson Cnty, IL 1910 Census ED 107 Sh 10B.*
1910. *Northern Twp., Franklin Cnty, IL 1900 Census ED 33 Sh 7A.*
1911. *Mount Vernon, Jefferson Cnty, IL 1910 Census ED 107 Sh 10B.*
1912. *Mount Vernon, Jefferson Cnty, IL 1920 Census ED 134 Sh 11A.*
1913. *Mount Vernon, Jefferson Cnty, IL 1910 Census ED 107 Sh 10B.*
1914. *Northern Twp., Franklin Cnty, IL 1900 Census ED 33 Sh 7A.*
1915. *Mount Vernon, Jefferson Cnty, IL 1920 Census ED 134 Sh 11A.*
1916. *Mount Vernon, Jefferson Cnty, IL 1910 Census ED 107 Sh 10B.*
1917. *Northern Twp., Franklin Cnty, IL 1900 Census ED 33 Sh 7A.*
1918. *Mount Vernon, Jefferson Cnty, IL 1920 Census ED 134 Sh 11A.*
1919. *Mount Vernon, Jefferson Cnty, IL 1910 Census ED 107 Sh 10B.*
1920. *Punxsutwaney, Jefferson Cnty, PA 1870 Census p. 293.*
1921. *Punxsutwaney, Jefferson Cnty, PA 1860 Census p. 293B.*
1922. *Punxsutawney, Jefferson Cnty, PA 1880 Census ED 203 Sh 34B.*
1923. *Punxsutwaney, Jefferson Cnty, PA 1870 Census p. 293.*
1924. *Punxsutawney, Jefferson Cnty, PA 1880 Census ED 203 Sh 34B.*
1925. *Punxsutwaney, Jefferson Cnty, PA 1870 Census p. 293.*
1926. *Punxsutwaney, Jefferson Cnty, PA 1860 Census p. 293B.*
1927. *Punxsutawney, Jefferson Cnty, PA 1880 Census ED 203 Sh 317C.*
1928. *Pitcairn, Allegheny Cnty, PA 1900 Census ED 473 Sh 5B.*
1929. *Punxsutwaney, Jefferson Cnty, PA 1870 Census p. 293.*
1930. *Pitcairn, Allegheny Cnty, PA 1900 Census ED 473 Sh 5B.*
1931. *Punxsutwaney, Jefferson Cnty, PA 1870 Census p. 293.*
1932. *Punxsutawney, Jefferson Cnty, PA 1900 Census ED 73 Sh 22B.*
1933. *Punxsutawney, Jefferson Cnty, PA 1880 Census ED 203 Sh 317C.*
1934. *Punxsutwaney, Jefferson Cnty, PA 1870 Census p. 293.*
1935. *Punxsutawney, Jefferson Cnty, PA 1900 Census ED 73 Sh 22B.*
1936. *Punxsutawney, Jefferson Cnty, PA 1930 Census ED 25 Sh 14A & B.*
1937. *Punxsutawney, Jefferson Cnty, PA 1900 Census ED 73 Sh 22B.*
1938. *Punxsutawney, Jefferson Cnty, PA 1930 Census ED 25 Sh 14A & B.*
1939. *Punxsutawney, Jefferson Cnty, PA 1900 Census ED 73 Sh 22B.*
1940. *Punxsutwaney, Jefferson Cnty, PA 1870 Census p. 293.*
1941. *Punxsutawney, Jefferson Cnty, PA 1920 Census ED 158 Sh 11B.*
1942. *Punxsutawney, Jefferson Cnty, PA 1880 Census ED 203 Sh 317C.*
1943. *Punxsutawney, Jefferson Cnty, PA 1910 Census ED 82 Sh 32A.*
1944. *Punxsutawney, Jefferson Cnty, PA 1930 Census ED 25 Sh 14A.*
1945. *Punxsutwaney, Jefferson Cnty, PA 1870 Census p. 293.*
1946. *Punxsutawney, Jefferson Cnty, PA 1920 Census ED 158 Sh 11B.*
1947. *Punxsutawney, Jefferson Cnty, PA 1910 Census ED 82 Sh 32A.*
1948. *Punxsutawney, Jefferson Cnty, PA 1930 Census ED 25 Sh 14A & B.*
1949. *Punxsutawney, Jefferson Cnty, PA 1920 Census ED 158 Sh 11B.*
1950. *Punxsutawney, Jefferson Cnty, PA 1910 Census ED 82 Sh 32A,   .*
1951. *Punxsutawney, Jefferson Cnty, PA 1910 Census ED 82 Sh 32A.*
1952. *South Mahoning Twp., Indiana Cnty, PA 1860 Census p. 334.*
1953. *Wendell, Thomas Cnty, KS 1900 Census ED 179 Sh 6B.*

1954. *Northern Twp., Franklin Cnty, IL 1880 Censes ED 14 Sh 50/52D.*
1955. *South Mahoning Twp., Indiana Cnty, PA 1860 Census p. 334.*
1956. *Wendell, Thomas Cnty, KS 1900 Census ED 179 Sh 6B.*
1957. *Wendell, Thomas Cnty, KS 1910 Census ED 216 Sh 7B.*
1958. *Northern Twp., Franklin Cnty, IL 1880 Censes ED 14 Sh 50/52D.*
1959. *Illinois Marriages 1851-1900*, "Electronic."
1960. *Wendell, Thomas Cnty, KS 1900 Census ED 179 Sh 6B.*
1961. *Illinois Marriages 1851-1900*, "Electronic."
1962. *Wendell, Thomas Cnty, KS 1900 Census ED 179 Sh 6B.*
1963. *Wendell, Thomas Cnty, KS 1910 Census ED 216 Sh 7B.*
1964. *Wendell, Thomas Cnty, KS 1930 Census ED 16 Sh 2A.*
1965. *Wendell, Thomas Cnty, KS 1900 Census ED 179 Sh 6B.*
1966. *Wendell, Thomas Cnty, KS 1930 Census ED 16 Sh 2A.*
1967. *South Mahoning Twp., Indiana Cnty, PA 1860 Census p. 334.*
1968. *Webbs Prairie, Franklin Cnty, IL 1870 Census p. 251.*
1969. *Northern, Franklin Cnty, IL 1880 Census ED 14 Sh 527C.*
1970. *South Mahoning Twp., Indiana Cnty, PA 1860 Census p. 334.*
1971. *Northern, Franklin Cnty, IL 1900 Census ED 33 Sh 14A.*
1972. *Northern, Franklin Cnty, IL 1880 Census ED 14 Sh 527C.*
1973. *Northern Twp., Franklin Cnty, IL 1910 Censes ED 37 Sh 2A.*
1974. *Northern, Franklin Cnty, IL 1900 Census ED 33 Sh 14A.*
1975. *South Mahoning Twp., Indiana Cnty, PA 1860 Census p. 334.*
1976. *Moores Prairie, Jefferson Cnty, IL 1880 Census ED 52 Sh 599A.*
1977. *South Mahoning Twp., Indiana Cnty, PA 1860 Census p. 334.*
1978. *Moores Prairie, Jefferson Cnty, IL 1880 Census ED 52 Sh 599A.*
1979. *Webbs Prairie, Franklin Cnty, IL 1870 Census p. 251.*
1980. *Northern Twp., Franklin Cnty, IL 1880 Censes ED 14 Sh 50/52D.*
1981. *Webbs Prairie, Franklin Cnty, IL 1870 Census p. 251.*
1982. *Northern, Franklin Cnty, IL 1900 Census ED 33 Sh 5A & B.*
1983. *Webbs Prairie, Franklin Cnty, IL 1870 Census p. 251.*
1984. *Northern, Franklin Cnty, IL 1930 Census ED 34 Sh 7B.*
1985. *Northern, Franklin Cnty, IL 1900 Census ED 33 Sh 7B.*
1986. *Northern, Franklin Cnty, IL 1910 Census ED 37 Sh 20B.*
1987. *Northern Twp., Franklin Cnty, IL 1880 Censes ED 14 Sh 50/52D.*
1988. *Webbs Prairie, Franklin Cnty, IL 1870 Census p. 251.*
1989. *Northern, Franklin Cnty, IL 1930 Census ED 34 Sh 7B.*
1990. *Northern, Franklin Cnty, IL 1900 Census ED 33 Sh 7B.*
1991. *Northern, Franklin Cnty, IL 1910 Census ED 37 Sh 20B.*
1992. *Northern, Franklin Cnty, IL 1930 Census ED 34 Sh 7B.*
1993. *Northern, Franklin Cnty, IL 1900 Census ED 33 Sh 7B.*
1994. *Northern, Franklin Cnty, IL 1910 Census ED 37 Sh 20B.*
1995. *Northern, Franklin Cnty, IL 1900 Census ED 33 Sh 7B.*
1996. *Northern, Franklin Cnty, IL 1910 Census ED 37 Sh 20B.*
1997. *Northern, Franklin Cnty, IL 1900 Census ED 33 Sh 7B.*
1998. *Northern, Franklin Cnty, IL 1910 Census ED 37 Sh 20B.*
1999. *Northern, Franklin Cnty, IL 1900 Census ED 33 Sh 7B.*
2000. *Northern, Franklin Cnty, IL 1910 Census ED 37 Sh 20B.*
2001. *Punxsutawney, Jefferson Cnty, PA 1900 Census ED 73 Sh 23B.*
2002. *Greenwood Twp., Clearfield Cnty, PA 1880 Census ED 269 Sh 28.*
2003. *Ferguson Twp., Clearfield Cnty, PA 1870 Census p. 163B.*
2004. "8 July 1908 Indiana Evening Gazette (Indiana, PA) Miriam Work Van Horn Obiturary."
2005. *Greenwood Twp., Clearfield Cnty, PA 1880 Census ED 269 Sh 28.*
2006. *Punxsutawney, Jefferson Cnty, PA 1900 Census ED 73 Sh 23B.*
2007. *Punxsutawney, Jefferson Cnty, PA 1910 Census ED 84 Sh 8B.*

2008. *Punxsutwaney Ward 6, Jefferson Cnty, PA 1920 Census ED 162 Sh 8B.*
2009. "Indiana Weekly Messenger (Indiana, PA) March 19, 1890."
2010. *Punxsutawney, Jefferson Cnty, PA 1910 Census ED 84 Sh 8B.*
2011. *6 March 1943 Indiana Evening Gazette (Indiana, PA) Death Notice of Sadie Kinnan Van Horn,* "Electronic."
2012. "Indiana Weekly Messenger (Indiana, PA) March 19, 1890."
2013. *Punxsutawney, Jefferson Cnty, PA 1900 Census ED 73 Sh 23B.*
2014. *Punxsutawney, Jefferson Cnty, PA 1910 Census ED 84 Sh 8B.*
2015. *Punxsutawney, Jefferson Cnty, PA 1900 Census ED 73 Sh 23B.*
2016. *Kentucky Death Certificate Volume 31 27560.*
2017. *Punxsutwaney Ward 6, Jefferson Cnty, PA 1920 Census ED 162 Sh 8B.*
2018. *Pennsylvania Veterans Burial Cards 1777-1999,* "Electronic."
2019. "Joseph O. Van Horn Obituary Indiana County Genealogical and Historical Society Newspaper Clippings."
2020. *Pennsylvania Veterans Burial Cards 1777-1999,* "Electronic."
2021. *Punxsutawney, Jefferson Cnty, PA 1910 Census ED 84 Sh 8B.*
2022. *Punxsutwaney Ward 6, Jefferson Cnty, PA 1920 Census ED 162 Sh 8B.*
2023. *Allegheny Ward, Allegheny Cnty, PA 1880 Census ED 14 Sh 472A.*
2024. *O'Hara Twp., Allegheny Cnty, PA 1910 Census ED 185 Sh 8A.*
2025. *O'Hara Twp., Allegheny Cnty, PA 1920 Census ED 297 Sh 20A.*
2026. *O'Hara Twp., Allegheny Cnty, PA 1930 Census ED 742 Sh 3B.*
2027. *Allegheny Ward, Allegheny Cnty, PA 1880 Census ED 14 Sh 472A.*
2028. *O'Hara Twp., Allegheny Cnty, PA 1910 Census ED 185 Sh 8A.*
2029. *O'Hara Twp., Allegheny Cnty, PA 1920 Census ED 297 Sh 20A.*
2030. *O'Hara Twp., Allegheny Cnty, PA 1930 Census ED 742 Sh 3B.*
2031. *O'Hara Twp., Allegheny Cnty, PA 1910 Census ED 185 Sh 8A.*
2032. *O'Hara Twp., Allegheny Cnty, PA 1920 Census ED 297 Sh 20A.*
2033. *O'Hara Twp., Allegheny Cnty, PA 1910 Census ED 185 Sh 8A.*
2034. *O'Hara Twp., Allegheny Cnty, PA 1920 Census ED 297 Sh 20A.*
2035. *O'Hara Twp., Allegheny Cnty, PA 1910 Census ED 185 Sh 8A.*
2036. *O'Hara Twp., Allegheny Cnty, PA 1920 Census ED 297 Sh 20A.*
2037. *O'Hara Twp., Allegheny Cnty, PA 1930 Census ED 742 Sh 3B.*
2038. *O'Hara Twp., Allegheny Cnty, PA 1910 Census ED 185 Sh 8A.*
2039. *O'Hara Twp., Allegheny Cnty, PA 1920 Census ED 297 Sh 20A.*
2040. *O'Hara Twp., Allegheny Cnty, PA 1930 Census ED 742 Sh 3B.*
2041. *O'Hara Twp., Allegheny Cnty, PA 1920 Census ED 297 Sh 20A.*
2042. SSN Death Index.
2043. *The Abridged Compendium of American Genealogy Vol. II, Lineage records,, P. 236,* "Electronic."
2044. *Glenfield, Allegheny Cnty, PA 1900 Census ED 391 Sh 3B .*
2045. *Pct. 1, Nueces Cnty, TX 1930 Census ED 11 Sh 23A.*
2046. *Justice Pct. 4, Jim Wells Cnty, TX 1920 Census ED 112 Sh 8A.*
2047. *Glenfield, Allegheny Cnty, PA 1900 Census ED 391 Sh 3B .*
2048. *The Abridged Compendium of American Genealogy Vol. II, Lineage records,, P. 236,* "Electronic."
2049. *Glenfield, Allegheny Cnty, PA 1900 Census ED 391 Sh 3B .*
2050. *Pct. 1, Nueces Cnty, TX 1930 Census ED 11 Sh 23A.*
2051. *Justice Pct. 4, Jim Wells Cnty, TX 1920 Census ED 112 Sh 8A.*
2052. *Glenfield, Allegheny Cnty, PA 1900 Census ED 391 Sh 3B .*
2053. *The Abridged Compendium of American Genealogy Vol. II, Lineage records,, P. 236,* "Electronic," 236.
2054. *Glenfield, Allegheny Cnty, PA 1900 Census ED 391 Sh 3B .*
2055. *Pct. 1, Nueces Cnty, TX 1930 Census ED 11 Sh 23A.*
2056. *Corpus Christi Ward 4, Nueces Cnty, TX 1920 Census ED 178 Sh 2A.*
2057. *Glenfield, Allegheny Cnty, PA 1900 Census ED 391 Sh 3B .*
2058. *East Mahoning Twp., Indiana Cnty, PA 1870 Census p. 210B.*
2059. *Green Twp., Indiana Cnty, PA 1860 Census p. 200.*

2060. *Grant Twp., Indiana Cnty, PA 1900 Census ED 54 Sh 10B.*
2061. *Cherry Hill Twp., Indiana Cnty, PA 1910 Census ED 68 Sh 15B.*
2062. *East Mahoning Twp., Indiana Cnty, PA 1870 Census p. 210B.*
2063. *Grant Twp., Indiana Cnty, PA 1900 Census ED 54 Sh 10B.*
2064. *Cherry Hill Twp., Indiana Cnty, PA 1910 Census ED 68 Sh 15B.*
2065. *Cherry Hill Twp., Indiana Cnty, PA 1920 Census ED 102 Sh 10A.*
2066. *Cherry Hill Twp., Indiana Cnty, PA 1910 Census ED 68 Sh 15B.*
2067. *Grant Twp., Indiana Cnty, PA 1900 Census ED 54 Sh 10B.*
2068. *Cherry Hill Twp., Indiana Cnty, PA 1910 Census ED 68 Sh 15B.*
2069. *Green Twp., Indiana Cnty, PA 1880 Census ED 140 Sh 14 & 15.*
2070. *East Mahoning Twp., Indiana Cnty, PA 1870 Census p. 210B.*
2071. *Green Twp., Indiana Cnty, PA 1860 Census p. 200.*
2072. *Canoe Twp., Indiana Cnty, PA 1900 Cenus ED 46 Sh 6A.*
2073. *Lohman, Hill Cnty, MT 1930 Census ED 10 Sh 1B.*
2074. *Lohman, Hill Cnty, MT 1920 Census ED 128 Sh 5A.*
2075. *Punxsutwaney, Jefferson Cnty, PA 1910 ED 83 Sh 4B.*
2076. *Green Twp., Indiana Cnty, PA 1880 Census ED 110 Sh 14 & 15.*
2077. *Canoe Twp., Indiana Cnty, PA 1900 Census ED 46 Sh 6A.*
2078. *Lohman, Hill Cnty, MT 1930 Census ED 10 Sh 1B.*
2079. *Lohman, Hill Cnty, MT 1920 Census ED 128 Sh 5A.*
2080. *Punxsutwaney, Jefferson Cnty, PA 1910 ED 83 Sh 4B.*
2081. *Green Twp., Indiana Cnty, PA 1880 Census ED 140 Sh 14 & 15.*
2082. *Canoe Twp., Indiana Cnty, PA 1900 Cenus ED 46 Sh 6A.*
2083. *Punxsutwaney, Jefferson Cnty, PA 1910 ED 83 Sh 4B.*
2084. *Canoe Twp., Indiana Cnty, PA 1900 Census ED 46 Sh 6A.*
2085. *Punxsutwaney, Jefferson Cnty, PA 1910 ED 83 Sh 4B.*
2086. *Canoe Twp., Indiana Cnty, PA 1900 Cenus ED 46 Sh 6A.*
2087. *Lohman, Hill Cnty, MT 1930 Census ED 10 Sh 1B.*
2088. *Punxsutwaney, Jefferson Cnty, PA 1910 ED 83 Sh 4B.*
2089. *Canoe Twp., Indiana Cnty, PA 1900 Cenus ED 46 Sh 6A.*
2090. *Lohman, Hill Cnty, MT 1930 Census ED 10 Sh 1B.*
2091. *East Mahoning Twp., Indiana Cnty, PA 1870 Census p. 210B.*
2092. *Green Twp., Indiana Cnty, PA 1860 Census p. 200.*
2093. *Sandy Twp., Clearfield Cnty, PA 1900 Census ED 97 Sh 26B.*
2094. *East Mahoning Twp., Indiana Cnty, PA 1870 Census p. 210B.*
2095. *Sandy Twp., Clearfield Cnty, PA 1900 Census ED 97 Sh 26B.*
2096. *Green Twp., Indiana Cnty, PA 1880 Census ED 140 Sh 14 & 15.*
2097. *East Mahoning Twp., Indiana Cnty, PA 1870 Census p. 210B.*
2098. *Grant Twp., Indiana Cnty, PA 1910 Census ED 76 Sh 4B.*
2099. *Grant Twp., Indiana Cnty, PA 1900 Census ED 54 Sh 6B&7A.*
2100. *Green Twp., Indiana Cnty, PA 1880 Census ED 140 Sh 14 & 15.*
2101. *Grant Twp., Indiana Cnty, PA 1910 Census ED 76 Sh 4B.*
2102. *Grant Twp., Indiana Cnty, PA 1900 Census ED 54 Sh 6B&7A.*
2103. *Grant Twp., Indiana Cnty, PA 1910 Census ED 76 Sh 4B.*
2104. *Grant Twp., Indiana Cnty, PA 1900 Census ED 54 Sh 6B&7A.*
2105. *Grant Twp., Indiana Cnty, PA 1910 Census ED 76 Sh 4B.*
2106. *Grant Twp., Indiana Cnty, PA 1900 Census ED 54 Sh 6B&7A.*
2107. *Grant Twp., Indiana Cnty, PA 1910 Census ED 76 Sh 4B.*
2108. *Grant Twp., Indiana Cnty, PA 1900 Census ED 54 Sh 6B&7A.*
2109. *Grant Twp., Indiana Cnty, PA 1910 Census ED 76 Sh 4B.*
2110. *Grant Twp., Indiana Cnty, PA 1900 Census ED 54 Sh 6B&7A.*
2111. *Grant Twp., Indiana Cnty, PA 1910 Census ED 76 Sh 4B.*
2112. *Grant Twp., Indiana Cnty, PA 1900 Census ED 54 Sh 6B&7A.*
2113. *Green Twp., Indiana Cnty, PA 1880 Census ED 140 Sh 14 & 15.*

2114. *East Mahoning Twp., Indiana Cnty, PA 1870 Census p. 210B.*
2115. *Cherry Hill Twp., Indiana Cnty, PA 1900 Census ED 49 Sh 3A.*
2116. *Cherry Hill Twp., Indiana Cnty, PA 1910 Census ED 67 Sh 3B.*
2117. *Cherry Hill Twp., Indiana Cnty, PA 1920 Census ED 102 Sh 11B.*
2118. *Green Twp., Indiana Cnty, PA 1880 Census ED 140 Sh 14 & 15.*
2119. *Cherry Hill Twp., Indiana Cnty, PA 1900 Census ED 49 Sh 3A.*
2120. *Cherry Hill Twp., Indiana Cnty, PA 1910 Census ED 67 Sh 3B.*
2121. *Cherry Hill Twp., Indiana Cnty, PA 1920 Census ED 102 Sh 11B.*
2122. *Cherry Hill Twp., Indiana Cnty, PA 1900 Census ED 49 Sh 3A.*
2123. *Cherry Hill Twp., Indiana Cnty, PA 1910 Census ED 67 Sh 3B.*
2124. *Cherry Hill Twp., Indiana Cnty, PA 1900 Census ED 49 Sh 3A.*
2125. *Cherry Hill Twp., Indiana Cnty, PA 1910 Census ED 67 Sh 3B.*
2126. *Cherry Hill Twp., Indiana Cnty, PA 1920 Census ED 102 Sh 11B.*
2127. *Cherry Hill Twp., Indiana Cnty, PA 1910 Census ED 67 Sh 3B.*
2128. *Cherry Hill Twp., Indiana Cnty, PA 1920 Census ED 102 Sh 11B.*
2129. *Green Twp., Indiana Cnty, PA 1880 Census ED 140 Sh 14 & 15.*
2130. *East Mahoning Twp., Indiana Cnty, PA 1870 Census p. 210B.*
2131. *Grant Twp., Indiana Cnty, PA 1900 Census ED 54 Sh 4B.*
2132. *Grant Twp., Indiana Cnty, PA 1910 Census ED 76 Sh 5B&6A.*
2133. *Grant Twp., Indiana Cnty, PA 1920 Census ED 109 8A.*
2134. *Hempfield Twp., Westmoreland Cnty, PA 1930 Census ED 52 Sh 8B.*
2135. *Green Twp., Indiana Cnty, PA 1880 Census ED 140 Sh 14 & 15.*
2136. *Grant Twp., Indiana Cnty, PA 1900 Census ED 54 Sh 4B.*
2137. *Grant Twp., Indiana Cnty, PA 1910 Census ED 76 Sh 5B&6A.*
2138. *Grant Twp., Indiana Cnty, PA 1900 Census ED 54 Sh 4B.*
2139. *Grant Twp., Indiana Cnty, PA 1910 Census ED 76 Sh 5B&6A.*
2140. *Hempfield Twp., Westmoreland Cnty, PA 1930 Census ED 52 Sh 8B.*
2141. WWI Civilian Draft Registration Index.
2142. *Grant Twp., Indiana Cnty, PA 1900 Census ED 54 Sh 4B.*
2143. *Grant Twp., Indiana Cnty, PA 1910 Census ED 76 Sh 5B&6A.*
2144. *Grant Twp., Indiana Cnty, PA 1900 Census ED 54 Sh 4B.*
2145. *Grant Twp., Indiana Cnty, PA 1910 Census ED 76 Sh 5B&6A.*
2146. *Grant Twp., Indiana Cnty, PA 1900 Census ED 54 Sh 4B.*
2147. *Grant Twp., Indiana Cnty, PA 1910 Census ED 76 Sh 5B&6A.*
2148. *Grant Twp., Indiana Cnty, PA 1900 Census ED 54 Sh 4B.*
2149. *Grant Twp., Indiana Cnty, PA 1910 Census ED 76 Sh 5B&6A.*
2150. *Green Twp., Indiana Cnty, PA 1880 Census ED 140 Sh 14 & 15.*
2151. *East Mahoning Twp., Indiana Cnty, PA 1870 Census p. 210B.*
2152. *White Twp., Indiana Cnty, PA 1930 Census ED 52 Sh 14 A.*
2153. *Cherry Hill Twp., Indiana Cnty, PA 1910 Census ED 67 Sh 10B.*
2154. *Green Twp., Indiana Cnty, PA 1880 Census ED 140 Sh 14 & 15.*
2155. *White Twp., Indiana Cnty, PA 1930 Census ED 52 Sh 14 A.*
2156. *Cherry Hill Twp., Indiana Cnty, PA 1910 Census ED 67 Sh 10B.*
2157. *White Twp., Indiana Cnty, PA 1930 Census ED 52 Sh 14 A.*
2158. *Indiana County Marriage Records Book 1 Page 459 Lic #459.*
2159. *White Twp., Indiana Cnty, PA 1930 Census ED 52 Sh 14 A.*
2160. "7 Nov 1933 Indiana Evening Gazette (Indiana,PA) Evan Wallace Shankle Death Notice."
2161. *White Twp., Indiana Cnty, PA 1930 Census ED 52 Sh 14 A.*
2162. *Indiana County Marriage Records Book 1 Page 459 Lic #459.*
2163. *Cherry Hill Twp., Indiana Cnty, PA 1910 Census ED 67 Sh 10B.*
2164. *Armstrong, Indiana Cnty, PA 1930 Census ED 2 Sh 7B.*
2165. "7 Aug 1964 Indiana Evening Gazette (Indiana, PA) Death Notice Myrtle Mae Mock."
2166. *Cherry Hill Twp., Indiana Cnty, PA 1910 Census ED 67 Sh 10B.*
2167. SSN Death Index.

2168. *Cherry Hill Twp., Indiana Cnty, PA 1910 Census ED 67 Sh 10B.*
2169. "14 Dec 1916 Indiana Evening Gazette (indiana, PA) Ralph Shankle Death."
2170. "10 Oct 1916 Indiana Evening Gazette (Indiana, PA) License Listing."
2171. "16 Oct 1916 Indiana Evening Gazette (Indiana, PA) Marriage Listing."
2172. "10 Oct 1916 Indiana Evening Gazette (Indiana, PA) License Listing."
2173. "16 Oct 1916 Indiana Evening Gazette (Indiana, PA) Marriage Listing."
2174. *White Twp., Indiana Cnty, PA 1930 Census ED 52 Sh 14 A.*
2175. *Cherry Hill Twp., Indiana Cnty, PA 1910 Census ED 67 Sh 10B.*
2176. SSN Death Index.
2177. "6 Dec 1969 Indiana Evening Gazette (Indiana, PA) Obit Mable Shnakle Wyland."
2178. "7 Aug 1964 Indiana Evening Gazette (Indiana, PA) Death Notice Myrtle Mae Mock."
2179. *White Twp., Indiana Cnty, PA 1930 Census ED 52 Sh 14 A.*
2180. SSN Death Index.
2181. *Green Twp., Indiana Cnty, PA 1880 Census ED 140 Sh 14 & 15.*
2182. *Rayne Twp., Indiana Cnty, PA 1900 Census ED 61 Sh 2B.*
2183. *Indiana, Indiana Cnty, PA 1920 Census ED 117 Sh 10B&11A.*
2184. *Armstrong, Indiana Cnty, PA 1930 Census ED 2 Sh 7B.*
2185. *Cherry Hill Twp., Indiana Cnty, PA 1910 Census ED 67 Sh 3B.*
2186. *Green Twp., Indiana Cnty, PA 1880 Census ED 140 Sh 14 & 15.*
2187. *Indiana, Indiana Cnty, PA 1920 Census ED 117 Sh 10B&11A.*
2188. *Armstrong, Indiana Cnty, PA 1930 Census ED 2 Sh 7B.*
2189. *Cherry Hill Twp., Indiana Cnty, PA 1910 Census ED 67 Sh 3B.*
2190. *Indiana, Indiana Cnty, PA 1920 Census ED 117 Sh 10B&11A.*
2191. *Rayne Twp., Indiana Cnty, PA 1900 Census ED 61 Sh 2B.*
2192. *Indiana, Indiana Cnty, PA 1920 Census ED 117 Sh 10B&11A.*
2193. *Cherry Hill Twp., Indiana Cnty, PA 1910 Census ED 67 Sh 3B.*
2194. *Rayne Twp., Indiana Cnty, PA 1900 Census ED 61 Sh 2B.*
2195. *Indiana, Indiana Cnty, PA 1920 Census ED 117 Sh 10B&11A.*
2196. *Cherry Hill Twp., Indiana Cnty, PA 1910 Census ED 67 Sh 3B.*
2197. "27 March 1929 Indiana Evening Gazette (Indiana, PA) Rosaline Lydick Obit."
2198. *Indiana, Indiana Cnty, PA 1920 Census ED 117 Sh 10B&11A.*
2199. "27 March 1929 Indiana Evening Gazette (Indiana, PA) Rosaline Lydick Obit."
2200. *Indiana, Indiana Cnty, PA 1920 Census ED 117 Sh 10B&11A.*
2201. *Armstrong, Indiana Cnty, PA 1930 Census ED 2 Sh 7B.*
2202. "27 March 1929 Indiana Evening Gazette (Indiana, PA) Rosaline Lydick Obit."
2203. *Indiana, Indiana Cnty, PA 1920 Census ED 117 Sh 10B&11A.*
2204. *Armstrong, Indiana Cnty, PA 1930 Census ED 2 Sh 7B.*
2205. "27 March 1929 Indiana Evening Gazette (Indiana, PA) Rosaline Lydick Obit."
2206. *Indiana, Indiana Cnty, PA 1920 Census ED 117 Sh 10B&11A.*
2207. *Green Twp., Indiana Cnty, PA 1880 Census ED 140 Sh 14 & 15.*
2208. *Green Twp., Indiana Cnty, PA 1900 Census ED 55 Sh 6A.*
2209. *Green Twp., Indiana Cnty, PA 1880 Census ED 140 Sh 14 & 15.*
2210. *Green Twp., Indiana Cnty, PA 1900 Census ED 55 Sh 6A.*
2211. *Indiana Marrige Records Book 8 Page 20 License #105.*
2212. *Green Twp., Indiana Cnty, PA 1900 Census ED 55 Sh 6A.*
2213. *Indiana Marrige Records Book 8 Page 20 License #105.*
2214. *Green Twp., Indiana Cnty, PA 1900 Census ED 55 Sh 6A.*
2215. *Green Twp., Indiana Cnty, PA 1880 Census ED 140 Sh 14 & 15.*
2216. *Grant Twp., Indiana Cnty, PA 1910 Census ED 76 Sh 11B.*
2217. *Indiana, Indiana Cnty, PA 1920 Census ED 116 Sh 2B.*
2218. *Ferndale, Cambria Cnty, PA 1930 Census ED 42 Sh 17B.*
2219. *Green Twp., Indiana Cnty, PA 1880 Census ED 140 Sh 14 & 15.*
2220. WWI Civilian Draft Registration Index.
2221. *Grant Twp., Indiana Cnty, PA 1910 Census ED 76 Sh 11B.*

2222. *Indiana, Indiana Cnty, PA 1920 Census ED 116 Sh 2B.*
2223. *Ferndale, Cambria Cnty, PA 1930 Census ED 42 Sh 17B.*
2224. Amos Berton Lydick Obit reproduced in notes source unknown.
2225. *Grant Twp., Indiana Cnty, PA 1910 Census ED 76 Sh 11B.*
2226. *Indiana, Indiana Cnty, PA 1920 Census ED 116 Sh 2B.*
2227. *Ferndale, Cambria Cnty, PA 1930 Census ED 42 Sh 17B.*
2228. Amos Berton Lydick Obit reproduced in notes source unknown.
2229. *Grant Twp., Indiana Cnty, PA 1910 Census ED 76 Sh 11B.*
2230. Amos Berton Lydick Obit reproduced in notes source unknown.
2231. *Indiana, Indiana Cnty, PA 1920 Census ED 116 Sh 2B.*
2232. *Ferndale, Cambria Cnty, PA 1930 Census ED 42 Sh 17B.*
2233. *Indiana, Indiana Cnty, PA 1920 Census ED 116 Sh 2B.*
2234. Amos Berton Lydick Obit reproduced in notes source unknown.
2235. *Grant Twp., Indiana Cnty, PA 1900 Census ED 54 Sh 9B.*
2236. "18 Jan 1979 Indiana Evening Gazette (Indiana, PA) Charles A. Lambing Obit."
2237. *Grant Twp., Indiana Cnty, PA 1900 Census ED 54 Sh 9B.*
2238. *South Mahoning Twp., Indiana Cnty, PA 1930 Census ED 42 Sh 7B.*
2239. *Rayne Twp., Indiana Cnty, PA 1910 Census ED 90 Sh 1B.*
2240. *Grant Twp., Indiana Cnty, PA 1900 Census ED 54 Sh 9B.*
2241. "18 Jan 1979 Indiana Evening Gazette (Indiana, PA) Charles A. Lambing Obit."
2242. *Grant Twp., Indiana Cnty, PA 1900 Census ED 54 Sh 9B.*
2243. *Indiana Marrige Records Book 8 Page 20 License #105.*
2244. *South Mahoning Twp., Indiana Cnty, PA 1930 Census ED 42 Sh 7B.*
2245. *Grant Twp., Indiana Cnty, PA 1900 Census ED 54 Sh 9B.*
2246. *Indiana Marrige Records Book 8 Page 20 License #105.*
2247. *Rayne Twp., Indiana Cnty, PA 1910 Census ED 90 Sh 1B.*
2248. *Grant Twp., Indiana Cnty, PA 1900 Census ED 54 Sh 9B.*
2249. *Rayne Twp., Indiana Cnty, PA 1910 Census ED 90 Sh 1B.*
2250. *Grant Twp., Indiana Cnty, PA 1900 Census ED 54 Sh 9B.*
2251. "11 Nov 1920 Indiana Evening Gazette (Indiana, PA) Martha Van Horn Obituary."
2252. *Indiana, Indiana Cnty, PA 1920 Census ED 117 Sh 10B&11A.*
2253. "11 Nov 1920 Indiana Evening Gazette (Indiana, PA) Martha Van Horn Obituary."
2254. *Indiana, Indiana Cnty, PA 1920 Census ED 115 Sh 7B.*
2255. *East Mahoning Twp., Indiana Cnty, PA 1870 Census p. 210B.*
2256. *East Mahoning Twp., Indiana Cnty, PA 1880 Census ED 145 Sh 14.*
2257. *Cherry Hill Twp., Indiana Cnty, PA 1910 Census ED 67 Sh 5B.*
2258. *East Mahoning Twp., Indiana Cnty, PA 1870 Census p. 210B.*
2259. *Cherry Hill Twp., Indiana Cnty, PA 1910 Census ED 67 Sh 3B.*
2260. *East Mahoning Twp., Indiana Cnty, PA 1870 Census p. 210B.*
2261. *East Mahoning Twp., Indiana Cnty, PA 1880 Census ED 145 Sh 14.*
2262. *Green Twp., Indiana Cnty, PA 1910 Census ED 78 Sh 18A.*
2263. *Green Twp., Indiana Cnty, PA 1930 Census ED 28 Sh 12B.*
2264. "23 October 1914 Indiana Evening Gazette (Indiana, PA) Obituary of Mary Van Horn Lydick."
2265. *East Mahoning Twp., Indiana Cnty, PA 1870 Census p. 210B.*
2266. *Green Twp., Indiana Cnty, PA 1910 Census ED 78 Sh 18A.*
2267. *Green Twp., Indiana Cnty, PA 1930 Census ED 28 Sh 12B.*
2268. *Green Twp., Indiana Cnty, PA 1910 Census ED 78 Sh 18A.*
2269. *Green Twp., Indiana Cnty, PA 1930 Census ED 28 Sh 12B.*
2270. *Green Twp., Indiana Cnty, PA 1910 Census ED 78 Sh 18A.*
2271. *Green Twp., Indiana Cnty, PA 1930 Census ED 28 Sh 12B.*
2272. *East Mahoning Twp., Indiana Cnty, PA 1880 Census ED 145 Sh 14.*
2273. *White Twp., Indiana Cnty, PA 1920 Census ED 132 Sh 11A.*
2274. *Rayne Twp., Indiana Cnty, PA 1910 Census ED 89 Sh 9A.*

2275. "23 October 1914 Indiana Evening Gazette (Indiana, PA) Obituary of Mary Van Horn Lydick."
2276. *East Mahoning Twp., Indiana Cnty, PA 1880 Census ED 145 Sh 14.*
2277. *White Twp., Indiana Cnty, PA 1920 Census ED 132 Sh 11A.*
2278. *Rayne Twp., Indiana Cnty, PA 1910 Census ED 89 Sh 9A.*
2279. *White Twp., Indiana Cnty, PA 1920 Census ED 132 Sh 11A.*
2280. *Rayne Twp., Indiana Cnty, PA 1910 Census ED 89 Sh 9A.*
2281. *White Twp., Indiana Cnty, PA 1920 Census ED 132 Sh 11A.*
2282. *Rayne Twp., Indiana Cnty, PA 1910 Census ED 89 Sh 9A.*
2283. *White Twp., Indiana Cnty, PA 1920 Census ED 132 Sh 11A.*
2284. *Rayne Twp., Indiana Cnty, PA 1910 Census ED 89 Sh 9A.*
2285. *White Twp., Indiana Cnty, PA 1920 Census ED 132 Sh 11A.*
2286. *Rayne Twp., Indiana Cnty, PA 1910 Census ED 89 Sh 9A.*
2287. *White Twp., Indiana Cnty, PA 1920 Census ED 132 Sh 11A.*
2288. *Rayne Twp., Indiana Cnty, PA 1910 Census ED 89 Sh 9A.*
2289. *East Mahoning Twp., Indiana Cnty, PA 1880 Census ED 145 Sh 14.*
2290. *Clymer, Indiana Cnty, PA 1910 Census ED 61 Sh 21B.*
2291. "23 October 1914 Indiana Evening Gazette (Indiana, PA) Obituary of Mary Van Horn Lydick."
2292. *East Mahoning Twp., Indiana Cnty, PA 1880 Census ED 145 Sh 14.*
2293. *Clymer, Indiana Cnty, PA 1910 Census ED 61 Sh 21B.*
2294. *East Mahoning Twp., Indiana Cnty, PA 1880 Census ED 145 Sh 14.*
2295. *Cherry Hill Twp., Indiana Cnty, PA 1910 Census ED 67 Sh 6B.*
2296. "23 October 1914 Indiana Evening Gazette (Indiana, PA) Obituary of Mary Van Horn Lydick."
2297. *East Mahoning Twp., Indiana Cnty, PA 1880 Census ED 145 Sh 14.*
2298. *Cherry Hill Twp., Indiana Cnty, PA 1910 Census ED 67 Sh 6B.*
2299. *Cherry Hill Twp., Indiana Cnty, PA 1920 Census ED 101 Sh 5B & 6A.*
2300. *Cherry Hill Twp., Indiana Cnty, PA 1910 Census ED 67 Sh 6B.*
2301. *Gerrardstown, Berkeley Cnty, WV 1870 Census p. 177.*
2302. *Gerrardstown, Berkeley Cnty, WV 1900 Census ED 12 Sh 11B.*
2303. *Hedgesville, Berkeley Cnty, WV 1910 Census ED 18 Sh 4A.*
2304. *Gerrardstown, Berkeley Cnty, WV 1870 Census p. 177.*
2305. *Gerrardstown, Berkeley Cnty, WV 1900 Census ED 12 Sh 11B.*
2306. *Hedgesville, Berkeley Cnty, WV 1910 Census ED 18 Sh 4A.*
2307. *Gerrardstown, Berkeley Cnty, WV 1900 Census ED 12 Sh 11B.*
2308. *Hedgesville, Berkeley Cnty, WV 1910 Census ED 18 Sh 4A.*
2309. *Gerrardstown, Berkeley Cnty, WV 1900 Census ED 12 Sh 11B.*
2310. *Hedgesville, Berkeley Cnty, WV 1910 Census ED 18 Sh 4A.*
2311. *Hedgesville, Berkeley Cnty, WV 1920 Census ED 24 Sh 12B.*
2312. *Hedgesville, Berkeley Cnty, WV 1910 Census ED 18 Sh 4A.*
2313. *Hedgesville, Berkeley Cnty, WV 1920 Census ED 24 Sh 8B.*
2314. *Hedgesville, Berkeley Cnty, WV 1910 Census ED 18 Sh 4A.*
2315. *Hedgesville, Berkeley Cnty, WV 1920 Census ED 24 Sh 12A.*
2316. *Hedgesville, Berkeley Cnty, WV 1910 Census ED 18 Sh 4A.*
2317. *Gerrardstown, Berkeley Cnty, WV 1880 Census ED 14 Sh 22.*
2318. *Mill Creek, Berkeley Cnty, WV 1910 Census ED 24 Sh 15A.*
2319. *Gerrardstown, Berkeley Cnty, WV 1900 Census ED 12 Sh 3A.*
2320. *Martinsburg, Berkeley Cnty, WV 1930 Census ED 13 Sh 10B.*
2321. *Martinsburg Ward 2, Berkeley Cnty, WV 1920 Census ED 28 Sh 15B.*
2322. *Gerrardstown, Berkeley Cnty, WV 1880 Census ED 14 Sh 22.*
2323. *Mill Creek, Berkeley Cnty, WV 1910 Census ED 24 Sh 15A.*
2324. *Gerrardstown, Berkeley Cnty, WV 1900 Census ED 12 Sh 3A.*
2325. *Martinsburg, Berkeley Cnty, WV 1930 Census ED 13 Sh 10B.*

2326. *Martinsburg Ward 2, Berkeley Cnty, WV 1920 Census ED 28 Sh 15B.*
2327. *Mill Creek, Berkeley Cnty, WV 1910 Census ED 24 Sh 15A.*
2328. *Gerrardstown, Berkeley Cnty, WV 1900 Census ED 12 Sh 3A.*
2329. *Mill Creek, Berkeley Cnty, WV 1910 Census ED 24 Sh 15A.*
2330. *Gerrardstown, Berkeley Cnty, WV 1900 Census ED 12 Sh 3A.*
2331. *Martinsburg Ward 2, Berkeley Cnty, WV 1920 Census ED 28 Sh 15B.*
2332. *Mill Creek, Berkeley Cnty, WV 1910 Census ED 24 Sh 15A.*
2333. *Martinsburg, Berkeley Cnty, WV 1930 Census ED 13 Sh 10B.*
2334. *Martinsburg Ward 2, Berkeley Cnty, WV 1920 Census ED 28 Sh 15B.*
2335. *Martinsburg, Berkeley Cnty, WV 1930 Census ED 13 Sh 10B.*
2336. *Gerrardstown, Berkeley Cnty, WV 1880 Census ED 14 Sh 22.*
2337. *Gerrardstown, Berkeley Cnty, WV 1910 Census ED 16 Sh 6A&B.*
2338. *Gerrardstown, Berkeley Cnty, WV 1900 Census ED 12 Sh 3A.*
2339. *Gerrardstown, Berkeley Cnty, WV 1930 Census ED 5 Sh 3A.*
2340. *Gerrardstown, Berkeley Cnty, WV 1920 Census ED 22 Sh 10B.*
2341. *Gerrardstown, Berkeley Cnty, WV 1880 Census ED 14 Sh 22.*
2342. *Gerrardstown, Berkeley Cnty, WV 1920 Census ED 22 Sh 10B.*
2343. *Gerrardstown, Berkeley Cnty, WV 1910 Census ED 16 Sh 6A&B.*
2344. *Gerrardstown, Berkeley Cnty, WV 1920 Census ED 22 Sh 10B.*
2345. *Gerrardstown, Berkeley Cnty, WV 1930 Census ED 5 Sh 3A.*
2346. *Gerrardstown, Berkeley Cnty, WV 1920 Census ED 22 Sh 10B.*
2347. *Gerrardstown, Berkeley Cnty, WV 1910 Census ED 16 Sh 6A&B.*
2348. *Gerrardstown, Berkeley Cnty, WV 1920 Census ED 22 Sh 10B.*
2349. *Gerrardstown, Berkeley Cnty, WV 1930 Census ED 5 Sh 3A.*
2350. *Gerrardstown, Berkeley Cnty, WV 1920 Census ED 22 Sh 10B.*
2351. *Email Rebekah Hutzler Malatt April 10, 2006,* "Electronic."
2352. *Brunswick, Frederick Cnty, MD 1920 Census ED 94 Sh 4B.*
2353. *Brunswick, Frederick Cnty, MD 1910 Census ED 83 Sh 4B.*
2354. *Brunswick, Frederick Cnty, MD 1930 Census ED 51 Sh 12A.*
2355. *Brunswick, Frederick Cnty, MD 1920 Census ED 94 Sh 4B.*
2356. "29 August 1949 The News (Frederick, MD) Obituary of M. P. Catlett."
2357. "13 Sept. 1954 The Frederick Post (Frederick, MD) Mary Edith Catlett Koogle Obituary."
2358. *Email Rebekah Hutzler Malatt April 10, 2006,* "Electronic."
2359. *Brunswick, Frederick Cnty, MD 1920 Census ED 94 Sh 4B.*
2360. *Brunswick, Frederick Cnty, MD 1910 Census ED 83 Sh 4B.*
2361. *Brunswick, Frederick Cnty, MD 1930 Census ED 51 Sh 12A.*
2362. *Brunswick, Frederick Cnty, MD 1920 Census ED 94 Sh 4B.*
2363. "29 August 1949 The News (Frederick, MD) Obituary of M. P. Catlett."
2364. "13 Sept. 1954 The Frederick Post (Frederick, MD) Mary Edith Catlett Koogle Obituary."
2365. *Brunswick, Frederick Cnty, MD 1920 Census ED 94 Sh 4B.*
2366. *Brunswick, Frederick Cnty, MD 1930 Census ED 51 Sh 12A.*
2367. *Brunswick, Frederick Cnty, MD 1920 Census ED 94 Sh 4B.*
2368. *Brunswick, Frederick Cnty, MD 1910 Census ED 83 Sh 4B.*
2369. "29 August 1949 The News (Frederick, MD) Obituary of M. P. Catlett."
2370. "13 Sept. 1954 The Frederick Post (Frederick, MD) Mary Edith Catlett Koogle Obituary."
2371. *Brunswick, Frederick Cnty, MD 1910 Census ED 83 Sh 4B.*
2372. "29 August 1949 The News (Frederick, MD) Obituary of M. P. Catlett."
2373. *Brunswick, Frederick Cnty, MD 1920 Census ED 94 Sh 4B.*
2374. *Brunswick, Frederick Cnty, MD 1910 Census ED 83 Sh 4B.*
2375. *Brunswick, Frederick Cnty, MD 1930 Census ED 51 Sh 12A.*
2376. "13 Sept. 1954 The Frederick Post (Frederick, MD) Mary Edith Catlett Koogle Obituary."
2377. *Brunswick, Frederick Cnty, MD 1920 Census ED 94 Sh 4B.*
2378. "29 August 1949 The News (Frederick, MD) Obituary of M. P. Catlett."
2379. *Brunswick, Frederick Cnty, MD 1920 Census ED 94 Sh 4B.*

2380. *Brunswick, Frederick Cnty, MD 1910 Census ED 83 Sh 4B.*
2381. "13 Sept. 1954 The Frederick Post (Frederick, MD) Mary Edith Catlett Koogle Obituary."
2382. *Brunswick, Frederick Cnty, MD 1920 Census ED 94 Sh 4B.*
2383. "13 Sept. 1954 The Frederick Post (Frederick, MD) Mary Edith Catlett Koogle Obituary."
2384. *Brunswick, Frederick Cnty, MD 1920 Census ED 94 Sh 4B.*
2385. *Brunswick, Frederick Cnty, MD 1910 Census ED 83 Sh 4B.*
2386. *Brunswick, Frederick Cnty, MD 1930 Census ED 51 Sh 12A.*
2387. "13 Sept. 1954 The Frederick Post (Frederick, MD) Mary Edith Catlett Koogle Obituary."
2388. *Brunswick, Frederick Cnty, MD 1920 Census ED 94 Sh 4B.*
2389. "13 Sept. 1954 The Frederick Post (Frederick, MD) Mary Edith Catlett Koogle Obituary."
2390. *Email Rebekah Hutzler Malatt April 10, 2006,* "Electronic."
2391. *Gerrardstown, Berkeley Cnty, WV 1920 Census ED 21 Sh 11B.*
2392. *Mill Creek, Berkeley Cnty, WV 1930 Census ED 18 Sh 4A.*
2393. *Gerrardstown, Berkeley Cnty, WV 1920 Census ED 21 Sh 11B.*
2394. *Email Rebekah Hutzler Malatt April 10, 2006,* "Electronic."
2395. *Gerrardstown, Berkeley Cnty, WV 1920 Census ED 21 Sh 11B.*
2396. *Mill Creek, Berkeley Cnty, WV 1930 Census ED 18 Sh 4A.*
2397. *Gerrardstown, Berkeley Cnty, WV 1920 Census ED 21 Sh 11B.*
2398. *Mill Creek, Berkeley Cnty, WV 1930 Census ED 18 Sh 4A.*
2399. *Gerrardstown, Berkeley Cnty, WV 1920 Census ED 21 Sh 11B.*
2400. *Mill Creek, Berkeley Cnty, WV 1930 Census ED 18 Sh 4A.*
2401. SSN Death Index.
2402. *Email Rebekah Hutzler Malatt April 10, 2006,* "Electronic."
2403. *Martinsburg Ward 4, Berkeley Cnty, WV 1910 Census ED 22 Sh 9A.*
2404. *Email Rebekah Hutzler Malatt April 10, 2006,* "Electronic."
2405. *Martinsburg Ward 4, Berkeley Cnty, WV 1910 Census ED 22 Sh 9A.*
2406. *Email Rebekah Hutzler Malatt April 10, 2006,* "Electronic."
2407. *Martinsburg Ward 5, Berkeley Cnty, WV 1900 Census ED 17 Sh 2A.*
2408. *Bath, Morgan Cnty, WV 1910 Census ED 85 Sh 10B.*
2409. *Bath, Morgan Cnty, WV 1920 Census ED 115 Sh 10B.*
2410. *Bath, Morgan Cnty, WV 1930 Census ED 3 Sh 19B.*
2411. *Martinsburg Ward 5, Berkeley Cnty, WV 1900 Census ED 17 Sh 2A.*
2412. *Email Rebekah Hutzler Malatt April 10, 2006,* "Electronic."
2413. *Martinsburg Ward 5, Berkeley Cnty, WV 1900 Census ED 17 Sh 2A.*
2414. *Bath, Morgan Cnty, WV 1910 Census ED 85 Sh 10B.*
2415. *Bath, Morgan Cnty, WV 1920 Census ED 115 Sh 10B.*
2416. *Bath, Morgan Cnty, WV 1930 Census ED 3 Sh 19B.*
2417. *Martinsburg Ward 5, Berkeley Cnty, WV 1900 Census ED 17 Sh 2A.*
2418. *Bath, Morgan Cnty, WV 1910 Census ED 85 Sh 10B.*
2419. *Bath, Morgan Cnty, WV 1920 Census ED 115 Sh 10B.*
2420. *Bath, Morgan Cnty, WV 1910 Census ED 85 Sh 10B.*
2421. *Bath, Morgan Cnty, WV 1920 Census ED 115 Sh 10B.*
2422. *Bath, Morgan Cnty, WV 1910 Census ED 85 Sh 10B.*
2423. *Bath, Morgan Cnty, WV 1920 Census ED 115 Sh 10B.*
2424. *Bath, Morgan Cnty, WV 1930 Census ED 3 Sh 19B.*
2425. *Bath, Morgan Cnty, WV 1910 Census ED 85 Sh 10B.*
2426. *Bath, Morgan Cnty, WV 1930 Census ED 3 Sh 19B.*
2427. *Bath, Morgan Cnty, WV 1910 Census ED 85 Sh 10B.*
2428. *Bath, Morgan Cnty, WV 1920 Census ED 115 Sh 10B.*
2429. *Bath, Morgan Cnty, WV 1910 Census ED 85 Sh 10B.*
2430. *Bath, Morgan Cnty, WV 1920 Census ED 115 Sh 10B.*
2431. *Bath, Morgan Cnty, WV 1930 Census ED 3 Sh 19B.*
2432. *Bath, Morgan Cnty, WV 1920 Census ED 115 Sh 10B.*
2433. *Email Rebekah Hutzler Malatt April 10, 2006,* "Electronic."

2434. *Gerrardstown, Berkeley Cnty, WV 1900 Census ED 12 Sh 4B.*
2435. *Gerrardstown, Berkeley Cnty, WV 1920 Census ED 21 Sh 2B.*
2436. *Mill Creek, Berkeley Cnty, WV 1930 Census ED 18 Sh 14A.*
2437. *Gerrardstown, Berkeley Cnty, WV 1900 Census ED 12 Sh 4B.*
2438. *Email Rebekah Hutzler Malatt April 10, 2006,* "Electronic."
2439. *Gerrardstown, Berkeley Cnty, WV 1920 Census ED 21 Sh 2B.*
2440. *Mill Creek, Berkeley Cnty, WV 1930 Census ED 18 Sh 14A.*
2441. *Gerrardstown, Berkeley Cnty, WV 1920 Census ED 21 Sh 2B.*
2442. *Mill Creek, Berkeley Cnty, WV 1930 Census ED 18 Sh 14A.*
2443. *Gerrardstown, Berkeley Cnty, WV 1920 Census ED 21 Sh 2B.*
2444. *Mill Creek, Berkeley Cnty, WV 1930 Census ED 18 Sh 14A.*
2445. *Gerrardstown, Berkeley Cnty, WV 1920 Census ED 21 Sh 2B.*
2446. *Mill Creek, Berkeley Cnty, WV 1930 Census ED 18 Sh 14A.*
2447. *Gerrardstown, Berkeley Cnty, WV 1920 Census ED 21 Sh 2B.*
2448. *Mill Creek, Berkeley Cnty, WV 1930 Census ED 18 Sh 14A.*
2449. *Gerrardstown, Berkeley Cnty, WV 1920 Census ED 21 Sh 2B.*
2450. *Email Rebekah Hutzler Malatt April 10, 2006,* "Electronic."
2451. *Gerrardstown, Berkeley Cnty, WV 1900 Census ED 12 Sh 4B.*
2452. "25 Feb 1939 Fredrick Post (Frederick, MD) Obituary Jennie T. Unger ."
2453. *Email Rebekah Hutzler Malatt April 10, 2006,* "Electronic."
2454. *Gerrardstown, Berkeley Cnty, WV 1900 Census ED 12 Sh 4B.*
2455. *Brunswick, Frederick Cnty, MD 1910 Census ED 83 Sh 11B.*
2456. *Harrisonburg, Rockingham Cnty, VA 1920 Census ED 101 Sh 7A.*
2457. *Ashby, Rockingham Cnty, VA 1930 Census ED 7 Sh 6A.*
2458. *Gerrardstown, Berkeley Cnty, WV 1900 Census ED 12 Sh 4B.*
2459. *Email Rebekah Hutzler Malatt April 10, 2006,* "Electronic."
2460. *Brunswick, Frederick Cnty, MD 1910 Census ED 83 Sh 11B.*
2461. *Ashby, Rockingham Cnty, VA 1930 Census ED 7 Sh 6A.*
2462. *Brunswick, Frederick Cnty, MD 1910 Census ED 83 Sh 11B.*
2463. *Harrisonburg, Rockingham Cnty, VA 1920 Census ED 101 Sh 7A.*
2464. *Brunswick, Frederick Cnty, MD 1910 Census ED 83 Sh 11B.*
2465. *Harrisonburg, Rockingham Cnty, VA 1920 Census ED 101 Sh 7A.*
2466. *Ashby, Rockingham Cnty, VA 1930 Census ED 7 Sh 6A.*
2467. *Email Rebekah Hutzler Malatt April 10, 2006,* "Electronic."
2468. *Gerrardstown, Berkeley Cnty, WV 1900 Census ED 12 Sh 4B.*
2469. *Charlestown District, Jefferson Cnty, WV 1920 Census ED 64 Sh 13A.*
2470. *Gerrardstown, Berkeley Cnty, WV 1900 Census ED 12 Sh 4B.*
2471. *Email Rebekah Hutzler Malatt April 10, 2006,* "Electronic."
2472. *Charlestown District, Jefferson Cnty, WV 1920 Census ED 64 Sh 13A.*
2473. *Martinsburg, Berkeley Cnty, WV 1930 Census ED 16 Sh 13A.*
2474. *Charlestown District, Jefferson Cnty, WV 1920 Census ED 64 Sh 13A.*
2475. *Martinsburg, Berkeley Cnty, WV 1930 Census ED 16 Sh 13A.*
2476. *East Mahoning Twp., Indiana Cnty, PA 1850 p. 247B.*
2477. *Liberty Twp., Fairfield Cnty, OH 1870 Census p.61B.*
2478. *Liberty Twp., Clarke Cnty, IA 1880 Census ED 40 Sh 114C.*
2479. "Indiana Weekly Messenger (Indiana, PA) 8 May 1895," Estate of Enoch Stear.
2480. "24 April 1895 Indiana Weekly Messenger (Indiana, PA)."
2481. *North Mahoning Twp., Indiana Cnty, PA 1870 Census p. 306B.*
2482. *Lowe, Kay Cnty, OK 1900 Census ED 88 Sh 6B.*
2483. *Pueblo Cnty, CO ED 88 Sh 3B.*
2484. *North Mahoning Twp., Indiana Cnty, PA 1870 Census p. 306B.*
2485. "Indiana Weekly Messenger (Indiana, PA) 8 May 1895," Estate of Enoch Stear.
2486. *North Mahoning Twp., Indiana Cnty, 1870 Census p. 303.*
2487. *Lowe, Kay Cnty, OK 1900 Census ED 88 Sh 6B.*

2488. *North Mahoning Twp., Indiana Cnty, 1870 Census p. 303.*
2489. *Lowe, Kay Cnty, OK 1900 Census ED 88 Sh 6B.*
2490. *Pueblo Cnty, CO ED 88 Sh 4A.*
2491. *Lowe, Kay Cnty, OK 1900 Census ED 88 Sh 6B.*
2492. *Pueblo Cnty, CO ED 88 Sh 3A.*
2493. *Lowe, Kay Cnty, OK 1900 Census ED 88 Sh 6B.*
2494. *Pueblo Cnty, CO ED 88 Sh 3A.*
2495. *Lowe, Kay Cnty, OK 1900 Census ED 88 Sh 6B.*
2496. *Pueblo Cnty, CO ED 88 Sh 3B.*
2497. *Pueblo Cnty, CO ED 88 Sh 3A.*
2498. "Indiana Progress (Indiana Cnty, PA) Jan. 8, 1936."
2499. "Indiana Weekly Messenger (Indiana, PA) 8 May 1895," Estate of Enoch Stear.
2500. *North Mahoning Twp., Indiana Cnty, PA 1870 Census p. 306B.*
2501. *Davidsville, North Mahoning Twp., Indiana Cnty, PA 1880 Census ED 146 Sh 358C.*
2502. *North Mahoning Twp., Indiana Cnty, PA 1910 Census ED 86 Sh 4A.*
2503. *North Mahoning Twp., Indiana Cnty, PA 1870 Census p. 306B.*
2504. "9 September 1936 Indiana Democrat (Indiana, PA) David Stear Obit."
2505. "Indiana Progress (Indiana Cnty, PA) Jan. 8, 1936."
2506. "9 September 1936 Indiana Democrat (Indiana, PA) David Stear Obit."
2507. "Indiana Progress (Indiana Cnty, PA) Jan. 8, 1936."
2508. "9 September 1936 Indiana Democrat (Indiana, PA) David Stear Obit."
2509. *North Mahoning Twp., Indiana Cnty, PA 1910 Census ED 86 Sh 4A.*
2510. "Indiana Progress (Indiana Cnty, PA) Jan. 8, 1936."
2511. "9 September 1936 Indiana Democrat (Indiana, PA) David Stear Obit."
2512. "Indiana Weekly Messenger (Indiana, PA) 8 May 1895," Estate of Enoch Stear.
2513. *Punxsutwaney Ward 1, Jefferson Cnty, PA 1920 Census ED 157 Sh 8A & B.*
2514. *Indiana, Indiana Cnty, PA 1930 Census ED 33 Sh 21B.*
2515. *Davidsville, North Mahoning Twp., Indiana Cnty, PA 1880 Census ED 146 Sh 358C.*
2516. *Punxsutwaney Ward 1, Jefferson Cnty, PA 1920 Census ED 157 Sh 8A & B.*
2517. *Indiana, Indiana Cnty, PA 1930 Census ED 33 Sh 21B.*
2518. *Punxsutwaney Ward 1, Jefferson Cnty, PA 1920 Census ED 157 Sh 8A & B.*
2519. *Indiana, Indiana Cnty, PA 1930 Census ED 33 Sh 21B.*
2520. *Punxsutwaney Ward 1, Jefferson Cnty, PA 1920 Census ED 157 Sh 8A & B.*
2521. WWI Civilian Draft Registration Index.
2522. *Punxsutwaney Ward 1, Jefferson Cnty, PA 1920 Census ED 157 Sh 8A & B.*
2523. *Ann Arundel, MD US Naval Academy and US Naval Hospital 1930 Census ED 10 Sh 1A.*
2524. *Punxsutwaney Ward 1, Jefferson Cnty, PA 1920 Census ED 157 Sh 8A & B.*
2525. *Indiana, Indiana Cnty, PA 1930 Census ED 33 Sh 21B.*
2526. *Punxsutwaney Ward 1, Jefferson Cnty, PA 1920 Census ED 157 Sh 8A & B.*
2527. "Indiana Weekly Messenger (Indiana, PA) 8 May 1895," Estate of Enoch Stear.
2528. *Davidsville, North Mahoning Twp., Indiana Cnty, PA 1880 Census ED 146 Sh 358C.*
2529. *North Mahoning Twp., Indiana Cnty, PA 1900 Census ED 58 Sh 12A & B.*
2530. DAR National Record Copy of Member Application # 800118.
2531. *Southwest Greensburg, Westmoreland Cnty, PA 1910 Census ED 199 Sh 11B.*
2532. *Davidsville, North Mahoning Twp., Indiana Cnty, PA 1880 Census ED 146 Sh 358C.*
2533. *North Mahoning Twp., Indiana Cnty, PA 1900 Census ED 58 Sh 12A & B.*
2534. *North Mahoning Twp., Indiana Cnty, PA 1930 Census ED 39 Sh 6A.*
2535. *North Mahoning Twp., Indiana Cnty, PA 1900 Census ED 58 Sh 12A & B.*
2536. DAR National Record Copy of Member Application # 800118.
2537. *North Mahoning Twp., Indiana Cnty, PA 1930 Census ED 39 Sh 6A.*
2538. *Southwest Greensburg, Westmoreland Cnty, PA 1910 Census ED 199 Sh 11B.*
2539. *North Mahoning Twp., Indiana Cnty, PA 1900 Census ED 58 Sh 12A & B.*
2540. DAR National Record Copy of Member Application # 800118.
2541. *North Mahoning Twp., Indiana Cnty, PA 1900 Census ED 58 Sh 12A & B.*

2542. DAR National Record Copy of Member Application # 800118.
2543. *North Mahoning Twp., Indiana Cnty, PA 1900 Census ED 58 Sh 12A & B.*
2544. DAR National Record Copy of Member Application # 800118.
2545. *North Mahoning Twp., Indiana Cnty, PA 1900 Census ED 58 Sh 12A & B.*
2546. *North Mahoning Twp., Indiana Cnty, PA 1920 Census ED 120 Sh 1B.*
2547. *Southwest Greensburg, Westmoreland Cnty, PA 1910 Census ED 199 Sh 11B.*
2548. *North Mahoning Twp., Indiana Cnty, PA 1900 Census ED 58 Sh 12A & B.*
2549. *North Mahoning Twp., Indiana Cnty, PA 1920 Census ED 120 Sh 1B.*
2550. *Southwest Greensburg, Westmoreland Cnty, PA 1910 Census ED 199 Sh 11B.*
2551. *North Mahoning Twp., Indiana Cnty, PA 1900 Census ED 58 Sh 12A & B.*
2552. *North Mahoning Twp., Indiana Cnty, PA 1920 Census ED 120 Sh 1B.*
2553. *Southwest Greensburg, Westmoreland Cnty, PA 1910 Census ED 199 Sh 11B.*
2554. *North Mahoning Twp., Indiana Cnty, PA 1920 Census ED 120 Sh 1B.*
2555. *Southwest Greensburg, Westmoreland Cnty, PA 1910 Census ED 199 Sh 11B.*
2556. *North Mahoning Twp., Indiana Cnty, PA 1930 Census ED 39 Sh 6A.*
2557. *North Mahoning Twp., Indiana Cnty, PA 1920 Census ED 120 Sh 1B.*
2558. *Southwest Greensburg, Westmoreland Cnty, PA 1910 Census ED 199 Sh 11B.*
2559. *North Mahoning Twp., Indiana Cnty, PA 1930 Census ED 39 Sh 6A.*
2560. *North Mahoning Twp., Indiana Cnty, PA 1920 Census ED 120 Sh 1B.*
2561. "Indiana Weekly Messenger (Indiana, PA) 8 May 1895," Estate of Enoch Stear.
2562. *Davidsville, North Mahoning Twp., Indiana Cnty, PA 1880 Census ED 146 Sh 358C.*
2563. *Perry Twp., Jefferson Cnty, PA 1900 Census ED 69 Sh 14B.*
2564. *Lake Charles, Calcasieu Parish, LA 1910 Census ED 38 Sh 1B.*
2565. *Lake Charles, Calcasieu Parish, LA 1920 Census ED 44 Sh 5B.*
2566. *Police Jury Ward 3, Calcasieu Parish, LA 1930 Census ED 13 Sh 6B.*
2567. *Davidsville, North Mahoning Twp., Indiana Cnty, PA 1880 Census ED 146 Sh 358C.*
2568. *Perry Twp., Jefferson Cnty, PA 1900 Census ED 69 Sh 14B.*
2569. *Lake Charles, Calcasieu Parish, LA 1910 Census ED 38 Sh 1B.*
2570. *Lake Charles, Calcasieu Parish, LA 1920 Census ED 44 Sh 5B.*
2571. *Police Jury Ward 3, Calcasieu Parish, LA 1930 Census ED 13 Sh 6B.*
2572. *Lake Charles, Calcasieu Parish, LA 1910 Census ED 38 Sh 1B.*
2573. *Perry Twp., Jefferson Cnty, PA 1900 Census ED 69 Sh 14B.*
2574. *Lake Charles, Calcasieu Parish, LA 1910 Census ED 38 Sh 1B.*
2575. *Lake Charles, Calcasieu Parish, LA 1920 Census ED 44 Sh 9B.*
2576. *Police Jury Ward 3, Calcasieu Parish, LA 1930 Census ED 13 Sh 6B.*
2577. *Lake Charles, Calcasieu Parish, LA 1910 Census ED 38 Sh 1B.*
2578. "Indiana Weekly Messenger (Indiana, PA) 8 May 1895," Estate of Enoch Stear.
2579. *Davidsville, North Mahoning Twp., Indiana Cnty, PA 1880 Census ED 146 Sh 358C.*
2580. *Punxsutawney Ward 3, Jefferson Cnty, PA 1920 Census ED 161 Sh 9B.*
2581. *Young Twp., Jefferson Cnty, PA 1910 Census ED 103 Sh 8A.*
2582. *West Mahoning Twp., Indiana Cnty, PA 1930 Census ED 50 Sh 6A.*
2583. *Davidsville, North Mahoning Twp., Indiana Cnty, PA 1880 Census ED 146 Sh 358C.*
2584. *Punxsutawney Ward 3, Jefferson Cnty, PA 1920 Census ED 161 Sh 9B.*
2585. *Young Twp., Jefferson Cnty, PA 1910 Census ED 103 Sh 8A.*
2586. *West Mahoning Twp., Indiana Cnty, PA 1930 Census ED 50 Sh 6A.*
2587. *Young Twp., Jefferson Cnty, PA 1910 Census ED 103 Sh 8A.*
2588. *Punxsutawney Ward 3, Jefferson Cnty, PA 1920 Census ED 161 Sh 9B.*
2589. *Young Twp., Jefferson Cnty, PA 1910 Census ED 103 Sh 8A.*
2590. *Punxsutawney Ward 3, Jefferson Cnty, PA 1920 Census ED 161 Sh 9B.*
2591. *Young Twp., Jefferson Cnty, PA 1910 Census ED 103 Sh 8A.*
2592. *West Mahoning Twp., Indiana Cnty, PA 1930 Census ED 50 Sh 6A.*
2593. *Punxsutawney Ward 3, Jefferson Cnty, PA 1920 Census ED 161 Sh 9B.*
2594. *Young Twp., Jefferson Cnty, PA 1910 Census ED 103 Sh 8A.*
2595. *Punxsutawney Ward 3, Jefferson Cnty, PA 1920 Census ED 161 Sh 9B.*

2596. *West Mahoning Twp., Indiana Cnty, PA 1860 Census p. 189B.*
2597. *North Mahoning Twp., Indiana Cnty, PA 1870 Census p. 305.*
2598. *Canoe Twp., Indiana Cnty, PA 1880 Census ED 149 Sh 398.*
2599. "21 October 1910 Indiana Evening Gazette (Indiana, PA) Jacob Coon Obiturary."
2600. *West Mahoning Twp., Indiana Cnty, PA 1860 Census p. 189B.*
2601. *Canoe Twp., Indiana Cnty, PA 1880 Census ED 149 Sh 398.*
2602. *Harrisburg, Ward 3, Dauphin Cnty, PA 1900 Census ED 48 Sh 4A.*
2603. *Harrisburg, Ward 3, Dauphin Cnty, PA 1910 Census ED 59 Sh 2A.*
2604. "21 October 1910 Indiana Evening Gazette (Indiana, PA) Jacob Coon Obiturary."
2605. *Canoe Twp., Indiana Cnty, PA 1880 Census ED 149 Sh 398.*
2606. *Harrisburg, Ward 3, Dauphin Cnty, PA 1900 Census ED 48 Sh 4A.*
2607. *Harrisburg, Ward 3, Dauphin Cnty, PA 1910 Census ED 59 Sh 2A.*
2608. *Harrisburg, Ward 3, Dauphin Cnty, PA 1900 Census ED 48 Sh 4A.*
2609. *Harrisburg, Ward 3, Dauphin Cnty, PA 1910 Census ED 59 Sh 2A.*
2610. *Harrisburg, Ward 3, Dauphin Cnty, PA 1900 Census ED 48 Sh 4A.*
2611. *Harrisburg, Ward 3, Dauphin Cnty, PA 1910 Census ED 59 Sh 2A.*
2612. *Harrisburg, Ward 3, Dauphin Cnty, PA 1900 Census ED 48 Sh 4A.*
2613. *Harrisburg, Ward 3, Dauphin Cnty, PA 1910 Census ED 59 Sh 2A.*
2614. *Harrisburg, Ward 3, Dauphin Cnty, PA 1900 Census ED 48 Sh 4A.*
2615. *Harrisburg, Ward 3, Dauphin Cnty, PA 1910 Census ED 59 Sh 2A.*
2616. *Harrisburg, Ward 3, Dauphin Cnty, PA 1900 Census ED 48 Sh 4A.*
2617. *North Mahoning Twp., Indiana Cnty, PA 1870 Census p. 305.*
2618. *Canoe Twp., Indiana Cnty, PA 1880 Census ED 149 Sh 398.*
2619. *North Mahoning Twp., Indiana Cnty, PA 1870 Census p. 305.*
2620. *Canoe Twp., Indiana Cnty, PA 1880 Census ED 149 Sh 398.*
2621. *North Mahoning Twp., Indiana Cnty, PA 1870 Census p. 305.*
2622. *Canoe Twp., Indiana Cnty, PA 1880 Census ED 149 Sh 398.*
2623. *North Mahoning Twp., Indiana Cnty, PA 1870 Census p. 305.*
2624. "26 Sept 1929 Indiana Weekly Messenger (Indiana, PA) A. Kimmel Coon Obituary."
2625. *Compton, Los Angeles Cnty, CA 1930 Census ED 895 Sh 16A.*
2626. *Milford, Star Pct., Beaver Cnty, UT 1920 Census ED 6 Sh 2A.*
2627. *Paint Twp., Somerset Cnty, PA 1900 Census ED 164 Sh 25A.*
2628. *Canoe Twp., Indiana Cnty, PA 1880 Census ED 149 Sh 398.*
2629. *Milford, Star Pct., Beaver Cnty, UT 1920 Census ED 6 Sh 2A.*
2630. *Paint Twp., Somerset Cnty, PA 1900 Census ED 164 Sh 25A.*
2631. WWI Civilian Draft Registration Index.
2632. *California Death Index 1940-1997*, "Electronic."
2633. *Compton, Los Angeles Cnty, CA 1930 Census ED 895 Sh 16A.*
2634. *Milford, Star Pct., Beaver Cnty, UT 1920 Census ED 6 Sh 2A.*
2635. *Paint Twp., Somerset Cnty, PA 1900 Census ED 164 Sh 25A.*
2636. *Compton, Los Angeles Cnty, CA 1930 Census ED 895 Sh 16A.*
2637. *Paint Twp., Somerset Cnty, PA 1900 Census ED 164 Sh 25A.*
2638. *Smicksburg, Indiana Cnty, PA 1870 Census p. 396A&B.*
2639. *Smicksburg, Indiana Cnty, PA 1880 Census ED 144 Sh 29.*
2640. *Punxsutawney, Jefferson Cnty, PA 1900 Censue ED 74 Sh 14B.*
2641. "14 Dec 1916 Indiana Evening Gazette (indiana, PA) Ralph Shankle Obit."
2642. *Smicksburg, Indiana Cnty, PA 1860 Census p 357.*
2643. *Smicksburg, Indiana Cnty, PA 1870 Censue p. 396A&B.*
2644. *The Colonial Society of Pennsylvania 1950 , Page 66*, "Electronic."
2645. *Smicksburg, Indiana Cnty, PA 1880 Census ED 144 Sh 29.*
2646. "4 June 1874 Indiana Progress (Indiana,PA)."
2647. *Smicksburg, Indiana Cnty, PA 1880 Census ED 144 Sh 29.*
2648. *Punxsutawney, Jefferson Cnty, PA 1900 Censue ED 74 Sh 14B.*
2649. *Punxsutawney, Jefferson Cnty, PA 1880 Census ED 203 Sh 317C.*

2650. *Punxsutawney, Jefferson Cnty, PA 1900 Censue ED 74 Sh 14B.*
2651. "4 June 1874 Indiana Progress (Indiana,PA)."
2652. *Punxsutawney, Jefferson Cnty, PA 1880 Census ED 203 Sh 317C.*
2653. *Smicksburg, Indiana Cnty, PA 1880 Census ED 144 Sh 29.*
2654. *Punxsutawney, Jefferson Cnty, PA 1900 Censue ED 74 Sh 14B.*
2655. *Punxsutawney, Jefferson Cnty, PA 1910 Censue ED 83 Sh 17B.*
2656. *Smicksburg, Indiana Cnty, PA 1880 Census ED 144 Sh 29.*
2657. *Punxsutawney, Jefferson Cnty, PA 1900 Censue ED 74 Sh 14B.*
2658. *Punxsutawney, Jefferson Cnty, PA 1910 Censue ED 83 Sh 17B.*
2659. *Punxsutawney, Jefferson Cnty, PA 1900 Censue ED 74 Sh 14B.*
2660. *Punxsutawney, Jefferson Cnty, PA 1910 Censue ED 83 Sh 17B.*
2661. *Punxsutawney, Jefferson Cnty, PA 1900 Censue ED 74 Sh 14B.*
2662. *Punxsutawney, Jefferson Cnty, PA 1910 Censue ED 83 Sh 17B.*
2663. *Punxsutawney, Jefferson Cnty, PA 1900 Censue ED 74 Sh 14B.*
2664. *Smicksburg, Indiana Cnty, PA 1870 Census p. 396A&B.*
2665. *Smicksburg, Indiana Cnty, PA 1880 Census ED 144 Sh 327C.*
2666. *Punxsutawney, Jefferson Cnty, PA 1900 Census ED 73 Sh 14A.*
2667. *Smicksburg, Indiana Cnty, PA 1860 Census p 357.*
2668. *Smicksburg, Indiana Cnty, PA 1870 Census p. 396A&B.*
2669. *Smicksburg, Indiana Cnty, PA 1880 Census ED 144 Sh 327C.*
2670. *Punxsutawney, Jefferson Cnty, PA 1900 Census ED 73 Sh 14A.*
2671. "10 January 1878 Indiana Progress (Indiana, PA)."
2672. *Smicksburg, Indiana Cnty, PA 1880 Census ED 144 Sh 327C.*
2673. "10 January 1878 Indiana Progress (Indiana, PA)."
2674. *Smicksburg, Indiana Cnty, PA 1880 Census ED 144 Sh 327C.*
2675. *Punxsutawney, Jefferson Cnty, PA 1900 Census ED 73 Sh 14A.*
2676. *Smicksburg, Indiana Cnty, PA 1880 Census ED 144 Sh 327C.*
2677. *Punxsutawney, Jefferson Cnty, PA 1900 Census ED 73 Sh 14A.*
2678. *Smicksburg, Indiana Cnty, PA 1880 Census ED 144 Sh 327C.*
2679. *Punxsutawney, Jefferson Cnty, PA 1900 Census ED 73 Sh 14A.*
2680. *Smicksburg, Indiana Cnty, PA 1870 Census p. 396A&B.*
2681. *Punxsutawney, Jefferson Cnty, PA 1910 Census ED 82 Sh 16B.*
2682. *West Mahoning Twp., Indiana Cnty, PA 1900 Census ED 63 Sh 12A.*
2683. *Smicksburg, Indiana Cnty, PA 1860 Census p 357.*
2684. *Smicksburg, Indiana Cnty, PA 1870 Census p. 396A&B.*
2685. *Punxsutawney, Jefferson Cnty, PA 1910 Census ED 82 Sh 16B.*
2686. *West Mahoning Twp., Indiana Cnty, PA 1900 Census ED 63 Sh 6A.*
2687. *Punxsutwaney Ward 1, Jefferson Cnty, PA 1920 Census ED 157 Sh 2A.*
2688. *Punxsutwaney Ward 1, Jefferson Cnty, PA 1930 Census ED 24 Sh 17A.*
2689. "6 October 1881 Indiana Progress (Indiana, PA)."
2690. *Punxsutawney, Jefferson Cnty, PA 1910 Census ED 82 Sh 16B.*
2691. "6 October 1881 Indiana Progress (Indiana, PA)."
2692. *Punxsutawney, Jefferson Cnty, PA 1910 Census ED 82 Sh 16B.*
2693. *West Mahoning Twp., Indiana Cnty, PA 1900 Census ED 63 Sh 6A.*
2694. *Punxsutwaney Ward 1, Jefferson Cnty, PA 1920 Census ED 157 Sh 2A.*
2695. *Punxsutwaney Ward 1, Jefferson Cnty, PA 1930 Census ED 24 Sh 17A.*
2696. *Punxsutawney, Jefferson Cnty, PA 1910 Census ED 82 Sh 16B.*
2697. *West Mahoning Twp., Indiana Cnty, PA 1900 Census ED 63 Sh 6A.*
2698. *Punxsutawney, Jefferson Cnty, PA 1910 Census ED 82 Sh 16B.*
2699. *West Mahoning Twp., Indiana Cnty, PA 1900 Census ED 63 Sh 6A.*
2700. *Punxsutawney, Jefferson Cnty, PA 1910 Census ED 82 Sh 16B.*
2701. *West Mahoning Twp., Indiana Cnty, PA 1900 Census ED 63 Sh 6A.*
2702. *Punxsutawney, Jefferson Cnty, PA 1910 Census ED 82 Sh 16B.*
2703. *West Mahoning Twp., Indiana Cnty, PA 1900 Census ED 63 Sh 6A.*

2704. *Punxsutawney, Jefferson Cnty, PA 1910 Census ED 82 Sh 16B.*
2705. *West Mahoning Twp., Indiana Cnty, PA 1900 Census ED 63 Sh 6A.*
2706. *Punxsutawney, Jefferson Cnty, PA 1910 Census ED 82 Sh 16B.*
2707. *West Mahoning Twp., Indiana Cnty, PA 1900 Census ED 63 Sh 6A.*
2708. *Punxsutwaney Ward 1, Jefferson Cnty, PA 1920 Census ED 157 Sh 2A.*
2709. *Punxsutwaney Ward 1, Jefferson Cnty, PA 1930 Census ED 24 Sh 17A.*
2710. *Punxsutawney, Jefferson Cnty, PA 1910 Census ED 82 Sh 16B.*
2711. *West Mahoning Twp., Indiana Cnty, PA 1900 Census ED 63 Sh 6A.*
2712. *Smicksburg, Indiana Cnty, PA 1880 Census ED 144 Sh 326A.*
2713. *Smicksburg, Indiana Cnty, PA 1870 Census p. 396A&B.*
2714. *Smicksburg, Indiana Cnty, PA 1910 Census ED 95 Sh 12A.*
2715. *Smicksburg, Indiana Cnty, PA 1930 Census ED 47 Sh 2A.*
2716. *Smicksburg, Indiana Cnty, PA 1880 Census ED 144 Sh 326A.*
2717. *California Death Index 1940-1997,* "Electronic."
2718. *Smicksburg, Indiana Cnty, PA 1910 Census ED 95 Sh 12A.*
2719. *Smicksburg, Indiana Cnty, PA 1930 Census ED 47 Sh 2A.*
2720. *Smicksburg, Indiana Cnty, PA 1910 Census ED 95 Sh 12A.*
2721. *Smicksburg, Indiana Cnty, PA 1880 Census ED 144 Sh 326A.*
2722. *Smicksburg, Indiana Cnty, PA 1870 Census p. 396A&B.*
2723. *Verona, Allegheny Cnty, PA 1920 Census ED 841 Sh 11B.*
2724. *Smicksburg, Indiana Cnty, PA 1880 Census ED 144 Sh 326A.*
2725. *Verona, Allegheny Cnty, PA 1930 Census ED 842 Sh 22A.*
2726. *Verona, Allegheny Cnty, PA 1920 Census ED 841 Sh 11B.*
2727. *Verona, Allegheny Cnty, PA 1930 Census ED 842 Sh 22A.*
2728. *Verona, Allegheny Cnty, PA 1920 Census ED 841 Sh 11B.*
2729. *Verona, Allegheny Cnty, PA 1930 Census ED 842 Sh 22A.*
2730. *Verona, Allegheny Cnty, PA 1920 Census ED 841 Sh 11B.*
2731. *Verona, Allegheny Cnty, PA 1930 Census ED 842 Sh 22A.*
2732. *Verona, Allegheny Cnty, PA 1920 Census ED 841 Sh 11B.*
2733. *Verona, Allegheny Cnty, PA 1930 Census ED 842 Sh 22A.*
2734. *Verona, Allegheny Cnty, PA 1920 Census ED 841 Sh 11B.*
2735. *Verona, Allegheny Cnty, PA 1930 Census ED 842 Sh 22A.*
2736. *Smicksburg, Indiana Cnty, PA 1880 Census ED 144 Sh 326A.*
2737. *Smicksburg, Indiana Cnty, PA 1870 Census p. 396A&B.*
2738. *Verona, Allegheny Cnty, PA 1920 Census ED 841 Sh 7A.*
2739. *Smicksburg, Indiana Cnty, PA 1880 Census ED 144 Sh 326A.*
2740. *Verona, Allegheny Cnty, PA 1920 Census ED 841 Sh 7A.*
2741. *Verona. Allegheny Cnty, PA 1920 Census ED 841 Sh 7A.*
2742. *Verona, Allegheny Cnty, PA 1920 Census ED 841 Sh 7A.*
2743. *Smicksburg, Indiana Cnty, PA 1880 Census ED 144 Sh 326A.*
2744. *Punxsutwaney, Jefferson Cnty, PA 1900 Census ED 74 Sh 12A.*
2745. *Smicksburg, Indiana Cnty, PA 1880 Census ED 144 Sh 326A.*
2746. *Punxsutwaney, Jefferson Cnty, PA 1900 Census ED 74 Sh 12A.*
2747. *Smicksburg, Indiana Cnty, PA 1880 Census ED 144 Sh 326A.*
2748. *Verona, Allegheny Cnty, PA 1900 Census ED 519 Sh 5B.*
2749. *Smicksburg, Indiana Cnty, PA 1880 Census ED 144 Sh 326A.*
2750. *Verona, Allegheny Cnty, PA 1900 Census ED 519 Sh 5B.*
2751. *Verona, Allegheny Cnty, PA 1920 Census ED 841 Sh 7A.*
2752. *Verona, Allegheny Cnty, PA 1900 Census ED 519 Sh 5B.*
2753. *Smicksburg, Indiana Cnty, PA 1910 Census ED 95 Sh 12A.*
2754. "22 March 1923 Indiana Weekly Messenger (Indiana, PA) Tirzah Van Horn Obituary."
2755. "George Logan Van Horn Obituary 21 Sept 1909 Indiana Evening Gazette (Indiana, PA)."
2756. *West Mahoning Twp., Indiana Cnty, PA 1880 Census ED 144 Sh 325C.*
2757. *Saltsburg, Indiana Cnty, PA 1910 Census ED 91 Sh 4B.*

2758. *Saltsburg, Indiana Cnty, PA 1900 Census ED 62 Sh 7B.*
2759. *Saltsburg, Indiana Cnty, PA 1930 Census ED 45 Sh 7A.*
2760. "Stella M. Van Horn Obituary Indiana County Genealogical and Historical Society Newspaper Clippings."
2761. *West Mahoning Twp., Indiana Cnty, PA 1880 Census ED 144 Sh 325C.*
2762. "22 March 1923 Indiana Weekly Messenger (Indiana, PA) Tirzah Van Horn Obituary."
2763. "George Logan Van Horn Obituary 21 Sept 1909 Indiana Evening Gazette (Indiana, PA)."
2764. *Saltsburg, Indiana Cnty, PA 1910 Census ED 91 Sh 4B.*
2765. *Saltsburg, Indiana Cnty, PA 1920 Census ED 127 Sh 5A.*
2766. *Saltsburg, Indiana Cnty, PA 1900 Census ED 62 Sh 7B.*
2767. *Saltsburg, Indiana Cnty, PA 1930 Census ED 45 Sh 7A.*
2768. "Stella M. Van Horn Obituary Indiana County Genealogical and Historical Society Newspaper Clippings."
2769. *Saltsburg, Indiana Cnty, PA 1910 Census ED 91 Sh 4B.*
2770. "George Logan Van Horn Obituary 21 Sept 1909 Indiana Evening Gazette (Indiana, PA)."
2771. *West Mahoning Twp., Indiana Cnty, PA 1880 Census ED 144 Sh 325C.*
2772. *Buffington, Indiana Cnty, PA 1900 Census ED 44 Sh 2A.*
2773. *West Mahoning Twp., Indiana Cnty, PA 1880 Census ED 144 Sh 325C.*
2774. *Buffington, Indiana Cnty, PA 1900 Census ED 44 Sh 2A.*
2775. "George Logan Van Horn Obituary 21 Sept 1909 Indiana Evening Gazette (Indiana, PA)."
2776. *Buffington, Indiana Cnty, PA 1900 Census ED 44 Sh 2A.*
2777. "22 March 1923 Indiana Weekly Messenger (Indiana, PA) Tirzah Van Horn Obituary."
2778. "George Logan Van Horn Obituary 21 Sept 1909 Indiana Evening Gazette (Indiana, PA)."
2779. *West Mahoning Twp., Indiana Cnty, PA 1900 Census ED 63 Sh 6A.*
2780. *Rural Valley, Jefferson Cnty, PA 1930 Census ED 45 Sh 1B.*
2781. *Armstrong Cnty, PA Miracode Index 1920 ED 42 Visit 6.*
2782. *WWI Draft Registration Card 1917-1918*, "Electronic."
2783. *West Mahoning Twp., Indiana Cnty, PA 1900 Census ED 63 Sh 6A.*
2784. *WWI Draft Registration Card 1917-1918*, "Electronic."
2785. "22 March 1923 Indiana Weekly Messenger (Indiana, PA) Tirzah Van Horn Obituary."
2786. "George Logan Van Horn Obituary 21 Sept 1909 Indiana Evening Gazette (Indiana, PA)."
2787. *West Mahoning Twp., Indiana Cnty, PA 1880 Census ED 144 Sh 325C.*
2788. *Cowanshonnock Twp., Armstrong Cnty, PA 1920 Census ED 5 Sh 4A .*
2789. *Cowanshonnock Twp., Armstrong Cnty, PA 1910 Census ED 9 Sh 1B .*
2790. "27 March 1964 Simpson's Leader-Times (Kittanning, PA) Owen DeLone Van Horn Obituary."
2791. *West Mahoning Twp., Indiana Cnty, PA 1880 Census ED 144 Sh 325C.*
2792. *West Mahoning Twp., Indiana Cnty, PA 1900 Census ED 63 Sh 6A.*
2793. *Cowanshonnock Twp., Armstrong Cnty, PA 1920 Census ED 5 Sh 4A .*
2794. *Cowanshonnock Twp., Armstrong Cnty, PA 1910 Census ED 9 Sh 1B .*
2795. "27 March 1964 Simpson's Leader-Times (Kittanning, PA) Owen DeLone Van Horn Obituary."
2796. *Cowanshonnock Twp., Armstrong Cnty, PA 1910 Census ED 9 Sh 1B .*
2797. *Cowanshonnock Twp., Armstrong Cnty, PA 1920 Census ED 5 Sh 4A .*
2798. *Cowanshonnock Twp., Armstrong Cnty, PA 1910 Census ED 9 Sh 1B .*
2799. *Cowanshonnock Twp., Armstrong Cnty, PA 1920 Census ED 5 Sh 4A .*
2800. *Cowanshonnock Twp., Armstrong Cnty, PA 1910 Census ED 9 Sh 1B .*
2801. *Cowanshonnock Twp., Armstrong Cnty, PA 1920 Census ED 5 Sh 4A .*
2802. *Rural Valley, Armstrong Cnty, PA 1910 Census ED 42 Sh 9A.*
2803. *WWII Civilian Draft Registration*, "Electronic."
2804. *West Mahoning Twp., Indiana Cnty, PA 1900 Census ED 63 Sh 6A.*
2805. *Cowanshonnock Twp., Armstrong Cnty, PA 1920 Census ED 4 Sh 16B.*
2806. *Armstrong Cnty, PA Miracode Index 1920 ED 42 Visit 166.*
2807. *Rural Valley, Armstrong Cnty, PA 1910 Census ED 42 Sh 9A.*

2808. *WWII Civilian Draft Registration*, "Electronic."
2809. *Rural Valley, Armstrong Cnty, PA 1910 Census ED 42 Sh 9A.*
2810. *Armstrong Cnty, PA Miracode Index 1920 ED 42 Visit 166.*
2811. *Rural Valley, Armstrong Cnty, PA 1910 Census ED 42 Sh 9A.*
2812. *PlumCreek, Armstrong Cnty, PA 1910 Census ED 37 Sh 9B.*
2813. *Cowanshonnock Twp., Armstrong Cnty, PA 1920 Census ED 5 Sh 2A.*
2814. *Erie, Erie Cnty, PA 1930 Census ED 88 Sh 7A.*
2815. *Armstrong Cnty, PA Miracode Index 1920 ED 42 Visit 166.*
2816. *PlumCreek, Armstrong Cnty, PA 1910 Census ED 37 Sh 9B.*
2817. *Rural Valley, Armstrong Cnty, PA 1910 Census ED 42 Sh 9A.*
2818. *Saltsburg, Indiana Cnty, PA 1920 Census ED 127 Sh 5A.*
2819. *Armstrong Cnty, PA Miracode Index 1920 ED 42 Visit 166.*
2820. *Saltsburg, Indiana Cnty, PA 1910 Census ED 91 Sh 4B.*
2821. *Rural Valley, Armstrong Cnty, PA 1910 Census ED 42 Sh 9A.*
2822. *Armstrong Cnty, PA Miracode Index 1920 ED 42 Visit 166.*
2823. *Rural Valley, Armstrong Cnty, PA 1910 Census ED 42 Sh 9A.*
2824. "Edna L. McMinn Van Horn Obituary Indiana County Genealogical and Historical Society Newspaper Clippings."
2825. *Falls Creek, Jefferson Cnty, PA 1920 Census ED 146 Sh 13A.*
2826. *Snyder Twp., Jefferson Cnty, PA 1910 Census ED 90 Sh 15A.*
2827. *Brockway, Snyder Twp., Jefferson Cnty, PA 1900 Census ED 58 Sh 14A.*
2828. *Falls Creek, Jefferson Cnty, PA 1930 Census ED 11 Sh 12A.*
2829. DAR National Record Copy of Member Application # 862524.
2830. *Snyder Twp., Jefferson Cnty, PA 1910 Census ED 90 Sh 15A.*
2831. WWI Civilian Draft Registration Index.
2832. DAR National Record Copy of Member Application # 862524.
2833. "Edna L. McMinn Van Horn Obituary Indiana County Genealogical and Historical Society Newspaper Clippings."
2834. *Snyder Twp., Jefferson Cnty, PA 1910 Census ED 90 Sh 15A.*
2835. WWI Civilian Draft Registration Index.
2836. *Falls Creek, Jefferson Cnty, PA 1920 Census ED 146 Sh 13A.*
2837. *Falls Creek, Jefferson Cnty, PA 1930 Census ED 11 Sh 12A.*
2838. DAR National Record Copy of Member Application # 862524.
2839. *Snyder Twp., Jefferson Cnty, PA 1910 Census ED 90 Sh 15A.*
2840. "Edna L. McMinn Van Horn Obituary Indiana County Genealogical and Historical Society Newspaper Clippings."
2841. DAR National Record Copy of Member Application # 862524.
2842. *East Mahoning Twp., Indiana Cnty, PA 1860 Census p. 170.*
2843. *East Mahoning Twp., Indiana Cnty, PA 1900 Census ED 53 Sh 5A.*
2844. Hamilton, Von Gail, *Work Family History: Twelve Generations of Work in America 1690-1969, Park City, Utah,* (Park City, Utah: Publishers Press, 1969, 614 pgs.).
2845. *East Mahoning Twp., Indiana Cnty, PA 1910 Census ED 73 Sh 5A.*
2846. *East Mahoning Twp., Indiana Cnty, PA 1880 Census ED 145 Sh 17/337.*
2847. *East Mahoning Twp., Indiana Cnty, PA 1860 Census p. 170.*
2848. *East Mahoning Twp., Indiana Cnty, PA 1900 Census ED 53 Sh 5A.*
2849. *East Mahoning Twp., Indiana Cnty, PA 1910 Census ED 73 Sh 5A.*
2850. *East Mahoning Twp., Indiana Cnty, PA 1880 Census ED 145 Sh 17/337.*
2851. *East Mahoning Twp., Indiana Cnty, PA 1900 Census ED 53 Sh 5A.*
2852. *East Mahoning Twp., Indiana Cnty, PA 1880 Census ED 145 Sh 17/337.*
2853. *East Mahoning Twp., Indiana Cnty, PA 1900 Census ED 53 Sh 5A.*
2854. *East Mahoning Twp., Indiana Cnty, PA 1910 Census ED 73 Sh 5A.*
2855. *East Mahoning Twp., Indiana Cnty, PA 1900 Census ED 53 Sh 5A.*
2856. *East Mahoning Twp., Indiana Cnty, PA 1910 Census ED 73 Sh 5A.*
2857. *East Mahoning Twp., Indiana Cnty, PA 1900 Census ED 53 Sh 5A.*

2858. *East Mahoning Twp., Indiana Cnty, PA 1910 Census ED 73 Sh 5A.*

2859. *East Mahoning Twp., Indiana Cnty, PA 1900 Census ED 53 Sh 5A.*

2860. *East Mahoning Twp., Indiana Cnty, PA 1910 Census ED 73 Sh 5A.*

2861. Hamilton, Von Gail, *Work Family History: Twelve Generations of Work in America 1690-1969, Park City, Utah,* (Park City, Utah: Publishers Press, 1969, 614 pgs.).

2862. *East Mahoning Twp., Indiana Cnty, PA 1900 Census ED 53 Sh 5B.*

2863. *East Mahoning Twp., Indiana Cnty, PA 1900 Census ED 53 Sh 6B.*

2864. "James I. Van Horn Obituary Indiana County Genealogical and Historical Society Newspaper Clippings."

2865. "Robert L. Claire Van Horn Obituary."

2866. *Indiana Ward 1, Indiana Cnty, PA 1910 Census ED 80 Sh 12 B.*

2867. "Van Horn, Bennett Work Obituary Indiana County Genealogical and Historical Society Newspaper Clippings."

2868. *South Mahoning Twp., Indiana Cnty, PA 1880 Census ED 143 Sh 26.*

2869. *Indiana Ward 2, Indiana Cnty, PA 1920 Census ED 114 Sh 16A.*

2870. "22 May 1953 Indiana Evening Gazette (Indiana, PA) Mrs. Adda M. McAdoo Obituary."

2871. *Indiana, Indiana Cnty, PA 1930 Census ED 32 Sh 13B.*

2872. *Indiana Ward 1, Indiana Cnty, PA 1910 Census ED 80 Sh 12 B.*

2873. "22 May 1953 Indiana Evening Gazette (Indiana, PA) Mrs. Adda M. McAdoo Obituary."

2874. "James I. Van Horn Obituary Indiana County Genealogical and Historical Society Newspaper Clippings."

2875. *Indiana Ward 1, Indiana Cnty, PA 1910 Census ED 80 Sh 12 B.*

2876. "Van Horn, Bennett Work Obituary Indiana County Genealogical and Historical Society Newspaper Clippings."

2877. *Indiana Ward 2, Indiana Cnty, PA 1920 Census ED 114 Sh 16A.*

2878. "22 May 1953 Indiana Evening Gazette (Indiana, PA) Mrs. Adda M. McAdoo Obituary."

2879. *Indiana, Indiana Cnty, PA 1930 Census ED 32 Sh 13B.*

2880. *Indiana Ward 1, Indiana Cnty, PA 1910 Census ED 80 Sh 12 B.*

2881. "Van Horn, Bennett Work Obituary Indiana County Genealogical and Historical Society Newspaper Clippings."

2882. *South Mahoning Twp., Indiana Cnty, PA 1880 Census ED 143 Sh 26.*

2883. *Plumville, South Mahoning Twp., Indiana Cnty, PA 1910 Census ED 92 Sh 1A.*

2884. *Cowanshonnock Twp., Armstrong Cnty, PA 1920 Census ED 4 Sh 7B.*

2885. *East Mahoning Twp., Indiana Cnty, PA 1900 Census ED 53 Sh 5A.*

2886. "4 Sept 1957 Simpson's Leader-Times (Kittanning, PA) Alma Florence Aul Shaffer Obituary, p.2."

2887. "23 April 1974 Simpson's Leader-Times (Kittanning, PA) Herbert Aul Obituary."

2888. "9 April 1951 The Progress (Clearfield, PA) Iva Hopkins Obituray."

2889. *South Mahoning Twp., Indiana Cnty, PA 1880 Census ED 143 Sh 26.*

2890. "Van Horn, Bennett Work Obituary Indiana County Genealogical and Historical Society Newspaper Clippings."

2891. *Plumville, South Mahoning Twp., Indiana Cnty, PA 1910 Census ED 92 Sh 1A.*

2892. *Cowanshonnock Twp., Armstrong Cnty, PA 1920 Census ED 4 Sh 7B.*

2893. *East Mahoning Twp., Indiana Cnty, PA 1900 Census ED 53 Sh 5A.*

2894. *WWI Draft Registration Card 1917-1918,* "Electronic."

2895. "15 Feb 1950 Indiana Evening Gazette (Indiana, PA) Obit Myrtle Aul Wagner."

2896. "26 Nov 1957 Indiana Evening Gazette (Indiana, PA) Lula Aul Obit."

2897. "20 June 1955 Indiana Evening Gazette (Indiana, PA) Laney Aul Death Announcement."

2898. *East Mahoning Twp., Indiana Cnty, PA 1880 Census ED 145 Sh 377A.*

2899. "26 April 1899 Indiana Weekly Messenger(Indiana, PA) Casper Aul Obituary."

2900. "4 Sept 1957 Simpson's Leader-Times (Kittanning, PA) Alma Florence Aul Shaffer Obituary, p.2."

2901. "23 April 1974 Simpson's Leader-Times (Kittanning, PA) Herbert Aul Obituary."

2902. "9 April 1951 The Progress (Clearfield, PA) Iva Hopkins Obituray."

2903. "Indiana Evening Gazette (Indiana, PA) 28 May 1895."
2904. *Plumville, South Mahoning Twp., Indiana Cnty, PA 1910 Census ED 92 Sh 1A.*
2905. *WWI Draft Registration Card 1917-1918*, "Electronic."
2906. "20 June 1955 Indiana Evening Gazette (Indiana, PA) Laney Aul Death Announcement."
2907. "Indiana Evening Gazette (Indiana, PA) 28 May 1895."
2908. *Plumville, South Mahoning Twp., Indiana Cnty, PA 1910 Census ED 92 Sh 1A.*
2909. "27 Dec. 1917 Indiana Evenin Gazette (Indiana, PA) Mable Mildred Aul Obit."
2910. *Plumville, South Mahoning Twp., Indiana Cnty, PA 1910 Census ED 92 Sh 1A.*
2911. *Cowanshonnock Twp., Armstrong Cnty, PA 1920 Census ED 4 Sh 7B.*
2912. "21 Feb 1950 Indiana Evening Gazette (Indiana, PA) Funeral Announcememt Mrs. J. E. Wagner."
2913. "20 June 1955 Indiana Evening Gazette (Indiana, PA) Laney Aul Death Announcement."
2914. "15 Feb 1950 Indiana Evening Gazette (Indiana, PA) Obit Myrtle Aul Wagner."
2915. "23 April 1974 Simpson's Leader-Times (Kittanning, PA) Herbert Aul Obituary."
2916. "James I. Van Horn Obituary Indiana County Genealogical and Historical Society Newspaper Clippings."
2917. "Robert L. Claire Van Horn Obituary."
2918. "Van Horn, Bennett Work Obituary Indiana County Genealogical and Historical Society Newspaper Clippings."
2919. *South Mahoning Twp., Indiana Cnty, PA 1880 Census ED 143 Sh 26.*
2920. *South Mahoning Twp., Indiana Cnty, PA 1900 Census ED 64 Sh 2B .*
2921. *South Mahoning Twp., Indiana Cnty, PA 1920 Census ED 124 Sh 5A.*
2922. *WWI Draft Registration Card 1917-1918*, "Electronic."
2923. *White Twp., Indiana Cnty, PA 1930 Census ED 53 Sh 4A.*
2924. "Indiana Evening Gazette (Indiana, PA) 20 and 21 September 1961 Cora Belle Shaffer Obituary."
2925. *South Mahoning Twp., Indiana Cnty, PA 1910 Census ED 92 Sh 2B.*
2926. "22 May 1953 Indiana Evening Gazette (Indiana, PA) Mrs. Adda M. McAdoo Obituary."
2927. *South Mahoning Twp., Indiana Cnty, PA 1880 Census ED 143 Sh 26.*
2928. "Indiana Evening Gazette (Indiana, PA) 20 and 21 September 1961 Cora Belle Shaffer Obituary."
2929. "James I. Van Horn Obituary Indiana County Genealogical and Historical Society Newspaper Clippings."
2930. "Van Horn, Bennett Work Obituary Indiana County Genealogical and Historical Society Newspaper Clippings."
2931. *South Mahoning Twp., Indiana Cnty, PA 1910 Census ED 124 Sh 5A.*
2932. *White Twp., Indiana Cnty, PA 1930 Census ED 53 Sh 4A.*
2933. "24 Nov 1941 Indiana Evening Gazette (Indiana, PA) Alber Shaffer Obit."
2934. "22 May 1953 Indiana Evening Gazette (Indiana, PA) Mrs. Adda M. McAdoo Obituary."
2935. *South Mahoning Twp., Indiana Cnty, PA 1920 Census ED 124 Sh 5A.*
2936. *WWI Draft Registration Card 1917-1918*, "Electronic."
2937. "Indiana Evening Gazette (Indiana, PA) 24 November 1941."
2938. *South Mahoning Twp., Indiana Cnty, PA 1920 Census ED 124 Sh 5A.*
2939. *South Mahoning Twp., Indiana Cnty, PA 1910 Census ED 92 Sh 2B.*
2940. "14 May 1945 Indiana Evening Gazette (Indiana, PA) Dorothy Bell Shaffer Obit."
2941. *South Mahoning Twp., Indiana Cnty, PA 1920 Census ED 124 Sh 5A.*
2942. "10 Jan 1977 Indiana Evening Gazette (Indiana, PA)."
2943. *White Twp., Indiana Cnty, PA 1930 Census ED 53 Sh 4A.*
2944. "10 Jan 1977 Indiana Evening Gazette (Indiana, PA)."
2945. "14 May 1945 Indiana Evening Gazette (Indiana, PA) Dorothy Bell Shaffer Obit."
2946. *White Twp., Indiana Cnty, PA 1930 Census ED 53 Sh 4A.*
2947. "James I. Van Horn Obituary Indiana County Genealogical and Historical Society Newspaper Clippings."
2948. "Robert L. Claire Van Horn Obituary."

2949. Hamilton, Von Gail, *Work Family History: Twelve Generations of Work in America 1690-1969, Park City, Utah*, (Park City, Utah: Publishers Press, 1969, 614 pgs.).
2950. "Van Horn, Bennett Work Obituary Indiana County Genealogical and Historical Society Newspaper Clippings."
2951. *South Mahoning Twp., Indiana Cnty, PA 1910 Census ED 93 Sh 3B.*
2952. *South Mahoning Twp., Indiana Cnty, PA 1920 Census ED 124 Sh 5A.*
2953. *South Mahoning Twp., Indiana Cnty, PA 1930 Census ED 48 Sh 12B.*
2954. "22 May 1953 Indiana Evening Gazette (Indiana, PA) Mrs. Adda M. McAdoo Obituary."
2955. "26 June 1961 Indiana Evening Gazette (Indiana, PA) Anne Johnston 80th Birthday."
2956. *South Mahoning Twp., Indiana Cnty, PA 1910 Census ED 93 Sh 3B.*
2957. "5 Jan 1972 Obituary of Ann Florence Van Horn Johnston Indiana Evening Gazette(Indiana, PA)."
2958. "James I. Van Horn Obituary Indiana County Genealogical and Historical Society Newspaper Clippings."
2959. Hamilton, Von Gail, *Work Family History: Twelve Generations of Work in America 1690-1969, Park City, Utah*, (Park City, Utah: Publishers Press, 1969, 614 pgs.).
2960. "Van Horn, Bennett Work Obituary Indiana County Genealogical and Historical Society Newspaper Clippings."
2961. *South Mahoning Twp., Indiana Cnty, PA 1910 Census ED 93 Sh 3B.*
2962. *South Mahoning Twp., Indiana Cnty, PA 1920 Census ED 124 Sh 5A.*
2963. *South Mahoning Twp., Indiana Cnty, PA 1930 Census ED 48 Sh 12B.*
2964. "22 May 1953 Indiana Evening Gazette (Indiana, PA) Mrs. Adda M. McAdoo Obituary."
2965. "5 Jan 1972 Obituary of Ann Florence Van Horn Johnston Indiana Evening Gazette(Indiana, PA)."
2966. *South Mahoning Twp., Indiana Cnty, PA 1910 Census ED 93 Sh 3B.*
2967. "5 Jan 1972 Obituary of Ann Florence Van Horn Johnston Indiana Evening Gazette(Indiana, PA)."
2968. "James I. Van Horn Obituary Indiana County Genealogical and Historical Society Newspaper Clippings."
2969. "Robert L. Claire Van Horn Obituary."
2970. *Plumville, South Mahoning Twp., Indiana Cnty, PA 1920 Census ED 123 Sh 1A.*
2971. *Plumville, South Mahoning Twp., Indiana Cnty, PA 1930 Census ED 42 Sh 7A&B.*
2972. "Van Horn, Bennett Work Obituary Indiana County Genealogical and Historical Society Newspaper Clippings."
2973. *South Mahoning Twp., Indiana Cnty, PA 1900 Census ED 64 Sh 2B .*
2974. WWI Civilian Draft Registration Index.
2975. *Plumville, South Mahoning Twp., Indiana Cnty, PA 1910 Census ED 92 Sh 1A.*
2976. *Plumville, South Mahoning Twp., Indiana Cnty, PA 1920 Census ED 123 Sh 1A.*
2977. *WWII Civilian Draft Registration*, "Electronic."
2978. "Floyd Van Horn Obituary Indiana County Genealogical and Historical Society Newspaper Clippings."
2979. WWI Civilian Draft Registration Index.
2980. *Plumville, South Mahoning Twp., Indiana Cnty, PA 1910 Census ED 92 Sh 1A.*
2981. "20 March 1907 Indiana County Gazette (iindiana, PA)."
2982. "14 March 1907 Indiana County Gazette (Indiana, PA)."
2983. *Plumville, South Mahoning Twp., Indiana Cnty, PA 1910 Census ED 92 Sh 1A.*
2984. "23 October 1913 Indiana Evening Gazette (Indiana, PA) Minnie Van Horn Death."
2985. "Wilbur Van Horn Obituary Indiana County Genealogical and Historical Society Newspaper Clippings."
2986. *Plumville, South Mahoning Twp., Indiana Cnty, PA 1930 Census ED 42 Sh 7A&B.*
2987. *Plumville, South Mahoning Twp., Indiana Cnty, PA 1920 Census ED 123 Sh 1A.*
2988. "Indiana Weekly Messenger (Indiana, PA) 11 November 1914."
2989. *South Mahoning Twp., Indiana Cnty, PA 1930 Census ED 42 Sh 7B.*
2990. "20 March 1907 Indiana County Gazette (iindiana, PA)."

2991. "14 March 1907 Indiana County Gazette (Indiana, PA)."
2992. "Indiana Weekly Messenger (Indiana, PA) 11 November 1914."
2993. *Plumville, South Mahoning Twp., Indiana Cnty, PA 1920 Census ED 123 Sh 1A.*
2994. "Robert L. Claire Van Horn Obituary."
2995. "Raymond L. Van Horn Obituary Indiana County Genealogical and Historical Society Newspaper Clippings."
2996. "Wilbur Van Horn Obituary Indiana County Genealogical and Historical Society Newspaper Clippings."
2997. *Plumville, South Mahoning Twp., Indiana Cnty, PA 1930 Census ED 42 Sh 7A&B.*
2998. *Plumville, South Mahoning Twp., Indiana Cnty, PA 1910 Census ED 92 Sh 1A.*
2999. *Plumville, South Mahoning Twp., Indiana Cnty, PA 1930 Census ED 42 Sh 7A&B.*
3000. "Floyd Van Horn Obituary Indiana County Genealogical and Historical Society Newspaper Clippings."
3001. *Plumville, South Mahoning Twp., Indiana Cnty, PA 1930 Census ED 42 Sh 7A&B.*
3002. "Raymond L. Van Horn Obituary Indiana County Genealogical and Historical Society Newspaper Clippings."
3003. "Wilbur Van Horn Obituary Indiana County Genealogical and Historical Society Newspaper Clippings."
3004. *Plumville, South Mahoning Twp., Indiana Cnty, PA 1930 Census ED 42 Sh 7A&B.*
3005. "Robert L. Claire Van Horn Obituary."
3006. "Wilbur Van Horn Obituary Indiana County Genealogical and Historical Society Newspaper Clippings."
3007. "Raymond L. Van Horn Obituary Indiana County Genealogical and Historical Society Newspaper Clippings."
3008. *South Mahoning Twp., Indiana Cnty, PA 1920 Census ED 24 Sh 8A.*
3009. "Van Horn, Bennett Work Obituary Indiana County Genealogical and Historical Society Newspaper Clippings."
3010. *South Mahoning Twp., Indiana Cnty, PA 1900 Census ED 64 Sh 2B .*
3011. *South Mahoning Twp., Indiana Cnty, PA 1910 Census ED 93 Sh 3A.*
3012. *WWI Draft Registration Card 1917-1918,* "Electronic."
3013. *South Mahoning Twp., Indiana Cnty, PA 1920 Census ED 24 Sh 8A.*
3014. WWI Civilian Draft Registration Index.
3015. *South Mahoning Twp., Indiana Cnty, PA 1920 Census ED 24 Sh 8A.*
3016. WWI Civilian Draft Registration Index.
3017. *South Mahoning Twp., Indiana Cnty, PA 1920 Census ED 24 Sh 8A.*
3018. *Interments of the Gilgal Cemetery, Gilgal Church, Indiana Cnty, PA.*
3019. "11 Sept 1971 Indiana Evening Gazette(Indiana, PA) Norman Clarence Van Horn Obituary."
3020. "James I. Van Horn Obituary Indiana County Genealogical and Historical Society Newspaper Clippings."
3021. "Robert L. Claire Van Horn Obituary."
3022. "Sprague L. Van Horn Obituary Indiana County Genealogical and Historical Society Newspaper Clippings."
3023. "Harry B. Van Horn Obituary Indiana County Genealogical and Historical Society Newspaper Clippings."
3024. "Van Horn, Harry 35 year Anniversary and Wedding Article Indiana County Genealogical and Historical Society Newspaper Clippings."
3025. "Van Horn, Bennett Work Obituary Indiana County Genealogical and Historical Society Newspaper Clippings."
3026. *South Mahoning Twp., Indiana Cnty, PA 1900 Census ED 64 Sh 2B .*
3027. *South Mahoning Twp., Indiana Cnty, PA 1910 Census ED 93 Sh 3A.*
3028. *South Mahoning Twp., Indiana Cnty, PA 1920 Census ED 24 Sh 8A.*
3029. *South Mahoning Twp., Indiana Cnty, PA 1930 Census ED 48 Sh 8A.*
3030. "22 May 1953 Indiana Evening Gazette (Indiana, PA) Mrs. Adda M. McAdoo Obituary."
3031. *Interments of the Gilgal Cemetery, Gilgal Church, Indiana Cnty, PA.*

3032. WWI Civilian Draft Registration Index.
3033. *Interments of the Gilgal Cemetery, Gilgal Church, Indiana Cnty, PA.*
3034. Harry Coulter Van Horn Obituary.
3035. *Interments of the Gilgal Cemetery, Gilgal Church, Indiana Cnty, PA.*
3036. *South Mahoning Twp., Indiana Cnty, PA 1930 Census ED 48 Sh 8A.*
3037. "Harry Bennett Van Horn Obituary Indiana County Genealogical and Historical Society Newspaper Clippings."
3038. *South Mahoning Twp., Indiana Cnty, PA 1920 Census ED 24 Sh 8A.*
3039. "Irene B. Simpson Van Horn Obiuary."
3040. "Harry B. Van Horn Obituary Indiana County Genealogical and Historical Society Newspaper Clippings."
3041. "Van Horn, Harry 35 year Anniversary and Wedding Article Indiana County Genealogical and Historical Society Newspaper Clippings."
3042. *South Mahoning Twp., Indiana Cnty, PA 1930 Census ED 48 Sh 8A.*
3043. "Van Horn, Harry 35 year Anniversary and Wedding Article Indiana County Genealogical and Historical Society Newspaper Clippings."
3044. *Interments of the Gilgal Cemetery, Gilgal Church, Indiana Cnty, PA.*
3045. *East Mahoning Twp., Indiana Cnty, PA 1900 Census ED 53 Sh 3A.*
3046. *Interments of the Gilgal Cemetery, Gilgal Church, Indiana Cnty, PA.*
3047. *South Mahoning Twp., Indiana Cnty, PA 1930 Census ED 48 Sh 8A.*
3048. "Van Horn, Harry 35 year Anniversary and Wedding Article Indiana County Genealogical and Historical Society Newspaper Clippings."
3049. *South Mahoning Twp., Indiana Cnty, PA 1930 Census ED 48 Sh 8A.*
3050. *South Mahoning Twp., Indiana Cnty, PA 1920 Census ED 24 Sh 8A.*
3051. "Merle Wayne Van Horn Obituary Indiana County Genealogical and Historical Society Newspaper Clippings."
3052. *South Mahoning Twp., Indiana Cnty, PA 1930 Census ED 48 Sh 8A.*
3053. SSN Death Index.
3054. Grave Stone
3055. SSN Death Index.
3056. *South Mahoning Twp., Indiana Cnty, PA 1930 Census ED 48 Sh 8A.*
3057. "Clair Van Horn Obituary Indiana County Genealogical and Historical Society Newspaper Clippings."
3058. "Merle Wayne Van Horn Obituary Indiana County Genealogical and Historical Society Newspaper Clippings."
3059. *South Mahoning Twp., Indiana Cnty, PA 1930 Census ED 48 Sh 8A.*
3060. "Clair Van Horn Obituary Indiana County Genealogical and Historical Society Newspaper Clippings."
3061. "Harry Bennett Van Horn Obituary Indiana County Genealogical and Historical Society Newspaper Clippings."
3062. "James I. Van Horn Obituary Indiana County Genealogical and Historical Society Newspaper Clippings."
3063. "Robert L. Claire Van Horn Obituary."
3064. "Van Horn, Bennett Work Obituary Indiana County Genealogical and Historical Society Newspaper Clippings."
3065. *South Mahoning Twp., Indiana Cnty, PA 1900 Census ED 64 Sh 2B .*
3066. *South Mahoning Twp., Indiana Cnty, PA 1910 Census ED 93 Sh 3A.*
3067. "Indiana Progress (Indiana Cnty, PA) 5 February 1913," Marriage License.
3068. "22 May 1953 Indiana Evening Gazette (Indiana, PA) Mrs. Adda M. McAdoo Obituary."
3069. "6 Feb 1963 Indiana Evening Gazette (Indiana, PA) 50th Wedding Story of Delbert and Pearl Good."
3070. *South Mahoning Twp., Indiana Cnty, PA 1930 Census ED 48 Sh 11B.*
3071. "James I. Van Horn Obituary Indiana County Genealogical and Historical Society Newspaper Clippings."

3072. *South Mahoning Twp., Indiana Cnty, PA 1930 Census ED 48 Sh 11B.*
3073. "Van Horn, Bennett Work Obituary Indiana County Genealogical and Historical Society Newspaper Clippings."
3074. "Indiana Progress (Indiana Cnty, PA) 5 February 1913," Marriage License.
3075. "22 May 1953 Indiana Evening Gazette (Indiana, PA) Mrs. Adda M. McAdoo Obituary."
3076. "6 Feb 1963 Indiana Evening Gazette (Indiana, PA) 50th Wedding Story of Delbert and Pearl Good."
3077. "Indiana Progress (Indiana Cnty, PA) 5 February 1913," Marriage License.
3078. "6 Feb 1963 Indiana Evening Gazette (Indiana, PA) 50th Wedding Story of Delbert and Pearl Good."
3079. *South Mahoning Twp., Indiana Cnty, PA 1930 Census ED 48 Sh 11B.*
3080. "Indiana Progress (Indiana Cnty, PA) 5 February 1913," Marriage License.
3081. "6 Feb 1963 Indiana Evening Gazette (Indiana, PA) 50th Wedding Story of Delbert and Pearl Good."
3082. "11 Sept 1971 Indiana Evening Gazette(Indiana, PA) Norman Clarence Van Horn Obituary."
3083. "Robert L. Claire Van Horn Obituary."
3084. Gravestone in Mt. Hope Cemetery, Logansport, Cass Cnty, IN.
3085. "Van Horn, Bennett Work Obituary Indiana County Genealogical and Historical Society Newspaper Clippings."
3086. "Van Horn, Effie Obituary Indiana County Genealogical and Historical Society Newspaper Clippings."
3087. *South Mahoning Twp., Indiana Cnty, PA 1900 Census ED 64 Sh 2B .*
3088. *South Mahoning Twp., Indiana Cnty, PA 1910 Census ED 93 Sh 3A.*
3089. "Wedding Anniversary Announcement of Norman and Effie Van Horn Indiana County Genealogical and Historical Society Newspaper Clippings."
3090. *Green Twp., Indiana Cnty, PA 1920 Census ED 110 Sh 18B.*
3091. *Plumville,South Mahoning Twp., Indiana Cnty, PA 1930 Census ED 42 Sh 3B.*
3092. "22 May 1953 Indiana Evening Gazette (Indiana, PA) Mrs. Adda M. McAdoo Obituary."
3093. "12 Oct 1961 Indiana Evening Gazette (Indiana, PA) Charles Brooks birthday announcement."
3094. "11 Sept 1971 Indiana Evening Gazette(Indiana, PA) Norman Clarence Van Horn Obituary."
3095. *WWII Civilian Draft Registration*, "Electronic."
3096. "11 Sept 1971 Indiana Evening Gazette(Indiana, PA) Norman Clarence Van Horn Obituary."
3097. Hamilton, Von Gail, *Work Family History: Twelve Generations of Work in America 1690-1969, Park City, Utah,* (Park City, Utah: Publishers Press, 1969, 614 pgs.).
3098. *Green Twp., Indiana Cnty, PA 1920 Census ED 110 Sh 18B.*
3099. "Indiana Evening Gazette (Indiana, PA) 26 July 1917."
3100. *Green Twp., Indiana Cnty, PA 1920 Census ED 110 Sh 18B.*
3101. "11 Sept 1971 Indiana Evening Gazette(Indiana, PA) Norman Clarence Van Horn Obituary."
3102. Hamilton, Von Gail, *Work Family History: Twelve Generations of Work in America 1690-1969, Park City, Utah,* (Park City, Utah: Publishers Press, 1969, 614 pgs.).
3103. "Glenn L. Van Horn Obituary Indiana County Genealogical and Historical Society Newspaper Clippings."
3104. "Van Horn, Effie Obituary Indiana County Genealogical and Historical Society Newspaper Clippings."
3105. "Wedding Anniversary Announcement of Norman and Effie Van Horn Indiana County Genealogical and Historical Society Newspaper Clippings."
3106. *Plumville,South Mahoning Twp., Indiana Cnty, PA 1930 Census ED 42 Sh 3B.*
3107. *WWII Civilian Draft Registration*, "Electronic."
3108. "Wedding Anniversary Announcement of Norman and Effie Van Horn Indiana County Genealogical and Historical Society Newspaper Clippings."
3109. "Van Horn, Effie Obituary Indiana County Genealogical and Historical Society Newspaper Clippings."
3110. "Glenn L. Van Horn Obituary Indiana County Genealogical and Historical Society Newspaper

Clippings."

3111. "Van Horn, Effie Obituary Indiana County Genealogical and Historical Society Newspaper Clippings."

3112. "Indiana Evening Gazette (Indiana, PA) 26 July 1917."

3113. "Wedding Anniversary Announcement of Norman and Effie Van Horn Indiana County Genealogical and Historical Society Newspaper Clippings."

3114. *Interments of the Gilgal Cemetery, Gilgal Church, Indiana Cnty, PA.*

3115. "11 Sept 1971 Indiana Evening Gazette(Indiana, PA) Norman Clarence Van Horn Obituary."

3116. "James I. Van Horn Obituary Indiana County Genealogical and Historical Society Newspaper Clippings."

3117. "Robert L. Claire Van Horn Obituary."

3118. *North Mahoning Twp., Indiana Cnty, PA 1930 Census ED 39 Sh 5A.*

3119. "Van Horn, Bennett Work Obituary Indiana County Genealogical and Historical Society Newspaper Clippings."

3120. *South Mahoning Twp., Indiana Cnty, PA 1900 Census ED 64 Sh 2B .*

3121. *South Mahoning Twp., Indiana Cnty, PA 1910 Census ED 93 Sh 3A.*

3122. WWII Civilian Draft Registration for Walter Byron Fetterhoff.

3123. "22 May 1953 Indiana Evening Gazette (Indiana, PA) Mrs. Adda M. McAdoo Obituary."

3124. "24 Nov 1965 Indiana Evening Gazette (Indiana, PA) 50th Anniversary Fetterhoffs."

3125. *South Mahoning Twp., Indiana Cnty, PA 1910 Census ED 93 Sh 3A.*

3126. "11 Sept 1971 Indiana Evening Gazette(Indiana, PA) Norman Clarence Van Horn Obituary."

3127. "James I. Van Horn Obituary Indiana County Genealogical and Historical Society Newspaper Clippings."

3128. Hamilton, Von Gail, *Work Family History: Twelve Generations of Work in America 1690-1969, Park City, Utah,* (Park City, Utah: Publishers Press, 1969, 614 pgs.).

3129. "Van Horn, Bennett Work Obituary Indiana County Genealogical and Historical Society Newspaper Clippings."

3130. *North Mahoning Twp., Indiana Cnty, PA 1930 Census ED 39 Sh 5A.*

3131. *WWII Civilian Draft Registration,* "Electronic."

3132. "22 May 1953 Indiana Evening Gazette (Indiana, PA) Mrs. Adda M. McAdoo Obituary."

3133. "24 Nov 1965 Indiana Evening Gazette (Indiana, PA) 50th Anniversary Fetterhoffs."

3134. *North Mahoning Twp., Indiana Cnty, PA 1930 Census ED 39 Sh 5A.*

3135. *WWII Civilian Draft Registration,* "Electronic."

3136. "24 Nov 1965 Indiana Evening Gazette (Indiana, PA) 50th Anniversary Fetterhoffs."

3137. *North Mahoning Twp., Indiana Cnty, PA 1930 Census ED 39 Sh 5A.*

3138. "8 Oct 1947 Indiana Evening Gazette (Indiana, PA) Marrige license listing of Elmer Byron Fetteroff and Loletta Arlene Shield."

3139. "15 Oct 1947 Indiana Evening Gazette (Indiana, PA) Marriage announcement of E. Byron and Loletta Arlene Shilelds."

3140. *North Mahoning Twp., Indiana Cnty, PA 1930 Census ED 39 Sh 5A.*

3141. "11 Sept 1971 Indiana Evening Gazette(Indiana, PA) Norman Clarence Van Horn Obituary."

3142. "James I. Van Horn Obituary Indiana County Genealogical and Historical Society Newspaper Clippings."

3143. "Robert L. Claire Van Horn Obituary."

3144. *Plumville, South Mahoning Twp., Indiana Cnty, PA 1930 Census ED 42 Sh 5B.*

3145. *South Mahoning Twp., Indiana Cnty, PA 1920 Census ED 24 Sh 8A.*

3146. "Van Horn, Bennett Work Obituary Indiana County Genealogical and Historical Society Newspaper Clippings."

3147. *South Mahoning Twp., Indiana Cnty, PA 1900 Census ED 64 Sh 2B .*

3148. *South Mahoning Twp., Indiana Cnty, PA 1910 Census ED 93 Sh 3A.*

3149. "22 May 1953 Indiana Evening Gazette (Indiana, PA) Mrs. Adda M. McAdoo Obituary."

3150. *South Mahoning Twp., Indiana Cnty, PA 1910 Census ED 93 Sh 3A.*

3151. "11 Sept 1971 Indiana Evening Gazette(Indiana, PA) Norman Clarence Van Horn Obituary."

3152. "James I. Van Horn Obituary Indiana County Genealogical and Historical Society Newspaper

Clippings."

3153. *Plumville, South Mahoning Twp., Indiana Cnty, PA 1930 Census ED 42 Sh 5B.*

3154. "Van Horn, Bennett Work Obituary Indiana County Genealogical and Historical Society Newspaper Clippings."

3155. "22 May 1953 Indiana Evening Gazette (Indiana, PA) Mrs. Adda M. McAdoo Obituary."

3156. "Indiana Weekly Messenger (Indiana, PA) 23 September 1920."

3157. "16 September 1920 Indiana Evening Gazette (Indiana, PA)."

3158. *Plumville, South Mahoning Twp., Indiana Cnty, PA 1930 Census ED 42 Sh 5B.*

3159. "Indiana Weekly Messenger (Indiana, PA) 23 September 1920."

3160. "16 September 1920 Indiana Evening Gazette (Indiana, PA)."

3161. "James I. Van Horn Obituary Indiana County Genealogical and Historical Society Newspaper Clippings."

3162. "Robert L. Claire Van Horn Obituary."

3163. *South Mahoning Twp., Indiana Cnty, PA 1920 Census ED 24 Sh 8A.*

3164. "Van Horn, Bennett Work Obituary Indiana County Genealogical and Historical Society Newspaper Clippings."

3165. *South Mahoning Twp., Indiana Cnty, PA 1910 Census ED 93 Sh 3A.*

3166. *South Mahoning Twp., Indiana Cnty, PA 1930 Census ED 48 Sh 2A.*

3167. "22 May 1953 Indiana Evening Gazette (Indiana, PA) Mrs. Adda M. McAdoo Obituary."

3168. Hamilton, Von Gail, *Work Family History: Twelve Generations of Work in America 1690-1969, Park City, Utah,* (Park City, Utah: Publishers Press, 1969, 614 pgs.).

3169. "James I. Van Horn Obituary Indiana County Genealogical and Historical Society Newspaper Clippings."

3170. "Van Horn, Bennett Work Obituary Indiana County Genealogical and Historical Society Newspaper Clippings."

3171. *South Mahoning Twp., Indiana Cnty, PA 1930 Census ED 48 Sh 2A.*

3172. *Perry, Jefferson Cnty, PA 1900 Census ED 69 Sh 12A.*

3173. "22 May 1953 Indiana Evening Gazette (Indiana, PA) Mrs. Adda M. McAdoo Obituary."

3174. *South Mahoning Twp., Indiana Cnty, PA 1930 Census ED 48 Sh 2A.*

3175. *Washington, Distict of Columbia, 1900 Census ED 120 Sh 7A.*

3176. *Washington Twp., Indiana Cnty, PA 1900 Census ED 65 Sh 1B.*

3177. *Washington, Distict of Columbia, 1900 Census ED 120 Sh 7A.*

3178. DAR National Record Copy of Member Application# 446865.

3179. *Utica, Oneida Cnty, NY 1900 Census ED 62 Sh 3B.*

3180. DAR National Record Copy of Member Application# 446865.

3181. *Utica, Oneida Cnty, NY 1900 Census ED 62 Sh 3B.*

3182. DAR National Record Copy of Member Application# 446865.

3183. *Washington, Distict of Columbia, 1900 Census ED 120 Sh 7A.*

3184. *Washington, District of Columbia, 1930 Census ED 321 Sh 30A.*

3185. *Washington, District of Columbia, 1920 Census ED 15 Sh 4B.*

3186. *Washington, Distict of Columbia, 1900 Census ED 120 Sh 7A.*

3187. *Washington, District of Columbia, 1930 Census ED 321 Sh 30A.*

3188. *Washington, District of Columbia, 1920 Census ED 15 Sh 4B.*

3189. *Washington, District of Columbia, 1930 Census ED 321 Sh 30A.*

3190. *Hillsboro, Montgomery Cnty, IL 1880 Census ED 148 Sh 18B.*

3191. *St Louis, St Louis Cnty, MO 1900 Census ED 314 Sh 11B.*

3192. *White Plains, Westchester Cnty, NY 1910 Census ED 128 Sh 9A.*

3193. *New Brunswick, Middlesex Cnty, NJ 1930 Census ED 48 Sh 8B.*

3194. *New Brunswick, Middlesex Cnty, NJ 1920 Census ED 22 Sh 12A.*

3195. *Hillsboro, Montgomery Cnty, IL 1880 Census ED 148 Sh 18B.*

3196. *St Louis, St Louis Cnty, MO 1900 Census ED 314 Sh 11B.*

3197. *New Brunswick, Middlesex Cnty, NJ 1930 Census ED 48 Sh 8B.*

3198. *New Brunswick, Middlesex Cnty, NJ 1920 Census ED 22 Sh 12A.*

3199. *New Brunswick, Middlesex Cnty, NJ 1930 Census ED 48 Sh 8B.*

3200. *Green Twp., Indiana Cnty, PA 1900 Census ED 55 Sh 9A.*
3201. *Vandergrift, Westmoreland Cnty, PA 1930 Census ED 187 Sh 6B.*
3202. "22 August 1913 Indiana Evening Gazette (Indiana, PA) Barr Miller Marriage Announcement."
3203. *Vandergrift, Westmoreland Cnty, PA 1920 Census ED 231 Sh 3B.*
3204. DAR National Record Copy of Member Application # 684102.
3205. *Green Twp., Indiana Cnty, PA 1900 Census ED 55 Sh 9A.*
3206. DAR National Record Copy of Member Application # 684102.
3207. *Vandergrift, Westmoreland Cnty, PA 1930 Census ED 187 Sh 6B.*
3208. "Indiana Progress (Indiana Cnty, PA) Jan. 1, 1936 Barr- Van Horn Golden Anniversay Announcement."
3209. "22 August 1913 Indiana Evening Gazette (Indiana, PA) Barr Miller Marriage Announcement."
3210. *Vandergrift, Westmoreland Cnty, PA 1920 Census ED 231 Sh 3B.*
3211. DAR National Record Copy of Member Application # 684102.
3212. "22 August 1913 Indiana Evening Gazette (Indiana, PA) Barr Miller Marriage Announcement."
3213. *Vandergrift, Westmoreland Cnty, PA 1930 Census ED 187 Sh 6B.*
3214. DAR National Record Copy of Member Application # 684102.
3215. "22 August 1913 Indiana Evening Gazette (Indiana, PA) Barr Miller Marriage Announcement."
3216. *Indiana, Indiana Cnty, PA 1930 Census ED 32 Sh 1B.*
3217. *Green Twp., Indiana Cnty, PA 1900 Census ED 55 Sh 9A.*
3218. *Green Twp., Indiana Cnty, PA 1930 Census ED 29 Sh 31B.*
3219. *Green Twp., Indiana Cnty, PA 1900 Census ED 55 Sh 9A.*
3220. *Green Twp., Indiana Cnty, PA 1930 Census ED 29 Sh 31B.*
3221. "Indiana Progress (Indiana Cnty, PA) Jan. 1, 1936 Barr- Van Horn Golden Anniversay Announcement."
3222. *Green Twp., Indiana Cnty, PA 1930 Census ED 29 Sh 31B.*
3223. *Green Twp., Indiana Cnty, PA 1900 Census ED 55 Sh 9A.*
3224. *Green Twp., Indiana Cnty, PA 1920 Census ED 110 Sh 22A.*
3225. "13 June 1941 Indiana Evening Gazette (Indiana, PA) Barr Ellsworth Marriage."
3226. "23 June 1941 Indiana Evening Gazette (Indiana, PA) Barr Mclaughlin Marriage."
3227. "22 March 1954 Indiana Evening Gazette (Indiana, PA) Nellie Hancocok BARR Obit."
3228. "Indiana Weekly Messenger (Indiana, PA) 16 September 1914."
3229. *Green Twp., Indiana Cnty, PA 1920 Census ED 110 Sh 22A.*
3230. "22 March 1954 Indiana Evening Gazette (Indiana, PA) Nellie Hancocok BARR Obit."
3231. "Indiana Weekly Messenger (Indiana, PA) 16 September 1914."
3232. *Green Twp., Indiana Cnty, PA 1900 Census ED 55 Sh 9A.*
3233. *Green Twp., Indiana Cnty, PA 1920 Census ED 110 Sh 22A.*
3234. *White Twp., Indiana Cnty, PA 1930 Census ED 31 Sh 4A.*
3235. *Green Twp., Indiana Cnty, PA 1900 Census ED 55 Sh 9A.*
3236. SSN Death Index.
3237. *White Twp., Indiana Cnty, PA 1930 Census ED 31 Sh 4A.*
3238. "Indiana Progress (Indiana Cnty, PA) Jan. 1, 1936 Barr- Van Horn Golden Anniversay Announcement."
3239. *White Twp., Indiana Cnty, PA 1930 Census ED 31 Sh 4A.*
3240. *Walden, Jackson Cnty, CO 1920 Census ED 59 Sh 3A & B.*
3241. *Loveland, Larimer Cnty, CO 1930 Census ED 16 Sh 9A.*
3242. *US Public Records Index,* "Electronic."
3243. *Walden, Jackson Cnty, CO 1920 Census ED 59 Sh 3A & B.*
3244. Hamilton, Von Gail, *Work Family History: Twelve Generations of Work in America 1690-1969, Park City, Utah,* (Park City, Utah: Publishers Press, 1969, 614 pgs.).
3245. *West Indiana Borough, Indiana Cnty, PA 1880 Census ED 127 Sh 21A.*

3246. *Des Moines, Ward 1, Polk Cnty, IA 1925 Iowa Census.*

3247. *West Indiana Borough, Indiana Cnty, PA 1880 Census ED 127 Sh 21A.*

3248. "8 March 1943 Indiana Evening Gazette (Indiana, PA) Notice of Dora Hood Smith Death."

3249. Hamilton, Von Gail, *Work Family History: Twelve Generations of Work in America 1690-1969, Park City, Utah,* (Park City, Utah: Publishers Press, 1969, 614 pgs.).

3250. *Des Moines, Ward 1, Polk Cnty, IA 1925 Iowa Census.*

3251. Hamilton, Von Gail, *Work Family History: Twelve Generations of Work in America 1690-1969, Park City, Utah,* (Park City, Utah: Publishers Press, 1969, 614 pgs.).

3252. "19 May 1954 Indiana Evening Gazette (Indiana, PA) Mary Work Steele Obit."

3253. *Berkeley, Alemeda Cnty, CA 1930 Census ED 319 Sh 5A.*

3254. *Sacramento, Sacramento Cnty, CA 1920 Census ED 93 Sh 9A.*

3255. *WWII Civilian Draft Registration,* "Electronic."

3256. *Wenatchee, Chelan Cnty, WA 1910 Census ED 25 Sh 4A.*

3257. *Ft. Morgan, Morgan Cnty, CO 1900 Census ED 185 Sh 9A.*

3258. *Berkeley, Alemeda Cnty, CA 1930 Census ED 319 Sh 5A.*

3259. *California Death Index 1940-1997,* "Electronic."

3260. Hamilton, Von Gail, *Work Family History: Twelve Generations of Work in America 1690-1969, Park City, Utah,* (Park City, Utah: Publishers Press, 1969, 614 pgs.).

3261. Sacramento, Sacramento Cnty, CA 1920 Census ED 93 Sh 9A.

3262. *Wenatchee, Chelan Cnty, WA 1910 Census ED 25 Sh 4A.*

3263. *Sacramento, Sacramento Cnty, CA 1920 Census ED 93 Sh 9A.*

3264. Hamilton, Von Gail, *Work Family History: Twelve Generations of Work in America 1690-1969, Park City, Utah,* (Park City, Utah: Publishers Press, 1969, 614 pgs.).

3265. *Berkeley, Alemeda Cnty, CA 1930 Census ED 319 Sh 5A.*

3266. *Sacramento, Sacramento Cnty, CA 1920 Census ED 93 Sh 9A.*

3267. *Wenatchee, Chelan Cnty, WA 1910 Census ED 25 Sh 4A.*

3268. *Berkeley, Alemeda Cnty, CA 1930 Census ED 319 Sh 5A.*

3269. *California Death Index 1940-1997,* "Electronic."

3270. Hamilton, Von Gail, *Work Family History: Twelve Generations of Work in America 1690-1969, Park City, Utah,* (Park City, Utah: Publishers Press, 1969, 614 pgs.).

3271. *Pueblo, Pueblo Cnty, CO 1900 Census ED 98 Sh 1A.*

3272. *Denver, Denver Cnty, CO 1930 Census ED 102 Sh 1B.*

3273. *Pueblo, Pueblo Cnty, CO 1900 Census ED 98 Sh 1A.*

3274. Hamilton, Von Gail, *Work Family History: Twelve Generations of Work in America 1690-1969, Park City, Utah,* (Park City, Utah: Publishers Press, 1969, 614 pgs.).

3275. *Denver, Denver Cnty, CO 1930 Census ED 102 Sh 1B.*

3276. Hamilton, Von Gail, *Work Family History: Twelve Generations of Work in America 1690-1969, Park City, Utah,* (Park City, Utah: Publishers Press, 1969, 614 pgs.).

3277. *US Veterans Gravesites 1775-2006,* "Electronic."

3278. Hamilton, Von Gail, *Work Family History: Twelve Generations of Work in America 1690-1969, Park City, Utah,* (Park City, Utah: Publishers Press, 1969, 614 pgs.).

3279. *Pueblo, Pueblo Cnty, CO 1900 Census ED 98 Sh 1A.*

3280. *Pueblo, Pueblo Cnty, CO 1920 Census ED 228 Sh 6B.*

3281. *Pueblo, Pueblo Cnty, CO 1900 Census ED 98 Sh 1A.*

3282. Hubert Work Passport Application 38090 Sept 13, 1910.

3283. *Pueblo, Pueblo Cnty, CO 1920 Census ED 228 Sh 6B.*

3284. Hamilton, Von Gail, *Work Family History: Twelve Generations of Work in America 1690-1969, Park City, Utah,* (Park City, Utah: Publishers Press, 1969, 614 pgs.).

3285. *Pueblo, Pueblo Cnty, CO 1900 Census ED 98 Sh 1A.*

3286. *Denver, Denver Cnty, CO 1930 Census ED 120 Sh 7A.*

3287. *Pueblo, Pueblo Cnty, CO 1900 Census ED 98 Sh 1A.*

3288. Hubert Work Passport Application 38090 Sept 13, 1910.

3289. *Denver, Denver Cnty, CO 1930 Census ED 120 Sh 7A.*

3290. *Kansas City, Jackson Cnty, MO 1880 Census ED 7 Sh 30.*

3291. *Blue Twp., Jackson Cnty, MO 1900 Census ED 2 Sh 7B.*
3292. *Kansas City, Jackson Cnty, MO 1910 Census ED 164 Sh 2B.*
3293. *Blue Twp., Jackson Cnty, MO 1920 Census ED 286 Sh 21A.*
3294. *Blue Twp., Jackson Cnty, MO 1930 Census ED 260 Sh 12A.*
3295. *Kansas City, Jackson Cnty, MO 1880 Census ED 7 Sh 30.*
3296. *Blue Twp., Jackson Cnty, MO 1900 Census ED 2 Sh 7B.*
3297. *Kansas City, Jackson Cnty, MO 1910 Census ED 164 Sh 2B.*
3298. *Blue Twp., Jackson Cnty, MO 1920 Census ED 286 Sh 21A.*
3299. *Blue Twp., Jackson Cnty, MO 1930 Census ED 260 Sh 12A.*
3300. *Blue Twp., Jackson Cnty, MO 1900 Census ED 2 Sh 7B.*
3301. *Kansas City, Jackson Cnty, MO 1910 Census ED 164 Sh 2B.*
3302. *Blue Twp., Jackson Cnty, MO 1920 Census ED 286 Sh 21A.*
3303. *Blue Twp., Jackson Cnty, MO 1930 Census ED 260 Sh 12A.*
3304. *Kansas City, Jackson Cnty, MO 1910 Census ED 164 Sh 2B.*
3305. C. S. Williams, Christian Barentsen Van Horn and His Descendants, 1911 NY.
3306. *Brookfield, Jefferson Cnty, PA 1880 Census ED 186 Sh 10C.*
3307. *Barnett Twp., Forest Cnty, PA 1900 Census ED 45 Sh 12A.*
3308. WWI Civilian Draft Registration Index.
3309. *Barnett Twp., Forest Cnty, PA 1920 Census ED 24 Sh 3A.*
3310. *Barnett Twp., Forest Cnty, PA 1910 Census ED 54 Sh 2B.*
3311. *Brookfield, Jefferson Cnty, PA 1880 Census ED 186 Sh 10C.*
3312. WWI Civilian Draft Registration Index.
3313. *Barnett Twp., Forest Cnty, PA 1910 Census ED 54 Sh 2B.*
3314. *Barnett Twp., Forest Cnty, PA 1920 Census ED 24 Sh 3A.*
3315. *Barnett Twp., Forest Cnty, PA 1910 Census ED 54 Sh 2B.*
3316. *Barnett Twp., Forest Cnty, PA 1920 Census ED 24 Sh 3A.*
3317. *Barnett Twp., Forest Cnty, PA 1910 Census ED 54 Sh 2B.*
3318. *Barnett Twp., Forest Cnty, PA 1920 Census ED 24 Sh 3A.*
3319. *Barnett Twp., Forest Cnty, PA 1910 Census ED 54 Sh 2B.*
3320. *Barnett Twp., Forest Cnty, PA 1920 Census ED 24 Sh 3A.*
3321. *Barnett Twp., Forest Cnty, PA 1910 Census ED 54 Sh 2B.*
3322. *Barnett Twp., Forest Cnty, PA 1920 Census ED 24 Sh 3A.*
3323. *Barnett Twp., Forest Cnty, PA 1910 Census ED 54 Sh 2B.*
3324. *Barnett Twp., Forest Cnty, PA 1920 Census ED 24 Sh 3A.*
3325. *Barnett Twp., Forest Cnty, PA 1900 Census ED 45 Sh 12A.*
3326. *Barnett Twp., Forest Cnty, PA 1910 Census ED 54 Sh 3A.*
3327. *Barnett Twp., Forest Cnty, PA 1920 Census ED 24 Sh 3A.*
3328. *Barnett Twp., Forest Cnty, PA 1900 Census ED 45 Sh 12A.*
3329. *Barnett Twp., Forest Cnty, PA 1910 Census ED 54 Sh 3A.*
3330. *Barnett Twp., Forest Cnty, PA 1920 Census ED 24 Sh 3A.*
3331. *Barnett Twp., Forest Cnty, PA 1910 Census ED 54 Sh 3A.*
3332. *Barnett Twp., Forest Cnty, PA 1920 Census ED 24 Sh 3A.*
3333. *Barnett Twp., Forest Cnty, PA 1910 Census ED 54 Sh 3A.*
3334. *Barnett Twp., Forest Cnty, PA 1920 Census ED 24 Sh 3A.*
3335. *Barnett Twp., Forest Cnty, PA 1910 Census ED 54 Sh 3A.*
3336. *Barnett Twp., Forest Cnty, PA 1920 Census ED 24 Sh 3A.*
3337. *East Mahoning Twp., Indiana Cnty, PA 1880 Census ED 145 Sh 338C.*
3338. *Barnett Twp., Forest Cnty, PA 1900 Census ED 45 Sh 12A.*
3339. *Barnett Twp., Forest Cnty, PA 1910 Census ED 54 Sh 4B.*
3340. *Charleston, Kanawha Cnty, WV 1930 Census ED 50 Sh 14B.*
3341. *Charleston, Kanawha Cnty, WV 1920 Census ED 112 Sh 8 A&B.*
3342. *East Mahoning Twp., Indiana Cnty, PA 1880 Census ED 145 Sh 338C.*
3343. *Barnett Twp., Forest Cnty, PA 1900 Census ED 45 Sh 12A.*
3344. *Barnett Twp., Forest Cnty, PA 1910 Census ED 54 Sh 4B.*

3345. *Charleston, Kanawha Cnty, WV 1930 Census ED 50 Sh 14B.*
3346. *Charleston, Kanawha Cnty, WV 1920 Census ED 112 Sh 8 A&B.*
3347. *Barnett Twp., Forest Cnty, PA 1900 Census ED 45 Sh 12A.*
3348. *Barnett Twp., Forest Cnty, PA 1910 Census ED 54 Sh 4B.*
3349. *Charleston, Kanawha Cnty, WV 1920 Census ED 112 Sh 8 A&B.*
3350. *Barnett Twp., Forest Cnty, PA 1900 Census ED 45 Sh 12A.*
3351. *Barnett Twp., Forest Cnty, PA 1910 Census ED 54 Sh 4B.*
3352. *Charleston, Kanawha Cnty, WV 1920 Census ED 112 Sh 8 A&B.*
3353. *Barnett Twp., Forest Cnty, PA 1910 Census ED 54 Sh 4B.*
3354. *Charleston, Kanawha Cnty, WV 1930 Census ED 50 Sh 14B.*
3355. *Charleston, Kanawha Cnty, WV 1920 Census ED 112 Sh 8 A&B.*
3356. *Barnett Twp., Forest Cnty, PA 1910 Census ED 54 Sh 4B.*
3357. *East Mahoning Twp., Indiana Cnty, PA 1880 Census ED 145 Sh 338C.*
3358. *Clarion, Clarion Cnty, PA 1910 Census ED 6 Sh 10B.*
3359. *Pittsburgh, Ward 23, Allegheny Cnty, PA 1920 Census ED 685 Ah 4B.*
3360. *East Wheatfield Twp,, Indiana Cnty, PA 1880 Census ED 135 Sh 146C.*
3361. *Clarion, Clarion Cnty, PA 1910 Census ED 6 Sh 10B.*
3362. *Pittsburgh, Ward 23, Allegheny Cnty, PA 1920 Census ED 685 Ah 4B.*
3363. *Clarion, Clarion Cnty, PA 1910 Census ED 6 Sh 10B.*
3364. *Pittsburgh, Ward 23, Allegheny Cnty, PA 1920 Census ED 685 Ah 4B.*
3365. *Clarion, Clarion Cnty, PA 1910 Census ED 6 Sh 10B.*
3366. *Pittsburgh, Ward 23, Allegheny Cnty, PA 1920 Census ED 685 Ah 4B.*
3367. *Barnett Twp., Forest Cnty, PA 1900 Census ED 45 Sh 12B.*
3368. *Barnett Twp., Forest Cnty, PA 1910 Census ED 54 Sh 3B.*
3369. *Kane, Wetmore Twp., McKean Cnty, PA 1930 Census ED 19 Sh 13B.*
3370. *Barnett Twp., Forest Cnty, PA 1900 Census ED 45 Sh 12B.*
3371. *Kane, Wetmore Twp., McKean Cnty, PA 1930 Census ED 19 Sh 13B.*
3372. *Springfield Twp., Fayette Cnty, PA 1900 Census ED 64 Sh 9B & 10A.*
3373. WWI Civilian Draft Registration Index.
3374. *Connellsville, Fayette Cnty, PA 1910 Census ED 14 Sh 9B.*
3375. *Crafton, Allegheny Cnty, PA 1920 Census ED 74 Sh 20B.*
3376. *Pittsburgh, Allegheny Cnty, PA 1930 Census ED 331 Sh 14A.*
3377. *Springfield Twp., Fayette Cnty, PA 1900 Census ED 64 Sh 9B.*
3378. WWI Civilian Draft Registration Index.
3379. *Connellsville, Fayette Cnty, PA 1910 Census ED 14 Sh 9B.*
3380. *Crafton, Allegheny Cnty, PA 1920 Census ED 74 Sh 20B.*
3381. *Pittsburgh, Allegheny Cnty, PA 1930 Census ED 331 Sh 14A.*
3382. *Connellsville, Fayette Cnty, PA 1910 Census ED 14 Sh 9B.*
3383. *Crafton, Allegheny Cnty, PA 1920 Census ED 74 Sh 20B.*
3384. *Pittsburgh, Allegheny Cnty, PA 1930 Census ED 331 Sh 14A.*
3385. *Connellsville, Fayette Cnty, PA 1910 Census ED 14 Sh 9B.*
3386. *Crafton, Allegheny Cnty, PA 1920 Census ED 74 Sh 20B.*
3387. *Pittsburgh, Allegheny Cnty, PA 1930 Census ED 331 Sh 14A.*
3388. *Crafton, Allegheny Cnty, PA 1920 Census ED 74 Sh 20B.*
3389. *Pittsburgh, Allegheny Cnty, PA 1930 Census ED 331 Sh 14A.*
3390. *Scottdale, Westmoreland Cnty, PA 1900 Census ED 132 Sh 1A & B.*
3391. *Scottdale Ward 1, Westmoreland Cnty, PA 1910 Census ED 191 Sh 12A.*
3392. *Scottdale, Westmoreland Cnty, PA 1900 Census ED 132 Sh 1A & B.*
3393. Willey, Gordon (Van Horn TREE) Husband of Jacqueline Marshal Granddaughter of Judson Van Horn.
3394. *Scottdale Ward 1, Westmoreland Cnty, PA 1910 Census ED 191 Sh 12A.*
3395. WWI Civilian Draft Registration Index.
3396. *Scottdale Ward 1, Westmoreland Cnty, PA 1910 Census ED 191 Sh 12A.*
3397. *Scottdale, Westmoreland Cnty, PA 1900 Census ED 132 Sh 1A & B.*

3398. *Scottdale Ward 1, Westmoreland Cnty, PA 1920 Census ED 201 Sh 8A.*
3399. *East Hunnington, Westmoreland Cnty, PA 1930 Census ED 24 Sh 10A.*
3400. *Scottdale Ward 1, Westmoreland Cnty, PA 1910 Census ED 191 Sh 12A.*
3401. *WWI Draft Registration Card 1917-1918*, "Electronic."
3402. SSN Death Index.
3403. *Georgia Deaths, 1919-98*, "Electronic."
3404. *Scottdale Ward 1, Westmoreland Cnty, PA 1920 Census ED 201 Sh 8A.*
3405. *East Hunnington, Westmoreland Cnty, PA 1930 Census ED 24 Sh 10A.*
3406. Willey, Gordon (Van Horn TREE) Husband of Jacqueline Marshal Granddaughter of Judson Van Horn.
3407. *Scottdale Ward 1, Westmoreland Cnty, PA 1920 Census ED 201 Sh 8A.*
3408. SSN Death Index.
3409. Willey, Gordon (Van Horn TREE) Husband of Jacqueline Marshal Granddaughter of Judson Van Horn.
3410. SSN Death Index.
3411. Willey, Gordon (Van Horn TREE) Husband of Jacqueline Marshal Granddaughter of Judson Van Horn.
3412. *WWI Draft Registration Card 1917-1918*, "Electronic."
3413. *Pittsburgh Ward 22, Allegheny Cnty, PA 1920 Census ED 674 Sh 2A.*
3414. *Scottdale Ward 1, Westmoreland Cnty, PA 1910 Census ED 191 Sh 12A.*
3415. *Scottdale, Westmoreland Cnty, PA 1900 Census ED 132 Sh 1A & B.*
3416. *Pittsburgh Ward, Allegheny Cnty, PA 1930 Census ED 332 Sh 4A.*
3417. "Indiana Evening Gazette (Indiana, PA) 20 October 1916."
3418. *WWI Draft Registration Card 1917-1918*, "Electronic."
3419. SSN Death Index.
3420. *Pittsburgh Ward, Allegheny Cnty, PA 1930 Census ED 332 Sh 4A.*
3421. *Pittsburgh Ward 22, Allegheny Cnty, PA 1920 Census ED 674 Sh 2A.*
3422. "Indiana Evening Gazette (Indiana, PA) 20 October 1916."
3423. *Pittsburgh Ward 22, Allegheny Cnty, PA 1920 Census ED 674 Sh 2A.*
3424. Stephens, Dallas Malone, *Old Allegheny: A Handbook of Information*, (The Tribune Publishing Company, Meadvile, PA, 1921).
3425. *Scottdale Ward 1, Westmoreland Cnty, PA 1910 Census ED 191 Sh 12A.*
3426. *Scottdale, Westmoreland Cnty, PA 1900 Census ED 132 Sh 1A & B.*
3427. *Meyersdale, Somerset Cnty, PA 1930 Census ED 31 Sh 7B.*
3428. *Meyersdale, Somerset Cnty, PA 1920 Census ED 184 Sh 13B.*
3429. *Scottdale Ward 1, Westmoreland Cnty, PA 1910 Census ED 191 Sh 12A.*
3430. Willey, Gordon (Van Horn TREE) Husband of Jacqueline Marshal Granddaughter of Judson Van Horn.
3431. *Meyersdale, Somerset Cnty, PA 1930 Census ED 31 Sh 7B.*
3432. *Williamsport Ward 3, Lycoming Cnty, PA 1870 Census p. 476B.*
3433. *Meyersdale, Somerset Cnty, PA 1920 Census ED 184 Sh 13B.*
3434. *Meyersdale, Somerset Cnty, PA 1930 Census ED 31 Sh 7B.*
3435. Willey, Gordon (Van Horn TREE) Husband of Jacqueline Marshal Granddaughter of Judson Van Horn.
3436. *Meyersdale, Somerset Cnty, PA 1930 Census ED 31 Sh 7B.*
3437. Willey, Gordon (Van Horn TREE) Husband of Jacqueline Marshal Granddaughter of Judson Van Horn.
3438. *Meyersdale, Somerset Cnty, PA 1930 Census ED 31 Sh 7B.*
3439. *Meyersdale, Somerset Cnty, PA 1920 Census ED 184 Sh 13B.*
3440. *Meyersdale, Somerset Cnty, PA 1930 Census ED 31 Sh 7B.*
3441. *Scottdale Ward 1, Westmoreland Cnty, PA 1910 Census ED 191 Sh 12A.*
3442. *Scottdale, Westmoreland Cnty, PA 1900 Census ED 132 Sh 1A & B.*
3443. *Butler, Butler Cnty, PA 1920 Census ED 9, Sh 6A.*
3444. *Scottdale Ward 1, Westmoreland Cnty, PA 1910 Census ED 191 Sh 12A.*

3445. Willey, Gordon (Van Horn TREE) Husband of Jacqueline Marshal Granddaughter of Judson Van Horn.
3446. WWI Civilian Draft Registration Index.
3447. *WWII Civilian Draft Registration*, "Electronic."
3448. *Butler, Butler Cnty, PA 1920 Census ED 9, Sh 6A.*
3449. Willey, Gordon (Van Horn TREE) Husband of Jacqueline Marshal Granddaughter of Judson Van Horn.
3450. *Scottdale Ward 1, Westmoreland Cnty, PA 1910 Census ED 191 Sh 12A.*
3451. *Scottdale, Westmoreland Cnty, PA 1900 Census ED 132 Sh 1A & B.*
3452. *Scottdale Ward 1, Westmoreland Cnty, PA 1920 Census ED 201 Sh 18B.*
3453. *Scottdale Ward 3, Westmoreland Cnty, PA 1930 Census ED 1471 Sh 8A.*
3454. *Scottdale Ward 1, Westmoreland Cnty, PA 1910 Census ED 191 Sh 12A.*
3455. Willey, Gordon (Van Horn TREE) Husband of Jacqueline Marshal Granddaughter of Judson Van Horn.
3456. *Scottdale Ward 3, Westmoreland Cnty, PA 1930 Census ED 1471 Sh 8A.*
3457. *WWII Civilian Draft Registration*, "Electronic."
3458. *Scottdale Ward 3, Westmoreland Cnty, PA 1930 Census ED 1471 Sh 8A.*
3459. *WWII Civilian Draft Registration*, "Electronic."
3460. SSN Death Index.
3461. *Scottdale Ward 3, Westmoreland Cnty, PA 1930 Census ED 1471 Sh 8A.*
3462. *Derry, Westmoreland Cnty, PA 1900 Census ED 89 Sh 1B.*
3463. *Edgewood, Allegheny Cnty, PA 1930 Census ED 585 Sh 14B.*
3464. *Derry, Westmoreland Cnty, PA 1900 Census ED 89 Sh 1B.*
3465. WWI Civilian Draft Registration Index.
3466. *Edgewood, Allegheny Cnty, PA 1930 Census ED 585 Sh 14B.*
3467. *Derry, Westmoreland Cnty, PA 1900 Census ED 89 Sh 1B.*
3468. *Derry, Westmoreland Cnty, PA 1910 Census ED 109 Sh 13A.*
3469. *Derry, Westmoreland Cnty, PA 1930 Census ED 13 Sh 26A.*
3470. *Derry, Westmoreland Cnty, PA 1900 Census ED 89 Sh 1B.*
3471. WWI Civilian Draft Registration Index.
3472. *Derry, Westmoreland Cnty, PA 1910 Census ED 109 Sh 13A.*
3473. *Derry, Westmoreland Cnty, PA 1930 Census ED 13 Sh 26A.*
3474. *Derry, Westmoreland Cnty, PA 1910 Census ED 109 Sh 13A.*
3475. *Derry, Westmoreland Cnty, PA 1930 Census ED 13 Sh 26A.*
3476. *Derry, Westmoreland Cnty, PA 1910 Census ED 109 Sh 13A.*
3477. *Derry, Westmoreland Cnty, PA 1930 Census ED 13 Sh 26A.*
3478. *West Wheatfield Twp., Indiana Cnty, PA 1900 Census ED 66 Sh 15A.*
3479. *West Wheatfield Twp., Indiana Cnty, PA 1910 Census ED 97 Sh 7A.*
3480. *New Florence, Westmoreland Cnty, PA 1920 Census ED 171 Sh 3B.*
3481. *New Florence, Westmoreland Cnty, PA 1930 Census ED 114 Sh 1B.*
3482. *West Wheatfield Twp., Indiana Cnty, PA 1900 Census ED 66 Sh 15A.*
3483. *New Florence, Westmoreland Cnty, PA 1920 Census ED 171 Sh 3B.*
3484. *New Florence, Westmoreland Cnty, PA 1930 Census ED 114 Sh 1B.*
3485. "25 June 1913 Indiana Weekly Messenger (Indiana, PA) Wedding License List."
3486. *New Florence, Westmoreland Cnty, PA 1920 Census ED 171 Sh 3B.*
3487. "25 June 1913 Indiana Weekly Messenger (Indiana, PA) Wedding License List."
3488. *New Florence, Westmoreland Cnty, PA 1920 Census ED 171 Sh 3B.*
3489. *New Florence, Westmoreland Cnty, PA 1930 Census ED 114 Sh 1B.*
3490. *New Florence, Westmoreland Cnty, PA 1920 Census ED 171 Sh 3B.*
3491. *West Wheatfield Twp., Indiana Cnty, PA 1900 Census ED 66 Sh 15A.*
3492. *West Wheatfield Twp., Indiana Cnty, PA 1910 Census ED 97 Sh 7A.*
3493. *Pittsburgh, Allegheny Cnty, PA 1930 Census ED 217 Sh 16A.*
3494. *West Wheatfield Twp., Indiana Cnty, PA 1900 Census ED 66 Sh 15A.*
3495. SSN Death Index.

3496. Lutz, June Schaull, A Historical Account of the Schall/Schaull Family, Grand Rapids, MI 1968.
3497. *Pittsburgh, Allegheny Cnty, PA 1930 Census ED 217 Sh 16A.*
3498. *Kanaranzi, Rock Cnty, MN 1885 MN Census p. 6.*
3499. *Little Rock, Nobles Cnty, MN 1895 MN Census p. 5.*
3500. *Center, Winnebago Cnty, IA 1870 Census p. 8.*
3501. *Minnesota, Roberts Cnty, SD 1910 Census ED 375 Sh 6A.*
3502. *Burke, Gregory Cnty, SD 1920 Census ED 64 Sh 6A.*
3503. *Minnesota, Roberts Cnty, SD 1900 Census ED 292 Sh 7A.*
3504. *Kanaranzi, Rock Cnty, MN 1885 MN Census p. 6.*
3505. *Minnesota, Roberts Cnty, SD 1910 Census ED 375 Sh 6A.*
3506. South Dakota Births 1856-1903 Record.
3507. *Minnesota, Roberts Cnty, SD 1900 Census ED 292 Sh 7A.*
3508. *Minnesota, Roberts Cnty, SD 1910 Census ED 375 Sh 6A.*
3509. *Minnesota, Roberts Cnty, SD 1900 Census ED 292 Sh 7A.*
3510. *Minnesota, Roberts Cnty, SD 1910 Census ED 375 Sh 6A.*
3511. South Dakota Births 1856-1903 Record.
3512. *Minnesota, Roberts Cnty, SD 1910 Census ED 375 Sh 6A.*
3513. *Franklin Twp., Allamakee Cnty, IA 1900 Census ED 3 Sh 4A&B.*
3514. *Township 160, Koochiching Cnty, MN 1910 Census ED 93 Sh 4A.*
3515. *Murphy, Koochiching Cnty, MN 1920 Census ED 54 Sh 1B.*
3516. *Murphy, Koochiching Cnty, MN 1930 Census ED 30 Sh 1B.*
3517. *Kanaranzi, Rock Cnty, MN 1885 MN Census p. 6.*
3518. *Franklin Twp., Allamakee Cnty, IA 1900 Census ED 3 Sh 4A&B.*
3519. WWI Civilian Draft Registration Index.
3520. *Franklin Twp., Allamakee Cnty, IA 1900 Census ED 3 Sh 4A&B.*
3521. *Franklin, Allamakee Cnty, IA 1910 Census ED 3 Sh 6A.*
3522. *Milnor, Sargent Cnty, ND 1920 Census ED 158 Sh 5A.*
3523. *Rawlings, Carbon Cnty, WY 1930 Census ED 1 Sh 1B.*
3524. *Kanaranzi, Rock Cnty, MN 1885 MN Census p. 6.*
3525. *Franklin Twp., Allamakee Cnty, IA 1900 Census ED 3 Sh 4A&B.*
3526. *Franklin, Allamakee Cnty, IA 1910 Census ED 3 Sh 6A.*
3527. *Milnor, Sargent Cnty, ND 1920 Census ED 158 Sh 5A.*
3528. *Rawlings, Carbon Cnty, WY 1930 Census ED 1 Sh 1B.*
3529. *Windsor, Clayton Cnty, IA 1880 Census ED 132 Sh 349C&D.*
3530. *Franklin, Allamakee Cnty, IA 1910 Census ED 3 Sh 6A.*
3531. *Milnor, Sargent Cnty, ND 1920 Census ED 158 Sh 5A.*
3532. *Franklin, Allamakee Cnty, IA 1910 Census ED 3 Sh 6A.*
3533. *Milnor, Sargent Cnty, ND 1920 Census ED 158 Sh 5A.*
3534. *Franklin, Allamakee Cnty, IA 1910 Census ED 3 Sh 6A.*
3535. *Millville, Cambria Cnty, PA 1880 Census ED 187 Sh 166C.*
3536. *Forman, Sargent Cnty, ND 1930 Census ED 7 Sh 1A.*
3537. *Dunbar Twp., Sargent Cnty, ND 1920 Census ED 154 Sh 3A.*
3538. *Millville, Cambria Cnty, PA 1880 Census ED 187 Sh 166C.*
3539. *ND Public Death Index,* "Electronic."
3540. *Forman, Sargent Cnty, ND 1930 Census ED 7 Sh 1A.*
3541. *Dunbar Twp., Sargent Cnty, ND 1920 Census ED 154 Sh 3A.*
3542. *ND Public Death Index,* "Electronic."
3543. *Forman, Sargent Cnty, ND 1930 Census ED 7 Sh 1A.*
3544. *ND Public Death Index,* "Electronic."
3545. *Forman, Sargent Cnty, ND 1930 Census ED 7 Sh 1A.*
3546. *Dunbar Twp., Sargent Cnty, ND 1920 Census ED 154 Sh 3A.*
3547. *ND Public Death Index,* "Electronic."
3548. *Forman, Sargent Cnty, ND 1930 Census ED 7 Sh 1A.*

3549. *Dunbar Twp., Sargent Cnty, ND 1920 Census ED 154 Sh 3A.*
3550. *Forman, Sargent Cnty, ND 1930 Census ED 7 Sh 1A.*
3551. *Dunbar Twp., Sargent Cnty, ND 1920 Census ED 154 Sh 3A.*
3552. *Forman, Sargent Cnty, ND 1930 Census ED 7 Sh 1A.*
3553. Handwritten Notes of Leafy Fern Van Horn Wolf.
3554. The Van Horn Family History by Francis M. Marvin 1929, The Press Publishing Co., p 373-4.
3555. *Dalhart, Dallam Cnty, TX 1930 Census ED 5 Sh 10B.*
3556. *East Wheatfield Twp., Indiana Cnty, PA 1900 Census ED 37 Sh 2B .*
3557. "21 Jan 1937 Indiana Weekly Messenger (Indiana, PA) S. C. Van Horn Obit."
3558. *East Wheatfield Twp., Indiana Cnty, PA 1900 Census ED 37 Sh 2B , ED 37, S 2.*
3559. *Dalhart, Dallam Cnty, TX 1930 Census ED 5 Sh 10B.*
3560. *Texas Death Index 1903-2000,* "Electronic."
3561. *Dalhart, Dallam Cnty, TX 1930 Census ED 5 Sh 10B.*
3562. *Texas Death Index 1903-2000,* "Electronic."
3563. SSN Death Index.
3564. Handwritten Notes of Leafy Fern Van Horn Wolf.
3565. The Van Horn Family History by Francis M. Marvin 1929, The Press Publishing Co., p 373-4.
3566. *East Wheatfield Twp., Indiana Cnty, PA 1900 Census ED 37 Sh 2B .*
3567. "21 Jan 1937 Indiana Weekly Messenger (Indiana, PA) S. C. Van Horn Obit."
3568. Nancy Bostic Hagenmaier, *Seneca County, Ohio, Birth Records, Volume 1-3,p. 324,* (P.O. Box 157, Tiffin, OH: Seneca Co. Ohio Genealogical Society, 2003).
3569. Handwritten Notes of Leafy Fern Van Horn Wolf.
3570. Social Security Application, SSN 288-07-4824.
3571. Social Security Application, SSN 302-07-3970.
3572. Handwritten Notes of Leafy Fern Van Horn Wolf.
3573. Social Security Application, SSN 302-07-3970.
3574. Broderbund Family Archive #110, Vol. 2, Ed. 3, Social Security Records: U.S., SS Death Benefit Records, Surnames Beginning with W, Date of Import: Dec 16, 1995, Internal Ref. #1.112.3.104816.77
3575. Brøderbund Family Archive #110, Vol. 2, Ed. 3, Social Security Records: U.S., SS Death Benefit Records, Surnames Beginning with W, Date of Import: Dec 16, 1995, Internal Ref. #1.112.3.104816.77
3576. Broderbund Family Archive #110, Vol. 2, Ed. 3, Social Security Records: U.S., SS Death Benefit Records, Surnames Beginning with W, Date of Import: Dec 16, 1995, Internal Ref. #1.112.3.104816.77
3577. Brøderbund Family Archive #110, Vol. 2, Ed. 3, Social Security Records: U.S., SS Death Benefit Records, Surnames Beginning with W, Date of Import: Dec 16, 1995, Internal Ref. #1.112.3.104816.77
3578. Brøderbund Family Archive #110, Vol. 2, Ed. 3, Social Security Records: U.S., SS Death Benefit Records, Surnames Beginning with W, Date of Import: Nov 30, 1998, Internal Ref. #1.112.3.104816.77
3579. Handwritten Notes of Leafy Fern Van Horn Wolf.
3580. *East Wheatfield Twp., Indiana Cnty, PA 1900 Census ED 37 Sh 2B , Ed 37, S 2.*
3581. *Justice Pct. 2, Dallam Cnty, TX 1910 Census ED 69 Sh 4B.*
3582. *Dalhart Ward 1, Dallam Cnty, TX 1920 Census ED 44 Sh 4B.*
3583. "21 Jan 1937 Indiana Weekly Messenger (Indiana, PA) S. C. Van Horn Obit."
3584. *Justice Pct. 2, Dallam Cnty, TX 1910 Census ED 69 Sh 4B.*
3585. Handwritten Notes of Leafy Fern Van Horn Wolf.
3586. Harry Coulter Van Horn Obituary.
3587. *Justice Pct. 2, Dallam Cnty, TX 1910 Census ED 69 Sh 4A.*
3588. *Dalhart Ward 1, Dallam Cnty, TX 1920 Census ED 44 Sh 4B.*
3589. "Indiana Progress (Indiana Cnty, PA) 3 February 1915."
3590. *Florda Twp., Parke Cnty, IN 1900 Census ED 58 Sh 9A.*
3591. "Indiana Progress (Indiana Cnty, PA) 3 February 1915."

3592. *Justice Pct. 2, Dallam Cnty, TX 1910 Census ED 69 Sh 4A.*
3593. *Florda Twp., Parke Cnty, IN 1900 Census ED 58 Sh 9A.*
3594. "Indiana Progress (Indiana Cnty, PA) 3 February 1915."
3595. "Indiana Progress (Indiana Cnty, PA) 6 August 1919."
3596. *Pittsburgh Ward 24, Allegheny Cnty, PA 1910 Census ED 604 Sh 17B.*
3597. *Jeanette, Westmoreland Cnty, PA 1930 Census ED 69 Sh 12B.*
3598. *Pittsburgh Ward 24, Allegheny Cnty, PA 1910 Census ED 604 Sh 17B.*
3599. *Jeanette, Westmoreland Cnty, PA 1930 Census ED 69 Sh 12B.*
3600. *Young Twp., Indiana Cnty, PA 1900 Census ED 69 Sh 2B.*
3601. *Young Twp., Indiana Cnty, PA 1910 Census ED 100 Sh 2B.*
3602. *Young Twp., Indiana Cnty, PA 1900 Census ED 69 Sh 2B.*
3603. *Young Twp., Indiana Cnty, PA 1910 Census ED 100 Sh 2B.*
3604. *Rayne, Indiana Cnty, PA 1880 Census ED 142 Sh 248A.*
3605. Nordick, Wilkin Cnty, MN 1895 Territorial Census p. 1.
3606. *Harmony, Forrest Cnty, PA 1900 Census ED 47 Sh 6B.*
3607. *Rayne, Indiana Cnty, PA 1880 Census ED 142 Sh 248A.*
3608. *Harmony, Forrest Cnty, PA 1920 Census ED 26 Sh 6A.*
3609. *Harmony, Forrest Cnty, PA 1910 Census ED 56 Sh 7A.*
3610. *Harmony, Forrest Cnty, PA 1920 Census ED 26 Sh 6A.*
3611. *Rayne, Indiana Cnty, PA 1880 Census ED 142 Sh 248A.*
3612. *Otter Tail, Otter Tail Cnty, MN 1905 Territorial Census ED 8.*
3613. *Nordick, Wilkin Cnty, MN 1895 Territorial Census p. 1 .*
3614. *Strathmore Langdon, Calgary, Alberta Canada 1911 Census p. 14.*
3615. *Rayne, Indiana Cnty, PA 1880 Census ED 142 Sh 248A.*
3616. *British Columbia Death Index 1872-1979*, "Electronic."
3617. *Otter Tail, Otter Tail Cnty, MN 1905 Territorial Census ED 8.*
3618. *Strathmore Langdon, Calgary, Alberta Canada 1911 Census p. 14.*
3619. *Otter Tail, Otter Tail Cnty, MN 1905 Territorial Census ED 8.*
3620. *British Columbia Death Index 1872-1979*, "Electronic."
3621. *Rayne Twp., Indiana Cnty, PA 1900 Census ED 60 Sh 3B.*
3622. *Rayne, Indiana Cnty, PA 1880 Census ED 142 Sh 248A.*
3623. *Bellingham, Whatcom Cnty, WA 1920 Census ED 229 Sh 1A.*
3624. *Bellingham, Whatcom Cnty, WA 1930 Census ED 8 Sh 3B.*
3625. *Strathmore Langdon, Calgary, Alberta Canada 1911 Census p. 9.*
3626. *Rayne Twp., Indiana Cnty, PA 1900 Census ED 60 Sh 3B.*
3627. *Bellingham, Whatcom Cnty, WA 1920 Census ED 229 Sh 1A.*
3628. *Bellingham, Whatcom Cnty, WA 1930 Census ED 8 Sh 3B.*
3629. *Strathmore Langdon, Calgary, Alberta Canada 1911 Census p. 9.*
3630. "6 Jan 1904 Indiana Gazette(indiana, PA)," Listing of Marriage Licenses.
3631. *Bellingham, Whatcom Cnty, WA 1920 Census ED 229 Sh 1A.*
3632. "6 Jan 1904 Indiana Gazette(indiana, PA)," Listing of Marriage Licenses.
3633. *Bellingham, Whatcom Cnty, WA 1920 Census ED 229 Sh 1A.*
3634. *Strathmore Langdon, Calgary, Alberta Canada 1911 Census p. 9.*
3635. *Bellingham, Whatcom Cnty, WA 1920 Census ED 229 Sh 1A.*
3636. *Strathmore Langdon, Calgary, Alberta Canada 1911 Census p. 9.*
3637. *Bellingham, Whatcom Cnty, WA 1920 Census ED 229 Sh 1A.*
3638. *Strathmore Langdon, Calgary, Alberta Canada 1911 Census p. 9.*
3639. *Bellingham, Whatcom Cnty, WA 1920 Census ED 229 Sh 1A.*
3640. *Rayne Twp., Indiana Cnty, PA 1900 Census ED 60 Sh 3B.*
3641. *Rayne, Indiana Cnty, PA 1880 Census ED 142 Sh 248A.*
3642. *Rayne Twp., Indiana Cnty, PA 1930 Census ED 43 Sh 19 A.*
3643. *Rayne Twp., Indiana Cnty, PA 1900 Census ED 60 Sh 3B.*
3644. WWI Civilian Draft Registration Index.
3645. *Rayne Twp., Indiana Cnty, PA 1930 Census ED 43 Sh 19 A.*

3646. *Rayne Twp., Indiana Cnty, PA 1900 Census ED 60 Sh 3B.*
3647. *Rayne, Indiana Cnty, PA 1880 Census ED 142 Sh 248A.*
3648. *Rayne Twp., Indiana Cnty, PA 1930 Census ED 43 Sh 19 A.*
3649. *Rayne Twp., Indiana Cnty, PA 1900 Census ED 60 Sh 3B.*
3650. *Rayne Twp., Indiana Cnty, PA 1930 Census ED 43 Sh 19 A.*
3651. *Rayne Twp., Indiana Cnty, PA 1900 Census ED 60 Sh 3B.*
3652. *British Columbia Marriage Index 1872-1924,* "Electronic."
3653. *Rayne Twp., Indiana Cnty, PA 1910 Census ED 89 Sh 2B.*
3654. *Blairsville, Indiana Cnty, PA 1920 Census ED 90 Sh 1B.*
3655. DAR National Record Copy of Member Application# 448771.
3656. *Blairsville, Indiana Cnty, PA 1910 Census ED 57 Sh 12A.*
3657. *Blairsville, Indiana Cnty, PA 1930 Census ED 7 Sh 14A.*
3658. *Blairsville, Indiana Cnty, PA 1920 Census ED 90 Sh 1B.*
3659. DAR National Record Copy of Member Application # 451294.
3660. *Blairsville, Indiana Cnty, PA 1920 Census ED 90 Sh 1B.*
3661. *Blairsville, Indiana Cnty, PA 1910 Census ED 57 Sh 12A.*
3662. *Blairsville, Indiana Cnty, PA 1930 Census ED 7 Sh 14A.*
3663. DAR National Record Copy of Member Application # 451294.
3664. *Blairsville, Indiana Cnty, PA 1920 Census ED 90 Sh 1B.*
3665. DAR National Record Copy of Member Application # 451294.
3666. *Blairsville, Indiana Cnty, PA 1920 Census ED 90 Sh 1B.*
3667. *Blairsville, Indiana Cnty, PA 1910 Census ED 57 Sh 12A.*
3668. *Blairsville, Indiana Cnty, PA 1920 Census ED 90 Sh 1B.*
3669. *Blairsville, Indiana Cnty, PA 1930 Census ED 7 Sh 14A.*
3670. DAR National Record Copy of Member Application # 451294.
3671. *Blairsville, Indiana Cnty, PA 1930 Census ED 7 Sh 14A.*
3672. *Blairsville, Indiana Cnty, PA 1920 Census ED 91 Sh 11A.*
3673. *Blairsville, Indiana Cnty, PA 1910 Census ED 57 Sh 19A & B.*
3674. "21 Feb 1972 Indiana Evening Gazette(Indiana, PA) Cliford Keil Obit."
3675. DAR National Record Copy of Member Application # 449599.
3676. "21 Feb 1972 Indiana Evening Gazette(Indiana, PA) Cliford Keil Obit."
3677. DAR National Record Copy of Member Application # 449599.
3678. "21 Feb 1972 Indiana Evening Gazette(Indiana, PA) Cliford Keil Obit."
3679. *East Mahoning Twp., Indiana Cnty, PA 1900 Census ED 53 Sh 7A.*
3680. *East Mahoning Twp., Indiana Cnty, PA 1920 Census ED 108 Sh 10B.*
3681. *East Mahoning Twp., Indiana Cnty, PA 1900 Census ED 53 Sh 7A.*
3682. *White Twp., Indiana Cnty, PA 1900 Census ED 67 Sh 1A.*
3683. *White Twp., Indiana Cnty, PA 1910 Census ED 98 Sh 4B.*
3684. *White Twp., Indiana Cnty, PA 1920 Census ED 132 Sh 9B.*
3685. *White Twp., Indiana Cnty, PA 1900 Census ED 67 Sh 1A.*
3686. *White Twp., Indiana Cnty, PA 1910 Census ED 98 Sh 4B.*
3687. *White Twp., Indiana Cnty, PA 1920 Census ED 132 Sh 9B.*
3688. *White Twp., Indiana Cnty, PA 1910 Census ED 98 Sh 4B.*
3689. "28 May 1975 Indiana Evening Gazette (Indiana, PA) Alta Blanche Burkley Obituary."
3690. *White Twp., Indiana Cnty, PA 1910 Census ED 98 Sh 4B.*
3691. "28 May 1975 Indiana Evening Gazette (Indiana, PA) Alta Blanche Burkley Obituary."
3692. *White Twp., Indiana Cnty, PA 1910 Census ED 98 Sh 4B.*
3693. *White Twp., Indiana Cnty, PA 1920 Census ED 132 Sh 9B.*
3694. *White Twp., Indiana Cnty, PA 1910 Census ED 98 Sh 4B.*
3695. *White Twp., Indiana Cnty, PA 1920 Census ED 132 Sh 9B.*
3696. "Jennie Van Horn Obituary."
3697. *Presho, Lyman Cnty, SD 1910 Census Ed 61 Sh 6B.*
3698. *Banks Twp., Indiana Cnty, PA 1870 Census p. 22.*
3699. *Presho, Lyman Cnty, SD 1930 Census ED 27 Sh 4A.*

3700. South Dakota Births 1856-1903 Record.

3701. *Banks Twp., Indiana Cnty, PA 1880 Census ED 150 Sh 405 A & B.*

3702. *Presho, Lyman Cnty, SD 1910 Census Ed 61 Sh 6B.*

3703. *Banks Twp., Indiana Cnty, PA 1870 Census p. 22.*

3704. South Dakota Death Index 1905-1955.

3705. *Presho, Lyman Cnty, SD 1910 Census Ed 61 Sh 6B.*

3706. *Presho, Lyman Cnty, SD 1930 Census ED 27 Sh 4A.*

3707. South Dakota Births 1856-1903 Record.

3708. *Presho, Lyman Cnty, SD 1910 Census Ed 61 Sh 6B.*

3709. South Dakota Births 1856-1903 Record.

3710. *Presho, Lyman Cnty, SD 1910 Census Ed 61 Sh 6B.*

3711. South Dakota Births 1856-1903 Record.

3712. "Jennie Van Horn Obituary."

3713. "23 Oct 1907 Indiana Evening Gazette (Indiana, PA) Van Horn, John N. Obituary ."

3714. *Brule, Brule Cnty, SD 1910 Census ED 71 Sh 6A.*

3715. *Chamberlain, Brule Cnty, SD 1920 Census ED 24 Sh 9B.*

3716. *Banks Twp., Indiana Cnty, PA 1880 Census ED 150 Sh 405 A & B.*

3717. *Brule, Brule Cnty, SD 1910 Census ED 71 Sh 6A.*

3718. *Chamberlain, Brule Cnty, SD 1920 Census ED 24 Sh 9B.*

3719. *Sioux Falls, Minnehaha Cnty, SD 1930 Census ED 39 Sh 8A.*

3720. *Brule, Brule Cnty, SD 1910 Census ED 71 Sh 6A.*

3721. *Chamberlain, Brule Cnty, SD 1920 Census ED 24 Sh 9B.*

3722. *Minneapolis, Hennepin Cnty, MN 1930 Census ED 146 Sh 2B.*

3723. *Brule, Brule Cnty, SD 1910 Census ED 71 Sh 6A.*

3724. *Minnesota Death Index 1908-2002 Records,* "Electronic."

3725. *Minneapolis, Hennepin Cnty, MN 1930 Census ED 146 Sh 2B.*

3726. *Brule, Brule Cnty, SD 1910 Census ED 71 Sh 6A.*

3727. *Chamberlain, Brule Cnty, SD 1920 Census ED 24 Sh 9B.*

3728. *Brule, Brule Cnty, SD 1910 Census ED 71 Sh 6A.*

3729. South Dakota Births 1856-1903 Record.

3730. "Jennie Van Horn Obituary."

3731. "23 Oct 1907 Indiana Evening Gazette (Indiana, PA) Van Horn, John N. Obituary ."

3732. *Kennebec Ward 1, Lyman Cnty, SD 1910 Census ED 52 Sh 7A.*

3733. *Kennebec, Lyman Cnty, SD1920 Census ED 130 Sh 7A.*

3734. *Kennebec, Lyman Cnty, SD 1930 Census ED 15 Sh 2A.*

3735. *Banks Twp., Indiana Cnty, PA 1880 Census ED 150 Sh 405 A & B.*

3736. *Kennebec Ward 1, Lyman Cnty, SD 1910 Census ED 52 Sh 7A.*

3737. DAR National Record Copy of Member Application # 486836.

3738. *Kennebec Ward 1, Lyman Cnty, SD 1910 Census ED 52 Sh 7A.*

3739. *Kennebec, Lyman Cnty, SD1920 Census ED 130 Sh 7A.*

3740. *Twp. 105, Lyman Cnty, SD 1900 Census ED 43 Sh 6A.*

3741. *Kennebec, Lyman Cnty, SD 1930 Census ED 15 Sh 2A.*

3742. DAR National Record Copy of Member Application # 486836.

3743. *Twp. 105, Lyman Cnty, SD 1900 Census ED 43 Sh 6A.*

3744. DAR National Record Copy of Member Application # 486836.

3745. *Kennebec Ward 1, Lyman Cnty, SD 1910 Census ED 52 Sh 7A.*

3746. *Twp. 105, Lyman Cnty, SD 1900 Census ED 43 Sh 6A.*

3747. DAR National Record Copy of Member Application # 486836.

3748. *Kennebec Ward 1, Lyman Cnty, SD 1910 Census ED 52 Sh 7A.*

3749. *Kennebec, Lyman Cnty, SD1920 Census ED 130 Sh 7A.*

3750. DAR National Record Copy of Member Application # 486838.

3751. *Kennebec Ward 1, Lyman Cnty, SD 1910 Census ED 52 Sh 7A.*

3752. *Kennebec, Lyman Cnty, SD1920 Census ED 130 Sh 7A.*

3753. DAR National Record Copy of Member Application # 486839.

3754. *Kennebec Ward 1, Lyman Cnty, SD 1910 Census ED 52 Sh 7A.*
3755. *Kennebec, Lyman Cnty, SD1920 Census ED 130 Sh 7A.*
3756. DAR National Record Copy of Member Application # 486840.
3757. *Kennebec, Lyman Cnty, SD1920 Census ED 130 Sh 7A.*
3758. "Jennie Van Horn Obituary."
3759. *Twp. 105, Lyman Cnty, SD 1900 Census ED 43 Sh 1B.*
3760. "23 Oct 1907 Indiana Evening Gazette (Indiana, PA) Van Horn, John N. Obituary ."
3761. *Dix, Schuyler Cnty, NY 1930 Census ED 7 Sh 2B.*
3762. *Catlin, Chemung Cnty, NY 1910 Census ED 5 Sh 8B & 9.*
3763. *Catlin, Chemung Cnty, NY 1920 Census ED 5 Sh 7A.*
3764. *Banks Twp., Indiana Cnty, PA 1880 Census ED 150 Sh 405 A & B.*
3765. *Dix, Schuyler Cnty, NY 1930 Census ED 7 Sh 2B.*
3766. "23 Oct 1907 Indiana Evening Gazette (Indiana, PA) Van Horn, John N. Obituary ."
3767. *Catlin, Chemung Cnty, NY 1910 Census ED 5 Sh 8B & 9.*
3768. *Catlin, Chemung Cnty, NY 1920 Census ED 5 Sh 7A.*
3769. *Catlin, Chemung Cnty, NY 1910 Census ED 5 Sh 8B & 9.*
3770. *Catlin, Chemung Cnty, NY 1920 Census ED 5 Sh 7A.*
3771. *Dix, Schuyler Cnty, NY 1930 Census ED 7 Sh 2B.*
3772. *Catlin, Chemung Cnty, NY 1920 Census ED 5 Sh 7A.*
3773. *Dix, Schuyler Cnty, NY 1930 Census ED 7 Sh 2B.*
3774. "Jennie Van Horn Obituary."
3775. *Twp. 105, Lyman Cnty, SD 1900 Census ED 43 Sh 1B.*
3776. "23 Oct 1907 Indiana Evening Gazette (Indiana, PA) Van Horn, John N. Obituary ."
3777. *Banks Twp., Indiana Cnty, PA 1880 Census ED 150 Sh 405 A & B.*
3778. *Earling, Lyman Cnty, SD 1910 Census ED 52 Sh 5A.*
3779. *Earling, Lyman Cnty, SD 1920 Census ED 127 Sh 13A.*
3780. *Presho, Lyman Cnty, SD 1930 Census ED 27 Sh 1A.*
3781. *Twp. 105, Lyman Cnty, SD 1900 Census ED 43 Sh 1B.*
3782. *Twp. 105, Lyman Cnty, SD 1900 Census ED 43 Sh 6B.*
3783. "23 Oct 1907 Indiana Evening Gazette (Indiana, PA) Van Horn, John N. Obituary ."
3784. *Earling, Lyman Cnty, SD 1910 Census ED 52 Sh 5A.*
3785. *Earling, Lyman Cnty, SD 1920 Census ED 127 Sh 13A.*
3786. *Twp. 105, Lyman Cnty, SD 1900 Census ED 43 Sh 1B.*
3787. *Earling, Lyman Cnty, SD 1910 Census ED 52 Sh 5A.*
3788. *Earling, Lyman Cnty, SD 1920 Census ED 127 Sh 13A.*
3789. *Earling, Lyman Cnty, SD 1910 Census ED 52 Sh 5A.*
3790. *South Dakota Births 1856-1903,* "Electronic."
3791. *Minnesota Death Index 1908-2002,* "Electronic."
3792. *South Dakota Marriage Certificate 90940 Stanley County, SD*, "Electronic."
3793. *Earling, Lyman Cnty, SD 1910 Census ED 52 Sh 5A.*
3794. *Earling, Lyman Cnty, SD 1920 Census ED 127 Sh 13A.*
3795. *Earling, Lyman Cnty, SD 1910 Census ED 52 Sh 5A.*
3796. *Rayne Twp., Indiana Cnty, PA 1920 Census ED 125 Sh 3B.*
3797. "Andrew G. Van Horn Obituary."
3798. "Oran Dent Van Horn Obituary Indiana County Genealogical and Historical Society Newspaper Clippings."
3799. "Mary Juart Van Horn Obituary Indiana County Genealogical and Historical Society Newspaper Clippings."
3800. *South Mahoning Twp., Indiana Cnty, PA 1880 Census ED 143 Sh 28.*
3801. *Marion Center, East Mahoning Twp., Indiana Cnty, PA 1910 Census ED 73 Sh 12B.*
3802. *WWI Draft Registration Card 1917-1918,* "Electronic."
3803. "25 Aug, 1921 Indiana Weekly Messenger(Indiana, PA) Harvey Van Horn Obit."
3804. *South Mahoning Twp., Indiana Cnty, PA 1900 Census ED 64 Sh 10 B&11 A.*
3805. *South Mahoning Twp., Indiana Cnty, PA 1900 Census ED 64 Sh 10B.*

3806. *Rayne Twp., Indiana Cnty, PA 1920 Census ED 125 Sh 3B.*
3807. "Andrew G. Van Horn Obituary."
3808. "Oran Dent Van Horn Obituary Indiana County Genealogical and Historical Society Newspaper Clippings."
3809. "Mary Juart Van Horn Obituary Indiana County Genealogical and Historical Society Newspaper Clippings."
3810. *Marion Center, East Mahoning Twp., Indiana Cnty, PA 1910 Census ED 73 Sh 12B.*
3811. "Calvn Austin Juart Obit 21 July 1937 Indiana Progress(Indiana, PA)."
3812. *South Mahoning Twp., Indiana Cnty, PA 1900 Census ED 64 Sh 10 B&11 A.*
3813. *South Mahoning Twp., Indiana Cnty, PA 1900 Census ED 64 Sh 11A.*
3814. "Oran Dent Van Horn Obituary Indiana County Genealogical and Historical Society Newspaper Clippings."
3815. "Mary Juart Van Horn Obituary Indiana County Genealogical and Historical Society Newspaper Clippings."
3816. *Marion Center, East Mahoning Twp., Indiana Cnty, PA 1910 Census ED 73 Sh 12B.*
3817. *Rayne Twp., Indiana Cnty, PA 1920 Census ED 125 Sh 3B.*
3818. *Meyersdale, Somerset Cnty, PA 1930 Census ED 31 Sh 7B.*
3819. *Rayne Twp., Indiana Cnty, PA 1920 Census ED 125 Sh 3B.*
3820. *Meyersdale, Somerset Cnty, PA 1930 Census ED 31 Sh 7B.*
3821. *Pennsylvania Veterans Burial Cards 1777-1999*, "Electronic."
3822. "Oran Dent Van Horn Obituary Indiana County Genealogical and Historical Society Newspaper Clippings."
3823. *Marion Center, East Mahoning Twp., Indiana Cnty, PA 1930 Census ED 36 Sh 5A.*
3824. *Marion Center, East Mahoning Twp., Indiana Cnty, PA 1910 Census ED 73 Sh 13A.*
3825. *East Mahoning Twp., Indiana Cnty, PA 1920 Census ED 108 Sh 8A.*
3826. *Marion Center, East Mahoning Twp., Indiana Cnty, PA 1900 Census ED 53 Sh 10A.*
3827. "25 Aug, 1921 Indiana Weekly Messenger(Indiana, PA) Harvey Van Horn Obit."
3828. *Marion Center, East Mahoning Twp., Indiana Cnty, PA 1910 Census ED 73 Sh 13A.*
3829. WWI Civilian Draft Registration Index.
3830. *East Mahoning Twp., Indiana Cnty, PA 1920 Census ED 108 Sh 8A.*
3831. "Charles Blaine Van Horn Obituary Indiana County Genealogical and Historical Society Newspaper Clippings."
3832. "Oran Dent Van Horn Obituary Indiana County Genealogical and Historical Society Newspaper Clippings."
3833. *Washington Twp., Indiana Cnty, PA 1920 Census ED 129 Sh 8B.*
3834. *White Twp., Indiana Cnty, PA 1930 Census ED 52 Sh 12A.*
3835. *Marion Center, East Mahoning Twp., Indiana Cnty, PA 1900 Census ED 53 Sh 10A.*
3836. *Washington Twp., Indiana Cnty, PA 1920 Census ED 129 Sh 8B.*
3837. "Charles Blaine Van Horn Obituary Indiana County Genealogical and Historical Society Newspaper Clippings."
3838. *Washington Twp., Indiana Cnty, PA 1920 Census ED 129 Sh 8B.*
3839. *White Twp., Indiana Cnty, PA 1930 Census ED 52 Sh 12A.*
3840. *Washington Twp., Indiana Cnty, PA 1920 Census ED 129 Sh 8B.*
3841. *White Twp., Indiana Cnty, PA 1930 Census ED 52 Sh 12A.*
3842. "Park Van Horn Obituary Indiana County Genealogical and Historical Society Newspaper Clippings."
3843. "Charles Blaine Van Horn Obituary Indiana County Genealogical and Historical Society Newspaper Clippings."
3844. *Marion Center, East Mahoning Twp., Indiana Cnty, PA 1910 Census ED 73 Sh 13A.*
3845. *Plumville, South Mahoning Twp., Indiana Cnty, PA 1930 Census ED 42 Sh 1A.*
3846. *Rayne Twp., Indiana Cnty, PA 1920 Census ED 125 Sh 3B.*
3847. *Marion Center, East Mahoning Twp., Indiana Cnty, PA 1900 Census ED 53 Sh 10A.*
3848. "25 Aug, 1921 Indiana Weekly Messenger(Indiana, PA) Harvey Van Horn Obit."
3849. *Marion Center, East Mahoning Twp., Indiana Cnty, PA 1910 Census ED 73 Sh 13A.*

3850. "Charles Blaine Van Horn Obituary Indiana County Genealogical and Historical Society Newspaper Clippings."
3851. *Plumville, South Mahoning Twp., Indiana Cnty, PA 1930 Census ED 42 Sh 1A.*
3852. *Rayne, Indiana Cnty, PA 1920 Census ED 125 Sh A.*
3853. "Indiana Weekly Messenger (Indiana, PA) 19 June 1919."
3854. *Plumville, South Mahoning Twp., Indiana Cnty, PA 1930 Census ED 42 Sh 1A.*
3855. "Indiana Weekly Messenger (Indiana, PA) 19 June 1919."
3856. D. Scott Van Horn Family Group Sheet, August 8, 1983.
3857. *East Mahoning Twp., Indiana Cnty, PA 1880 Census ED 145 Sh 20.*
3858. *South Mahoning Twp., Indiana Cnty, PA 1900 Census ED 64 Sh 3A.*
3859. *Youngstown, Mahoning Cnty, OH 1920 Census ED 78 Sh 20B.*
3860. D. Scott Van Horn Family Group Sheet, August 8, 1983.
3861. *East Mahoning Twp., Indiana Cnty, PA 1880 Census ED 145 Sh 20.*
3862. D. Scott Van Horn Family Group Sheet, August 8, 1983.
3863. "LeRoy Van Horn Obituary Indiana County Genealogical and Historical Society Newspaper Clippings."
3864. "Indiana Evening Gazette (Indiana, PA) 17 February 1954."
3865. D. Scott Van Horn Family Group Sheet, August 8, 1983.
3866. "LeRoy Van Horn Obituary Indiana County Genealogical and Historical Society Newspaper Clippings."
3867. *Youngstown, Mahoning Cnty, OH 1920 Census ED 78 Sh 20B.*
3868. D. Scott Van Horn Family Group Sheet, August 8, 1983.
3869. "Sprague L. Van Horn Obituary Indiana County Genealogical and Historical Society Newspaper Clippings."
3870. *Ambridge, Beaver Cnty, PA 1930 Census ED 18 Sh 8A.*
3871. *East Mahoning Twp., Indiana Cnty, PA 1880 Census ED 145 Sh 20.*
3872. *South Mahoning Twp., Indiana Cnty, PA 1900 Census ED 64 Sh 3A.*
3873. "Sprague L. Van Horn Obituary Indiana County Genealogical and Historical Society Newspaper Clippings."
3874. *East Mahoning Twp., Indiana Cnty, PA 1880 Census ED 145 Sh 20.*
3875. "Sprague L. Van Horn Obituary Indiana County Genealogical and Historical Society Newspaper Clippings."
3876. "Indiana Progress (Indiana Cnty, PA)."
3877. *Ambridge, Beaver Cnty, PA 1930 Census ED 18 Sh 8A.*
3878. "Indiana Progress (Indiana Cnty, PA)."
3879. "LeRoy Van Horn Obituary Indiana County Genealogical and Historical Society Newspaper Clippings."
3880. *South Mahoning Twp., Indiana Cnty, PA 1900 Census ED 64 Sh 3A.*
3881. *South Mahoning Twp., Indiana Cnty, PA 1910 Census ED 93 Sh 2A.*
3882. "LeRoy Van Horn Obituary Indiana County Genealogical and Historical Society Newspaper Clippings."
3883. *SSN Death Index at Ancestry.com*, "Electronic."
3884. DAR National Record Copy of Member Application # 835192.
3885. "Indiana Progress (Indiana Cnty, PA) 22 August 1906."
3886. *South Mahoning Twp., Indiana Cnty, PA 1910 Census ED 92 Sh 4A.*
3887. "LeRoy Van Horn Obituary Indiana County Genealogical and Historical Society Newspaper Clippings."
3888. *South Mahoning Twp., Indiana Cnty, PA 1900 Census ED 64 Sh 3A.*
3889. WWI Civilian Draft Registration Index.
3890. *Aliquippa, Beaver Cnty, PA 1930 Census ED 13 Sh 29B.*
3891. *Aliquippa, Beaver Cnty, PA 1920 Census ED 1 Sh 12A.*
3892. "13 Jan 1965 Indiana Evening Gazette (Indiana, PA) George Percy Van Horn Obit."
3893. WWI Civilian Draft Registration Index.
3894. *WWII Civilian Draft Registration*, "Electronic."

3895. "13 Jan 1965 Indiana Evening Gazette (Indiana, PA) George Percy Van Horn Obit."

3896. *Aliquippa, Beaver Cnty, PA 1930 Census ED 8 Sh 1A.*

3897. *Aliquippa, Beaver Cnty, PA 1920 Census ED 1 Sh 12A.*

3898. "LeRoy Van Horn Obituary Indiana County Genealogical and Historical Society Newspaper Clippings."

3899. *Homer, Indiana Cnty, PA 1920 Census ED 112 Sh 13B.*

3900. *South Mahoning Twp., Indiana Cnty, PA 1910 Census ED 93 Sh 2A.*

3901. *South Mahoning Twp., Indiana Cnty, PA 1900 Census ED 64 Sh 3A.*

3902. "Indiana Progress (Indiana Cnty, PA) 5 March 1913."

3903. *Homer, Indiana Cnty, PA 1930 Census ED 30 Sh 14B.*

3904. Delayed Birth Certificate Indiana Cnty, PA.

3905. "LeRoy Van Horn Obituary Indiana County Genealogical and Historical Society Newspaper Clippings."

3906. *Homer, Indiana Cnty, PA 1920 Census ED 112 Sh 13B.*

3907. "Indiana Progress (Indiana Cnty, PA) 5 March 1913."

3908. *Homer, Indiana Cnty, PA 1930 Census ED 30 Sh 14B.*

3909. "Indiana Progress (Indiana Cnty, PA) 5 March 1913."

3910. *Homer, Indiana Cnty, PA 1920 Census ED 112 Sh 13B.*

3911. "Indiana Progress (Indiana Cnty, PA) 5 March 1913."

3912. "LeRoy Van Horn Obituary Indiana County Genealogical and Historical Society Newspaper Clippings."

3913. *Akron, Summit Cnty, OH 1920 Census ED 147 Sh 10B.*

3914. *South Mahoning Twp., Indiana Cnty, PA 1910 Census ED 93 Sh 2A.*

3915. *South Mahoning Twp., Indiana Cnty, PA 1900 Census ED 64 Sh 3A.*

3916. *Akron, Summit Cnty, OH 1930 Census ED 23 Sh 20B.*

3917. *Akron, Summit Cnty, OH 1920 Census ED 147 Sh 10B.*

3918. "LeRoy Van Horn Obituary Indiana County Genealogical and Historical Society Newspaper Clippings."

3919. *Akron, Summit Cnty, OH 1920 Census ED 147 Sh 10B.*

3920. *Akron, Summit Cnty, OH 1930 Census ED 23 Sh 20B.*

3921. "Indiana Weekly Messenger (Indiana, PA) 26 April 1916."

3922. *Akron, Summit Cnty, OH 1920 Census ED 147 Sh 10B.*

3923. "Indiana Weekly Messenger (Indiana, PA) 26 April 1916."

3924. "LeRoy Van Horn Obituary Indiana County Genealogical and Historical Society Newspaper Clippings."

3925. *South Mahoning Twp., Indiana Cnty, PA 1910 Census ED 93 Sh 2A.*

3926. *South Mahoning Twp., Indiana Cnty, PA 1900 Census ED 64 Sh 3A.*

3927. *Akron, Summit Cnty, OH 1920 Census ED 147 Sh 10B.*

3928. *Aliquippa, Beaver Cnty, PA 1930 Census ED 1 Sh 44B.*

3929. *South Mahoning Twp., Indiana Cnty, PA 1910 Census ED 93 Sh 2A.*

3930. *Aliquippa, Beaver Cnty, PA 1930 Census ED 1 Sh 44B.*

3931. *Cowanshannock Twp., Armstrong Cnty, PA 1900 Census ED 3 Sh 3A.*

3932. *Chino, San Bernardino Cnty, CA 1930 Census ED 11 Sh 1A.*

3933. *Cowanshannock Twp., Armstrong Cnty, PA 1900 Census ED 3 Sh 3A.*

3934. *Chino, San Bernardino Cnty, CA 1930 Census ED 11 Sh 1A.*

3935. *Cowanshannock Twp., Armstrong Cnty, PA 1900 Census ED 3 Sh 3A.*

3936. *Cowanshannock Twp., Armstrong Cnty, PA 1910 Census ED 9 Sh 7A.*

3937. "Indiana Evening Gazette (Indiana, PA) 2 April 1960."

3938. *Cowanshannock Twp., Armstrong Cnty, PA 1930 Census ED 11 Sh 2B.*

3939. "2 April 1960 Simpson's Leader-Times (Kittanning, PA) Bertha A. Lukehart Neal Obituary."

3940. *Cowanshannock Twp., Armstrong Cnty, PA 1900 Census ED 3 Sh 3A.*

3941. "2 April 1960 Simpson's Leader-Times (Kittanning, PA) Bertha A. Lukehart Neal Obituary."

3942. "Indiana Evening Gazette (Indiana, PA) 2 April 1960."

3943. *Cowanshannock Twp., Armstrong Cnty, PA 1910 Census ED 9 Sh 7A.*

3944. *Cowanshannock Twp., Armstrong Cnty, PA 1930 Census ED 11 Sh 2B.*
3945. "2 April 1960 Simpson's Leader-Times (Kittanning, PA) Bertha A. Lukehart Neal Obituary."
3946. *Cowanshannock Twp., Armstrong Cnty, PA 1910 Census ED 9 Sh 7A.*
3947. "Indiana Evening Gazette (Indiana, PA) 2 April 1960."
3948. "2 April 1960 Simpson's Leader-Times (Kittanning, PA) Bertha A. Lukehart Neal Obituary."
3949. *Cowanshannock Twp., Armstrong Cnty, PA 1910 Census ED 9 Sh 7A.*
3950. "Indiana Evening Gazette (Indiana, PA) 2 April 1960."
3951. "2 April 1960 Simpson's Leader-Times (Kittanning, PA) Bertha A. Lukehart Neal Obituary."
3952. *Cowanshannock Twp., Armstrong Cnty, PA 1910 Census ED 9 Sh 7A.*
3953. "2 April 1960 Simpson's Leader-Times (Kittanning, PA) Bertha A. Lukehart Neal Obituary."
3954. *Cowanshannock Twp., Armstrong Cnty, PA 1910 Census ED 9 Sh 7A.*
3955. *Cowanshannock Twp., Armstrong Cnty, PA 1930 Census ED 11 Sh 2B.*
3956. "2 April 1960 Simpson's Leader-Times (Kittanning, PA) Bertha A. Lukehart Neal Obituary."
3957. *Cowanshannock Twp., Armstrong Cnty, PA 1910 Census ED 9 Sh 7A.*
3958. "2 April 1960 Simpson's Leader-Times (Kittanning, PA) Bertha A. Lukehart Neal Obituary."
3959. *Cowanshannock Twp., Armstrong Cnty, PA 1900 Census ED 3 Sh 3A.*
3960. *Cowanshannock Twp., Armstrong Cnty, PA 1910 Census ED 9 Sh 7A.*
3961. *Wayne Twp., Armstrong Cnty, PA 1930 Census ED 52 Sh 2A.*
3962. *Cowanshannock Twp., Armstrong Cnty, PA 1900 Census ED 3 Sh 3A.*
3963. *Wayne Twp., Armstrong Cnty, PA 1930 Census ED 52 Sh 2A.*
3964. *Wayne Twp., Armstrong Cnty, PA 1870 Census p. 535.*
3965. *Porter Twp., Jefferson Cnty, PA 1880 Census ED 197 Sh 191A.*
3966. *West Millville, Clarion Cnty, PA 1900 Census ED 22 Sh 12B.*
3967. *Hawthorn, Clarion Cnty, PA 1910 Census ED 25 Sh 1A.*
3968. *Hawthorn, Clarion Cnty, PA 1920 Census ED 65 Sh 8A.*
3969. "19 June 1976 The Oil City Derrick (Oil City, PA) Obituary of Lula VanHorn."
3970. *Wayne Twp., Armstrong Cnty, PA 1870 Census p. 535.*
3971. *Hawthorn, Clarion Cnty, PA 1930 Census ED 13 Sh 2B.*
3972. *West Millville, Clarion Cnty, PA 1900 Census ED 22 Sh 12B.*
3973. *Hawthorn, Clarion Cnty, PA 1910 Census ED 25 Sh 1A.*
3974. *Hawthorn, Clarion Cnty, PA 1920 Census ED 65 Sh 8A.*
3975. *Hawthorn, Clarion Cnty, PA 1930 Census ED 13 Sh 2B.*
3976. "19 June 1976 The Oil City Derrick (Oil City, PA) Obituary of Lula VanHorn."
3977. *West Millville, Clarion Cnty, PA 1900 Census ED 22 Sh 12B.*
3978. *Hawthorn, Clarion Cnty, PA 1910 Census ED 25 Sh 6B.*
3979. *West Millville, Clarion Cnty, PA 1900 Census ED 22 Sh 12B.*
3980. WWI Civilian Draft Registration Index.
3981. "19 June 1976 The Oil City Derrick (Oil City, PA) Obituary of Lula VanHorn."
3982. *Hawthorn, Clarion Cnty, PA 1910 Census ED 25 Sh 6B.*
3983. *West Millville, Clarion Cnty, PA 1900 Census ED 22 Sh 12B.*
3984. *Hawthorn, Clarion Cnty, PA 1910 Census ED 25 Sh 1A.*
3985. *Hawthorn, Clarion Cnty, PA 1920 Census ED 65 Sh 8A.*
3986. *Hawthorn, Clarion Cnty, PA 1930 Census ED 13 Sh 2B.*
3987. *West Millville, Clarion Cnty, PA 1900 Census ED 22 Sh 12B.*
3988. *WWI Draft Registration Card 1917-1918*, "Electronic."
3989. "19 June 1976 The Oil City Derrick (Oil City, PA) Obituary of Lula VanHorn."
3990. *Porter Twp., Jefferson Cnty, PA 1880 Census ED 197 Sh 191A.*
3991. *Kingsley Twp., Forest Cnty, PA 1910 Census ED 60 Sh 8B.*
3992. *Wetmore, McKean Cnty, PA 1900 Census ED 125 Sh 9A.*
3993. *Porter Twp., Jefferson Cnty, PA 1880 Census ED 197 Sh 191A.*
3994. *Kingsley Twp., Forest Cnty, PA 1910 Census ED 60 Sh 8B.*
3995. *Wetmore, McKean Cnty, PA 1900 Census ED 125 Sh 9A.*
3996. *Kingsley Twp., Forest Cnty, PA 1910 Census ED 60 Sh 8B.*
3997. *Wetmore, McKean Cnty, PA 1900 Census ED 125 Sh 9A.*

3998. *Kingsley Twp., Forest Cnty, PA 1910 Census ED 60 Sh 8B.*
3999. *Wetmore, McKean Cnty, PA 1900 Census ED 125 Sh 9A.*
4000. *Kingsley Twp., Forest Cnty, PA 1910 Census ED 60 Sh 8B.*
4001. *Wetmore, McKean Cnty, PA 1900 Census ED 125 Sh 9A.*
4002. *Kingsley Twp., Forest Cnty, PA 1910 Census ED 60 Sh 8B.*
4003. *Wetmore, McKean Cnty, PA 1900 Census ED 125 Sh 9A.*
4004. *Kingsley Twp., Forest Cnty, PA 1910 Census ED 60 Sh 8B.*
4005. *Wetmore, McKean Cnty, PA 1900 Census ED 125 Sh 9A.*
4006. *Kingsley Twp., Forest Cnty, PA 1910 Census ED 60 Sh 8B.*
4007. *Wetmore, McKean Cnty, PA 1900 Census ED 125 Sh 9A.*
4008. *Kingsley Twp., Forest Cnty, PA 1910 Census ED 60 Sh 8B.*
4009. *Sandy, Clearfield Cnty, PA 1930 Census ED 64 Sh 7A.*
4010. *Troutville, Clearfield Cnty, PA 1900 Census ED 55 Sh 9B.*
4011. *Luthersburg Pct., Brady Twp., Clearfield Cnty, PA 1910 Census ED 55 Sh 12A.*
4012. *Falls Creek, Jefferson Cnty, PA 1920 Census ED 146 Sh 1A.*
4013. Sandy Ruppell Genforum Posting 12/2/1998 Robert the American Imigrant.
4014. *Sandy, Clearfield Cnty, PA 1930 Census ED 64 Sh 7A.*
4015. *Troutville, Clearfield Cnty, PA 1900 Census ED 55 Sh 9B.*
4016. *Luthersburg Pct., Brady Twp., Clearfield Cnty, PA 1910 Census ED 55 Sh 12A.*
4017. *Falls Creek, Jefferson Cnty, PA 1920 Census ED 146 Sh 1A.*
4018. *Luthersburg Pct., Brady Twp., Clearfield Cnty, PA 1910 Census ED 55 Sh 12A.*
4019. *Sandy, Clearfield Cnty, PA 1930 Census ED 64 Sh 7A.*
4020. *Luthersburg Pct., Brady Twp., Clearfield Cnty, PA 1910 Census ED 55 Sh 12A.*
4021. *Troutville, Clearfield Cnty, PA 1900 Census ED 55 Sh 9B.*
4022. *Luthersburg Pct., Brady Twp., Clearfield Cnty, PA 1910 Census ED 55 Sh 12A.*
4023. *Troutville, Clearfield Cnty, PA 1900 Census ED 55 Sh 9B.*
4024. *Luthersburg Pct., Brady Twp., Clearfield Cnty, PA 1910 Census ED 55 Sh 12A.*
4025. *Falls Creek, Jefferson Cnty, PA 1920 Census ED 146 Sh 1A.*
4026. *Luthersburg Pct., Brady Twp., Clearfield Cnty, PA 1910 Census ED 55 Sh 12A.*
4027. *Falls Creek, Jefferson Cnty, PA 1920 Census ED 146 Sh 1A.*
4028. *Luthersburg Pct., Brady Twp., Clearfield Cnty, PA 1910 Census ED 55 Sh 12A.*
4029. *Falls Creek, Jefferson Cnty, PA ED 146 Sh 1A.*
4030. *Falls Creek, Jefferson Cnty, PA 1920 Census ED 146 Sh 1A.*
4031. *Luthersburg Pct., Brady Twp., Clearfield Cnty, PA 1910 Census ED 55 Sh 12A.*
4032. *Falls Creek, Jefferson Cnty, PA 1920 Census ED 146 Sh 1A.*
4033. *Luthersburg Pct., Brady Twp., Clearfield Cnty, PA 1910 Census ED 55 Sh 12A.*
4034. *Falls Creek, Jefferson Cnty, PA 1920 Census ED 146 Sh 1A.*
4035. *Luthersburg Pct., Brady Twp., Clearfield Cnty, PA 1910 Census ED 55 Sh 12A.*
4036. *Falls Creek, Jefferson Cnty, PA 1920 Census ED 146 Sh 1A.*
4037. *Luthersburg Pct., Brady Twp., Clearfield Cnty, PA 1910 Census ED 55 Sh 12A.*
4038. *Troutville Pct., Brady Twp., Clearfield Cnty, PA 1900 Census ED 55 Sh 7B.*
4039. *Dayton, Armstrong Cnty, PA 1920 Census ED 12 Sh 6A.*
4040. *Plumville, South Mahoning Twp., Indiana Cnty, PA 1910 Census ED 92 Sh 1A.*
4041. *Dayton, Armstrong Cnty, PA 1930 Census ED 13 Sh 4B.*
4042. *Troutville Pct., Brady Twp., Clearfield Cnty, PA 1900 Census ED 55 Sh 7B.*
4043. *South Mahoning Twp., Indiana Cnty, PA 1910 Census ED 92 Sh 1A.*
4044. *Dayton, Armstrong Cnty, PA 1920 Census ED 12 Sh 6A.*
4045. *Plumville, South Mahoning, Indiana Cnty, PA 1910 Census ED 92 Sh 1A.*
4046. *Dayton, Armstrong Cnty, PA 1930 Census ED 13 Sh 4B.*
4047. *Marion, Indiana Cnty, PA 1880 Census ED 146 Sh 348C.*
4048. WWI Civilian Draft Registration Index.
4049. *South Mahoning Twp., Indiana Cnty, PA 1910 Census ED 92 Sh 1A.*
4050. *Dayton, Armstrong Cnty, PA 1920 Census ED 12 Sh 6A.*
4051. WWI Civilian Draft Registration Index.

4052. *South Mahoning Twp., Indiana Cnty, PA 1910 Census ED 92 Sh 1A.*
4053. *Dayton, Armstrong Cnty, PA 1920 Census ED 12 Sh 6A.*
4054. *Dayton, Armstrong Cnty, PA 1930 Census ED 13 Sh 4B.*
4055. "12 Feb 1913 Indiana Progress (Indiana, PA) birth announcemet of the birth of twins last week to William Gearhart."
4056. "6 Jan 1937 Indiana Progress (Indiana, PA) Wedding Announcement of Marriage of L M Gearhart to A J DeHaven."
4057. *Dayton, Armstrong Cnty, PA 1920 Census ED 12 Sh 6A.*
4058. "6 Jan 1937 Indiana Progress (Indiana, PA) Wedding Announcement of Marriage of L M Gearhart to A J DeHaven."
4059. *Dayton, Armstrong Cnty, PA 1930 Census ED 13 Sh 4B.*
4060. SSN Death Index.
4061. *Troutville Pct., Brady Twp., Clearfield Cnty, PA 1900 Census ED 55 Sh 7B.*
4062. *Luthersburg Pct., Brady Twp., Clearfield Cnty, PA 1910 Census ED 55 Sh 12A.*
4063. *DuBois, Clearfield Cnty, PA 1920 Census ED 84 Sh 16A.*
4064. *DuBois, Clearfield Cnty, PA 1930 Census ED 29 Sh 4B.*
4065. *Troutville Pct., Brady Twp., Clearfield Cnty, PA 1900 Census ED 55 Sh 7D.*
4066. *DuBois, Clearfield Cnty, PA 1920 Census ED 84 Sh 16A.*
4067. *DuBois, Clearfield Cnty, PA 1930 Census ED 29 Sh 4B.*
4068. *Luthersburg Pct., Brady Twp., Clearfield Cnty, PA 1910 Census ED 55 Sh 12A.*
4069. *DuBois, Clearfield Cnty, PA 1930 Census ED 29 Sh 4B.*
4070. *DuBois, Clearfield Cnty, PA 1920 Census ED 84 Sh 16A.*
4071. *Luthersburg Pct., Brady Twp., Clearfield Cnty, PA 1910 Census ED 55 Sh 12A.*
4072. *DuBois, Clearfield Cnty, PA 1930 Census ED 29 Sh 4B.*
4073. *Luthersburg Pct., Brady Twp., Clearfield Cnty, PA 1910 Census ED 55 Sh 12A.*
4074. *DuBois, Clearfield Cnty, PA 1920 Census ED 84 Sh 16A.*
4075. *DuBois, Clearfield Cnty, PA 1930 Census ED 29 Sh 4B.*
4076. *Luthersburg Pct., Brady Twp., Clearfield Cnty, PA 1910 Census ED 55 Sh 12A.*
4077. *DuBois, Clearfield Cnty, PA 1920 Census ED 84 Sh 16A.*
4078. *DuBois, Clearfield Cnty, PA 1930 Census ED 29 Sh 4B.*
4079. *DuBois, Clearfield Cnty, PA 1920 Census ED 84 Sh 16A.*
4080. *Falls Creek, Jefferson Cnty, PA 1920 Census ED 146 Sh 1A.*
4081. *Canoe Twp., Indiana Cnty, PA 1930 Census ED 13 Sh 20 A&B.*
4082. *Troutville Pct., Brady Twp., Clearfield Cnty, PA 1900 Census ED 55 Sh 7B.*
4083. *Luthersburg Pct., Brady Twp., Clearfield Cnty, PA 1910 Census ED 55 Sh 12A.*
4084. *Falls Creek, Jefferson Cnty, PA 1920 Census ED 146 Sh 1A.*
4085. *Troutville Pct., Brady Twp., Clearfield Cnty, PA 1900 Census ED 55 Sh 7B.*
4086. *WWII Civilian Draft Registration,* "Electronic."
4087. *Falls Creek, Jefferson Cnty, PA 1920 Census ED 146 Sh 1A.*
4088. *Canoe Twp., Indiana Cnty, PA 1930 Census ED 13 Sh 20 A&B.*
4089. "2 November 1971 The Progress (Clearfield, PA) Presley Marsh Obituary."
4090. *Falls Creek, Jefferson Cnty, PA 1920 Census ED 146 Sh 1A.*
4091. *Canoe Twp., Indiana Cnty, PA 1930 Census ED 13 Sh 20 A&B.*
4092. *Falls Creek, Jefferson Cnty, PA 1920 Census ED 146 Sh 1A.*
4093. *Falls Creek, Jefferson Cnty, PA 1920 Census ED 146 Sh 4b.*
4094. *Canoe Twp., Indiana Cnty, PA 1930 Census ED 13 Sh 20 A&B.*
4095. *Troutville Pct., Brady Twp., Clearfield Cnty, PA 1900 Census ED 55 Sh 7B.*
4096. *Luthersburg Pct., Brady Twp., Clearfield Cnty, PA 1910 Census ED 55 Sh 12A.*
4097. *WWI Draft Registration Card 1917-1918,* "Electronic."
4098. *Troutville Pct., Brady Twp., Clearfield Cnty, PA 1900 Census ED 55 Sh 7B.*
4099. *Canoe Twp., Indiana Cnty, PA 1930 Census ED 13 Sh 20 A&B.*
4100. *Falls Creek, Jefferson Cnty, PA 1920 Census ED 146 Sh 4b.*
4101. *Canoe Twp., Indiana Cnty, PA 1930 Census ED 13 Sh 20 A&B.*
4102. *Falls Creek, Jefferson Cnty, PA 1920 Census ED 146 Sh 1A.*

4103. *Troutville Pct., Brady Twp., Clearfield Cnty, PA 1900 Census ED 55 Sh 7B.*
4104. *Luthersburg Pct., Brady Twp., Clearfield Cnty, PA 1910 Census ED 55 Sh 12A.*
4105. *Sandy, Clearfield Cnty, PA 1930 Census ED 64 Sh 7A.*
4106. WWI Civilian Draft Registration Index.
4107. *Falls Creek, Jefferson Cnty, PA 1920 Census ED 146 Sh 1A.*
4108. *Troutville Pct., Brady Twp., Clearfield Cnty, PA 1900 Census ED 55 Sh 7B.*
4109. WWI Civilian Draft Registration Index.
4110. "2 May 1917 Clearfield Progress (Clearfield, PA) Marriage License."
4111. *Wayne Twp., Armstrong Cnty, PA 1900 Census ED 9 Sh 9B&10A.*
4112. *Wayne Twp., Armstrong Cnty, PA 1910 Census ED 49 Sh 7B.*
4113. *West Mahoning Twp., Indiana Cnty, PA 1920 Census ED 128 Sh 5A.*
4114. *Wayne Twp., Armstrong Cnty, PA 1900 Census ED 9 Sh 9B&10A.*
4115. *West Mahoning Twp., Indiana Cnty, PA 1920 Census ED 128 Sh 5A.*
4116. DAR National Record Copy of Member Application # 614578.
4117. *Punxsutawney, Jefferson Cnty, PA 1910 Census ED 82 Sh 32A.*
4118. *Punxsutawney, Jefferson Cnty, PA 1930 Census ED 24 Sh 12A.*
4119. *Punxsutawney, Jefferson Cnty, PA 1910 Census ED 82 Sh 32A.*
4120. *Punxsutawney, Jefferson Cnty, PA 1930 Census ED 24 Sh 12A.*
4121. *Wendell, Thomas Cnty, KS 1900 Census ED 179 Sh 6B.*
4122. *Northern Twp., Franklin Cnty, IL 1880 Censes ED 14 Sh 50/52D.*
4123. *Rexford, Smith Twp., Thomas Cnty, KS 1930 Census ED 12 Sh 3B.*
4124. *Wendell, Thomas Cnty, KS 1900 Census ED 179 Sh 6B.*
4125. *Rexford, Smith Twp., Thomas Cnty, KS 1930 Census ED 12 Sh 3B.*
4126. *Rexford, Smith Twp., Thomas Cnty, KS 1920 Census ED 232 Sh 3A.*
4127. *Rexford, Smith Twp., Thomas Cnty, KS 1930 Census ED 12 Sh 4A.*
4128. *Northern Twp., Franklin Cnty, IL 1880 Censes ED 14 Sh 50/52D.*
4129. *Rexford, Smith Twp., Thomas Cnty, KS 1920 Census ED 232 Sh 3A.*
4130. *Rexford, Smith Twp., Thomas Cnty, KS 1930 Census ED 12 Sh 4A.*
4131. *Rexford, Smith Twp., Thomas Cnty, KS 1920 Census ED 232 Sh 3A.*
4132. *Rexford, Smith Twp., Thomas Cnty, KS 1930 Census ED 12 Sh 4A.*
4133. *Dorothy M. McAfoos Miller Obituary reproduced in notes source unknow,* "Electronic."
4134. *Rexford, Smith Twp., Thomas Cnty, KS 1920 Census ED 232 Sh 3A.*
4135. *Dorothy M. McAfoos Miller Obituary reproduced in notes source unknow,* "Electronic."
4136. *Rexford, Smith Twp., Thomas Cnty, KS 1920 Census ED 232 Sh 3A.*
4137. *Rexford, Smith Twp., Thomas Cnty, KS 1930 Census ED 12 Sh 4A.*
4138. *Dorothy M. McAfoos Miller Obituary reproduced in notes source unknow,* "Electronic."
4139. *Rexford, Smith Twp., Thomas Cnty, KS 1920 Census ED 232 Sh 3A.*
4140. *Rexford, Smith Twp., Thomas Cnty, KS 1930 Census ED 12 Sh 4A.*
4141. *Dorothy M. McAfoos Miller Obituary reproduced in notes source unknow,* "Electronic."
4142. *Rexford, Smith Twp., Thomas Cnty, KS 1930 Census ED 12 Sh 4A.*
4143. *Dorothy M. McAfoos Miller Obituary reproduced in notes source unknow,* "Electronic."
4144. *Rexford, Smith Twp., Thomas Cnty, KS 1930 Census ED 12 Sh 4A.*
4145. *Dorothy M. McAfoos Miller Obituary reproduced in notes source unknow,* "Electronic."
4146. *Northern Twp., Franklin Cnty, IL 1880 Censes ED 14 Sh 50/52D.*
4147. Cook, Decatur Cnty, KS 1910 Census ED 9 Sh 5A.
4148. *Prairie Dog, Sheridan Cnty, KS 1920 Census ED 194 Sh 9B.*
4149. *Rexford, Smith Twp., Thomas Cnty, KS 1930 Census ED 12 Sh 1A.*
4150. Cook, Decatur Cnty, KS 1910 Census ED 9 Sh 5A.
4151. *Cook, Decatur Cnty, KS 1910 Census ED 9 Sh 5A .*
4152. *Prairie Dog, Sheridan Cnty, KS 1920 Census ED 194 Sh 9B.*
4153. *Rexford, Smith Twp., Thomas Cnty, KS 1930 Census ED 12 Sh 1A.*
4154. Cook, Decatur Cnty, KS 1910 Census ED 9 Sh 5A.
4155. *Rexford, Smith Twp., Thomas Cnty, KS 1930 Census ED 12 Sh 1A.*
4156. Cook, Decatur Cnty, KS 1910 Census ED 9 Sh 5A.

4157. WWI Civilian Draft Registration Index.
4158. Cook, Decatur Cnty, KS 1910 Census ED 9 Sh 5A.
4159. *Prairie Dog, Sheridan Cnty, KS 1920 Census ED 194 Sh 9B.*
4160. Cook, Decatur Cnty, KS 1910 Census ED 9 Sh 5A.
4161. *Prairie Dog, Sheridan Cnty, KS 1920 Census ED 194 Sh 9B.*
4162. Cook, Decatur Cnty, KS 1910 Census ED 9 Sh 5A.
4163. *Prairie Dog, Sheridan Cnty, KS 1920 Census ED 194 Sh 9B.*
4164. Cook, Decatur Cnty, KS 1910 Census ED 9 Sh 5A.
4165. *Prairie Dog, Sheridan Cnty, KS 1920 Census ED 194 Sh 9B.*
4166. *Wendell, Thomas Cnty, KS 1900 Census ED 179 Sh 6B.*
4167. *Wendell, Thomas Cnty, KS 1910 Census ED 216 Sh 7B.*
4168. *Wendell, Thomas Cnty, KS 1930 Census ED 16 Sh 3A.*
4169. *Wendell, Thomas Cnty, KS 1900 Census ED 179 Sh 6B.*
4170. *Wendell, Thomas Cnty, KS 1930 Census ED 16 Sh 3A.*
4171. *Wendell, Thomas Cnty, KS 1900 Census ED 179 Sh 6B.*
4172. *Wendell, Thomas Cnty, KS 1910 Census ED 216 Sh 7B.*
4173. *Rexford, Smith Twp., Thomas Cnty, KS 1930 Census ED 12 Sh 3B.*
4174. *Wendell, Thomas Cnty, KS 1900 Census ED 179 Sh 6B.*
4175. *Rexford, Smith Twp., Thomas Cnty, KS 1930 Census ED 12 Sh 3A.*
4176. *Rexford, Smith Twp., Thomas Cnty, KS 1930 Census ED 12 Sh 3B.*
4177. SSN Death Index.
4178. *Rexford, Smith Twp., Thomas Cnty, KS 1930 Census ED 12 Sh 3B.*
4179. *Northern, Franklin Cnty, IL 1900 Census ED 33 Sh 14A.*
4180. *Northern, Franklin Cnty, IL 1880 Census ED 14 Sh 527C.*
4181. *Northern Twp., Franklin Cnty, IL 1920 Censes ED 41 Sh 8A.*
4182. *Northern Twp., Franklin Cnty, IL 1930 Censes ED 34 Sh 5A&B.*
4183. *Northern, Franklin Cnty, IL 1900 Census ED 33 Sh 14A.*
4184. *Northern Twp., Franklin Cnty, IL 1920 Censes ED 41 Sh 8A.*
4185. *Northern Twp., Franklin Cnty, IL 1930 Censes ED 34 Sh 5A&B.*
4186. *Northern Twp., Franklin Cnty, IL 1920 Censes ED 41 Sh 8A.*
4187. *Northern Twp., Franklin Cnty, IL 1930 Censes ED 34 Sh 5A&B.*
4188. *Northern Twp., Franklin Cnty, IL 1920 Censes ED 41 Sh 8A.*
4189. *Northern Twp., Franklin Cnty, IL 1930 Censes ED 34 Sh 5A&B.*
4190. *Northern Twp., Franklin Cnty, IL 1920 Censes ED 41 Sh 8A.*
4191. *Northern Twp., Franklin Cnty, IL 1930 Censes ED 34 Sh 5A&B.*
4192. *Northern Twp., Franklin Cnty, IL 1920 Censes ED 41 Sh 8A.*
4193. *Northern Twp., Franklin Cnty, IL 1930 Censes ED 34 Sh 5A&B.*
4194. *Northern, Franklin Cnty, IL 1900 Census ED 33 Sh 14A.*
4195. *Northern Twp., Franklin Cnty, IL 1910 Censes ED 37 Sh 2A.*
4196. *Northern, Franklin Cnty, IL 1900 Census ED 33 Sh 14A.*
4197. *Northern, Franklin Cnty, IL 1900 Census ED 33 Sh 5A & B.*
4198. *Northern, Franklin Cnty, IL 1910 Census ED 37 Sh 19A.*
4199. *Moores Priarie, Jefferson Cnty, IL 1920 Census ED 126 Sh 7B.*
4200. *Northern, Franklin Cnty, IL 1900 Census ED 33 Sh 5A & B.*
4201. *Moores Priarie, Jefferson Cnty, IL 1920 Census ED 126 Sh 7B.*
4202. *Northern, Franklin Cnty, IL 1930 Census ED 34 Sh 8A,* "Electronic."
4203. *Northern, Franklin Cnty, IL 1900 Census ED 33 Sh 5A & B.*
4204. *Northern, Franklin Cnty, IL 1920 Census ED 41 Sh 11A.*
4205. *Northern, Franklin Cnty, IL 1910 Census ED 37 Sh 19A.*
4206. *Northern, Franklin Cnty, IL 1930 Census ED 34 Sh 8A,* "Electronic."
4207. SSN Death Index.
4208. *Northern, Franklin Cnty, IL 1930 Census ED 34 Sh 8A,* "Electronic."
4209. *Northern, Franklin Cnty, IL 1920 Census ED 41 Sh 11A.*
4210. *Northern, Franklin Cnty, IL 1930 Census ED 34 Sh 8A,* "Electronic."

4211. *Northern, Franklin Cnty, IL 1900 Census ED 33 Sh 5A & B.*
4212. *Northern, Franklin Cnty, IL 1910 Census ED 37 Sh 19A.*
4213. *Northern, Franklin Cnty, IL 1930 Census ED 34 Sh 2B.*
4214. *Northern, Franklin Cnty, IL 1900 Census ED 33 Sh 5A & B.*
4215. *Northern, Franklin Cnty, IL 1930 Census ED 34 Sh 2B.*
4216. *Punxsutawney, Jefferson Cnty, PA 1900 Census ED 73 Sh 23B.*
4217. "Anna Stafford Van Horn Obituary."
4218. *O'Hara Twp., Allegheny Cnty, PA 1910 Census ED 185 Sh 8A.*
4219. *O'Hara Twp., Allegheny Cnty, PA 1920 Census ED 297 Sh 20A.*
4220. *O'Hara Twp., Allegheny Cnty, PA 1930 Census ED 742 Sh 3B.*
4221. *O'Hara Twp., Allegheny Cnty, PA 1910 Census ED 185 Sh 8A.*
4222. *O'Hara Twp., Allegheny Cnty, PA 1920 Census ED 297 Sh 20A.*
4223. *O'Hara Twp., Allegheny Cnty, PA 1930 Census ED 742 Sh 3B.*
4224. *O'Hara Twp., Allegheny Cnty, PA 1920 Census ED 297 Sh 20A.*
4225. SSN Death Index.
4226. *O'Hara Twp., Allegheny Cnty, PA 1920 Census ED 297 Sh 20A.*
4227. *O'Hara Twp., Allegheny Cnty, PA 1930 Census ED 742 Sh 3B.*
4228. *O'Hara Twp., Allegheny Cnty, PA 1920 Census ED 297 Sh 20A.*
4229. SSN Death Index.
4230. *Aspinwall, Allegheny Cnty, PA 1930 Census ED 490 Sh 2B.*
4231. SSN Death Index.
4232. *O'Hara Twp., Allegheny Cnty, PA 1930 Census ED 742 Sh 3B.*
4233. *O'Hara Twp., Allegheny Cnty, PA 1910 Census ED 185 Sh 8A.*
4234. *O'Hara Twp., Allegheny Cnty, PA 1920 Census ED 297 Sh 20A.*
4235. *Aspinwall, Allegheny Cnty, PA 1930 Census ED 492 Sh 17B.*
4236. *O'Hara Twp., Allegheny Cnty, PA 1910 Census ED 185 Sh 8A.*
4237. SSN Death Index.
4238. *Aspinwall, Allegheny Cnty, PA 1930 Census ED 492 Sh 17B.*
4239. The Abridged Compendium of American Genealogy.
4240. *Glenfield, Allegheny Cnty, PA 1900 Census ED 391 Sh 3B .*
4241. *Pct. 5, Greenup Cnty, KY 1870 Census p. 50.*
4242. *Justice Pct. 4, Jim Wells Cnty, TX 1920 Census ED 112 Sh 6B.*
4243. *Glenfield, Allegheny Cnty, PA 1900 Census ED 391 Sh 3B .*
4244. *Pct. 1, Nueces Cnty, TX 1930 Census ED 11 Sh 23A.*
4245. *Justice Pct. 4, Jim Wells Cnty, TX 1920 Census ED 112 Sh 6B.*
4246. *The Abridged Compendium of American Genealogy Vol. II, Lineage records,, P. 236,* "Electronic."
4247. *Pct. 1, Nueces Cnty, TX 1930 Census ED 11 Sh 23A.*
4248. WWI Civilian Draft Registration Index.
4249. *Grant Twp., Indiana Cnty, PA 1900 Census ED 54 Sh 10B.*
4250. *Cherry Hill Twp., Indiana Cnty, PA 1920 Census ED 102 Sh 10A.*
4251. *Cherry Hill Twp., Indiana Cnty, PA 1910 Census ED 67 Sh 7A.*
4252. *Cherry Hill Twp., Indiana Cnty, PA 1920 Census ED 102 Sh 10A.*
4253. *Grant Twp., Indiana Cnty, PA 1900 Census ED 54 Sh 10B.*
4254. *Cherry Hill Twp., Indiana Cnty, PA 1910 Census ED 67 Sh 7A.*
4255. *Cherry Hill Twp., Indiana Cnty, PA 1920 Census ED 102 Sh 10A.*
4256. *Cherry Hill Twp., Indiana Cnty, PA 1910 Census ED 67 Sh 7A.*
4257. *Youngstown, Mahoning Cnty, OH 1930 Census ED 11 Sh 7A.*
4258. *Cherry Hill Twp., Indiana Cnty, PA 1920 Census ED 102 Sh 10A.*
4259. *Grant Twp., Indiana Cnty, PA 1900 Census ED 54 Sh 10B.*
4260. *Cherry Hill Twp., Indiana Cnty, PA 1930 Census ED 17 Sh 6A.*
4261. *Cherry Hill Twp., Indiana Cnty, PA 1920 Census ED 102 Sh 11A&B.*
4262. *Grant Twp., Indiana Cnty, PA 1900 Census ED 54 Sh 10B.*
4263. *Cherry Hill Twp., Indiana Cnty, PA 1930 Census ED 17 Sh 6A.*
4264. *Cherry Hill Twp., Indiana Cnty, PA 1920 Census ED 102 Sh 11A&B.*

4265. *Cherry Hill Twp., Indiana Cnty, PA 1930 Census ED 17 Sh 6A.*
4266. *Indiana County Marriage Records Book 12 Page 587 Lic #846.*
4267. *Cherry Hill Twp., Indiana Cnty, PA 1930 Census ED 17 Sh 6A.*
4268. *Indiana County Marriage Records Book 12 Page 587 Lic #846.*
4269. *Cherry Hill Twp., Indiana Cnty, PA 1930 Census ED 17 Sh 6A.*
4270. *Cherry Hill Twp., Indiana Cnty, PA 1920 Census ED 102 Sh 11A&B.*
4271. *Cherry Hill Twp., Indiana Cnty, PA 1930 Census ED 17 Sh 6A.*
4272. *Cherry Hill Twp., Indiana Cnty, PA 1920 Census ED 102 Sh 11A&B.*
4273. *Cherry Hill Twp., Indiana Cnty, PA 1930 Census ED 17 Sh 6B.*
4274. *Cherry Hill Twp., Indiana Cnty, PA 1920 Census ED 102 Sh 11A&B.*
4275. *Cherry Hill Twp., Indiana Cnty, PA 1930 Census ED 17 Sh 6B.*
4276. *Cherry Hill Twp., Indiana Cnty, PA 1920 Census ED 102 Sh 11A&B.*
4277. *Grant Twp., Indiana Cnty, PA 1900 Census ED 54 Sh 10B.*
4278. *Cherry Hill Twp., Indiana Cnty, PA 1910 Census ED 68 Sh 15B.*
4279. *Cherry Hill Twp., Indiana Cnty, PA 1920 Census ED 102 Sh 10A.*
4280. *Grant Twp., Indiana Cnty, PA 1900 Census ED 54 Sh 10B.*
4281. WWI Civilian Draft Registration Index.
4282. "Indiana Evening Gazette (Indiana, PA) Sylvia Harmon Lydic Obit."
4283. SSN Death Index.
4284. "Indiana Evening Gazette (Indiana, PA) Sylvia Harmon Lydic Obit."
4285. *WWI Darft Registration for James Robert Lambing*, "Electronic."
4286. *Rayne Twp., Indiana Cnty, PA 1900 Census ED 60 Sh 6A.*
4287. *Cheekside Twp., Indiana Cnty, PA 1910 Census ED 72 Sh 4A.*
4288. *Rayne Twp., Indiana Cnty, PA 1900 Census ED 60 Sh 6A.*
4289. *Cheekside Twp., Indiana Cnty, PA 1910 Census ED 72 Sh 4A.*
4290. *Rayne Twp., Indiana Cnty, PA 1900 Census ED 60 Sh 6A.*
4291. *Cheekside Twp., Indiana Cnty, PA 1910 Census ED 72 Sh 4A.*
4292. *Rayne Twp., Indiana Cnty, PA 1900 Census ED 60 Sh 6A.*
4293. *Cheekside Twp., Indiana Cnty, PA 1910 Census ED 72 Sh 4A.*
4294. *Grant Twp., Indiana Cnty, PA 1900 Census ED 54 Sh 4B.*
4295. *Grant Twp., Indiana Cnty, PA 1910 Census ED 76 Sh 5B&6A.*
4296. "2 Feb 1970 Indiana Evening Gazette (Indiana, PA) Harry I. Myers Obit."
4297. *Grant Twp., Indiana Cnty, PA 1900 Census ED 54 Sh 4B.*
4298. *Grant Twp., Indiana Cnty, PA 1910 Census ED 76 Sh 5B&6A.*
4299. *Cooperstown, Westmoreland Cnty, PA 1920 Census ED 85 Sh 1A.*
4300. *Grant Twp., Indiana Cnty, PA 1910 Census ED 76 Sh 5B&6A.*
4301. *Hempfield Twp., Westmoreland Cnty, PA 1930 Census ED 52 Sh 8B.*
4302. *Grant Twp., Indiana Cnty, PA 1900 Census ED 54 Sh 4B.*
4303. *Grant Twp., Indiana Cnty, PA 1910 Census ED 76 Sh 5B&6A.*
4304. *White Twp., Indiana Cnty, PA 1930 Census ED 53 Sh 6A.*
4305. *Green Twp., Indiana Cnty, PA 1920 Census ED 110 Sh 16A.*
4306. *White Twp., Indiana Cnty, PA 1920 Census ED 133 Sh 9A.*
4307. *White Twp., Indiana Cnty, PA 1930 Census ED 53 Sh 6A.*
4308. *Green Twp., Indiana Cnty, PA 1920 Census ED 110 Sh 16A.*
4309. *Cherry Hill Twp., Indiana Cnty, PA 1910 Census ED 67 Sh 10B.*
4310. *White Twp., Indiana Cnty, PA 1930 Census ED 53 Sh 6A.*
4311. "7 Aug 1964 Indiana Evening Gazette (Indiana, PA) Death Notice Myrtle Mae Mock."
4312. *Cherry Hill Twp., Indiana Cnty, PA 1910 Census ED 67 Sh 10B.*
4313. *Young Twp., Indiana Cnty, PA 1930 Census ED 55 Sh 6A.*
4314. "6 Dec 1969 Indiana Evening Gazette (Indiana, PA) Obit Mable Shnakle Wyland."
4315. "7 Aug 1964 Indiana Evening Gazette (Indiana, PA) Death Notice Myrtle Mae Mock."
4316. *Cherry Hill Twp., Indiana Cnty, PA 1910 Census ED 67 Sh 10B.*
4317. *Young Twp., Indiana Cnty, PA 1930 Census ED 55 Sh 6A.*
4318. *Cherry Hill Twp., Indiana Cnty, PA 1920 Census ED 102 Sh 11A&B.*

4319. "7 Aug 1964 Indiana Evening Gazette (Indiana, PA) Death Notice Myrtle Mae Mock."
4320. *Cherry Hill Twp., Indiana Cnty, PA 1930 Census ED 17 Sh 7A.*
4321. *Cherry Hill Twp., Indiana Cnty, PA 1920 Census ED 102 Sh 11A&B.*
4322. "6 Dec 1969 Indiana Evening Gazette (Indiana, PA) Obit Mable Shnakle Wyland."
4323. *Cherry Hill Twp., Indiana Cnty, PA 1920 Census ED 102 Sh 11A&B.*
4324. "6 Dec 1969 Indiana Evening Gazette (Indiana, PA) Obit Mable Shnakle Wyland."
4325. *Cherry Hill Twp., Indiana Cnty, PA 1930 Census ED 17 Sh 7A.*
4326. *Cherry Hill Twp., Indiana Cnty, PA 1920 Census ED 102 Sh 11A&B.*
4327. "6 Dec 1969 Indiana Evening Gazette (Indiana, PA) Obit Mable Shnakle Wyland."
4328. *Cherry Hill Twp., Indiana Cnty, PA 1920 Census ED 102 Sh 11A&B.*
4329. "6 Dec 1969 Indiana Evening Gazette (Indiana, PA) Obit Mable Shnakle Wyland."
4330. *Cherry Hill Twp., Indiana Cnty, PA 1920 Census ED 102 Sh 11A&B.*
4331. "6 Dec 1969 Indiana Evening Gazette (Indiana, PA) Obit Mable Shnakle Wyland."
4332. *Cherry Hill Twp., Indiana Cnty, PA 1920 Census ED 102 Sh 11A&B.*
4333. *Cherry Hill Twp., Indiana Cnty, PA 1930 Census ED 17 Sh 7A.*
4334. *Cherry Hill Twp., Indiana Cnty, PA 1920 Census ED 102 Sh 11A&B.*
4335. *Cherry Hill Twp., Indiana Cnty, PA 1930 Census ED 17 Sh 7A.*
4336. "6 Dec 1969 Indiana Evening Gazette (Indiana, PA) Obit Mable Shnakle Wyland."
4337. *Cherry Hill Twp., Indiana Cnty, PA 1930 Census ED 17 Sh 7A.*
4338. *Cherry Hill Twp., Indiana Cnty, PA 1920 Census ED 102 Sh 11A&B.*
4339. *Cherry Hill Twp., Indiana Cnty, PA 1930 Census ED 17 Sh 7A.*
4340. "6 Dec 1969 Indiana Evening Gazette (Indiana, PA) Obit Mable Shnakle Wyland."
4341. *Cherry Hill Twp., Indiana Cnty, PA 1930 Census ED 17 Sh 7A.*
4342. *Cherry Hill Twp., Indiana Cnty, PA 1910 Census ED 67 Sh 10B.*
4343. "7 Aug 1964 Indiana Evening Gazette (Indiana, PA) Death Notice Myrtle Mae Mock."
4344. *Penn, Westmoreland Cnty, PA 1930 Census ED 135 Sh 25B.*
4345. *Penn, Westmoreland Cnty, PA 1920 Census ED 192 Sh 5A.*
4346. *Cherry Hill Twp., Indiana Cnty, PA 1910 Census ED 67 Sh 10B.*
4347. "7 Aug 1964 Indiana Evening Gazette (Indiana, PA) Death Notice Myrtle Mae Mock."
4348. *Penn, Westmoreland Cnty, PA 1930 Census ED 135 Sh 25B.*
4349. *Center Twp., Indiana Cnty, PA 1880 Census ED 129 Sh 57A.*
4350. *Penn, Westmoreland Cnty, PA 1920 Census ED 192 Sh 5A.*
4351. *Penn, Westmoreland Cnty, PA 1930 Census ED 135 Sh 25B.*
4352. "7 Aug 1964 Indiana Evening Gazette (Indiana, PA) Death Notice Myrtle Mae Mock."
4353. *Penn, Westmoreland Cnty, PA 1930 Census ED 135 Sh 25B.*
4354. *Penn, Westmoreland Cnty, PA 1920 Census ED 192 Sh 5A.*
4355. *Penn, Westmoreland Cnty, PA 1930 Census ED 135 Sh 25B.*
4356. "7 Aug 1964 Indiana Evening Gazette (Indiana, PA) Death Notice Myrtle Mae Mock."
4357. *Penn, Westmoreland Cnty, PA 1930 Census ED 135 Sh 25B.*
4358. *Penn, Westmoreland Cnty, PA 1920 Census ED 192 Sh 5A.*
4359. *Penn, Westmoreland Cnty, PA 1930 Census ED 135 Sh 25B.*
4360. "7 Aug 1964 Indiana Evening Gazette (Indiana, PA) Death Notice Myrtle Mae Mock."
4361. *Penn, Westmoreland Cnty, PA 1930 Census ED 135 Sh 25B.*
4362. *Penn, Westmoreland Cnty, PA 1920 Census ED 192 Sh 5A.*
4363. *Penn, Westmoreland Cnty, PA 1930 Census ED 135 Sh 25B.*
4364. "7 Aug 1964 Indiana Evening Gazette (Indiana, PA) Death Notice Myrtle Mae Mock."
4365. *Penn, Westmoreland Cnty, PA 1930 Census ED 135 Sh 25B.*
4366. "7 Aug 1964 Indiana Evening Gazette (Indiana, PA) Death Notice Myrtle Mae Mock."
4367. *Penn, Westmoreland Cnty, PA 1930 Census ED 135 Sh 25B.*
4368. "7 Aug 1964 Indiana Evening Gazette (Indiana, PA) Death Notice Myrtle Mae Mock."
4369. *Cherry Hill Twp., Indiana Cnty, PA 1910 Census ED 67 Sh 10B.*
4370. *Kittanning, Armstrong Cnty, PA 1920 Census ED 29 Sh 9A.*
4371. *Center Twp., Indiana Cnty, PA 1930 Census ED 16 Sh 4B.*
4372. "6 Dec 1969 Indiana Evening Gazette (Indiana, PA) Obit Mable Shnakle Wyland."

4373. "7 Aug 1964 Indiana Evening Gazette (Indiana, PA) Death Notice Myrtle Mae Mock."
4374. *Cherry Hill Twp., Indiana Cnty, PA 1910 Census ED 67 Sh 10B.*
4375. *Kittanning, Armstrong Cnty, PA 1920 Census ED 29 Sh 9A.*
4376. *Center Twp., Indiana Cnty, PA 1930 Census ED 16 Sh 4B.*
4377. "6 Dec 1969 Indiana Evening Gazette (Indiana, PA) Obit Mable Shnakle Wyland."
4378. *Kittanning, Armstrong Cnty, PA 1920 Census ED 29 Sh 9A.*
4379. *Center Twp., Indiana Cnty, PA 1930 Census ED 16 Sh 4B.*
4380. *Cherry Hill Twp., Indiana Cnty, PA 1910 Census ED 67 Sh 10B.*
4381. *White Twp., Indiana Cnty, PA 1930 Census ED 53 Sh 6A.*
4382. "7 Aug 1964 Indiana Evening Gazette (Indiana, PA) Death Notice Myrtle Mae Mock."
4383. *Cherry Hill Twp., Indiana Cnty, PA 1910 Census ED 67 Sh 10B.*
4384. *Grant Twp., Indiana Cnty, PA 1900 Census ED 54 Sh 4B.*
4385. *Grant Twp., Indiana Cnty, PA 1910 Census ED 76 Sh 5B&6A.*
4386. *White Twp., Indiana Cnty, PA 1930 Census ED 53 Sh 6A.*
4387. *Green Twp., Indiana Cnty, PA 1920 Census ED 110 Sh 16A.*
4388. *White Twp., Indiana Cnty, PA 1920 Census ED 133 Sh 9A.*
4389. *White Twp., Indiana Cnty, PA 1930 Census ED 53 Sh 6A.*
4390. *South Mahoning Twp., Indiana Cnty, PA 1930 Census ED 42 Sh 7B.*
4391. *Cherry Hill Twp., Indiana Cnty, PA 1910 Census ED 67 Sh 10B.*
4392. "6 Dec 1969 Indiana Evening Gazette (Indiana, PA) Obit Mable Shnakle Wyland."
4393. "15 Dec 1972 Indiana Evening Gazette (Indiana, PA) Evan Shankle Birthday Announcement."
4394. "7 Aug 1964 Indiana Evening Gazette (Indiana, PA) Death Notice Myrtle Mae Mock."
4395. "21 July 1921 Indiana Weekly Messenger (Indiana,PA) Marriage Announcement of Shankle Lambing."
4396. "18 Jan 1979 Indiana Evening Gazette (Indiana, PA) Charles A. Lambing Obit."
4397. *South Mahoning Twp., Indiana Cnty, PA 1930 Census ED 42 Sh 7B.*
4398. *Cherry Hill Twp., Indiana Cnty, PA 1910 Census ED 67 Sh 10B.*
4399. *South Mahoning Twp., Indiana Cnty, PA 1930 Census ED 42 Sh 7B.*
4400. *Rayne Twp., Indiana Cnty, PA 1910 Census ED 90 Sh 1B.*
4401. "18 Jan 1979 Indiana Evening Gazette (Indiana, PA) Charles A. Lambing Obit."
4402. *South Mahoning Twp., Indiana Cnty, PA 1930 Census ED 42 Sh 7B.*
4403. "21 July 1921 Indiana Weekly Messenger (Indiana,PA) Marriage Announcement of Shankle Lambing."
4404. *South Mahoning Twp., Indiana Cnty, PA 1930 Census ED 42 Sh 7B.*
4405. "21 July 1921 Indiana Weekly Messenger (Indiana,PA) Marriage Announcement of Shankle Lambing."
4406. SSN Death Index.
4407. *South Mahoning Twp., Indiana Cnty, PA 1930 Census ED 42 Sh 7B.*
4408. SSN Death Index.
4409. *Green Twp., Indiana Cnty, PA 1930 Census ED 29 Sh 13A.*
4410. *Cherry Hill Twp., Indiana Cnty, PA 1910 Census ED 67 Sh 3B.*
4411. "27 March 1929 Indiana Evening Gazette (Indiana, PA) Rosaline Lydick Obit."
4412. *White Twp., Indiana Cnty, PA 1930 Census ED 52 Sh 3B.*
4413. "27 March 1929 Indiana Evening Gazette (Indiana, PA) Rosaline Lydick Obit."
4414. *White Twp., Indiana Cnty, PA 1930 Census ED 52 Sh 3B.*
4415. *Indiana, Indiana Cnty, PA 1920 Census ED 117 Sh 10B&11A.*
4416. *Cherry Hill Twp., Indiana Cnty, PA 1910 Census ED 67 Sh 3B.*
4417. "27 March 1929 Indiana Evening Gazette (Indiana, PA) Rosaline Lydick Obit."
4418. *Indiana, Indiana Cnty, PA 1920 Census ED 117 Sh 10B&11A.*
4419. *Green Twp., Indiana Cnty, PA 1900 Census ED 55 Sh 6A.*
4420. I. Paul Wilt Obituary.
4421. *South Mahoning Twp., Indiana Cnty, PA 1930 Census ED 42 Sh 7B.*
4422. *Rayne Twp., Indiana Cnty, PA 1910 Census ED 90 Sh 1B.*

4423. "18 Jan 1979 Indiana Evening Gazette (Indiana, PA) Charles A. Lambing Obit."
4424. *South Mahoning Twp., Indiana Cnty, PA 1930 Census ED 42 Sh 7B.*
4425. *Cherry Hill Twp., Indiana Cnty, PA 1910 Census ED 67 Sh 10B.*
4426. "6 Dec 1969 Indiana Evening Gazette (Indiana, PA) Obit Mable Shnakle Wyland."
4427. "15 Dec 1972 Indiana Evening Gazette (Indiana, PA) Evan Shankle Birthday Announcement."
4428. "7 Aug 1964 Indiana Evening Gazette (Indiana, PA) Death Notice Myrtle Mae Mock."
4429. "21 July 1921 Indiana Weekly Messenger (Indiana,PA) Marriage Announcement of Shankle Lambing."
4430. "18 Jan 1979 Indiana Evening Gazette (Indiana, PA) Charles A. Lambing Obit."
4431. *South Mahoning Twp., Indiana Cnty, PA 1930 Census ED 42 Sh 7B.*
4432. "21 July 1921 Indiana Weekly Messenger (Indiana,PA) Marriage Announcement of Shankle Lambing."
4433. *South Mahoning Twp., Indiana Cnty, PA 1930 Census ED 42 Sh 7B.*
4434. *Cherry Hill Twp., Indiana Cnty, PA 1910 Census ED 67 Sh 10B.*
4435. "21 July 1921 Indiana Weekly Messenger (Indiana,PA) Marriage Announcement of Shankle Lambing."
4436. *Rayne Twp., Indiana Cnty, PA 1910 Census ED 90 Sh 1B.*
4437. "18 Jan 1979 Indiana Evening Gazette (Indiana, PA) Charles A. Lambing Obit."
4438. *Green Twp., Indiana Cnty, PA 1910 Census ED 78 Sh 18A.*
4439. *Clymer, Indiana Cnty, PA 1910 Census ED 61 Sh 21B.*
4440. *Gerrardstown, Berkeley Cnty, WV 1900 Census ED 12 Sh 11B.*
4441. *Hedgesville, Berkeley Cnty, WV 1910 Census ED 18 Sh 4A.*
4442. *Falling Waters, Berkeley Cnty, WV 1920 Census ED 20 Sh 14B.*
4443. *Gerrardstown, Berkeley Cnty, WV 1900 Census ED 12 Sh 11B.*
4444. *Falling Waters, Berkeley Cnty, WV 1920 Census ED 20 Sh 14B.*
4445. *Gerrardstown, Berkeley Cnty, WV 1930 Census ED 6 Sh 12B.*
4446. *Falling Waters, Berkeley Cnty, WV 1920 Census ED 20 Sh 14B.*
4447. *Gerrardstown, Berkeley Cnty, WV 1930 Census ED 6 Sh 12B.*
4448. *Gerrardstown, Berkeley Cnty, WV 1900 Census ED 12 Sh 11B.*
4449. *Hedgesville, Berkeley Cnty, WV 1910 Census ED 18 Sh 4A.*
4450. *Falling Waters, Berkeley Cnty, WV 1920 Census ED 20 Sh 14B.*
4451. *Hedgesville, Berkeley Cnty, WV 1930 Census ED 8 Sh 3B.*
4452. *Gerrardstown, Berkeley Cnty, WV 1900 Census ED 12 Sh 11B.*
4453. *Falling Waters, Berkeley Cnty, WV 1920 Census ED 20 Sh 14B.*
4454. *Hedgesville, Berkeley Cnty, WV 1930 Census ED 8 Sh 3B.*
4455. *Falling Waters, Berkeley Cnty, WV 1920 Census ED 20 Sh 14B.*
4456. *Mill Creek, Berkeley Cnty, WV 1910 Census ED 24 Sh 15A.*
4457. *Gerrardstown, Berkeley Cnty, WV 1900 Census ED 12 Sh 3A.*
4458. *Martinsburg Ward 2, Berkeley Cnty, WV 1920 Census ED 28 Sh 15B.*
4459. *Martinsburg, Berkeley Cnty, WV 1930 Census ED 13 Sh 10B.*
4460. *Martinsburg Ward 2, Berkeley Cnty, WV 1920 Census ED 28 Sh 15B.*
4461. *Martinsburg, Berkeley Cnty, WV 1930 Census ED 13 Sh 10B.*
4462. *Mill Creek, Berkeley Cnty, WV 1910 Census ED 24 Sh 15A.*
4463. *Martinsburg Ward 2, Berkeley Cnty, WV 1920 Census ED 28 Sh 15B.*
4464. *Mill Creek, Berkeley Cnty, WV 1910 Census ED 24 Sh 15A.*
4465. *Martinsburg Ward 2, Berkeley Cnty, WV 1920 Census ED 28 Sh 15B.*
4466. *Martinsburg, Berkeley Cnty, WV 1930 Census ED 13 Sh 10B.*
4467. *Gerrardstown, Berkeley Cnty, WV 1920 Census ED 22 Sh 10B.*
4468. *Gerrardstown, Berkeley Cnty, WV 1910 Census ED 16 Sh 6A&B.*
4469. *Gerrardstown, Berkeley Cnty, WV 1920 Census ED 22 Sh 10B.*
4470. *Brunswick, Frederick Cnty, MD 1920 Census ED 94 Sh 4B.*
4471. *Brunswick, Frederick Cnty, MD 1910 Census ED 83 Sh 4B.*
4472. *Brunswick, Frederick Cnty, MD 1930 Census ED 51 Sh 6B.*

4473. *Brunswick, Frederick Cnty, MD 1920 Census ED 94 Sh 4B.*
4474. "29 August 1949 The News (Frederick, MD) Obituary of M. P. Catlett."
4475. "13 Sept. 1954 The Frederick Post (Frederick, MD) Mary Edith Catlett Koogle Obituary."
4476. *Brunswick, Frederick Cnty, MD 1930 Census ED 51 Sh 6B.*
4477. "29 August 1949 The News (Frederick, MD) Obituary of M. P. Catlett."
4478. *Brunswick, Frederick Cnty, MD 1930 Census ED 51 Sh 6B.*
4479. "13 Sept. 1954 The Frederick Post (Frederick, MD) Mary Edith Catlett Koogle Obituary."
4480. *Martinsburg Ward 5, Berkeley Cnty, WV 1900 Census ED 17 Sh 2A.*
4481. *Bath, Morgan Cnty, WV 1910 Census ED 85 Sh 10B.*
4482. *Martinsburg, Berkeley Cnty, WV 1930 Census ED 15 Sh 3B.*
4483. *Martinsburg Ward 5, Berkeley Cnty, WV 1900 Census ED 17 Sh 2A.*
4484. *Martinsburg, Berkeley Cnty, WV 1930 Census ED 15 Sh 3B.*
4485. *Gerrardstown, Berkeley Cnty, WV 1920 Census ED 21 Sh 2B.*
4486. *Charlestown District, Jefferson Cnty, WV 1920 Census ED 64 Sh 13A.*
4487. *Martinsburg, Berkeley Cnty, WV 1930 Census ED 16 Sh 13A.*
4488. SSN Death Index.
4489. *Lowe, Kay Cnty, OK 1900 Census ED 88 Sh 6B.*
4490. *Stillwater, Payne Cnty, OK 1930 Census ED 29 Sh 22B.*
4491. *Bartlesville, Washington Cnty, OK 1920 Census ED 271 Sh 29A.*
4492. *Lowe, Kay Cnty, OK 1900 Census ED 88 Sh 6B.*
4493. *Bartlesville, Washington Cnty, OK 1920 Census ED 271 Sh 29A.*
4494. *Stillwater, Payne Cnty, OK 1930 Census ED 29 Sh 22B.*
4495. *Bartlesville, Washington Cnty, OK 1920 Census ED 271 Sh 29A.*
4496. *Stillwater, Payne Cnty, OK 1930 Census ED 29 Sh 22B.*
4497. *Bartlesville, Washington Cnty, OK 1920 Census ED 271 Sh 29A.*
4498. *Stillwater, Payne Cnty, OK 1930 Census ED 29 Sh 22B.*
4499. *Lowe, Kay Cnty, OK 1900 Census ED 88 Sh 6B.*
4500. *Pueblo Cnty, CO ED 88 Sh 3A.*
4501. *Lowe, Kay Cnty, OK 1900 Census ED 88 Sh 6B.*
4502. *Pueblo Cnty, CO ED 88 Sh 3A.*
4503. *Lowe, Kay Cnty, OK 1900 Census ED 88 Sh 6B.*
4504. *Pueblo Cnty, CO ED 88 Sh 3A.*
4505. *Lowe, Kay Cnty, OK 1900 Census ED 88 Sh 6B.*
4506. *Pueblo Cnty, CO ED 88 Sh 3A.*
4507. "9 September 1936 Indiana Democrat (Indiana, PA) David Stear Obit."
4508. *North Mahoning Twp., Indiana Cnty, PA 1910 Census ED 86 Sh 4A.*
4509. *Rayne Twp., Indiana Cnty, PA 1930 Census ED 43 Sh 3A.*
4510. *North Mahoning Twp., Indiana Cnty, PA 1910 Census ED 86 Sh 4A.*
4511. *Rayne Twp., Indiana Cnty, PA 1930 Census ED 43 Sh 3A.*
4512. "9 September 1936 Indiana Democrat (Indiana, PA) David Stear Obit."
4513. *Rayne Twp., Indiana Cnty, PA 1930 Census ED 43 Sh 3A.*
4514. "9 September 1936 Indiana Democrat (Indiana, PA) David Stear Obit."
4515. *Rayne Twp., Indiana Cnty, PA 1930 Census ED 43 Sh 3A.*
4516. *Perry Twp., Jefferson Cnty, PA 1900 Census ED 69 Sh 14B.*
4517. *Lake Charles, Calcasieu Parish, LA 1910 Census ED 38 Sh 1B.*
4518. *Lake Charles, Calcasieu Parish, LA 1920 Census ED 44 Sh 9B.*
4519. *Perry Twp., Jefferson Cnty, PA 1900 Census ED 69 Sh 14B.*
4520. *Compton, Los Angeles Cnty, CA 1930 Census ED 877 Sh 3A.*
4521. *Milford, Star Pct., Beaver Cnty, UT 1920 Census ED 6 Sh 2A.*
4522. *Paint Twp., Somerset Cnty, PA 1900 Census ED 164 Sh 25A.*
4523. *Compton, Los Angeles Cnty, CA 1930 Census ED 877 Sh 3A.*
4524. *Paint Twp., Somerset Cnty, PA 1900 Census ED 164 Sh 25A.*
4525. *Compton, Los Angeles Cnty, CA 1930 Census ED 877 Sh 3A.*
4526. *Milford, Star Pct., Beaver Cnty, UT 1920 Census ED 6 Sh 2A.*

4527. *Compton, Los Angeles Cnty, CA 1930 Census ED 877 Sh 3A.*
4528. *Milford, Star Pct., Beaver Cnty, UT 1920 Census ED 6 Sh 2A.*
4529. *Paint Twp., Somerset Cnty, PA 1900 Census ED 164 Sh 25A.*
4530. *Santa Barbara, Santa Barbara Cnty, CA 1930 Census ED 4 Sh 17A.*
4531. *Milford, Star Pct., Beaver Cnty, UT 1920 Census ED 6 Sh 2A.*
4532. *Paint Twp., Somerset Cnty, PA 1900 Census ED 164 Sh 25A.*
4533. *Santa Barbara, Santa Barbara Cnty, CA 1930 Census ED 4 Sh 17A.*
4534. *Milford, Star Pct., Beaver Cnty, UT 1920 Census ED 6 Sh 2A.*
4535. *Milford, Star Pct., Bever Cnty, UT 1930 Census ED 8 Sh 11A.*
4536. *Milford, Star Pct., Beaver Cnty, UT 1920 Census ED 6 Sh 2A.*
4537. *Californis Marriage Index 1960-1985,* "Electronic."
4538. *Milford, Star Pct., Bever Cnty, UT 1930 Census ED 8 Sh 11A.*
4539. *Californis Marriage Index 1960-1985,* "Electronic."
4540. *West Mahoning Twp., Indiana Cnty, PA 1900 Census ED 63 Sh 6A.*
4541. *Creekside, Indiana Cnty, PA 1920 Census ED 107 Sh 3B.*
4542. *Creekside, Indiana Cnty, PA 1930 Census ED 23 Sh 4A.*
4543. *West Mahoning Twp., Indiana Cnty, PA 1900 Census ED 63 Sh 6A.*
4544. *Creekside, Indiana Cnty, PA 1920 Census ED 107 Sh 3B.*
4545. *Creekside, Indiana Cnty, PA 1930 Census ED 23 Sh 4A.*
4546. *Creekside, Indiana Cnty, PA 1920 Census ED 107 Sh 3B.*
4547. *Creekside, Indiana Cnty, PA 1930 Census ED 23 Sh 4A.*
4548. *Creekside, Indiana Cnty, PA 1920 Census ED 107 Sh 3B.*
4549. *Punxsutawney, Jefferson Cnty, PA 1910 Census ED 82 Sh 16B.*
4550. *West Mahoning Twp., Indiana Cnty, PA 1900 Census ED 63 Sh 6A.*
4551. *O'Hara Twp., Allegheny Cnty, PA 1920 Census ED 297 Sh 1A.*
4552. *O'Hara Twp., Allegheny Cnty, PA 1930 Census ED 742 Sh 5B.*
4553. *Punxsutawney, Jefferson Cnty, PA 1910 Census ED 82 Sh 16B.*
4554. *West Mahoning Twp., Indiana Cnty, PA 1900 Census ED 63 Sh 6A.*
4555. WWI Civilian Draft Registration Index.
4556. *O'Hara Twp., Allegheny Cnty, PA 1920 Census ED 297 Sh 1A.*
4557. *O'Hara Twp., Allegheny Cnty, PA 1930 Census ED 742 Sh 5B.*
4558. *O'Hara Twp., Allegheny Cnty, PA 1920 Census ED 297 Sh 1A.*
4559. *Verona, Allegheny Cnty, PA 1920 Census ED 841 Sh 7A.*
4560. *Verona, Allegheny Cnty, PA 1930 Census ED 842 Sh 22B.*
4561. *Verona, Allegheny Cnty, PA 1920 Census ED 841 Sh 7A.*
4562. *Punxsutawney, Jefferson Cnty, PA 1900 Census ED 74 Sh 1A.*
4563. *Verona, Allegheny Cnty, PA 1920 Census ED 841 Sh 7A.*
4564. *Verona, Allegheny Cnty, PA 1930 Census ED 842 Sh 22B.*
4565. *Punxsutawney, Jefferson Cnty, PA 1900 Census ED 74 Sh 1A.*
4566. *Saltsburg, Indiana Cnty, PA 1910 Census ED 91 Sh 4B.*
4567. *Saltsburg, Indiana Cnty, PA 1930 Census ED 45 Sh 4B.*
4568. *Saltsburg, Indiana Cnty, PA 1920 Census ED 127 Sh 5A.*
4569. "Stella M. Van Horn Obituary Indiana County Genealogical and Historical Society Newspaper Clippings."
4570. *Saltsburg, Indiana Cnty, PA 1900 Census ED 62 Sh 7B.*
4571. *Saltsburg, Indiana Cnty, PA 1910 Census ED 91 Sh 4B.*
4572. "Owen Meridith Serene Obituary Date and Newspaper Unknown."
4573. *Saltsburg, Indiana Cnty, PA 1930 Census ED 45 Sh 4B.*
4574. *Saltsburg, Indiana Cnty, PA 1910 Census ED 91 Sh 4B.*
4575. *Florida Death Index 1877-1998,* "Electronic."
4576. *Rural Valley, Jefferson Cnty, PA 1930 Census ED 45 Sh 1B.*
4577. *Armstrong Cnty, PA Miracode Index 1920 ED 42 Visit 6.*
4578. *Rural Valley, Jefferson Cnty, PA 1930 Census ED 45 Sh 1B.*
4579. *Cowanshonnock Twp., Armstrong Cnty, PA 1920 Census ED 5 Sh 4A .*

4580. *Cowanshonnock Twp., Armstrong Cnty, PA 1910 Census ED 9 Sh 1B* .

4581. *Niles, Trumbull Cnty, OH 1930 Census ED 60 Sh 8A.*

4582. *Cowanshonnock Twp., Armstrong Cnty, PA 1920 Census ED 5 Sh 4A* .

4583. "Van Horn-Patterson Wedding Article Indiana County Genealogical and Historical Society Newspaper Clippings."

4584. *Plumville, South Mahoning Twp., Indiana Cnty, PA 1930 Census ED 52 Sh 10B.*

4585. "27 March 1964 Simpson's Leader-Times (Kittanning, PA) Owen DeLone Van Horn Obituary."

4586. "Van Horn-Patterson Wedding Article Indiana County Genealogical and Historical Society Newspaper Clippings."

4587. "27 March 1964 Simpson's Leader-Times (Kittanning, PA) Owen DeLone Van Horn Obituary."

4588. SSN Death Index.

4589. *Cowanshonnock Twp., Armstrong Cnty, PA 1920 Census ED 5 Sh 4A* .

4590. "Edna L. McMinn Van Horn Obituary Indiana County Genealogical and Historical Society Newspaper Clippings."

4591. *Snyder Twp., Jefferson Cnty, PA 1910 Census ED 90 Sh 15A.*

4592. *Brockway, Jefferson Cnty, PA 1930 Census ED 5 Sh 13A.*

4593. *Snyder Twp., Jefferson Cnty, PA 1910 Census ED 90 Sh 15A.*

4594. *Brockway, Jefferson Cnty, PA 1930 Census ED 5 Sh 13A.*

4595. "Edna L. McMinn Van Horn Obituary Indiana County Genealogical and Historical Society Newspaper Clippings."

4596. *Snyder Twp., Jefferson Cnty, PA 1910 Census ED 90 Sh 15A.*

4597. DAR National Record Copy of Member Application # 862524.

4598. *Snyder Twp., Jefferson Cnty, PA 1910 Census ED 90 Sh 15A.*

4599. DAR National Record Copy of Member Application # 862524.

4600. *East Mahoning Twp., Indiana Cnty, PA 1900 Census ED 53 Sh 5A.*

4601. *East Mahoning Twp., Indiana Cnty, PA 1880 Census ED 145 Sh 17/337.*

4602. *Limestone, Clarion Cnty, PA 1910 Census ED 14 Sh 4A.*

4603. *East Mahoning Twp., Indiana Cnty, PA 1900 Census ED 53 Sh 5A.*

4604. *WWII Civilian Draft Registration,* "Electronic."

4605. *Limestone, Clarion Cnty, PA 1910 Census ED 14 Sh 4A.*

4606. *East Mahoning Twp., Indiana Cnty, PA 1900 Census ED 53 Sh 5A.*

4607. *East Mahoning Twp., Indiana Cnty, PA 1930 Census ED 24 Sh 6A.*

4608. *East Mahoning Twp., Indiana Cnty, PA 1900 Census ED 53 Sh 5A.*

4609. SSN Death Index.

4610. *East Mahoning Twp., Indiana Cnty, PA 1930 Census ED 24 Sh 6A.*

4611. *Indiana Ward 1, Indiana Cnty, PA 1910 Census ED 80 Sh 12 B.*

4612. *Indiana Ward 2, Indiana Cnty, PA 1920 Census ED 114 Sh 16A.*

4613. "22 May 1953 Indiana Evening Gazette (Indiana, PA) Mrs. Adda M. McAdoo Obituary."

4614. *Indiana, Indiana Cnty, PA 1930 Census ED 32 Sh 7B.*

4615. *Indiana Ward 2, Indiana Cnty, PA 1920 Census ED 114 Sh 16A.*

4616. "22 May 1953 Indiana Evening Gazette (Indiana, PA) Mrs. Adda M. McAdoo Obituary."

4617. *Indiana, Indiana Cnty, PA 1930 Census ED 32 Sh 7B.*

4618. *Indiana Ward 1, Indiana Cnty, PA 1910 Census ED 80 Sh 12 B.*

4619. *Indiana Ward 2, Indiana Cnty, PA 1920 Census ED 114 Sh 16A.*

4620. *Indiana, Indiana Cnty, PA 1930 Census ED 32 Sh 9A.*

4621. "22 May 1953 Indiana Evening Gazette (Indiana, PA) Mrs. Adda M. McAdoo Obituary."

4622. "9 April 1987 Indiana Gazette (Indiana, PA) Charles Ferrier Obit."

4623. "Ethyl McAdoo Ferrier Obituary from Indiana Historical and Genealogical Society file dated 3/31/1998."

4624. *Indiana, Indiana Cnty, PA 1930 Census ED 32 Sh 9A.*

4625. "22 May 1953 Indiana Evening Gazette (Indiana, PA) Mrs. Adda M. McAdoo Obituary."

4626. *Indiana, Indiana Cnty, PA 1900 Census ED 56 Sh 6B.*

4627. "8 Jan 1938 Indiana Evening Gazette (Indiana, PA) Sarah Jane Shearer Ferrier Obit."
4628. "Ethyl McAdoo Ferrier Obituary from Indiana Historical and Genealogical Society file dated 3/31/1998."
4629. "News Clipping from Indiana Historical and Genealogical Society dated 9/19/1922."
4630. *Indiana, Indiana Cnty, PA 1930 Census ED 32 Sh 9A.*
4631. *Indiana, Indiana Cnty, PA 1900 Census ED 56 Sh 6B.*
4632. "9 April 1987 Indiana Gazette (Indiana, PA) Charles Ferrier Obit."
4633. "News Clipping from Indiana Historical and Genealogical Society dated 9/19/1922."
4634. *Indiana Ward 1, Indiana Cnty, PA 1910 Census ED 80 Sh 12 B.*
4635. *Indiana Ward 2, Indiana Cnty, PA 1920 Census ED 114 Sh 16A.*
4636. "22 May 1953 Indiana Evening Gazette (Indiana, PA) Mrs. Adda M. McAdoo Obituary."
4637. "8 Sept 1954 Indiana Evening Gazette (Indiana, PA)."
4638. "8 July 1907 Indiana Evening Gazette (Indiana, PA)."
4639. "Ethyl McAdoo Ferrier Obituary from Indiana Historical and Genealogical Society file dated 3/31/1998."
4640. "22 May 1953 Indiana Evening Gazette (Indiana, PA) Mrs. Adda M. McAdoo Obituary."
4641. "6 June 1924 Indiana Evening Gazette (Indiana, PA) Marriage Article."
4642. "Ethyl McAdoo Ferrier Obituary from Indiana Historical and Genealogical Society file dated 3/31/1998."
4643. *WWII Civilian Draft Registration,* "Electronic."
4644. "6 June 1924 Indiana Evening Gazette (Indiana, PA) Marriage Article."
4645. "8 Sept 1954 Indiana Evening Gazette (Indiana, PA)."
4646. *WWII Civilian Draft Registration,* "Electronic."
4647. "8 Sept 1954 Indiana Evening Gazette (Indiana, PA)."
4648. *WWII Civilian Draft Registration,* "Electronic."
4649. "6 June 1924 Indiana Evening Gazette (Indiana, PA) Marriage Article."
4650. *Indiana Ward 1, Indiana Cnty, PA 1910 Census ED 80 Sh 12 B.*
4651. *Indiana Ward 2, Indiana Cnty, PA 1920 Census ED 114 Sh 16A.*
4652. "22 May 1953 Indiana Evening Gazette (Indiana, PA) Mrs. Adda M. McAdoo Obituary."
4653. *Apollo, Armstrong Cnty, PA 1920 Census ED 2 Sh 5B.*
4654. "22 May 1953 Indiana Evening Gazette (Indiana, PA) Mrs. Adda M. McAdoo Obituary."
4655. *Apollo, Armstrong Cnty, PA 1930 Census ED 1 Sh 5A.*
4656. *Apollo, Armstrong Cnty, PA 1920 Census ED 2 Sh 5B.*
4657. *Plumville, South Mahoning Twp., Indiana Cnty, PA 1910 Census ED 92 Sh 1A.*
4658. *Cowanshonnock Twp., Armstrong Cnty, PA 1920 Census ED 5 Sh 7A.*
4659. *Cowanshannock Twp., Armstrong Cnty, PA 1930 Census ED 11 Sh 13A.*
4660. *East Mahoning Twp., Indiana Cnty, PA 1900 Census ED 53 Sh 5A.*
4661. "27 Dec. 1917 Indiana Evenin Gazette (Indiana, PA) Mable Mildred Aul Obit."
4662. *Plumville, South Mahoning Twp., Indiana Cnty, PA 1910 Census ED 92 Sh 1A.*
4663. *Cowanshannock Twp., Armstrong Cnty, PA 1930 Census ED 11 Sh 13A.*
4664. "23 April 1974 Simpson's Leader-Times (Kittanning, PA) Herbert Aul Obituary."
4665. *Cowanshonnock Twp., Armstrong Cnty, PA 1920 Census ED 5 Sh 7A.*
4666. *Cowanshannock Twp., Armstrong Cnty, PA 1930 Census ED 11 Sh 13A.*
4667. *Cowanshonnock Twp., Armstrong Cnty, PA 1920 Census ED 5 Sh 7A.*
4668. *Cowanshannock Twp., Armstrong Cnty, PA 1930 Census ED 11 Sh 13A.*
4669. "23 April 1974 Simpson's Leader-Times (Kittanning, PA) Herbert Aul Obituary."
4670. *Cowanshannock Twp., Armstrong Cnty, PA 1930 Census ED 11 Sh 13A.*
4671. "23 April 1974 Simpson's Leader-Times (Kittanning, PA) Herbert Aul Obituary."
4672. *Plumville, South Mahoning Twp., Indiana Cnty, PA 1910 Census ED 92 Sh 1A.*
4673. *Cowanshonnock Twp., Armstrong Cnty, PA 1920 Census ED 4 Sh 7B.*
4674. *Cowanshannock Twp., Armstrong Cnty, PA 1930 Census ED 12 Sh 17A.*
4675. *East Mahoning Twp., Indiana Cnty, PA 1900 Census ED 53 Sh 5A.*
4676. "21 Feb 1950 Indiana Evening Gazette (Indiana, PA) Funeral Announcememt Mrs. J. E. Wagner."

4677. "20 June 1955 Indiana Evening Gazette (Indiana, PA) Laney Aul Death Announcement."
4678. "27 Dec. 1917 Indiana Evenin Gazette (Indiana, PA) Mable Mildred Aul Obit."
4679. *Plumville, South Mahoning Twp., Indiana Cnty, PA 1910 Census ED 92 Sh 1A.*
4680. WWI Civilian Draft Registration Index.
4681. *Cowanshannock Twp., Armstrong Cnty, PA 1930 Census ED 12 Sh 17A.*
4682. *Plumville, South Mahoning Twp., Indiana Cnty, PA 1910 Census ED 92 Sh 1A.*
4683. *Cowanshannock Twp., Armstrong Cnty, PA 1930 Census ED 12 Sh 5B.*
4684. *East Mahoning Twp., Indiana Cnty, PA 1900 Census ED 53 Sh 5A.*
4685. "20 June 1955 Indiana Evening Gazette (Indiana, PA) Laney Aul Death Announcement."
4686. "27 Dec. 1917 Indiana Evenin Gazette (Indiana, PA) Mable Mildred Aul Obit."
4687. "23 April 1974 Simpson's Leader-Times (Kittanning, PA) Herbert Aul Obituary."
4688. *Plumville, South Mahoning Twp., Indiana Cnty, PA 1910 Census ED 92 Sh 1A.*
4689. *Cowanshannock Twp., Armstrong Cnty, PA 1930 Census ED 12 Sh 5B.*
4690. *Cowanshannock Twp., Armstrong Cnty, PA 1900 Census ED 2 Sh 6B.*
4691. "29 Dec 1948 Indiana Evening Gazette ((Indiana, PA) Engagement Anouncement."
4692. "21 Feb 1950 Indiana Evening Gazette (Indiana, PA) Funeral Announcememt Mrs. J. E. Wagner."
4693. "1 Dec 1972 Indiana Evening Gazette (Indiana, PA) Callie Johnsoton Obit."
4694. *Cowanshannock Twp., Armstrong Cnty, PA 1930 Census ED 12 Sh 5B.*
4695. *Cowanshannock Twp., Armstrong Cnty, PA 1900 Census ED 2 Sh 6B.*
4696. *Plumville, South Mahoning Twp., Indiana Cnty, PA 1910 Census ED 92 Sh 1A.*
4697. *Cowanshonnock Twp., Armstrong Cnty, PA 1920 Census ED 4 Sh 7B.*
4698. "27 Dec. 1917 Indiana Evenin Gazette (Indiana, PA) Mable Mildred Aul Obit."
4699. "9 April 1951 The Progress (Clearfield, PA) Iva Hopkins Obituray."
4700. *Plumville, South Mahoning Twp., Indiana Cnty, PA 1910 Census ED 92 Sh 1A.*
4701. "9 April 1951 The Progress (Clearfield, PA) Iva Hopkins Obituray."
4702. "15 Feb 1950 Indiana Evening Gazette (Indiana, PA) Obit Myrtle Aul Wagner."
4703. "9 April 1951 The Progress (Clearfield, PA) Iva Hopkins Obituray."
4704. *Plumville, South Mahoning Twp., Indiana Cnty, PA 1910 Census ED 92 Sh 1A.*
4705. *Cowanshonnock Twp., Armstrong Cnty, PA 1920 Census ED 4 Sh 7B.*
4706. "20 June 1955 Indiana Evening Gazette (Indiana, PA) Laney Aul Death Announcement."
4707. "27 Dec. 1917 Indiana Evenin Gazette (Indiana, PA) Mable Mildred Aul Obit."
4708. "4 Sept 1957 Simpson's Leader-Times (Kittanning, PA) Alma Florence Aul Shaffer Obituary, p.2."
4709. *Plumville, South Mahoning Twp., Indiana Cnty, PA 1910 Census ED 92 Sh 1A.*
4710. "4 Sept 1957 Simpson's Leader-Times (Kittanning, PA) Alma Florence Aul Shaffer Obituary, p.2."
4711. "21 Feb 1950 Indiana Evening Gazette (Indiana, PA) Funeral Announcememt Mrs. J. E. Wagner."
4712. "20 June 1955 Indiana Evening Gazette (Indiana, PA) Laney Aul Death Announcement."
4713. "4 Sept 1957 Simpson's Leader-Times (Kittanning, PA) Alma Florence Aul Shaffer Obituary, p.2."
4714. *Plumville, South Mahoning Twp., Indiana Cnty, PA 1910 Census ED 92 Sh 1A.*
4715. *Cowanshonnock Twp., Armstrong Cnty, PA 1920 Census ED 4 Sh 7B.*
4716. "21 Feb 1950 Indiana Evening Gazette (Indiana, PA) Funeral Announcememt Mrs. J. E. Wagner."
4717. "20 June 1955 Indiana Evening Gazette (Indiana, PA) Laney Aul Death Announcement."
4718. "27 Dec. 1917 Indiana Evenin Gazette (Indiana, PA) Mable Mildred Aul Obit."
4719. "23 April 1974 Simpson's Leader-Times (Kittanning, PA) Herbert Aul Obituary."
4720. *Plumville, South Mahoning Twp., Indiana Cnty, PA 1910 Census ED 92 Sh 1A.*
4721. "21 Feb 1950 Indiana Evening Gazette (Indiana, PA) Funeral Announcememt Mrs. J. E. Wagner."
4722. "20 June 1955 Indiana Evening Gazette (Indiana, PA) Laney Aul Death Announcement."
4723. "22 Sept 1955 Indiana Evening Gazette (Indiana, PA)."

4724. *Plumville, South Mahoning Twp., Indiana Cnty, PA 1910 Census ED 92 Sh 1A.*
4725. *Cowanshonnock Twp., Armstrong Cnty, PA 1920 Census ED 4 Sh 7B.*
4726. "27 Dec. 1917 Indiana Evenin Gazette (Indiana, PA) Mable Mildred Aul Obit."
4727. *Plumville, South Mahoning Twp., Indiana Cnty, PA 1910 Census ED 92 Sh 1A.*
4728. "21 Feb 1950 Indiana Evening Gazette (Indiana, PA) Funeral Announcememt Mrs. J. E. Wagner."
4729. "15 Feb 1950 Indiana Evening Gazette (Indiana, PA) Obit Myrtle Aul Wagner."
4730. *Cowanshonnock Twp., Armstrong Cnty, PA 1920 Census ED 4 Sh 7B.*
4731. "21 Feb 1950 Indiana Evening Gazette (Indiana, PA) Funeral Announcememt Mrs. J. E. Wagner."
4732. "20 June 1955 Indiana Evening Gazette (Indiana, PA) Laney Aul Death Announcement."
4733. "27 Dec. 1917 Indiana Evenin Gazette (Indiana, PA) Mable Mildred Aul Obit."
4734. "23 April 1974 Simpson's Leader-Times (Kittanning, PA) Herbert Aul Obituary."
4735. *Cowanshonnock Twp., Armstrong Cnty, PA 1920 Census ED 4 Sh 7B.*
4736. "12 August 1941 Indiana Evening Gazette (Indiana, PA) Wedding Announcemnt."
4737. *Cowanshonnock Twp., Armstrong Cnty, PA 1920 Census ED 4 Sh 7B.*
4738. "31 May 1969 Indiana Evening Gazette (Indiana, PA)."
4739. "20 June 1955 Indiana Evening Gazette (Indiana, PA) Laney Aul Death Announcement."
4740. "27 Dec. 1917 Indiana Evenin Gazette (Indiana, PA) Mable Mildred Aul Obit."
4741. "17 May 1945 Indiana Evening Gazette (Indiana, PA)."
4742. "23 April 1974 Simpson's Leader-Times (Kittanning, PA) Herbert Aul Obituary."
4743. *Cowanshonnock Twp., Armstrong Cnty, PA 1920 Census ED 4 Sh 7B.*
4744. "31 May 1969 Indiana Evening Gazette (Indiana, PA)."
4745. "17 May 1945 Indiana Evening Gazette (Indiana, PA)."
4746. *21 Dec 1937 Indiana Evening Gazette (Indiana, PA).*
4747. *South Mahoning Twp., Indiana Cnty, PA 1920 Census ED 124 Sh 5A.*
4748. *South Mahoning Twp., Indiana Cnty, PA 1910 Census ED 92 Sh 2B.*
4749. "14 May 1945 Indiana Evening Gazette (Indiana, PA) Dorothy Bell Shaffer Obit."
4750. "11 April 1955 Indiana Evening Gazette (Indiana, PA) report of family.."
4751. *South Mahoning Twp., Indiana Cnty, PA 1920 Census ED 124 Sh 5A.*
4752. *Plumville, Indiana Cnty, PA 1920 Census ED 123 Sh 4B.*
4753. "11 April 1955 Indiana Evening Gazette (Indiana, PA) report of family.."
4754. "15 Feb 1923 Indiana Weekly Messenger (Indiana, PA)."
4755. *Plumville, Indiana Cnty, PA 1920 Census ED 123 Sh 4B.*
4756. SSN Death Index.
4757. "15 Feb 1923 Indiana Weekly Messenger (Indiana, PA)."
4758. "11 April 1955 Indiana Evening Gazette (Indiana, PA) report of family.."
4759. *South Mahoning Twp., Indiana Cnty, PA 1920 Census ED 124 Sh 5A.*
4760. *South Mahoning Twp., Indiana Cnty, PA 1910 Census ED 92 Sh 2B.*
4761. *Indiana, Indiana Cnty, PA 1930 Census ED 34 Sh 4B.*
4762. *South Mahoning Twp., Indiana Cnty, PA 1920 Census ED 124 Sh 5A.*
4763. "14 May 1945 Indiana Evening Gazette (Indiana, PA) Dorothy Bell Shaffer Obit."
4764. *Indiana, Indiana Cnty, PA 1930 Census ED 34 Sh 4B.*
4765. "14 May 1945 Indiana Evening Gazette (Indiana, PA) Dorothy Bell Shaffer Obit."
4766. *South Mahoning Twp., Indiana Cnty, PA 1920 Census ED 124 Sh 5A.*
4767. *South Mahoning Twp., Indiana Cnty, PA 1910 Census ED 92 Sh 2B.*
4768. "10 Jan 1977 Indiana Evening Gazette (Indiana, PA)."
4769. *Rayne Twp., Indiana Cnty, PA 1930 Census ED 43 Sh 21A.*
4770. "14 May 1945 Indiana Evening Gazette (Indiana, PA) Dorothy Bell Shaffer Obit."
4771. *South Mahoning Twp., Indiana Cnty, PA 1920 Census ED 124 Sh 5A.*
4772. "10 Jan 1977 Indiana Evening Gazette (Indiana, PA)."
4773. *Rayne Twp., Indiana Cnty, PA 1930 Census ED 43 Sh 21A.*
4774. *South Mahoning Twp., Indiana Cnty, PA 1920 Census ED 124 Sh 5A.*
4775. *White Twp., Indiana Cnty, PA 1930 Census ED 53 Sh 4A.*

4776. "10 Jan 1977 Indiana Evening Gazette (Indiana, PA)."
4777. "14 May 1945 Indiana Evening Gazette (Indiana, PA) Dorothy Bell Shaffer Obit."
4778. *South Mahoning Twp., Indiana Cnty, PA 1920 Census ED 124 Sh 5A.*
4779. "17 March 1933 Indiana Evening Gazette (Indiana, PA) Obituary of Gladys Shaffer Marshall."
4780. *South Mahoning Twp., Indiana Cnty, PA 1920 Census ED 124 Sh 5A.*
4781. *White Twp., Indiana Cnty, PA 1930 Census ED 53 Sh 4A.*
4782. "10 Jan 1977 Indiana Evening Gazette (Indiana, PA)."
4783. "24 May 1950 Indiana Evening Gazette (Indiana, PA) list of marriage licenses.."
4784. "14 May 1945 Indiana Evening Gazette (Indiana, PA) Dorothy Bell Shaffer Obit."
4785. *South Mahoning Twp., Indiana Cnty, PA 1920 Census ED 124 Sh 5A.*
4786. SSN Death Index.
4787. "24 May 1950 Indiana Evening Gazette (Indiana, PA) list of marriage licenses.."
4788. SSN Death Index.
4789. "24 May 1950 Indiana Evening Gazette (Indiana, PA) list of marriage licenses.."
4790. *South Mahoning Twp., Indiana Cnty, PA 1910 Census ED 93 Sh 3B.*
4791. *South Mahoning Twp., Indiana Cnty, PA 1920 Census ED 124 Sh 5A.*
4792. *South Mahoning Twp., Indiana Cnty, PA 1910 Census ED 93 Sh 3B.*
4793. *South Mahoning Twp., Indiana Cnty, PA 1920 Census ED 124 Sh 5A.*
4794. *South Mahoning Twp., Indiana Cnty, PA 1910 Census ED 93 Sh 3B.*
4795. "30 Sept 1969 Indiana Evening Gazette (Indiana, PA) Irene Johnston OBITUARY."
4796. Hamilton, Von Gail, *Work Family History: Twelve Generations of Work in America 1690-1969, Park City, Utah,* (Park City, Utah: Publishers Press, 1969, 614 pgs.).
4797. "26 June 1961 Indiana Evening Gazette (Indiana, PA) Anne Johnston 80th Birthday."
4798. "30 Sept 1969 Indiana Evening Gazette (Indiana, PA) Irene Johnston OBITUARY."
4799. *South Mahoning Twp., Indiana Cnty, PA 1910 Census ED 93 Sh 3B.*
4800. *South Mahoning Twp., Indiana Cnty, PA 1920 Census ED 124 Sh 5A.*
4801. "26 June 1961 Indiana Evening Gazette (Indiana, PA) Anne Johnston 80th Birthday."
4802. *South Mahoning Twp., Indiana Cnty, PA 1910 Census ED 93 Sh 3B.*
4803. "26 June 1961 Indiana Evening Gazette (Indiana, PA) Anne Johnston 80th Birthday."
4804. "30 Sept 1969 Indiana Evening Gazette (Indiana, PA) Irene Johnston OBITUARY."
4805. *South Mahoning Twp., Indiana Cnty, PA 1920 Census ED 124 Sh 5A.*
4806. *South Mahoning Twp., Indiana Cnty, PA 1930 Census ED 48 Sh 12B.*
4807. "26 June 1961 Indiana Evening Gazette (Indiana, PA) Anne Johnston 80th Birthday."
4808. *17 Aug 1967 Indiana Evening Gazette (Indiana, PA).*
4809. *South Mahoning Twp., Indiana Cnty, PA 1920 Census ED 124 Sh 5A.*
4810. *17 Aug 1967 Indiana Evening Gazette (Indiana, PA).*
4811. "9 Nov 1965 Indiana Evening Gazette (Indiana, PA)."
4812. *South Mahoning Twp., Indiana Cnty, PA 1920 Census ED 124 Sh 5A.*
4813. *South Mahoning Twp., Indiana Cnty, PA 1930 Census ED 48 Sh 12B.*
4814. "26 June 1961 Indiana Evening Gazette (Indiana, PA) Anne Johnston 80th Birthday."
4815. *South Mahoning Twp., Indiana Cnty, PA 1920 Census ED 124 Sh 5A.*
4816. "Floyd Van Horn Obituary Indiana County Genealogical and Historical Society Newspaper Clippings."
4817. *Plumville, South Mahoning Twp., Indiana Cnty, PA 1920 Census ED 123 Sh 1A.*
4818. "Robert L. Claire Van Horn Obituary."
4819. "Raymond L. Van Horn Obituary Indiana County Genealogical and Historical Society Newspaper Clippings."
4820. "Wilbur Van Horn Obituary Indiana County Genealogical and Historical Society Newspaper Clippings."
4821. *Plumville, South Mahoning Twp., Indiana Cnty, PA 1930 Census ED 42 Sh 7A&B.*
4822. *Plumville, South Mahoning Twp., Indiana Cnty, PA 1910 Census ED 92 Sh 1A.*
4823. "Floyd Van Horn Obituary Indiana County Genealogical and Historical Society Newspaper Clippings."
4824. *Plumville, South Mahoning Twp., Indiana Cnty, PA 1930 Census ED 42 Sh 7A&B.*

4825. "Floyd Van Horn Obituary Indiana County Genealogical and Historical Society Newspaper Clippings."

4826. Ohio Deaths, 1908-1932, 1938-1944, and 1958-2002.

4827. "Floyd Van Horn Obituary Indiana County Genealogical and Historical Society Newspaper Clippings."

4828. *Ohio Deaths, 1908-1932, 1938-1944, and 1958-2002* , "Electronic."

4829. "Robert L. Claire Van Horn Obituary."

4830. "Joseph L. Van Horn Obituary Indiana County Genealogical and Historical Society Newspaper Clippings."

4831. "Raymond L. Van Horn Obituary Indiana County Genealogical and Historical Society Newspaper Clippings."

4832. *Plumville, South Mahoning Twp., Indiana Cnty, PA 1920 Census ED 123 Sh 1A.*

4833. *Plumville, South Mahoning Twp., Indiana Cnty, PA 1930 Census ED 42 Sh 7A&B.*

4834. "Indiana Progress (Indiana Cnty, PA) November 22, 1933."

4835. *Plumville, South Mahoning Twp., Indiana Cnty, PA 1910 Census ED 92 Sh 1A.*

4836. "Wilbur Van Horn Obituary Indiana County Genealogical and Historical Society Newspaper Clippings."

4837. *Plumville, South Mahoning Twp., Indiana Cnty, PA 1930 Census ED 42 Sh 7A&B.*

4838. "Wilbur Van Horn Obituary Indiana County Genealogical and Historical Society Newspaper Clippings."

4839. SSN Death Index.

4840. "Joseph L. Van Horn Obituary Indiana County Genealogical and Historical Society Newspaper Clippings."

4841. "Indiana Progress (Indiana Cnty, PA) November 22, 1933."

4842. "Katheen Nesbit Van Horn Obituary Indiana County Genealogical and Historical Society Newspaper Clippings."

4843. "Joseph L. Van Horn Obituary Indiana County Genealogical and Historical Society Newspaper Clippings."

4844. "Robert L. Claire Van Horn Obituary."

4845. *Rayne Twp., Indiana Cnty, PA 1920 Census ED 125 Sh 3B.*

4846. *Plumville, South Mahoning Twp., Indiana Cnty, PA 1920 Census ED 123 Sh 1A.*

4847. "Wilbur Van Horn Obituary Indiana County Genealogical and Historical Society Newspaper Clippings."

4848. *Plumville, South Mahoning Twp., Indiana Cnty, PA 1930 Census ED 42 Sh 7A&B.*

4849. "Robert L. Claire Van Horn Obituary."

4850. "Wilbur Van Horn Obituary Indiana County Genealogical and Historical Society Newspaper Clippings."

4851. "Raymond L. Van Horn Obituary Indiana County Genealogical and Historical Society Newspaper Clippings."

4852. "Robert L. Claire Van Horn Obituary."

4853. *South Mahoning Twp., Indiana Cnty, PA 1920 Census ED 24 Sh 8A.*

4854. "Raymond L. Van Horn Obituary Indiana County Genealogical and Historical Society Newspaper Clippings."

4855. "Wilbur Van Horn Obituary Indiana County Genealogical and Historical Society Newspaper Clippings."

4856. *Plumville, South Mahoning Twp., Indiana Cnty, PA 1930 Census ED 42 Sh 5A.*

4857. *South Mahoning Twp., Indiana Cnty, PA 1920 Census ED 24 Sh 8A.*

4858. "Floyd Van Horn Obituary Indiana County Genealogical and Historical Society Newspaper Clippings."

4859. *Plumville, South Mahoning Twp., Indiana Cnty, PA 1920 Census ED 123 Sh 1A.*

4860. *Plumville, South Mahoning Twp., Indiana Cnty, PA 1930 Census ED 42 Sh 7A&B.*

4861. "Robert L. Claire Van Horn Obituary."

4862. "Raymond L. Van Horn Obituary Indiana County Genealogical and Historical Society Newspaper Clippings."

4863. "Wilbur Van Horn Obituary Indiana County Genealogical and Historical Society Newspaper Clippings."

4864. "Indiana Progress (Indiana Cnty, PA) 10 April 1918."

4865. *Plumville, South Mahoning Twp., Indiana Cnty, PA 1930 Census ED 42 Sh 7A&B.*

4866. "Robert L. Claire Van Horn Obituary."

4867. "Raymond L. Van Horn Obituary Indiana County Genealogical and Historical Society Newspaper Clippings."

4868. "Robert L. Claire Van Horn Obituary."

4869. *Plumville, South Mahoning Twp., Indiana Cnty, PA 1920 Census ED 123 Sh 1A.*

4870. *Plumville, South Mahoning Twp., Indiana Cnty, PA 1930 Census ED 42 Sh 7A&B.*

4871. "Wilbur Van Horn Obituary Indiana County Genealogical and Historical Society Newspaper Clippings."

4872. *Plumville, South Mahoning Twp., Indiana Cnty, PA 1930 Census ED 42 Sh 7A&B.*

4873. *Plumville, South Mahoning Twp., Indiana Cnty, PA 1920 Census ED 123 Sh 1A.*

4874. *Plumville, South Mahoning Twp., Indiana Cnty, PA 1930 Census ED 42 Sh 7A&B.*

4875. "Raymond L. Van Horn Obituary Indiana County Genealogical and Historical Society Newspaper Clippings."

4876. "Robert L. Claire Van Horn Obituary."

4877. "Wilbur Van Horn Obituary Indiana County Genealogical and Historical Society Newspaper Clippings."

4878. *Plumville, South Mahoning Twp., Indiana Cnty, PA 1930 Census ED 42 Sh 7A&B.*

4879. SSN Death Index.

4880. *Plumville, South Mahoning Twp., Indiana Cnty, PA 1930 Census ED 42 Sh 7A&B.*

4881. "Floyd Van Horn Obituary Indiana County Genealogical and Historical Society Newspaper Clippings."

4882. "Raymond L. Van Horn Obituary Indiana County Genealogical and Historical Society Newspaper Clippings."

4883. "Robert L. Claire Van Horn Obituary."

4884. "Wilbur Van Horn Obituary Indiana County Genealogical and Historical Society Newspaper Clippings."

4885. *Plumville, South Mahoning Twp., Indiana Cnty, PA 1930 Census ED 42 Sh 7A&B.*

4886. "Robert L. Claire Van Horn Obituary."

4887. *Plumville, South Mahoning Twp., Indiana Cnty, PA 1930 Census ED 42 Sh 7A&B.*

4888. "Wilbur Van Horn Obituary Indiana County Genealogical and Historical Society Newspaper Clippings."

4889. *Plumville, South Mahoning Twp., Indiana Cnty, PA 1930 Census ED 42 Sh 7A&B.*

4890. "Floyd Van Horn Obituary Indiana County Genealogical and Historical Society Newspaper Clippings."

4891. *Plumville, South Mahoning Twp., Indiana Cnty, PA 1930 Census ED 42 Sh 7A&B.*

4892. "Raymond L. Van Horn Obituary Indiana County Genealogical and Historical Society Newspaper Clippings."

4893. "Robert L. Claire Van Horn Obituary."

4894. "Van Horn, Margaret Obituary Indiana County Genealogical and Historical Society Newspaper Clippings."

4895. "29 June 1949 Indiana Evening Gazette (Indiana, PA) Marriage License."

4896. *Plumville, South Mahoning Twp., Indiana Cnty, PA 1930 Census ED 42 Sh 7A&B.*

4897. "Van Horn, Margaret Obituary Indiana County Genealogical and Historical Society Newspaper Clippings."

4898. "29 June 1949 Indiana Evening Gazette (Indiana, PA) Marriage License."

4899. "Van Horn, Margaret Obituary Indiana County Genealogical and Historical Society Newspaper Clippings."

4900. "29 June 1949 Indiana Evening Gazette (Indiana, PA) Marriage License."

4901. *Plumville, South Mahoning Twp., Indiana Cnty, PA 1930 Census ED 42 Sh 7A&B.*

4902. "Raymond L. Van Horn Obituary Indiana County Genealogical and Historical Society

Newspaper Clippings."
4903. "Robert L. Claire Van Horn Obituary."
4904. "Wilbur Van Horn Obituary Indiana County Genealogical and Historical Society Newspaper Clippings."
4905. *Plumville, South Mahoning Twp., Indiana Cnty, PA 1930 Census ED 42 Sh 7A&B.*
4906. "Robert L. Claire Van Horn Obituary."
4907. "Raymond L. Van Horn Obituary Indiana County Genealogical and Historical Society Newspaper Clippings."
4908. "Floyd Van Horn Obituary Indiana County Genealogical and Historical Society Newspaper Clippings."
4909. *South Mahoning Twp., Indiana Cnty, PA 1920 Census ED 24 Sh 8A.*
4910. *Rayne Twp., Indiana Cnty, PA 1930 Census ED 44 Sh 3A.*
4911. "22 July 1971 Indiana Evenng Gazette (Indiana, PA) Obituary Deloris Belle Van Horn Weaver."
4912. *South Mahoning Twp., Indiana Cnty, PA 1920 Census ED 24 Sh 8A.*
4913. "31 Aug 1970 Indiana Evenng Gazette (Indiana, PA) Alex Lambing Obituary."
4914. *Rayne Twp., Indiana Cnty, PA 1930 Census ED 44 Sh 3A.*
4915. "31 Aug 1970 Indiana Evenng Gazette (Indiana, PA) Alex Lambing Obituary."
4916. *South Mahoning Twp., Indiana Cnty, PA 1920 Census ED 24 Sh 8A.*
4917. *White Twp., Indiana Cnty, PA 1930 Census ED 52 Sh 10B.*
4918. *South Mahoning Twp., Indiana Cnty, PA 1920 Census ED 24 Sh 8A.*
4919. "22 July 1971 Indiana Evenng Gazette (Indiana, PA) Obituary Deloris Belle Van Horn Weaver."
4920. *South Mahoning Twp., Indiana Cnty, PA 1920 Census ED 24 Sh 8A.*
4921. *Rayne Twp., Indiana Cnty, PA 1930 Census ED 44 Sh 3A.*
4922. "22 July 1971 Indiana Evenng Gazette (Indiana, PA) Obituary Deloris Belle Van Horn Weaver."
4923. "9 July 1964 Indiana Evenng Gazette (Indiana, PA) Obituary Gary Lee Stewart."
4924. *South Mahoning Twp., Indiana Cnty, PA 1920 Census ED 24 Sh 8A.*
4925. "22 July 1971 Indiana Evenng Gazette (Indiana, PA) Obituary Deloris Belle Van Horn Weaver."
4926. "9 July 1964 Indiana Evenng Gazette (Indiana, PA) Obituary Gary Lee Stewart."
4927. *South Mahoning Twp., Indiana Cnty, PA 1930 Census ED 48 Sh 8A.*
4928. *South Mahoning Twp., Indiana Cnty, PA 1920 Census ED 24 Sh 8A.*
4929. "Merle Wayne Van Horn Obituary Indiana County Genealogical and Historical Society Newspaper Clippings."
4930. "Van Horn, Margaret Obituary Indiana County Genealogical and Historical Society Newspaper Clippings."
4931. "Van Horn, John S. Obituary Indiana County Genealogical and Historical Society Newspaper Clippings."
4932. *South Mahoning Twp., Indiana Cnty, PA 1930 Census ED 48 Sh 8A.*
4933. "Van Horn, John S. Obituary Indiana County Genealogical and Historical Society Newspaper Clippings."
4934. "Van Horn, Marion Obiuary Indiana County Genealogical and Historical Society Newspaper Clippings."
4935. "Van Horn, John S. Obituary Indiana County Genealogical and Historical Society Newspaper Clippings."
4936. "Van Horn, Marion Obiuary Indiana County Genealogical and Historical Society Newspaper Clippings."
4937. *South Mahoning Twp., Indiana Cnty, PA 1930 Census ED 48 Sh 8A.*
4938. *South Mahoning Twp., Indiana Cnty, PA 1920 Census ED 24 Sh 8A.*
4939. "Merle Wayne Van Horn Obituary Indiana County Genealogical and Historical Society Newspaper Clippings."
4940. *South Mahoning Twp., Indiana Cnty, PA 1930 Census ED 48 Sh 8A.*

4941. SSN Death Index.

4942. *South Mahoning Twp., Indiana Cnty, PA 1930 Census ED 48 Sh 8A.*

4943. "Harry Bennett Van Horn Obituary Indiana County Genealogical and Historical Society Newspaper Clippings."

4944. *South Mahoning Twp., Indiana Cnty, PA 1920 Census ED 24 Sh 8A.*

4945. "Merle Van Horn Obituary Indiana County Genealogical and Historical Society Newspaper Clippings."

4946. *South Mahoning Twp., Indiana Cnty, PA 1930 Census ED 48 Sh 8A.*

4947. "Indiana Evening Gazette (Indiana, PA) 4 September 1948."

4948. "Glennetta Campbell Van Horn Obituary Indiana County Genealogical and Historical Society Newspaper Clippings."

4949. *South Mahoning Twp., Indiana Cnty, PA 1930 Census ED 48 Sh 8A.*

4950. "Clair Van Horn Obituary Indiana County Genealogical and Historical Society Newspaper Clippings."

4951. "Merle Wayne Van Horn Obituary Indiana County Genealogical and Historical Society Newspaper Clippings."

4952. *South Mahoning Twp., Indiana Cnty, PA 1930 Census ED 48 Sh 8A.*

4953. "Clair Van Horn Obituary Indiana County Genealogical and Historical Society Newspaper Clippings."

4954. "Merle Wayne Van Horn Obituary Indiana County Genealogical and Historical Society Newspaper Clippings."

4955. *South Mahoning Twp., Indiana Cnty, PA 1930 Census ED 48 Sh 8A.*

4956. *Social Security Records Ancestry.com,* "Electronic."

4957. "Clair Van Horn Obituary Indiana County Genealogical and Historical Society Newspaper Clippings."

4958. *Social Security Records Ancestry.com,* "Electronic."

4959. *South Mahoning Twp., Indiana Cnty, PA 1930 Census ED 48 Sh 8A.*

4960. "Merle Van Horn Obituary Indiana County Genealogical and Historical Society Newspaper Clippings."

4961. "Van Horn, Harry 35 year Anniversary and Wedding Article Indiana County Genealogical and Historical Society Newspaper Clippings."

4962. "Wedding Announcements for Blaine Van Horn and Ruth Waltz Indiana County Genealogical and Historical Society Newspaper Clippings."

4963. *South Mahoning Twp., Indiana Cnty, PA 1930 Census ED 48 Sh 8A.*

4964. Blaine W. and Ruth Waltz Van Horn Tombstone.

4965. "Van Horn, Harry 35 year Anniversary and Wedding Article Indiana County Genealogical and Historical Society Newspaper Clippings."

4966. "Wedding Announcements for Blaine Van Horn and Ruth Waltz Indiana County Genealogical and Historical Society Newspaper Clippings."

4967. "Van Horn, Harry 35 year Anniversary and Wedding Article Indiana County Genealogical and Historical Society Newspaper Clippings."

4968. "Wedding Announcements for Blaine Van Horn and Ruth Waltz Indiana County Genealogical and Historical Society Newspaper Clippings."

4969. "Van Horn, Harry 35 year Anniversary and Wedding Article Indiana County Genealogical and Historical Society Newspaper Clippings."

4970. "Wedding Announcements for Blaine Van Horn and Ruth Waltz Indiana County Genealogical and Historical Society Newspaper Clippings."

4971. "Melinda Van Horn Obituary Indiana County Genealogical and Historical Society Newspaper Clippings."

4972. "Kenneth Allan Van Horn Obituary Indiana County Genealogical and Historical Society Newspaper Clippings."

4973. "Clair Van Horn Obituary Indiana County Genealogical and Historical Society Newspaper Clippings."

4974. "Merle Wayne Van Horn Obituary Indiana County Genealogical and Historical Society

Newspaper Clippings."
4975. "Clair Van Horn Obituary Indiana County Genealogical and Historical Society Newspaper Clippings."
4976. *South Mahoning Twp., Indiana Cnty, PA 1930 Census ED 48 Sh 11B.*
4977. "6 Feb 1963 Indiana Evening Gazette (Indiana, PA) 50th Wedding Story of Delbert and Pearl Good."
4978. *South Mahoning Twp., Indiana Cnty, PA 1930 Census ED 48 Sh 11B.*
4979. "6 Feb 1963 Indiana Evening Gazette (Indiana, PA) 50th Wedding Story of Delbert and Pearl Good."
4980. *South Mahoning Twp., Indiana Cnty, PA 1930 Census ED 48 Sh 11B.*
4981. "6 Feb 1963 Indiana Evening Gazette (Indiana, PA) 50th Wedding Story of Delbert and Pearl Good."
4982. *South Mahoning Twp., Indiana Cnty, PA 1930 Census ED 48 Sh 11B.*
4983. "6 Feb 1963 Indiana Evening Gazette (Indiana, PA) 50th Wedding Story of Delbert and Pearl Good."
4984. *South Mahoning Twp., Indiana Cnty, PA 1930 Census ED 48 Sh 11B.*
4985. "6 Feb 1963 Indiana Evening Gazette (Indiana, PA) 50th Wedding Story of Delbert and Pearl Good."
4986. "25 May 1949 Indiana Evening Gazette (Indiana, PA) Birth announcement of Terry Good."
4987. *South Mahoning Twp., Indiana Cnty, PA 1930 Census ED 48 Sh 11B.*
4988. "25 May 1949 Indiana Evening Gazette (Indiana, PA) Birth announcement of Terry Good."
4989. "11 Sept 1971 Indiana Evening Gazette(Indiana, PA) Norman Clarence Van Horn Obituary."
4990. "Van Horn, Effie Obituary Indiana County Genealogical and Historical Society Newspaper Clippings."
4991. "11 Sept 1971 Indiana Evening Gazette(Indiana, PA) Norman Clarence Van Horn Obituary."
4992. "Van Horn, Effie Obituary Indiana County Genealogical and Historical Society Newspaper Clippings."
4993. "11 Sept 1971 Indiana Evening Gazette(Indiana, PA) Norman Clarence Van Horn Obituary."
4994. "Van Horn, Effie Obituary Indiana County Genealogical and Historical Society Newspaper Clippings."
4995. *Plumville,South Mahoning Twp., Indiana Cnty, PA 1930 Census ED 42 Sh 3B.*
4996. "11 Sept 1971 Indiana Evening Gazette(Indiana, PA) Norman Clarence Van Horn Obituary."
4997. "Van Horn, Effie Obituary Indiana County Genealogical and Historical Society Newspaper Clippings."
4998. "Wedding Announcement dated 3/6/1953 in the Indiana Evening Gazette(Indiana, PA)."
4999. "Glenn L. Van Horn Obituary Indiana County Genealogical and Historical Society Newspaper Clippings."
5000. SSN Death Index.
5001. *North Mahoning Twp., Indiana Cnty, PA 1930 Census ED 39 Sh 5A.*
5002. "24 Nov 1965 Indiana Evening Gazette (Indiana, PA) 50th Anniversary Fetterhoffs."
5003. *North Mahoning Twp., Indiana Cnty, PA 1930 Census ED 39 Sh 5A.*
5004. "24 June 1953 Indiana Evening Gazette (Indiana, PA)."
5005. "24 Nov 1965 Indiana Evening Gazette (Indiana, PA) 50th Anniversary Fetterhoffs."
5006. *North Mahoning Twp., Indiana Cnty, PA 1930 Census ED 39 Sh 5A.*
5007. "24 June 1953 Indiana Evening Gazette (Indiana, PA)."
5008. Hamilton, Von Gail, *Work Family History: Twelve Generations of Work in America 1690-1969, Park City, Utah,* (Park City, Utah: Publishers Press, 1969, 614 pgs.).
5009. *Denver, Denver Cnty, CO 1930 Census ED 120 Sh 7A.*
5010. *Clarion, Clarion Cnty, PA 1910 Census ED 6 Sh 10B.*
5011. *Pittsburgh, Ward 23, Allegheny Cnty, PA 1920 Census ED 685 Ah 4B.*
5012. *Pittsburgh, Ward 3, Allegheny Cnty, PA 1930 Census ED 664 Sh 5A.*
5013. *Clarion, Clarion Cnty, PA 1910 Census ED 6 Sh 10B.*
5014. *Pittsburgh, Ward 3, Allegheny Cnty, PA 1930 Census ED 664 Sh 5A.*
5015. *Connellsville, Fayette Cnty, PA 1910 Census ED 14 Sh 9B.*

5016. *Crafton, Allegheny Cnty, PA 1920 Census ED 74 Sh 20B.*

5017. *Pittsburgh, Allegheny Cnty, PA 1930 Census ED 331 Sh 14A.*

5018. *Connellsville, Fayette Cnty, PA 1910 Census ED 14 Sh 9B.*

5019. *Pittsburgh, Allegheny Cnty, PA 1930 Census ED 331 Sh 14A.*

5020. *Scottdale Ward 1, Westmoreland Cnty, PA 1910 Census ED 191 Sh 12A.*

5021. *Meyersdale, Somerset Cnty, PA 1930 Census ED 31 Sh 7B.*

5022. *Scottdale Ward 1, Westmoreland Cnty, PA 1910 Census ED 191 Sh 12A.*

5023. *Scottdale Ward 1, Westmoreland Cnty, PA 1920 Census ED 201 Sh 18B.*

5024. *Scottdale, Westmoreland Cnty, PA 1930 Census ED 147 Sh 11A.*

5025. *Scottdale Ward 1, Westmoreland Cnty, PA 1910 Census ED 191 Sh 12A.*

5026. *Scottdale Ward 1, Westmoreland Cnty, PA 1920 Census ED 201 Sh 18B.*

5027. *Scottdale, Westmoreland Cnty, PA 1930 Census ED 147 Sh 11A.*

5028. *East Hunnington, Westmoreland Cnty, PA 1930 Census ED 24 Sh 10A.*

5029. Willey, Gordon (Van Horn TREE) Husband of Jacqueline Marshal Granddaughter of Judson Van Horn.

5030. *East Hunnington, Westmoreland Cnty, PA 1930 Census ED 24 Sh 10A.*

5031. Willey, Gordon (Van Horn TREE) Husband of Jacqueline Marshal Granddaughter of Judson Van Horn.

5032. *East Hunnington, Westmoreland Cnty, PA 1930 Census ED 24 Sh 10A.*

5033. Willey, Gordon (Van Horn TREE) Husband of Jacqueline Marshal Granddaughter of Judson Van Horn.

5034. *East Hunnington, Westmoreland Cnty, PA 1930 Census ED 24 Sh 10A.*

5035. Willey, Gordon (Van Horn TREE) Husband of Jacqueline Marshal Granddaughter of Judson Van Horn.

5036. *Scottdale Ward 3, Westmoreland Cnty, PA 1930 Census ED 1471 Sh 8A.*

5037. *NC Death Collection 1908-2004,* "Electronic."

5038. *Edgewood, Allegheny Cnty, PA 1930 Census ED 585 Sh 14B.*

5039. *New Florence, Westmoreland Cnty, PA 1920 Census ED 171 Sh 3B.*

5040. *New Florence, Westmoreland Cnty, PA 1930 Census ED 114 Sh 1B.*

5041. *New Florence, Westmoreland Cnty, PA 1920 Census ED 171 Sh 3B.*

5042. *New Florence, Westmoreland Cnty, PA 1930 Census ED 114 Sh 1B.*

5043. *New Florence, Westmoreland Cnty, PA 1920 Census ED 171 Sh 3B.*

5044. SSN Death Index.

5045. Handwritten Notes of Leafy Fern Van Horn Wolf.

5046. Haas, Rodney personal information on family.

5047. Broderbund Family Archive #110, Vol. 1, Ed. 3, Social Security Records: U.S., SS Death Benefit Records, Surnames Beginning with H, Date of Import: Dec 16, 1995, Internal Ref. #1.111.3.86160.32

5048. Brøderbund Family Archive #110, Vol. 1, Ed. 3, Social Security Records: U.S., SS Death Benefit Records, Surnames Beginning with H, Date of Import: Dec 16, 1995, Internal Ref. #1.111.3.86160.32

5049. Broderbund Family Archive #110, Vol. 1, Ed. 3, Social Security Records: U.S., SS Death Benefit Records, Surnames Beginning with H, Date of Import: Dec 16, 1995, Internal Ref. #1.111.3.86160.32

5050. Brøderbund Family Archive #110, Vol. 1, Ed. 3, Social Security Records: U.S., SS Death Benefit Records, Surnames Beginning with H, Date of Import: Dec 16, 1995, Internal Ref. #1.111.3.86160.32

5051. Haas, Rodney personal information on family.

5052. Brøderbund Family Archive #110, Vol. 1, Ed. 3, Social Security Records: U.S., SS Death Benefit Records, Surnames Beginning with H, Date of Import: Dec 1, 1998, Internal Ref. #1.111.3.86160.32

5053. Direct Personal Information.

5054. Broderbund Family Archive #110, Vol. 2, Ed. 3, Social Security Records: U.S., SS Death Benefit Records, Surnames Beginning with M, Date of Import: Dec 16, 1995, Internal Ref.

#1.112.3.22017.196
5055. Handwritten Notes of Leafy Fern Van Horn Wolf.
5056. Broderbund Family Archive #110, Vol. 1, Ed. 3, Social Security Records: U.S., SS Death Benefit Records, Surnames Beginning with C, Date of Import: Dec 16, 1995, Internal Ref. #1.111.3.37757.29
5057. *Jeanette, Westmoreland Cnty, PA 1930 Census ED 69 Sh 12B.*
5058. *Buffalo, Erie Cnty, NY 1930 Cenus ED 229 Sh 2A.*
5059. *Harmony, Forrest Cnty, PA 1910 Census ED 56 Sh 7A.*
5060. *Harmony, Forrest Cnty, PA 1900 Census ED 47 Sh 6B.*
5061. *Buffalo, Erie Cnty, NY 1930 Cenus ED 229 Sh 2A.*
5062. *Harmony, Forrest Cnty, PA 1920 Census ED 26 Sh 6A.*
5063. *Harmony, Forrest Cnty, PA 1910 Census ED 56 Sh 7A.*
5064. *Pittsburgh, Allegheny Cnty, PA 1930 Census ED 293 Sh 15B.*
5065. *Harmony, Forrest Cnty, PA 1920 Census ED 26 Sh 6A.*
5066. *Pittsburgh, Allegheny Cnty, PA 1930 Census ED 293 Sh 15B.*
5067. *Otter Tail, Otter Tail Cnty, MN 1905 Territorial Census ED 8.*
5068. *Strathmore Langdon, Calgary, Alberta Canada 1911 Census p. 14.*
5069. *Los Angeles, Los Angeles Cnty, CA 1930 Census ED 493 Sh 97B.*
5070. *Otter Tail, Otter Tail Cnty, MN 1905 Territorial Census ED 8.*
5071. SSN Death Index.
5072. *California Death Index 1940-1997,* "Electronic."
5073. *Tuscon, Pima Cnty, AZ 1910 Census ED 107 Sh 8A.*
5074. *Los Angeles, Los Angeles Cnty, CA 1930 Census ED 276 Sh 2A.*
5075. *Tuscon, Pima Cnty, AZ 1910 Census ED 107 Sh 8A.*
5076. *Otter Tail, Otter Tail Cnty, MN 1905 Territorial Census ED 8.*
5077. *Strathmore Langdon, Calgary, Alberta Canada 1911 Census p. 14.*
5078. *Otter Tail, Otter Tail Cnty, MN 1905 Territorial Census ED 8.*
5079. *Strathmore Langdon, Calgary, Alberta Canada 1911 Census p. 14.*
5080. *British Columbia Death Index 1872-1979,* "Electronic."
5081. *Rayne Twp., Indiana Cnty, PA 1930 Census ED 43 Sh 19 A.*
5082. *White Twp., Indiana Cnty, PA 1920 Census ED 132 Sh 9B.*
5083. *Presho, Lyman Cnty, SD 1910 Census Ed 61 Sh 6B.*
5084. *Presho, Lyman Cnty, SD 1930 Census ED 27 Sh 5A.*
5085. *Presho, Lyman Cnty, SD 1910 Census Ed 61 Sh 6B.*
5086. SSN Death Index.
5087. *Presho, Lyman Cnty, SD 1930 Census ED 27 Sh 5A.*
5088. *Brule, Brule Cnty, SD 1910 Census ED 71 Sh 6A.*
5089. *Chamberlain, Brule Cnty, SD 1920 Census ED 24 Sh 9B.*
5090. *Queens, Queens Cnty, NY 1930 Census ED 567 Sh 25A.*
5091. *Brule, Brule Cnty, SD 1910 Census ED 71 Sh 6A.*
5092. *Queens, Queens Cnty, NY 1930 Census ED 567 Sh 25A.*
5093. *Brule, Brule Cnty, SD 1910 Census ED 71 Sh 6A.*
5094. *Chamberlain, Brule Cnty, SD 1920 Census ED 24 Sh 9B.*
5095. *Sioux Falls, Minnehaha Cnty, SD 1930 Census ED 39 Sh 8A.*
5096. *Brule, Brule Cnty, SD 1910 Census ED 71 Sh 6A.*
5097. *Elsworth, Elsworh Cnty, KS 1905 Kansas Census P. 1-6.*
5098. *Kennebec Ward 1, Lyman Cnty, SD 1910 Census ED 52 Sh 7A.*
5099. *Kennebec, Lyman Cnty, SD1920 Census ED 130 Sh 7A.*
5100. *Kennebec, Lyman Cnty, SD 1930 Census ED 15 Sh 2A.*
5101. DAR National Record Copy of Member Application # 486836.
5102. *Kennebec Ward 1, Lyman Cnty, SD 1910 Census ED 52 Sh 7A.*
5103. DAR National Record Copy of Member Application # 486836.
5104. *Kennebec Ward 1, Lyman Cnty, SD 1910 Census ED 52 Sh 7A.*
5105. *Kennebec, Lyman Cnty, SD1920 Census ED 130 Sh 7A.*

5106. *Kennebec, Lyman Cnty, SD 1930 Census ED 15 Sh 2A.*
5107. DAR National Record Copy of Member Application # 486837.
5108. *Kennebec Ward 1, Lyman Cnty, SD 1910 Census ED 52 Sh 7A.*
5109. *Kennebec, Lyman Cnty, SD1920 Census ED 130 Sh 7A.*
5110. *Kennebec, Lyman Cnty, SD 1930 Census ED 15 Sh 2A.*
5111. Nellie Mae Clower Van Horn Obituary.
5112. *South Mahoning Twp., Indiana Cnty, PA 1900 Census ED 64 Sh 10B.*
5113. "Andrew G. Van Horn Obituary."
5114. "Oran Dent Van Horn Obituary Indiana County Genealogical and Historical Society Newspaper Clippings."
5115. "Mary Juart Van Horn Obituary Indiana County Genealogical and Historical Society Newspaper Clippings."
5116. *South Mahoning Twp., Indiana Cnty, PA 1900 Census ED 64 Sh 11A.*
5117. *Marion Center, East Mahoning Twp., Indiana Cnty, PA 1910 Census ED 73 Sh 12B.*
5118. *Punxsutawney, Jefferson Cnty, PA 1930 Census ED 25 Sh 14A & B.*
5119. *Punxsutwaney Ward 2, Jefferson Cnty, PA 1920 Census ED 158 Sh 4B & 5A.*
5120. *Quaker Records of the Miami Valley of Ohio, 1980.*
5121. *South Mahoning Twp., Indiana Cnty, PA 1900 Census ED 64 Sh 10B.*
5122. Nellie Mae Clower Van Horn Obituary.
5123. *Punxsutwaney, Jefferson Cnty, PA 1930 Census ED 25 Sh 14A & B.*
5124. "Andrew G. Van Horn Obituary."
5125. *Punxsutwaney Ward 2, Jefferson Cnty, PA 1920 Census ED 158 Sh 4B & 5A.*
5126. "28 May 1975 Indiana Evening Gazette (Indiana, PA) Alta Blanche Burkley Obituary."
5127. Nellie Mae Clower Van Horn Obituary.
5128. *Punxsutwaney Ward 2, Jefferson Cnty, PA 1920 Census ED 158 Sh 4B & 5A.*
5129. *Punxsutwaney, Jefferson Cnty, PA 1930 Census ED 25 Sh 14A & B.*
5130. *Punxsutwaney Ward 2, Jefferson Cnty, PA 1920 Census ED 158 Sh 4B & 5A.*
5131. Nellie Mae Clower Van Horn Obituary.
5132. *Punxsutawney, Jefferson Cnty, PA 1930 Census ED 25 Sh 14A & B.*
5133. Nellie Mae Clower Van Horn Obituary.
5134. *Punxsutawney, Jefferson Cnty, PA 1930 Census ED 25 Sh 14A & B.*
5135. *South Mahoning Twp., Indiana Cnty, PA 1900 Census ED 64 Sh 10B.*
5136. "Oran Dent Van Horn Obituary Indiana County Genealogical and Historical Society Newspaper Clippings."
5137. "Mary Juart Van Horn Obituary Indiana County Genealogical and Historical Society Newspaper Clippings."
5138. *Marion Center, East Mahoning Twp., Indiana Cnty, PA 1910 Census ED 73 Sh 12B.*
5139. "6 Jan 1936 Indiana Evening Gazette (Indiana, PA) Listing of marriages 20 years ago."
5140. *Creekside, Indiana Cnty, PA 1920 Census ED 107 Sh 1A.*
5141. *Washington, Indiana Cnty, PA 1930 Census ED 23 Sh 1B.*
5142. *South Mahoning Twp., Indiana Cnty, PA 1900 Census ED 64 Sh 10B.*
5143. "Mary Juart Van Horn Obituary Indiana County Genealogical and Historical Society Newspaper Clippings."
5144. "6 Jan 1936 Indiana Evening Gazette (Indiana, PA) Listing of marriages 20 years ago."
5145. *Creekside, Indiana Cnty, PA 1920 Census ED 107 Sh 1A.*
5146. *Washington, Indiana Cnty, PA 1930 Census ED 23 Sh 1B.*
5147. "6 Jan 1936 Indiana Evening Gazette (Indiana, PA) Listing of marriages 20 years ago."
5148. SSN Death Index.
5149. *Creekside, Indiana Cnty, PA 1920 Census ED 107 Sh 1A.*
5150. SSN Death Index.
5151. "6 Jan 1936 Indiana Evening Gazette (Indiana, PA) Listing of marriages 20 years ago."
5152. SSN Death Index.
5153. *Creekside, Indiana Cnty, PA 1920 Census ED 107 Sh 1A.*
5154. "Oran Dent Van Horn Obituary Indiana County Genealogical and Historical Society

Newspaper Clippings."
5155. *South Mahoning Twp., Indiana Cnty, PA 1900 Census ED 64 Sh 10B.*
5156. *Marion Center, East Mahoning Twp., Indiana Cnty, PA 1910 Census ED 73 Sh 12B.*
5157. *Marion Center, East Mahoning Twp., Indiana Cnty, PA 1920 Census ED 108 Sh 14B.*
5158. "Mary Juart Van Horn Obituary Indiana County Genealogical and Historical Society Newspaper Clippings."
5159. *Punxsutwaney Ward 3, Jefferson Cnty, PA 1930 Census ED 26 Sh 11A.*
5160. *WWI Draft Registration Card 1917-1918,* "Electronic."
5161. *South Mahoning Twp., Indiana Cnty, PA 1900 Census ED 64 Sh 11A.*
5162. *Punxsutwaney Ward 3, Jefferson Cnty, PA 1930 Census ED 26 Sh 11A.*
5163. WWI Civilian Draft Registration Index.
5164. *Marion Center, East Mahoning Twp., Indiana Cnty, PA 1920 Census ED 108 Sh 14B.*
5165. "Indiana Progress (Indiana Cnty, PA) 4 September1918."
5166. *Punxsutwaney Ward 3, Jefferson Cnty, PA 1930 Census ED 26 Sh 11A.*
5167. "Indiana Progress (Indiana Cnty, PA) 4 September1918."
5168. D. Scott Van Horn Family Group Sheet, August 8, 1983.
5169. "LeRoy Van Horn Obituary Indiana County Genealogical and Historical Society Newspaper Clippings."
5170. *Youngstown, Mahoning Cnty, OH 1920 Census ED 78 Sh 20B.*
5171. "Indiana Progress (Indiana Cnty, PA) 11 September 1912."
5172. D. Scott Van Horn Family Group Sheet, August 8, 1983.
5173. Ohio Deaths, 1908-1932, 1938-1944, and 1958-2002.
5174. D. Scott Van Horn Family Group Sheet, August 8, 1983.
5175. Ohio Deaths, 1908-1932, 1938-1944, and 1958-2002.
5176. "Sprague L. Van Horn Obituary Indiana County Genealogical and Historical Society Newspaper Clippings."
5177. *South Mahoning Twp., Indiana Cnty, PA 1910 Census ED 92 Sh 4A.*
5178. DAR National Record Copy of Member Application # 835192.
5179. *South Mahoning Twp., Indiana Cnty, PA 1910 Census ED 92 Sh 4A.*
5180. DAR National Record Copy of Member Application # 835192.
5181. "13 Jan 1965 Indiana Evening Gazette (Indiana, PA) George Percy Van Horn Obit."
5182. *Aliquippa, Beaver Cnty, PA 1920 Census ED 1 Sh 12A.*
5183. *Aliquippa, Beaver Cnty, PA 1930 Census ED 8 Sh 1A.*
5184. *Aliquippa, Beaver Cnty, PA 1920 Census ED 1 Sh 12A.*
5185. "13 Jan 1965 Indiana Evening Gazette (Indiana, PA) George Percy Van Horn Obit."
5186. *Aliquippa, Beaver Cnty, PA 1920 Census ED 1 Sh 12A.*
5187. *Aliquippa, Beaver Cnty, PA 1930 Census ED 8 Sh 1A.*
5188. *Aliquippa, Beaver Cnty, PA 1920 Census ED 1 Sh 12A.*
5189. *California Death Index 1940-1997,* "Electronic."
5190. *Homer, Indiana Cnty, PA 1920 Census ED 112 Sh 13B.*
5191. *Homer, Indiana Cnty, PA 1930 Census ED 30 Sh 14B.*
5192. *Homer, Indiana Cnty, PA 1920 Census ED 112 Sh 13B.*
5193. SSN Death Index.
5194. *Homer, Indiana Cnty, PA 1930 Census ED 30 Sh 14B.*
5195. SSN Death Index.
5196. *Cowanshannock Twp., Armstrong Cnty, PA 1910 Census ED 9 Sh 7A.*
5197. *Cowanshannock Twp., Armstrong Cnty, PA 1930 Census ED 11 Sh 2B.*
5198. "2 April 1960 Simpson's Leader-Times (Kittanning, PA) Bertha A. Lukehart Neal Obituary."
5199. "27 Jan 2005 News Leader (Pittsburgh, PA) Obituary Shirley Mae Barrett."
5200. *Cowanshannock Twp., Armstrong Cnty, PA 1910 Census ED 9 Sh 7A.*
5201. "27 Jan 2005 News Leader (Pittsburgh, PA) Obituary Shirley Mae Barrett."
5202. *Cowanshannock Twp., Armstrong Cnty, PA 1930 Census ED 11 Sh 2B.*
5203. *Cowanshannock Twp., Armstrong Cnty, PA ED 11 Sh 2B.*
5204. *West Millville, Clarion Cnty, PA 1900 Census ED 22 Sh 12B.*

5205. *Hawthorn, Clarion Cnty, PA 1910 Census ED 25 Sh 1A.*
5206. *New Bethlehem, Clarion Cnty, PA 1930 Census ED 22 Sh 11B.*
5207. *West Millville, Clarion Cnty, PA 1900 Census ED 22 Sh 12B.*
5208. "19 June 1976 The Oil City Derrick (Oil City, PA) Obituary of Lula VanHorn."
5209. *New Bethlehem, Clarion Cnty, PA 1930 Census ED 22 Sh 11B.*
5210. "19 June 1976 The Oil City Derrick (Oil City, PA) Obituary of Lula VanHorn."
5211. *New Bethlehem, Clarion Cnty, PA 1930 Census ED 22 Sh 11B.*
5212. "19 June 1976 The Oil City Derrick (Oil City, PA) Obituary of Lula VanHorn."
5213. *Kingsley Twp., Forest Cnty, PA 1910 Census ED 60 Sh 8B.*
5214. *Wetmore, McKean Cnty, PA 1900 Census ED 125 Sh 9A.*
5215. *Howe, Forrest Cnty, PA 1930 Census ED 5 Sh 2B.*
5216. *Kingsley Twp., Forest Cnty, PA 1910 Census ED 60 Sh 8B.*
5217. *Wetmore, McKean Cnty, PA 1900 Census ED 125 Sh 9A.*
5218. *Howe, Forrest Cnty, PA 1930 Census ED 5 Sh 2B.*
5219. *Erie, Millcreek Twp., Erie Cnty, PA 1930 Census ED 54 Sh 13A.*
5220. *Erie, Ward 3, Erie Cnty, PA 1920 Census ED 89 Sh 16A.*
5221. *Kingsley Twp., Forest Cnty, PA 1910 Census ED 60 Sh 8B.*
5222. *Wetmore, McKean Cnty, PA 1900 Census ED 125 Sh 9A.*
5223. *Erie, Millcreek Twp., Erie Cnty, PA 1930 Census ED 54 Sh 13A.*
5224. *Kingsley Twp., Forest Cnty, PA 1910 Census ED 60 Sh 8B.*
5225. *Wetmore, McKean Cnty, PA 1900 Census ED 125 Sh 9A.*
5226. *Erie, Millcreek Twp., Erie Cnty, PA 1930 Census ED 54 Sh 13A.*
5227. *Erie, Ward 3, Erie Cnty, PA 1920 Census ED 89 Sh 16A.*
5228. *Erie, Millcreek Twp., Erie Cnty, PA 1930 Census ED 54 Sh 13A.*
5229. *Erie, Ward 3, Erie Cnty, PA 1920 Census ED 89 Sh 16A.*
5230. *Erie, Millcreek Twp., Erie Cnty, PA 1930 Census ED 54 Sh 13A.*
5231. *Dayton, Armstrong Cnty, PA 1920 Census ED 12 Sh 6A.*
5232. *Dayton, Armstrong Cnty, PA 1930 Census ED 13 Sh 4B.*
5233. "12 Feb 1913 Indiana Progress (Indiana, PA) birth announcemet of the birth of twins last week to William Gearhart."
5234. *Dayton, Armstrong Cnty, PA 1920 Census ED 12 Sh 6A.*
5235. SSN Death Index.
5236. "12 Jan 1962 Simpson's Leader-Times (Kittanning, PA) Pvt Hartzell visist parents Mr and Mrs Delbert Hartzell."
5237. *Falls Creek, Jefferson Cnty, PA 1920 Census ED 146 Sh 1A.*
5238. *Canoe Twp., Indiana Cnty, PA 1930 Census ED 13 Sh 20 A&B.*
5239. *Falls Creek, Jefferson Cnty, PA 1920 Census ED 146 Sh 1A.*
5240. *Rexford, Smith Twp., Thomas Cnty, KS 1930 Census ED 12 Sh 4A.*
5241. *Dorothy M. McAfoos Miller Obituary reproduced in notes source unknow*, "Electronic."
5242. *Rexford, Smith Twp., Thomas Cnty, KS 1930 Census ED 12 Sh 4A.*
5243. SSN Death Index.
5244. *Lawrence, Cloud Cnty, KS 1930 Census ED 15 Sh 2B.*
5245. *Dorothy M. McAfoos Miller Obituary reproduced in notes source unknow*, "Electronic."
5246. *Lawrence, Cloud Cnty, KS 1930 Census ED 15 Sh 2B.*
5247. SSN Death Index.
5248. *Dorothy M. McAfoos Miller Obituary reproduced in notes source unknow*, "Electronic."
5249. Cook, Decatur Cnty, KS 1910 Census ED 9 Sh 5A.
5250. *Guymon, Texas Cnty, OK 1920 Census ED 191 Sh 16A.*
5251. *Dalhart, Dallam Cnty, TX 1930 Census ED 5 Sh 1A.*
5252. Cook, Decatur Cnty, KS 1910 Census ED 9 Sh 5A.
5253. *Texas Death Index 1903-2000*, "Electronic."
5254. *Guymon, Texas Cnty, OK 1920 Census ED 191 Sh 16A.*
5255. *Dalhart, Dallam Cnty, TX 1930 Census ED 5 Sh 1A.*
5256. SSN Death Index.

5257. *Dalhart, Dallam Cnty, TX 1930 Census ED 5 Sh 1A.*
5258. SSN Death Index.
5259. Cook, Decatur Cnty, KS 1910 Census ED 9 Sh 5A.
5260. *Prairie Dog, Sheridan Cnty, KS 1920 Census ED 194 Sh 9B.*
5261. Cook, Decatur Cnty, KS 1910 Census ED 9 Sh 5A.
5262. "Indiana Evening Gazette (Indiana, PA) Sylvia Harmon Lydic Obit."
5263. WWI Civilian Draft Registration Index.
5264. *Cheekside Twp., Indiana Cnty, PA 1910 Census ED 72 Sh 4A.*
5265. *Rayne Twp., Indiana Cnty, PA 1900 Census ED 60 Sh 6A.*
5266. *Young Twp., Indiana Cnty, PA 1930 Census ED 54 Sh 17B.*
5267. WWI Civilian Draft Registration Index.
5268. *Rayne Twp., Indiana Cnty, PA 1900 Census ED 60 Sh 6A.*
5269. SSN Death Index.
5270. *Young Twp., Indiana Cnty, PA 1930 Census ED 54 Sh 17B.*
5271. SSN Death Index.
5272. *Young Twp., Indiana Cnty, PA 1930 Census ED 54 Sh 17B.*
5273. WWII Young American Patriots 1941-1945 Pennsylvania.
5274. *Young Twp., Indiana Cnty, PA 1930 Census ED 54 Sh 17B.*
5275. Ohio Deaths, 1908-1932, 1938-1944, and 1958-2002.
5276. SSN Death Index.
5277. *Cheekside Twp., Indiana Cnty, PA 1910 Census ED 72 Sh 4A.*
5278. *Young Twp., Indiana Cnty, PA 1930 Census ED 55 Sh 6A.*
5279. *Kittanning, Armstrong Cnty, PA 1920 Census ED 29 Sh 9A.*
5280. *Center Twp., Indiana Cnty, PA 1930 Census ED 16 Sh 4B.*
5281. *Kittanning, Armstrong Cnty, PA 1920 Census ED 29 Sh 9A.*
5282. SSN Death Index.
5283. *Center Twp., Indiana Cnty, PA 1930 Census ED 16 Sh 4B.*
5284. *15 Oct 1947 Indiana Evening Gazette (Indiana, PA) Robert Scott Birth Announcement.*
5285. *Center Twp., Indiana Cnty, PA 1930 Census ED 16 Sh 4B.*
5286. *Creekside, Indiana Cnty, PA 1920 Census ED 107 Sh 3B.*
5287. *Creekside, Indiana Cnty, PA 1930 Census ED 23 Sh 4A.*
5288. *Creekside, Indiana Cnty, PA 1920 Census ED 107 Sh 3B.*
5289. *Limestone, Clarion Cnty, PA 1910 Census ED 14 Sh 4A.*
5290. *East Mahoning Twp., Indiana Cnty, PA 1930 Census ED 24 Sh 6A.*
5291. SSN Death Index.
5292. *Indiana, Indiana Cnty, PA 1930 Census ED 32 Sh 9A.*
5293. "8 Jan 1938 Indiana Evening Gazette (Indiana, PA) Sarah Jane Shearer Ferrier Obit."
5294. "5 Dec 1960 Indiana Evening Gazette (Indiana, PA)."
5295. "Ethyl McAdoo Ferrier Obituary from Indiana Historical and Genealogical Society file dated 3/31/1998."
5296. "9 April 1987 Indiana Gazette (Indiana, PA) Charles Ferrier Obit."
5297. *Indiana, Indiana Cnty, PA 1930 Census ED 32 Sh 9A.*
5298. "5 Dec 1960 Indiana Evening Gazette (Indiana, PA)."
5299. *Cowanshannock Twp., Armstrong Cnty, PA 1930 Census ED 12 Sh 5B.*
5300. "29 Dec. 1960 Indiana Evening Gazette (Indiana, PA) Engagement Anouncement."
5301. *Cowanshannock Twp., Armstrong Cnty, PA 1930 Census ED 12 Sh 5B.*
5302. "23 Nov 1953 Indiana Evening Gazette (Indiana, PA)."
5303. *Cowanshannock Twp., Armstrong Cnty, PA 1930 Census ED 12 Sh 5B.*
5304. SSN Death Index.
5305. *Cowanshannock Twp., Armstrong Cnty, PA 1930 Census ED 12 Sh 5B.*
5306. "29 Dec 1948 Indiana Evening Gazette ((Indiana, PA) Engagement Anouncement."
5307. "6 Dec 1952 Indiana Evening Gazete (Indiana, PA)."
5308. "1 March 1954 Indiana Evening Gazette (Indiana, PA)."
5309. "6 March 1958 Indiana Evening Gazette (Indiana, PA)."

5310. "11 April 1955 Indiana Evening Gazette (Indiana, PA) report of family.."
5311. "30 Sept 1969 Indiana Evening Gazette (Indiana, PA) Irene Johnston OBITUARY."
5312. "26 June 1961 Indiana Evening Gazette (Indiana, PA) Anne Johnston 80th Birthday."
5313. "30 Sept 1969 Indiana Evening Gazette (Indiana, PA) Irene Johnston OBITUARY."
5314. "Katheen Nesbit Van Horn Obituary Indiana County Genealogical and Historical Society Newspaper Clippings."
5315. "Wilbur Van Horn Obituary Indiana County Genealogical and Historical Society Newspaper Clippings."
5316. "Van Horn-Marshall Wedding Newpaper Article."
5317. "Katheen Nesbit Van Horn Obituary Indiana County Genealogical and Historical Society Newspaper Clippings."
5318. "Van Horn-Marshall Wedding Newpaper Article."
5319. "Katheen Nesbit Van Horn Obituary Indiana County Genealogical and Historical Society Newspaper Clippings."
5320. "Indiana Evening Gazette (Indiana, PA) 2 December 1977."
5321. "Katheen Nesbit Van Horn Obituary Indiana County Genealogical and Historical Society Newspaper Clippings."
5322. "Joseph L. Van Horn Obituary Indiana County Genealogical and Historical Society Newspaper Clippings."
5323. "Van Horn-Marshall Wedding Newpaper Article."
5324. "Katheen Nesbit Van Horn Obituary Indiana County Genealogical and Historical Society Newspaper Clippings."
5325. "Joseph L. Van Horn Obituary Indiana County Genealogical and Historical Society Newspaper Clippings."
5326. "Katheen Nesbit Van Horn Obituary Indiana County Genealogical and Historical Society Newspaper Clippings."
5327. "Joseph L. Van Horn Obituary Indiana County Genealogical and Historical Society Newspaper Clippings."
5328. "Wilbur Van Horn Obituary Indiana County Genealogical and Historical Society Newspaper Clippings."
5329. "Van Horn, Margaret Obituary Indiana County Genealogical and Historical Society Newspaper Clippings."
5330. "2 July 1964 Indiana Evening Gazette (Indiana, PA) Birth Announcement."
5331. "19 April 1961 Indiana Evening Gazette (Indiana, PA) Engagement Announcement."
5332. "31 Aug 1970 Indiana Evenng Gazette (Indiana, PA) Alex Lambing Obituary."
5333. "22 July 1971 Indiana Evenng Gazette (Indiana, PA) Obituary Deloris Belle Van Horn Weaver."
5334. "19 Nov 1959 Indiana Evening Gazette (Indiana, PA)."
5335. Willey, Gordon (Van Horn TREE) Husband of Jacqueline Marshal Granddaughter of Judson Van Horn.
5336. *Sheldon Schimmel Funeral Service Brochure.*
5337. Marriage Announcement in Newspaper.
5338. *Sioux Falls, Minnehaha Cnty, SD 1930 Census ED 39 Sh 8A.*
5339. Nellie Mae Clower Van Horn Obituary.
5340. "Richard Van Horn Obituary Indiana County Genealogical and Historical Society Newspaper Clippings."
5341. *Punxsutawney, Jefferson Cnty, PA 1930 Census ED 25 Sh 14A & B.*
5342. *Pennsylvania Veterans Burial Cards 1777-1999*, "Electronic."
5343. "Richard Van Horn Obituary Indiana County Genealogical and Historical Society Newspaper Clippings."
5344. *Punxsutawney, Jefferson Cnty, PA 1930 Census ED 25 Sh 14A & B.*
5345. "Richard Van Horn Obituary Indiana County Genealogical and Historical Society Newspaper Clippings."
5346. "Richard G. Van Horn, III Obituary Indiana County Genealogical and Historical Society

Newspaper Clippings."

5347. *Pennsylvania Veterans Burial Cards 1777-1999*, "Electronic."

5348. Nellie Mae Clower Van Horn Obituary.

5349. "Frank O. Van Horn Obituary Indiana County Genealogical and Historical Society Newspaper Clippings."

5350. *Punxsutawney, Jefferson Cnty, PA 1930 Census ED 25 Sh 14A & B.*

5351. "Frank O. Van Horn Obituary Indiana County Genealogical and Historical Society Newspaper Clippings."

5352. *Creekside, Indiana Cnty, PA 1920 Census ED 107 Sh 1A.*

5353. *Washington, Indiana Cnty, PA 1930 Census ED 23 Sh 1B.*

5354. SSN Death Index.

5355. *Creekside, Indiana Cnty, PA 1920 Census ED 107 Sh 1A.*

5356. SSN Death Index.

5357. "11 June 2004 Daily Courier (Pittsburgh, PA) Janice Louise Rankin Obituary."

5358. SSN Death Index.

5359. "11 June 2004 Daily Courier (Pittsburgh, PA) Janice Louise Rankin Obituary."

5360. *California Death Index 1940-1997*, "Electronic."

5361. "27 Jan 2005 News Leader (Pittsburgh, PA) Obituary Shirley Mae Barrett."

5362. *Howe, Forrest Cnty, PA 1930 Census ED 5 Sh 2B.*

5363. *Erie, Millcreek Twp., Erie Cnty, PA 1930 Census ED 54 Sh 13A.*

5364. *Erie, Ward 3, Erie Cnty, PA 1920 Census ED 89 Sh 16A.*

5365. *Erie, Millcreek Twp., Erie Cnty, PA 1930 Census ED 54 Sh 13A.*

5366. SSN Death Index.

5367. *Erie, Millcreek Twp., Erie Cnty, PA 1930 Census ED 54 Sh 13A.*

5368. *Erie, Ward 3, Erie Cnty, PA 1920 Census ED 89 Sh 16A.*

5369. *Erie, Millcreek Twp., Erie Cnty, PA 1930 Census ED 54 Sh 13A.*

5370. Ohio Deaths, 1908-1932, 1938-1944, and 1958-2002.

5371. SSN Death Index.

5372. "Katheen Nesbit Van Horn Obituary Indiana County Genealogical and Historical Society Newspaper Clippings."

5373. "Van Horn-Marshall Wedding Newpaper Article."

5374. "Katheen Nesbit Van Horn Obituary Indiana County Genealogical and Historical Society Newspaper Clippings."

5375. "Joseph L. Van Horn Obituary Indiana County Genealogical and Historical Society Newspaper Clippings."

5376. "Van Horn-Marshall Wedding Newpaper Article."

5377. Lori Van Horn Marshall Review of Family Data Sheets.

5378. "Katheen Nesbit Van Horn Obituary Indiana County Genealogical and Historical Society Newspaper Clippings."

5379. "Joseph L. Van Horn Obituary Indiana County Genealogical and Historical Society Newspaper Clippings."

5380. "Van Horn-Marshall Wedding Newpaper Article."

5381. "Katheen Nesbit Van Horn Obituary Indiana County Genealogical and Historical Society Newspaper Clippings."

5382. "Richard Van Horn Obituary Indiana County Genealogical and Historical Society Newspaper Clippings."

5383. "Richard G. Van Horn, III Obituary Indiana County Genealogical and Historical Society Newspaper Clippings."

5384. "Alberti, Barbara Obituary Indiana County Genealogical and Historical Society Newspaper Clippings."

5385. "Richard G. Van Horn, III Obituary Indiana County Genealogical and Historical Society Newspaper Clippings."

Ancestors of Emma Ellen HUMMEL

Generation No. 1

1. Emma Ellen HUMMEL[1,2,3,4,5], born 1854 in Sandusky Cnty, OH[6]; died 04 Jan 1887 in Seneca Cnty, OH[7]. She was the daughter of **2. Christian HUMMEL** and **3. Margaret Ann FISHER**. She married **(1) Samuel Cornelius VAN HORN**[8,9,10,11,12,13,14] 24 Apr 1883 in Fremont, OH Reformed Church, Sandusky Cnty, OH. He was born Bet. 31 Dec 1857 - 1858 in Near Armagh, Indiana Cnty, PA[15,16,17,18], and died 06 Jan 1937 in Dalhart, Dallam Cnty, TX[19,20]. He was the son of Henry Coulter VAN HORN and Ellen HUTCHISON.

Notes for Emma Ellen HUMMEL:
In 1880 Emma is a servant in the John King home in Jackson Twp., Sandusky Cnty, OH. She is 24 and born OH. She says her father was born in Germany and mother in PA.
According to the Fremont Weekly Journal of 7 January 1887 Mrs. Emma Van Horn of Bettsville, died on Tuesday. She formerly lived in the family of James Kridler of this city.

More About Emma Ellen HUMMEL:
Burial: 1887, Liberty Cemetery, Bettsville, OH
Occupation: 1880, Housekeeper

Notes for Samuel Cornelius VAN HORN:
Emma Hummel Van Horn died shortly after the birth of her second child Leafy Fern Van Horn. Samuel C. Van Horn then married Emma's sister Jennie Hummel.
In 1920 living in Dalhart,TX on Keeler Street in a home they own free and clear.

An article in the Indiana Progress(Indiana, PA) of 23 July 1874 H. C. Van Horn writes that Samuel Van Horn has Run Away. He is 16 years of age and is 5 feet 6 or 7 inches tall brown hair, light complexion, grayish blue eyes. He asks that no one harbor Samuel and is willing to pay expenses for his return.
15 March 1899 the Indiana Weekly Messenger (Indiana, PA) reports that S. C. Van Horn is elected from East Wheatfield Twp. to the county committee.
7 June 1899 Indiana Progress (Indiana, PA) states that S C. Van Horn is building a coal, wash and wood house.
9 Aug 1899 Indiana Progress (Indiana, PA) reports that Hubert Van Horn of Wilkinsburg visited his brother S. C. Van Horn. In the same paper it is reported that S. C. and his wife visited the Free Methodists camp meeting at Blairsville the latter part of the previous week.
24 June 1903 Indiana Progress (Indiana, PA) reported that S. C. Van Horn in a delegation from East Wheatfield participated in the county's centennial activities by exhibiting a pair of millstones from the Findley Mill constructed at Cramer in 1784-85.
From the Indiana County 175th Anniversary History by Clarence D. Stephenson quotes an article for the Indiana County Gazette (Indiana, PA) of 24 June 1903 states that in the Great Industrial Parade " The Plumville band led North and south Mahoning. North Mahoning was led by Marshall S. C. Van Horn, followed by a number of cavalrymen."
1 March 1905 S. C. Van Horn election as constable in East Wheatfield Twp., Is reported in the Indiana Progress (Indiana, PA) and the Indiana Weekly Messenger (Indiana, PA) of the same date.
24 April 1907 the Indiana Progress (Indiana, PA) reports that Constable Samuel C. Van Horn of East Wheatfield Twp. was at the county seat.
27 November 1907 Indiana Progress (Indiana, PA) reports a sale by S. C. Van Horn to John B. Taylor of 116 acres in East Wheatfield for $29.
13 May 1908 S. C. Van Horn sells 2 acres in East Wheatfield to C. G. and W. H. Dick for $10 as reported in the Indiana Progress(Indiana, PA).
11 November 1908 the Indiana Weekly Messenger (Indiana, PA) reports that Mr. and Mrs. S. C. Van Horn have purchased a ranch in the Lone Star State and are leaving soon to raise cattle. Their friends in and about Armagh have gathered to say they good byes and wish them well in their new home.
11 Nov 1908 the Indiana Evening Gazette (Indiana, PA) reports that the S. C. Van Horn family of Armagh left this day for their new home in Dalhart, TX.
25 November 1908 the Indiana Weekly Messenger (Indiana, PA) reports that Ex-Patrolman Riggs of Johnstown has purchased the Van Horn farm of 116 acres near Armagh and has taken possession. the Van Horn

577

family has moved to a cattle ranch in Texas.

More About Samuel Cornelius VAN HORN:
Burial: 1937, Elmwood Cemetery, Dalhart. Dallam Cnty, TX
Occupation: Farmer, Labor Foreman Round House

Generation No. 2

2. Christian HUMMEL[21,22,23,24,25,26,27], born Abt. 1821 in Bavaria, Germany[28]; died Bet. 1880 - 1886 in Sandusky Cnty, OH. He married **3. Margaret Ann FISHER** Abt. 1845.
3. Margaret Ann FISHER[29,30,31,32,33,34,35,36], born Apr 1826 in VA/WV/MD[37]; died 19 Aug 1903 in Fremont, Sandusky Cnty, OH[38]. She was the daughter of **6. William FISHER** and **7. Jane ANDERSON**.

Notes for Christian HUMMEL:
　　Name spellings 1850 Hoomel, 1860 Humel, 1870 Hamel, 1880 Humel and 1900 Hommel.
　　In the 1850 Mortality Index a John Hoomel age 56 born Germany died in Sandusky Cnty, OH from Palsy.
　　A Christian F. Hummel is listed in the Wuerttenberg immigration records born 4 April 1821 in Niederstotzingen with application date of Feb 1854, According to the records immigrants often left with out permission and then sent back word of their change of residence.
　　A Christian Humel age 24 arrived in 1846 in New Orleans from Bremen, Germany on the Peter Hattrick. Arrival before 1850 is essential as by 1850 he is married and has 2 children. He likely arrived in 1844.
　　In 1850 Christian is a farmer and has real estate worth about $550. He is married with a son and a daughter. A Frederick Hoomel born Germany age 25 is also living with the family. this is likely a brother or other relative. Christin born Germany and Margaret VA.
　　In 1860 Christian is born Bavaria and Margaret VA. The ages change by 7 years with her being born in 1832 rather than 1825. There are now 7 children including Elizabeth (Jennie) and Emmy (Emma). Christian is a farmer with real estate worth $3000 and person effects or $600.
　　In 1870 Christian is born Wuerttenberg and Margret VA. The ages are 48 and 44. There are now 10 children that include Elizabeh and Emma. He is a farmer and his land is worth $7,500 and person affects worth $1500.
　　In 1880 he is 58 and Margaret is 54. He is born Wutenburg and Margeret is erroneously also listed as born in Wuerttenberg. There are 3 daughters living in the home as the others have left home with Emma and Jennie living in other families and working as servants. Alvin Lewis is living next door and is married with a wife and two children a son and daughter. Lewis states his father was born in 'Wuerttenberg and mother in VA.
　　In 1910 and 1920 Jennie states her father was born in Germany and in 1910 her mother was born in MD and in 1920 in VA. In 1900 she states Germany and MD for the birth places.

Notes for Margaret Ann FISHER:
　　Margaret's family was in Sandusky Cnty, OH before 1840 as her father is in in the 1840 Census of Jackson Twp., Sandusky Cnty, OH. This would suggest that Christian Hummell came to OH between 1840 and their marriage date of 1845
　　In 1873 Margaret and her husband as heirs to the estate of William Fisher receive from the probate of his estate on March 7, 1873 $70. In the probate papers Christian signs and Margaret places her mark as receiving this distribution.
　　In 1900 Margaret is widowed and is born April `1826 in WV with both parents born in WV which would have been VA when she was born. She owns her farm and is a landlord. She is living alone and states she is the mother of 11 with 9 living in 1900. One of the children that is not living is Emma first wife of Samuel C. Van Horn. She is living in Jackson Twp so she must be living right on the home place.

Children of Christian HUMMEL and Margaret FISHER are:
　　　　i.　Mary B. HUMMEL[39,40,41,42], born Abt. 1847 in OH[43]; died 10 Apr 1903 in Toledo State Hospital Toledo, OH; married John B. GEPHART Abt. 1870; born Dec 1846 in OH[44]; died Unknown.

　　　　　　Notes for Mary B. HUMMEL:
　　　　　　11 April 1903 Fremont Daily News p2 c6 Obit of Mary Hummel
　　　　　　" Mrs. Mary Gephart died Friday morning at 9 o'clock at the Toledo state hospital, where she has been a patient for the past fifteen years. The remains were brought to Fremont Saturday morning by Undertaker Will Tschumy, who went after the body. The funeral services will be held Sunday afternoon at 2 o'clock at the Bethlehem Church followed by Internet at Oakwood cemetery. The deceased was 55 years of age and leaves a husband J. B. Gephart, and two sons, Jesse C. and Chanuncey N. Gephart."

Notes for John B. GEPHART:
Mary is missing in 1900 but John says he is married. He has two of his unmarried single sisters living with him in the home. His 3 male children are living at home and single.

ii. Alvin Lewis HUMMEL[45,46,47,48], born Abt. Apr 1850 in OH[49]; died Bet. 1900 - 1930; married Elsie Lavina GAMBY Abt. 1874; born Feb 1858 in OH[50]; died 25 Jan 1937 in Litchfield, Hillsdale Cnty, MI.

Notes for Alvin Lewis HUMMEL:
In 1880 Benjamin Gamby is a servant in the home. It could be assumed that this person is a relative of Alvin's wife Else and likely a brother since their parents birthplaces are the same.

Notes for Elsie Lavina GAMBY:
In 1900 Elsie is living with her 3 sons. She indicates she is divorced. She is the mother of 6 children of which only the 3 sons with her are living.
In 1910 Elsie is living in Scott Twp., Sandusky Cnty, OH with 3 sons. She is widowed and is farming. The 2 older sons are working in the oil field and the younger is working on the farm. Elsie is the mother of 6 children of whom 3 are living and are listed in the census.
In 1920 she states she is divorced which would indicate that Alvin is still living. All 3 sons are single and living with her. They all work in the oil fields.
In 1930 she states she is widowed. She lives with her oldest son William in Litchfield, MI.

iii. Clarissa Ann HUMMEL[51,52,53,54,55,56], born 15 Apr 1851 in Jackson Twp., Sandusky Cnty, OH[57]; died 15 Dec 1933 in Fremont, Sandusky Cnty, OH[58]; married Perry Franklin ROSENBERGER 19 Feb 1874; born 15 Mar 1850 in OH[59]; died 23 Apr 1939 in Fremont, Sandusky Cnty, OH.

Notes for Clarissa Ann HUMMEL:
Her death certificate verifies her parents their place of birth her husband, her birth date and place and death date and place as well as cause.

More About Clarissa Ann HUMMEL:
Burial: 18 Dec 1933, Oakwood Cemetery
Cause of Death: Cerebrial Hemmorage complicated by arteial scerosis
Religion: United Brethren Church

Notes for Perry Franklin ROSENBERGER:
In 1920 living on Oak Harbor Rd in Sandusky Twp., Sandusky Cnty, OH. He is retired.

More About Perry Franklin ROSENBERGER:
Occupation: Farmer

iv. Jennie E. HUMMEL[60,61,62,63,64], born 11 Aug 1852 in OH[65,66,67,68]; died 14 Aug 1929 in Dalhart, Dallam Cnty, TX[69]; married Samuel Cornelius VAN HORN Abt. 1889 in OH[70]; born Bet. 31 Dec 1857 - 1858 in Near Armagh, Indiana Cnty, PA[71,72,73,74]; died 06 Jan 1937 in Dalhart, Dallam Cnty, TX[75,76].

Notes for Jennie E. HUMMEL:
In 1880 Jennie is a servant in the John Stierwalt home in Fremont, Sandusky Cnty, OH. She is 27 born OH and says her father was born in OH and mother in VA.
9 May 1900 Indiana Progress (Indiana, PA) reports that Mrs. S. C. Van Horn spent the day in Armagh.
25 Dec 1901 Indiana Progress (Indiana, PA) newspaper: "Mrs. Trombel of Fremont, is visiting her daughter, Mrs. S. C. Van Horn."
9 Oct. 1907 the Indiana Progress (Indiana, PA) reports that Mrs. S. C. Van Horn and daughter Nellie were traveling to Ohio and Michigan to visit friends.
In 1910 and 1920 Jennie states her father was born in Germany and in 1910 her mother was born in MD and in 1920 in VA. In 1900 she states Germany and MD for the birth places.
In 1910 Jennie, Samuel and Nellie are living two doors from her sister Ida and her family in Dallam Cnty, TX. both families are farming.

More About Jennie E. HUMMEL:

Burial: 15 Aug 1929, Elmwood cemetery, Dalhart. Dallam Cnty, TX

Notes for Samuel Cornelius VAN HORN:
Emma Hummel Van Horn died shortly after the birth of her second child Leafy Fern Van Horn. Samuel C. Van Horn then married Emma's sister Jennie Hummel.
In 1920 living in Dalhart,TX on Keeler Street in a home they own free and clear.

An article in the Indiana Progress(Indiana, PA) of 23 July 1874 H. C. Van Horn writes that Samuel Van Horn has Run Away. He is 16 years of age and is 5 feet 6 or 7 inches tall brown hair, light complexion, grayish blue eyes. He asks that no one harbor Samuel and is willing to pay expenses for his return.
15 March 1899 the Indiana Weekly Messenger (Indiana, PA) reports that S. C. Van Horn is elected from East Wheatfield Twp. to the county committee.
7 June 1899 Indiana Progress (Indiana, PA) states that S C. Van Horn is building a coal, wash and wood house.
9 Aug 1899 Indiana Progress (Indiana, PA) reports that Hubert Van Horn of Wilkinsburg visited his brother S. C. Van Horn. In the same paper it is reported that S. C. and his wife visited the Free Methodists camp meeting at Blairsville the latter part of the previous week.
24 June 1903 Indiana Progress (Indiana, PA) reported that S. C. Van Horn in a delegation from East Wheatfield participated in the county's centennial activities by exhibiting a pair of millstones from the Findley Mill constructed at Cramer in 1784-85.
From the Indiana County 175th Anniversary History by Clarence D. Stephenson quotes an article for the Indiana County Gazette (Indiana, PA) of 24 June 1903 states that in the Great Industrial Parade " The Plumville band led North and south Mahoning. North Mahoning was led by Marshall S. C. Van Horn, followed by a number of cavalrymen."
1 March 1905 S. C. Van Horn election as constable in East Wheatfield Twp., Is reported in the Indiana Progress (Indiana, PA) and the Indiana Weekly Messenger (Indiana, PA) of the same date.
24 April 1907 the Indiana Progress (Indiana, PA) reports that Constable Samuel C. Van Horn of East Wheatfield Twp. was at the county seat.
27 November 1907 Indiana Progress (Indiana, PA) reports a sale by S. C. Van Horn to John B. Taylor of 116 acres in East Wheatfield for $29.
13 May 1908 S. C. Van Horn sells 2 acres in East Wheatfield to C. G. and W. H. Dick for $10 as reported in the Indiana Progress(Indiana, PA).
11 November 1908 the Indiana Weekly Messenger (Indiana, PA) reports that Mr. and Mrs. S. C. Van Horn have purchased a ranch in the Lone Star State and are leaving soon to raise cattle. Their friends in and about Armagh have gathered to say they good byes and wish them well in their new home.
11 Nov 1908 the Indiana Evening Gazette (Indiana, PA) reports that the S. C. Van Horn family of Armagh left this day for their new home in Dalhart, TX.
25 November 1908 the Indiana Weekly Messenger (Indiana, PA) reports that Ex-Patrolman Riggs of Johnstown has purchased the Van Horn farm of 116 acres near Armagh and has taken possession. the Van Horn family has moved to a cattle ranch in Texas.

More About Samuel Cornelius VAN HORN:
Burial: 1937, Elmwood Cemetery, Dalhart. Dallam Cnty, TX
Occupation: Farmer, Labor Foreman Round House

1 v. Emma Ellen HUMMEL, born 1854 in Sandusky Cnty, OH; died 04 Jan 1887 in Seneca Cnty, OH; married Samuel Cornelius VAN HORN 24 Apr 1883 in Fremont, OH Reformed Church, Sandusky Cnty, OH.

  vi. Hannah Mahala HUMMEL[77,78,79,80], born 27 Jan 1856 in Sandusky Cnty, OH[81]; died 11 Oct 1925 in Warren, Trumbull Cnty, OH[82]; married James William DICKEN Abt. 1882; born Feb 1847 in OH[83]; died Aft. 1925.

Notes for Hannah Mahala HUMMEL:
Th informant for her death certificate was Mrs. Elmer Parker of Warren, OH. this may be Anna her daughter. the certificate verifies birth dates, death dates, parents and fathers birth country as well as cause of death and husband.

More About Hannah Mahala HUMMEL:
Burial: 13 Oct 1925, North Bristol, OH

Cause of Death: Cerebral Hemorage contributed to by arterial scerosis

Notes for James William DICKEN:
In 1920 lives on Oakfield Rd in Bristol, Twp., Trumbull Cnty, OH. He is a general farm laborer and owns his place free and clear.

vii.   Harriet Rowena HUMMEL[84,85], born Abt. 1858 in OH[86]; died Dec 1896 in Sandusky Cnty, OH; married George F. KEEFER Abt. 1879; born Mar 1858 in PA[87]; died 14 Dec 1916 in Ballville, Sandusky Cnty, OH[88].

Notes for Harriet Rowena HUMMEL:
25 Dec 1896 Fremont Weekly Journal p3 c7 " The wife of Hon George F. Keefer died at her home in Ballville township on Thursday December 17th, from cancer. Mrs Keefer suffered long and painfully from the disease, but bore her suffering with Christian patience and fortitude. Her death is mourned by the husband and little son and a large circle of friends. The funeral occurred Saturday, an the body was interred in Oakwood cemetery."

More About George F. KEEFER:
Politics: State Represenative

viii.   Sarah C. HUMMEL[89,90,91,92], born 24 Jun 1863 in Fremont, Sandusky Cnty, OH[93,94]; died 12 Feb 1938 in Fremont, Sandusky Cnty, OH[95,96]; married Florian YOUNG Abt. 1890 in Millersvlle, OH[97]; born Oct 1867 in Fremont, Sandusky Cnty, OH[98]; died 06 Mar 1942 in Euclid, OH[99].

Notes for Sarah C. HUMMEL:
The information in her death certificate confirms her parents, birth and death date, as well as her husband. Her birth is stated as 24 Aug 1863 even though the 1910 census suggests Jan 1865.
Sarah's obituary gives her parents and the name of her husband and son as well as her only living sister Ida of Dalhart, TX.

More About Sarah C. HUMMEL:
Burial: 15 Feb 1938, Oakwood Cemetery
Cause of Death: Pathelogical fracture of left femure due to sarcoma of the uterus
Medical Information: Tripped on rug at home and fractured the femure
Religion: United Brethren Church

Notes for Florian YOUNG:
In 1920 living in Fremont on Rowan Road in a home he owns free and clear. He is a pumper for the Ohio Oil company. both he and Sarah say they were born in Fremont, OH.
In 1930 he owns his house worth $3000 and has a radio. He is employed as a pumper for an oil company. Living on Rawson Place in Fremont, OH.

More About Florian YOUNG:
Employment: Foreman Gas Company

ix.   Rosina M. HUMMEL[100,101,102,103], born 07 Jun 1865 in near Freemont, Sandusky Cnty, OH[104]; died 23 Mar 1908 in Quincy, MI[105]; married William Joseph KISER 29 Oct 1891[105]; born Aug 1866 in OH[106]; died Unknown.

Notes for Rosina M. HUMMEL:
27 March 1908 Fremont Daily News p2 c6 Died at her late residence in Qunicy, Mich. "The funeral of Mrs. W. J. Kiser a former resident of this county was held at Qunicy, Mich., Wednesday conducted by rev George Laubach of the Free Methodist Church. The deceased whose maiden name was Rosina Hummel, was born near Fremont June 7, 1865, and died March 23, aged 42 years, 9 months and 16 days. She was married to W. J. Kiser October 29, 1891. Seven children were the fruits of this union, three sons and four daughters, but only four survive their mother. One son and three daughters. Her husband and one brother and two sisters also survive. She was converted to God in 1887 and always lived a consistent Christian life. The deceased is well remembered by many relatives and friends in this vicinity."

Notes for William Joseph KISER:

Moved to Quincy, MI from Sandusky county, OH after marriage. Name might be Keiser/Kaiser

More About William Joseph KISER:
Occupation: Farmer, Factory Sawyer

x.   Ida E. HUMMEL[107,108,109,110,111,112,113], born Nov 1867 in OH[114]; died Aft. 1930; married Michael William LUDWIG 22 Oct 1890[115]; born Oct 1857 in OH[116]; died 13 Nov 1941 in Dalhart, Dallam Cnty, TX[117,118].

Notes for Ida E. HUMMEL:
In 1900 she indicates she is the mother of 1 chid living. Since in 1910 we learn that Michael has 2 marriages the two older children in the family in 1900 are by his first wife.
In 1910 living 1 farm away from sister Jennie and her family. In 1920 living in the same county with her sister Jennie but not near as Jennie and Samuel have moved to Dalhart. She and Michael are living alone and farming. Ida states her father was born in Germany and mother in VA giving another item of proof of her relationship to Jennie and the Hummel family of Sandusky Cnty, OH.

Notes for Michael William LUDWIG:
In 1930 living with wife in Dallam Cnty, TX owns his farm free and clear and does not have a radio.

More About Michael William LUDWIG:
Occupation: Farmer

xi. Rhoda T. HUMMEL[119,120,121], born 03 Oct 1871 in OH[122]; died 04 Aug 1912 in Grafton, OH or Elyria, OH[123,124]; married Joseph G. RUMPLER Jan 1890[125,126]; born Nov 1869 in OH[127]; died Aft. 1912.

Notes for Rhoda T. HUMMEL:
Rhoda's death certificate confirms her parents and husband.

More About Rhoda T. HUMMEL:
Burial: 06 Aug 1912, Eaton Twp. Cemetery, Loriane Cnty, OH
Cause of Death: Uremic Coma complication nephritis

Notes for Joseph G. RUMPLER:
In 1910 living on Center Rd in Eaton, OH. Joe G. is a farmer and he and Rhoda have one child Lester.

Generation No. 3

6. William FISHER[128,129,130,131,132], born 15 Apr 1789 in Near Staunton, Augusta Cnty, VA[133]; died 08 Mar 1872 in Sandusky Cnty, OH. He was the son of **12. Daniel FISCHER** and **13. Nancy Ann JONES**. He married **7. Jane ANDERSON** 30 Sep 1817 in Augusta Cnty, VA.
7. Jane ANDERSON[134], born 1795; died Bet. 1831 - 1833 in Perry Cnty, OH[134].

Notes for William FISHER:
In 1840 already in Jackson Twp., Sandusky Cnty, OH the family is 3,1,0,0,2,0,0,1 males and 0,1,2,1,1. This places him in the 50 to 60 ranges which is correct and his wife Mary in the 20 to 30 range. Margaret would be there at 15 to 20. THE $ MALES ARE SONS OF William and Mary. This data indicates many more children of William and Jane in addition to Margaret likely 2 boys and 3 girls.
By 1860 moved to Washington Twp., Sandusky Cnty, OH from Jackson Twp. of the same county where the family lived in 1850 and is a farmer with land worth $3000 and person effects of $500. He is born in Va and Mary in PA.
In 1870 still in Washington Twp. Sandusky Cnty, OH farming with 2 children (Peter and Sarah) and a grandson(Charles) in the family. He is 81 and has property worth $4000 with $1000 in personal effects.
From the History of Sandusky County, Ohio with portraits and Biographies of Prominent Citizens and Pioneers, H. Z. Williams & Bro. 1882, p. 750
"William Fisher a soldier of the War of 1812 was born in Virginia in 1789. He settled in Jackson township in 1836.

He had previously lived in Perry county, where his first wife, whose maiden name was Jane Anderson, died in 1833, leaving five children living: James A. in Colorado; George W; Harriet H (Fought); Magaret (Hummel) and Mary E. (Hufford), this county. Mr. Fisher married for his second wife, in 1833, Mary McCullough. the fruit of this union was eleven children, six of who are living, vis: Belinda (Miller), William T., Thomas H., Perter B., Sarah (Klotz0, and Flora. Six of Mr. Fisher's sons served in the army-William T. Thomas H., John and Austin T., in the Seventy-second Ohio volunteer Infantry, and Sardis B. and Perter B. in the one hundred days' service. Mr. Fisher died in 1872. George W. the oldest son living in this county was born in 1819. In 1844 he married Clara Black, and has a family of three children living-Rhoda J. (Hathaway), John C. and William F. John C. Fisher was born in 1848. they have five children- Claude, Guy, Webb, James, and Maud"

More About William FISHER:
Burial: Unknown, Washington Chapel, Washington Twp., Sandusky Cnty, OH
Military service: 1812, War of 1812

Children of William FISHER and Jane ANDERSON are:
      i.   James A. FISHER[134,135,136,137], born 1818 in VA[138]; died 24 May 1887 in Georgetown, CO; married Levancha; born Abt. 1834 in MI[138]; died Unknown.

          Notes for James A. FISHER:
          In 1870 he is listed as born in NY he is married and his wife is Lavantia and a son Morill which we learn in 1880 is his step son.
          In 1880 he is married and has a step son and his brother Peter B. Fisher living with him. They are working as miners.

      ii.   George W. FISHER[139,140,141], born 1819 in VA[142]; died 09 Jun 1899 in Ballville Twp., Sandusky Cnty, OH; married Clarica; born Abt. 1825 in OH; died Unknown.
      iii.   Harriet H. FISHER[143], born 1822 in VA; died Unknown; married (1) George FOUGHT; born Abt. 1813; died Unknown; married (2) SKINNER; died Unknown.
3   iv.   Margaret Ann FISHER, born Apr 1826 in VA/WV/MD; died 19 Aug 1903 in Fremont, Sandusky Cnty, OH; married Christian HUMMEL Abt. 1845.
      v.   Mary E. FISHER[144,145], born 1828; died Unknown; married James HUFFORD; died Unknown.

Generation No. 4

12. Daniel FISCHER, born 1745 in Philadelphia, PA; died Jan 1817 in Shenandoah Valley, Augusta Cnty, VA. He was the son of **24. Adam FISCHER** and **25. Nancy HULL.** He married **13. Nancy Ann JONES** 1777.
    13. Nancy Ann JONES, born 1747; died Unknown. She was the daughter of **26. Benjamin JONES** and **27. Lydia**.

Children of Daniel FISCHER and Nancy JONES are:
6   i.   William FISHER, born 15 Apr 1789 in Near Staunton, Augusta Cnty, VA; died 08 Mar 1872 in Sandusky Cnty, OH; married (1) Jane ANDERSON 30 Sep 1817 in Augusta Cnty, VA; married (2) Mary MCCULLOUGH 1833 in Perry Cnty, OH.
      ii.   Peter FISHER, died Unknown.
      iii.   Daniel FISHER, died Unknown.
      iv.   Adam FISHER, born 12 Mar 1788 in Middle River, Augusta Cnty, VA; died 18 Apr 1877 in Robb, Posey Cnty, IN; married Elizabeth BALSLEY; died Unknown.
      v.   Henry FISHER, died Unknown.

Generation No. 5

24. Adam FISCHER, born 1690 in Germany; died 1757 in PA. He was the son of **48. VON FISCHERBACH**. He married **25. Nancy HULL.**
    25. Nancy HULL, born 1719; died Unknown.

Notes for Adam FISCHER:
I got my information of Ancestry World tree. Johann Adam Fischer Von Fischerbach Was born in Silesia Germany in 1684. He had a son Adam Fisher Born in 1710 in Germany and died 1757 in Pennsylvania of small poxs. His

wife was Nancy Hull. She was born in 1719. Their Children was Jacob Abraham Infant Fisher Louis Daniel and Adam. They list another Jacob but thats in question. Jacob Was born in 1741 Pa. And died 1785 in Maryland. His wife was Mary Bish. There Children was Mary, Philip Jacob Jr. Elizabeth, and David. Jacob and Mary bish married in 1770 in Franklin, Va. Abraham was Born in 1730 in Penn. Died ? in Yanceyville, Casswell, NC. He married a Rhoda Layton. Haven't found a list of there children yet! Infant Fisher was born in 1731. I have nothing on this one. Louis was born in 1743 in Penn. I have nothing else on this one.Adam was Born on sept. 29 1750 in Philadelphia Penn. and He died on May 7 1827 Indian Creek, Washington Twp., Clermont. OH. He married Suzzannah Jones in 1777.There children are the ones you listed for me. Daniel is my 4th great grandfather! He was born1745 in Philadelphia Penn. And died Jan 1817 Shenndoah Valley, Augusta Va, He married Nancy Jones. Which I believe to be Suzannas Sister. They had Daniel 11, Jacob Absalom, Adam, Salley, Samual,Andrew,William, John, Polly,Peggy, And Henry which is my 3rd. Henry married Pooly culp and Then Frankey Jane Shifflet.Farnkey and him had William, Catherine Charles Clinton Joseph John Elizabeth and Nannie. My 2nd Great grandfather was William B he married a Nannie,They had Jim, Huse Mary, Nannie Emma And Tom which was my great grandfather.His real name was William Mitchell but he was Know as Tom. He married Alberta Craig and had Clara Emma Carrie Tommy Lionel James Jake And Dennis which was my Grandfather.William Dennis married a Virginia Margaret Fisher from over the mountain. Her Parents name was Clinton And Mattie. Dennis and Margaret had Nellie Sylvia Franklin Hawthrone Vida Wayne Carl, Alice and Vastine which is my father. He married a Virginia Fay Fridley and had Nellie, Vastine Jack11, Dennis, Julie and Ellen which is me!. Nancy and Daniel was respected people in Augusta county Va. And Fishersville Va. Was named after them. My father still owns the home place which lies below the blue ridge parkway. It is called Calf Mt. and it is still Full of Fisher today. There is a old cementary on the mountain which most of the fishers are buried there is also one on top the mountain that my father knows of. Would like to here more from you. I am getting the book Legacy of Adam Fisher on a Library loan in hope that it helps in my research . If there is any thing I can help you with let me know.I find new stuff everyday. Hope I helped. Ellen Campbell

---

Adam FISCHER and his Descendants
Posted by: Janice Mauldin Castleman Date: October 04, 1999 at 14:12:27
I have posted here previously, but have noticed that many of you are interested in the lineage of Adam FISHCER of PA & Rockingham Co., VA. Here are the first 3 generations in my line. Can you add to or correct any of this data?
Descendants of Adam Fischer, Sr.

1 Adam FISCHER, Sr. b: Abt. 1690 in Germany d: 1757 in Schuylkill Co, PA
...... 2 Abraham FISHER b: Abt. 1728 in Germany d: in Yanceyville, Guilford, NC
.... +Rhoda LAYTON m: 1773 in VA b: Abt. 1745 d: in North Carolina m: 1773 in VA
.... 3 Prudence FISHER b: Abt. 1775
.... +David STRAEDER b: Abt. 1772
.... 3 Caleb FISHER b: Abt. 1776 in VA d: 1845 in Tipton, MO
.... +Mary HEITHER m: 1793 in MD b: Abt. 1776 m: 1793 in MD
.... 3 Trustrum FISHER b: Abt. 1778 d: in Tipton, MO
.... +Catherine GOLDEN m: in NC b: Abt. 1780 m: in NC
.... 3 Mary FISHER b: Abt. 1780
.... +Samuel DRISCOLL b: Abt. 1775
.... 3 Mahala FISHER b: Abt. 1782 d: in Tipton, MO
.... +Unk ALLEN b: Abt. 1780
.... 3 Celia FISHER b: Abt. 1783
.... 3 Rachel FISHER b: Abt. 1784 d: in Tipton, Moniteau, MO
.... +Furness ADAIR b: Abt. 1780
.... 3 Milcah FISHER b: Abt. 1785
.... +Miss DILL b: Abt. 1790
...... 2 Jacob FISHER b: Abt. 1742 in PA d: 1785 in Frederick Co, MD
.... +Mary M. BISH m: 1765 in Franklin Co., VA b: Abt. 1744 m: Abt. 1765 in Franklin Co., VA
.... 3 Peter FISHER b: July 06, 1771 in Franklin Co., VA d: January 17, 1840 in Franklin Co., VA
.... +Elizabeth ALTICK m: March 12, 1792 in Grayson Co., VA b: 1773 d: December 15, 1841 in Franklin Co., VA Father: John Altick m: March 12, 1792 in Grayson Co., VA
.... 3 Phillip FISHER b: Abt. 1772 in VA d: February 08, 1839 in OH
.... +Margaret ALBRECHT m: Abt. 1785 in Franklin Co., VA b: Abt. 1770 m: Abt. 1785 in Franklin Co., VA
.... 3 Jacob FISHER, Jr. b: October 07, 1775 in VA d: 1852 in Wythe Co., VA
.... +Elizabeth ROBINSON b: Abt. 1785
.... *2nd Wife of Jacob Fisher, Jr.:
.... +Susannah PETERS m: December 17, 1798 in Rockingham Co., VA b: November 09, 1777 m: December 17, 1798 in Rockingham Co., VA

.... 3 David FISHER b: November 08, 1777 in VA d: August 26, 1855 in Wythe Co., VA
.... +Rachel PETERS m: February 26, 1798 in Rockingham Co., VA b: 1776 d: July 16, 1833 in Wythe Co., VA m: February 26, 1798 in Rockingham Co., VA
.... 3 Mary Eva FISHER b: Abt. 1778
.... +Peter COBER m: 1795 b: Abt. 1772 m: 1795
.... 3 Elizabeth FISHER b: Abt. 1779
.... +Jacob CUMMER m: Abt. 1795 b: Abt. 1775 m: Abt. 1795
...... 2 Daniel FISHER b: Abt. 1745 d: January 1817
.... +Nancy Ann JONES b: Abt. 1760 Father: Benjamin Jones Mother: Lydia
.... 3 Jacob FISHER b: Abt. 1778 in Augusta Co., VA d: in Highland, OH
.... +Mary PAINTER m: December 27, 1798 in Rockingham Co., VA b: Abt. 1778 in Rockingham Co., VA m: December 27, 1798 in Rockingham Co., VA
.... 3 Peggy FISHER b: January 13, 1783 in Augusta Co., VA
.... +Benjamin RANSBARGER b: June 07, 1777
.... 3 Daniel FISHER b: November 28, 1784 in Augusta Co., VA d: October 22, 1858 in Howard Co., MO
.... +Elizabeth CORNALL m: March 25, 1806 in Augusta Co., VA b: May 27, 1785 in Augusta Co., VA d: April 12, 1858 in Howard Co., MO m: March 25, 1806 in Augusta Co., VA
.... 3 John FISHER b: Abt. 1786 in Augusta Co., VA
.... +Polly Ann LONG m: August 1823 b: Abt. 1798 m: August 1823
.... 3 Adam FISHER b: March 12, 1788 in VA d: April 18, 1877 in Robb Twp., Posey, IN
.... +Elisabeth BALSLEY m: December 17, 1811 in Augusta Co., VA b: March 28, 1790 in Carlisle, Cumberland Co., PA d: 1844 in McLeansboro, Hamilton Co., IL Father: Christian Balsley Mother: Anna Elizabeth Keinadt (my line)
.... *2nd Wife of Adam Fisher:
.... +Salome SCHNEE m: August 20, 1846 in Poseyville, IN b: April 17, 1809 in PA d: June 12, 1883 Father: Jacob Schnee m: August 20, 1846 in Poseyville, IN
.... 3 Mary Polly FISHER b: Abt. 1789 d: in IL?
.... +Daniel JOHNSTON m: Abt. 1806 b: Abt. 1780 m: Abt. 1806
.... 3 William FISHER b: April 15, 1789 in Augusta Co., VA d: March 09, 1872 in Sandusky Co., OH
.... +Jane ANDERSON m: September 30, 1817 in Augusta Co., VA b: Abt. 1795 d: 1831 m: September 30, 1817 in Augusta Co., VA
.... *2nd Wife of William Fisher:
.... +Mary MCCULLOUGH m: Abt. 1833 b: Abt. 1810 d: 1866 m: Abt. 1833
.... 3 Henry FISHER b: Abt. 1794 d: in Howard Co., MO
.... +Polly CULP m: December 01, 1825 b: Abt. 1809 m: December 01, 1825
.... 3 Andrew FISHER b: Abt. 1796 in Augusta Co., VA
.... +Polly SORRELLS m: August 08, 1822 b: Abt. 1802 m: August 08, 1822
.... 3 Absolom FISHER b: Abt. 1803
.... +Margaret RANKIN m: November 01, 1826 in Augusta Co., VA b: Abt. 1806 m: November 01, 1826 in Augusta Co., VA
.... 3 Salley FISHER b: Abt. 1803 in Augusta Co., VA
.... +Abraham FREED m: December 22, 1823 in Augusta Co., VA b: Abt. 1803 in VA m: December 22, 1823 in Augusta Co., VA
.... 3 Samuel FISHER b: Abt. 1805
.... +Martha C. FISHER b: Abt. 1810
...... 2 Adam FISHER, Jr. b: September 29, 1750 in PA d: May 07, 1827 in Clermont Co., OH
.... +Susannah JONES m: 1777 in VA b: March 03, 1758 in MD d: December 17, 1842 in Clermont Co., OH Father: Benjamin Jones Mother: Lydia m: 1777 in VA
.... 3 Margaret FISHER b: April 08, 1778 in MD d: August 11, 1837
.... +Lewis MILLER m: December 05, 1800 in Pendleton Co., KY b: Abt. 1775 m: December 05, 1800 in Pendleton Co., KY
.... 3 Jacob FISHER b: June 22, 1779 in MD d: September 18, 1835 in Rush Co., IN
.... +Jennette SUTTON b: September 13, 1783 d: October 29, 1856 in Rush Co., IN
.... 3 John FISHER b: November 02, 1781 d: August 29, 1868
.... 3 Henry FISHER b: October 05, 1783 d: May 25, 1866
.... 3 Peter FISHER b: November 17, 1785 d: August 18, 1869
.... 3 Barbary FISHER b: December 17, 1788 d: March 23, 1876
.... 3 Elizabeth FISHER b: October 15, 1790 d: May 18, 1875
.... 3 George FISHER b: March 03, 1792 d: August 28, 1863
.... 3 David FISHER b: December 03, 1794 d: May 07, 1886
.... 3 Daniel FISHER b: April 05, 1797 d: October 10, 1858
.... 3 Samuel FISHER b: August 11, 1800 d: September 21, 1872

More About Adam FISCHER:
Cause of Death: Small Pox

Children of Adam FISCHER and Nancy HULL are:

12   i.   Daniel FISCHER, born 1745 in Philadelphia, PA; died Jan 1817 in Shenandoah Valley, Augusta Cnty, VA; married Nancy Ann JONES 1777.

          ii.   Adam FISHER, JR, born 1750; died Unknown; married Susannah JONES; died Unknown.

Notes for Adam FISHER, JR:
1. Adam2 Fisher, Jr. (Adam1 Fischer, Sr.) was born September 29, 1750 in PA, and died May 07, 1827 in Clermont Co., OH. He married Susannah Jones 1777 in VA, daughter of Benjamin Jones and Lydia Unknown. She was born March 03, 1758 in MD, and died December 17, 1842 in Clermont Co., OH.

Notes for Adam Fisher, Jr.:
As a young child, because of the circumstances of his family, Adam Jr. was bound out to try to help the dire financial hardships facing his family. He was ill treated by cruel masters and finally his mother got him back to the family. This information was written by James S. Fisher in his "Legacy Of Adam Fischer".
In the Rev. War, Adam served as Adjutant of the First Battalion of the Lancaster County Militia under Col. Philip Greenawalt. After the war his family moved to Bedford Co., PA, where six children were born. About 1797 this family moved to Portsmouth, Scioto Co., OH, then moved to Kentucky for about two years. By 1800 they were settled at their permanent home on Indian Creek in Clermont Co., OH. Here Adam and Susannah are buried on the old home site. Of their eleven children, two were ministers, and one served a term in congress as a Representative from the state of Ohio.
This line has been entered into Ancestry.com by robins69@hotmail.com. E-mail was sent regarding this submission (also lists Nancy Hull as the wife of Adam FISCHER).

26. Benjamin JONES, born Abt. 1738; died Unknown. He was the son of **52. Robert JONES** and **53. Mary**. He married **27. Lydia**.
    27. Lydia, died Unknown.

Notes for Benjamin JONES:
Benjamin Jones, b. c1738, served in the Rev. War as a Lt., and lived in Augusta Co., VA. A deed dated Sept 21, 1798, by Benjamin John and Lydia of Washington Co., to Thomas Pierce of Wythe Co., VA, an iron ore bank on South Fork Holstein River, was proved in Washington Co., VA. His name was variously spelled Jones/John/Johns in different records.
A deed was delivered to Nancy, wife of Daniel Fisher, of Rockingham Co., dated 18 Aug 1800 (DEED BOOK No. 27). Nancy and her sister Susannah (who married Adam Fisher, Jr.), were daughters of Benjamin and Lydia Jones/Johns. Benjamin's parents were Robert and Mary Jones. Mary Jones was believed to be a native American Indian. Robert had a fur trading company on the James River in Amherst Co., VA. Benjamin was a Lieutenant in the American Revolutionary War from Augusta County. Early Virginia records show the following: "Pierce vs. Razor--O.S. 157, N. S. 55--Bill, Dec. 1807. Complainants are, viz: George, Moses, Aaron, Isaac Pierce; Seth Hendrick (?), and by Hepsaba, their mother and next friend. Joshua Jones, Peter Razor and Ben. John owned ironworks in Wythe Co., and on 12th April 1794 sold to father of orators and oratrixes. Joshua Jones left the commonwealth. He had sold to James Doughterty, who died, and same descended to his son Daniel. Peter Razor died leaving widow Anna, and children viz: Edward Caleham (?:0 and his wife; John, Ann, Christy, Daniel, and Christiana Razor. Deed 21st Sept 1798, by Benjamin John and Lydia, of Washington County, to Thomas Pierce of Wythe Co., an iron ore bank on South Fork Holstein River. Proved in Washington Co., Sept. 1798".
1810 Augusta Co., VA:
JONES, Isaiah 32001-30010
JONES, Enoch 00210-00210
JONES, Amos 20010-10010
JONES, Robert 12101-11211-02
JONES, Peter 21011-25110
JONES, Nancy 30000-10010
JONES, Salley 00000-01010
Would you please list the URL for the Internet site that lists David Jones of Clermont Co. OH as a parent to

Isaiah Van Horn Pioneer of Indiana County, Pennsylvania

Susannah? I don't have a lot of data on these lines and would love to know more.

More About Benjamin JONES:
Military service: Lt. Virginia Revolutionary War

Children of Benjamin JONES and Lydia are:

13   i.   Nancy Ann JONES, born 1747; died Unknown; married Daniel FISCHER 1777.

      ii.   Susannah JONES, died Unknown; married Adam FISHER, JR; born 1750; died Unknown.

Notes for Adam FISHER, JR:
1. Adam2 Fisher, Jr. (Adam1 Fischer, Sr.) was born September 29, 1750 in PA, and died May 07, 1827 in Clermont Co., OH. He married Susannah Jones 1777 in VA, daughter of Benjamin Jones and Lydia Unknown. She was born March 03, 1758 in MD, and died December 17, 1842 in Clermont Co., OH.

Notes for Adam Fisher, Jr.:
As a young child, because of the circumstances of his family, Adam Jr. was bound out to try to help the dire financial hardships facing his family. He was ill treated by cruel masters and finally his mother got him back to the family. This information was written by James S. Fisher in his "Legacy Of Adam Fischer".
In the Rev. War, Adam served as Adjutant of the First Battalion of the Lancaster County Militia under Col. Philip Greenawalt. After the war his family moved to Bedford Co., PA, where six children were born. About 1797 this family moved to Portsmouth, Scioto Co., OH, then moved to Kentucky for about two years. By 1800 they were settled at their permanent home on Indian Creek in Clermont Co., OH. Here Adam and Susannah are buried on the old home site. Of their eleven children, two were ministers, and one served a term in congress as a Representative from the state of Ohio.
This line has been entered into Ancestry.com by robins69@hotmail.com. E-mail was sent regarding this submission (also lists Nancy Hull as the wife of Adam FISCHER).

Generation No. 6

48. VON FISCHERBACH, died Unknown.

Child of VON FISCHERBACH is:

24   i.   Adam FISCHER, born 1690 in Germany; died 1757 in PA; married Nancy HULL.

52. Robert JONES, died Unknown. He married **53. Mary.**
53. Mary, died Unknown.

Child of Robert JONES and Mary is:

26   i.   Benjamin JONES, born Abt. 1738; died Unknown; married Lydia.

Endnotes

1. Handwritten Notes of Leafy Fern Van Horn Wolf.
2. Social Security Application, Application of daughter Leafy Fern Van Horn.
3. *Jackson Twp., Sandusky Cnty, OH 1860 Census p. 232.*
4. *Jackson Twp., Sandusky Cnty, OH 1870 Census p. 147.*
5. *Jackson Twp., Sandusky Cnty, OH 1880 Census ED 75 Sh 95A.*
6. *Jackson Twp., Sandusky Cnty, OH 1860 Census p. 232.*
7. *Grave Stone Liberty Cemetery Bettsville, OH,* "fig."
8. *East Wheatfield Twp., Indiana Cnty, PA 1900 Census ED 37 Sh 2B* .
9. The Van Horn Family History by Francis M. Marvin 1929, The Press Publishing Co., p 373-4.

10. Social Security Application, Application of daughter Leafy Fern VanHorn.
11. *East Wheatfield Twp., Indiana Cnty, PA 1860 Census p. 374.*
12. *Dalhart, Dallam Cnty, TX 1920 Census ED 46 Sh 5A.*
13. *Justice Pct. 2, Dallam Cnty, TX 1910 Census ED 69 Sh 4B.*
14. *East Wheatfield Twp., Indiana Cnty, PA 1870 Census p. 22B.*
15. Handwritten Notes of Leafy Fern Van Horn Wolf.
16. The Van Horn Family History by Francis M. Marvin 1929, The Press Publishing Co., p 373-4.
17. *Dalhart, Dallam Cnty, TX 1920 Census ED 46 Sh 5A.*
18. *East Wheatfield Twp., Indiana Cnty, PA 1860 Census p. 374.*
19. *Texas Death Index 1903-2000,* "Electronic," Certificate # 1279.
20. "21 Jan 1937 Indiana Weekly Messenger (Indiana, PA) S. C. Van Horn Obit."
21. *Christian Hummel's Will Sandusky Cnty, OH probate records #3259.*
22. *Jackson Twp., Sandusky Cnty, OH 1850 Census p. 46B.*
23. *Jackson Twp., Sandusky Cnty, OH 1860 Census p. 232.*
24. *Jackson Twp., Sandusky Cnty, OH 1870 Census p. 147.*
25. *Jackson Twp., Sandusky Cnty, OH 1880 Census ED 75 Sh 91A.*
26. *Texas Death Index 1903-2000,* "Electronic," Jennie Hummel # 39246.
27. *Probate Records William Fisher March 30, 1872 Daniel C. Miller Administrator.*
28. *Jackson Twp., Sandusky Cnty, OH 1850 Census p. 46B.*
29. *Margaret's Fisher Hummmel Will Sandusky Cnty, OH #4804.*
30. *Jackson Twp., Sandusky Cnty, OH 1850 Census p. 46B.*
31. *Jackson Twp., Sandusky Cnty, OH 1860 Census p. 232.*
32. *Jackson Twp., Sandusky Cnty, OH 1870 Census p. 147.*
33. *Jackson Twp., Sandusky Cnty, OH 1880 Census ED 75 Sh 91A.*
34. *Texas Death Index 1903-2000,* "Electronic," Jennie Hummel # 39246.
35. H. Z Willimas & Bro., *History of Sandusky County, Ohio with Protrails and Biographies of Prominent Citizens and Pioneers,* (Cleveland, Ohio 1882).
36. *Probate Records William Fisher March 30, 1872 Daniel C. Miller Administrator,* Soource Data 1889 Rutherford B. Hayes Presidential Library.
37. *Jackson Twp., Sandusky Cnty, OH 1850 Census p. 46B.*
38. "Margaret Fisher Hummel's Obituary 20 Aug 1903 Fremont Daily News p3. c3."
39. *Jackson Twp., Sandusky Cnty, OH 1850 Census p. 46B.*
40. *Jackson Twp., Sandusky Cnty, OH 1860 Census p. 232.*
41. *Jackson Twp., Sandusky Cnty, OH 1870 Census p. 147.*
42. *Jackson Twp., Sandusky Cnty, OH 1880 Census ED 75 Sh 4D.*
43. *Jackson Twp., Sandusky Cnty, OH 1850 Census p. 46B.*
44. *Jackson Twp., Sandusky Cnty, OH 1880 Census ED 75 Sh 4D.*
45. *Jackson Twp., Sandusky Cnty, OH 1850 Census p. 46B.*
46. *Jackson Twp., Sandusky Cnty, OH 1860 Census p. 232.*
47. *Jackson Twp., Sandusky Cnty, OH 1870 Census p. 147.*
48. *Jackson Twp., Sandusky Cnty, OH 1880 Census ED 75 Sh 91A.*
49. *Jackson Twp., Sandusky Cnty, OH 1850 Census p. 46B.*
50. *Scott, Sandusky Cnty, OH 1900 Census ED 87 Sh 5A.*
51. *Jackson Twp., Sandusky Cnty, OH 1860 Census p. 232.*
52. *Jackson Twp., Sandusky Cnty, OH 1870 Census p. 147.*
53. *Sandusky, Sandusky Cnty, OH 1920 Census ED 91 Sh 4B.*
54. *Sandusky, Sandusky Cnty, OH 1910 Census ED 126 Sh 1B.*
55. *Sandusky, Sandusky Cnty, OH 1900 Census ED 86 Sh 9A.*
56. *Sandusky, Sandusky Cnty, OH 1880 Census ED 79 Sh 159C.*
57. *Jackson Twp., Sandusky Cnty, OH 1860 Census p. 232.*
58. *OHio Death Certificate 71663.*
59. *Sandusky, Sandusky Cnty, OH 1930 Census ED 22 Sh 24A.*
60. *Dalhart, Dallam Cnty, TX 1920 Census ED 46 Sh 5A.*
61. *Justice Pct. 2, Dallam Cnty, TX 1910 Census ED 69 Sh 4B.*
62. *East Wheatfield Twp., Indiana Cnty, PA 1900 Census ED 37 Sh 2B .*
63. *Jackson Twp., Sandusky Cnty, OH 1860 Census p. 232.*
64. *Jackson Twp., Sandusky Cnty, OH 1870 Census p. 147.*
65. *East Wheatfield Twp., Indiana Cnty, PA 1900 Census ED 37 Sh 2B ,* ED 37, S 2.
66. *Dalhart, Dallam Cnty, TX 1920 Census ED 46 Sh 5A.*
67. *Justice Pct. 2, Dallam Cnty, TX 1910 Census ED 69 Sh 4A.*
68. *Jackson Twp., Sandusky Cnty, OH 1860 Census p. 232.*
69. *Texas Death Index 1903-2000,* "Electronic," Certificate # 39246.
70. *Justice Pct. 2, Dallam Cnty, TX 1910 Census ED 69 Sh 4B.*

71. Handwritten Notes of Leafy Fern Van Horn Wolf.
72. The Van Horn Family History by Francis M. Marvin 1929, The Press Publishing Co., p 373-4.
73. *Dalhart, Dallam Cnty, TX 1920 Census ED 46 Sh 5A.*
74. *East Wheatfield Twp., Indiana Cnty, PA 1860 Census p. 374.*
75. *Texas Death Index 1903-2000,* "Electronic," Certificate # 1279.
76. "21 Jan 1937 Indiana Weekly Messenger (Indiana, PA) S. C. Van Horn Obit."
77. *Jackson Twp., Sandusky Cnty, OH 1870 Census p. 147.*
78. *Bristol, Trumbull Cnty, OH 1910 Census ED 206 Sh 3A.*
79. *Bristol, Trumbull Cnty, OH 1920 Census ED 249 Sh 10A.*
80. *Mecca, Trumbull Cnty, OH 1900 Census ED 114 Sh 7B.*
81. *Jackson Twp., Sandusky Cnty, OH 1870 Census p. 147.*
82. *Ohio Death Certificate 60296.*
83. *Bristol, Trumbull Cnty, OH 1910 Census ED 206 Sh 3A.*
84. *Jackson Twp., Sandusky Cnty, OH 1870 Census p. 147.*
85. *Sandusky, Sandusky Cnty, OH 1880 Census ED 79 Sh 156A.*
86. *Jackson Twp., Sandusky Cnty, OH 1870 Census p. 147.*
87. *Sandusky, Sandusky Cnty, OH 1880 Census ED 79 Sh 156A.*
88. Rutherford B. Hayes Obituary Archives.
89. *Jackson Twp., Sandusky Cnty, OH 1870 Census p. 147.*
90. *Fremont, Sandusky Cnty, OH 1930 Census ED 5 Sh 17B.*
91. *Jackson Twp., Sandusky Cnty, OH 1900 Census ED 81 Sh 14A.*
92. *Lorain, Lorain Cnty, OH 1910 Census ED 91 Sh 12A.*
93. *Jackson Twp., Sandusky Cnty, OH 1870 Census p. 147.*
94. "14 Feb. 1938 Fremont Daily News p2 c6 Sarah Hummel Obit."
95. *Ohio Death Certificate 11790.*
96. Rutherford B. Hayes Obituary Archives.
97. "14 Feb. 1938 Fremont Daily News p2 c6 Sarah Hummel Obit."
98. *Fremont, Sandusky Cnty, OH 1930 Census ED 5 Sh 17B.*
99. Rutherford B. Hayes Obituary Archives.
100. *Jackson Twp., Sandusky Cnty, OH 1870 Census p. 147.*
101. *Jackson Twp., Sandusky Cnty, OH 1880 Census ED 75 Sh 91A.*
102. *Scott, Sandusky Cnty, OH 1900 Census ED 87 Sh 5A.*
103. "27 March 1908 Fremont Daily News p2 c 6 Obit of Rosina Hummel."
104. *Jackson Twp., Sandusky Cnty, OH 1870 Census p. 147.*
105. "27 March 1908 Fremont Daily News p2 c 6 Obit of Rosina Hummel."
106. *Scott, Sandusky Cnty, OH 1900 Census ED 87 Sh 5A.*
107. *Jackson Twp., Sandusky Cnty, OH 1870 Census p. 147.*
108. *Jackson Twp., Sandusky Cnty, OH 1880 Census ED 75 Sh 91A.*
109. *Justice Pct. 2, Dallam Cnty, TX 1910 Census ED 69 Sh 4B.*
110. *Justice Pct. 2, Dallam Cnty, TX 1920 Census ED 43 Sh 5B.*
111. *Justice Pct. 2, Dallam Cnty, TX 1930 Census ED 8 Sh 4A.*
112. *Ballville Twp., Sandusky Cnty, OH 1900 Census ED 73 Sh 16A.*
113. Rutherford B. Hayes Obituary Archives.
114. *Jackson Twp., Sandusky Cnty, OH 1870 Census p. 147.*
115. Rutherford B. Hayes Obituary Archives.
116. *Justice Pct. 2, Dallam Cnty, TX 1910 Census ED 69 Sh 4B.*
117. *Texas Death Index 1903-2000,* "Electronic."
118. Rutherford B. Hayes Obituary Archives.
119. *Jackson Twp., Sandusky Cnty, OH 1880 Census ED 75 Sh 91A.*
120. *North Eaton, Lorain Cnty, OH 1900 Census ED 76 Sh 9A.*
121. *Eaton, Lorain Cnty, OH 1910 Census ED 104 Sh 10B.*
122. *Jackson Twp., Sandusky Cnty, OH 1880 Census ED 75 Sh 91A.*
123. *Ohio Death Certificate 44543.*
124. Rutherford B. Hayes Obituary Archives.
125. *North Eaton, Lorain Cnty, OH 1900 Census ED 76 Sh 9A.*
126. Rutherford B. Hayes Obituary Archives.
127. *North Eaton, Lorain Cnty, OH 1900 Census ED 76 Sh 9A.*
128. *Jackson Twp., Sandusky Cnty, OH 1850 Census p. 40.*
129. *Washington Twp., Sandusky Cnty, OH 1870 Census p. 273.*
130. *Washington Twp., Sandusky Cnty, OH 1860 Census p. 207B.*
131. H. Z Willimas & Bro., *History of Sandusky County, Ohio with Protraits and Biographies of Prominent Citizens and Pioneers,* (Cleveland, Ohio 1882).
132. *Probate Records William Fisher March 30, 1872 Daniel C. Miller Administrator.*

133. *Jackson Twp., Sandusky Cnty, OH 1850 Census p. 40.*
134. H. Z Willimas & Bro., *History of Sandusky County, Ohio with Protraits and Biographies of Prominent Citizens and Pioneers,* (Cleveland, Ohio 1882).
135. *Georgetown, Clear Creek Cnty, CO 1880 Census ED 112 Sh 20D.*
136. *Georgetown, Clear Creek Cnty, CO 1870 Census p. 125B.*
137. *Probate Records William Fisher March 30, 1872 Daniel C. Miller Administrator.*
138. *Georgetown, Clear Creek Cnty, CO 1880 Census ED 112 Sh 20D.*
139. H. Z Willimas & Bro., *History of Sandusky County, Ohio with Protraits and Biographies of Prominent Citizens and Pioneers,* (Cleveland, Ohio 1882).
140. *Probate Records William Fisher March 30, 1872 Daniel C. Miller Administrator.*
141. *Ballville Twp., Sandusky Cnty, OH 1870 Census p. 12.*
142. H. Z Willimas & Bro., *History of Sandusky County, Ohio with Protraits and Biographies of Prominent Citizens and Pioneers,* (Cleveland, Ohio 1882).
143. *Probate Records William Fisher March 30, 1872 Daniel C. Miller Administrator.*
144. H. Z Willimas & Bro., *History of Sandusky County, Ohio with Protraits and Biographies of Prominent Citizens and Pioneers,* (Cleveland, Ohio 1882).
145. *Probate Records William Fisher March 30, 1872 Daniel C. Miller Administrator.*

Family Map

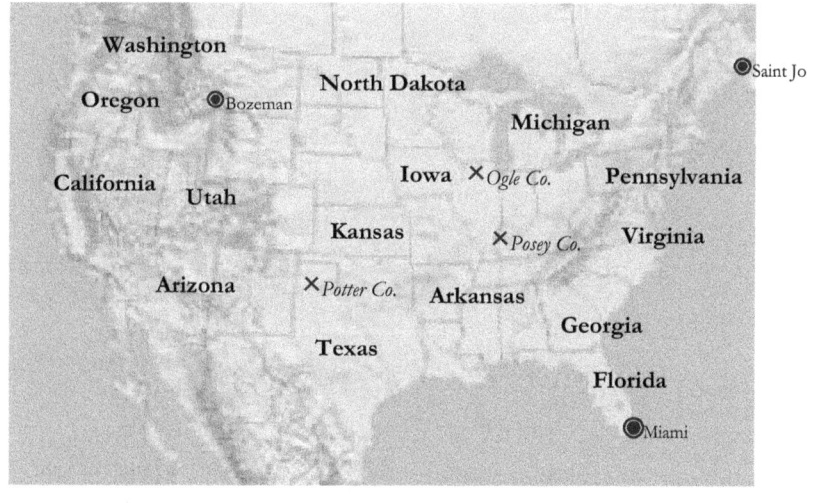

Family Map

Abilene, Taylor Co., TX

Grace GOODLOE Died: 23 Oct 1965

Abington, Montgomery Co., PA

Cornelius CORSON, SR and Annetje VAN HOORN Married: 06 Aug 1735

Aiken, Aiken Co., SC

Otto William MARSHALL, JR and Mary Ella VAN HORN Married: 19 Sep 1941

Marvin Harold TARPLEY and Eunice Matilda VAN HORN Married: 31 Aug 1951

Akron, Summit Co., OH

Wilmer Todd DIXSON and Zula L. VAN HORN Married: 25 Dec 1915

William Washington GEARHART Died: 08 Feb 1945

Myrtle Olive LAMBING Died: 25 Jun 1984

Thelma Imogene ASHCOM Died: Abt. 2003

Alabama (NW of Georgia)

Edith Rae CROSSMAN Born: Abt. 1893

Albany, Albany Co., NY

Evert WYNKOOP

Johannes WYNKOOP

Maria WYNKOOP

Elizabeth Strudles GABRIELS Born: 1689

Albuquerque, Bernalillo Co., NM (268 Mi SW of Potter Co.)

Joseph Jefferson VAN HORN Died: 28 Sep 1857

Aliquippa, Beaver Co., PA

Edward Dale VAN HORN Born: Apr 1940

Allamakee Co., IA

Albert A. VAN HORN Died: 25 Oct 1869

William VAN HORN Died: 09 Nov 1886

Mariah Died: 06 Mar 1912

Samuel R. VAN HORN Died: 24 Mar 1916

Allegheny Co., PA

Nancy VAN HORN Died: 1916

Allendale, Bergen Co., NJ

Cornelius VAN HORN and Lavina VANDERVECK

Lavina VANDERVECK Born: 14 Feb 1789

Alma, Wabaunsee Co., KS

Warren Alfred MILLER and Dorothy M. MCAFOOS Married: 14 Sep 1940

Altoona, Blair Co., PA

Roseannah VAN HORN Born: 24 May 1850

Eugene R. HARKCOM VAN HORN Died: 10 Mar 2007

Amarillo, Potter Co., TX (Potter Co.)

Ella Mary MCAFOOS Died: 14 Dec 1955

Ambridge, Beaver Co., PA

Sprague L. VAN HORN Died: 30 Mar 1951

Amsterdam, Montgomery Co., NY

Cornelis Christiansen VAN HOORN Born: 03 Aug 1653

Family Map

Myrtie ROELOFS Died: 1676

Dirk CLAUSSEN Died: 1686

Annapolis, Anne Arundel Co., MD

John Dwight WEEKS and Betty Jane O'ROURKE Married: 10 Jan 1948

Arcadia, Indiana Co., PA

Wallace Evan SHANKLE Born: Bet. 22 Nov 1853 - 1856

Arizona

Anna Sampson BENT Born: 04 Oct 1901

Arkansas

Florence Van Horn BOWSER Born: Dec 1891

Marion VAN HORN Born: Abt. Mar 1909

Christopher Columbus VAN HORN Died: 1932

See Also Tennessee, and Mississippi.

Armstrong Co., PA

John W. MCAFOOS Born: Bet. 1811 - 1813

Rosalie L. KERNS Born: 20 Mar 1859

John Martin COGLEY Born: 19 Mar 1861

Mary Blanche ROWE Born: 27 Feb 1866

William Gillespie MORROW, MD Born: 20 Dec 1868

Robert Enos NEAL Born: 28 Nov 1869

Nora Ethel LUKEHART Born: 25 Feb 1876

Luther Merle LUKEHART Born: 21 Nov 1877

Alice Leone NEAL Born: 18 Jul 1878

Bertha Agnes LUKEHART Born: Bet. 02 - 12 Aug 1880

Tirzah Theresa WADDING Born: 14 Dec 1882

William Presley DONALDSON Born: 16 Apr 1883

Homer Boyd LUKEHART Born: 17 Sep 1888

Christian VAN HORN Died: 24 Jan 1904

Turner Thompson LUKEHART Died: 03 Mar 1905

Nelson Blair VAN HORN Born: 13 Aug 1913

Mae V. REEFER Born: 05 Jun 1919

Arnold Wilton VAN HORN Died: 1929

Imogene Mildred AUL Born: Abt. May 1929

Shirley Mae NEAL Born: 01 Dec 1930

James Edward HARTZELL Born: 19 Jun 1943

Howard Paul BLACK Born: 30 Apr 1955

Owen DeLone VAN HORNE Died: 26 Mar 1964

Dale Robert LAMBING Died: 16 Sep 1967

John Aldous STEELE Died: Jul 1972

Iva C. HILTY Died: 09 Oct 1973

Lena Christine VAN HORN Died: 16 May 1993

Mae V. REEFER Died: 06 Mar 1998

Donald Reid MCCAUSLAND Died: 22 Nov 2003

Herbert BOWSER Died: 12 Feb 2004

Delbert Clair HARTZELL Died: 21 Jan 2006

Athens, Athens Co., OH (321 Mi NE of Posey Co.)

Family Map

Adela Honeywood COOLEY Born: 18 Jan 1826

Augusta, Richmond Co., GA

Beatrice Elizabeth BARTON Born: Bet. 01 Mar 1898 - 1899

Otto William MARSHALL, JR Born: 08 Feb 1923

Charles Lee GRAVES Died: Abt. 1942

Judson Tannehill VAN HORN Died: 27 May 1967

Beatrice Elizabeth BARTON Died: 23 Oct 1977

Otto William MARSHALL, JR Died: 08 Nov 1980

Augusta Co., VA

Adam FISHER Born: 12 Mar 1788

William FISHER and Jane ANDERSON Married: 30 Sep 1817

Baltimore, Baltimore Co., MD

Elizabeth CHAPEZE Born: 1800

Marion Beatrice BAKER Born: 14 May 1908

Eugene Monroe WAGNER Died: 27 Oct 1967

Henry Logan VAN HORN Died: 1981

Battle Creek, Calhoun Co., MI (212 Mi NE of Ogle Co.)

Marion Earl MAUK Died: 23 Sep 1949

Beavercreek, Greene Co., OH (317 Mi SE of Ogle Co.)

Sheldon Henry SCHIMMEL and Norma Davene HUDSON Married: 31 Dec 1949

Bedford, Bedford Co., PA

Jacob SINK Born: 15 May 1827

Clyde Wallace HINES Died: 27 Aug 1971

Benton, Franklin Co., IL (59 Mi SW of Posey Co.)

Henry Oliver CARLTON Died: 21 Aug 1966

Golda May DIXON Died: 25 May 1975

Benton Co., WA

Esther G. VAN HORN Born: Oct 1893

Bergen, Genesee Co., NY

Aeltie BANTE Born: 1684

Bergen Co., NJ

Christian Barentsen VAN HOORN Born: Bet. 24 Oct 1680 - 21 Oct 1681

Dirck Barentsen VAN HOORN Born: 23 Jan 1680

Pieter Barentsen VAN HOORN Born: 19 Apr 1686

Nickolas Barentsen VAN HOORN Born: 03 Feb 1688

Barent Barentsen VAN HOORN Born: 03 Apr 1691

Johannes Barentsen VAN HOORN Born: 05 Feb 1692

Jannetje JANS Died: 13 Jul 1694

Abraham Barentsen VAN HOORN Born: 12 Sep 1695

Jannetje Barents VAN HOORN Born: 18 Apr 1697

Isaac Barentsen VAN HOORN Born: 02 Jan 1699

Jacob Barentsen VAN HOORN Born: 18 Nov 1702

Benjamin Barentsen VAN HOORN Born: 10 Jan 1705

Family Map

Barent Barentsen
VAN HOORN
and Jannetje
PIETERS
Married: 23 Feb
1712

Barent
Christiansen VAN
HOORN Died:
1726

Barent Barentsen
VAN HOORN
and Elizabeth
KLINKENBER
G Married: 11
Nov 1726

Cornelius VAN
HOORN Died:
12 Mar 1733

Andries VAN
BOSKERK Died:
1738

Peter VAN
BOSKERK Died:
1738

Jacob Barentsen
VAN HOORN
Died: 14 Apr
1775

Cornelius VAN
HORN Born: 17
Dec 1790

Thomas VAN
BOSKERK Died:
Unknown

Berkeley Co.,
WV

Charles
Thompson
GAGEBY Born:
22 Sep 1867

David Brown
GAGEBY Born:
20 Dec 1869

Delia VAN
HORN Born:
1871

Sarah VAN
HORN Born:
Abt. 1872

Florida Anna
Vrginia VAN
HORN Born: 05
Jun 1878

Jeremiah M.
UNGER Born: 14
Feb 1881

Mary Agnes
NESMITH Born:
21 Aug 1882

Lillian DUNHAM
Born: 06 Jun 1884

Laura B.
SHROADS Born:
20 Sep 1884

George Drury
CATLETT and
Mary Pearl
HUTZLER
Married: 18 Dec
1888

Frances Margaret
PALMER Born:
09 Feb 1892

John Wesley
VAN HORN
Born: 07 Oct
1893

George W.
MCBEE and
Nannie Mae
HUTZLER
Married: 23 Jun
1897

James Allen
GAGEBY Born:
Feb 1900

Charles Strother
HUTZLER and
Mary B. LYNN
Married: 10 Jul
1900

William Logan
HUTZLER and
Odessa
MCCARTY
Married: 17 Feb
1901

Charles
Thompson
GAGEBY and
Florida Anna
Vrginia VAN
HORN Married:
12 Feb 1902

Rosalie
HUTZLER Died:
1903

Mary B. LYNN
Died: 1903

Ida May
GAGEBY Born:
08 Jul 1904

Dorothy
HUTZLER Born:
12 Jul 1904

Dorothy
HUTZLER Died:
12 Oct 1904

John Harland
HUTZLER Born:
03 May 1905

Harwood
Chapman
HUTZLER and
Mary Agnes
NESMITH
Married: 20 Dec
1906

Edgar Leroy
GAGEBY Born:
26 Jan 1907

Hugh Samuel
HUTZLER Born:
22 Apr 1907

John Milton
HUTZLER and
Olive B. FUSS
Married: 06 Nov
1907

Ward Irvin
HUTZLER Born:
12 Jan 1909

William Brown
GAGEBY Born:
03 Oct 1909

Virginia Rose
HUTZLER Born:
03 Aug 1910

Adeline
HUTZLER Born:
16 Apr 1912

Family Map

George Sherman HUTZLER and Frances Margaret PALMER Married: 16 Apr 1912

John Henry GAGEBY Born: 01 Jun 1913

Bertha Melissa GAGEBY Died: 15 Aug 1919

Carl Pitkin SCHULTZ and Margaret Picolla Van Horn GAGEBY Married: Abt. 1920

Alan Porterfield GAGEBY Born: 08 Mar 1921

Alan Porterfield GAGEBY Died: 07 Mar 1925

Harwood Chapman HUTZLER Died: 15 May 1929

George Sherman HUTZLER Died: 1931

Jane Narcissa LONG Died: 25 Jan 1932

Charles Strother HUTZLER Died: 19 Jul 1936

John Henry GAGEBY and Lila Mae BILLMYER Married: 08 Dec 1945

Ernest Irvin HUTZLER Died: 1948

Frances Margaret PALMER Died: 01 Feb 1955

Nellie Mae DEARING Died: Apr 1967

Virginia Rose HUTZLER Died: Jul 1979

Edgar Leroy GAGEBY Died: 03 Jun 1980

Berkeley Springs, Morgan Co., WV

Nannie Mae HUTZLER Died: 1948

Berks Co., PA

Jesse WILLETS Born: Nov 1770

Bethel Park, Allegheny Co., PA

Robert Eugene KINTER Died: 30 Nov 1988

Beverly Hills, Los Angeles Co., CA

James Maitland STEWART Died: 02 Jul 1997

Biglerville, Adams Co., PA

John Henry GAGEBY Died: 19 Sep 1981

Lila Mae BILLMYER Died: 03 Nov 1989

Biloxi, Harrison Co., MS

John Raymond ASHCOM, JR Died: 08 Feb 2000

Blairsville, Indiana Co., PA

Henry Milton DILTS Died: 15 Nov 1932

Daniel G. BEERS Died: 05 Oct 1941

Charlotte Susan HAMILTON Died: 21 Feb 1954

George Percy VAN HORN Died: 12 Jan 1965

Janice Louise RANKIN Died: 09 Jun 2004

Boston, Suffolk Co., MA

George R. LEGHORN Died: 03 Apr 1939

Mary VAN HORN Died: 16 Jun 1950

Boulder, Boulder Co., CO

Thelma Evelyn VAN HORN Born: 12 Oct 1908

Bound Brook, Somerset Co., NJ

Leigh S. BACHE

Bozeman, Gallatin Co., MT

Mary Gladys VAN HORN Died: 15 Aug 1985

See Also Choteau, and Helena.

Family Map

**Braddock,
Allegheny Co.,
PA**

John VAN
HORN Born: Oct
1868

Clarence E. VAN
HORN Born: Jul
1879

John VAN
HORN Died:
Bef. 1920

Alpha Retta
WEAMER Died:
21 Sep 1920

**Bremerton,
Kitsap Co.,
WA**

Norman Clayton
BOWERS Died:
10 Dec 2008

**Bristol, Bucks
Co., PA**

Moses WRIGHT
Born: 1767

**Brockway,
Jefferson Co.,
PA**

Samuel Redding
VAN HORN and
Elizabeth Odessa
CRAFT Married:
Bet. 1870 - 1875

Samuel Redding
VAN HORN
Died: Bet. 13 - 23
May 1906

Elizabeth Odessa
CRAFT Died: 28
Jul 1932

Edward Harry
VAN HORN
Died: 28 Jan 1951

**Brookville,
Jefferson Co.,
PA**

Elizabeth Odessa
CRAFT Born: 10
Jan 1865

John Chester
TRAINER Born:
15 May 1894

Jeremiah Johnson
BREWER Died:
26 Jan 1933

Minnie VAN
HORN Died: 08
Aug 1953

Michael W.
STEELE Born:
23 Feb 1957

Lulu V. VAN
HORN Died: 18
Jun 1976

Clair W. STEELE
Died: 07 Nov
2007

Brule Co., SD

William Burton
VAN HORN and
Jennie Elizabeth
BAIREY Married:
25 Nov 1895

Jesse Garrett
VAN HORN
Born: 03 Oct
1896

Joy Avis VAN
HORN Born: 29
Jan 1898

Henry Logan
VAN HORN
Born: 09 Sep 1901

Jennie Elizabeth
VAN HORN
Born: 29 Sep 1903

**Brunswick,
Frederick Co.,
MD**

Mary Pearl
HUTZLER Died:
28 Aug 1949

Mary Edith
CATLETT Died:
11 Sep 1954

**Buckingham,
Bucks Co., PA**

Mary BETTS
Born: 02 Oct
1760

Bucks Co., PA

Benjamin C.
BENNETT

Isaac GILLAM
and Mary VAN
HORN

Annetje VAN
HOORN Born:
19 Jul 1716

Garret VAN
HOORN Born:
Bet. 1725 - 1834

Bernard VAN
HOORN Born:
12 Jul 1727

Helleka
WYNKOOP
Born: 1730

Adrian
WYNKOOP
Born: Bet. 1730 -
1736

Gerardus
WYNKOOP
Born: 1732

Elizabeth VAN
ZANT Born:
1736

Johannis
WYNKOOP
Born: 1736

Isaac VAN
HOORN Born:
05 Nov 1745

Christian
Barentsen VAN
HOORN Died:
Bet. 23 Nov 1751
- 25 Nov 1753

Isaac VAN
HOORN Born:
13 Jan 1754

Isaac VAN
HORNE Born:
13 Jan 1754

Dorothy JOHN
Born: 30 Sep 1755

Family Map

Dorothy MARPLE Born: 30 Sep 1755

Joseph VAN HORNE Born: 1757

Henry B. VAN HORN and Elizabeth VAN ZANT Married: 10 Aug 1758

Joshua VAN HORN Born: 21 Feb 1759

Aaron WINDER Born: 14 Sep 1759

Isaac GILLAM Born: 1760

Isaac Barentsen VAN HOORN Died: Feb 1760

Isaiah VAN HORN Born: Bet. 02 - 24 Oct 1760

Martha HOWELL Born: 05 Jul 1763

Mary VAN HORN Born: 05 May 1764

Christian VAN HORN Born: 13 Jul 1766

Catherine SUBER Born: Bet. 1769 - 1773

Elizabeth VAN HORN Born: Bet. 06 May 1770 - 1774

Mary NEAL Died: 13 Jan 1776

Barent Barentsen VAN HOORN Died: Bet. 1776 - 22 Oct 1779

Susanna VAN VLECK Died: Jun 1776

Henry B. VAN HORN Died: Dec 1777

Bernard VAN HOORN Died: 11 Jan 1778

Hannah REEDER Born: Bet. 11 Mar 1781 - 1786

Mary VAN HOORN Died: 1781

Jane VAN HORN Born: 04 Sep 1785

Sarah VAN HORN Born: 1786

Isaiah VAN HORN and Dorcas LOGAN Married: 01 Jan 1787

Henry VAN HORN Born: Bet. 11 Nov 1787 - 25 Jan 1788

William L. REEDER Born: 08 Feb 1788

Alexander VAN HORN Born: Bet. 17 Dec 1789 - 1790

Isaac VAN HORN, JR Born: 18 Aug 1789

Jonathan SMITH Born: 18 Apr 1790

Dorothea VAN HORN Born: 1791

Samuel VAN HORN Born: 1792

Patience VAN HOORN Born: 17 Sep 1794

Cynthia VAN HORN Born: 04 Feb 1796

Sarah VAN HORN Born: 29 Feb 1796

Henry VAN HORN, JR and Hannah REEDER Married: Bet. Feb 1798 - 01 May 1800

Bernard VAN HORN Born: 22 Jan 1798

Jesse WILLETS and Susanna VAN HORN Married: Abt. 1802

Isaiah VAN HORN Died: 1802

Joseph Jefferson VAN HORN Born: 21 Apr 1802

Elizabeth VAN ZANT Died: 25 Nov 1807

Mary BETTS Died: 15 Dec 1810

William L. REEDER and Jane VAN HORN Married: 19 Aug 1811

Lucinda B. REEDER Born: 1812

Elijah REEDER Born: 1813

Mary WINDER Born: 18 Jul 1814

Josiah REEDER Born: 1815

Christian V. REEDER Born: 1817

Family Map

Charles REEDER
Born: 1819

John VAN
HOORN Died:
15 Feb 1819

Charles VAN
HORN Born: 05
Jan 1820

Catherine SUBER
Died: Dec 1820

William H.
REEDER Born:
1821

David VAN
HORN Born: 04
Oct 1821

Christian VAN
HORN Died: Bet.
18 Apr 1823 - 14
Aug 1833

James VAN
HORN Born: 01
Dec 1823

Amy Ann
REEDER Born:
1824

Aaron WINDER
Died: 02 Jul 1824

Abraham
REEDER Born:
1826

Emily A. VAN
HORN Born: 30
May 1829

Charles
THOMPSON
Born: 18 Jul 1829

Margery VAN
HORN Born:
Abt. 1831

Christian VAN
HORN Born: 18
Oct 1831

Isaac VAN
HOORN Died:
27 Dec 1831

Sarah VAN
HORN Born: 29
Sep 1833

Thomas Gaine
VAN HORN
Born: Bet. 1835 -
29 Jan 1837

Edith VAN
HORN Born:
Abt. 1837

Sarah VAN
HORN Died: 27
Jan 1838

Isaiah VAN
HORN Born:
Abt. 1842

Phebe VAN
HORN Born:
Abt. 1844

Dallas L. VAN
HORN Born: 18
Feb 1845

Samuel
Scattergood VAN
HORN Born: 28
Oct 1848

Henry VAN
HORN, JR Died:
Feb 1849

George H.
THOMPSON
Born: 05 Mar
1857

Hannah
REEDER Died:
17 Sep 1867

William L.
REEDER Died:
01 Jan 1870

Jane VAN
HORN Died: 21
Jan 1876

George V. BOOZ
Born: Feb 1885

Florence Van
Horn BOOZ
Born: 09 Jul 1892

**Buffalo,
Harding Co.,
SD**

Mary Gladys
VAN HORN
Born: 30 Apr
1910

Charles W.
MELANEY and
Mary Gladys
VAN HORN
Married: 07 Mar
1934

**Buffalo,
Washington
Co., PA**

George Curtis
AUL Died: 21
Apr 1933

**Burlington,
Burlington
Co., NJ**

William D. VAN
HOORN and
Sarah
RUDDERROW
Married: 21 May
1757

Sarah
CHIDESTER
Born: 20 Dec
1771

**Butler, Butler
Co., PA**

Cliford J. KEIL
Born: 17 Jun 1894

Evelyn
STEWART Born:
06 Jan 1916

Lawrence Moyes
VAN HORN
Died: 11 Apr
2004

**Calhoun Co.,
MI**

Edna Mabel VAN
HORN Died: 06
Jan 1980

California

Ralph B.
LUKEHART
Born: Abt. 1907

Mary B.
LUKEHART
Born: Abt. 1909

599

Family Map

Vincent VAN HORN Born: Abt. 1913

Charles Merle MCELHOES and Anna Sampson BENT Married: Mar 1924

Fred William BENISH Died: 1950

Mae STILLWAGON Died: 1961

Herbert Jolly LYTLE Died: 14 Feb 1962

Steven Edward MARINKO Born: 10 Dec 1967

Donald Alvin HUTZLER Died: 23 Apr 1981

Margaret Eliabeth VAN HORN Died: 1988

Edward Dale VAN HORN Died: Sep 2002

Calimesa, Riverside Co., CA

Charles Merle MCELHOES Died: 03 Feb 1970

Cambria Co., PA

James Donald ASHCOM Born: 16 Apr 1890

Francis Martha MANNING Born: 13 Feb 1900

Celina, Mercer Co., OH (266 Mi SE of Ogle Co.)

Lula Belle VAN HORN Born: 07 Mar 1894

Howard Gaine VAN HORN Born: 03 Jan 1897

Arthur Lee VAN HORN Born: 28 Nov 1898

Ethel May VAN HORN Born: 14 Apr 1901

Thomas Gaine VAN HORN Died: 29 Jul 1904

Central City, Gilpin Co., CO

Ethel Reed SPOONER Born: 17 Jul 1872

Centre Co., PA

James HOPKINS Born: 18 Jul 1816

Edward Patrick DALY Born: 05 Apr 1889

Chamberlain, Brule Co., SD

William Burton VAN HORN Died: 12 Oct 1924

Chambersburg, Franklin Co., PA

Phillip HUTCHISON Born: 14 Apr 1824

John HUTCHISON Died: 1855

Chicago, Cook Co., IL (86 Mi SE of Ogle Co.)

Eliza YARDLEY

Alva Marco VAN HORN and Mable Chloe CURTIS Married: 21 Dec 1895

Choteau, Teton Co., MT (157 Mi NW of Bozeman)

Pearl Ruth VAN HORN Born: 23 Oct 1912

Churchville, Bucks Co., PA

Christian VAN HOORN and Elizabeth PLUMMER Married: Bet. 13 - 18 Aug 1761

Peter VAN HOORN and Priscilla VAN BOSKIRK Married: 26 Mar 1768

Clara City, Chippewa Co., MN

Neva Emma ANDERSON Died: 14 Jan 1998

Clarion, Clarion Co., PA

Helen N. STEELE Born: Abt. 1905

Harold C. STEELE Born: 25 Apr 1908

Bertha Olive STEELE Born: 29 Mar 1912

Dorothy Marie SMITH Born: 10 Apr 1921

Eleanor SMITH Born: 04 Mar 1923

Family Map

Clair W. STEELE Born: 12 Oct 1923

Rosco Thomas SMITH Died: 25 Mar 1975

Harold C. STEELE Died: Apr 1985

Bertha Olive STEELE Died: 14 Oct 1991

Michael W. STEELE Died: 04 Jul 2005

Dorothy Marie SMITH Died: 05 Feb 2008

Clark Co., OH (253 Mi NE of Posey Co.)

Peter Smith VAN HORN Born: 30 May 1830

John Black VAN HORN Born: 04 Jun 1832

Clarksburg, Harrison Co., WV (412 Mi NE of Posey Co.)

Job VAN HORN, JR Born: 04 Jun 1807

Clay Co., MO (325 Mi SW of Ogle Co.)

Robert Thompson VAN HORN Died: Bet. 02 - 03 Jan 1916

Clayton, Clayton Co., IA (111 Mi NW of Ogle Co.)

Exenia M. WHITE Born: Jul 1879

Clearfield, Clearfield Co., PA

Norman Ernest VAN HORN and Fae WOODWARD Married: May 1917

Iva Bell AUL Died: 09 Apr 1951

Clair LUCE Died: 27 Aug 1975

Clearwater, Pinellas Co., FL (220 Mi NW of Miami)

Leslie Metrezat BROOKS Died: 12 Mar 1976

Cleveland, Cuyahoga Co., OH

Stephen DEDON Born: 23 Sep 1927

Verna M. SHAFFER Died: 12 Dec 1994

Clinton, Clinton Co., IA (46 Mi SW of Ogle Co.)

John Black VAN HORN and Martha BABCOCK Married: 08 Apr 1856

Clinton, Vermillion Co., IN (192 Mi SE of Ogle Co.)

James Overton SMITH Born: 29 May 1893

Clymer, Indiana Co., PA

Freda WYLAND Born: 13 Feb 1913

Jesse Clark MCMANUS and Eva Jane SHANKLE Married: 02 Apr 1913

Emerson Ralph SHANKLE and Edna LAMBING Married: 11 Oct 1916

Arthur James LYDICK Born: 13 Jul 1938

Elizabeth Pearl PALMER Died: 23 Jul 1966

John Torrence LYDICK Died: Dec 1975

James M. LAMBING Died: 17 Jan 1994

Coldwater, Branch Co., MI (221 Mi SE of Ogle Co.)

Zella May GEPHART Died: 03 Feb 1978

Colorado (W of Kansas)

Caroline Blanche Born: Abt. 1889

Helen Hortense LYTLE Born: 26 Jan 1897

Mary Ellen DOUGLAS Born: Feb 1898

Irma Mary WEICKER Born: Abt. 1903

Family Map

Gail Leigh DOUGLAS Born: Abt. Jun 1903

Margaret Van Horn DOUGLAS Born: Bet. 1903 - 1906

Dorcas Grace LYTLE Born: 04 Aug 1905

Colorado Springs, El Paso Co., CO

Shirley Louise CHRISTIANSEN Died: 29 Jan 2005

Columbia, Richland Co., SC

Marvin Harold TARPLEY Died: 07 Jun 1991

Eunice Matilda VAN HORN Died: 18 Dec 2006

Columbus, Franklin Co., OH (358 Mi SE of Ogle Co.)

Thomas Budd VAN HORNE, JR Died: 05 Apr 1895

Compton, Los Angeles Co., CA

Don Mitchell COON Died: Mar 1962

Connecticut (NE of Pennsylvania)

Thomas Edward CLEWS Born: Bet. 10 Sep 1890 - 1891

Crafton, Allegheny Co., PA

William Lynn BROOKS Born: 26 Apr 1922

Cranford, Union Co., NJ

Thomas Edward CLEWS Died: 15 Apr 1972

Florence Irene VAN HORN Died: 09 Mar 1982

Cumberland Co., PA

John WORK Born: Bet. 1758 - 1762

William WORK Born: 21 Feb 1760

Elizabeth WORK Born: Abt. 1763

Mary EAKEN Born: Abt. 1764

Alexander WORK Born: Abt. 1765

James WORK Born: 31 Dec 1768

Susannah WORK Born: Abt. 1770

Letitia WORK Born: Abt. 1775

Miriam SCROGGS Born: 30 Jun 1775

James WORK Died: 1783

John MCELHOES Born: 1785

William WORK and Mary EAKEN Married: 01 Mar 1785

Letita SCOTT Died: 1790

Jane VAN HORN Born: Bet. 25 Feb - 05 Mar 1792

Elizabeth WORK Born: 17 Apr 1793

Rachel Ireland WORK Born: 06 Oct 1793

Joshua VAN HORN Born: Bet. 17 Aug 1794 - 19 Aug 1795

John VAN HORN Born: Bet. 28 Nov 1796 - 07 May 1797

Johnston LIGHTCAP Born: 02 Oct 1811

Dalhart, Dallam Co., TX (57 Mi NW of Potter Co.)

Davis Macy WOLF and Leafy Fern VAN HORN Married: 21 Dec 1910

Emma Elizabeth WOLF Born: 25 Sep 1911

? SMITH Born: Abt. Dec 1917

? SMITH Died: Abt. Aug 1919

Jennie E. HUMMEL Died: 14 Aug 1929

Samuel Cornelius VAN HORN Died: 06 Jan 1937

Family Map

Michael William
LUDWIG Died:
13 Nov 1941

Henry Coulter
VAN HORN
Died: 27 Jul 1960

Ethel Mae Died:
08 Oct 1973

**Dallas, Dallas
Co., TX (343
Mi SE of
Potter Co.)**

Betty Jane
O'ROURKE
Died: 23 May
1980

**Davis, Tucker
Co., WV**

George Preston
VAN HORN
Died: 21 Jan 1902

**Dayton,
Armstrong
Co., PA**

Daniel G. BEERS
Born: 07 Apr
1864

Cora BOSSARD
Born: 02 Mar
1883

Nana Pearl
COGLEY Born:
20 Apr 1890

Robert Merle
NEAL Born: 10
Nov 1902

Florence
KIRKPATRICK
Born: 08 Feb
1920

Lester M.
GEARHART
Born: 19 May
1920

Margaret Ann
SLONINGER
Born: 30 Jul 1931

Laurence Robert
FREDERICK
and Olive Marion
VAN HORN
Married: 25 May
1932

A. J. DEHAVEN
and Lottie Mae
GEARHART
Married: 24 Dec
1937

Robert Enos
NEAL Died: 13
Jan 1953

Homer Boyd
LUKEHART
Died: 19 Feb
1956

Bertha Agnes
LUKEHART
Died: 01 Apr
1960

Dorsey Clinton
VAN HORN
Died: Aug 1978

**Dayton,
Montgomery
Co., OH (309
Mi SE of Ogle
Co.)**

Davis Macy
WOLF Born: 02
May 1886

Malcolm Berger
FRANK Born: 01
Oct 1910

Marianna WOLF
Born: Bet. 08 Feb
1916 - 1917

Avis Ruth WOLF
Born: 21 Sep 1919

Thelma Louise
WOLF Born: 24
Sep 1921

John A. VAN
HORN Died: 12
Apr 1922

Norma Davene
HUDSON Born:
23 Jul 1929

Leafy Fern VAN
HORN Died: 18
Nov 1969

Marianna WOLF
Died: 13 Feb
1974

Chad Michael
LINDSEY Born:
22 Nov 1977

Walter Clarence
CECIL, JR Died:
31 Dec 1987

Malcolm Berger
FRANK Died: 30
Jul 2001

Thelma Louise
WOLF Died: 14
Mar 2006

Chad Michael
LINDSEY Died:
14 Nov 2007

**Deadwood,
Lawrence Co.,
SD**

Leah VAN
HORN Born: 09
Aug 1895

Jane VAN
HORN Born: 13
Jan 1904

**Decatur,
Macon Co., IL
(153 Mi SE of
Ogle Co.)**

John Steele
HUTCHISON
Died: 03 Sep 1873

**Deer Creek,
Otter Tail Co.,
MN**

Sarah Viola
TRAVER Born:
24 Mar 1871

**Delaware (NE
of Virginia)**

Nickolas
Barentsen VAN
HOORN Died:
Unknown

Family Map

**Delaware Co.,
PA**

Tyron LEWIS

**Delmont,
Westmoreland
Co., PA**

Jeremiah Johnson
BREWER Born:
23 Sep 1856

**Denver,
Denver Co.,
CO**

Helen Taylor
TUTTLE Born:
15 Mar 1890

George H. VAN
HORN and Belle
COLEMAN
Married: 22 May
1902

George Henry
VAN HORN and
Marie
WHITFORD
Married: 20 Sep
1926

Hubert Van Horn
WORK III Born:
01 Sep 1928

Harold Barney
VAN HORN
Born: Bet. 1934 -
1942

Robert Van Horn
WORK Died: 23
Aug 1935

Sarah Steele
WORK Died: 27
Sep 1938

Hubert Robert
WORK Died: 14
Dec 1942

Wallace Logan
HINES Died: 03
Sep 1955

Hubert Van Horn
WORK III Died:
04 Aug 2007

**Des Moines,
Polk Co., IA
(223 Mi SW of
Ogle Co.)**

Oliver Ortho
SMITH Born: 01
Dec 1867

Edna Elizabeth
SMITH Born: 04
Dec 1893

Ethel Mae Born:
20 May 1902

Joseph
Henderson
HOOD Died: 07
Jan 1908

Elizabeth Francis
WORK Died: 02
Apr 1926

**Doylestown,
Bucks Co., PA**

Robert
YARDLEY

**DuBois,
Clearfield Co.,
PA**

Albert Martin
SHAFFER Born:
26 Aug 1875

Mary Elizabeth
BROWN Born:
Bet. 30 Jan 1894 -
31 Jan 1896

Lester Leona
VAN HORN
Born: 05 Apr
1895

Mary Ann
HOPKINS Died:
22 Feb 1898

Jonica VAN
HOORN Died:
Unknown

**Durham,
Durham Co.,
NC**

Mildred Heavlyn
BOBBITT Born:
20 Apr 1917

**Economy,
Beaver Co.,
PA**

Sprague L. VAN
HORN and
Hattie STOFFLE
Married: 25 Jan
1911

Elk Co., PA

Tirzale E. VAN
HORN Died: 11
Mar 1923

**Elkton,
Brookings Co.,
SD**

Walter Duval
VAN HORN
Died: Apr 1965

Nan C.
CORCORAN
Died: Jun 1975

**Elkton,
Rockingham
Co., VA**

Nellie Mae
DEARING Born:
19 Jan 1912

**Equality,
Gallatin Co.,
IL (36 Mi SW
of Posey Co.)**

William Vinson
CARLTON Born:
02 Dec 1846

**Erie, Erie Co.,
PA**

Geraldine
STANTON Born:
21 May 1921

Beverly
STANTON Born:
11 Dec 1941

Raymond Walter
STANTON. JR
Born: 03 Jul 1952

Raymond Walter
STANTON Died:
08 May 1971

Family Map

Beverly STANTON Died: 08 Dec 2000

Margaret STANTON Died: 02 Dec 2002

Hilda MILLER Died: 21 Mar 2006

Raymond Walter STANTON. JR Died: 31 Jul 2007

Erie Co., NY

Howard Lee VAN HORN Died: Jan 1984

Euclid, Cuyahoga Co., OH

Florian YOUNG Died: 06 Mar 1942

Evanston, Cook Co., IL (84 Mi E of Ogle Co.)

Dora Myrtle HOOD Died: 28 Feb 1933

Evansville, Vanderburgh Co., IN (16 Mi SE of Posey Co.)

Garrett DEAN Born: 08 Jul 1892

Export, Westmoreland Co., PA

Marion Catherine LEARN Died: 31 Jan 2000

Fairfield Co., OH (304 Mi NE of Posey Co.)

Susannah ANDRICK Died: Aug 1875

Falls Creek, Jefferson Co., PA

Emery Ernest VAN HORN Born: Bet. 08 Jan - Feb 1915

Farmington, Fulton Co., IL (98 Mi SW of Ogle Co.)

Peter Smith VAN HORN and Mary RANDALL Married: 25 Dec 1855

Fayette Co., PA

Lois VAN HOORN Born: 08 Aug 1798

Charles K. BROOKS Born: 06 Mar 1858

Sarah Jane VAN HORN Born: 13 Mar 1859

Clarence Wilbur BROOKS Born: 04 Sep 1882

Mae STILLWAGON Born: Abt. 1884

Sarah Jane VAN HORN Died: 03 Jun 1942

Charles K. BROOKS Died: Abt. 1949

Clarence Wilbur BROOKS Died: 1958

Fayetteville, Washington Co., AR (373 Mi SW of Posey Co.)

William Grant VAN HORNE Born: 1854

Feasterville, Bucks Co., PA

Dorcas LOGAN Born: Bet. 1765 - 02 Apr 1771

Findlay, Hancock Co., OH (300 Mi SE of Ogle Co.)

Jacob HIESTAND Died: 12 Dec 1866

John W. HUMMEL Died: 04 May 1909

Elias Winfield HUMMEL Died: 24 Oct 1915

Susannah HIESTAND Died: 08 Sep 1916

Florida

Joseph ORESIK Died: Abt. 2001

Forest City, Winnebago Co., IA (235 Mi NW of Ogle Co.)

Charles CUMMINGS Born: 01 May 1879

Forest Co., PA

Jay Miller BURKET Born: 21 Feb 1885

Fort Morgan, Morgan Co., CO

Phillip WORK Born: 20 Jun 1888

Family Map

Frances Mary WORK Born: 10 Aug 1890

Tabitha Logan VAN HORN Died: 10 Dec 1890

Frances Mary WORK Died: 08 Aug 1891

Hubert Robert WORK, JR Died: 1895

John Miller LYTLE Died: 15 Jul 1928

Fort Pierre, Stanley Co., SD

Theodore WAGNER and Neva Emma ANDERSON Married: 22 Dec 1922

Fort Smith, Sebastian Co., AR (407 Mi SW of Posey Co.)

William C. ADAMS Died: 06 Jun 1925

Fort Worth, Tarrant Co., TX (320 Mi SE of Potter Co.)

Frank Phillip MARKLEY Died: 14 Feb 1922

Franklin, Warren Co., OH (312 Mi SE of Ogle Co.)

Sarah T. SCHENCK Died: 03 Feb 1888

Frederick, Frederick Co., MD

Charles William GRUBB Died: 16 Aug 1977

Naomi Jane GAGEBY Died: 25 Nov 1979

Frederick Co., VA

Isaac L. VAN HORN Born: 01 Jan 1815

Elizabeth A. MCDONALD Born: 13 Nov 1816

Fremont, Sandusky Co., OH (323 Mi SE of Ogle Co.)

Sarah C. HUMMEL Born: 24 Jun 1863

Florian YOUNG Born: Oct 1867

Samuel Cornelius VAN HORN and Emma Ellen HUMMEL Married: 24 Apr 1883

Margaret Ann FISHER Died: 19 Aug 1903

James Marcus ROSENBERGER Born: 18 Dec 1905

Clarissa Ann HUMMEL Died: 15 Dec 1933

Sarah C. HUMMEL Died: 12 Feb 1938

Perry Franklin ROSENBERGER Died: 23 Apr 1939

Ermie A. ROSENBERGER Died: 06 May 1961

Medina Emma WOLFE Died: 26 May 1970

Fresno, Fresno Co., CA

Gladys Mabel POINTER Died: 20 Apr 1996

Friendsville, Garrett Co., MD

Effie A. HUMBERSON Born: 19 Sep 1902

Norman Clarence VAN HORN and Effie A. HUMBERSON Married: 15 Aug 1925

Garwin, Tama Co., IA (172 Mi W of Ogle Co.)

Nancy Ann AMBLER Born: 24 Nov 1868

William Lawson VAN HORN and Nancy Ann AMBLER Married: 28 Aug 1899

Peter Smith VAN HORN Died: 21 Aug 1909

Georgetown, Clear Creek Co., CO

James A. FISHER Died: 24 May 1887

Georgia

Sarah VAN HOORN Died: 16 Nov 1874

Family Map

Marvin Harold TARPLEY Born: 26 Oct 1912

See Also Alabama, and South Carolina.

Gloucester Co., NJ

John VAN HOORN Born: 03 Jun 1792

Goodland, Sherman Co., KS

Samuel Fred POINTER Died: 12 Oct 1940

Greensboro, Guilford Co., NC

Walter M. EDGE, JR Died: 25 Aug 1999

Greensburg, Westmoreland Co., PA

Olive Mae VAN HORN Died: 12 Jul 1981

Grove City, Mercer Co., PA

Enoch Blair STEAR Born: 31 Oct 1874

John Dilts LEWIS Died: 08 Feb 1946

Lilly May STEAR Died: 14 Sep 1954

Hackensack, Bergen Co., NJ

Margaret VAN HOORN

Cornelis Christiansen VAN HOORN and Margaret VANDERBURG H Married: 04 Mar 1665

Cornelius VAN HOORN Born: 1671

Lucas VAN HOORN Born: 1680

Barent VAN HOORN Born: 08 Sep 1705

Gerret VAN HOORN Born: 01 Oct 1706

Gertje VAN HOORN Born: 17 Dec 1710

Cornelius VAN HOORN and Jacomina DEMAREST Married: 16 Jul 1711

Margaret VAN HOORN Born: 28 Apr 1712

John VAN HOORN Born: 12 Jan 1717

Leah VAN HOORN Born: 06 Jun 1720

Nelsie VAN HOORN Born: 22 Oct 1723

Cornelius VAN HOORN Born: Nov 1747

Lucas VAN HOORN Died: 1760

Dirck Barentsen VAN HOORN Died: Dec 1763

Haddam, Washington Co., KS

Wallace Logan HINES Born: 28 Dec 1887

Hagerstown, Washington Co., MD

Ernest Irvin HUTZLER and Lillian DUNHAM Married: 10 Feb 1903

Charles Strother HUTZLER and Laura B. SHROADS Married: 07 Sep 1907

Hampshire Co., WV

Isaac Lindsay VAN HORN Born: 10 Apr 1853

Hancock Co., OH

William H. HUMMEL Died: 22 May 1930

Hannastown, Westmoreland Co., PA

Sarah Aldo GRINDLE Born: 28 Feb 1916

Harpers Ferry, Jefferson Co., WV

Martha Virginia MOLER Born: 05 Mar 1900

Harrisburg, Dauphin Co., PA

Edith R. COON Died: 03 Apr 1922

Harrison Co., VA

Jacob DAVIS and Sarah HOFFMAN Married: 03 Oct 1816

Family Map

Job VAN HORN,
JR and Prudence
DAVIS Married:
20 Sep 1828

**Harrison Co.,
WV (410 Mi
NE of Posey
Co.)**

Bernard Harrison
VAN HORN
Born: 26 May
1804

Ai VAN HORN
Born: 03 Dec
1823

**Harrisonville,
Cass Co., MO
(355 Mi NW of
Posey Co.)**

Kate TIMMEY
Born: 29 Jun 1857

**Hartsville,
Darlington
Co., SC**

George Kenneth
KUEHNER
Died: 14 Jul 1987

**Hastings,
Adams Co.,
NE**

Clifford Austin
HINES Died: 24
Apr 1985

**Hedgesville,
Berkeley Co.,
WV**

Olive B. FUSS
Born: 17 Jul 1885

**Helena, Lewis
and Clark Co.,
MT (79 Mi
NW of
Bozeman)**

Roy VAN HORN
Died: 21 Jan 1969

**Hoboken,
Hudson Co.,
NJ**

Albert West
BISSELL Born:
04 Mar 1891

**Holton,
Jackson Co.,
KS**

Charles Austin
MCAFOOS Died:
29 Jan 1962

**Homer City,
Indiana Co.,
PA**

George Robert
LAMBING Born:
28 Nov 1919

Myrtle Olive
LAMBING Born:
23 Sep 1922

William L.
JOHNSTON
Born: 21 Sep 1928

Alexander Milton
VAN HORN
Died: 28 May
1944

**Hoxie,
Sheridan Co.,
KS**

Clarence Everett
MCAFOOS Died:
21 Feb 1970

**Hudson Co.,
NJ**

Jacob Cornelius
VREELAND
Born: 07 Nov
1835

**Hunterdon
Co., NJ**

Henry N.
GODOWN
Born: Jun 1861

**Hyattsville,
Prince
Georges Co.,
MD**

Ira Van LYDICK
Died: 11 Feb
1951

James Arthur
ROSENBERGE
R Died: 06 Apr
1967

**Idaho (E of
Oregon)**

Kenneth V.
DOUGLAS
Born: Abt. Oct
1909

**Illinois (SE of
Iowa)**

Mary RANDALL
Born: 23 Jul 1839

Martha Born: Feb
1840

Francis Marion
VAN HORN
Born: 08 Feb
1848

John R. BURNS
Born: Apr 1850

Theodore Julian
VAN HORN
Born: Bet. 1856 -
1858

Rhoda Emaline
SMITH Born:
Bet. Apr 1862 - 30
Mar 1863

William Sherman
COCKRUM
Born: Jan 1866

Lora Bell CLARK
Born: Jun 1873

Peregrine Stewart
WHITHAM
Born: 21 Sep 1875

Calvin SINK
Born: Sep 1879

John Wesley
WITTERS Born:
Abt. 1880

Calvin C. HECK
Born: Oct 1880

Ellen SINK Born:
Sep 1881

Family Map

Wiley Scribner ACKEN Born: Oct 1882

Althia SINK Born: Nov 1883

Lucy Born: Abt. 1885

Ella E. SINK Born: Apr 1886

Cora SINK Born: May 1886

Norma SINK Born: Mar 1888

Stella SINK Born: Jan 1890

Oscar COCKRUM Born: Oct 1892

Goldie VAN HORN Born: Sep 1893

William Jacob SINK Born: Jun 1894

Rhoda L. Born: 1896

William Raymond VAN HORN Born: Nov 1896

Eddie COCKRUM Born: Dec 1897

Owen COCKRUM Born: Dec 1899

Coral Opal BOYER Born: Abt. 1900

Roy Louis VAN HORN Born: Feb 1900

Clara R. Born: Abt. 1901

Clyde COCKRUM Born: Abt. 1902

Everett VAN HORN Born: 1902

Carleton George ALBRIGHT Born: 08 Jan 1903

Nola VAN HORN Born: 1904

Ora SINK Born: Abt. 1905

Ethel SINK Born: Abt. 1906

Omar SINK Born: Abt. 1908

Lloyd VAN HORN Born: Abt. Oct 1908

Roy SINK Born: Abt. 1910

William SINK Born: Abt. 1911

Frank P. ALBANO Born: Abt. 1912

Shirley Louise CHRISTIANSEN Born: 29 Jan 1930

Indiana (SW of Pennsylvania)

Margaret Mitchell DYE Born: Nov 1827

Martha GAST Born: Abt. 1843

Melinda Finch DAVIS Born: 28 Jun 1850

William F. FISHER Born: Abt. 1857

James SMITH Born: Abt. 1859

Matilda Born: Abt. 1864

Edward VAN HORN Born: Nov 1869

Rilla HUBER Born: Abt. 1882

Pearl VAUGHN Born: Apr 1883

Rosco VAUGHN Born: May 1885

Frank SMITH Born: Abt. 1899

James Arthur ROSENBERGER, JR Born: Abt. 1910

Indiana, Indiana Co., PA

Miriam Scroggs HAMILTON

Marion Earl MAUK

Earl Eugene SCOTT

Alice C. VAN HORN

William R. MCELHOES Born: 28 Jan

Robert HUTCHISON Born: 10 Jan 1789

Joseph VAN HORNE and Martha EWING Married: 22 Nov 1792

Ann HUTCHISON Born: 1795

Matthew Bennett WYNCOOP Born: 13 Jan 1795

Mary LYDICK Born: 30 Apr 1800

William G. VAN HORN Born: Bet. 01 Mar 1800 - 1802

Mary Ann HOPKINS Born: Bet. 1800 - 1816

Family Map

John LYDICK
Died: Bet. Jul -
Aug 1803

Nancy VAN
HORN Born: 02
Oct 1804

Sarah S. WORK
Born: 17 Apr
1805

Isaac VAN
HORN Born:
Bet. 20 May 1806
- 11 Apr 1810

Aaron WORK
Born: 26 Oct
1806

Isabella KINTER
Born: 31 May
1807

Robert Alexander
THOMPSON
Died: 13 Oct
1809

Mary MAY Died:
1810

Miriam WORK
Born: 25 Jul 1810

William
STEWART Died:
07 Dec 1810

Henry D.
KINTER Born:
08 Jun 1812

Moses Thompson
WORK Born: 05
Dec 1812

George Logan
VAN HORN
Born: Bet. 06 - 16
Jan 1813

James Ross
KINTER Born:
05 Apr 1814

William DILTS
Born: 25 Apr
1814

Mary Brady
WYNCOOP
Born: Bet. 08 - 11
Dec 1814

Mary CANNON
Died: 25 Jan 1815

Cornelius
HUTCHISON
Born: 04 Feb
1815

Isaiah
MCELHOES
Born: 25 Jun 1815

Susan WORK
Born: 30 Sep 1815

Mary C. VAN
HORN Born:
Abt. 1817

David STEAR
Born: 03 Aug
1817

Elijah Ireland
WORK Born: 23
Nov 1818

Hugh
HAMILTON and
Nancy VAN
HORN Married:
Apr 1819

Robert
HAMILTON and
Rachel Ireland
WORK Married:
Apr 1819

Alexander VAN
HORN and Mary
WHERRY
Married: 13 May
1819

James Thompson
VAN HORN
Born: 15 Aug
1819

Benjamin Briggs
VAN HORN
Born: Bet. 1819 -
1822

William W.
HAMILTON
Born: Abt. 1820

Susan
MCELHOES
Born: Bet. 22 Feb
1820 - 1821

Isaiah VAN
HORN Born: 22
May 1820

Agnes M.
WYNCOOP
Born: 20 Aug
1820

Christian VAN
HORN Born: 05
Aug 1821

Hugh Hunter
HAMILTON
Born: 09 Oct
1821

Tabitha Logan
VAN HORN
Born: Bet. 27 Sep
1821 - 1822

Mary Ann VAN
HORN Born:
Abt. 1822

John Work
WYNCOOP
Born: 06 May
1822

Isaiah
MCELHOES
Died: 1823

John D. TOMB
Born: 06 Sep 1823

James Alexander
HAMILTON
Born: 04 Dec
1823

Robert
Thompson VAN
HORN Born:
Bet. 10 - 19 May
1824

Jane F.
WYNCOOP
Born: 02 Aug
1824

Robert W.
HAMILTON
Born: Abt. 1825

Ellen
HUTCHISON
Born: 12 Apr
1825

Penine RICE
Died: 06 Jul 1826

Family Map

Elizabeth J. WYNCOOP Born: 22 Jul 1826

John HAMILTON Born: Abt. 1827

Tabitha Dorcas VAN HORN Born: 02 Dec 1827

William WORK Died: 01 Aug 1828

Lucinda HUTCHISON Born: 12 Jan 1830

Allen HAMILTON Born: 14 Feb 1830

James Monroe WORK Born: 08 Apr 1830

Sarah VAN HORN Born: 30 Apr 1830

Robert Porter WARDEN Born: Jan 1832

Margaret HAMILTON Born: 15 Mar 1833

Robert A. MCELHOES Born: 15 May 1833

Dorcas VAN HORN Born: 06 Aug 1833

Miriam Waiver HAMILTON Born: Abt. 1834

Stuchell LYDICK Born: 23 Mar 1834

Miriam VAN HORN Born: Bet. 1834 - 1840

Thaddeus C. WORK Born: 13 Feb 1835

Jane Elizabeth VAN HORN Born: 22 Oct 1835

Elizabeth WORK Died: 08 Dec 1835

Milton WORK Born: 10 Nov 1836

Ellen H. MEANOR Born: Jun 1837

James W. STEELE Born: Abt. 1838

Arabella WORK Born: 14 Apr 1839

Mary P. VAN HORN Born: 27 Apr 1839

John Alexander STEWART Born: 04 May 1839

William Wesley LYDICK Born: 05 Sep 1839

Peter Watson DILTS Born: Abt. 1840

Henry AUL Died: 18 Jun 1840

George Logan VAN HORN Born: 29 Dec 1840

Elizabeth Canon STEWART Born: Bet. 1840 - 1843

Eleanor MCGUIRE Died: 1841

Jane MCELHOES Born: Mar 1841

Asenath WORK Born: 20 Nov 1841

Henry Van Zandt STEWART Born: Bet. 1841 - 1848

John Scott DILTS Born: Abt. 1842

Madison W. MCLAUGHLIN Born: 01 Jan 1842

George Logan VAN HORN and Mary Brady WYNCOOP Married: 07 Apr 1842

John Neff VAN HORN Born: 13 Aug 1842

Cornelius HUTCHISON and Katherine FRY Married: 10 Oct 1842

Margaret Huston THOMPSON Born: 10 Nov 1842

Elizabeth VAN HORN Born: 26 Jun 1843

Ruth WORK Born: 20 Nov 1843

James Coulter DILTS Born: Abt. 1844

Aaron Work STEELE Born: 14 Jul 1844

Elizabeth VAN HORN Died: Bet. 17 Aug 1844 - 1848

Isaiah VAN HORN Died: Bet. 06 - 27 Aug 1844

611

Family Map

Thomas WAKEFIELD Died: 20 Nov 1844

William C. DILTS Born: Abt. 1845

Archibald J. STEWART Born: Abt. 1845

Andrew Jackson LIMERICK Born: 08 Jan 1845

John Kinter MCELHOES Born: 16 Mar 1845

Elizabeth MORTON Died: 09 May 1845

Melissa Jane VAN HORN Born: 27 Jul 1845

Robert STEWART and Mary Ann VAN HORN Married: 24 Aug 1845

John LYDICK Died: 11 Mar 1846

Jane DILTS Born: Abt. 1847

Jane T. LIGHTCAP Born: 1847

Roseanna PATTERSON Died: 15 Jan 1847

Jacob LYDICK, SR Died: 28 Feb 1847

Mazella I. VAN HORN Born: 27 Mar 1847

James Steele MCELHOES Born: 04 Apr 1847

Moses Thompson WORK and Tabitha Logan VAN HORN Married: 13 May 1847

Jane Narcissa LONG Born: 05 Aug 1847

Bennett Work VAN HORN Born: Bet. 13 May 1847 - 1851

Margaretta T. STEWART Born: 25 Jun 1848

Elizabeth Francis WORK Born: 01 Sep 1848

Mary THOMPSON Died: 05 Sep 1848

Catherine Araminta TRAVIS Born: Bet. 06 Apr - May 1848

Alice Roselia VAN HORN Born: Bet. 21 - 22 Mar 1848

James THOMPSON Died: 13 Feb 1849

Kate STEWART Born: Abt. 1850

Lucinda LIGHTCAP Born: 1850

Elizabth MCELHOES Born: Abt. Jan 1850

William Alexander VAN HORN Born: 21 Mar 1850

Samuel Taylor ROBINSON Born: 11 May 1850

George SINKS Died: Jul 1850

Miriam SCROGGS Died: 28 Jul 1850

Miriam WORK Died: 11 Aug 1850

Miriam Waiver HAMILTON Died: Aft. 1850

Samuel Redding VAN HORN Born: Bet. 15 Feb 1850 - 1851

Frances A. WORK Born: Bet. 30 Aug 1850 - 1852

Mary C. VAN HORN Died: Bet. 1850 - 1860

James Harvey VAN HORN Born: Abt. 1851

Alexander Milton VAN HORN Born: 20 Jan 1851

John Miller LYTLE Born: 27 May 1851

Henry Scott KINTER Born: 09 Jun 1851

William Allen STEELE and Dorcas HAMILTON Married: 11 Jun 1851

Mary Ellen SINK Born: 17 Sep 1851

John Scott LIGHTCAP Born: 21 Sep 1851

Mary Agnes VAN HORN Born: Bet. 04 - 13 May 1851

Family Map

Mary Agnes VAN HORN Born: 20 Nov 1851

Mary BARBER Born: 04 Mar 1852

Elijah Work STEELE Born: 26 Apr 1852

Margaret Emily VAN HORN Born: 01 Nov 1852

Mary S. WORK Born: Bet. 05 Oct 1852 - 1854

John HAMILTON Died: 15 Jun 1853

Turner Thompson LUKEHART Born: 26 Aug 1853

Sarah Dorcas SINK Born: 15 Sep 1853

Samuel Gates VAN HORN Born: 14 Dec 1853

Sarah S. VAN HORN Born: 27 Dec 1853

Sarah Isabella MCELHOES Born: Bet. 1853 - 1855

Laura Jane CONDRON Born: Bet. 24 Oct 1854 - 1855

Alice Amelia STEELE Born: 27 Feb 1854

Clara Lucinda VAN HORN Born: 27 Apr 1854

Stuchell LYDICK and Jane Elizabeth VAN HORN Married: 04 May 1854

Nancy Ann LIGHTCAP Born: 14 Sep 1854

Dorcas LOGAN Died: 22 Sep 1854

Robert W. VAN HORN Born: 19 Jan 1855

Rhoda Haseltine WORK Born: 22 Jan 1855

John Albert LYDICK Born: Feb 1855

Henry Coulter VAN HORN Born: 12 Mar 1855

Henry D. KINTER Died: 10 Jun 1855

John Alexander LYDICK Died: Bef. 18 Jun 1855

Ruth WORK Born: 07 Nov 1855

Austin Addison SINK Born: Abt. 1856

James Melantheon CONDRON Born: Mar 1856

Jacob L. COON and Catherine VAN HORN Married: 05 May 1856

James Irvin LYDICK Born: 11 Jul 1856

Mary C VAN HORN Born: 02 Aug 1856

Clara Frances WORK Born: 11 Sep 1856

Peter DILTS, SR Died: 04 Oct 1856

Lettice Jane STEELE Born: 15 Nov 1856

James O'CONNER Born: Abt. 1857

Augustus Gilbert SINK Born: Abt. 1857

John MCELHOES Died: 17 Jan 1857

Charles Fremont VAN HORN Born: 15 Mar 1857

Martha Belle NICHOL Born: 17 May 1857

John M. LAFFERTY Born: 27 May 1857

Samuel K. LYDICK Born: 22 Oct 1857

Samuel Cornelius VAN HORN Born: Bet. 31 Dec 1857 - 1858

Thaddeus VAN HORN Born: Feb 1858

Sarah Steele WORK Born: 09 Feb 1858

Thaddeus VAN HORN Died: 17 Mar 1858

Robert HOPKINS Died: 17 Apr 1858

William Madison CONDRON Born: 18 Apr 1858

Family Map

Elizabeth THOMPSON Died: Bet. 13 Feb - 16 Apr 1858

Jeremiah Walter WORK Born: 12 May 1858

William VAN HORN Born: Bet. 1858 - 1859

Wilson T. LYDICK Born: 27 Mar 1859

John THOMPSON Died: 27 Mar 1859

Henry Milton DILTS Born: 10 May 1859

Elizabeth VAN HORN Born: Bet. 14 Jun 1859 - 1860

Mary Agnes VAN HORN Died: 03 Dec 1859

Margaret Emily VAN HORN Died: 28 Dec 1859

Emma Jane WIDDOWSON Born: Abt. 1860

Samuel H. VAN HORN and Miriam Work STEELE Married: 07 Mar 1860

Zoe Frances O'CONNER Born: May 1860

Melissa J. SINK Born: Jun 1860

Carl Hamilton WORK Born: 15 Sep 1860

Ester Emma VAN HORN Born: 19 Sep 1860

Samuel Lydick BARR Born: 18 Nov 1860

Melissa Jane VAN HORN Died: Bet. 13 - 15 Mar 1860

Ida Jane O'CONNER Born: Abt. 1861

James W. VAN HORN Born: 1861

Mary A. LYDICK Born: 01 Apr 1861

Anderson T. VAN HORN Born: 03 Jun 1861

Wilson T. LYDICK Died: 09 Jun 1861

Infant LIGHTCAP Born: 02 Oct 1861

William DILTS Died: 27 Oct 1861

Cornelius Elsworth CONDRON Born: 17 Nov 1861

Elmer E. SINK Born: Bet. 29 Jul 1861 - 1863

Nancy Jane TOMB Born: 12 Feb 1862

Jacob Leroy CONDRON Born: Mar 1862

Jessie Fremont WORK Born: 01 Aug 1862

Tabitha Logan VAN HORN Born: 14 Oct 1862

Jennie Myrtle WORK Born: Bet. 02 Dec 1862 - 1864

Charlotte Susan HAMILTON Born: 15 Jan 1863

Elmer E. LYDICK Born: 25 Feb 1863

Hugh Clark STEELE Born: 27 Feb 1863

son VAN HORN Born: Mar 1863

son VAN HORN Died: Mar 1863

Hugh Dixon TOMB Born: 19 Nov 1863

John Scott DILTS Died: 12 Jan 1864

William Wesley LYDICK and Mary P. VAN HORN Married: 15 Mar 1864

Margaret VAN HORN Born: Apr 1864

Harry Johnson LIGHTCAP Born: Sep 1864

Margaret THOMPSON Died: Bet. 13 - 23 Feb 1864

Jacob CONDRON Died: 1865

Hugh Clark STEELE Died: Apr 1865

Marion M. CONDRON Born: 07 Apr 1865

Melissa B. ALLISON Born: 08 Jun 1865

Ellen Caroletta VAN HORN Born: 30 Jun 1865

Family Map

Martha Jane LYDICK Born: 03 Sep 1865

Margaret Emma SINK Born: Bet. 02 Jul 1865 - 1867

Edsell Hale WORK Born: 08 Sep 1865

Jane VAN HORN Died: 13 Sep 1865

Minnie VAN HORN Born: 27 Jan 1866

David Blanchard STEAR Born: 05 May 1866

Harry Logan LYDICK Born: 20 May 1866

Alvord Hamilton STEELE Born: 11 Jun 1866

Charles Gillis CONDRON Born: Abt. 18 Nov 1867

Rachel VAN HORN Born: Abt. 1868

John Neff VAN HORN and Mary Jane CAMPBELL Married: 1868

John Kinter MCELHOES and Margaret Huston THOMPSON Married: 11 Mar 1868

Milton Crawford LYDICK Born: 11 Apr 1868

Ida Mae LYDICK Born: 11 May 1868

daughter VAN HORN Born: Sep 1868

daughter VAN HORN Died: Sep 1868

George Stockholm WYNKOOP and Jane T. LIGHTCAP Married: 23 Sep 1868

Elizabeth Estella WORK Born: 30 Oct 1868

Ida Sarah STEELE Born: 15 Nov 1868

Lilly May STEAR Born: 1869

Claude Duval VAN HORN Born: 21 Feb 1869

Gertrude MCELHOES Born: 24 Mar 1869

Lottie Nancy WORK Born: 21 Sep 1869

Howard William MCLAUGHLIN Born: Abt. Dec 1869

Hubert Earl VAN HORN Born: Bet. 21 Aug 1869 - 1870

Fanny BRIGGS Died: Bef. 1870

George H. VAN HORN Born: Abt. 1870

Peter Watson DILTS Died: 1870

Dora Myrtle HOOD Born: 14 Feb 1870

George A. CONDRON Born: Mar 1870

Tirzale E. VAN HORN Born: Bet. Jan - May 1870

Rachel STEWART Died: Bet. 1870 - 1872

Ira Van LYDICK Born: 16 Jan 1871

Thomas McCord MCLAUGHLIN Born: 25 Feb 1871

Stella M. VAN HORN Born: 28 Feb 1871

Alexander VAN HORN Died: 27 Jul 1871

William Burton VAN HORN Born: 20 Nov 1871

Nancy Ellen NEAL Born: 22 Nov 1871

Albert LYDICK Born: Abt. 1872

John A. L. MCLAUGHLIN Born: Abt. 1872

Clara Lucinda VAN HORN Died: 26 Jan 1872

Robert Elmer STEELE Born: 16 Apr 1872

Alexander Maitland STEWART Born: 19 May 1872

Ester Emma VAN HORN Died: 20 Jun 1872

Olive Florence CONDRON Born: 02 Jul 1872

Family Map

Mary Carothers WORK Born: 07 Aug 1872

Lizzie A. VAN HORN Born: 26 Aug 1872

Anna B. VAN HORN Born: Oct 1872

John Graham GALENTINE Born: Nov 1872

Lula M. SHIELDS Born: 04 Nov 1872

Ellen HUTCHISON Died: 26 Dec 1872

Frank Thomas MCELHOES Born: Bet. 06 - 16 Sep 1872

Bennett Work VAN HORN and Mary Belle WARDEN Married: Bet. 01 Jan 1872 - 1873

Ada Myrtle VAN HORN Born: 29 Aug 1873

Joseph Bell LYDICK Born: 30 Aug 1873

Ruth E. LYDICK Born: Bet. 12 Oct 1873 - 1876

Mary Lois MCLAUGHLIN Born: Abt. 1874

Samuel Taylor ROBINSON and Laura Jane CONDRON Married: 21 May 1874

Orin Denton VAN HORN Born: 11 Aug 1874

Margaret Hamilton WORK Born: 01 Sep 1874

Margaret HAMILTON Died: 07 Sep 1874

James Estep TOMB and Mary E. HUTCHISON Married: 01 Oct 1874

Turner Thompson LUKEHART and Sarah S. VAN HORN Married: 08 Oct 1874

William Hastings STEELE Born: 13 Oct 1874

Laney Lawrence AUL Born: Bet. 03 - 13 Sep 1875

Angus Blanchard CONDRON Born: Jan 1875

Robert Campbell VAN HORN Born: 03 Feb 1875

George Preston VAN HORN Born: 16 May 1875

Margaret Jane LYDICK Born: 07 Nov 1875

Margaret Jane FULMER Born: 08 Nov 1875

Mand F. SIMPSON Born: Abt. 1876

Minnie A. VAN HORN Born: Abt. 1876

Jane DILTS Died: 27 Mar 1876

Edward G. LYDICK Born: 07 Jul 1876

Robert Roy MCELHOES Born: 13 Jul 1876

Edward G. LYDICK Died: 27 Jul 1876

John Scott LIGHTCAP and Maria Lucinda BENCE Married: 16 Nov 1876

Dorcas VAN HORN Died: Bet. 15 Mar 1876 - 1889

Ida A. MCLAUGHLIN Born: Abt. 1877

James C. SIMPSON Born: Abt. 1877

Edward Telford STEELE Born: Abt. 1877

Elmer Monroe VAN HORN Born: 13 Jan 1877

Emma VAN HORN Born: 21 Jan 1877

Mary Caroline VAN HORN Born: 11 Apr 1877

Myrreel VAN HORN Born: Jun 1877

Margaret Ellen STEELE Born: 26 Jun 1877

Henry VAN HORN Died: 18 Sep 1877

Robert HUTCHISON Died: Oct 1877

Sarah VAN HORN Died: 12 Nov 1877

616

Family Map

Alexander Milton VAN HORN and Rosalie L. KERNS Married: 18 Dec 1877

James Melantheon CONDRON and Mary Agnes GALBRAITH Married: 01 Jan 1878

Rachel Ireland WORK Died: 08 Apr 1878

John Miller LYTLE and Sarah Steele WORK Married: 07 May 1878

Amos Burton LYDICK Born: 24 May 1878

Arnold Wilton VAN HORN Born: Jul 1878

LeRoy Kerns VAN HORN Born: 08 Jul 1878

David Wade WAKEFIELD Died: 18 Dec 1878

Isabella KINTER Died: 31 Jan 1879

Clark SIMPSON Born: Feb 1879

Jennie B. LYDICK Born: Mar 1879

Joseph Isaiah MCELHOES Born: 18 May 1879

Cora Belle VAN HORN Born: 03 Jun 1879

Nora VAN HORN Born: 03 Aug 1879

Sprague L. VAN HORN Born: 23 Sep 1879

Clark Lewis STEELE Born: 08 Oct 1879

Linda Maude HOUCK Born: 06 Aug 1880

Angus Vanzant VAN HORN Born: 26 Aug 1880

Isaiah VAN HORN Died: 15 Nov 1880

Roy Harvey MCLAUGHLIN Born: 11 Dec 1880

George W. COLLINS and Jane MCELHOES Married: Abt. 1881

Mary Brady WYNCOOP Died: 07 Feb 1881

Anna Florence VAN HORN Born: 20 Jun 1881

Mary LYDICK Died: 15 Jul 1881

William Madison CONDRON and Margaret Cymisca KUNKLE Married: Oct 1881

Emma Evans WYNCOOP Born: 21 Jan 1882

Harry Stanley HOUCK Born: 09 Jun 1882

Martha Belle MCELHOES Born: Bet. 31 Oct - 01 Nov 1882

Robert Lee Claire VAN HORN Born: 25 Jul 1882

Mary Mae VAN HORN Born: 12 Sep 1882

William G. VAN HORN Died: Bet. 10 - 17 Aug 1882

Nettie Alice WALTERMIRE Born: 23 Nov 1882

Samuel S. MCLAUGHLIN Born: Feb 1883

George Percy VAN HORN Born: Bet. 06 Sep 1883 - 1884

Henry VAN HORN Died: Bet. 26 Aug 1883 - 19 Jul 1896

William D. LYDICK Born: 06 Mar 1884

Samuel J. LIGHTCAP Died: 29 Mar 1884

Silas Edgar LIGHTCAP Born: Bet. 1884 - 16 Dec 1885

John Aldous STEELE Born: 02 May 1884

William R. MCELHOES Died: 28 Aug 1884

James Ira VAN HORN Born: 26 Apr 1885

Henry Milton DILTS and Charlotte Susan HAMILTON Married: 03 Jun 1885

George G. MCLAUGHLIN Born: Aug 1885

Family Map

Samuel Lydick BARR and Mary C VAN HORN Married: 31 Dec 1885

Etta VAN HORN Born: 21 Jan 1886

Elva Floid DILTS Born: 01 Mar 1886

Allen Ester STEELE Born: 09 Jun 1886

James HOPKINS Died: 14 Jul 1886

David STEAR Died: 25 Aug 1886

James Lucas KINTER Born: 23 Jan 1887

Stella BARR Born: 31 Mar 1887

Wallace Evan SHANKLE and Ida Mae LYDICK Married: 03 May 1887

Amanda JAMES Died: 06 Jun 1887

Harry Bennett VAN HORN Born: 17 Jun 1887

Benjamin Briggs VAN HORN Died: 29 Aug 1887

Hansel Clark MCLAUGHLIN Born: Sep 1887

Henry A. VAN HORN Died: Bet. 27 - 28 Apr 1887

Joshua VAN HORN Died: 02 Nov 1887

Daniel Clair FREEDLINE Born: 1888

Samuel H. VAN HORN Died: 1888

James Buckley RANKIN Born: 07 Sep 1888

Clare Clawson STEELE Born: 18 Oct 1888

Eva BARR Born: 06 Nov 1888

Elmer E. LYDICK and Anna FULMER Married: Abt. 1889

Irene Bertha SIMPSON Born: 09 Jul 1889

Pearl Agnes VAN HORN Born: 24 Jul 1889

James Ross KINTER Died: 14 Dec 1889

George Leroy CONDRON Died: Aft. 1889

Rachel POUNDS Died: Bet. 02 - 12 Apr 1889

Homer Park VAN HORN Born: Bet. 26 Mar 1889 - 20 Mar 1890

Anderson T. VAN HORN and Sadie A. KINNAN Married: 14 Mar 1890

Charles Blaine VAN HORN Born: Bet. 01 - 02 Aug 1890

John VAN HORN and Alpha Retta WEAMER Married: 30 Oct 1890

Cornelius HUTCHISON Died: Jun 1891

John Graham GALENTINE and Alice C. VAN HORN Married: 13 Jun 1891

Harry Melbourn MOCK and Mary Emma LYDICK Married: 16 Oct 1891

Annie P. VAN HORN Born: Bet. 20 Jul 1891 - 1893

Norman Clarence VAN HORN Born: 22 Oct 1891

Harry M. WILT and Ruth E. LYDICK Married: Abt. 1892

Maude U. STEFFY Born: 06 Mar 1892

J. A. WALTER and Olive Florence CONDRON Married: 12 May 1892

Alexander Thomas LAMBING Born: 18 May 1892

Mabel BARR Born: 28 May 1892

Ernest MCLAUGHLIN Born: 07 Jun 1892

Family Map

Harry Logan LYDICK and Mary LONG Married: 09 Jun 1892

Goldie Esther LYDICK Born: 02 Apr 1893

Mary WHERRY Died: 30 Jun 1893

Samuel Taylor ROBINSON Died: 10 Jul 1893

Nancy MCELHOES Died: 14 Jul 1893

Helen Irene HUTCHISON Born: 25 Jul 1893

John Raymond ASHCOM Born: 12 Oct 1893

Harry Arlington ALLISON Born: 16 Oct 1893

Lester Donald STEELE Born: 07 Nov 1893

Carleton Van Horn BARR Born: 23 Nov 1893

Joseph Bell LYDICK and Margaret Jane FULMER Married: 07 Dec 1893

Dollie Ethel VAN HORN Born: 20 Apr 1894

Wesley Long LYDICK Born: 23 Apr 1894

Clair J. LYDICK Born: 11 Jul 1894

Paul BUTTERBAUG H Born: 25 Jul 1894

Andrew Glenn VAN HORN Born: 24 Aug 1894

Mary Ada VAN HORN Born: Sep 1894

Mary Jane FERRIER Born: Dec 1894

James W. VAN HORN and Melissa B. ALLISON Married: 1895

Laney Lawrence AUL and Mary Caroline VAN HORN Married: Bet. 15 - 21 May 1895

Cornelius HUTCHISON Died: Apr 1895

Mabel Marie HUTCHISON Born: 20 Apr 1895

John Bion TOMB Born: 29 May 1895

William M. MCADOO and Ada Myrtle VAN HORN Married: 25 Sep 1895

Hazel B. MCADOO Born: 02 Nov 1895

James Monroe WORK Died: 23 Nov 1895

Thomas A. LAMBING and Jennie B. LYDICK Married: Abt. 1896

Herbert Riggle AUL Born: 22 Feb 1896

Dorcas MCELHOES Died: 10 Apr 1896

Catherine Isabelle VAN HORN Born: 25 Apr 1896

Charles Andrew FERRIER Born: 05 May 1896

Alice Elsie VAN HORN Born: Jun 1896

Anna HUTCHISON Died: 05 Jul 1896

Isaiah MCELHOES Died: 02 Oct 1896

Cyrus B. DILTS Born: 05 Oct 1896

Helen C. BARR Born: 22 Oct 1896

Winifred Hazel HUTCHISON Born: 30 Oct 1896

Blair James LYDICK Born: 15 Nov 1896

Johnston LIGHTCAP Died: Dec 1896

Bessie M. STEELE Born: Jan 1897

Lulu Leona LYDICK Born: 10 Feb 1897

Talmage VAN HORN Born: 24 Feb 1897

James Alexander HAMILTON Died: 23 Apr 1897

Esther M. MCADOO Born: 20 May 1897

Lucy Adelia CONRAD Died: 15 Jun 1897

Family Map

George Stockholm WYNKOOP Died: 02 Oct 1897

Lucinda LIGHTCAP Died: 22 Oct 1897

Edna Gertude VAN HORN Born: 26 Apr 1898

? VAN HORN Born: 28 May 1898

? VAN HORN Died: 31 May 1898

John D. TOMB Died: 18 Jul 1898

Henry Coulter VAN HORN Died: 19 Jul 1898

Tero Fulmer LYDICK Born: 03 Mar 1899

Casper AUL Died: 21 Apr 1899

Charles Boyd VAN HORN Born: 09 Jul 1899

Norman Hamilton STEELE Born: Abt. 1900

Mary Elizabeth LYDICK Born: 15 Jan 1900

James Robinson HUTCHISON Born: 20 Jan 1900

Katherine FRY Died: 03 Jun 1900

Verna Viola VAN HORN Born: 21 Aug 1900

James Thompson VAN HORN Died: 17 Oct 1900

Iva Bell AUL Born: Bet. 11 - 12 Nov 1901

Susan MCELHOES Died: 1901

George Logan VAN HORN Died: 27 Feb 1901

William Clair JOHNSTON Born: 28 Apr 1901

Edna Alpha JUART Born: 18 May 1901

Margaret Huston THOMPSON Died: 14 Feb 1902

Robert Porter WARDEN Died: 20 Sep 1902

Sylvia Bell HARMON Born: 31 Oct 1902

Wilda Jeanette LYDICK Born: 12 Nov 1902

Emma Mable LAMBING Born: 15 Dec 1902

Alma Florence AUL Born: 14 Apr 1903

Milton Crawford LYDICK and Nettie Alice WALTERMIRE Married: 12 May 1903

Ernest Torrence LYDICK Born: 01 Oct 1903

John GRIFFITH and Mary Lucetta MCELHOES Married: 28 Dec 1903

Isaac M. HADDEN and Alice M. LYDICK Married: 1904

Ruth E. LYDICK Died: 1904

Harry M. VAN HORN Born: 09 Oct 1904

Charles A. LAMBING Born: 14 Oct 1904

Irene Mae JOHNSTON Born: 21 Oct 1904

John Neff VAN HORN and Martha Belle NICHOL Married: 23 Nov 1904

Phoebe NEFF Died: 05 Feb 1905

Margaret J. VAN HORN Died: 04 Mar 1905

Mary Jane AUL Born: 04 Sep 1905

Robert A. MCELHOES Died: Dec 1905

Velma A. JOHNSTON Born: Abt. 1906

Agnes Marie SHAFFER Born: 02 Jan 1906

Harry S. KUEHNER and Mary Mae VAN HORN Married: 19 Aug 1906

Jacob L. COON and Elizabeth CARR Married: 13 Sep 1906

John Crawford LYDICK Born: 08 Oct 1906

Family Map

Dorothy MORROW Died: Bet. 29 Aug - 01 Sep 1906

Robert Lee Claire VAN HORN and Mary Ella KROH Married: 13 Mar 1907

Grace Sylvia LIVINGSTON Born: 17 Mar 1907

Walter Laird VAN HORN Born: 29 Aug 1907

Charles JEWART Died: 01 Dec 1907

Jane Elizabeth VAN HORN Died: 11 Feb 1908

John Kinter MCELHOES Died: 18 Feb 1908

Hansel Clark MCLAUGHLIN Died: 11 Mar 1908

George Clair MABON and Virginia C. MCHENRY Married: 25 Mar 1908

Zelda Mae SHAFFER Born: 07 Apr 1908

James Maitland STEWART Born: 20 May 1908

Miriam Work STEELE Died: 03 Jul 1908

Floyd Albert VAN HORN Born: 08 Oct 1908

David Seba WAKEFIELD Died: 01 May 1909

Eugene H. VAN HORN Born: 16 Sep 1909

Wilbur Bennett VAN HORN Born: 24 Feb 1910

Louise Grace LYDICK Born: 12 Mar 1910

Claude Ellsworth SHAFFER Born: 21 Jun 1910

William Marshall LIAS and Inez Ethel STEAR Married: 02 Nov 1910

Stuchell LYDICK Died: 05 Feb 1911

William Wesley LYDICK Died: 05 Feb 1911

Lester Carl JOHNSTON Born: 23 Nov 1911

Olive Marion VAN HORN Born: 24 Dec 1911

Harry Brown VAN HORN Born: Abt. 1912

James Estep TOMB Died: 1912

John Albert LYDICK Died: 20 May 1912

Harry Bennett VAN HORN and Irene Bertha SIMPSON Married: 25 Dec 1912

Jay MCELHOES Born: 1913

Caroline MCQUOWN Died: 27 Jan 1913

Lois Fae GEARHART Born: 05 Feb 1913

Lottie Mae GEARHART Born: 05 Feb 1913

James Buckley RANKIN and Nellie Gertrude VAN HORN Married: 27 Feb 1913

Susan WILEY Died: 14 Jul 1913

David Paul MILLER and Stella BARR Married: 19 Aug 1913

Robert VAN HORN Born: 29 Sep 1913

Mary Ella KROH Died: 22 Oct 1913

Gladys Rossett SHAFFER Born: Bet. 07 Jan - 26 Feb 1913

Blane C. MILLER Born: Abt. 1914

Lawrence Kenneth GOOD Born: Abt. 29 Jan 1914

John Simpson VAN HORN Born: 24 Feb 1914

Stella E. PLUTO Born: 12 May 1914

Katherine Belle JUART Born: 12 Jul 1914

621

Family Map

Carleton Van Horn BARR and Nellie M. HANCOCK Married: Abt. 16 Sep 1914

Mary P. VAN HORN Died: 17 Oct 1914

Violet Mae GAMBEL Born: 1915

June Louise VAN HORN Born: 08 Jun 1915

Deloris Belle VAN HORN Born: 04 Sep 1915

Laura Jane CONDRON Died: 08 Oct 1915

Edward Patrick DALY and Della Gloria LYDICK Married: 17 Oct 1915

James Rogers RANKIN Born: 21 Nov 1915

Walter Byron FETTERHOFF and Dollie Ethel VAN HORN Married: 08 Dec 1915

Catherine Araminta TRAVIS Died: 24 Dec 1915

Oran E. BREWER and Catherine Isabelle VAN HORN Married: 05 Jan 1916

Clair Wilson SHAFFER Born: 14 Feb 1916

Clair Wilson SHAFFER Died: 14 Feb 1916

Martin W. FETTERHOFF Born: 26 May 1916

James Lucas KINTER, JR Born: 08 Jun 1916

Marion Catherine LEARN Born: 09 Jul 1916

Wilbur Dale GOOD Born: 16 Jul 1916

Ralph Emerson VAN HORN Born: 18 Oct 1916

Emerson Ralph SHANKLE Died: 13 Dec 1916

Walter L. VAN HORN Born: 14 Mar 1917

Norman Clarence VAN HORN and Edna LANEY Married: 25 Jul 1917

Rosalie L. KERNS Died: 29 Aug 1917

Alice Belle VAN HORN Born: 24 Oct 1917

Delsie Pearl HEBERLING Born: 08 Nov 1917

Lester Roy SHANKLE Born: Bet. 07 Dec 1917 - 1919

Ellen H. MEANOR Died: 06 Feb 1918

Dean Ray KEPHART and Annie P. VAN HORN Married: 20 Feb 1918

Arlene May VAN HORN Born: 29 Mar 1918

Thomas Wilson KINTER Born: 15 Jul 1918

Walter R. JOHNSTON Born: 27 Sep 1918

Clyde Sylvester SHAFFER Born: Bet. 07 Dec 1918 - Jan 1919

Merle Wayne VAN HORN Born: 24 Feb 1919

Arthur Glenn BLACK Born: 20 Apr 1919

Homer N. MONTGOMERY and Alice Elsie VAN HORN Married: 19 Jun 1919

Donald J. BREWER Born: 22 Jul 1919

Ronald J. BREWER Born: 22 Jul 1919

Charles B. VAN HORN and Mae GEARHART Married: Oct 1919

Howard Lee VAN HORN Born: 14 Dec 1919

Mary Belle VAN HORN Born: Abt. 1920

Cyrus B. DILTS and Edna Gertude VAN HORN Married: 13 Sep 1920

Robert Eugene KINTER Born: 14 Sep 1920

Donald J. BREWER Died: 20 Jan 1921

Family Map

Ford Russell SHANKLE and Mildred Grace LAMBING Married: 19 Jul 1921

James Harvey VAN HORN Died: 20 Aug 1921

William Clyde VAN HORN Born: 24 Jan 1922

Aaron Work STEELE Died: 03 Aug 1922

Betty Jane MCMANUS Born: 29 Aug 1922

Mildred Ann SHANKLE Born: 29 Aug 1922

Paul Benett SHAFFER Born: 30 Dec 1922

Nelson Ernest SHAFFER and Margaret E. DOUDS Married: Feb 1923

Effie V. BARNETT Born: 26 Mar 1923

Alice Belle GOOD Born: 14 Apr 1923

Claire L. VAN HORN Born: 22 Jul 1923

James Steele MCELHOES Died: 08 Aug 1923

Bennett Wesley VAN HORN Born: 1924

John Chester TRAINER and Nellie E. MCADOO Married: 06 Jun 1924

Hillary Leroy VAN HORN Born: 10 Oct 1924

Bennett Work VAN HORN Died: 01 Feb 1925

Talmage VAN HORN Died: 02 Jul 1925

Lola Stella GOOD Born: 17 Oct 1925

Helen Louise VAN HORN Born: Bet. 13 Jun - Jul 1926

Donald Charles VAN HORN Born: 21 Feb 1927

Elmer E. LYDICK Died: 30 Jul 1927

Verna M. SHAFFER Born: 07 Oct 1927

? VAN HORN Born: Abt. 1928

? VAN HORN Died: 1928

Blaine W. VAN HORN Born: 26 Jan 1928

Evelyn Jane STEELE Born: 23 Mar 1928

William T. JUART Died: 24 Jul 1928

Joseph ORESIK Born: Abt. 1929

Alice May MCMANUS Born: 18 Jan 1929

Henry Scott KINTER Died: 07 Mar 1929

Infant MILLER Born: 12 Mar 1929

Rosaline LYDICK Died: 26 Mar 1929

Harry Arlington ALLISON and Helen C. BARR Married: 20 May 1929

Richard Max VAN HORN Born: 12 Nov 1929

John Scott LIGHTCAP Died: 29 Nov 1929

Lulu A. STEELE Born: 09 Dec 1929

Infant MILLER Died: Bef. 1930

Theadore RUPERT Born: Abt. 1930

Melissa B. ALLISON Died: 06 Jun 1930

George Eugene VAN HORN Born: 02 Sep 1931

John Ray WEAVER and Deloris Belle VAN HORN Married: 11 Sep 1931

Raymond LaVern VAN HORN Born: Bet. 19 Sep 1931 - 1932

Sarah S. VAN HORN Died: 29 Jan 1932

James E. HARE and Pluma Ruth VAN HORN Married: 04 Feb 1932

Family Map

Betty M. WEAVER Born: 04 Aug 1932

Mary Belle WARDEN Died: 13 Aug 1932

Wallace Evan SHANKLE Died: 07 Nov 1932

Gladys Rossett SHAFFER Died: 17 Mar 1933

Blair I. SHANK, JR Born: 28 Mar 1933

James COON and June Louise VAN HORN Married: 1934

Joseph Lee VAN HORN Born: 04 Apr 1934

Dale Robert LAMBING Born: 05 Jun 1934

Annabelle WEAVER Born: 06 Sep 1934

Milton Crawford LYDICK Died: 17 Nov 1934

William Francis LUKEHART Died: Jan 1935

Earl Clark STEELE Born: 25 Feb 1935

Carl Eugene JOHNSTON Born: 28 Nov 1935

Mary E. VAN HORN Died: 1936

Mary E. HUTCHISON Died: 21 May 1936

Calvin Austin JUART Died: 1937

Margaretta T. STEWART Died: 06 Feb 1937

Blair James LYDICK, JR Born: 06 Mar 1937

John Simpson VAN HORN and Marion Catherine LEARN Married: 21 Aug 1937

Wilbur Dale GOOD and Delsie Pearl HEBERLING Married: 10 Nov 1937

Arthur Glenn BLACK and Theda Agnes MCMANUS Married: 06 Jul 1938

Samuel Lydick BARR Died: 20 Jan 1939

Donna Jean GOOD Born: 08 Feb 1939

Robert JOHNSTON Died: 24 Nov 1939

Stella M. VAN HORN Died: 02 May 1940

Mary Caroline VAN HORN Died: 13 May 1940

Senita Doris GOOD Born: 16 Jun 1940

Senita Doris GOOD Died: Bet. 16 Jun 1940 - 1941

Infant GOOD Born: 14 Mar 1941

Infant GOOD Died: 14 Mar 1941

Edith Lee VAN HORN Died: 23 Aug 1941

Hugh Dixon TOMB Died: Nov 1941

Albert Martin SHAFFER Died: 23 Nov 1941

William James VAN HORN Born: Abt. 1942

William M. MCADOO Died: Apr 1942

Walter R. JOHNSTON and Gail MILLER Married: 14 Nov 1942

John William SHAFFER Born: 07 Dec 1942

Earl Eugene SCOTT Died: 22 Jan 1943

Nancy Mary LAMBING Born: 03 Apr 1943

Nancy Ann LIGHTCAP Died: 21 Aug 1943

Harold Wilbur GOOD Born: 19 Mar 1944

Harold Wilbur GOOD Died: 21 Mar 1944

William J. LIVINGSTON Died: 27 Nov 1944

Rachel A. MCCRACKEN Died: 20 Oct 1945

Infant GOOD Born: 22 Oct 1945

Family Map

Infant GOOD Died: 22 Oct 1945

Anna L. KLINE Died: 05 Nov 1946

Raymond VAN HORN Born: Abt. 1947

Mary C VAN HORN Died: 29 Apr 1947

Raymond VAN HORN Died: 20 Oct 1947

Mary Elizabeth JUART Died: 27 Oct 1947

Grace Sylvia LIVINGSTON Died: 01 May 1948

Gary Lee STEWART Born: 24 Dec 1948

John HOUCK Died: 21 May 1949

Donald Charles VAN HORN and Margaret Ann SLONINGER Married: 29 Jun 1949

Clyde Sylvester SHAFFER and Ferne Ellen AIRGOOD Married: May 1950

Beryl Emerson SHAFFER Born: 01 Dec 1950

Samuel Andrew OLSON Died: 31 May 1951

James Ira VAN HORN Died: Bet. 10 - 26 Mar 1951

Robert Lee Claire VAN HORN Died: 05 Jul 1951

Blair James LYDICK and Carrie Emma CARNAHAN Married: 23 Aug 1952

Ada Myrtle VAN HORN Died: 21 May 1953

Elizabeth Ruth JACKSON Died: 02 Aug 1953

Lorenzo Peter LAMBING Died: 27 Sep 1953

Nellie M. HANCOCK Died: 21 Mar 1954

Mary S. WORK Died: 18 May 1954

John Chester TRAINER Died: 07 Sep 1954

Laney Lawrence AUL Died: 18 Jun 1955

Alma Florence AUL Died: 03 Sep 1957

Lula M. SHIELDS Died: 25 Nov 1957

Robert Roy MCELHOES Died: 25 Feb 1958

William Thomas LUKEHART Died: 26 Jun 1958

James Lucas KINTER Died: 08 Oct 1959

Patricia Ann RUPERT Born: 18 Nov 1959

Bonnie Lu DUNCAN Born: 02 Dec 1960

Bonnie Lu DUNCAN Died: 04 Dec 1960

Cora Belle VAN HORN Died: 19 Sep 1961

Alexander Maitland STEWART Died: 28 Dec 1961

Daniel Clair FREEDLINE Died: 1964

David WYLAND Died: 1964

Myrtle Mae SHANKLE Died: 06 Aug 1964

Nellie Gertrude VAN HORN Died: 22 Aug 1964

Emma Evans WYNCOOP Died: 02 Jun 1965

Etta MOTTARN Died: 23 Oct 1965

Charles Blaine VAN HORN Died: 01 Nov 1965

James Buckley RANKIN Died: 24 Sep 1966

Matt William VAN HORN Died: 15 Jul 1967

Pearl Agnes VAN HORN Died: 03 Oct 1967

George Clair MABON Died: 03 Dec 1967

Walter Byron FETTERHOFF Died: 26 Feb 1969

James Robert LAMBING Died: 07 May 1969

Family Map

Elizabeth Mabel SHANKLE Died: 04 Dec 1969

Harry Irvin MYERS Died: 31 Jan 1970

Alexander Thomas LAMBING Died: 30 Aug 1970

Blair James LYDICK Died: 17 Sep 1970

Anna Florence VAN HORN Died: 04 Jan 1971

Cliford J. KEIL Died: 20 Feb 1972

Wallace Glenn SHANKLE Died: 08 Sep 1972

Norman Clarence VAN HORN Died: 11 Sep 1972

Thomas Roy SHANKLE Died: 07 Jan 1974

Herbert Riggle AUL Died: 22 Apr 1974

Joseph Isaiah MCELHOES Died: 06 Sep 1974

Inez Ethel STEAR Died: Mar 1975

John Bion TOMB Died: 24 Apr 1975

Alta Blanche CLOWER Died: 26 May 1975

Arlene May VAN HORN Died: 19 Dec 1975

Emma Mable LAMBING Died: 08 Feb 1976

Dollie Ethel VAN HORN Died: Bet. 30 - 31 Aug 1976

Harry Bennett VAN HORN Died: 19 Feb 1976

Homer Park VAN HORN Died: 01 Dec 1976

Mary Jane FERRIER Died: 21 May 1977

Arthur James LYDICK Died: 17 Jul 1977

Francis Martha MANNING Died: 25 Feb 1978

Margaret E. DOUDS Died: Sep 1978

Richard G. VAN HORN III Born: 21 Nov 1978

Irene Bertha SIMPSON Died: 06 Jan 1979

John Delbert GOOD Died: 07 Oct 1980

Oran E. BREWER Died: 27 Feb 1982

Ira Paul WILT Died: 15 May 1982

Joseph Lee VAN HORN Died: 31 Mar 1985

Cyrus B. DILTS Died: 28 Oct 1985

Helen C. BARR Died: Dec 1985

Harry Arlington ALLISON Died: 03 Feb 1987

Ford Russell SHANKLE Died: 07 Mar 1987

Charles Andrew FERRIER Died: 07 Apr 1987

Claire L. VAN HORN Died: 18 Jun 1988

Mary Elizabeth BROWN Died: 02 May 1989

Thomas BANKS Died: 22 Jun 1989

Nancy Mary LAMBING Died: Sep 1989

Florence KIRKPATRICK Died: 22 Mar 1990

Wilbur Dale GOOD Died: 15 Sep 1991

Blair James LYDICK, JR Died: 15 Sep 1991

Ferne Ellen AIRGOOD Died: 03 Jul 1992

Eva Jane SHANKLE Died: 03 Jul 1992

Martin W. FETTERHOFF Died: 05 Nov 1993

Agnes Marie SHAFFER Died: 26 May 1994

Walter R. JOHNSTON Died: 05 Jul 1994

Effie A. HUMBERSON Died: 26 Sep 1997

Sylvia Bell HARMON Died: 06 Jan 1998

Clyde Sylvester SHAFFER Died: 06 Mar 1998

Isaiah Van Horn Pioneer of Indiana County, Pennsylvania

Family Map

Esther M.
MCADOO Died:
28 Mar 1998

Wilbur Bennett
VAN HORN
Died: 11 Jul 1998

Lulu A. STEELE
Died: 02 Jun 1999

Mildred
RUDDOCK
Died: 20 Mar
2000

Delsie Pearl
HEBERLING
Died: 06 Feb
2001

Kathleen
NESBIT Died: 06
Nov 2001

Earl Clark
STEELE Died:
01 Apr 2002

Ronald J.
BREWER Died:
11 May 2002

Evelyn Jane
STEELE Died:
14 Nov 2004

Margaret Ann
SLONINGER
Died: 20 Feb
2005

Gilbert D.
BRIGHTBILL
Died: 10 Oct
2005

John William
SHAFFER Died:
26 Jun 2006

Theda Agnes
MCMANUS
Died: 17 Aug
2007

Elizabeth
LOCKHARD
Died: Unknown

Nancy SCOTT
Died: Unknown

**Inglewood,
Los Angeles
Co., CA**

Anna Sampson
BENT Died: 04
Nov 1977

**Inwood,
Berkeley Co.,
WV**

Fred Likens
HUTZLER Born:
06 Mar 1921

David Brown
GAGEBY Died:
11 Dec 1944

Lillian DUNHAM
Died: 15 Jun 1945

John Harland
HUTZLER Died:
29 Apr 1975

Hugh Samuel
HUTZLER Died:
14 Mar 1980

Ward Irvin
HUTZLER Died:
22 May 1987

Iowa

Sylvanus D. VAN
HORN Born: 19
Jan 1857

Samuel R. VAN
HORN Born: 08
Nov 1857

Orin VAN
HORN Born: 19
Mar 1858

Athelia VAN
HORN Born:
Abt. 1859

Joseph J. VAN
HORN Born: 31
Jan 1859

Albert A. VAN
HORN Born: 31
Jul 1859

Minnie VAN
HORN Born:
Abt. 1860

Hannah M. VAN
HORN Born: Jul
1860

Jesse Erwin VAN
HORN Died: 03
Jan 1861

Calista T. VAN
HORN Born: 23
Aug 1861

Sherman VAN
HORN Born:
Abt. 1863

Edson Grant
VAN HORN
Born: Feb 1863

Leon VAN
HORN Born:
Abt. 1865

Orel VAN
HORN Born:
Abt. 1865

Cordelia VAN
HORN Born:
Abt. 1866

Anna C. WHITE
Born: Abt. 1866

Albert VAN
HORN Born:
Abt. 1867

Clara VAN
HORN Born:
Abt. 1868

Cora VAN
HORN Born:
Abt. 1868

Joseph Jay VAN
HORN Born:
Abt. 1868

Marhta WHITE
Born: Abt. 1868

Alva Marco VAN
HORN Born:
1868

Emmett W.
CUMMINGS
Born: Feb 1868

Frank
CUMMINGS
Born: Sep 1869

Leonard VAN
HORN Born:
Abt. 1870

627

Family Map

Bell WHITE
Born: Abt. 1870

Ernest VAN
HORN Born: Jul
1870

Wilomina VAN
HORN Born: Feb
1871

Thomas Patrick
CUMMINGS
Born: Bet. 14 Aug
1872 - 1874

Mable Chloe
CURTIS Born:
Abt. 1872

Loyal VAN
HORN Born:
Abt. 1872

Ruth VAN
HORN Born:
Abt. 1872

Willard Manley
VAN HORN
Born: Abt. 1872

Edward WHITE
Born: Abt. 1872

Edith B. VAN
HORN Born:
Abt. 1873

Elizabeth VAN
HORN Born:
Abt. 1875

Frank VAN
HORN Born:
Abt. 1875

Sarah WHITE
Born: Abt. 1875

Etta Jane
HOPKINS Born:
Abt. 1877

Ansel VAN
HORN Born:
Abt. 1877

Laura M. Born:
Abt. 1878

William A.
HOPKINS Born:
Dec 1879

Rachel Amaranda
VAN HORN
Born: Jun 1880

Nellie B. Born:
1882

Myrtle L. VAN
HORN Born: Jul
1882

Agnes Born: Abt.
1885

Orra L. VAN
HORN Born: Sep
1888

Elsie A. FRICK
Born: Abt. 1901

Evelyn Maxine
CUMMINGS
Born: 15 May
1904

Wilmer LaVerne
DAVIS Born:
Abt. 1905

Thomas E.
CUMMINGS
Born: 07 Feb
1906

Oscar Arlie
DAVIS Born:
Abt. 1914

Duane Ardes
DAVIS Born:
Abt. 1916

Wesley B. DAVIS
Born: Abt. 1918

Mable Chloe
CURTIS Died:
1927

Wilmer LaVerne
DAVIS and
Thelma Evelyn
VAN HORN
Married: 25 Oct
1927

See Also Illinois,
South Dakota, and
Wisconsin.

**Jamestown,
Chautauqua
Co., NY**

Walter Edward
VAN HORN
Died: 14 Sep 1994

Marion Isabelle
CREE Died: 02
Mar 2001

**Janesville,
Rock Co., WI
(47 Mi NE of
Ogle Co.)**

Rachel Amaranda
VAN HORN
Died: 25 Oct
1962

Buena Geraldine
DAVIS Died: 21
May 1975

Oscar Rex
BOWERS Died:
24 Jan 1978

**Jefferson Co.,
WV**

George W.
MCBEE Born: Jul
1869

Harwood
Trammell
HUTZLER Born:
17 Nov 1918

**Jersey City,
Hudson Co.,
NJ**

John
HUTCHISON
Born: 1788

George Herbert
JONES Born: Jul
1855

Elizabeth
BANNON Born:
01 Nov 1863

Robert A. BELL
Born: Bet. Aug
1877 - 1879

George Herbert
JONES and Clara
VAN HORN
Married: 18 Nov
1877

Mabel VAN
HORN Died: 01
Feb 1879

Family Map

Frank Wesley JONES Born: Nov 1886

George Mallory LEGHORN Born: 16 Jan 1888

Florence Irene VAN HORN Born: 09 Sep 1895

Clarence VAN HORN Born: 30 Aug 1899

William Bell VAN HORN Died: 15 Jul 1905

Grace BRENNAN Born: 06 Nov 1907

George Herbert JONES Died: 11 Jan 1926

Elizabeth BANNON Died: 11 Apr 1934

William Frederick VAN HORN Died: 07 Nov 1939

Frank Wesley JONES Died: 27 Sep 1961

Johnstown, Cambria Co., PA

Dorothy Bell SHAFFER Died: 13 May 1945

Donna Jean GOOD Died: 03 Jan 1946

Cora Pearl MILLER Died: 08 Oct 1953

Amos Burton LYDICK Died: 21 Jun 1954

James Donald ASHCOM Died: 03 Mar 1968

William WINEBRENNER Died: 09 Aug 1986

Kane, McKean Co., PA

George H. SHEPHARD Born: 14 Feb 1893

Laurence Robert FREDERICK Died: 14 Feb 1999

Kansas

Mae B. Born: Abt. 1875

Grace J. SNYDER Born: Abt. 1879

Henry K. DILTS Born: 01 May 1879

John DILTS Born: 14 Aug 1881

Arthur DILTS Born: 10 Mar 1888

Eva Born: Abt. 1889

Clara Estella HOFFMAN Born: Abt. 1889

Grace GOODLOE Born: Bet. 1890 - 1892

Thomas DILTS Born: 12 Sep 1891

Alvin Everett POINTER Born: 04 May 1900

Virgie Bernice POINTER Born: Abt. 1901

Elmer MCAFOOS Born: Abt. 1902

Perry Amos POINTER Born: Abt. 1904

Viola Born: Abt. 1904

Lawrence M. DILTS Born: Abt. 1906

Freida M. Born: Abt. 1907

Ferma Dorcas POINTER Born: Abt. 1909

Ira MCAFOOS Born: Abt. 1911

Delphia Mae POINTER Born: Abt. 1911

Charles Raymond MCAFOOS Born: Abt. 1912

George E. MCAFOOS Born: Abt. 1915

Clifford Austin HINES Born: 1916

Harold A. MCAFOOS Born: Abt. 1919

Clyde Wallace HINES Born: 1919

Clarence A. MCAFOOS Born: Abt. 1924

Cleo H. MCAFOOS Born: Abt. 1927

See Also Oklahoma, Missouri, Nebraska, and Colorado.

Kansas City, Jackson Co., MO (371 Mi NW of Posey Co.)

Caleb Henry VAN HORN Died: 12 Jun 1858

Family Map

Charles C. VAN HORN Born: 17 Feb 1861

Adela C. VAN HORN Born: 03 Oct 1876

Henry Kirkwood VAN HORN Born: 25 Feb 1878

Robert Cannon VAN HORN Died: 12 Nov 1918

Kenmore, Erie Co., NY

Berdeen Boylan BRAYMER Died: 19 Apr 1984

Kennebec, Lyman Co., SD

Mary Jane CAMPBELL Died: 28 Feb 1898

Fred William BENISH and Inez Vernal VAN HORN Married: 05 Jul 1938

Robert Campbell VAN HORN Died: 05 Apr 1943

Kentucky (W of Virginia)

?

Henry VAN HORN Born: Bet. 23 Jan 1823 - 1826

Jane Born: Abt. 1883

Keota, Keokuk Co., IA (143 Mi SW of Ogle Co.)

Jonathan SMITH Died: 08 Dec 1871

Kingston, Ulster Co., NY

Nickolas WYNKOOP Born: 16 Oct 1668

Catherine WYNKOOP Born: 18 Jun 1671

Benjamine WYNKOOP Born: 18 Apr 1675

Cornelius C. WYNKOOP Died: 1676

Maria Janse LANGEDYCK Died: 1679

Maria WYNKOOP Born: 03 Jun 1694

Jacoba WYNKOOP Born: 02 Mar 1696

Ann WYNKOOP Born: 21 Aug 1698

Cornelius WYNKOOP Born: 01 Jan 1701

Gerrit WYNKOOP Born: 19 Nov 1702

Nicholas WYNKOOP Born: 18 Feb 1705

Henry WYNKOOP Born: 19 Oct 1707

Phillip WYNKOOP Born: 11 Sep 1709

Tobias WYNKOOP Born: 03 May 1713

Kittanning, Armstrong Co., PA

Mary E. HUTCHISON Born: 21 May 1852

Phillip HUTCHISON Died: 03 Jan 1866

Mary Jane HUTCHISON Died: 30 Nov 1887

Henry BUSH Died: 04 Feb 1894

Theda Agnes MCMANUS Born: 21 May 1918

Nelson Ernest SHAFFER Died: 12 Jan 1959

Cora BOSSARD Died: 28 Jan 1962

Barbara Ann ALBERTI Born: 12 Apr 1967

Deloris Belle VAN HORN Died: 21 Jul 1971

Raymond LaVern VAN HORN Died: 21 Oct 1974

James Edward HARTZELL Died: 19 Feb 1988

Lois Fae GEARHART Died: 18 May 1995

Charlotte Marie MCMASTERS Died: 11 May 1996

Stella E. PLUTO Died: 23 Jun 1997

Betty M. WEAVER Died: 30 Jul 1999

Family Map

Berdella
GOLDSTROHM
Died: 05 Jan 2000

Howard Paul
BLACK Died: 09
Dec 2003

Barbara Ann
ALBERTI Died:
02 Apr 2005

**Koochiching
Co., MN**

Thomas Patrick
CUMMINGS
Died: Bet. 1930 -
1940

**Ladysmith,
Rusk Co., WI**

Oscar Rex
BOWERS Born:
11 Nov 1889

**Lancaster,
Lancaster Co.,
PA**

Alexander
WORK Born:
Abt. 1702

Henry WORK
Died: Abt. 1738

Alexander
WORK Died: 17
Mar 1749

John KINTER
Born: 1755

**Lancaster,
Lancaster Co.,
VA**

Jacob
HIESTAND
Born: 1736

**Las Cruces,
Dona Ana Co.,
NM (352 Mi
SW of Potter
Co.)**

Phillip WORK
Died: 02 Jul 1952

**Latrobe,
Westmoreland
Co., PA**

Lester Roy
SHANKLE Died:
05 Jul 1988

**Lawton,
Comanche
Co., OK (206
Mi SE of
Potter Co.)**

Frank COON
Died: 02 Nov
1912

**Lebanon,
Lebanon Co.,
PA**

David Paul
MILLER Born:
21 May 1885

**Lebanon,
Warren Co.,
OH (322 Mi
SE of Ogle
Co.)**

William Alexander
VAN HORNE
Born: 23 Dec
1808

Thomas Budd
VAN HORNE,
JR Born: 06 Jul
1821

Lavinia BUDD
Died: 28 Dec
1837

Enos FRENCH
and Harietta J.
VAN HORNE
Married: 23 Sep
1840

Enos FRENCH
Died: 15 Oct
1856

**Leetsdale,
Allegheny Co.,
PA**

Arthur Palmer
VAN HORN
Born: 17 Jul 1887

**Lewes, Sussex
Co., DE**

Arthur James
YOUNG Died:
29 Dec 1987

Lewis Co., NY

John L. MOORE,
DD Born: 17 Feb
1803

**Lewis Co., VA
(400 Mi NE of
Posey Co.)**

Sarah
HOFFMAN
Died: 26 Nov
1857

**Ligonier,
Westmoreland
Co., PA**

William H.
BOWSER Born:
04 Aug 1846

Mary Elizabeth
ASHCOM Died:
24 Aug 2002

**Litchfield,
Hillsdale Co.,
MI (234 Mi E
of Ogle Co.)**

Harold Demary
WADE Born:
1906

Elsie Lavina
GAMBY Died: 25
Jan 1937

Harold Demary
WADE Died:
1965

Chauncey Wilber
GEPHART Died:
20 Feb 1974

Family Map

Lodi, San Joaquin Co., CA

Dorcas Grace LYTLE Died: 25 May 1985

Lorain, Lorain Co., OH (369 Mi SE of Ogle Co.)

Agnes Mary WEBER Born: 02 May 1896

Lester J. RUMPLER and Agnes Mary WEBER Married: 18 May 1920

Agnes Mary WEBER Died: 10 Jun 1960

Lester J. RUMPLER Died: 18 Dec 1966

Los Angeles, Los Angeles Co., CA

Bowen VAN HORN Died: 17 May 1941

Wade Blair COON Died: 17 Jun 1943

Harry C. VAN HORN Died: 04 Jun 1944

Cornelius Elsworth CONDRON Died: 07 Jul 1946

Myrtle Irene HARDY Died: Mar 1962

Bessie Irene MITCHELL Died: Aug 1965

Victor Von LYTLE Died: 14 Nov 1969

Kimmel B. COON and Myrtle HORTON TANNER Married: 02 Jul 1971

Frank P. ALBANO Died: 12 Oct 1980

Gloria Hatrick MCLEAN Died: 16 Feb 1994

Oliver Sidney GOTTLIEB Born: 08 Jul 2004

Oliver Sidney GOTTLIEB Died: 11 Jul 2004

Lost Creek, Harrison Co., WV (410 Mi NE of Posey Co.)

William D. VAN HOORN Born: Abt. 1735

William D. VAN HOORN Died: Bet. 1807 - 1809

William Barnard VAN HOORN Died: 1831

Elizabeth VAN HOORN Died: 1834

Sarah CHIDESTER Died: 30 Jun 1839

Loveland, Larimer Co., CO

George Henry VAN HORN Born: 02 Jun 1903

Dorthea VAN HORN Born: Abt. 1905

Naomi VAN HORN Born: Abt. 1907

Paul H. VAN HORN Born: Abt. 1912

Lyman, Lyman Co., SD

Susan Nova VAN HORN Born: 06 Mar 1897

Florence Loretta VAN HORN Born: 02 Aug 1900

Claude Duval VAN HORN Died: 23 Jun 1937

Mahaffey, Clearfield Co., PA

Joseph W. VAN HORN Born: Bet. 24 Mar 1890 - 1893

Manhattan, Riley Co., KS

Harietta J. VAN HORNE Died: 15 Jan 1886

Martinsburg, Berkeley Co., WV

John William HUTZLER and Roseannah VAN HORN Married: 23 Feb 1869

Samuel Lindsay VAN HORN Born: 17 Jun 1886

John Albert VAN HORN Born: 09 Feb 1888

Joseph Earl VAN HORN Born: 06 Jan 1891

Paul Garland VAN HORN Born: 15 Dec 1896

Family Map

Jame Link COFFINBERGER Born: 21 Feb 1905

Charles William GRUBB Born: 23 Jun 1923

John Harland HUTZLER and Marion Beatrice BAKER Married: 30 Jun 1923

Naomi Jane GAGEBY Born: 25 Oct 1924

Isaac Lindsay VAN HORN Died: 02 Aug 1930

Mary Ellen FETZER Died: 1933

Thettie Jane HUTZLER Died: 20 Feb 1939

Nora Mary Agnes VAN HORN Died: 24 Oct 1957

William Logan HUTZLER Died: 09 Dec 1957

Martha Virginia MOLER Died: 16 Mar 1959

James Allen GAGEBY Died: 08 Aug 1966

Adeline HUTZLER Died: 29 Nov 1973

William Brown GAGEBY Died: 31 Dec 1974

Jame Link COFFINBERGER Died: 11 Dec 1982

Ida May GAGEBY Died: 14 Nov 1983

Mary Virginia WILSON Died: 27 Apr 1987

Marion Beatrice BAKER Died: 19 Aug 1987

Edgar McLaren RICE Died: 13 Feb 1989

Harwood Trammell HUTZLER Died: 08 Jul 1993

Maryland (SE of Pennsylvania)

Peter DILTS, SR Born: 1785

Margaret Ann FISHER Born: Apr 1826

Mary Ellen VAN HORN Born: 21 Sep 1847

George W. H. VAN HORN Born: Abt. 1850

Mary E. VAN HORN Born: Abt. Feb 1850

Hannah VAN HORN Born: Abt. 1854

Elengenet VAN HORN Born: Abt. 1855

Ida VAN HORN Born: Abt. 1856

Mary E. VAN HORN Born: Abt. 1858

Abraham VAN HORN Born: Abt. 1861

Hugh HAMILTON Died: Abt. 1875

Raymond W. CATLETT Born: Abt. 1892

Harley S. CATLETT Born: Abt. 1894

John H. CATLETT Born: Abt. 1894

Maryland GOURLEY Born: Jul 1895

Harry Samuel CATLETT Born: 01 Oct 1895

George Grayson KOOGLE Born: Abt. 1897

Mary Edith CATLETT Born: Abt. 1898

Bertha L. CATLETT Born: Abt. 1902

Helen V. CATLETT Born: Abt. 1906

Donald Alvin HUTZLER Born: 11 Jun 1909

Dorthea M. HUTZLER Born: Abt. 1911

Massachusetts (NE of Pennsylvania)

Pauline F. WOODBERRY Born: Abt. 1890

Meadville, Crawford Co., PA

Berdeen Boylan BRAYMER Born: 26 Mar 1889

Mary Mae VAN HORN Died: 31 Oct 1967

John Dick VAN HORN Died: 14 Apr 1982

633

Family Map

Mercer Co., IL

Susanna VAN HORN Died: 06 Jun 1839

Jesse WILLETS Died: 07 Jul 1842

Mercer Co., OH (243 Mi NE of Posey Co.)

Thomas Gaine VAN HORN and Elizabeth HANELINE Married: 07 Feb 1864

Mexico Beach, Bay Co., FL

Mildred Ann SHANKLE Died: 25 Mar 1995

Miami, Dade Co., FL

James W. VAN HORN Died: 21 Sep 1947

See Also Saint Petersburg, Clearwater, Venice, Sebring, Sarasota, Miami Beach, and Pinellas Park.

Miami Beach, Dade Co., FL (4 Mi NE of Miami)

Rollin Weber VAN HORN Died: Feb 1964

Michigan

Levancha Born: Abt. 1834

Morrell A. CLARK Born: Abt. 1859

Weltha J. Born: 1866

Susan VAN HORN Died: 05 Sep 1872

Ray C. KANKLE Born: Abt. 1902

Infant VAN HORN Born: 22 Dec 1904

Middletown, Butler Co., OH (310 Mi SE of Ogle Co.)

Lester George HAAS Born: 06 Oct 1908

Middletown, Frederick Co., MD

Harry Samuel CATLETT Died: May 1976

Millersville, Lancaster Co., PA

James Lucas KINTER, JR Died: 07 Dec 2003

Millville, Butler Co., OH (305 Mi SE of Ogle Co.)

Joseph VAN HORNE Died: 1833

Milnor, Sargent Co., ND

William H. BOWSER Died: 11 Mar 1926

Sarah Viola TRAVER Died: 10 Mar 1938

Milton, Rock Co., WI (55 Mi NE of Ogle Co.)

Lottie Belle DAVIS Born: 20 Jun 1863

Milwaukee, Milwaukee Co., WI (100 Mi NE of Ogle Co.)

Edward Churchill THOMAS Born: 07 May 1909

Minneapolis, Hennepin Co., MN

Jesse Garrett VAN HORN Died: Bet. 02 Sep - 12 Nov 1967

Minnesota (SE of North Dakota)

Jennie Elizabeth BAIREY Born: 17 Dec 1867

Clara A. DAHL Born: May 1876

Ellen M. CUMMINGS Born: Jul 1887

Huberta BAKER Born: Oct 1899

Robert Allan MCELHOES Born: Bet. 21 Jun 1907 - 1908

Mississippi (SE of Arkansas)

Chessiah VAN HORN Born: Abt. 1882

Theodore Leigh VAN HORN Born: 1903

Missouri (E of Kansas)

Family Map

Margaret KIRKWOOD Born: Jan 1851

Mary Frances MCCLURE Born: Aug 1878

Robert VIVION Born: Abt. 1882

Robert T. VAN HORN Born: 08 Aug 1900

Florence Born: Abt. 1901

Adela Honeywood COOLEY Died: 24 Jul 1910

Vernon W. RIEKE Born: 25 Oct 1915

Monroeville, Allegheny Co., PA

Hazel B. MCADOO Died: 07 Sep 1985

Montana (SE of Washington)

Emmitt VAN HORN Born: Abt. 1911

Montclair, Essex Co., NJ

Clara VAN HORN Died: 02 Aug 1940

Florence Dorothy JONES Died: 23 Mar 1961

Montgomery Co., MD

Pearl SPICHER Died: 31 May 1956

Joseph Lucas MYERS Died: 19 Apr 1975

Morristown, Morris Co., NJ

Sophia CARMICHAEL Born: 06 May 1784

Thomas Budd VAN HORNE and Sophia CARMICHAEL Married: 06 May 1807

Mount Kisco, Westchester Co., NY

Charles B. UPJOHN Died: 14 Apr 1953

Louise VAN HORNE Died: 31 Dec 1957

Mount Pleasant, Isabella Co., MI (254 Mi NE of Ogle Co.)

Esther VAN HORN

Lena Marie VAN HORN

John Duncan VAN HORN Born: 24 Feb 1908

Mount Pleasant, Westmoreland Co., PA

Judson Tannehill VAN HORN Born: 02 Aug 1887

Mount Vernon, Linn Co., IA (108 Mi SW of Ogle Co.)

Fred William BENISH Born: 18 Apr 1886

Murphy, Cherokee Co., NC (293 Mi SE of Posey Co.)

Emma Elizabeth WOLF Died: 13 May 1982

Lester George HAAS Died: 17 Sep 1984

Murrysville, Westmoreland Co., PA

Walter L. VAN HORN Died: 21 Feb 2008

Natrona Heights, Allegheny Co., PA

Charles A. LAMBING Died: 17 Jan 1979

Navasota, Grimes Co., TX

Harry Vernon POINTER Died: 24 Dec 1995

Nebraska (NW of Kansas)

Edgar Delbert VAN HORN Born: Mar 1874

Elsie Born: Abt. 1889

Viola V. BABCOCK Born: 10 Mar 1889

Mae B. Born: Abt. 1892

Family Map

Nan C. CORCORAN Born: 19 Feb 1893

Emmerson HALL Born: Abt. 1894

Mary Lorraine DVORK Born: 02 Jul 1912

New Auburn, Chippewa Co., WI

Virginia Audrey BOWERS Born: 03 Feb 1922

New Bethlehem, Clarion Co., PA

Tallie Amberson VAN HORN Born: Bet. 19 Jul 1892 - 1893

New Brighton, Beaver Co., PA

Helen HILL Died: 1996

New Castle, Lawrence Co., PA

Freeman Blondell VAN HORN Born: 25 Jul 1891

LeRoy Wadding VAN HORN Born: 20 May 1903

David Paul MILLER Died: 22 Nov 1947

Lawrence Kenneth GOOD Died: 20 Jan 1968

Vincent VAN HORN Died: 1977

New Florence, Westmoreland Co., PA

William WINEBRENNER Born: 16 Sep 1910

Benjamin Frank ASHCOM Died: Abt. 1930

Nana Pearl COGLEY Died: 24 Dec 1967

New Jersey (SE of Pennsylvania)

Dirk VAN HOORN Born: 29 Sep 1729

Jannecke VAN HOORN Born: 17 Nov 1730

William VAN HOORN Born: 08 Jul 1747

Antje BERDEN Born: 19 Jul 1761

Johannis BERDEN Born: 24 Jun 1764

Mary VAN HOORN Born: 26 Dec 1775

Johannis VAN HOORN Born: 08 Sep 1777

Catherine VAN HOORN Born: 28 Feb 1779

Johannis HARRIS Born: 16 Jun 1779

Dirk VAN HOORN Born: 27 Nov 1780

Elizabeth VAN HOORN Born: 17 Nov 1781

Marritje HARRIS Born: 09 Aug 1782

Isaac HARRIS Born: 26 Apr 1784

Margaret VAN HOORN Born: 20 Dec 1784

Jacob VAN HOORN Born: 20 Jan 1786

Jacob HARRIS Born: 20 Jul 1786

Cornelius HUTCHISON and Eleanor MCGUIRE Married: Bet. 1786 - 1787

William Barnard VAN HOORN and Sarah CHIDESTER Married: 03 Dec 1787

Johannes VAN HOORN Born: 20 Dec 1787

Phillip HUTCHISON Born: 16 Oct 1790

Margaret VAN HOORN Born: 03 Apr 1791

Johannes VAN HOORN Born: 10 Sep 1793

Maria HARRIS Born: 15 May 1794

Margaret JURIANSS Born: 12 Jun 1799

Margaret JURIANSSE Born: 21 Jan 1800

John VAN HOORN Born: 25 Jul 1800

John JURIANSS Born: 07 Oct 1801

Family Map

Annatje JURIANSSE Born: 15 Jan 1802

Elizabeth DAVIS Born: Bet. 05 Oct 1804 - 1806

Dirck JURIANSSE Born: 19 Jan 1804

William VAN HOORN Born: 23 Jan 1804

Dirck JURIANSS Born: 04 Jul 1805

Sarah S. Born: Abt. 1806

Thomas VAN HOORN Born: 09 Jan 1806

Christofel JURIANSSE Born: 09 Nov 1806

Abraham VAN HOORN Born: 13 Feb 1808

Christofel JURIANSSE Born: 27 Feb 1808

Hendrick JURIANSS Born: 16 Jul 1808

Margaret VAN HOORN Born: 31 Dec 1808

Syntie JURIANSS Born: 16 Dec 1810

Hessel JURIANSSE Born: 25 Nov 1811

Paggy VAN HOORN Born: 21 Jun 1812

Gabriel VAN HOORN Died: 1815

Rebecca SCATTERGOOD Born: 07 Feb 1820

Edward WHITE Born: Abt. 1843

Cornelius VAN HORN Died: 09 Nov 1845

Jennie Sophia MILLER Born: Bet. 1857 - Apr 1860

William Frederick VAN HORN Born: 27 Sep 1860

George VAN HORN Born: 26 Nov 1862

Mary VAN HORN Born: Nov 1864

Cora Belle VAN HORN Born: Sep 1867

Sarah Bell VAN HORN Born: Bet. 1871 - Apr 1875

Mabel VAN HORN Born: 30 May 1877

Florence Dorothy JONES Born: Nov 1878

Herbert George JONES Born: Jul 1884

Sarah VAN HORN Born: 19 Apr 1886

Frank VAN HORN Born: Abt. 1891

Helen M. LEGHORN Born: 09 Feb 1891

Lawrence VAN HORN Born: Abt. 1896

Clarence VAN HORN and Grace BRENNAN Married: Abt. 1924

Grace BRENNAN Died: 06 Jan 1971

Clarence VAN HORN Died: 31 Aug 1972

New Kensington, Westmoreland Co., PA

Dorsey Clinton VAN HORN and Berdella GOLDSTROHM Married: 06 Oct 1926

Melinda VAN HORN Died: 30 Oct 1953

Herman Eber VAN HORN Died: May 1980

Rosemary RANKIN Died: Jun 1992

Vernon W. RIEKE Died: 29 Apr 2003

New London, Huron Co., OH (363 Mi SE of Ogle Co.)

George Milton KECK Died: 02 Jul 1918

New Market, Shenandoah Co., VA

Olive B. FUSS Died: 16 Sep 1959

Family Map

**New York
(NE of
Pennsylvania)**

George R.
LEGHORN
Born: Jun 1858

Arthur VAN
HORN Born:
Mar 1860

Ralph W.
GOULD Born:
Abt. 1866

F. Edwina
HORNE Born:
Abt. 1878

Harley G.
BENTLEY Born:
Abt. 1888

William ORR
Born: Abt. 1897

Florence
GOULD Born:
Abt. 1902

Helen J. GOULD
Born: Abt. 1906

Myrreel VAN
HORN Died: Aft.
1907

Madeline
MACLENNAN
Born: 27 Jan 1908

John D. GOULD
Born: Abt. 1911

Marion Isabelle
CREE Born: 22
Jul 1911

Robert C.
GOULD Born:
Abt. 1915

Lyle Bennett
VAN HORN
Born: 16 Feb
1943

Myrtle Linda
AUL Died: 13
Feb 1950

Hillary Leroy
VAN HORN
Died: 24 Oct
1973

Lawrence David
AUL Died: 07 Jan
1984

**New York,
NY**

Geertje Dircks
CLAUSSEN
Born: 05 Feb
1662

Moses WRIGHT
Died: 20 Oct
1815

Gloria Hatrick
MCLEAN Born:
10 Mar 1918

**Newtown,
Bucks Co., PA**

Henry VAN
HORN Born:
Bet. 15 Sep 1704 -
1707

Christian VAN
HORN Born: 29
Aug 1728

Henry B. VAN
HORN Born: 02
Oct 1734

Henry VAN
HORN Died: Jun
1761

Isaiah VAN
HORN Born:
1768

Susanna VAN
HORN Born: 09
Oct 1768

Elizabeth
BURLEY Born:
Bet. 16 Mar 1770
- 1777

Sarah VAN
HORN Born: 07
Feb 1773

Henry VAN
HORN, JR Born:
05 Apr 1777

Isaac VAN
HOORN and
Mary BETTS
Married: 05 Apr
1786

Christian VAN
HORN and
Elizabeth
BURLEY
Married: 29 Mar
1787

Isaiah VAN
HORN and
Catherine SUBER
Married: 31 Dec
1794

Sarah VAN
HORN Died:
1799

John
WYNKOOP and
Catherine SUBER
Married: 31 Jan
1805

Jonathan SMITH
and Martha VAN
HOORN
Married: 10 Aug
1819

Amos VAN
HORN Died: 05
Sep 1823

Cornelius S. VAN
HORN Born:
Abt. 1849

Elizabeth
BURLEY Died:
Bet. 23 Jul 1851 -
1854

Elizabeth VAN
HORN Died: 12
May 1868

**Niles,
Trumbull Co.,
OH**

Lester M.
GEARHART
Died: 17 Mar
1982

Katherine Belle
JUART Died: 13
Apr 2001

Family Map

North Carolina (SW of Virginia)

Thomas Budd VAN HORNE Died: 19 Mar 1865

Dale Robert LAMBING, JR Born: 22 Dec 1956

North Dakota

Hansine Bergetha GULSTAD Born: 15 Aug 1888

Bowen VAN HORN Born: 10 Jul 1889

Theodore CYANET Born: Abt. 1890

Bertha C. BOWSER Born: Jun 1893

Frank Thomas MCELHOES and Patience Ann ANDERSON Married: 15 Jan 1901

Roy Melvin VAN HORN Born: Abt. 1914

See Also Minnesota.

North Loup, Valley Co., NE

Cordella Adeline VAN HORN Born: 1875

Edwin Burtel VAN HORN and Lottie Belle DAVIS Married: 17 Apr 1883

Ernest L. VAN HORN Born: 09 Jul 1884

Beecher Lynn VAN HORN Born: 20 Jun 1886

Merril Warrn VAN HORN Born: 03 Jun 1888

Harry Russel VAN HORN Born: 11 Oct 1889

Bertha Mae VAN HORN Born: 03 May 1891

Cordella Adeline VAN HORN Died: 1895

Obadiah Davis VAN HORN Died: 27 Nov 1895

Edwin Burtel VAN HORN Died: 01 Apr 1907

Lottie Belle DAVIS Died: 12 Jun 1909

Ernest L. VAN HORN and Viola V. BABCOCK Married: 03 Jan 1911

Northampton, Northampton Co., PA

Abraham Barentsen VAN HOORN and Mary DUNGAN Married: 06 Jul 1718

Abraham Barentsen VAN HOORN and Mary VAN SCRIVER Married: Abt. 1751

Northumberland, Northumberland Co., PA

Samuel WILLETS Born: Apr 1791

Elisha WILLETS Born: 27 Feb 1794

Hiram Benson MCPHERSON Born: 18 Mar 1843

Nortonville, Jefferson Co., KS

Mary RANDALL Died: 27 Feb 1930

William Lawson VAN HORN Died: 14 Oct 1957

Norwood, Norfolk Co., MA

Nellie KLINGENSMITH Died: 12 Feb 1998

Nutley, Essex Co., NJ

Christiana APPO Died: 28 Jul 1935

Oakland, Alameda Co., CA

Earl VAN HORN Died: 21 Nov 1961

Hansine Bergetha GULSTAD Died: 15 Mar 1974

Roy Melvin VAN HORN Died: 24 Dec 1981

Louis Albert LININGER Died: 19 Aug 1984

Mary Lorraine DVORK Died: 16 Feb 2000

Pearl Ruth VAN HORN Died: 26 Oct 2003

Family Map

Oakmont, Allegheny Co., PA

Frank W. MCLAUGHLIN Born: Abt. 1875

Olive Florence CONDRON Died: 09 Jul 1977

Oberlin, Decatur Co., KS

Gladys Mabel POINTER Born: 11 Aug 1906

Ogle Co., IL

Martha VAN HOORN Died: 03 Jan 1857

See Also Clay Co., Vigo Co., Chicago, Milwaukee, Welton, Dayton, Fremont, Celina, Lebanon, Des Moines, Toledo, Lorain, Litchfield, Findlay, Garwin, Piqua, Mount Pleasant, Janesville, Decatur, Warsaw, Port Huron, Quincy, Waldron, Beavercreek, Evanston, Coldwater, Middletown, New London, Forest City, Milton, Farmington, Franklin, Battle Creek, Mount Vernon, Clinton, Waynesville, Ridgeway, Millville, Columbus, Keota, Clayton, Clinton, and Wabash.

Ohio (SW of Pennsylvania)

Anna D. HALL

PARKILL

Prudence DAVIS Born: 27 Mar 1808

John H. VAN HORNE Born: 02 Apr 1812

Sarah T. SCHENCK Born: Abt. 1815

Isaac VAN HORNE Born: Abt. 1817

Harietta J. VAN HORNE Born: 29 Jan 1817

Ann HONAS Born: 1820

Alice Elizabeth VAN HORN Born: 06 Jun 1820

Rebecca Anna SCHIRRA Born: Abt. 1821

Clarissa Ross VAN HORNE Born: 23 Apr 1824

Clarica Born: Abt. 1825

Sophia CARMICHAEL Died: 20 Sep 1828

Maria VAN HORN Born: Abt. 1830

Amaranda Rachel LOOFBURROW Born: 01 Jun 1830

Almarine VAN HORN Born: Abt. 1832

Elizabeth Born: Abt. 1833

Elizabeth Born: Abt. 1833

Mary Elizabeth HAYNES Born: 09 Jan 1834

Thomas H. FISHER Born: Abt. 1835

Obadiah Davis VAN HORN Born: 13 Feb 1835

Martha BABCOCK Born: Bet. 1835 - 1837

James Romine VAN HORN Born: Abt. 1836

John FISHER Born: Abt. 1837

Lucy Jane VAN HORN Born: Abt. 1838

Catherine A. VAN HORNE Born: Abt. 1838

Emiline VAN HORN Born: 1838

Austin T. FISHER Born: Abt. 1839

Sallie VAN HORNE Born: Abt. 1839

Sardis B. FISHER Born: Abt. 1840

Jefferson VAN HORN Born: Abt. 1840

Mary VAN HORN Born: Abt. 1840

Francis J. VAN HORNE Born: Abt. 1840

Thomas Budd VAN HORNE Died: 21 Sep 1841

Cornelia VAN HORNE Born: Abt. 1842

William VAN HORNE Born: Abt. 1842

Mary FISHER Born: Abt. 1843

Margaret VAN HORN Born: Abt. 1843

Alice VAN HORNE Born: Abt. 1843

Family Map

Jacob Davis VAN
HORN Born:
1843

Sarah C. VAN
HORNE Born:
Abt. 1844

Peter B. FISHER
Born: Abt. 1845

Rhoda J. FISHER
Born: Abt. 1845

Sarah FISHER
Born: Abt. 1845

Joshua VAN
HORN Born:
Abt. 1845

Sarah VAN
HORN Born:
Abt. 1845

Moses Stout
VAN HORN
Born: 1845

Eliza VAN
HORNE Born:
Abt. 1846

John VAN
HORNE Born:
Abt. 1846

Daniel L. VAN
HORN Born: 29
Apr 1846

John B.
GEPHART Born:
Dec 1846

Flora FISHER
Born: Abt. 1847

John C. FISHER
Born: Abt. 1847

Mary B.
HUMMEL Born:
Abt. 1847

James William
DICKEN Born:
Feb 1847

John William
HUTZLER Born:
Bet. 24 Jul 1847 -
Jan 1848

Martha VAN
HORNE Born:
Abt. 1848

Mattie Born: 1848

Holdridge
Chidester VAN
HORN Born:
1848

Mary VAN
HORNE Born:
Abt. 1849

Lucy Ann VAN
HORN Born: 04
Feb 1849

Jefferson VAN
HORNE Born:
Abt. Sep 1849

Perry Franklin
ROSENBERGE
R Born: 15 Mar
1850

Alvin Lewis
HUMMEL Born:
Abt. Apr 1850

Samuel VAN
HORN Born:
Abt. Apr 1850

Alfred VAN
HORNE Born:
May 1850

Mary M. FISHER
Born: Abt. 1851

Thomas VAN
HORNE Born:
Abt. 1851

Arthelia VAN
HORN Born: 07
Jul 1851

Hannah R. Born:
Aug 1851

William L. VAN
HORN Born:
Nov 1851

Elias Winfield
HUMMEL Born:
13 Nov 1851

William VAN
HORNE Born:
Abt. 1852

Jennie E.
HUMMEL Born:
11 Aug 1852

George W.
HUMMEL Born:
Abt. 1853

Ella F. Born: Apr
1853

Sarah M. VAN
HORN Born: 03
Jan 1854

Christopher
Columbus VAN
HORN Born: 19
Jul 1854

John W.
HIESTAND
Born: Abt. 1856

L. M. SKINNER
Born: Abt. 1856

Malinda
FULERTON
Born: Jan 1856

Rosanna A. VAN
HORN Born: 25
Apr 1857

Michael William
LUDWIG Born:
Oct 1857

George W.
HIESTAND
Born: Abt. 1858

Harriet Rowena
HUMMEL Born:
Abt. 1858

Elsie Lavina
GAMBY Born:
Feb 1858

Magdaline
HUMMEL Born:
Dec 1859

Frank EBERT
Born: Sep 1860

Annie Mary
HUMMEL Born:
Abt. 1861

Levint Leveritt
VAN HORN
Born: 08 Jul 1862

Laura Jane
HUMMEL Born:
Abt. 1863

Family Map

Nellie HUMMEL
Born: Abt. 1864

William Joseph
KISER Born: Aug
1866

Ida E. HUMMEL
Born: Nov 1867

Mary E. DAVID
Born: Apr 1868

Elizabeth
Rebbeca
DEEMER Born:
Dec 1868

Joseph G.
RUMPLER Born:
Nov 1869

Rhoda T.
HUMMEL Born:
03 Oct 1871

Edwin E.
GEPHART Born:
Jan 1873

Cornelius
WALKER Born:
Abt. 1874

James Arthur
ROSENBERGE
R Born: Dec 1874

John Calvin VAN
HORN Born: 27
Dec 1875

Minnie B.
HUMMEL Born:
Abt. 1876

Jesse C.
GEPHART Born:
Jul 1876

Abeca HUMMEL
Born: Abt. 1878

Edna
PATTERSON
Born: Abt. 1879

Chauncey Wilber
GEPHART Born:
27 Sep 1879

Medina Emma
WOLFE Born: 12
Dec 1879

Elizabeth M.
MILLER Born:
Jan 1880

Sara G. Born:
Abt. 1881

Ella M.
OVERMIER
Born: Abt. 1881

Ermie A.
ROSENBERGE
R Born: Mar 1881

Alvin C.
KEEFER Born:
Oct 1882

William F.
HUMMEL Born:
Dec 1882

Nellie MOONEY
Born: Abt. 1883

Hazel B.
LUDWIG Born:
Sep 1883

George
Washington
ROSENBERGE
R Born: 25 Sep
1883

Anna M.
DICKEN Born:
Jan 1884

Pearsy L.
HUMMEL Born:
Oct 1885

Harry A.
STROHL Born:
Abt. 1886

Mazie L.
SWANGER
Born: Abt. 1886

Levint Leveritt
VAN HORN and
Mary E. DAVID
Married: 20 Oct
1886

Harvey T.
HUMMEL Born:
01 Oct 1887

Oliver Perry
ROSENBERGE
R Born: 13 Oct
1887

Walter J.
LUDWIG Born:
Dec 1887

Ada EBERT
Born: Aug 1888

Samuel Cornelius
VAN HORN and
Jennie E.
HUMMEL
Married: Abt.
1889

Minnie VAN
HORN Born: 18
Mar 1889

Florian YOUNG
and Sarah C.
HUMMEL
Married: Abt.
1890

William H.
ROSENBERGE
R Born: Nov 1890

Amy VAN
HORN Born:
Bet. 13 Nov 1890
- 1891

Sylvia M. Born:
1892

Ethel V.
LUDWIG Born:
Nov 1892

Roy VAN HORN
Born: Bet. 01 May
1892 - 1893

Nellie Vidella
VAN HORN
Born: Nov 1893

Lester J.
RUMPLER Born:
18 Nov 1894

Lilia Born: Abt.
1895

Alva YOUNG
Born: Feb 1895

Luella P. Born:
Abt. 1896

Walter Othel
VAN HORN
Born: 27 May
1897

Family Map

Jefferson VAN HORN Died: 1898

Ada LUDWIG Born: Abt. 1900

Iva B. GEPHART Born: Abt. 1902

Ida Mae KISER Born: 22 Mar 1902

Chauncey Wilber GEPHART and Nellie MOONEY Married: Abt. 1903

Lida KISER Born: Abt. 1903

Edna N. GEPHART Born: Abt. 1904

Franklin ROSENBERGE R Born: 05 Apr 1904

Wilbur L. GEPHART Born: Abt. 1906

Elizabeth Born: Abt. 1908

Howard J. GEPHART Born: Jan 1908

Audry E. GEPHART Born: Abt. 1911

Kennard W. GEPHART Born: Abt. 1911

Gwendolyn D. ROSENBERGE R Born: Abt. 1911

Wilbur James STROHL Born: Abt. 1911

Floyd OVERMYER Born: Abt. 1912

Earl O. ROSENBERGE R Born: Abt. 1913

Sheldon Henry SCHIMMEL Born: 12 Mar 1928

Howard Calvin HUTZLER Died: Aft. 1949

William H. GRINDLE Died: Aft. 10 Oct 1969

Oil City, Venango Co., PA

Joseph W. VAN HORN Died: 27 Jun 1976

Oklahoma (SE of Kansas)

Frederick DILTS Born: 17 Aug 1893

Daniel W. DILTS Born: 10 Jul 1896

Lillie M. DILTS Born: 28 Dec 1898

Robert VAN HORN Born: Abt. 1902

Ailod VAN HORN Born: Abt. 1907

Lloyd VAN HORN Born: Abt. 1911

Freeman Verne VAN HORN Born: Abt. 1915

Walter Othel VAN HORN and Eva Zelpha SMITH Married: 1921

Harry Vernon POINTER Born: Abt. 1925

Olean, Cattaraugus Co., NY

Hilda MILLER Born: 12 Apr 1917

Omaha, Douglas Co., NE

Betty Jane O'ROURKE Born: 06 Oct 1928

John Dwight WEEKS Born: 06 Oct 1928

Orchard Park, Erie Co., NY

Carl Eugene JOHNSTON Died: 08 Nov 1965

Oregon

Georgia MILLER Born: Aug 1870

Franklin L. STEWART Died: Aft. 1941

See Also Idaho.

Ottertail, Otter Tail Co., MN

Charles Merle MCELHOES Born: 22 Jan 1902

Waldo Steele MCELHOES Born: 15 Jan 1905

John Gordon MCELHOES Born: 16 Sep 1906

Page Co., VA

Jacob HIESTAND and Mary BLOSSER

Samuel HIESTAND Born: 1781

Penn Hills, Allegheny Co., PA

Family Map

Rachel POUNDS
Born: Bet. 03 May
1802 - 1805

Martha VAN
HORN Born:
Bet. May 1835 -
1837

**Pennington
Co., SD**

Anna Burel VAN
HORN Born: 02
May 1893

Pennsylvania

?

?

Mae
GEARHART

Joseph HILTY

HUMMEL

James
KEPHART

Mary

? MCAFOOS

Dorothy VAN
HORN

Lavona VAN
HORN

William E. VAN
HORN

Christena
WHITACRE

Gerritje VAN
HOORN Born:
19 Mar 1713

Elizabeth VAN
HOORN Born:
19 Sep 1714

Christian VAN
HOORN Born:
24 Dec 1738

Johannes VAN
HOORN Born:
11 Oct 1741

Isaiah
MCELHOES
Born: 1743

Peter VAN
HOORN Born:
03 Apr 1746

Bernard VAN
HOORN and
Sarah VAN PELT
Married: Bet. 17
Jan 1752 - 1753

Adam FISCHER
Died: 1757

Gertje Charity
VAN HOORN
Died: Abt. 1769

Margaret
REDDING
Born: 1778

John Ford
KINTER Born:
02 Jun 1786

Phoebe VAN
HORN Born: 25
Oct 1787

Jacob BURKET
Born: Abt. 1788

Agnes Born: 1789

Jane VAN
HORN Born: 29
Mar 1789

Nancy STEELE
Born: 09 Apr
1789

David VAN
HORN Born: 05
Jun 1789

John Alexander
LYDICK Born:
16 Jul 1790

James
HUTCHISON
Born: 1791

Samuel
HUTCHISON
Born: 1792

Mary
HUTCHISON
Born: 1794

William
HUTCHISON
Born: 1794

Fanny BRIGGS
Born: 17 Nov
1795

Henry VAN
HORN Born:
Bet. 1795 - 27
Nov 1798

Elizabeth
HUTCHISON
Born: 1796

Florence
HUTCHISON
Born: 1797

George SINKS
Born: 1798

Elizabeth GAINE
Born: 17 Nov
1798

Matthew
STEELE Born:
Abt. 1799

David
WYNCOOP
Born: 15 Aug
1800

Abraham VAN
HORN Born:
Abt. 1801

Sarah BELL
Born: Abt. 1803

Elizabeth Born:
Abt. 1804

Christian VAN
HORN Born:
Bet. 04 Jan 1804 -
1807

Elizabeth VAN
HORN Born:
Abt. 1804

Mary
MCCULLOUGH
Born: Bet. 1805 -
1808

Cornelius SLACK
Born: 1806

Thressa
HASTINGS
Born: 14 Sep 1806

Family Map

Charlotte Born: Abt. 1807

William CUNNINGHAM Born: Bet. 1807 - 1810

Eleanor H. VAN HORN Born: Abt. 1810

Catherine Born: 1810

Hester HUTCHISON Born: 1810

Moses H. VAN HORN Born: 15 Jan 1812

John Steele HUTCHISON Born: Bet. 03 Feb 1813 - 1824

Elizabeth SPEACE Born: 1813

Margaret Born: Abt. 1814

Christian VAN HORN Born: 1814

Susannah MCELROY Born: Abt. 1815

Elizabeth MCCOMB Born: Abt. 1816

Mary A. VAN HORN Born: Abt. 1816

Dorcas MCELHOES Born: 08 Sep 1816

Seneca BARNETT Born: Abt. 1817

Katherine FRY Born: Abt. 1817

William HUTCHISON Born: Abt. 1817

Isaac KECK Born: Abt. 1817

Mary Elizabeth SAMSEL Born: Abt. 1817

Cornelius HUTCHISON Born: Abt. 1819

Samuel HUTCHISON Born: Oct 1819

Aaron HOPKINS Born: Abt. 1820

Ann THOMPSON Died: Abt. 1820

John R. VAN HORN Born: Abt. 1820

Phoebe NEFF Born: Oct 1820

Robert STEWART Born: Abt. 1821

Annie L. STOUT Born: Bet. 23 Jul 1821 - 1832

James Wherry VAN HORN Born: 31 Oct 1821

Joseph KISSINGER Born: Abt. 1822

Elizabeth Born: Abt. 1823

Sarah Born: Abt. 1823

Samuel VAN HORN Born: Abt. 1823

Rachael PEIRCE Born: Abt. 1824

Isabella SUTTON Born: Abt. 1824

George Leroy CONDRON Born: 29 Apr 1824

Eliza A. ROSE Born: Bet. 26 Mar 1824 - 1829

John Hastings VAN HORN Born: Bet. 1824 - 1827

Mary D. VAN HORN Born: 20 Jul 1825

Eliza Born: Bet. 1825 - 1829

Martha WARREN Born: Abt. 1826

Isaiah VanZant VAN HORN Born: 1826

Mary D. VAN HORN Died: 27 Jun 1826

William A. VAN HORN Born: Bet. 1826 - 1832

William VAN HORN Born: Bet. 1827 - 31 Dec 1833

Robert C. HAMILTON Born: Abt. 1828

Martha VAN HORN Born: 20 Feb 1828

Ann Caroline NEIGHLY Born: Mar 1828

Casper AUL Born: 28 Nov 1828

Henry A. VAN HORN Born: Bet. 1828 - 1829

Charlotte HUTCHISON Born: Abt. 1829

Jane Born: Abt. 1829

Family Map

William E. NICHOL Born: Abt. 1829

John VAN HORN Born: Abt. 1829

Rachel STEWART Born: 1829

William G. VAN HORN, JR Born: 11 Sep 1829

John Dick VAN HORN Born: Dec 1829

Joshua LYDICK Born: Abt. 1830

Christine VAN HORN Born: Abt. 1830

Susan WILEY Born: Abt. 1830

Christina WRIGHT Born: Abt. 1830

Charles JEWART Born: Feb 1830

Dorcas HAMILTON Born: Abt. 1831

Jacob B. O'CONNER Born: Abt. 1831

Sarah Born: Abt. 1831

J. J. HENDERSON Born: Apr 1831

Margaret J. VAN HORN Born: 19 Jul 1831

Martha WELLS Born: Abt. 1832

Julia Ann HUTCHISON Born: 1832

Alexander VAN HORN, JR Born: 18 Jan 1832

Catherine MCHENRY Born: Feb 1832

Catherine VAN HORN Born: Bet. 11 Sep 1832 - 1838

Amanda JAMES Born: Bet. 1832 - 1834

Robert CUNNINGHAM Born: Abt. 1833

Margaret Born: Abt. 1833

Mary A. SHAFFNIC Born: Abt. 1833

Caroline MCQUOWN Born: Jan 1833

Caroline Born: Abt. 1834

Elizabeth Born: Abt. 1834

Elizabeth ROBINSON Born: Abt. 1834

Kinsley VAN HORN Born: Abt. 1834

Mary E. Born: 1834

James Devin VAN HORN Born: 1834

Elizabeth C. BAKER Born: Jan 1834

Miriam Work STEELE Born: 02 Mar 1834

David Seba WAKEFIELD Born: Bet. 1834 - 15 Jan 1835

John H. CUNNINGHAM Born: Abt. 1835

George W. COLLINS Born: Jan 1835

Nancy VAN HORN Born: Bet. 18 Aug 1835 - 1836

John KINTER Died: 1836

Robert Alexander STEELE Born: 07 Feb 1836

Daniel CUNNINGHAM Born: Abt. 1837

Catherine LYDICK Born: Abt. 1837

Oliver VAN HORN Born: Abt. 1837

Andrew Jackson MCGAUGHEY Born: 23 Feb 1837

Isaiah VAN HORN Born: 24 Oct 1837

Eliza Arminda HARKNESS Born: Abt. 1838

George VAN HORN Born: Nov 1838

Samuel CUNNINGHAM Born: Abt. 1839

Jane HAMILTON Born: Abt. 1839

Robert Clark MCGAUGHEY Born: Abt. 1839

Amos RANDAL Born: Abt. 1839

Senica VAN HORN Born: Abt. 1839

Caroline B. Born: Abt. 1840

Family Map

Sarah Jane TAYLOR Born: 1840

Mariah Born: 11 Apr 1840

Joseph CUNNINGHAM Born: Abt. 1841

Margaret VAN HORN Born: Abt. 1841

John F. HEISLEY Born: Apr 1841

Martha A. HAMILTON Born: Bet. 1841 - 1844

George NEALE Born: Abt. 1842

Moses T. STEELE Born: 08 May 1842

Sarah VAN HORN Born: Bet. 25 Dec 1842 - 1846

Albert CUNNINGHAM Born: Abt. 1843

Jacob Vanderbilt VAN HORN Born: Abt. 1843

Richard Henry VAN HORN Born: Abt. 1843

Agnes HUTCHISON Born: Abt. 1844

John VAN HORN Born: Abt. 1844

W. H. CUNNINGHAM Born: Feb 1844

Charles J. VAN HORN Born: 11 Nov 1844

Mary Lucinda VAN HORN Born: Bet. 23 Feb 1844 - 1846

James CUNNINGHAM Born: Abt. 1845

Martha R. HAMILTON Born: Abt. 1845

Mary Ann VAN HORN Born: Abt. 1845

John Miles VAN HORN Born: Sep 1845

John A. VAN HORN Born: Bet. 1845 - 1855

Mary E. Born: Abt. 1846

Margaret HUTCHISON Born: Abt. 1846

Richard HUTCHISON Born: Abt. 1846

George VAN HORN Born: Abt. 1846

James VAN HORN Born: Abt. 1846

Regina Anna Born: Feb 1846

George Stockholm WYNKOOP Born: 26 Dec 1846

Fanny VAN HORN Born: 28 Dec 1846

Abram VAN HORN Born: Aft. 1846

George E. FAIR Born: Abt. 1847

Robert A. HAMILTON Born: Abt. 1847

William H. HOUCK Born: Abt. 1847

Alice VAN HORN Born: Abt. 1847

Mariah VAN HORN Born: Abt. 1847

Joseph KISSINGER Born: 1847

John M. DILTS Born: 27 Mar 1847

James PALMER Born: Oct 1847

Martha I. HOPKINS Born: Abt. 1848

Francis HUTCHISON Born: Abt. 1848

William H. VAN HORN Born: Abt. 1848

Jacob C. MOCK Born: 1848

Mary Jane CAMPBELL Born: 04 Jan 1848

Mary V. VAN HORN Born: Jul 1848

Charles Milton VAN HORN Born: 19 Sep 1848

Agnes DILTS Born: Abt. 1849

Abraham GEARHART Born: Abt. 1849

Ann E. HOUCK Born: Abt. 1849

Family Map

Ester E.
HUTCHISON
Born: Abt. 1849

Lois NICHOL
Born: Abt. 1849

Caroline
RICHNER Born:
Abt. 1849

Jacob BURKET,
JR Born: 1849

Robert Clair
MABON Born:
Nov 1849

Samuel BARKER
Born: Abt. 1850

Mary E.
BEIGHEL Born:
Bet. 1850 - May
1853

Alphonse
CUNNINGHAM
Born: Abt. 1850

Nancy
HUTCHISON
Born: Abt. 1850

Kate Born: Abt.
1850

James W. VAN
HORN Born:
Abt. 1850

Joseph L. VAN
HORN Born:
Abt. 1850

Thirza VAN
HORN Born:
Abt. 1850

Nancy
HOPKINS Born:
Mar 1850

Wesley C.
SIMPSON Born:
Mar 1850

James N.
HOPKINS Born:
Abt. Jun 1850

Florence M. VAN
HORN Born:
Nov 1850

John Taylor
HOPKINS Born:
Bet. 1850 - 1852

Clara Born: Abt.
1851

Samuel DILTS
Born: Abt. 1851

William
HUTCHISON
Born: Abt. 1851

Caroline Widmina
STEAR Born:
Abt. 1851

Melissa VAN
HORN Born:
Abt. 1851

Nathan VAN
HORN Born:
Abt. 1851

William T. VAN
HORN Born:
Abt. 1851

James M.
ASHBAUGH
Born: Jun 1851

John
HUTCHISON
Born: Abt. 1852

Theodosia Born:
Abt. 1852

Augustus VAN
HORN Born:
Abt. 1852

Caroline VAN
HORN Born:
Abt. 1852

Daniel HOUCK
Born: Apr 1852

Hugh Albert
MCAFOOS
Born: 14 Jul 1852

Calvin W. BOOZ
Born: 02 Sep 1852

Emma ALDOUS
Born: Oct 1852

Emma VAN
HORN Born:
Bet. 1852 - 1853

Scott HOPKINS
Born: Bet. 1852 -
1854

Charles Edwin
BENT Born: Abt.
1853

Fanny HOUCK
Born: Abt. 1853

John P.
HUTCHISON
Born: Abt. 1853

Mary Belle
WARDEN Born:
27 Feb 1853

Anna I. VAN
HORN Born: Jun
1853

Frances F. HAAS
Born: Aug 1853

Elizabeth VAN
HOORN Died:
09 Nov 1853

Kate VAN
HORN Born:
Bet. 1853 - 1855

Cornelius A.
HUTCHISON
Born: Abt. 1854

Julia A.
HUTCHISON
Born: Abt. 1854

Mary C.
NICHOL Born:
Abt. 1854

Robert
STEWART Born:
Abt. 1854

Hannah VAN
HORN Born:
Abt. 1854

Susannah J. VAN
HORN Born:
Abt. 1854

Levina C.
WARDEN Born:
Abt. 1854

Anna M. VAN
HORN Born: Feb
1854

George L. VAN
HORN Born: 09
Feb 1854

Family Map

George L. COON
Born: 26 Jun 1854

John Wesley
BALLANTYNE
Born: 07 Jul 1854

Ida VAN HORN
Born: 30 Oct
1854

Mary Agnes
GALBRAITH
Born: Dec 1854

Martha AUL
Born: Abt. 1855

Tabitha DILTS
Born: Abt. 1855

Jennie Born: Abt.
1855

Julian Born: Abt.
1855

George VAN
HORN Born:
Abt. 1855

Susannah VAN
HORN Born:
Abt. 1855

William W. VAN
HORN Born:
Abt. 1855

Ellen
WAKEFIELD
Born: Abt. 1855

Alice Lucetta
VAN HORN
Born: 1855

George J.
BOSSARD Born:
May 1855

Reuben H.
GOURLEY
Born: Jul 1855

Theophilus Albert
COON Born:
Bet. 1855 - 1856

Addie VAN
HORN Born:
Bet. 1855 - 1856

Anna
HUTCHISON
Born: Bet. 1855 -
1858

William Worth
AUL Born: Abt.
1856

Alice Melissa
COON Born:
Bet. 1856 - 28 Apr
1858

Mary COON
Born: Abt. 1856

Franklin L.
STEWART Born:
Abt. 1856

Hannah Ella
VAN HORN
Born: Abt. 1856

Margaret
WAKEFIELD
Born: Abt. 1856

Anna Margaret
WARDEN Born:
Abt. 1856

Alexander M.
VAN HORN
Born: 1856

Lowery
HUGHES Born:
Apr 1856

Christian VAN
HORN Born: 12
May 1856

Louisa W. Born:
Jul 1856

John A MYERS
Born: Aug 1856

Kate Born: Oct
1856

Silas W.
LIGHTCAP
Born: Oct 1856

Caroline E. VAN
HORN Born:
Dec 1856

Samuel
HUTCHISON
Born: Abt. 1857

Emma VAN
HORN Born:
Abt. 1857

John E. F. VAN
HORN Born:
Abt. 1857

Maggie VAN
HORN Born:
Abt. 1857

Isabelle FRY
Born: Jan 1857

Clara VAN
HORN Born:
Bet. 12 May 1857
- 06 May 1858

Irene VAN
HORN Born:
May 1857

Harriett
STEWART Born:
Abt. 1858

Anna M. VAN
HORN Born:
Abt. 1858

Francis VAN
HORN Born:
Abt. 1858

Sarah R. VAN
HORN Born:
Abt. 1858

Mary
WAKEFIELD
Born: Abt. 1858

Adella VAN
HORN Born:
1858

George F.
KEEFER Born:
Mar 1858

William D.
SHIELDS Born:
May 1858

Lizzie C. VAN
HORN Born: 21
Jun 1858

John HOUCK
Born: 25 Jun 1858

Maria Lucinda
BENCE Born:
Sep 1858

Family Map

Amelia E.
HUTCHISON
Born: Bet. Jan
1858 - 1866

Emma STIVER
Born: Sep 1858

Hannah J.
PALMER Born:
Oct 1858

Kate HOUCK
Born: Abt. 1859

Matilda HOUSER
Born: Abt. 1859

Silas
HUTCHISON
Born: Abt. 1859

Marion VAN
HORN Born:
Abt. 1859

Robert James
WARDEN Born:
Abt. 1859

Robert Logan
VAN HORN
Born: 1859

Lanieann COON
Born: 16 Jun 1859

Elizabeth H.
Born: Bet. 1859 -
1867

Malinda AUL
Born: Abt. 1860

Mary C. GRACE
Born: Abt. 1860

Ianthus
STEWART Born:
Abt. 1860

Benjamin Franklin
VAN HORN
Born: Abt. 1860

John H. VAN
HORN Born:
Abt. 1860

Millie VAN
HORN Born:
Abt. 1860

J. A. WALTER
Born: Feb 1860

Lavina
WAKEFIELD
Born: Abt. Apr
1860

Martha J. Born:
Jun 1860

Mary E. VAN
HORN Born: Jun
1860

John Hastings
VAN HORN
Born: Aug 1860

Henry D. Foster
VAN HORN
Born: 12 Sep 1860

Adessa Levina
VAN HORN
Born: Oct 1860

George Curtis
AUL Born: Abt.
1861

Margaret C.
HOUSER Born:
Abt. 1861

Edward R.
STEWART Born:
Abt. 1861

Frank VAN
HORN Born:
Abt. 1861

Mary Ida LYTLE
Born: Jan 1861

Harry T.
BATEMAN
Born: Aug 1861

E. Susan
WAKEFIELD
Born: Bet. 1861 -
1862

John
WAKEFIELD
Born: Bet. 1861 -
1862

Albert G. CRAFT
Born: Abt. 1862

Robert Parnold
O'CONNER
Born: Abt. 1862

Alice VAN
HORN Born:
Abt. 1862

Emma L. VAN
HORN Born:
Abt. 1862

Sidney VAN
HORN Born:
Abt. 1862

Emma
WARDEN Born:
Abt. 1862

S. Lem BROCK
Born: 1862

Charles Barclay
COON Born: 03
Feb 1862

Edith Lee VAN
HORN Born: 23
Feb 1862

Margaret Cymisca
KUNKLE Born:
Jun 1862

Sarah B.
HOUSER Born:
Abt. 1863

James M.
NICHOL Born:
Abt. 1863

Mansfield
STEWART Born:
Abt. 1863

William VAN
HORN Born:
Abt. 1863

Jacob B. A.
O'CONNER
Born: Apr 1863

Matilda
TANNEHILL
Born: 19 Apr
1863

Means A.
GRUBE Born:
Sep 1863

Anna FULMER
Born: Dec 1863

James Harold
BEATTY Born:
Abt. 1864

Sarah Ida
MCGAUGHEY
Born: Abt. 1864

650

Family Map

Mary Rachel NEAL Born: Abt. 1864

Ida VAN HORN Born: Abt. 1864

Tabitha VAN HORN Born: Abt. 1864

Clarence WARDEN Born: Abt. 1864

Rachel Margaret PIERCE Born: May 1864

Albert VAN HORN Born: May 1864

Fannie E. Born: Nov 1864

Sarah E. HUTCHISON Born: Bet. 1864 - Feb 1870

Mc Henry AUL Born: Abt. 1865

Edith BOYLAN Born: Abt. 1865

John C. MCGAUGHEY Born: Abt. 1865

Minerva MCKILLIP Born: Abt. 1865

Orpha RUPPERT Born: Abt. 1865

A. Judson TANNEHILL Born: Abt. 1865

Emma VAN HORN Born: Abt. 1865

Ida VAN HORN Born: Abt. 1865

Sarah Isabel PALMER Born: Mar 1865

Ella Born: Jun 1865

George Steele HUTCHISON Born: 28 Jun 1865

James Johnson HUTCHISON Born: 28 Jun 1865

Lucy Adelia CONRAD Born: 21 Jul 1865

Abner Briggs VAN HORN Born: Bet. 24 Jul 1865 - 1867

Mack James AUL Born: Abt. 1866

Albert HUTCHISON Born: Abt. 1866

Zoe Wilemina NEAL Born: Abt. 1866

Flora VAN HORN Born: Abt. 1866

Frank WAKEFIELD Born: Abt. 1866

Ida M. WYNCOOP Born: Apr 1866

Samuel A. VAN HORN Born: Aug 1866

Edward J. DURBIN Born: Abt. 1867

Andrew MCGAUGHEY Born: Abt. 1867

Edward P. O'CONNER Born: Abt. 1867

Rebecca S. Born: Abt. 1867

Elizabeth VAN HORN Born: Abt. 1867

Thomas VAN HORN Born: Abt. 1867

Martha Jane Born: May 1867

Harry COON Born: 29 May 1867

John GRIFFITH Born: Dec 1867

Benjamin Frank ASHCOM Born: Abt. 1868

Olive NICHOL Born: Abt. 1868

William A. VAN HORN Born: Abt. 1868

Jennie WAKEFIELD Born: Abt. 1868

John WARDEN Born: Abt. 1868

Margaret Mary VAN HORN Born: Mar 1868

William VAN HORN Born: Jul 1868

Belle COLEMAN Born: Abt. 1869

Charles Andrew HUTCHISON Born: Abt. 1869

Nancy Loretta LNU Born: Abt. 1869

Mary Annie WYNKOOP Born: Abt. 1869

Richard Henry VAN HORN and Lydiana Beatty WARNER Married: 1869

Alpha Retta WEAMER Born: Jan 1869

Family Map

Lycenges M. MCGAUGHEY Born: Abt. Aug 1869

Ruth NEAL Born: Abt. Aug 1869

Francis VAN HORN Born: Abt. Sep 1869

Harry M. WILT Born: Nov 1869

Samuel S. MCGAUGHEY Born: Abt. 1870

Susan L. WYNKOOP Born: Abt. 1870

Mary A. HOUCK Born: Feb 1870

Robert JOHNSTON Born: Bet. 07 Jul 1870 - 1874

William M. MCADOO Born: 01 Feb 1870

Henry E. VAN HORN Born: 21 Apr 1870

Dallas F. VAN HORN Born: 24 May 1870

W. H. WEISS Born: Jun 1870

Harry Melbourn MOCK Born: 22 Jun 1870

James VAN HORN Born: Jul 1870

Alice HOUCK Born: Abt. 1871

Anna MCCALL Born: Abt. 1871

Sedora B. PARKILL Born: Abt. 1871

Arthur VAN HORN Born: Abt. 1871

David M. VAN HORN Born: Abt. 1871

Edward VAN HORN Born: Abt. 1871

William H. VAN HORN Born: Abt. 1871

Etta WARDEN Born: Abt. 1871

Ambrose Kelly STEAR Born: Mar 1871

Ida May STEWART Born: Apr 1871

John Rochester FRAMPTON Born: May 1871

James W. VAN HORN Born: 23 Oct 1871

Mary Emma LYDICK Born: 06 Nov 1871

George B. WAKEFIELD Born: Dec 1871

Frank COON Born: 16 Dec 1871

Danks AUL Born: Abt. 1872

Rose C. Born: Abt. 1872

Mattie HEISLEY Born: Abt. 1872

James L. MCGAUGHEY Born: Abt. 1872

Mavina WAKEFIELD Born: Abt. 1872

Sadie Born: Sep 1872

Bessie Irene MITCHELL Born: 08 Oct 1872

Wade Blair COON Born: Bet. 26 Aug 1873 - 1874

Mary E. KECK Born: Abt. 1873

Robert J. WYNKOOP Born: Abt. 1873

Edwin J. DILTS Born: 08 Mar 1873

Bertha Katherine Born: May 1873

Annie VAN HORN Born: 10 Aug 1873

Charles H. HUTCHISON Born: Dec 1873

Blanch Born: Abt. 1874

Amos F. HOUCK Born: Abt. 1874

Joseph A. HOUCK Born: Abt. 1874

Albert M.PARKILL Born: Abt. 1874

Wilber MCGAUGHEY Born: Abt. 1874

Lizzie ROBINSON Born: Abt. 1874

Gertrude VAN HORN Born: Abt. 1874

William A. VAN HORN Born: Abt. 1874

Melissa WARDEN Born: Abt. 1874

Family Map

David WYLAND
Born: Abt. 1874

Harry V. VAN
HORN Born: 02
Feb 1874

Mary Lucetta
MCELHOES
Born: 01 Dec
1874

Nora Mary Agnes
VAN HORN
Born: 29 Dec
1874

Ellen BOWSER
Born: Abt. 1875

Kitty A.
BURKET Born:
Abt. 1875

Laura
HOFFMAN
Born: Abt. 1875

Myrtle M.
MOORE Born:
Abt. 1875

Agnes B. MOYES
Born: Abt. 1875

Alice V. VAN
HORN Born:
Abt. 1875

Elizabeth VAN
HORN Born:
Abt. 1875

Charles
WIDDOWSON
Born: Abt. 1875

Thomas A.
LAMBING Born:
Mar 1875

Elizabeth Ruth
JACKSON Born:
16 Mar 1875

William R. DILTS
Born: 12 Jul 1875

Carrie Adella
VAN HORN
Born: 16 Aug
1875

Dessia A. VAN
HORN Born: Oct
1875

Ernie Born: Abt.
1876

David G. KECK
Born: Abt. 1876

Maud Belle
MCGAUGHEY
Born: Abt. 1876

William Carl
MOCK Born:
Abt. 1876

Ada Leona
O'CONNER
Born: Abt. 1876

Annie T. Born:
Abt. 1876

William
WAKEFIELD
Born: May 1876

Charles W.
ASHBAUGH
Born: Sep 1876

Homer
LAFFERTY
Born: 18 Sep 1876

Cora Estella
WILLIAMS Born:
26 Oct 1876

Maggie DILTS
Born: Abt. 1877

Jessie
HUTCHISON
Born: Abt. 1877

Theressa
WEAVER Born:
Feb 1877

Richard E.
BARKER Born:
Mar 1877

Emma
RITCHEY Born:
22 Jul 1877

John A.
BOWSER Born:
07 Aug 1877

Merril VAN
HORN Born:
Nov 1877

Guy Wiseman
VAN HORN
Born: 22 Nov
1877

Van Horn
STEAR Born:
Bet. 1877 - 1879

Robert E.
CONDRON
Born: Abt. 1878

Gertrude S.
KECK Born:
Abt. 1878

Samuel A.
MOCK Born:
Abt. 1878

William C.
WYNKOOP
Born: Abt. 1878

Vernie Born: 1878

William B.
LIGHTCAP
Born: 18 Jan 1878

William Alexander
BURKET Born:
06 Aug 1878

Mary Gertude
BALLANTYNE
Born: Sep 1878

Mary R.
HUTCHISON
Born: Sep 1878

Oila May
ROBINSON
Born: Oct 1878

Harry Burk VAN
HORN Born: Oct
1878

Ada Born: Nov
1878

Florence May
VAN HORN
Born: Bet. Feb -
18 Apr 1878

Elizabeth R.
GROCE Born:
Abt. 1879

Martha LYDICK
Born: 1879

Family Map

Nora Ellie VAN HORN Born: May 1879

Edmori E. VAN HORN Born: Oct 1879

Susana LIGHTCAP Born: 05 Nov 1879

Wilmer Todd DIXSON Born: Bet. 1879 - 1887

Phillip Lisle BLYSTONE Born: Abt. 1880

Irene HENDERSON Born: Abt. 1880

E. W. VAN HORN Born: Abt. 1880

Martha LYDICK Died: 1880

Maude Born: Feb 1880

George L. CONDRON Born: Apr 1880

Frank MCGAUGHEY Born: Apr 1880

Margaret BOWSER Born: May 1880

Alfred VAN HORN Born: May 1880

Bertha VAN HORN Born: May 1880

John R. SOWERS Born: Aug 1880

Emma H. VAN HORN Born: Nov 1880

Omer Victor BROOKS Born: Bet. 1880 - 1900

Florence M. FUCHHART Born: Abt. 1881

Harry S. KUEHNER Born: Abt. 1881

Louise Born: Abt. 1881

Bertha L. REISH Born: 1881

Annie LYDICK Born: 11 Feb 1881

Silas Merle MABON Born: Mar 1881

Euena Margaretta CRAIG Born: 07 Apr 1881

Larsa Jane LYDICK Born: May 1881

Joseph Laurie ROBINSON Born: May 1881

Samuel J. LIGHTCAP Born: 26 Jun 1881

Charissa B. CALDWELL Born: Abt. 1882

Laura E. FAIR Born: Abt. 1882

Hattie Born: Abt. 1882

Lola Irene SMITH Born: Abt. 1882

Hattie STOFFLE Born: Abt. 1882

Carrie Emma CARNAHAN Born: 1882

Clair CONDRON Born: Jan 1882

Elizabeth Pearl PALMER Born: Jan 1882

Joseph M. COLLINS Born: Feb 1882

Rollin Weber VAN HORN Born: 18 Feb 1882

Blaine Keller STEWART Born: 14 Mar 1882

John Ford KINTER Died: 27 Mar 1882

Mary M. BOWSER Born: Apr 1882

Minnie Myrtle CONDRON Born: May 1882

Stella Marilla VAN HORN Born: May 1882

Laura A. VAN HORN Born: Nov 1882

Nora E. LYDICK Born: Dec 1882

May E. CRAFT Born: Abt. 1883

Elsie M. CUNNINGHAM Born: Abt. 1883

Isaac M. HADDEN Born: Abt. 1883

Mary J. LIGHTCAP Born: 26 Feb 1883

John Earle BATEMAN Born: 07 Mar 1883

Boyd A. HOOVER Born: Jun 1883

Mary Ella KROH Born: Bet. 03 Aug 1883 - 1885

Family Map

Myrtle J. PALMER Born: Jul 1883

Virginia C. MCHENRY Born: Abt. 1884

Helen WILSON Born: Abt. 1884

Olive Florence CONDRON Born: 1884

Lizzie B. SIMPSON Born: Jan 1884

Elliot BOSSARD Born: Feb 1884

Iva C. HILTY Born: 22 Mar 1884

Clara Mabel LIGHTCAP Born: Bet. 29 Mar 1884 - 1887

Dolly ROBINSON Born: Jun 1884

Edward Harry VAN HORN Born: 05 Jul 1884

Merle John MCELHOES Born: 23 Jul 1884

Harry K. CUNNINGHAM Born: Abt. 1885

Laura KONSER Born: Abt. 1885

Louise Born: Abt. 1885

Laura Born: 1885

Claude BATEMAN Born: Jan 1885

George Edward COLLINS Born: Feb 1885

Carney Vance HARKCOM Born: 01 Feb 1885

Moses H. VAN HORN Died: 13 Feb 1885

Nellie GOURLEY Born: Jun 1885

Manda LYDICK Born: Jun 1885

Samuel V. SHIELDS Born: Aug 1885

Van E. BROOKS Born: Oct 1885

Nellie Gertrude VAN HORN Born: 06 Nov 1885

Urbin Melvin VAN HORN Born: Bet. 17 Aug 1885 - 1886

William L. CUNNINGHAM Born: Abt. 1886

Estella F. Born: Abt. 1886

Rudolph Hazen NYE Born: Abt. 1886

Anna C. BREWER Born: Mar 1886

Laura Elizabeth CONDRON Born: Jun 1886

John Martin COGLEY and Mary Blanche ROWE Married: 24 Jun 1886

Calvin C. BOSSARD Born: Oct 1886

Alfred Roland VAN HORN Born: Oct 1886

Martha Elizabeth DILTS Born: Abt. 1887

Lattie Mae Born: Abt. 1887

Harvey J. MYERS Born: Abt. 1887

Alice M. LYDICK Born: Mar 1887

Zula L. VAN HORN Born: Mar 1887

M. Blair GOURLEY Born: May 1887

Leone E. KECK Born: Sep 1887

Annie J. SIMPSON Born: Sep 1887

John Delbert GOOD Born: 21 Oct 1887

Frank FERGUSON Born: Abt. 1888

Elva VAN HORN Born: Abt. 1888

Clarence Reed CONDRON Born: 1888

Viola Sophia LODING Born: 1888

Florence BALLANTYNE Born: Jun 1888

Nellie M. HANCOCK Born: 16 Jul 1888

George Clair MABON Born: Aug 1888

Burton S. PALMER Born: Aug 1888

Harry Christopher BREWER Born: 10 Aug 1888

Miller LYDICK Born: Sep 1888

Family Map

Hugh W. CONDRON Born: 1889

Ellis P. GOURLEY Born: Jan 1889

Arthur Bell MYERS Born: 31 Jan 1889

Lulu V. VAN HORN Born: 29 Jul 1889

Norma C. KECK Born: Oct 1889

Florence Maggie LIGHTCAP Born: 04 Nov 1889

Bertha LIGHTCAP Born: Dec 1889

Mary Verne BARR Born: Abt. 1890

Richard L. BOUCHER Born: Abt. 1890

Hazel B. CONDRON Born: Abt. 1890

Scott E. CUNNINGHAM Born: Abt. 1890

Howard E. GAYLEY Born: Abt. 1890

Inez Ethel STEAR Born: Abt. 1890

John Torrence LYDICK Born: Feb 1890

Laura VAN HORN Born: Feb 1890

Charlotte WHITACRE Born: Feb 1890

Callie S. MCCAUSLAND Born: 16 Mar 1890

Dollie Irene CONDRON Born: Apr 1890

Minnie M. MYERS Born: Oct 1890

Andrew F. COOK Born: Abt. 1891

Bertha Mae Born: Abt. 1891

Clark W. MILLER Born: Abt. 1891

Bob HENDERSON Born: Mar 1891

Flora WEISS Born: Apr 1891

Russell L. BATEMAN Born: May 1891

Lilla L. VAN HORN Born: May 1891

Roy L. SIMPSON Born: Jul 1891

Glenn Shields BREWER Born: 06 Jul 1891

Ruby M. KECK Born: Aug 1891

Sarah Isabel VAN HORN Born: Aug 1891

Russel LYDICK Born: Sep 1891

Clark S. LIGHTCAP Born: Oct 1891

Fay R. LIGHTCAP Born: 29 Nov 1891

Lou GRUBE Born: Dec 1891

Charles H. GOODNOW Born: Abt. 1892

David Myrl LYDICK Born: Abt. 1892

Beulah E. Born: 1892

Eugene Wesley ASHCOM Born: 21 Jan 1892

Etta J. GALENTINE Born: Apr 1892

Florence ROBINSON Born: Apr 1892

Edgar L. MYERS Born: 19 Apr 1892

Dorothy MOCK Born: 29 May 1892

Calvin WILT Born: Jul 1892

Percy A. KECK Born: Dec 1892

Mildred L. DILTS Born: Abt. 1893

Andrew C. FERRIER and Sarah Jane SHEARER Married: Abt. 1893

Goldie HILL Born: Abt. 1893

Edna MARSH Born: Abt. 1893

Homer N. MONTGOMERY Born: Abt. 1893

George VAN HORN Born: Abt. 1893

Harvey S. BOSSARD Born: Mar 1893

Family Map

Elvie E. VAN HORN Born: Mar 1893

Claude WEISS Born: Mar 1893

Bryston Milton MOCK Born: 14 May 1893

Ira Sloan CONDRON Born: 05 Jul 1893

Budd E. LIGHTCAP Born: Aug 1893

Maud VAN HORN Born: Aug 1893

Theodore VAN HORN Born: Aug 1893

Erwin GODOWN Born: Nov 1893

Lee GRUBE Born: Nov 1893

Augusta BREWER Born: Dec 1893

Pluma Ruth VAN HORN Born: Dec 1893

Dean Ray KEPHART Born: Abt. 1894

Eunice W. KIFFER Born: 19 Jan 1894

Harry Irvin MYERS Born: 06 Feb 1894

Levi LYDICK Born: Mar 1894

Anna V. SHEPHARD Born: Mar 1894

Marion E. KECK Born: Apr 1894

Laura Cornelia SIMPSON Born: Apr 1894

David Edward PALMER Born: Aug 1894

Jean May VAN HORN Born: Aug 1894

Roxie May MOCK Born: Sep 1894

Alta Blanche CLOWER Born: 21 Sep 1894

Harry V. VAN HORN, JR Born: 15 Oct 1894

Annie E. LYDICK Born: Nov 1894

Wade Blair COON and Bessie Irene MITCHELL Married: Abt. 1895

Mary R. CUNNINGHAM Born: Abt. 1895

Daniel HOUCK and Ella Married: Abt. 1895

Raymond Merle NEVILLE Born: Abt. 1895

Hazel V. HENRY Born: 1895

Ellsworth E. CONDRON Born: Jan 1895

Frank VAN HORN Born: Mar 1895

Glenn F. STEELE Born: Apr 1895

Ira Paul WILT Born: Apr 1895

Lulu Blanche MYERS Born: 22 May 1895

John Irven LIGHTCAP Born: 11 Jun 1895

Charles Dean LYDICK Born: Aug 1895

Walter Merle CONDRON Born: Sep 1895

Helen FRAMPTON Born: Sep 1895

Ethel L. BOSSARD Born: Nov 1895

Helen R. GRUBE Born: Nov 1895

Lulu L. BREZGER Born: Abt. 1896

Edwin CONDRON Born: Abt. 1896

Helen Born: Abt. 1896

Anna L. KLINE Born: Abt. 1896

Harry D. LIGHTCAP Born: Bet. 22 Oct 1896 - 1897

Agnes M. Born: Abt. 1896

Mary N. VAN HORN Born: Jan 1896

Clara WEISS Born: Mar 1896

Homer Wilford MOCK Born: 19 Jun 1896

Eleanor D. WALTER Born: Jul 1896

Lottie P. MYERS Born: Oct 1896

Cecile H. SHEPHARD Born: Nov 1896

Family Map

Curtis Edwin AUL Born: Bet. Nov 1897 - 21 Sep 1898

Ethel WIDDOWSON Born: Abt. 1897

Pearl June HALL Born: 1897

Louise Ernestine YANHKE Born: 1897

Walter Byron FETTERHOFF Born: 21 Jan 1897

Elizabeth B. WALDER Born: 08 Feb 1897

William HOUCK Born: Mar 1897

Katherine VAN HORN Born: Mar 1897

Marion VAN HORN Born: Apr 1897

Albert B. STEELE Born: Jul 1897

Allen BATEMAN Born: Aug 1897

Warren H. VAN HORN Born: Aug 1897

Joseph WILT Born: Aug 1897

Esther L. LIGHTCAP Born: Sep 1897

Dorcas Belle CONDRON Born: Nov 1897

Donald Michael VAN HORN Born: 28 Nov 1897

Margaret BECK Born: Abt. 1898

George L. CONDRON Born: Abt. 1898

Elma Born: Abt. 1898

Edna LANEY Born: Abt. 1898

Pearl SPICHER Born: Abt. 1898

Alvord Boyd STEELE Born: 1898

Mary Edna LAMBING Born: Mar 1898

Byron L. STEAR Born: Mar 1898

Joseph Lucas MYERS Born: 14 Mar 1898

Eva M. BARKER Born: May 1898

Harry L. COON Born: Jun 1898

Mabel J. SHEPHARD Born: Jun 1898

Alverta STEAR Born: Jun 1898

Florence V. ASHCOM Born: Jul 1898

John Reid MCCAUSLAND Born: Jul 1898

Cora Pearl MILLER Born: 25 Aug 1898

James Robert LAMBING Born: 02 Sep 1898

Anna SCHIRRA Born: 10 Oct 1898

Alva WIDDOWSON Born: Abt. 1899

Annie LYDICK Died: 1899

Alice VAN HORN Born: Jan 1899

Dorcas Jane CONDRON Born: Mar 1899

Benjamin VAN HORN Born: Apr 1899

Benjamin O. WILT Born: Apr 1899

Leonard GRUBE Born: May 1899

Florence E. BREWER Born: Jun 1899

Mildred L. VAN HORN Born: Jun 1899

Margaret MORROW Born: 06 Jun 1899

Rosaline LYDICK Born: Abt. 09 Jul 1899

Bertha Della AUL Born: 06 Aug 1899

Lowery HUGHES, JR Born: Sep 1899

Norris Glenn LAMBING Born: Sep 1899

Russell E. VAN HORN Born: Oct 1899

Charles Berton LEWIS Born: 13 Oct 1899

Norman Ernest VAN HORN Born: 16 Oct 1899

Mable GODOWN Born: Nov 1899

Carl PALMER Born: Nov 1899

Family Map

Samuel S. BARKER Born: Abt. 1900

Wilma M. BURKET Born: Abt. 1900

Agnes Culshaw COOLEY Born: Abt. 1900

Annie LAMBING Born: Abt. 1900

Ethel LAMBING Born: Abt. 1900

Eva V. LYDICK Born: Abt. 1900

Nellie E. MCADOO Born: Abt. 1900

William T. SHEPHARD Born: Abt. 1900

John M. WOLFE Born: Abt. 1900

June GRUBE Born: Feb 1900

Moana STEAR Born: Feb 1900

Virginia LYDICK Born: Apr 1900

Nellie Mae CLOWER Born: 19 Apr 1900

Jay McKinley MOCK Born: 03 May 1900

Ralph Hastings VAN HORN Born: 14 Aug 1900

Alice L. BREWER Born: Abt. 1901

Kimmel B. COON Born: Abt. 1901

Emerson C. DILTS Born: Abt. 1901

Laura Born: Abt. 1901

Sloan B. LIGHTCAP Born: Abt. 1901

Sadie MCHANNA Born: Abt. 1901

Vera MUMAN Born: Abt. 1901

Mary ROHAN Born: Abt. 1901

Orcett STEAR Born: Abt. 1901

Charles VAN HORN Born: Abt. 1901

Charles R. WEAVER Born: Abt. 1901

Vada WEAVER Born: Abt. 1901

Blanche WIDDOWSON Born: Abt. 1901

Thomas BANKS Born: 01 May 1901

John Dick VAN HORN Died: 17 Oct 1901

Ula BAILEY Born: Abt. 1902

Lois I. BARKER Born: Abt. 1902

Darrell C. BURKET Born: Abt. 1902

James B. BURKET Born: Abt. 1902

George L. CONDRON Born: Abt. 1902

Loretta Margaret CONDRON Born: Abt. 1902

Jesse C. JACKSON Born: Abt. 1902

John K. McElhoes MORROW Born: Abt. 1902

Clarence R. MYERS Born: Abt. 1902

Adessa M. SHEPHARD Born: Abt. 1902

Vera STEAR Born: Abt. 1902

Arveta T. STEELE Born: Abt. 1902

Inez B. VAN HORN Born: Abt. 1902

Doris V. VAN HORN Born: 02 Jan 1902

Margaret E. DOUDS Born: 27 Aug 1902

Frank Noble LEWIS Born: 27 Sep 1902

Arthur Lee BOSSARD Born: Abt. 1903

Lester V. BROCK Born: Abt. 1903

Lillian A. BURKET Born: Abt. 1903

Zella LAMBING Born: Abt. 1903

Maude LYDICK Born: Abt. 1903

Marion M. MCELHOES Born: Abt. 1903

Loretta E. SHEPHARD Born: Abt. 1903

Family Map

Faye STEAR
Born: Abt. 1903

Weird A. STEAR
Born: Abt. 1903

Homer E. VAN
HORN Born:
Abt. 1903

Minnie VAN
HORN Born:
Abt. 1903

Martha
WEAVER Born:
Abt. 1903

Donald
WIDDOWSON
Born: Abt. 1903

Emma
RITCHEY Died:
21 Mar 1903

Muriel Ruth
BARKER Born:
Abt. 1904

William DOLBY
Born: Abt. 1904

Ralph E.
DURBIN Born:
Abt. 1904

Leo F. GERBER
Born: Abt. 1904

Edna HADDEN
Born: Abt. 1904

Charles G.
LYDICK Born:
Abt. 1904

Lena V. NEAL
Born: Abt. 1904

Walter C.
SHEPHARD
Born: Abt. 1904

Annie C. VAN
HORN Born:
Abt. 1904

Caroline VAN
HORN Born:
Abt. 1904

Edith L. VAN
HORN Born:
Abt. 1904

Ruth
WIDDOWSON
Born: Abt. 1904

Viola Agnes VAN
HORN Born: 09
Oct 1904

Angus Blanchard
CONDRON
Died: 25 Nov
1904

Olive LAMBING
Born: Abt. 1905

Jane E.
MCADOO Born:
Abt. 1905

Dorothy STEAR
Born: Abt. 1905

Jennie VAN
HORN Born:
Abt. 1905

Mary Isabel VAN
HORN Born:
Abt. 1905

Cleone I.
LUKEHART
Born: 1905

Fred W.
BURKET Born:
Abt. Jul 1905

George L. COON
and Minnie Bell
BURKETT
Married: 03 Jul
1905

Bruce Guy
MOCK Born: 06
Dec 1905

Dorothy
MORROW Born:
Bet. 12 Feb - 23
Mar 1905

Dan S. BROCK
Born: Abt. 1906

Harry W.
BURKET Born:
Abt. 1906

Margaret
CONDRON
Born: Abt. 1906

Nova HADDEN
Born: Abt. 1906

Tirza L. VAN
HORN Born:
Abt. 1906

Jennie B.
LYDICK Died:
1906

Edward Harry
VAN HORN and
Edna Leona
MCMINN
Married: 27 Jan
1906

Thelma I. VAN
HORN Born:
Bet. 1906 - 1908

Ellis V. BARKER
Born: Abt. 1907

Clarence Wilbur
BROOKS, JR
Born: Abt. 1907

Paul GRUBE
Born: Abt. 1907

Eva Grace
LIGHTCAP
Born: Abt. 1907

Frayne C.
LYDICK Born:
Abt. 1907

Edward L.
REDPATH Born:
Abt. 1907

Loyd N.
SHEPHARD
Born: Abt. 1907

Dotha C. VAN
HORN Born:
Abt. 1907

Mary Emma
VAN HORN
Born: Abt. 1907

H. Van
KUEHNER
Born: Abt. 1907

Edith
WIDDOWSON
Born: Abt. 1907

Mary WYLAND
Born: Abt. 1907

Family Map

Lawrence Moyes
VAN HORN
Born: 01 Jul 1907

Mable Mildred
AUL Born: 08
Sep 1907

Alma Gertrude
BEATTY Born:
Abt. 1908

Lenora E. BOSH
Born: Abt. 1908

Ruth BROCK
Born: Abt. 1908

Raymond
BURKET Born:
Abt. 1908

Herman
HADDEN Born:
Abt. 1908

Robert G.
MABON Born:
Abt. 1908

Edna MOCK
Born: Abt. 1908

Lysle SHORT
Born: Abt. 1908

Sylvada Born:
Abt. 1908

Chester A. VAN
HORN Born:
Abt. 1908

Estella Laura
VAN HORN
Born: Abt. 1908

Anna Pearl DILL
Born: 1908

Merl F.
COLLINS Born:
Feb 1908

Dorsey Clinton
VAN HORN
Born: 01 Mar
1908

Eleanor
GRIFFITH Born:
Jun 1908

Blaine A.
LYDICK Born:
Abt. Aug 1908

William Thomas
LUKEHART
Born: 07 Nov
1908

Helen BROCK
Born: Bet. 1908 -
1909

Anderson T.
VAN HORN
Died: Bet. 1908 -
1910

Charles Gillis
CONDRON, JR
Born: Abt. 1909

Eleanor Lucile
LEWIS Born:
Abt. 1909

Jay Miller
BURKET and
Irene
HENDERSON
Married: 1909

Mary C. LYDICK
Born: Jan 1909

Cloyd LAMBING
Born: Abt. Mar
1909

Lena Christine
VAN HORN
Born: 02 Jul 1909

Ernest P.
BARKER Born:
Abt. Aug 1909

James K.
MCELHOES
Born: 02 Oct
1909

William Wright
VAN HORN
Born: 24 Oct
1909

Mary G.
ASHCOM Born:
Abt. Dec 1909

Myrtle Linda
AUL Born: Bet.
03 Nov - Dec
1909

George Kenneth
KUEHNER
Born: Bet. Jun -
04 Oct 1909

Lila GEARHART
Born: Bef. 1910

Marie
HAMILTON
Born: Bef. 1910

Norman
HAMILTON
Born: Bef. 1910

Wilber Lightcap
BEATTY Born:
Abt. 1910

William Alexander
BURKET, JR
Born: Abt. 1910

Gertrude
GEARHART
Born: Abt. 1910

Helen HADDEN
Born: Abt. 1910

Blaine MABON
Born: Abt. 1910

Gertrude MOCK
Born: Abt. 1910

Paul R.
REDPATH Born:
Abt. 1910

Charles STEELE
Born: Abt. 1910

Blaine Keller
STEWART Born:
Abt. 1910

Audrey VAN
HORN Born:
Abt. 1910

Gretchen
BROOKS Born:
Abt. Jan 1910

Harry Paul
BURKET Born:
Jan 1910

Myrtle MOCK
Born: Abt. Feb
1910

Bella E.
SHEPHARD
Born: Abt. Feb
1910

Family Map

Harold L. NEAL
Born: Feb 1910

Dorothy Virginia
BALLANTYNE
Born: 10 Aug
1910

Delbert Clair
HARTZELL
Born: 16 Nov
1910

Clyde Burnell
HOOVER Born:
Dec 1910

Charles B.
BROOKS Born:
Abt. 1911

Nellie J.
BURKET Born:
Abt. 1911

Russell GRUBE
Born: Abt. 1911

Naomi
LAMBING Born:
Abt. 1911

Lenore B. LIAS
Born: Abt. 1911

Myrna E.
LYDICK Born:
Abt. 1911

Roberta Born:
Abt. 1911

Minta STEAR
Born: Abt. 1911

Edith Nadine
STEWART Born:
Abt. 1911

Albert J.
WYLAND Born:
Abt. 1911

Lois Mildred
BEATTY Born:
Abt. 1912

Clarence J.
CONDRON
Born: Abt. 1912

Bernice A.
LYDICK Born:
Abt. 1912

Leola
M.LUKEHART
Born: Abt. 1912

Donald E.
STEAR Born:
Abt. 1912

Mary STEELE
Born: Abt. 1912

Evaline VAN
HORN Born:
Abt. 1912

Hazel M. VAN
HORN Born:
Abt. 1912

Sophia VAN
HORN Born:
Abt. 1912

James C.
BALLANTYNE
Born: 07 Sep 1912

Walter Morris
VAN HORN
Born: Bet. 19 Mar
- Dec 1912

Wilmer C.
MABON Born:
Abt. 1913

Emerson MOCK
Born: Abt. 1913

Helen HILL
Born: 1913

Frank Martin
ASHCOM Born:
Abt. 1914

James Harold
BEATTY Born:
Abt. 1914

Lloyd E.
HOOVER Born:
Abt. 1914

Ira M.
LUKEHART
Born: Abt. 1914

Thomas MOCK
Born: Abt. 1914

Charlotte
Elizabeth
REDPATH Born:
Abt. 1914

Carrie Etta VAN
HORN Born:
Abt. 1914

Charles VAN
HORN Born:
Abt. 1914

Frances
WYLAND Born:
Abt. 1914

Marjorie May
RANKIN Born:
1914

Marjorie May
RANKIN Died:
1914

Lucinda
HUTCHISON
Died: 23 Mar
1914

William G.
MORROW, JR
Born: Abt. Oct
1914

Robert Lee Claire
VAN HORN and
Mary Elizabeth
BROWN
Married: Nov
1914

James Van Horn
BALLANTYNE,
JR Born: 24 Nov
1914

Paul LAMBING
Born: Bet. 1914 -
1925

Deane A.
BENTLEY Born:
Abt. 1915

Vincent K.
BROOKS Born:
Abt. 1915

Bert M. MABON
Born: Abt. 1915

Delores Ariel
SHEPHARD
Born: Abt. 1915

Beryl VAN
HORN Born:
Abt. 1915

Family Map

William Rowe PRICE Born: 1915

Gwendolyn E. REARICH Born: 1915

Thelma Imogene ASHCOM Born: Abt. Dec 1915

Eugene Wesley ASHCOM and Beulah E. Married: Abt. 1916

Harry W. VAN HORN Born: 14 Jan 1916

Audrey M. LYDICK Born: Feb 1916

Lisa WYLAND Born: Abt. Mar 1916

Owen DeLone VAN HORNE Born: 06 Mar 1916

Charles WIDDOWSON Died: Bet. 1916 - 1929

Genieve VAN HORN Born: Abt. 1917

Edith Marie KECK Born: 1917

Oliver G. LYDICK Born: 19 Mar 1917

Dale VAN HORN Born: 26 Jun 1917

Mable Mildred AUL Died: 26 Nov 1917

Naomi MOCK Born: Abt. 1918

Carl Rigg BALLANTYNE Born: 10 Mar 1918

Ruby L. FETTERHOFF Born: 27 Mar 1918

Raymond Walter STANTON Born: 28 Aug 1918

Elmer Byron FETTERHOFF Born: Abt. 1919

Martha E. REDPATH Born: Abt. 1919

Ida VAN HORN Born: Abt. 1919

Phillip HUTCHISON Died: 1919

Helen WYLAND Born: Jan 1919

Marion L. EGGERS Born: 10 Jul 1919

Margaret STANTON Born: 14 Oct 1919

Jesse MOCK Born: Abt. 1920

Margaret Mary VAN HORN Died: Abt. 1920

Donald Lloyd KECK Born: 1920

Rosemary RANKIN Born: 01 Apr 1920

Edna Faye WYLAND Born: Abt. 1921

Wanda Louise KECK Born: 1921

Margaret Eliabeth VAN HORN Born: 02 Feb 1921

Florence Jane MCCAUSLAND Born: 26 Dec 1921

Robert E. VAN HORN Born: 28 Jan 1922

Charles Andrew FERRIER and Esther M. MCADOO Married: 18 Sep 1922

Charles MOCK Born: Abt. 1923

James N. REDPATH Born: Abt. 1923

Richard Glenn VAN HORN Born: 08 Jan 1923

Arthur Melvin AUL Born: Abt. 1924

Pearl M. FETTERHOFF Born: Abt. 1924

Oliver WYLAND Born: Abt. 1924

Donald Reid MCCAUSLAND Born: 14 May 1924

Michael RUSNICA Born: 29 Jun 1924

Donald Paul BUTTERBAUGH Born: 26 Oct 1924

Theodore Blaine KECK Born: 1925

Athelia Grace SHANKLE Born: 1925

Hubert VAN HORN Born: 09 May 1925

Walter M. EDGE, JR Born: 17 Jun 1925

Family Map

Ferne Ellen AIRGOOD Born: 26 Sep 1925

Mary Jane FERRIER Born: Abt. Nov 1925

Raymond E. VAN HORN Born: Apr 1926

Virginia E. VAN HORN Born: 10 Aug 1926

William S. BUTTERBAUGH Born: Abt. 1927

Robert C. VAN HORN Born: Mar 1928

Ambrose Kelly STEAR Died: 24 Nov 1928

Herbert BOWSER Born: 04 Mar 1929

James M. LAMBING Born: 27 May 1929

Richard WYLAND Born: Abt. Jul 1929

Harry MOCK Born: Feb 1930

William H. VAN HORN Born: Feb 1930

Grace Lucille MCCAUSLAND Born: 08 Aug 1930

Richard MOCK Born: Aft. 1930

Dorothy M. KLINGENSMIT H Born: 27 Jun 1931

Nancy Jane TOMB Died: 22 May 1933

Glenn LeRoy VAN HORN Born: 20 Aug 1933

Wilbur Bennett VAN HORN and Mildred Wenona ADAMSON Married: 16 Nov 1933

Joyce Eleanor KECK Born: 1934

Dorothy Jean MCCAUSLAND Born: 10 Sep 1934

Clara Jane KECK Born: 1935

David Blanchard STEAR Died: 04 Sep 1936

Shirley Ann MCCAUSLAND Born: 16 Sep 1936

William D. LYDICK Died: 1937

Blaine W. VAN HORN and Ruth WALTZ Married: 25 Dec 1947

James Van Horn BALLANTYNE Died: 07 Jan 1948

Melinda VAN HORN Born: 30 Oct 1953

Harry V. VAN HORN Died: 11 Nov 1953

Kenneth Allan VAN HORN Born: 05 Apr 1955

Kenneth Allan VAN HORN Died: 06 Apr 1955

Harold V. HARKCOM VAN HORN Died: Abt. 1958

Agnes B. MOYES Died: Aft. 1961

Gary Lee STEWART Died: 08 Jul 1964

John Raymond ASHCOM Died: 14 Jul 1965

Delsa Joan SHANKLE Died: 14 Feb 1968

Carrie Etta VAN HORN Died: 03 Dec 1968

Donald Michael VAN HORN Died: 1970

Lester Carl JOHNSTON Died: 17 Sep 1975

Effie Golda VAN HORN Died: 22 Sep 1980

Hazel V. HENRY Died: 1985

Glenn LeRoy VAN HORN Died: 31 Jan 1988

Helen Louise VAN HORN Died: 08 Sep 1990

Elizabeth B. WALDER Died: Mar 1991

Anna SCHIRRA Died: 03 Dec 1993

Robert E. VAN HORN Died: 30 May 1995

William L. JOHNSTON Died: 10 Jul 1996

Dorothy M. KLINGENSMIT H Died: 14 May 1997

Family Map

Blair I. SHANK, JR Died: 05 Apr 2003

Michael RUSNICA Died: 11 Apr 2007

See Also Ohio, New Jersey, West Virginia, Maryland, New York, Indiana, Connecticut, Rhode Island, and Massachusetts.

Perry Co., OH (322 Mi NE of Posey Co.)

Jane ANDERSON Died: Bet. 1831 - 1833

William FISHER and Mary MCCULLOUGH Married: 1833

Philadelphia, Philadelphia Co., PA

Marion HILTON

William M. MEHLHORN and Marion HILTON

Paulus VAN VLECK and Jannetje VAN DYKE Married: 11 Jul 1711

Johannes Barentsen VAN HOORN and Rebecca VANDEGRIFT Married: 20 Apr 1718

Isaiah VAN ZANT and Margaret THOMPSON Married: 06 Jun 1732

Isaiah VAN ZANT and Gertje Charity VAN HOORN Married: Bet. 06 Apr - Jun 1732

Gabriel Pieterson VAN HOORN and Martha BREISFORD Married: 04 Mar 1737

Joseph JACKSON and Eleanor VAN HOORN Married: 17 Jun 1737

Bernard VAN HOORN and Patience HELLINGS Married: 13 Jul 1737

Barent VAN HOORN and Patience HELLINGS Married: 13 Jul 1737

Peter Peterson VAN HOORN and Grace STACKHOUSE Married: 23 Oct 1740

Daniel FISCHER Born: 1745

Johannes Barentsen VAN HOORN Died: 15 Feb 1758

Johannes VAN HOORN and Margaret PEARSON Married: 01 Mar 1762

John MCELHOES Died: 1791

Alfred Roland VAN HORN Born: 1829

William Bell VAN HORN Born: Apr 1830

Matilda VAN HORN Born: 1834

Christiana APPO Born: 20 Apr 1836

Maria VAN HORN Born: 1837

Lawrence JOHNSON and Mary WINDER Married: 29 May 1837

Lawrence JOHNSON Died: 26 Apr 1860

Harry C. VAN HORN Born: 22 Sep 1867

Horace Miller VAN HORN Born: 14 Oct 1888

Silas W. LIGHTCAP Died: 13 Feb 1911

Jennie Elizabeth BAIREY Died: 29 Dec 1953

Pierre, Hughes Co., SD

Carl S. KITTLESON and Inez Vernal VAN HORN Married: 1952

Inez Vernal VAN HORN Died: 21 Oct 1985

Carl S. KITTLESON Died: 31 Mar 1996

Family Map

Pinellas Co., FL

Tabitha Logan VAN HORN Died: 1950

Pinellas Park, Pinellas Co., FL (210 Mi NW of Miami)

Ruth Loraine BERRY Died: 12 Feb 2001

Piqua, Miami Co., OH (293 Mi SE of Ogle Co.)

Thomas Budd VAN HORNE and Elizabeth CHAPEZE Married: 31 Dec 1830

Enos Van Horne FRENCH Born: 03 Apr 1848

Elizabeth CHAPEZE Died: 10 Jan 1858

Pittsburgh, Allegheny Co., PA

William VAN HOORN Died: 13 Oct 1807

Charles Barclay COON Died: 14 Mar 1904

Mary Elizabeth ASHCOM Born: 24 Jun 1917

Frank Phillip MARKLEY and Jean May VAN HORN Married: Bef. 1920

John Raymond ASHCOM, JR Born: 03 May 1924

Augustus Kimmel COON Died: 19 Sep 1929

Walter Morris VAN HORN and Evelyn Florence HUSTON Married: 16 Nov 1932

Walter Morris VAN HORN Died: 21 Sep 1968

Norman Hamilton STEELE Died: Jul 1970

Walter Malcolm EDGE Died: Aug 1972

Callie S. MCCAUSLAND Died: 28 Nov 1972

Laura B. SHROADS Died: 1979

Paul BUTTERBAUG H Died: 18 Aug 1980

Robert Clark MCCAUSLAND Died: 11 Mar 1992

Fred Likens HUTZLER Died: 30 Mar 1994

Annabelle WEAVER Died: 22 Jul 1996

Ralph Hastings VAN HORN Died: 06 Apr 1997

James Van Horn BALLANTYNE, JR Died: 28 Dec 1999

Effie V. BARNETT Died: 11 Jul 2000

Piute Co., UT

Myrtle Irene HARDY Born: 28 Jun 1896

Pomeroy, Meigs Co., OH (320 Mi NE of Posey Co.)

Robert Thompson VAN HORN and Adela Honeywood COOLEY Married: 22 Dec 1848

Caleb Henry VAN HORN Born: 24 May 1850

Richard VAN HORN Born: 15 Nov 1851

Robert Cannon VAN HORN Born: 26 Jul 1853

Port Angeles, Clallam Co., WA

Thelma Evelyn VAN HORN Died: 18 Oct 1994

Port Huron, Saint Clair Co., MI (356 Mi NE of Ogle Co.)

Laurence Robert FREDERICK Born: 09 Dec 1908

Portage Co., OH

Carney Vance HARKCOM Died: Dec 1969

Family Map

Portland, Multnomah Co., OR

Geraldine STANTON Died: 21 May 2008

Portsmouth, VA

Olive Marion VAN HORN Died: 19 Mar 2000

Posey Co., IN

Adam FISHER Died: 18 Apr 1877

Golda May DIXON Born: 18 Aug 1888

See Also Harrison Co., Clark Co., Perry Co., Lewis Co., Mercer Co., Fairfield Co., Kansas City, Zanesville, Lost Creek, Pomeroy, Rolla, Benton, Murphy, Wilkesboro, Equality, Springfield, Evansville, Athens, Williamstown, Clarksburg, Harrisonville, West Frankfort, Fayetteville, and Fort Smith.

Potter Co., TX

Homer Vernon POINTER Died: 13 Feb 1948

Alvin Everett POINTER Died: 20 Feb 1959

See Also Dallas, Dalhart, Rocky Ford, Lawton, Santa Fe, Amarillo, Fort Worth, Roy, Albuquerque, Richardson, Walters, Wichita, and Las Cruces.

Presho, Lyman Co., SD

Walter Duval VAN HORN Born: 06 Jan 1893

Carl S. KITTLESON Born: 1904

Walter Duval VAN HORN and Nan C. CORCORAN Married: 01 Jun 1926

Pueblo, Pueblo Co., CO

Hubert Robert WORK, JR Born: 22 May 1894

Dorcas Logan WORK Born: 30 Sep 1896

Robert Van Horn WORK Born: 23 Apr 1898

Quincy, Branch Co., MI (227 Mi E of Ogle Co.)

Rosina M. HUMMEL Died: 23 Mar 1908

Randolph Co., WV

Grace GRIFFITH Born: 01 Feb 1905

Ravenna, Portage Co., OH

Lyle Bennett VAN HORN Died: 20 Apr 1986

Rexford, Thomas Co., KS

Homer Vernon POINTER Born: 17 Mar 1895

Sarah Dorcas SINK Died: Bet. 25 Aug 1925 - 1926

Elsie Estelle MCAFOOS Died: 08 Apr 1940

Hugh Albert MCAFOOS Died: 03 Mar 1942

Rhode Island (NE of Pennsylvania)

Harriett Wells CARPENTER Born: Abt. 1865

Richardson, Dallas Co., TX (340 Mi SE of Potter Co.)

John Dwight WEEKS Died: 15 Oct 1991

Richboro, Bucks Co., PA

Williamtje VAN DYKE Died: 06 May 1760

Richland Co., SC

Mildred Heavlyn BOBBITT Died: 19 Oct 2000

Ridgeway, Winneshiek Co., IA (161 Mi NW of Ogle Co.)

Elmira Solle ARMSTRONG Born: 27 Aug 1878

Rochester, Beaver Co., PA

Family Map

Lawrence David AUL and Nova Jane MINSER Married: 08 Aug 1941

Annie P. VAN HORN Died: 07 Apr 1969

William Clair JOHNSTON Died: 19 Oct 1986

Rockingham Co., VA

Jacob HIESTAND Born: Bet. 03 Nov 1787 - 1791

Rockland Co., NY

Sarah BLAUVELT Born: 1756

Rocky Ford, Otero Co., CO (207 Mi NW of Potter Co.)

Robert M. DOUGLAS Born: 09 Dec 1901

Margaret Van Horn DOUGLAS Died: 16 Nov 1906

Gail Leigh DOUGLAS Died: 30 Nov 1906

Rolla, Phelps Co., MO (214 Mi SW of Posey Co.)

Avis Ruth WOLF Died: 04 Oct 1980

Phillip Michael BORTHACYRE II Born: 17 Apr 1987

Phillip Michael BORTHACYRE II Died: 15 Mar 2006

Roy, Harding Co., NM (134 Mi NW of Potter Co.)

Henry Coulter VAN HORN and Ethel Mae Married: 1921

Rutherford, Bergen Co., NJ

Robert A. BELL Died: 30 Jun 1957

Sarah VAN HORN Died: 21 Jun 1970

Sagamore, Armstrong Co., PA

Lawrence David AUL Born: 27 Jul 1912

Floyd William AUL Born: Abt. 1914

Ralph Lee AUL Born: Bet. Nov 1917 - 18 Jan 1918

Ruby Mae MCCAUSLAND Born: 15 Feb 1919

Robert Clark MCCAUSLAND Born: 12 Jul 1920

Ernest Glenn GOOD Born: 11 Dec 1920

Clair Eugene MCCAUSLAND Born: 27 Jun 1926

Eugene Monroe WAGNER Born: 14 Apr 1931

Saint Cloud, Osceola Co., FL

Anna STAFFORD Died: 17 Apr 1966

Saint John, Canada

Patience Ann ANDERSON Born: 29 Oct 1876

Saint Marys, Elk Co., PA

Emery Ernest VAN HORN Died: 02 Sep 1996

Saint Marys, Pottawatomie Co., KS

Dorothy M. MCAFOOS Born: 01 Feb 1922

Warren Alfred MILLER Died: 14 Apr 2003

Dorothy M. MCAFOOS Died: 01 Jan 2010

Saint Petersburg, Pinellas Co., FL (206 Mi NW of Miami)

Mary Verne BARR Died: 28 Feb 1966

James C. BALLANTYNE Died: 30 Jun 1993

Carl Rigg BALLANTYNE Died: 17 Aug 1993

Salem, Salem Co., NJ

Peter Peterson VAN HOORN Died: 10 Sep 1789

Family Map

**Salt Lake City,
Salt Lake Co.,
UT**

David VanHorn
BENNETT Died:
27 Mar 1895

**Saltsburg,
Indiana Co.,
PA**

James Clifford
SERENE Born:
Oct 1870

Owen Meridith
SERENE Born:
15 Jul 1899

Ruth Margaret
JOHNSTON
Born: 10 May
1903

Owen Meridith
SERENE Died:
14 Jan 1951

James Clifford
SERENE Died:
Aft. 1951

**Sampson Co.,
NC**

Archibald J.
STEWART Died:
18 Mar 1865

**San
Bernardino,
San
Bernardino
Co., CA**

Dale VAN
HORN Died: 10
Jun 1992

**San Francisco,
San Francisco
Co., CA**

Louis Albert
LININGER
Born: 23 Jul 1901

**Santa Clara,
Santa Clara
Co., CA**

Frank P.
ALBANO and
Anna Sampson
BENT Married:
09 Jun 1962

**Santa Fe,
Santa Fe Co.,
NM (228 Mi
NW of Potter
Co.)**

Oscar Alvin
MCAFOOS Died:
Sep 1974

**Sarasota,
Sarasota Co.,
FL (180 Mi
NW of Miami)**

Gertude Agnes
SULLEY Died:
27 Oct 1988

**Sargent Co.,
ND**

Roy H. BOWSER
Born: Abt. 1899

Ralph R.
BOWSER Born:
29 Nov 1900

Lillie V.
BOWSER Born:
Abt. 1907

Frank A.
BOWSER Born:
Abt. 1910

Ralph R.
BOWSER Died:
10 Mar 1929

**Scotch Plains,
Union Co., NJ**

Thomas Budd
VAN HORNE
Born: 01 Jun 1783

**Seaside,
Clatsop Co.,
OR**

Virginia Audrey
BOWERS Died:
30 Jul 2007

**Sebring,
Highlands
Co., FL (142
Mi NW of
Miami)**

Shirley Mae
NEAL Died: 24
Jan 2005

**Seneca Co.,
OH**

Leafy Fern VAN
HORN Born:
Bet. 17 Dec 1885
- 1886

Emma Ellen
HUMMEL Died:
04 Jan 1887

**Shanghai,
Berkeley Co.,
WV**

Mary Pearl
HUTZLER Born:
1870

Charles Strother
HUTZLER Born:
21 Aug 1872

William Logan
HUTZLER Born:
1874

Nannie Mae
HUTZLER Born:
14 Mar 1877

Ernest Irvin
HUTZLER Born:
13 Jul 1879

Thettie Jane
HUTZLER Born:
Bet. 30 Nov 1881
- 1882

John Milton
HUTZLER Born:
18 Jul 1884

Harwood
Chapman
HUTZLER Born:
Bet. 26 Jan - Jun
1887

Howard Calvin
HUTZLER Born:
Bet. Jan - 26 Jun
1887

George Sherman
HUTZLER Born:
11 Jul 1889

Family Map

John William HUTZLER Died: 19 Jan 1914

Roseannah VAN HORN Died: 02 May 1926

Jeremiah M. UNGER Died: 14 Jul 1945

Shippenville, Clarion Co., PA

Eleanor SMITH Died: Oct 1980

Shrewsbury, Monmouth Co., NJ

Jacob DAVIS Born: 04 Nov 1769

Sarah HOFFMAN Born: 15 Dec 1796

Somerset, Somerset Co., NJ

Fanny CONINE Born: Abt. 1801

South Carolina (NE of Georgia)

Sophia A. Born: Abt. 1817

South Dakota (NW of Iowa)

R. Vandall VAN HORN

Frank Avery VAN HORN Born: 14 Sep 1884

Marguerita E. VAN HORN Born: Abt. 1887

Jeannette M. VAN HORN Born: Jul 1894

Aura CUMMINGS Born: Aft. 1894

Katherine V. VAN HORN Born: Abt. 1895

Gustave N. ANDERSON and Nora VAN HORN Married: Abt. 1897

Martin Harry CUMMINGS Born: 14 Jan 1899

Neva Emma ANDERSON Born: 18 Dec 1902

Mabel VAN HORN Born: 1903

Ruth B. CUMMINGS Born: Abt. 1904

Iva Verone VAN HORN Born: Abt. 1904

Ralph MITCHELL Born: Abt. 1905

Wilhemina VAN HORN Born: 1905

Inez Vernal VAN HORN Born: 06 Apr 1905

J. Alfred ANDERSON Born: Abt. 1906

Marion F. FRICK Born: Abt. 1906

Ward VAN HORN Born: 1906

Rhoda A. CUMMINGS Born: Abt. 1907

Mildred D. VAN HORN Born: Abt. 1907

Francis VAN HORN Born: 1909

Opal Leone VAN HORN Born: Abt. 1910

Nora VAN HORN Died: Aft. 1930

Joy Avis VAN HORN Died: Unknown

Southampton, Bucks Co., PA

Isaiah VAN ZANT

Isaiah VAN ZANT Born: 1712

Isaiah VAN ZANT Died: 1786

Spokane, Spokane Co., WA

Levint Leveritt VAN HORN Died: 09 Dec 1944

Springfield, Greene Co., MO (304 Mi SW of Posey Co.)

Thomas CLARK Died: 1862

Stanislaus Co., CA

Steven Edward MARINKO Died: 27 Jul 1990

Stanley Co., SD

Theodore WAGNER Born: Abt. 1899

Family Map

Staten Island, Richmond Co., NY

Williamtje VAN DYKE Born: 04 Jul 1681

Sarah VAN PELT Born: 06 Dec 1719

Sun City, Maricopa Co., AZ

Florence Loretta VAN HORN Died: Unknown

Swissvale, Allegheny Co., PA

George Edward MILLIKEN Born: 13 Jul 1910

Tarentum, Allegheny Co., PA

Merle Wayne VAN HORN Died: 28 Aug 1948

Teaneck, Bergen Co., NJ

Marytje VAN HOORN Born: 02 Jul 1705

Tennessee (NE of Arkansas)

William M. HECK Born: Abt. 1855

Alice Born: Abt. 1887

Texas

Hubert WRIGHT Born: Abt. 1900

Samuel Cornelius VAN HORN and Teressa Married: Abt. 1932

Thomas Co., KS

Oscar Alvin MCAFOOS Born: 27 Jun 1887

Clarence Everett MCAFOOS Born: 31 Aug 1890

Ella Mary MCAFOOS Born: Bet. 19 Aug 1893 - 1896

Roy Harold MCAFOOS Born: 09 Sep 1900

Tioga, Tioga Co., PA

Anna STAFFORD Born: 1891

Toledo, Lucas Co., OH (297 Mi SE of Ogle Co.)

Mary B. HUMMEL Died: 10 Apr 1903

Bruce Douglas SCHIMMEL Born: 20 Dec 1956

Bruce Douglas SCHIMMEL Died: Bet. 29 - 30 Jan 1958

Sheldon Henry SCHIMMEL Died: 05 Oct 2001

Norma Davene HUDSON Died: 27 May 2007

Toms River, Ocean Co., NJ

Marion L. EGGERS Died: 25 Sep 1990

Harry W. VAN HORN Died: 24 Sep 1992

Tonawanda, Erie Co., NY

Frank O. VAN HORN Died: 08 Jul 1971

Topeka, Shawnee Co., KS

John L. MOORE, DD Died: 23 Jan 1878

Trenton, Mercer Co., NJ

James R. COOPER, MD

Trumbull Co., OH

Alta J. DICKEN Born: 13 Jul 1886

Tucson, Pima Co., AZ

Floyd William AUL Died: 02 Dec 1977

Violet Mae GAMBEL Died: 10 Sep 1979

Twin Falls, Twin Falls Co., ID

Margaret VAN HORN Died: 21 Oct 1909

Tyrone, Blair Co., PA

William Francis LUKEHART Born: 19 Oct 1888

Family Map

Utah

Idonna Born: Abt. 1899

Mildred Agnes MARTIN Born: Abt. 1904

Don Mitchell COON and Myrtle Irene HARDY Married: Bef. 1920

Kimmel B. COON and Mildred Agnes MARTIN Married: Abt. 1925

Utica, Oneida Co., NY

William C. ADAMS Born: Bet. 08 Jan 1874 - 1875

Valdosta, Lowndes Co., GA

Margaret Jeane BROYLES Born: 24 Jul 1943

Margaret Jeane BROYLES Died: 15 Jul 2006

Vandergrift, Westmoreland Co., PA

Stella BARR Died: 06 Jun 1961

Venice, Sarasota Co., FL (167 Mi NW of Miami)

Ruth Margaret JOHNSTON Died: 28 May 1981

Verona, Allegheny Co., PA

Olive Florence CONDRON Born: 25 Aug 1892

Charles Gillis CONDRON Died: 09 Aug 1928

Belle Clifford HILL Died: 03 Jul 1950

Vigo Co., IN (203 Mi SE of Ogle Co.)

William Lynn BROOKS Died: 03 Mar 1993

Virginia

Jacob HIESTAND Born: 1760

Susannah ANDRICK Born: Bet. 1797 - 1799

Mary A. Born: 30 Apr 1808

James A. FISHER Born: 1818

George W. FISHER Born: 1819

Harriet H. FISHER Born: 1822

Hannah A. WILLIAMS Born: Aug 1828

James Devin VAN HORN Died: 1864

Alexander VAN HORN, JR Died: 27 Jun 1866

George Drury CATLETT Born: 1867

Mary B. LYNN Born: 1879

Odessa MCCARTY Born: Abt. 1881

James E. HARE Born: Abt. 1888

Lila Mae BILLMYER Born: 02 Aug 1920

Eli TANNEHILL Died: 1964

See Also Kentucky, North Carolina, and Delaware.

Wabash, Wabash Co., IN (200 Mi SE of Ogle Co.)

Margaret Alice ANDERSON Born: 08 Apr 1922

Waldron, Hillsdale Co., MI (252 Mi SE of Ogle Co.)

Harvey T. HUMMEL Died: 1948

Walker Co., GA

Gertude Agnes SULLEY Born: 04 Mar 1895

Walters, Cotton Co., OK (216 Mi SE of Potter Co.)

Davis Macy WOLF Died: 14 Dec 1973

Warren, Trumbull Co., OH

Hannah Mahala HUMMEL Died: 11 Oct 1925

Alta J. DICKEN Died: 22 Feb 1938

Family Map

Harry A. STROHL Died: 25 Mar 1966

Warren, Warren Co., PA

Belle Clifford HILL Born: 26 Apr 1872

William Gillespie MORROW, MD Died: 01 Feb 1932

Warsaw, Gallatin Co., KY (322 Mi SE of Ogle Co.)

Malcolm Berger FRANK and Marianna WOLF Married: 05 Jul 1937

Washington

Elizabeth E. VAN HORN Born: Feb 1891

Henry Coulter VAN HORN Died: 01 Dec 1919

See Also Montana.

Washington, DC

Susannah G. CALDWELL Born: Abt. 1856

Reberta E. VAN HORN Born: Abt. 1878

Roberta STEWART Born: 23 Mar 1886

John G. STEWART Born: 30 Dec 1890

William G. STEWART Died: Bet. 12 Jan - 02 Nov 1890

Mary Mabel STEWART Born: Aug 1892

John Alexander STEWART Died: 09 Jan 1899

Laura May ARBUCKLE Died: May 1924

Mary BARBER Died: 15 Feb 1940

Jennie Elizabeth VAN HORN Died: 01 Apr 1952

Washington, Washington Co., PA

Enos FRENCH Born: 21 Jun 1810

Nancy MCELHOES Born: 06 Mar 1817

Washington Co., MD

Hugh Samuel HUTZLER and Mary Virginia WILSON Married: 26 Jun 1930

Washington Co., RI

Theodore Julian VAN HORN and Harriett Wells CARPENTER Married: 19 Jul 1898

Amy Doris VAN HORN Born: 24 Oct 1899

Theodore Julian VAN HORN Died: Aft. 1930

Waynesville, Warren Co., OH (323 Mi SE of Ogle Co.)

Henry Coulter VAN HORN Born: Bet. 07 Sep 1884 - 1885

Wellsburg, Brooke Co., WV

Andrew Glenn VAN HORN and Nellie Mae CLOWER Married: 01 Jan 1917

Wellsville, Allegany Co., NY

George H. SHEPHARD Died: 17 Mar 1973

Eunice W. KIFFER Died: 01 Jun 1983

Welton, Clinton Co., IA (66 Mi SW of Ogle Co.)

Obadiah Davis VAN HORN and Eliza Arminda HARKNESS Married: 11 Nov 1855

George VAN HORN Born: Abt. 1858

Jesse Erwin VAN HORN Born: Abt. 1860

Lewis Alexander VAN HORN Born: 31 Oct 1860

Edwin Burtel VAN HORN Born: Bet. 1860 - 1861

William Lawson VAN HORN Born: 02 Feb 1862

673

Family Map

Calista T. VAN HORN Died: 15 Nov 1863

Orin VAN HORN Died: 25 Nov 1863

Sylvanus D. VAN HORN Died: 29 Nov 1863

Joseph J. VAN HORN Died: 13 Dec 1863

Ulysess Sherman VAN HORN Born: 1865

Frank E. VAN HORN Born: 04 Jan 1865

Prudence DAVIS Died: 14 Jan 1867

Francis Marion VAN HORN and Melinda Finch DAVIS Married: 06 Jun 1867

Effie VAN HORN Born: 08 Jul 1868

Effie VAN HORN Died: 23 Jul 1868

Maleta Alice HURLY Born: 14 Nov 1868

Job VAN HORN, JR Died: 25 Dec 1869

Ernest VAN HORN Died: 13 Aug 1871

Nettie M. VAN HORN Born: 01 Feb 1872

Elizabeth DAVIS Died: 22 Dec 1872

Bernard Harrison VAN HORN Died: 08 Jan 1874

Edson Grant VAN HORN Died: 05 Apr 1877

Edna Mabel VAN HORN Born: 20 Dec 1888

Amaranda Rachel LOOFBURROW Died: 25 Jun 1889

Ai VAN HORN Died: 09 Jul 1889

John Black VAN HORN Died: 1900

Francis Marion VAN HORN Died: 20 Nov 1902

Buena Geraldine DAVIS Born: 09 Feb 1903

Martha BABCOCK Died: 1916

West Frankfort, Franklin Co., IL (61 Mi SW of Posey Co.)

Mazella I. VAN HORN Died: 30 Jun 1951

West Hickory, Forest Co., PA

Gertrude MCELHOES Died: 26 Mar 1907

West Orange, Essex Co., NJ

Frank Wesley JONES and Lenora Deborah SCHWARZ Married: 15 Oct 1919

West Virginia (SW of Pennsylvania)

Arienne A. COMEGIST Born: Abt. 1826

Luther Brainard WHITHAM Born: 28 Mar 1840

Margaret A. Born: Abt. 1861

Martha V. Born: Abt. 1861

Mary Ellen FETZER Born: Bet. Feb 1866 - 1870

Wesley D. SLONAKER Born: Abt. 1867

Lucy Born: Aug 1872

Florence E. VAN HORN Born: Dec 1878

Roberta E. VAN HORN Born: Dec 1880

William Clark PRICE Born: 1882

August VAN HORN Born: 28 Feb 1882

Charles VAN HORN Born: Sep 1884

Frank VAN HORN Born: Sep 1884

Carla VAN HORN Born: Jul 1885

Virginia GAGEBY Born: Jun 1888

Goldie A. CROWL Born: Abt. 1889

Family Map

Ethel VAN
HORN Born:
Abt. 1889

Vallie V. Born:
Abt. 1893

Margaret Picolla
Van Horn
GAGEBY Born:
Abt. 1894

Daniel H. VAN
HORN Born: Sep
1895

William H.
STANLEY Born:
Abt. 1896

Hazel G. Born:
Abt. 1897

Rose Jane
GAGEBY Born:
Jan 1897

Forest W.
MCBEE Born:
Mar 1898

Sadie A. VAN
HORN Born: Feb
1899

Anna M. MCBEE
Born: Abt. 1900

Nellie Born: 1900

Henry G.
MCBEE Born:
Abt. 1901

Rosalie
HUTZLER Born:
1901

Alonzo Curtis
VAN HORN
Born: Abt. 1902

Bertha Melissa
GAGEBY Born:
20 Jan 1902

Lebben W.
MCBEE Born:
Abt. 1903

John D.
GAGEBY Born:
Abt. 1904

Herbert L.
MCBEE Born:
Abt. 1905

Dora F. VAN
HORN Born:
Abt. 1905

Adrian
HUTZLER Born:
Abt. 1907

Berta Blanche
VAN HORN
Born: Abt. 1907

Eual B. MCBEE
Born: Abt. Mar
1909

Evelyn I. VAN
HORN Born:
Abt. 1910

Mildred VAN
HORN Born:
Abt. 1910

George William
Francis
GAGEBY Born:
Abt. 1911

Evelyn V. Born:
Abt. 1911

Earl W. VAN
HORN Born:
Abt. 1911

Katherine V.
HUTZLER Born:
Abt. 1912

Ira G. MCBEE
Born: Abt. 1912

Daniel H. VAN
HORN and Hazel
G. Married: Abt.
1919

John Milton
HUTZLER Died:
24 Jul 1965

**Westmoreland
Co., PA**

Martha
THOMPSON
Born: 1770

David Wade
WAKEFIELD
Born: 03 Feb
1796

William WORK
Born: 10 Dec
1800

Martha
HAMILTON
Born: 02 Jun 1803

David Wade
WAKEFIELD
and Susan
WILSON
Married: 25 Aug
1818

Robert
HAMILTON
Died: 15 Sep 1829

Ann
HUTCHISON
Died: 1840

Lida Carrie RIGG
Born: 06 Aug
1880

James Van Horn
BALLANTYNE
Born: 13 Oct
1881

Charles Franklin
REDPATH Born:
25 Sep 1883

Howard Covode
ASHBAUGH
Born: 30 Jun 1885

John Wesley
BALLANTYNE
Born: 21 Jul 1885

Annie VAN
HORN Born: 11
Apr 1886

John Dick VAN
HORN Born: 19
May 1889

Viola Virginia
VAN HORN
Born: 25 Dec
1890

Hazel Foster
VAN HORN
Born: 15 Jul 1892

Olive Mae VAN
HORN Born: 14
Jul 1894

Family Map

Isaiah VAN HORN Died: 01 Mar 1895

John Dick VAN HORN and Berdeen Boylan BRAYMER Married: Abt. 1903

Harold V. HARKCOM VAN HORN Born: Abt. 1906

Phyllis M. BALLANTYNE Born: Aug 1908

Eugene R. HARKCOM VAN HORN Born: 17 Dec 1908

James Van Horn BALLANTYNE and Lida Carrie RIGG Married: 13 Oct 1909

Caroline E. VAN HORN Died: Bet. 1910 - 1920

John Edwin BALLANTYNE Born: 03 Oct 1912

Ruth Loraine BERRY Born: 24 Oct 1913

Judson Tannehill VAN HORN, JR Born: 12 Mar 1920

Eunice Matilda VAN HORN Born: 06 Apr 1922

Mary Ella VAN HORN Born: 28 Feb 1925

George Edward MILLIKEN and Dorothy Virginia BALLANTYNE Married: 13 Oct 1934

Zelda Mae SHAFFER Died: 06 Jan 1977

Hubert VAN HORN Died: 16 Nov 2002

Wichita, Sedgwick Co., KS (298 Mi NE of Potter Co.)

Carleton George ALBRIGHT Died: 02 May 1962

Wilderness, Spotsylvania Co., VA

Henry Van Zandt STEWART Died: 05 May 1864

Wilkesboro, Wilkes Co., NC (389 Mi SE of Posey Co.)

Gilbert Lee MCGLAMERY Born: 01 May 1923

Gilbert Lee MCGLAMERY Died: 13 Mar 2000

Wilkinsburg, Allegheny Co., PA

Elizabeth Jane GILLESPIE Born: 15 May 1910

Martin Luther KECK Died: Jun 1923

Williamsport, Lycoming Co., PA

John F. HEISLEY and Mary Frances LYON Married: 1863

John F. HEISLEY Died: 25 Jan 1915

Williamstown, Wood Co., WV (356 Mi NE of Posey Co.)

Richard S. LAMBING Died: 05 Jun 2000

Willoughby, Lake Co., OH

Nelson Blair VAN HORN Died: 02 Feb 1993

Winchester, VA

Charles Lee GRAVES Born: 1918

Charles Lee GRAVES and Eunice Matilda VAN HORN Married: 1939

Wisconsin (NE of Iowa)

Fannie F. AVERY Born: Abt. 1860

Gertrude M. Born: Abt. 1871

Sophia Christina HELLEKSON Born: Nov 1871

Winifred A. VAN HORN Born: Abt. 1899

Family Map

Chloe Alberta
VAN HORN
Born: Abt. 1901

Maurice Alva
VAN HORN
Born: Abt. 1902

Willlis M. VAN
HORN Born:
Abt. 1904

Francis J VAN
HORN Born:
Abt. 1911

Oscar Rex
BOWERS and
Buena Geraldine
DAVIS Married:
31 Jul 1921

**Wooster,
Wayne Co.,
OH**

Frank Phillip
MARKLEY
Born: 28 Nov
1890

**Yankton,
Yankton Co.,
SD**

Elmira Solle
ARMSTRONG
Died: 18 Jan 1956

**Yardley,
Bucks Co., PA**

John YARDLEY

**Yatesboro,
Armstrong
Co., PA**

Berdella
GOLDSTROHM
Born: 13 Apr
1903

Nelson Earnest
SHAFFER, JR
Died: 15 Oct
1999

**Youngstown,
Mahoning
Co., OH**

LeRoy Kerns
VAN HORN
Died: 16 Feb
1954

Tirzah Theresa
WADDING
Died: 11 Feb
1967

LeRoy Wadding
VAN HORN
Died: 03 Mar
1987

Floyd Albert
VAN HORN
Died: 24 Jul 1987

Evelyn
STEWART Died:
26 Sep 1988

John Edwin
BALLANTYNE
Died: 07 Nov
2002

**Zanesville,
Muskingum
Co., OH (338
Mi NE of
Posey Co.)**

Bernard VAN
HORNE Born:
22 Jan 1789

Mary Ann
MORROW Born:
1808

Joseph J. VAN
HORNE Born:
19 Mar 1820

Isaac VAN
HORNE Died:
1823

Isaac VAN
HOORN Died:
02 Feb 1834

Isaac VAN
HORNE Died:
02 Feb 1834

Elizabeth GAINE
Died: 17 Jan 1838

Bernard VAN
HORNE and
Mary Ann
MORROW
Married: 05 Sep
1839

Jefferson VAN
HORNE Born:
26 Oct 1840

Sydney E.
CULBERTSON
Born: 16 Sep 1842

Dorothy JOHN
Died: 15 Sep 1843

Dorothy
MARPLE Died:
15 Sep 1843

Joseph J. VAN
HORNE and
Ann HONAS
Married: 03 Aug
1845

Bernard VAN
HORNE Died:
14 Jan 1861

Henry VAN
HORN Died: 08
Aug 1861

Jane VAN
HORN Died:
1866

Bernard VAN
HORN Died: 14
Jan 1866

Bernard Van
Horne
SCHULTZ Born:
24 Jul 1866

Jefferson VAN
HORNE and
Sydney E.
CULBERTSON
Married: 04 Nov
1869

Alice Elizabeth
VAN HORN
Died: Abt. 1876

Mary Ann
MORROW Died:
1877

Louise VAN
HORNE Born:
19 Feb 1877

Mary A. Died: 06
Nov 1877

Family Map

John H. VAN
HORNE Died:
24 May 1884

Earl VAN
HORN Born: 24
Sep 1887

Sarah Francis
SCHULTZ Born:
18 Jan 1888

Lucretia
SCHULTZ Born:
15 Dec 1890

Jefferson VAN
HORNE Died:
27 Apr 1898

David VAN
HORN Died: 08
Mar 1900

Sydney V. H.
UPJOHN Born:
25 Apr 1905

Sidney Ellen
CULBERTSON
Died: 1930

Sydney E.
CULBERTSON
Died: 27 Oct
1930

Index of Individuals

664
John Raymond , JR: 281, 596, 666
Kelly Ann: 435, 459
Mary Elizabeth: 281, 387, 435, 631, 666
Mary G. (aka: Grace M. ASHCOM): 188, 661
Sandra Lee: 386, 435
Thelma Imogene: 281, 592, 663
Tina Marie: 435, 459, 460
Vickie Lynn: 435

ASHCORN -
Frank (name: Benjamin Frank ASHCOM): 187, 636, 651

ATKINSON -
R. W.: 232

AUL -
?: 354
Alma Florence: 253, 352, 620, 625
Arthur Melvin: 350, 663
Bertha Della: 253, 351, 413-415, 449-456, 465-468, 658
Casper: 253, 620, 645
Charles K.: 354
Curt Edward (name: Curtis Edwin AUL): 253, 350, 351, 413, 658
Curtis Edwin (aka: Curt Edward AUL): 253, 350, 351, 413, 658
Danks: 652
Floyd William (aka: Lloyd W. AUL): 254, 354, 668, 671
George Curtis: 599, 650
Henry: 611
Herbert H. (name: Herbert Riggle AUL): 253, 349, 350, 619, 626
Herbert Riggle (aka: Herbert H. AUL): 253, 349, 350, 619, 626
Imogene Mildred: 350, 593
Iva Bell: 253, 351, 352, 601, 620
James E.: 350
James M. (name: Mack James AUL): 651
Laney Lawrence: 253, 616, 625
Larry Arthur: 354
Larue Bernadine: 351, 413
Lawrence David: 254, 353, 638, 668
Liola: 354
Lloyd W. (name: Floyd William AUL): 254, 354, 668, 671
Mable Mildred: 253, 661, 663
Mack James (aka: James M. AUL): 651
Malinda: 650
Martha: 649
Mary Jane: 253, 352, 620
Mc Henry: 651
Merle: 351
Myrtle Linda: 253, 352, 353,

638, 661
Norman L.: 354
Ralph Lee: 254, 668
Raymond Curtis: 354
Robert: 350
Ronals: 354
Ruth Ann: 354
Twila Ethel: 254
William L.: 350
William Worth: 649

AVERY -
Fannie F.: 676

AZEVEDO -
Lucy: 442

B

B. -
Caroline: 646
Mae: 337, 629
Mae (aka: Mae E.): 635
Mary: 372
Melissa (name: Melissa B. ALLISON): 171, 172, 614, 623
Nellie: 312, 313, 628

B.WHITTAM -
Luther (name: Luther Brainard WHITHAM): 168, 169, 674

BABCOCK -
Martha: 640, 674
Viola V.: 635

BABER -
Sarah Margaret: 389

BACHE -
Leigh S.: 596

BAERTS -
Mary: 67, 74

BAILETT -
Catherine Work: 381
Francis Dwight: 381
James Dwight: 381
Susan Dwight: 381

BAILEY -
Ann: 235
Ethel (name: Ethel LAMBING): 659
Ula: 659
Zella (name: Zella LAMBING): 659

BAIR -
Ellen Marie: 339

BAIREY -
George: 294
Jane Elizabeth (name: Jennie Elizabeth BAIREY): 294, 634, 665
Jennie Elizabeth (aka: Jane Elizabeth BAIREY): 294, 634, 665

BAKER -
Anna Mary: 342
David Paul: 456
Edgar Stanley: 336
Elizabeth C.: 646

Gerald David: 456
Huberta: 634
Lindsay Marie: 456
Marion Beatrice: 336, 594, 633
Michael Scott: 456

BALCZUM -
Unnamed: 465
?: 465
?: 465
?: 465
?: 465

BALENTINE/BALLENTYNE -
John W. (name: John Wesley BALLANTYNE): 186, 187, 649

BALLANTYNE -
?: 386
?: 386
?: 386
?: 386
?: 386
?: 386
?: 386
?: 386
?: 386
Carl Rigg: 279, 386, 663, 668
Dorothy Virginia: 279, 385, 662
Florence (aka: Flora BALLENTYNE): 187, 655
James C.: 280, 662, 668
James Van Horn: 187, 279, 385, 386, 664, 675
James Van Horn , JR: 279, 386, 662, 666
John Edwin: 279, 385, 386, 676, 677
John Wesley (aka: John W. BALENTINE/BALLEN TYNE): 186, 187, 649
John Wesley (aka: Weslie BALLENTYNE): 187, 279, 280, 675
Mary Gertude: 187, 653
Phyllis M.: 280, 676

BALLENTYNE -
Flora (name: Florence BALLANTYNE): 187, 655
Weslie (name: John Wesley BALLANTYNE): 187, 279, 280, 675

BALSLEY -
Elizabeth: 583

BANKS -
Helen: 356, 417
Louise: 356
Rosemary: 356
Thomas: 355, 356, 626, 659

BANNON -
Bessie (name: Elizabeth BANNON): 628, 629
Elizabeth (aka: Bessie BANNON): 628, 629

BANTE -
Aeltie: 594

680

681

682

683

CHMELAR -
Charles: 374, 375
Christa -
Unnamed: 314
CHRISTIANSEN -
Shirley Louise: 381, 382, 602, 609
CHRISTIE -
Jane: 391
Christina -
Unnamed: 168
Christine -
Unnamed: 321
Clara -
Unnamed: 310
Unnamed: 309
Unnamed: 210, 648
Clarica -
Unnamed (aka: Clarra): 583, 640
CLARK -
George Joseph: 417, 418
Herbert Fargo: 434
Lora Bell: 209, 608
Lorraine: 394
Morill (name: Morrell A. CLARK): 634
Morrell A. (aka: Morill CLARK): 634
Thomas: 670
Clarra -
(name: Clarica): 583, 640
CLAUSSEN -
Dirk: 60, 73-75, 593
Geertje Dircks: 56, 60, 62, 63, 73, 74, 638
CLAWSON -
Daniell Renee: 454
Donald Ward: 454
Joseph Edward: 454
Nicole Susette: 454
CLAYPOOLE -
Marianne S.: 344
CLEWS -
Thomas Edward: 602
CLOWER -
Alta Blanche: 626, 657
Frank (aka: Frank CLOWES): 397
Nellie Mae (aka: Nellie Mae CLOWES): 397, 398, 659
CLOWES -
Frank (name: Frank CLOWER): 397
Nellie Mae (name: Nellie Mae CLOWER): 397, 398, 659
COALMER -
Amanda G.: 447
Richard M.: 447
Ryan P.: 447
COCHRAN -
Unnamed: 429
COCKRUM -
Unnamed: 214
Clyde: 214, 609
Eddie: 214, 609

Oscar: 214, 609
Owen: 214, 609
William Sherman: 214, 608
COFFINBERGER -
Ann V.: 335
David: 335
Jame Link: 334, 335, 633
COGLEY -
Unnamed: 309
Rev. John Martin: 280, 593
Nana Pearl: 280, 281, 603, 636
COLEMAN -
Belle: 174, 175, 651
J. Nelson: 174
Linda: 448
COLLINS -
George Edward: 196, 655
George W.: 196, 646
Joseph M.: 196, 287, 288, 654
Merl F.: 288, 661
COMEGIST -
Ari A. (name: Arienne A. COMEGIST): 674
Arienne A. (aka: Ari A. COMEGIST): 674
CONCETTA -
Argie: 287
CONDRON -
Angus Blanchard: 160, 247, 616, 660
Charles: 374
Charles Gillis: 160, 245, 246, 342, 615, 672
Charles Gillis , JR: 246, 661
Clair: 244, 654
Clarence J.: 246, 662
Clarence Reed: 245, 655
Cornelius Elsworth: 160, 245, 614, 632
Dollie Irene: 245, 341, 410, 656
Dorcas Belle: 247, 658
Dorcas Jane: 245, 658
Edwin: 246, 657
Ellsworth E.: 247, 657
George A.: 160, 246, 615
George L.: 244, 654
George L.: 245, 658
George L.: 246, 659
George Leroy (aka: George CONDRUM): 159, 160, 618, 645
Hazel B.: 246, 656
Hugh W.: 245, 656
Ike: 247
Ira Sloan: 245, 341, 657
Jacob: 159, 614
Jacob Leroy: 160, 614
James Melantheon: 160, 244, 613
Laura Elizabeth: 245, 655
Laura Jane: 160, 243, 244, 613, 622
Loretta Margaret: 247, 659
Margaret: 246, 660
Marion M. (aka: Uriah CONDRON): 160, 614

Minnie Myrtle: 245, 654
Olive Florence (aka: Ollie F. CONDRON): 160, 246, 615
Olive Florence: 245, 655
Olive Florence: 246, 342, 640, 672
Ollie F. (name: Olive Florence CONDRON): 160, 246, 615
Robert: 341
Robert E.: 244, 653
Uriah (name: Marion M. CONDRON): 160, 614
W. F. (name: William Madison CONDRON): 160, 244, 245, 341, 410, 613
Walter Merle: 245, 657
William Madison (aka: W. F. CONDRON): 160, 244, 245, 341, 410, 613
CONDRUM -
George (name: George Leroy CONDRON): 159, 160, 618, 645
CONINE -
Fanny: 125, 670
Peter: 125
CONNELL -
Ann: 364, 365
CONNER -
Jacob Park (name: Jacob B. A. O'CONNER): 161, 650
Martha: 366
Robert P. A. (name: Robert Parnold O'CONNER): 161, 650
CONRAD -
Lucy Adelia: 619, 651
COOK -
Andrew B. (name: Andrew F. COOK): 182, 656
Andrew F. (aka: Andrew B. COOK): 182, 656
COOLEY -
Adela Honeywood: 132, 134, 594, 635
Agnes Culshaw: 390, 659
COON -
Unnamed: 313
?: 242
?: 243
Alice Melissa: 159, 241, 339, 649
Allan: 363
Augustus Kimmel: 159, 242, 666
Bertha: 242
Carol Sue: 363
Catherine: 242
Cecil: 242
Charles Barclay: 159, 242, 339, 650, 666
Cynthia: 363
Daniel B.: 341
Don Mitchell: 243, 340, 602
Edith R.: 159, 607
Edna: 242

Stephen , JR: 379
Trudy: 379
DEEMER -
Elizabeth Rebbeca: 642
DEHAVEN -
A. J.: 309
DELONG -
Unnamed: 318
DEMPSEY -
Unnamed: 312
DESPAIN -
Billie Burnetta: 440, 463
Bonnie Christine (aka: Bonnie
   Christine HEY): 440
Robert Edward: 440
Ronald Wendell: 440
DEVAUGHN -
Wayne Lee: 404
DEVERS -
Nancy: 324
DICK -
Emma: 393
Mary Louisa: 119
DICKEN -
Alta J.: 671, 672
Anna M.: 642
James William: 580, 581, 641
DICKEY -
Jim: 416
DILL -
Anna Pearl: 402, 661
William Alexander: 402
DILTS -
Agnes: 143, 647
Arthur: 237, 629
Barbara: 264
Betty J.: 264
Cye (name: Cyrus B. DILTS):
   263, 264, 619, 626
Cyrus B. (aka: Cye DILTS): 263,
   264, 619, 626
Daniel W.: 237, 337, 338, 643
Deloris Louise: 338
E. Floyd (name: Elva Floid
   DILTS): 198, 292, 618
Edwin J.: 237, 652
Elva Floid (aka: E. Floyd
   DILTS): 198, 292, 618
Emerson C.: 198, 659
Frederick: 237, 337, 643
Glennabelle: 360
Helen L.: 264
Henry K.: 237, 629
Henry Milton: 143, 197, 198,
   292, 596, 614
Isabella: 238
J. LaRetta: 338
James Coulter: 143, 611
Jane: 143, 612, 616
John: 237, 629
John Frederick: 337
John M.: 237, 647
John Scott: 143, 611, 614
Lawrence M.: 337, 629
Lillie M.: 237, 238, 643
Lola Fern: 338

Maggie: 237, 653
Marjorie: 264, 379
Martha Elizabeth: 198, 292, 655
Mildred L.: 198, 656
Novell B.: 338
Peter: 237
Peter Watson: 143, 611, 615
Peter , SR: 143, 613, 633
Samuel: 143, 648
Tabitha: 143, 649
Thomas: 237, 629
William: 143, 610, 614
William C.: 143, 612
William R.: 237, 337, 653
Wilson: 263
DIMAIO -
Anthony: 467
Chelsea Marie: 467
Manda Sue: 467
DINGER -
Melanie: 457
Mindi: 457
Mysti: 457
Roger: 457
DIPLANTIS -
Mary Clare: 434
DIXON -
Golda May: 311, 312, 594, 667
DIXSON -
Unnamed: 303
Clifford T.: 303
Margaret: 122
Mildred E.: 303
Wilmer Todd: 303, 654
DOLBY -
Alice: 256
William: 343, 660
William , JR: 343
DOLLISON -
Mary Jean: 453
DONAHUE -
Daniel Edward: 432
DONALDSON -
Foster V.: 278
Richard P.: 278
Virginia M.: 278
William Perry: 278
William Presley: 278, 593
Donna -
Unnamed: 402
Doris -
Unnamed: 378
DOUDS -
Unnamed: 354
Margaret E.: 354, 355, 626, 659
DOUGLAS -
Gail Leigh: 173, 602, 668
James: 173
Kenneth B. (name: Kenneth V.
   DOUGLAS): 173, 174,
   608
Kenneth V. (aka: Kenneth B.
   DOUGLAS): 173, 174,
   608
Margaret Van Horn: 173, 602,
   668

Mary Ellen: 173, 601
Robert M.: 173, 668
Thomas J. (aka: Thomas
   DUGLAS): 173
DOWDEN -
Ruth Virginia Madaline: 407
DOWN -
Unnamed: 429
DUDZINSKI -
Gertude Genowefa: 439
Joseph Michael: 439
DUFF -
Grace Elizabeth: 448
DUFFY -
Owen: 325
DUGLAS -
Thomas (name: Thomas J.
   DOUGLAS): 173
DUNCAN -
Betsy: 413
Bonnie Lu: 413, 625
Charles H.: 412, 413
Laurel: 413, 449
DUNGAN -
Mary: 65
DUNHAM -
Lillian: 234, 595, 627
Samuel Smith: 234
DUNMIRE -
Mary Elizabeth: 211
DURBIN -
Edward J.: 345, 651
Keith E.: 345
Ralph E.: 345, 660
DVORK -
Mary Lorraine: 636, 639
DYE -
Margaret Mitchell: 609

E
E. -
Beulah: 188, 656
Fannie: 185, 651
Kathryn (name: Catherine
   LYDICK): 170, 646
Mae (name: Mae B.): 635
Mary: 140, 646
Mary: 647
EAKEN -
Mary: 602
EBERT -
Ada: 642
Frank: 641
EDGE -
Judy: 385
Kimberly: 385
Mary: 385
Moses H.: 385
Samuel: 278
Walter M. , JR: 279, 385, 607,
   663
Walter Malcolm: 278, 279, 666
EGGERS -
Marion L.: 318, 663, 671
Eliza -

686

689

690

691

654
Arthur Konser: 293
Bertha: 200, 656
Budd E.: 200, 657
Charles Bence: 199
Clara Mabel: 199, 655
Clark S.: 200, 656
Esther L.: 200, 658
Eva Grace: 293, 660
Fay R. (aka: rennie Fern
      LIGHTCAP): 199, 656
Florence Maggie (aka: Margaret
      Florence LIGHTCAP):
      199, 656
Harry D.: 199, 657
Harry Johnson: 145, 200, 614
Infant: 145, 614
Jane T.: 144, 199, 612
John Irven: 199, 657
John Leonard: 293
John Scott: 145, 199, 293, 612,
      623
Johnston: 144, 602, 619
Lucinda: 144, 612, 620
Margaret Florence (name:
      Florence Maggie
      LIGHTCAP): 199, 656
Mary J.: 199, 654
Nancy Ann (aka: Nannie
      LIGHTCAP): 145, 200,
      293, 395, 613, 624
Nannie (name: Nancy Ann
      LIGHTCAP): 145, 200,
      293, 395, 613, 624
rennie Fern (name: Fay R.
      LIGHTCAP): 199, 656
Samuel J.: 199, 617, 654
Silas Edgar: 199, 293, 617
Silas W.: 145, 649, 665
Sloan B.: 200, 659
Susana (aka: Anna Susannah
      LIGHTCAP): 199, 293,
      654
William B.: 199, 293, 653
Lilia -
    Unnamed: 642
Lilly -
    Unnamed: 278
LIMERICK -
    Andrew Jackson: 612
LINDSEY -
    Chad Michael: 439, 603
    Matthew Dawson: 439
    Ronnie D.: 439
LININGER -
    Louis Albert: 639, 669
LINSENBIGLE -
    Emma: 250
LITTLE -
    Rose: 367
LITTLE/LYTLE -
    Effie (name: Effie A.
      HUMBERSON): 261,
      262, 606, 626
LIVINGSTON -
    ?: 407, 408

Grace Sylvia: 331, 621, 625
William J.: 407, 624
LLOYD -
    Gilbert: 208
LNU -
    Gertrude Elise: 341
    Nancy Loretta: 245, 651
LOCKHARD -
    Elizabeth: 159, 627
LOCKHART -
    Charles: 458
    Theresa Anne: 458
LODING -
    Viola Sophia: 346, 655
LOGAN -
    Dorcas: 79, 117, 605, 613
LOKSTAD -
    Lois Jean: 440
LONG -
    Unnamed: 367
    Alice (name: Jane Narcissa
      LONG): 154, 155, 596,
      612
    Daniel: 154
    Elmer: 428
    Jane Narcissa (aka: Alice
      LONG): 154, 155, 596,
      612
    Louella Madge: 428
    Mary (aka: Melissa LONG): 226
    Melissa (name: Mary LONG):
      226
LONGSHORE -
    Euclides: 54
LOOFBURROW -
    Amaranda Rachel: 640, 674
Lou -
    Mary: 357
Louise -
    Unnamed: 654
    Unnamed: 186, 655
LOVE -
    Rose: 399
LOWERY -
    Charles: 316
    Sarah M.: 293
LOWMAN -
    ?: 428
    Worth: 428
LUBERS -
    Catherine (name: Catherine
      SUBER): 598, 599
LUCAS -
    ?: 446
    ?: 446
    ?: 446
    ?: 446
    ?: 446
    ?: 446
    ?: 446
    ?: 446
    ?: 446
    ?: 446
    ?: 446
    ?: 446
    ?: 446
    Nicholas George: 446

Paul Ray: 436, 437
LUCE -
    Clair (aka: Red LUCE): 375, 601
    Connie Eileen: 375, 432
    Denis Renee: 432
    Red (name: Clair LUCE): 375,
      601
    Terry Lee: 375, 432
    Tina Diane: 432
    Tracy Autumn: 432
LUCKHART -
    Jacob (name: Jacob
      LUKEHART): 206
    Turner (name: Turner
      Thompson
      LUKEHART): 206, 593,
      613
LUCUS -
    Paula Diane: 437, 460
Lucy -
    Unnamed: 228, 674
    Unnamed: 315, 609
LUDWIG -
    Ada: 643
    Ethel V.: 642
    Hazel B.: 642
    Michael William: 582, 603, 641
    Walter J.: 642
LUKEHART -
    Albert Anthony: 371
    Bertha Agnes: 207, 304, 402,
      443, 593, 603
    Clayton: 371
    Cleone I.: 304, 660
    Clifford J.: 305
    Dianne Lynne: 371
    Donna: 371
    Effie: 373
    Gloria Jane: 371
    Helen R.: 305
    Herbert (name: Herbert
      BOWSER): 371, 593, 664
    Homer Boyd: 207, 305, 593, 603
    Ira M.: 341, 662
    Jacob (aka: Jacob LUCKHART):
      206
    James Albert: 371
    James Francis: 410
    Jane M.: 341
    Leone M.: 305
    Linda Lee: 371
    Luther Merle (aka: Mearle
      LUKEHART): 207, 304,
      593
    Mary B.: 304, 599
    Mearle (name: Luther Merle
      LUKEHART): 207, 304,
      593
    Nora Ethel: 206, 207, 593
    Ralph B.: 304, 599
    Richard M: 410
    Roy R.: 341
    Turner Thompson (aka: Turner
      LUCKHART): 206, 593,
      613
    William Francis: 341, 624, 671

697

703

Lucille (name: Dolly
    ROBINSON): 244, 655
Oila May (aka: Olie May
    ROBINSON): 244, 653
Olie May (name: Oila May
    ROBINSON): 244, 653
Samuel Taylor: 243, 244, 612,
    619
RODKEY -
Grace C. (name: Grace C.
    RADKEY): 324
Jacob Snyder: 324
ROELOFS -
Myrtie (aka: Wyntje ROELOFS):
    60, 73-75, 593
Wyntje (name: Myrtie
    ROELOFS): 60, 73-75,
    593
ROHAN -
Unnamed: 303
Mary: 303, 304, 659
ROMANO -
Unnamed: 382
ROOF -
Martha Emma: 398
ROSE -
Eliza A.: 645
ROSENBERGER -
Earl O.: 643
Ermie A. (aka:
    Irma/Emma/Imma
    ROSSENBERGER):
    606, 642
Franklin: 643
George Washington: 642
Gwendolyn D.: 643
James Arthur: 608, 642
James Arthur , JR: 609
James Marcus: 606
Oliver Perry: 642
Perry F. (name: Perry Franklin
    ROSENBERGER): 579,
    606, 641
Perry Franklin (aka: Perry F.
    ROSENBERGER): 579,
    606, 641
William H.: 642
ROSS -
Sarah: 144
ROSSENBERGER -
Irma/Emma/Imma (name:
    Ermie A.
    ROSSENBERGER): 606,
    642
ROUSH -
Hannah: 314
ROWE -
Mary Blanche: 280, 593
ROWLEY -
Martha Jane: 322
ROWSE -
Unnamed: 284
RUDDOCK -
Mildred (aka: Mildred
    RUDDUCK): 401, 627
RUDDUCK -

Mildred (name: Mildred
    RUDDOCK): 401, 627
RUGH -
Samuel: 165
RUMPLER -
Joseph G.: 582, 642
Lester J.: 632, 642
RUPERT -
Beverly Jean: 372, 430
Connie: 372
Earl: 352
H. Lester: 372
Jeffery Allen: 373
Kathy Lynn: 373
Larry A.: 372, 430
Lisa Kaye: 373
Michael Shawn: 430
Patricia Ann (aka: Patty
    RUPERT): 372, 430, 458,
    625
Patty (name: Patricia Ann
    RUPERT): 372, 430, 458,
    625
Sara: 352
Theadore: 372, 623
RUPP -
Annette Carol: 451, 467
Arthur Wayne: 451
Beverly Sue: 451, 467
Christine Marie: 451, 466, 467
Cynthia Mae: 451, 467
Henry: 208
Kelvin Arthur: 451, 468
Kevin Wayne: 451
Taylor Cathline: 468
RUPPERT -
Orpha: 197, 651
RUSNICA -
Carol: 416
Michael: 416, 663, 665
Thomas: 416
Tom: 416
RUSSELL -
Elsie: 330, 331
RUZBARSKY -
Frank: 369

S
S. -
Rebecca: 155, 156, 651
Sarah: 637
Sadie -
Unnamed: 252, 652
SAHYONNE -
Mary: 362
SALVAGGIO -
Antoinette: 441
SAMSEL -
Mary Elizabeth: 645
Sandra -
Unnamed: 458
Unnamed: 420
Unnamed: 430
Sarah -
Unnamed: 207, 645

Unnamed (aka: Sarah
    HOUSER): 146, 646
SCARLETT -
H. B.: 235
SCARRY -
Isabelle: 430
SCATTERGOOD -
Rebecca: 637
SCHALTZ -
Pamela: 438
SCHENCK -
Sarah T.: 606, 640
SCHEUCH -
Minnie Martha: 396
SCHIMMEL -
Bruce Douglas: 436, 671
Bruce Douglas II: 460
Melanee Sue: 436, 460
Rusty (name: Sheldon Henry
    SCHIMMEL): 435, 436,
    643, 671
Shelda Lynn: 436, 460
Sheldon Henry (aka: Rusty
    SCHIMMEL): 435, 436,
    643, 671
SCHIMPF -
Unnamed: 249
SCHIRRA -
Anna: 318, 319, 658, 664
Rebecca Anna: 640
SCHOEMANN -
Unnamed: 405
SCHOFFSTALL -
Unnamed: 370
SCHOFIELD -
Hattie (name: Hattie
    STOFFLE): 300, 301,
    654
SCHRECKENGOST -
Frances Evelyn: 423
SCHUETTE -
Unnamed: 459
Alysa Janell: 459
SCHULTZ -
Bernard Van Horne: 677
Carl Pitkin: 335
Lucretia: 678
Sarah Francis: 678
SCHURR -
?: 378
Carl (name: Harold Wallace
    SCHURR): 378
Harold Wallace (aka: Carl
    SCHURR): 378
Martha: 291, 292
SCOTT -
Earl E.: 409
Earl Eugene: 409, 609, 624
Howard L.: 409
Joyce Eileen: 341
Letita (aka: Letitia SCOTT): 602
Letitia (name: Letita SCOTT):
    602
Nancy: 120, 627
Robert Clair: 409
SCROGGS -

704

705

706

709

180, 189, 649

Alice Lucetta (aka: Alice L. VAN HORN): 135, 179, 180, 189, 649

Alice Roselia: 139, 188, 281, 282, 612

Alice V.: 207, 653

Allan: 423

Allison: 441

Almarine: 640

Alonzo Curtis: 228, 675

Alva Marco: 627

Amos: 638

Amos C.: 333

Amy: 642

Amy Doris: 673

Anderson T. (aka: Andrew R. VAN HORN): 150, 214, 215, 317, 614, 661

Andrew Glenn: 297, 397, 398, 440, 441, 463, 619

Andrew R. (name: Anderson T. VAN HORN): 150, 214, 215, 317, 614, 661

Angus Vanzant (aka: Ingus V. VAN HORN): 162, 250, 617

Anna B.: 162, 248, 616

Anna Burel: 644

Anna Florence (aka: Annie VAN HORN): 166, 255, 256, 358-360, 419-422, 457, 617, 626

Anna I. (aka: Annie VAN HORN): 138, 185, 186, 648

Anna M.: 135, 179, 272, 273, 648

Anna M. (aka: Sadie VAN HORN): 136, 649

Anna Mary (name: Annie VAN HORN): 184, 275, 382, 383, 675

Annie (name: Anna I. VAN HORN): 138, 185, 186, 648

Annie: 652

Annie (name: Anna Florence VAN HORN): 166, 255, 256, 358-360, 419-422, 457, 617, 626

Annie (aka: Anna Mary VAN HORN): 184, 275, 382, 383, 675

Annie C.: 249, 660

Annie P.: 203, 204, 618, 668

Ansel (aka: Ansle VAN HORN): 628

Ansle (name: Ansel VAN HORN): 628

Arlene May: 258, 368, 622, 626

Arnold Wilton (aka: Wilson Arnold VAN HORNE): 162, 249, 343, 344, 593, 617

Arthelia: 641

Arthur: 638

Arthur: 652

Arthur Lee: 600

Arthur Palmer: 217, 631

Asbury Boyd (name: Charles Boyd VAN HORN): 298, 399, 620

Ashley: 464

Athelia: 627

Audrey: 249, 661

Augus (name: August VAN HORN): 674

August (aka: Augus VAN HORN): 674

Augustus: 152, 648

Barbara: 406

Barnet (name: Bernard VAN HOORN): 597, 598

Beecher Lynn: 639

Belle: 146

Benjamin: 658

Benjamin Briggs: 122, 145, 200, 202, 204, 206, 294-305, 395-402, 439-443, 463, 464, 610, 618

Benjamin Franklin: 650

Bennett Wesley: 260, 623

Bennett Work (aka: Benett Wyncoop.VAN HORN): 126, 165, 166, 252-256, 258, 260-264, 346-379, 412-423, 426-433, 449-458, 465-468, 612, 623

Bernard: 598, 677

Bernard: 333

Bernard Harrison: 608, 674

Bert (name: William Burton VAN HORN): 202, 294, 395, 396, 439, 600, 615

Berta Blanche: 229, 675

Bertha: 209, 654

Bertha Mae: 639

Beryl: 662

Beth (name: Elizabeth E. VAN HORN): 191, 673

Betty J.: 301, 400

Bill (name: William Clyde VAN HORN): 258, 364, 427, 623

Bill (name: William James VAN HORN): 362, 426, 624

Billy Joe: 426

Blaine W.: 260, 371, 372, 623

Blaine W. , JR: 372

Bonnie: 427

Bowen: 191, 632, 639

Brian Edward: 427

Bula (name: Zula L. VAN HORN): 205, 303, 655

Burt (name: Amos Burton LYDICK): 153, 224, 225, 617, 629

Caleb Henry: 134, 629, 666

Calista T.: 627, 674

Carla: 674

Carol: 369

Carol: 404

Caroline: 146, 648

Caroline: 185, 660

Caroline E. (aka: Carrie VAN HORN): 138, 186, 187, 279, 385, 386, 649, 676

Carrie (name: Caroline E. VAN HORN): 138, 186, 187, 279, 385, 386, 649, 676

Carrie (name: Mary Caroline VAN HORN): 166, 253, 349-354, 413-415, 449-456, 465-468, 616, 624

Carrie Adella: 653

Carrie Etta: 258, 366, 428, 662, 664

Catherine: 124, 158, 159, 241-243, 339, 340, 646

Catherine Isabelle (aka: Katherine I. VANHORN): 297, 398, 399, 441, 619

Charles: 599

Charles: 674

Charles: 195, 287, 389, 659

Charles: 662

Charles: 423

Charles Blaine: 203, 298, 618, 625

Charles Boyd (aka: Asbury Boyd VAN HORN): 298, 399, 620

Charles C.: 135, 630

Charles Fremont: 140, 613

Charles G. (name: Charles J. VAN HORN): 647

Charles J. (aka: Charles G. VAN HORN): 647

Charles Kuras: 377

Charles Lee: 361, 423

Charles Milton: 124, 647

Charles , JR: 287

Charlotte Ann: 384

Chessiah: 634

Chester A.: 277, 661

Chloe Alberta: 677

Christian: 55, 56, 638

Christian: 80, 598, 599

Christian: 644

Christian: 645

Christian: 122, 146, 207, 208, 305, 307-311, 402-404, 444-446, 464, 465, 593, 610

Christian: 599

Christian: 649

Christine: 122, 646

Christopher Columbus: 593, 641

Christy Lynn (aka: Kristilyn VAN HORN): 426

Claire L.: 260, 623, 626

Clara: 635, 649

Clara (aka: Clarie VAN HORN): 627

Clara Emmagina: 310

Clara Lucinda: 139, 190, 613,

713

714

715

719

720

Dr. J. Derald Morgan is an accomplished author, genealogist, family historian and expert witness.

Dr. Morgan was a University Professor and Administrator for 46 years. He served as Vice President and Executive Director of the UAH Foundation at The University of Alabama in Huntsville, was Dean at New Mexico State University, and was Department Head and the ALCOA and Emerson Electric Chaired Professors at University of Missouri-Rolla now Missouri Science and Technology during his academic career.

Dr. Morgan is a Fellow of the Institute of Electrical Engineers and the National Academy of Forensic Engineers and Associate Editor of the Power Systems Research Journal. In addition to being a successful researcher, professor and university administrator, he is a forensic engineer with an active practice.

Dr. Morgan has been an adult Boy Scout Leader for over 48 years, a leader in the United Methodist Church and a member of numerous professional and civic organizations.

The father of four children and grandfather to 9 he has been an avid family historian for over 40 years. He believes that knowing your roots is essential to developing a perspective on who you are and what your role is in society. Knowing your roots gives a foundation for a successful and fulfilling life.

As a member of the Sons of the American Revolution Dr. Morgan also believes that every American needs more knowledge about their family and its contribution to the development of this great nation. Out of this knowledge grows an appreciation for the freedoms we have and a commitment to sustaining a free society.